LOCI THEOLOGICI

CHEMNITZ'S WORKS

VOLUME 8

LOCI THEOLOGICI

PART II

MARTIN CHEMNITZ

TRANSLATED BY J. A. O. PREUS

CONCORDIA PUBLISHING HOUSE · SAINT LOUIS

15-5129
0-7586-1547-7
978-0-7586-1547-3
Theology & Doctrine / Historical Theology

This work is dedicated to my devoted
and talented wife, Delpha.

 Copyright © 1989, 2008 Concordia Publishing House
3558 S. Jefferson Ave., St. Louis, MO 63118-3968
1-800-325-3040 • www.cph.org

Some quotations from the Lutheran Confessions are taken from *The Book of Concord*, translated and edited by Theodore G. Tappert, copyright © 1959 Fortress Press. Used by permission.

Manufactured in the United States of America

Library of Congress Cataloging-in-Publication Data
Chemnitz, Martin, 1522–1586.
[Loci theologici. English]
Loci theologici / Martin Chemnitz ; translated by J. A. O. Preus.
    p. cm. — (Chemnitz's works ; v. 7)
ISBN 978-0-7586-1547-3
1. Lutheran Church—Doctrines—Early works to 1800. 2. Theology, Doctrinal—Early works to 1800. 3. Melanchthon, Philipp, 1497–1560. Loci communes rerum theologicarum. I. Preus, Jacob A. O. (Jacob Aall Ottesen), 1920–94 II. Title. III. Series.
BT8064.C4613 2007
230'.41—dc22

                                                                    2007028769

    3 4 5 6 7 8 9 10 11   26 25 24 23 22 21 20 19 18 17

Second part of the Loci Theologici of the reverend and notable theologian Dr. Martin Chemnitz, at one time most faithful superintendent of the church of Brunswick

Edited in the name of his heirs by Polycarp Leyser doctor of sacred theology and successor to Dr. Chemnitz

Published by Johannes Spies, Frankfurt am Main, 1594[1]

---

[1] Tome 2 was prepared by Leyser about six months after Tome 1, in 1592. The form is the same, and the work proceeds according to Melanchthon's order.

Contents

[PART II]

[Dedicatory Epistle by Polycarp Leyser]   xi

[Poem in Praise of Polycarp Leyser]   xxvi

Locus [VIII]: The Divine Law

[Melanchthon's Text]   589

[A.] The Law of God

Chapter I. The Word "Law" or the Definition of the Term   591

Chapter II. Definition of the Law   596

Chapter III. The Perfect Obedience Which the Law Requires, Fulfillment of the Law   599

Chapter IV. Classification of the Laws [Melanchthon's Text]   611

Classification of the Laws   612

Chapter V. Abrogation of the Law   621

Chapter VI. Promulgation of the Decalog   632

[B.] Exposition of the Decalog

[Melanchthon's Text]   637

Chapter [I]. How We Are to Investigate the True Meaning . . . of the Decalog   638

[Chapter II]. The Decalog

[Melanchthon's Text]   655

The First Commandment   662

The Second Commandment [Melanchthon's Text]   682

The Second Commandment   684

The Third Commandment [Melanchthon's Text]   699

The Third Commandment   701

The Second Table [Melanchthon's Text]   715

The Commandments of the Second Table   716

The Fourth Commandment [Melanchthon's Text]   718

The Fourth Commandment   721

The Fifth Commandment [Melanchthon's Text]   734

The Fifth Commandment   735

The Sixth Commandment [Melanchthon's Text]   749

The Sixth Commandment   750

The Seventh Commandment [Melanchthon's Text]   760

The Seventh Commandment   760

The Eighth Commandment [Melanchthon's Text]   770

The Eighth Commandment   770

The Ninth and Tenth Commandments [Melanchthon's Text]   778

The Ninth and Tenth Commandments   780

[C.] The Fulfilling of the Decalog . . .   789

[D.] Natural Law

   [Melanchthon's Text]   793

   Natural Law   798

[E.] The Use of the Law

   [Melanchthon's Text]   800

   The Use and Purpose of the Law   803

[F.] The Honored Position of the Law, Against the Antinomians   808

[Locus IX]: The Difference Between Precepts and Counsels

   Omitted   811

[Locus X]: Revenge

   Omitted   811

[Locus XI]: Poverty

   Omitted   811

[Locus XII]: Chastity

   Omitted   811

Locus [XIII]: Justification

   [A.] Introductory Remarks   813

   [B.] The Gospel

   [Melanchthon's Text]   816

   [Chapter] I. The Gospel   818

   [Chapter] II. The Proper Doctrine of the Gospel, That Is,
      the Definition of the Subject   822

   [Chapter] III. The Common Definition That the Gospel
      Is the Preaching of Repentance and the Forgiveness of Sins   828

   [C.] The Need for the Promise of the Gospel

   [Melanchthon's Text]   833

   [Chapter I]. The Need for the Promise of the Gospel
      . . . and the Similarity Between the Law and the Gospel   837

[Chapter II]. All the Saints in All Ages . . . Have Been Saved
    by One and the Same Gospel   838
[D.] Grace and Justification
[Melanchthon's Text]   846
Chapter I. The Controversies   850
Chapter II. The True and Proper Point at Issue in This Topic   874
Chapter III. The Vocabulary of Justification   876

[E.] **The Word "Faith"**
[Melanchthon's Text]   898
[Chapter I]. The Word "Faith"   906
[Chapter II]. The Definition of Justifying Faith   925
[Chapter III]. Faith Is a Sure Confidence, Contrary to the Popish
    Dogma of Doubt   937

[F.] **The Word "Grace"**
[Melanchthon's Text]   955
[Chapter I]. The Word "Grace"   965
[Chapter II]. The Term "Freely"   979
[Chapter III]. The Word "Imputation"   982
[Chapter IV]. The Works of the Law   988
[Chapter V]. The Exclusive Expressions   1003
[Chapter VI]. The Term *Sola*   1006
[Chapter VII]. The Testimonies of Scripture   1018

[Dedicatory Epistle by Polycarp Leyser]   1044

Locus [XIV]: Good Works
[Melanchthon's Text]   1051
Good Works   1071
The First Question. Which Works Must Be Done?   1074
The Second Question. What Kind of Good Works
    Should the Regenerate Perform, and How Can They Be Done?   1086
The Third Question. Whether, Why, and How the Good Works
    of the Regenerate Please God   1088
The Fourth Question. Why Are Good Works to Be Done?   1091
The Controversy as to Whether the Good Works of the Regenerate
    Are Necessary [Leyser's Comments]   1110
[The Controversy: Are Good Works Necessary?]   1111
The Arguments of the Adversaries [Melanchthon's Text]   1185
The Arguments of the Adversaries   1202

[Locus XV]: The Difference Between the Old and New Covenants
  [Melanchthon's Text]   1225
  The Difference Between the Old and New Covenants   1240

Locus [XVI]: The Difference Between Mortal and Venial Sin
  [Melanchthon's Text]   1255
  The Difference Between Mortal and Venial Sin in the Regenerate   1263
  Chapter I. The Scripture Passages Underlying This Doctrine   1264
  Chapter II. The Terms by Which This Difference Is Explained 1266
  Chapter III. Definition of the Matter   1271
  Chapter IV. The Bases of the Definitions   1280
  Chapter V. The Use of This Doctrine   1282
  Chapter VI. The Antithesis to This Doctrine   1284

Locus [XVII]: The Church
  [Melanchthon's Text]   1287
  The Church   1301
  Chapter I. The Terminology   1302
  Chapter II. Question: Is There a Church?   1306
  Chapter III. Definition of the Church   1307
  Chapter IV. Teachers and Hearers in the Church   1312

Locus [XVIII]: The Sacraments
  [Melanchthon's Text]   1355
  The Sacraments in General   1361

Locus [XIX]: Baptism
  [Melanchthon's Text]   1363
  Baptism   1370

Locus [XX]: The Lord's Supper
  Omitted   1374

Locus [XXI]: Marriage
  Omitted   1374

Theses [On Various Subjects]
  Omitted   1374

Scripture Index   1375

Subject Index   1423

To Our Most Admirable and Generous Lords Who Excel in Piety, Virtue, Wisdom, and Learning, Members of the Councils and of the Senate of the Renowned Republics of Lübeck, Hamburg, Lüneberg, Rostock, and Wismar, Honorable Rulers and Benefactors, Greetings in Christ from Polycarp Leyser:

Six months ago, at the request of his heirs, I humbly offered to the illustrious leaders, the dukes of Brunswick and Lüneburg, the first volume of the Loci Theologici *of Dr. Martin Chemnitz, of blessed memory. The reason for this has been given in the preface, namely, that it is a great blessing of God for the church to have had from the very beginning the chief loci of the heavenly doctrine summarized in brief fashion according to the norm by which the rest of the teaching can be more properly examined and more correctly explained. And at the same time I have shown that this method of teaching was not discovered by men but was introduced into the church by God Himself and preserved by Him up to this present time. In His name it is most appropriate that we give special thanks to Dr. Chemnitz. For in this very act he has pointed out the best method of teaching, and if our younger men will also maintain it, they can easily understand what must be taught, what omitted, what received, and what rejected in the teaching of the Christian religion, and by which testimonies of sacred Scripture the correct doctrine can be confirmed or false doctrine refuted, so that the pure and uncorrupted tradition of the true religion may be transmitted to our distant posterity. Therefore, just as many faithful teachers of the church have occupied themselves with this kind of writing to their own credit and for the fruitful development of their students, so I hope that from his first volume of sound theology those who are eager for more of the same kind of teaching have learned that our Chemnitz yields first place to none of them, but that he has so skillfully prepared his studies on these subjects that it was most proper even after his death to publish them and share them with the church.*

And now, after this passage of time, most worthy and prudent men, at the urging of the same heirs, I am dedicating this second volume to your Excellencies. I believe that I would be amply rewarded if in a few remarks I might demonstrate how ungrateful the world has shown itself in all times for this highest blessing of God, a world which with its vigorous and constant defections, which we can note from the very beginning of time, has made itself unworthy of the grace of God and has absolutely deserved that God should take away all light of the truth and drown the whole world in the eternal darkness of error. I shall make only a few remarks on this matter and beg that there be no inconvenience for your Excellencies or that you be detained for too long a time. For it is my hope that this brief presentation will not be lacking in value for you.

How great a blessing of God it is that, even after our tragic fall, God comes forth from His secret dwelling place and reveals His will to us in His Word, and has deigned to procure eternal salvation for the human race. This is something which can never be sufficiently praised or celebrated. And this great kindness ought to move man to put a higher value on this treasure and more diligently preserve it. And if man, even with his corrupted reason, would show at least some good judgment, he would pronounce that this is beyond description and horrible to hear, that the creature is departing from the will of his Creator as expressed in His Word, that he is following other paths than those which God has revealed. And yet from the very beginning man has always done this very thing, as we shall now hear.

After God had given children to Adam and Eve, the first founders of our race, there is no doubt that they very diligently set before them the heavenly doctrine of our salvation and that they were instructed above all concerning the promise of the Seed of the woman and the coming Redeemer.[1]

Yet despite all their diligence they were not able to prevent their firstborn, who yielded to the urgings of the devil, in total contempt for God, from being the first not only to depart from the divinely taught doctrine but also to persecute and murder his own brother in satanic hatred, and finally in the exile (into which he was sent by God in order that he might come to himself) to lose all hope. What sorrow Cain in his apostasy brought to his parents! Who can describe it in words? For he brought great anguish into the church. But how much damage he did by his example when he rejected the Word of God Himself by his superficial, offhanded folly is seen in this one point to which Moses so strongly testified concerning the progeny of Adam, "Then men began to call upon the name of God" [Gen. 4:26]. And from this we understand that the worship of the true God was so adulterated and corrupted by the cursed offspring of Cain, to which doubtless many also from the posterity of Adam and Seth were added on account of the good fortune which they enjoyed, that finally in the times of Enoch, around the 300th year of the world, it was restored to its integrity and thus began to grow and flourish in the world again.

But this vigor did not last long. For within scarcely five or six generations, their posterity, whom God had chosen for Himself as sons, after leaving the true faith and the true worship of God and all godliness, threw themselves into every kind of sin to such a degree and so polluted the whole world with their crimes, that God undertook to purge the whole world by a universal flood.

We can see that by the Flood the church was purged from error and wickedness. For there remained only one man with his small family, the race reduced to eight souls, so that it might be hoped that this seed of the future church, which had witnessed the horrendous wrath of God against all ungodliness, would bring forth nothing in

---

[1] This paragraph illustrates the great dependence of Chemnitz and Leyser on Luther. Chemnitz's handling of the early history of mankind resembles that of Luther in his *Lectures on Genesis*. For example, note Amer. Ed., 1.243ff. and many other places.

God's field except pure holiness. But what happened? Scarcely had the ground dried up and men again had begun gradually to multiply, when immediately in Ham, the author of all fornication both spiritual and bodily, the third part of the human race was cut off. And a little later the posterity of Japheth was washed away and lost the true doctrine of God. And not long afterward also the family of Shem, which was the particular, holy possession of God, was nearly completely swallowed up by this new kind of piety and this flood of impiety which was worse than the previous kind, except for Melchizedek, who along with a few others held on to the pure worship of God and among the countless defections of the rest stood straight and uncorrupted. Why, because not even Abraham, the father of all believers, along with his leading people, was immune to the abomination of idolatry, but when God wanted to keep him safe, He was compelled to call him from the deep mire of idolatry [Joshua 24:2].

And almost all of these things took place while Noah was still alive, serving both as ruler and father as well as high priest. Thus how often can we imagine that the good father groaned, how often did he wet his grey beard with tears, when he saw his sons and grandsons so swiftly after the rebirth of the human race falling back into the old wickedness and vices (on account of which the world had perished in the Flood)? Think of what kind of corruptions of teaching, what cleverly devised lying vanities, the wicked progeny of the wicked Ham produced! What about the kingdom of Nimrod, what kind of morals did it have in which the king did not present himself as a king and a father as he should have done, but as a hunter of men, that is, he did not protect men as men for their true salvation, but like wild beasts he subjected them to himself on account of his desires and forced them to a godlessness by which they were made subject to eternal death![2] How did the eyes and the mind of our first parent view all these things? What words and threats did he use to condemn these things! We must believe that he in no way remained silent, as a dumb dog, in the face of these profane defections. But he accomplished less than he had hoped, sad to say. Men are indeed flesh, and by the cunning and the malice of the devil they sought vanity and loved the darkness of error more than the light of truth [John 3:19].

Yet lest the sacred seed entirely perish and the worship of God be completely done away, God Himself explicitly repeated to Abraham the heavenly doctrine, and the great diligence of himself and his family was so commendable that He gave oaths that it would be impossible for his posterity ever to lose the doctrine. But even then there was no constancy in holding to their father's religion among them, so that soon Ishmael in the time of Abraham and Esau in Isaac's time, while the patriarchs were still alive, fell away and almost completely lost the knowledge of the true God, or so obfuscated it that very few of their posterity had even a small taste of it. Likewise, the posterity of Jacob the heirs of the unique promise of blessing, in addition to the

---

[2]   Here compare Luther on Nimrod, Amer. Ed., 2.197ff.

great crimes and vices by which they offended God in incredible ways, while in Egypt fell away from the pure religion and little by little took on the idolatrous practices of the Egyptians, in which they would have perished unless under the divinely created leadership of Moses they had been delivered from them.

But now after the family of Israel, by the miraculous power of God and with stupendous miracles which exceed all human belief, had been delivered from Egypt and with the crossing of the Red Sea had come into their inheritance, who would not believe that this family would offer to their God a noted and ongoing obedience in the face of His marvelous works toward them? But they for whose deliverance God had shown such remarkable examples of His power, turned around and so clearly demonstrated their own unfaithfulness that it almost could appear that the people were in a contest to see whether God with His longsuffering and patience could prevail over them or the people with their wickedness and desire to sin would prevail over God. It would almost stupefy a person when he considers that when God with horrendous thunder and threatening lightning had with His own voice proclaimed the Law and expressly prohibited the Israelites from worshiping any other God besides Jehovah or making any graven image, yet before the passing of 40 days the same people who shortly before had promised that they would do all that God had said to them had defiled all true religion with their shameful defection in the vile worship of the calf. Who would believe that the people of God could commit so heinous a crime, if sacred history had not recorded it? Who would think that when the sound of the clarion voice of God Himself had scarcely ceased to resound in their ear they went straight on to so great a crime? What folly!

It did not stop here but went on and on. What shall I say of the repeated revolts against Moses and Aaron, the total opposition to the true religion? What shall I say of the factiousness of Korah? In brief, their hearts were never right with God. They were never found faithful to His covenant. They never made an end to their defection and their sinning, until finally in the desert all but two of them perished.

Finally, their sons came into the promised inheritance and under the leadership of Joshua occupied the land of Canaan. But here it cannot be said strongly enough how often God in leading His people repeated the signs by which He tried to cultivate in them constancy and worship. And indeed, while Joshua lived, who like a helmsman directed the course of Israel, they were sufficiently observant of the divine law. But with the death of Joshua and the older men who had known all the works which Jehovah had performed with Israel, immediately the descendents began to fall away from the Lord God of their fathers, and they followed foreign gods, the gods of the people in whose lands they were dwelling [Joshua 24:1ff., Judg. 2:7–12]. And this took place within so brief a time that scarcely 10 years passed (calculated on the basis of correct suppositions) from the time of the solemn and celebrated obligation placed on them by Joshua until their deliverance under Othniel [Judg. 3:9]. Within this space of time the people had called down the wrath of God upon themselves because of their shameful idolatry. But why waste many words describing the obvious? What does history record as the judgment against all these continuous defections? As a result of them they fell into the hands of their enemies, by whom they were compelled to endure a thousand evils. To be sure, God often had mercy on His people and, moved by their repentance and their prayers, made the state of their religion and their nation bearable, but they repeatedly troubled Him with their wicked folly. Neither did they remember the deliverance of their ancestors nor the oft-repeated punishments which were designed to chastise them, nor the present instances of punishment, nor the oft-given permission to maintain their position if only they would seek to carry out the prescriptions of the divine law from which they could obtain the renewal of their religion.

And because the origin and fount of all this capriciousness seemed to lie in the fact that there was no king in Israel and everyone did what seemed right to him in his own eyes, finally the very form of their government itself was changed, and the people of Israel established the monarchy. But soon they found themselves in trouble again. For in all the days of Saul, the Ark of the Covenant, before which alone the true worship of God was to take place, was not used. Afterward when David succeeded to the throne, for some time religion was in a strong position. But with his death Solomon, the strongest and wisest of all the kings, befouled himself and his kingdom with shameful idolatry and thus opened the way for that final schism whereby the 10 tribes were alienated from the body of the kingdom. I would have to write a whole history if I were to describe in proper detail all the turnings from light to darkness which befell each kingdom and to give honor to the glorious goodness of God in preserving the church and in repeatedly purging the saving doctrine from corruptions. But it is sufficient to touch on these matters lightly in passing. For some things must be left for the consideration of the pious and assiduous reader of the sacred Scriptures. He can note these examples of fickleness for himself in his reading.

It is certain that the kingdom of Israel very quickly totally degenerated into heathen rites. And as a result of this the nation completely departed from the family of God, except for those under Elijah, Elisha, and a few others to whom, as prophets and godly men, God from time to time granted a few rays of light. But the kingdom of Judah, although more receptive to the true religion, had a change of religion almost every time there was the death of a king. For as often as a godly king who desired to promote the true worship of God came to the end of his reign, just as often a king succeeded who was ungodly and given over to superstitions. Thus only once were there two kings in a row who loved the pure faith, namely, Asa and Jehoshaphat, but more often ungodly and idolatrous men were chosen in turn to succeed. Indeed Moses had predicted that this would happen, that having become fat and well-nourished they would rebel [Deut. 32:15]. And as a result, God's anger so burned against this people that He delivered them over to be punished through Nebuchadnezzar and to be led away into a wretched captivity. For if this constant evil of falling away and rebelling had not driven them headlong into direct opposition, this calamity would never have come upon them.

And thus the chosen people of God, earning their just punishment for their defections, were carried away into Babylon, a condition not unlike being buried in the grave. Yet after the passage of 70 years they were delivered; and this deliverance was in a sense a rebirth. After this experience, they very properly should have clung completely to God and, moved by the punishments of their ancestors, been more faithful interpreters of the divine law, more constant hearers of it, and more observant worshipers. But there was still no end of the defections. For as soon as they had returned home, they forgot the divine blessings and began to go aside into different corruptions. Some polluted themselves with profane marriages. Others neglected to participate in the rebuilding of the temple and were occupied only in building and furnishing their own homes. Others withheld the proper sacrifices from God Himself. This lack of gratitude was disgraceful, and God strongly condemned it not only through the preaching of the later prophets but also by the invasions of barbarian kings, especially when He severely punished them through Antiochus. And the purpose was that in this ebb and flow of numerous defections the church could seem to be almost destroyed and yet be miraculously and powerfully preserved by God, so that, although not only were the institutions of God destroyed and the profane rites of the gentiles brought into the temple of God, and on top of this the sacred books cast into the fire, by which the knowledge of the true God and His worship were to be completely burned out of the memory of all men—yet by the unique blessing of God the sacred seed of the church always remained in such turbulent times, and the truth of God was never entirely extinguished.

And then the time finally came which had been for so long anxiously awaited and hoped and prayed for by all the fathers, in which the Son of God Himself, the Author of all truth and goodness, the one and only Benefactor, was manifested in the flesh. Of Him the prophets had spoken long before, that "the Lord shall come to His temple . . . where He shall purify the sons of Levi, as a refiner of gold and silver" [Mal. 3:1–3], for even among the ancient people the conservation both of sound teaching as well as of true worship centered at the temple. But both of these things had been corrupted by the Pharisees and the scribes before the coming of the Messiah, partly through the traditions of the elders and partly through the popularly accepted arguments of philosophy. And thus the Messiah, after the almost countless instances of apostasy, put His own hand to work and purged His temple from the corruption of doctrine and ceremonies, reintroduced the proper understanding of the Law, brought the saving faith in the Gospel, and thus distinctly showed the correct road to salvation.

And He confirmed His teaching with such divine miracles that all the people hung on Him and the whole world seemed as if it would follow Him.

But how stable and how lasting was this fervor toward the teaching of Christ? It took only three days for the lies of the Pharisees and the priests to persuade the minds of all the people, with the exception of very few who hid themselves for fear. The people became so stirred up and alienated from the one Author of truth and peace, that they demanded the death of the cross for Him, a foul and horrible death. I couldn't believe that such folly could befall men, unless that sacred Scripture, concerning the credibility of which it is improper to have doubt, had testified to the fact. For what more shameful apostasy from the truth could be imagined or where could one find a description of it within the memory of man?

And still God offered a cure for this wickedness, and after the resurrection of Christ from the dead, even to the very people who were guilty of killing Christ, He offered through the preaching of the apostles the remission of their crime. Many with thankful mind received this forgiveness, so that Jerusalem became a kind of common fountain of salvation from which the knowledge of Him went forth to the uttermost parts of the earth. Here a person could persuade himself that a firm and perpetual base for spreading the truth could be established, after the Lord Himself took up His rule over the gentiles from the cross.

But the matter turned out quite differently. Within 40 years this very city which for so many centuries had been the home base and the mother of true teaching about God and the genuine worship of Him, was destroyed to the foundations and together with the whole region was reduced to a waste land. And the cause of this calamity is not hard to find, for it is well known to all, that Christ was held in contempt and His Gospel rejected, because the Jews could in no way endure it and tried to drive it together with His servants (ministri) from their territory, for they wanted to be vindicated. Therefore when the Jews could make no end of their defections, God imposed upon them an end to their political freedom. And so horrendously did God's wrath finally lay hold upon them, that to this day, they are scattered and dispersed throughout the world, lamenting the just punishments of the countless defections, so that they might be an example to all men by which they might learn that they must cling with stronger faith and piety to the religion revealed in the Word of God, and at the same time hold constantly to the truth which has been received in the heavenly teaching, so that they do not make themselves worthy to receive a similar punishment for their sin.

Up to this point I have shown what twists and turnings of their religion they [the Jews] permitted, not the gentiles who soon after the beginning of creation by God fell away and remained in the perpetual darkness of ignorance, but that nation who possessed the adoption and the glory, the covenant and the established law and the worship and the promises, that is, the nation which had been ordained and established

by God to be the faithful guardian of the true faith up to the time of the coming of the Messiah. Furthermore we have seen the varied waves of changes which point up the inconstancy of the human mind in the matter of religion, yet brevity of space permits us to touch upon only a tenth of the evidence. It would be trying to empty the sea if I were to try to examine or recite in order also those twists and turnings which have occurred in the world from the time when the gentile regions came to the knowledge of Christ and submitted themselves to His rule. And so, lest I be compelled to put together a complete treatise (which is unnecessary for our present purposes), I am cutting off the thread of this discussion and leave to pious minds the consideration of how the unexpected and calamitous confusions of the true religion have over and over again arisen if, when pious rulers have died off, heretics and wicked men under irreligious princes have gained power over things; when godly and faithful pastors by force and often with great shame have become fugitives from their churches and were compelled to become exiles in unknown lands. At home in the meantime the wretched and grieving flock under the violence of atrocious persecution, as under the feet of wolves, lies prostrate, so that it could seem to be near death. And since these things are sufficiently known to those who have some acquaintance with the history of the church, I shall not dwell further on them, but rather I will show to what purpose I want to direct their consideration.

It is well known throughout the Christian world how God in His unique kindness visited us in the time of our fathers, restored to us in purified form the complete body of heavenly doctrine, purged of corruptions through His faithful servant Martin Luther and his coworkers. They declared, confirmed, and spread the correct teaching with many great writings. And because the works of God are such that no human power can resist them or impede them, it happened that many thousands of people rejected the papacy and most eagerly adopted the name "Evangelical," and so the purer teaching again triumphed through the whole world. And here would it not be completely appropriate to acknowledge with grateful mind the indescribable goodness of God and to declare the gratitude of our hearts with the genuine constancy which would rather have life and all things be taken away than lose this truth? But because the minds of men are absolutely fickle and always more prone to evil than to good, partly while Luther was still alive and partly shortly after his death, it happened that sharp controversies and contention arose regarding doctrine, and many sects began and factions surfaced. Nor is this to be wondered at. For the world under the papacy had lain like an uncultivated field into which, after God through His ministers had sown the seed of the Gospel, immediately Satan sowed his tares and produced a field filled with many different kinds of errors. And he was able to do this more easily because it is well known that at that time many sought only to sink into every kind of lasciviousness in their new freedom after the yoke and fearful tyranny of the papacy had been broken.

However, there were still those who in the midst of these storms were anxious to preserve uncorrupted the sound teaching. Among these our Chemnitz held an important position, and as in his other writings he sought to use his midnight studies to produce this unique commentary on the Loci Communes, so that without acrimony and with the rejection of both ancient as well as modern errors we might possess the individual doctrines of Christian teaching pure and in all respects consistent with the Word of God. Nor was the blessing of heaven absent from this godly endeavor. For not only in this church but also elsewhere many were found who strongly confessed that if they had not been strengthened and preserved in the way of truth by the writings and treatises of Chemnitz, they would undoubtedly have been taken in by the blandishments of the sophists and misled into the bypaths of error.

But at this point another even greater benefit of God appeared. For He raised up "the shields of the earth," as He called David, and brought it about that, by the godly and providential care of those most notable princes and leaders of the empire, the Book of Christian Concord was written and published, in which all those controversies were decided and settled in keeping with the norm and prescription of the divine Word and thus peace was restored to the Christian world in keeping with the truth.

But the world does not endure harmony and truth, and with great uproar rejected this great blessing. For scarcely 10 years went by between the time of the publication of this book and its being held in contempt by many and its ignominious rejection by many others. Rejected, I say, even by those who had in their own handwriting received and approved it, and by those in places from which it had either been particularly produced for publication and in which it should have been most strongly defended over against the fanatics. What ingratitude! What detestable fickleness! Men would really have experienced how sure and blessed the truth and peace of our churches would have been, if they had been willing to keep constantly in their midst the doctrine contained in that book. For we have been concerned not only about the book or our contention for it, but it is the doctrine itself about which we are concerned and our knowledge as to the genuine truth (which can overcome all the gates of hell) which is contained in it and our hope to spread this message to our children.

Therefore when prominent and learned people began to reject this book, two kinds of men emerged. Some with boldness and insults snatched the helm as a result of this and ridiculed us as if we were cherishing some kind of a stillborn child. And with this kind of ridicule simple people were so offended that they actually thought about a defection from this book on the grounds that it was accused of being a field filled with errors. In the case of other people their faith was tottering, and they were in despair over preserving the genuine teaching in the church, and they feared that it might be driven away from sounder teaching. What then? Shall we also reject this book, so that we are not ridiculed for the inconstancy of others? God forbid! Are we not willing to lay down our life for the preservation and spreading of the doctrine *contained in that book? Rather let us fix our eyes on that clear glass which has been placed in a higher position and there we will find a remedy prepared against all temptation.*

Why this ungodly and sacrilegious defection by many from the acknowledged and subscribed truth which has taken place within these past few years? Will it bring shame upon us, since we know that this happened to the ancient world and that the present is in no way similar but is far worse? Was it shameful for Moses that Aaron and the people of Israel before 40 days had gone by after the giving of the Law, had again rejected it and followed after idolatry? Was it shameful for Christ that He was dishonored and rejected by the builders? Absolutely not, but rather the ignominy rests on the defectors themselves, and to them came the ultimate destruction. Therefore it shall be that we shall witness within the next 40 years more shameful defections than the historians of all nations and times have ever recorded. Yet their inconsistencies have not proved false the doctrine which is built upon the immovable and incontrovertible foundations of Scripture. Therefore if the Book of Concord is despised by some only because many have rejected it, for our part it is evident that they have fashioned for themselves something new, not only a new Book of Concord, but a new Gospel, a new Christ; but we desire to have no other Christ than as Scripture describes Him, nor do we desire any portion of His teaching except that which the sacred Scriptures set forth. And of Christ the Scriptures testify that He is the stone which was rejected by the builders. But because the leaders of the Jews rejected Him, shall we do the same? God forbid. For we know that He is the chosen of God and the head of the corner on whom are to be laid those who are the living stones who desire to grow into a living temple, pleasing to God. And concerning the teaching of Christ, the apostles have proclaimed that "the Spirit expressly says that in the latter times some shall depart from the faith, giving heed to seducing spirits" [1 Tim. 4:1]. And again, "In those days there were false prophets among the people, even as there shall be false teachers among you who will bring in destructive heresies, denying the Lord who bought them" [2 Peter 2:1]. And Christ Himself says, "False prophets shall arise and give signs, so as to deceive (if it were possible) even the very elect" [Matt. 24:24].

Since these things have been so clearly predicted, whom, I pray, will even a thousand defections hurt? To be sure, there will be perverse Christians who will try to repudiate that teaching which has been purged and carefully explained in the Book of Concord against the corruptions of the fanatics and against the common understanding of the Gospel on the excuse that some people have turned against this book, that is, they see that what was predicted by the prophets and apostles has been fulfilled. But what would they do if they had happened to live with Christ? Good God, how quickly they would have fled from Christ with the people of Capernaum! How they would have been horrified lest they be infected with some disease! How much differently Peter together with the Eleven acted, who, even if the whole world left Him, wanted to cling to Christ! For to whom should he go, for he recognized that Christ truly had the words of eternal life [John 6:68].

But at this point some hairy beast who is devouring the Book of Concord may growl at me, screaming: "But we deny that in the are Book of Concord contained the words of eternal life, nor do we concede that the doctrine of Christ is contained in this book, and further, those things which you have said up to this point regarding Christ and His teaching make up very little of that book." To clowns of this sort let this reply be briefly given: unless a person with clear passages of Scripture and firm lines of argument has shown the Book of Concord to be false in any of its articles, which up to this time has been attempted by godless Jesuits as well as blasphemous Calvinists, and now by that noisy Manichaean Flaccius, and a few other sophists with their flights of words, his clamors will be no more to us than the brutish buzzing of some gnats.

If someone should be irritated that I have said so much about this defection and apostasy, as if I should be subjected to criticism for it, let him get irritated, and I want to say to him that defection is indeed a shameful thing, hateful to steady minds, but yet it is such a thing as can be honorably averted, if a person desires to do so. That teaching which is handed down to us by the ministry of Luther has already for many years been judged not only as a true and saving doctrine, but also countless thousands of people with calm and constant mind have strengthened their certainty of it in their journey from the valley of tears. Therefore, why do they now so frivolously, almost the very next day, reject and repudiate it? What ingratitude to tread under their feet this inestimable treasure! When Staphylus or someone like him departs from the known truth to the papistic idolatry, everyone is indignant. Thus when Adam Neuser[3] at the beginning became an Arian, and then soon deserted to the Turks, everyone condemned him. But when entire regions open their doors to Zwinglian Calvinism (which first had admitted the Arian heresy) and then drive into exile the staunch defenders of the religion of their fathers, are we going to praise these actions as a good work?

But let us look at those who are making these statements, as to whether the number of defectors (daily on the increase) ought to move us to doubt the possibility of preserving the church in the truth. Let us look again at the glass which was set before us previously and call to our own attention that this ought to be the same solid foundation for our greatest comfort. From the very beginning has the condition of the church not always been unstable? And has not the ship for this very reason always been tossed in the stormy sea by the various waves and tempests? Yet it has never been swamped, but always with almost the whole world against it and attacking it,

---

3   Adam Neuser, d. 1576, born a Lutheran, became a Reformed pastor, defected to Socinianism, was persecuted by the Reformed in the Palatinate; fled to Constantinople and became a Moslem.

has it not escaped as from a shipwreck? And who with open eyes does not see this as a marvelous work of the miraculous providence of God Himself? "But if God be for us, who can be against us?" If the church were forever to be flourishing and the mood which flowed through the church were one of continuous peace, its joy could indeed be described with great encomiums of praise, but the great acts of salvation performed by God would then not be so clearly recognized. But because God seriously wills that the church not be understood in a human sense but as something ruled by Him and that this is His greatest work, that in the midst of its enemies, who are raging against it from the gates of hell, He gathers and preserves the church in the great weakness of the believers, and thus abandons it, as it were, to countless attacks and yet snatches it away from them. So that if He has preserved His church for so many ages against all adversities, so also may we not believe in all reverence that He will again preserve it?

Indeed, a new and beautiful treatise ought to be undertaken which would not be any briefer than the previous one, if I were willing to demonstrate fully how admirably God's providence has, among the greatest apostasies in the world, always preserved a small remnant of His people, so that from the fiercest storms and disturbances His people again might emerge. But my prefatory remarks have already dealt at length with this thought. Therefore I leave to the study of the reverent reader to meditate on this for himself by running through all the ages of the world from the beginning as to how the church of God has been protected and always prevailed in its suffering. This power of God has not been diminished, nor can anything, not even unbelief joined with impenitence, keep it from being exercised also in our age.

The voice of God is, "Hear Me, O house of Jacob and all the remnant of the house of Israel, who are carried by My bowels, who are borne up by My womb, even to your old age I am He, and even to your grey hairs will I carry you. I have made and I will bear" [Is. 46:3–4]. And now extreme old age has fallen upon the church, and all its powers seem to be declining, but we trust in God who is faithful in keeping His promises, and He will grant that we can sing with David, "Many a time have they afflicted me from my youth. May Israel now say, 'Many a time have they afflicted me from my youth, yet they have not prevailed against me.' " [Ps. 129:1–2].

At this point there is still need for the patience and confidence of the saints. For even though the church will be saved, yet in the meantime some of its members suffer and some even die. Those very members upon whom God has imposed the burden that they must remain under a mountain of persecutions shall strengthen themselves with the consolations of the divine Word and the hope of the reward which they shall have in eternal life. We are not the first whom the great indignity of defeat must consume. For we know that the same afflictions are fulfilled by our brethren who are in the world.

Holy men, and indeed holy women, the old along with the young, who labored before us in this struggle, who time after time were compelled to wander for many years through long and many paths of evils, also finally broke through and constantly preserved the profession of their faith. Their courageous struggle reflects on our weakness and should move us to remember that we must walk through this valley of tears zealous of preserving the treasure of pure doctrine and retaining our faith and a good conscience. Then, having struggled through a thousand obstacles, we "receive the end of our faith, the salvation of our souls" [1 Peter 1:9].

There remains for me, O illustrious and prudent men, the task of indicating briefly to you why the heirs and I wanted this second part of the Loci Theologici to appear before the public under your illustrious patronage. And although I could cite many reasons, both important and honorable, which I would consider as appropriate for your Excellencies and for others, yet they all involve this unique feature. We seek (to put it candidly) patrons for works of this kind who love and are anxious to preserve the memory of Chemnitz and the blessing which he brought and the kind of doctrine in which he continued steadfast up to his death. For we know and fully realize that he, as long as he lived, had his patrons in other quarters, yet nowhere did he have followers who were more attached to him and more faithful than the people in your cities. Nor is this good will going to die with him, but that it is still vigorous and enduring can be understood because of the many arguments still going on. Therefore, in order that he may be preserved even more strongly and established increasingly, the heirs of these works judge that we must work even more diligently, and they are convinced that the publication of this book will be beneficial.

His heirs remember that some of your cities used the works of their father in the difficult and sensitive negotiations concerning our religion and that these works brought significant benefits to them afterward. They also remember that their father of pious memory often praised your Saxon cities above others and that he had this one thing in his prayers, that from time to time he could for some particular reason declare his personal affection for them.

Therefore because their most excellent father, partly because he was hindered by his other activities and finally because he was prevented by death, could not complete this work, his heirs have determined to present it to you posthumously.

Wherefore, most noble lords, just as you highly regarded, honored, and gave greatest tribute to Chemnitz while he was alive, so also now when he is dead please receive with kindness and promote the writings of this man and defend them as they deserve, against the malicious attacks of malevolent and destructive men.

And for my part, I have great joy in my own role that there has been offered to me the opportunity of editing this material for your Excellencies. For I also love your cities and your churches and the close relationship with their ministers, just as I know was the case with Chemnitz while he was alive and desired to nourish them in Christ. Nor have I forgotten the great kindness with which I have been received and treated by them these past two years as I have gone in and out among them whenever I came to your cities for a visit or rather for strengthening friendship and brotherliness with your theologians. I freely confess that greater acts of kindness and hospitality have been shown to me than I could possibly describe or repay.

At this point I would be delighted to mention those things in your cities which are worthy of being seen and discovered. But because these too are more numerous than I can describe, and already so well known throughout the Christian world that they do not need my commendation, and finally above all, because your Excellencies do not seek profuse praise, I believe that I now must pass over those matters.

However, I must touch on one more matter because the honor of the true religion is involved, which is properly considered the highest among the gifts of God, and it will correctly explain what moves me to regard your churches above others. If there was any special reason why the most holy King David should love Zion, it was that the Lord was especially known there and His name was great in Jerusalem. Who will deny that that is a good reason why I myself and all good men with me should also especially love your cities? For there God is also known, and His name is also great and held in honor among you. Among human beings (as we have said previously) it is rare, from that time in which God introduced into your noble cities the Gospel of His kingdom so that He blessed your churches, that even in perilous times they have preserved inviolate the honor of the pure doctrine and now for a very long time have enjoyed happy and calm days and have many pastors and teachers, and all of them pious and faithful men among whom is a most enviable consensus. This happy state is so rare and comes to so few cities (although our Brunswick also, by the blessing of God, up to the present time has also preserved its good reputation for this quality) that it excites the minds of good men so that they may see who are pleasing to God and love, respect, and honor them. And I certainly must confess that this has happened to your cities. Hence I call upon God in my daily prayers that He would preserve this blessed situation for your cities and our city forever, that He may admonish us with kindness so that our descendants never sully or lose this reputation for steadfastness. I believe these prayers are very necessary, for we all know how hard the bald-faced[4] herd of fanatics are working to foist their entire theology upon these churches and schools. Up to this point they have been free of this poison, under the blessing of God, and we must pray most fervently that they are never infected with this cancer.

O how often I have happily reported not only the fervent discourses which I have heard from your theologians against various kinds of fanatics, but also and especially

---

4   The term "bald-faced" in Latin is *calvus*, a rather rarely used word usually meaning "bald." The way Leyser uses the term might indicate that he is pointing to Calvin, who along with other errorists is mentioned in the next paragraph.

the excellent speech which I heard delivered by the old and revered Master Andreas Puchenius, the most honorable superintendent of the church of Lübeck, a most praiseworthy man by the common consent of all the ministry. This man reported to me that he could state in all truthfulness that in the whole city and among such a large population of citizens not one person could be found whom they could even suspect of being attached to any sect, Anabaptist, Schwenkfelder, Sacramentarian, or Calvinist (as they are now called). Indeed they all held with such constancy to that old and once-for-all received Augsburg Confession, that when any people came from outside who adhered to another kind of doctrine, and they were noted or noticed, they compelled them to flee and turned them away. A piety worthy of praise and emulation!

Irenaeus gave this kind of report concerning the ancient race of the Germans, that they fled and closed their ears lest any people come to them who were trying to impose upon them any other doctrine than that which they had received (he spoke this way of the Creed as embracing the sum and substance of our faith) from the apostles. And would that the same could be stated regarding other populous cities! For in almost all of those cities which are given over to trade and commerce, along with foreign merchants a foreign religion and foreign practices are brought to them. And the sneakiness of the old heretics is so great that the guardians of the truth must possess watchful eyes, so that the people are not caught by stealth or against their will and their minds are taken over. But since this serpentine evil moves secretly, the provident and dutiful concern of the magistrates merits our praise in that it brings help to the ministers of the Word through their sound pronouncements and helps to suppress the lust of proud minds, so that they do not rudely disturb the churches which have been so correctly established in the faith and so that heresies and false teachings do not dare return. It goes badly here for those servants of Beelzebub who seek permission to believe whatever they wish and to persuade others of the same. But because such license, by which a confusion of religion is drawn into the church, is in no way approved by God, therefore the Christian ruler rightly uses the law by which he has been established as guardian of both tables, and he is earnestly concerned that truth and public peace be preserved in the churches. And what was carefully done in your cities was rightly appreciated and honored by all good men. And as I mentioned above, this also moved me to work most harmoniously with the ministers of your churches, and as we publicly professed in our subscription to the Book of Concord, I still desire to hold with them most firmly to this doctrine.

Please accept my love toward your cities and hear the appeal which I am bringing to you and the ministers of your churches. Perhaps from our mutual cooperation some good can come to the church of God. And nothing but good can come from this, at least no new evil will arise to create further divisions among the professors. What will happen to the church if we do not stand firm in that alliance which our fathers so faithfully preserved and if we do not publicly confess that we will continue to support the Book of Concord? In part the church has been deprived of some very outstanding men who are greatly deserving of our gratitude, as, sad to say, has happened recently to the celebrated theologian Dr. Simon Paulus, whose name was noted for his great zeal and constancy. In part some faithful pastors have been ruthlessly driven from their office in many places by godless wolves; in part the Epicurean contempt for the pure Gospel has been gradually and destructively growing among the people. To these evils are added a thousand injuries by which the vigor and eagerness in the faithful preachers of the Word has been blunted, together with the hatred and insults of those who have been lukewarm in defense of the truth and who should have been with us as our energetic and watchful comrades. It certainly seems that these evils will destroy the church, for humanly speaking, there is no protection against them. And thus we must seek comfort in the mutual conviction of our minds and affirm and strengthen one another through earnest exhortations until we arrive safe and happy at the harbor of our eternal homeland, free of all the dangers from the raging sea. At the same time let us implore God with our earnest prayers that the great and courageous Michael would fight for us and protect our little ship against the storms created by our adversaries and the reefs of our defectors, and that we may finally enter into our eternal home with songs of thanksgiving.

May Our Lord Jesus Christ see to it that your cities, most noble lords and fathers of your states, may abound in every spiritual blessing. May there be sweet concord among you and us, both teachers and learners. May He adorn our rulers with the Spirit of wisdom and righteousness. May He preserve the pious progress of our schools. May He not permit godless doctrine or our peace to be disturbed by arms, a peace which He Himself can bestow upon us. May there be "peace within your walls and prosperity within your palaces" [Ps. 122:7]. May mercy and truth come upon you and "righteousness and peace kiss you" [Ps. 85:10], May "truth spring forth from the earth and righteousness look down from heaven" [Ps. 85:11]. May the Lord strengthen the bolts of your doors and bless your sons forever. Amen.

Written at Brunswick in the month of August, in the year of our Lord 1591.

[POEM IN PRAISE OF POLYCARP LEYSER]

To the reverend and notable gentleman, Master Polycarp Leyser, doctor of sacred theology and most worthy superintendent of the church of Brunswick, a man worthy of the honor of his brothers.

You, dear brother, with the greatest possible effort have continued to publish the revered writings of Chemnitz, treasures which are of greater value than silver or gold, which the whole world does not possess. You are lamenting the fate of the Word of God and the lot of pious men who were well deserving of honor both from the church and even God Himself. This [work] should certainly be celebrated among the saints for the sake of the world which has this treasure from the beginning of time. But the fact is that if anyone has sown the godly seeds of the divine Word and has been a guardian of the true religion, him the great men of the world receive with harsh ridicule; he receives as his sole reward hatred and envy. Why marvel if in this age of ours there is this same lack of gratitude toward those men who are now so well-deserving for their piety? How much does all of Germany owe for his great achievements to the great Luther, who restored the true religion? What thanks was shown and what was given to this great man? They besmirched his name, they befouled the writings of Luther, O that ungrateful mob of men, utterly wicked! Who will deny that Chemnitz has defended the Holy Scriptures of the prophets, given by the voice of God, and that in his simple and direct way showed their true meaning and did it with great ability? What does the ungrateful world do? What rewards does the accursed mob give to so great a man for his merits? Reluctantly his enemies marvel at the gifts which God bestowed upon him and honor his genius and his learning. What about us? We forget him, one and all, utterly unconcerned about the brilliant writings of such a great man. There are those who have a great desire to gnaw away with their nasty tongues at innocent men whom death has taken from this world, lying men who shamefully damage the reputation of others who deserve so much from the world. But you, Brother Polycarp, are now reintroducing, after the death of your predecessor, his works posthumously, and for this action posterity owes you great thanks from wise men. And if the present world does not bestow this thanks upon you, someday God Himself in the heavenly mansions will do so. Therefore, my honorable brother, continue zealously, may many writings of the sainted Chemnitz follow, as monuments to an old man.

Melchior Neofanius,
Pastor of St. Peter's Church, Brunswick

LOCUS [VIII]

The Divine Law

[MELANCHTHON'S TEXT]

The Law is a teaching given by God, which directs what we are to be like, what we are to do, what we must omit. The Law requires perfect obedience toward God. It pronounces that God is angry and punishes with eternal death those who do not present perfect obedience. This definition is taken from the law of God itself and from many statements of Christ. The Law contains precepts and promises to which are added the condition of complete fulfillment of the Law. Likewise, the threats. Precepts are spoken regarding complete obedience: "You shall love the Lord your God with all your heart, with all your mind, and with all your strength," Deut. 6:5. Likewise, "You shall love your neighbor as yourself," Lev. 19:18. Again, "You shall not covet," Ex. 20:17. And the warning says, "Cursed is he who does not abide by the words of the Law to do them," Deut. 27:26. Again Christ says in Matt. 25:41, "Depart from Me, you cursed, into everlasting fire."

First it is necessary to give this warning, that there is a great and immeasurable difference between human law and divine law. But just as the people could not see the shining face of Moses and looked at him behind a veil, so the minds and eyes of all men see the law of God from a distance. Nor do they understand what the nature of the judgment is, but they universally think that the teaching pertains to outward works in the same way that they consider the precepts of Phoclydes or Theognis. But there are more reasons for giving and revealing the divine law than this, as shall be mentioned later. Thus we should not regard the law of God as the Decemvirales tables of the Romans, which perished many centuries before, along with their legal system and their courts. But the law of God is an eternal and immovable rule of the divine mind and a judgment against sin, a judgment impressed on human minds, often proclaimed by the voice of God, of which Christ says, "I have not come to destroy the Law, but to fulfill it" [Matt. 5:17].

Therefore we must consider the difference. Human law only demands or forbids external works. Philosophy sometimes teaches that more is required, such as that the action be an honorable one and not merely external or simulated, but an upright judgment in the mind and in the will a free choice or decision for acting correctly. Therefore the Law demands a certain prudence or moderation of the emotions and the actions, which is properly called "ethics." But this law does not accuse our natural uncleanness, nor does it pronounce judgment on all the sins which are in conflict with the First Table—the doubting of God, the heart which lacks fear and love for God, our weakness of faith, and evils like this which cling in our nature.

But the law of God not only requires outward action or that love which comes from bridled emotions, of which the philosophers speak, but it commands that our nature obey God perfectly, have an unshaken knowledge of God, true or constant fear of Him, firm trust in God, and a burning love for Him. But because the nature of man is not such, the voice of the Law is the judgment of God, condemning the sin in our nature. Paul is expressing this concept when he says, "The Law is spiritual" [Rom. 7:14], that is, it is not only a civil wisdom giving commandments concerning our outward actions in our life in society, but it is a far different teaching, which demands spiritual actions, strong knowledge concerning God, a burning and perfect love, as the Law says, "You shall love the Lord your God with all your heart" [Deut. 6:5].

But the monks speak of the law of God as they do of civil righteousness; they say that the law of God is satisfied through this civil or philosophical training, that is, through outward works and whatever the will attempts to do, even though in the mind doubts remain and in the will and heart many evil inclinations still exist. And they taught that these doubts and corrupt desires are not sins.

Therefore they imagine that men are righteous and pleasing to God because of the works which they think satisfy the law of God; they have not taught that men are righteous in the sense of having been reconciled to God and pleasing to Him by faith for the sake of our Mediator, Christ. But Paul refutes these pharisaic errors and affirms that this weak nature of man cannot satisfy the law of God nor placate the wrath of God nor take away sin through the works of the Law. But he affirms that the Son of God, our Lord Jesus Christ, has been sent to take away our sins and give us righteousness and eternal life, as we shall discuss more fully under the proper locus.

[A.] THE LAW OF GOD

First of all, let the sequence and order of the loci be considered. For since sin is *anomia*, that is, whatever is in conflict with the law of God, it is necessary that those loci concerning the Law and sin be very closely joined together. For it is useless to deal with the doctrine of sin, nor can we understand what sin is, unless it is shown that what is not in conformity with the rule of righteousness in the mind of God is sin. Also concerning free choice, there are too many philosophical arguments in the church where the doctrine of the Law is not involved as the true object of human efforts.

Furthermore, this doctrine precedes the locus on justification if we follow the best and most necessary order. For the Gospel consists in the proclamation of the merits and benefits of the Son of God, but these are defined in terms of the fulfillment of the righteousness of the Law and deliverance from the curse of the Law. What, therefore, does a person understand in the article of justification who has not learned and seriously considered with what great severity the Law acts and what perfect obedience it demands of all and what the curse of the Law is? For there is absolutely no way that a person can understand how great the work of the Mediator is unless he learns from the law to what kind of obedience and to what kind of punishment all of us are obligated. And the free imputation cannot be correctly understood unless the Law first shows the inability of the flesh, Rom. 8:3. Thus we are rather cold in our consideration of the benefits of the Son of God because we do not carefully or seriously learn the Law.

Nor must this order, that the doctrine of the Law precede, be preserved merely in teaching, but also in serious exercises of piety. For unless the stony heart is first broken and brought low by the hammer of the Law, Jer. 23:29, it is not able to receive the teaching of the Gospel, but new wine is simply being poured into old bottles, Matt. 9:17. And Paul says earnestly, "that the promise of grace might be given to those who believe, it is necessary that through Scripture all things should first be confined under sin," Gal. 3:22. Therefore when we feel either Epicurean indifference or pharisaic pride in regard to the doctrine of justification, we must go back to the doctrine of the Law.

But we shall call careful attention to the value and importance of this doctrine at the end of this locus. But now I have only shown in a brief way why and how this doctrine of Law should precede the article of justification. For unless this order is preserved both in our teaching and our practice of repentance, our minds are rendered either Epicurean or pharisaic. Further, in order that the treatment of the doctrine of the Law may be simpler, we shall divide the subject into certain main points.

CHAPTER I: THE WORD "LAW" OR THE DEFINITION OF THE TERM

Because the term "law" is used in different senses in Scripture, we need to gather the principal meanings which the word has in Scripture and establish what the term "law" means in this locus. This concern pertains not only to the grammar but is useful and necessary for the substance of the matter also. For this equivocation in the meaning of the term "law" has produced many significant and pernicious errors.

The monks changed the doctrine of the Gospel into law, because the Gospel is called "the law of the Spirit of life," Rom. 8:2; and they imagined that the Gospel differed in no way from the law of Moses, except that it gave precepts which demanded greater perfection and were more arduous to obey.

The Anabaptists, because the whole of Scripture of the Old Testament is called the Law, dreamed up the notion that the patriarchs believed nothing about the Gospel or the promises of eternal life, but had only external and physical promises such as fattened pigs, because they are said to have been "in the Law," Rom. 3:19, and "under the Law," Gal. 4:5.

The Antinomians, because in Matt. 11:13 it says that "the Law was until John," contend that the teaching of the Decalog has no place under the new covenant.

The Libertines say that believers "are not under the Law," Gal. 5:18, and therefore they have the idea that believers ought not learn from the Law concerning the good works in which they should walk, but rather let each do as the Spirit suggests to him (as they figure it for themselves).

These controversies are important matters, for they have arisen concerning things which are in themselves important. The principle meanings of the word "law" can be divided into the following categories:

I

In a general sense. In Paul the term is used with reference to a moving, impelling force or impetus or efficacy as, "the law of sin," Rom. 7:25; "the law in my members," Rom. 7:23; "the law of death," and "the law of the Spirit of life," Rom. 8:2.

II

There is also the general meaning, when under the term "law" is understood the teaching which has been universally revealed, as in Ps. 19:8, 9 and Psalm 119, where the Law is said to comfort and make happy the heart. Isaiah speaks this way of the Gospel in 2:3, "The Law comes from Zion." Rom. 8:2, "The law of the Spirit of life"; Rom. 3:27, "The law of faith"; Gal. 2:19, "Therefore I through the Law am dead to the Law." There is also the Hebrew expression in which the Law (thōrah) has its name from establishing and teaching. Thus Paul speaks of "the law of works" and "the law of faith," Rom. 3:27.

III

Often the term "law" is used to describe the sacred books in which the Christian doctrine is set forth under the old covenant; and sometimes indeed for all the books of the Old Testament. Thus John 10:34, based on Ps. 82:6, uses the word "law" in a comprehensive manner, "It is written in your law 'I said you are gods.'" And again John 15:25, citing Ps. 35:19, "It is written in the Law, 'They hated me without a cause,'" and in 1 Cor. 14:21 Paul cites the statement from Is. 28:11–12, "For in the Law it is written . . ." Sometimes the term is used for the books of Moses and distinguished from the prophets and the psalms, cf. Luke 24:44; Rom. 3:21; Matt. 7:12. In Gal. 4:21ff. the book of Genesis is called the Law. And the Jews popularly called the books of Moses the Torah or the Law. Sometimes this term seems to be understood of those books of Moses in which the Law is described, Luke 10:26ff., cf. Matt. 22:36ff., "What is the first commandment in the Law, what is written?" For if Genesis is included, the first commandment would be either that which was given in Paradise concerning the forbidden tree, or that command which was given in regard to circumcision, cf. Gal. 3:10; Acts 7:53.

IV

The term "law" is used with reference to the old covenant inasfar as it is opposed to the new covenant, signifying the entire form of the political life and the establishment of the priesthood which God through Moses had instituted for the people of Israel. Thus in the entire Epistle to the Hebrews [this use of the Law is evident, especially in] 7:12, where it points out that "With the changing of the priesthood it was also necessary that the Law be changed." Again in 10:1, "The Law having a shadow of the things to come . . ." Matt. 11:13, "The Law and the prophets prophesied until John." On the basis of this usage the term "law" refers to ceremonies, as in Luke 2:22, "The days of her purifying according to the Law," and sometimes to judicial matters, as in John 19:7, "We have a law according to which He must die," cf. Acts 23:3.

V

The term "law" is used in opposition to "Gospel" or "faith," referring to the teaching of the Decalog which prescribed works to be done, Rom. 10:4–6, in whatever books there are, whether Old Testament or New Testament.

VI

The term "law" is used in opposition to grace, referring to the reign of the Law which is correctly said to consist in these three things: (1) The Law gives its approval to no obedience except that which is pure, perfect, and perpetual. And it rejects and condemns all obedience to which clings any filth, imperfection, or omission, in keeping with the statement, "He who falls in one point is guilty of all," James 2:10. (2) The law promises life and salvation to no one except upon the condition of perfect fulfillment. (3) The Law subjects to condemnation all whom it can accuse of any weakness, without any mitigation or gentleness. Thus Gal. 5:18, "If you are led by the Spirit, you are not under the Law." Rom. 6:14–16, "You are not under the Law but under grace." Here Paul is clearly saying that the term "law" does not mean obedience, but rather the strength of the curse: "Shall we sin because we are not under the law but under grace? God forbid! Do you not know that to whom you yield yourselves as servants to obedience, his servants you are whom you obey, whether sin unto death or obedience unto righteousness?" From these passages the definition of the term "law" can easily be established. For the term "law" is used in this passage principally under the last two categories, namely with reference to the Decalog and the power of the curse. And many serious controversies can be settled by the use of this distinction.

Furthermore, to the definition of the term pertains also the collecting of the various terms which in Scripture are attributed to the one and the same subject. For the Holy Spirit is accustomed to describe the same thing by different names so that the nature of the matter can be better understood. Thus in the names for the Decalog this point is of particular interest: that when there is a comparison of Law and Gospel, especially under the article of justification, then Paul attributes demeaning names to the Law, as Luther shows. For he calls it a "schoolmaster and something that imprisons us," Gal. 3:23–24; "the yoke of servitude," Gal. 5:1; "the power of sin," 1 Cor 15:56; "the working of wrath and death," Rom. 4:15 and 7:5; "the weak and poverty-stricken elements of the world," Gal. 4:9; "the ministration of death and condemnation, the letter which kills," 2 Cor. 3:6–7, 9; "the handwriting against us," Col. 2:14; "the covenant giving birth in bondage," Gal. 4:24; "the unbearable yoke," Acts 15:10.

The doctrine of the Decalog has these terms applied to it in comparison with the Gospel (as Paul clearly says in 2 Cor. 3:16), in part because of the excelling glory of the new covenant. But when this law in itself is considered as a doctrine given by God, then it has the most wonderful names, as in Rom. 7:12, "The Law is holy, and the commandment is holy and good." In Acts 7:38 Stephen calls the Law "the living Word," in the same way that Paul speaks in Rom. 7:10, "The commandment which was given to produce life was found to be for me unto death."

Also there are some especially beautiful terms applied to the Law in Psalms 119 and 19, but concerning the doctrine and the applicability of these passages there was no agreement among the learned Hebrews, because the rabbis were confused even in regard to Scripture. They counted 613 precepts and did not want the whole doctrine of the Law to be described under all these different names. They said that there were peculiar names for certain commandments, such as *chuqīm*, the explanation for which could be called *piqūdīm*, but which arose and was demonstrated from natural justice. Thus they referred *chuqīm* to matters of ceremony and *mishpātīm* to judicial matters.

I am not going to make my point of dispute only an argument of grammarians, but simply accept this: The Holy Spirit attributes to the Law many names in order that He may show us more clearly the nature and duties of the Law. Therefore if these terms in the psalms are applied in this way—that certain terms refer to the definition and certain ones to the division and certain ones to the duties of the Law—then there is no danger concerning grammar. It will be productive to consider how the Holy Spirit has involved the whole doctrine of the Law in these simple words. Therefore I shall review, as they stand, the expressions used in Psalm 119, because the Greek words which correspond to the Hebrew have been taken over from the LXX into the New Testament and thus can be correctly understood from their sources.

[dābār], *logia*, *logos* (the oracles, words, or word of God). These terms refer to His revelation and pronouncement; they show that God Himself is the author of the Law and that it is not the uncertain opinion of men. Thus Stephen in Acts 7:38 uses *logos*, and Rom. 3:2 uses *"logia* of God."

thorāh, *nomos* (law). The rationale for this name is that just as rain is prepared in the clouds and showered down so that it soaks and gives fertility to the earth, so God gives the teaching of the Law, not that He may hide it in books, but that by teaching He may sow it abroad and write it in our hearts, "so that one shall have and obey it" (*Dass mans haben und treiben soll*).

ʿēdūth, *martyrion* (witness). For just as witnesses by their testimony make something known and certain, to a judge and jury, that was unknown and in doubt, to a judge and jury, so God by sure and clear testimonies has revealed His will, which was partly unknown and partly received with weak assent in our hearts. This term is applied in a general way to the Word of God. Hence the apostles often call the Gospel a witness. The word "testimony" is used because it convinces the conscience. Thus in Rom. 2:15, "Their conscience bearing witness to them and their thoughts accusing or excusing them. . . ." Thus Matt. 24:14 and Mark 13:9 speak of a "testimony to them" because they do not have an excuse.

piqūd. The rabbis took the etymology of this word from the concept of depositing something, that God in writing the natural law had deposited it, as it were, in the heart of man. Some of them interpret it as a commission or a command, something which God requires. For the word *pāqad* means both to commit to a course of action or to command something, thus to require it through a visitation, that is, to demand an account. The LXX renders it by *entolē* (an order), or *epitagē* (a command). Related to this is the word *mitswāh* (a command), which binds one to observe it. The LXX likewise translates this with *entolē*. Therefore these two terms mean that the law binds men.

tsedek, *dikaiosynē*, and *dikaiōma* (righteousness and requirement). For the Law is the rule of righteousness in God. Other good works are not to be sought, because the quintessence of righteousness is prescribed in the Law. And therefore it is called the "law," because it prescribes this kind of righteousness: "He who does the Law shall live in it," Deut. 8:1.

mishpātīm, krimata (judgments). Because the Law is the perpetual judgment of God condemning sins and crushing them with His eternal wrath, those who do not conform to it are judged by the statement in Deut. 27:26, "Cursed is everyone who does not continue in all the works of the Law."

bᵉrith, Jer. 31:31–33, *diathēkē* (covenant, treaty, testament), because in the Law God makes peace with His people and the Law contains promises with conditions attached.

derek (the way), because the Law is a guide for our path, showing the good works in which we ought to walk.

chuqōth. The LXX translates this with *dikaiōmata*, referring to ceremonies which have been established by God, which represent something. Those who were learned in Hebrew customs observed that when these two terms the "ceremonies" and "judgments" are joined together, the first refers to the ceremonial laws and the second to the civil laws.

Thus Heb. 9:1 uses the word *dikaiōmata*, and adds the word *latreia* for the sake of explanation, i.e., "regulations for worship." In the New Testament this term is generally used for the regulations which God prescribed in His law, Rom. 8:4; and the LXX also translates *tsedek* by the word *dikaiōma*.

I have called to your attention this list of names for the Law for two special reasons: (1) That the words which are taken over from the usage of the LXX into the New Testament may be more carefully considered and so that the etymological reason can be better understood by going back to the sources themselves. (2) Because by using these different terms the entire definition of the law is given by looking at its various parts, as it were, and a beneficial application is made to the individual parts of the definition. And there ought to be this kind of observation regarding those terms which the Holy Spirit willed to use in His own language.

CHAPTER II: DEFINITION OF THE LAW

In the definition of the Law it is not asked what the Law is in a general sense, nor what is human law or natural law. But the proper question is this: What does the word "law" mean in this locus, that is, what is the moral law?

Many definitions of the Law have been given, some of them imperfect, some improper, because those who wrote them were speaking only of the Law in a general sense.

We have cited from Augustine, *De Lib. Arb.* [1.6.15, MPL 32.1229], this definition: "The Law is the eternal, highest reason, which must always be observed, on account of which those who are evil deserve an evil life and those who are good a good life." Again [ibid.], "The Law is a supernatural measure and rule governing the actions of men in order that they may come to eternal blessedness."

Thomas Aquinas says, "The Law is the measure and the rule, directing what must be done. It is a particular direction to our reason for the common good, promulgated by Him who has care for the community of men."[1] Again [ibid.], "The eternal law is the eternal concept of divine wisdom, according to which the Law has been ordained for the governance of things foreknown by Him." Again [ibid.], "It is the reasoning of divine wisdom, according to that which is the directing force of all actions and emotions."

The philosophers can also develop such definitions of the law. For Cicero, *De Legibus* 1 [6.18; cf. 2.48] says, "The law is the highest reasoning implanted in nature, which commands the things which ought to be done and prohibits the contrary. The same reasoning, when it is confirmed and takes place in the mind of man, is law." Again in *De Legibus* 2 [48.78], "The law is neither concocted by the genius of men, nor is it some decree of the people, but it is something eternal which governs the whole world by the wisdom of commanding and forbidding." *De Natura Deorum* [2.31.78], "The law is the commanding of that which is right and the rejection of what is evil."

Varinus also cites this kind of definition of the philosophers: "The law is the word asserting the things which must be done and prohibiting what must not be done."

Likewise, there are those, who have not advanced far beyond the definition of the philosophers, who say that the Law has these aspects: (1) to command; (2) to oppose; (3) to permit; (4) to grant rewards; (5) to punish.

But because only the church has the full teaching of the Law, we must construct a definition of "law" which is suitable for the church, that is, one which will more fully explain and show the meaning, work, and use of the moral law than the philosophic definitions do and particularly include those things which in the teaching of the Law are unknown to human reason. Now, there are two definitions given by Philipp: one in his *Loci* and the other in the *Examination of the Ordinands*, which if they are compared with each other will show how his later thoughts were wiser, that is, his treatment of the same matter was very careful and diligent. He teaches many things and shows many points which were not evident in the first study of the subject, especially how the many parts could be more carefully described.

Early definition: "The law of God is the teaching given by God which prescribes what we are to be and what we are to do and not do, requiring perfect

---

[1]   *Summa* 1a2ae90.1ff. These citations from Thomas are all part of a very long definition, stretching over many pages. The citations here are only a small part of the total. See Blackfriars Ed., Vol. 29, s.v.

obedience toward God and pronouncing that God is angry and punishes with eternal death those who do not present perfect obedience."

Later definition: "The moral law is the eternal and unmovable wisdom of God and the rule of righteousness in Him distinguishing right from wrong, revealed to men at creation and afterward often repeated and explained by the divine voice, so that we may know that God exists, what He is like, that He binds all rational creatures and demands that they conform to God, and destroys all who do not conform to God unless there be forgiveness and reconciliation with God for the sake of His Son the Mediator."

We should note the difference between these two definitions. (1) "The teaching given by God" distinguishes the Decalog from human laws. But because the ceremonial and civil laws have also been given by God, under the second definition, it is more explicitly called "eternal and unmovable." (2) We should not have the notion that the Law was first given on Mt. Sinai, as if before Moses there had been no Law, but it is said to be first "revealed in creation" and "often repeated," namely on Mt. Sinai, and in a third way, "explained," not only in the Decalog but wherever it is found in the prophetic and apostolic Scriptures. (3) What is said in the later definition, "distinguishing right from wrong," is said more clearly in the first definition, "what we are to be and what we are to do and not do" and that it "requires perfect obedience." This constitutes the particular and principal difference between the philosophic and churchly definitions, namely that the divine law speaks not only of actions, whether external or internal, but also of our nature and the corruption of all our powers and of uprightness. Likewise, that the Law requires perfect and unending obedience; it is not the kind of obedience which this nature of ours can present. (4) The words are added in the later definition, "unless there be forgiveness." For the Law in its true use must be defined as "a schoolmaster" to bring us to Christ, "For Scripture has imprisoned all under sin, so that the promise of grace might be given to those who believe," Gal. 3:22–24. How the Law is a universal judge is explained more clearly in the definition of the *Examination*, which indicates that even the angels were bound to obedience to the Law and were also punished because of their stubborn disobedience against that ordinance of the righteousness in God.

Furthermore, we must note from which testimonies of Scripture the definition in the *Loci* has been developed and explained. But this question is not to be passed over lightly: Since the Law puts before us both promises of life and threats of death, why is only the one part included in the definition?

Some criticize this definition as being unsatisfactory and they believe that we must add the words, "promising (and also bestowing) eternal life to those who observe the Law." But my judgment is that only with very serious reasoning should this definition be so stated. A consideration of this point may be helpful.

The Law given by God should be considered in two ways, either in itself, as in Deut. 11:26 and 30:19, "I have set before you life and death, a blessing and a curse"; or as it is referred to our nature corrupted and weakened by sin, as in Rom. 7:10, "The commandment which was ordained unto life has been found for me to be unto death." In this context Paul is not speaking in terms of distinctions. The Law works either mercy or wrath. Those who are of the works of the Law are under either a blessing or a curse. Likewise, he does not call it the ministration of life and of death, nor does he say that the knowledge of righteousness is from the Law, that is, over against God and sin, but he simply says that "the Law works wrath," Rom. 4:15. See 2 Cor. 3:7; Gal. 3:10, 21; Rom. 3:20. Thus it is correct that the Law is defined not according to its own capability but in such a way that it is related to this corrupt nature of ours, and when that point regarding righteousness and the promise of eternal life is added in the definition, then we must also posit this: The Law, to be sure, promises eternal life, but under the condition of perfect fulfillment; yet because no human being in this life can produce it, the Law as a universal judge accuses and condemns all.

Therefore the definition of the moral law must contain these points: (1) It is a teaching given and revealed by the voice of God. (2) It warns not only about our actions, but it speaks about our very nature itself and the corruption of all our powers. (3) It does not require only outward and imperfect and tarnished obedience, but a perfect and constant obedience, with all our powers and absolute purity. (4) No one can perfectly produce this kind of obedience in the corruption of our nature. (5) The Law, indeed, sets before us life and blessing, but because no one observes and fulfills the Law, we neither can nor ought to seek life in it. (6) Therefore the Law is properly the ministration of death, the knowledge of sin, working wrath. (7) And it is correct in the definition when mention is made of the true use of the Law, namely that it "imprisons all under sin, that the promise of grace might be given," Gal. 3:22, again, that it might show to the regenerate "those good works which God has prepared that they should walk in them," Eph. 2:10. If these points are taken together at the same time, there is no danger as to the form or terminology by which this definition is established. For the rationale is very simple, that in preparing a definition we must gather together the points which pertain to the nature of the subject to be defined.

CHAPTER III: THE PERFECT OBEDIENCE WHICH THE LAW REQUIRES, FULFILLMENT OF THE LAW

[I.] In days gone by this part of the definition was called into question by the Manichaeans, namely, that it was "a teaching given by God." For they blasphemously asserted that the doctrine of the law was given by an evil god who arose from and came from the devil. But in our day there are no controversies over the other parts of this definition.

However, there is controversy over the clause "by which He requires perfect obedience," an obedience in the proper evaluation of which there is established not only the correct meaning of the divine law but on which depends also the chief articles of the Christian doctrine, for example, justification and good works.

At all times, both in antiquity and now, the doctrine of perfect obedience which the law of God requires has been corrupted by various errors and this corruption has always brought with it great harm to the article of justification. For in the very proclamation of the Law, the people said to Moses, "We will do all the things which the Lord says," Ex. 19:8. God, in order that He might hold them to this persuasion, set forth His law in a terrifying way, so that in their fear they said, "Do not let the Lord speak to us. For if we hear His voice anymore, we shall die," Deut. 5:25. When they repeated this "Hearing it, we shall do it," God replied, "They have spoken correctly." But who was to give them this mind?

Later on the Pharisees were fully persuaded that the fulfilling of the Law was easy and possible, as is manifest from Matt. 19:20 and Luke 10:25, "All these things I have kept from my youth: what do I still lack?" In Luke 18:11–12, the Pharisee boasts in the fact that he has done much more than the law of God demands. It is notable that Christ in Matt. 5:20ff. tells those whom the corruptions of the Pharisees had misled that regarding the doctrine of perfect obedience which the law of God requires, they have devised a distinction for themselves whereby there are great commandments such as the grosser sins of murder, adultery, perjury and also certain minor ones, the committing of which does not concern God. These are minor aberrations from the law of God. But Christ in all seriousness says, "Whosoever breaks one of the least of these commandments and teaches men to do so shall be called least in the kingdom of heaven," Matt. 5:19. The expression "to break the law" which is a common Greek expression, refers not only to private violation of the Law, as used in John 7:23, but particularly also to the public abrogation by which the obligation of the Law is taken away. But Christ does not wish that this kind of washing out of the minor commandments of God be taught. For the same God who says, "Do not kill," also has said, "Do not covet." There is a plausible opinion regarding the possibility of implementing the Law. For there is an axiom of human reason which Plutarch cites in his *Solon* [20.89ff.], "The Law must be capable of fulfillment." We all know this by nature as is said in the rude verse, "God does not require man to do what is beyond his powers."

The fathers also, even before the Pelagian controversies arose, used philosophic language with considerable confidence and brought it into the church.

Roffensis[2] cites from Augustine, *De Temp. Serm.*, 6, "God cannot command any-thing which is impossible because He is just; nor will He condemn a person for that which he cannot avoid, because He is kind." This statement must be exam-ined in the light of the circumstances under which the ancients spoke rather improperly and unclearly regarding this doctrine. Since the Manichaeans taught that certain men were unredeemable, in whom no obedience to the command-ments could even be begun through the Spirit of God, this statement attributed to Jerome was used in opposition to them: "If anyone says that God has com-manded the impossible, let him be anathema." But later on the Pelagians threw up statements of this kind even to Jerome himself, as is evident in his *Epist. ad Ctesiphontem* [MPL 22.1155]. Augustine in many places tells us that the Pelagians had taken on this old axiom as an immovable and established princi-ple of the faith; that is, that God would not command what He knew could not be accomplished by man. For they gathered principally from books, which had been written against the Manichaeans, all these unclear statements and things which were incorrectly explained, as Augustine cites in his *Contra Julian.*, 1 [MPL 44.650–51], a statement from Basil the Great: "Sin can very easily be sep-arated from the will of man, so that it becomes pure in all respects and so that no sign of any evil remains." To this Augustine gives a sufficient reply to the Manichaeans: "What he says is easy is not easy for the human will but for the nature of God; and what he says ('pure in all respects') then becomes a reality, when in the next life God will be all in all."

In ancient times this dispute was corrupted in this way. In our day it is done differently. Erasmus says that God with brutal sarcasm would only be playing with the misery of men if those things which He commands in the Law can-not be fulfilled by us with perfect obedience, as if a person should promise to a lame man mountains of gold if he would walk properly, when he knows that he cannot do it. This is only a mockery. But now another subtle sophistry has been created. For they cannot deny that the Law preaches about perfect obe-dience, which in this life cannot be accomplished even by a regenerate man. This is what Augustine is demonstrating by clear testimonies of Scripture in many of his writings. Therefore they draw this distinction from Augustine, *De Litera et Spiritu*, 36 [MPL 44.243–44], "There is one perfection in this life and another in the future." Then they proceed later on to twist this statement in this way, namely, that the Law does not require that absolute and completely per-fect obedience from men in this life, because this precept pertains only to the future age. Therefore [they say] Augustine has figured that the Law demands of men no more perfect obedience than that which can be achieved in this life and

---

[2]   John Fisher (ca. 1459–1535), cf. T1, L6, FN 177.

therefore what is lacking from this absolute perfection, including the filthiness which Paul confesses still clings to his obedience, is not under the accusation of the Law in this life. Therefore, they say that regenerate men in this life can perfectly fulfill the Law in their status as pilgrims.

Eck in the Colloquy of Ratisbon was unwilling to permit the expression *obedientia inchoata* (obedience which has begun), but argued that we must say that the obedience of the regenerate is perfect in proportion to their status as pilgrims. But the argument not only deals with the terminology, but strikes at the very nerve center of papal powers, namely, that man can perfectly fulfill the commands of God: A man who walks in obedience to the commands of God has no need of the remission of sins and the intercession of a mediator; good works can be placed in opposition to the judgment and wrath of God; the Law renders worthy of eternal life those who observe it to the degree that they are pilgrims on the way. Thus speaks Asotus. Likewise: Man can do something beyond what is asked, that is, he can accomplish more and greater things than the Law demands of man in this life.

I have gone into these matters at some length in order that the true teaching on this part of the definition can be more readily understood, namely, that "the Law requires a perfect obedience and accuses all who do not present a perfect obedience." This historical summary will sharpen our awareness of how at different times and in many ways this doctrine has been corrupted, and with what danger there is to the chief articles of faith in this and how necessary it is that this doctrine be correctly and properly explained in the church. For the sake of order and teaching it will be seen that this entire doctrine can be easily divided into categories.

Passages from Scripture can be gathered which manifestly assert that the law of God requires such continuous and perfect obedience as is impossible for us to fulfill in this life, John 7:19. "Moses gave you the Law and no one of you keeps the Law." Acts 7:38–39, "Moses received the living word to give it to you, but our fathers were unwilling to obey him." Again, v. 53, "You have received the Law that was put into effect through angels, but you have not obeyed it," that is, in observing you have not observed it, and in doing it you have not done it.

Lest someone object that the Jews indeed did not obey the Law yet they could have if they had been willing to strive to do it, these passages are pertinent for they clearly speak of these matters: Acts 13:39, ". . . from all things for which you could not be justified by the law of Moses"; Acts 15:10, "A yoke which neither you nor your fathers could bear"; Rom. 8:3; Gal. 3:21; 2 Cor. 3:7; Rom. 8:7.

In addition to these testimonies of Scripture there are two very convincing demonstrations in the writings of the apostles that no one in this life can satisfy the Law with perfect obedience. The first demonstration: "The Law is spiritual but we are carnal . . . in whose flesh dwells no good thing . . . we are sold into slavery under sin," Rom. 7:14, 18, "when I will to do good, sin increases," v. 21, that is, the demonstration is shown by the corruption and depravity of all the powers in man; and when this corruption is compared to the perfect obedience which the Law demands, then it is manifest that as long as the flesh remains, no one can satisfy the law of God. The second demonstration is shown in the sending and sacrifice of the Son of God. [See] Gal. 2:21; Rom. 8:3; Matt. 5:17.

II. Not only must we preach in a general way about the impossibility of the Law, but we must add from Scripture the teaching as to how impossible the perfect fulfillment of the Law is for us in this life, namely, not in the sense that men cannot in some way present an outward compliance, (even the unregenerate), nor in the sense that in the justified and regenerate there must be no beginning of the new obedience, according to the commands of God; but in the sense that the Law is incapable because it demands a conformity not only in external actions but also inwardly. Nor is it sufficient to say to a person that the Law is satisfied by the inner endeavor of his will, but it requires love, that is, the most burning desires which come from the whole heart, the whole mind and all our powers.

Paul as the interpreter is most assuredly explaining this in Rom. 7:14, "The law is spiritual," that is, it demands such complete and perfect obedience, that there be nothing carnal or anything felt in any powers of men which either leans in another direction or draws them that way, James 1:14, or hinders the total man in any way from being spiritual and on fire with the desire of love. There must be no law of sin in our members in conflict with the law of our mind which wishes only to do good and adds nothing of evil, so that whatever the regenerate man wills under the law of God, he can perform. And Augustine, *De Perfecta Justitia*, 8 [MPL 44.301], is correct when he says, "As long as there is still some carnal concupiscence which must be held in check by continence or self-control, we do not love God with our whole heart. Only when there will be no law in our members will we love God with our whole heart." Again, he says in his learned way that the rule and measure of obedience in the affirmative precepts is, "You shall love with your whole heart"; and in the negative precepts the measure is, "You shall not covet." Since both are impossible for us in this life, it is manifest why and in what way no one can satisfy the Law [MPL 44.296–97].

This comparison will shed a great deal of light on this teaching as to what kind of obedience the laws of men require and those in which philosophy goes beyond civil laws and in which degrees the righteousness of the divine law is more excellent and more perfect. Aristotle, *Ethics*, 7.1, names three degrees: beastliness, wickedness, and lack of self-control. The first two of these levels pertain to civil laws; the third, which concerns our inner desires and actions, is the proper domain of philosophy.

III. When it is said that this weak nature of men cannot satisfy the Law, this must not be understood only of the natural powers in the unregenerate man. For Paul even after his renewal or conversion, when he is "led by the Spirit," Gal. 5:18, is now no longer a neophyte, but for over 20 years he has labored through the Spirit in putting to death his "old man," Rom. 8:13, in crucifying his flesh, Gal. 5:17, and in purging out the old leaven, 1 Cor. 5:7. Yet he brings in a lengthy lament that he is still far distant from that perfect obedience which the Law requires, Romans 7. Because of this imperfection he says, "Evil is present with me," Rom. 7:21; that he "has been sold into slavery under sin," Rom. 7:14; that he is "wretched and in the body of death," Rom. 7:24; so that he "does what he does not want to do," Gal. 5:17; "not as though I have already obtained this or were already perfect," Phil. 3:12. It is clear that this imperfection is accused by the Law of being sin, Romans 7. 1 John 1:8, "If we say that we have no sin, we deceive ourselves"; cf. Ps. 32:6; 130:3; 1 Cor. 4:3–4; Prov. 20:9.

The adversaries get around these testimonies in this way: Scripture is speaking of different works of the saints, of which some are good and satisfy the Law, and some are bad and in conflict with the Law, as David in one place spares his enemy Saul and in another place commits adultery. So that the sense is: The saints, although they satisfy the Law with some of their good works, yet sometimes fall into evil deeds which are against the Law. But Paul clearly is speaking of one and the same work which is good, "For," he says, "with the mind I serve the law of God," Rom. 7:25. Again, "I delight in the law of God according to the inner man, and with the good works evil is present, and to perform that which is good that I do not find," Rom. 7:18–22.

IV. We must also demonstrate the true use of this doctrine. We should not use the pretext that because the Law is impossible to fulfill, therefore we should excuse our carnal security, sloth, heedlessness, or assumed omission. Epicureans corrupt the doctrine by saying that no one can satisfy the law of God; therefore, let us not follow the leading of the Holy Spirit; let us not be zealous for good works; there is no need for any obedience on the part of the regenerate. But God at the very beginning has revealed this teaching in His Word and forever after it has been necessary that it always be set forth and taught in the church for these very important, correct, and necessary reasons:

First, to show where the true and perfect fulfillment of the Law is to be sought. For God is not so hapless a law-giver as men imagine and picture Him, but before "one jot or tittle in the divine law is done away, it is necessary that heaven and earth must perish," Matt. 5:18. But to those who think that they can present to the Law that perfect obedience which it requires, Paul says in Rom.

9:31, "Although they pursued the law of righteousness, they have not attained it"; Gal. 3:10, "Those who rely on the works of the Law are under the curse." Therefore we must set forth the teaching that "What was impossible for the law because it was weak through the flesh, God supplied by sending His Son in order that He might be the fulfillment of the Law for righteousness to every one who believes," Rom. 8:3. The perversions in the article of justification among the Pharisees arose primarily from the fact that when the teaching regarding the perfect fulfillment of the Law is lost, it is necessary that this understanding be fully explained in the church in order that the purity of the article of justification be preserved.

Second, because it is absolutely necessary that there be a beginning of obedience of the Law, as it says in Ezek. 36:27, "I will write My law in their hearts." We must deal with this doctrine which shows that the Law does not require only outward discipline and is not content with the kind of effort described by the philosophers. We must also teach how to begin this obedience, on what foundations to build it and where to seek it, that is, not from the natural effort of our free choice but from the Spirit of renewal. In this way and in this order faith comes first, which accepts or receives the remission of sins and offers peace and joy of conscience. As a result of this, by the same faith we receive the promise of the Spirit who creates the new man unto good works and turns our hearts to obedience: When we will be led by the Spirit, that is, follow the leading of the Spirit.

Third, this doctrine has been revealed so that we do not fall into Pharisaism when we have made a beginning of obedience; so that boasting about our good works may be excluded; so that they are not placed in opposition to the judgment and wrath of God on the grounds that they fall far short of the perfection demanded by the divine law, but that "we may always humble ourselves under the mighty hand of God," 1 Peter 5:6, and with Isaiah we may say, "All our righteousnesses are as filthy rags," Is. 64:6; and with Paul remain under the shadow of His mercy and the remission of sins, "Who shall deliver me from this body of death? I thank God through our Lord Jesus Christ," Rom. 7:24–25. This obedience is so necessary that to the Galatians who had begun under faith and later wanted to finish this course by their works, Paul says, "You have been alienated from Christ, you have fallen away from grace when you try to be justified by the Law," Gal. 5:4.

Fourth, this teaching also is useful so that we might know how and why this obedience which has been begun by the faithful is pleasing to God, that is, not in the sense that it perfectly satisfies the law of God, but because it is covered by the imputation of Christ's obedience, as the subject is dealt with under the locus on good works. Thus always when this subject is treated, we must get rid of the abuses of the Epicureans. Then we must show the purposes of the doctrine, for this is beneficial; and it is apparent that the ancients, offended by the Epicurean abuse of this doctrine, preferred to preach about the possibility of obeying the divine law but in a way contrary to Scripture. What kind of disturbance followed in the church is amply demonstrated by the Pelagian controversy. Therefore, just as we should not do evil that good may come, so false ideas must not be taught in order that wickedness and abuses may be corrected. But the correct teaching has been demonstrated and the abuses have been removed, and he who is ignorant, let him remain ignorant and "he who is filthy, let him become filthier," Rev. 22:11.

V. The correct understanding of this matter having been established and proved, it is also useful to consider with which arguments the Pelagians in the past and now more recently the papists have tried to overthrow this doctrine concerning the fulfillment of the Law. These studies of the history of this subject are of great interest to me since they show how, in the contentions against the Pelagians, more and more light began to be thrown on this doctrine and as a result it began to be explained more correctly and more expeditiously.

For at first Jerome, when objections were raised against him (e.g. for his statement, "If anyone says that God demands the impossible, let him be anathema") simply replied in his *Dialog. adv. Pel.*, Bk. 2 [MPL 23.577], "These things are impossible for our nature but possible for grace." And he understood grace only in the sense of the aid and renewal of the Holy Spirit. Also Augustine in his first argument with the Pelagians said many things like this: "Grace restores the will so that the restored will fulfills the Law."

But afterward Coelestius, the disciple of Pelagius, attacked this axiom and began to spread his [erroneous] opinion, namely, that even though by nature man cannot perfectly satisfy the Law by the power of his free choice, yet he can by the acceptance of the Spirit of renewal fulfill the Law with perfect obedience, so that he can be without sin. Because when a person satisfies the Law, when he is not guilty of breaking any commandment of God, when the Law cannot accuse him of any sin against man, then he is without sin, because sin is lawlessness or the breaking of the Law. At this point Augustine was compelled to study more carefully the testimonies of Scripture concerning this article and to teach the doctrine more carefully; that is, that even the regenerate who are led by the Holy Spirit cannot in this life arrive at that perfection which the Law requires, but that the elect will obtain it for the first time in the life to come, cf. his *De Litera et Spiritu*, 36, *Epistola 15 ad Hieron.* [MPL 44.243–44]. "Grace" is interpreted not only in the sense of the aid of the Holy Spirit, but he adds, "The grace of God forgives, even if something is minimally observed in the commandments of God."

Again, "Then the whole law is fulfilled when something is forgiven, whatever it may be."[3] He opposed a particular book of Coelestius for corruptions concerning the perfection of our righteousness under the Law in this life. He cites these testimonies from Scripture which Coelestius had wrongly opposed in support of his opinion, e.g., Deut. 18:13; Matt. 5:48; 2 Cor. 13:11; Col. 1:28; Phil. 2:15; Col. 1:22; Eph. 5:27; Ps. 15:2.

Augustine shows the correct source for the solution to this matter and deals with three ways of explaining these and similar passages:

The first way. There are certain mandates which require perfection, yet it is not a question whether it has been commanded but whether this thing which obviously has been commanded can be fulfilled in this life when the flesh lusts against the Spirit. Certain passages point out the goal toward which we are tending in our course. For we do not run properly if we do not know where we are to run. Yet the goal in this life is not reached before the course is completed. Finally, there are certain passages which speak of spiritual blessings which have been begun and certain which will be consummated in eternal life and have only begun here in this life. Thus Paul clearly says in Phil. 3:12, "Not that I have already attained or am already perfect . . . ." In Eph. 5:27 he says, ". . . that she may stand";[4] he does not say, "she stands," but "that she may stand." Thus he also says to the Colossians, 1:22, "that we may present you perfect."

The second way. Whatever imperfection and filthiness still cling to us is covered by the prayer, "Forgive us our trespasses." In this way the regenerate are said to be perfect in Christ, Col. 1:22ff., by the beginning [of righteousness] and by the imputation [of Christ's righteousness].

The third way. The words "perfect," "complete," "pure," and "blameless" mean, in the language of Scripture, that a person has a good conscience, that is, as Augustine says, a person does not have damnable crimes and does not neglect to cleanse himself of those venial sins by daily praying, "Forgive us our trespasses."

I have cited these points regarding the chief arguments of Coelestius and their refutation because the papists do not hesitate to repeat again the statements about perfection, which in the past were refuted by Augustine, in order to establish their Pelagian errors now. Therefore the correct understanding as developed by Augustine can very correctly be used in opposition to these errors.

But the papists also have certain other arguments which they hold in

---

[3] Cannot locate this quotation.

[4] There is no such construction in Eph. 5:27 or elsewhere in the NT as *ut sistat*. Perhaps Chemnitz misread *ut sit sancta*.

common with Stenckfeld[5] and other enthusiasts. Their most plausible argument is this: Scripture not only commands love from the whole heart, that is, perfect obedience, but it also gives to the regenerate in this life the witness that they have "fulfilled the Law with their whole heart." For of Josiah it is said in 2 Kings 23:25, "There was before him no king like him who turned to the Lord with all his heart and with all his soul and with all his might according to all the law of Moses"; cf. 1 Sam. 7:3; 1 Chron. 29:9; 2 Chron. 15:15; Ps. 111:1; 119:34, 69; Acts 8:37, "If you believe with your whole heart. . . ." Therefore, because the perfect obedience which the Law requires is described in the expression "with the whole heart," and because Scripture gives this witness to the regenerate in this life, then it is wrong to say that in this life no one can satisfy the Law.

Reply: The expression "with my whole heart" is used in many places in Scripture in opposition to hypocrisy and outward pretense and particularly to certain kinds of obedience. For Scripture describes this hypocrisy in this way: Ps. 12:2, "Men speak with a double heart"; In James 1:8, such a man is called "double-minded"; Is. 29:13, "They draw near to Me with their lips, but their heart is far from Me"; 1 Chron. 12:33, "They were prepared to fight—they were not of double heart," which Jerome translates *non in corde duplici*, and later on this text explains what the words "prepared to fight" mean, namely, "with a perfect heart," v. 38. Therefore it is manifest that the expression "with all your heart" or "with a perfect heart" is used in opposition to the idea of a double heart. Thus in the case of Abijam, 1 Kings 15:13, who destroyed the golden calves of Jeroboam, Scripture says, 1 Kings 15:3, "His heart was not perfect with God." If we understand the precept of the Law, "You shall love with all your heart" in the sense that the regenerate truly do love God with all their hearts, because this means nothing else than that the regenerate do not have any outward hypocrisy because of their good works, but the Holy Spirit is renewing their minds, creating a new heart and thus out of the good treasure of the heart bringing forth good works "that they might be a people zealous of good works," Titus 2:14, then Paul is the surest interpreter of the divine will, for in Romans 7 he explains this addition to the Law "with all your heart" in a very different way. For he draws his interpretation from the law, "You shall not covet or lust." And with a long lament he affirms that the Law requires not only zeal for good works but absolute spiritual obedience or obedience from the heart, as has been shown above. In this way also Augustine in many places explains the words "with all your heart," that in this life it cannot be fulfilled.

---

[5]   Kasper Schwenkfeld, 1489–1561, Silesian who first supported Luther and later broke with him and all organized churches. He is regarded as the father of the enthusiasts. Chemnitz follows Luther in calling him Stenckfeld.

1 John 5:3, "The commandments of God are not burdensome." Much less must they be called impossible.

Reply: Scripture affirms both and both are true. The commandments of God are "a yoke which no one can bear," Acts 15:10. "The flesh" (as Paul also says he himself is carnal) "cannot be subject to the law of God," Rom. 8:7. And the commandments of God are not burdensome, viewed from another aspect. For while it is impossible in this life for the commandments of God to lead to perfect obedience, as has been demonstrated above, yet on the other hand believers have absolutely perfect fulfillment of all the commandments of God from the standpoint of imputation. For Christ who has absolutely and completely fulfilled the Law is given to believers with all His righteousness. Therefore the commandments of God are not burdensome, but not because they can be perfectly fulfilled in this life by the works of the regenerate. For thus in this way a person could be without sin, which according to 1 John 1:8–10 is nothing else than to make God a liar. But it is possible in a twofold sense: (1) by the beginning of obedience, that is, because the Spirit of renewal works a willingness of this kind in the believers so that they delight in the law of God, Rom. 7:22; Ps. 1:2 and 119:14, and are "zealous of good works," Titus 2:14; (2) by imputation, that is, the commandments of God are not burdensome to the believers because they have the remission of sins applied to them. They are not under the Law but "under grace," Rom. 6:14. They are free from the demands of the Law "with their whole heart," and from the stricture that "he who offends in one point is guilty of all," James 2:10. Therefore when they confess their sins they have a ready remedy, namely, the remission of their sins from whence they can make up their deficiency, and thus in this sense the commandments of God are not burdensome for believers.

The papists argue: Deut. 32:4, "The works of God are perfect." The obedience of the regenerate is the work of the Holy Spirit. Therefore his obedience is not defective, mutilated, foul, or imperfect. For this would be an insult to God Himself, the author of good works.

Reply: The works which God performs in Himself (*per se*) are holy and perfect, and it is evident that Moses is speaking about these in Deuteronomy 32 since God is without any iniquity, He is just and righteous. But those things which the Holy Spirit works in our body of sin and death in the regenerate, these things the Spirit Himself affirms are imperfect because of our flesh which has not yet been completely destroyed, Rom. 6:6.

Nor is it blasphemy to say that the goodness of the Holy Spirit is to be admired because in this miserable and shameful body of our sin the Holy Spirit deigns to bring forth His fruit, even though His work is hindered and befouled by our flesh and often crushed and destroyed. Therefore the things which God performs in themselves are perfect, the things which are done not only in man but also in other creatures have their beginning, progress, and increase until they are finally brought to perfection. Just as a sapling which divine power produces is not immediately a perfect tree but must grow to maturity, so the works of the regenerate are perfect by (1) imputation and (2) future completion.

Stenckfeld uses this argument: All things are possible for the believer; therefore also perfect fulfillment of the Law is possible.

Reply: It is true that he, to whom the righteousness of Christ has been imputed by faith, perfectly fulfills the Law. But that is not what the fanatic is trying to say, but rather that the Law can be fulfilled by our obedience and our works. The answer to this is that for the believer, all those things which he believes according to the Word of God are possible, for there is only one proper object for our faith, that is, the revealed Word of God. For the believer it is not possible to make God a liar, because then faith would not have His Word as its object. But for the believer this is impossible because the Word of God says, Heb. 6:18, "It is impossible for God to lie." Thus the fallacies of this argument can easily be seen. For the believer all things are possible; therefore even though the Word of God says it is impossible that the Law can be perfectly fulfilled in this life by our obedience, yet for the believer it is possible. But for the believer it is actually impossible because the object of his faith must not be his imagination, but the Word of God.

Finally some statements from Augustine's book, *Contra Duas Epistolas Pelag.* 3.7 [MPL 44.602], are raised in objection, where he says that the obedience of the regenerate is perfect in the sense of our being pilgrims. He says, "We can say that a traveler has completed his journey when it has been well begun, even though his goal has not been reached, unless something prevents its completion. . . ." Again [ibid.], "According to the capacity of mortal man and in keeping with the standards of this life, we are perfect . . ." The papists immediately add: Therefore what is lacking from the perfection which the Law requires is not sin, nor do pious men need to confess that this lack of perfection is sin, but they can put up their own good works in the face of the judgment and wrath of God.

But they do a manifest injustice to Augustine, for in this very same writing he says [ibid.], "The goodness which is now in a righteous man is called perfect to this extent that both its perfection and its imperfection pertain to it, both recognition in the truth and confession in humility. For then in keeping with this weakness this poor righteousness is perfect to a degree, when it understands what it lacks. In this sense the apostle says he is perfect and imperfect." Again he says [ibid.], "The grace of God produces this zeal for keeping the commandments and the same grace forgives even if the keeping of these commandments is less than perfect." And in his *Epist. 26 to Jerome* [MPL 33.739] he clearly says,

"Because of this weakness of our imperfection, 'if we say that we do not have sin, we deceive ourselves and the truth is not in us'; and for this reason, even if we do make some progress, it is necessary for us to say, 'Forgive us our trespasses,' since, although in baptism they have all been forgiven, yet because of this weakness, 'no living being will be justified before God.'"

Thus all of these statements regarding perfection can be answered. For in this life in the saints there is some degree of good conscience (as when they offer their members as arms of righteousness and do not permit errors against the foundation or lapses against conscience) according to which they are also in Scripture called "perfect," Phil. 3:15; 1 Cor. 2:6, but not however in such a way as if in this life they owe nothing more to the Law or are perfectly satisfying it; but by the beginning of obedience and by imputation, they have through the Spirit some degree of good conscience, they recognize their own imperfection and they seek to be ruled by the imputation of Christ's obedience, and in this kind of imperfect perfection (as Jerome calls it) the saints clearly recognize their imperfection as being sin and because of this weakness of this imperfection they confess that they are miserable sinners, Romans 7. This is the *status controversiae*: Do the regenerate in this life with their own obedience perfectly fulfill the Law? I have dealt at some length with this section regarding the fulfilling of the Law since in our time a great number of controversies turn on this question; and it is useful always to have an overview of the entire summary of this doctrine before us.

CHAPTER IV: CLASSIFICATION OF THE LAWS

[MELANCHTHON'S TEXT]

First we shall review these classifications: The divine law, the natural law, and human law. Divine laws are those which have been given by God at some particular time and are found in written form in the writings of Moses and the books of the Gospel. The natural law, as I shall indicate below, is the natural knowledge of God and of the governance of our conduct, or the difference between honorable and shameful behavior, which has been divinely implanted in the human race, just as our knowledge of numbers has been divinely implanted in the minds of men. Therefore, it agrees with the part of the Law which is called the natural law, as we shall show below. For first we must distinguish the classifications of the divine law.

Although from the beginning of the world there has sounded in the church the voice of the Law and the voice of the promise of grace, yet in a certain sense when the nation of Israel was established, the law of God was promulgated, for God willed by a public and manifest testimony to set forth that knowledge which at creation He had instilled in the minds of men, so that He might show His judgment against sin. But because an entire civil structure was being established, not only were laws set forth regarding the moral conduct of individuals, but also there were added laws regarding civil matters and other ceremonies.

Thus there are three general divisions of the Mosaic law: the moral laws, the ceremonial, and the civil or judicial laws. This distinction must be carefully studied because even though the political structure established by Moses has now been destroyed, yet the distinction of the laws must be taken into consideration. The ceremonial laws of Moses and the civil laws are not commanded to the other nations, nor are they binding upon us. They were given to the people of Israel for that time in order that the political structure might continue for a definite period of time, so that there might be a specific place in which the Christ should be born and reveal Himself, be proclaimed, and become the sacrifice and openly complete the work of our eternal life.

But there is still another classification of laws which are called moral laws, which are the eternal mind and rule of God and are not changed by the passing of time. Always and from all eternity God has willed that His creatures should love and fear God and that the rational creature be pure. There are also moral laws which give commands concerning the acknowledgment of God in our hearts and our obedience toward God and concerning good works toward men, as well as concerning righteousness, chastity, truthfulness, and temperance. The moral laws have been summarized by God in a remarkable way on one small table, which is called the Decalog. It is common to call it the Decalog when we are referring to the moral law, a term which can be easily understood without any war of words. Therefore, there are moral laws and those which are contained in the Decalog, as we shall indicate below, and there are repetitions and explanations of the Decalog wherever we read them in the writings of the prophets and apostles. Since these laws are the eternal rule of the mind of God, they always sounded forth in the church, even before the time of Moses, and they shall remain in force forever and apply also to the gentiles. There are also many natural laws in the civil and ceremonial laws which also are perpetual, such as the law which prohibits incestuous practices, Leviticus 18, because the reverence for blood relationships pertains to these virtues. God has clearly said that the Canaanites should be destroyed because of their incestuous lusts. Therefore when the gentiles, even before the promulgation of the law of Moses, were condemned for this crime, it is certain that they were condemned by the eternal law of God and the judgment of nature.

CLASSIFICATION OF THE LAWS

All law is either divine or human. The divine law is either revealed by the voice of God Himself, promulgated or repeated and given to us in sacred writings, or it is divinely ingrafted into the minds of men in creation. Sirach in Ecclus. 17:6 points out this division, and most clearly of all, Paul sets it forth in Rom. 2:14–16, where he asserts that there is need for the divine law written by nature in the hearts of all men, so that there may be a witness to their conscience, that is, a judgment concerning what they have done or ought to have done, through their thoughts which either accuse or excuse them, or concerning the difference between upright and dishonorable actions. Because he adds the words "on the day when God will judge the secrets of men," he is clearly showing that the judgment of the natural law is a divine judgment.

Human laws are either civil ordinances set forth by a magistrate who has the power to establish laws which have been instituted for good reasons and for civil purposes. To such people Peter in his First Epistle 2:13 says that they are to be obeyed for the Lord's sake. Paul in Rom. 13:5 adds the idea of conscience. Or human laws are the practices or traditions which have been established by men in order that there may be the worship of God. Christ calls these "the commandments of men," Matt. 15:9, and He adds the words, "In vain do they worship Me." Paul says in Col. 2:16, "Let no one judge you."

But this locus deals only with the divine law as it is in written form. It is divided into three classifications: the moral, the ceremonial, and the civil or judicial. This division is commonly known and accepted. And yet, just as modesty befits the pious not rashly or impatiently to reject or overturn accepted distinctions which have been used in the explanation of the doctrine of the church, so this diligence befits the learned that they seek and consider with careful observation the Scriptural foundations from which these teachings are developed. For the Jews, as tenacious adversaries, will not allow this division to be used in this way. But logic compels us to admit that the divine law in general prescribes concerning the worship of God and concerning morality and determines these matters through certain external circumstances, and that this takes place either toward God in worship or toward men in the exercise and administration of morality. Thus there are certain moral laws, and certain which are ceremonial, and certain which are civil.

Furthermore, we should add the testimonies from Scripture by which this division is established. (1) Often in one and the same sentence the divine law is designated by different names. Deut. 6:1, "These are the commandments and the ceremonies and the civil laws which the Lord has commanded you." Again, v. 17, "You shall diligently keep the commandments of the Lord, and the testimonies and the ceremonies. . . ." Among the Hebrews the rule is that when "statutes and judgments" are joined together in the same place, as happens in many instances, the first is understood as applying to ceremonial laws and the second to civil laws. It is apparent that the terms "ceremonial" and "civil" laws are derived from these and similar passages. (2) God in the very act of promulgating the Law shows this very helpful distinction. For He Himself first recites the Decalog while all of the people were listening. Then Moses alone is ordered to approach the darkness where God was and there he received the civil (*iudicia*) laws to be given to the people. Then, after the giving of the civil laws (*forensium*), in Exodus 24 Moses again ascends alone into the mountain and there receives the ceremonial laws. Thus, this division is nicely demonstrated in the very order and progress of their promulgation. For this act was divided into three episodes because of the three parts of the Law. (3) In this way there is also demonstrated the different parts of the Mosaic law. Knowledge of the Decalog is commanded of all men, Deuteronomy 6. But concerning the civil law there was particularly established the Consistory of Jerusalem, the higher court before whom the people would come "if any case is too difficult for you to decide between one kind of homicide or another, between one kind of lawsuit or another, and between one kind of assault or another," Deut. 17:8. In regard to the ceremonial laws, although Malachi, in 1:7ff. speaks of them, yet in 2:7 he says, "The lips of the priest should preserve knowledge, and men should seek law from his mouth." Likewise the ark of the covenant was dedicated to protect the Decalog. But the second giving of the Law was ordered to be kept under royal control, 2 Chron. 35:3. The Book of the Law is found in the house of the Lord, 2 Kings 22:8. (4) Also from the New Testament this division can be demonstrated. For Christ who explains the moral law and commands that it be taught, Matt. 5:17ff., when someone asked Him concerning the division of his inheritance, in Luke 12:14, replies, "Who has made Me a judge?" And in Matt. 9:13 and again in 12:7 He says, "I will have mercy and not sacrifice, and obedience rather than burnt offering." Therefore there is a difference between the ceremonial and the moral laws. Likewise He does not lay upon religious people the ceremonial or civil laws, but only the Decalog, Acts 15:28, as the Jews themselves testify in their histories. See the Preface, "Ph. M. in the Acta Wormatiensia."[6]

In the second place, we are adding here definitions of the ceremonial and civil laws which we have cited in the *Examen*, which are better understood when they are divided into certain classifications. Thus a description of the ceremonial law includes these points: (1) Because the moral law on the First Table warns concerning the worship of God, we must include in a description of the differences the fact that the ceremonial laws are precepts given by God which deal with external rituals by which are governed the external actions in the sacrifices and other external practices, as for example in matters of food and clothing. (2) Then we must add a brief list of the types or parts of the ceremo-

---

[6] *Corpus Reformatorum*, 4.723–24.

nial law. I shall add here a more detailed distinction of the parts, as it has been handed down to us by the scholastic writers in a rather helpful way. For it can be a kind of commentary on the whole book of Leviticus.

Thus the ceremonial laws contain commandments regarding either sacrifices or sacred rites as to times and places, regarding such matters as the temple, the altar, the vessels, religious rituals, or such sacred practices as the Passover lamb, circumcision, washings, or concerning the observance regarding food, vestments, etc. These ceremonial laws are placed under four categories

The first category describes the differences of the sacrifices.

1. There is a difference concerning the material involved, which is called the *causa materialis*. Animals were offered or products grown from the ground. Sacrifices were made from four kinds of animals: first, from the cow family, a calf, a bull, or a heifer. Second, from the goat family, the ram or a kid. Third, from the sheep family, a lamb or a ram. Fourth, from the bird family, such as a pigeon or a turtledove. Things which are produced by the earth were offered: either dry items, such as bread baked in a pan, a bowl, or a griddle; or similar things like grain, fruit, incense, salt; or liquids such as wine and oil, Lev. 2:4ff.

2. There are differences in sacrifices regarding the purpose (*causa finalis*) for which they were offered. First, the burnt offering was burned out of reverence for the divine majesty. Second, the sin offering was offered for the forgiveness of sin. Third, a peace offering was made, which was an act of thanksgiving for a benefit received or petition for a benefit to be received.

3. Origen suggests that there is a difference based on who is making the sacrifice (*causa efficiens*), for they were offered either by the high priest (*pontifex*) or by the priests (*sacerdotes*), by the ruler or by the people as a whole or by a private person. Likewise one sacrifice was commanded to be offered for the sin of the priest, another for the sin of the ruler, another for the sin of the people, and another for the sin of a private person.

4. This kind of difference was also indicated: The burnt offering held first place because the whole animal was consumed by the fire and none of it was eaten. The sin offering held second place. This was eaten only at the entrance by the priests and on the day of the sacrifice. The peace offerings held third place in holiness and importance. They were eaten on the very day of the sacrifice but not everywhere, only in Jerusalem. The fourth level was that of the votive peace offering, which could be eaten also on the following day.

5. The difference is this: The one kind is the sacrifice of a domestic yoke animal, the other involved a matter of choice.

The second category of ceremonial laws describes the sacred places or times.

1. The tabernacle and the temple are sacred places with some differences:

(a) The tabernacle was portable, but the temple was fixed in one place. (b) God willed to be present with only the tabernacle or the temple. (c) The tabernacle or temple were divided into three parts: one, the Holy of Holies, into which once a year the high priest alone entered; the second, the holy place where the priests entered daily; the third, the porch or courtyard, the place of the people; the fourth, the site of the temple was important, for they put the Holy of Holies at the west end in order that they might worship facing toward the west. For in Ezek. 8:16, idolatry is described as when certain men in their worship "had their backs to the temple of God and their faces toward the east" [to worship the sun]; the fifth, in the inner part of the temple which they called the "Holy of Holies," there were three things: [first,] the manna, the rod of Aaron, and the tables of the Decalog; second, the two cherubim, Ex. 25:18; third, the cover of the ark, which is called the place of propitiation or mercy seat, Ex. 25:17. But in the second part of the temple which was called the holy place, there were also three things: (a) The altar of incense which was directly in front of the veil of the ark. (b) The table of showbread in the north side [Ex. 25:23ff. and 40:22–23]. (c) The candelabra in the south side [Ex. 40:24 and 25:31]. The tabernacle in addition had four coverings: (a) curtains of four colors; (b) lavender skins; (c) ram skins, Ex. 39:34, dyed red; and (d) goat hair vestments [Ex. 26:7].

2. The Levitical rites pertain to the altar. There were four aspects of this: (a) an earthen altar outside the tabernacle, Ex. 20:24; (b) a portable wooden altar under brass, Ex. 27:2; (c) a bronze altar of burnt offerings and sacrifices in the courtyard of the holy place, Ex. 40:5; (d) a golden altar of incense in the holy place of the tabernacle, Ex. 40.

3. Here are pertinent the legal holy days or festivals which are eight in number: (a) the sabbath; (b) new moons; (c) the passover; (d) Pentecost; (e) the festival of trumpets on the first day of the seventh month; (f) the festival of propitiation or the day of atonement on the tenth day of the same month; (g) the feast of tabernacles on the nineteenth day of the seventh month; (h) the feast of ingathering on the eighth day of the following month. Thus some include this festival with the preceding.

The third category involves sacred rituals (*sacramenta*), of which some pertain to the whole populace and some to the priests and Levites. Here we list the following categories:

(1) Circumcision; (2) the eating of the passover lamb; (3) the eating of the showbread; (4) purification from certain impurities; (5) expiation of sins. Included here are eight kinds of impurity: (1) one who has touched a dead person, Num. 19:13; (2) leprosy, Lev. 13:2ff.; (3) the clothing or home of a leper, Lev. 13:45ff.; 14:33ff.; (4) childbirth, Leviticus 15; (5) menstruation; (6) flow of

semen, Lev. 15:2ff.; (7) one who suffers a nocturnal pollution, Lev. 15:18; (8) a vessel not having a cover, Num. 19:15.

Furthermore, certain impurities are expiated by a sacrifice for sin and others simply by sprinkling with the water of purification, Num. 19:20.

To this kind of ceremonial laws pertain also the consecration of priests, which is described under these categories:

1. There is a separation or selection, Num. 8:6, "Take the Levites from among the people of Israel." This was first done through the sign of the flowering bush, just as in the New Testament Matthias was chosen by lot. But in the election of a priest, the whole multitude was called together, Lev. 8:3; Num. 8:9. And a man who had a blemish was prohibited from being chosen, Lev. 21:17.

[2.] They were sprinkled with water of expiation, shaved, and bathed, Num. 8:7.

[3.] They were dressed in special clothes. The vestments of the high priest were these: (1) a linen garment; (2) a blue robe with bells; (3) a coat; (4) a turban or headdress; (5) a sash; (6) a cap; (7) a golden breastplate; (8) linen breeches. But the lesser priests had only four of these items: the linen tunic, breeches, sash, and the cap.

4. Following the consecration [Ex. 29:19ff.] they were anointed with oil: the high priest on the head, Lev. 8:12, but the rest of the priests were only anointed on the hands, Lev. 21:10. Kings were anointed on the shoulders or upper arms. The Levites were not anointed but only commended to the ministry.

5. The sacrifices were offered, a heifer for sin, a ram for a burnt offering, a sheep for a peace offering, and a basket of bread. The right ear, the thumb of the right hand, and the toe of the right foot were touched with blood [Ex. 29:20].

6. They were received into the ministry. The duties of the priests were, first, to teach concerning the Law and to answer questions about it; to judge and settle controversies; Lev. 14:35; Deut. 17:9; Mal. 2:7. Second, they were to pray, Lev. 4:20; Num. 15:25. Third, to make sacrifices and offerings, Lev. 24:4. And fourth, to cleanse, Leviticus 14.

The fourth category of sacrifices concerns the different external observances or practices and some of these pertain peculiarly to the priests, such as not being contaminated by contact with the dead, Lev. 21:1, or not making their heads bald or shaving the edges of their beard, nor making any cuttings in their flesh [v. 5]. Nor were they to marry a harlot, a widow, or a divorced woman. Certain regulations pertained to the entire population with regard to food and certain prohibited animals, Deut. 14:6, and certain foods and the eating of blood, Lev. 17:12 and 19:26; the eating of fat, Lev. 3:17; the eating of an animal which dies of itself, Deut. 14:21; cf. Ex. 22:31; the eating of the sinew of the hip, Gen. 32:32. Furthermore, in Scripture there are three kinds of fat: that which covers the vital organs, the heart or the stomach; the skin around the liver; the fat of the kidneys.

To agriculture and vestments pertain Deut. 22:5, 10–11; 25:4; 22:9; Lev. 19:19; Ex. 23:19; Lev. 19:23; Deut. 22:6. I have rather copiously cited this list of only a part of the ceremonial laws in order that we might get a brief overview of it. Now let us return to the subject at hand. We have finished the first two parts of the definition.

In the third place, it is also useful to mention the purpose (*causa finalis*) of the ceremonial laws. From Scripture we note three general purposes: (1) Col. 2:17, "They are a shadow of what is to come, but the real thing is Christ Himself." Cf. Heb. 10:1; 8:5. (2) Gal. 3:24, "The Law is our guardian until Christ." (3) Heb. 10:3, "In these sacrifices there is a reminder (*eine Erinnerung*) of sin."

These general purposes then are subdivided by the scholars into the following categories:

1. They were reminders or warnings concerning sin, the wrath of God, and condemnation. For in various ways this legal uncleanness was a guardian which signified and in a sense demonstrated the uncleanness of the sin which inheres in man, in his entire nature, in all men, in individual men and the actions of men. When a person offered some animal to God to be sacrificed for his sin, this was a public confession that in the eyes of God sin was not mere child's play or a matter of indifference, but if He should wish to enter into judgment with us, we should all in this way be sacrificed by an eternal death.

2. They were reminders of the coming sacrifice of the Mediator because the death which the sinner deserved was poured out upon the animal to be sacrificed in the manner described in Lev. 16:5ff., which was in a sense a visible demonstration that it is impossible for us to free ourselves from death and condemnation, but it is necessary that there be another victim which "is wounded for our transgressions" so that by His bruising we might be healed, Is. 53:5. But this manifold variety and frequent repetition of the sacrifices signified not that sins are expiated by the blood of cattle but rather that a different and more perfect sacrifice is pointed to.

3. They were figures and shadowy descriptions of the person, the work, and the benefits of the Mediator, just as the entire tabernacle, the cleansings of the sacrifices, the odor of the incense were. For the various sacrifices were instituted in order that the manifold blessings of the Mediator might be impressed upon them by this visible instruction.

4. They were symbols of the church itself and of the spiritual union between God and the church showing the fact that the church should have access to God and how it takes place and the fact that God would communicate Himself and His blessings to the elect. Thus the incense symbolizes prayer, Ps. 51:17, "The

sacrifice to God is a broken spirit." Thus a certain part of the sacrifice was offered to God and a certain was eaten by those who offered it.

5. They were sacred acts by the godly people in which faith applies the forgiveness of sins to each individual who was making the offering. Such was the sacrifice of Abel, of Noah, and others.

6. They were works of confession of the true teaching and also exercises in obedience to God.

7. They were guardians by which the unregenerate were compelled not to imitate the idolatry of the gentiles, Deuteronomy 12.

8. They were symbols which distinguished the government of Moses from all other nations. For God willed by a very graphic difference that His people from whom the Messiah was to be born were to be conspicuously different.

9. They were bonds binding the members of this nation together, or the cords of the public unity of this people. Finally, there was also this purpose that there should be concern for the sustenance of the Levites.

In the fourth place, in the same way the definition of the civil law must include three categories: (1) Because both moral as well as judicial or civil laws are concerned with precepts concerning morals, we must make the distinction in the definition that the civil laws were given as commandments by God out of His eternal concern to defend and instruct His people in keeping with the entire Decalog. In other words, the civil law is a particularization of the general precepts of the Decalog in order to produce a certain kind of outward behavior by which the civil society might be best governed among the people of Israel. (2) There is inserted into the description a listing of the special subjects with which the civil laws of Moses deal, namely magistrates, the order of judges, contracts, property rights, inheritances, marriage rights, slavery, the order and laws pertaining to military matters, wills, punishments, blasphemy, perjury, profanation of the Sabbath and its ceremonies, treason, disobedience, murder, payment of damages; either in fines or corporal punishment for adultery and theft. That is to say, the civil law shows how all external crimes against the individual precepts of the Decalog are to be punished.

Of some help also is the division of the scholastics: Certain civil laws command, certain forbid, certain defend and certain punish. All these laws teach and demonstrate what is good and what is evil. But some permit something which in itself and by nature is not good: not that they approve of it, but for the prevention of an even greater evil, such as the law concerning divorce and the acceptance of usury from aliens, Deut. 23:19–20. We must observe that, although such things were permitted in the law of Moses in a civil way, yet they were severely criticized by the prophets on the basis of the moral law, for example, divorce, Mal. 2:14ff. In Matt. 19:8, the Pharisees are condemned because they interpreted this law as if in itself and before God divorce were a good thing. Thus also regarding usury the prophets speak without exception, e.g., Ps. 15:5, "He will not dwell in the holy mountain of God, nor will he live who gives his money to usury," cf. Ezek. 18:17. Our own Luther correctly distinguishes in this way: "Some laws are for instruction, some are for protection."

This division is still clearer: (1) Certain civil laws govern the arrangement of society: regarding slaves, Ex. 21:2ff.; Deut. 15:12; others deal with marriage, Deut. 25:5ff.; 22:13ff.; Ex. 22:16–17; Lev. 18:6ff.; Num. 5:12ff.; Deut. 7:3ff.; concerning parents and children, cf. Deut. 21:15ff. concerning a stubborn son. (2) Certain laws govern the civil aspects of society between citizens, magistrates, judges, contracts, settlement of property rights, and punishments. The punishments were either capital or payment of damages, either "an eye for an eye" (*lex talionis*), or some shameful punishment such as prison, or whipping, or slavery for a thief, Ex. 22:3, or exile for murderers. However, "They shall not be left outside the land of promise lest they fall into idolatry," Num. 35:6ff. (3) Certain laws speak of external matters, such as military regulations and foreigners, Ex. 23:9. Those who were to be denied honors in public offices in the state, Deut. 23:2, 8, were not, however, put out of the country nor prohibited from the public worship of God, Ex. 12:45ff. In regard to eunuchs, Is. 56:4–5, the law was dispensed with in the case of Achior, Judith 6:18, Ruth 4.

In this description we must also mention that the purpose of the civil law had been set by God: (1) in keeping with the conditions of the place, the time, and His people; (2) in order that there might be a clear distinction between the Mosaic civil state where the Messiah was to be born and all other nations.

But from these principles many points can be correctly dealt with and decided, e.g., how and to what extent in the civil laws certain of them are natural or moral laws. For many of these belong to the category of moral laws, such as actions which upset human society, theft, murders, and which are to be punished.

However, the determination of the punishment is the province of the civil laws. Thus Paul from the ceremonial laws, "They who serve at the altar should have their food from the altar," 1 Cor. 9:13, draws his principle that therefore those who minister with the Gospel should live from the Gospel. But by what method physical care should be provided for their ministers, he leaves to free choice. Thus also from the Law, "You shall not muzzle the ox which treads out the grain," Deut. 25:4, Paul puts into the category of a natural or moral law, "The laborer is worthy of his hire," Luke 10:7; Matt. 10:10. Here again the principle has been laid down by God, but the application is accommodated to the condition of the person; yet it shows how and to what extent the positive laws are approved by God and what laws could be established with good conscience.

Thus because the law of Moses in Deut. 22:20–21 orders a woman convicted of adultery to be stoned, the husband is thereby freed. Therefore the Christian magistrate, although there is no obligation that a husband must be freed in this way, yet in some other way with good conscience in such a situation he can absolve the husband.

On the basis of these principles it is possible to understand why the civil laws of Moses have not been reintroduced into our present situation. For we use Roman laws and civil regulations not because we believe that Scaevola and other lawmakers established their laws with greater wisdom than God Himself, who alone is wise, Rom. 16:27; or as if we were to put the civil laws which God Himself gave for the people of Israel in the same position as the Spartan law whereby it was permitted to make an agreement with a husband for the prostitution of his wife. But the Mosaic civil law is far preferable to other legal systems, not by simple comparison but because of the circumstances of the times and situations, or because of the different conditions of the nations and the dissimilar form of government. For God did not give civil laws which corresponded to the customs of all nations, but He accommodated them: (1) to the customs of His people; (2) to the conditions of the land because of the surrounding regions; (3) to the political circumstances of that time when the Messiah was expected and into which He was to be born; (4) to the form and status of their existing governmental structure.

Then we must learn from the civil laws of Moses that they were not promulgated in such a way as to be binding on all nations, but that they might produce differentiation or separation of the Mosaic nation from all others and that with the coming of Christ they were abrogated, so that they could be entirely omitted and that they might be rendered extinct. It was good that this happened because our freedom can be demonstrated by public example. Thus when the idea of the necessity of civil laws has been removed, then certain of them can be used and applied to the form of our present civil life, such as the laws concerning tithing. These descriptions and distinctions are also profitable in determining which are moral precepts, which are ceremonial, and which are civil, as in Leviticus 19 and Deuteronomy 4–6.

CHAPTER V: ABROGATION OF THE LAW

In other matters generalization produces confusion and obfuscation. But in the teaching concerning the abrogation of the Law, such statements are absolutely perilous unless they are clearly and carefully explained as to which parts of the Law have been abrogated and how. For many in all ages have gone astray by trying to imitate these laws of Moses. It is certain that because of brutish people there is a need for some external and structured regulations in the church. It is also manifest that no government can be without established laws. Therefore since God Himself, who is the highest wisdom, has presented a certain form of rites in the ceremonies of the church and has in the civil laws established a certain form for the defense of external discipline, it would be insane for a person to think that he could invent a better method in the ceremonies and could establish wiser judgments than God's. It would be an affront to God to prefer the laws of Rome and the traditions of men above the civil and ceremonial laws which God Himself has given and sanctified. Hence the papists have established their theatrical ceremonies in imitation of the Levitical worship, as is openly confessed in their manual of worship. Certain fanatics in our time, deceived by these ideas, are contending that in our public courts controversies ought to be judged in keeping with the Mosaic law and that, e.g., thieves should not be hanged. In a certain duchy there were at one time great uproars which were aroused by the clergy. Because according to the law of Moses tithes were to be paid to the priests, therefore neither the citizens nor the nobles nor the princes could with good conscience accept tithes. But seditious peasants, because they had heard in a general way about the abrogation of the civil and ceremonial laws of Moses, were unwilling to pay their tithes to the magistrate, because, they said, the law regarding tithes is among those which have been abrogated. Thus the antinomians in a general way declaim about the abrogation of the Law, so that they contend that at the same time both the teaching of and obedience even to the moral law must be removed from the churches.

In antiquity there were various errors concerning the abrogation of the Law. Marcion, Valintinus, and others, when they read in the writings of the apostles that there had been a repudiation of the prior commandment because of its weakness and uselessness, Heb. 7:18, imagined that the Law had been abrogated because it was evil and given by an evil god. Even in the time of the apostles this question produced various arguments. Converted gentiles despised the Jews for retaining these laws without need or right. Thus Paul in Rom. 14:5 contends that it is a matter of indifference. But later, when the liberty was taken away and the idea of necessity and works-righteousness set in, Paul opposed it strongly, Gal. 2:14. Likewise, the observance of days, Gal. 4:10–11, "I am afraid that I have bestowed labor on you in vain"; Gal. 5:2, "If you are circumcised, Christ will profit you nothing."

I have pointed out these matters in order that when we have considered the causes, the doctrine may be taught with greater care. Thus the true and accepted teaching about the abrogation of the Law is this: (1) that it impinges on justification in the same way that we must understand regarding all parts of the Mosaic law, namely, that a person is not righteous or accepted for eternal life on account of the works of the moral law or other works; (2) that it relates to obedience, but we must separate the parts of the Mosaic law, for the civil and ceremonial have been abolished in such a way that they can be absolutely omitted and are extinct. But in order that this statement can be correctly understood, these three points need to be shown: (1) We must gather testimonies which prove that the two parts of the Law have been abrogated in such a way that absolutely nothing pertains to us; (2) that we must show why they have been abrogated; and (3) how they are abolished.

First. There is a beautiful testimony in the Old Testament in Jer. 31:31–32, "Behold, the day is coming and I will make a new covenant . . . not according to the covenant which I made with your fathers. . . ." In Deut. 18:18, God promises that He will raise up another prophet after Moses, and "I will put My words in His mouth and you shall hear Him." Therefore the laws of Moses were given in such a way that they were going to endure until that time when "that prophet" should come and promulgate a new law. This is the line of argumentation in Heb. 8:13, that "in speaking of the new covenant the first became obsolete and growing old and is ready to vanish away."

Likewise these clear examples prove that as long as the nation of Israel stood, the ceremonial and civil laws would still stand even though they were not imposed upon converted gentiles, such as Nebuchadnezzar, the Ninevites, Darius, Cyrus, etc. Therefore these laws were not imposed upon other nations and not even made obligatory for all people of that era, even though they had not yet been abrogated by the coming of Christ; but they were given only to the Jews. Therefore much less are they now to be mandated to the gentiles.

In regard to the civil laws there is a passage in Gen. 49:10, "I will not take the scepter from Judah and the lawgiver from the midst of this people until the Messiah comes." He joins together the scepter and the lawgivers, who in the writings of the New Testament are called "scribes," people who answered questions concerning the civil law of Moses. For they got their name from the Hebrew *choq* about which we have already spoken in this locus. Therefore it clearly affirms that with the advent of the Messiah this state together with its laws was to be abrogated.

In regard to the ceremonial laws there is a very clear passage that the Messiah with His coming was going to bring an end to them, namely Dan. 9:27, where the Messiah will confirm a covenant, that is, the new covenant of which Jeremiah 31 speaks. But in the New Testament the testimonies are still clearer. For in Acts 15:6ff. the council of Jerusalem was called to consider the question of whether the observance of circumcision and the other Mosaic laws were to be required of the gentiles, and it was decided under the guidance of the Holy Spirit that the gentiles were not to be disturbed by the imposition of the burdens of these laws. 1 Peter 1:18, "Since you know that you were not redeemed by perishing things from the futile efforts which you received from the tradition of your fathers." This statement is not speaking about their life according to the moral law, but about the two other parts of the Law. In Eph. 2:14–15, Paul says that those laws which made a distinction between Jews and other people have been abrogated, "He has made us both one and broken down the dividing wall, abrogating the law of commandments contained in ordinances." Matt. 11:13, "The Law and the prophets were until John."

But regarding the form of the abrogation of the ceremonies, these points have been made: Col. 2:16, "Let no one judge you in food or in drink or in holy days"; Gal. 4:10, "You observe days and years"; Gal. 5:2, "If you are circumcised, Christ profits you nothing." In Gal. 2:11 Peter is criticized for making a distinction of foods. In the Epistle to the Hebrews the chief point is that the ceremonies of the old law have been abrogated. Heb. 7:11–12, "When the priesthood is changed, there must also be a change of the law." But the Messiah is a priest of the order of Melchizedek, v. 17, not of Aaron. Therefore in the coming of the Messiah there had to be a change in the Levitical laws.

Regarding the abrogation of the civil laws we read these statements: Gal. 3:28, "There is neither Jew nor Greek. For you are all one in Christ Jesus"; Col. 3:11, "There is neither gentile nor Jew, barbarian or Scythian, slave or free; but Christ is all and in all." It is certain that Paul is speaking of the customary and ordinary conditions of different political nations, because in the same places the people are free, that is, the laws were gentle and in other places they are slaves, that is, the laws were harsh, and he says that it is a matter of indifference in Christ Jesus. Thus 1 Peter 2:13 says, "Be subject to every ordinance or institution of man," that is, to things established by man. For this word is used in this sense by Plutarch in *Publicola* [4.100] when Brutus established a new form of government with precise laws. Therefore the Christian can use the proper laws of all forms of government and is not bound to the Mosaic structure. This is what Stephen was saying in Acts 6:10.

However, the clearest demonstration of the abrogation of these laws is the actual destruction of the temple and the government, which was done so that no one should think that these practices were necessary, as was predicted in Hos. 3:4, "For many days shall the children of Israel abide without a king, without a prince, without a priest, without an altar."

Second. We must consider the question of why these two parts of the Law were to be utterly abrogated. For it was not done as if they in themselves were evil or harmful, as in the case of the Saxon law where many laws were abrogated. Nor were they abrogated because they had come from an evil god, as the Marcionites blasphemously asserted. But the reason for the abrogation can be correctly understood when we consider the purposes for which the Mosaic civil law was originally established. They are the following: (1) in order that there might be a civil structure for the revelation of God, that is, a definite place in which, with His mighty Word and with additional wondrous miracles, God might reveal Himself and bear witness concerning His teaching; (2) that there might be an academy or school, that is, a definite place for teaching or education in which all men could hear and learn the doctrine which had been given by God; (3) that there might be a library in which were preserved the books of the prophets and the proper interpretation of the Law and the Gospel; (4) that there might be a definite place and a definite family in which the Messiah might be born, bear His witness, teach, proclaim, make His sacrifice, and rise again.

When these purposes have been correctly considered, the answer is easy as to why the civil and ceremonial laws, which were the strength of that government, were abrogated. For after the coming of the Messiah the heavenly doctrine was to be spread through all the nations and throughout all the world, and with the birth of the Messiah there was no longer a use for this government, that is, the ceremonial and civil laws had to point to His origin and birthplace.

Scripture lists these causes: (1) Gal. 3:19, "The Law was given till the Seed should come"; Heb. 9:10, "The ceremonial law was imposed until the time of the new order." Therefore those laws were given not that they might be in force forever, but that they might continue to a certain time and then be abrogated along with the state itself. (2) The dividing wall had been constructed by God through certain rituals in order that this people, among whom the Messiah was to be born, might be separated from all other nations by a conspicuous difference. But in His flesh "He broke down this dividing wall," Eph. 2:14. Thus God did not institute these rituals in order that all nations should use them. Indeed, because there had to be a distinction even before the coming of the Messiah, He did not want these rites to be common property with other nations, as is repeatedly said in the Law, "You shall not do as other nations do." (3) The ceremonies were figures and shadows of Christ and His blessings. But with His coming in the body and His own actual appearance, the shadows vanished and the figures ceased, Col. 2:17. Heb. 10:18, "Where there is forgiveness of sins there is no longer any offering for sin." (4) Heb. 7:18–19, "The commandment which preceded is abrogated because of its weakness and uselessness, for the Law made nothing perfect, but it introduced a better hope."

Third. We must also consider how the abrogation is to be understood, namely, has the reading of a certain portion of the Old Testament been prohibited as something useless and harmful, as the Marcionites contended, or have the civil and ceremonial laws by their abrogation been made evil or detrimental in themselves? Jerome vigorously disputed against Augustine that the ceremonies of the Jews were both harmful and destructive for Christians, so that whoever observed them, whether he was of Jewish or gentile background, would be cast into the pit of the devil. He added that to observe the ceremonies of the Law cannot be a matter of indifference, but is either good or evil. He cites from the Epistle of Ignatius to the Philippians, "Whoever eats the passover with Jews participates with those who killed the Lord and His apostles," etc., while, however, the *Canon of the Apostles* and the *Ecclesiastical History* say the opposite.[7]

Therefore the apostolic Scriptures teach that these laws in being abrogated are not thereby made evil in themselves, nor do they bring death, but are matters of indifference which, without the burden of necessity and righteousness, can be used with freedom. 1 Cor. 7:19, "Circumcision is nothing and uncircumcision is nothing." Cf. 1 Cor. 8:8; Rom. 14:6. Thus in the very earliest years, because of weaknesses, the apostles at times did observe the ceremonial laws, as in Acts 16:3, where Timothy, although a gentile, is circumcised; or Acts 21:24–26, where Paul shaved his head because of a vow, and in 1 Cor. 9:20, "To the Jews I became as a Jew."

But later, when the Jews assumed the attitude of necessity for salvation, the apostles by their example showed that the Law had been abrogated, Gal. 2:11 and 5:4, where Paul says that this idea makes the law of Moses something that brings death. However, this notion did not only render the civil and ceremonial laws as dangerous to faith and as death-dealing, but also the moral law itself, Luke 18:14. Therefore the apostles, after the abrogation, even though they did not want the teaching of these laws to be retained in the church in such a way as to make them as well as the Decalog to be necessary, yet they did not reject or prohibit the reading of Moses where the text describes these laws, as the Manichaeans did. But often they took their proof passages from the Mosaic law. And Paul, when he says, "Those things which were written in the past were written for our learning," Rom. 15:4, certainly is including also this part of Scripture.

Now the apostles cite these abrogated laws in two ways. (1) They use statements from the civil or ceremonial laws to establish general natural or moral principles, as "They who serve at the altar shall get their living from the altar," 1 Cor. 9:13. (2) They interpret the Mosaic ceremonies in an allegorical sense, such as the sacrifices and offerings in Rom. 12:1 and Heb. 13:11–15; the priesthood in 1 Peter 2:9; the Passover in 1 Cor. 5:7; circumcision in Rom. 2:25ff. and Phil. 3:3.

But concerning the observance of the Law the apostles teach that before the abrogation the Jews were obligated to the observance of these laws as they applied to the external worship commanded by the Word of God. But after the abrogation they say that no one is to be compelled to observe them and no one

---

[7] Reference is to Pseudo-Ignatius in MPG 5 and to Eusebius.

forced to reject them, but rather that the observance is a matter of free choice and a matter of indifference, yet with these distinctions: (1) The Jews who grew up with these ceremonies may retain them without the belief that it was a worship form or a matter of necessity, but they were not to be imposed upon the gentiles, e.g., 1 Cor. 7:18, "Was a man already circumcised when he was called? He should not become uncircumcised." (2) They can freely draw from the civil laws those which are beneficial to our own legal system. For when Paul speaks about civil matters, he says, "There is neither Jew nor Greek," Gal. 3:28 and again, "There is neither gentile nor Jew," Col. 3:11. But the ceremonies which were "shadows and figures of the coming Christ," Heb. 8:6, which were fulfilled with the coming of the Christ, cannot be observed unless we wish with the Jews to deny that the Messiah has come. Heb. 10:18, "Where there is remission of sins there is no longer offering for sin." But the other ceremonies, which were educational, such as the festivals and the special foods, etc., these the apostles say are matters of indifference, if they are not made matters of worship or necessity or righteousness, yet in such a way that when believers worship in the knowledge or confession of Christ they are not converted to the "weak and miserable principles of the world," Gal. 4:9; or Col. 2:20, "If you have died with Christ to the base elements of this world, why do you live as if you still belonged to the world?" 1 Peter 1:18, "You were redeemed from that empty way of life by the blood of Christ." Martin Luther, in ch. 2 of his commentary on Galatians, says of this argument, "I believe that if believing Jews had observed the Law and circumcision on the condition which the apostles permitted, Judaism would still stand and that the whole world would have accepted the ceremonies of the Jews. But because they argued that the Law and circumcision were necessary for salvation and established their worship on this basis, God could not endure this and therefore He overturned the temple, the Law, the worship, and Jerusalem."

For this reason the ceremonial and civil laws have been abrogated. But because Scripture, when it speaks of the abrogation, speaks in a general way, it is necessary under the teaching concerning the abrogation also to include the most important and most difficult part of the Law, namely the moral law. But again, because the moral law was not given for only one particular time, as the other laws were, but is the eternal wisdom and rule of the righteousness in God, unto the obedience of which both Christ and the apostles teach that believers should be renewed, therefore it is necessary that we determine the difference between the abrogation of the moral law and the others. For the moral law has not been abolished in such a way that it can be entirely omitted, nor put away as the other laws of Moses, but it has been abrogated: (1) as pertaining to justification. Indeed in Gal. 3:21, we read, "A law was not given which could give life, so that righteousness might be from the Law"; (2) as pertaining to the curse, Gal.

3:13, "Christ has redeemed us from the curse of the Law"; (3) as pertaining to the rigor of its demands. For example, the Law does not recognize our obedience unless it is perfect, pure, and unending; and if it has any stains or defects, it adds the curse of James 2:10, "He who is guilty in one point is guilty of all." From these rigorous demands we have been set free, Gal. 5:18, "If you are led by the Spirit, you are not under the Law." But this abrogation applies only to believers "who are in Christ Jesus," Rom. 8:1, and who "are led by the Spirit," Gal. 5:18; Rom. 8:4.

But as it pertains to teaching and obedience the moral law has not been abrogated but is eternal and, as Urbanus Rhegius [*Luther's Works*, Amer. Ed., 26.125] so beautifully puts it, the abrogation of the moral law did not cause any change in the eternal wisdom and rule of righteousness in God. But because the Son of God took upon Himself the obligation of the Law as it pertains both to the obedience to the law and the punishment of the Law, by this abrogation there is produced for us such a change that we are freed from the curse and harsh demands of the Law.

This distinction between the abrogation of the moral law and that of the other laws is not the invention of ingenious men, but this is what Scripture teaches. For Christ in speaking of the moral law in Matt. 5:17 clearly says, "I have not come to destroy the Law." The Greek expression "to destroy the Law" does not mean to remit privately something in the Law, but with public authority to abolish the law so that it is plainly no longer in existence and nothing of it pertains to those to whom it was given. The term is used this way in the *Thalia* of Herodotus [*History*, 3.82]. But in regard to the other laws which were signs and distinctive marks of the Mosaic state in contradistinction to the gentiles, Paul says in Eph. 2:14 that Christ "has broken down the dividing wall." In the same chapter, v. 15, he clearly states that Christ "has abrogated the law of commandments contained in ordinances." In 2 Cor. 3:11, "If that which is abrogated was glorious . . ." But concerning the law of works, that is, the Decalog, he raises this objection in Rom. 3:31, "Do we then abrogate the Law through faith? God forbid. But we uphold the Law."

We should note the words dealing with the abrogation of the ceremonial and civil laws. The Scripture uses these words: *lyein*, to break or destroy; *katargein*, to abolish; *metatithesthai*, to change, Heb. 7:12; *palaiōthai*, to become old; *gēraskein*, to decay; *aphanizein*, to vanish, Heb. 8:13; *athetēsis*, "There is an annulment of the commandment which preceded," Heb. 7:18. These statements are not used with reference to the moral law, as we have said concerning the two prior kinds, but "He has freed me from the law of sin and death," Rom. 8:2, that is, "He has redeemed us from the curse of the Law," Gal. 3:13; cf. Rom. 7:4; Gal. 2:19; Rom. 7:6; 6:14; Gal. 5:18. "The Law is not laid upon a righteous man," that is, it does not press down upon the righteous man with its condemnation and accusation; 1 Tim. 1:9. As 1 John 5:19 says, "The whole world lies pressed down under sin." Col. 2:14, Christ "destroyed the record of debt which stood against us and set it aside." Note also how precisely Paul speaks. He mentions the curse, the written charge against us, death and sin, when he speaks about the abrogation of the moral law. Likewise he does not say that the moral law is dead or abrogated, but that we are dead, delivered from the Law, Rom. 7:6, so that he refers to the fact that a change has taken place, not in the standing rule of the righteousness of God, but in us, as we have said before. This consideration of the grammar of the words is useful.

Now that the moral law was not given only for a particular time, as the other laws of Moses were, but to be the eternal statement and standard of God which is not changed by the circumstances and that it pertains to doctrine and obedience in the way that has been said is proved by these arguments: (1) Because it is the eternal and immovable wisdom and standard of the righteousness of God. (2) Because from the beginning of the world it has always proclaimed in the church, even before Moses. Christ uses it with this understanding, for example, in Matt. 19:7, "Moses commanded that they give a certificate of divorce, but from the beginning it was not this way"; Rom. 4:9–11, Abraham was justified before circumcision was instituted. Therefore, circumcision was not an unalterable ceremony necessary for salvation. (3) Because the knowledge of the moral law in the very act of creation was placed by God into the minds of men, they cannot abolish this knowledge while it remains in force. (4) The apostles clearly teach that believers are renewed by the Holy Spirit unto obedience of the precepts of the moral law. (5) In life eternal there will be a true and perfect conformity of the elect with the moral law. Therefore the law will endure to all eternity. In this way the teaching concerning the abrogation of the Law has been correctly and definitively established. But the Jews vigorously contend that no part of the Law has been abrogated, but that the entire Law with its individual parts is eternal, unalterable, and immovable. And although this group of people is accustomed in other areas also to hang on like a bulldog to their presumptuous notions out of unreasoning stubbornness and to defend them, yet in this dispute they have such plausible arguments that they can mislead simple and unwary people. Therefore I shall cite their principal arguments and add the correct understanding:

1. There is one and the same author for the ceremonial, civil, and moral laws. For He who said, "You shall have no other gods" is the same as He who said, "You shall make sacrifices." And the entire Law with all its individual parts was even promulgated at the same time. Therefore either the whole Law with its individual parts should be abolished in the same way or the whole retained. For

we must not grant to men such license that just as the Roman Decemvirs had a choice among the laws of Solon, so we also from the divine laws, which were promulgated by the same God and at the same time, must not omit the ceremonial and civil laws as in no way pertaining to us and only retain the teaching of the Decalog.

Reply: Burgensis[8] has brilliantly refuted this argument by proving that God in the very act of promulgating the Law showed that He did not place the ceremonial and the civil on the same level with the Decalog. (1) The precepts of the Decalog were given first in point of place and time and in a much more solemn manner, cf. Exodus 19. (2) God gave the Decalog to the whole nation directly, cf. Deut. 5:22, where the Lord spoke these words to the whole multitude. But with regard to the other laws God says to Moses alone in v. 31, "You stand here with Me and I will speak to you all the commandments both ceremonial and civil, which you shall teach them." (3) The precepts of the Decalog were written by God Himself on tables of stone, but the rest of the laws were written by Moses, Ex. 24:14, "Moses wrote all the words of the Lord"; Deut. 31:9, "Moses wrote this law." (4) The tables of the Decalog were placed in the ark of the covenant, 1 Kings 8:9; Heb. 9:4. But the book of Deuteronomy, which included the rest of the laws written by Moses, was placed into the custody of the priests and the king, Deut. 17:14ff. and 31:9.

2. Deut. 4:2, when Moses speaks specifically concerning the ceremonial and civil laws, he says, "You shall not add to the word which I will speak to you, nor shall you take away from it." Therefore, just as the Pharisees were deservedly criticized because through their traditions they added something to the law of God, so Christians have not acted properly in taking away the ceremonial and civil aspects of the law of God and retaining only the Decalog.

Reply: God Himself established a certain term of duration within which there should be nothing added or taken away; but when the new covenant was promulgated, then not only should something be taken away, but it will be absolutely made obsolete, Jer. 31:31–33; Dan. 9:27.

3. God is not like a man that He should lie, nor like a son of man that He should be changed," Num. 23:19. Therefore the ceremonial and civil laws which have come from God are not subject to change.

Reply: God gave the laws in such a way that they were not to continue in perpetuity but to a certain time, until the Seed should come, and then be abrogated, Heb. 9:10, "imposed until the time of reformation." Therefore, because God willed these laws to be subject to change, it was necessary that they be abrogated so that their mutability might be consistent with the will of God.

---

[8] Paul of Burgos (ca. 1351–1435), convert from Judaism, bishop of Burgos, Spain.

4. In regard to circumcision, Gen. 17:7, "I will establish My covenant between Me and you . . . with an eternal covenant." Regarding the Sabbath, Ex. 31:16, "They shall observe the Sabbath . . . as a perpetual covenant." Concerning the Passover, Ex. 12:14, "You shall celebrate it as a permanent ordinance," cf. Lev. 23:14, 21, 31 and 41. Concerning the festivals, "there is a permanent ordinance in your generation," Lev. 24:3. Regarding the lights, "with perpetual rites and worship." Concerning the showbread, it is by perpetual law, Ex. 29:9, 42. Regarding the entire Levitical priesthood, it is a constant religious duty, with ongoing prayer and sacrifice.

Reply: These appear to be very good arguments to those who are inexperienced, but the question can easily be evaluated by the use of a figure of speech. For in the Hebrew language there are two ways to express permanence or perpetuity. Some terms refer to a continuance or permanence of duration which has no end. Others to a circumscribed or limited period of time. For example, the word *'ōlām* is used when it is connected with a term signifying a thing the duration of which is limited to the life of a person, as in Deut. 15:17, "He will be your servant forever"; Ex. 21:6, "He will serve forever"; 1 Sam. 1:22, Hannah says of Samuel, "He will dwell there forever"; Rabbi Solomon explains this to mean for the lifetime of the Levites, that is, to age 50; Eccl. 3:14, "Everything which God made will remain," that is, in some way it has its course in the period of its duration as determined by God; 1 Sam. 27:12, "He will be My servant forever." Thus when the Scripture speaks about the permanence of the Mosaic law, it does not use the term indicating an absolute permanence, but the term *lᵉ 'ōlām*.

But again they raise the objection that the term *'ōlām* is used in such verses as these: Ps. 145:13, "Your kingdom and Your domain endure through all generations"; Gen. 21:33, "There Abraham called the name of God *'ōlām*, that is, the everlasting God"; Is. 40:28, "Have you not heard, God is the Lord of eternity?" Here it is certain that *'ōlām* signifies endless perpetuity. Therefore it also means this when it is used with reference to the Law.

Reply: It is said that *'ōlām* refers to perpetuity according to the condition of the thing with which it is joined. Therefore, when it is used with reference to God, it means an absolute perpetuity, but when it is used with reference to the Law whose duration was to come to an end with the advent of the Messiah, it refers to a limited duration, to a certain designated point in time. Therefore Moses often adds this limitation, e.g., "forever in your generations and in your house."

5. God Himself has prescribed certain rituals in these ceremonial laws and a certain form of government. Therefore not without dishonoring God can ordinary civil laws be preferred above the civil laws of Moses. But we have spoken

above concerning the answer to this argument, and thus there is no need to say more.

CHAPTER VI: PROMULGATION OF THE DECALOG

Therefore, although the ceremonial and civil laws are absolutely extinct, yet the moral law remains in force in regard to teaching. Now we shall speak about the promulgation of the Decalog. Three questions arise. (1) Since it is certain that the Decalog was promulgated on Mt. Sinai on the 50th day after the departure from Egypt in the 2449th year after the foundation of the world, did the knowledge and the teaching of it begin thus for the first time, or had this taken place before Moses? (2) Because in the very act of creation itself the moral law had been grafted into the hearts of men, why did God afterward with such great solemnity promulgate it on Sinai? (3) How did this promulgation take place?

1. That this knowledge of the Law and the teaching of it did not begin for the first time under Moses is manifest from the fact that moral law had been written in the hearts of men in the act of creation, Rom. 2:15. Even this is not the first beginning of the moral law. For when it is said, "You shall be holy in your entire life," as it is written, "You shall be holy because I am holy," 1 Peter 1:15–16, and "You must be perfect as your Father in heaven is perfect," Matt. 5:48, it means that the Law is eternal, just as God Himself is eternal. Furthermore, the moral law was not only known by nature by the fathers before the time of Moses, but it had always been taught from the very beginning of the world, as it was proclaimed in the church, because it was revealed by the voice of God even before Moses. It is interesting to consider how the Decalog was revealed by the voice of God during the first two millennia before the promulgation by Moses.

It will be helpful to compare how, as time went on, God revealed more clearly His will in the Law. But I wish to make only a few brief remarks regarding the antediluvian era, so that it might serve as a guide for noting the other points in the text.

Thus the First Commandment, concerning the recognition, love, and fear of God and the obedience and worship prescribed by the Word, was given and revealed in Paradise itself by the voice of God. Thus the breaking of His command shows what it means to have "other gods."

The Second Commandment is first implied in Gen. 4:26, when the hallowing or sanctifying of the name of God had been profaned by the sons of Cain, and then "Enosh began to call upon the name of God."

The Third Commandment regarding the sanctifying of the Sabbath was clearly suggested by God in Gen. 2:3, because at a certain time the fathers were to gather together to hear the Word and establish the worship of God. This is clear from Gen. 4:3–4, 26, in regard to praying in the name of the Lord and making sacrifices. Nor is that true what Thomas says, that the first patriarchs created the idea of sacrifices without any definite word of God purely by the dictates of their own reason. For in Heb. 11:4 it is written, "By faith Abel made a sacrifice"; and in Rom. 10:17 faith has as its object the Word of God. Therefore, just as later God Himself commanded what Abraham should sacrifice and how it should be done, so without doubt they also had a word from God relative to sacrifices, because from the very beginning God condemned self-made or self-imposed religions, Col. 2:23. That the practice of making sacrifices first began under the institution of God is manifest from the fact that afterward God through Moses, with His own voice, placed into the regular order those things which had been in use by the first fathers for the purpose of sacrifices. The violation of the Third Commandment was listed among the causes of the Flood, Gen. 6:3, which clearly mentions a ministry of the Spirit of God in condemning the world. Is not this the teaching of the Third Commandment as it stands in the Decalog?

There is a rather veiled reference to the Fourth Commandment in the statement in Gen. 2:24, "A man shall leave his father and his mother," etc., in Gen. 6:4–5 it says that the oppression by giants over their subjects, that is, a violation of the Fourth Commandment, was a cause of the Flood.[9]

The Fifth Commandment was not only engrafted into the minds of our first parents in Creation, but was clearly repeated by the divine voice in the story of Cain, Gen. 4:10, "Your brother's blood cries to Me." And it is worthy of remembrance that He is not speaking only of Abel's physical blood, but He says in v. 6, "Why are you angry and why has your countenance fallen?" Therefore even before the Flood there was this understanding of the Fifth Commandment, "Whoever is angry with his brother . . . who says 'Raca . . . you fool,' etc.," Matt. 5:22. Likewise God in Genesis 4 also clearly prohibits private revenge, even though the cause may not seem unjust. For Cain, because he knew that for the killing of his brother he deserved death, yet says, "Whoever finds me will kill me." But God answers, "No," Gen. 4:13–15.

The Sixth Commandment was established by the divine voice in Paradise itself, as the Son of God shows in Matt. 19:5, "He who created them said, 'For this reason a man shall leave,' etc." Promiscuous lusts are punished in the Flood, Gen. 6:2ff.

The Seventh Commandment, which prescribes that we labor and work at our calling, is expressed by the voice of God in Gen. 3:15, "In the sweat of your brow you shall eat your bread." In Gen. 2:15, even before the Fall, God commands Adam that he shall cultivate the garden of Paradise and work in it.

The Eighth Commandment, that we avoid lying and love the truth, not only

---

[9] Cf. Luther, *Lectures on Genesis*, Amer. Ed., 2.32ff.

was known by nature before the Flood but was also repeated by the voice of God. For when Cain in response to God's question about Abel answers falsely, he is severely reprimanded by the divine voice, Gen. 4:9ff.

In regard to the Ninth and Tenth Commandments, there are now great contentions. The scholastics conclude that the law of Moses involves only a physical action but in the New Testament for the first time Christ prohibits the lust of the heart and [they say] that this only takes place with the full consent of man's will. But the story of Genesis shows that even before the Flood God with His own voice had set forth these two commandments which were to accuse the root of human sin, our concupiscence and the very depravity of our nature, without any notion of the addition of the consent of our will. For God warns Cain about the sin which lies at the door or in wait, which David calls the secret or hidden sin, and he clearly says that the desire or appetite for sin increases in man and God commands him to master it, cf. Gen. 4:7. Yet He says that it is sin, Gen. 6:5, "The intention of man's heart is evil continually." Therefore also before the Flood, in the Ninth and Tenth Commandments, there is the accusation against the depravity of our nature, that is, original sin.

The foregoing is the pre-Flood Decalog. And by a similar line of reasoning we can demonstrate the Decalog from the Flood to the public promulgation under Moses and show how the individual commandments were repeated and explained by the voice of God, before they were engraved on tablets of stone. But this would take a great deal of time. For afterward we would have to add also the Decalog of the prophets, the Decalog of Christ, and the Decalog of the apostles. Therefore it suffices for the present that we have shown that the teaching of the Decalog did not first begin at the time of Moses, nor was it only under the natural law, but always from the beginning it has been proclaimed in the church.

2. Because the moral law is, first, the eternal and unaltered rule of righteousness in God; and, second, inscribed in the minds of men in the act of creation; and, third, from the beginning the divine voice has always been revealed and repeated in the church, therefore this question is not unworthy of our consideration: Why did God after so many years again publicly and with solemn testimony promulgate the Decalog and willed to inscribe it on stone with His own fingers? For His revelation on Mt. Sinai was not merely an empty and worthless spectacle for us to admire, but many serious reasons are given to illustrate the importance of the Law, so that we might use it properly and love it more.

(1) Because in this state of corruption of ours many depraved inclinations to wickedness cling to our nature, by which the judgment of our mind is often perverted, therefore God in a public way has promulgated the Decalog in order that there might be a clear testimony that the natural promptings of the Law concerning the difference between honorable and shameful actions have been

divinely ingrafted into the human race and are in agreement with that eternal rule of righteousness which is in God.

(2) Because the human mind on account of sin was darkened with many thick shadows and even the natural knowledge of the Law was rendered more obscure and the principal part of the Law had been lost in its efforts to expose our inward sin, and because many shameful things and evil practices had been received and confirmed by long custom and were now of greater importance than the natural law, therefore God with this solemn promulgation restored the complete knowledge of the Law in order that He might again reveal with His own voice and correctly explain those things in the natural law which had been forgotten because of sin, rejecting those which under false pretenses had been received into the understanding of the natural law, and that He might show again the points wherein the natural law was in agreement with the eternal standard of righteousness which is in God.

(3) Because even in that knowledge of the Law which is clear and sure the assent is weak, so that our conscience could easily avoid "thoughts which accuse or excuse," as Paul says in Rom. 2:15, therefore with great solemnity God promulgated the Decalog, so that when divine authority is set forth, the reason for the testimony of our conscience might be considered more carefully. In support of this thinking, Augustine writes on Psalm 58 [Vulgate 57] [MPL 36.673], "The Law was given not because it had not been written in our hearts, but because you were running away from your heart, which through the Law was calling you back to your own inner promptings." And again, "By the same hand with which He formed us He wrote the truth in our hearts, 'What you do not wish to have happen to you, do not yourself do to another'" [Luke 6:31; Matt. 7:12]; but because men through sin have been exiled from their very selves, the Law was given them in written form.

(4) Because men greatly admire outward discipline and because of their longing for honor, they cannot recognize their wretched condition by the natural law so that they would seek a physician, therefore God with His own voice has solemnly repeated His law in order to show what sin is and make known His judgment against sin and thus lead us to a correct understanding of our misery, so that we healthy people who do not seem to need a physician may as sick people seek our Redeemer and Liberator.

(5) The most important reason that God at all times with His own voice has repeated the teaching of the Law is this, that it might be the means or instrument through which the Holy Spirit convicts the world of sin and leads it to "a recognition of sin," Rom. 3:20; cf. Jer. 23:29; Rom. 4:15; Gal. 3:22; 2 Cor. 7:10; John 8:37ff.; Gal. 3:24.

3. The third question deals with historical matters. How was the Decalog

promulgated? For from it is shown how much God attributes to the teaching of the Law in its proper use. In Num. 12:6 God says that He reveals His Word through the prophets either in visions or through dreams or through some occult inner communication by the Holy Spirit, but when He promulgated the Decalog, He used none of these methods. He even says in v. 8 that Moses is greater than the other prophets in that He spoke to him mouth to mouth, or face to face. But He did not promulgate the Decalog in the way that He gave the rest of the laws to Moses alone in the darkness of the cloud, but in a peculiar manner and with many amazing miracles. Therefore Moses also says in Deut. 5:3, "The Lord did not make such a covenant as this with our fathers," that is, before the birth of Christ no teaching was ever revealed in the church with such great miracles and testimonies as the promulgation of the Law. Thus this account pertains to the strengthening of the authority of the teaching of the Law and is divided into three parts: (1) What miracles preceded? (2) What miracles occurred in the actual promulgation? (3) What miracles followed? For God in the Decalog attaches so much importance to the leading out from Egypt that He performs all these miracles from the exodus up to the entrance into the Promised Land.

Therefore, in the first place, many terrifying plagues preceded the promulgation of the Decalog in the land of Egypt, and many remarkable signs took place in the presence of Pharaoh. Likewise the column of cloud and of fire was the leader on the journey, and there was the incredible miracle at the Red Sea in the drowning of Pharaoh and the standing apart of the water on the left and the right, so that there was a space of over 4,000 feet in width which existed until the great multitude was able to cross with dry feet. Likewise, there was prepared for them a table for food in the wilderness, the manna was given from heaven, water came forth from a rock. These miracles preceded as a way of arousing a desire to receive the teaching of the Decalog.

In the second place, what miracles were done in the act of promulgating the Law are described in Exodus 19–20 and Hebrews 12. Among these certainly one of the most prominent was when the multitude of 600,000 men stood at the base of Mt. Sinai, which undoubtedly occupied a great expanse of space, that the voice of God who was reciting the Decalog could be equally well heard by all, for there was need for a very loud voice.

In the third place, pertaining to the confirmation of the authority of the Decalog were miracles which followed both in the desert and upon their entrance into the land of promise, Deut. 8:2–4; 29:5–6, "He led you for 40 years in the wilderness, yet your clothes were not worn out nor the shoes on your feet. You have not eaten bread, nor have you drunk wine or strong drink. . . ."

[B.] Exposition of the Decalog

A reverent consideration of the Decalog is most useful and spiritually uplifting. For it contains so complete and sublime a teaching that it can never be satisfactorily understood or exhausted. More and more we must come to detest the ravings of those who imagine that they can satisfy the law of God or even do more than it requires. These are not the voices of men, but they have been sown by the devil, who by this kind of bitter humor plays with the human race which has fallen from its dignity and purity. For when God shows in His law the condition in which human nature was created, from whence we have fallen, and into what miseries and darkness we have been degraded, the devil, as if playing with us, spreads abroad voices which ironically try to minimize the law of God. Therefore the reverent should know that the errors of the Pharisees and the monks are not inconsequential, and they should pray God that the veil of our hearts, which hinders us from seeing the law of God properly, might be drawn away, for we must seriously consider it as being the voice of God which contains far greater things than we can completely comprehend.

Above all we must consider these four points concerning the Law.

In the first place, the Law instructs as to the purpose for which human nature was created and what the dignity and purity of man was like in which he was created. For human nature would have been as this Law describes him, with full knowledge of God, always worshiping Him, always obedient to Him, always in all his works looking to His presence and guidance, observing the righteous order of things in all his actions, without any wickedness or calamities or death.

In the second place, the Law instructs us concerning our present wretched state. For we now see that our nature has fallen from its original honorable position, is in conflict with the Law, is filled with darkness and contempt for God, without any order, filled with corrupt desires of every kind. We also recognize that our sin is the cause of death and immeasurable disasters. But yet we do not understand our wretchedness, nor do we really hear the Law unless with true terror and suffering we recognize the wrath of God against sin. When this happens, we begin to a slight degree to understand the Law of God and the wretchedness of our human condition. As David cries, the wrath of God could not be endured if God wished to punish sin in keeping with our merits. "If You should mark iniquities, O Lord, Lord, who shall stand?" Ps. 130:3. Our sins are more numerous and greater in each of us than can be understood. Furthermore, note the emphasis of the passage, "Who shall stand?" No one has such strength that he can bear the calamity of our human condition, which is the punishment for our sins. Just as David felt the penalties of his adultery— the killing of his sons, the treason of a son, the marriages which were polluted by incest, the exile, the overthrow of his cities, and other incalculable evils—so in his punishments he learned to understand this verse, "Who shall stand?" Yet these present evils are not worthy to be compared with eternal punishments. Thus, as often as we recite this verse, "If You should mark iniquities, O Lord, Lord, who shall stand?" we should understand that the wrath of God against sin is real and beyond measure, and we should regard the whole law, and consider what mountains of punishment have been laid upon the human race, and regard our own and our common troubles and pray God that He would mitigate His wrath which no one can endure or bear. If He put forth His wrath, men would have to crumble and perish in present and eternal punishments. Likewise, similar passages in the psalms warn us concerning the true understanding of the Law and the knowledge of our sin and the wrath and punishments of God.

In the third place, the Law by implication quietly instructs us concerning the restoration of the human race and concerning eternal life. It further points out to what greater excellence we are recalled. For because God has repeated the word of the Law after the fall of our nature, He surely wills that the Law in some way be fulfilled. Therefore there will be a restoration of the human race and there will be an eternal life. Because we see that in this life the law of God is not satisfied, the teaching concerning this restoration is more clearly set forth in the promises.

In the fourth place, when we have thus considered how great is the misery of the human race under the oppression of sin, the wrath of God, and death, and have understood that the voice of the Law is a sentence, a chain, a witness, and the messenger of His unspeakable wrath, we must always turn from this area to the Son of God and consider His sacrifice, which alone has endured this wrath for us, undergone the burden of the Law, and pleased the Father. We must consider the benefits of the Son of God, which He poured out to cover our sin. Also we should know that we are called by the Son of God Himself in order that once again that purity described in the Law might begin to take root in us, as we shall indicate later in the proper locus.

Chapter [I]: How We Are to Investigate the True Meaning . . . of the Decalog

So great is the brevity in the individual precepts of the Decalog that Moses called them "words" (*verba*), Deut. 4:12; 10:4; Ex. 34:28. Yet within this brevity is included whatever pertains to loving God and our neighbor, and these brief statements should be the rule and measure by which we recognize what sins are, Rom. 3:20. Similarly Christ in Matt. 15:3, when His disciples were transgressing the traditions of the Pharisees, defended them as not sinning, because they were not committing anything against the Decalog. In 1 John 3:4 it says, "Whatever is not lawlessness is not sin." Paul says in Col. 2:16, "Let no one judge you in food or in drink." Thus it is manifest from Matthew 5 alone that the precepts of the

Decalog are synecdochical, that is, they represent the ordering and prohibiting of more things than are expressly mentioned in the Decalog.

As a result of this at all times there have arisen great controversies concerning the correct explanation of this subject, with some interpreting the synecdoche in a broad sense and others in a narrow. For which of the prophets did not contend with hypocrites concerning the proper meaning of the Law? In the time of the ministry of Christ the Pharisees were continuing the synecdoche of the precepts of the Decalog as if only those were great sins and worthy of death which were expressly mentioned in the Decalog. But the rest of the sins, such as anger, jealousy, and things of this kind, were minimized, things which God would not punish with hellfire. In our own times certain men have argued that simple fornication is not a sin, because the Sixth Commandment says only, "You shall not commit adultery." Eck contends that an act of concupiscence is sin only when the desire is obeyed with full consent, because the Tenth Commandment says, "You shall not covet the servants, fields. . . ." The more recent Jews restrict idolatry, which is forbidden in the First Commandment, only to the use of statues and images, because of an appendix which had been added to the First Commandment. Likewise, when they do not pronounce the great name of God, Jehovah, and will not write it with all the letters, they think that they are completely fulfilling the Second Commandment. How widespread this notion is even among Christians, that the Sabbath is sanctified by outward laziness, because the Decalog says, "You shall not labor!" On the other side, certain people extend this synecdoche too widely and try to include everything under it. Thus in days gone by the Pharisees under the pretext of the commandments of God pushed their traditions onto the people, on the grounds that they thus might be more easily observed. Likewise now in our age the papists try to include their Masses and their theatrical worship system under the Third Commandment.

Thus it is right and necessary to add that the Decalog must always be understood as its explanation is given to us in the prophetic and apostolic Scriptures. For God in 10 words has summarized all the wisdom of the moral law, not in such a way that each person is free to devise whatever interpretation he wishes, but with His own voice He has included His own synecdoche of the Decalog with definite boundaries in the explanations given in the prophetic and apostolic Scriptures.

Because there is no opportunity for each person to gather these explanations which are spread around in the prophetic and apostolic Scriptures and to apply them properly to the precepts of the Decalog, learned men have given us certain rules which demonstrate the basic principles for a smooth and methodical way whereby a definite and complete explanation of the individual commandments of the Decalog can be constructed. Then we can be certain of the things which God, according to His own explanation of each individual precept, wishes us to understand. I shall take them up in their particular order.

In the first place, in the case of the individual commandments, we must make such an antithesis that when something is commanded by express affirmation, then the negative is added. If the negative prohibition is expressly stated in the precept, then the affirmative must be added which commands the opposite. The reason and principle of this rule is that the use of the Law in the church is twofold, to show our sin and to give direction for the new life. Therefore through the use of antitheses to individual sins, the opposite virtues must be added also.

In the second place, among the several reasons for the promulgation of the Law there is this, that the Law reveals those sins the knowledge of which has been eradicated in the natural law because of sin. Therefore in the explanation of the Decalog we must not only describe those external points which are expressly set forth in most of the commandments, but they involve at the same time both external and internal aspects, both sins and good works. But in regard to the internal aspects we should note not only those points which in some way were known to the philosophers, but especially those hidden diseases which cling to the depraved condition of all the powers of man. Thus there is a threefold thrust in the individual precepts: (1) the external aspect; (2) the internal, which even human reason to some degree can see; and (3) the internal and hidden aspects, which only the church on the basis of the Word of God can recognize. The reason for this rule is that the law of God is not only a civil thing, or something philosophical, but it is spiritual, Rom. 7:14. Heb. 4:12, "The Word of God penetrates to the dividing of soul and spirit, and members and marrow, and is able to judge the thoughts and intentions of the heart." This statement is very helpful, for under the term "members" it includes the external and under the term "soul" (*anima*) the internal desires and actions about which man as a rational being can make a judgment. Under the term "spirit" it understands that uncleanness which is unknown to our reason, for it says that in the heart two entities are accused by the Law, our thoughts and our intentions, as in Gen. 6:5 and 8:21, where it argues that not only the thoughts but also the imagination of the heart is evil. There is no doubt that the apostles rendered the word *yētzer* with two different words, either *ennoia* (insight) or *enthymēsis* (thought). The LXX used *dianoia* (mind or understanding). Thus it is often repeated in Scripture that God searches the inner nature of man (*renes*) or the heart. Those learned in Hebrew have noted that by the term *renes* we are to understand the crasser desires and by "heart" (*cor*) the secret evils which human reason does not see, as it is said, "The heart of man is desperately wicked. Who can know it?" Jer. 17:9.

In the third place, in explaining the Decalog we must show not only the sins which are present in evil actions, but also that evil which still clings in the regenerate even when they wish to do good. For Paul says that he finds in the Law that sins still inhere in the good works of the regenerate, either in multiple faults, since "the flesh is lusting against the Spirit," or in powerlessness or inability whereby they cannot find how to achieve perfection even though through the Holy Spirit the desire to do good is present with them, Rom. 7:18. Martin Luther in a very learned way observes that the civil laws, because they served to produce outward discipline, which is possible, were often stated in an affirmative way. Thus in Cicero we read, "Worship the gods, preserve the sacred rites of our ancestors." But in the Decalog, when God wants both to prohibit sins and command good works, He sets forth all but two of the commandments in a negative way, in order to show that the law of God was given not only for external discipline, as in the case of civil sanctions, but that the chief end and use of the moral law is that it might reveal the knowledge of sin and charge us with failing to conform to the Law. He even willed to include the affirmative precepts concerning good works under the negative prohibition of sin, so that He might show that the good works of believers in this life are not perfect and that we should be admonished regarding the misery of this life when we learn from the negative precepts the teaching concerning good works. Almost the same commands are set forth in other places affirmatively, "You shall love God and your neighbor," Matt. 22:37–39, in order that there might be a reference to eternal life where the human race is so restored that the Law can be perfectly fulfilled.

In the fourth place, Paul in Rom. 7:7 is not speaking only of the Decalog when he says, "I would not have known sin except through the Law," and he adds in v. 13, "that sin might become utterly sinful through the commandment," that is, from the Decalog must be learned not only a listing of our sins, but especially must we learn the enormity of sin and what a great abomination sin is before the judgment of God. Therefore we must consider in an explanation of the Decalog (since God promulgated His law for this reason) that from our internal sins which are unknown to our reason can be understood why, in the case of individual precepts, certain elements are reckoned to be external and very serious. For it seems to us, for example, that under the Fifth Commandment it should have said, "You shall not be angry," rather than "You shall not kill." But by the example of 1 John 3:15, the reason can be established which shows the way to interpret all the rest of the commandments. For when we condemn the inner wickedness of the sin against the Fifth Commandment, such as anger, hatred, jealousy, ill-will, etc., human temerity can excuse these things in wondrous ways, as when the Pharisees called them small commandments, cf. Matt. 5:19. Therefore the Decalog includes all of these things under the name of homicide. And all sane people know and confess, says John, that a murderer does not have eternal life "remaining in him." The Decalog affirms that "He who hates his brother is a murderer." Therefore, "He who does not love remains in death."

On the basis of this passage in John we can clearly understand that God, when He particularly willed in the Decalog to reveal the knowledge of those sins of which Paul is speaking when he says, "I would not have known lust unless the Law had said . . ." [Rom. 7:7], used words which describe the crassest sins, in order to admonish us that not only the names or terms, but especially the magnitude and seriousness of our inner sins must be recognized on the basis of the Decalog. For the fact that these sins are condemned under its designation of murder, adultery, etc., shows how great an abomination before the judgment of God these secret sins are which human reason either ignores or excuses. Thus in Matt. 5:28 Christ says, "He who looks at a woman to lust after her has committed adultery in the eyes of God." And Paul in Eph. 5:5, in demonstrating the magnitude in God's eyes of the sin of avarice, calls it idolatry. There is a clear example of this in 1 Sam. 15:7ff. when Saul tried to excuse his sin in not killing, according to God's command, the king of the Amalekites and his best flocks. Samuel replied, v. 23, "Rebellion against God is as bad as the sin of witchcraft, and unwillingness to obey as the crime of idolatry." He shows that in his disobedient way the rule he broke was the Second Commandment. For he says that in the eye of God, he, Saul, is not innocent when he uses His name in vain. Much more the case with him who blasphemes!

In the fifth place, because the entire Law obligates us either to obedience or punishment, therefore in the explanation of the Decalog we must not only show what terrible names God gives to sins, but in the case of the individual precepts we must add the warnings regarding punishment. They are of four kinds:

1. Certain punishments are added in general to the entire Law, and they pertain to all the commandments, as in Deut. 28:15ff.

2. Certain punishments were special, which in a particular way were added to certain commandments, and this difference God shows in the Decalog itself: For to the First Commandment He adds the general threat which pertains to the whole Law and to all its precepts. To the Second Commandment in addition to the general threat He adds a special point, showing to us the method that in the explanation there are added to the individual commandments both general and special threats.

3. The difference in the threats is that some involve external or corporal punishments.

4. Some threaten spiritual and eternal punishments, such as, "Cursed is he who does not continue in them," Gal. 3:10.

Further, the chief part of the teaching regarding threats consists in the examples of punishments which God shows, so the witness "of their sound might be heard throughout the whole world" concerning the greatness of God's anger against our sins, Rom. 10:18. The most notable examples which the Holy Spirit has wanted to be seen in Scripture must be gathered under the individual precepts.

By the same line of reasoning God in the Decalog not only prescribes and commands good works, but He also adds promises of rewards when to the First Commandment He adds a general reward and to the Fourth a special one. There is almost the same division of promises in the laws as there is of threats:

(1) There are some general promises. (2) Some are special ones. (3) Some rewards are external or physical, dealing with this life. (4) Some are spiritual and deal with this life and the life to come, Matt. 5:12, "Your reward will be great in heaven"; 1 Tim. 4:8, "Godliness has the promise of life and of the life to come." (5) Some rewards are promises added to the Law, concerning eternal life.

But we must carefully observe the difference between the promises and the threats. For because of the fact that the promises of the Law require the condition of perfect fulfillment and this is impossible for us in this life, therefore the promise of the Law regarding eternal life is for us simply vain and useless (for thus it says in Heb. 7:18); cf. Gal. 3:21. This does not take place because of a fault in the Law, as if its promises were unsure or false, but because of a fault in our flesh, through which the condition added to the promise is impossible for us to fulfill. The threats of the Law regarding eternal death remain over the unbelievers so that even when they are performing the works of the Law, they are still under the curse, Gal. 3:10. But for believers these threats have been abolished, not because God has capriciously changed His eternal will but because the Son of God has taken upon Himself the wrath which we had to endure, and those who by faith apply this benefit of Christ to themselves are freed from the threats of the Law regarding eternal life, Gal. 3:13.

Therefore this is the summary of the promises and the threats of the Law: The rewards are eternal life, and the punishments are eternal death.

The promises and the external or physical threats remain firm, and their interpretation must be taken from the Gospel. There is a difference when they are applied to the ungodly or to believers and those who have been reconciled by faith. For the ungodly must always and immediately be subject to all these physical punishments in keeping with the rigor of the Law. But the Gospel shows two reasons for the difference in punishment: (1) Rom. 2:4, "The goodness of God leads men to repentance"; (2) Jer. 12:3, "Let them be fattened as sheep for the day of slaughter," that is, the testimony remains sure that there is another life in which the particular punishments which the Law threatens will be meted out to the ungodly. But when the physical promises are applied to the believers and those who have been reconciled, because they are said to have the added condition of perfect fulfillment, the promises become vain even for the regenerate. But the Gospel shows the interpretation of such promises and threats as being wonderfully mitigated and tempered if applied to the believers. For because the regenerate still have sinned against the Law, therefore these punishments also remain, e.g., physical death; but because their sins have been forgiven and covered, the punishments are mitigated, Ps. 89:32–33, "I will punish their iniquities with the rod, but I will not take away My mercy from them." Punishments are warnings of the sins which cling in the flesh of believers. For example, Jer. 30:11, "I will correct you in judgment so that you do not think that you do not deserve punishment."

Therefore there is a universal rule that the threats of the Law must be understood as being under the exception of our conversion and repentance, by which the eternal penalties are removed and the temporal penalties reduced. There is the same condition regarding the external promises in the Law as over against the regenerate. For because their obedience, albeit impure and imperfect, is accepted by God and pleasing to Him because of His Son the Mediator, therefore the promises of rewards for obedience to them are also fulfilled. But because there are still many imperfections clinging to us which God seriously wishes to be confessed by believers and put to death by them, therefore these promises connected with the Law must always be considered under the condition of our cross and our chastisement, Mark 10:30, "They shall receive a hundredfold in this life . . . but with tribulation."

The Gospel adds another reason, namely, that it is ordained by God that special punishments on the ungodly and special rewards on the regenerate will be deferred to the life to come. Therefore, because also in this life God wills to preserve His church, He bestows certain rewards on the godly. But what the degrees are of reducing the punishments in the threats, and exceptions in the cross and chastisements in the promises, this cannot and must not be established with certainty, but rather all this is commended to the will of God, who governs these matters because of the intercession of His Son, for some with less and others with more, because some modify the body of sin more and others less, 1 Cor. 11:31, "If we should judge ourselves, we would not be judged by the Lord." For some people there is a necessary admonition against the sin which dwells in them, so that they do not exalt themselves, 2 Cor. 12:7. Some are "to be led to repentance by the goodness of God," Rom. 2:4. Some must be forced to do their duty by the chastening of punishments, Is. 26:16. Some who are stronger must be shown the hope of eternal life by delaying those rewards and laying a cross upon them, Rom. 8:23. This entire subject can be very correctly explained by the example of the rewards which God shows to the godly in this life.

In the sixth place, in order that by a sure and certain method we can set up a list of the sins as well as the good works included under each of the commandments, we must first determine the definite and general goal for each of God's precepts. Then we must consider of what things this goal consists, and what things are joined with it and appointed for it. Likewise [to be considered are] the contraries, which are in conflict with this purpose or impede it, according to the dictum, "To flee sin is to flee the occasion for sin." It is certain that this statement pertains to the same precept, and thus the catalog or list can be put together with some kind of definite order. Likewise, the interpretations of others can thus be more easily understood and evaluated, than when each follows his own reasoning, as is shown in the history of this rule.

This rule has sure foundations in Scripture. For Paul says of the entire Decalog in 1 Tim. 1:5, "The purpose of the commandment is love which comes from a pure heart and a good conscience and sincere faith." He adds, v. 7 ". . . teachers of the Law who do not draw their lectures from this purpose and direct them to this end have turned aside and do not understand either what they are talking about or what they are affirming." Christ also, when He was criticized by the Pharisees for profaning the Sabbath, showed from the purpose of the Third Commandment that works which increased the ministry or service were not only not forbidden but commanded. Likewise He defended the disciples when they wanted to pick grain on the Sabbath day in this way: Only those works conflict with the Third Commandment which hinder ministry to our neighbor. Thus Luther in disputing against the image-breakers established the purpose of the First Commandment, namely, the true God is only to be worshiped according to the prescription of His Word, and those things which conflict with the true worship are prohibited in the First Commandment. Hence, he later determined which things were images, how and why they were prohibited, and what things are free for us.

In the seventh place, therefore, because the correct and undoubted explanation of the Decalog ought not be established only on the basis of dialectical precepts concerning method, we must, when a catalog is put together on the basis of the purpose of the commandments, always show the testimonies which demonstrate and prove which sins and which good works Scripture itself, when it deals with the explanation of the Decalog, applies to the individual commandments. In this way we can take notice when Scripture changes the terminology on the basis of the Decalog and applies the terms to other sins or virtues than those expressly specified in the Decalog. Therefore in undertaking an explanation we must always carefully stipulate the terms in the individual precepts. This is the surest basis for investigating the correct explanation, as the examples show. Thus, for example: To what persons and relationships does Scripture attribute the title of parents and children, terms which Scripture shows pertains to the Fourth Commandment? Likewise the sins to which Scripture gives the name "idolatry" surely pertain to the First Commandment, as we shall show under the locus of each commandment.

In the eighth place, we must not, however, investigate these matters with too much anxiety. For there is no danger to faith, if in applying these points there be some variation or even an error, as in the case of the knowledge of God when one person applies it to the First Commandment and another to the Second. The correct preaching of sound doctrine some people put under the Second Commandment and others under the Third. Things of this kind do not destroy the foundation of faith, as long as a correct understanding of sins and good works remains. God Himself so summarized the entire First Table under the general statement, "You shall love the Lord your God," that there is no danger when the reason for our position is not so clear, whether something is referred to the First or to the Second or the Third Commandment, just as long as it is included under the general precept, "You shall love the Lord." In Rom. 13:9 Paul shows that the catalog of good works of the Second Table is more easily established from the general statement, "You shall love your neighbor," than by any kind of strained accommodation to the individual precepts of the Decalog.

This observation beautifully shows many things: that certain sins and good works cannot be referred to one particular commandment, but are distributed through many precepts, so that the magnitude and enormity of sin may be demonstrated, just as the sins which conflict with the knowledge of God are not only against one commandment but against the whole First Table. Likewise, the work of the Word of God applies not only to the First but also to the Second and Third Commandments, and also in the Fourth Commandment on the Second Table, under the name "parents," God should be honored.

In the ninth place, when the teaching of the Law is set before the regenerate, this division is useful and helpful: (1) In the individual precepts we must show those sins which violate conscience, grieve the Holy Spirit, and thus conflict with faith, lest the regenerate who do such things lose their inheritance in the kingdom of God and so that the faithful should take warning to seek to be protected from lapses of this kind; or if they have been overtaken by a sin of this kind, that they would return to God through repentance. (2) To those who have been received into the grace of God we must show what good works God has prepared in the individual precepts, so that His children may walk in them. (3) But when the regenerate by the aid of the Holy Spirit have begun the new obedience and avoid lapses against conscience, then we must demonstrate to them out of the Decalog those sins which are called venial.

This is the correct doctrine of the church, which must be taught very carefully in its own place for several reasons: (1) As Paul also says, "I am not conscious of any evil on my own part," 1 Cor. 4:4, yet he recognizes that in his own flesh he finds nothing but the law of sin, which is not idle but in a state of rebellion against the law of his mind and lusting against the Spirit which often takes the believers captive in their desire to do good, so that they cry out, "Who can understand his sin?" Ps. 19:12. For in many respects we all offend and must seek to have our many offenses covered because of the Mediator. (2) That they may learn to acknowledge how impure, defective, and imperfect is our new obedience, what imperfection and uncleanness still cling to our good works, how little they can stand before the judgment of God, lest they fall into the arrogance of the Pharisees; but even when they live the most holy lives, they must know that they have to pray, "Forgive us our trespasses." (3) That they may learn from this catalog that they must contend against many different kinds of evil lusts in the individual commandments, so that sin does not invade the Kingdom and drive out the Holy Spirit and faith.

In the 10th place, because God on Mt. Sinai promulgated the Decalog in such a way that He clothed it with certain wrappings which pertained only to the civil nation of Israel, which the apostles showed had already ceased and been abrogated, as is manifest under the First, Third, Fourth, Ninth and Tenth Commandments, therefore we must carefully distinguish in the Decalog those matters which pertain to all men and those which were binding only on the people of Israel, while that nation still existed, so that, having separated and removed the Mosaic wrappings, we might have the pure Decalog of the New Testament so that these points can be distinguished and certain specific rules handed down. Those points which are simply Mosaic can be recognized by these marks, namely, those precepts which have not been received specifically in the writings of the New Testament or those which the apostles clearly showed had been abrogated and definitely do not pertain to the Decalog of the New Testament.

But those points in the Decalog which are binding on all people can be ascertained by three rules: (1) Those points which concur with the natural knowledge which in creation was implanted in the minds of all men. (2) Because the natural knowledge has been badly obscured and darkened on account of sin, so that human reason does not realize that concupiscence is sin and that the Law commands the impossible, therefore there is added this rule, that in the New Testament whatever applies to the gentiles, and is repeated and commanded, is binding on all. (3) Those points shown by Moses himself and to the prophets as pertaining not only to the Israelites but to all nations, such as the law regarding respect for consanguinity in marriage, Leviticus 18. And when the prophets on the basis of the Law warn against these sins among the Gentiles, it is certain that these points pertain also to us in the New Testament era.

The observance of these rules sheds light on many disputations. For Karlstadt[10] in our time stirred up some terrible troubles by saying that we should confess to a great crime because in the common recitation of the Decalog the appendix regarding images, Ex. 20:4, was omitted. Among the Zwinglians certain people screamed that our people were mutilating and castrating the Decalog in the commonly used catechisms, where the appendixes to the First and Third Commandments were not completely recited. Paul by his own example shows that among the Christians in the New Testament it was not necessary that there be the same form of the Decalog as was used among the Jews, but that the Mosaic wrappings had to be removed because we retain the doctrine of the Decalog in the New Testament, not because of Moses but for the reasons cited above. For Paul in Eph. 6:3 in citing the promise added to the Fourth Commandment says, "That you may live long on the earth," but he deletes the words "which the Lord your God will give you," Ex. 20:12, because these words pertain only to the children of Israel in regard to the land of Canaan. Therefore, it is not a falsification or a mutilation when we do not recite the complete Decalog as it was given by Moses. But those points which apply only to Moses we relegate to the civil law; but we receive those things in the Decalog which pertain to all people. Thus let us consider, according to the order of the commandments, what are Mosaic wrappings in the individual commands and what points have been abrogated in the New Testament.

In the First Commandment the expression, "I who led you out of the land of Egypt, from the house of bondage," Ex. 20:1, clearly does not pertain to us but to that people who either themselves or through their parents had served "in the house of bondage" in Egypt. Jer. 23:7 clearly predicts, "Behold, the days are coming, says the Lord, when men no longer shall say, 'as the Lord lives who brought the children of Israel out of the land of Egypt.'" Therefore, we are correct in reciting the First Commandment [thus]: "I am the Lord your God; you shall have no other gods before Me."

But concerning the appendix which was added to the First Commandment, "You shall not make for yourself a graven image . . . ," there is a very hot argument that this pertains also to us Christians in the New Testament. Those people say that no images are to be tolerated in the church buildings and those who keep them without any feeling of superstition are sinning and thus blaspheme the name of God because it is one of the commandments of the Decalog which

---

[10] For an example of Luther against Karlstadt, see his "Against the Heavenly Prophets," *Luther's Works*, Amer. Ed., 40.86ff.

was written with the finger of God which says, "You shall not make a graven image. . . ." This controversy has been stirred up not only by the Jews but in the church itself, both in ancient times and in the present; but the solution is easy on the basis of the rules set forth previously. For (1) in the apostolic writings this appendix has not been repeated because, just as for the Jews images were forbidden, so that they should not make them or possess them, so also in the New Testament: there is no punishment for having images, if there is no superstition attached. (2) There are statements of Paul such as 1 Cor. 8:4, that an idol is nothing; and in a different connection, 1 Cor. 7:19, he says, "circumcision is nothing," that is, it is an adiaphoron. And "things which have been sacrificed to idols," which in the beginning under the law of Christian love had been forbidden by the apostles, Acts 15:29 and Rev. 2:20, yet are permitted by Paul in 1 Cor. 8:1ff. under the free law of faith. Therefore at this point this appendix about not making or possessing ceremonial images has been abrogated in the New Testament. But the expression, "You shall not bow down or serve them" is moral law and pertains to all the gentiles, and the rules show this for (1) in many places of the Old Testament the gentiles are condemned for using images for the purpose of worship or for having them as objects of religious admiration. (2) In the New Testament this prohibition is repeated in Rom. 1:23; 1 Cor. 10:7; 1 John 5:21, where the author calls idols those things which are worshiped in place of God. For this reason there is the appendix which is partly moral law and partly ceremonial. And in the Decalog under the New Testament we must recite the First Commandment this way, "I am, the Lord your God; you shall have no other gods before Me; you shall not worship or adore any likeness or image."

The threat added to the Second Commandment is not ceremonial but moral. Therefore it pertains not only to the Israelites but to all nations. The reason is that also among the gentiles in the Old Testament blasphemy of the name of God was punished, Is. 37:23; and also in the New Testament, Acts 19:37.

In the Third Commandment is a lengthy appendix regarding work on the seventh day. If the question is asked whether this pertains also to the Decalog of the Christians in the New Testament, the correct and proper reply is: yes, if the rules are applied. For (1) the reason for the appendix which is added in Deut. 5:13 shows very clearly that it pertains only to those people who had been in bondage in Egypt. (2) The apostles say clearly that the circumstances regarding the seventh day have been abrogated in the New Testament, Col. 2:16; Gal. 4:10; Is. 66:23. And indeed, when they repeat the substance of the Third Commandment, they do not speak of "sanctifying the Sabbath." Although the reason added in Ex. 20:11 seems to be universal and eternal, namely, that God even before giving the Law to Moses had sanctified the seventh day because He at that time rested from the work of Creation; yet the apostles clearly say that the

Sabbath was a shadow of things to come, Col. 2:16; Heb. 4:9; Gal. 3:23–25, "We are no longer under the custodian." (3) There is no precept in the New Testament prohibiting labors other than those which hinder service and ministry. But that part of the Sabbath concerning the external rest on the Sabbath is treated allegorically, Heb. 4:4. Therefore it is ceremonial just as those things which are set forth in Ex. 16:23, 29 concerning the Sabbath day's journey and cooking are, beyond controversy, ceremonial laws. Therefore the appendix of itself is ceremonial. But it is moral law to this degree: (1) For the sake of good order, it is necessary that some day be designated for religious gatherings. (2) Insofar as there is the natural necessity for some rest for both men and work animals. (3) Those works are forbidden which hinder ministry and service.

In the Fourth Commandment we have the example of Paul, Eph. 6:3, that that statement which pertains to the children of Israel alone must be deleted in the New Testament Decalog.

Paul quotes the Eighth Commandment in Rom. 13:9 thus, "You shall not bear false witness" because in a general way concern and love for the truth are commanded.

Again when Paul cites the last two commandments, he simply omits the reference to house, wife, servants, and cites as a generalization, "You shall not covet." This occurs in two places, Rom. 7:7 and 13:9, and the reason for this is manifest: (1) The rest are Mosaic wrappings which have now ceased. For God distinguished the possessions and property of the Israelites in such a way that they were not to be transferred from tribe to tribe but in the year of jubilee they were to be returned to their owners. He surely did not require this civil ordinance of Moses to be imposed upon the other nations. So also the permission of divorce, which was in the law of Moses, is withdrawn because Christ clearly abrogates it. And the law of slavery, which was in the Mosaic civil law, is not binding on all nations; therefore Paul is acting correctly in cutting off the Mosaic wrappings. (2) Lust or covetousness which is forbidden in the Decalog, seems through the appendix of Moses to be restricted only to the Sixth and Seventh commandments. However, Paul says that this is extended to all the commandments, even those on the First Table, e.g., "The flesh lusts against the Spirit" [Gal. 5:17]. "Therefore I see in my members another law contending with the law of my mind" [Rom. 7:23]. Likewise, "Sin worked in me all concupiscence" [Rom. 7:8], that is, against all the commandments. And Luther, although he retained the customary terminology for the last two commandments, against the Sabbatarians, yet it is clear that he explained them as I have noted above.

The 11th rule is that the division of the Decalog into 10 commandments was commonly observed. For it is certain that there were 10 precepts. Scripture speaks this way in Ex. 34:28; Deut. 4:13; 10:4. It is also certain that these 10 precepts were divided by God Himself into two tables. But what and how many were written on the First Table and what on the Second is not expressly stipulated in Scripture.

Philo and Josephus cut the Decalog in the middle with five commandments on each table. But this is wrong and we can understand from this how fully the light of teaching had been extinguished among the Jews even in small points. But we on the basis of the New Testament can clearly understand what kind of division there was. For Paul in Eph. 6:2 says that the precept regarding honoring our parents is "the first with a promise." It is manifest that to the First Commandment of the First Table a promise has been added, namely, "showing mercy. . . ." Therefore Paul calls the fourth, concerning honoring parents, the first commandment with promise because it is the beginning of the Second Table. When it has been established that this commandment was the first on the Second Table, the entire matter becomes clear and free of doubt. For Christ clearly shows that this was the division of the Decalog. For what Moses calls the two tables He Himself calls the First and Second Commandments. When He says that the first commandment is this, "You shall love the Lord your God . . . ," Matt. 22:37, He is showing that on the First Table were written those precepts by which we directly deal with God. On the second were those which are the bonds of human society by which we deal directly with our neighbor, because He says, "The second is this, You shall love your neighbor . . . ," Matt. 22:39. Therefore, it is erroneous according to the notion of Philo and Josephus to say that the precept regarding honoring parents was written on the First Table. On this division all Christian writers are in agreement.

The dissension regarding this question is not a new one but was stirred up in ancient times. For the Chaldean translators, along with Josephus [*Antiquities*, 3.91–92], Origen *In Exodium*, Gregory of Nazianzus, Jerome [MPL 26.271], and Ambrose [MPL 17.422], on Ephesians 6, contend that four commandments were to be listed on the First Table. For they make a special second commandment out of the appendix concerning images. On the Second Table they join into one the ninth and 10th regarding coveting house, wife, etc. But even Deut. 5:21 puts the precept on coveting the wife first while Ex. 20:17 puts it second. In the Hebrew there is only one verse, not divided in two. Therefore, according to the opinion of these men, the Second Table, beginning with "Honor your father . . ." contains six commandments. But Augustine and others include the appendix on images with the First Commandment and divide the First Table into three precepts and the second into seven, because two different words for coveting are used in the ninth and tenth. Clearly, it is not of great importance how the commandments are listed (for in Rom. 13:9 the precept regarding adultery is placed ahead of the one on murder), as long as we retain the fact that to the First Table pertain those commandments which deal directly with the divine worship of God.

There is great value to this division of the Decalog into two parts and each table has its own rules. To the first pertains a passage such as Acts 5:29, "We must obey God rather than man," that is, obedience to the First Table takes precedence over the Second when it is not possible to obey both. For God did not will to put all the commandments on one table, but those which govern the direct worship of God He separated from the rest and placed on the First Table, because Christ in Matt. 22:38 says, "This is the first and great commandment." Indeed, it is so "great" that when something on the Second Table hinders the worship commanded on the First, or where both cannot at the same time be obeyed, then the following rule applies: The First Commandment is greater than the Second, as Christ says, "No one can serve two masters," Matt. 6:24, that is, contrary commands; "If a person does not hate his father, wife, children, and his own life, he cannot be My disciple," Luke 14:26. Thus when Abraham received the command on the First Table, he is praised regarding the killing of his son because he was willing to break the Fifth Commandment. The Israelites in receiving the command from God to despoil the Egyptians, did the right thing in breaking the Seventh Commandment, because the First Table takes precedence over the Second. Moreover, the First Commandment is of such a nature that the obedience to all the commandments must be undertaken out of the First Table. For the carrying out of the other commandments cannot take place without the First Table, that is, without knowing, loving, and fearing God under the First Commandment, without calling upon Him under the Second Commandment and without the Word which is the ministration of the Spirit under the Third. But when our conscience is contaminated by sin contrary to the First Table, it cannot fail to happen that there follow tragic lapses under the Second Table. Even when the greatest degree of observance of the Second Table is demonstrated, yet it is not pleasing to God without the First Table, that is, if it does not take place principally for the purpose of pleasing God and confessing Christ.

Here is relevant the definition of the worship of Christ, which must include three elements: (1) There must be the commandment of God. (2) It must be done in faith by a reconciled person, in the confidence that the work is pleasing to the Father for the sake of Christ. (3) [It must be done] to the end that we present to God obedience and honor. Therefore the descriptions of all the commandments must be referred back to the First Commandment, "We must fear and love God and by trust in our Mediator not kill, not steal, etc." These are the rules for understanding the First Table.

In regard to the Second Table, Christ gives us this rule: The command to love your neighbor is like the first great commandment but it is not like it in such a sense as though God is not to be loved more than man, Luke 14:26. But the likeness consists in two points: (1) We owe it, for the Second Table demands obedience in the same way that obedience to the First is necessary. (2) The two tables are similar in their purpose because the works of the Second Table are also the worship of God, if they are presented to Him in faith because of His command.

Furthermore, Christ used this rule in opposition to the false persuasions of the Pharisees. For when they made sacrifices, fasted, offered gifts in the temple and did other such works, they believed that God did not care if they neglected their parents, Matt. 15:5–6, or cheated their neighbors, Is. 58:4. Therefore there are four rules for the Second Table: (1) Obedience to the Second Table is as necessary as to the First. (2) The works of the Second Table are also done as worship of God, as has been said. (3) Outward worship in keeping with the First Table, unless it also has attached to it obedience to the Second Table, does not please God, Micah 6:7ff.; 1 John 4:20, "He who says that he loves God and hates his brother is a liar." (4) Outward worship of God, when it takes place while there is violation of love of one's neighbor, where the Second Table does not hinder or conflict with the First, is not accepted by God, Matt. 5:19ff.; Is. 1:15, "When you reach out your hand to pray, I will hide My eyes from you."

In the 12th place it is useful and necessary in the individual commandments to show how and to what degree even in the regenerate in this life perfect fulfillment is impossible. Then we must also consider in addition how in this weakness of ours obedience to the individual precepts can be achieved by believers and must be begun by faith and the Spirit of renewal, namely by the beginning and imputation of righteousness; and these things must be carefully taught with reference to the individual precepts so that the regenerate do not fall into the presumptuousness of the Pharisees by cultivating security under the pretext of the impossibility of fulfillment or by excusing lapses against conscience and thus becoming hardened to every good work.

Finally, because the Decalog was not promulgated for the sake of idle sophistries but that it might be a means through which the Holy Spirit leads us to an acknowledgment of our sin, works repentance, and keeps us in the fear of God, therefore in explaining the Decalog we must not dispute about the Law in such a way that in the meantime we live without the Law, as Paul says, that although he himself had been schooled in the Law at the feet of Gamaliel, Acts 22:3, yet he had lived for a time without the Law. But we must always consider and show how the individual precepts are to be applied to that use of the Law of which we shall speak shortly.

To this end it is useful and necessary that you love and meditate upon the Decalog. For there is one unique way and salutary method for the correct and beneficial use of Scripture and for learning theology, as the ancients have said, namely by utilizing these four aids; reading, meditating, praying, and being tested. For it is one thing to dispute many points with great learning and brilliance; it is another to make Scripture useful to oneself "for teaching, for reproof, for correction and for edification," as Paul says [2 Tim. 3:16]. In regard to the teaching of the Decalog, Scripture expressly says that it is not correctly learned only by reading and hearing, but "the words shall be upon your hearts and you shall meditate upon them when you sit down in your house, as you walk on your journey, when you lie down, and when you rise up, and you shall bind them as a sign upon your hand, and they shall be as frontlets between your eyes; you shall write them upon the doorposts of your house and on your gates," Deut. 6:7ff.; 11:18ff. In regard to the value of meditation on the Law, the whole of Psalm 119 proclaims that your meditation must not be hypocritical but joined with prayer, as God through His Spirit has written that He will put His law in our hearts, Jer. 31:33. The reason for this reverent and salutary meditation on the Decalog is beautifully described by Paul in the passage in Eph. 4:26–30, "Be angry and do not sin. Do not let the sun go down on your wrath. Give no opportunity to the devil. Let him who stole steal no more, but let him labor. . . . Do not grieve the Holy Spirit." For because he says, "Do not let the sun go down on your wrath," he is showing that every single day must be approached with earnest meditation in the mirror of the Decalog, in which we view the polluted image of our corrupt birth, James 1:2–3. [Paul] teaches first that we must meditate daily on the individual commandments, so that we ponder how we may desire to put our life in order and not permit such lapses as grieve the Holy Spirit. If by chance we become involved on that day with a particular sin, that through repentance we return to God and seek His mercy. Second, [Paul] also wills that in our meditation on the individual commandments we acknowledge and consider our inner wickedness and the terrible conflict between the flesh and the Spirit and how our lust keeps hold on us by enticing us and drawing us away in disobedience to individual commandments. Therefore he calls it a *parorgismos*, that is, an angry mood [Eph. 4:26], or the first emotion of anger, as also the Hebrew word in Ps. 4:5 signifies. He warns that we must resist the first movements of concupiscence, lest they put down roots. For, he says, "Let not the sun go down . . ." and he shows what a great peril it is to live without this kind of meditation. For he says this is giving place to the devil. There is no doubt that sin itself follows such security and such lapses against consciences. When Paul makes the third point, "Let him not steal but do good works," Eph. 4:28, he is showing that in the individual commandments we must daily undertake our new obedience, that is, so that our meditation on the Decalog may demonstrate the exhortation to good works. If we have the beginnings of renewal, we should give thanks to

God for beginning in us the restoration of His image, and we should pray that these beginnings be increased and finally brought to perfection. We should also consider how sluggishly we follow the Holy Spirit as He helps and leads us into new obedience, and if we stumble or undo the work of the Holy Spirit, we must confess our wretchedness and seek mercy. I think this method is useful not only for teaching and learning, but particularly for serious practices of piety in which also those things which have been said about meditating on the Decalog can be correctly and fully understood.

Here are pertinent also to these rules those four points about the Law which are cited under the *Loci*.

I have cited these rules before I approach the Decalog because they demonstrate the foundations of the correct explanation and give an introduction as to how the accounts found in the prophetic and apostolic Scriptures must be applied to the Decalog, in order that the sure and complete explanation can be set forth. Now we shall, according to these rules, speak about the individual commandments.

[Chapter II]: The Decalog

[MELANCHTHON'S TEXT]

There are two tables. The First Table contains the works by which we deal with God directly and properly, that is, the principal union and outward worship of God. The Second Table contains the works toward men which are the bond linking human society together, and yet become also the worship of God; for God in His Word commands and enunciates that this is true worship if they are performed because of God's command, as Isaiah says in 1:10ff., and again in 54:13ff. Samuel says [1 Sam. 15:22], "Obedience is better than sacrifices." Hosea 6:6 says, "I will have mercy rather than sacrifice." Christ says that the commandment to love our neighbor "is like the First Commandment" [Matt. 22:39], that is, He demands the required obedience in the same way that obedience to the First Commandment is necessary. These points must be noted in order that we may learn what the true worship of God is and that the works of all the commandments must be related to the first one, and that the purpose must be determined in each of the individual commandments so that they may be done principally in order to give obedience and honor to God. For the worship of God is the work commanded by God, which consists primarily in this, that obedience and honor be given to God and that, along with the confession or acknowledgment of Christ by faith, we please the Father for Christ's sake, just as Peter commands us to offer "spiritual sacrifices acceptable to God through Jesus Christ" [1 Peter 2:5].

The First Commandment

The First Commandment prescribes concerning the highest and most important work, that is, the true knowledge of God, and concerning the true and perfect obedience toward God in perfect fear, trust, and love of God. The two most important elements here are the knowledge of God and the true worship of God. The way of knowing Him is through His Word and testimony. For because God is invisible, it is necessary that there be a testimony about Him, through which He might be recognized and understood, with the result that the human mind is caught up with the workmanship of the world and thinks about God its Creator, but this knowledge, which also the gentiles and the Mohammedans hold, is not sufficient, since these thoughts are driven out of many people by the devil. But even when God is most closely present, yet doubt remains as to whether God the Creator is concerned, hears our prayers, whether He wants to be worshiped, and how. At this point there is need for a word and testimony from God. Therefore here is set forth the sure Word and testimony: "I am the Lord your God, who led you out of the land of Egypt," Ex. 20:2. Thus the human mind should establish that He is the God who has revealed Himself by this word given on Mount Sinai and who asserts that He is your God, that is, the One who is concerned about you, sees you, judges you, defends and punishes you.

The glorious liberation and defense of this people when they were led out of Egypt is an added testimony. Therefore, although God is invisible, yet the human mind knows that He is the true God who reveals Himself by His marvelous testimonies and shows how He wishes to be worshiped. Thus, in the beginning the Word was given to Adam in Paradise, and the whole nature of things, which was a testimony about God, was set before him. But afterward, when he had fallen, he needed comfort concerning the forgiveness of his sin. Therefore another Word was given, namely, the promise of grace; and signs were added by the use of burnt offerings. So also to us the Word of the Gospel has been given and a sure testimony, namely the crucifixion and resurrection of the Son of God. He shows us the Father, John 14:8ff. When the Son is acknowledged, then we evoke the eternal Father who has revealed Himself in His Son, as it says in John 1:18, "No one has ever seen the Father. The Son who is in the bosom of the Father, He has declared Him." Likewise John 14:9, "He who has seen Me has seen the Father." Matt. 11:27, "No one knows the Father except the Son and he to whom the Son reveals Him." Through Him the Father is pleased, and for His sake He hears our prayers. Christ Himself says in John 16:23, "Whatsoever you ask the Father in My name, He will give it to you." Therefore we have established that He is God, who has revealed Himself by the giving of His Son, sent to be a sacrifice and to be raised again in order that He might be our Mediator, Intercessor, Helper, and Savior. Likewise it is He who gave to His Son the Gospel of the remission of sins and life everlasting. This invocation, which recognizes the eternal and almighty God by trust in Christ through the Gospel that has been given to us, distinguishes the worship of the true church from the worship of all the gentiles. Therefore, as often as the human mind cries out to God, it should call upon the God who is the Father of our crucified and risen Lord Jesus Christ and in faith meditate on the good news given through this Son: "Whatsoever you ask the Father in My name, He will give it to you," John 16:23. This method of knowing God Paul repeatedly commends to us, cf. 1 Cor. 1:21, "Because in the wisdom of God the world in its wisdom did not know God, it pleased God through the foolishness of preaching to save those who believe." Likewise the doctrine of Christ the High Priest entering the Holy of Holies teaches the same thing. The remainder of mankind does not know the invisible God, but into the secret Holy of Holies the Son of God entered alone. Therefore we who are about to come near to God should recognize Him as our High Priest who leads us to the Father and carries our requests to Him, as it says in Heb. 4:16, "Having this high priest, let us come near to the throne of grace." Men must learn this way of knowing God in order that He may be properly worshiped.

Moreover, the worship commanded here is the knowledge of God, belief in His Word, true fear, true faith or trust, and true love. For He is requiring fear when He says, "I am the mighty God, jealous, visiting the iniquities . . ." Ex. 20:1ff. Likewise, "You shall fear the Lord your God, and Him only shall you serve," Deut. 6:13. He is requiring trust and love when He says, "I am your almighty God, who sees you, cares for you, defends you, and saves you," Ex. 20:1ff. Again, ". . . Showing mercy to them that love Me," Ex. 20:6. And again, "You shall love the Lord your God with your whole heart," Deut. 6:5. For these statements, wherever we read them, are explanations of the First Commandment.

Because this commandment requires perfect obedience, these words in Deut. 6:5 are a testimony, "You shall love the Lord your God with your whole heart, mind, and strength." Thus it requires fear, trust, and love for God above all things; and this is the case in order that these virtues are to be pure, sweet-smelling, and perfect without any mixture of sin and lust. But the corrupt nature of man in this life cannot produce this perfect obedience. Doubts concerning both the anger and mercy of God cling in his heart. No one fears God as he ought. No one is so on fire with love as he ought to be, and [we have] many corrupt lusts. Therefore Paul says, "The carnal mind is enmity against God," Rom. 8:7. Nor does our evil nature easily understand when we speak of "enmity against God." Thus this law always accuses and condemns all men in their corrupt nature, because they cannot produce perfect obedience.

Now someone will ask, Is it necessary that those who want to please God must obey the Law? I reply: The first beginnings of obedience cannot take place without the knowledge of Christ in the Gospel. For because the Law accuses and condemns all, and we acknowledge that we are guilty and full of stubborn opposition to this Law, therefore our hearts flee from God, do not love Him, and do not dare to ask good things from Him. But when the Gospel has been heard, when we understand that our sins have been remitted to us because of Christ and that we have been truly received into His grace and have been made His children, even though we are unworthy, then in the knowledge of the mercy of God we call upon Him, begin to submit ourselves to Him, to fear Him, to meditate on the promise of His mercy, and to love Him, not in a vain way but as our Father who truly cares for us and saves us, as He says, "I am your God" [Ex. 20:2]. Thus the beginning of keeping the commandments is the acknowledgment of Christ. Then, although obedience ought to increase, yet not even the regenerate ever satisfy the law, and yet the rest of their sins are overlooked for those who, as we shall point out under the proper locus, are reputed righteous for the sake of Christ our Mediator, as it is written, "Christ is the completion of the Law" [Rom. 10:4]. And since they are righteous by this imputation which is accomplished for the sake of the Son of God, their beginning obedience is pleasing to God, even if it is not perfect. The regenerate carry out the law by beginning to obey it and by believing that for the sake of Christ they are regarded as righteous and that for His sake the sins which still cling to them are pardoned.

Furthermore, it is helpful for the sake of teaching this doctrine to include all of the works of the First Commandment under two terms, fear and faith. For although love is of necessity joined to faith or trust in God's mercy, yet the word "love" is less clear than the word "fear" or "faith." For it is necessary that we experience fear in our repentance and trust in our consolation.

I have summarized the works of the First Commandment as the knowledge of God, belief in His word, fear, faith, trust, and love of God. To these points I have added that we must show patience in the face of affliction, either when we are troubled by the unrighteous violence of tyrants or other evil men or when common calamities befall us: sickness, death, the loss of personal property, etc. In each of these difficulties God requires obedience of the heart. The work of the First Commandment is also the worship of God and the obedience of the church in every kind of affliction. Such was the obedience of Abel in his murder, the obedience of the martyrs in their torments, the obedience of Job, of David in his family tragedies. For concerning the first kind it is clearly written, "He who wishes to follow Me, let him take up his cross . . ." Matt. 16:24. Likewise it is necessary that we "be conformed to the image of His Son," Rom. 8:29. Again, "Precious in the sight of the Lord is the death of His saints," Ps. 116:15. Thus there are clear commandments concerning this obedience, and God wills to be feared more than tyrants. Further, He wills that we in these very punishments do not fall into despair in our sorrow nor think that we are forgotten by God, but rather cling to the comfort that God is lovingly inclined toward us and will direct the outcome.

In regard to the calamities that befall us it is written: "Judgment begins at the house of God," 1 Peter 4:17; therefore whether they are punishments or testings, God wills that the church be subjected to such afflictions because human nature by reason *of the sin which clings in our flesh is subject to death, and many of the actual sins of the church, even of the saints, are punished. Thus God wills that the church be admonished by these troubles to repent, to render obedience, to practice faith, worship, and hope, and not to fall into despair or think that we are forgotten or cast off by God. Rather we should cling to the consolation that God is favorable toward us and will direct the final outcome. Here are pertinent the statements which command us to be obedient in our common calamities and be hopeful through faith: "Do not murmur," 1 Cor. 10:10, that is, do not be angry with God as if He were treating us cruelly or neglecting us. Likewise, "Humble yourselves under the mighty hand of God," 1 Peter 5:6. Again, "A broken spirit is a sacrifice to God . . ." Ps. 51:17. "Commit your way unto the Lord, trust also in Him," Ps. 37:5. Again, "Offer the sacrifice of righteousness and put your trust in the Lord," Ps. 4:5.*

See how many good works relate to this obedience which also at the same time pertain to the First Commandment. First, the very obedience of looking to God is of itself a good work, and in this precept it is commanded that God be feared more than tyrants. Likewise, the precept commands us to bear divinely imposed punishments, such as death and the like, as it is said, "Judgment begins at the house of God," 1 Peter 4:17, or "We are chastened by the Lord that we should not be condemned with the world," 1 Cor. 11:32. It is necessary to add faith to this obedience which determines that God does not neglect us, nor cast us off in our affliction, but even now is regarding you and is favorable toward you and will direct the outcome, as David believed when he was in exile. The faith and hope are works of the First Commandment. From all these things comes the virtue which is called patience, that is, the obedience which is given to God with a kind of tranquility of soul or an obedient will which comes from the comfort of our faith. All of these things Paul calls "peace," as in Phil. 4:7, "The peace of God which surpasses all understanding shall keep your hearts and minds," that is, there shall be in you such peace or tranquility of mind that you can sustain and strengthen your minds by the consolation of obedience to God and the comfort of faith and can bear adversities by keeping your eyes on the promise of God by which, when we see the marvelous goodness and mercy of God, we also love Him.

Antithesis

Now we should consider the stubborn resistance of the human race in opposition to the First Commandment, in order that we may acknowledge our frailty and to some extent learn to distinguish the kinds or degrees of sins against this precept.

The first kind is the sin of the Epicureans and academic philosophers who deny or doubt whether there is a God or whether He is concerned about human matters or whether the Word which the church has was given to us by God. For such is the great majority of mankind everywhere, who have completely banished from their

1

minds every thought about God, who are filled with doubt and increase in it. Thus the greatest darkness followed the fall of our first parents; the wickedness of men later on confirmed the darkness, and the devil aids it also.

The second kind of sin against the First Commandment belongs to those who worship idols, that is, those who devise many gods and attribute different powers to them individually, as when the gentiles attribute divine honor, that is, invoke a creature or call upon dead saints. For this invocation attributes omnipotence to the creature or limits God to certain images, even though He does not will to be bound to anything without His Word. For it is evident that the world has always been full of idols and is still given to idolatry. Nor does this invoking of the saints and the worship of statues differ from the practices of the heathen.

The third kind belongs to magicians who make pacts with devils, the enemies of God, and those who consult magicians, and those who are given over to other superstitious observances to which powers are attributed without the ordinance of God. If some effects do result from these practices, the devil is the author of them, and trust is placed in him. All these things are forbidden in Lev. 20:6, "The person who turns to mediums and wizards plays the harlot after them. I will turn My face against him and cut him off from the midst of his people."

Fourth, the Jews, philosophers, heretics, and Mohammedans all devise for themselves their own gods and are unwilling to acknowledge that He is God who reveals Himself in His Word through His Son, Christ, since He wills to be known and worshiped only in this way. Therefore the Manichaeans violated the First Commandment when they created the notion that there were two gods, one good and one evil and both equally eternal. Likewise Paul of Samosata, who argued that in Christ there was only the human nature, just as Mohammedans irreverently believe. The Arians also broke this commandment in denying that the Son of God is of the substance of the Father. Likewise others who say that the Holy Spirit is only an emotion created in men.

Fifth, there are those who do not worship and call upon God through Christ the Mediator, but imagine other mediators such as the saints, Masses, satisfactions, and other works. Also those who say that we must remain in doubt about the grace of God.

Sixth, the deserters who have fallen away from the true doctrine of the Gospel because of fear or hatred, such as Judas and Julian the Apostate.

Seventh, those who have lost hope, such as Saul, and of necessity all people will fall into this state who do not know the Gospel of faith in Christ.

Eighth, those who refuse to learn the Gospel and are not aroused to hear or understand the teaching of Christ, even though the heavenly Father has commanded, "Hear Him," Matt. 17:5.

Ninth, the hypocrites, who even though they profess the truth and are not polluted by worship of idols, yet in their heart are without fear of God, without faith, and they love their pleasures or their treasures more than they love God, men such as Nabal, 1 Sam. 25:3ff. This is the way the great majority of people in the church are, even when the church possesses the pure doctrine, as the parable of the sower teaches [Matt. 13:3ff.].

Tenth, pride, that is, an admiration for and trust in one's own power, wisdom, or virtues, without the admission of our own weakness, without acknowledging our need of or praying for divine help, as was the case with Alexander, who after so many great things had been accomplished, believed that this beautiful empire of his had come into being by his own decision and military might and took great delight in his own wisdom and his own courage, and began to despise and oppress his subordinates and did not recognize that these great achievements had been made by the help of God, who took the rule away from the Persians that He might punish them, just as afterward Alexander was reduced to nothing and punished. The same is recorded of Nebuchadnezzar who, when he was chastened for his arrogance, repented, Dan. 4:3ff. Sennacharib in the same way was puffed up in his own self-confidence and did not repent and was killed, 2 Kings 18–19. History shows that many men of heroic proportions were finally brought low by tragic circumstances. This happens because they sin in their self-admiration and trust in their own talents without recognizing their human frailty and without acknowledging and seeking divine aid. They often create dangerous situations and even evil ones out of their own desires, because of confidence in their own power, as Pompey did. Thus they add other vices—love of wealth, despising and oppressing other people, as Alexander did when in his false security he became intoxicated and killed his most deserving generals and thus brought down punishments upon himself. Poetry also refers to this same kind of thing in the case of Ajax, whom Sophocles describes as being punished with madness because, when his father Telamon had said to him in his departure that he should fight with all his might but seek his victory from God, Ajax replied that even a coward could be victorious with the help of God but that he would win without him. From examples of this kind we can easily understand why heroic men are finally destroyed by evil circumstances. It is written of this pride and self-confidence, "Everyone who is proud in heart before men is an abomination before the Lord," Prov. 16:5. Although this evil can more clearly be seen in heroic people, yet all are subject to the disease. The trust of many people leans more heavily on riches, friends, and their own industry than on God. We must learn to recognize this disease in order that we may amend ourselves and place our trust truly in God, as David cried, "Look upon me and be merciful to me, for I am desolate and afflicted," Ps. 25:16. Again he says, "When my father and my mother forsake me, then the Lord will take me up," Ps. 27:10.

Here we must also mention those hypocrites who put their trust in their own righteousness before God, as the Pharisees in Luke 18:10ff. Upon such people falls the guilt of many sins, because they do not recognize their own weakness, they do not *recognize that in the eyes of God they are worthy of punishment because they have a false confidence and do not call upon God through Christ the Mediator. Indeed, they put their own works forward in the place of the Mediator's. I have described their attributes above under the fifth degree.*

Eleventh, unwillingness to suffer, which in the proper sense of the word is a violation of the First Commandment because our will refuses to be obedient to God in our punishments. Sometimes it even becomes angry at God as being a harsh master or an unjust judge, an emotion against which Scripture often cautions us, for example, "Be angry and do not sin" [Eph. 4:26], that is, rule over your sorrow and bend your mind so that you may willingly be obedient to God in your anguish, as has been said in Ps. 4:4.

I have gathered together the kinds of sins which in themselves are violations of the First Commandment, which can easily be recognized and evaluated. Because the Decalog is the sum of the teaching of all virtues, we should distribute also these virtues among the individual commandments. To the first pertains the virtue sometimes called "piety," sometimes "religion," but it is more easily understood as fear of God, faith or trust, love of God. Of necessity this virtue called piety includes these aspects. Here we consider also the willingness to suffer. Another name for piety is almost equivalent to the term "universal righteousness," if we define it as that obedience which is given to God in all His commandments, as we shall later discuss, to this end, that we humble ourselves before God and do all our works for Him. Therefore we shall discuss also that virtue called "universal righteousness."

The First Commandment:
"I Am Jehovah Your God. You Shall Have No Other Gods before Me."

At the outset we must speak about the terminology. I shall not rehearse all the arguments about the name "Jehovah," but shall only add the simplest point, namely that God has willed that by this special name "Jehovah" He separates Himself from all false deities, that He is the true God who has revealed His essence and will among His people, with a sure Word and clear testimonies. We must not believe anything concerning God except what He has revealed. Therefore there is added the plural *'elohīm* with the singular attached to it, showing the mystery of the Trinity and of the unity in the divine nature.

This phrase "You shall have no other gods" Paul also imitates in 1 Cor. 8:5–6, "Although there are many who are called gods . . . but to us there is only one God." And John expresses this through the word "to have," "He who denies the Son does not have the Father," 1 John 2:23, and in 2 John 9, "He has both the Father and the Son." Hence the phrase "You shall not have" is used. Moreover, He does not call any alien god by name, but simply uses the plural "gods" to indicate that the idolatry which clings in our hearts is multiple and immeasurable.

Further, Scripture says four things about alien gods, a consideration of which will cast light on the First Commandment. In Ex. 20:3, the word *ʾachērīm* is used, derived from the preposition "after," meaning later gods who after the true, first, and highest God were devised by men or devils; or those who are worshiped after the true God, *neben Götter*. Ps. 81:9, "There shall be no strange gods among you" because they have nothing in common with the true God, or because they steal you away from and alienate you from the true God, *Abgötter*. In the same verse they are called illegitimate, spurious gods, that is, those who "by nature are not gods," Gal. 4:8. In Deut. 32:17 they are called "new gods," namely those whom your fathers did not worship, that is, gods who have been received outside of and contrary to the Word and the established worship. Hence they can be judged from such German words as "other" (*andere*), "strange" (*fremde*), "gods alongside of the true God" (*Nebengötter*), "spurious gods" (*Afftergötter*).

We must also examine the expression "before My face" or "before Me" (*ʿal-pānī*). The LXX translates it in Ex. 20:3 "beside Me" and in Deut. 5:7 "before My face"; Luther renders it "beside Me" (*neben mir*) and "before Me" (*für mir*) respectively. The "before Me" of the First Commandment is explained this way in Deut. 4:35; 32:39; Is. 44:6; 45:21: "Beside Me," that is, according to the true God we must not at the same time also worship other gods. For He wills that divine worship be offered to Him alone and that He be loved above all other things. Therefore He condemns those who "halt between two opinions," 1 Kings 18:21, and those "who are neither hot not cold," Rev. 3:15. But God through the term "before Me" is pointing out that in the First Commandment He is accusing not only outward idolatry which is carried out in the eyes of the world, which the philosophers also ridiculed, but especially the inner idolatry of the heart, which often has the appearance of the greatest piety in the eyes of men but before God is an abomination. The grammatical description of these terms has great value, as we shall see.

The rules set forth earlier should now be utilized for investigating and confirming the explanation of the First Commandment. Because the statement is put negatively, "You shall have no other gods," you shall not adore or worship them, we must also add from Scripture other similar negative expressions. Note Ps. 81:9, "You shall not worship any strange gods." Deut. 7:16, "You shall not reverence new gods." On the opposite side we note affirmative statements of the First Commandment, as in Deut. 32:39, "See that I am He alone, and there is no other God beside Me," cf. Is. 45:21; John 17:3; Deut. 6:4. These antitheses can be understood in the sense of alien gods, cf. Deut. 6:5; 10:20; Matt. 4:10.

Furthermore, there is one external kind of idolatry mentioned in the Decalog in regard to graven images. But because He says, "Before Me," therefore the inner idolatry of the heart, as well as many other sins are forbidden which are in conflict with the First Commandment. Rom. 2:22, "You who condemn idolatry, are you guilty of sacrilege?" Ezek. 14:7, "They placed idols in their hearts." Furthermore, the various kinds of idolatry are mentioned by name, in order that we might be warned as to the place where sins against the First Commandment are regarded as sins before the judgment of God. From these words of the First Commandment we can very nicely develop a catalog, first, from the affirmative side. Clearly this was the way the ancients explained it, as we can gather from Augustine's *Enchiridion* [117, MPL 40.286], namely that under the First Commandment we ought to worship God in true faith, with sincere hope, and with perfect love. From these fundamental points we can more precisely draw these conclusions:

(1) Because He says, "I am Jehovah," He is showing that He has the rule over us, the right to give us commandments, and that we owe Him obedience—therefore, as often as we confess that the Lord is our God, we are bearing witness that we are obligated to obey His commandments. (2) Because He describes what He is like, namely the one and only God, separated from all spurious gods, and indeed Jehovah who has revealed Himself with His sure Word and the testimony of the exodus, He therefore wills to be known as He has revealed Himself. (3) Because He not only says that He is God and Lord, the Creator and Sustainer of all things, but adds testimony concerning the blessing which belongs in a peculiar and proper way to the church: "I am your God who led you out of Egypt," Ex. 20:2, He therefore is recalling to our memory the many blessings by which He daily shows Himself to us as our God, and by this name He requires even from individuals—for He does not use "your" (*vester*), in the plural, but "your" (*tuus*) in the singular—love, trust, and hope. (4) Because to the First Commandment is added the element of jealousy, He therefore requires fear, as Jer. 10:7, 6 says, "Who would not fear You? For there is none like unto You." These points are clear.

Moreover, it is pleasant to see how these matters are proved and confirmed in the accounts of the prophets, that is, how the very words are borrowed from the First Commandment. Jer. 9:24, "I am the Lord who practices loving-kindness and judgment." There one can recognize the words of the First Commandment, also because He adds, "Let him glory in this, that he understands and knows Me." Thus the knowledge of God pertains to the First Commandment. John 17:3, "That they may know You the only true God," and these words borrowed from the First Commandment show to what precept the knowledge of God pertains. Deut. 6:5, "You shall love the Lord your God." That the love of God pertains to the First Commandment is clear because these words precede (v. 4), "The Lord your God is one God," words which definitely have been taken from the First Commandment. Again in vv. 13–14, "You shall not go after alien gods, but fear the Lord your God," cf. 1 Sam. 15:23; Deut. 10:20–21; Is. 45:22; Ps. 7:1; 1 Tim. 6:17. In these and similar statements the words of the First Commandment re-echo and demonstrate the setting of these virtues in the Decalog. The most beautiful passage is Mal. 1:6, which shows the true explanation. For the Jews were vehement in asserting that the Lord is God and He is our Father. But, says God, "If I am your Father, where is My honor? If I am your Lord, where is My fear?" These are the sure, firm, and clear foundations of the meaning of the First Commandment. A listing or catalog of the virtues that pertain to the First Commandment can be set forth in definite order:

I. The knowledge of God. To its definition pertains: (1) to understand and believe correctly concerning the essence and will of God; (2) that we draw this understanding from the revelation of the divine Word which is confirmed by miracles; (3) that this knowledge is kindled in us by the Holy Spirit.

II. The fear of God. Scripture attributes these qualities to this fear: (1) It attributes to it the word concerning the will of God, Deut. 4:10, "I will make them to hear My words in order that they may learn to fear Me all their days." (2) It attributes to the fear of God the warnings of the wrath of God and the examples of His punishments, Deut. 9:19; Ps. 52:6; Zech. 9:5. (3) By the dread of the wrath of God it shuns evil pleasures, Prov. 8:13, "The fear of the Lord is to hate evil, pride, and the evil way," or it causes repentance which desists from evil. Cf. Prov. 3:7; Ex. 1:17; Gen. 22:12; Ex. 20:20. (4) Pertinent also to the fear of God is filial reverence by which we are warned not to offend our father. This is the way the idea is used in Lev. 19:3, "You shall each fear your mother and your father." (5) By the word "fear" Scripture often describes the entire worship we owe to God.

III. The love of God. (1) This takes into consideration the many blessings of God which have been shown to us in both spiritual and material matters, Deut. 6:12; 1 John 4:10; Ps. 18:1; 116:1. (2) Scripture attributes to the love of God His promises concerning this life and the life to come, Ps. 40:16; 31:23. (3) And in turn a person subjects himself to God out of gratitude and obedience, in keeping with the order which has been instituted by God, John 14:21, 23; 1 John 5:13.

IV. Trust in God. In this locus we shall not speak of the faith which lays hold on the forgiveness of sins, for this properly pertains to the doctrine of the Gospel. But that kind of trust which properly pertains here is related to hope, as, for example: (1) that we flee to the true God and do not go after alien or foreign gods; (2) that we establish the fact that God is both willing and able to help us; (3) that we in keeping with His Word and His promises look to Him for help, either success in good things or lightening of our burdens in evil things; (4) that we leave things entirely in the counsel of God; (5) that we do not do anything against God out of fearfulness, but in confidence in His promises remain in obedience to the commandments of God; (6) that whatever happens in present or eternal matters, we always keep our trust in the grace and mercy of God and our hope for eternal life, as the words of the First Commandment proclaim, "I am the Lord your God."

These are the kinds of good works under the First Commandment; and the virtues which in a sense are bound together with them manifestly are pertinent at this point. With reference to patience: (1) It is developed out of the faith which believes that God does not neglect us in our affliction but is favorably inclined toward us, James 1:3. (2) It is developed out of the hope which is certain that God will govern the outcome of our trials and lessen our calamities, Rom. 5:4; 8:25. (3) Patience comes out of love so that we do not murmur against God, as if He were treating us cruelly or neglecting us, but rather we offer to God obedience in our calamities with quiet mind or obedient will which grows out of faith and love, when we consider the reason why the cross is laid upon us. Thus also in Rom. 15:4 these concepts are joined together, "That we through patience and comfort of the Scriptures might have hope." And 2 Peter 1:5–7 points out the close connection between patience and many other virtues: "Strive to add to your faith moral excellence or virtue, and to virtue knowledge, and to knowledge self-control, and to self-control patience, and to patience godliness, and to godliness love of the brethren, and to love of the brethren charity."

Humility also includes many virtues: (1) The knowledge of God and of our own weakness, 1 Peter 5:6. (2) Fear of God because He resists the proud, lest we exalt our own merits, Ps. 130:4. (3) Humility includes also obedience, so that we do not seek a greater calling but content ourselves within the boundaries of our calling. (4) Trust and hope, that is, in the hope of divine aid we carry out the duties of our office, and know that no one is happy in his work unless God is aiding him, and if anything good befalls us, we should not do homage to our own endeavors but confess that it is a gift of God. Hope likewise comes from confidence in the promises and long-suffering of God, Gal. 5:5; Rom. 5:4.

Now having established the affirmative aspect of the First Commandment and having proved it on the basis of correct foundations, it is a simple thing to add the antithesis, namely those sins which are in conflict with the First Commandment. Because the affirmative is better known, as that which is more often and more clearly taught in Scripture, it is useful on the basis of the antithesis to draw up a list of sins. Those who under the papacy wrote their explanations of the Decalog, under the First Commandment listed primarily these people as sinners: (1) those who worship men in place of gods; (2) those who worship the moon and the stars; (3) those who through magic call upon the devil; (4) soothsayers; (5) those who put their trust in dreams; (6) those who are guilty of sacrilege. But they do not even mention the greatest sins against the First

Commandment. We can understand the list better if we consider it from the standpoint of the negative. The following people are in conflict with:

The knowledge of God: the Epicureans, together with the academicians and others who deny or doubt that there is a God, Ps. 14:1; also the Jews, Turks, and heretics who believe differently about the essence of God than has been revealed in the Word of God; also those who invent many gods; likewise all those who devise other mediators than Christ and have their own self-chosen religious beliefs, who do not believe correctly concerning the will of God.

The fear of God: carnal security conflicts with the fear of God, and we can learn what this security is from the things which it raises in opposition, such as devising something against God because of a useless fear either of men or of human disasters. Likewise, because the fear, as the term is used in Scripture, includes the entire worship which we owe to God. Therefore in conflict with the fear of God are the magicians and those who invent their own peculiar religions outside the Word. For Christ clearly affirms that such people are contending against the fear of God, Matt. 15:9, likewise those people who attribute to creatures or created things the honor and worship due to God.

The love of God: being an enemy or hater of God, also [those showing] ingratitude and disobedience toward God, especially in loving pleasure or wealth more than God.

Trust: despair and the loss of hope, as it was written of the Israelites in the wilderness that they tempted God, that is, out of their lack of confidence, or that because of trust in their own wisdom they departed from the Word and from obedience to God and sought means which had been prohibited by God.

Humility: the hypocrisy of bragging of one's own righteousness and the pride, which is either the trust in one's own ideas and powers, so that the person does not seek the aid of God, or an admiration of one's own virtue without the knowledge of his weakness, and refusing to acknowledge that his successes are blessings of God but rather attributing them to his own counsels and ability. Here is pertinent also the tempting of God, as when the means which He has ordained are neglected because of human pride.

Patience: murmuring against God, which is a form of impatience, when the human will refuses to obey God in its punishments, or is angry with God, as if under an unfair judgment which does not rightly distribute either the successes or the penalties, and does not consider the true causes of the cross.

In this way almost a list of transgressions against the First Commandment can be rehearsed in the various loci. But I have said that the correct understanding of the subject, on the basis of the foundations of the other points which are in the Decalog, can be evaluated. Therefore I wish to add only a few more items.

Brenz has made a list of sins against the First Commandment, not on the basis of the antithesis, but by establishing the purpose, which he has done by using the very words of the First Commandment: "You shall not adore or worship any image, because you did not see any likeness on Mt. Horeb." Therefore the purpose is that this one true God alone is to be worshiped according to His Word. Thus Christ in Matt. 4:10 is speaking of the First Commandment when He says, "You shall worship the Lord your God, and Him only shall you serve." Or Rom. 1:21, "They did not glorify Him as God," that is, according to His revealed Word. Therefore the sins against the First Commandment are those which are in conflict with this purpose or end: (1) when men deny that there is a God, or when divine honors are not given to the one true God but to idols, Hos. 13:4; (2) when He alone is not worshiped, but we also seek other gods, saviors, deliverers, and helpers in addition to the true God, that is, when we seek and search elsewhere for the blessings which alone are given by God; (3) when other religious practices have been invented, and we put our trust in these rather than in what has been established in the Word of God, or think that because of these acts of worship God will be well-disposed toward us and bless us, as when they sought after certain idols, Num. 15:39–40. We sin in the worship of God in three ways: (1) when in place of the true God we worship those things which by nature are not gods; (2) when we worship the true God, to be sure, but not according to the Word; (3) when we worship the true God but He is not worshiped solely. All these concepts are comprehended under the one term "idolatry." Thus from this purpose is developed almost the same list as above: (1) the gentiles with their idols; (2) the Jews with their high places and their sacred groves; (3) the Pharisees with their traditions; (4) the Mohammedans; (5) the rites of the papists, which have been instituted without the Word of God, either in order to merit salvation or to obtain some physical deliverance; (6) the invocation of the saints; (7) the adoration of statues; (8) the sins of magicians; etc.

This method of investigating the true meaning of the First Commandment is in accord with Scripture, which includes all sins contrary to the First Commandment under the name of idolatry and fornication. It attributed names to certain idols in order that it might show by the very words themselves that there is not only one kind of idolatry, but that it is committed in as many different ways as there are names for it.

Therefore I shall cite the principal words because, as has been said above under the rules, in this way Scripture is accustomed to set forth the description of the commandments of God through key words. (1) *'elīl*. Some people wish to describe it from the concept of vanity or foolishness. Others say that it is a breaking of the Law. The word *'ēl* refers to the true God, and *'elī* to a fictitious god or idol (*Mittgott/Götzen*), that is, to invent something as being God and to worship as God that which is by nature not God; as if one were to say that God (*'ēl*) is not God. (2) *ba'al*, "lord," because he is considered as such by his worshipers, or because they said that they did not worship idols but that they were carrying on this worship in honor of the true God, Hos. 2:16, "She will no longer call Me Baal or Lord. Therefore forms of worship not commanded by the Word of God, even though offered to the true God, are idols, contrary to the First Commandment. (3) *gelālīm*, "dung," "filth." Thus Paul in Phil. 3:8 says that even his good works are dung when they are placed in opposition to the judgment of God. (4) *hakamīm*, so named from the concept of glowing, because of the warmth of the devotion of the heart, when the worshipers have a good intention, that is, a zeal for God but not according to knowledge. (5) *mōlak*, "God rules." (6) *sēmel*, "image, statue." Therefore those who attribute to graven images certain power, or think that in connection with certain images God gives greater heed to their prayers or is more efficacious than elsewhere, commit idolatry. (7) *miplezeth*, from "fear" or "terror," that is, that when the fear which is due God alone is given to another, that is idolatry—or whatever form of worship is established without the Word, out of some kind of fear. (8) *zirim*, from "anxiety" and "sorrow," because they cannot give a peaceful conscience; but even if people think that in this way they are worshiping the true God, they still are leading the worshipers to the sorrows of hell. (9) *thohū*, from "confusion" or "devastation," because the person who goes after idols is cursed.

This simple consideration of the terms contains a great warning. For the first seven describe the various kinds of idolatry which, in keeping with the meaning of the words, can be stipulated in order. The last two show the penalties, even of inward idolatry, which often has the appearance of piety. For human reason neither understands nor believes that these arbitrarily chosen forms of worship, which are undertaken with great zeal and not with the intention of worshiping the devil or any creature but of honoring the true God, are actually idolatrous. During the reigns of the emperors Valentinian, Theodosius, and Arcadius, when paganism had been abolished and the religion of Christ everywhere restored, the Roman senate sent to the emperors asking for the freedom either to accept the Christian religion or to retain the sacred rites of their ancestors if they preferred. The orator Symmachus, among other points, used this argument: God is something immeasurable and infinite, whose nature cannot be perfectly understood, and therefore it would be fair that He be worshiped in different ways, as each man perceives and understands Him. A decree of this kind from Emperor Maximinus is cited in Eusebius, 9.9 [MPG 825–27], "No Christian shall be compelled, against his will, to take part in the worship of the gods, but each man may choose by what rite he wishes to worship God." But Paul says, "The things which the gentiles sacrifice according to their own opinion, they do not sacrifice to God but to demons," 1 Cor. 10:20. The Israelites were not so foolish as to think that the golden calf was the eternal and infinite divine essence. For they had seen, since it had been melted down recently, that it had not previously been a calf, much less God. But because they remembered that the Egyptians who worshiped god by this kind of ritual lived in the greatest affluence, they also wanted by the use of this kind of rite to worship the God who had led them out of Egypt, so that He might be kind to them, as He had been to the Egyptians. Nor did they think that in this kind of worship they were having other gods. But we know well how viciously God condemned this act of idolatry.

This method of seeking the negative meaning of the First Commandment has been given to us by the Holy Spirit Himself, in order that under the name of idolatry all sins might be included which conflict with the First Commandment and that the varieties of such sin might be listed, as we have shown. What kind of sins they should include can be understood from the fact that the word "fornication" is used to designate them: First, because new rites come from the wantonness and lustfulness of the flesh. Second, therefore also when the marriage covenant with God has been violated, people quickly fall away into new religious rites. Third, just as harlots are purchased for their bodies, so also those who rely on and trust in their own powers or human aid, as well as those who wish to earn their salvation by their own works, are said to be guilty of fornication.

Scripture also in this way explains the First Commandment from the definition of what God is, and thus a catalog is produced showing how and in what ways we have other gods. Luther and Rhegius followed this line of reasoning. The definition is made up of two parts:

1. To whatever thing is attributed the glory which belongs to God alone, from this comes another god. The rationale and foundation of this definition is in Gen. 30:1–2, when Rachel said, "Give me children, or else I will die." Jacob replied, "Am I in the place of God, who has withheld from you the fruit of the womb?" 2 Kings 5:7, when the king of Syria had written to the king of Israel that he should cure Naaman from his leprosy, the king of Israel cried out, "Am I God that I can kill and make alive?" Is. 42:8, "I am the Lord; that is My name. I will give My glory to no other, nor My praise to graven images." There you will recognize the words of the First Commandment and see this added explanation, that is, that to have other gods is to give to another the glory which is owed only to God. Two points are expressly mentioned here: (1) glory, when we seek other saviors, helpers, and deliverers rather than God Himself in the way He has revealed His will in His Word; (2) praise, when we have received blessings and do not attribute them to God but to other creatures. Scripture expressly teaches that this glory and praise must be given to God alone, Jer. 17:5; 10:5–7; 2 Tim. 3:4.

2. The second part of the definition is this: Whatever creatures are placed above God in respect to obedience, fear, love, trust, etc., are made alien gods in the same way as when we so fear or love something that we obey and trust it so much that we depart from and violate the Word and commands of God. This part of the definition has clear witness in Scripture, Acts 5:29; Matt. 10:28; 1 Peter 3:14–15; Ps. 118:8; Matt. 10:37. Thus it is manifest that, when fear, obedience, and love of God and a created thing are in conflict, then we either violate or keep the First Commandment. Matt. 6:24, "No one can serve two masters."

The apostles attribute the name "god" to various things so that as though pointing with the finger, they are giving an explanation of the First Commandment. In 2 Cor. 4:4; Satan is called "the god of this world," because men are more obedient to his promptings than to God. Likewise, because the devil has put forth this message, "I will give you all things, if you will worship me," Matt. 4:9, and experience shows that the ungodly often prosper, Ps. 73:3ff., hence the Word of God is despised, His commands broken, [and people feel that] there is no good reason for being godly; but even though our conscience cries out in opposition, we fall into sins. Thus the devil becomes another god. In Phil. 3:19 the belly is called god, as is further explained in Rom. 16:18, where they do not serve Christ but their own belly, that is, servants or ministers who do not seek the glory of God but only the comforts of their own belly. Or those who for the sake of their belly either deny the teaching or do something else contrary to the Word of God, and thus make another god out of their own belly. 2 Thess. 2:4 says that the Antichrist makes himself God because he commands that in the church his own decrees be obeyed rather than the Word of God. Likewise as God he tries to bind consciences to his own traditions. Eph. 5:5 and Col. 3:5 teach that avarice is idolatry. Indeed avarice is also a sin contrary to the Second Table; but when in seeking and grasping riches the commandments of God are violated, then it becomes a command contrary to the First Commandment, because avarice loves, fears, and serves mammon more than God. Also when one so trusts in riches, 1 Tim. 6:9ff., that in his false security he no longer cares about God and His Word and does not fear the wrath of God nor pray to Him, then his avarice has become an idolatry and by definition is another god.

These descriptions seem to be diverse, to be sure, yet they all definitely go in the same direction and render the explanation of the Decalog more certain. But because so much wisdom is included here which cannot fully be treated, we must set forth for consideration the various ways in which the testimonies are given in Scripture, so that what is given in one line of reasoning in a rather obscure way can be made clearer in another, lest we omit something. The Holy Spirit has dealt especially fully and in different ways with the discussion of the First Commandment, because it is the foundation stone of the entire Decalog.

Now having established both positively and negatively the correct meaning of the First Commandment, it is easy hereafter to apply the various distinctions about which we have spoken in the rules: (1) what are the internal, what are the external and actual sins about which we can in some way make a rational judgment; (2) the distinction between moral and venial sins, for these can be distinguished in keeping with our definition; (3) how and to what degree perfect fulfillment is impossible for us in this life, and still how obedience can be begun toward the First Commandment. This will be explained in the third section.

Therefore there remains only that we say something about the threats and promises under this commandment and give some examples. We have also spoken earlier about the distinctions of these matters. Therefore we shall gather only a rudimentary list.

Threat and promise; The words in Ex. 20:5, "I am a jealous God . . ." pertain to the whole Decalog, which explains what He means when He says, "Keep My commandments," v. 6. This is added to the First Commandment, because it derives from it, both with reference to keeping as well as violating the rest of the commandments. There is also at the same time both the spiritual and the material aspect.

Further, "the sins of the parents shall be visited unto the third and fourth generation," v. 5, in both spiritual and physical punishments in this life, as in the case of Solomon because of his sin of the worship of the calf, 1 Kings 11:11, or the permanent punishment which was meted out to the kings of Israel. So also with the rewards. The eternal rewards and punishments do not befall us, however, because of the sins and works of others.

The punishment of idolatry is dealt with in Deut. 4:25–26 and 8:19–20, "If you worship other gods, I call upon heaven and earth to witness that you will utterly perish just as those other nations." Jer. 5:25 threatens them with war and exile; Deut. 11:17 with famine; in Deut. 17:2–5 idolatry is punished with physical punishment; in Deut. 27:15ff., a curse is threatened; cf. Deut. 28:15ff. and v. 32; Lev. 26:14ff.; Zephaniah 1; Deuteronomy 30–31; Jeremiah 23; Obadiah 1.

Threats against those who do not love God: Ps. 11:5; 109:17; John 3:19; 1 Cor. 16:22; John 12:25; 14:24; 1 John 3:14.

Threats against those who do not trust in God: Ps. 49:6ff.; 115:8; Prov. 11:28; Is. 59:4; 42:17; Jer. 17:5; 7:8; Luke 18:14; Mark 10:23.

Threats against those who do not hope in God: Job 8:13; 11:20; Prov. 11:28; Is. 20:5; 28:13.

Threats against those who do not fear God: Prov. 29:25; Hos. 10:3; Deut. 11:28; 2 Cor. 10:6; 2 Thess. 1:8.

Promises connected with love: Deut. 11:5–7; Ex. 23:20ff.; Is. 64:4; Prov 4:6; 8:17; John 14:23; 1 Cor. 8:3; John 16:27.

Promises connected with trust in God: Ps. 125:1; Jer. 17:7; Ps. 37:5; 56:11; 91:14; 31:1; Prov. 29:25; Is. 40:31; Rom. 5:5.

Promises connected with the fear of God: Ps. 34:10; 115:13; 111:5; 145:19; 15:4; Luke 1:50; Prov 1:7; 9:10; 14:27; 15:33; 22:4; Ps. 111:10; Ecclus. 1:2.

The general promises of the First Commandment: Luke 16:10; Matt. 25:29; Ex. 20:6.

Examples of punishments for breaking the First Commandment: Ex. 32:28; 1 Cor. 10:7, idolatry is punished. Deut 7:2ff.; 20:16–18, the Canaanites are exterminated. In Judg. 8:27ff., the house of Gideon is punished. In 1 Kings 14:9–10 Jeroboam is punished. In 2 Chronicles 36 the entire people of Israel are cast out of the Promised Land. The Jews perished in the desert because of their unbelief, Num. 14:36–37; Heb. 3:18. In 2 Peter 2:4 the apostate angels are driven out of heaven. In 1 Sam. 15:24 Saul says, "I have sinned because I feared the people." In Gen. 6:5–7 false security is punished by the Flood. In 2 Chron. 16:12 Asa put his trust in doctors, and in the same chapter he puts his trust in the king of Syria and is punished. Ps. 52:7, "Behold the man who made not God his strength, but trusted in the abundance of his riches." In Luke 12:16ff. we read of the rich man who placed his trust in the fullness of his wealth. In 1 Sam. 2:29 Eli loves his sons so much that he is unconcerned about profaning God. In 1 Sam. 13:11ff. Saul out of fear of danger breaks the command of God. In 1 Kings 11:4 Solomon loves his wives so much that he falls into idolatry. In Is. 7:2 Ahaz is so terrified that "his heart was moved as the trees of the forest are moved with the wind." In 1 Kings 12:26ff. Jeroboam out of love for his royal power instituted idolatry. In 1 Kings 13:21ff., in regard to the prophet who was disobedient in a matter which seems unimportant, we read that a lion killed him on the road. 2 Kings 18:21, "Because you trust in this bruised reed, Egypt. . . ."

Examples of the blessings for keeping the First Commandment: See Hebrews 11; Ecclesiasticus 44–50, Daniel 3 concerning the fiery furnace in Babylon. In 2 Chron. 15:15 when Israel sought the Lord, peace was given to them. In 2 Kings 22:18–20 Josiah is promised that before he dies he shall see no evil come. Note 2 Peter 2:7–8 regarding Lot. Ex. 1:21, "Because the midwives feared God He blessed them and built homes for them." Job 1:9–10, because Job feared the Lord, God built a wall around him. Genesis 22 and 26 describe the obedience of Abraham and Isaac. Other instances can be observed in our daily reading, and these must be noted.

Images

Because it is necessary to say something about the appendix which has been added to the First Commandment, I shall at this point note the chief points at issue concerning images, as to what things have been brought into great contention both in the past and in our own time. It is certain that God, both in other precepts as well as in the First Commandment, has taken note of one special kind of idolatry which is so crass and manifest that it was even ridiculed by the more sensible philosophers. Under this kind of idolatry God has willed that there also be included the inner and outward idolatry of the heart, so that the enormity of this sin may be put before our very eyes. It is clear from Romans 1 that God in this appendix was looking particularly at the idolatry of the gentiles, as well as that of the Israelites who, as they saw the worshipers of idols abounding in all respects, dared to imitate them. For this reason the names of so many idols are recorded in Scripture. . . . Joshua also in 24:14 is clearly saying that the Israelites in Egypt were accustomed to the practice of idolatry: "Put away the gods which your fathers served in Mesopotamia and Egypt."

Therefore God, when it seemed that His people were turning to this heathen idolatry, absolutely forbade the making and use of images of every kind, whether of heavenly things or earthly or aquatic, which either existed or did not exist in the realm of nature. Origen makes a distinction between an image and a likeness. Some people interpret the term "likeness" as anything, in addition to statues and graven images, which is used for divine worship without the Word of God, such as the heavens, light, the altar of a foreign god, the course of the sun. But that it was absolutely forbidden to the Jews to place images or carved objects in the temple can indeed be understood just from this one example: when Pilate wanted to bring into the temple a statue of Caesar, of which Josephus speaks [in *Bellum Judaicum*,] 18.5 [new 2.164–74]. Therefore, just as many other rites of the heathen, which in themselves and by their nature were matters of indifference, were forbidden to the Jews in the ceremonial laws lest they give them an occasion for godlessness and idolatry, so, because images and graven figures did give occasion for the true religion, even among the members of the people of God, little by little to become corrupted under the appearance of godliness (as we read in Gen. 11:31, where Nahor and Abraham with their father Terah gave up the idolatry of the Chaldeans, but Laban the son of Nahor, Gen. 31:30, called his idolatrous images "gods," and Rachel [in stealing them] attributed some power to them, and this after more than 200 years), God absolutely forbade that they make them, or that they gather images made by others into a place where they were to carry on divine worship.

Yet at the same time God showed that this was prohibited not by the moral law but by the ceremonial. For before the law of Moses, Jacob had set up a stone for a statue or for worship, Gen. 28:18 and 31:45, something which is prohibited in Lev. 26:1. In the very promulgation of the Law God Himself commands that two cherubim be placed on top of the ark of the covenant, and the form of the cherubim was described in 1 Kings 7:36 and 2 Chron. 3:10. After Moses, when the sons of Reuben, Gad, and Manasseh had built an altar across the Jordan (Joshua 22), there arose a controversy over the meaning of the appendix of the First Commandment. Some contended that this was absolutely not permitted. When they replied that they had not set up this altar with the intention or purpose of dishonoring God or departing from Him, this was pleasing in the eyes of Phinehas and the rest of the people. Joshua, as he was about to die, erected a stone for a testimony, 24:26, although already the explanation of the First Commandment might seem to prohibit it. In 1 Sam. 7:12 Samuel erects a stone for a memorial, and in 1 Kings 7:36 and 2 Chron. 4:3 Solomon engraved lions and cherubim on the tablets and panels of the temple. There was also there the likeness of graven oxen. In 2 Chron. 7:1 the divine Majesty filled the temple. Therefore He did not disapprove of the work of Solomon. In 2 Chron. 9:18 Solomon made two lions for his ivory throne and 12 small lions for the steps. This example established the civil use of images.

In the New Testament, 1 Cor. 8:4, Paul puts idols and the matter of eating things sacrificed to idols into the realm of indifferent matters, unless they are connected with causing the conscience of a neighbor to stumble. For he says, "There is no such thing in the world as an idol," that is, if you remove the idea of worship or adoration or prayer, an idol is nothing. Moses did not speak like this, for at that time graven images were prohibited. At that time they were not "nothing," just as circumcision, which in the Old Testament was so necessary that he who was not circumcised on the eighth day, his soul was cut off from the people, Gen. 17:14, in the New Testament is "nothing." In the Old Testament a foreskin was an abomination, but in the New Testament it is "nothing," that is, it has no significance, Gal. 5:6; it does no harm but is a matter of indifference. Thus an idol is nothing, and in 1 Cor. 10:19 it is not a thing which can either sanctify or contaminate. Surely if anyone had taken an idol into the Jewish temple, that would have been something which God had forbidden. But Paul adds, because the gentiles had set up idols and were eating meats sacrificed to idols with the intention and purpose that they might through this worship cause their gods to be favorable to them and that they might obtain something good: These things, he says, are idolatry, which Christians ought to flee. Those things which Scripture condemns in the Old Testament in regard to the images and statues of the gentiles certainly pertain to all men and are matters of the moral law.

Thus, from the 10 rules which have been demonstrated it is clear that the appendix to the First Commandment is in part moral and in part ceremonial. The moral aspects which bind all men also in the New Testament are these: (1) Images are universally forbidden which manifestly in themselves are used for heathen superstition and open godlessness in opposition to the Word of God. (2) Images of whatever kind which are set up for worship and adoration in any way are idolatrous, and Christians must flee them. For this is the moral law, Lev. 26:1, "You shall not make idols in order to worship them." (3) To adore or worship graven images, that is, to consider them gods and to render to them the worship which belongs alone to God, such as praying to them, trusting in them, or to imagine that images possess some peculiar sanctity or powers, or to think that God is so bound to any image that He hears our prayers and is more efficacious in the place where the image is than elsewhere, these are not matters of the ceremonial law, which applied only to the Jews, but they pertain to all people. (4) It is moral law in this appendix that images which at one time were matters of indifference and in legitimate use, when in the progress of time they are approached with the idea of worship must no longer be tolerated, as Hezekiah says in 2 Kings 18:4–5. (5) It is also a matter of the moral law that when images are involved, all opportunities which could arise for idolatry must be avoided. It was for this reason that God prohibited this to the Israelites. Paul says, "All things are lawful for me, but not all things are expedient," 1 Cor. 6:12; 10:23. The experiences of all periods in both the Old and New Testaments show that images and statues give opportunity and contain the seeds of idolatry; and always from the indifferent use of images in the progress of time there arise corruptions in divine worship. (6) Paul advises Christians that they not knowingly provoke God in their use of images, 1 Cor. 8:1ff. Therefore this also is moral law.

However, some bitter controversies were stirred up regarding images between the Eastern and Western churches about the year 728. The dispute was carried on not only with great wars of words but also with force of arms for more than 60 years, from the time of Leo the Isaurian to the seventh general council [Nicaea, A.D. 787]. As is the case in other controversies, the actual events and what truly happened can scarcely be understood from the historical records.

Suidas notes that Constantinus, the son of Leo, contended that we must not implore the intercessions and help of the saints. Thus it seems proper that there was a rejection of the godless worship which was given to images in opposition to the First Commandment. Suidas adds that Constantinus spoke in a shameful way regarding the saints and the mother of the Lord. But I think that this was fabricated by his enemies. From the proceedings of the seventh council this much is evident: Those who were called image-haters or iconoclasts not only condemned the worship and adoration of images but contended in general that Christians out of the binding nature of the commandment should have no images or pictures at all. They alleged this on the authority of Epiphanius, bishop of Constantia in Cyprus, who tells that he had discovered a veil in a certain church on which had been depicted the picture or image of Christ or of some holy person, and that he had destroyed it because it was contrary to the authority of Scripture. He says, "When in the church of Christ, contrary to the authority of the Scripture, I saw a picture of a man, I tore it up." He adds, "Remember that you should not bring images into the church, nor statues into cemeteries of the saints, but always carry Christ about in your hearts. These things should not even be allowed in the home. For it is not lawful that He be suspended before the eyes of Christians but that He be the great concern of their minds." He also cited from the letter of Eusebius of Pamphilia to Constantia Augusta begging that the image of Christ be sent to him: "I wish you would write to me as to what image of Christ you are thinking about, whether that immutable image or that which He assumed for us? But I do not think you are concerned about the divine image. Therefore you are looking entirely for the image of a servant. We have learned that even this human image has been joined to the glory of the Godhead. Who can with human colors and shadowy picture depict the flashing splendor of this kind of glory, when the disciples on the mountain were unable to gaze upon it?"

It always happens this way in controversies, according to Basil, Epistle 41 [MPG 32.369–70], "Just as farmers, when they try to correct a bend in the branch of a tree, err in bending it too much in the other direction . . ." For it has already been demonstrated that when the idea of worship and adoration is taken away, there is no prohibition of historical images in the New Testament. There are three kinds of images: the superstitious kind which either in the picture itself have some element of godlessness or which contribute toward [idolatrous] worship and adoration. The typical kinds were the bronze serpent, the cherubim, etc. But because the types now have lost their force, they are not to be used as images which foreshadow or signify true reality, because the light of the Gospel has been so revealed and illuminated, just as also it was necessary that the foreshadows instituted by God must come to an end.

Thus we are only arguing about the use of historical images which are used either for a memento of things which have been done or for the sake of decoration. These uses are in no way prohibited in Scripture, and it can be a perfectly legitimate use for them: (1) as a reminder of a historical event. Thus Gregory says, "For this reason we have had painted in the churches pictures of the Gospel stories, so that they might remind illiterate man of the things which Christ said while He was in the flesh." He adds, "Can it be that the sky, the earth, plants, or any other thing, whether through colors or pictures or by voice, could tell or describe the true reality of Christ?" Cyril speaks this way about images in his *Contra Julianum*, Bk. 6 [MPG 76.795–99]. Julian had said, "You Christians worship the wood of the cross." To which Cyril replied, first by enumerating the blessings which have been given to us in the cross by Christ, and then he says,

"To record all of these things causes us to preserve the wooden cross and convinces us to believe that just as one man died for all and rose again, so we who live should no longer live unto ourselves. Is it your desire that we should now reject the wood which leads us to a record of all this good, and should we prefer to have pictures of Ganymede or the Danae?" Again he says that parables are like images to us to put the doctrine before our eyes. (2) The sight of the picture as a present thing arouses our holy desires. Thus Gregory of Nyssa says in a sermon on the Song of Solomon [MPG 44.776], "I have often seen a picture of the suffering of Christ, and I have not been able to get through the Scripture account of it without tears." Again in a certain oration he says, "I have often seen a picture of the inscription on the cross and could not pass it by without tears, since the picture puts the story before my eyes in so effective a way. For Isaac was kneeling before the altar . . ." [ibid.]. Chrysostom, *In Meletium*: "In their rings, on their cups, and on their walls they paint pictures of St. Meletius, so that they not only hear the sacred name, but wherever they see the form of his body, they have a twofold comfort in their pilgrimage."[11] Basil, *In Quadraginta Martyres* [Homily 19, MPG 31.503–09]: "The trophies of war, the writers of history, and painters often show pictures very beautifully. Some people adorn their work with their prayers, and others depict it on tablets, but both add many blessings to their good works." The scholastics put it this way: Images serve (1) for the instruction of the unlearned; (2) to recall things to memory; (3) to cause thoughts of meditation and devotion.

These things said about the legitimate use of images must be understood in the sense of belonging among those outward exercises which Paul says profit but little, 1 Tim. 4:8. For God has given His Scripture in order that there might be a means of instruction, reminding and producing the desire for devotion. In no way are mute images to be compared with this means. But if someone is lacking in edification, admonition, or instruction, let him seek it in the Word of God. The power and efficacy of God is the Gospel, Rom. 1:16. Therefore to have images is not a matter of the commandment but of adiaphora, and Scripture gives us examples of how we should use the historical and the ornamental aspects of images. We must see to it that for the uninstructed or for our posterity images do not become an occasion for offense or idolatry, or that money which ought to be given to living men who are the image of God should be squandered on mute images.

Furthermore the Seventh Council, Nicaea II, which condemned the image breakers, did not itself deal correctly with the doctrine of images, but was guilty of many errors. The proceedings of this synod, as they have been edited, contain such crass and impudent falsehoods that even Pighius is critical of it.

---

[11] *Homilia Encomiastica*, MPG 50.516. Meletius was a bishop of Antioch.

For: 1. In a ridiculous, inept, and shameful way the council twists certain testimonies to suggest that it has been commanded by the Word of God to have images. If the Old Testament had cherubim overshadowing the ark of the covenant, then we also will have images overshadowing our altars. David says, "Praise and beauty are before Him," Ps. 96:6. "Your face, O Lord, will I seek," Ps. 27:8. "The light of Your countenance, O Lord, has shined upon us," Ps. 4:7 [Vulgate]. Therefore we ought to have images and lights in our temples. Likewise, God made man in His own image. Adam called all the animals by their correct names. Noah constructed an altar and sacrificed animals on it which had form, figure, and lines. Therefore Christians ought to have images on their altars. John of Damascus: "Then they will see the sign of the Son of man, that is, the cross." Therefore the wood of the cross is to be adored, for where there is the sign of Christ, there He is also present Himself. 2. The members of the council clearly say that they are defending images which not only have the historical use, but for the sake of veneration, worship, and adoration. They play games with such words as adoration, salvation, and *dulia* as opposed to *latreia*, but what they are contending for is that we must seek intercession and protection in images, and they believe that this worship is pleasing to God, that the saints sought this grace, and that those who are called upon in this way can give us aid. Likewise they believe that images and relics have some power to help us. For it is manifest from the first and third session of the council that they were at that time defending images for the sake of retaining the invocation of saints, as they state in some of their confessions. In the fourth session they praise this practice. In the great city of Rome they placed small images of Simeon even in all the entrances to workshops, as things which promised a kind of guardian protection and security for what went on there. It is customary in the writings of all the scholastics to mitigate and excuse the invocation of saints and adoration of images by distinguishing between the words *doulia* and *latreia*. Augustine in his *De Civitate Dei*, 10.1 [MPL 41.278], deals with this distinction properly: "It is one thing that God be worshiped (*colo*) with that honor which is due to Him alone; but it is another thing that men be worshiped, when rather we should celebrate (*frequento*) them with respect for a past or present deed." The Latin language does not have words to make this distinction, but the Greeks use terms such as *latreia*, *thrēskeia*, and *theosebeia* to refer to the worship that is due to God alone. But because Scripture commands us to honor our parents, elders, magistrates, those placed above us, and to venerate or respect other gifts of God among men, there has been attributed to this kind of veneration which applies to men the word *doulia*. These terms have been used properly. But the papists under a false manipulation or twisting of the words think that they can cover up all these idolatrous abuses. They say that we adore the saints but not with the adoration of *latreia* but of *doulia*. They are clearly perverting the definitions. They give to the saints invocation and say they are heard because of their merits and intercessions; they trust in them, fear them, hope in them, and credit the benefits which they receive to the saints. Scripture cries out that these are acts of worship which belong to God alone. Therefore, whether they are called by the name of *latreia* or of *doulia*, God is not deceived by words, but wills that these honors not be given to any creature. But these points pertain to the locus on the invocation of saints. 3. They want to prove the adoration of images. But it is worth the effort to note the argument by which they prove it. Jacob worshiped facing the top bough of a tree, Is. 17:4–7.[12] Therefore they argued that it was right that images be adored. If we believe that the people of Israel were saved from the plague by looking at the bronze serpent [they say], why should we hesitate to believe that we are serving God by looking at and venerating images of Christ and all the saints? Then they cite many testimonies from the fathers of the Greek church in the use of which they clearly practiced deception. They cite Basil, "I acknowledge the holy apostles, prophets, and martyrs, who make supplication for me before God and through whose mediation God is made favorable to me and freely bestows remission of sins. For this reason I honor the accounts of their images and openly adore them." They quote Chrysostom, "I have loved a picture cast out of melted wax, a picture filled with devotion. For I saw an image or likeness of an angel pursuing the troop of barbarians." But in all the writings of Basil and Chrysostom these words are not found. In the city of Beirut there is an account of a picture of the crucifixion attributed to Athanasius. But *The History of the Lombards* says that this picture was produced about A.D. 750. Basil says, "The honor shown to the image is referred to the prototype Himself." These words were said with regard to the Son of God, in keeping with the passage, "He who does not honor the Son does not honor the Father," John 5:23. But these people in an underhanded way twist the matter to prove the adoration of images.

Therefore in the papal realm there is not the historic and legitimate use of images, but the simple idolatrous practice, as the prayers and pilgrimages to the statues of the saints demonstrate. One can find in the papist literature instances as to how the wood of the cross is blessed: "We ask You that You would deign to bless this wood of the cross, so that to all who bend their knees at this place and beseech Your Majesty there may be remorse of the heart, and that remission of the sins which they confess might be granted them." Likewise, "Let this wood be sanctified in the name of the Father, etc., in order that as they adore and turn themselves for the sake of God before this cross, they may find cleansing for

---

[12] This is an obscure reference to Is. 17:4–7.

body and soul." In this way they taught that the prayer which took place before an altar was more acceptable and efficacious because of the relics which were on the altar. These practices are in direct opposition to the statement, "You shall not adore or worship them."

Certain arguments are used in opposition to this clear testimony.

1. In the proper sense of the word, the honor is not given to the stones or the wood, but applies to God Himself. Reply: The gentiles also used to defend their idols by the same kind of subterfuge, as we can read in Lactantius, Athanasius, and Augustine. The rule is certain and firm: No worship is pleasing to God except that which He Himself has instituted in His own Word. Matt. 15:9, "In vain do they worship Me. . . ." Col. 2:23 condemns self-made religion. They also use this argument: Honor which is given to His friends cannot be displeasing to God. Reply: God says, "I will not give My glory to another," Is. 42:8. How He wishes His friends to be honored He shows in His Word.

2. This practice was handed down by the apostles and was always observed in the first church. Reply: This is manifestly false. For the first church had absolutely no images, and the ancient writers recall nothing about images. Those stories which are told about Veronica, about Nicodemus painting a picture of Christ, or of Luke painting Mary are unfounded fables. Gelasius dreamed up the story about Veronica. . . . The Greek church even in the time of Jerome did not have images. Gregory in Bk. 9, Epistle 9 [MPL 77.1128], strongly forbids adoration of images, and *De Consec.*, dist. 4, supports this.[13] Eusebius in 7.18 [MPG 20.680], in discussing the picture of Christ and the woman who suffered from the issue of blood, clearly indicates whence the use of images descended upon the church. He says, "It is not at all surprising that the gentiles who long ago received such benefits from our Savior should have shown their gratitude in this way, for the features of His apostles Paul and Peter, and indeed of Christ Himself, have been preserved in portraits which I have examined. How could it be otherwise, when the ancients followed their own gentile practice of honoring for posterity those whom they consider worthy of their true love?" Thus Eusebius.

3. Many miracles have taken place in connection with statues and images. Reply: This argument would establish also the universal mania for idols which the heathen have. But we have a sure and certain rule about miracles, Deut. 13:1ff.; 2 Thess. 2:2; Matt. 24:24, where it is predicted that it would come to pass that errors would be corroborated by many signs and wonders.

Augustine, *De Symbolo et Fide*, ch. 7 [MPG 40.188], "We believe that He sits

---

[13] Cf. *Corpus Iuris Canonici*, dist 3, ch. 27, p. 1360. The reference to Gelasius and Veronica can also be found here, in *Sancta Romana*, dist. 15.

at the right hand of God the Father, but not in such a way, however, as if we are to think that God the Father is limited by a human form, so that to those who think about Him there comes to mind the right or left side; or that because the Father is said to be sitting, we fall into the sacrilege for which the apostle condemned those who 'changed the glory of the incorruptible God into the likeness of corruptible man,' Rom. 1:23. It is sinful for a Christian to place this kind of likeness of God in the temple, and much more sinful to have it in the heart, which is truly the temple of God." Thus Augustine.

Deut. 4:15–16, "You did not see the form of God that day as He spoke to you . . . nor should you make an image for yourselves." Is. 40:18, "To whom will you liken God, or what likeness will you give to Him?" Rom. 1:23, "They changed the glory of the incorruptible God into the likeness of the image of corruptible man." Therefore it is ungodly to paint a picture of God the Father in the form of a bearded and grizzled man. Reply: That we can paint a picture of Christ or the human nature there is no doubt. The Holy Spirit is depicted in the form of a dove, not because we believe that this is His essence; but because at the Jordan He revealed Himself in this kind of bodily form, it cannot be said that by this mode of appearance His glory was changed, Romans 1. Furthermore, Daniel in 7:9, in a vision sees "thrones set up and the Ancient of Days sitting, and His hair as pure wool." The result is that God is pictured this way, not because this is His essence but because He has revealed Himself this way in the vision to Daniel. But if anyone thinks that God in His essence and nature is like this, he has truly changed the "glory of the immutable God," Romans 1. However, it is simplest, surest, and safest to think about God not according to images, but according to His revealed Word.

The Second Commandment [Melanchthon's Text]

Under the First Commandment we have spoken regarding the desires of the heart toward God, which are the highest and innermost worship, because God requires obedience from the heart and not something pretended, in keeping with the passage, "You shall love the Lord your God with all your heart," Deut. 6:5, or "The true worshipers are those who worship the Father in spirit and in truth," John 4:24. Now we move on to a discussion of the Second Commandment from the standpoint of its outward observance. For God wills that we know Him and call upon Him with our voice. Just as He has revealed Himself through the Word, so He wills that this Word be proclaimed. Therefore, after He has spoken about the desires of the heart, He then gives a command concerning that proclamation in which the name of God and the Word of God sounds forth.

"You Shall Not Take the Name of God in Vain"

Under the First Commandment we have placed affirmative and negative statements: "I am the Lord your God who led you out of the land of Egypt." This is the affirmative, to which are added also other affirmative statements: "You shall love the Lord your God with all your heart," Deut. 6:5. Likewise, "You shall fear the Lord your God," Deut. 6:13. When we have established the affirmative aspects, then we must add the negative statements, always bearing in mind that under the First Commandment the affirmative is expressed first. Here in the Second Commandment God forbids the misuse of His name, and wills that it be proclaimed and made known: "I am the Lord your God," Ex. 20:2. There are, therefore, true uses for the name of God: true preaching, true invocation, the giving of thanks, and confession. We should understand here that these four kinds of work are commanded, and at this place we should bring in the affirmative passages regarding these works. For example, "Go and teach all nations," Matt. 28:19; "Call upon Me in the day of trouble, and I will deliver you, and you will glorify Me," that is, give Me thanks, Ps. 50:15; "With the heart it is believed unto righteousness and with the mouth confession is made unto salvation," Rom. 10:10. These statements very properly give command concerning things of this kind. Relative to invocation also is the matter of taking an oath. For in swearing, a person calls upon God to be a witness of his will that he does not want to lie, and he prays that God will take vengeance and punish him if he lies, and he subjects himself to this punishment. From this we can understand how great a bond an oath is. A person calls upon God to pour out His wrath upon him if he is lying. What more terrible thing can a man bring down upon himself, or how can he bind a greater punishment upon himself! Therefore the final outcome is that this obligation is sanctified and confirmed by a divine oath in keeping with this passage, "God will not hold him guiltless who takes His name in vain," Ex. 20:7. Also in this life horrible punishments come to perjurers.

How Can This Commandment Be Carried Out?

As we have said above, the works of the First Commandment cannot be carried out without the knowledge of the Son of God and faith. We must understand the same thing regarding this commandment. It is thoroughly evident that there can be no invocation unless there be knowledge of Christ the Mediator, and the same applies to the giving of thanks. Again it is certainly necessary in regard to the ministry that the Gospel of the Son of God be taught. Finally, as we have said above, it is necessary first that we lay hold on the reconciliation given to us through the Son of God, but after this to determine to make a beginning of obedience. The same must be understood regarding the other commandments. The works of the other commandments are thus pleasing to God and become the worship of God when the works of *the First Commandment precede, namely fear and faith. Thus [the work of] the rest of the commandments becomes sacrifices of praise and are pleasing to God, but this is particularly true in the case of the Second Commandment. As it has been written especially about this kind of obedience, "I will sacrifice to You the sacrifice of praise, and I will call upon the name of the Lord," Ps. 116:17.*

Sins Against the Second Commandment

The antithesis is the same as for the preceding commandment, since the sins of the heart, as we have reviewed them above, are made known. In conflict with this commandment are epicurean words; words of outward godless worship; godless invocation of demons, idols, the dead; false doctrine, perjury, unjust condemnations; the words of those who proclaim arrogance and impudence as in the case of Ajax, who said that he could conquer even without God. Likewise the very common evil of attaching the name of God, religion, and the Gospel to sinful desires, ambitions, greed, lust, and hatred conflicts with the Second Commandment. The pope under the title of "minister" or "servant" seeks power and starts unjust wars. He has set up idols and laid snares for catching immeasurable amounts of money and other things. Now this generation of ours under the title of the "Gospel" often covers up the avarice of private citizens. Here pertain also all the snares which either wound the simple or weaken faith or turn the wills of some people away from the Gospel.

Frightful threats have been added to this precept; they speak of physical punishments and also refer to eternal wrath, because the Law does not announce the remission of sins, but in the Gospel God's eternal wrath is declared against those who do not repent: "Depart from Me, you wicked people, into everlasting fire," Matt. 25:41. For what is said here regarding the punishments "unto the third and fourth generation of those who hate" God, Ex. 20:5, should be understood in the physical sense. Just as penalties were added to previous generations, so we should understand that they have also been added to succeeding generations, and in Deut. 27:15ff. curses are added to all the commandments. Nor should we doubt that the calamities of this world are punishments for the sins of the whole race, as it says in Ps. 39:11, "Because of iniquity You have corrected the sons of men."

The Second Commandment

The very words of the Decalog in the individual commandments show how the true meaning can be properly studied. When we have determined what is actually in Scripture, it is worthwhile to consider how God in these very few words of the Decalog has beautifully covered the basics of all the explanations of the Law made by the prophets and the apostles.

Therefore our first task is to explain the words of the Second Commandment. Because it speaks about the name of Jehovah, the Jews played childish games with this, namely that when they wrote the four-letter name for God (tetragrammaton, as they called it in Greek), they did not write it with all its vowel points and in complete form, but wrote for it the words "Jehovah" or *Elohim*. Or in reading they would not utter the word, but at that place used the term *Adonai*, or they only used the letters, thinking that they were satisfying the commandment most perfectly and fully, even though they were committing the sheerest blasphemies and perjuries. For they understood and interpreted the Second Commandment as forbidding the uttering of the name of Jehovah and the touching with bare hands of the book in which His name was written, and as commanding it to be treated in all ways in the purest possible way. But God is not speaking about letters and syllables.

Others more correctly say that the name of God signifies His glory, His splendor, His majesty, etc., just as in Gen. 6:4 people are called "men of renown" (*viri nominis*) and Deut. 26:19 says, ". . . the nations which He has made to His praise and name and glory" (Vulgate).

[1.] But it is the least complicated to derive our interpretation from the nature of correlative statements. For Scripture often speaks this way. Ex. 6:3, "I have not made My name known to them"; John 17:6, "I have manifested Your name to men"; Ps. 22:22; Acts 9:15; John 1:18; Deut. 4:12; Matt. 11:27. Thus coming out of unapproachable light, He revealed and manifested Himself by voice and word. To this revelation of Himself in His Word is correlated the name of God. Thus His name signifies that which is revealed in His Word concerning the essence and will of God, or that which is proclaimed in Scripture about God. Here pertain all miracles and works by which God bore witness to Himself and His will. Ex. 9:16, "I have raised you up . . . that My name might be declared throughout all the earth."

[2.] Furthermore, in the Second Commandment the word "to take up" or "to lift up" (*elevandi* or *assumendi*) is used, which we more correctly render in German by *Du sollst nicht führen* rather than the Latin *non assumes* (You shall not take). Ps. 50:16, "What right have you to take My covenant upon your lips?" Jer. 7:16, "Do not lift up a prayer for them." Luke renders it correctly in Acts 9:15, "That he might carry My name." Therefore He is showing by the word "lifting up" that He has manifested His name to men, not in order that it might be hidden under a bushel or buried in silence, but that He wills that His name be lifted up, but not for improper uses. Thus the purpose of the Second Commandment deals with the use and misuse of God's name.

3. He forbids that His name be lifted up for vain, improper, or thoughtless purposes. For the term "to use in vain" has this meaning: When the words are used in a thoughtless, hasty, and rash way, as when it is a matter of an insignificant thing, something of no importance, which does not glorify God but

rather despises His name through joking, contempt or in thoughtlessness. The words are not thought out (*wie man davon reden wolle*), but they come out as bombast.

4. God does not say "My name," but "the name of the Lord your God." This distinction very beautifully shows two lines of thinking: (1) At the mention of some great king whose power we admire, we either uncover our heads or show some other sign of respect, by which we demonstrate what honor we give to his powers. Therefore—because here is the name of Jehovah, which is "great" in Jer. 10:6; "worthy of praise," Ps. 113:3; "holy," Ps. 111:9; "terrible," Ps. 99:3—therefore you should not use it in vain. (2) When He says, "the name of your God," He is asking us to consider all the benefits that come to us through the name of the Lord. In the case of spiritual blessings, "There is not given to men any other name by which they can be saved," Acts 4:12. Joel 2:32, "Whosoever shall call upon the name of the Lord shall be saved." In the case of physical blessings, Ps. 20:1, "The name of the God of Jacob defend you," also Ps. 91:14. Therefore because the revelation and knowledge of the name of the Lord have made you a son of God, because He is your God, "You shall not take His name in vain."

This explanation of the terms beautifully demonstrates the whole area of the Second Commandment. For God wills that we not only believe reverently concerning His name but that we also do not take it in vain. And just as in the case of the other precepts He speaks of one kind of sin as being especially gross in order that He may illustrate the abomination of other sins, so also here under the negative aspect He wants us to consider the subject from the less to the greater. For people think they are really innocent and guiltless in their idle and vain use of God's name, as long as it is not manifest blasphemy. But because the Second Commandment says, "The Lord will not hold him guiltless . . ." therefore those who do profane or blaspheme will be much more guilty. For this line of reasoning is used in Scripture, for example in Matt. 12:36, where an accounting must be rendered for every idle word; therefore it is much more the case when it is a matter of malicious talking and blasphemy. Matt. 10:42, "Whoever gives a drink of cold water to one of these little ones shall not lose his reward," and Matt. 25:40, "What you have done for the least of these My brethren, you have done it unto Me," indicate that greater actions [shall also be rewarded—or punished].

Moreover, Christ Himself gives us the affirmative side of this precept in the Lord's Prayer, "Hallowed be Thy name." He also gave us the Second Commandment in the negative form, in order to show that that shameful sin of ingratitude toward the name of God still clings to our human nature. Paul in a skillful way gives the reason why most of the commandments are stated negatively. For the Law was not given that it might take away sins and give the new obedience, but that "sin might abound," Rom. 5:20. "Sin taking occasion by the

Law worked in me all manner of concupiscence," Rom. 7:8. Hence the Law is called "the strength of sin," 1 Cor. 15:56. "Sin was in the world," up to the time of Moses. Rom. 5:13. "The Law made nothing perfect," Heb. 7:19. But because in this prayer we are asking and imploring, therefore in the Lord's Prayer it is put positively, "Hallowed be Thy name."

But if the question is asked what is the correct and complete catalog of the sins and the good works under the Second Commandment, this can be properly determined either by the purpose for using God's name, as indicated above, or by the testimonies of Scripture which clearly utilize the terminology of the Second Commandment, both regarding the honoring and the profaning of the divine name. Indeed, this line of reasoning is more certain. But now for the sake of brevity, having given above an explanation of the terms, we shall summarize the meaning of the Second Commandment.

1. God commands in the Second Commandment our inner desires, so that we consider and think about how great a blessing there is that in the great darkness of our depraved nature God has revealed the knowledge of His name by which we are to be saved, so that our mind may have fear and reverence toward the divine name. For it is the name of "the Lord Jehovah your God," Ex. 20:7.

2. Because He is speaking of the taking or lifting up of the name, He wills that we not only believe reverently and respectfully in our heart about this name, but also that we use it this way with our mouth, our tongue, in our speaking and our public life. Thus the second use of the name of God is in prayer. For Scripture clearly speaks this way. Joel 2:32, "Whosoever shall call upon the name of the Lord . . ."; John 16:23, "Whatsoever you ask in My name"; Ps. 20:7; Prov. 18:10; Col. 3:17. We should observe that the Holy Spirit speaks this way (to call upon the name of the Lord) in this sense, that it is our prayer to seek eternal and present blessings from the God who has revealed Himself in the promises of the Gospel and the sending of the Son and has determined to hear us according to those promises, for the sake of Christ our Mediator. This is the very name of the Lord.

3. The giving of thanks. [We give thanks] when we confess with mind and voice that good things have been given to us not only by accident or secondary causes, but that God is truly the Giver of all benefits, and in our own confession and acknowledgment of the blessings of God we invite others to know and call upon Him, because we bear witness that God is concerned about the godly and truly hears their prayers when they come to Him in faith in His Son. From these points it is clear in what way the giving of thanks pertains to hallowing the name of God.

4. True proclamation, so that the doctrine which has been revealed by God in His Word, not only in the public ministry (which pertains properly to the

Third Commandment), may be set forth, but that each person, in whatever station or calling he has, may meditate on the law of the Lord and speak of His testimonies, Psalm 119, reverently and sincerely, and may flee all corruptions and refute them. 1 Peter 3:15 gives us the rules for this kind of proclamation: "Be ready to give an answer to every man who asks you the reason for the hope that is in you, with meekness and respect, having a good conscience."

5. Confession. When in dangers, terrors, and persecutions we do not reject the true teaching of the Gospel because of hatred and punishments but confess it with our mouths, to this end that obedience toward God and the knowledge of God might be retained in the land and spread abroad. Cf. Acts 9:14; Matt. 24:9; Luke 21:12.

6. Glorifying or honoring of the name of God. This can be done by voice, Ps. 34:3, "Let us exalt His name"; 2 Sam. 22:50; Ps. 66:2. Here is pertinent the fact that the name should be used with great reverence and we should feel such great honor toward it that we do not take it into our mouth without very good reason, either for the glory of God or our own salvation or the upbuilding of our neighbor. For this is not taking His name in vain. We also glorify Him by our lives, when all our actions relate to Him, so that our example may give light to others, may adorn the glory of God, and may render His teaching more pleasant and worthy of commendation.

7. Testifying to the name of God in the proper taking of an oath and swearing for the sake of the faith. More on this later.

Now the antithesis will easily show what sins are in conflict with the Second Commandment. For there are certain outward things which God in His Law has commanded also to the civil magistrate for punishment, such as blasphemy, Lev. 24:16, perjury, etc. In Scripture the sins against the Second Commandment are summarized under three headings: (1) not to use the name of God at all, Ps. 79:6; (2) to profane the name of God, Lev. 20:3; Ezek. 20:9, 14, for the word *ʾālāh* is used in opposition to the concept of sanctifying or hallowing, that is, treating something as profane or unclean; (3) to blaspheme. But we shall simply give the antithesis of the affirmative statements.

1. Not to realize the great blessing the revelation of God's name is, not to love it, not to be concerned about it, to feel irreverent and frivolous about it.

2. Not to use the name of God at all, or make mention of it, or speak of Him, or gladly hear about the name of God.

3. To neglect prayer or to be sluggish and negligent in prayer, or repetitious in prayer, praying to the saints, or to pray with confidence in one's own merits, shouting out the name of God in church without any understanding, because in such a situation the name of God is not really being called upon.

4. To use the gifts of God without giving thanks, or to think that such things come to us only by accident or secondary causes.

5. To spread or defend false doctrine or to corrupt true doctrine, to create divisions and schisms. Jer. 14:14, "They prophesy lies in My name." Luke 21:8, "Many shall come in My name. . . ."

6. To fail to confess the correct doctrine when we are questioned; to conceal or deny our faith. Out of either hope or fear to be unwilling to endure persecutions for the sake of the name of the Lord.

7. Many things conflict with the glorifying of the name of God: (1) Epicurean statements, or joking and ridiculing uses of the words of Scripture. Paul in Eph. 5:4 speaks of "coarse joking." Ecclus. 23:10, "Let not the naming of God be a matter of habit." (2) The use of the name of God in the incantations of exorcisms, or in superstitions, either in writing or orally. For He does not say, "You shall not blaspheme," but, "You shall not take or use His name in vain." But there is a true and permissible use of the name of God which is pleasing to Him, which He Himself in His Word has prescribed. He wills that among us there only be reverence for His name, so that we do not only not use it in a way that is contrary to this precept, but in a way that is beside it. For He charges us with sin when we use it in vain. (3) Abuses of the name of God and whatever use is made of God's name for curses as in Lev. 24:10–11, where in an argument between two men one blasphemed the name of the Lord, that is, he misused the name by cursing the other man. In the Hebrew language the word ʾālāh describes both taking an oath and uttering a curse to show that both ideas pertain to the same precept.

These things are in opposition to the Second Commandment: (1) To use the name of God irreverently or disrespectfully out of anger or in a purposeless manner. (2) Because God has revealed His name in order that He might aid, defend, and save us, therefore it is against His commandment to call upon Him in vain. (3) Michael did not dare to bring the charge of blasphemy against the devil, Jude 9. (4) Blasphemy is in direct opposition to honoring the name of God. Lev. 24:16, "He who blasphemes the name of the Lord shall die." Ambrose, De Paradiso [MPL 14.303], says that it is blasphemy when one attributes to God that which is not appropriate for Him or takes away from Him that which does belong to Him. Another difference is added when we attribute to the creature that which belongs to God alone. Thus the Jews said that Christ was blaspheming in Matt. 9:3; 26:65; and John 10:33. Blasphemies are curses and ungodly words raised against God and His Word, the curses of those who have no hope, and all statements by which the glory of God is minimized and the faith of the weak is shaken, cf. Acts 13:45; 18:6; 26:11. (5) All scandals of a wicked life, by whose example harm is done to others, are in conflict with the glorifying or honoring of the name of God, cf. Rom. 2:24; 1 Tim. 6:1; Titus 2:5. Likewise, when sacred things are treated lightly, irreverently, and improperly, the Lord says that His name is being polluted, Lev. 20:3; Ezek. 20:31; Mal. 1:6, which pertains to using the name of God as a cover for ungodly avarice.

Finally, in conflict with the Second Commandment are perjury, false swearing, godless and irresponsible prayers.

To the Second Commandment there is clearly added the warning which we must note: (1) The precepts of the Decalog contain threats which are not only general and common to all the commandments, such as the one in the First Commandment; but the individual precepts have special warnings which can be determined from Scripture. Therefore, although to the Second Commandment pertains also that which was added to the First Commandment wherein God says, "Those who keep My commandments," yet it also has a particular warning, and by this example God shows that the same must be understood in the case of the other commandments. (2) Because in the hearts of all people the notion clings that we are not guilty before God, even if we do not invoke and glorify the name of God, therefore God by means of this warning is showing His very clear opposition to these ideas when He says, "I will not hold him guiltless." Thus also Jer. 30:11 should be treated, ". . . that you may not seem to yourself to be innocent," (Vlg.). (3) Because the general warning speaks about the visitation of God, that is, concerning external and physical punishments, no one should think, because these punishments are slow in coming, that the transgressors are guiltless. Thus God in the Second Commandment clearly expresses the fact that the punishment of the wrath of God is involved in these warnings, and He describes this with the judicial word *nāqāh*, to show that the chief punishments have been held back to Judgment Day. Therefore He adds this warning to the Second Commandment: Lev. 24:16, "He shall die the death." And, "He shall not hold him guiltless," Ex. 20:7. (4) It is manifest to a person who studies the matter that this warning is used as an antithesis to the promises about knowing, invoking, and honoring the name of God, e.g., "Whosoever shall call upon the name of the Lord shall be saved," Joel 2:32. To receive remission through His name means that we pray: "Have mercy, deliver, help us for Your name's sake." Therefore those who take His name in vain do not have remission, mercy, salvation, etc. Thus God is showing that not only must the warning be added, but that the promises have been given to those who honor the name of the Lord. Ps. 145:18, "The Lord is near to all who call upon Him"; Ps. 34:17, "The Lord hears their cry"; Ps. 50:23; Matt. 10:32; 5:11–12. Here are pertinent the examples of punishment: Lev. 24:14; Num. 22:31, [where] the angel of the Lord meets Balaam with drawn sword when he is on his way to curse the people of Israel. 2 Kings 19:35 and 2 Chron. 32:20 deal with the destruction of Sennacherib.

Acts 12:23 tells of Herod's punishment; Dan. 4:28, Nebuchadnezzar's insanity; and 5:3, Belshazzar's overthrow; 1 Kings 20:28, the Syrians; Judith 6:2, Holofernes. Examples of rewards: Ps. 22:4–5, "Our fathers cried unto You and were saved." See the examples of Sirach in Ecclesiasticus 46–48. Note also victory songs in Exodus 15; Jude 5; 1 Samuel 2; Deuteronomy 32; 2 Samuel 22. All these songs give us an example of thanksgiving and honoring the name of God.

The Question of Taking Oaths

It is clear from the above that the doctrine of oathtaking pertains to the Second Commandment, for it is said in Deut. 6:13, "You shall swear by His name." 2 Cor. 1:23, "Upon my soul, I call upon God as a witness." In the Old Testament there was never any doubt that in a proper, just, and necessary cause it was permissible to swear by the name of God. But in the New Testament because Christ says, "Swear not at all," Matt. 5:34 (and James 5:12 repeats the same idea), this subject has been under dispute in different ways at all times. For many of the martyrs around A.D. 200 refused to give the oath demanded by the government, and then contended that it was not permitted to Christians to swear under any circumstances. The Manichaeans rejected the Old Testament because it both used and approved of taking oaths, which they imagined was totally forbidden. Within recent memory there was a controversy with the Anabaptists on this same question. Jerome, *In Matt.* [5:34, MPL 26.41], says, "This was a kind of concession by the Law to the 'little ones,' so that just as in times past men had sacrificed victims to God but should not now sacrifice them to idols, so also in our time they are permitted to take an oath with God as witness, not because they were doing the right things, but because it was better to call God as a witness than demons."

Therefore we must seek the correct foundation on which our conscience can rest with certainty. It is absolutely certain that Christ in His sermon in Matthew 5 does not reprehend or abrogate or take away the moral law which had been laid down in the Old Testament. He Himself clearly says this in His little preface, "Do not think that I have come to destroy the Law," Matt. 5:17, but rather He was trying to purify the corruptions of Pharisaic errors and restore the original meaning. Now the testimonies of the Old Testament are entirely clear. Deut. 6:13 and 10:20, "You shall swear by His name." In Ex. 22:11, He commands that in doubtful controversies over facts the matter is to be put to an oath. Ps. 62:12, "All they shall be praised that swear by Him" (Vulgate). And it is certain that these statements pertain to the moral law. For Ps. 15:4 says, "He shall dwell in the tabernacle of the Lord who swears to his neighbor and does not deceive." There are other examples of godly people. In Joshua 14:9, "Moses swears, saying . . . ." In 2 Chron. 15:14, "The children of Israel swore to the Lord." In Judg. 11:10 the

Israelites took an oath to Jephthah. In 2 Sam. 21:7, 17 David and his co-work-ers took an oath. In Gen. 14:22 Abraham swore an oath to the king of Sodom. In Gen. 24:2 Abraham demanded an oath from his household servant. In Gen. 42:15 Joseph demanded an oath from his brothers. In Gen. 21:23ff. and 26:28 a treaty is confirmed by an oath. In 1 Sam. 20:3 David in an oath said to Jonathan in making a covenant, "As the Lord lives . . ." And in Dan. 12:7 an angel lifts up his hands to heaven and swears. Indeed, Scripture attributes to God Himself the taking of an oath. Gen. 22:16, "I have sworn by Myself." See Ps. 110:4; Jer. 44:26; Amos 4:2; Luke 1:73; Ps. 132:11. Certainly it cannot be said to come out of evil when God beyond a simple assertion adds an oath.

The strongest argument is that there is no doubt that Christ and the apostles correctly understood the statement "Swear not at all." Christ repeatedly uses the expression, "Verily, verily, I say to you," and it is manifest from Heb. 6:13–14 that this is a formula for an oath. In Matt. 26:63–64, although Christ first remained silent after the high priest had adjured Him or put Him under oath by the living God, He gave His confession, cf. Phil. 1:8; 2 Cor. 11:31; Rom. 9:11; 2 Cor. 12:19; 1:23. The evidence is very clear that Paul is using the words of Christ when He says, 2 Cor. 1:17, ". . . that with Me there should be yea, yea and nay, nay." He goes on to add an oath in vv. 22–23, and says that he "has been sealed by the Holy Spirit in his heart." Thus this does not come out of evil. It is unfortunate that the Anabaptists say that a Christian can certainly call on God against his soul as a witness to his words, but cannot take an oath; for an oath is nothing else than this kind of corroborating witness. New Testament Scripture uses the same vocabulary for taking an oath. Rev. 10:6, "The angel swore by Him who lives forever." Heb. 6:16 the text clearly says, "Men swear by One greater than themselves, and an oath for confirmation is the end of every controversy." He does not say that this was permitted to the Jews as only a lesser evil, that they might avoid the worse, but he introduces the example of God Himself confirm-ing His promises by an oath.

From these testimonies and examples it is manifest that Matt. 5:34 does not abrogate the taking of oaths as being something only ceremonial; nor is it abolished as the practice of divorce is repudiated in Matt. 19:8. Therefore what is the meaning of the statement of Christ in Matt. 5:34, "Swear not at all"? The answer is to be most certainly determined out of antithesis to the corruptions of the Pharisees. For because in Lev. 19:12 it is written, "You shall not swear by My name falsely," the Pharisees manipulated it to mean that only perjury was prohibited, and that it was permissible, indeed a worshiping of God, to use the name of God in taking an oath in daily speech, in public business dealings, for frivolous and vain matters, as long as it was not done to support a lie. Christ is criticizing this, as is manifest. For He is speaking about business negotiations, which can be transacted with a simple yes or no. In the solemn oath-taking among the Jews they never used such formulas as "by my head," or "by heaven," but [they were used] in familiar speech. Thus Christ is speaking of this and is not bringing in some new law. For this kind of swearing is condemned as futile and rash: Ecclus. 23:9ff.; 27:15; Hos. 4:15; and Jer. 44:26 forbid swearing by those who cannot hallow the name of God. Thus Christ draws the correct interpretation of the commandment about taking oaths from the statement, "You shall not take His name in vain." For we are of such a state of mind that when some business matter serves our comfort, even though it does not take place for the glory of God or the welfare of our neighbor, when we cannot obtain a person's confidence, we quickly use the name of God. Because we do not realize how holy and terrible the name of God is, Christ therefore condemns futile and foolish oaths, when the business could be transacted by a simple yes or no. Because the name of God must be held in such great reverence among us, we not only should not use it to support a lie but also we should not use it in trivial matters.

We shall divide [the treatment of] this subject into different parts:

I. What is taking an oath? It is a calling upon the name of God in which we ask that God be a witness of our intention, because we do not wish to deceive men in that matter about which we are making an assertion. At the same time, we are asking that God punish us if we are lying, and that we are obligating ourselves to punishment with Him as our witness, according to His own warning. The Hebrew word ʾālāh, "to swear," plainly means this. Note the formula: "May the Lord do this to me and add these things to me. . . ." Here a manifold, serious, and careful consideration is required lest in taking even permissible oaths, we profane the name of God or take it in vain. Jerome is correct when he says that he who takes an oath either honors or loves the one by whom he swears. For in Deut. 10:20 these concepts are joined together, "You shall fear the Lord your God and serve Him and cling to Him and swear by His name." Note that he who in a legitimate oath does not want to take the name of God in vain must have fear toward God, piety, faith, etc. For unless the name of God is used this way in an oath, it is being taken in vain. Deut. 6:12–13, "Beware that you do not forget the Lord . . . and you shall swear by His name." Deut. 10:21, "He is your praise." Note that in taking an oath we must consider the blessings which we both have received and expect through the name of God, and that by this confession the name of God may be glorified. Otherwise it is being used in vain. Jer. 4:1–2, "If you will return to Me, O Israel . . . then you will swear . . . in truth." Is. 45:23–24, "I have sworn by Myself . . . that every tongue shall swear . . . in the Lord I have righteousness." Hos. 4:15 and Jer. 44:26 teach that He does not want an oath to be taken in His name by the ungodly and the apostate, because His name is being taken in vain and it is a very great matter to call upon God to be a witness of our intention and word, when our desires are improper and it is easy for our tongue to deceive, James 3:2, and indeed to bind Him with so great an obligation.

Therefore, because the matter of swearing is so difficult and it can so easily happen that even in legitimate situations the name of God is used in vain, Augustine says that Christ was critical of the habit of easy, quick, rash, and ill-considered swearing, lest we fall swiftly into perjury or into a vain use of the name of God.

Now I want to add these testimonies to the definition. For from these one can properly judge what correct swearing is which does not conflict with the law of God and how we ought to worship God. For Scripture clearly says that to take an oath in the name of God is worshiping Him. Is. 19:18–19; 45:23; and 65:16 show how we are to regard worship. An oath is a confession that He is the true God by whom we are swearing. For this reason God has severely forbidden swearing by idols. In Joshua 22:7 the praise of truth is attributed to God, the power to punish, both because He is the judge and the weigher of the hearts. There is also the confession of our fear toward God because we believe that His threats are true and we do not wish to fall under them. Likewise, there is the testimony that the name of God is dear to us because we do not want Him to be evilly inclined toward us. Because even the saints have and feel the fires of evil desires, through taking an oath they are brought back into line, so that they can mortify their evil lusts and speak the truth. Controversies are also settled by taking an oath, and peace and harmony restored, Heb. 6:16. It is most certain that these actions constitute worship of God and hence I believe we can correctly understand the religious aspects involved in taking an oath.

II. There are many kinds of swearing, of which we shall review only a few. There is the oath of assertion, as when a person asserts something or denies something regarding a present or past matter. There is the oath of promise regarding something in the future which is possible and legitimate. This kind of oath is either voluntary or forced; and it is correct to say that in such an oath there is an obligation which cannot be ignored because it takes place before God.

Swearing is also categorized according to the subject, for example, swearing about godless and forbidden matters. There is the kind which deals with something permissible, to be sure, but impossible; swearing about uncertain and dubious matters, as the oath of Herod, Matt. 14:7, and the prayer of Jephthah, Judg. 11:30ff. These oaths could not be kept without either blaspheming or taking God's name in vain. But with regard to something possible, permissible, right, and good, Scripture says, "You shall swear by His name," Deut. 6:13. Likewise, it is one thing to take an oath when a person calls upon God as a witness for his soul. It is another thing to swear when something is sworn to by calling upon the true God, that if he is lying, God will be the judge. Thus in Num. 5:19ff. there is a good illustration of this. In 1 Sam. 14:24 Saul adjured the people. In 1 Kings 22:16 Micaiah is adjured. In Matt. 26:63 Christ is adjured. Here pertains this kind of swearing: 1 Cor. 1:10, "I beseech you by the name of our Lord Jesus Christ"; Rom. 12:1, "I beseech you by the mercies of God."

There is another kind of oath, one which is imposed on another person as in Gen. 24:2; Joshua 2:12; 1 Esdras 10:5 (Vulgate); Ex. 22:11. Another oath is taken voluntarily out of one's calling. Likewise, sometimes in taking an oath the name of God is clearly invoked; and sometimes a dear and beloved thing is offered as a pledge. Thus Joseph swears by the life of Pharaoh in Gen. 42:15. In 1 Sam. 17:55 Abner swears by his soul, cf. 1 Sam. 25:34; 1 Cor. 15:31. Augustine is correct in saying that this is a formula for an oath, Epistle 89.

Condemned are oaths by created things, and this for two reasons: (1) When there is attributed to creatures or idols by whom one swears some divine quality or deity whereby they can do something either good or evil, Jer. 5:7; Amos 8:14; Ex. 23:13. (2) In Matt. 5:34 and James 5:12 such swearing is condemned because the Pharisees had the notion that as long as they did not use the name of God, they could without risk in their common speech swear by created things such as by their head or by heaven, cf. Matt. 5:34–36, and still not sin against the Second Commandment. If they asserted anything in swearing by created things, they did not consider themselves guilty of perjury if they broke their vow, because it is written, "You shall pay your vows unto the Lord," Matt. 5:33. This figment of Pharisaic imaginings can be seen from Matthew 5. But Christ replies that some vestiges of the Deity exist in created things, as seen in God's creation and governance, in the heavens, in the earth, in the head of man, that is, in the temple and on the altar where the glory of the revelation of God shines forth in a special way. Therefore God Himself is pointed to and recognized in His works, as it were, when we swear by heaven and the temple, etc. Thus Christ absolutely prohibits swearing by heaven. All swearing by heaven or by the earth is absolutely forbidden. But He did not need to add the name of God which is self-evident, just as in the case of St. Paul when he says, "All things are lawful for me . . ." 1 Cor. 6:12, and "I am made all things to all men," 1 Cor. 9:22, where this principle of universality must not be extended to filthiness, adultery, idolatry, etc., but is restricted to those subjects of which Paul is speaking.

III. Because useless and rash oaths are forbidden, the question arises: In what situation is it permissible to take an oath and for what reason may we swear? The correct answer is that it is permissible to take an oath either when the magistrate demands and requires it or when our calling requires it. This principle can be clearly and easily understood from the Scriptural examples cited for the use of oaths, as godly men may read in Gen. 21:23, "Now swear by God that you will not harm me or my children," says Abimelech to Abraham. Gen. 26:28, the king of Gerar says to Isaac, "Let there be an oath between us and let us make a covenant"; Gen. 31:52–53, Jacob swears to Laban that he will keep friendship with him and do him no mischief. In Judges 11:10, by an oath the people pledged Jephthah their loyalty, obedience, and subjection, cf. Deut. 21:1–7; Ex. 22:11. Here pertain also the passages and examples which were previously cited. Likewise Christ and Paul give oaths to harmonize their faith and authority with their words.

Therefore it is lawful to require and give an oath when all human proof is absent, when a controversy can be settled in no other way, when the welfare or salvation of one's neighbor is seriously endangered, when by taking an oath he may receive good counsel, or when the glory of the name of God is involved in the matter for which the oath is taken.

IV. The question is how an oath is lawful and how does one swear lawfully? Jerome in regard to Jer. 4:2, "You will swear in truth, in justice, and righteousness," says that an oath must have three conditions and "if these are lacking, it is not an oath but perjury."[14] (1) Swearing in truth is taken on behalf of something which conscience dictates is true. (2) Swearing in justice refers to not swearing regarding an uncertain thing and where one should not swear to an unproved thing. Here justice or judgment is exhibited because it should take place with deliberate intention. Thus we should consider in such a case what our duty is in making an oath. (3) Swearing in righteousness takes place by confirming a promise by an oath regarding a righteous matter, something which is lawful and can possibly be done, which is not in conflict either with faith or love. Here pertains those matters which have been mentioned in the definition of an oath.

V. The duty of taking an oath must involve a matter of great obligation in accord with the definition. There are examples of this among the godly. Joshua, although deceived by the Gibeonites, yet was unwilling to break the promise he had given with an oath, Josh. 9:18. Saul, after he had broken his oath, was punished in his children, 2 Sam. 2:6. Antiochus broke his oath and was punished, 2 Macc. 9:5. David swore to Jonathan and his descendants and therefore he was unwilling to kill Shimei, even though he had cause, 1 Sam. 20:16ff., cf. 2 Sam. 19:23. What great seriousness the children of Israel showed in their treatment of the oath which they had taken against the Benjaminites can be read in Judges 21, cf. Ps. 15:4, "He who swears even to his own hurt (that is, that afterward he sees trouble for his own concerns) and takes care of his affairs, he shall dwell

---

[14] Epistle 89 (157) to Hilarion, re 1 Cor. 15:31, MPL 33.693.

in the holy hill of the Lord." Oaths which have been given to our enemies must be kept, as we see in the example in 2 Kings 25:6 and Ezek. 17:13.

VI. Thus those things which by an oath are in conflict with the Second Commandment can easily be determined from the points which have been stated, namely: (1) Rash and futile oaths given in insignificant matters, where the business could have been handled with a simple yes or no. (2) Perjury, which is either confirming a lie by oath or by breaking an oath and a false oath in which, in the very act of swearing, a person knows that he will not keep his oath. (3) When an oath is not accompanied by a righteous cause, but is itself wrong, as when David swears that he will kill Nabal, in 1 Sam. 25:22; or when an oath is taken which is impossible to keep, such as the vow of celibacy by those who do not have the gift; or an oath regarding an uncertain thing or something about which we have incomplete information. (4) When an imprudent oath is taken, that is, an ill-considered matter when there is a duty involved, as has been seen in the definition. (5) To swear by created things in the manner mentioned above, cf. Jer. 5:7, "They swear by them that are not gods"; Zeph. 1:5, "Who swear by the name of God and of Molech. . . ." (6) The magistrate also is guilty of sin who demands an oath while seeing the name of God profaned. Even more does a private person sin when in using an oath, he provides an occasion for perjury. Thus Augustine says, "If any private citizen calls upon a person to take an oath when he knows he is going to swear falsely, he is guilty of murder." (7) Those who use a shameful formula in swearing by God, for example, those who swear by the beard, the nose, or the private parts of God. These people are punished for their oath. (8) Those who like Herod swear to something wrongfully act irreverently and destructively. This is a double sin, both in the swearing and in the action involved.

Concerning Magic, Incantation, and Superstition

Because the name of God and sacred words are commonly used in incantations, I shall make a few brief remarks at this point on matters commonly disputed concerning magic superstitions. They are divided into the following categories:

1. The purpose (*causa finalis*). They are used to gain knowledge of future events and hidden things, or for the cure and other helps; to do evil things; to perform magic tricks, as in the case of Pharaoh's magicians.

2. The efficient or material cause. First, sometimes there is the manifest invocation or worship of devils, either through certain verbal formulas, sacrifices, fastings and other rituals, or through the writings of known individuals whom they call characters or magic symbols or images; and when an express covenant is made with the devil, it is evident that this is a frightful sin against

the First Commandment. Second, sometimes the invocation or worship of the devil is not manifest, nor is there an express covenant with him, but they use either the verbal formula, whether known or unknown, but still vain and blasphemous, or the characters or images either tied up or suspended, of certain of these, or they employ other vain observances without mentioning the pact or the worship of the devil. Augustine tells that superstitions of this kind wanted to be called magic, but he said that they had physical causes. He is correct when he says, "All such observances which do not have their cause either in nature or divine institutions, arise out of and constitute a pestilent alliance between men and devils, a kind of pact and friendship of unbelief." That is, in the case of the original developers of superstitions, the person made a pact with the devil that he would do such works in keeping with superstitious practices of this kind. Thus there comes to be a tacit worship and an implied pact with the devil, and the devils rejoiced that they were receiving these vain observances, as the minds of the people were involved in vanity and they fell into other more vile practices. Thus Augustine is correct in saying that practices of this kind must be absolutely avoided and rejected by Christians.

3. The name of God or certain words from Scripture are often used in these observances. Sometimes the words are used by themselves and sometimes they are mixed with unknown, vain, and irreverent names and symbols. We should recall the wiles of the devil at this point. In the early church the elders were called to the beds of the sick and prayed there, cf. James 5:14–15, "The prayer of faith relieved the sick." Thus, when the devil saw that by open trickery he could not in the light of the Gospel impose his will on Christians against the First Commandment, under the pretext of the name of God, he fabricated a new form of magic against the Second Commandment. As Augustine says in his seventh sermon on John, "When the evil spirits cannot lead Christians astray, so that they can poison them, then they add some honey, so that through something sweet they may hide their bitter poison." All agree that it is a great profanation of the divine name, when the name of God is tied in with superstitious words, notes, or symbols. But when only the words of Scripture are used for this purpose, so that something is performed with a set form and mode of words and constant repetition of them, for example, to stop the flow of blood, if these words are recited, such as "May your blood remain in your veins as Christ in His Supper. . . ." Again, if a symbol such as the Lord's Prayer or words from the Gospel are used or written on behalf of the sick and placed upon him or over his heart, or hung from his neck . . . this is clearly permitted under canonical law, quest. 26, ch. 5. It is not permitted under the question in ch. 7, nor should it be observed. Augustine, because he was rather indulgent toward those who were pressured to do such things, says in Epistle 119 [MPL 24.706], "Many things of

this kind I do not dare to disapprove as scandals which must be avoided, because of some who are either holy people or those who are troublesome." He says the same thing in *In Joh. Hom.*, 7 [MPL 35.1440], "When your head aches, I strongly urge that you put the Gospel on your head." But Chrysostom, *In 23 Matt.* [MPL 33.221], in a long discourse criticizes these superstitious practices and gives his reason, "Because the power of the Gospel is in the mind and not in figures or images." And Jerome also rejects these ideas and says that they are "the actions of superstitious old women."

It is not difficult to evaluate this question when we apply the Second Commandment. For God prohibits not only blasphemy and the profanations of His name, but also using His name in vain. Therefore He approves only of that use of His name which He prescribes in His Word. But when we apply it to another use, even if it is not blasphemous, then a great threat is added, "For He will not hold him guiltless who takes His name in vain." In Matt. 23:14, we read, "You devour widows' houses and make long prayers; for this you shall receive the greater damnation." Therefore, even if they did not blaspheme, nevertheless, He says that they would receive condemnation.

Therefore Scripture condemns also those who practice things of this kind, Deut. 18:10–11; Lev. 20:6, "Those who consult them (wizards, necromancers, etc.) and use their services," cf. Leviticus 10; 19:31; 20:6; 1 Sam. 28:7ff.; 2 Kings 1:3; 2 Chron 33:6; Acts 19:13, the example of the Ephesian exorcists who used the name of Jesus.

The Third Commandment

[MELANCHTHON'S TEXT]

In the First Commandment are taught the inner works of the mind, will, and heart toward God; in the Second, the outward profession; in the Third Commandment is taught the precept regarding the divinely instituted ceremonies. We must understand the purpose of these. Ceremonies were given for the service of teaching and serve this function. Thus the precept regarding the Sabbath speaks principally of the service of teaching and administering the divinely instituted ceremonies or rites. Thus the text is not speaking only in a general way but specifically of sanctification. The commandment intends that on that holy day good works are to take place, that is, properly those things which God has commanded, that the people are to be taught and the divinely established rites be observed. For this purpose a certain day was set aside. This principal point in the commandment pertains to all men and to all times, because it is natural law. But in regard to the observance of the seventh day, it is obvious that after the Levitical ceremonies were abrogated, this observance has also been changed, as Col. 2:14ff. clearly teaches. Thus it is correct to say that in the

Third Commandment there are two parts, one a natural, moral, or general law, and the other part is the ceremonial which applied properly to the people of Israel specifically with reference to the seventh day. Of the first part it is correct to say that as a natural or general law it is in effect for all time and cannot be abrogated, that is, it is a commandment for the preservation of the public ministry, so that there be a day on which the people may be taught and the divinely instituted rites observed. But the specific reference to the Jews by name and the specific reference to the seventh day have been abrogated.

Therefore we should learn with certainty that here is commanded the preservation of the public ministry and the rites which God has instituted, because God wills to preserve them in order that His church may remain and be planted, as it says in Eph. 4:11ff., "He gave some apostles, some prophets, some pastors, some teachers, that the body of Christ may be built . . . that we be not tossed to and fro and carried about by every wind of teaching," that is, He gave a sure word to be spread among people through the prophets and apostles, with certain witnesses added. He established the public ministry by which this Word is preached, so that we might have the sure teaching about God and not devise new religions and new worship, as the gentiles do. Each person in his own place ought to love and respect this gift of God and support it, as Christ says, "He who hears you hears Me and he who despises you despises Me," Luke 10:16. The prophets deplored the desolation of the Sabbath (2 Chron. 36:21, cf. Jer. 27:2) and lamented that the ministry of teaching had been abolished. Therefore the works demanded by this commandment and the reverent performance of this ministry are: to hear those who teach correctly and use the Sacrament reverently and to support their use also by Christian example and frequent attendance; to obey those who teach correctly and honor and support them and defend true teachers and to aid with zealous works the needs of the church. I do not require any allegory for this commandment but rather give the proper and particular meaning. For it is no easy and insignificant task to preserve the divinely established ministry. The sins against this commandment are these: to omit or abolish the work of correct teaching, to teach falsely, to corrupt the sacred rites, never or rarely to attend public services in the congregation where the churches are correctly taught; to lead others away from the public ministry which is not corrupted by ungodliness, as when the Donatists led their congregations out. Or not to obey the ministry of pure teaching, to carry on useless works, that is, works which hinder religious services on days set aside for public worship, or to spend those days in games and gormandizing or other vices, or to despise and bring humiliation on godly pastors, or being unwilling to give them financial support and to defend them, or to be unwilling to cover their faults if they are sound in doctrine, as when Ham ridiculed his naked father; or not to give eager support to the church.

Furthermore, as we have said above, the First Commandment must be included *in all the others, for, since they are the commandments of God, He must be recognized as their author and obedience must be given Him. Therefore, the fear of God and trust in God are the life of the other commandments and must be present in all of the works of all the remaining commandments. Thus, in order that the works of this precept may be accomplished, we must add the recognition of the Son of God, so that we can in faith and worship of God obey this command. Likewise, since this precept speaks of the ministry and the rites, it has to include the Gospel because the ministry of the Law is only the ministry of death, but the Gospel proclaims the remission of sins and life everlasting for the sake of the Son of God. Likewise, the divinely established ceremonies are a type of Christ. Thus, the Jews cannot correctly perform the works of this commandment without the true knowledge of Christ, and the monks and those who sacrifice the mass (because the doctrine of faith, true worship and true prayer is unknown among them) pile up many sins in their own ceremonies. They wrongly think that the works of human traditions are worship. They pervert the Lord's Supper in many ways and actually bring the rites themselves into question by their corruptions. These errors are in conflict with this commandment and they defile the Sabbath.*

The titles for the good works which pertain to the First Commandment also apply to the Second and Third.

The Third Commandment

Because the Third Commandment is partly moral and partly ceremonial, we must first note on which sure Scripture passage it is established; which are the Mosaic portions in the Third Commandment which applied only to the people of Israel while that nation still existed and those which have been abrogated in the New Testament and no longer apply to us; and which portions are moral and pertain to all men. The Third Commandment is made up of three chief parts: (1) the seventh day; (2) physical rest; (3) the sanctifying of the day.

To the first part is added the reason, given in Gen. 2:3, which pertains not only to the Jews but is seen to be a universal and continuing precept which shall not change, and because at the very beginning of the world, long before the law of Moses, God set aside the seventh day, the observance of this day is not only ceremonial. This point greatly disturbed Burgensis and he struggles with it in various ways. First, he says that the sanctifying of Genesis 2 pertains only to that one day on which God rested after completing the works of creation. But the words of the Decalog, Ex. 20:11, clearly refer the sanctification to each individual seventh day. Finally, he comes to the point of saying that it is a moral and everlasting principle that the number seven must be involved in counting the days and from this began the erroneous notion that the day which in order and number is the seventh must be observed, because in six days God created the heaven and the earth.

The scholastics argued that the Sabbath had not been abrogated in such a way that it has been taken away. For they say that that just as the Jews were bound to the seventh day, so we are bound to the first day, which is called the Lord's Day (*Dominica*), and we must observe it with the same strictness as required in the Third Commandment. Thus it is explicitly ordered that all Lord's Days apart from feast days must be observed from evening to evening, just as the Jews observe the Sabbath. Some argue about barbers who often on the eve of the Lord's Day extend their working hours until late at night. They say that the barbers must stop working, and yet they themselves cannot be condemned for a mortal sin if after a feast day they drag out their celebrating for over 24 hours, as if 24 hours of feasting were perfectly moral. This is in clear conflict with Paul, in Gal. 4:10 and Col. 2:16, who says that the Sabbath was abrogated because we are not bound to a particular day because of the number seven. For as Isaiah predicted in 66:23, "Men will come from Sabbath to Sabbath." Therefore, there is no necessity in the New Testament to observe the commandment regarding the number seven.

We can clearly prove from the New Testament that the addition to the Third Commandment is not moral law but typical and pedagogical. For Col. 2:17 includes the Sabbath among "the shadows of things to come," and it is a type and shadow of a certain thing, as Heb. 4:4 explains. Even in the Old Testament God called the Sabbath a "sign," Ex. 31:13; Ezek. 20:20. Nor is it some mysterious matter as to what kind of teaching is involved in the Sabbath. (1) Regarding the article of creation, the very day should be a reminder that the world did not arise by accident, nor is it ruled by accident, but the Sabbath should lead to the recognition of the Creator. The Sabbath also teaches what benefits men receive in the article of the six days of creation, so that they should also remember them on the seventh day. [2] The Sabbath was a sign that men were not only created for the activities and duties of this life, but there is coming a time when they shall be translated to the eternal Sabbath where God will be "all in all," Eph. 1:23, and "all tears shall be dried," Rev. 21:4. (3) The Sabbath was a sign of sanctification, that it is not the work of our powers but the gift of God. (4) It was a sign of mortification, that we should rest from all our works, Heb. 4:4.

There is no doubt that in the New Testament the signs, shadows, and figures have been abrogated and that the teaching role of the Sabbath has ceased, Gal. 4:2. Therefore the rationale which has been added to the Third Commandment is not moral and continuing, but typical and pedagogical. "It has been imposed along with other things until the time of correction," Heb. 9:10. Nor does it follow that because the observance of the Sabbath was instituted before the law of

Moses, therefore it is part of the moral law and is ongoing. Otherwise the sacrifices and circumcisions would be obligatory for us even in the New Testament. But the whole time up until the coming of the Messiah was a time of shadows, signs, and teaching, and this applies also to those practices before the law of Moses.

Therefore the circumstances surrounding the seventh day have already been abrogated, so that we "can judge every day," Rom. 14:5. However, it is not as if the seventh day, which previously was set aside, should now be cursed, so that it is no longer permissible to rest on this day and call together the congregations for worship, as certain students of the *Summa* incorrectly assert, saying that on the Sabbath there should be no ceasing of labor before sunset lest we be guilty of Judaizing. For the apostles often gathered on the Sabbath and taught, etc., and in Rom. 14:5 Paul clearly says that in the early period the apostles did not contend against those who wanted to retain a legal distinction of days, not out of legal necessity but as a free observance. Thus at first they held their services on the Sabbath. But later, Gal. 2:4, when they were trying to make it a matter of necessity that no other day could be set aside under the Third Commandment and said that those who did not observe the Sabbath (seventh day) were guilty of mortal sin, then the apostles and Christians, not only by word but also by practice and example, showed Christian liberty and would not hold their services on the Sabbath, lest they seem to be corroborating the Jewish opinion regarding the necessity of the law of Moses.

Furthermore, they used the first day of the week, Acts 20:7 and 1 Cor. 16:2, on which Christ had arisen, not with the idea that just as God had in creation sanctified the seventh day, so that the soul which did not observe it should die the death, and thus that Christ by His resurrection had set aside the first day of the week so that upon peril of one's salvation this day must be observed. For they said that the rules which Paul lays down in Gal. 4:10 and Col. 2:16 must be firmly retained in the New Testament. Thus they set aside the day on which Christ arose because through the resurrection of Christ the abrogation of all the shadows of the Law was accomplished and among these shadows the Sabbath itself was included, Col. 2:17. They called it the Lord's Day, Rev. 1:10, because they wanted the change from the Sabbath to the Lord's Day to be a public confession that Christians had been freed from the necessity of distinguishing days through Christ's resurrection and thus they taught that in the New Testament the Lord's Day was not to be observed out of necessity as in the case of the Sabbath under the Law, but with that liberty with which Christ by His resurrection has abolished the shadow of the distinction of days and only for the sake of order and propriety has willed that there be a certain day on which the people gather. Yet this can freely be changed as long as there is no scandal or disorder. Perhaps the apostles in this change of the days also had in mind the point raised in Deut. 5:15 that to the Sabbath was joined the memorializing of God's leading them out of Egypt. Jeremiah in 16:14–15 predicts that "the day is coming in which there will come to them the memory of greater blessing, when the prisoners shall be led out of the pit," cf. Zech. 9:11, which was completed in the resurrection of Christ.

The heathen set aside the ninth day. As the poet says, "It is he who always in the ninth day returns." The Turks, in order to shame Christ and the day on which He was crucified, celebrated the fifth day. Thus the apostles wished to separate themselves from the Jews and from all other nations in this external practice.

The second part of the commandment pertains to the abstinence from work. Deut. 5:15 adds the reason: "Remember that you yourself were a slave in Egypt and the Lord your God brought you out with a mighty hand and an outstretched arm. Therefore He commanded you to keep the Sabbath." This manifestly pertains to the people of Israel, namely, that the Sabbath is a memorial that they had been led out of the harshest slavery by the strong hand of God and were put in a place of rest in the land of Canaan, as Hebrews 4 so beautifully explains the reference in Psalm 44. For this memorializing of His blessing God commanded that not only free men but also slaves, foreigners, and even beasts of burden cease from their labors. Certainly this part of the commandment does not apply to us. Thus in the New Testament there is no repetition of this mandate: "You shall not labor, neither your slaves nor your ox," Ex. 23:12. Indeed, Paul in the Book of Acts sometimes journeyed for several continuous days even though the command about ceasing from travel, Ex. 16:29, was still in effect. Jerome concluded on the basis of Acts 18 that Paul labored with his hands on the Lord's Day when he was not able to preach to the people in public worship, for Luke says in Acts 18:3–4 that Paul on every Sabbath engaged in religious debates and on the other days he labored. Christ with very notable zeal performed many deeds on the Sabbath day in order to show the abrogation of the Mosaic Sabbath and to demonstrate the real meaning of the Sabbath in the New Testament.

The Pharisees added many superstitious corruptions to the observance of the Sabbath, of which the Jews have many even to this day, such as not cooking vegetables, peeling garlic, killing lice, etc. Christ Himself sharply criticized these practices in many places and shows that the true meaning of the Third Commandment had been perverted. In addition to this He also shows that those ceremonies which sanctified the name of the Sabbath or the seventh day which God established through Moses were abrogated in the New Testament. Jeremiah 17:21 severely condemns carrying a burden on the Sabbath day, but in John 5:8 Jesus orders the man to carry his bed and defends the action. In Matt. 12:8 He adds the reason: "The Son of man is Lord also of the Sabbath," indicating that by His very presence the Sabbath of the Law has been abrogated. He adds that in the Old Testament this refers to the priests in the temple performing the sacrifices on the Sabbath, v. 5, but "I say to you, that One greater than the temple is here," Matt. 12:6.

Furthermore, it is profitable to consider in the examples of Christ which works are permissible on the Sabbath and which prohibited. (1) Work performed in case of necessity is not in conflict with the Third Commandment, for example, in Matt. 12:1, when the disciples were hungry and picked the heads of grain; Luke 13:15, ". . . to loose the beast of burden and lead him to water"; Luke 14:5, "If your donkey falls into a pit . . ." (2) Works which are undertaken for the benefit and help of one's neighbor, so that service is not denied them, are not prohibited on the Sabbath. Matt. 12:12, "It is lawful to do good on the Sabbath"; cf. Mark 3:4, "Is it lawful to save a life or to kill?" Christ on the basis of the statement, "I will have mercy and not sacrifice," Matt. 12:7, gives this precept. Necessary works of love must be placed ahead of ceremonies, but not in such a way that public worship is abolished. (3) Works which serve to the glory of God are not prohibited, as in John 5:7ff. and 9:1ff. (4) Works which pertain to the conservation of the ministry do not violate the Sabbath, such as circumcision, John 7:11; the performance of sacrifices in the temple, Matt. 12:5. In the Old Testament, to be sure, God makes specific mention of "servile works," Lev. 23:8. But He shows that it is not simply work or labor which is prohibited on the Sabbath, but the interpretation of Christ clearly shows by antithesis that only those works are in conflict with the Third Commandment which are not necessary or are undertaken out of greed, vanity and/or contempt for public worship, which either interfere with public worship or cause a scandal to others so that they are led away from divine worship.

The third part of this commandment speaks of sanctifying the day, which was fulfilled through the ministry of the Levitical ceremonies. These have obviously been abrogated.

Thus we have removed the Mosaic wrappings in which God clothed the nation of Israel until the time of the new order, Heb. 9:10. Thus it still is correct and Biblical to say that the part of the Third Commandment which pertains to the human race is moral law and always in effect. Thus we should consider what the general meaning of this commandment is, and what is changeless and pertains to all men.

1. The portion related to the sanctuary, the ceremonies, the tithes, etc., is specifically Mosaic. But the general aspect which applies to all men is the preservation of public worship, the doctrine, and the divinely instituted cere-

monies. Likewise, included are such things as reverence and obedience toward the ministry.

2. The circumstances of the seventh day pertain to the specifically Mosaic aspects of the commandment. But the general teaching is that among the activities of this world we in this earthly life must have some opportunity to attend the ministry of the Word and the ceremonies, and that for the sake of decency and order stipulated days are beneficial for this purpose.

3. In regard to the Sabbath day's journey of Ex. 16:29, the kindling of a fire in Ex. 35:3, or bearing burdens out of your house in Jer. 17:22—these are matters of ceremonial law. But the general principle is: Do not perform works which hinder the ministry or stubbornly carry on needless labor. For if we are to support the practice of public worship, then we must give up those activities which hinder this worship.

4. This aspect is also moral, although not properly or principally a part of the Third Commandment, namely, that the duties of humanitarianism should be shown toward servants, strangers, and even the very beasts of burden whose labors we employ in our work, so that they are not burdened beyond their powers, but may be refreshed by proper rest. For we recall how God does not allow us to be "tried beyond our powers," but rather renews us through His comfort, 1 Cor. 10:13. Conversely, through the practice of cruelty toward animals is fostered also inhumanity toward our neighbor.

Thus it is customary and possible on the basis of the purpose of the Third Commandment to determine the true meaning which pertains to all of us. But for my part far more convincing is the study of the account itself, from the very words, as from those which are the closest and surest foundations for the points which God makes in each of the commandments. For there is no doubt that the individual words are used in the Decalog with great wisdom. There is no surer way to learn the ongoing and immutable doctrine of the Third Commandment, which is binding upon all men, than from these precise words. Then it will be easier to apply the Scripture passages which occur in various parts of Scripture to the explanation of this precept. Therefore we shall consider the terminology.

1. We must note the form of the precept. It does not simply say, "Sanctify the Sabbath," in the way that it says, "Honor your father"; but it says, "Remember to sanctify." It is spoken in the indefinite, as when we say, "Remember to sanctify or set aside" (*zu gedencken dass du heyligest*). Certain people are trying to say that God spoke this way because the Sabbath was not at that time first established, but there should be a remembrance of that day which had then perhaps begun to fall into disuse, and it was now renewed. Thus, they say, that God commanded that they should remember that in the very act of creation God had sanctified the seventh day. These facts are certainly true, but God doubtlessly

looks at the matter more deeply. For He foresaw that in the future there would be hypocrisy in the external observance of the Sabbath and therefore He provided for the use of the Sabbath at the very beginning by making it a part of His recorded Word, so that He might thereby demonstrate that the true sanctifying of the Sabbath does not consist principally in taking one's case, in one's clothing, or in external ceremonies, but in remembrance, that is, in the action of our mind, our will, and our heart; so that our mind which is distracted with cares and occupied with the necessary activities of this life might be given the opportunity to recall and meditate on this sanctifying of the day, that it is God who has set it aside. In the brevity of the Decalog God universally observes this point, that what is included in each individual precept, even when it is not repeated in each, yet can and must be applied to it correctly. For Ex. 13:9 and Deut. 6:8 speak of the entire Law, "It shall be a sign to you, upon your hand and for a memorial between your eyes. . . ." Likewise, Ps. 103:18, ". . . who remember His commandments to do them." The word "to remember," according to the interpretation of Holy Scripture, must be applied to the individual precepts, namely, that God does not require so much an outward work as the thoughts of the mind and the inner emotions or desires. Likewise, to forget the commandments of God is the source of all transgressions, just as on the other hand the remembrance or meditation upon the precepts (of which clear testimonies are evident, for example, Joshua 1:8 and Psalm 119) is the means through which the Holy Spirit writes the Law in our hearts. He warns us that we are not to treat the precepts of God lightly or contemptuously, as if they can be neglected without peril and buried in forgetfulness, but rather our soul must be so guided that thoughts of the commandments of God always are in our minds.

2. "That you may sanctify the Sabbath day." Origen correctly says that the term "sanctify" indicates the separation of something from a profane or common use for the worship of God or for divine things. In the first two commandments God has already described the inner sanctification and spiritual worship which He demands. Therefore, because He adds a precept governing the setting aside of the Sabbath by external rites, He is showing that the spiritual worship of God among men should have in this life some external exercise or practice of public worship services. For that we as individuals ought to meditate on the law of God is taught in Ps. 1:2, or to speak of His testimonies in Ps. 119:46. But these points pertain to the Second Commandment. Thus the Third is speaking of public worship. God adorns these services with the loveliest name when He speaks of them as a sanctification. This is not done in the way an unbelieving husband is "sanctified" by the wife in 1 Cor. 7:14, or food is "sanctified" in 1 Tim. 4:5, or as works of one's calling done in faith are called "holy." But in the Third Commandment the sanctifying has been instituted by

God for the purpose of being a means through which God wills to sanctify His church, as it is written in Ex. 31:13 and Ezek. 20:12, where He says, "It is the Sabbath of the Lord your God," that is, it has been established because He wills in this way to show Himself to you through the sanctification of the day. Or as Isaiah says in 58:13, "Let not our own will be done on the Sabbath day," for it is the Lord's day. Further, just as God did not permit to the people of Israel freely to choose their own method of observing the Third Commandment, according to their own ideas, but He gave the day its name and prescribed definite cere-monies; and when they set up their own groves and high places and performed works of their own choosing, God said that His Sabbath was being profaned and not sanctified, Ezek. 20:27–28. Likewise in the New Testament we must teach on the basis of the Gospel what those practices of public worship are through which God wishes to sanctify His church. For the Levitical ceremonies have not been abrogated in such a way that under the Third Commandment we have been granted the right of making our own religion, Col. 2:23, as some argue in regard to hearing mass and lighting candles on the Sabbath.

3. "Six days shall you labor." It is a beautiful thought that God in His Word not only wills to consecrate our external worship but also our common labors and the works of our calling, so that in this way we might discern the true mean-ing of the worship of God. For just as God set aside the seventh day for rest, so also God says that the other six days on which we perform our heavy labor have also been consecrated, because in six days God made heaven and earth. Therefore the faithful must not have the opinion that they are not serving God when they are involved in their daily tasks, or that they are less acceptable to God because they cannot like the Levites conduct daily ceremonies or services. It is worth our consideration that six days are given for common labors and only one for the sanctifying of the Sabbath, not because the labors to be done are more important than the public service, but because God knows very well that the increase of idleness is dangerous in this corrupt nature of ours. Therefore He wills that our flesh be held in subjection by our labors. He shows the differ-ence, because He calls the works of the Sabbath "sanctifying" but the works of the other six days He calls servile or the works of our hands. This great wisdom is imbedded in these few words.

4. Because neither the nature of man nor that of beasts of burden can endure continuous labors, but must have some change of activity, therefore God shows that there must not be any other way, and that the idleness which is given to rest the body can be put to no better use than in the public services of worship. Thus God wills us to use both our leisure and labor in keeping with His Word. When we are distracted by cares and the burdens of this life, God in a sense pulls our ear in the Third Commandment and says, "Remember to sanctify the

Sabbath," that is, do not give ourselves over to physical or servile work to such a degree that we forget to sanctify the day. He joins together the leisure for men and animals, signifying thereby that men should observe the Sabbath along with their beasts of burden, when men without remembering to sanctify the holy day only indulge in idleness.

5. We must also note the words, "You and your son and your servant," which are spoken to the head of the household. He enumerates: (1) children who are subject to their parents; (2) servants who have their particular masters; (3) foreigners and visitors who dwell within the gates and over whom the government has authority. Therefore it is clearly expected of the parents, family heads, and rulers that not only should they keep the Sabbath holy, but it is also their duty to see that it be sanctified by the rest of the people, and that it not be profaned, and that those who do so be punished. He says, "That they may rest, as you do." Therefore they ought to set an example, cf. Deut. 6:7; Ps. 78:5. God has shown that the ruler must be concerned that the strangers who dwell within the gates must conform themselves to the true religion, so that no scandals arise from them.

6. In the Third Commandment He remembers the beasts of burden, not because the sanctifying of the Sabbath pertains to the brute animals, but because the labor of yoke animals requires the guidance of men. Thus God is showing that under this specific instance there is the general rule that we must beware not only of things which expressly conflict with His mandates but also of things which hinder obedience to them. Therefore in the Third Commandment He specifically names yoke animals and forbids not only evil things but lawful works when they are a hindrance to sanctifying the day. This rule applies also in the case of other commandments.

7. God has willed that in the observance of the Sabbath there be a memorial of the article of creation, that just as God created all things in six days and then rested on the seventh day and looked at all the things He had made, so He commanded that on the Sabbath day we give thought and thanks for the benefits we have received throughout the other six days under the article of creation, that the people may be instructed by this teaching device to pray to God and to await His blessings, and that thus faith be strengthened. In Deut. 5:15 He mentions that He had led them from Egypt, which is a blessing proper and peculiar to the church. To be sure, the circumstances of that time have been set aside, but the same general principle remains, namely that in the meetings of the congregation people should remember and celebrate the general and special blessings of God. Thus, just as God saw all the things which He had made, so also we should note the work of the Lord and consider the works of His hands, Is. 5:12.

8. That we should do works of love particularly on the Sabbath is indicated

when He speaks of showing humanitarian consideration for servants, strangers and beasts of burden on the Sabbath day. It is worth noting how the Son of God constructed His arguments on the basis of the Third Commandment: (1) He brings in the example of God's working and resting, and then says that works which serve the glory of God ought to be performed particularly on the Sabbath. (2) Setting aside the day is commanded. Therefore work which pertains to the public ministry must be performed on the Sabbath. (3) Because the commandment speaks of servants and beasts of burden, therefore it commands that works of love be performed on the Sabbath. (4) Because the Third Commandment says that your servant and the stranger should rest just as you do, therefore the Sabbath was made for men and man's needs take precedence. A person might not easily notice these basic points in these words. But we must not despise the brevity of the Decalog, but rather note with sincere hearts how carefully God has covered matters of the profoundest meaning with the briefest words.

With these observations we have covered the chief part of the description of this commandment. But because God Himself through His prophets and apostles has instructed that the brevity of the Decalog should not lead us to neglect the matter, it is useful to make a comparison as to how the prophetic and apostolic handling of this commandment agree and refer us back to those fundamentals laid down in the Decalog. We have already said that the reader should note when the words of the Decalog are used in other passages, although with a change of terminology. For example, in the New Testament the apostles, when they speak of matters pertaining to the Third Commandment, because it has been abrogated, do not often use the actual words of the commandment. But the Old Testament Scripture, in describing a rite of the people of God who have been called together and have gathered in a public meeting to hear the preaching of the Law and the prophets, or for prayers or other acts of worship, do use the words of the Third Commandment. Joel 2:15–16, "Sanctify a fast. Call a solemn assembly. Gather the people, sanctify the congregation"; cf. 2 Kings 10:20; Job 1:5. Therefore pertinent here are the testimonies written regarding the meeting and gathering of the faithful for public services, as those which have been repeated in the Acts of the Apostles. Compare also 1 Cor. 11:17ff. and 14:26ff.; Matt. 18:20. In Heb. 10:25 it is commanded that "We be together gladly, and not forsake the assembling of ourselves together."

The following passages show with what spirit the public gatherings of the church were to be approached and how the people were to behave in them: 1 Cor. 11:17; Matt. 18:20; 1 Cor. 5:4; Lev. 26:2; Is. 1:13; 1 Cor. 14:26, 40. The words of the Decalog teach us that the soul must be called away from all other concerns and give itself entirely over to the public divine services. In Matt. 18:20 Christ repeats the promise given in Ex. 25:8 and Ezek. 37:26, "I will be in the midst of them and I will hear." In 1 Cor. 14:24–25: "A person who comes into the church should be convinced, so that he will report that God truly is among us."

At this point we might add testimonies which show what pious people should be doing in the public meetings of the church. They include the following: (1) Acts 13:14–15, the words of the prophets are read every Sabbath; cf. Acts 15:21; 20:7; 13:44ff. (2) There were prayers, Acts 16:13; Luke 1:10; 1 Tim. 2:1, 8. (3) They praised God with psalms and encouraged one another, Col. 3:16; 1 Cor. 14:26; Ps. 42:5. (4) The Lord's Supper was administered, 1 Cor. 11:20ff.; Acts 2:42; 20:7. (5) They collected alms, 1 Cor. 16:1–2. Some explain the breaking of bread in Acts as referring to the alms.

The statement in the New Testament which is particularly pertinent to the Third Commandment is Eph. 4:11–13, "He gave some apostles, some teachers . . . for the work of ministry, for the edifying of the body of Christ, until we all come into the unity of the faith and the knowledge of the Son of God. . . ." Therefore it is correct to deal with the duties of ministers and their hearers under this commandment.

Paul, to be sure, describes the duty of ministers in one word when he says in 1 Cor. 4:2, "It is required in servants that they be faithful." To this faithfulness pertains the fact that they should have at least a fair knowledge of those things which are required for service or ministry and that they show diligence and constancy in performing their duties. There are several aspects of ministry: (1) The preaching of the Word, for which is required: (a) that "he speak as the oracles of God," 1 Peter 4:11. (b) that he "not teach false doctrine," 1 Tim. 1:3; but "guard the treasure which has been put into your charge," 2 Tim. 1:13; "rightly dividing" the Law and the Gospel, 2 Tim. 2:15. (2) The proper administration of the sacraments. (3) The use of the keys in absolution and excommunication. (4) Praying for the whole church. (5) An example to the believers, 1 Tim. 4:12; Titus 2:7, 1 Peter 5:3, "that the ministry be not discredited," 2 Cor. 6:3. (6) The care of the poor, such as visiting the sick, comforting the afflicted, etc.

Furthermore, Paul divides the handling of the Word or preaching into different categories. At one point the Word is dealt with in meetings of the learned. Paul seems to be referring to these meetings in 1 Cor. 14:6 when he lists such things as tongues, revelation, interpretation (v. 26), and knowledge. But "when the whole church," which Paul describes as consisting of both unlearned and learned, "comes together it is foolish," he says, if they all speak in tongues, v. 23. But for meetings of this kind he proposes instruction (*katēchēsis*), prophecy (*prophēteia*), and teaching (*didachē*), 1 Cor. 14:19, 22, 26. These terms can be distinguished: *Katēchēsis* refers to teaching the basic principles to the unlearned and partially instructed, Luke 1:4; Heb. 6:1; 1 Cor. 3:1, while *prophēteia* is interpreted of those who have advanced to a higher knowledge of Scripture. *Didachē*, applies the teachings of Scripture to regular statements of doctrine (*loci communes*), which it explains in keeping with a logical method. To these three terms Paul adds the following kinds of teaching in 2 Tim. 3:16: *Didaskalia* is correct teaching; *elegchos* refutes false teachings; *paideia* guides our life and morals; and *epanorthōsis* condemns and refutes wickedness and evil morals in order to correct them. In Rom. 15:4 *paraklēsis* means comfort; *hypomonē* is an exhortation to perseverance and patience. In 1 Cor. 10:11 *nouthesia* signifies either a warning or reminder (*Erinnerung*) which is impressed upon the mind or thoughts, or the application of certain examples. 1 Cor. 14:3 has *oikodomē*, (upbuilding), *paraklēsis* (comfort), and *parathymia* (encouragement). Again in v. 24 he uses the concept of convicting and judging which seems to point to the rule according to which judgments in doctrine are to be made. Likewise 1 Peter 3:15 gives a general description of the practice of apologetics. And 2 Tim. 4:2 says that certain exhortations are to be "with all long-suffering," while 1 Peter 3:16 says that this must take place with "meekness." 1 Thess. 2:7, "Gentle as a nurse cherishing her children." But when "they will not endure sound doctrine," 2 Tim. 4:3, then "be prepared in season and out of season to rebuke and encourage." 1 Tim. 1:3 and 4:11, "command them" and condemn them by the authority of your office. Titus 2:15, "Rebuke with all authority." Titus 1:13, "Reprove them severely." In 1 Cor. 14:29 Paul directs that when two or three prophets have spoken that the rest then judge their teaching. Acts 15:6, when controversies arise, then the elders come together for discussion. Acts 20:28, 31, be on guard against wolves; tend the flock. Titus 1:9, "Convince the gainsayers." 2 Tim. 2:25, "Instruct those who stand in opposition." Titus 1:5, "Appoint elders," 2 Tim. 2:2, "committing them to faithful men." 1 Corinthians 14; establish order in the church. See also 1 Timothy 3; Titus 1; and 2 Corinthians 6.

The duties of the hearers are: Gladly to be present at public services, Heb. 10:25; to hear and to learn, 1 Cor. 14:28, 31. Luke 8:15, to keep (*retineo*) the Word. John 14:23, to protect (*servare*) the Word. Rom. 10:9, to confess the Word. 1 Cor. 11:20, to use the sacraments. Titus 2:10, "To make attractive the profession of the doctrine by an upright life"; cf. Rom. 2:24. 1 Tim. 2:1, to add our prayers, cf. Acts 2:42. 1 Cor. 16:1, to bestow alms. To love, esteem, and obey the ministry, 1 Thess. 5:13; Heb. 13:17; 1 Tim. 5:17; Phil. 2:2. Likewise to be zealous in support of sincere preachers, 2 Cor. 7:7. To imitate the faith and examples of godly teachers, Phil. 3:17; Heb. 13:7. To pray for the ministers, Eph. 6:18; 2 Thess. 3:1; Heb. 13:18. To chime in with the amen, 1 Cor. 14:16. To test the spirits, 1 John 4:1; 1 Thess. 5:21. To give gifts to support those who teach and those who learn in the churches and schools, Gal. 6:6; 1 Cor. 9:14; 2 Cor. 11:9; 2 Thess. 3:8; Phil. 4:14ff.; 1 Tim. 5:17; Matt. 10:42. To uphold and help also those who serve in other churches, Rom. 16:1–2; 3 John 5; Phil. 4:3. To refrain from bidding godspeed to those who have been excommunicated, 2 John 10; 1 Cor. 5:11. To do the other things which are set forth in the preceding passages, cf. Is. 49:23.

The antitheses are shown partly in the preceding verses and partly are manifest in themselves. Therefore for the sake of brevity I shall note only a few points. To observe the Sabbath according to the Jewish understanding is to change and corrupt the doctrine and the ceremonies, Gal. 4:10; Col. 2:16. Ezek. 23:38, "They have profaned My Sabbaths when they have sacrificed their children to idols," cf. Jer. 23:11; Is. 58:3–4; 1 Thess. 5:19–20; 1 Cor. 14:39; Deut. 12:19. Note Nehemiah 13; Amos 2:11–12. In the time of Elisha, when the government had transferred the payment owed to the sons of the prophets and given it to the Baalites, the godly were supporting the students with alms, as is related in 2 Kings 4:38ff., cf. 1 Tim. 5:22; 1 Cor. 14:9; 2 Tim. 4:3; 1 Cor. 5:11; 2 Thess. 3:6; 1 Cor. 1:12; 3:4; 2 Cor. 6:16. Particularly pertinent here are the scandals against the Third Commandment which shall be shown. A scandal against the individual commandments is a sin. It is not necessary to give antitheses in each case.

We should still say something regarding the warnings, promises, and examples related to this matter. Warnings are such passages as Ex. 31:14 and 35:2; Jer. 17:27; cf. Ezek. 20:47; 22:21; 23:47; Amos 8:10–11; 5:22–23; Lev. 26:14ff.; Jer. 8:9; Matt. 10:15. To avoid lengthiness I do not want to talk further about the bodily and spiritual punishments, temporal and eternal, which apply to this precept. I want to add only what will make these warnings more easily understood.

Examples of punishments: Num. 15:32, the man who gathered sticks unnecessarily and out of stubbornness on the Sabbath. In this chapter it is speaking of sins of ignorance and stubbornness, and this story is added as an example. In Ezek. 20:12ff. God tells of the punishments which He shall inflict upon the people of Israel because of their violations of the Sabbath. In 2 Chron. 36:14ff. a long catalog is given. Antiochus profaned the Sabbath, 1 Macc. 1:50, and received his punishment, 1 Macc. 9:29. Pashhur is punished in a similar way in Jer. 20:4–6, cf. 52:24. See also Neh. 13:15ff. Ahaz, to accommodate the king of Assyria, removed the Sabbath canopy which had been constructed in the temple of the Lord, 2 Kings 16:18; and in 2 Chron. 18:25 Ahab imprisoned Micaiah. In 1 Sam. 2:22ff. the sons of Eli.

The promises: Lev. 26:2–4; Jer. 17:25; Is. 56:4–7; 58:13–14; Matt. 10:41. Note also the promises implicit antithetically in the threats.

Examples of rewards: Ex. 16:29, the gathering of the manna in double portions for the Sabbath. Ex. 34:24, "When you go up and appear before the Lord three times in the year, no man will try to take over your land." 2 Chronicles 23 and 24 concerning King Josiah and the priest Jehoiada. Likewise the examples of Jehoshaphat, Josiah, David, Solomon, Jehu, and Hezekiah, which are not necessary to consider individually, since their stories are told at length in their proper setting in Scripture. Note also Luke 10:42, where Christ tells Martha that her sister Mary has chosen the "better part." Luke 5:3, where Peter contributes the use of his boat to Christ for His preaching, and he himself is chosen to be a fisher of men, that is, an apostle.

The Allegorical Understanding of the Sabbath

Scripture clearly allegorizes the Third Commandment in regard to the Sabbath, Heb. 4:1ff.; Is. 56:4; 58:11; 66:23. Thus we must note this general rule: Allegorical interpretations of the commands of the Decalog must not be blown out of proportion so as either to obscure or abolish the principal meaning which is called the literal one, as some are doing who declaim regarding spiritual adultery in connection with the Sixth Commandment and tacitly permit the fornication forbidden by the Sixth Commandment. But when the proper and simple meaning of the commandment has been set forth first, then it is permissible to speak of the allegorical side. Thus Rom. 2:21–22, "Do you who teach that we must not steal . . . do you rob temples?" Again, Wisd. of Sol. 1:11, "A lying tongue is man's destruction." Spiritual adultery does not pertain to the Sixth but to the First Commandment.

The term "Sabbath" is used in Scripture in four different senses. (1) In connection with Creation, Gen. 2:2, "God rested on the seventh day." (2) In the Mosaic law, in Ex. 20:10 in the Decalog. (3) In the spiritual sense, that in this life the concept of a Sabbath rest is included among those things which comprise the beginning of a new and eternal life. This new life is described in Is. 56:2, "He keeps the Sabbath and keeps his hand from all evil," cf. Is. 58:13; also Hebrews 4 and 10, he who keeps the Sabbath shall rest from his labors just as God rested from His. It is correct to refer this allegory to the Third Commandment, because the means through which God begins in us that spiritual Sabbath is the external preaching of His Word. (4) There is the eternal Sabbath, Is. 66:23, in which we shall rest both in soul and body from the labors of this present life. This refers to the status of our renewed nature after the resurrection in which they will cease from their physical labors, their civil duties, their troubles, and their sins. As it is written, "They shall neither eat nor drink nor marry, but they shall be like the angels," Matt. 22:30, cf. 24:38. Likewise, "The Lord shall wipe away every tear," Is. 25:8; Rev. 21:4. This allegory is correctly referred to the Third Commandment because it instructs us that eternal life will be the kind of peace and quiet in which men may rejoice in the knowledge of God and in glorifying Him.

The Second Table

Even if only civil life is established in this table, yet it is necessary that the human mind understand that here is set forth the best form of life for man in his society. In the first place, government is established as a divine institution and obedience is commanded. In the second place, peace is protected: "Thou shalt not kill." Marriage is protected: "Thou shalt not commit adultery." Ownership of property is protected: "Thou shalt not steal." Later on courts of justice were established and the truth was verified by oaths in the case of contracts and covenants: "Thou shalt not bear false witness." These are all sources for the laws of human society. We should know, to be sure, that life in society is taught to us, but two other points have been added. First, we must remember that God is the Maker both of these laws and of civil life. Thus we must know that we must be obedient for the sake of God, and we should include the First Commandment in all things in order that fear and respect for God and faith in Him may govern our obedience in all areas. Second, we should understand not only the outward works of the precept but also the inner obedience. Thus the nature of man must be ordered so that it does not have inclinations, desires, and works which run counter to this order in which it has been established, which is also set forth and commanded in the Law.

The opposition and confusion in the order in man's nature is especially apparent in this life of man in society. The arrogance in government, the multitude of unjust killings, the unjust wars, the hatred and the envy! Uncontrolled lusts, improper desires, the ravings of the demented are beyond calculation. Thievery is clearly beyond measure in illegal business practices, in usury, and the like. Who works without greed? Who is content with what he has? Who piously and properly handles his property? Finally, everyone deplores double-talk and lying in treaties, contracts, and courts of justice. In these examples we can clearly see the confusion in the order established by God. Thus we must learn that His law is speaking not only about external actions, but also is accusing the whole stubborn opposition of human nature and the confusion of His order, both internal and external. Thus were added at the end of the commandments the precepts regarding coveting, which speak directly to our inner opposition.

Therefore let us now run through the rest of the commandments, which even though they pertain to civil matters, you must know were first given by God in order that we might live in this societal life in which He wills to be known; in which He wills to develop our faith and worship in the midst of our common perils and labors; in which He wills that love be demonstrated toward our fellow men, and that individuals be subject to the common service for His sake; in which He wills that the light of our confession shine forth, so that others may be taught and invited to know and fear

God, as it is written, "Let your light shine before men . . . ," Matt. 5:16. He does not will that Samuel or David lie hidden in solitude and spend their time in some cave performing secret ceremonies, but He wills that they live in the midst of the floods and storms of governing and there spread the divinely given teaching. He wills that they exercise their faith in the midst of dangers and teach others; and that they be known as witnesses of the doctrine which God shows through them. He wills that they be subject to the common service for the sake of the obedience they owe to God. Thus, the Law treats all alike, setting forth the duties in which each individual serves other individuals, when they carry out their own duties, since we are all members of one body, in mutual love, joined together in our mutual duties, in order to obey God. Therefore let us learn here to be ruled so that we may bear the common burdens of our entire life and carry out our common service, that we may contribute our works and remember that we have been made by God for their life in human society. For the first law does not say: seek solitude, or your pleasure, or take your ease, but it says, "Honor your father and your mother, respect your government, and render obedience." Therefore we should learn that the works of the Second Table are truly the worship of God, as this worship has been described above, that is, when our works are guided by the fear of God and by faith. Thus it is common in the prophets, when a choice must be made, that civil obligations should be placed ahead of ceremonies, e.g. Is. 1:17, "Defend the orphan . . ." Is. 58:7, "Divide your bread with the hungry." Cf. also Hosea 6 and Zechariah 7: Be just in your judgment. Christ adorns these duties in the most beautiful way when He tells us that loving our neighbor is like the First Commandment, that is, God demands obedience in both categories at the same time and that both kinds of obedience are the worship of God.

The Commandments of the Second Table

It is clear that the entire Second Table deals with man in society. For it establishes the duties which take place in the common interrelationships of this life. The Second Table must be carefully obeyed because of the results which follow from it. For many people in all ages have given great approval to the solitary life, and it has seemed logical that a man should be freed from the cares and burdens of life in society and be able to devote himself entirely to the exercises of private piety; not called away by the din of family affairs or public problems which constantly occur in our daily lives; not tempted or led into conflict; not drawn away by the forbidden pleasures of the world or the various opportunities for sinning which we meet in our busy daily lives; and not be corrupted. This certainly seems to be the angelic life, and for this reason many zealously sought after it and withdrew from the world and extolled the solitary life to the shame of normal human social relationships. But to these extravagant praises we must place in opposition this fundamental and immovable fact, that the worship which is pleasing to God, internally and externally, both in our spiritual and outward life, is summed up in the Decalog. In the Second Table not even one word calls attention to the solitary life; but concerning our duties toward our fellowman in society in our common life together, not one or two or three precepts are used, but the entire Second Table had to be set forth to protect and enhance our common life. Just as in the case of creation God gave to each individual part of the human body its own peculiar function whereby they are joined together in performing their duties, so under the Second Table He has carefully established the various duties in which individuals in mutual love serve other individuals, share their tasks, and bear together the common burdens of their entire life, in order that they may be obedient to God. No greater praise for man's life in society can be imagined than that God by so many glorious and marvelous testimonies, on Mt. Sinai, gave the entire Second Table of the Law dealing with the duties of our common life together. With a mighty voice which could be heard by more than 600,000 people, He confirmed the fact that, after the worship of the First Table, men were to establish this common society together.

Moreover, we must note that the teaching of the Second Table differs from the civil precepts, which have been given by the philosophers, particularly in three respects: (1) The obedience to the Second Table must be included under the First Commandment, so that we are governed by the fear of God and faith, and subject ourselves to the common burdens of our life together because of the obedience which we owe God. (2) The Decalog relates not only to external works but also to inner obedience which is so perfect in its effects, indeed in its very inclinations, that the Second Table is a judgment of God which accuses the stubborn resistance of human nature in which there is great confusion over the political order as God has established it. (3) The works of the Second Table are actually a worship of God when they are guided by the fear of God and faith, according to the definition of the worship of God.

In order that we may understand more correctly and love the honored position of civil life, we must consider the reasons why God willed that we should live in a social structure with other people. The principal reasons are these: (1) That in a great multitude we might see more clearly the testimonies to the providence, goodness, and righteousness of God, since He covers and protects not only private individuals in their own quiet lives, but entire families and great states in the midst of the storms and tempests of statesmanship. (2) That serious and compelling occasions might be given for the exercise of faith, prayer, obedience, patience, and when for the sake of God we are subject to one another in service, things which the solitary life in its tranquility does not afford. Therefore, hermits, when they have deserted the true and serious practices of piety which are commanded with the voice of God in the Decalog, devise childish and foolish notions not commanded in the Word of God. (3) That we may carry on the charitable works which really cannot be truly performed in the solitary life, where the members are cut off from the body and are not joined together in their mutual duties. (4) That we might invite one another to the knowledge and fear of God, in keeping with the statement, "Let your light shine before men," Matt. 5:16; or, "That thanks may be given to God by many persons," 2 Cor. 1:11; and Ps. 22:25, "I will praise You in the great assembly (*ecclesia*)."

The Fourth Commandment

[MELANCHTHON'S TEXT]

The Fourth Commandment is established at the first level of authority, namely our parents, and thus ought to be the rule for other forms of governance, as in Romans 13. Likewise the highest degree of obedience is commanded, namely honor. Honor has three aspects: The first is the recognition of God, who is the author of the laws for human society both in marriage and in the state. In these ordinances we see the wisdom of God, His goodness toward us, His righteousness, His anger against wrongdoers, and His defense of the innocent. Therefore honoring our parents is recognizing that this human state is a divine work, a testimony to God's providence, beneficial for the human race, good and honorable; loving this ordinance for the sake of God and the common good; and seeking with godly prayers that He would preserve this state.

The second involves external obedience, so that we may observe our common duties in society and not destroy them.

The third involves equity by which in the great weakness of mankind we pardon certain wrongs in our government and restore or repair them with our sense of fairness, gentleness, and concern, and yet in such a way that we do not act contrary to the commandments of God.

The substance of the matter must be distinguished from the personalities. This threefold concept of honor which I have mentioned is always owed to those in authority, that is to the estate of matrimony and to civil government, and committed and bound to the honored and respected laws which God has grafted into the minds of men, and to other just laws. Thus the patriarchs, the prophets, Christ, and the apostles always respected matrimony and the civil order as being the works and benefits of God, just as they considered changes in movements and times and the many miraculous outcomes of events in civil life, and considered them as being the concern of God toward the human race. In the meantime, however, they made a distinction between the things themselves from the persons and from the works of the devil who furiously tries to ruin, overturn, and disrupt the greater works of God. Thus Paul loved and obeyed the government, that is, the laws of the Roman empire, but he did not love Caligula and Nero. Indeed, he execrated them as instruments of the devil, cursed by God, by whose crimes the entire nature of things appeared to be contaminated. This distinction between the subjects themselves and the personalities involved must be kept in mind, so that the works of God can be kept separate from the works of the devil. He who can distinguish between the matters themselves and the personalities will love and revere his government and its laws more, as he looks at the great confusion of rulers which comes from the devil and his agents. For what can be imagined as more monstrous, more shameful, and more abominable than the tyrants of all ages, and how few kindly rulers there have been in any age! We must understand and lament these evils and pray God that He Himself will correct and preserve our governments. Nor are iniquities to be excused or defended under the pretext of godly work; nor are the manifest and horrible injuries, impieties, and indescribable lusts of tyrants to be tolerated on the ground of the dignity of their rank, when there is no end to their raging, but rather other elements of government, to whom God has given the sword, also are doing the right thing when they remove monsters like Caligula and Nero from the power of governing. As the most honorable Trajan said to his master of the horse when he was giving him his sword, "Use this sword to support me, if I rule justly; but if I rule unjustly, use it against me."

If rulers are faithful, that is, if they try at least to some degree to carry out their duties and act as justly as possible, and are mindful of failing, then we must forgive them and either overlook or correct their mistakes. Such men were David, Solomon, and Jehoshaphat, who although they were excellent rulers, also had their lapses, which are described in Scripture in order that we might be warned that governing is a most difficult and dangerous activity. For the devil, since he is a murderer, causes the destruction of statesmen and either overturns their governments or has his henchmen among their people, as he did in the case of Saul, whom he totally destroyed, although Saul at the beginning had done some fine and useful things. David fell into some traps from which he was barely extricated. Then the devil incited Absalom, whose crime brought immeasurable ruin. The devil stirs up the civic realm and the nature of man in itself is weak both in the case of rulers and their people. Both, by nature, love license and hate laws and the iron fetters of discipline. That among the great traps of the devil and the manifold weakness of men even a modicum of stability remains is a great and remarkable gift of God, as Solomon clearly says, "That the eye sees and the ear hears, the Lord has done both," Prov. 20:12, that is, that a ruler rules wisely and that obedience is the response of his subjects each in their station, this is the work of God and He bestows it through faithful rulers, some of whom pass it on to others. No human wisdom, watchfulness, or power is equal to these great tasks. Thus Paul says in 2 Cor. 3:5, "Our sufficiency is from God; not that we are able of ourselves to consider anything as coming from ourselves." But in the people themselves faithfulness is required, that is, a desire to do the right things, 1 Cor. 4:2, "But this is required in stewards that they be faithful." Therefore, when the state of political affairs is reasonably good, we should understand that it is a blessing of God which He imparts to others through His faithful servants and we should obey God through the authority of our rulers.

Furthermore, we should give honor to these rulers for their faithfulness and the heavy labors which accompany all governance, that is, we should confess that they are aided by God and are the instruments through which God supplies good things to us; we should love them and be subject to them. We ought to express gratitude to them for their hard work and overlook their failures, as long as it is not contrary to the commandments of God. This equity is a great and difficult virtue. I have briefly noted the things included under the word "honor," and we must carefully consider these things. I have also spoken of the distinction between the concept itself and the people involved.

Furthermore, this precept deals with the interrelationships between the rulers and the ruled. The duties of the rulers are indicated in such terms as "father" and "mother." Likewise in the entire Decalog, which is the complete statement regarding governance, are included all the virtues and the duties of a good father and a good ruler. Xenophon says it correctly: "A good prince differs in no way from a good father." The first concern of a good ruler deals with the First Table, that is, he is anxious that the churches teach correctly. A father is concerned that his children are taught about God. In the second place, he must be just and strong in his defense of his people; he must be chaste, helpful in aiding the good, he must have zeal, and a strong hatred for wickedness; he must be honest in his words and actions, open, not given to suspicion, etc. He must be diligent in using his resources so that there is no lack of necessities. Then, as I have said, the entire Decalog is a model for governance, and if a ruler will have the attitude of a father, he will have a desire and the ability to do these things.

In turn, the subject must give honor to his ruler, that is, he must recognize that government is a work of God, he should obey for the sake of God and he overlooks some of the errors of his ruler. Here pertain such virtues as universal justice, which is legitimate obedience to a magistrate. There must likewise be a concern about our calling. Likewise, reasonableness in overlooking and correcting the errors of our rulers so that the public peace is not disturbed. But vices which we oppose and sins are more easily seen, so that there is a stubbornness against rulers, which is called disobedience and is a universal unrighteousness, or sedition, neglect of the duties of one's calling, that is, injecting oneself into the responsibilities of others. Both rulers and ruled often fall into this kind of sin. Thus Peter in 1 Peter 4:15 forbids meddling in the government of someone else.

Besides, just as we have said above in the case of governments that we must distinguish between the subject itself and the personalities, so also we must observe a distinction in the kinds of government. In the case of many kingdoms there was particular concern for the defense of honorable civil society, even if religion was unknown. But in the kingdom of the Antichrist there are continuing and particular laws regarding the new religion which [it is said] brings shame to Christ and is condemned by God, and the principal purpose of his kingdom is to destroy the name of Christ, and his kingdom itself is established on the pretext that to extirpate the name and doctrine of Christ is for the glory of God. Such also is the kingdom of Mohammed. The very law of Mohammed is in manifest contempt of Christ. In the second place, it is a law of violence, in which he commands that those who believe that Christ is the Son of God are to be killed, and he commands his followers to propagate his errors by the sword. These kingdoms were predicted in Daniel 7 in connection with the little horn, v. 8ff., "Who speaks words against God and crushes His saints," v. 25. In the third place, the law of Mohammed allows manifold shameful lusts. In fact, there is no real marriage among Mohammedans, because they permit marriage, divorce, and the receiving of divorcés, according to their private decisions, without cause; and by law they allow shameful perversions on account of which God destroyed Sodom and many other cities. In this kingdom the law is not from God but from the ragings of the devil which God permits to continue until the last time, in order that He may punish the world. By the same token, as sins increased from the very beginning, slavery increased, and also the harshness and confusion of rulers. Thus the difference between the rest of the kingdoms and the rule of Mohammed must be noted. Daniel was able to be a magistrate in the kingdom of Babylon. The Jews could serve in Alexander's army. Christians could fight under the Roman emperors, such as when under the believing Marcus Antoninus a great victory was won by Christian soldiers in Pannonia, because the purpose of the military action was the establishment of good government. But it is not right to serve under the Turks, whose purpose is not good political order but the strengthening and spreading of the law they profess. It is permitted for Christians to suffer slavery under them, but not to enter military service with the Turks, because the text clearly says, "He shall crush the saints of God," Dan. 7:25.

The Fourth Commandment

[I.] We shall divide our explanation into certain categories. First, let us speak about the terminology. To be sure, names such as father and mother are so well known that they need no explanation. But we must note these two points, when we deal with the Fourth Commandment: (1) that there be an order, whether social, civil, or domestic, which is distinguished by honorable laws; (2) that people are to administer this order because God clearly refers to persons and indeed in such a way that He does not make reference only to famous people who are deserving of being parents but simply your father, whatever kind he may be, is to be honored if he is your father. For example, 1 Peter 2:18 says,

"Servants owe their masters obedience, not only good and gentle masters, but also harsh ones." With remarkable wisdom God designates who these persons are. Evil men pretend to love and honor the social and domestic order, but for an improper reason they withhold honor which they owe to the persons involved. But Scripture, when it sets forth the account of this precept, as for example the political order in Rom. 13:1, tells us to "be subject to the governing authorities who have been constituted by God." 1 Peter 2:13, "Obey the law of your government." The persons are mentioned in 1 Tim. 2:2, 8–9; 1 Peter 2:13ff., and in many places.

Furthermore, Matt. 15:4 cites the Fourth Commandment: "Honor father and mother." In various places in Proverbs it is the same. In many other places the pronoun "your" is added, as in Matt. 19:19 (Textus Receptus); Mark 7:10 and 10:19; Luke 18:20; Eph. 6:2; etc. These pronouns are added for good reason. For God willed to show clearly in the brevity of the Decalog the persons to whom they are bound. The person who bears the name "father" by virtue of having produced one son, does not have paternal power over all men, but the commandment says, "Honor your own father." It is clearly with the same rationale that Paul in Rom. 13:1 speaks of the "powers of government," that is, those who are our own magistrates, to whose law and authority we are subject.

In the second place God has willed in this commandment not only to sanctify the authority of those above us but also to bind us to certain duties as regards those who are beneath us. Thus He not only says, "Honor the father," but "Honor your father." For He wills not only that there be fathers, that is, that they have the prerogative of power and supremacy, but He also wills that they be and show themselves as the fathers of those by whom they desire to have honor and obedience given. It is a great dignity to be a father under the commandment, but it is a great responsibility to be "your" father. Thus the words in the Decalog are very instructive and worthy of the consideration of pious people.

For this reason also it is significant that, in the great brevity of the Decalog, God mentions not only the father but also names the mother, who could certainly have been included under the generic term "father," as often is the case in other places in Scripture. But because she is beneath the father (for the husband is "the head of the wife," 1 Cor. 11:3), and is weaker by nature and by sex (hence she is called the "weaker vessel," 1 Peter 3:7), therefore God willed to make special mention of the mother in the Decalog, lest sons feel less concerned about their mothers because of the weakness of [the female] sex and think that they have fully carried out their duty if they show their fathers due honor, as if it were not equally important in the same passage that their mothers have the same honor. Therefore He established an equality of honor for both father and mother, and yet according to the laws the power of the father can extend farther.

The same verse commands respect to the other orders of the Fourth Commandment, that we not only freely submit ourselves to those who are above us in authority and other prerogatives, but as 1 Peter 2:13–14 says, "Whether it be to the king as supreme, or to governors as commissioned by him." Again in v. 18 he says, "Servants, be submissive to your masters, not only the kind and gentle, but also the overbearing."

Finally we must consider the word "honor." For it does not say, "Fear, love, obey or be subject to your parents," even though He certainly wills that these concepts be understood in keeping with the interpretation of the prophets and apostles, but He says, "Honor." This word *kābad* is very significant, for it refers to the excellence and loftiness of a thing to which something is attributed either for good or for evil. Thus He wills first of all that we acknowledge in our superiors and revere in them the authority and dignity which God has vested in them. For God in the Decalog regulated not only external actions but above all He turns the heart itself toward obedience, so that we do not regard those who are above us in some human rank as being people who only seek after a high position because of ambition and therefore there is no obligation to respect them; but we should acknowledge that God has placed them in their station and that it is His institution and order which we should recognize and honor in our superiors, so that we are subject to them because of the obedience which we owe to God. Paul emphasizes and explains this in Eph. 6:1, "Obey your parents in the Lord." Col. 3:22, "Doing the will of the Lord, as serving the Lord and not men." Again in the same verse, "Fearing the Lord," cf. Eph. 3:15; Rom. 13:1, 2; 1 Peter 2:13; Ps. 144:2; Is. 45:1; Deut. 25:19; Jer. 27:6ff. Therefore, since these passages are the fountains from which arise true and genuine obedience, God uses the term "honor," which excludes pretenses, neglect, and contempt, and requires that our mind should think honorable thoughts regarding our parents because it leads our thoughts to the will and ordinance of God Himself, which He wants to be honored in those people whom God has placed in that position.

II. Because synecdoche is used in the precepts of the Decalog, we must consider which persons, which stations, orders, or offices in our civil and domestic structure pertain to the Fourth Commandment. It is noteworthy that although it is certain that God in the Fourth Commandment willed to give honor to every ordinance in our civil and domestic life, yet He did not name kings or lords, but father and mother. Many learned reasons are cited and many useful warnings given as to why God willed to include all those in authority, who have been placed in some high position, under the title or category of parents. (1) This is the first degree of authority, the font and seed of all society, and as children are accustomed to conduct themselves first in the society of the home, so they will later act as citizens, lords, magistrates, etc. (2) Because nearly all of us try to escape the dangers of our common life, the burdens of being in subjection and the labors of governing in the various turns of fortune, therefore God included the society of our common life in which He wills us to live under the form of parental authority and filial obedience, so that these burdens might be easier for us. (3) Because the human mind is by nature exceedingly proud in that it cannot quietly endure someone in authority and bears subjection with much complaint, therefore God gave as an example of governance that which is the least unpleasant and as an example of subjection that which is pleasant and enjoyable for reasonable men, so that our minds for the sake of God might be turned toward obedience to other orders in society. (4) Because those to whom God has given some degree of preeminence above others often abuse their power either by oppressing those who are subject to them or by seeking their own private comfort, therefore God has willed to instruct them in their duties by comparing them to a father, so that this very title may under the Fourth Commandment restrain the lust for power.

Therefore it is certain that, just as under the Fifth Commandment not only outward murder is prohibited so the Fourth is not speaking only of our parents according to the flesh. The common designations have been noted. It is useful and worthwhile in the testimonies of Scripture to see how the Holy Spirit clearly gives the name of parents also to other orders in society, not only to the domestic order, but also to the civil. This point will develop reverence toward all those persons who are included under the Fourth Commandment, when we see that the Holy Spirit as with a finger is showing that your master, your magistrate, your tutor, etc., in the Decalog is called your father.

First, therefore, "the fathers of our flesh," Heb. 12:9, are thus called.

Second, all those who are above us, in ascending order, are called fathers—something which in Scripture is quite common. John 6:58, "Your fathers ate manna," although this had been done 1,500 years previously. Luke 11:47, "You build the tombs of the prophets whom your fathers killed," although they had had no prophet for over 500 years. 1 Tim. 5:4, "If a widow has nephews, let them learn to support their needy parents." These words seem to include not only those who are in the direct line of descent, but also collateral relatives, cf. 1 Tim. 5:8; Judg. 9:1.

Third, the disciples of the prophets are called "the sons of the prophets." In 2 Kings 2:12 Elisha cries after his preceptor Elijah, "My father." Not only did the disciples apply the title of "Father" to their teachers, but also the hearers applied it to their instructors. In 2 Kings 13:14 the king called the prophet "my father," cf. 1 Cor. 4:15; Gal. 4:19. Nor is there any confusion in the fact that the teachers of the church are dealt with under both the Third and the Fourth Commandment, but they are shown to be "worthy of double honor," as Scripture says in 1 Tim. 5:17, where they come under both the First and the Second Table of the Law.

Fourth, in Scripture the name of "father" is also attributed to those who are in government. In Gen. 41:43, when Joseph was announced as the ruler representing the king, a herald went before him crying "Abrek," that is, "father." In 1 Sam. 24:11–12 David calls king Saul "my father," cf. Ezra 1:5; Num. 1:4; 17:2. Hence Joseph gives the loveliest names to the father and the king in Gen. 45:8, "The Lord has appointed me as the father of Pharaoh." Therefore counselors or government officials and those who are commissioned with power from the highest rulers are also included under the name of "father."

Fifth, the servants of Naaman of Syria said to him in 2 Kings 5:13, "Father, if the prophet had said to do some great thing . . . ," cf. Ex. 12:3; Judg. 6:11, Vulgate. In the same way the Latins called their heroes or lords the *paterfamilias* or the father of the family, and the head of state is called the *pater patriae* or the father of the country. For they understood that the families under the natural law shared in the name and functions of a father.

Sixth, older men are called fathers, as in 1 Tim. 5:1–2, "Treat an older man as a father and older women as mothers."

Seventh, Christ Himself commended His own mother into the hands of John to protect and care for her, John 19:26–27, saying, "Behold your mother, behold your son," cf. Gal. 4:1–2. Job 29:16, "I was a father to the poor, and I saw to it that even strangers received fair treatment." Thus the word "father" is applied also to patrons and those who advocate a cause.

Eighth, Gen. 4:20–21, "He was the father of those who play the harp and have cattle." Thus artisans with their apprentices come under the Fourth Commandment. The nation also relates to the Fourth Commandment. Thus Joab says in 2 Sam. 10:12, "Let us fight for our people and for the city of God," cf. 1 Macc. 3:20–21; Jer. 29:7.

In these examples, because the Holy Spirit uses the name "father" in a metaphorical sense with reference to the Fourth Commandment and applies it to other persons in a most beautiful way, we have a catalog of the persons who relate to the Fourth Commandment. And for the same reason, because "honor" is a word appropriate for the Fourth Commandment, Scripture orders us to give honor to these people and lists them under the rubric of parents. Thus Ex. 20:12, "Honor parents and magistrates," cf. 1 Peter 2:17; Rom. 13:7; 1 Tim. 5:17; Phil. 2:29; 1 Tim. 6:1; Lev. 19:32; 1 Tim. 5:3.

III. After we have determined which people come under the Fourth Commandment, there is still need to see what the duties of the individuals are. The Decalog gives a brief indication of this. To those in authority it lays down this rule, that they be fathers to those by whom they wish to be honored. Thus it says, "your father and your mother." But to those who are in the lower position, their duty is covered with the one word "honor." Although there are many arguments for reverence toward parents on the basis of birth, education, status, etc., Prov. 23:22; Ecclus. 7:27; Tobit 4:4; and others, yet the Decalog establishes as the source of obedience the fact that we are to understand that it is the will of God that we honor His ordinance in our parents. Thus in 1 Tim. 5:4 Paul says that parents are to be "supported fittingly," and not as a matter of human opinion, but that this is "good and acceptable before God." We acknowledge this also in the case of our rulers and honor the ordinance of God because through these people He does good toward us by punishing evildoers. Paul says, "We are servants through whom you believed," 1 Cor. 3:5. "Little children, with whom I am in travail until Christ be formed in you . . . ," Gal. 4:19. This is the source of our reverence toward the ministry of the Gospel when we acknowledge this ordinance and will of God. As is the case in the other situations, all the duties of those in subjection are covered with the word "honor." But the prophets and apostles as interpreters of the Decalog explain this very general doctrine in specific ways in their writings. Therefore we shall briefly note in summary fashion some of their explanations.

[A.] Paul in Eph. 6:4 describes the duties of parents under three headings: (1) The upbringing [of children], which includes both their nurture and their protection. In 2 Cor. 12:14, "Parents should accumulate wealth for their children." (2) Disciplining them, which includes directing their morals, and this is done by training, instructing, and chastening, cf. Prov. 23:13; Heb. 12:7. Paul wills that moderation be demonstrated, so that the minds of the children are not alienated from their parents by too strict a treatment, since the minds of children must be directed toward love for their parents. This is the thrust of the word "discipline" (*paideia*), Eph. 6:4, cf. Titus 3:14. (3) The instruction of the Lord. For because people are born in order that the knowledge of God might be spread and celebrated, therefore not only must the bodies of those who are born be nourished, not only must their financial welfare be regarded, but particularly we must take care that they be instructed in the teaching which has been given by God, and He calls it an admonition, because He wills that this commandment be given to parents, so that their children may live in prayer and the other practices of godliness.

The antithesis is obvious. 1 Tim. 5:8, "He who does not provide for those of his own household . . ."; Prov. 13:24, "He that spares the rod . . ."; Eph. 6:4, "Do not provoke your children to wrath."

[B.] Sirach in Ecclus. 3:8–9 sets forth the duties of children: "He who fears the Lord honors his parents, who brought him into the world . . . in work, in word, and in all patience." A list of such activities can be gathered from other places in Scripture also: (1) Honor, Ex. 20:12; love and reverence, Mal. 1:6; Matt. 10:37; Prov. 10:1. (2) Obedience, Eph. 6:1; Col. 3:20. Sirach explains this obedience in Ecclesiasticus 3. Solomon in Prov. 3 and 6:20 says, "Heed the discipline of your father and do not despise the teaching of your mother," cf. Lev. 19:3. In Titus 1:6 and 1 Tim. 3:4 the term "in subjection" is used to indicate that children are under the will of their parents and that sons should hold themselves in subjection to the command of their parents, cf. Luke 2:51. (3) Gratitude, 1 Tim. 5:4, "Let them learn to support their needy parents." In Matt. 15:4–6 Christ commands us to aid our parents by generosity toward them. (4) Patience in enduring the weaknesses of our parents, Prov. 23:22, "Do not despise your mother when she is old." Here is pertinent the example of Shem, Ham, and Japheth. See also Ecclesiasticus 3.

Christ also teaches definite rules of obedience toward parents, Matt. 10:37; Luke 14:26; likewise, Eph. 6:1. The antitheses are clearly and unequivocally stated in Scripture. 1 Tim. 1:9 refers to patricide and matricide, cf. 2 Tim. 3:2; Rom. 1:31; Ecclus. 3:15; Prov. 23:22; Lev. 20:2, 9; Deut. 27:16; Ex. 21:15; Deut. 21:18ff.; Prov. 19:26; Prov. 26:17; 15:5; Mark 7:12; Prov. 28:24. An example of filial reverence is found in Jonathan, the son of Saul, who did not argue as to whether his father was worthy or unworthy but honored him even when he knew that Saul had been rejected by God, 1 Sam. 19ff. Also in regard to the actions of his father he excused them, endured, and tried to explain them, but he did not support the iniquity of his father. When his father wanted to attack him with force, he did not oppose him or resist but fled.

[C.] At a later point we shall have a special locus regarding government. [There is no such locus in the editions we have.] At this point, therefore, we shall make only a brief explanation regarding the duties of government officials. The Decalog prescribes that they are to be the fathers of those who are subject to them, cf. 1 Peter 2:14; Rom. 13:3–4. These are general principles. The specifics can be very easily determined from the list which has been drawn up, as they are categorized in 1 Tim. 2:2;

[1.] The first duty of a ruler is to care for those who are subject to him, so that they may "live in godliness," that is, his first concern must be for their religion, that the true doctrine may be taught to the people and they may be instructed in the true worship, kept from outward blasphemies and godless forms of worship and whatever else is a detriment to piety. In Judg. 17:5–6 the account of the idolatry of Micah is described when there was no king in Israel and "every man did what was right in his own eyes," cf. Is. 49:23. For this reason it is the duty of government officials to be supportive of churches and schools, to provide for them and protect them, cf. Ps. 2:11–12; 47:9. Therefore the ruler must by his own confession be a good example to others. Here note the examples of David, Solomon, Jehoshaphat, Hezekiah, and others.

2. The duty of the ruler is to see that the people "live in honesty," that is, they are to establish and defend external order and not tolerate anything in conflict with it. The ruler must establish discipline, as it is written in Deut. 17:18, "Let the king receive a copy of this book (Deuteronomy) and let him write a copy of it and read it all the days of his life," that is, let him rule according to the Decalog. And 1 Peter 2:13, "Let him rule according to the ordinance of men," that is, in keeping with laws which are favorable and which are in keeping with the law of nature.

3. It is the duty of the ruler to see that the people "lead a quiet life," that is, he must be concerned about the physical welfare of his subjects, as Joseph was, and not burden them down, disturb them, or jeopardize their property but rather nurture them, love them, and shower them with all good things, 1 Peter 2:14; Rom. 13:3. They must not be a terror for those who are good.

[4.] It is the duty of rulers to see that the people lead "a peaceable life." This refers to the fact that rulers are to defend the bodies and properties of their subjects against violence and injustice and thus protect the peace.

5. The ruler is to "execute wrath upon evildoers," Rom. 13:4, that is, he is to compel them with force and physical punishments to obey the laws and he is to chastise the stubborn by court judgments, legal penalties, or wars. For "he does not bear the sword in vain," Rom. 13:4.

6. He is to execute judgment. There is a description of a good judge in Deut. 1:16–17; Exodus 23; and 2 Chronicles 19.

[D.] The duties of subjects: (1) There should be "prayers and the giving of thanks for kings and all who are in authority," 1 Tim. 2:1–2. (2) "Fear to whom fear, honor to whom honor," Rom. 13:7, cf. Prov. 24:21. 1 Peter 2:17, "Honor the king," that is, we should show reverence or respect to their persons, and respect the fact that God has established their office and recognize that a good ruler is the gift of God, cf. 2 Sam. 14:20. [3] Be subject to your rulers. Rom. 13:5; Titus 3:1; 1 Peter 2:18; Titus 3:1; Rom. 13:2, 5, he who resists them resists the ordinance of God and will receive judgment. They are to be obeyed for conscience' sake, that is, the conscience which is guilty before God deserves the wrath of God and is cut off from the grace of God when it resists just laws and good rulers, cf. Jer. 27:8 (4) They are to be subject to rulers in the performance of their lawful duties which they undertake for the public good and tranquility, such as military duty, etc. (5) "Therefore pay your taxes, for magistrates are God's servants, attending to this very matter," that is, "for the punishment of evildoers and the praise of those who do good. Therefore render to them all that is due to them, tribute to whom tribute, revenue to whom revenue is due," Rom. 13:6–7.

In these passages the reasons are given for paying taxes and why subjects should give money to support their government. Boundaries are drawn around the duties of rulers, so that they may know the rights of their subjects and do not use their power for greed or graft, but to serve the public need. (6) We must be open in judging the actions of our rulers lest we in seeking out the reasons for their decisions subject them to slander. We should endure minor weaknesses and errors in our rulers with an upright mind and rejoice in our common peace, and yet not in such a way as to approve of any wickedness.

Likewise the obedience of subjects has its limits. Acts 5:29, "We must obey God rather than men." Matt. 22:21, "Render unto Caesar the things that are Caesar's and unto God the things that are God's." Prov. 24:21, "Fear the Lord and the king." Scripture makes this kind of distinction: When something is commanded contrary to the command of God, then we must not obey ungodly edicts, as Daniel with his friends in Daniel 3. But when subjects are burdened down by their rulers with injustice and violence, it is not the will of God that people be aroused to rebellion by private seditions, but that unjust wickedness be endured. Matt. 5:40, "If someone takes you into court. . . ." But because God has willed that there be degrees in the power of government, so that there are some ranks above private citizens, which are part of the public governing body, 1 Peter 2:13–14, "Whether to the king as supreme or governors as sent by him"; 1 Tim. 2:2, "For kings and all other constituted authorities," therefore the higher orders by virtue of their office must give counsel and perform works for the maintenance of discipline and the common safety, and they do not fulfill their duties when they tolerate injustice and violence. But they are obligated to reprehend this and resist it in their realms. Thus regarding all of these orders it is said, Prov. 24:11, "Deliver those who are being taken to their death," cf. Micah 7:3. But these points properly belong under the locus on government.

[E.] The duty of masters or lords toward their servants is described thus:

[1.] Paul in Eph. 6:9 and Col. 4:1 urges that the minds of masters toward their servants should be fair and just because they should understand that God in heaven is equally the Lord both of servants and masters, and that men are brought to the position of serving not only by human practice, but, as Paul says in Col. 3:23, "Whatever you do, work heartily as unto the Lord and not to men . . . knowing that you are serving the Lord Christ." He thus makes certain men lords because just as in their station they approve the diligence of their servants, so they themselves shall render an account.

2. The Decalog attributes to masters the duty of seeing to it that their servants and their relatives observe the Sabbath, that is, that they be instructed in the teaching of religion and are directed to the exercise of piety.

[3.] Ecclus. 33:25, among those things which masters owe to their servants, lists instruction, that masters be concerned about the morals of their servants as to how they live, and that they establish instruction, admonition, and chastisements.

4. Paul in Col. 4:1 requires equity, so that masters not demand only the things that are owed to themselves and treat their servants as cattle or complete strangers, but that they know and understand that their duties are to be human toward their servants out of that fellowship to which they are obligated in order that there be this equality.

5. Sirach in Ecclus. 33:25 [v. 3 in some mss. of LXX] says that it is just that servants for their lawful labor be given food, training, and what a servant needs. James 5:4 speaks of "the wages of the workers," cf. Ecclus. 7:23. Jer. 34:11 deals with those who had been freed and were again brought back into slavery. Paul wills not only that we give our servants what is owed them by law, but also that they be treated equally, Col. 4:1, cf. Ecclus. 7:23; 33:31; Prov. 30:10; Deut. 23:15. In the Decalog it is commanded that times of rest be given to servants, e.g., 5:13–14.

6. Scripture shows that servants are to be treated more harshly than sons. See Ecclus. 33:27, 30; Prov. 29:19, 21.

[F.1.] But the duties of slaves were even more carefully set forth, because their condition was extremely harsh and it seems to be unworthy of the profession of Christianity that those who have been freed by the blood of Christ should remain under the yoke of slavery to their fellowmen. Thus Paul describes the obedience of slaves in such a way that he leads them to understand that this slavery has not been imposed upon them by accident or by some unjust violence of men, but that God Himself has distributed the vocations of men in this way. Therefore they should submit themselves to their masters for the sake of the will of God. Since in a sense the Lord has placed them to work in this calling of slaves, they should not doubt that God accepts their service as done to Him. He adds that as far as salvation before God is concerned, there is no difference between a free man and a slave.

2. If servants have unbelieving masters, they should not refuse to obey them but consider them as worthy of all honor, lest the name of the Lord and His teaching be blasphemed, 1 Tim. 6:1–2; 1 Peter 2:18.

3. The duty of servants is called "obedience" in Eph. 6:5, "subjection" or "submissiveness" in Titus 2:9, "service" in Col. 3:22, "work" or "labor" in Ecclus. 33:25. Because the servile mind does not obey from the heart but out of fear of punishment, obedience must be coerced from it. Thus Paul does not will that the obedience of the Christian servant be such as is approved by men, but it should come from the heart alone, which is not from fear of punishment or doing its duty only because of the present opinions of men, but with fear and trembling

in sincere diligence because of the love of the Lord, as Col. 3:22 says, and indeed with heartiness, lest our hearts do their duty unwillingly, unworthily, and complainingly. Indeed the verse says to obey "in all things," lest in their response they question the commands of their masters.

4. The antithesis in Eph. 6:6–8 correctly shows that not only in outward appearance and pretense, when in the presence of their masters, or only for fear of punishment should they show diligence, or look only at the amount of money they receive or the gratitude of their masters, because the Lord will repay them; nor are they to nurse anger or hatred against the commands of their masters. Such sins as this are specifically noted; not rendering eye-service, pleasing men; Titus 2:9–10, "not defying them, nor defrauding them, but showing them all fidelity."

[G.] The duties of the other orders in society which pertain to the Fourth Commandment in keeping with these examples can easily be added. Regarding old men and widows, see Titus 2:2 and 1 Tim. 5:3–6; regarding young people, 1 Peter 5:5 and Titus 2:6; regarding instructors, Gal. 3:24 and 1 Cor. 4:15; regarding guardians, Gal. 4:2 and John 19:26.

IV. We must also consider the promise added to the Fourth Commandment, for in the Decalog not only are certain outward varieties of activity demanded, but they must be done out of faith and in fear of God, just as Paul says point by point regarding the Fourth Commandment in Eph. 6:1ff. under the rubric "obey in the Lord." Also 1 Peter 2:13, "for the Lord's sake"; and Eph. 6:5, "with fear and trembling"; Col. 3:20, "for this pleases the Lord." Therefore promises and threats are added to the precepts, so that by thinking of these things we may be led to the fear of God and the exercise of our faith.

The promise attached to this commandment consists of the following: (1) Long life. (2) Prosperity and blessing which pertain to the comforts of this life. For this is the way Eph. 6:3 explains it with the words, "That it may be well with you and you may live long on the earth." For an unhappy long life is not a benefit, but a long torment, as Ecclus. 41:3 says. (3) Peace and tranquility. The Canaanites because of the sin of Ham were cast out from the land of promise, Gen. 9:25, and by the mere mention of them God warns the Israelites that if they are unwilling to destroy their enemies they will be cast into exile and the earth devastated, as did happen to the Canaanites; but they would possess the land in peace and tranquility and leave it for the possession of their posterity, and therefore they should not imitate the example of Ham, whose sin God visited unto the tenth generation, but they should honor their parents. He is referring to the land of promise when he says, "Which God shall give to you," Ex. 20:12. But because the New Testament does not have a special promise concerning a specific place, Paul gives a general promise, "that it may be well with you and you may live long on the earth," Eph. 6:3.

It is manifest that this promise is an external or temporal one. But we must add the spiritual dimension and those things which speak of the life to come. A very appropriate division has been made in keeping with the brevity of the Decalog. Since it would be tedious to add to each case the promises and warnings peculiar to it, certain points have been added to some instances, not because there is lacking in the other precepts the element of rewards for obedience and punishments for transgression, but as is often the case in summaries, a warning is given by certain kinds of examples as to what will happen also in other cases. Since the brevity which has been set up for the Decalog does not permit a triple order of rewards—physical, spiritual, and eternal—to be established for each individual case, a division of this kind has been made: To the First Commandment has been added a warning about temporal punishments. To the Second Commandment a warning concerning being guilty of the wrath of God, which is a spiritual punishment, and this warning has been added to the whole Law, "Cursed is he who does not continue in all . . . ," Deut. 27:26; Col. 3:10. Thus the promise of the First Commandment speaks of the mercy of God which involves a spiritual reward. But in the Fourth Commandment it speaks of physical rewards; and just as in the First Commandment physical promises are not excluded, so in the Fourth Commandment spiritual promises are not excluded but must be added in.

Therefore we should gather examples of this promise which are found in other passages of Scripture and the special promises which are applied to individual orders or ranks among people, in keeping with the triple order mentioned above, because some are physical, some spiritual, and others pertain to the life of the future.

Certain promises are given to children: Eph. 6:3; Gen. 9:27; Ecclus. 3:6; Col. 3:20; Ps. 128:3; Gen. 9:27; Jer. 35:19; Prov. 1:9; 6:23–24. To parents apply the promise in Prov. 10:1 and in 23:14.

This promise is given to those who are subject to a ruler: Jer. 29:7; Matt. 5:5; Rom. 13:3; 1 Peter 2:13–15; Rom. 13:5.

Certain special promises are also given to servants: Prov. 17:2; Ecclus. 10:28; Col. 3:24; Eph. 6:8. We must note that among these promises the same line of reasoning applies to all orders of society who come under the Fourth Commandment, and the promise given to each rank can properly also be referred to another. Thus, for example, what is said to servants in Col. 3:24 is correctly also applied to sons or subjects.

We must also add some warnings by way of antithesis under the Fourth Commandment: Ex. 21:15–16; Lev. 20:9; Deut. 21:21; 27:16; Prov. 15:5; 19:26;

20:20; 30:17; Ecclus. 3:18; 41:9. In Rom. 1:30 those who are "disobedient to parents" are included in the list of those who have been "given over to a reprobate mind." And 2 Tim. 3:1–2 speaks of "the punishments of the last times, which those who "are disobedient to parents" will suffer.

To those who are subjects Prov. 24:21–22 says, "Do not join yourselves to seditious movements, for their destruction is swift"; Rom. 13:2, "Those who resist authority bring judgment upon themselves," cf. Matt. 26:52; Jer. 27:8; Rom. 13:5, "One must be subject not only for the sake of God's wrath but also for conscience sake," that is, grace and the Holy Spirit are involved.

To servants Col. 3:25 says, "He who does wrong will be paid back for the wrong he has done," cf. Ps. 108:10; 1 Tim. 5:8.

Examples of the rewards: Gen. 9:26–27, Shem and Japheth; Gen. 49:1ff., Jacob predicts blessings for his sons who were obedient. Jeremiah 35 regarding the Rechabites. Tobit 5:15, Tobit is led by an angel when he undertakes a journey in obedience to his father. Ruth honors her mother-in-law and becomes a member of the people of God and is placed into the lineage of Christ. Luke 2:51–52, Christ "subjected Himself to His parents and increased in wisdom and grace." Gen. 48:5, since Joseph had respectfully received his father, his two sons were taken into the number of the patriarchs and became possessors of the promises of Abraham. When Esau caused suffering to his parents and took two heathen women as wives, he lost the blessing. But Jacob honored his parents and was blessed with great rewards by God, defended in the midst of his enemies, enriched, and as an old man saw his son Joseph in his greatness. When Jonathan in dutiful wisdom in keeping with the First Table honored Saul as his father and king, even when his father killed himself, and Jonathan's posterity flourished up to the time of the Babylonian Captivity, 1 Chron. 8:34ff., even though all the rest of Saul's posterity had perished right after he did. See in 1 Kings 2:19 how Solomon received his mother. 1 Sam. 24:7 shows how David yielded to Saul and spared him, as he would Christ the Lord; and how he was elevated to the position of king later on, as Saul himself said in v. 19, "May the Lord reward you with good for what you have done for me this day." Joseph in Egypt and Daniel in Babylon, even though in slavery, faithfully performed the will of God for which they were rewarded and marvelously delivered. The children of maidservants are included in the number of the 12 patriarchs.

As examples of punishments see Gen. 9:25, where Ham is cursed in his youngest son, who was his favorite, and his posterity is punished. In Gen. 49:3–4 Reuben is cursed, even though he is the oldest son; 1 Sam. 2:34 and 4:11, the sons of Eli are punished; 2 Sam. 18:9, Absalom the traitor; 1 Kings 1:5ff., Adonijah against Solomon; 2 Sam. 20:21, Seba against David; 2 Sam. 17:23, Ahithophel; 1 Kings 16:18, Zimri; 2 Kings 11:20, Athaliah; 2 Kings 15:14, Shallum the son of Jabesh; Num. 16:32, Korah, Dathan, and Abiram; Judg. 9:53–55, Abimelech; Judg. 12:4, the men of Ephraim against Jephthah; Acts 5:36–37, Theudas and Judas the Galilean; 1 Kings 13:4, Jeroboam does not properly carry out his duty; Gen. 21:10, Hagar the maidservant is cast out; 2 Kings 5:27, Gehazi is stricken with leprosy; 2 Kings 2:24, the children who mocked Elisha are torn by the bears; Ezek. 22:7, 15, "They afflicted their father and mother with shamefulness and therefore I have given them over to shame among the nations and the ridicule of all people."

This is a fairly complete description of the Fourth Commandment. The purpose of this commandment is the establishment, approval, and preservation of society both in the nation and in the home. Therefore pertinent here are both the persons and the duties upon which deliverance and safety, both public and domestic, depend. From this purpose one can develop a description by using synthesis.

The Fifth Commandment: "Thou Shalt Not Kill"

[MELANCHTHON'S TEXT]

This commandment forbids not only external injuries to the body and private outward revenge, but also hatred in the heart, evil intention, jealousy, and hidden desire for revenge. Christ clearly explains this commandment in Matt. 5:21ff. On the contrary, it demands benevolence toward all men, mercy, concern, kindness which is opposed to all evil intention; it demands gentleness, long-suffering, equity which forgives something out of a higher law for the sake of probable causes, that is, that those who can be restored should be called back to the right way. Likewise, the commandment demands that public disagreements should not arise out of private discord. For we know that the strong command regarding private offenses is, "Forgive and it shall be forgiven you." Again, revenge is not a matter of one's own private attack, but God demands that it be left to Him and He sets boundaries for it. Therefore He says, "Vengeance is Mine," Rom. 12:19. For it is evident what great commotions the desire for personal revenge often arouses. Thus we should learn what vengeance God prescribes and how we are to obey the divine mandate.

Here we must also add that the government official has a divine mandate to take legitimate vengeance. The duty of an official pertains to this statement: "Vengeance is Mine; I will repay"—I will punish, either by my own hand or by permission or by the lawful office of the magistrate. For God has established powers and governments, He retains and changes them, as Daniel says in 2:37. God transfers and establishes the powers of government. Therefore lawful punishments are divine vengeance by which the magistrate chastises murderers, adulterers, perjurers, and idlers who have been condemned by the courts. To the office of ruler also pertains the matter of just wars, as when Constantine repressed the savagery of Licinius by force of arms. But just as war is the highest degree of political power, so also it is the most abused, and just and lawful wars are very rare. The devil, since he is a murderer and opposed to good political order and discipline, often stirs up great wars on the most flimsy pretexts, with the minds of men on both sides enflamed by sinful desires. God tolerates these villainies in order that the crimes of both parties may be punished. Just as the Peloponnesian War, which was the most destructive war of all Greece, was stirred up by the most insignificant causes, by a quarrel over the destruction of a certain grove which was considered sacred for some heathen rites and which Pericles had burned down because he was offended at things they had said against Aspasia. Nor is the highest law, especially in an insignificant case, a sufficiently just cause for initiating war, as it is said: Often the highest law is the highest injury. But let us employ equity which, even if offense has been given, is more concerned to bring peace than to destroy the innocent and bring immeasurable harm to the churches and the nation because of the errors of the few. Rulers should know that wars must be divine punishment and not serve human greed or rash anger. As Abigail says to David in 1 Sam. 25:28, "Because you are fighting the battles of the Lord, evil shall not be found in you."

The Fifth Commandment

The order of the precepts in the Decalog is well arranged. In the Fourth Commandment those persons who are bound to their obligations in the state and the home are established in their offices as superiors and inferiors. But because in our common life together we live among many people who are not our superiors, nor are subject to us under the Fourth Commandment, therefore God in the Fifth Commandment sets a pattern for this common life as to how those who are neither superior nor inferior in their relationships with one another ought to live among themselves as those who in their state or family duty, as is stated in the Fourth Commandment, and are not bound by the tie of charity or bound together in their mutual duty. This order is certainly most lovely. On this basis the Fifth Commandment is established. For God wills that the mutual duties of love and charity be applied not only to the rulers and the ruled but also to all people in general.

Thus the explanation of the Fifth Commandment is the longest and most definite of all the precepts of the Second Table, cf. Matt. 5:21ff.; Eph. 4:26, 31; Gal. 5:20–21; 1 John 3:15, because our inner wickedness which is in conflict with the Fifth Commandment is more noticeable and more easily seen than it is in the other commandments. For the Holy Spirit calls to our attention in each table that in one particular precept He has shown the rationale and fundamental way in which we are to seek the true meaning also of the rest of the commandments. Thus on the First Table we should carefully seek the explanation of the First

Commandment, and on the Second Table the Fifth Commandment. Thus the explanation of the fifth precept is plain and simple, because it has been shown and given by the Son of God Himself, who shows in His explanation of the precepts of the Decalog that there is a synecdoche to be observed, that is, that there are many more kinds of sins which are in conflict with individual commandments than are mentioned specifically in the Decalog. Under this heading the Pharisees are condemned because they imagined that only external murder was in conflict with the Fifth Commandment and that the warnings against this precept which were added in the Scripture applied only to a homicide, which is actually committed, but that anger is something much less important (for in Matt. 5:19 the errors of the Pharisees are described) and certainly not worthy of God's eternal wrath. For the fact that He says, "It has been said by them of old time . . . but I say unto you . . . ," Matt. 5:21, does not mean that He is opposing His doctrine to Moses and is rejecting and condemning him, as the Manichaeans raved; or that He is trying to hand down commandments which are better, more perfect, or of greater importance than those of Moses, as the scholastics dream. For Moses was clearly giving the same interpretation to the Fifth Commandment in Lev. 19:17, "You shall not hate your brother in your heart." Indeed, Moses clearly commands that we are to love our brother, Ex. 23:4, "If you see the donkey of one who hates you . . ."; cf. Lev. 19:18; Prov. 25:21. For this reason Christ condemns and rejects the errors of the Pharisees, who through the passage of a long period of time had gained a high authority, but Christ brings back to mind the oldest interpretation, which had been given by Moses and the prophets. He says for the sake of emphasis, "But I say to you," Matt. 5:21. Paul affirms in 1 Cor. 10:4 that the Lord God who led the children of Israel out of Egypt was Christ. He also says that He who led them out also gave the Law, 1 Cor. 10:5ff. Therefore Christ is asserting by this mode of speaking ("I say to you") that He who promulgated the Decalog possesses the absolutely surest explanation of it. In this way, when the Pharisees tried to protect their long-standing errors by appealing to antiquity or the long passage of time, Christ opposed them by saying, "But I who first promulgated the Decalog, I say to you. . . ."

Therefore there is no need for seeking some exotic rationale or searching out the genuine meaning of the Fifth Commandment. For it has been clearly given by the Son of God and indeed in such a way that it is evident that He wills this example to be applied to the interpretation of the rest of the commandments also. Therefore we shall adapt the interpretation of Christ to the words of the Decalog, for in this way the method can more easily be called to our attention and the fundamental points more correctly considered.

Thus the first point must be stated in a general way without reference to the circumstances of any particular person: "Thou shalt not kill." A person is forbidden to kill. In the Fourth Commandment parents are mentioned and honor for them required on the part of their children. But in this case it is not only men, servants, friends, strangers, enemies, acquaintances, rich, old, etc., who are mentioned specifically, but to all people in general it is said: "Thou shalt not kill." Therefore to no one is granted the privilege of killing a man with impunity. Although masters could get the idea that they are not bound by this law if they kill their own slaves, God clearly adds this explanation in Ex. 21:20, "If a person strikes his slave, male or female, and they die under his hand, he is guilty of a crime." It is necessary to consider who is prohibited from killing under the Fifth Commandment, for God by His own ordinance has given the sword to the magistrate, so that "he does not bear it in vain . . . to execute punishment on the wrongdoer." Thus we must distinguish between public officials to whom has been given the commandment to kill (Ex. 22:18–20; Gen. 9:6) and private individuals to whom the commandment is given, "Thou shalt not kill." Indeed the very order of the Decalog shows this distinction clearly enough. For in the Fourth Commandment their offices are established for public officials and the sword is given to the magistrate. Afterward it passes to private individuals. Therefore the words, "Thou shalt not kill," do not apply to the office of the magistrate, but forbid the use of the sword to private parties in a general sense, so that not only do they not injure innocent people but also do not destroy criminals by their own private authority, indeed, they are to resist unlawful violence, as shall be further explained under the locus on taking revenge.

At this point this observation is in order, that it does not say only to the hand, "Thou shalt not kill," but to the whole man. Therefore sins against the Fifth Commandment are inherent in all our powers. The warning is given equally, without distinction, to the godly and regenerate as well as to the godless and unregenerate. Indeed, the Decalog spoke to those who had been taken into the people of God, who had been received into the covenant of grace by circumcision. Thus the Fifth Commandment is a universal judgment which brings accusation against the corruption of the nature in all men. For the purpose of the Law which was promulgated was that we might be led to a recognition of our sin. And Paul in Rom. 3:15 says that so great is the corruption of the nature in all men that "their feet are swift to shed blood." For he is demonstrating that human nature is so deplorably depraved that we are not restrained by the fear of punishment, nor by any kind of secret rein of God's providence; we not only deceive by our actions but we do not even spare the life or blood of our fellow men. He is showing that this poison has invaded all human powers, so that he mentions not only the hands but also the feet. By referring to the speed of our feet he is indicating the strong inclination, as is described in Rom. 7:23 and

James 1:14. It is useful to consider why the general command is made, without any kind of qualification, "Thou shalt not kill."

The second point to consider is what is meant by the killing prohibited in the Fifth Commandment. The word "kill" of itself means to destroy, to snuff out, or to cut off the life of a man. But Christ in His interpretation shows that to kill under the Fifth Commandment refers not only to the act itself but also to the inner attitudes of the heart, to our deeds and to our words. He shows that the Pharisees, in their ignorance of the grammar of the Holy Spirit, were insane in their understanding of the Fifth Commandment.

Christ lists four kinds of homicide, and a more proper catalog of sins which are in conflict with this precept cannot be drawn up. Indeed, from this list we must draw the rule that in the case of each of the individual commandments four kinds of sin are to be noted: (1) the inner emotions of the heart or mind; (2) sins of gesture; (3) sins of words; (4) sins of deeds.

The first and most heinous kind is the external deed itself. Scripture speaks of the shedding of blood, Rom. 3:15; Gen. 9:6. In Ex. 21:18–20 and Num. 25:7 certain instruments or weapons are mentioned, such as iron, rock, or club. Rev. 18:23 and Gal. 5:20 mention sorcery. But in the Decalog it simply says, "Thou shalt not kill," without mentioning either the instruments or the circumstances of the crime. In Judg. 20:5 the wife of the Levite who was ravished by a mob of Gibeanites was said to have been "murdered." Pertinent here also are those things which hinder conception, Gen. 38:9; likewise, the matter of destroying the fetus in the womb, Ex. 21:22, "If a pregnant woman is struck. . . ." 1 Kings 3:19 refers to those who in their sleep lie on and smother their children. Applicable also to the Fifth Commandment are wounds or mutilations to parts of the body, Ex. 21:24ff.; 22:2. There is a universal rule pertaining to all of the commandments in Rom. 1:32: "They who do such things deserve to die, not only those who do them, but also those who give their approval to those who are doing them." Therefore they who give aid or approval or add injuries of their own, whether by advice, command, betrayal, or false witness, are also involved in this first kind of homicide. Thus Saul says in 1 Sam. 18:17, "Let it not be my hand upon him, but that of the Philistines." In 2 Tim. 3:4 are listed "traitors." In Deut. 19:21 concerning the lying witness it is written, "life for life." The same applies to him who gives occasion whereby the body or life is injured, or for one who digs a pit, Ex. 21:23, and in the law of Moses there is a warning concerning goring by a bull, Ex. 21:29. Also pertinent here is the sin of omission, that is, not defending those whom we ought to protect. 1 John 3:16 teaches that we ought to lay down our lives for our brothers. Prov. 24:11, "Rescue those who are being taken away to death." Prov. 28:24, "He who robs his father is a partaker in his murder." Thus the statement of Ambrose: "Feed him who is dying of hunger;

if you have not fed him you have killed him." Thus the rich man at his feast is the murderer of Lazarus.

The second kind of murder consists in the inner thoughts of the heart against one's neighbor. Christ speaks of anger and is saying that all desires of the heart against our neighbor are involved here. In 1 Cor. 13:5 thoughts of the mind are mentioned: "Love thinks no evil." Likewise in Matt. 9:4, Jesus says, "Why do you think evil in your hearts?" In Gen. 27:41 the intention or the advance decision to do harm is described. It is in the will: "Then I will kill my brother." Thus the root of murder clings in all our inner powers. We must consider how the apostles, on the basis of the foundation laid down by Christ in Matt. 5:22, developed fuller explanations: Gal. 5:20, "Hatreds, contention, jealousy, strifes, dissensions"; Col. 3:8, "anger, wrath"; bitterness, desire for revenge. See fuller explanations in the long lists in Rom. 12:19; 1 Thess. 5:15; and 2 Cor. 12:20. Likewise James 3:14; Rom. 1:29, 31, "filled with contention and maliciousness, faithless, unforgiving"; 1 John 3:15, "hatred"; 2 Tim. 3:3, "pitiless." These depraved desires can be categorized thus: Some arise out of sorrow and impatience over an injury; some are born out of jealousy toward a neighbor's happiness; some out of our natural wickedness and desire to be disagreeable.

These points are very well taken and have a great deal of value in demonstrating how the Holy Spirit, by examples of the Fifth Commandment, is teaching what is necessary for an explanation of the whole Decalog. For Christ in Matthew 5 makes a distinction between venial and mortal sins and very properly shows this in regard to the Fifth Commandment. Regarding the Pharisees who considered the inner corrupt desires as either nothing at all or only minor sins, Christ says in v. 20, "You shall not enter into the kingdom of heaven." Concerning those who "while there still is time will not lay aside their anger and become reconciled," He says in v. 26, "You will not get out until . . . ." But because these lusts which are contrary to the Fifth Commandment cling in this corrupt nature of ours, so that no one is free of them, He teaches this doctrine in v. 24: First let us be reconciled and then let us go to the altar, that is, let us seek forgiveness. Paul in Eph. 4:26 gives us useful advice concerning the different degrees of anger. He speaks of the first feelings, when out of the misery provoked by some injury, a hot anger boils up in the heart and the blood. In Col. 3:8 he uses the word *thymos*, "wrath" or "outburst of passion." This term refers to something caused by a violent impulse. The Greeks use it to describe a kind of pounding around the heart involving many blood vessels wherein the emotion of anger is strongly felt, as when blood bursts out of the lips. Thus Paul says in Eph. 4:26, "Be angry but do not sin," that is, the first emotion or feeling cannot be stopped or avoided (as the Hebrew word in Ps. 4:4 meaningfully describes this agitation), but see to it that this does not continue on to become sin by which "the Holy Spirit is grieved" and "place is given to the devil," as Paul says in vv. 30 and 27. Therefore he commands that we fight against this so that "the sun does not go down on our wrath," v. 26, but rather that the heat of anger be cooled and we seek forgiveness from God. But of those who do not calm their angry heart and allow the sun to set and keep nursing the flames, Paul says that they are giving place to the devil and have fallen into such a great sin that the Holy Spirit is grieved. The second degree or level of anger he calls *orgē*, when the mind devises and plans evil and burns with desire for revenge. The third level is hatred, long-standing anger. The fourth which follows is jealousy, dissension, quarreling, contentions, and other outward actions, as James 1:20 says, "Man's anger does not work the righteousness of God." The Holy Spirit has made these distinctions so that we may learn what great efforts we must make in order to control the inner desires of our mind and what great evil follows when we give free rein to these lusts. We must also note that this doctrine applies to the other commandments.

The third kind of murder includes external action or gesture by which is demonstrated, as by signs and pointers, the evil intention of the heart against one's neighbor. Christ uses the term *raca* in Matt. 5:22. Phil. 2:14 speaks of "murmurings." 1 Cor. 13:5, "love is not arrogant or rude," *sich ungebärdig stellen*. 2 Cor. 12:20 refers to being "puffed up with conceit," so that when a person arrives at a certain state, he regards his neighbor as unworthy. James warns against despising the poor and elevating the rich. Gen. 4:6, "Why are you angry and why has your face fallen?" Gen. 31:2, "Jacob noticed Laban's face and that he did not regard him with favor as before."

The fourth kind of murder is committed by the tongue, as when a person says, "you fool," out of anger, evil intent, or with the intention of doing him harm. Paul adds many terms to this list: "contentions," 2 Tim. 2:14; "quarrels," Titus 3:2; "disputings," Phil. 2:14; and in 2 Cor. 12:20 he refers to strife, contentions, and seditions. 1 Tim. 6:5 speaks of "wranglings," which, however, speak more of the Eighth Commandment. Rom. 1:29–30 refers to "whisperers and backbiters." Rom. 12:14, "Do not curse your neighbor." Matt. 7:1 speaks of judging and condemning. Gal. 5:15 mentions "biting, devouring, and consuming one another."

Christ Himself teaches this division of the various kinds of homicide. It is useful and helpful to see how this division is carried through in the writings of the prophets. Lev. 19:17–18, "You shall not hate your brother in your heart . . . you shall not take vengeance or bear a grudge." The words used are from the Fifth Commandment, cf. Jer. 18:18; Ps. 57:4; Prov. 25:18; Jer. 9:8. We must also consider how the apostles modeled their warnings regarding the Fifth

Commandment on the basis of Christ's division and with accuracy and care referred back to it.

This is almost unique to the Fifth Commandment, that the things which are prohibited, such as wrath, saying *raca*, calling a person a "fool," killing, etc., can also in a certain sense be done lawfully and with benefit. Thus Christ adds, Matt. 5:22, "Whoever is angry rashly (*eikē*), without a true and righteous cause . . ." for the word *eikē* means this, as in Prov. 28:25, "The unbelieving man judges rashly." When the magistrate puts a wrongdoer to death, he not only is not sinning against the Fifth Commandment but he is doing a work commanded by God. When the Levites bore the sword of Moses and killed 3,000 men, they received a blessing, Ex. 32:25ff. Therefore killing is sin when it is the act of a private person under his own authority and when a public official acts on his own, without the authority of the Law where by reason of his own lust he destroys innocent people.

Thus when Jacob became angry at Rachel in Gen. 30:2, he did not sin. Compare Ex. 11:8; 16:20; 32:19; Num. 16:15; 31:14; 2 Kings 13:19; Prov. 29:9; Matt. 18:34. Regarding hatred Ps. 6:5 says, "I have hated the company of evildoers," cf. Ps. 139:21–22; 119:113. Often in the Psalms the idea of "hating without a cause" is added, e.g., 35:19; 69:4. 2 John 10 commands us not to bid heretics Godspeed. This pertains to external actions. Christ in Luke 24:25 calls His disciples "fools." Paul in Gal. 3:1 speaks of the "foolish Galatians." Thus these terms can at times be properly and lawfully used.

But the question is: When is anger sin and what is righteous wrath? The scholastics replied that "a man can have hatred for his brother, but a person cannot without sin hate the nature of his brother." Chrysostom [Sermons 72–73, MPG 58.668ff.] says, "We must hate sins but not men." Gregory's statement is: "There must be a punishment for sin, but compassion for man's nature." This is a correct distinction, but it is a little too obscure. For Phinehas killed the person in Num. 25:8. And David says in Ps. 139:22, "I hate them." Therefore the better explanation is that of Philipp, that it is a case of being angry for the sake of God's glory and love of righteousness, and that anger against ungodliness and wickedness is not a sin but a virtue. Luke 14:26, "He who does not hate his father . . ." In the case of public officials there must be direct action taken to defend the glory of God and righteousness, for punishing wrongdoing and for protecting the state. Thus in Scripture a particular term is used. Num. 25:11, ". . . concerned about My zeal." 2 Kings 10:16, "See my zeal for the Lord." In John 11:33, "Jesus was deeply moved and groaned in the spirit." On the other hand, anger is a sin against the Fifth Commandment when we are angry at our neighbor for personal reasons. This comes from either impatience when some personal comfort has been taken from us or when pleasures have been interrupted or when we are aroused over some other personal desire, and not angry primarily for the sake of God's glory or the love of righteousness or the hatred of sin, or it arises out of the jealousy or envy of our nature, as David complains when he says, "They hate me without a cause," Ps. 35:19. To this anger is joined the desire for revenge. Thus he who does not "bid Godspeed" so that his neighbor might be brought to tears of repentance is not guilty of sin. For the carrying out of the duties of a ministry or for the sake of correcting a brother, to call a man a fool is not a breaking of the Fifth Commandment.

Now when we have established the negative meaning, namely those points at which we are in conflict with the Fifth Commandment, then we must add by way of antithesis the affirmative side, that is, the good works which this commandment prescribes. For in certain commandments the affirmative meaning takes first place, as in the case of the First Commandment, and the negative side follows. But here the negative is most noteworthy, because it has been taught by Christ and He refers to the desires which conflict with this precept. But the antithesis to the Fifth Commandment has been clearly set forth by Moses, Christ, and Paul, namely, "You shall love your neighbor." We must note that since the negative speaks of an external action, "Thou shalt not kill," God in the affirmative does not want to talk only about benefits, lest the commandment be understood as speaking only of external works, but He uses the term "love," which includes the innermost desires of the heart, so that when we compare the prohibitions and the commands we might see the true meaning and understand the Fifth Commandment as not referring only to external actions but also inner desires, as Christ teaches in the parable of the wounded man, where the priest and the Levite, as they journeyed by, showed a kind of mercy but without any action, while the Samaritan showed both.

It is worthwhile to consider how John adds positive aspects to the example which Christ explains negatively. (1) Note 1 John 3:18, "Let us not love only in word and speech, but in deed and in truth." The concept of "truth" includes the true desire of the inner emotions in the heart, such things as mercy, sympathy, and gentleness, being pleasing to God, giving up hatred and evil intentions, not tenaciously holding to an offensive position, not being vindictive, etc. (2) Under the term "speech" are included also external actions or gestures. 1 Peter 3:8, "Be sympathetic"; Eph. 4:32, "Be kind." (3) He also says, "Let us love in word." He is referring to words of comfort and helpful advice. Rom. 12:14, "Bless those who persecute you." (4) "Let us love in deed," that is, demonstrate kindness, Heb. 13:16. All the virtues under the Fifth Commandment can be covered by this division.

Paul in Rom. 12:9ff., using another rationale, gives us a very useful division of the virtues under the Fifth Commandment. In general, all people should show love and kindness, having a desire for harmony with all men. Give no one offense; provide good things, not only before God but also before people. Gal. 6:10: There should be love of the brethren, toward those of the household of faith; thankfulness toward deserving friends; toward our enemies patience, kindness, understanding in our common weaknesses; generosity toward the poor and afflicted; mercy and benevolence; tears with those who weep, providing for the necessities of the saints; rejoicing with the fortunate who are rejoicing; reverence toward superiors; desire for harmony with our peers and those of the same mind; respect for those beneath us; kindness toward the humble; hospitality toward strangers. "If a person be overtaken in a fault, restore him," Gal. 6:1; Matt. 18:15; 1 Thess. 5:14. Correct the erring, comfort the frightened, support the weak, be patient toward all. Affirmative statements are used for three reasons: (1) by way of antithesis, as to lay aside hatred, malice, and desire for revenge; (2) in keeping with John's division, 1 John 3:18; (3) in keeping with Paul's categories.

Clearly applicable to these distinctions is the catalog of virtues attached to the Fifth Commandment, such as righteousness, particularly not injuring people. There is the benefit in works of charity, Mark 14:7, "The poor you have always with you and you can do good to them," cf. Rom. 12:20. Kindness and long-suffering soften anger and the desire for revenge, 2 Tim. 2:24. Being kind toward all people, enduring with gentleness even those who are evil, 1 Tim. 6:11. Having patience, gentleness, kindness, forgiving offenses, and overlooking injury, Eph. 4:32; Col. 3:12. Friendship and gratitude, rendering kindness for kindness. Showing mercy toward the evils of others, having warm love which is shown toward and rejoices in the good deeds of others. Fairness which bears many weaknesses in others. Showing friendship and kindness, which demonstrates the signs of good intention in our deeds and words.

This list, aside from the sins mentioned above, shows still other things by way of antithesis, so that it is correct to say, "Who can understand his sins?" Ps. 19:12. Ingratitude, cf. Prov. 17:13, "When a man returns evil for good." Rejoicing in another's trouble, Prov. 24:17, "Do not rejoice at your enemy's destruction"; cf. Prov. 17:5. Peevishness, abrasiveness, love of conflict which is opposed to a desire for harmony, a pretended love, 2 Corinthians 6; Rom. 12:9; 1 Peter 1:22. This is "loving only in word and speech," 1 John 3:18. "Let not each seek only his own," 1 Cor. 10:24. To desert a friend in a time of difficulty, 2 Tim. 4:16. "Slow to wrath," James 1:19, cf. Eccl. 7:9.

The third point to consider under the Fifth Commandment is who is prohibited from killing. For in the Fourth Commandment the words are clearly added, "Honor your father. . . ." But the Fifth simply says, "Thou shalt not kill." The Manichaeans had ridiculous notions on this matter. They had heard from the philosophers that all things which are produced and grown on the earth are called animate substances and thus they were unwilling to cut vegetables or even pick an apple, lest they sin against the Fifth Commandment. They tried to twist 1 Cor. 15:36, where the seed is described as being made alive, to prove their point. See also Ps. 78:47. The followers of Tatian abstained from meats because they thought that a living creature could not be changed without violating the commandment, "Thou shalt not kill." Some of the hermits even said that it was a sin to kill lice and other insects which were infesting them, such as worms which are born in wounds. But Scripture manifestly declares that the Fifth Commandment is not talking about beasts or birds or fish. For in Gen. 9:2–3 it stipulates (1) that they were to hunt and kill beasts, "The fear of you shall be upon them." (2) Beasts were to be eaten, Acts 10:13, "Kill and eat." But he who beats a pack animal to death sins against the Seventh Commandment. God has willed that, in the very act of killing, all cruelty be avoided. This is true to such a degree that He prohibited eating the flesh with the blood, lest anyone should be influenced by this example to become accustomed to inhumanity toward his neighbor, and that the gifts of God might be used with reverence. Thus the Fifth Commandment does not pertain properly to the birds of the air, the fish of the sea, or the beasts of the field, but in the Law mention is made of one's brother and one's neighbor for whose protection the precept "Thou shalt not kill" was given. It is not to be understood only of friends and those who deserve kindness, as the Pharisees later corrupted it to mean, nor is an exception to be made in the killing of one's own self. Scripture simply says in other places that the pouring out of human blood is prohibited, cf. Gen. 9:6 and 1 John 3:15, where he speaks of a "murderer."

Thus it is forbidden for a man to kill a man, either himself or another. Augustine [*De Civitate Dei*, 1.17, MPL 41.31] is correct when he says, "He who kills himself surely kills a man, and much less will he who tries to kill himself spare another person, for it is written, 'Thou shalt love thy neighbor as thyself,'" Matt. 5:43. In Col. 2:23 those people are condemned who abuse their own body. This is even more the case with those who kill themselves. Here arises the question of suicide. The heathen honor the practice of laying hands on oneself as a sign of great bravery. Lyra reports that the Hebrews teach that not only is it permitted to kill oneself, but that it is even meritorious: (1) if you are afraid that you may be unable to bear the torment; (2) if you are afraid that in contempt of God you may be led into a life of wantonness. Among the Donatists there were the *circumcelliones*, who considered it to their glory if they could be thrown off a cliff, cast into the fire, or given to death in some other way, because it was written that the flesh must be mortified, Col. 3:5. They also cited, "He who hates his life shall find it," Matt. 10:39, cf. John 12:25. Augustine dealt with this question at great length in his *De Civitate Dei*, 1 [20, MPL 41.34], and laid down this fundamental point, that there is in Scripture neither precept nor example to imitate this practice, whereby it can be proved that suicide is pleasing to God, but rather the Fifth Commandment plainly forbids killing a human being. Then with a lengthy discussion he gives the reasons why people bring death upon themselves and shows that there is no lawful reason for suicide. He cites as examples (1) despair, as in the case of Judas and Ahithophel; (2) unwillingness to bear or accept calamities, real or impending; (3) when the torments of the wretched seem tragic and inescapable, and they think that by ending their life they will bring an end to their troubles; (4) in order to avoid a scandal, as in the case of Lucretia [ibid. MPG 41.32]; (5) out of vain ambition for glory, as in the case of Empedocles; (6) out of a desire for a better life, as Cicero writes of Cleombrotus, *Tuscul. Disputationes*, 1 [34.84], who, when he had finished reading Plato's book on the immortality of the soul, immediately threw himself over a wall; (7) because of the weakness of the flesh, as when certain people feared that they would fail in the time of persecution. The Donatists thought that they could voluntarily kill themselves without sin. See Augustine, *Contra Gaudentium*, 2.22 [MPL 43.728–29]: God has not given or approved this remedy, but rather 1 Cor. 10:13 says that "God is faithful who will not permit you to be tried beyond your powers." In 2 Cor. 12:9 he says, "My strength is made perfect in weakness." (8) in order to avoid sin, as is written of Apollonia, that she threw herself into the fire rather than be forced to worship heathen gods. Augustine writes of certain women that they threw themselves into a river rather than be ravished by their persecutors. "But if this was a lawful reason," says Augustine correctly, "there would be nothing more blessed or useful than to commit suicide immediately after Baptism" [*De Civit. Dei*, 1.27, MPL 41.40, paraphrase]. It is plain that none of these reasons is lawful or capable of proof on the basis of the Word of God. In 2 Sam. 1:15 the young man who reported that he had fallen upon Saul at Saul's own command was ordered to be killed. No one has said that the example of Judas and Ahithophel should be imitated.

In 2 Macc. 14:37–46 there is a description of how Razis killed himself. And Augustine, *Contra Gaudentium*, 1.31.38 [MPL 43.729], after he has dealt at some length with this passage, finally comes down to the correct solution: "The Jews do not regard the writings of the Maccabees as witnesses in the way law, prophets, and psalms are stipulated in Luke 24:44, in which the Lord gives His prohibitions, but these books have been received by the church for its use, if they are read or heard with care." The author of this account in Maccabees praises this example rather gently, as an instance of choosing to die nobly rather than be subject to sinners and bring upon his countrymen injuries which were unworthy of them. Augustine is correct in saying [ibid.], "The history of the gentiles was accustomed to praise their brave men in this way, but the church does not treat the martyrs of Christ thus."

But in Judg. 16:30 Samson, in order that he might punish his enemies, said, "Let me die with the Philistines," and he even prayed the Lord for this. The answer to this objection is that Samson was not a private individual but a judge over the people of God who, when he realized that it was not only he himself who as a captive was being mocked, but that God Himself was also treated this way, prayed of the Lord, from whom he had his mandate, for the public punishment of the Philistines so that he might be able to avenge himself on the enemy. Just as a ruler in punishing the enemy in a lawful war, when he exposes himself to the danger of death, is not sinning, neither did Samson. Furthermore, Samson was a type of Christ, who in dying must destroy death in keeping with the statement of Hos. 13:14, "I will be your death, O death." Therefore it came about in the hidden guidance of the Holy Spirit that Samson in his death killed more than he had killed while living. So much for this question. Let us move on to the next division of the subject.

The Fifth Commandment forbids that a man kill either himself or another person whom Scripture calls his neighbor. The Pharisees corrupted the meaning of the word "neighbor," as if kindness was to be shown only to friends and those who were particularly deserving, but it was not a sin if a person persecuted his enemy in hatred or returned evil for evil. Therefore Christ taught the correct interpretation of what should be understood by the term "neighbor." Moses long before had taught the same thing, Ex. 23:5; Deut. 22:2. From Scripture we can draw a threefold application: (1) to love our friends, Prov. 3:29, "Do not plot against your friend, since he has confidence in you," cf. Prov. 11:12; Ps. 35:12; 37:21; (2) to "love your enemies, pray for those who persecute you, do good to those who do evil, bless those who curse," Matt. 5:44; Rom. 12:14; (3) with regard to those who have done neither good nor evil, as far as you know, note Prov. 3:30, "Do not contend with a man for no reason, when he has done you no harm." Paul nicely develops this general division in Rom. 12:9ff., as we have shown.

Pertinent here also is the parable of the Samaritan in Luke 10:30ff., in which Christ is making a clear reply to the question, "Who is my neighbor?" For because it is written, "Love your neighbor," therefore because he is my neighbor, is it a sin on my part when in some other place, without my knowing about it, some person dies of hunger? Or is it necessary for me to run around to find my neighbor over whom destruction is impending? In the schools they reply that the affirmative precepts are always in force but not on every occasion. But this question can be more simply and correctly understood on the basis of the Biblical foundations. For Christ, as if painting a picture of our neighbor, said that when, in our interpersonal relationships in the home or in some other business, whether by accident or in some other way, God puts before us a person who in his necessity needs our help and love, and you can help him, this person is your neighbor whom you are commanded to love, nor are you to argue as to whether he is your friend, your enemy, known to you, a stranger, of a different religion or language. Thus Lazarus is neighbor to the rich man. So the wounded man was to the Samaritan. Therefore we must not love only those who are near to us whom we want to help, but those whom God for whatever reason puts before us, these we must recognize as our neighbors.

Furthermore, love for our neighbor has degrees or order, as is clear from Scripture, Gal. 6:10; 1 Tim. 5:8; Deut. 15:7–8; Lev. 23:22. Therefore we should maintain this rule: (1) that we acknowledge as our neighbors those whom God has placed next to us; (2) that we show to them willingly our works of love. For "a person is accepted by God according to what he has and not what he does not have," 2 Cor. 8:12.

We should also consider the fact that God with His great wisdom wills to lump all men together under the designation of neighbor or brother. The term "neighbor" is derived from the association among citizens or the people of a community, (1) because God willed to show that man was not created for a solitary existence, nor should a person be concerned only about himself and seek only his own things, but that we should show ourselves as neighbors to all men, just as the members in one body or the citizens in one state. (2) He uses the term "brothers" because of our common origin. Our neighbor is our brother and flesh of our flesh. Likewise, "A man does not despise his own flesh," Eph. 5:29. (3) Because God is the same over all, the same Creator, the same Redeemer, the same Sanctifier, there is one faith, one salvation, Eph. 4:4. Therefore God uses this term "neighbor" in opposition to those who argue as to whether the person is known to us, a stranger, an enemy, a friend, deserving, etc. For He wills that only this point be considered, that the person is a neighbor in the sense just discussed.

Finally, we must say something about the threats and promises which have been added to the Fifth Commandment. In this area Christ also has shown us the way. For He has shown that for the correct understanding of the Decalog it is required that not only must the sins be listed in keeping with a proper cataloging of those that are in conflict with the individual precepts, but we must also add the threats to the individual varieties of sins. "He who is angry is guilty . . ."; Matt. 5:22, "whoever says, 'you fool,' shall be guilty. . . ." For to discuss sins without talking about the punishment is not to teach the Law but to break it. We must carefully note in Christ's sermon the errors of the Pharisees. For because certain statements in Scripture threaten eternal punishments, certain spiritual ones, and others physical punishments, the Pharisees imagined that not all sins merited the eternal wrath of God, that some were expiated by physical punishments, so that he who paid the judicial punishment of Moses was not guilty before God; and thus certain sins did not deserve any punishment. It is apparent that the Pharisees developed four degrees of threats or penalties: (1) the gehenna of fire, to which they referred the sins of blasphemy, profanation of the Sabbath, etc.; (2) judgment, to which were added the punishments for sins as stipulated in the law of Moses; (3) punishment by the council (Sanhedrin) took place when the law of Moses gave no specific punishment, and then the judges imposed an arbitrary penalty, as in Deut. 17:8ff. and 25:1. (4) The Pharisees also established certain minimum sins or errors which were punished neither by the judges nor by the council, and they believed that they were much less worthy of eternal wrath. Thus they dreamed that these minimal sins, such as getting angry, saying *raca*, carried no guilt at all and merited no punishment. Thus Christ is condemning these ideas and uses such terms as "judgment," "Sanhedrin," and the fire of hell, which were familiar in the teaching of the Pharisees, but He applied them far more extensively than did the Pharisees. For He ascribes the greatest punishment, gehenna, to a sin which in their eyes was minimal and carried no guilt. By the application of these threats which seemed novel to the Pharisees, He gives a very useful warning: (1) Of no sin, even one which seemed minor, should we speak without a threat. (2) External or physical punishments do not expiate sins or satisfy the judgment of God, nor are these threats to be understood as if the eternal wrath of God is not something to be feared, but rather that the testimonies and warnings concerning eternal punishments and the eternal wrath of God do apply, as is written in Matt. 10:15 in regard to the Sodomites. (3) The admonitions concerning the eternal wrath of God and hellfire pertain not only to external and crass sins but also to inner sins, which the Pharisees called minor sins. The warning in Matthew 5 is best understood in keeping with this judgment.

This doctrine is absolutely necessary in the individual precepts as to how the warnings are to be applied to our sins and in what ways, so that we do not dream up this difference or distinction as the Pharisees did. Christ shows by this example in the one commandment that the principle is to be applied to the rest of them. Therefore, because we have definite rules drawn from Christ's teaching concerning the application of these warnings, we shall gather statements from Scripture, some of which speak of physical or outward punishments and others of spiritual, and still others of eternal punishments.

Gal. 5:21; 1 John 3:14–15; James 2:13; Matt. 6:15; 18:35; 7:2; 5:25; Gen. 4:10; Rev. 6:9–10; Matt. 26:52; Rev. 13:10; Ex. 21:12, 14; Num. 35:16; Lev. 24:17; Gen. 9:6; Deut. 27:24; Prov. 14:30; 17:13; 24:17–18; Mal. 3:5; Hos. 4:3; Matt. 5:22. See also Ecclesiasticus 27 and 28; Gen. 9:5; Ps. 10:13; 55:23; Job 5:2; Ecclus. 30:26;

Prov. 19:19; 22:24–25; Ps. 68:30. And there is a warning for each of us in the Lord's Prayer when we say, "As we forgive those who trespass against us."

Examples of punishments: Gen. 4:12, Cain wandering, a fugitive, and because of his actions "the earth no longer yielded to him its strength." 2 Sam. 4:12, they were killed because of a murder. Gen. 34:30 and 49:5–7, Simeon and Levi are cursed because of their taking revenge on their own initiative. Judg. 9:53, Abimelech. The title of Psalm 52 describes the curse upon Doeg and Saul because of the killing of the priests in Nob, cf. 1 Sam. 22:9. In 1 Kings 21:1ff. the sin of Jezebel is described and in 2 Kings 9:33 she is punished. 2 Kings 11:16, the punishment of Athaliah. In Esther 7:10 Haman, who had not yet committed the murder but had given counsel in favor of it, received his just punishment. In Jer. 38:4 they took counsel regarding Jeremiah, but they themselves were thrown into prison and later on punished, cf. 2 Kings 25. In 1 Kings 2:29ff. Joab is punished. Judg. 8:21, the punishment of Zebah and Zalmunna. 2 Chronicles 24–25, Joash. Dan. 14:21 (Vulgate), the elders. Numbers 21, Arad is conquered in an unjust war. 2 Kings 14:8ff. Amaziah starts an unjust war. Numbers 22–23, Balaam curses the Israelites and gives evil counsel, but in Joshua 13:22 he is slain. Matt. 18:23ff., the unmerciful servant.

Promises are added to the Fifth Commandment in 1 John 4:16, "He who abides in love abides in God and God abides in him," cf. Matt. 6:14; 25:40; Prov. 25:21–22; Matt. 5:5, 7, 9; Prov. 14:29; 16:32; Ecclus. 1:29 (Vulgate); James 1:4; Psalm 9; 25:9; 37:11; 147:6; Ecclus. 3:19, (Vulgate); Prov. 12:20; Ps. 133:1; Luke 6:37–38, 35; Ps. 112:5; Prov. 20:7, 22; 21:3, 21; Is. 33:16–17; Eccl. 10:4.

Examples of rewards: Matt. 25:34; Esther 6:11, Mordecai, although he was walking into a trap, yet was honored by the king; Ex. 1:21, homes were built for the midwives; 2 Sam. 21:7, Jonathan's love for David brought it about that his posterity remained; 2 Sam. 16:11–12. See the examples of David in 1 Sam. 24:20 and 26:25 and how his enemy Saul blessed him. In Jer. 38:7ff. and 39:17 the eunuch frees Jeremiah from his imprisonment and is saved in the destruction of Jerusalem. In Gen. 13:14–15 Abraham yields to Lot and the Lord immediately says to him, "All the land which you see I will give to you." In Gen. 28:1ff. Jacob yields to his brother Esau and the Lord blesses him.

The Sixth Commandment: "Thou Shalt Not Commit Adultery"

[MELANCHTHON'S TEXT]

There is a great confusion among all people as to what God has actually prohibited in this commandment. Christ adds an explanation in Matthew 5 which shows that not only are outward sins prohibited but also our depraved lusts and wandering and erring desires which are against this commandment. As we have said above, with the prohibitions are included also certain affirmative concepts such as the sanctifying and strengthening of lawful wedlock, which is protected under this commandment and which gives approval to marriage in the common sense of that term. On the contrary, it condemns all cohabitation outside of legitimate marriage and sets forth penalties in this life and eternal torments after this life. As it says in Heb. 13:4, "God will punish fornicators and adulterers." Likewise Eph. 5:5, "No fornicator or unclean man has any inheritance in the kingdom of Christ and of God . . . because of these things comes the wrath of God upon the children of disobedience." It says that marriage is protected by these laws because even when the world does not punish adultery or other lusts, yet God punishes them and does not allow His commands to be taken lightly, as the examples of all ages show, even those which are not put in writing. But God has willed that certain things be written so that we may be cautioned regarding the rule that God is angry at all impurities and He either severely chastises or completely destroys those who do not respect [this commandment], as the Sodomites were destroyed. Not only were those five cities destroyed for this reason, but the evil desires of every nation gave occasion for the destruction of many others, as happened to the Greek cities Thebes, Athens, and Sparta. Not only was Troy punished because of adultery, but many kings perished in tragic accidents because of their lusts, as in the case of the king of Egypt, Clytemnestra, nearly all the kings of Macedonia, Archelaus, Philip, Alexander, Demetrius, Ptolemy, and most of the Caesars. Often also in great wars kingdoms were changed because of this, so that almost the entire tribe of Benjamin was wiped out over the rape of the Levite's wife [Judges 19–20]. We should study these examples, apply them to ourselves as warnings from God, and resolve to be obedient to this precept and to fight against the flames of illicit desire. In obedience to this commandment are required virtues such as modesty, chastity, continence, a sense of shame, temperance, and sobriety. For without temperance no person can protect chastity.

The Sixth Commandment

[I.] We must first speak about synecdoche. The word *nāʾaph*, which is used in this commandment, generally refers to a shaking or a wallowing and is used with reference to an unlawful mixing up between persons who are not free and where one or both have already been joined in marriage. For there is a different word in the Hebrew language (*zānāh*) that refers to simple fornication, as in Greek we distinguish between *moicheia* and *porneia*, and among the Latins we speak of *adulterium* on the one hand and *scortatio* or *fornicatio* on the other. But certain fanatics are contending on the basis of the grammatical meaning of the word that only a certain kind of dissipation is forbidden in the Sixth Commandment but that the other kinds of intercourse, such as simple fornication, can be done without sin. To prove this foul opinion, from which the common sense in all sane men recoils, they quote Hos. 1:2 where, they assert, God not only permits but orders and commands the prophet to commit fornication. But they are doing manifest harm to God, to the prophet, and to the text. For God in clear words adds the statement as to why He is speaking of a "wife of whoredom and children of whoredom," because, He says, "the land is committing great whoredom by forsaking or committing harlotry against the Lord." Therefore the term is used here in an allegorical or metaphorical sense. The point should be strongly emphasized that this woman had previously lived in fornication, and yet it is certain, from the perfectly clear words of the text, that the prophet had not carried on the shameful practice of fornication with her outside of lawful wedlock. For God says to him, "Take to yourself a wife." The text continues with the words, "The prophet took her." These words are used in Scripture with reference to the lawful taking of a wife. Therefore it is an error to say that God has given a mandate to practice fornication, as something legitimate and permitted, when in so many places in Scripture it is condemned and harshly punished.

Now because the Decalog must be understood according to the interpretation given by the prophets and apostles, it is completely clear from the testimonies of Scripture, some of which we shall shortly hereafter study, that all intercourse outside of marriage is prohibited under the Sixth Commandment, not only outward sins but our inner flames of desire. For Christ in Matt. 5:32, in discussing the precepts of the Second Table, joins adultery with fornication. Therefore, just as in the other precepts other sins are also included under one item which is mentioned by name, so also in the Sixth Commandment we must discuss not only adultery, because it is so severely noted in the Julian law, but we must also learn the many different ways in which God holds us guilty of adultery, if there is not forgiveness for the sake of Christ the Mediator.

We must also now consider why God has willed in the Sixth Commandment to speak especially by name of the sin of adultery. The Son of God Himself shows the reason for this in Matt. 5:28, when He says, "He has already committed adultery in his heart," that is to say, that God in this way has willed to demonstrate the enormity of sin, because just as the Julian law recognizes that the crime of adultery is a great disgrace and worthy of severe punishment, so are the wandering flames of lust considered to be before God's judgment. And because human wickedness is accustomed to give mild and innocent names to sins of dissipation, therefore God accuses all of these practices with a harsh name, so that we are not deceived by extenuations and excuses, but rather will acknowledge our impurity and deplore it, seek forgiveness through the Mediator, and put to death our acts of the flesh by the Holy Spirit, so that they do not rule over us. There is another reason why God does not specify any other particular kind of unlawful intercourse in the Sixth Commandment but simply uses a term which signifies a violation of the conjugal union. For by prohibiting this He is showing that He is sanctifying, approving, and protecting marriage, its practice, custom, and conjugal union. God with His own finger willed in the Decalog that this word should prohibit the violation of lawful marriage in opposition to the teaching of demons who condemn the institution of marriage. For He is showing that He is not only the author but also the defender of marriage. These points in a very expert way demonstrate the synecdoche of the Sixth Commandment.

[II.] Next we must develop a catalog of sins against the Sixth Commandment. For since the knowledge of sin always comes through the Law, we should not recite the commandments without any understanding and in only a general way, but when we recite the individual sins, we are clearly and specifically accused. Therefore we must inquire which external and which internal sins the Sixth Commandment condemns in us, and we must seek forgiveness for them and with the power of the Holy Spirit fight against them, and we must do this on the basis of the principles laid down in the prophets and apostles. For the conscience must not be burdened down by the opinion of men regarding sin, whether against the Sixth Commandment or any other. We have stated that there must be established a definite purpose in the use of the individual precepts. We have in this precept the example of the apostles for this rule. Paul sets forth the purpose of the Sixth Commandment in a learned and appropriate way in 1 Cor. 6:18–20, "He who fornicates sins against his own body . . . your body is the temple of the Holy Spirit whom you have from God. You are not your own. You were bought with a price. Therefore glorify God in your body and in your spirit"; 1 Thess. 4:4–5 [cf. KJV], "Let each of you know how to possess his vessel in sanctification, not in the passion of lust." From the establishment of this purpose we can correctly put together a catalog. For it is certain that all kinds of shamefulness and dissipation, by which the body and soul are polluted, are in conflict with the Sixth Commandment.

We must observe that the Holy Spirit does not want us to use our own ideas, so that we draw up a catalog of sins only on the basis of the purpose of the arrangement according to our own notions. For human boldness is accustomed to make sins out of things which God has made matters of liberty, and those things which are true sins under the judgment of God we either defend, explain away, or excuse. Therefore the Holy Spirit takes to Himself the task of clearly listing by name the individual kinds of sins. Indeed, the Son of God Himself gives us a brief explanation of this precept, cf. Matt. 5:27–28. For it is the custom and practice of Scripture to handle the commandments in a general way and give the particulars in the form of examples. Thus when Scripture wants to speak about bearing an injury, it says, "If anyone strikes you on the right cheek . . ." Matt.

5:39. Likewise Christ, in teaching how the true understanding of the precepts of the Decalog are to be studied and established, takes as an example the Fifth Commandment and tries to apply this rationale to the other precepts. Therefore the points which were made under the Fifth Commandment, although they may be pertinent to the Sixth Commandment, He does not repeat, such as the matter of the four degrees of sins and threats, but gives a brief explanation in which He deals with many kinds of sins. (1) He mentions the outward sin of adultery itself. (2) He mentions the woman in a general way, whether she be single or married. (3) He speaks of the eyes. (4) He mentions lusting. (5) Adultery in the heart. Thus in this brief statement are seen the basics of the entire subject, it is worth the consideration of godly people as to how the apostles expanded this brief statement of Christ with their own explanation.

Thus we here present the list of sins against the Sixth Commandment, of which some are external and others internal. Among the external are:

The first kind: An actual sexual union outside of marriage, as Augustine correctly says, under the title of adultery, is prohibited, as is every unlawful sexual union and the illicit practice of these things. Furthermore, Scripture sometimes includes all external, unlawful unions under the general title of uncleanness. But sometimes it goes into great detail, and thus various degrees of sins may be observed: (1) Fornication or defilement which is committed between single persons. Some make the distinction that *stuprum* is the violation of a virgin, and *scortatio* takes place simply with unmarried women, cf. Deut. 23:17; Lev. 19:29. (2) Rape, as when this sin is forced upon a woman by violence. For Scripture makes this distinction. See Ex. 22:16; Deut. 22:25; Gen. 34:2; 2 Sam. 13:11. (3) Adultery. See Lev. 20:10. The rabbis say that there is no adultery unless it is with the wife of a particular man. For they believe that adultery is committed with a married woman, but there is no adultery if a married man has intercourse with some unmarried woman. The lawyers use this definition: Adultery is the violation of another person's marriage bed. Alcandes of Hales [Tome 1, line 8, note 53] also says that properly speaking adultery occurs only when a man makes an approach to the wife of another. But it is certain that adultery is the violation of the bond and faith of marriage.

The lawful union of husband and wife consists in this, as Paul says in 1 Cor. 7:4, "The husband does not have power over his own body, nor does the wife." Therefore it is adultery whether a husband does not keep the marriage vow toward his wife or a wife toward her husband, but permits his or her body to be put in the power of another person. Therefore the Decalog simply says, "You shall not commit adultery," And Hostiensis[15] is entirely correct when he

---

[15] Henry of Segusio, 1200–1271, noted canonist.

says that adultery is the violation of another person's marriage bed or the defiling of what belongs to him alone. Simply put, adultery takes place when either a married man has such a relationship with a single woman, or when a single man pollutes the wife of another man. The adultery is twofold when a married man corrupts the wife of another. For there is both the violation of the marriage bed of another man and the shaming of his own private parts. (4) Incest is intercourse with relatives and kinsmen in degrees of relationship which are forbidden in the divine law. See Lev. 18:6ff.; 20:11ff.; Deut. 27:20–23. Paul refers to it under the general title of *porneia*, 1 Cor. 5:1. Scripture speaks strongly about this practice. Lev. 18:25, "The land vomited out its inhabitants." Lev. 20:14, "When this crime has been committed, they shall be burned with fire, that there be no wickedness among you." Deut. 27:20, "Cursed is he . . . and all the people shall say 'Amen.'" Lest anyone think that this was only the ceremonial law, Paul in 1 Cor. 5:5 "hands over the incestuous man to Satan" and shows that it is a matter of natural law. For he says, "Such things are not even heard of among the gentiles," v. 1. (5) Intercourse with males or with beasts. Paul speaks of sin which is "contrary to nature," or unnatural, by which the natural use is perverted, Rom. 1:26. Others call such people Sodomites and it is called an unspeakable sin, because by the very mention of it the mouth and ears are polluted. Some of these sins are dealt with by name in Lev. 18:22–23; Rom. 1:26–27; 1 Cor. 6:9; 1 Tim. 1:10. It is noteworthy that where these vices are known and practiced, as in great cities and empires, there Paul lists them by name. But in places where they were not generally known, lest they offend godly ears or where the very naming of such things causes sin, he speaks of uncleanness only in a general way, Gal. 5:19; Eph. 4:19; Col. 3:5; 1 Thess. 4:7.

The second variety is shamefulness or filthiness in speech. Col. 3:8, "filthy communication out of your mouth." Eph. 4:29, "Let no foul language come out of your mouth . . . lest you grieve the Holy Spirit."

Third are shameful, lewd, and obscene gestures or symbols which indicate lewdness. Jer. 5:8, those who are "amorous horses" and their emissaries, "each whinnying after his neighbor's wife." Prov. 5:20, "Do not embrace a loose woman. Why are you caressing in your bosom a strange woman?" Prov. 7:10–13, "A woman in the dress of a harlot meets the young man and kisses him and flatters him with her impudent face." See Ecclesiasticus 9 and Ezekiel 23. Here we are speaking about such things as gestures, dress, causing or exciting lust. Scripture has precise terms to describe this: "wantonness" (*aselgeia*), Rom. 13:13; Gal. 5:19; Eph. 4:19; 2 Peter 2:7. There is also the word "licentiousness," where all shame has been lost and there is delight in open shamelessness. 1 Tim. 5:11 and Rev. 18:7 use the word *strēniaō*, which refers to unbridled lasciviousness which acts as if the bridle of modesty has been shamelessly removed. 1 Tim. 5:6 and James 5:5 use the word "self-indulgence" (*spatalaō*).

Fourth is the lust of the eyes, 1 John 2:16; Matt. 5:28; Ezek. 23:16. The lust of the eyes rages over them, 2 Peter 2:14, ". . . having eyes full of adultery." Ecclus. 9:8, "Do not gaze upon the beauty of a woman who is not yours." Gen. 39:7, "She cast her eyes upon Joseph." Ecclus. 26:12, "The fornication of a woman is known in her eyes and her eyelids." Job 31:1, "I have made a covenant with my eyes that I not look upon a maiden." See also Ecclesiasticus 9. God wills that the light of chastity shine in our entire body and all of our members.

The fifth includes all unlawful occasions or opportunities for uncleanness. Paul is referring particularly to the Sixth Commandment in Eph. 5:18, "Do not be drunk with wine, in which is debauchery." Rom. 13:14, "Do not make provision for the flesh to fulfill its desires"; in v. 13 reveling and drunkenness are associated with wantonness and chambering. Prov. 23:30, 33, "Those who tarry long over the wine . . . their eyes shall see strange women." For this reason drunkenness is contrary to the Sixth Commandment. In this state Lot committed incest, Gen. 19:33. In another context, insofar as drunkenness destroys the health of the body, it is against the Fifth Commandment. Is. 5:11, "You who run after wine"; cf. Prov. 23:29, where sorrow fills the eyes of those who "linger over wine." We should also consider the terms given to drunkenness in the Old and New Testaments. But we will take this up in another place. But there can be godly celebrations and honorable pleasures, as are described in Jer. 31:13, 1 Kings 4:20; 8:65; Neh. 8:10–12; Deut. 8:9. But to return to the occasions for sin against the Sixth Commandment, we must also include idleness, luxury, and false security. Jer. 5:7, "They were fed to the full, and then they committed adultery." 1 Cor. 10:7, "They sat down to eat and to drink and rose up to play." Ezek. 16:49, God, in explaining the causes of the crimes of Sodom says, "pride, gluttony, and idleness." In 2 Sam. 11:4, when David was no longer struggling in exiles and wars, but rather was indulging in an afternoon nap and wandering glances, he fell into adultery. In Gen. 34:1–2 Dinah was raped while strolling around. In 2 Sam. 13:9ff. Amnon was alone with his sister in his bedroom. These examples are given in Scripture, and others like them could be added.

The sixth variety: In this commandment there is also this general rule, Rom. 1:32, "They are worthy of death, not only those who do such things, but also those who give their approval." Therefore they are guilty of [violating] the Sixth Commandment who defend or aid or do not prohibit, or in other circumstances share in another's sin, as has been said under the locus on sin, cf. Lev. 19:29; Ps. 50:18; Ecclus. 26:13; 42:11.

These are the varieties of outward sins against the Sixth Commandment which Scripture seems more carefully to stipulate here than in the other commandments. Because original sin with its poison infects primarily the very noble work of procreation, therefore immediately after the Fall our first parents did not cover their hands or their feet but their reproductive organs. In order that we might thereby learn what the works of the flesh are and how they are to be put to death, Scripture gives us a list of these works by name.

The inward sins Christ calls "concupiscence" and locates them in the heart. There are two kinds, in keeping with the distinction between the sin of the regenerate and the sin of the unregenerate. (1) It is the disease itself or the depraved inclination which suggests lustful thoughts which are against the Sixth Commandment. In believers, indeed, who by the power of the Spirit mortify these actions of the flesh and pray that the obedience of the Son of God will cover them, these are venial sins. Yet Paul warns of the drives and impulses which are so strong, so uncontrolled and violent, that they consume a person like a fire and a person is so likely to fall that Paul says in 1 Cor. 7:9, "It is better to marry than to burn with lust." He does not want us to attribute too much to our own power to resist, for he says in v. 5, "Come together again, since Satan is testing you because of your lack of self-control." He calls this desire a disease (*morbus*) when: (2) The inner lust occupies the throne. In Eph. 4:19 Paul speaks of *apēlgēkotes*, that is, those who have "surrendered themselves to impurity in working all uncleannesses." In 1 Thess. 4:5 and Col. 3:5 he calls lusts "passion," that is to say, when the flames of lust under some power take hold of the emotions and thoughts of the heart, so that no serious thought is given to restraining these untamed desires. We should also note the degrees in inner sins: (1) There are teasing suggestions of our thoughts, erring drives of our emotions. (2) Satan tempts us. (3) Pleasure rears its head, 2 Tim. 3:4, "They love pleasure more than God." (4) Following this, "They become slaves to their passions and various kinds of pleasures," Titus 3:3.

[III.] Third, by way of antithesis to sin we must show what the virtues are or the good works of the Sixth Commandment. In a general sense such things are named as modesty, purity, chastity, or continence. Paul uses the term *hagiasmos* or "sanctification," 1 Thess. 4:4; cf. Heb. 12:14, which progresses through the same degrees, sins of deed, of word, of the eye, of gestures, and of the heart. Matt. 15:19, "Out of the heart come wicked thoughts . . ."; cf. 1 Cor. 7:34; 1 Tim. 2:9. James 3:17 pertains primarily to actions. Paul uses the terms "temperance" and "sobriety" interchangeably in reference to food, drink, idleness, and other causes for lust, 1 Cor. 9:27, "I chasten my own body" cf. 1 Thess 5:22; 1 Peter 5:8.

Here is pertinent virginity or widowhood, that is, life in the unmarried state, without the fires of lust which Paul calls a "burning," living without any cohabitation or misuse of the seed; 1 Cor. 7:34, ". . . that she may be holy in body and spirit."

It is obvious that marriage refers properly to the virtues of the Sixth Commandment, for God prohibits the violation of marriage and the purpose of chastity is to preserve order in the conjugal union established by God, cf. Heb. 13:4; 1 Cor. 7:2, 5, 27, 29, 39.

At this point it is wise and proper to consider the duties of godly spouses. For there is no doubt that God, who has forbidden the violation of marriage, antithetically has commanded that in marriage the conjugal order, instituted by His will, should be preserved. Therefore the duties of husbands are: (1) "to love your wives as your own bodies, just as Christ loved the church. For no one ever hated his own flesh, but nourishes and cherishes it," Eph. 5:28–29. (2) "A man shall leave his father . . . and cling to his wife and the two shall be in one flesh," Gen. 2:24; Matt. 19:5; Mark 10:7; Eph. 5:31. Therefore the union must be indissoluble, the wife must not depart from the man, but preserve the marriage troth so that the union of the two may be a sharing of both the good and the difficult things of life. (3) Forbearance or consideration is demanded; 1 Peter 3:7 "Husbands, dwell with your wives according to knowledge, or considerately, as with the weaker vessel, since you are joint heirs of the grace of life"; cf. Col. 3:19. (4) 1 Cor. 14:35, "If they wish to learn anything, let them ask their husbands at home"; 1 Peter 3:7, ". . . in order that your prayer be not hindered." There ought to be common prayers by husband and wife, 1 Cor. 7:5 (Textus Receptus), ". . . that you may devote yourselves to fasting and prayer." Likewise v. 12, "If a man has an unbelieving wife . . . he should not divorce her." (5) The man should be the head of the woman, so that "her desire is to her husband," Gen. 3:16, 1 Cor. 11:3. Therefore the life and action of the woman must be governed according to his direction and she must be reprimanded by his authority when she errs. (6) Eph. 5:29, "The husband must nourish and cherish her." Therefore he must provide for her support. 1 Tim. 3:4, "He must manage his household well and keep his children submissive and respectful." (7) The husband must render to his wife the conjugal rights which are owed to her, "A man does not have power over his own body . . . do not refuse one another, except by agreement," 1 Cor. 7:3–5.

The duties of wives are the following: They are to be subject to their husbands, as Sarah was obedient to Abraham, 1 Peter 3:5–6; ". . . as is fitting in the Lord," Col. 3:18; ". . . as the church is subject to Christ," Eph. 5:22, 24, cf. v. 33. She must recognize that her husband is her head and her lord, 1 Peter 3:6; Eph. 5:23, cf. 1 Tim. 2:12. "She is bound to this marriage as long as her husband lives," and while her husband is alive, if she is with some other man, "she will be called an adulteress," Rom. 7:2–3. "She should not be separated from her husband, but if she does depart, she shall either remain unmarried or be reconciled with her husband" [1 Cor. 7:10–11]. She should give to her husband his conjugal rights, 1 Cor. 7:3. "She will be saved through bearing children," 1 Tim. 2:15. "I want the younger widows to marry and bear children," 1 Tim. 5:14, cf. Titus 2:4; 1 Cor. 7:34; Titus 2:5; 1 Tim. 5:4. The industriousness of the mother of the household is described in Prov. 31:10ff., cf. 1 Cor. 14:35; 1 Peter 3:1; 1 Cor. 7:16.

In other passages we have a fuller description of godly women. 1 Peter 3:2 refers to having a "holy and chaste behavior joined together with their reverence." 1 Tim. 2:11 says a wife should "be silent." 1 Peter 3:4 and 1 Tim. 2:9, "adorned in modest attire," cf. 1 Cor. 14:34; 11:5; 1 Tim. 2:15; Titus 2:5; 1 Tim. 3:11; 5:13; 1 Peter 3:6.

Furthermore, it is noteworthy that Christ includes two kinds of sins under the Sixth Commandment: (1) [those stated] from the negative standpoint; and (2) because the order of marriage is the obedience or fulfillment of the Sixth Commandment and because divorce is in conflict with this order, He says it is the sin of adultery. Likewise, the apostles in antithesis to the affirmative aspect develop, in a sense, a new catalog of sins. Thus in 1 Tim. 4:3 Paul speaks of those who "forbid to marry." In Col. 3:19 he says, "Do not be harsh with your wife." 1 Tim. 2:9, ". . . not adorned with braided hair," etc. These antitheses are in part added by the apostles themselves and are self-evident. Also in the Proverbs of Solomon there are many statements about bad women. This rule should therefore be observed because it is also used in the other commandments.

[IV.] We must add certain warnings. In Scripture many threats of different kinds are applied to this precept. For this corrupt nature of ours is so infested and blinded by the poison of lust that many people overlook it and many excuse the sins of the Sixth Commandment as if it were only something like eating or sleeping. Hence the apostles also were compelled to send out special directives to the gentiles to avoid fornication. Therefore when these sins become of less and less concern, God adds more and greater threats and a person should observe this order because the punishments follow more quickly than in the case of the other commandments. In other cases God's wrath moves to punishment with slow foot. But in the case of drunkenness and fornication, punishment follows immediately and manifestly. Therefore it is useful to keep always in view certain statements of warnings as examples. These statements are made concerning the spiritual and eternal punishments: 1 Cor. 6:13, where not only is the prohibition and warning against fornication baldly stated, but because in the great [Roman] empire it was not considered a sin and was in keeping with the practices of the region, even Christians were lured away into it, therefore with many arguments Paul demonstrates the seriousness of this sin and what punishments it brings: Gal. 5:21; Eph. 5:5; Col. 3:6, cf. Heb. 12:14; 13:4. In Rom. 1:28 and Eph. 4:18 lust is punished with "a reprobate mind." See Eccl. 7:26; Ecclus. 19:2; Prov. 22:19; 1 Peter 3:7.

There are general outward warnings: Jer. 5:29; Mal. 3:5; Prov. 6:29. Scripture in case after case and by name threatens various punishments, (1) to the soul, as above; (2) to body and life, Prov. 6:32–33, "It ruins his life; he hurts himself"; (3) to property, Prov. 29:3, "He who keeps company with a harlot squanders his substance"; (4) to reputation, Prov. 6:33, "He brings dishonor upon himself, and his disgrace will not be wiped away"; (5) to mental abilities, Hos. 4:11, "Wine takes away the understanding"; (6) to life, Prov. 2:18, "Her house sinks down to death," cf. 5:5; (7) to posterity, cf. Job 31:10–12; Wisd. of Sol. 3:16–17. In Prov. 7:22–23, he compares the harlot and the adulterer to "an ox which goes to the slaughter . . . and a bird which hastens to a snare." In Lev. 20:10 and Deut. 22:22 the adulterer is commanded to be punished with death, cf. Lev. 21:9; Job 24:18. See Ecclus. 19:2–3 and 23:24ff.; Prov. 2:16ff.; 5:3ff.; 6:24ff.; 23:27–28. God sets forth these various kinds of punishment in order to show His wrath against these sins which are not even considered important.

Examples of punishments: Gen. 6:4, where they are listed among the causes of the Flood. In Genesis 19, Sodom. In Genesis 34, the Shechemites. Paul in 1 Cor. 10:8 cites the example of the punishment of the tribe of Benjamin in Num. 25:1; Judg. 15:6, when the wife of Samson was given to another man, she was burned to death. The sons of Eli in 1 Sam. 2:22; David's adultery, 2 Samuel 11. In Jer. 29:22–23 Zedekiah and Ahab are punished; in Gen. 12:17 and 20:3 the entire family of the king is punished; in Gen. 38:10, Onan; Judges 16, Samson; 2 Sam. 3:27, Abner; 2 Sam 20:10, Amasa; 2 Sam. 13:28, Amnon is killed by his brother; Gen. 49:4, Reuben; 2 Sam. 16:2, Absolom; Gen 26:10, fornication and adultery bring harm to the ungodly.

The Epicureans talk nonsense in saying that Christ in John 8:11 has abrogated the severity of punishment which had been imposed upon adulterers by the law of Moses, when He says, "Neither do I condemn you. Go and sin no more." But Christ Himself testifies in John 3:17 that in His first advent into the world He had not come to condemn the world but that it might be saved. Just as He says in another place, Luke 12:14, "Who has made Me a judge?" in the meantime He has not abolished the punishment of the Law and therefore He asks the woman, "Who has condemned you?" When she replies, "No one, Lord," He then says, "Neither do I condemn you."

The promises attached to the Sixth Commandment: Gal. 5:22–23, chastity is a "fruit of the Spirit, and against such there is no law." 1 Cor. 6:19, "Your bodies are the temples of the Holy Spirit," Ezek. 18:6, 9, "He who does not defile his neighbor's wife . . . shall surely live," cf. Ecclus. 26:20. Many promises are given in opposition to the threats. Examples of rewards: In Gen. 39:8 and 41:40 Joseph is exalted, has children who are included in the number of the patriarchs, cf. Gen. 48:5; Judith 15–16. In Gen. 12:17 and 20:3 the marriage of Abraham is protected by God; Dan. 13:45, Susanna.

The Seventh Commandment: "Thou Shalt Not Steal"

[MELANCHTHON'S TEXT]

Here we must assert the affirmative aspects of this commandment, for the distinction of ownership is sanctified by God, a distinction which the very word of the commandment asserts has been ordained by God. Because He forbids theft, He thereby wills that individuals should possess their own property. By this testimony are refuted the ravings of fanatical men who contend under the great and dangerous error that in the Gospel the holding of private property has been abolished. In the second place, the prohibitory aspect of the precept must be kept in mind also, lest we covet the property of others. Because the arrangement has been divinely established that men among themselves in the natural performance of their duties should demonstrate their obedience toward God and honorably carry out their duties, God also punishes inequity in the performance of these relationships, not only with the punishments of magistrates but also with other disasters, as Isaiah says in 33:1, "Woe to you who despoil . . . for you will be despoiled." Deut. 25:15, "You shall have an honest measure . . . that your days may be prolonged." And experience proves the well-known rule: "Divide dishonestly and your goods will dishonestly disappear." This commandment demands many virtues which are in conflict with greed, jealousy, and wastefulness, such as uprightness in our business affairs, generosity, industriousness, and thrift. Thus the lazy and wasteful are all thieves, for unless they take from someone else they cannot sustain their laziness and costly habits.

The Seventh Commandment

The teaching of the Seventh Commandment is very involved, but we shall speak under the locus on poverty[16] concerning ownership of property, begging, almsgiving, contracts, and usury. Therefore we shall briefly summarize those matters which properly pertain to a description of the Seventh Commandment. We have already noted that the Son of God, in His practice of explaining the Decalog, has shown in His handling of the Fifth Commandment what use He wills also to be applied to the other precepts. Thus the explanation of the Seventh Commandment has been given to us in Scripture itself, but not in only one particular passage whereby it could be easily comprehended, as is the case with the Fifth Commandment. Therefore those points which we have noted in Christ's explanation must be applied here also, so that those matters which are scattered in Scripture regarding the Seventh Commandment can be utilized according to a definite method.

First, we must consider the terminology. The word *gānab* refers to taking

---

[16] We have not translated that locus.

away the property of another person without the knowledge of the owner and in so stealthy a way that the action is not noticed: Matt. 24:43ff., "If the owner of the house had known in what hour the thief was coming . . ."; likewise 1 Thess. 5:2; 2 Peter 3:10. The term is used metaphorically in Job 21:18, "They are like chaff which the wind carries away, or steals." In Gen. 31:26, Jacob is said to have stolen away the heart [daughters] of Laban, who was unaware, unsuspecting, and absent. 2 Sam. 15:6, "Absalom stole the hearts of the men of Israel," that is, under the pretext of doing something else, he won their hearts to his cause so that they did not notice his treachery. Thus the word refers to doing something in a secretive, underhanded, and deceptive way, so that those with whom we are dealing are deceived and the fraudulent act is not noticed or brought to their attention.

Now, since it is certain that robbery, plundering, forcible seizure, etc., are prohibited in the Seventh Commandment, as these passages clearly show, 1 Cor. 6:10; Ezek. 18:7, 10, 12, 16, why did God not write, "You shall not be a plunderer or a robber," instead of "You shall not steal"? This consideration will show how great the wisdom of the Decalog is. Human reason recognizes that robbery is a clear violation of the Law and reproves and condemns it, but when we increase our possessions at the expense of our neighbor through hidden deceptions or under the pretext of legality, so that we cheat other people so that they do not realize and understand that we are defrauding them, there we find no fear of God [to keep us from] growing rich. Yet we are all well acquainted with these sins, either excusing or extenuating or even defending them. Therefore God has used this particular word with a definite purpose in mind, as we have said, to show that in the eyes of God's judgment not only are robbers to be regarded as guilty, whom even the civil law punishes, but even if your fraud escapes the knowledge of all, yet God will punish you. For because plundering is a public matter, it is punished by the sword of the magistrate, or at least it ought to be punished. But the stealthy kinds of thievery, because they elude the knowledge of the judge, are still subject to the judgment of God under the Decalog. Thus the explanation, as in the case of the Second Commandment, proceeds from the lesser to the greater. We shall shortly show how this takes place.

In the second place, we must establish the scope of this precept. For there are certain people who argue philosophically that because Scripture often encourages us to despise temporal goods, therefore God did not make external regulations of this kind so that for the sake of protecting them He wrote the Seventh Commandment with His own finger on the Second Table, but they contend that under the term "to steal" we must understand something more important than merely laying hands on external property. In other words they refer this precept to the stealing of spiritual things, such as the Word, the sacraments, and the souls of people. To be sure, these things are condemned in Scripture under the term "stealing," and they are most grievous sins. But we must observe this general rule in all of Scripture, that we first establish the simple and proper meaning of the words on the basis of their grammatical sense; and when this has been done, then allegorical meanings can be added, but yet the meaning of these terms must be based on other passages of Scripture. Thus Scripture first gives us the simple and proper explanation of each precept and then it deals with the allegorical meaning of certain of them, as the Third Commandment deals with the Sabbath, and the Sixth with spiritual fornication. Likewise the Seventh Commandment applies allegorically to spiritual things, cf. Jer. 23:30; Rom. 2:21–22; 2 Cor. 2:17; Is. 1:22; John 10:1. Yet these sins are not properly against the Seventh Commandment but they are horrible sins because they violate the entire First Table and the idea of a spiritual thief is not derived properly from the Seventh Commandment but from the First Table. Because of similarity of circumstance, the name "thief" is given to such a person. These allegories are appropriate and correct if dealt with at the proper place, namely after the simple and proper meaning of the precept has been established. But when allegorical interpretations of the Decalog are put in the primary position as being the main thrust of the precept, or when the proper and the simple meanings are confused, then it often results in loss of the literal meaning, or those things which pertain literally to what is commanded and forbidden are disregarded. This is also the case with the many who despise public church organization and the support of the public ministry. The allegorizing of the Third Commandment which they can observe privately seems to have been raised to the higher position.

Thus, for example, Sebastian Frank [Tome 1, line 5, note 101] philosophized a great deal regarding spiritual fornication under the Sixth Commandment, but he did not regard physical fornication as any enormous crime. Therefore it is incorrect reasoning to assert that outward matters are not of such importance that God would have deigned to write with His finger, "You shall not steal," but there is clear testimony that the very opposite is the case, namely that God did not regard the private ownership, acquisition, possession, use, and sharing of outward or physical goods as something unworthy of His concern, because with His own finger He wrote both "You shall have no other gods" as well as "You shall not steal." In the same way Paul in 1 Thess. 4:6 says, "The Lord is the avenger in all these things." Prov. 16:11, "A just weight and balance are the Lord's, and all the weights in the bag are the Lord's works." In Luke 16:1ff. the parable of the householder shows that God as the Father of the family gives to men, as His dispensers, the possession of physical goods to use and to share according to the word of His will and indeed in such a way that He affirms that He will demand an accounting of their stewardship. This, therefore, is the closest objective of the

Seventh Commandment, that it bears witness that it is the will and ordinance of God that in the society of men there be a definite distinction of ownership, the lawful acquisition of goods and benefits, and the possession, sharing, and use of them. He shows that this must be maintained not only because of human regulations, but that lawful exchange of property is approved by Him in human society and defended by Him, and He even threatens that He will be an avenger when we violate this lawful practice. For it is not merely an action of chance or blind fortune that each has lawful possession of his property, but it has come about by the distribution of the Lord. Therefore, for the sake of God, we must keep our hands off the property of others, both because He prohibits theft and because as the father of the family He has given to each his own.

In the third place, we must consider which sins God wishes us to understand under the synecdoche of the thief. Just as Christ derives His interpretation of the Sixth Commandment from the Tenth, that because it speaks of lust for our neighbor's wife He says that in the Sixth not only is the outward act of adultery prohibited but He also condemns the lust in the heart, thus because the Ninth Commandment speaks of coveting our neighbor's house, He shows that in the Seventh we must issue warnings not only regarding external pleasures but also regarding the very root of these evils, namely the inherited greed of our heart. Therefore there is use for a word of this kind which refers to underhanded machinations which escape the notice of another person, in order to show that inner sins also are included here. In Matt. 15:19 Christ wants us to recognize that inward sins of the heart must also be considered under the Seventh Commandment, as the source and root of stealing, for He says, "from the heart come . . . thefts."

Therefore the inward sins in conflict with the Seventh Commandment are called "avarice" or "covetousness." But it is not covetousness when someone in his vocation labors hard or works at a legitimate business, and in doing so, seeks and awaits a blessing from God whereby he might be enriched. For, says Paul in 1 Cor. 9:10, "He who plows should plow in hope." And "the blessing of God is given to the woman who reveres the Lord," Prov. 31:30. Nor is that man working in a covetous manner who, aside from inclusion in the kingdom of heaven, is so constituted that if God gives him more, he accepts it with thanks. For Paul says in Phil. 4:12, "I know how to live simply and how to enjoy prosperity." But covetousness is condemned when it stands in opposition to self-sufficiency, that is, when a person is not content with the lot in life which God in His kindness has given to him, but murmurs against God, is jealous of the prosperity of others, and desires to have more than the blessing of God has granted him through lawful means. Thus Phil. 2:4, "Neither must each look out only for his own interests but also for those of others." In 1 Tim. 6:10 he calls it "the love of money" when people seek after riches not to use them properly and share them, but when they love riches for themselves. This is a lack of confidence from which arises an anxiety about one's physical sustenance. Matt. 13:22; "The care of the world" does not truly and from the heart entrust our path to God, that is, such a person in doing the work of his calling does not have the confidence and hope that, if he does his duty, God will bestow upon him an abundance of the necessities of life, but rather his heart compels him to think only about his desire for money, even unjustly obtained. We must note the progression of these inner sins: (1) sinful desires, greediness or covetousness, lack of confidence in God and despair, which by nature inheres in all men because of the root of our corrupt mass. First they entertain the idea in their mind and then under a certain compulsion they begin to steal, as James 1:14 says. (2) When men no longer fight against this lust and begin to enjoy it, as Paul says, 1 Tim. 6:10, "Some people eagerly seek money," and in Prov. 9:17 and 20:17 Solomon says, "Bread which is stolen in secret is sweet," that is, if we can have it, we do not care whether we get it by lawful means or at the disadvantage of our neighbor. (3) When the premeditated desire for unlawful gain has obviously taken possession of us. (4) The person plots and plans frauds and evil schemes, Micah 2:1–2, "Woe to you who plot evils on your bed and in the morning you carry them out. You covet fields and take them by violence." 1 Tim. 6:17, "Do not put your trust in riches"; Ps. 62:11, "Set not your heart upon riches . . . so that you forget the fear of God."

Scripture divides the external sins against the Seventh Commandment into two general categories: unlawful thievery (*furtus*) and robbery (*rapina*), Luke 8:11ff.; 1 Cor. 6:8–9. For when someone's property is taken from him, whether by stealth or openly and by force, this is called robbery (*rapina*). And in Scripture are listed the various categories in which it is shown how one sin is more serious than another: (1) Theft (*furtus*) which is laying hands upon the property of another, contrary to the will of God, for the sake of making money. (2) Stealing or robbery (*rapina*) which takes place openly and by force. Furthermore, it is correct to say that robbery is committed also by extortion, tribute, or plundering. In many passages of Scripture robbery is condemned: Job 29:9; Luke 3:14; Ezek. 18:10; Hab. 2:8. (3) Embezzlement, a theft which is committed against the government either by withholding or by not paying money which is owed to the commonwealth. Those who falsify accounts or debase the coinage are called thieves of the state. Pertinent here also are those who plunder the public treasury, Micah 3:2–3; 1 Sam. 8:3; 1 Kings 21:2ff. Related to this is cheating or purloining, Titus 2:10, cf. Acts 5:2–3, where it applies to matters of our faith, also 2 Cor. 8:20–21. (4) Sacrilege in those matters which pertain to the support of the ministry and the maintenance of the poor, Acts 5:2, Ananias and Sapphira.

2 Chron. 28:21, Ahaz took away all the vessels of the temple. In Neh. 13:5 the public room for sacrifices in the temple had been turned to the use of a private citizen, and in v. 10, "The portions for the Levites had not been given to them." 2 Macc. 3:7, the treasures of the temple were plundered. (5) Kidnapping, 1 Tim. 1:10–11; Ex. 21:7; Deut 24:7; Gen. 37:28; 40:15. (6) Prov. 22:28; Deut. 19:14; 27:17, "You shall not remove the ancient landmarks."

These things, whether secret or open, are cases of withholding, because the word *gānab* refers to this kind of machination which is done without the knowledge of the other person, so that he does not realize that he is being defrauded. Thus Paul lays the charge of unrighteousness against robbers. The word "unrighteousness" covers all sins in the matter of financial relationships, as Paul says in 1 Thess. 4:6, "Let no man overstep the bounds and take advantage of his brother in business." Therefore all unfair and illegal contracts are forbidden, such as usury and other illegal practices. Indeed in lawful contracts and business affairs all unfairness, fraud, thievery, and pretense are forbidden, as Moses in Lev. 19:11–15, 35–36 clearly makes such a distinction in interpreting the Seventh Commandment, cf. Lev. 19:35–36.

The prophets also speak of these varieties of stealing: Sin is committed in business matters and contracts (1) by use of debased money, Is. 1:22; Amos 8:6; (2) by unfair prices, Amos 8:6; Job 31:39–40; (3) by false measure, weight, or money, Deut. 25:13–15; Prov. 20:23; Lev. 19:35; Micah 6:10–11; Amos 8:5; (4) by dishonesty in wording and other deceptions, Jer. 5:27; Micah 6:12; Jer. 9:4–5; (5) by seeking only our own things, without love for our neighbor, Is. 5:8; (6) by refusing to take the time and opportunity for acts of charity, Amos 8:5; Prov. 11:26; (7) by making pretext and appearance of fulfilling the Law, Luke 3:14; Micah 2:2; Lev. 19:13; Is. 10:1–2; Zeph. 3:3; Is. 1:23.

Further, the general rule is stated in Eph. 5:11, "Have no part in the sins of others." Likewise Rom. 1:32, "Not only those who do wrong but also those who give approval. . . ." This rule has established another new category of sins against the Seventh Commandment. Scripture clearly notes, Is. 1:23, that "the princes are the companions of thieves." Ps. 50:18, "When you saw a thief, you were his friend." Prov. 29:24, "He who has a thief for his partner hates his own soul." Here are pertinent the circumstances of being party to another person's sins, of which we have spoken in the locus on sin, namely that we do so by committing the sin, commanding it, advising it, consenting or hiding it, as is the case with those who give shelter to robbers, thus sharing in their crimes, or those who buy stolen goods, or in bad faith keep back part of the merchandise, or by giving permission when they could have stopped the robbery, or by keeping silence they aid and abet and contribute to their sins. Here are also pertinent the sins of commission or neglect, as when a person gives opportunity for a loss or injury to be suffered, or seems to have given this opportunity, Ex. 22:6, "If a fire breaks out . . ."; or v. 10, "If a man has agreed to keep an ox or an ass for another person . . ."; v. 7, the case of a person who has agreed to keep some money for another person. If some property is found and not restored . . . such a case applies to this category. Augustine's opinion is: "If you find a certain thing and do not return it, you have stolen it. If you cannot find the owner, you have done what you could, you cannot do more. He who keeps the property of another, if he can return it, has stolen it. For God examines the heart and not the hand." And in the *Digests* regarding thieves it says: "He who for profit picks up what another man throws on the ground is guilty of theft whether he knows it or not."[17] For the definition of thievery fits the person who does not restore property which he has found. However, it is another matter when it concerns something considered as thrown away or something which is not among the possessions of the neighbor, such as the birds of the air or the things which grow at large on the land.

Here we have made a listing on the basis of the negative terms under this precept. Later we shall list the virtues or good works which apply to the Seventh Commandment. The antithesis will show that there are many sins involved here. In this way the list can be divided, as Christ does under the Fifth and Sixth Commandments. There is thievery in the heart and in the eye: Prov. 23:5, "Do not set your eyes on wealth which you cannot possess"; 27:20, "The eyes of men are never satisfied." [There is thievery] with the tongue and with words, by deception and by deed. Likewise some sins are committed in the acquisition of wealth, others in retaining it, others in its use, and still others in distributing it. It is useful to list the various ways these sins occur, for the human mind is beclouded by so great a darkness that Psalm 19:12 speaks correctly when it says, "Who can understand his errors?" Yet, because we must have some understanding of our sin, it is useful to look at some of them in different ways.

In the fourth place, we must determine the positive or affirmative side of this precept, that is, the virtues or the good works of the Seventh Commandment. Under this precept these points should be stressed primarily, which we have also emphasized under the Sixth on the basis of Christ's explanation, namely: (1) The sins which have been stipulated from the negative aspect must be listed. (2) The affirmative statement regarding the good works must be placed in opposition. (3) Again, other and more sins can be demonstrated and recognized on the basis of the affirmative by way of antithesis. Also we must begin from the point of inner obedience, that is, our conscience, which has been reconciled with God

---

[17] The reference to *Digests* probably applies to the Pandects of Justinian, a remnant of which still applied in Chemnitz's time to the remains of the empire.

through faith in the Mediator, must be sure that its calling pleases God, or is in agreement with His Word and His way, that is, when the person faithfully performs the duties of his calling, commends himself to God, seeks His blessing, and, trusting in His promises, awaits from Him a happy outcome, the support and the other necessities of life. And there must also be present self-sufficiency, cf. 1 Tim. 6:8, namely that our heart should be content with its lot and receive with gratitude and joy the blessing which God has given and not look with jealous eyes on the fortunes of others and despise its own. Phil. 4:11, "I have learned in whatsoever state I am, therein to be content." Heb. 13:5, "Be content with what you have." The antithesis is the person who carries out his calling without specific testimony in the Word of God or is in conflict with Him. Likewise those who are discontented, who are always dissatisfied with their present lot and who are tossed about by impatience of vain hopes, are always flitting from one kind of life to something new, the kind of people Solomon is describing in Ecclesiastes. Rather, we should obey God in our poverty and patiently and honorably bear ill fortune in regard to our property. Phil. 4:12, "I know how to be abased and how to abound, how to be full and how to be hungry, how to be rich and how to be poor," cf. Heb. 10:34; Prov. 30:8–9.

In the external works of the Seventh Commandment (such as the prohibition, "Thou shalt not steal," where the antithesis is already given) the first place, belongs to:

[1.] The just exchange of property, where the distinctions of property holding and ownership are not upset by acts of robbery and other such things and which maintains equity and truthfulness in business matters.

2. Industriousness in performing the duties of our calling, Eph. 4:28; 2 Thess. 3:10–12; 1 Thess. 4:11–12. It is worthwhile to consider how the apostles also add the antithesis to the affirmative side of the precept. (1) They vigorously opposed slothfulness, of which Solomon says a great deal in his Proverbs. Paul calls it "not working." He also opposes unnecessary begging when he says, "Let them eat their own bread," and again, "Be dependent on nobody." They command us to have a calling which is in keeping with the Word of God, that is, to work in an honorable manner. In Eph. 4:8 he speaks of "performing that which is good." In 1 Tim. 6:18 the one word, *agathoergein*, "being rich in good works," he puts in opposition to the busybodies of 2 Thess 3:11, people who carry on activities which have no useful purpose in life, practices such as being meddlesome, treasonous, or hypocritical. In 1 Tim. 3:3, 8, he opposes those who are "greedy of filthy lucre." Paul here also refers to quietness, which applies to the proper performance of the duties of one's calling, and he puts it in opposition to these sins. In 1 Peter 4:15, "Busybodies in other men's affairs" is a popular term for *polypragmosynē* (meddlesomeness), which refers to injecting oneself

into someone else's calling and causing a disturbance by neglecting the necessary duties of one's own calling.

3. Paying to all what we owe them, such as tribute or taxes, Rom. 13:7. 1 Tim. 5:18, "The laborer is worthy of his pay"; cf. Tobit 4:14; 1 Cor. 9:7; James 5:4; Jer. 22:13; Lev. 19:13; Ecclus. 34:22. Also pertinent here are the statements concerning lazy and diligent workmen. Ecclus. 19:1 and 40:18; cf. 2 Cor. 11:13, "deceitful workers," and Phil. 3:2, "evil workers."

4. Many virtues are involved with the true and godly use of riches: 1 Cor. 7:30–31, "Those who buy as though they had no goods and those who use this world as though not using it"; cf. 1 Tim. 5:8; 6:17; Mark 10:24; Matt. 13:22; Ps. 62:10; Eccl. 5:10–17. At this point we think of thrift which tries to save money and use it properly, which does not squander it in unnecessary purchases.

5. Scripture also gives directions regarding the sharing of our resources through contributions, loaning, and pledging: Ps. 37:21, "The righteous man every day shows mercy and shares"; 112:5, "Blessed is the man who lends and shows mercy"; cf. Deut. 15:8; Luke 6:35. The antithesis is: Do not refuse to give a loan when you can, Deut. 15:9; Luke 6:34; Ex. 22:25–26; Ezek. 33:15; Isaiah 28; Ps. 37:21; Ecclus. 29:4, 25; Prov. 22:7.

6. In Eph. 4:28 Paul clearly shows that kindness and generosity pertain to the Seventh Commandment, "so that the person can give to him who has need"; 1 Tim. 6:18; Heb. 13:16, 2. The antithesis is seen in 1 John 3:17, "He who has this world's goods . . . and closes his heart to his brother who is in need . . ."; James 2:16; Prov. 21:13; 3 John 10; 2 Cor. 8:13; 1 Thess. 2:9; 2 Thess. 3:8; 1 Tim. 5:16; Ecclus. 34:21. I shall speak further regarding almsgiving under that locus.

7. Luke 19:8, "If I have defrauded anyone, I restore it fourfold"; Ezek. 33:14, "If he gives back what he has taken by robbery . . . he shall surely live." Augustine, Epistle 54 [153M] *ad Macedonium* [MPL 33.662], "The worst thing about the human race is that a man to whom the medicine of repentance has been of no benefit still wants the punishment of his crime to be removed on the grounds that he has confessed it. For if he has not returned the other person's property on account of which the crime was committed, even though he could have done so, he has not really repented but only pretended to do so. But if he really has repented, there is no remission of sin unless he has made restitution.

Thus there is an order of good works relating to the Seventh Commandment: Some apply to the acquisition of wealth, some to the way an individual spends it, some to the sharing and giving of it which takes place either in our normal civil life (as in the payment of debts, contracts and loans) or in generous giving.

[V.] In the fifth place, in order that we may recognize the enormity of the sins against the Seventh Commandment, God adds certain warnings. Some passages of Scripture seem to excuse the sin of theft, such as Prov. 6:30–32, "A thief is not despised if he steals to satisfy his hunger . . . but an adulterer destroys his own soul"; cf. Ecclus. 5:14; 20:25. But these passages are speaking of a comparison in which one sin is greater than another, but this does not simply absolve a thief from his guilt. Thus Ecclus. 20:25 adds, "Both will come to the same bad end." Many warnings testify to this: 1 Cor. 6:10; Eph. 5:5; and Col. 3:5, "Make no mistake, neither thieves nor greedy men . . . nor extortioners shall inherit the kingdom of God"; cf. Deut. 27:17; Is. 5:8; Prov. 20:23; Ezek. 18:10–13; 1 John 3:17; Prov. 21:13; Hab. 2:6ff.; Job 20:19ff.; 27:8; also Jer. 7:7; Micah 4:3, 6:13; Prov. 11:1, 26; 20:23; 21:6–7; 22:16; 23:5; 28:8, 22, 28; 27:4. Regarding envy, Prov. 6:11; 24:30ff.; Ecclus. 5:1; 10:9; 11:10; 31:5; Luke 12:15; 1 Thess. 4:6; Ps. 15:5; Is. 33:1; Hab. 2:8; Ex. 21:16; Deut. 24:7; Ex. 22:1–3.

At this point, the question is asked whether it is lawful to suspend the punishment of a thief even though the divine law has not called for a lessening of the punishment. The correct answer is that the regulations of Moses do not govern our civil laws in a binding way as to what punishments we can lay upon criminals, in keeping with the rule that there be general peace and tranquility and that wickedness be deterred and violence curbed, so that others might fear the Law. For there is need of an example for many shiftless people. God Himself in the civil law of Moses shows that the punishment for a thief could be lessened or increased in keeping with the circumstances of the case and that some things were to be returned fourfold and others fivefold; in some cases the thieves were to be sold and in others put to death. Likewise, the Mosaic law determined that a thief who was thought to be dangerous could be lawfully put to death even without a trial. It is noteworthy that Solomon in Prov. 6:31 shows that in the passing of time even in the law of Moses thieves could not be compelled to undergo the punishment of the Mosaic law but that the magistrates had determined that certain people must make a sevenfold restitution and that certain were to be punished by the confiscation of all their goods. These basic principles show the rationale that the punishment for theft could be made harsher and the statement of Chrysostom is cited: Where a loss can be repaid a man must not pay with his life. But under the Mosaic law a man who was guilty of kidnapping must be put to death, even if he could make restitution.

As examples of punishments see Joshua 7:24ff., the case of Achan; 2 Kings 5:27, Gehazi; 2 Macc. 1:16–17 and 4:24, the penalty of sacrilege; 1 Sam. 25:38, Nabal denies the kindness of David; Luke 16:22ff., the rich man and Lazarus; Matt. 25:41, the final judgment; cf. James 5:2. Furthermore Eccl. 5:10, 6:1ff.; Ecclus. 14:3ff. show that the experience of all ages bears witness to the punishment of greedy people; 1 Sam. 15:23, Saul against the command of God retains the booty; 2 Macc. 10:22, Maccabaeus killed those who were corrupted by money.

We must note that there are so few examples cited in Scripture because we see so many examples in our own daily life, cf. Ecclesiastes 6 and Ecclesiasticus 14.

As examples of promises see Heb. 13:16; Matt. 5:7; Deut. 15:10; 24:13; Ex. 23:11; Deut. 24:19; 26:12; Is. 58:8; Ezek. 18:9; Dan. 4:27; Tobit 4:11; Ecclus. 4:1; 7:36; 14:13; Prov. 11:26; 19:17; 11:3, 21; 22:9; 28:27; Ecclus. 11:22–26; 12:2, 29:15; 35:4; 41:26 (Vlg.); Ps. 15:5; 112:6; 112:3; Matt. 6:4; 10:42; Luke 6:38; 11:41; 14:14; 18:22; 1 Peter 5:7; Ps. 55:22; 34:10; 128:2; 2 Cor. 9:10; Job 31:20; Prov. 3:10.

Examples of rewards: Ruth 2:12; 3:10; Luke 5:6, Peter's catch of fish; 2 Kings 4:13, the Shunammite woman; Matt. 25:34, the last judgment; Luke 16:9, "They shall be received into everlasting habitations"; Acts 10:4, Cornelius's works of charity; Gen. 30:43, Jacob is blessed; Ex. 12:36, the children of Israel receive as a reward for their labors the spoils of the Egyptians; Ex. 23:11; Deut. 24:19; 26:15, their fields are blessed; Acts 9:36, 40, Tabitha "filled with good works."

The Eighth Commandment: "Thou Shalt Not Bear False Witness"

[MELANCHTHON'S TEXT]

This Law protects judgments and treaties and contains the most beautiful of all virtues, truth, the value of which is most widely evident in teaching, in legal judgments, in treaties or contracts, and in our daily life. For all corruptions of doctrine which take place through fraud or the pride of human reason are violations of this commandment, as well as all spoken slanders, verbal game-playing, falsifications regarding human activities, all sophistries, all statements made either out of hypocrisy or are insinuated in some other manner and do not clearly demonstrate what the person believes or what his nature really is. These things which are manifest in our daily life must be carefully considered, so that we truly and earnestly learn to hate all sophistry and double-talk.

The Eighth Commandment

[I]

The first thing to be considered is the synecdoche. "Thou shalt not bear false witness against thy neighbor." It is manifest that these words have their origin in the legal system which God had established in the government of Moses, "In the mouth of two or three witnesses every word must stand," Matt. 18:16; Deut. 17:6 and 19:15. Thus this particular kind of lying is mentioned by name; when a witness is given in court and questions are being asked about a certain case, a person must answer truthfully. We must note that the judicial system itself and the office of judge are established and formalized under the Fourth Commandment. But the Eighth Commandment approves, establishes, and strengthens these judicial activities, such as prosecutions, accusations, defenses, testimonies, and other judicial duties for whatever reason. Thus by this very ordering of things the Decalog refutes those who even though they do not dare to condemn the judicial system yet disapprove if someone takes a case to court.

Furthermore it is clear that there is here as in the other commandments a synecdoche whereby under one classification which is expressly designated there is included a general hatred of lying, because Christ in Matt. 19:18 and Mark 10:19 and Paul in Rom. 13:9 simply include the Eighth Commandment under the simple expression "You shall not bear false witness." The concept of a testimony or bearing witness in Scripture are not only courtroom words, but have the general meaning of affirming something with great seriousness. The witness of the Baptist is called a testimony in John 1:7, 8, 15, 19, 32 and 34. 1 Cor. 15:15 says, "We are found false witnesses of God, because we bore witness against God that He raised Christ from the dead. . . ." In Titus 1:13 the testimony of Epimenides is true. Likewise when Scripture uses the joint expression "He replied and said," this is a very strong assertion. Therefore, the apostles, when they are giving an explanation of the Eighth Commandment, speak in a general sense, e.g., Eph. 4:25, "Lay aside falsehood and let each speak the truth with his neighbor."

[II]

Second, it is certain that many more sins are in conflict with the Eighth Commandment than only bearing false witness in court.

But the question is: By what line of reasoning can a catalog of the sins against the Eighth Commandment be established? God in the Decalog itself shows the correct method. Because He clearly designates that particular kind of lying which takes place in courts and involves legal actions, He therefore is indicating that the explanation or interpretation of the Eighth Commandment can be properly divided into various categories by the subject matter under discussion as to whether it is the truth or a lie. Moses himself seems to be pointing to this method when he says in Lev. 19:16, "You shall not act against the life of your neighbor, lest you be an accuser or a tale-bearer." A person shall not deceive his neighbor, that is, in contracts or other business matters. But the Decalog adds the words "against your neighbor," which seems to indicate the final purpose of the Eighth Commandment, namely that we dutifully cultivate the truth, not only in those matters which pertain to the name of God under the Second Commandment or in areas where legal requirements necessitate the use of an oath, but in our normal life in society, in our daily conversations, and our ordinary dealings with our neighbor, for God abominates lying and demands that we be zealous for the truth. These are the main points in explaining this commandment.

The first kind of lying which is specifically mentioned in the Decalog is concerned with legal judgments. Because giving testimony is a part of the legal process, all these fraudulent activities are involved here: lying, flattery, slander, and other forms of perversity in court. For He who prohibits a false witness, certainly does not give His approval to a participant in a trial giving a false accusation or a judge handing down an unjust verdict. Although courtroom sophistries are almost limitless, yet they can be categorized into matters pertaining to the legal aspects of the case.

1. We have the judge who brings forward false and unjust evidence, or who makes a judgment when the case has not been completely explored or all evidence has not been heard. Lev. 19:15–16, "Judges must be just in their sentences, neither being partial to the poor nor showing deference to the powerful; you are to judge your neighbor fairly . . . you are not to act against the life of your neighbor. I am the Lord." In this passage you will note that Moses is clearly referring to the Eighth Commandment, cf. Deut. 27:19, 25; 16:18–20; Prov. 17:15; Is. 5:23; Acts 16:37; Luke 18:4.

2. We have the participant in the trial who makes a false and slanderous accusation against someone, as in 1 Kings 21:9–10, where Jezebel accuses Naboth. In Luke 23:2 the priests accuse Christ before Pilate on the grounds that He was prohibiting paying tribute to Caesar. Acts 24:5, Tertullus the orator accuses Paul of sedition. 1 Cor. 6:6ff., Paul makes reference to those who out of an inordinate desire for litigation, for any kind of reason, immediately go to law against their neighbor, even when other remedies are at hand.

3. We have the instance of the guilty party who by his lying commits a crime or glosses over his case in a way that is contrary to good conscience. Joshua 7:19, "Give glory to God and confess your sins and receive your judgment."

4. Then there are false witnesses who are clearly mentioned by name in the Decalog. False witnesses are not only those who devise falsehoods, but also those who pervert the truth, as "He spoke of destroying the temple," Matt. 26:61, where they either affirmed something of which they had no information or were maliciously withholding the truth. Thus in 1 Kings 21:14; Matt. 27:13; Acts 5:6; Dan. 6:13 and 13:36 (Vlg.); and Prov. 25:18, "A man who bears false witness against his neighbor is a war club, a sword, or a sharp arrow."

5. There are lawyers who accept false accusations or slanderous defenses, even when the law is clear. Likewise there are those who cover up good evidence. Ex. 23:3, 6, "You shall neither show partiality toward the poor in his case . . . nor deprive him of justice," cf. Job 29:16; Is. 5:23.

The second kind of sin against this commandment is dishonesty in giving counsel. Ecclus. 8:20 (Vlg.), "Do not take counsel with fools." And 37:9, "Keep your heart from an evil counselor." Particularly pertinent here are those who offer bad counsel to rulers, as in Dan. 6:6ff.; as Doeg in 1 Sam. 22:9; the Ziphites in 1 Sam. 26:1; Ahithophel in 2 Sam. 17:1.

The third kind of sin is lying and breaking promises in covenants, treaties, and contracts. Rom. 1:31 includes covenant breakers and those who will not be reconciled. Jeremiah 37 cites the example of Zedekiah. 2 Kings 3:5 cites Moab. There is a notable instance of fidelity in the keeping of a pact and promises in Joshua 9:18 in the case of the Gibeonites. In 1 Tim. 1:10 lying and perjury are included in the same list. And perjury with respect to the name of God is contrary to the Second Commandment, but insofar as it is a violation of an oath on the part of our neighbor, it is deceitful and wrong, contrary to the Eighth Commandment.

The fourth kind of sin is the spreading of false ideas about matters of faith. This pertains to the Second Commandment, but corruptions of other practices and teachings which are useful and necessary in our common life together are in conflict with the Eighth Commandment because they give false witness against our neighbor. This kind of sophistry is harmful to our common life. Note Rom. 1:25; when it speaks of "natural knowledge," it says, "They have turned the truth of God into a lie."

The fifth kind. Any lie which in our life and conversation is committed in our daily speaking either with our neighbor or against him is forbidden. Col. 3:9, "Do not lie to one another." Eph. 4:25, "Speak the truth with your neighbor." Scripture also lists various kinds of lying, such as tale-bearing in Lev. 19:16; backbiting, Rom. 1:30; slandering, 1 Cor. 5:11; reviling, 1 Cor. 6:10; gossiping, Lev. 19:16. Rom. 12:14, "Do not curse a person." Eph. 4:31, "Put away all slander." James 3:2ff. speaks at great length about the tongue as being deceptive. Ps. 12:2, "They speak with double heart," these disputants. Prov. 18:6, "The lips of a fool bring strife." Ecclus. 8:4, "Do not argue with a long-winded man." 1 Peter 2:23, "When He suffered He did not threaten." Prov. 10:18, "He who speaks slander is a fool." Boasters, Rom. 1:30; 2 Cor. 10:12, "He who tells you how good he is." Flatterers, Acts 12:22, "It is the voice of a god and not of a man." Likewise Matt. 7:1; Luke 6:37, "Do not judge or condemn." He who imputes some evil to his neighbor, even if it is true, but if he does not make the accusation by reason of his office or out of a desire to see the person amend his ways or that there might be some consultation with others, but acts either out of ambition or vanity or some other evil intention of his mind, is sinning. Note Luke 6:41; Prov. 20:19; 25:9; Ecclus. 4:30. Revilers, as the boys who ridiculed Elisha with shameful words, 2 Kings 2:23. Michal, in 2 Sam. 6:20, 16. Also at this point pertain those who interpret ambiguous and unlikely statements in a slanderous way. Likewise 2 Cor. 3:1, those who deal in false letters of recommendation.

Sixth. Just as in the Fifth and Sixth Commandments there are sins of gesture, so also a person can lie by his body language, his nodding and his actions, such as expressions which insinuate and seem secretive in his life and his practices. Prov. 6:12–13, "A wicked man speaks with crooked speech, winks with his eyes, scrapes with his feet, and signals with his finger." Luke 20:47, "Making long prayers for appearance sake . . . they shall receive the greater condemnation." Augustine says that pretended piety is a double evil. In 1 Kings 14:2 the wife of Jeroboam tries to deceive the prophet by putting on a disguise. In 2 Sam. 20:9, Joab, as he was about to kill Amasa, kissed him. The same is the case with Judas and Christ in Matt. 26:49; Mark 14:45; Luke 22:47. Here we should also consider such things as suspiciousness, 1 Cor. 13:7, "Love is not suspicious."

Seventh are sins of omission and those things which are called alien, which can easily be understood in individual cases, such as not defending an innocent person, refraining from harming him, etc.; likewise those who consent to people who are doing such things.

These are largely external sins against the Eighth Commandment. But Christ also warns in Matt. 15:19 that the root must be sought within man. For He says, "Out of the heart come . . . false witnesses." Thus it is very easy to note the inward sins against the Eighth Commandment, if we consider the reasons for which lies pour out of us, namely, out of anger, hatred, jealousy, greed, desire for pleasure and approval, or the desire to harm someone, hope or fear, or out of the vanity of our nature which does not seek the welfare of either ourselves or our neighbor, but rather takes pleasure only in his "desire to lie" or the scurrility of reproaches, Ecclus. 7:14, "Refuse ever to tell a lie, for it is a habit from which no good comes." Prov. 24:28, "Do not be a witness against your neighbor without cause." Also there is self-love, so that a person sees the speck in his neighbor's eye, Luke 6:41.

[III]

In the third place, because at this point the question of ordinary lying is pertinent, we shall note the main categories of this subject. Scripture in a general sense prohibits all lying. Eph. 4:25; Ps. 5:6, "You destroy all those who speak lies." Wisd. of Sol. 1:11, "A lying tongue is a man's destruction." 1 John 2:21, "No lie is of the truth." Ecclus. 7:14, "Refuse ever to tell a lie."

But there are in Scripture certain examples of holy people whose lying must not be rashly condemned. Abraham in Gen. 12:13 and 20:2; Jacob in Gen. 27:19; Joseph dissimulated before his brothers in Gen. 42:7 and 44:15. Of the midwives in Ex. 1:19 and in v. 21 it says, "The Lord built them houses." Luke 24:28, Christ pretended that He was going farther on. 1 Sam. 21:13, David pretended to be insane. 1 Sam. 16:5, when Samuel was about to anoint David so that Saul would not find out, he pretended that he must go to Bethlehem to make a sacrifice. 2 Kings 10:19, when Jehu was about to kill the prophets of Baal, he pretended that he was going to make a solemn sacrifice to Baal. Thus also Judith in 11:4ff.; Jael in Judg. 4:18. Joshua in 8:5 pretends to flee, and in Joshua 2:4, Rahab deceives. Ex. 5:3, "We shall make a three-day journey to sacrifice." 1 Sam. 19:13, Michal, the wife of David, frees her husband by lying. 1 Sam. 20:28, Jonathan saves David's life by saying something misleading.

From this arises an argument. Augustine simply says [De Mendacio, 21, MPL 40.516], "Anyone who thinks that there is any kind of lie which is not sin is foolishly deceiving himself." Again [ibid., 6, MPL 40.494], "There is no arrangement, no good purpose, no dispensation whereby permission, human or divine, can be given to tell a lie." Again [ibid., MPL 40.495], "Even if someone flees to you who can be saved from death by your lie, you shall not lie. For it is written, 'The mouth which lies kills the soul,' Wisd. of Sol. 1:11. Thus, since eternal life is lost by lying, we must never lie for the sake of someone's temporal life." And Augustine gives his reasons: (1) Scripture simply and in an all-inclusive way prohibits and condemns all lying. (2) Words have been established, not in order that through them men might deceive one another, but in order that through them they might communicate their thoughts to the understanding of another person. Therefore, to use words for a purpose for which they have not been established, but to deceive, is a sin. Likewise, the commandment of God is that man speak in no other way than he believes in his heart. John says in his First Epistle, 2:21, "He who loves a lie is not of the truth." (3) If a person excuses lying on the ground that sometimes we can help someone by lying, then by the same line of reasoning murders and robberies can take place because sometimes we can help a person by these sins. But when he comes to an explanation for the instances in Scripture which we have mentioned above, he is involved in all kinds of contortions. Sometimes, he says, that for those who are not perfect it is only a venial sin. Sometimes he sets up degrees of lies whereby one lie is more serious than another and yet none is without guilt, although some are not of great guilt. Somewhere he says that things which are said in joking should not be included as sins. Gregory says that it is permitted in the Old Testament but prohibited only in the New Testament. Thus in the case of the midwives in Ex. 1:19, because of the guilt of their lying, their eternal reward was commuted to a temporal compensation in that God caused houses to be built for them. Ambrose brings up this question: God gave Abraham the command to sacrifice his son, yet because he did not want to do it, was that a lie? Jerome gets closer: Sometimes dissimulation is useful and lawful because Christ Himself pretended in Luke 24:28. Even Augustine says [ibid., 4, MPL 40.489], "To conceal the truth is one thing; to say something false or to speak a lie is something else." Others, in order to excuse Abraham for dissimulating before his servants in Gen. 22:5, refer to the mystical sense of the passage. There are many such opinions on this subject in Gratian, Question 22,[18] and in Lombard 3.38 [MPL 192.833–35].

It is manifest that this question is not answered by this variety of opinions, but rather consciences are only more disturbed. Thus we must seek a proper explanation from the true sources which can be correctly applied to all cases. This can be properly done on the basis of the definition of lying. We must note how perilous generalizations can be when used as definitions, as when someone says that it is a lie not to tell the truth. Augustine is correct when he says [*De Mendacio*, 4, MPL 40.491], "A lie is a false indication of the voice with the willful intention of deceiving." The meaning of the Eighth Commandment can be derived from these very words. For the definition of lying which is forbidden and condemned in Scripture, these points are required: (1) Something false must be presented. (2) This arises out of a "double heart," as it says in Ps. 12:2, that is, when the conscience is persuaded that the matter is false which is given out as the truth. For when someone says that he believes a certain thing to be true, even though in itself it is false, this is still not a lie, because it is not done against conscience. Conversely, when someone says something which he believes is false, even though in itself it is true, it is still a lie, because it is said contrary to the conscience of the one saying it. On this basis they make a distinction between lying (*mentiri*) and a lie (*mendacium dicere*). (3) There must be some will or intention of deceiving. A violation of the Eighth Commandment involves speaking against one's neighbor. (4) It is also a lie, when, although there is no desire to harm one's neighbor, a person speaks out of the vanity or pride of his mind and does not have a credible or honest reason. Statements of this kind are the lies of flattery, boasting, and things of this kind. Chrysostom, *In Matt.*, says, "Even if they do not have lies, whom do they deceive, for they are lying to themselves?" Under the heading of a sin of omission is the case of lying by wickedly withholding the truth when it would be right, useful, and necessary to speak it, with the intention of deceiving and harming someone.

From these basic points we can easily settle the question as to whether every lie is a mortal sin. It is a lie to speak falsely when the truth has been covered up, whether because of evil desire to work harm or because of the empty pride of one's own mind. Therefore not every hiding of the truth is a lie. For a lie is not only hiding something, but it involves telling a falsehood instead of the truth. Thus it is not only the concealing of a thing but rather the corrupting of a certain matter, contrary to conscience, something which ought to be said, which

---

[18] Gratian wrote his famous *Decreta* at Bologna about 1148. His work marks the high point of canon law. See his writing on lying, *causa* 22, *quaestio* 2, col. 1310–12. The title is *Concordia Discordantium Canonum*.

constitutes a lie. Therefore this rule is sure and correct: To conceal something for an honest and just cause in matters which need not be said for reasons of right or usefulness, is not a lie. Again, when a willful revelation of something would be a sin, it is not a lie to say or show something else which is indirect, but it is lawful to use figurative language which does not reveal the points under discussion. For example, see 2 Sam. 17:19.

All cases can be evaluated by the use of this rule. Yet the examples of various godly people ought not be imitated indiscriminately. For often in these cases they have fallen into sin out of fear or stupidity. From the basic teaching of the Eighth Commandment we can draw the principle that it does prohibit hiding or distorting that which ought to be said.

This definition is supported by dividing the matter of lying into certain varieties. Augustine lists eight kinds of lying which are cited at great length in Gratian and Lombard:[19] (1) Lying in the teaching of religion. (2) That which not only benefits no one but hurts someone. (3) That which benefits one person in such a way that it hurts someone else. (4) That which is done purely out of the desire to lie and deceive. (5) That which is done from a desire to please. (6) That which hurts no one and profits someone, that is, to avoid hurting his person. (7) That which harms no one and benefits someone in order to avoid harm to his property. (8) That which hurts no one and benefits no one, as in the case of protecting a person from some ailment of his body. Augustine himself correctly brings in this distinction in commenting on Matthew 5, and the scholastics draw from this the commonly held distinction that there are three kinds of lying: malicious, purposeful, and jesting. Thomas adds this distinction, "Certain lies are sinful in that they say too much and others that they say too little."

[IV]

Now that we have established the categories of sins, we must consider the antitheses, or those things which are done in obedience to the Eighth Commandment. Scripture sums this up in one word—truth. Eph. 4:25, "Putting aside lying, let us speak the truth." There is no need for a long list because the same subject revolves around each instance in which lying is dealt with. We must note that Scripture applies the same concept of truth to each of these instances. For example, in regard to judges, Jethro says to Moses in Ex. 18:21, "Provide us with men who have the truth in them." In regard to our civil life together Jeremiah says in 9:5, "They do not speak the truth." Regarding treaties Jer. 5:1 says, "See if you can find a man who seeks the truth." Of our daily speech, Eph.

---

[19] For the eight kinds of lying see his *De Mendacio,* 14, MPL 40.505ff.

4:25, "Let us speak the truth, every man with his neighbor." Matt. 5:37; James 5:12, "Let your speech be 'yes, yes; no, no.'"

A second general virtue under the Eighth Commandment is the careful use of the tongue, concerning which many passages in Scripture instruct us. The commonly mentioned virtues in this category are quietness, courteousness, friendliness, refinement. 1 Peter 3:10 on the basis of Ps. 34:14 says, "Let him refrain his tongue from evil." Prov. 21:23, "He who guards his mouth and his tongue . . ."; Ps. 39:1, ". . . that I may not sin with my tongue; I will guard my mouth"; Prov. 10:19; James 1:19, 26; Eph. 4:29. This virtue again shows other virtues by antithesis, such as Matt. 12:36, "rendering an account for every idle word." See Ecclesiasticus 21 concerning talking too much and ch. 28 regarding rash statements, as we have already noted. I am citing these briefly because they are clear in themselves as statements of antithesis.

[V]

Finally, we must add some warnings and promises along with examples: Zech. 8:17; Prov. 6:16; 12:22; John 8:44; 1 John 2:21; Ps. 5:6; Wisd. of Sol. 1:11; Rev. 21:8; Prov. 19:5, 9; 21:28; 12:13, 27; 13:3, 5; Matt. 7:2; Prov. 21:6; Jer. 9:9; Micah 6:13. See also Ecclus. 6:1; 7:14; 20:26; 20:28; 27:28; Prov. 17:5.

Examples of punishments: Ps. 15:1–2; 1 Peter 3:10; Luke 6:37; Gen. 12:3; Prov. 12:14, 19, 22; 13:2–3; 18:20; 20:15; 22:1; Ecclus. 6:5.

Examples of rewards: Rahab not only gained the preservation of her life, but she was included in the number of the people of God, Joshua 2:14 and 6:25. Likewise Joshua 7:19, "Give glory to God and tell me what you have done." Thus there is a reward after this life. A person should not wonder that there are so few examples of rewards for obedience to this precept recorded in sacred Scriptures. For the statements of promises are given in such a way that they do not lead us to a consideration of the examples of the ancients so much as to a view of the blessing of God in our daily experience and in all ages.

The Ninth and Tenth Commandments

[MELANCHTHON'S TEXT]

The Ninth and Tenth Commandments add an explanation in order that by the law of God we may know not only regarding the outward works of a particular commandment, but also that the evil which clings in the depraved nature of man, which they call concupiscence, is also under accusation and condemnation. For not only does the Law here condemn these wicked desires to which we give consent, as they call it, but it also condemns this wicked inclination itself which is a kind of continual turning away from God and a stubbornness which is in conflict with the law of

God and which produces an infinite confusion of desires, even if consent is not always given. Concerning this constant evil Paul says in Rom. 8:7, "the mind of the flesh is hostile to God; it does not submit to God's law and it cannot do so." Nor should this hostility toward God be regarded as a trifling evil, for it includes many troublesome qualities, such as doubt concerning God, turning away from Him, and raging against Him when we are punished. This hostility also includes innumerable vagrant and erring desires and feelings which are against the law of God, such as confidence in our own wisdom or powers, contempt for other people, jealousy, ambition, avarice, the flames of lust, desire for revenge. All of these concepts Paul includes under the term "hostility," in which we must also understand guilt. These qualities are in conflict with God, and God in turn is angry at these evils, even though for the sake of His Son He overlooks them in the believers. What Paul here calls hostility toward God in other places he calls "concupiscence," which describes the corrupt inclination and depravity of all our desires. From this it becomes clear that no man who is born in this state of corruption fulfills the law of God, because of this wicked concupiscence, which Paul in Romans 7 testifies is sin and which remains in our mortal nature. Later on, in ch. 8 he calls it enmity against God and adds that it cannot be made subject to the law of God, and for this reason it is condemned in the Decalog. At this point we must give this warning in order that the greatness of God's grace may be seen and the doctrine of faith can be understood.

Furthermore we must also add this: Although in the individual commandments mention is not made of rewards and punishments, yet we must understand that the promises and threats do pertain to the individual precepts and are repeated over and over again. The summary of the promises is expressed in these words, "He who does these things shall live in them," Lev. 18:5. The summary of the threats is, "Cursed is he who does not continue in all the things which are written in the Law," Lev. 27:26; Gal 3:10. But we must understand that all the promises of the Law are conditional, that is, they require the condition that a person does nothing against the Law. But since the Law always accuses us, these promises would be vain unless we learn from the Gospel how we are to be accounted righteous and how our incipient obedience to the Law is pleasing to God. The promises attached to the Law are accounted to the righteous by faith for the sake of Christ, because God has accepted this obedience. Therefore He gives both temporal and spiritual rewards in keeping with this statement: "Give and it shall be given to you," Luke 6:38. Likewise, Ps. 33:19, ". . . to deliver their soul from death and to nourish them in famine." Later on we must speak fully concerning the difference between Law and Gospel and between the promises attached to the Law and those which belong to the Gospel. Also remember this, that the social or political order is truly a work of God, just as much as the order of the movement of the heavenly bodies, and therefore God regularly is presenting both His promises and His threats in the area of civil justice among men. Outward heinous crimes are threatened with clear punishments, even if the public officers fail to do their duty. Even if murderers escape from the hands of the magistrate, yet they are still in a miraculous way brought to their punishment. Even if the civil law fails to punish perjurers, adulterers, or those corrupted by the lusts of incest, yet history and our daily experience bear witness that they are weighed down by all kinds of misfortunes. The Law is witness that these things have happened by God's intervention, as it says in Ex. 20:7, "The Lord will not hold him guiltless." Again, Heb. 13:4, "God will judge fornicators and adulterers." On the other hand, God aids upright rulers, as the good order and freedom from wars in their nations constantly demonstrate. Therefore the material promise is added to the Fourth Commandment, which deals with man in society, ". . . that you may live long on the earth."

The Ninth and Tenth Commandments

The meaning of these last two commandments is not as clear as the others and for this reason there have been many arguments and disagreements about the true understanding of them. The rest of the commandments have some aspect which pertains to outward discipline; to these two commandments principally applies the statement of Paul in Rom. 7:14, "The law is spiritual." 1 Cor. 2:14 says, "The natural man does not receive the things which are of the Spirit of God because they are spiritually discerned." The Jews interpreted concupiscence as occurring when a sin is not actually committed but there are clear and definite signs of the intent to commit sin, as when a man is caught with his neighbor's wife, alone with her. Luther cites this case in his description of Exodus 20. This opinion is in keeping with human reason and judgment. For even the civil laws say that no one should suffer punishment for his thoughts, that is, when they are held within boundaries. But when a person's mind progresses on to making an attempt to commit a serious or very great crime, such as rape, or murder, or arson, then his attempt is treated as an action. Eck in discussing this affirms that original concupiscence in the regenerate, when it is not obeyed, cannot be sin which is against the law of God, and that in these two commandments only the act of concupiscence is forbidden, that is to say, when by a complete and deliberate previous determination we give obedience to our concupiscence so that a person's desires are brought to completion. He alleges that Luther explains it this way in his *Catechism* and elsewhere. The scholastic writers and others limit the discussion to only one's home, his ox, and his ass, and assert that inclinations against the First Table are only deformities which are not against but irrelevant to the law of God because the Decalog speaks only of the home, wives, cattle, etc.

It is plain that someone may dare to affirm, or may wish to believe a person who does affirm, that when the Decalog says, "You shall not covet the home, wife, etc.," we are only being accused of evil desires to which we may give assent, but this corrupt inclination itself is contrary to the individual commandments. But because "the law is spiritual," consisting of things which are "spiritually discerned," it is our duty to seek and hold fast to that interpretation which the Spirit Himself has given us. The Son of God Himself shows that the two last commandments must be interpreted in this way so that they are applied to all the precepts of the Decalog. For example, in regard to the Sixth Commandment He gives a very clear instance in Matt. 5:28, and then He immediately adds in vv. 29–30 the general principles, "If your eye or your hand offend. . . ." When in Luke 8:14 He includes among the tares, which are the cares of this life, the deceptiveness of riches and pleasures, He also adds in Mark 4:19 [which is a parallel account], "the desire for other things." Therefore the objects of our sinful lusts are not only the things which are specified in the Decalog, such as home, wife, cattle, etc., but anything which one covets contrary to the law of God. Paul illustrates this point with an even clearer treatment of the sinfulness of concupiscence. I am not sure whether an interpretation of the commandment concerning concupiscence could be developed out of the other passages of Scripture if Paul had not dealt with the matter, so greatly has the understanding of this sin been obscured by the darkness of this corrupted nature of ours. Therefore in order that we may give correct and careful consideration to the fundamental points of Paul's teaching, we shall note the principal points of his position.

1. He says in Rom. 7:7, "I would not know covetousness (*concupiscentia, epithymia*) if the Law did not say, 'You shall not covet.' " But Paul was not a cyclops[20] who "held the truth of God in unrighteousness," or suppressed the truth, Rom. 1:18. Rather, he had been "brought up from childhood in the Law," Acts 22:3, and in this respect he was "blameless," Phil. 3:6. Thus, would he be in ignorance or doubt as to whether it is a sin when someone with deliberate forethought or choice plans and proposes something evil, or when the will proceeds to making the attempt? Even the Philosopher in discussing incontinence speaks clearly in his *Ethics* on this subject [*Nicomachean Ethics*, 7.1.1145a]. He even defines it as being an evil disposition or attitude of the will. Therefore, when Paul says such a sin as concupiscence is condemned in these precepts, which he says that he himself did not know how to understand before he learned the Law in a spiritual sense, it is certain that not only is this concupiscence condemned which even the philosophers recognize and include among the vices of men, as when

---

[20] The reference to a cyclops is first of all a reference to the cyclops of Greek mythology. However, according to the Oxford English Dictionary, s.v., in the time of Chemnitz (perhaps based on the idea of only one eye) the term was applied to "Epicureans who made war on God." Calvin used the term in this way.

a man adds consent to his wicked desires; but particularly that kind of concupiscence is condemned which not only the philosophers but even the Pharisees, who wanted to be doctors of the Law, had to recognize as sin.

2. Still more clearly he notes and describes what concupiscence is of which the commandments specifically speak. For he shows the difference between concupiscence in itself and when it obeys the desires of the flesh. Rom. 6:12 and Gal. 5:16, "You shall not fulfill the lusts or concupiscence of the flesh." Thus also in James 1:14–15 concupiscence is present and twists us in every direction, pushes us, and finally "when the desire has been conceived, gives birth to sin."

3. When he wishes to show that our original evil is sin which conflicts with the law of God, he takes his terminology from these two precepts and calls it "concupiscence."

4. He clearly shows that there is a synecdoche in these commandments. He says that concupiscence not only conflicts with the Sixth and Seventh Commandments as the words seem to say in the Decalog, but it is against the entire Law, Rom. 7:22–23, "I delight in the law of God in my inmost self, but I see another law in my inner being which is in conflict with my mind"; Gal. 5:17, "The flesh lusts (*concupiscit*) against the Spirit." Then in v. 19, he lists "the works of the Spirit" against which "the flesh is lusting," and these are not only from the Second Table but such things as faith, peace, joy, etc., from the First Table, just as among the "works of the flesh" are listed heresies, idolatry, etc.

This description by Paul is sure and clear. But the question is how to accommodate or apply it correctly to the words of the Decalog which speak of coveting or lusting after our neighbor's home, wife, servants, or beasts of burden. Paul in an expert way shows the rationale. For just as Moses includes other elements in the Fourth Commandment, so Paul brings in the last commandments and does not limit them to home and wife, etc., but simply without adding any attendant circumstances says in a general way, "You shall not covet," and he does this in two passages, Rom. 7:7 and 13:9. Therefore, just as it is said, "You shall not kill, you shall not commit adultery," so also Paul says, "You shall not covet." In 1 Cor. 10:6 he adds the general term "that we not be lustful for evil things." But he uses this general statement (so to speak) to lead us through the individual precepts of each Table, as is seen. Thus Paul's line of reasoning is this: wife, home, servants, etc., are mentioned not because coveting these alone is a sin, but as is the case with the individual precepts, one variety (*species*) of sin is mentioned, not because it alone is to be understood, but in order that through synecdoche all other kinds (*genera*) of evils which the Holy Spirit in the interpretations of the prophets and apostles shows are to be included. In other languages this concept of synecdoche is less clear. But in Hebrew it is well known and familiar that general principles are laid down through specific examples, as in Matt.

5:39, the smiting of the cheek. This is a case of moving from the lesser to the greater. For He who condemns coveting a servant, an ox, or an ass which belong to one's neighbor, certainly does not approve of coveting the life, reputation, or honor of one's neighbor, and much less coveting those things which pertain to the First Table. Luther says the same thing in his *Against the Sabbatarians* when he speaks of the Mosaic additions regarding home, wife, servants, etc. [*Luther's Works*, Amer. Ed., 47.65–98]. For in that civil arrangement there was the kind of distinction between ownership of property and inheritance laws which did not permit transference from one tribe to another. Likewise under Mosaic law the condition of servitude was that in the seventh year slaves were either set free or would bind themselves to their master for life. Therefore a man in an underhanded way could entice to himself the slave of another man if the slave was perhaps going to be set free in the seventh year by his own master. In the same way, because it had been permitted to give a bill of divorcement, they looked for excuses for divorce. Since these practices are not permitted in other societies, Paul is correct and shows wisdom when he separates the attendant circumstances of the Mosaic law and cites only the basic principle, "You shall not covet," just as he does in the case of the Fourth Commandment. In the case of the other commandments the synecdoche is more easily understood, but in the last two it is less clear and less easily noticed, because the inner reason of man neither knows nor understands the sinfulness of this concupiscence.

These points are useful, necessary, and well-reasoned. For it is clear that erroneous ideas have arisen regarding these two commandments, because concupiscence or covetousness is restricted only to those objects which are specifically stipulated in the Decalog. But when that statement "You shall not covet" is given as a general principle, then the meaning is clear and undebatable.

It is absolutely necessary that this explanation of the Ninth and Tenth Commandments be maintained and taught, and this for many reasons: (1) Because it is necessary that original sin be clearly included in each precept of the Decalog, therefore Paul on the basis of these precepts gives it the name of coveting or concupiscence. (2) Even the saints who observe the law of God and walk in His commands need to be encouraged to be concerned about their sins, Ps. 32:6. (3) Even in the good works of the regenerate these last two commandments call attention to the faults, blemishes, sordidness, and imperfection whereby they "war against the judgment of God," Rom. 7:23. For these serious reasons Paul's interpretation must be maintained and we must not allow any sophistry to take it from us. For when this is removed from the Decalog many grave errors are created.

Now having been aided by the light which Paul has shed on these last two commandments by his discussion, we will find it beneficial to consider how

God points out the same things in the Decalog itself, even though in a less direct manner. For in the case of the Fifth Commandment Christ says in Matt. 5:22 that anger is forbidden, which is a desire or lust which hopes for vengeance and thinks evil of the neighbor. Under the Sixth Commandment He clearly says that lusting after or coveting our neighbor's wife is condemned, cf. v. 28. Regarding the Seventh Commandment, Micah 2:1 says, "They lie awake at night plotting evil and rise at dawn to carry out their schemes." Now if the argument is made that since coveting our neighbor's house or wife is prohibited in the Sixth and Seventh Commandments, then what is meant in the Ninth and Tenth when they say, "You shall not covet"? Certainly in the very great brevity of the Decalog it is impossible, isn't it, to have such a repetition that what has already been forbidden in the earlier precepts is now said over again not only once but twice? The answer is that God wanted to show us that the lusting after the wife condemned in the Sixth is a different thing from the coveting condemned in the Tenth Commandment. Likewise the coveting of our neighbor's house which pertains to the Seventh commandment is something different from that which is spoken of in the Ninth. The Sixth Commandment condemns those desires to which we add our intention. For He says, "He who sees a woman to lust after her . . ." Therefore in the last two commandments the coveting does not refer to a situation in which the will has determined and is compelled and moved to do something. This is taken care of in the earlier commandments. But Scripture speaks of two kinds of coveting or concupiscence: the one is that which includes the desires of the heart combined with the intention of the will; the other consists of the first movements, as they call them in the schools, which the Greeks call *propatheia*, the first stage of emotion. This must be understood in the last commandments as the original concupiscence or the corrupt inclination which produces the infinite confusion of the desires, even if it does not always lead to the intention, but it is something which must be crucified or mortified. Human reason does not understand that this kind of concupiscence is in itself guilty of sin and the wrath of God, indeed even in the church the scholastics argue strongly that these first emotions are not sin. Jerome favors the position of the Stoics that this *propatheia* is not a sin. But for this very reason God repeats twice, "You shall not covet"; and not only in one but in two commandments He condemns and rejects this concupiscence. These precepts are stated negatively because the Law was given not to take away sin but to make it "abound," Rom. 5:20. "The strength of sin is the Law," 1 Cor. 15:56; "Sin taking occasion by the commandment worked in me all kinds of concupiscence," Rom. 7:8; "Sin was in the world until Moses," Rom. 5:13; "The law made nothing perfect," Heb. 7:19. Until the clear light of Paul's teaching had been shed on the matter it was not strange that these ideas, which to some degree can be observed in the Decalog, had not been noticed by the Jews, on whose eyes a veil had been placed in their reading of the Old Testament. Let each of us consider whether without Paul as a guide we would dare or be able (since the interpretation of Paul is very clear) to escape and elude error and come to Paul's conclusion. From this one instance we can understand how great a gift of interpretation had been given to the apostles. But in the Decalog it is very clear that the coveting of the last two commandments is not to be limited to the home, the wife, and the beast of burden, for it says, ". . . and all things which are his." Therefore it is clear that He wills that as objects of covetousness there be placed before us everything which belongs to our neighbor, that is, we must consider all the precepts of the Second Table which pertain to our neighbor. But that also to the First Table must be referred this concupiscence in the words of the Decalog is not quite so clear unless we remember that we are commanded to love God with our whole heart, and therefore no coveting must conflict with this love. But Paul deals with this matter much more clearly, as we have shown.

The grammatical meaning of the words sheds some additional light on this matter. Moses writes in Deut. 5:21 and Ex. 20:17 in a way which shows that God in the last two commandments used two words which referred to concupiscence or lusting. The Latin translator tried to show this, for he translates Ex. 20:17a and b, "You shall not covet . . . you shall not desire." But the Latin does not clearly show the distinction between the terms. It is clear in the Hebrew in Deuteronomy. The first is the word 'āwāh, whence is derived the word 'awāh, which refers to the original coveting of concupiscence. It is used in the fourth conjugation or the reflexive, "You shall not cause yourself to covet." For he was trying to show the evil root which has produced this flood of desires. The examples show that 'awāh refers to concupiscence or the corrupt inclination of our nature which produces evil desires, even if the intention has not been made. Ps. 119:133, "Let not iniquity have dominion over me"; Prov. 6:18, ". . . a heart that devises wicked schemes"; Ps. 7:14, "The wicked man conceives evil (concupiscentia), he is pregnant with mischief and he brings forth lies"; cf. Job 15:35. Thus James 1:15 sums up this picture by saying, "Lust (concupiscentia) when it conceives. . . ." The second word is chāmad, which refers to the delight which we take in pleasant, useful, and valuable things. Thus it is a concupiscence or coveting to which is added pleasure along with consent.

There is no doubt that God has willed to show that this concupiscence itself has varying levels, as we have said in the locus on sin regarding the distinction of sins, namely, (1) the urging to sin, as in Romans 7 where the first stirrings are described; (2) the pleasure; (3) the consent or intention; (4) the offering of the members as instruments of unrighteousness. For Scripture by the term "concupiscence" understands not only the first inclination but also the consent and the efforts to consummate the sin. Acts 20:33, "I have desired or coveted (*concupivi*) no man's money"; 1 Cor. 10:6 refers to the lusting of the Israelites. Prov. 6:25; Ecclus. 25:21 and 42:12 refer to the actual lusting after a woman. Zech. 7:10 and 8:17 deal with thinking evil of one's neighbor; Prov. 21:10, "The soul of the wicked desires evil"; 24:15, "Do not lie in wait against the dwelling of the righteous." Lombard in Bk. 2, dist. 24, on the basis of Augustine's *De Trinitate*[21] lists these degrees of covetousness: (1) There are the urgings or promptings which do not arise out of a proposal or deliberate intention but out of a kind of hidden source, so to speak. (2) When the will is not present to carry out these urgings and does not intend to proceed to the act itself, but still for a long period of time toys with the pleasure of some corrupt action, that is, it does not sorrow over these foul ideas but recalls them and enjoys them. (3) When the will thinks of actually performing the act or when the will to do it is present if the opportunity is given. Augustine is correct when he says, if this takes place without prior intention, then it is venial sin. But this is still not to be understood as if the sin in itself were a minor matter unworthy of the wrath of God; but rather in believers who pray that these sins might be covered by the obedience of the Son of God these are venial sins, whereas in the unregenerate they are mortal sins. Even the saints themselves must understand the nature of this concupiscence against which, by the Holy Spirit, they must fight, so that they may deplore this uncleanness and seek to have it covered.

Now after this explanation it is quite possible to understand what kind of concupiscence is forbidden in the last two commandments. For there is such a thing as a holy desire (*concupiscentia*) as in Ps. 119:40, "I long for Your precepts." Luke 10:24, "Many prophets have desired (*concupiverunt*) to see . . ."; 1 Tim. 3:1, "He desires (*desiderat*) a good work"; Luke 22:15, "With desire I have desired. . . ." It is certain that this is not the meaning when the Law says, "You shall not covet." There is also a desire or a coveting of the natural appetites, such as for food, drink, sleep, etc., Luke 15:16, "He would gladly have filled his stomach with the husks"; Luke 16:21, Lazarus desired (*desiderat* or *cupiebat*) to be fed with the crumbs. It is certain that this kind of desiring (*concupiscentia*) is not condemned by the Law because it was present even when our nature was undamaged, as when Adam desired Eve. God uses a word which they call a middle term to show that the desires of our minds and appetites in our nature, our social intercourse, and the spiritual aspects of our lives must be kept in check, and that disorder is condemned. Paul for the sake of showing this distinction, speaks in Col. 3:5 of "evil concupiscence or desire."

On this basis it is possible to set forth a description of this evil concupiscence

---

[21] MPL 192.703.5. He cites Augustine *De Trinitate*, 11.11, MPL 42.996ff.

as being a disorderly "desire of the mind," (*animus* or *mens*), Eph. 2:3; or in the "heart," Gen. 8:21; or in the "will," Eph. 2:3, which is burning or working against the law of God, Rom. 7:23, that is, against each of the commandments of the Decalog, and moving us toward all evil. This doctrine of coveting or concupiscence is not taught for the first time in the New Testament, but God from the very beginning has censured the evil thoughts which are strengthened by the consent of the will. Prov. 6:18, "A heart that devises wicked thoughts"; 15:26, "The thoughts of the wicked are an abomination to the Lord," and "man's very thoughts and inclinations are evil when they are moved and his mind is evil when it devises evil things," Gen. 6:5 and 8:21. Jer. 17:9, "The heart of man is deceitful . . . it cannot be understood." Is. 1:16, "Put away the evil of your thoughts."

We have gone into more detail concerning the sources and fundamental points of the correct interpretation of the last two commandments because in the darkness of our nature the matter is very obscure and difficult, and it is important that this understanding remain firm in the church. For Paul confesses that he himself had learned from the precept "You shall not covet" what he had otherwise not understood, namely that the saints need to pray for the forgiveness of sins, and why the good works of the regenerate cannot be put in the balance over against the judgment of God. Since the Decalog is a rule which shows the knowledge of sin, the locus on original sin must be included under one of the precepts of the Decalog. Paul for this reason calls it concupiscence.

It is noteworthy that God, when He foresaw the coming corruptions in the doctrine of the Law, as if it were only a thing to be warned against out of a philosophic desire for good order, placed in the Decalog itself the norm for interpreting the commandments of God, namely, "You shall not covet." In the same way Augustine also says that the sum of all the negative commandments lies in the words, "You shall not covet." It is obvious that this is the case with the Second Table, for it says, "nor anything which is his." But if some argumentative person says that the precepts of the Second Table are not to be mixed with those of the First Table, the end result is the same in any event. For where in the First Table anything is believed to belong to an opposing desire or concupiscence, then God is simply not being loved "with one's whole heart," and this is something which God demands in the First Table.

If the question is raised as to how we are to draw up a list of sins which are in conflict with these two precepts, the answer is at hand in the things which have already been said. For the Decalog itself shows that the listing of the sins which fall under these precepts must be based on everything which pertains to our neighbor, that is, everything stipulated in the Second Table. When Paul in Rom. 7:24 refers to "another law at war with the law of my mind," and in

Gal. 5:17 says that the "desires of the flesh are against the Spirit," he is trying to say that a catalog of our sinful desires or concupiscence involves the precepts of the First Table, in order that we may know that here there is an accusation against whatever thoughts, emotions, inclinations, desires, pleasures, intentions, temptations, in short, every longing which we feel contrary to any of God's commandments. Degrees of lust or concupiscence have been established, as we have said. Therefore a great catalog shall become evident, based on the order of the individual commandments.

In the same way we can set up a list of the good works required under these precepts, if we refer back to these two points: (1) That is, if we recognize this uncleanness, this depravity, this disorder in the desires of our mind and confess that we cannot satisfy the law of God but rather must deplore these iniquities and pray to have them covered for the sake of the Son our Mediator. (2) Rom. 6:12, "Let not sin reign in your mortal bodies to obey its lusts." Gal. 5:16, "Do not fulfill the desires of the flesh"; 24, "To crucify the flesh with its lusts"; cf. Rom. 6:6; 8:13; 1 Peter 1:14; 2 Peter 2:20; Titus 2:12; Heb. 12:1; Jude 23; Rom. 7:24. Passages such as these should be applied to each of the commandments. For the Holy Spirit through these passages has tried to show by what kind of strategems we are to contend against our lusts; and Scripture shows the very serious reasons why we must not obey our concupiscence. Eph. 4:30, "Do not grieve the Holy Spirit"; Rom. 8:13, "If we live according to the flesh we shall die"; Matt. 5:30 and 18:9, "It is better to enter into the kingdom of heaven having one eye than with two eyes to be cast into hell." Just as Paul in Rom. 6:13 and Col. 3:5 calls the powers of the soul "our members," so Christ also describes our desires by the term "members," Matt. 5:29–30. Here are some warnings: James 1:15, "Concupiscence, when it has conceived, brings forth sin and later death"; Eph. 4:27, "Give no opportunity to the devil"; cf. 2 Peter 2:9; Prov. 17:11; 1 Tim. 6:9; Micah 2:2.

Promises: 2 Peter 1:4, "He has given to us precious and very great promises that we may be partakers of the divine nature, fleeing from the corruption of our concupiscence"; Matt. 5:8; James 4:5–6; 2 Cor. 12:9.

I have not wanted to extend this list because I did not want to weary the reader, for we went through the same passages in connection with the individual commandments. But there is this one reason that in the individual precepts are included both the sins and the good works, and these last two commandments pertain to both falling into these sins and turning away from or rejecting good works, which occurs through our thoughts, inclinations, desires, emotions, love of pleasures, and intentions. For because in the catalog we have placed by name the outward kinds of sins which are involved, it is evident that God has willed through these last commandments to separate the Decalog from the civil laws and from the arguments of philosophers and questions of the natural law. Christ by His example in the case of the Sixth Commandment has shown that the individual precepts of the entire Decalog must be explained through the statement, "You shall not covet."

[C.] THE FULFILLING OF THE DECALOG . . .

The proper order of things would have demanded that the teaching concerning the fulfillment of the Law be attached to the individual precepts, but because this is a general teaching which applies in the same way to each of the commandments, I preferred to place it all under one [chapter] so as to keep the explanation from becoming too lengthy. For this reason we shall be rather brief in speaking of the perfect obedience which the law of God requires and which is impossible for us in this life, as has been said. Therefore are true both "what the law . . . could not do . . ." Rom. 8:3, and "that the righteousness of the law might be fulfilled in us who walk . . . according to the Spirit . . ." v. 4. This doctrine must be zealously taught under each of the individual precepts, both that the Law cannot possibly be fulfilled and yet how we can have the fulfillment of the Law. For in both cases there is danger, and this does not come from ignorance but from pride and arrogance. The Pharisees, because it is written in Ezek. 36:27, "I will cause you to walk in My commandments," imagine that as a result they can satisfy the individual precepts with perfect obedience. The Epicureans, on the other hand, when they hear that no one in this life can give perfect obedience to the law of God, cover up all lapses against conscience with an excuse and imagine and believe that a person neither can nor ought keep anything in the commandments of God. This dream is just as false as the delirium of the Pharisees, for the statements of Scripture regarding the regenerate are clear. Ezek. 36:27, "I will cause you to walk in My commandments"; Jer. 31:33, "I will write My law in their hearts"; Rom. 8:4; 3:31. Therefore in each of the commandments we must show how and to what extent the Law is impossible to fulfill or how it can be fulfilled. We must speak of the distinction between the regenerate and the unregenerate.

Thus for the unbelievers the Law is not so impossible that they cannot to a degree present a kind of outward conformity, for Scripture does speak of a kind of righteousness according to the flesh, as in Heb. 9:10, where mention is made of free choice. But it is impossible for the unregenerate in two ways: (1) The inner obedience of the heart cannot be begun, presented, or completed without faith and the Holy Spirit. (2) This outward obedience itself is not pleasing to God in the unregenerate, nor is it a good work because their hearts are impure and "without faith it is impossible to please God," Heb. 11:6.

When we speak of the regenerate it is correct to say that the Law is fulfilled by them in two ways: (1) by faith and imputation; (2) by the beginning of the new obedience which comes from faith. At the same time it is true that the saints must recognize that they are far away from a perfect fulfillment of the Law in this life.

We must consider each of the individual commandments as to how and to what degree the law of God is impossible for the regenerate in this life. It is not as if with the aid of the Holy Spirit they cannot avoid external lapses or as if the inner desires of the heart to live in conformity with the law of God are not beginning. For the Holy Spirit is given to "renew the mind," Rom. 12:2; "Create in me a pure heart," Ps. 51:10; "He will write His law upon their hearts," Jer. 31:33. But it is impossible because the regenerate in this life, even when they are led by the Holy Spirit, cannot satisfy the first or the last of the commandments, they cannot remove their concupiscence, and thus cannot give obedience from their whole heart. For nothing contrary must be felt in the mind, the will, the heart, or the members. This is impossible. In each of the individual precepts we must demonstrate the concupiscence which renders perfect obedience impossible in this life even among the regenerate, so that they do not in a mindless and impudent way say that they can satisfy the law of God.

Yet the perfect fulfillment of the Law is absolutely necessary, for it is written in Matt. 5:18, "Heaven and earth shall pass away before one jot or tittle passes from the Law." But because this is impossible for us, Scripture says in Rom. 8:3–4 and v. 1, "What was impossible for the Law because it was weak through the flesh, God accomplished by sending His Son . . . for sin, and condemned sin, in order that the just requirement of the Law might be fulfilled in us, so that . . . there might be no condemnation for those who are in Christ Jesus." Matt. 5:17, "I have not come to destroy the Law but to fulfill." To the believers through faith the Father "gives along with His Son all things," Rom. 8:32. Again, Gal. 3:13, "Christ has redeemed us from the curse of the Law"; Gal. 4:4–5, "God sent forth His Son, made under the Law, to redeem those who were under the Law"; Rom. 10:4, "Christ is the fulfillment of the Law to righteousness for everyone who believes." Therefore those who repent and by faith lay hold on Christ as mediator, to them is imputed the perfect obedience to the Law which Christ has accomplished, as if they themselves had satisfied the Law. In this way they have full, perfect, and complete obedience to the Law by imputation through faith. But this imputation through faith is not given to us in order that we might "live according to the flesh," Rom. 8:12. But the Spirit of renewal is given who causes us to walk in the commandments of God. Thus Paul attributes a twofold fulfillment of the Law to the regenerate: (1) "unto righteousness to everyone who believes," Rom. 10:4, so that "there is no condemnation," Rom. 8:1, because God in sending His Son has shown and condemned sin. (2) "That the just requirement of the Law might be fulfilled in us who do not live according to the flesh but according to the Spirit," Rom. 8:4.

The Holy Spirit works the new obedience in the regenerate, which applies not only to external works, for Christ says in Matt. 5:20, "Unless your righteousness exceeds that of the Pharisees . . ." The Spirit crucifies the inner lusts of the heart, puts to death the actions of the flesh, contends against our corrupt inclinations, and begins new desires in us which are in keeping with the law of God. This obedience is called the beginning obedience because it is still far removed from perfect fulfillment, as has been said. But it is called "the fulfilling of the law," Rom. 8:4, and "righteousness," Deut. 24:13, because it is pleasing to God for the sake of Christ, 1 Peter 3:18. Luther says in the Smalcald Articles [13] that just as a believing person is reckoned as righteous because of his faith, even though sin clings in his flesh, so also the good works of believers are reckoned as righteous and holy, out of grace and for the sake of Christ.[22] Therefore when the works of the regenerate are considered in themselves, they are called "beginning obedience" rather than the "perfect fulfillment or satisfaction of the Law."

We can get a correct understanding of the nature of this new obedience under the individual precepts and what defects it has if we divide the subject. (1) It avoids external lapses and performs outward works which are in keeping with the Law. (2) It begins new desires in the heart, the mind, the will, and all our members according to the individual commandments. (3) It contends against concupiscence and lusts and mortifies the inclinations which are contrary to the Law. But the defect or lack in it is that in these three respects it does not perform as much as the Law demands, namely from the whole heart. As Rom. 7:21 says, "Evil lies close at hand to the person who wants to do good."

We must also consider what things are required in order that our new obedience may be pleasing to God, that it may be a true worship of God and be regarded as the fulfillment of the Law. (1) We must acknowledge our uncleanness and by faith determine that God is favorably inclined toward us for the sake of Christ, that is, that the imputed fulfillment of the Law through faith comes first and leads the way. (2) We should pray that we may be ruled and governed by the Holy Spirit. Ps. 119:35, "Lead me in the paths of Your commandments"; cf. 2 Cor. 13:7. In all the epistles he prays that they may increase in love. (3) We must follow the lead of the Spirit of renewal. Rom. 8:4; Gal. 5:18, "Let us walk by the Spirit"; cf. Acts 7:51; Rom. 14:20. (4) Not only should we perform some work which has been commanded in the Decalog, but all the commandments must be related to the First Commandment, that they be performed out of fear

---

[22] Tappert, p. 315. Not an exact quotation.

and love for God, to this end that honor and obedience be given to God, and that is to do something for the sake of God. (5) Our obedience must proceed from faith, that is, we must acknowledge the imperfection and uncleanness which inhere in our good works, grieve over them, and pray to have them covered by the imputation of Christ's obedience. We must consider under each of the individual precepts how many and how great are our failures. The points are beneficial for us, so that we not only speak in a general way about the imperfection and uncleanness of our good works but that we examine ourselves according to each of these precepts.

Here also are pertinent the questions as to how, under the individual commandments, the regenerate are to stir themselves to obedience. As Paul says in 2 Tim. 1:6, we are "to fan into flame the gift of God" and those things which are the means by which zeal for well-doing is kindled, fostered, encouraged, increased, enlarged, etc. Now I only want to note briefly the main points which have been explained more fully by learned men. (1) The command proceeds from a faith which hates sins and desires to be unburdened and freed from them and seeks the grace of God in order to be pleasing to Him; therefore if it is a true faith, it will tirelessly encourage us to avoid sin and do things pleasing to God. (2) Because the Spirit who is received by faith is given along with the forgiveness of sins, this great benefit to us should rouse us to well-doing, because we have been made temples of the Holy Spirit and are renewed, led, and supported by Him. We should certainly be careful that we do not "grieve" Him who dwells within us as our guest, Eph. 4:30. We must not disturb or vex Him, Is. 63:10; nor "resist Him," Acts 7:51; nor "outrage the Spirit of grace," Heb. 10:29. (3) This exhortation is taken from the idea of love, namely that we should be mindful of the countless blessings of God, both spiritual and physical, which He loads upon us and with which He adorns us. We should look to His promises that He has decreed to crown our poor and imperfect obedience out of His bounty with the most fulsome rewards. Moved by these thoughts we should rouse ourselves to thankfulness, so that our mind is directed to showing obedience to our good Father. For it is the nature of love to follow and be obedient to the beloved one and to show gratitude toward Him, as John says in his First Epistle, 5:3, "This is the love of God that we keep His commandments." (4) Filial fear earnestly avoids offending the Father who deserves so much from us and whose kindness we desire to enjoy in all eternity. Likewise love keeps in mind the divine warnings and the examples of punishments in order to mortify the flesh and keep it in subjection as by a bridle. (5) The hearing and meditating upon the Word of God is a ministry of the Spirit through which He works efficaciously in our hearts, as David in Ps. 119:105 shows that by meditation on the Law a new light and new desires are kindled. (6) Serious worship begins. Ps. 119:133, "Direct my steps according to Your Word." (7) All things which in any way can offer an opportunity for sin must be carefully avoided. On the other hand, those things which can move the mind to obedience and keep it there must not be neglected. These points pertain to the individual precepts, and because the application is simple, I wanted to add these general statements at this place.

[D.] Natural Law

[MELANCHTHON'S TEXT]

As light has been set before our eyes by God, likewise certain knowledge has been implanted in the minds of men by which they understand and evaluate many things. The philosophers call this light the knowledge of the first principles, which they also call common notions or preconceptions. In popular speech a distinction is made: one category consists of principles visible to observation, such as the knowledge of numbers, order, logical syllogism, the principles of geometry, and physics. They grant that all of these are definite and the sources of the most useful things in this life. For what kind of life would we have without numbers or order? The second category consists of principles which relate to our actions, such as the natural difference between things which are honorable and those which are base. The matter of obedience to God comes under this category. To be sure, these principles governing our conduct ought to be as clear to us as the knowledge of numbers, and yet because of our original fall, a certain darkness has come over us and the human heart has conflicting desires over against the distinction between the upright and the immoral. For this reason men do not give their unequivocal assent to such areas of knowledge as the following: We must obey God, adultery must be shunned, contracts must be kept, in distinction to the fact that two times four is eight. The knowledge of the Law remains, but our assent to it is weak because of the stubbornness of our heart. This knowledge is a testimony that we have had our origin in God and that we owe obedience to Him and that He accuses our disobedience. But our hesitancy and stubbornness are clear signs that the nature of man is divided. The fact that we die points to the same thing, as well as the countless calamities which befall the human race and man's many incredibly evil actions. Paul is dealing with this in Rom. 1:18 when he says that men "suppress the truth in unrighteousness," that is, that even though the knowledge of the truth has been strongly impressed upon men that there is one God who is the eternal mind, the creator and preserver of things, who is wise, good, just, etc., and that this God is to be obeyed in keeping with the difference between honorable and evil things, yet this knowledge of the truth is suppressed and rejected in unrighteousness, that is, it is held captive and does not have the rule, but rather unrighteousness rules in opposition to this knowledge, by turning away man's will from God, by contempt for Him, by confidence in human abilities, and finally by various desires which conflict with the light which has been divinely kindled within our minds. Thus our assent is weak and—

> *"The charioteer is carried along by the horses and does not heed the direction of the chariot."*

Thus the philosophers (when they saw that the assent of man was very weak and that men were carried away with great force to different pleasures) asked whether what was right and what was wrong were to be determined by nature or merely by human opinion. To have doubt on such a matter is shameful and disgraceful, just as if one were to ask whether two times four is eight is a matter of nature or merely an accident. The divine light in the minds of men must not be extinguished; rather, the mind must be stirred up and strengthened in order that it may recognize the first principles of action and embrace them and to determine that the immutable decrees of God are just as sure and certain as the visible principles. This is what Paul is stressing in Rom. 1:19 when he says, "God has shown it to them"; and again in Rom. 2:15, when he says, "The work of the Law was written in their hearts." He calls this knowledge the divine decree or judgment, Rom. 1:32, ". . . who though they knew God's judgment . . . ." Therefore the correct definition of the law of nature is this: The law of nature is the knowledge of the divine law which has been grafted into the nature of man. For this reason man is said to have been created in the image of God, because in him shone the image, that is, the knowledge of God and the likeness to the mind of God, that is, the understanding of the difference between the honorable and the shameful; and the powers of man concurred or agreed with this knowledge. The will had been turned to God before the Fall, the true knowledge of God glowed in man's mind, and in his will was love toward God. His heart assented to the true knowledge of God without any doubt. This knowledge established for us that we had been created to know and worship God and to obey Him as our Lord who had made us, cared for us, and had impressed His image upon us, who demanded and gave His approval to what was righteous, and on the contrary condemned and punished unrighteousness. Although in this corruption of our nature the image of God has been so deformed that the knowledge of Him does not shine forth like it did, yet the knowledge does remain, but our heart contends against it and our doubts arise because of certain things which seem to conflict with this knowledge. For because punishments are deferred and evil befalls the good and good the evil, the human mind is uncertain regarding God's providence, that is, about the very first law, as to whether God really does bless the good and punish the wicked. Likewise all men by nature doubt that their prayers are heard. Yet the natural knowledge of God is not entirely extinct. Thus the first law of nature itself acknowledges that there is one God, who is eternal mind, wise, just, good, the Creator of things, kind toward the righteous and punitive toward the unrighteous, by whom there has been ingrafted into us the understanding of the difference between good and evil, and that our obedience is based on this distinction; that this God is to be invoked and that good things are to be expected from Him. Paul is citing this law of nature in Romans 1 and explaining it. It is obvious that it is in agreement with the First Commandment, and to this touchstone may be referred the discussion of Xenophon, Cicero, and men like them who followed their natural judgment and taught and often defended this law in opposition to atheists.

To the Second Commandment pertain laws and decrees concerning the taking of oaths and the penalties for perjury and also the punishments of those who curse God. For even human reason judges that punishments follow this, and the experience of all ages shows many examples. Here also pertain the countless statements regarding the punishments for perjury as we see them in Tibullus [I. 10.3]—

"Ah, poor man who first hides his perjuries;
For punishment comes slowly on silent feet."

To the Third Commandment pertain any proven or well-known statements which have been published regarding religious ceremonies, for example, when the citizens of Athens used to swear this: I will defend the sacred rites both alone and with the help of others, because we believe these rites have come down to us from our fathers who understood what oaths should be taken regarding things which have been divinely transmitted to us. Then their godless posterity rashly devised new ceremonies and new ideas, with the result that men lost the rule of God which forbade new religions to be undertaken by human authority. To ungodly rites of this kind this ancient statement should not have been applied.

Up to this point I have discussed the laws of nature which apply to the First Table, and these are not as clear as those which follow which refer to civil life. This is natural, because human reason understands that there is a difference between the life of men and that of animals, and it also understands righteousness, chastity, truthfulness, moderation, kindness, and other virtues. Likewise the race of men understands that these qualities have been established for a lawful society and that virtues are to be developed for the sake of worshiping God, and even if we are not motivated by any sense of their usefulness, God has added manifest values in this society.

Thus our human reason first recognizes that in this society of ours there is need for order and direction. The first source of this direction is the authority of our parents. To this authority figure later on is added the power of the rulers who govern and defend the entire society.

To the Fifth Commandment pertains the statement which prohibits all evil violence which harms anyone. Although the value of this precept is clear (for the safety of human existence cannot be maintained if violence is permitted to go unrestrained), yet human reason not only teaches that these injuries must be avoided for the sake of expedience, but also the mind of man must be educated to this for the sake of justice.

As justice commands that all innocent people are to be protected, so also it orders that violence be held in check by the magistrate and that the harmful members of society be removed. Nor is it difficult for prudent men to understand the many natural reasons for these statements, but the chief reason is that the understanding of justice has been divinely instilled into men just as the knowledge of numbers has been, even if our assent to it is weaker because of our stubborn heart, which does not heed the warnings of our reason and burns with anger because of hatred and desire for revenge. Nor was this law regarding doing an unjust murder written first on the tables of Moses. But immediately at the very beginning God by the judgment of nature added a clear testimony when He cursed and punished Cain because he killed his brother. Later on the Law was given in Gen. 9:6 which forbids murder and commands that it be punished by the magistrate. These are the words in the text, "Whosoever sheds man's blood, by man shall his blood be shed," Gen. 9:6, that is, through the magistrate. Man was made in the image of God, that is, that he might understand God, call upon Him, worship Him, and be righteous. God does not want this worship or the priesthood to be violated, but rather defended and supported, so that he may worship and call upon God. God Himself is the one who protects and avenges His violated image, His violated worshiper and priest. Because of this God has added clear testimonies to the laws of nature so that these things are not forgotten in the darkness of the human heart.

To the Sixth Commandment pertains the judgment of human reason which distinguishes the life of man from that of the beast and commands that men establish marriage in keeping with certain laws. He disapproves of adultery and moving from one bed to another. The existence of marriage proves that this judgment is inherent in human reason. Although this commandment is broken in many different ways contrary to this order because of the corruption of our nature, yet God immediately in Paradise sanctified the law concerning marriage. Later on He punished men's wandering lusts by the Flood and in other ways, in order to teach us by the law of nature.

To the Seventh Commandment applies the statement: to give to each his own property. Human reason is aware that the distinction of ownerships applies to man's very nature and that property must be transferred by legal methods and that men are obligated to one another to practice justice and honorable treatment toward one another through their mutual duties. This natural judgment the philosophers call the law or right of nature for which there is a great mountain of proofs and many grades or degrees. Thus the lawyers speak a little differently, even though the laws of the gentiles have no other meaning except the common judgment of men, that is, the normal principles and examples drawn from them. Nor does the "communism" advocated by Plato[23] apply to this aspect of the nature of men in which there must be a distinction between the laws of empires and those of particular states, whereby evil men may be punished, and also distinctions of property ownership must be noted. Thus in carrying out these duties we should learn not only to consider the useful-ness of the Law but also the fact that the order which has been established by God and demonstrated in nature must be preserved by us, both for the sake of God and also for keeping proper regulations to our contractual relationships, so that we do not defraud others but rather help them to keep their own property. Regarding this equality of the rights of ownership we have the most learned discourses of the philos-ophers and lawyers, which serve as testimonies to the law of nature or the natural law, that is, to the judgment of human nature on this matter.

In regard to the Eighth Commandment it is obvious that there has been grafted into human reason a power of judging which establishes that we should love and maintain the truth and avoid lying. Here again the value of this law and the duties related to it are very obvious, because, if trust in such contracts were taken away, there would be no lasting business relationships, no alliances or peace treaties; and court decisions would be made in vain if the truth were not required in areas of work-manship such as medicine and other arts. How evil life would be if the false were traded for the truth, poison given for remedies! God always adds countless values to His laws. We must not only consider the values but much more the fact that this has been ordained by God and that this order, namely the preservation of the concept of truth, must constantly be observed because we love God.

In reviewing the laws of nature I have followed the order of the Decalog, for this order is clearest and shows the way which our own reason points out for us to follow. But regardless of the order and the number, the substance is the same, if something foreign does not confuse things. Further, it is beneficial to follow this order so that the agreement of the laws of nature with the Decalog may be evident, and it is useful for many reasons that this be kept in view: First, in order that we may understand that the laws of nature themselves are also divinely instituted and that we may stress and correctly understand that the philosophers and law-givers approve of them and agree with them, and in order that we may reject statements contrary to this. It was for this reason that the divine law was proclaimed from heaven so that God might testify that He is the author of this natural knowledge and that He demands obe-dience in accordance with this knowledge and that He is accusing the human race because of its stubbornness. For God willed that the voice of His judgment against sin be known. Afterward, it was also for the benefit of the saints that there be a well-defined testimony from God as to which works He requires and approves, so that in

---

[23] See Plato's *Republic* and his *Laws.*

the weakness of our flesh human reason must not wander away, as has happened in the case of many law-givers who have made some iniquitous laws.

Natural Law

The comparison of the laws of nature with the Decalog has been given in [Melanchthon's] *Loci* in such a plain and clear explanation that there is no need for a longer discussion, unless a person wishes to gather from the ancient poets, philosophers, and law-givers statements similar to the individual precepts of the Decalog. Discussions of this kind have been raised by many people, such as the philosophers of whom Paul warned in Col. 2:8, "Beware that no one spoil your faith through philosophy and empty deceit." But we must be frank in speaking on this matter so that by an improper use of the term "philosophy" we do not disturb and overturn things which have been correctly and profitably taught among us. For this reason we should consider why it is useful to note the consensus of the natural law with the Decalog. We must show the limits which such a comparison must observe. For if a person wants to use this comparison in such a way that he twists it into an interpretation of the Decalog and restricts it only to the laws we know by natural knowledge, so that he may argue that the law of God accuses only those sins known by nature and that the Decalog is satisfied by the kind of obedience which human reason dictates and can present to God, such a person, because he has stepped beyond the proper boundaries, is rightly described as "captivated" in Col. 2:8. Nor is there any doubt as to the Pharisaic origin of these errors. For it is a plausible opinion that the interpretation of the Decalog should be derived from the natural law. This fantasy has seized upon many in the church who have imagined that the fathers before the time of Moses were saved through the natural law. For this reason we should use careful judgment in our discussion of the natural law.

In the *Loci* the correct reasoning is shown as to how the agreement between the law of nature and the Decalog can be considered in a right and useful way. These reasons are given:

1. Paul is manifestly dealing with this subject in Romans 1 and 2 and attributes to the law of nature some very honorable names. In Rom. 1:18 he calls it "the truth of God"; in v. 19, "the revelation of God"; in v. 17, "the righteousness of God"; in Rom. 2:15, "the work of the Law written in their hearts" at the creation itself. Indeed, the very term "natural law" is taken from 2:14, "The gentiles do by nature what the law requires." We gratefully recognize this blessing that He did not will that the entire light of the Law should be extinguished through the Fall, but willed that there be certain vestiges of it which remained, so that there could be the civil association of men, in which God through the voice of

the Gospel might gather His church. The words of Paul admonish us that these vestiges should be highly prized.

2. This comparison is useful in order that we may learn to love, to venerate, and to value all moral statements in agreement with the law of nature, wherever they may exist or be read among the poets, historians, philosophers, or law-givers, because the "righteousness of God" and the "truth of God" have been divinely revealed. Thus Paul in 1 Cor. 15:33 does not hesitate in a most serious statement to cite Menander, "Evil companions corrupt good morals."

3. There is value also in attaching a higher importance to the testimony of conscience, even in the case of the unregenerate, as it pertains to "accusing thoughts" (which Paul mentions in Rom. 2:15) when we experience them; and they are blunted in our imagining, as if they were only some kind of ridiculous fantasy which would be of concern only to a woman. But we should realize that this is truly the judgment of God contending against our sins.

4. From this comparison we can see in which areas the natural knowledge of the Law has been obscured, where our judgment has become corrupt, and what those works are, whether sinful or good, which in the Decalog are shown to be unknown to human reason. In this way the comparison of the laws of nature with the Decalog can be used correctly and with value and to some degree the true understanding illuminated.

To those proofs which have been so learnedly and clearly explained in the *Loci* I shall add nothing. I make only this observation, that just as the Decalog is divided into two tables, so also Scripture, when it speaks of the law of nature, in a sense divides it into two tables. The first table is beautifully described in Romans 1, as it deals with different precepts, namely with reference to God who is the eternal mind, omnipotent, invisible, the creator and sustainer of the world. Him we must acknowledge as God, for he says, Rom. 1:28. "They did not like to retain the knowledge of God." Him we must obey, in keeping with the truth of the natural law, for Paul says, Rom. 1:18–19, "They suppress the truth of God in unrighteousness; they know the righteous law of God," but they do not do it. Likewise Him we must glorify as God, to Him we must give thanks, as the text says, Rom. 1:21. Jer. 2:10–11, "Cross over to the islands and see if there has been such a thing: has a nation changed its gods?" That is, it is the law of nature that God be worshiped by the practice of religion and that the sacred rites of the ancestors be retained. The second table of the natural law has been stated in a negative way by the philosophers, namely what you do not wish done to you do not do to someone else. But Christ puts it affirmatively in Matt. 7:12, "Whatever you wish that men would do to you, do so to them." He is here clearly showing the agreement of this statement with the Decalog, for He says, "This is the law and the prophets," that is, the Second Table. Thus, just as

Moses had made God the subject of the First Table and our neighbor the subject of the Second, so Scripture affirms that the natural law is speaking either about God or about our fellow men.

[E.] THE USE OF THE LAW

There is no doubt that the law of God demands both inner and outward obedience, as it says, "You shall love the Lord your God with all your heart," Deut. 6:5. But since this corrupted nature of men cannot produce perfect obedience, as Paul so clearly testifies in Romans 7–8, and since this sin remains in us in this life in the form of doubt, lack of faith and insufficient fear and love of God, and countless desires which run counter to the law of God, it follows that men are not pronounced righteous, that is, accepted before God by reason of the Law. Therefore Paul in this controversy argues vigorously and separates the matter of justification from the Law. Even if human reason judges differently concerning sin and righteousness, even though controversies have arisen over the difference between human judgment and the Gospel, yet we must heed the voice of the Gospel which has been proclaimed from the very beginning that sins are forgiven to men and that they are reconciled and become pleasing to God, or righteous, that is, they are accepted for the sake of our Mediator, the Son, as it says in Rom. 5:2, "Through Him we have access to the Father by faith."

Thus the question arises: What is the use or purpose of the Law, if the works of the Law do not merit the remission of sins or if we are not righteous by the Law? At this point we need to understand that there are three uses or duties for the Law.

The first is the pedagogical or civil use, for God wills that all men be compelled by the discipline of the Law, even the unregenerate, not to commit outward sins. Paul speaks of this use in 1 Tim. 1:19, "The law was laid down for the unrighteous," that they might be compelled to obey. That this discipline might be strongly supported, God established magistrates or governments over the human race; He wills that men be governed by laws and sound teaching; He wills that the wild ravings of men be held in check and be punished by the penalties imposed by their rulers, as it says in Deut. 19:19ff., "You shall put the evil man out of your midst, so that the rest of the people shall hear of it and fear, and you shall have no pity on him." Previous to this God had established a much more unhappy prison, namely the universal calamities which afflict the human race, as Ps. 32:9 says regarding the causes of the troubles of mankind, "Their mouths must be held in with a bit and bridle that they will not come near to you." Men must be diligently taught regarding this discipline and these four reasons must be set before them:

1. It is necessary to show this to man because of the commandment of God to whom we owe obedience.

2. To avoid the penalties by which either the magistrate or God punishes our horrible crimes.

3. To preserve the public peace and order, for God demands discipline so that we do not practice violence against the person or property of others; He wills that peace and tranquility be maintained, so that men can be governed and taught. At this point we must speak a warning that we must preserve the life and property not only of ourselves but also of others and be mindful of the many crimes not only against the lives and fortunes of others but also in corrupting the minds of others. These injuries are not repaired, but the divine punishment for them follows.

4. The discipline of the Law is our "schoolmaster to Christ." The nobler gentiles have also seen other reasons for man's troubles, and there has been a great rage over the fact that nothing is improved by man's fear of calamities and punishments. But this fourth reason is more important and there is great praise for the discipline of the Law because it is called a schoolmaster unto Christ, that is to say, that for those who do not cease corrupting themselves by sins against their own conscience, Christ is of no effect, as it clearly says in 1 Cor. 6:9–10, "Fornicators, idolaters, adulterous people . . . shall not inherit the kingdom of God." Along the same line is the statement in 1 John 3:8, "Everyone who commits sin is of the devil." Thus it is necessary to curb our lusts so that we do not fight against the Holy Spirit when He moves our hearts. It also comes to this, that it is a part of discipline to hear and learn the Gospel through which the Holy Spirit is effective in us. It is very important that we remember these uses for the discipline of the Law, and yet not devise the errors of those who have taught that this discipline merits the forgiveness of sins or that it is without sin and is the fulfilling of the Law or the righteousness which avails before God.

Up to this point we have spoken of the civil or pedagogical use of the Law. Now we must say something regarding the second use of which Paul speaks so clearly in order to correct the errors of human judgment regarding sin and righteousness. Thus it is a second and very important use of the law of God to show our sin and to accuse, to terrify, and to condemn all men in this misuse of human nature. For the law of God which has been revealed to men is a perpetual judgment which condemns sin in the entire human race. Because the knowledge of the divine law has been grafted into our minds, and because it has been revealed in different ways by voice and examples as, for instance in Paradise, where God demanded obedience, and added the punishment, namely, death and other sorrows, in order that there might be testimonies of His judgment against sin. Afterward many warnings and examples followed, such as the matter of Cain, the Flood, the destruction of the Sodomites, and others. And the immutable judgment of God, whose eternal wrath presses upon all who are not freed through the knowledge of the Son of God. Therefore we should never get the idea that the law of God is a light matter and something changeable, as was the Laconic law, so that they used only iron money in the land of Laconia. But it is the judgment of God in which His horrible anger against sin is shown at all times, because it is always proclaimed and believed in the church even more than in the rest of the world, just as from the very beginning in Paradise and afterward in the sermons of the patriarchs the voice of the Law sounded forth condemning sin and preaching repentance. Paul says in Rom. 1:18, "The wrath of God has been revealed from heaven against all wickedness of men who oppress the truth in unrighteousness." Here it is witnessed that the voice of God rings out in the church announcing the wrath of God against the sins of men.

As I have said, the voice of the Law resounds in the church, but even more the thunderbolts are felt by men such as Adam, Abraham, Jacob, David, Hezekiah, and Paul. They felt the terrors of knowing their own sins. For example, Hezekiah says in Is. 38:13, "As a lion He will break all my bones." The Psalms are full of these laments. In order that this judgment may be felt and sin recognized, the church has been placed under the cross, while in the meantime the blind and raging world despises the judgment of God. Therefore there is no doubt that the voice of the Law condemning sins must constantly be set forth and taught in the church, and indeed it would be a monstrous crime to conceal God's judgment and His voice which announces His wrath against sin, as it says in Jer. 1:9–10, "Behold, I have put My words in your mouth. See, I have set you over the nations to overthrow and destroy." But in the church there is an argument over this question: Hypocrites think that the Law was laid down in order that it might merit reconciliation or take away sin. Paul calls us back from these errors and teaches a position foreign to the judgment of men. Indeed, he says, "Through the Law is the knowledge of sin," Rom. 3:20, as much as to say that the Law was laid down that it might accuse and condemn sin, but not take it away. Likewise Rom. 4:15, "The Law works wrath." Again, Rom. 7:13, "Through the Law sin became sinful beyond measure." Again, 1 Cor. 15:56, "The sting of death is sin and the strength of sin is the Law." It would be absurd to apply these statements to civil matters, they contain warnings not about civil practices but about the judgment of God which we feel in times of true terror and true repentance, for the Law does not have this use for carnally secure men, as Paul says in Rom. 7:9, "I was once alive apart from the Law," that is, I was secure and unaware of the judgment of God; but afterward I became terrified, recognized my own weakness and my sins. The Law had this use in the life of David when he was condemned by the prophet and became terrified over his adultery. Then the contrition, as they call it, can be clearly understood in his repentance, if we understand that it consisted of terrors of this kind. But the proclamation of the Gospel must be added which points to the Lamb of God who takes away the sin of the world and reveals the indescribable mercy of God who, although He is genuinely angry against sin and judges sin, to be sure, yet wills to free *those who believe in His Son, whom He made a victim for us. Thus Paul says that we are terrified, not that we may perish but that we may flee to the Mediator, for "He includes all under sin that He may have mercy on all," Rom. 11:32.*

The third use of the Law pertains to the regenerate. Insofar as the regenerate have been justified by faith, they are free from the Law. This must be said under this locus. For they are freed from the Law, that is, from the curse and the condemnation and the wrath of God which is set forth in the Law, that is to say, if they remain in the faith and fight against sin in confidence in the Son of God and overcome the terrors of sin. Yet in the meantime it must be said that the Law which points out the remnants of sin, in order that the knowledge of sin and repentance may increase, and the Gospel also must proclaim Christ in order that faith may grow. Furthermore, the Law must be preached to the regenerate to teach them certain works in which God wills that we practice obedience. For God does not will that we by our own wisdom set up works or worship, but He wills that we be ruled by His Word, as it is written, "In vain do they worship Me by the commandments of men," Matt. 15:9. Again, "Your Word is a lamp unto my feet," Ps. 119:105. When human reason is not directed by the Word of God it is very likely to lack something. For it is seized by wicked desires or gives its approval to iniquitous works, as is apparent in the laws of the gentiles. The divine order that we are to obey God remains unchangeable. Therefore, even though we are free from the Law, that is from damnation, because we are righteous by faith for the sake of the Son of God, yet because it pertains to obedience, the Law remains, that is, the divine ordinance remains that those who have been justified are to be obedient to God. Indeed, they have the beginning of obedience which we shall discuss under its own locus as to how it is pleasing to God. These comments suffice to give instruction briefly regarding the threefold use of the Law. We shall return later to the second and third uses.

THE USE AND PURPOSE OF THE LAW

The principal doctrine of the Law deals with the true use of the Law. For if this teaching is obscured or corrupted, all other aspects of the subject are not only taught in vain and become matters of argument but, as Paul says in Gal. 3:10, "Those who rely on the works of the Law are under the curse"; 2:21, "If righteousness comes by the Law, then Christ has died in vain"; again, Rom. 9:31, "Israel by pursuing after the righteousness which is based on the Law did not succeed in fulfilling the Law." It is easy to stray from the correct teaching on this matter because human reason demands a different judgment on the use and purpose of the Law than is taught in Scripture.

Therefore many different controversies have been stirred up in all ages regarding the use of the Law. The Pharisees contended that the Law was given in order that there might be certain works through which man might seek and obtain righteousness, salvation, and eternal life. They used specious arguments. For it is certain that the Law which God had corroborated by such severe punishments had not been promulgated with such stupendous miracles all in vain. For the Law clearly says, "He who does them shall live by them," Lev. 18:5; Ezek. 20:11; Gal. 3:12; Rom. 10:5. Paul by many arguments separates justification from the Law ("A law was not given which can make alive," Gal. 3:21) because the Law was weak through the flesh, and therefore he comes to this conclusion: "Those who rely on the works of the Law are under the curse," Gal. 3:10.

Later on, Cerdo, Marcion, Valentinus, and those who followed the teaching of the Manichaeans, since they did not correctly understand Paul's arguments, burst forth with the blasphemous statements that the doctrine of the Law did not come from the good God but from the devil. It was apparent in the time of Paul that certain people had misinterpreted his writings to the effect that the Law was to be removed from the church, since there was no use for it. This is what the word *katargoumen*, "do away with," means in Rom. 3:31. Likewise they argued that the Law was not good, that it had an evil purpose. Thus Paul says in 1 Tim. 1:8, "The Law is good, if a person uses it lawfully." Rom. 7:7, "Is the Law sin? God forbid!"

In our time the antinomians are contending that the use of the Law refers only to external civil life since God, in the very act of promulgating the public or civil laws, distinguished them from the Decalog in order to show that there is one use for the Decalog and another for the civil law. Therefore it is absolutely necessary that the teaching about the use of the Law be established upon the correct Scriptural foundations and be taught rightly and clearly in the church. It is by the blessing of God so clearly taught in our day on the basis of the apostolic writings and so clearly explained in the *Loci* by an excellent method and with clear-cut divisions, that it is neither useful nor necessary to produce a long commentary. For we shall see that those who by their desire for dissent do not appear to have anything in common with others whom they are ashamed to describe as belonging to the same party, as long as they are trying to set forth this doctrine by another line of reasoning and another method, are actually accomplishing nothing else than obscuring the clear light by the darkest shadows.

There is great value in this method of learning whereby in plain and clear loci we may consider both sides of a matter to see how the same doctrine is handled by other people in a less clear and effective manner, and how this difficulty produced these arguments, and how with such clarity, light was shed on the matter so that now the doctrine of the threefold use of the Law can be known to anyone. For if all the disputations of the fathers were gathered into one place, the summary of the entire matter can be reduced to this: Through the Law is shown sin and the weakness of our nature, so that we may seek the Physician by whose grace our nature may be healed, so that the new obedience is able to satisfy the Law and we thus be saved, as it is written, "This do, and you shall live," Luke 10:28. But they do not clarify the issue clearly and precisely enough. With regard to the disciplinary function of the Law in the unregenerate, many things were written in times past which are confused, and from this have arisen false and dangerous arguments about the matter of the merit of those who seek righteousness. If we would compare the things under dispute at the time of the beginning of the rebirth of the Gospel concerning the use of the Law, the reader would learn only about the one use, namely that the Law shows sin. Even now certain fanatics are claiming that there is no true use for the Law to show the regenerate how they may learn good works.

Luther in a very learned way sought the foundations of this doctrine in the Epistle to the Galatians, and divided the use of the Law into one aspect which was civil and one which was theological. Likewise in Galatians 5 there is one use of the Law in justification and another for those who have been justified. From this Luther constructed the threefold division of the uses of the Law. We must note the passages in Scripture in which the foundations of this doctrine are located. In regard to the civil law, Paul speaks very clearly in 1 Tim. 1:8–9; Rom. 2:1; Gal. 3:19. Regarding the second use, Paul instructs us in Rom. 3:20; 5:20; 7:7; Gal. 3:24. That there is a use for the Law even among the regenerate he teaches clearly in Rom. 13:8 and Gal. 5:14; cf. Jer. 31:33 and Psalm 119.

Thus the first use of the Law is the civil use. Properly the question is not whether the magistrate has the power to establish laws to which we must give obedience. But regarding the Decalog or the divine law the question is whether its teaching is to be set forth to those who are not truly repentant or whether it is useful to compel the unregenerate to obey or be forced under the doctrine of the divine law, so that they do not commit outward sins. The teaching of the civil law must be dealt with primarily to give an explanation to the very difficult argument which has arisen over the use of the Law over the unregenerate. This has caused a serious disturbance. For Scripture simply affirms, "Whatsoever is not of faith is sin," Rom. 14:23; again, "An evil tree cannot bring forth good fruit," Matt. 7:7. But because God does not will iniquity, therefore they seem to be doing wrong who do not warn or force the unregenerate not to commit outward sins, for no person should be encouraged to sin and it is a sin to ignore discipline in the unregenerate. At this point voices are raised that it is more advisable that the unregenerate wallow around in every kind of crime rather than to some degree control their habits by any kind of morality, for "it is easier for the harlots and the publicans to enter into grace than for the Pharisees," Matt. 21:31. It is correct to say this if we attach the concept of works-righteousness to this discipline under the article on the remission of sins; but, on the other hand, it is certain that God earnestly demands obedience or discipline even from the unregenerate, so that even in this life He punishes the violation of His law with terrifying penalties and gives external rewards to those who live under His discipline, even the unregenerate.

In opposition to this the scholastics say that it is a cruel idea found in the Master of the *Sentences* [Lombard] when he says, "The whole life of the unbeliever is sin." They say that to the man who does the best that is in him, God always gives His grace. This argument greatly disturbed Erasmus, for he says: "Is it all the same whether Socrates lives an honorable life or gives his mother poison or dishonors his sister?" Again, "If discipline does not merit the remission of sins, at least it renders the mind more open to grace. Socrates will be better prepared and more suited to receive grace than Phalaris will." There is no doubt that this is a difficult argument. It cannot be settled more simply, more correctly, and more easily than on the basis of the doctrine of the civil use of the Law. We must be careful that we do not apply the pedagogical use of the Law to this point, as if there is in the unregenerate a certain preparation for grace; but the matter must remain within the boundaries of the civil use because in this way men can be taught about the Gospel, through which later on the Holy Spirit is efficacious. For the doctrine of the Word of God cannot be taught when crime rules. Likewise, because in those who try to govern their morals by honorable discipline, there are many shameful lapses and their hearts remain impure. Therefore outward discipline instructs us to find out where righteousness comes from. This can most correctly be discovered in 1 Timothy 1 and Romans 1 and 2.

The second use of the Law relates to the matter of justification. Rom. 3:20, "Through the Law is the knowledge of sin"; Rom. 4:15, "The Law works wrath." The Law shows our sin and works repentance in four ways: (1) By accusing our sins, even the hidden ones which are unknown to our reason, such as, "I would not have known what it is to covet or lust, if the Law had not said, 'You shall not covet,'" Rom. 7:7; likewise by condemning a person's whole life which is not "of faith." Thus it leads man to the knowledge of himself. For just as mad men wildly imagine that they are very strong, so also this nature of ours, through the Fall, has been blinded so that it can easily become presumptuous about its own powers and does not fear to put its own kind of discipline or righteousness in opposition to the judgment of God. Therefore the Law shows what a stern examination of our good works we must make in the light of God's judgment, so that we may be led into a knowledge of our miserable condition and weakness and come to understand that we must seek another kind of righteousness. (2) The Law not only lists a catalog of sins, but it shows the magnitude and wickedness of sin and adds warnings regarding the wrath of God and eternal punishments, so that sin may be "exceeding sinful by the law," Rom. 7:13.

(3) Not only does the Law show sin in the sense of pointing to it, but it is the medium or instrument through which God works efficaciously; it terrifies secure hearts and works contrition, 1 Cor. 15:56, "The power of sin is the Law"; Rom. 4:15, "The Law works wrath." (4) The Gospel adds to the Law this interpretation, that the Law by its scourgings urges us to seek the promises of grace and forces us to Christ, and thus is profitable, so that grace can have access to us, so that the Law is a minister and preparer for grace. Thus Luther on Galatians 3 [Amer. Ed., 16.346].

The third use of the Law pertains to those who have been justified or born again. Controversies have been raised by arrogant minds under the pretext and in the name of Christian liberty. Rom. 6:14, "We are not under the Law . . ." Gal. 4:5, "We have been redeemed from the Law"; Gal. 3:25, "We are no longer under the schoolmaster. . . ." Therefore, they argue, the regenerate has no use for the Law, not even for teaching, because "His anointing will teach you all things," 1 John 2:27. Again, Rom. 12:2, "Be transformed by the renewing of your mind, that you may approve the things which God wills," not by encouragement or urgings because the new obedience ought to be voluntary, just as there is no need to give a good tree commandments to bear good fruit, but of itself and by its own nature it does this. They can expand on this idea in a marvelous and popular manner. But finally these extravagant statements leave in our minds the seeds which the Anabaptists, who have declared themselves as libertines, have adopted, increased, and brought to flourishing maturity, namely the notion that it is not necessary for a regenerate person to govern his life according to the norm of the divine law, from which he has been liberated; but rather whatever he decides and thinks of and does is by the Spirit, and when the Law says, "You shall love your neighbor," it is a matter of liberty for the regenerate whether he wants to do this or not.

Therefore we must preserve the "form of sound words," 2 Tim. 1:13, which must serve "that the church may be edified," 1 Cor. 14:5. It is a true and correct statement of Pauline theology that the regenerate are not under the Law. But it absolutely does not follow from this that therefore the Law is not useful for the regenerate. We must explain in what way they are not under the Law, namely for justification, accusation, condemnation, compulsion, perfect obedience. But there is a second proposition, namely that the Law does have a certain use in the case of the regenerate. For Paul says in Gal. 5:13–14, "You have been called unto liberty; but do not use your liberty as an opportunity for the flesh, but through love by the Spirit serve one another." He adds the definite rule of love, according to which the Spirit renews and leads the believers: "For the whole Law is fulfilled in one word, 'You shall love your neighbor as yourself.'" He says the same thing in Rom. 13:8 and 8:4, "In those who walk according to the Spirit the righteousness or requirement of the Law is fulfilled." The apostles everywhere preach about the new obedience of the regenerate and clearly seek the description of this new obedience in the Decalog. Christ also in John 13:34 says, "This is My commandment that you love one another."

Therefore it is the true and correct "form of sound words" that there is a use for the Law in the regenerate. It is threefold: (1) It pertains to doctrine and obedience that the regenerate should know, as they perform their worship, what kind of works are pleasing to God, so that they do not devise new forms of worship without the Word and may learn that it is the will of God that they make a beginning in obeying the commandments of the Decalog. (2) It is important that they know that this norm of the Law shows the imperfection and uncleanness which still clings to their good works, for otherwise they might easily fall into Pharisaism. (3) Because in this life the renewal of the Spirit does not wholly take away our old nature, but at the same time the old and the new man remain (the outward and the inner man), therefore there is a use for the Law in the regenerate that it may contend against and coerce their old man; and the beginnings of the new obedience are weak and are not supported by our whole spirit and mind. But Rom. 7:25 shows that "with the mind I serve the law of God but with the flesh the law of sin"; and again, vv. 22–23, "I delight in the law of God in my inmost self, but I see another law. . . ." Therefore these weak beginnings must not only be encouraged by the earnest entreaties of the Gospel, but also fostered by the precepts, exhortations, warnings, and promises of the Law. For we experience that the new obedience is not so voluntary a thing as a good tree which brings forth its new fruit without any command or exhortation. How much David as a regenerate man attributed to meditation on the doctrine of the Law is seen in Psalm 119, where the word "Law" involves the complete teaching of the Word of God, both Law and Gospel.

[F.] THE HONORED POSITION OF THE LAW, AGAINST THE ANTINOMIANS

Finally, we shall conclude this locus with a brief discussion of why it is useful and necessary to retain the teaching of the Law in the church and why we must treasure using it and give it a position of honor. We shall be brief because many things pertaining to this subject have already been said. Therefore, just as at Sinai the people first replied, "All the things which the Lord has spoken we shall do," Ex. 19:8; but later on when the Law was recited with the divine voice, they cried, "Do not let God speak to us . . ." Ex. 20:19, thus the Pharisees threw a kind of shade over the Law, for by nature we all are alienated from the true teaching of the Law and it is easy to instill in us a hatred of it. Nor is it a surprise that the Law of God is opposed and disputed. For even the civil laws, the knowledge and value of which are manifest, are opposed in various ways by proud minds. Luther says in his commentary on Galatians, "He who says he loves the Law is a liar and does not know what he is saying. For we love the Law as much as a murderer loves his prison." Thus there have arisen many antinomian controversies. The Pharisees put the Law under the locus on justification, and when Christ refuted this notion, light-minded men dreamed up the notion that Christ was trying to abolish the Law, Matt. 5:17, that is, that He was trying to establish a religion in which there was no use at all for the teaching of the Law. Thus at the time of Paul the Law went beyond its proper boundaries and arrogated to itself the honor which was due to Christ as the mediator. When the apostle vigorously rejected this idea and under this misuse of the Law gave to the Law a diminished reputation by such terms as "beggarly and weak elements," Gal. 4:9, and "the ministration of death," 2 Cor. 3:7, then followed the Valentinians and others, as we have mentioned above. Likewise, in our own time, when the false opinions of the Manichaeans concerning the Law had been refuted, then arose the antinomians. Now their ideas have been refuted, but still the opinion clings in the minds of all that we may sin because we are not under the Law, but under grace. But Paul is correct when he says that the "Law is holy, righteous, and good, if a person uses it lawfully," 1 Tim. 1:8. Thus in the correct use of the Law it is appropriate that the Law be a good thing for us. And there is a very beautiful dictum that the Law must not be used in an evangelical sense but in a legal sense. Therefore we must fortify our minds against antinomian opinions and ideas so that we may learn to appreciate the value of the doctrine of the Law in its own proper use.

It is useful to consider frequently the primary reasons for the value and usefulness of the Law. Thus I shall mention some of them. (1) The Law should be greatly honored because God instituted it with such solemnity, as is described in Ex. 19:6ff. and in ch. 20; again in Deut. 4:11ff.; Heb. 12:18–19; Acts 7:38. God with His own voice recited the Ten Commandments and in so loud a voice that He could be heard by 600,000 men for several miles. (2) All the prophets, in addition to explaining the promise of grace, were interpreters of the Law. Mal. 4:4, "Remember the Law of Moses." In the New Testament John the Baptist condemns sins on the basis of the Decalog and gives rules for the new obedience on the same basis as did the Son of God Himself and the apostles. Thus this doctrine must be of great importance. (3) It is likewise important that we understand correctly both the doctrine of sin and the doctrine of free choice. There is no doubt that the correct explanation of these subjects depends upon a true understanding of the doctrine of the Law. (4) The article of justification cannot be understood, rightly used, or retained in its purity unless the doctrine of the Law is carefully and precisely treated. For the Gospel consists in the preaching of the merits and benefits of Christ, but these are defined as the fulfilling of the righteousness of the Law and the liberation from the curse of the Law. Likewise the use of the article of justification consists in our laying hold on this freedom from the curse of the Law. For what does he understand about these matters who does not seriously consider what the Law is and what the curse of the Law is? We would become cold toward meditating on the blessings of Christ. Furthermore, we would not think about how serious a matter our redemption is, because we have not learned seriously or carefully about the Law or the degree to which the teaching of the Law and its correct use may be obscured as well as the Gospel lost. (5) The Law is a schoolmaster or custodian to Christ, in this sense, as Paul says in Gal. 3:22, "In order that the promise might be given to them that believe, all were imprisoned under sin," that is, through the Law.

There are more statements of this kind in Luther's Commentary on Galatians—The Law is profitable for this that it makes grace accessible to us. The Law is a servant and preparer for grace. Consequently, the Law in its relationship to justification does not justify but pushes us to the promise of grace and makes it sweet and desirable. The Law in its correct use and purpose humbles and prepares man so that he seeks and longs for grace. Thus the Law renders us capable of receiving Christ, capable of receiving grace and the benefits of Christ. Thus Luther. The other points which pertain to the honored position of the doctrine of the Law have been explained in earlier chapters.

The Difference Between Precepts and Counsels

Omitted

=====

Revenge

Omitted

=====

Poverty

Omitted

=====

Chastity

Omitted

=====

LOCUS [XIII]

Justification

[For this locus we are reprinting *Justification: The Chief Article of Christian Doctrine as Expounded in* Loci Theologici, trans. J. A. O. Preus (St. Louis: Concordia, 1985). That book has sizable omissions. We are restoring most of this material and are supplying footnotes. Those who wish to consult any parts still omitted should get the microfiche or its text from Concordia.]

[A.] INTRODUCTORY REMARKS

A consideration of the order shows a great deal. We have previously considered: 1. What God is and what His nature is. 2. How man was created in the image and likeness of God. 3. How he fell. 4. What horrible corruption followed, coming upon all human powers. 5. The voice of the Law, which before the judgment seat of God reveals, accuses, and condemns this depraved nature together with all its fruits. Next in correct and good order follows the locus on justification, dealing with the redemption, restitution, or reconciliation of the human race that has been lost and condemned because of sin.

This unique locus in a special way distinguishes the church from all other nations and religions. As Augustine says: "The church distinguishes the just from the unjust not by the standard of works but by the standard of faith." Indeed, this locus is the pinnacle and chief bulwark of all teaching and of the Christian religion itself; if this is obscured, adulterated, or subverted, it is impossible to retain purity of doctrine in the other loci. On the other hand, if this locus is securely retained, all idolatrous ravings, superstitions, and other corruptions are thereby destroyed under almost every locus, as the parallel example in 1 Sam. 5:1–4 shows. When the ark of the Lord was set up in the temple of the Philistines beside the idol Dagon, immediately the idol was moved from its position and fell down, and although it was replaced several times, as long as the ark of the Lord stood there, the idol could not stand and was finally completely broken apart. Our adversaries have noticed this fact and have confessed it. . . .

We must devote far more effort to retaining the genuine meaning and apostolic purity of the doctrine of justification, to handing it on to our posterity, and to preventing its being torn away from us or being adulterated by sophistic trickery or fraud. With the aid of God we can prevail more easily because we "have inherited the labors of others," John 4:38. For it was a labor far greater than those of Hercules to rescue the true light from the unspeakably dense darkness and the putrid filth and cesspools of the Antichrist and to restore the apostolic purity to the fountains of Israel. Nor could it have been done if the Holy Spirit had not led the way in kindling the light of the Word. Therefore it would be shameful and ungodly cowardice on our part if these teachings, which as a result of such great labor and the marvelous blessing of God have in this article been handed down and shown to us from the foundations of the prophets and apostles, were to be lost to us because of negligence in learning and cold formality in teaching, or that we would allow even a grain of it to be taken from us in controversy.

Nor must we think that with this great light we need not fear the shadows. For we have this treasure not in iron or brass vessels but in earthen ones, 2 Cor. 4:7, and the road on which we walk has many stumbling blocks where we may easily fall in our weakness. I am often horrified that Luther with some kind of foreboding often repeated this statement in his commentaries on Galatians and Genesis: "After my death this doctrine will again be brought into obscurity."

There are two reasons why, especially at this time, a consideration of these points must arouse us from our unconcern, so that we may exercise greater care to learn and teach this article and contend vigilantly against all corruptions of it: 1. The crafty serpent knows very well from what stronghold and fortress, as it were, those weapons were prepared and hurled by which his kingdom was weakened and almost destroyed. There is no doubt that, because he understands that the Day of Judgment is close at hand, he is undermining the doctrine of this locus with greater wrath [Rev. 12:12] and more dangerous deception. 2. The Son of God predicted that in the last times there would be great dangers (Matt. 24:24), so that even the elect, if possible, would be misled into error (cf. 2 Thess. 2:11; Luke 18:8).

The teaching regarding faith is dealt with chiefly under the locus of justification. It is worthy of note that God only a few years ago revealed, uncovered, and wonderfully overthrew the various tactics and tricks of the devil, whereby he was trying, under the appearance of moderation, to destroy the foundations of this article, as in the various formulas for reconciliation proposed by the papists, in the Ratisbon Book, in the Augsburg Interim, in the Osiandrian controversy, and in the statement that good works are necessary for salvation. God brought these insidious activities to light for our great benefit, so that in the future we might be both more diligent and more careful.

May the Son of God, our Lord Jesus Christ, by His Holy Spirit guide and enlighten the minds of both those who teach and those who learn and bestow upon them a true love for sound doctrine and keep our mind within the boundaries of the simple truth, so that we may learn, teach, and ever hold fast the true, simple teachings which are pleasing to God and salutary for the churches, and so that we may refuse to back away from any controversies necessary in order to protect and preserve the correctness and purity of this locus.

Therefore let us begin with a repetition of this doctrine of justification, which has been restored in our time to the form of the apostolic doctrine on the basis of the true, firm, and clear foundations of Scripture by the singular blessing of God through the work of Luther and others.

The Method of Dealing with This Locus

Some people are of the opinion that the points in this locus are disconnected, because only the terminology seems to require explanation. But a more careful consideration will show that a most beautiful method is observed. For Paul sums up the doctrine of justification thus: "The righteousness of God, without the Law, has been revealed . . ." in the Gospel, namely, that we are "justified freely by His grace, through the redemption which is in Christ Jesus, whom God set forth as a propitiation through faith, in His blood . . . without the works of the Law" [Rom. 3:21–28]. There is then a precise way to deal with this teaching in a methodical and orderly way, because the entire locus is divided into points in keeping with the order of this statement of Paul.

1. In the first place, we must explain what the Gospel is, in which is revealed and in which we must seek the doctrine of the righteousness of faith, and how it may be distinguished from the Law, because Paul says: "The righteousness of God is revealed in the Gospel without the Law" [Rom. 3:21]. We must also explain the boundaries of both the doctrine of the Law and that of the Gospel.

2. Then we must show in the Gospel the meaning of the words "to justify" (*justificare*), "righteousness" (*justitia*), and "to be righteous" (*iustus*).

3. Because we are justified freely through the grace of God, the terms "freely" and "the grace of God" must be explained.

4. Because this free or gracious righteousness of the Gospel is apprehended by faith, the explanation tells what justifying faith is and what is included with it.

5. Because the works of the Law must clearly be removed from the article of justification, we need to show which works Paul here understands.

Paul's statement on justification is made up of these parts, which summarize the entire doctrine.

Nor must we judge that this is mere childish zeal for the definition of terms. For just as the substantive matters in this locus are far above and beyond our reason, so also the Holy Spirit has certain terms in the teaching on justification that are not found in common usage. The church must be concerned about language, that is, it ought not devise new ideas or produce new dogmas, but those things which have been given us by the Holy Spirit it must learn from the correct meaning of the words that Scripture uses in teaching the heavenly doctrine. Later on we shall show that the neglect of correct language was the source and spring of all errors under this article.

[B.] THE GOSPEL

[MELANCHTHON'S TEXT]

There is no doubt that the apostles with remarkable wisdom gave such a sweet and pleasant name to their teaching to distinguish the Law from the promise of reconciliation. The prophets also in their proclamation used the peculiar term bāsar, which meant "to announce good news." Further, euangelion is an old word which even in Homer [Odyssey, 14.152] signifies that a gift is to be given to the one who brings good news, while elsewhere in the Greek language it refers to a message announcing good and happy things, just as the apostles used the term. And there are clear instances of this usage in Plutarch's Life of Artaxerxes *[14 (1.1018b)], where the words eu-aggeliōn misthon are used and the word euangelium must be understood as a speech which announces good news. In the same writer there are many instances of this.[1] There is also extant a witness to its use in his* Life of Pompey, *"Letter carriers came from the sea bearing good tidings" [cf.* Pompey, *66 (1.654b)]. Cicero says the same thing to Atticus [*Ad Atticum, *2.3.1 or 13.40.1].*

Therefore the sweetness of the name should alert the pious to a new kind of teaching and the difference between the Law and the Gospel. Nor are we creating new terminology more precise than necessary, as many hypocrites are now caviling. John the apostle at the beginning of his gospel [1:17] sets forth this clear distinction: "The Law was given through Moses, but grace and truth came through Jesus Christ." For it is necessary to distinguish precepts from the remission of sins and from promises; likewise, the free promise from promises that are not free. The Law, as we have said above, is a teaching that requires perfect obedience toward God, does not freely remit sins, and does not pronounce people righteous, that is, acceptable before God, unless the Law be satisfied. Although it has promises, yet they have the condition that the Law must be fulfilled. On the contrary, the Gospel, even when it makes its proclamation about repentance and good works, nevertheless contains the promise of the benefits of Christ, which is the proper and primary teaching of the Gospel, and this must be separated from the Law. For the Gospel freely forgives sins and pronounces us righteous even if we do not satisfy the Law. How these can be reconciled—that the Gospel along with the Law preaches about repentance and yet is a gracious promise—this we shall explain below. But first we must warn the reader that he must observe the difference between these promises, for the Law also has promises.

---

[1] Cf. Kittel, *Theological Dictionary of the New Testament*, 2.722–23.

We must understand that in the divine Scriptures there are two kinds of promises. Certain of them are added to the Law and have the condition of the Law, that is, the promise is given subject to the fulfillment of the Law. Such are promises of the Law. The Law teaches that God is good and merciful, but to those who are without sin. Human reason also teaches the same thing, for our reason does have some knowledge of the Law. Here let each person consult his own experience. For we know by nature that God is merciful, but only toward those who are worthy, that is, those who are without sin. Yet a person cannot be certain that he is pleasing God, since he is unworthy and unclean. Thus the Law and the promises of the Law, since they are conditional, leave our consciences in doubt.

The second kind of promise belongs to the Gospel. It does not have the condition of the Law as a cause for its fulfillment, that is, it does not make its promises on the condition that the Law be fulfilled, but freely for the sake of Christ. This is the promise of the remission of sins, or reconciliation or justification, concerning which the Gospel primarily speaks, so that these benefits are sure and do not depend upon the condition of fulfilling the Law. For if we are to believe that we will have remission of sins only when we have satisfied the Law, then we will have to despair of the remission of our sins. Therefore remission and reconciliation or justification are given freely, that is, not because of our worthiness. Yet there had to be some sacrifice for us. Therefore Christ was given and made a sacrifice for us, so that for His sake we might be assured that we are pleasing to the Father.

Thus this Gospel promise of reconciliation is different from the promise of the Law, because it is promised freely for the sake of Christ. Therefore Paul carefully and repeatedly sets before us this term "freely," as Rom. 4:16 says: "Therefore it is freely by faith, that the promise might be sure." The term "freely for the sake of Christ" spells the difference between the Law and the Gospel. For if we do not see this word concerning the free promise, doubt remains in our hearts, the Gospel is transformed into Law, and it renders our consciences just as uncertain regarding the remission of our sins or our justification as the Law or the natural judgment of our reason do.

Thus our adversaries, no matter how vociferously they protest that they are teaching the Gospel, nevertheless, because they do not teach about free reconciliation, still leave our consciences in doubt, and in place of the Gospel they are teaching the Hesiodic law, that is, the judgment of natural reason. Thus our mind and eyes must turn their attention to this term "freely." It is necessary to teach regarding this free promise in order that the matter may be certain, so that doubt may be banished from our consciences and they may have firm comfort in the face of the real terrors that afflict us. In their midst we can correctly judge how necessary this gracious promise is. And it is to this struggle that this doctrine is especially to be referred.

We must also understand that the promise has to be received by faith, as Paul teaches in Rom. 4:16: "Therefore it is freely by faith, that the promise might be sure. . . ." And in 1 John 5:10: "He who does not believe God makes Him a liar." Thus the word "freely" does not exclude faith, but it does exclude our worthiness as a condition, and it transfers the cause of this blessing from ourselves to Christ. It does not exclude our obedience, but it only transfers the cause of our blessing away from the worthiness of our own obedience and attributes it to Christ, in order that the blessing may be certain. Thus the Gospel speaks of repentance, but in order that the reconciliation may be certain, it teaches that sins are forgiven and that we are pleasing to God not because of the worthiness of our repentance or our renewal. This is necessary comfort for pious consciences. From this we can judge how to reconcile our statement that the Gospel speaks about repentance and yet freely promises reconciliation. Later we shall speak more fully on this paradox.

Christ defines the Gospel in the last chapter of Luke as clearly as an artist when He commands us to teach "repentance and remission of sins in His name" [v. 47]. Therefore the Gospel is the preaching of repentance and the promise. Human reason does not by nature comprehend this, but it is divinely revealed that God has promised that for the sake of Christ, His Son, He will remit sins and pronounce us righteous, that is, accepted by Him; and He gives the Holy Spirit and eternal life, if only we believe, that is, trust that these blessings come to us for the sake of Christ. These things are promised freely, that they may be sure.

This is the definition of the Gospel in which we lay hold on three Gospel blessings: that for the sake of Christ our sins are freely remitted; that we are freely pronounced righteous, that is, reconciled or accepted by God; that we are made heirs of eternal life. These three parts we shall explain later on. Only keep this in mind, that these blessings belong to the Gospel and are otherwise summed up in the one word "justification."

[CHAPTER] I: THE GOSPEL

The doctrine of free reconciliation or of the benefits of the Mediator is called the Gospel. Therefore we must first inquire as to the reason for this designation. To explain the meaning of words, which the grammarians call its etymology and the dialecticians call a definition of the term, there is pertinent not only a relationship of one word to another, as Augustine says, Contra Faustum, 2.2 [MPL 42.210], "The Gospel is called the good news or the good announcement," but we must also consider whence the word gets its name, why it is applied to the teaching of the new covenant, and what is the rationale of the term.

It is certain that the word "Gospel" was not used for the first time by ecclesiastical writers after the time of the apostles, as is the case with certain words under the article of the Trinity, such as homoousion, ousia, hypostasis. Christ Himself gave His doctrine this name, and the apostles called it "the ministration of the new covenant" [cf. 2 Cor. 3:6].

The name is derived from the Septuagint. For the prophets, when they foretold the preaching of grace or the new covenant, used a particular word, *bāsar*, which is translated in the Septuagint by the word *euangelizesthai* (cf. Is. 40:9–10; 41:27). Is. 52:7, "How beautiful are the feet of those who bring good tidings." Paul clearly interprets this passage in Rom. 10:15 as a description of the new covenant. Is. 61:1, "He has sent me to preach good tidings to the afflicted." Christ applies this statement to His own ministry in Luke 4:18. Ps. 40:9, "I will proclaim glad tidings of righteousness in the great congregation." This passage [Ps. 40:6–7] is applied to Christ in Heb. 10:5. Ps. 68:11, "He will give His Word to those who preach the good news." Again, Ps. 96:1–2, "Sing a new song. Tell the good tidings of His salvation from day to day." In these passages which unquestionably foretell the future preaching in the era of the new covenant, the word used is *bāsar*, which in all of these passages is rendered into Greek by the term *euaggelitzesthai*. In some places the words *euaggelion* and *euaggelia* are repeated more than once, as in 2 Sam. 18:22, 25, 27.

From this we can understand why Christ and the apostles called the ministry of the new covenant the Gospel. It is also called *thōrah* (law) in a general sense, as in Is. 2:3 and Micah 4:2 (cf. Rom. 3:27, "the law of faith"; Rom. 8:2, "the law of the Spirit of life"). But they did not want to designate the public title (so to speak) of their doctrine by the word "law," in order that the difference between the teaching of Moses and the teaching of Christ might be clearer and in order that they might show that these two kinds of teaching must be distinguished even in their very names. Therefore they gave a special and peculiar name to this teaching of free reconciliation. Because the Jews of the dispersion in that era spoke both Syriac and Greek, as the apocryphal books in the Old Testament and the language of the Septuagint show, and because Scripture was read, used, and known by many in that language [Greek], the apostles called the doctrine of grace they had received from Christ "the Gospel," in order to show that they had not brewed up a new kind of doctrine but that they were referring to the happy proclamation of the grace of the new covenant so often promised and foretold in the prophets under the term and designation "Gospel." Thus Paul in Rom. 1:2 says that he is proclaiming that Gospel which had been promised previously through the prophets, cf. Gal. 3:8, which "the Scripture preached beforehand (*proeuaggelisato*) to Abraham."

The reasoning behind this designation is abundantly clear. For among the Hebrews the word *bāsar* and in the Septuagint the word *euangelizesthai* are not used for the indiscriminate announcing of any kind of good and happy news. Rather, when news came that their enemies, by whom they were threatened with a great and dangerous crisis, had fled or been scattered, this announcement of liberation from enemies, restoring peace and tranquility, which was brought to them in their anxious waiting, was designated by this word, as in 2 Sam. 18:24ff., when David, in anxiety and worry, awaited news about the outcome of the battle with the seditious army of Absalom. Cf. Nah. 1:15; 2 Kings 7:10; Is. 61:1–2; Jer. 20:15; 2 Sam. 4:10; Zech. 9:11. And this rationale for designating applies beautifully to the preaching concerning the benefits of the Son of God. Cf. Zech. 9:11; 1 Cor. 15:55–57; Col. 2:15; Eph. 4:8; Ps. 68:18; Luke 1:74. Col. 1:13, "He has delivered us from the kingdom of darkness . . . ," as Chrysostom in his *Homilia 1 in Matt.* [MPG 57.15] so beautifully describes in his oratorical style, when the age-old battle is ended, the strong man overcome, his spoils taken from him, and messengers sent into the whole world announcing the joyous news of liberation; not because we have worked for it but because we have been loved by God. Luther has a similar description in his *Preface to the New Testament* [1541], [Amer. Ed., 35.358ff.]. This consideration of the grammatical aspects of the subject is lovely and casts much light on the teaching of the New Testament.

Furthermore, because this doctrine had to be preached not only to the Jews but to all nations on earth, they adopted a word that not only was known to the Jews from the Septuagint but had been in common usage among the Greeks. Thus we must consider the meaning of this word also among secular writers. . . .

In ordinary speech in the Greek this term has three meanings. First, it means the happy announcement itself about good and pleasant things, cf. Plutarch, *Marius* [22 (1.418b)]. Particularly is it used of the felicitous outcome of a battle. The same usage occurred among the Hebrews. Cf. Plutarch, *Sertorius* [11]; *Pompey* [41 (1.640)]; *Phocion*; *Artaxerxes*. Second, it refers to the reward and gift given to the bearer of good tidings, cf. Homer, *Odyssey* [14.152, cf. par. 1 of Melanchthon's text]. Third, it refers to the sacrifice and prayers which are observed because of the announcement of good news or something faithfully carried out, cf. Plutarch, *Phocion* [23 (752b)], "to celebrate a festival and make sacrifice because of the good tidings."

It is notable that these meanings agree almost completely with the Scriptural use of the word. For there are announcements of good news and happy events in the prophets, as we have noted above. The term is even used for the reward or gift for the one who bears the good news, 2 Sam. 4:10; 18:22. Also Paul, when he speaks in Rom. 15:16 of "the service of the Gospel," is undoubtedly taking into consideration the meaning commonly used among the Greeks, who by means of their sacrifices and supplications gave thanks for the blessings they had received or were seeking, in order that the deity might be placated. Therefore, he says, "I preach among the Gentile's the true Gospel and I establish a true sacrifice, because of the joyous message which has been received." Thus it is clear that the apostles were happy with the comparable meanings for these terms, which they used in teaching their doctrine.

Furthermore, to the definition of a term pertains also this consideration, whether other names or designations are attributed to this doctrine in Scripture. There ought to be no doubt that the Holy Spirit has knowledge of words, Wisd. of Sol. 1:7. The words He uses in treating the heavenly doctrine are very emphatic or significant, and there are serious underlying reasons why various names are used for the same concept. These points also are certainly worthy of our careful study. For Scripture wants to place before our eyes one and the same concept but using different words, in order that by comparison a sure and certain meaning can be gathered for the subject at hand and so that with the words, which because of brevity we can retain more easily than lengthy discussions, we can always carry around the doctrines themselves and keep them before us. But because a great many terms are applied to the doctrine of the Gospel, we divide them into categories in the following manner, in order that the rationale of each can be more easily and properly considered.

1. Some of these terms are of a general nature. For example, the Gospel is called "the Word," Is. 2:3; "the doctrine," Rom. 6:17; 15:4; 16:17; "the Law," Gal. 2:19: "Through the Law I am dead to the Law"; cf. Is. 2:3; 42:4; 51:4; Jer. 31:33; Micah 4:2; Ps. 19:7; "the testimony," Ps. 19:7; 1 Tim. 2:6; "the testimony of God," 1 Cor. 2:1; "the commandment," 1 John 3:23: "This is His commandment, that we should believe . . ."; 1 Tim. 1:18: "This commandment I commit to you . . . ." These general designations the apostles gave to the teaching of the Gospel because in the Old Testament it had been described by the same terms, as in Ps. 2:7; 19:8. Psalm 119 uses terms such as "law," "word," "testimony," and others.

2. Certain terms denote a kind of notation, paraphrase, or explanation of the word "Gospel," as when it is called "the good Word of God," Heb. 6:5, or "the good doctrine," 1 Tim. 4:6. These terms are taken from the Old Testament, cf. Ps. 45:1; Jer. 33:14, "the good Word." "Sound speech," Titus 2:8; "sound teaching," Titus 1:9; 2 Tim. 4:3. The Gospel is also called "proclamation" (*kērygma*) in Rom. 16:25; 1 Cor. 2:4; 2 Tim. 4:17, etc., to signify that this doctrine must be preached with a strong voice, like a trumpet, clearly, from the heart, earnestly, cheerfully. Thus it says in Titus 1:3 that God "has manifested His Word through preaching." And "I was appointed a preacher (*kēryx*)," 1 Tim. 2:7; 2 Tim. 1:11.

3. Certain terms for "Gospel" speak of its author or origin, namely that it is not a teaching known by nature to human reason but is a mystery, hidden from the ages, which the Son of God has told us; likewise, that it is not a new teaching but was set forth by the divine will, decreed before the times of this age, and promulgated by the ministry of the apostles through all the earth. [Chemnitz here refers to numerous passages: Matt. 13:52; Mark 1:27; Acts 2:42; 8:4, 14, 25; 10:36; 17:19; Rom. 1:9; 2:16; 16:25; 1 Cor. 1:21, 25; 2:1; 2:7, 13; 2 Cor. 2:17; 4:3;

11:7; Gal. 1:12; Eph. 1:9–11; 3:4; 6:17; Col. 1:5; 4:3; 1 Tim. 3:9; 2 Tim. 1:8; 2:15; 1 Peter 4:17; 2 Peter 2:2; 1 John 5:6; Rev. 12:17; 14:6; 19:10.]

4. Certain terms point to and describe the subject matter of the Gospel. [Chemnitz cites Jer. 31:31; Matt. 13:19; Mark 1:14; Luke 1:77; Acts 6:7; 13:12; 20:24, 25; Rom. 1:9, 16; 4:13–16; 9:9; 16:25; 1 Cor. 1:18; 2 Cor. 3:6; Gal. 3:16–22; Col. 3:16; Titus 2:10; 1 John 2:25.]

5. Certain terms refer to the effects of the Gospel. [Chemnitz cites John 6:68; Acts 5:20; 13:26; Rom. 1:16; 4:13; 8:2; 2 Cor. 3:8–9; 4:4; 5:18–19; Eph. 1:13; 6:15, 17; Phil. 2:16; 1 Tim. 1:11; James 2:12.]

6. Certain terms pertain to the instrument by which the promise of the Gospel is apprehended, e.g., "the Word of faith," Rom. 10:8; 1 Tim. 4:6; "the hearing or preaching of faith," Gal. 3:2; "the law of faith," Rom. 3:27; "the faith of the Gospel," Phil. 1:27.

7. Certain terms are metaphorical. [Chemnitz cites Ps. 23:2, 4, 5; Matt. 9:17; 13:24, 27; 24:45; John 4:14, 34; 6:55; 2 Cor. 2:15; Eph. 6:15, 17.]

[CHAPTER] II: THE PROPER DOCTRINE OF THE GOSPEL, THAT IS, THE DEFINITION OF THE SUBJECT

There are many testimonies in Scripture clearly affirming that the doctrine of justification before God must not be taught, learned, or sought in the Law but in the Gospel, e.g., Rom. 1:16–17; 3:21; 4:13; 10:4; Gal. 3:21–22; John 1:17. The object of justifying faith is not the doctrine of the Law but the voice of the Gospel, which is therefore called the Law and Word of faith. It must therefore be determined, on the basis of clear and firm testimonies of Scripture, what is the proper doctrine of the Gospel, which is to be separated from the Law and which reveals the righteousness of faith before God, upon which faith lays hold unto righteousness and eternal salvation. In this teaching we must seek reconciliation and the forgiveness of sins.

It is exceedingly important to have a carefully and correctly drawn up definition of what the true doctrine of the Gospel is. For Paul pays this tribute to the Jews, that they zealously sought righteousness; but because they sought it in the Law and not in the Gospel, they failed to find it. Instead they offended and stumbled in their blindness, Rom. 10:2–3; 11:17.

In order that we may more diligently seek and examine the true foundations of this doctrine and retain those things that have been correctly taught and are necessary, it is worthwhile to consider what pernicious hallucinations regarding the article of justification have occurred at all periods because it was not correctly established, on the basis of true foundations, and what the proper doctrine of the Gospel is, in which faith must seek righteousness before God.

It was the occasion of many errors that, as people limited the Law to the prophetic books in the Old Testament, so they limited the Gospel to the apostolic writings in the New Testament.

From this delusion proceeded the idea, found even in Justin, Tertullian, Clement, and Epiphanius, that before the time of Moses, because the writings of the prophets did not yet exist, men were justified and saved without either the divine law or the Gospel, but only by the natural law; but that after Moses, when the prophets had written their books, then men, because they did not have the books of the apostles or evangelists, were justified and saved by the law of Moses alone; but that now, after the apostolic books have been delivered to the church, we are justified and saved by the evangelical law.

The scholastics cannot deny that Paul clearly asserts that the righteousness of God, or of faith, has been revealed without the Law, in the Gospel, Rom. 1:17; 3:22. But because they have seen in the books of the apostles, to which, as we have said, they have limited the Gospel, that certain commands are given for good works, they have devised this kind of distinction between Law and Gospel: the [old] law, with these commands to do the good works that it teaches, now after the revelation of the Gospel does not justify, because it taught imperfect precepts which dealt only with outward works that were to be performed out of fear and had promises pertaining only to physical and temporal rewards. But under the new law there are given more perfect, more excellent, and more severe commands, which bring abundant righteousness to those who perform them, beyond the righteousness of the Pharisees and scribes, and which have the promise of salvation and eternal life.

They say that the Law and the Gospel differ in these respects: (1) as to the time; (2) as to the precepts; (3) as to the promises; (4) as to the sacraments. Or, that the old law was a matter of fear, the new law a matter of love. Thus, under the new law obedience is easier because the laws are few in number, and they are made easy through love or charity.

If the question is asked, "What is faith?" they reply that faith believes that the things written in the new law are true. But what about Christ? Some reply that He only brought these new commandments. Others, who attribute a little more to Christ, say that He gives us the grace to fulfill the commandments, and through this comes righteousness and eternal life. This idea appears very appropriate, but Paul clearly denies that Christ came in order that we might be justified through precepts of works.

The scholastics did not set these traps all by themselves, but even Augustine himself, who in other respects sheds light beyond all others in defining the Gospel, was in error on this point, and thus also on the doctrine of justification he was not in agreement with Scripture nor consistent with himself. He says in his *De Vera Innocentia*,[2] "The Gospel is a lovely fragrance and the preaching of the truth, and by this fragrance he lays hold on life who keeps the Gospel with his good works and lives according to it." Again in his *De Fide et Operibus* [9, MPL 40.206] he argues that properly speaking the doctrine of the Gospel is not only a matter of faith, but also of the good works of the faithful.

Eusebius in his *De Preparatione Evangelica* [1.1, MPG 21.23] has a description which is summarized thus: The doctrine of the Gospel brings to us the religion by which our souls are converted to God and to living a life in keeping with His commandments. From this life comes a friendship between God and men, and this friendship is a blessed condition.

Again in his *Demonstratio Evangelica* [9, MPG 22.689ff.] he raises the question as to why almost the same precepts are given under the Gospel as under the Law, and therefore what is the difference between the Law and Gospel. He gives the same answer as the scholastics did, as we have said above.

Jerome, in his prologue to the Gospel of Mark [*Prolog, Super Marcum*, MPL 30.590], says that there are four ingredients which make up the structure of the holy gospels: the precepts which command us to turn away from evil; the commandments which order us to do good; the testimonies which show what we are to believe about Christ; and the witnesses to examples that show perfect obedience, such as, "Learn of Me" [Matt. 11:29].

These men and others could not correctly teach the doctrine of justification; or even if they had some light, they could not be consistent with one another. But this foundation is clear: "The righteousness of God is revealed, without the Law, in the Gospel," Rom. 1:17; 3:21. Therefore if the correct doctrine of the Gospel is as they have defined it, then it follows that the righteousness of faith consists not only in the application of the free promise of the remission of sins for the sake of the Mediator, but that also an essential part of the Gospel is the new obedience or good works.

The adversaries, the papists, have seen this clearly. Consequently they are seeking various destructive tactics whereby they may confuse, obscure, and remove this necessary distinction, which makes the Gospel in the proper sense the doctrine that reveals the righteousness of faith availing before God. They see that this way is very easy: If it is established that the proper teaching of the Gospel is not only a matter of faith in the gracious promise for the sake of Christ but also deals with renewal or good works, then it immediately follows that good works have entered into the matter of justification as a partial cause. Because "the righteousness of God has been revealed in the Gospel," Rom. 1:17, therefore the Cologne theologians contend that in the definition of the Gospel we must

---

2   There is no work by this name attributed to Augustine.

add the statement of Matt. 28:20, "Teaching them to observe all things whatsoever I have commanded you," that is, the commandment to love.

Vicelius[3] contends that there are other good works of which the Gospel is speaking. And because the Gospel is the teaching of justification, therefore good works are required for justification.

But Gropper[4] is really playing a sneaky game. He says that the benefit of Christ is not only reconciliation but also sanctification or renewal. And the Gospel, because it reveals the righteousness of faith, consists of and is completed in these two parts, remission of sins and the inner renewal of the will, from whence come good works as the fruit of the Spirit. This was plainly the delusion of Osiander.

I have mentioned these points so that you may understand that these are not idle speculations when we are discussing the foundation of this matter, that is, what the proper teaching of the Gospel is in which "the righteousness of God is revealed from faith to faith," Rom. 1:17. It is impossible that the purity of the article of justification can be retained if we permit the kind of fantasizing in this fundamental point that we have shown in these examples.

Therefore, because Paul clearly says that "the righteousness of God has been revealed in the Gospel without the Law," it follows that the principal point in this matter is that the true and clear distinction between Law and Gospel be established and carefully retained. Luther, on Gal. 2:14, truly and elegantly says: "Whoever knows well how to distinguish between Law and Gospel should give thanks to God and should know that he is a theologian. In temptations I certainly do not know it as I ought. You should distinguish the righteousness of the Gospel from the righteousness of the Law as diligently as heaven is distinguished from earth, light from darkness, day from night . . . and would that we could separate them even farther!" [*Lectures on Galatians*, 1535; cf. *Luther's Works*, Amer. Ed., 26.115]. And what other light can cut through the dense darkness of the kingdom of the papacy except this because it shows the real difference between Law and Gospel? And now leaving out the points which Paul makes in 2 Cor. 3:6ff. and the statements of Hebrews 8 and other passages which compare the old and the new covenant, concerning the promulgation, the time, and the place (because properly these are not relevant), we shall review only the

---

[3] Vicelius (Georg Witzel), 1501–73, one of those characters found commonly in the Reformation period who wandered from Catholicism to Lutheranism to the Anabaptists and back to Rome. He was, of course, distrusted by all and failed to find acceptance anywhere.

[4] Johann Gropper (1503–59). Roman Catholic adherent of Erasmus. Later became vicious opponent of Luther and the Reformation.

main differences by which the doctrine of the Gospel must be distinguished from the Law.

1. The doctrine of the Law to a certain degree is known to human reason. But the Gospel is a mystery hidden from the world, revealed only by the ministration of the Spirit.

2. Luther correctly and elegantly says that both the doctrine of the Law and the doctrine of the Gospel deal with the subject of sin, but in a different way. The Law shows sin, accuses, imputes guilt, and condemns sin; but the Gospel remits, covers, and does not impute sin, because it points to "the Lamb of God, who takes away the sin of the world" [John 1:29].

3. Paul in Rom. 3:21; 4:5; and 10:5ff. shows this difference. The doctrine of the Law is the law of works, which talks about doing: "He who does these things . . ." It imputes a reward to the one who does the Law. But the Gospel is the law of faith, because "to one who does not work but believes in Him who justifies the ungodly" He imputes faith for righteousness.

4. The Law prescribes and demands of each individual perfect obedience to all the commandments of God, and it threatens a curse on those who do not have such conformity with the will of God. But the Gospel, because the Law is weakened through the flesh, Rom. 8:3, shows Christ, who was made sin and a curse, "made under the Law," Gal. 4:4, and is "the fulfillment of the Law unto righteousness to everyone who believes," Rom. 10:4.

5. The promises of the Law are conditional. But the promise of the Gospel concerning the remission of sins is free.

6. "The Law imprisons all under sin," Gal. 3:22; "makes the whole world guilty before God," Rom. 3:19; "works wrath," Rom. 4:15; "puts us under the curse," Gal. 3:10; is "the ministration of death" and damnation [2 Cor. 3:7, 9 KJV]. But the Gospel is the word of salvation, peace, reconciliation, etc. It frees from the law of sin and death and is "the ministration of" righteousness and "the Spirit" [2 Cor. 3:8 KJV].

7. The Law shows what the good works are in which God wants the regenerate to exercise obedience. But the Gospel teaches how they can demonstrate this obedience. For the Gospel contains the promise of the Spirit of renewal, who writes the Law into the hearts of believers, Jer. 31:33. It also teaches how the beginnings of obedience, although imperfect and contaminated in many ways, are pleasing to God in those who are righteous for the sake of Christ.

8. The Law speaks to hypocrites, the secure, the old Adam. The Gospel, however, speaks to the contrite, the broken, the captives, and keeps the new man in a state of grace.

I believe that these are the main points of difference. The true foundations are now clear in regard to the question: What is the correct doctrine of the Gospel which must be distinguished from the Law? For because Paul says that "the righteousness of God is revealed in the Gospel without the Law," Rom. 1:17, therefore, although in the teaching of Christ and the apostles many statements are found regarding sin and good works, yet these are not the doctrine of the Gospel in the proper sense of the word, inasfar as it is distinguished from the Law. We shall explain shortly why the precepts of the Law are repeated in the preaching of the Gospel.

But when in this way we have separated those things properly pertaining to the ministration of the Law, the answer is easy and simple as to what is the proper doctrine of the Gospel, which is to be distinguished from the Law, seeing that it speaks of the benefits of Christ and reveals the righteousness of faith before God.

Therefore we shall divide these passages into certain categories in order to expedite their explanation.

1. The Gospel is preached to those who are repentant, and it deals with the gracious promise of reconciliation, remission of sins, righteousness before God, salvation, and acceptance unto eternal life. This promise is established in God's grace, mercy, and love, Eph. 1:6–9; 2:8; 1 Tim. 1:15; Titus 2:11.

2. In defining the Gospel we must always include the person of Christ, in His office as Mediator. For "in Him all the promises of God are Amen," 2 Cor. 1:20. "The covenant is confirmed in Christ," Gal. 3:17.

Here it is absolutely necessary that the benefits of Christ on account of which we receive remission of sin and are received unto eternal life be distinguished from the benefits of sanctification or renewal which follow justification. We are not justified for the sake of the latter, that is, we do not receive remission of sins nor are we received unto eternal life because of this renewal which follows justification, although it is also a benefit of Christ.

The benefits of reconciliation are these: (1) Christ has taken upon Himself our sins and the punishments for our sins and has made satisfaction to the Father for them. (2) He "is the fulfillment of the Law for righteousness to everyone who believes," Rom. 10:4. Because of this benefit of Christ, we believers are reconciled to God and received unto eternal life. (3) The Gospel teaches that these benefits of the Mediator are apprehended by faith and apply to those who repent. (4) The Gospel teaches that these benefits are offered through the Word and the sacraments, through which instruments the Holy Spirit is efficacious, illumines our hearts, works faith, pours life-giving consolation into our hearts, raises them up, and sustains them. (5) After the benefit of grace or justification the Gospel also contains the promise of "the free gift through grace," Rom. 5:15, or of the "truth," John 1:17, namely that the Spirit of renewal is poured into believers, the Spirit who writes the Law in their hearts so that we may be "His workmanship, created in Christ Jesus for good works, which God prepared in advance, that we should walk in them," Eph. 2:10. (6) The Gospel speaks not only of present benefits we receive by faith for the sake of Christ in this life, but it has also the promise of "the hope of the righteousness which we await," Gal. 5:5, where "God will be all in all," 1 Cor. 15:28, and the hope of "the glory of God which shall be revealed in us" in the life to come, Rom. 5:21; 8:18–21. (7) The promise of the Gospel is universal, pertaining to all, both gentiles as well as Jews, who repent and receive the promise by faith.

These fundamental points regarding the distinctive doctrine of the Gospel are true, and it is necessary that they be diligently retained in the church; for otherwise the purity of the doctrine of justification cannot be preserved. If some insane notion is admitted regarding this question, then there will immediately follow a corruption of the article of justification, as we showed briefly at the beginning of this discussion.

[CHAPTER] III: THE COMMON DEFINITION THAT THE GOSPEL IS THE PREACHING OF REPENTANCE AND THE FORGIVENESS OF SINS

This form of speaking is repeated several times in the Augsburg Confession and its Apology. Nor ought it simply be rejected or condemned, as if no true or helpful explanation were possible. For Christ, when after the Resurrection He committed to the apostles the ministry of teaching, referred to teaching and baptizing and added, ". . . teaching them to observe all that I have commanded you," Matt. 28:20. And the sum and substance of this ministry He calls the Gospel, Mark 16:5, where He clearly adds, "Whoever does not believe will be condemned." And in Luke 24:47 He says, ". . . preaching repentance and remission of sins in His name."

But at this point we must consider what we have mentioned previously, namely, how the papists on the basis of definitions of this kind spread their traps for the truth, so that we should walk with careful steps. For Islebius[5] with devious intentions tries to build his antinomian error on the basis of this definition, as his theses clearly show. And here indeed Luther would have had cause to reject and condemn the common definition completely and without further ado if he had believed that it was a corruption of the true and correct teaching. But because he preferred to explain the matter correctly and properly and to refute an underhanded interpretation or abuse, it is manifest by Luther's example what

---

[5] Islebius is John Agricola of Eisleben. Luther called him Magister Islebius. He was the father of the Antinomian error and the following controversy among Lutherans. Cf. F. Bente, *Historical Introductions to the Symbolical Books of the Evangelical Lutheran Church*, p. 162.

must be done in a godly and correct way. Therefore they are in error and do not act properly who so defend this accepted definition [that is, Melanchthon's definition, in the second last paragraph of the quoted section some pages back] that they necessarily obscure and bury that foundation which is the proper doctrine of the Gospel. Likewise they also err who say that the Law is the preaching of contrition, but only for deadly or hopeless sins such as the sin of Judas, but that the preaching of saving contrition must be taught and learned not by the ministration of the Law but of the Gospel.

There are those who argue that the Gospel properly speaking not only contains the promise of grace but also the teaching of good works. Such people do not understand what they are saying. For in this way the distinction between Law and Gospel is confounded, as Paul has established in Rom. 3:27, "the law of faith" and "the law of works" [KJV], and the Gospel is changed into Law. Once these foundations are overturned, the purity of the doctrine of justification cannot stand. Philipp Melanchthon himself, the author of this definition, accurately warns that although in the teaching of Christ and the apostles there are many statements regarding repentance and the Law, the question remains as to what is the proper doctrine of the Gospel, which must be distinguished from the Law. We shall therefore note certain points as to how this common definition, which is repeated several times in the Augsburg Confession and the Apology, can be correctly and properly understood and explained, so that it may retain its saving and uncorrupted character and teaching regarding the necessary distinction between Law and Gospel, that is to say, there is a proper doctrine of the Gospel, which must be distinguished from the Law, and it speaks of the benefits of the Son of God in order to reveal the righteousness of faith before God. This must be the norm for our explanation.

I. When "Gospel" is used in a general sense as the summary of the entire teaching delivered and propagated through the ministry of Christ and the apostles, this is indeed a correct definition. In Acts 20:21 Paul says that it was his ministry to testify to the Gospel of the grace of God, and he reviews the primary points, namely, "testifying of repentance toward God and faith in Christ." Likewise Mark, in 1:1, 4, calls "the beginning of the Gospel . . . the baptism of repentance for the remission of sins." And when Christ taught repentance and remission of sins, the evangelists say that He preached the kingdom of God. And yet the doctrine of the Gospel in the proper sense of the word remains distinct from the Law. Mark 1:15, "Repent and believe the Gospel." There is a synecdoche when the name of something is taken from the most important part and attributed to the entire ministration. Our great Martin Luther speaks this way in his *Disputation 30 Against the Antinomians*,[6] namely that Christ from time to time through the Gospel condemns, upbraids, threatens, terrifies and exercises similar duties of the Law. Thus in his *Preface to Romans* Luther says, "Through the Gospel the wrath of God shall be revealed (*Es werde offenbaret durchs Evangelium Gottes Zorn*)."

II. Because the Gospel announces grace not to the secure and the hypocrites but to the penitent—that is, to those who, with recognition of their sins and a sense of the wrath of God, are humbled and contrite—in this sense it is proper to say that the Gospel is the preaching of repentance. There is no doubt that in the Augsburg Confession this form of speaking is repeatedly used in order to oppose the clamors of the papists, who were loudly proclaiming that the doctrine of the Gospel was strengthening carnal security and giving a license to sin in the minds of men. Therefore it was said that the gracious promise of the remission of sins requires repentance, that is, a contrite and humble heart. Yet the statement of Paul remained fixed: "Through the Law comes the knowledge of sin," Rom. 3:20. From where knowledge of sin and contrition is to be taught and learned is another question—certainly from the ministration of the Law. Luther often replies in this way to objections in his disputations with the Antinomians: "The Gospel preaches repentance, but through the ministration of the Law."[7] Philipp says the same thing in his next-to-last disputation.[8] And it is said in the same way in the Smalcald Articles [3.3.1, Tappert, p. 303], "This function of the Law [to accuse sin and prosecute it] is retained and taught by the New Testament." The Wittenberg Confession says, "The explanation of the Law is repeated in the Gospel of Christ in order that by showing the severity of the divine Law and the corruption of our nature, we may be moved to see Christ as He is revealed in the Gospel."[9] These are excellent statements.

III. The Gospel by its very nature, because it teaches that "there is no name given to men whereby they can be saved," except the name of Jesus Christ, Acts 4:12, antithetically shows that "all have been imprisoned under sin" [Gal. 3:22]. "To justify" is a judicial term presupposing a conscience accused and terrified by the fear of God's judgment. Luther says. "When God says, 'In your seed shall all nations be blessed,' He is showing that all nations in themselves have been

---

[6]   Luther, *Disputatio 3 Contra Antinomos*, untranslated. Cf. WA 39 (1) 364. Also note Amer. Ed., 47.101ff., and note 8 on p. 103.

[7]   Luther, *Preface to the Epistle to the Romans*, Amer. Ed., 35.372.

[8]   This statement refers to a quotation from Melanchthon made by Luther in one of Luther's own disputations on this subject. Cf. WA 39 (1) 576. Note also Luther, *Against the Antinomians*, Amer. Ed., 47.102, Fn 8. Also cf. our Fn 6.

[9]   The reference here is to the Wittenberg Confession of 1570. For details see Bente, p. 135.

condemned. And thence, how and why they have been condemned is learned from the Law." Luther speaks distinctly in *Disp. 4 Contra Antinomos*, Proposition 24, "Paul in effect, when he teaches that all must be justified in Christ, is arguing that all are sinners. This is the work of the Law."

IV. It is certain and clear that the Gospel teaches and demonstrates certain explanations of the Law which we cannot easily and clearly gather from Moses alone. Because the Law is the doctrine of repentance, in this sense it is not improper to say that the Gospel is the preaching of repentance, just as long as the distinctive doctrine of the Gospel remains the promise of grace. Thus Luther says in his *Lectures on Galatians* [of 1535] on ch. 2 [v. 17; Amer. Ed., 26.150], "Although there are commandments in the Gospel, they are not the Gospel; they are expositions of the Law and appendices to the Gospel." We must note these explanations which the Gospel adds to the Law, for in this way the treatment of the common definition can be used with benefit and value. In regard to the use of the Law Luther writes this concerning Galatians 3 [ibid., p. 315], "[The] function and use [of the Law] is not only to disclose the sin and wrath of God but also to drive us to Christ. None but the Holy Spirit is intent on this use of the Law or preaches the Gospel, because nothing but the Gospel says that God is present with those who are contrite in heart." Thus Luther.

[Chemnitz continues to quote from Luther's Galatians, pp. 314ff. and 398.]

When we learn this from the explanation of the Gospel, then we can also see the foundation in the Law itself and how perfect fulfillment of it is impossible for us.

There is also this one further point: The law of faith adds to the law of works [cf. Rom. 3:27 KJV], namely, that not only those vices in direct conflict with the law of God, but also that the outward honorable discipline in the unregenerate is a sin before God, as it says: "Without faith it is impossible to please God," Heb. 11:6, and "Whatever is not of faith is sin," Rom. 14:23. John 16:8–9: The Holy Spirit "will reprove the world of sin" [KJV], even the most upright lives, because the world does not believe in Christ. Indeed, there are some points of the Law which without the explanation of the Gospel, which is the doctrine of faith, would not be understood in the Law.

In addition, it is also a certainty and worthy of note that only the doctrine of faith shows the difference between mortal and venial sin. For the Law does not teach this but is in fact opposed to it. For the Law says: "He who is lacking in one point is guilty of all," James 2:10. Likewise: "Cursed is he who does not continue in all . . . ," Deut. 27:26; Gal. 3:10. It is a fountain of error among the scholastics that without respect to faith, and only on the basis of the Law, they have created the distinction between mortal and venial sin. . . .

Concerning the Law Moses says, Deut. 29:4, "You have heard and seen, but to this day God has not given you an understanding heart and seeing eyes." But in regard to the new covenant the prophet says: "I shall write My law in their hearts," Jer. 31:33. But how this beginning obedience in believers, even though imperfect and polluted in many ways, can be pleasing to God is not the teaching of the Law. For the Law teaches that our obedience is pleasing to God only when it is perfect and is rendered with our whole heart, without concupiscence, as the Law itself prescribes, and when no violation of the Law remains anywhere.

Furthermore, since the promises of the Law concerning the rewards for good works are conditioned absolutely on our doing nothing contrary to the Law, they would be rendered vain and meaningless for us if we did not learn from the Gospel how we are declared righteous and how this beginning obedience in keeping with the Law is pleasing to God. Therefore the promises of the Law are in force for those who have been justified through faith for the sake of Christ, because God accepts this obedience. But these points can be treated in a useful and beneficial way in the explanation of the commonly accepted definition. Nevertheless, there remains and of necessity ought to remain a salutary difference between these appendices of the Gospel (as Luther calls them) and the doctrine of the Gospel properly speaking, which reveals the righteousness of faith before God.

V. The Law, in the First Table, accuses as sin all unbelief over against the Word of God. But the Gospel, when it sets up the antithesis to the doctrine of faith, explains this unbelief specifically as being a rejection of the gracious promise of reconciliation, and he who does not believe in the Son of God is the greatest sinner because he thus keeps all the rest of his sins, if they are not remitted. Even if he lives a most upright life, it is a sin before God. Many passages prove this point: "The wrath of God remains upon him," John 3:36. Likewise: "Whoever does not believe will be condemned," Mark 16:16. Again: "This is the condemnation of the world," John 3:19. It is certain that the Law, insofar as it is Law, does not speak of the free and gracious promise of reconciliation or of the benefits of Christ the Mediator. Thus these antithetical statements have to do with the doctrine of the Gospel and not of the Law. For the affirmative statements concerning trust in God's gracious mercy for the sake of Christ are not the voice of the Law, as Paul clearly says in Gal. 3:12: "The Law is not of faith." The trust (*fiducia*) of which the First Commandment teaches, as the voice of the Law, properly speaking, is not that statement of Gospel: "Son, be confident; your sins are forgiven you," Matt. 9:2. It states that God is indeed good and merciful, but to those who render to the Law perpetual and perfect obedience. "Both the necessity for faith in Christ and the sin of unbelief which opposes God are reduced to the First Commandment," as Luther writes regarding Genesis 22.

Again, "Because the Law is proclaimed in a general way, we must believe the Word of God, and not to believe it is a sin." Again, "Because the Gospel gives to believers in Christ, through imputation, that perfect obedience which we owe under the First Commandment, therefore, the antithetical nature of the Gospel shows specifically that unbelief which is prohibited in the First Commandment." Thus what Luther says remains true, "Whatever shows sin, wrath, or death is carrying out the work of the Law, whether it occurs in the Old or the New Testament."[10] These statements are true and clear and free of all sophistry. But if a person takes pleasure in arguing, he can play games with these statements and also with some that are even clearer.

VI. Luther in his *First Disputation Against the Antinomians* [WA 39 (1) 345–46] through certain theses shows in what sense and for what reasons it is correct to say that the Gospel is the preaching of repentance. I shall cite only a few of these. He says in Thesis 1 that repentance, by the testimony of all, is sorrow over sin plus the intention to live a better life. Thesis 4: The first part of repentance, the sorrow, comes only from the Law. The second part, namely, the intention to do good, cannot come from the Law. 8. Repentance only from the Law is a half repentance or the beginning of repentance, or it is called repentance by the use of synecdoche, but it lacks the good intention. 9. If a person continues in this "half" repentance, it is the repentance of Cain, Saul, Judas, and other hopeless people. 21. Therefore, against these useless teachers of despair, the Gospel begins to teach that repentance must not be only despair. 22. But those who are repentant must take hope, and out of love for God they must hate sin. This is the truly good intention. 23. Some who do not understand the reasons for speaking this way, or the subject matter, used to think that the Law of God was being denigrated. I believe that this is a simple, true, useful, and salutary conclusion to this controversy regarding the definition of the Gospel.

[C.]: THE NEED FOR THE PROMISE OF THE GOSPEL

[MELANCHTHON'S TEXT]

After human nature has become oppressed by sin and death because of the fall of Adam, even though some knowledge of the Law remains, yet because sin inheres in our nature, our consciences cannot understand that God is willing to forgive if they hear nothing except the Law. For the Law does not teach that sins are forgiven freely. We know that we are not without sin, and we perceive it very clearly when

---

[10] Chemnitz has many citations from Luther which are difficult if not impossible to locate. Often he cites the Wittenberg Edition of Luther's works, or a certain folio in that edition, but time and unavailability of the sources make it impossible to give the exact location of the citation in a modern edition of Luther. In some instances no location at all is indicated.

our minds are really terrified by the judgment of God. Therefore there is need for a gracious and free forgiveness, and God has revealed through His mercy that He is willing to forgive us and restore eternal life to us. He has also supplied the Sacrifice for us, His own Son, that we may know that these blessings have been given for the sake of His Son and not because of our worthiness or merit. This Gospel promise was revealed immediately after the fall of Adam, so that there was no lack of comfort for that first church.

This is the one and the same Gospel by which all the saints from the beginning of the world have been saved in all periods of history—Adam, Noah, Abraham, Jacob, the prophets, and the apostles. Therefore we must not imagine that the patriarchs were saved by the natural law and the Jews by the law of Moses and that we are saved by some kind of law of our own. There is absolutely only one Law, the moral law of all ages and of all peoples, as we have said above; but neither the patriarchs nor the Jews nor the gentiles nor we ourselves are saved by satisfying this Law. No one satisfies the Law. The Law leaves our consciences in doubt.

The difference between the patriarchs and Xenophon, Cicero, and other good men like them is that although they all knew the Law, they did not all know the Gospel. Thus Xenophon, Cicero, and the others were in doubt as to whether God cared about them, whether God was favorably inclined toward them, whether they were heard by God. For since they knew the Law, they saw that they were not innocent; but the Law taught them that God was kindly disposed toward those who are without sin. They did not know the Gospel about the free remission of sins. On the other hand, Abraham, Jacob, and men like them, because they knew the Gospel, knew that their sins were forgiven them, that they had a God who was favorable toward them, that God cared about them, that they were heard by God, even though they were unworthy. Therefore it is written: "Abraham believed God, and it was imputed to him for righteousness" [Gen. 15:6; Rom. 4:3].

There is one Law, known by nature to all peoples and ages; and there is one Gospel, but it is not known by nature but only by divine revelation. Thus Paul calls it a "hidden mystery" [1 Cor. 2:7]. And John [1:18] says that "the Son, who is in the bosom of the Father, has revealed Him to us." All of these points will be explained more fully when we speak a little later about grace and about justification. . . .

The promise concerning Christ and His benefits was first revealed to Adam immediately after the Fall, so that, even though he had fallen under death and the wrath of God, he yet might have the consolation by which he could know both that God was again and would continue to be favorably inclined toward him and that death at some point would be overcome. That first promise clearly sets forth these two benefits, even though it seems to be rather obscure to us; but to Adam in his status at that time it was not obscure. "I will put enmity between you and the woman, and between your seed and her seed; He shall crush your head, and you shall lie in wait for His heel," Gen. 3:15.

This is a marvelous account, one that can seem ridiculous and fabulous to the ungodly. But the pious will see that the most important matters are here dealt with in the briefest possible way. Here is a description of the beginning of the punishment for sin, that because of sin the devil with his cruel tyranny is going to oppress the human race with sins and death, as the very history of the world testifies and which is all shown in the terrible sentence laid upon Adam.

Then there is added in this verse a brief description of the reign of Christ, that it is in the future, that the seed of the woman is going to crush the head, that is, the kingdom, of the serpent; that is, that He will destroy sin and death. This consolation raises Adam up; he recognizes that he is at peace with God, even though he sees that he is unworthy and unclean. He sees what he has lost, but he awaits that Seed by whom his lost righteousness and eternal life are to be restored to him. This trust in His mercy pleases God. The words that are added, that the devil "will lie in wait for the heel of the Seed," Adam understood to mean that Christ and the saints will be afflicted in this life but that Christ will nevertheless overcome the kingdom of the devil.

Later on the promise was renewed to Abraham: "In your Seed shall all the nations be blessed," Gen. 12:3. This means that all the nations are now under the curse, that God is angry at all nations, and that they all are oppressed by sin and death. But the time is coming when through the Seed of Abraham they shall again be freed from these evils. The apostles interpreted this promise in this way, as is evident from the Book of Acts and from Paul.

Furthermore, in this same account of Abraham is added the idea of justification. God comforts Abraham by saying: "Do not be afraid; I am your Protector," Gen. 15:1. Then He adds the promise concerning the Seed, and Abraham believes this word, that is, although he sees and realizes that he is unclean and unworthy, yet he understands that he has a God who is favorable toward him for the sake of His own mercy and the promise of the Seed, and thus he is pronounced righteous. This example teaches that we obtain reconciliation through the promise and faith, for faith does not rely on our own worthiness but only on the mercy of God.

Gradually many other statements and examples followed concerning the remission of sins. The clearest statements are in the Psalms and the prophets. The Gospel is set forth very clearly in some of these. In the Psalms, David seeks forgiveness of his sins for the sake of God's mercy and not on the grounds of his own worthiness or merit, for example, "Do not enter into judgment with Your servant, for no one living shall be justified in Your sight," Ps. 143:2. It is certainly not the preaching of the Law which seeks mercy and confesses sins; indeed, the Law condemns all, in order that we all may know that our sins are freely forgiven. Again, "If You should mark iniquities, O Lord, who will stand?" Ps. 130:3. Or, "I said I will confess against myself my unrighteousness, and You have forgiven the wickedness of my heart," Ps. 32:5. Or the passage which describes Christ as a priest, Ps. 110:4, "You are a priest forever," which testifies that this priest will propitiate God and restore eternal righteousness and eternal life, for it calls Him "a priest forever."

We must apply similar passages in the Psalms to this teaching concerning the gracious forgiveness of sins. For these lovely songs sing sweetly to us about this and bring us great comfort. If we believe that these promises depend upon our worthiness, when the Psalms command us to rejoice and trust in God's mercy, then our consciences would always remind us that we are unworthy and that these promises in no way apply to the unworthy. Therefore we must guard our minds against this doubt and be aware that these very words which command us to rejoice have been spoken in order that they may relieve this doubt which has arisen from our unworthiness.

If we believe that reconciliation has been freely promised to us, then faith will be certain and we will rejoice in God's mercy and give Him thanks. But so great is the weakness and frailty of the human mind that it cannot grasp the greatness of this mercy. We are so burdened down under works-righteousness and the judgment of the Law that we cannot be persuaded that the Gospel freely offers mercy to all. Therefore faith must always struggle with this weakness of ours in order that we may take courage and learn to trust in God and truly invoke and worship Him.

In Isaiah there are many statements which deal with Christ, the remission of sins, and eternal life. Ch. 53 clearly bears witness to the promise of the remission of sins for the sake of Christ and not because of our own worthiness. The Lord "has laid upon Him the iniquities of us all," v. 6. And lest the Jews get the idea that they merited the remission of their sins by reason of the Levitical sacrifices, Isaiah testifies that there is still another sacrifice by which sin is truly absolved: "He shall make His soul an offering for sin," v. 10. Again, He condemns all, for he says, "All we like sheep have gone astray," v. 6, in order that we know that we have received the benefits of Christ because of His mercy and not because of our own worthiness. And finally he adds the clearest testimony of all, "By His knowledge He shall justify many," v. 11. This means that we must definitely establish the fact that we are pronounced righteous if we confess Christ, that is, if we confess that God is favorable toward us for the sake of Christ. Therefore there must be no doubt regarding our own unworthiness and no feeling that we are righteous because of the Law. But I shall cite no more testimonies, for I have cited these for the sake of example so that the readers can see in Scripture which passages are speaking properly of the Law and which properly of the Gospel, and thus can note the difference between the Law and the promise of the Gospel. For these two particular loci are the chief teaching of Scripture, to which all parts of Scripture must be wisely compared. . . .

We must retain this universal promise against dangers we might imagine regarding predestination, so that we do not argue that this promise pertains only to a *certain few others, but not to ourselves. There is no doubt that this thought troubles the minds of all people. From this have arisen many useless controversies by writers on the subject of predestination. But we must make up our minds that the promise of the Gospel is universal. For just as the preaching of repentance is universal, so also is the preaching of the remission of sins universal. Under this heading belong the various statements of Scripture pertaining to the universality of the Gospel, such as John 3:16: "God so loved the world that He gave His only begotten Son, that whoever believes in Him should not perish . . . ." Likewise in Paul, "God has imprisoned all under sin that He might have mercy upon all" [Rom. 11:32; cf. Gal. 3:22]. This is sufficient instruction for the moment. . . .*

That not all obtain the Gospel promise comes from the fact that they do not all believe. For the Gospel, even though it promises freely, yet requires faith; it is necessary that the promise be received by faith. The term "freely" does not exclude faith, but it does exclude our worthiness as a condition, as we have said above; and it demands that we accept the promise, and this cannot take place except through faith.

[CHAPTER I]: THE NEED FOR THE PROMISE OF THE GOSPEL, AND THE SIMILARITY BETWEEN THE LAW AND THE GOSPEL

The Law has not only material or temporal promises but also the promise of righteousness and eternal life, Rom 2:13; 7:10. Lev. 18:5, "If a man keeps the laws he shall live by them." And Christ interprets this statement as applying to eternal life, Luke 10:28. Deut. 30:19, "I have set before you life and blessing." Because both the doctrine of the Law and the doctrine of the Gospel have the promise of salvation and eternal life, some have imagined that God has set forth two roads to eternal life: one in the Law for those who govern their life and morality with great diligence, and the other in the Gospel for those who either are more sluggish in their zeal for a virtuous life or have been overtaken in sins. But that there is only one way to justification before God, to eternal life, will be shown later. The promise of the Law which speaks of eternal life, because it requires as a condition that the entire Law be perfectly fulfilled, is absolutely useless to us in this flesh, as Heb. 7:18 says.

Thus it is not by the weakness of the Law, as if its promises were unsure or false, but by the weakness of our flesh that the condition which has been added to the promise of the Law has been rendered impossible for us, Rom. 8:3; Gal. 3:11. Therefore a change has taken place (Heb. 7:12) in the promise of salvation and eternal life, namely that it must be sought not in the Law but only in the Gospel; and those who seek it in the Law, even if with great zeal, are still under the curse, Rom. 10:2–3; Gal. 3:10. On this basis many objections from statements of the Law, contrary to the righteousness of faith, are removed.

Although, as we have said, the Law must carefully be distinguished from the Gospel, yet the Law is not contrary to the promise of the Gospel, Gal. 3:21; nor is the Law destroyed through faith, but rather established, Rom. 3:31. Therefore both points must be considered: the difference between the Law and the Gospel, of which we have spoken above, and also that Law and Gospel are so connected that it is impossible to use a mathematical parallel to describe their similarity, as Luther says on Galatians 3. The convergence of Law and Gospel consists particularly in this, that the benefits of Christ of which the Gospel speaks are nothing else than satisfaction for the guilt and punishment we owe to the Law and that completely perfect obedience which the righteousness of the Law demands. These two things which the Law requires and demands are given to believers and imputed in Christ for righteousness.

There is no way we can understand the greatness of the benefits of Christ unless they are thus compared with the rigor and severity of the Law. This righteousness of which the Law speaks, impossible for us because of the flesh, the Gospel shows and points out in Christ, who was made under the Law, in order that the righteousness of the Law might be fulfilled in us (1) by imputation through faith; (2) by the beginning stage when the Law through the Spirit is written in our hearts; (3) in eternal life, when our obedience to the law of God will be brought to completion.

Therefore the righteousness of the Law and of the Gospel is different, and it is also the same. In respect to us it is different, cf. Phil. 3:9, "a righteousness which is not of the Law." But with respect to Christ it is the same; for what the Law demands and requires, this Christ supplies and gives. So also reconciliation is called redemption with respect to Christ, because the compensation has been paid; but with respect to us it is called the gracious remission of sins. How Law and Gospel are very closely joined in daily use, in the same heart, Luther shows most beautifully in his comments on Galatians 3 [*Lectures on Galatians*, on 3:23, Amer. Ed. 26.343].

[Chapter II]: All the Saints in All Ages ... Have Been Saved by One and the Same Gospel

We have spoken previously about the statement used by many ancient writers, that some people are justified before God and saved only by the observance of the natural law and others by observing the law of Moses without any knowledge of or faith in the Gospel. Pelagius even used this statement as the consensus of all antiquity in order to prejudice people against the doctrine of grace. But Augustine rejected, refuted, and condemned this notion as Pelagian by citing by name writers who had spoken previously and by showing that it was in conflict with many clear and firm testimonies of Scripture concerning the grace of God.

Afterward the doctrine of the Gospel was again obscured. The scholastics began to turn to this line of thought: Because these ideas inhere by nature in the minds of all men, therefore whatever form of worship they offer to God with a good intention, insofar as within them lies, must consider them pleasing and acceptable to Him.

It is apparent that this question gave considerable trouble to the apostles themselves as they spread the doctrine of the Gospel throughout the world. For the gentiles raised in opposition the honorable behavior of their great men; and the Jews "the burden and heat of the day" [Matt. 20:12] in their observance of the Law. The apostles therefore gathered passages that were repetitions of the most ancient statements, from the very beginning of time, to show that the doctrine of the Gospel was not something new, Mark 1:27; Acts 17:19, but that it is one and the same Gospel by which all the saints in all ages, from the beginning of the world, have been justified and saved.

The line of reasoning used in gathering these testimonies is prescribed and shown in Luke 24:27; Acts 7:2ff.; Rom. 4:1ff.; and Heb. 11:3ff. If we follow this rationale, we will be able, with the singular pleasure supplied by the Spirit, and not without fruit, to examine and observe in the history of all periods from the beginning of the world these two points: (1) The same teaching and belief concerning righteousness before God and eternal life has always been in the church among all the saints. (2) In succeeding ages, by the repetition of this same doctrine, the Gospel has little by little been more clearly revealed. Just as with the rise of Lucifer there was a gradual darkness which surrounded us, so now more and more the sky is brightening until, after the day star, the sun itself shall arise. The arrangement of these times is described in the Old Testament with this kind of simile, cf. Mal. 4:2 and 2 Peter 1:19. Thus briefly and in chronological order I shall note the passages in which the most important repetitions of the Gospel are set forth and described.

I: From the Fall of Adam to the Flood

Immediately after the Fall the doctrine of the Gospel concerning the gracious reconciliation through faith for the sake of a Mediator was revealed to Adam in the promise of the Seed of the woman, Gen. 3:15. And when Eve named her son "a man, Jehovah," Gen. 4:1,[11] she showed how she understood the promise of the Seed. As the manner of contrition the promise mentions the bruising of the heel, which is explained through the sacrifice, by the killing of the Seed.

---

[11] Compare Luther's *The Last Words of David*, Amer. Ed., 15.319ff.

And then in Gen. 4:4 and 7 God Himself interprets the promise, namely through the taking away or the remission of sin, and God has respect for this in the case of Abel. In Heb. 11:4 it says, "Through faith Abel received the testimony that he was righteous before God, and indeed through this faith he spoke even after his death," that is, that he was living and was in God's care.

And what this faith is Moses shows in the clear revelation which took place in the case of Enosh, when he says in Gen. 4:26, "This man began to call on the name of the Lord" (Vulgate).

Enoch received "the testimony that through faith he was pleasing to God," Heb. 11:5. And God showed that the purpose of faith was not only the acceptance of the person in this life, but also salvation in eternal life. This is what it means when it says, "Enoch was translated," Gen. 5:24.

In Gen. 5:29 it seems that Lamech is speaking of the promise of grace when he says, "He will comfort us or give us rest on the earth which God has cursed."

When the wrath of God poured out over the whole earth, Noah was made "the heir of righteousness which is by faith," Heb. 11:7. Because Scripture says that Noah was a "preacher of righteousness," 2 Peter 2:5, and "through faith he condemned the world," Heb. 11:7, it is manifest that the patriarchs down to the time of the Deluge repeated and explained the first promise concerning the Seed which had been given in Paradise. Indeed there was a controversy concerning this teaching, particularly at the time of Noah. It is pleasant to note how down to the time of the Flood individual parts of the first promise were developed and explained, that is to say, what the Seed is, what the head of the serpent is, what contrition is, and how this promise is received. And from the names which are recorded in Genesis 5 we can learn many things.

II: From the Flood to Moses

After the Flood to Gen. 8:21, when God "smelled a sweet-smelling and pleasant odor" from the sacrifice of Noah, so that He said in His heart that He would "never again curse the earth for man's sake," even though his nature is so corrupted that "the imagination of man's heart is evil from his youth," this demonstrates a beautiful explanation of the first promise.

In Gen. 9:26, when Noah says, "Blessed be the Lord God of Shem," he is unquestionably referring to the promise. He is saying two things: (1) He is speaking of the blessing, and (2) "The Lord will be your God." As a result of this Shem is called "the king of righteousness" and "the king of peace," Heb. 7:1–2.[12]

---

[12] Note Luther's reference to Shem in regard to Gen. 14:18 in Amer. Ed., 2.381f.

But particularly illustrative is the repetition of the promise of the Gospel to Abraham, which took place over and over again and in various ways. Note Gen. 12:1–3 concerning the blessing; concerning the place in Canaan, Gen. 15:18; concerning Melchizedek, Gen. 14:18–20, who is called priest and king, terms which Hebrews 7 applies to the Messiah on the basis of this passage in Genesis. In Gen. 15:6 such terms as "faith," "righteousness," and "imputation" are used. In Gen. 17:9–10 the promise is called a "covenant," and circumcision is given as a sign of the righteousness of faith. And He shows that this method of justification pertains to all races who wish to be saved when He says in Gen. 17:5, "I have made you the father of many nations." Again in v. 14 the negative side is given when He says, "That soul shall be cut off from His people; he has broken My covenant." Gen. 21:10 mentions the inheritance from which the son of the bond woman is excluded. In Gen. 22:17–18 He mentions "the gates of his enemies," and He describes how this shall take place when He says, "All nations shall bless you in your Seed."

The promise is repeated to Isaac, Gen. 26:3–4, and here the promise is called an oath. God adds that He will confirm this oath, Gen. 27:27–29. And "by faith Isaac handed on the blessing to Jacob," Heb. 11:20.

The repetition of the promise is given to Jacob in Gen. 28:13–15. And for the sake of clarification there is added the expression, "I am with you, I will take care of you, I will not forsake you." And the reference to the word "vow" in v. 20 is explained in Gen. 32:10. Here for the first time "mercy" and "truth" are mentioned. The struggle of faith in temptation is first described in v. 24ff. In Gen. 35:2–4 Jacob cleans idolatry from the church, and in v. 9–12 the promise is repeated. Along with prayer is placed as a correlative the fact that God answers or hears our prayer, Gen. 48:15–16, cf. 49:1ff. where Jacob blesses his sons. In Heb. 11:21 it is said to have taken place by faith in the promise. In the blessing of Judah in Gen. 49:10–12 the promise is not repeated but the promise of God concerning the Seed is beautifully illuminated. For it refers to the time of the coming of the Seed, and the new name of Shiloh is applied to the Seed. The preaching of the Gospel is metaphorically described.

Concerning Joseph the Epistle to the Hebrews, 11:22, says, "By faith Joseph made mention of the exodus from Egypt and gave command concerning his bones." After the death of Joseph the teaching of the promise of liberation through the blessed Seed sounded forth among the children of Israel, as we can conclude from the fact that in Ex. 1:16 and 22 Pharaoh commanded that the male seed of the Israelites should be killed.

This is the chronology from the time of the Flood down to Moses, and it is most comforting to consider which parts of the promise have been more and more clearly and plainly revealed and explained in this period.

III: From Moses to the Prophets

In the third place the period of time from Moses to the prophets must be considered. Indeed the Epistle to the Hebrews, 11:23, bears witness concerning the faith of the parents of Moses. And in regard to Moses himself the epistle says in v. 26 that he considered "the reproach of Christ to be of greater value than the treasures of Egypt." But at this point we want to ask the question how in the public ministry of all ages the voice of the Gospel has rung out and been illuminated by so many repetitions. The ministry of Moses, although it must be distinguished from the ministry of the Gospel, yet in the final analysis shows and reveals Christ; John 5:46, "Moses wrote of Me." Concerning the ceremonial laws Heb. 9:9–10 says that they were "shadows, types, and figures" of Christ and the new covenant. Regarding the Passover, Heb. 11:28 says clearly that Moses kept it "by faith." Regarding the moral laws, however, Paul says in 2 Corinthians 3 and Rom. 10:4, "Christ is the completion of the Law unto righteousness for him who believes." The figures of Christ in the New Testament are taken from Ex. 25:17, the mercy seat, cf. Rom. 3:25, Heb. 5:5–7; and the Passover is interpreted in 1 Cor. 5:7 and Heb. 11:28. The Epistle to the Hebrews treats the entire Book of Leviticus. The lifting up of the serpent in Num. 21:9 is explained in John 3:14. And most worthy of memory is the statement in Deut. 18:15ff. which is cited in Acts 3:22. For when the people had answered proudly, "All the things which God has commanded we will do," Ex. 19:8, God restrains this arrogance by manifesting their sin and His wrath by the voice of the Law. Then the people complained that they could not bear this voice, Ex. 20:19, and therefore sought another prophet. In this passage in Deuteronomy, God with a clear repetition further develops His promise concerning Christ. And what the Father says from heaven [in Matt. 3:17], "hear Him," is taken from this passage in Moses.

Then the books of Joshua and Judges give examples of faith, as Heb. 11:32ff. shows. But we are now discussing the repetitions wherein the promise of the Gospel is clearly given. Joshua, by his very name as well as in his work, was a figure of Christ, Heb. 4:8. In Judg. 13:5 the term "Nazarite" is used, cf. Matt. 2:23.

IV: From the Prophets to Christ

In the fourth place, the same situation prevails through the period of the prophets. A beginning is made with Samuel, Acts 3:24 and 13:20. In regard to Samuel himself there is no particularly significant statement except what is said in 2 Sam. 7:12–14, which is written about David, but this relates to the period after the death of Samuel. But to David was given a particularly clear repetition of the promise, 2 Sam. 7:12–14; 1 Chron. 22:9–10 (Vulgate); Ps. 89:20ff.; 132:11ff. Here for the first time we encounter the expressions "in the fullness of time," and "Son of God," likewise, "fruit of the womb" (Vulgate), not of the "loins," as Scripture is accustomed to say elsewhere. And David in the Psalms repeats, explains and illuminates the promise of the Gospel more fully than all the others before him. He developed most fully the figure of Melchizedek and in Ps. 2:6 and 8 calls him a king whose inheritance and possession included not only the Jews but the gentiles and the uttermost parts of the earth. He calls him "a priest forever," Ps. 110:4; "the Son of God," not as the other saints are sons of God, but bar, the chosen Son, begotten of the Father, Ps. 2:7. And in Ps. 45:6 he calls Him "God." The term "Messiah" is first in the Psalms attributed to the Seed, Ps. 45:7; 2:2, "Against the Lord and His anointed One." In Ps. 105:15 people are called "anointed ones" from the word "messiah" (in the singular), in the same way that they were called Christians from the word "Christ." Likewise in the Psalms for the first time the word *yāsha*, from which is derived the name "Jesus" begins to be used in reference to the matter of salvation, cf. *yᵉshū'ath* in Ps. 98:3, "They have seen the salvation of our God." Also Ps. 119:41, 81, 123, 166, and 174. Ps. 8:6 speaks of the humiliation of Christ. David for the first time in Scripture begins to speak more clearly and openly regarding the death and resurrection of Christ, Ps. 8:6; 16:10; 22:1ff.; 40:13; 41:11; 69:1ff. On the Ascension see Ps. 47:7; 68:18; 110:2. Concerning the reign of Christ also over the gentiles see Ps. 2:8; 8; 24:7; 72:1ff.; 45:13ff.; 99; 102:16; 110:6–7. On the scandal of the cross, Ps. 118:22.

Matt. 12:42 shows that Solomon was a figure of Christ, cf. Ps. 72:1ff. Certain statements of Solomon also seem to speak of the Incarnation, e.g. Prov. 8:22ff.

Jonah lived in the time of Jereboam shortly before Isaiah, 2 Kings 14:25. He is a remarkable figure showing how Christ was an off scouring (*katharma*). Likewise, "Just as Jonah was three days and three nights in the belly of the fish . . ." Matt. 12:40.

Isaiah cast such brilliant light on the promise of the Seed, which in 5:1 he calls his "cousin" (Vulgate), that Jerome says he is not a prophet but an evangelist. He clearly interprets statements regarding the Seed of the woman and the fruit of the womb, as he says in 7:14, "Behold a virgin shall conceive . . . ." There was not so much light as this before the time of Isaiah. He beautifully describes the union of the two natures by his use of the name "Immanuel," 7:14. In 4:2 he speaks of "the branch of the Lord" and "the fruit of the earth." In 7:14–15 he describes the humiliation in the birth and development of Christ, "He eats butter in order that He may learn to refuse the evil and choose the good." 11:1, "the rod of Jesse." 53:2, "the root out of dry ground." Isaiah is the first to prophesy concerning the forerunner of the Messiah, 40:3; the first to speak of miracles, 35:5–6; the first to speak clearly of the burial, 11:10. In 53:9 he not only clearly describes the suffering and Resurrection but also explains the reason for the suffering and the fruit of the Resurrection, 43:24–25; 50:6; 53:2ff.; 63:1ff. He describes the ministry of Christ in 61:1ff. He makes reference to the place at which Christ begins His reign and whence His reign is to be proclaimed, 2:2–3. The reign itself in this world and in the world to come is described in 11:3ff. and in chs. 4, 25, 26, 27, 32, 35, 40, 42, 44, 49, 52, 54, 55, 59, 60, 62, 65, and 66. He predicts that this kingdom shall be governed amidst various offenses and troubles, 8:14 and ch. 28.

Hosea was a contemporary of Isaiah. In 6:6 he speaks of a different sacrifice. In 3:4–5 the people will sit without a king, without an altar, and without a sacrifice. He calls the Messiah David. In 13:14 he describes His death; in 6:2 he notes the Resurrection on the third day; in 11:1 the flight into Egypt; in 2:18ff. and 14:5ff. he speaks of the kingdom of Christ.

Amos lived during the same period. James in Acts 15:16–17 cites his prophecy given in 9:11–12.

Micah also prophesied at this time. He is the first and only one to note the place of Christ's birth, 5:2. He also speaks of the place of Christ's ministry, Jerusalem, 4:2; of Christ's reign under the figure of the shepherd, 5:4; and in 7:19 of the water in which sins would be drowned.

After them, in the period of Manasseh, Joel, Nahum, and Habakkuk prophesied. Joel 2:28 has a clear prophecy of the signs and mission of the Spirit. He calls Christ "the teacher of righteousness" in v. 23 (Vulgate). Nahum 1:15 repeats the words of Isaiah 40:9 regarding those who preach the Gospel of peace. Hab. 2:3–4 says that although Jerusalem must be destroyed and the people carried away, yet it is certain that the prophecy concerning Christ will be fulfilled. And by faith in this promise the just man will live, and the unbelievers will have all kinds of evils.

Zephaniah lived in the reign of Josiah. In 3:9ff. he brings in a reference to Christ by repeating preceding prophets.

Jeremiah lived before the carrying away into Babylon. In 16:16 he speaks of "fishers of men," and in 23:5 and 33:15–16 of the raising up of the Branch to David who shall be called "the Lord our righteousness." In 30:9 he speaks of "raising up King David," and in 31:31 of the new covenant.

Ezekiel describes the reign of Christ in 11:17ff., and in 36:25 he speaks of "sprinkling with water"; in 34:23 of David as the Shepherd; and in 37:12 of the resurrection of the dead.

Daniel is more specific in pointing to the time than the other prophets are. He speaks of definite periods of time. Ch. 2 deals with the time of the four monarchs. Ch. 9:24ff. speaks of the 70 weeks and the length of time in which Christ will preach, even fractions of the 70 weeks. In ch. 7:13–14 he mentions the Son of Man, to whom all things have been given by the Father. In 9:26–27 the Messiah is killed; the results of this action mark the end of the sacrifices and the destruction of Jerusalem. In 12:1ff. he speaks of the blessed consummation of things in the life to come. David and Daniel both use the term "Messiah."

Haggai in 2:6ff. says the time is near, "Yet one little while . . ." (Vulgate). He prophesies that the Christ as "the second temple shall be filled with glory," as He comes, presents Himself, and ministers.

Zechariah in 3:1 describes the priesthood of Christ under the figure of Jesus [Joshua] as a priest. In 8:7 the Servant is called *zerach*, a term which the Septuagint renders by "the east" (*anatolē*). Hence in Luke 1:78 Zechariah is cited in the expression "the light of dawn has visited us." This same concept is repeated in Zech. 6:12 (Vulgate). The kingdom of Christ is described in a figurative way in chs. 2, 8, 12, 13, 14. In addition to the other points Zechariah has these which are unique to him: He clearly predicts Jesus' riding on an ass into Jerusalem, 9:9; the flight of the disciples, 13:7; the 30 pieces of silver, 11:12; His being pierced by the spear, 12:10; the fountain against sin, 13:1.

Malachi in 1:11 prophesies regarding the sacrifice among all the gentiles. In 3:1 he describes the forerunner and says that the Lord Himself will soon come to the second temple. He also speaks in this verse of "the messenger of the covenant," who is called the Mediator of the new covenant for the Hebrews, vv. 3–4. In 4:2 he calls Christ "the Sun of righteousness" and says, "Salvation is under His wings." He prophesies concerning the glorious coming of Christ and predicts the end of the law of Moses and that Elijah will come. A fuller explanation may be found in the *Dialog* of Urbanus.[13]

Thus we have established four categories: (1) from the fall of Adam to the Flood; (2) from the Flood to Moses; (3) from Moses to the prophets; (4) from the prophets to Christ. We should note not only when and how often the promise is repeated, but how it is gradually revealed more and more clearly, what the various parts of the promise are, and how they were explained in different eras. Such careful study will be valuable for us.

It is clear that there is one and the same voice and doctrine of the Gospel; by knowledge of it and faith in it the saints of all ages have been justified and saved.

Some try to make the subtle distinction that the doctrine concerning the future coming of the Messiah recorded in the Old Testament is not properly called the Gospel, but the promise, and that only that is called Gospel which is preached in the New Testament regarding the Christ who has been manifested. To be sure, when Scripture speaks of the mode of His revelation, it does retain the distinction in vocabulary between the coming and the accomplished

[13] Urbanus Rhegius (Rieger), 1489–1541, strong supporter of Luther and notable polemicist.

manifestation of the Messiah. Gal. 3:16, "To Abraham were spoken the promises." Rom. 1:1–2, "The Gospel was promised beforehand through the prophets." Rom. 15:8, ". . . to confirm the promises given to the fathers."

The prophets foretold that the preaching under the new covenant would have its own name. And the apostles say that the Gospel was promulgated with the coming of Christ. In this way the distinction between the promise and the Gospel can be usefully employed. For they believed in the Messiah who was to come, and we in the One who has been manifested.

But when we are speaking of the subject itself, it is certain that the doctrine of gracious reconciliation, of the remission of sins, of righteousness, salvation, and eternal life through faith for the sake of the Mediator is one and the same in the Old and in the New Testament. This is a useful rule which we must retain at all costs: The doctrine, wherever we read it, in either the Old or the New Testament, which deals with the gracious reconciliation and the remission of sins through faith for the sake of God's mercy in Christ, is the Gospel.

Therefore we must consider this distinction as only a technicality for the sake of shedding light and as an aid in teaching. Otherwise, points which have all been handled very well can be overturned by arguments. For also in the New Testament the Gospel is called the promise, 2 Tim. 1:1: ". . . according to the promise of life in Christ"; Gal. 3:14: ". . . that we might receive the promise of the Spirit"; and again, ". . . that the promise might be given to believers by faith" [cf. Eph. 1:13]. And Gal. 3:8 says of Abraham: "The Gospel was preached beforehand" to him.

Someone can also cavil that it was not faith, in the proper sense of the word, which the ancients had in the coming Christ, because the expectation of something in the future is not faith but hope. But how do such subtle arguments edify? Therefore we must insist that distinctions serve to edify.

[D.] GRACE AND JUSTIFICATION

[MELANCHTHON'S TEXT]

This locus contains the sum and substance of the Gospel. It shows the benefit of Christ in the proper sense, it offers a firm comfort to pious minds, it teaches the true worship of God, true invocation, and it especially distinguishes the church of God from other people—the Jews, the Mohammedans, and the Pelagians, that is, from all who imagine that man is righteous by the Law or by discipline and who want us to be in doubt regarding the remission of our sins. There is great dissension of opinions about this subject, for many follow human judgments and neglect the simple teaching of the prophets, Christ, and the apostles. They change this teaching into a philosophy, minimize the sin in our nature, and believe that only discipline is required by the law of God. From here they go on to imagine that there is no difference between the teaching of the philosophers and that of Christ.

In all periods of history these ungodly and human fabrications have obscured the true doctrine of the church. For example, the Pharisees believed that they were righteous by the Law. Then, because it became necessary to ask why the Messiah was going to come, they dreamed up the idea that He was going to come to establish His rule over the world, not understanding that He had to become a sacrifice for the human race in order to satisfy the wrath of God against sin and that another kind of righteousness was going to be given to men. Even before the Pharisees, hypocrites in the church in the period of the patriarchs had believed the same things.

But the prophets attacked these errors and cried that sin is not taken away by the righteousness of the Law, that sin still remains in this mortal nature of ours, but that believers are righteous, their prayers are heard, and eternal life is given to them by God because of the promised Savior (cf. Ps. 143:2; 2:11; Is. 53:11). Thus, when Christ and the apostles revived this teaching, immediately human opinions regarding discipline began to be spread abroad, because it is something great to govern external morals. As a result, fanatical spirits arose who drastically changed the Gospel into Law, or Pharisaism, and imagined that people are righteous by the Law. Lest Christ seem to have brought in nothing new, they said that He handed down some new laws regarding celibacy and not taking revenge.

These ridiculous notions were spawned immediately after the apostles. It is no wonder that darkness also followed. Although some godly people did retain the true understanding, yet there was a great difference among writers, with one speaking more accurately than another. But we shall speak elsewhere regarding these writers. At this point I only want to say as a preface that the pious reader should understand that it is necessary to explain this locus of justification and with a grateful mind receive this blessing of God which the light of the Gospel has again restored.

It cannot be denied that there were errors in the teaching of the monks, and although they have corrected some of them, their substance remains. In regard to the remission of sins they still vociferously assert that it is not correct to teach that remission of sins is received by faith, freely, for the sake of Christ, and they do not admit that the term "by faith" means to trust in the mercy of God. Indeed, they want us always to be in doubt as to whether we are in grace. Then they add that we merit the remission of sins because of contrition and love. When they speak of a contrition or sorrow or shame which is without trust in God's mercy, the stronger it is the more it drives a person to despair, as Paul says: "The Law works wrath" [Rom. 4:15].

Then they say, further, that the regenerate satisfy the law of God and are righteous because of their fulfillment of the Law, and that this very thing is a merit and the reward is eternal life, and that in the regenerate there is no remaining disobedience in conflict with the law of God. They add that the regenerate still must be in doubt as to whether they are in grace, and they must remain in this doubt.

This kind of doubt is plainly heathenish. Nor are these errors only minor matters, but rather they cast darkness over the Gospel, hide the benefits of Christ, take away true comfort of conscience, and destroy true prayer. Therefore it is necessary that the church be warned about these important matters. For this reason I shall explain the sum of this matter as clearly and plainly as possible.

First. In regard to discipline, we loudly proclaim that all human beings must be trained by discipline, that is, by that righteousness which even the unregenerate must and can produce. As Paul says, "The Law was laid down for the unrighteous" [1 Tim. 1:9]. And God punishes the violation of discipline with temporal and eternal punishments. It is a great proclamation of discipline when Paul says: "The Law is our schoolmaster unto Christ" [Gal. 3:24], because the Gospel is not effective in those who do not cease to go against conscience.

Although no human activity is more beautiful than discipline, as Aristotle correctly says: "Righteousness is more lovely than the evening or morning star," yet we must not accept the notion that it is the fulfillment of the Law, that it merits remission of sins, and that because of it a person is righteous, that is, reconciled with God. Paul says that the Jews look upon the face of Moses under a veil [2 Cor. 3:13], that is, not correctly understanding the law of God, which is a voice condemning sin in man's nature and showing God's wrath against sin and arousing true terrors.

When the Gospel speaks of this understanding of the Law and the knowledge of sin, many people who are puffed up with their own wisdom think that these are Stoic exaggerations for which we have no need. Since discipline in itself is a sufficiently difficult matter. they contend that nothing further is required and that this degree of diligence merits the remission of sins and is righteousness before God. Origen and the monks have badly distorted Paul in order to favor these human notions. Therefore we must learn the true meaning of Paul from Paul himself and from the consensus of the rest of the prophetic and apostolic Scripture, and not from human opinions.

Second. After we have given this caution regarding discipline, we must now turn to the matter itself. The message of the church is the same from the beginning, after it was received by Adam, down to the end of time. The ministry of preaching repentance was instituted immediately in Paradise [Gen. 3:15], and the promise of the coming Liberator was given, which our first parents understood they had received. This promise was gradually more fully revealed, down to the preaching of Christ, who also Himself performed this ministry. To the apostles He committed the same ministry, saying: "Preach repentance and remission of sins in My name" [Luke 24:47].

Thus in the church the preaching of repentance must always sound forth. It is the voice of the Law through which God condemns our sins, both outward and inward, which are that we do not fear, do not love God, do not trust in God. The voice of the

Gospel also is sounded, accusing the world because it does not listen to the Son of God, is not moved by His suffering and resurrection, etc. Therefore Christ says: "The Holy Spirit will convict the world of sin because they do not believe," John 16:8–9. Cf. Rom. 1:18: "The wrath of God is revealed from heaven against all ungodliness and unrighteousness of men" [KJV].

Thus Adam (or David), upon hearing the voice of God accusing, since his mind was not hard or stubborn, grew terrified and acknowledged that God was really angry against sin and would punish sin. These terrors are often described in the Psalms (cf. Ps. 38:3). Indeed, just as the Law declares this anger to the human race, so all calamities of mankind are in a sense the voice of the Law admonishing us regarding the wrath of God and calling all to repentance.

Third. When the mind of man becomes terrified by this voice condemning sin, it hears the promise given in the Gospel and determines that its sins are freely remitted for the sake of Christ through mercy, not because of contrition or love or any other works. In this way, when the mind raises itself up by faith, remission of sins and reconciliation are given. For if the judgment must be made that we will have remission of sins only when our contrition and love are sufficient, our mind will be driven to despair. Thus, in order that our mind might have certain and firm comfort, the blessing of God does not depend upon the condition of our worthiness but only on the mercy promised for the sake of Christ. And when God forgives sins, at the same time He gives us the Holy Spirit, who begins new powers in the godly, as it says in Gal. 3:22: ". . . that we might receive the promise of the Spirit through faith."

These points are not complicated and are clearly understood by godly minds in the church that are acquainted with spiritual exercises, anxieties, comforts, and prayer. Therefore we must now bring forward some passages from Scripture, but the terminology must first be carefully explained.

We have spoken previously regarding sin and the Law, but now we shall speak of some other matters, such as the words "justification," "faith," and "grace."

"Justification" means the remission of sins, reconciliation, or the acceptance of a person unto eternal life. To the Hebrews "to justify" is a forensic term, as if I were to say that the Roman people "justified" Scipio when he was accused by the tribunes, that is, they absolved him or pronounced him to be a righteous man. Therefore Paul took the term "justify" from the usage of the Hebrew word to indicate remission of sins, reconciliation, or acceptance. All educated people understand that this is the thrust of the Hebrew expression, and examples are encountered frequently.

Although, as we have said above, when God remits sins He at the same time gives the Holy Spirit, who begins new powers within us, yet the terrified mind first seeks the remission of sins and reconciliation. About this it is troubled; about this it struggles in true terrors. It makes no argument over which powers are infused; even if these accompany reconciliation, yet we must never reach the conclusion that our *worthiness or purity are the cause for the remission of our sins. For this reason we must strongly stress the term "freely."*

CHAPTER I: THE CONTROVERSIES

The first chapter of this locus warns that the history of the controversies which have arisen over difference of opinions in all ages concerning the doctrine of justification, and which have greatly hurt the church, must be noted and studied. For this clash of opinions adds a great deal of light to this locus: It forms a judgment concerning the controversy before us; it sharpens diligence in preserving the purity of sound doctrine and in warding off all corruptions of every kind.

Further, those who have written catalogs of heresies do not give a great deal of help in this area. For in their time they adhered to the great darkness which shrouded the doctrine of justification. The same will be the case if we consider the history of the church of all ages from the beginning down to the present. We shall note only certain matters, for the sake of example and reminder.

Because this historical review covers a great deal of territory, and because it does not contribute to our stated purpose to pursue each individual point, I believe that the most expeditious method will be to make a list under certain categories, which will lead us through the chief historical accounts of all periods.

We shall deal with these main points:

1. We shall note whatever public controversies, manifest errors, or heresies have arisen and have been noted in opposition to the doctrine of justification; what their nature was; how very many errors there have been; from which causes, occasions, or sources they had their origin.

2. Particularly useful is the observation that when Satan could not extinguish the light of the true teaching on justification through the controversies aroused by heretics, he spread in the church examples or traditions or unauthentic scriptures under the names of prophets, apostles, or those who had heard the apostles speak, so that corruptions, in conflict with the genuine prophetic and apostolic writings, were thrust upon the churches by false pretenses.

3. We must also add this point, that often even great saints, disturbed by judgments of human reason and the Law, had wild notions on this article. Particularly the ecclesiastical writers, since they were occupied with controversies concerning other articles of faith, did not always use the proper care and circumspection in their handling of the doctrine of justification. On some occasions some very unfortunate statements concerning this article were made, which later on were the cause of the long and gradual process of departing from the purity of this doctrine.

4. We must also note when, through whom, and how God corrected the corruptions in this article and for a time rekindled the light of true purity.

Under these points, I believe, this entire historical discussion can be covered. We shall take up only certain individual points for the sake of instruction.

1. Controversies, Corruptions, and Heresies
in the Period of the Old Testament

In the fall of our first parents there is a most illustrative example of the judgment of human reason without an understanding of the Gospel in regard to this article. For when the worm of conscience after the Fall troubled them and they saw that they were naked, that is, that they had lost the image of God, they were filled with confusion because they felt the law of sin in their members. There was a question in their hearts concerning justification, that is, how they could stand before God and not "surely die" [KJV], according to the sentence of God, Gen. 2:17. But because the doctrine of the Gospel of the Seed had not yet been revealed, their reason judged that they could cover the depravity of their sin in the sight of God by fig leaves, that is, by external discipline. But when the voice of God condemning their sin tore away their fig-leaf clothing and brought their conscience down to hell, they began to excuse their sin and its guilt and indirectly tried to lay the blame on God Himself. But because they noticed that their sin was only aggravated more by their rationalization, in terror of conscience they fled from God and hid themselves from Him. They would have fallen into eternal despair, if the Son of God by the hidden decree of the promise of the Seed had not through faith raised them up and given them life. . . .

It should be noted that God did not immediately after the Fall reveal the promise of grace, but first He led them into serious recognition of sin and divine wrath, permitted them to struggle with sin, to try all their own powers. After they had tried everything, when they saw that they could not by their own powers be freed from the curse, then only was the doctrine of the Gospel revealed to their hearts, which had thus been prepared for it.

These were the opinions concerning the article of justification when the doctrine of faith had not yet been revealed. Now let us look at the dissensions that followed, when the doctrine of the Gospel, which then had first been revealed, was proclaimed and taught. Our first parents not only understood and grasped the concept of the righteousness of faith from the promise of the Seed, but also set forth this teaching to their children and educated them in it. This is manifest, for Heb. 11:4 says of Abel: "He received the testimony that he was righteous by faith."

The record in Genesis, however, testifies that not only were there sad dissensions but that a horrible persecution arose between the first two brothers,

Cain and Abel. The Epistle to the Hebrews shows that this conflict was not political or financial, but the cause and occasion for the dissension and persecution was the article of justification by faith.

We must note that this controversy between Cain and Abel was not only a general argument over the article of justification, but the precise nature of the conflict must be studied. We can conclude from Genesis 4 and Hebrews 11 that the point at issue, or the *status controversiae*, was not the question whether justification occurs, but rather what it is, namely, how and for what reason God regards man (who is guilty because of sin) so that "he may receive the testimony" that he is righteous before God, Heb. 11:4. Abel indeed believed that he was justified by having his sins lifted from his shoulders, that is, by the remission of sin, Gen. 4:7, and this by faith in the promise for the sake of the Seed, Heb. 11:4. And this faith is explained later, in Gen. 4:26, "Enosh began to call upon the name of the Lord." But Cain denied that the righteousness before God is a lifting off[14] or a remission of sins by faith for the sake of the Seed but judged that he could by his own sacrifices and other works remove and take away his sin, and he even grew angry that God did not have regard for him and his sacrifices because of the worthiness of his works, Gen. 4:5. It is worthy of note that God Himself in Gen. 4:6–7 shows the sources of his error to Cain: (1) He is not concerned about the removal of his sin through faith because he does not acknowledge how great and what kind of burden his sin is, especially when sin is quiet and appears dead.[15] (2) While sin is quiet, Cain can be persuaded regarding the discipline of the Law and thus have even less concern for the promise of grace. (3) He permits himself to be dominated by the lust of sin, and yet thinks that he is righteous because of his sacrifices merely by performing them (*ex opere operato*). (4) But when by the coming of the Law sin revives, then Cain cries out, "My sin is too great to be forgiven" [Gen. 4:13, Vulgate]. From this erroneous interpretation of the Law came these controversies regarding the article of justification between Cain and Abel.

Later, at the time of the Flood, there were conflicts and the whole world opposed the doctrine of the righteousness of faith, as we can gather from Heb. 11:7, "By faith Noah condemned the world." And what this is is more clearly explained in 2 Peter 2:5, where Noah is called "a preacher of righteousness"— the righteousness which through faith brings the inheritance, Heb. 11:7. In 1 Pet. 3:19–20 it is written that Christ, in connection with His resurrection, showed the power of His redemption for the confounding of those spirits who in the

---

14 Compare Luther on Gen. 4:7, Amer. Ed., 1.265–66.

15 Ibid., pp. 266–67.

time of Noah were unwilling to believe the doctrine of the promise of the Seed. Further, Scripture says that the source of this controversy in the time of the Flood was their carnal security whereby, although they had manifestly joined themselves to ungodly and idolatrous people, they were unwilling to bear the Spirit of God when He convicted them of sin out of the Word. And Scripture says that the cause of this security was that they would not admit that "the imagination of man's heart was evil."

After the Flood, Shem retained the true doctrine of the righteousness of faith, and hence he was called Melchizedek, that is, the king of righteousness, Heb. 7:2. But among his posterity in the seventh generation the light of the doctrine of justification had become entirely extinct, as we see from Joshua 24:2, "Terah the father of Abraham and Nahor served other gods." But when the true worship of God had become corrupted, it is a certain sign that the article of justification had also been corrupted. It is important to note that even while the bright lights of the church were still alive, even though Noah was a preacher of righteousness and Melchizedek was the king of righteousness, the shadows quickly descended over this article. For 100 years after the Flood there was the division of languages at the tower of Babel. Epiphanius says that idolatry had reared its head again at the time of Serug, Gen. 11:20ff., and he was born 163 years after the Flood. By the time of Terah, 200 years after the Flood, even in the family of the saints the doctrine of justification was almost gone.

At the time of Abraham God again kindled the light of the doctrine of faith in the Seed, Gen. 12:3; Heb. 11:8. The story of Abraham clearly shows how the doctrine of the Gospel was clarified and propagated, but to record all this here would take too long.

But even in the household of Abraham there were conflicts, between Ishmael and Isaac, as we can see in Genesis 21. Paul in Gal. 4:22ff. explains that this controversy did not deal with political or domestic affairs but with this article, because Ishmael claimed for himself, on the basis of the Law which later on was repeated at Sinai, the heritage of the blessing and ridiculed, even persecuted, Isaac, who by faith in the promise of the Seed was confident that he was going to be the heir.

It is worth the effort, moreover, to consider carefully that Abraham, the father of faith himself, by the judgment of reason almost went astray concerning the matter of righteousness before the Law. By reason he judged that Ishmael was not to be excluded from the inheritance, as if Ishmael could by the righteousness of the Law gain the inheritance which belonged to Isaac by the righteousness of faith. But God refuted this opinion of Abraham and corrected him by His word, and did so to such a degree that, although it diminished the authority of Abraham's person, yet He ordered him to follow the judgment of Sarah, even though she was of lesser authority, because she was keeping the words and understanding of the promise more precisely, namely that Isaac was the son of the promise and that Ishmael could not simultaneously be an heir on the basis of the Law.

The same thing later happened also to Isaac, for because of external obedience to the Law he wanted to transfer the blessing from Jacob to Esau.

These points must be noted, so that we can observe that the judgment of reason confuses even the most godly of people, so that even those who are like bright lights of the true church are blinded, just as Isaac was; and although they do not totally reject the gracious promise, yet because of their rationalizations they include something that belongs to the Law. But God vigorously rebukes and rejects such assumptions.

But while these pillars are tottering and drawing the majority with them, those in the despised and weaker part, such as Sarah and Isaac, Rebekah and Jacob, retain the simple teaching of the promise. God finally confirms the judgment of the weaker element, but in the meantime the righteous suffer.

We must remember in these accounts how God repeatedly brought this doctrine to light, namely in the fire of testing, Ps. 12:6; Mal. 3:3. He purges and separates the opinions of reason and the Law that have intruded themselves into the doctrine of justification. We must also bear in mind that when both Ishmael and Esau were removed from the church by the voice and judgment of God because of this article, they made peace and an alliance between themselves, cf. Gen. 28:9, so that by joining forces they could raise opposition to the doctrine of the church and by giving the appearance of harmony they could overturn the agreement of the people.

In Egypt, later on, the people of Israel, under the influence of the Egyptian religion, under which they observed all things flourishing and affluent, almost lost the true knowledge of God by turning to idols, Acts 7:39ff.; Amos 5:26; Ezek. 20:8ff. But what the principal and most important part of the true knowledge of God is, that is described in 1 Cor. 1:30; John 17:3; and Is. 53:11. There is therefore no doubt that at that time the doctrine of the benefits of the Messiah had become extinct or at least badly obscured.

But it is notable how God purged and restored this teaching to the people of Israel, namely by showing it to their understanding and by the use of the Law. The whole story is worth careful study, for in Ex. 19:8 the people were so puffed up by the feeling of their own righteousness in the Law that they did not hesitate to reply, "All that the Lord has spoken we will do," that is, as Augustine says of the Pelagians, "There is no lack of someone to do it, but there is a lack of someone to command."

Indeed, God allows it to happen that, after they have made the final effort, they are to learn by experience whether and how, when God enters into judgment, they can stand in His sight by their own righteousness. For they sanctified and prepared themselves for three days [vv. 11, 15], that is, as Paul says in Rom. 9:31, "They sought the righteousness of the Law," and in 10:2, "They had a zeal for God." But in Exodus 20, when the Law came with its true work producing "the knowledge of sin" and "the wrath of God," Rom. 3:20 and 4:15, this whole persuasion of their own ability fell to pieces. In fright and terror they came back and cried that they could not bear the judgment of the Law when God willed to enter into judgment.

Thus they recognized that they needed a mediator. It is noteworthy that Scripture itself carefully unfolds this story. For the people begged that Moses be the mediator, Ex. 20:19, but in Heb. 12:21 the text says that Moses, who at that time was the holiest of men, could not undertake and bear the office of mediator under the article of justification; for he himself, like the rest, was "trembling with fear."

Therefore, when minds have in this way been prepared and crushed by the Law, then God explains and repeats His promise about raising up another prophet and about another kind of teaching, namely the Gospel. Moses himself states this in his account, Deut. 18:15, 18. This observation is a most useful admonition. Although the doctrine of justification was explained by the voice of God in this way, yet Paul says in 2 Cor. 3:14 that the veil over the face of Moses signified that the Israelites pursued a kind of shadow of the Law and did not see the true end of the Law, which is Christ, Rom. 10:4.

Later on, in the period of the prophets, there were continuous controversies regarding the doctrine of justification, and it would take a long time to relate the entire history. Thus we shall present only a summary in this way: There were three primary errors regarding the article of justification against which the prophets contended. (1) Certain people attributed justification before God to the Mosaic ceremonial laws by merely performing them (*ex opere operato*) without any repentance. See Is. 1:11ff.; 58:2ff.; Jer. 7:21–23; Ps. 50:8ff. (2) There were those who piled up worship forms of their own choosing and uncalled-for works (*opera supererogationis*) with the opinion that this would bring merit and righteousness, Micah 6:6–7; Is. 58:3–5; Ezek. 20:18ff., where we see the refutation: "Do not walk in the path of your fathers . . . but walk in My precepts." (3) Others, who seemed to be in the majority, sought righteousness before God and eternal life in the moral law as given on Mt. Sinai. For this law promised those who performed it righteousness and eternal life.

It is worth the effort to consider in the prophets the sources of their refutations of this specious opinion. In the article of justification they confess that they only offer sins to God and therefore they cannot be justified in the sight of God, Ps. 143:2, and that they cannot endure the judgment of God, Ps. 130:3. Therefore they ask mercy and remission not for the sake of their works but for the sake of God's name, as David is accustomed to say; "for His own sake," as Isaiah says; and as Daniel expressly says in 9:17, "for the Lord's sake" [KJV]. Jer. 31:32ff. explains the reason why we are not justified by the Law. He says that the covenant of the Law had been rendered useless by us, and for this reason there was need for the new covenant, whose sum and substance is, "I will forgive their iniquity, and remember their sin no more." In Ezek. 20:25, when He says, "I gave them statutes that were not good and ordinances by which they could not live," He is saying the same thing that Paul says in Gal. 3:21, "If a law had been given that could make alive, then righteousness would surely be by the Law."

The story of Solomon relates to this point, 1 Kings 11; and the account of Jereboam's calves in 1 Kings 12; and the mixing with the religion of the Samaritans in 2 Kings 17.

After the Babylonian captivity, when there were no more prophets, the doctrine of justification not only was obscured but almost extinguished, as we can witness from the history of such sects as the Pharisees, the Sadducees, and the Essenes, whose ideas about justification can be understood from the writings of the New Testament, where mention is made of "the righteousness of the Pharisees," that is, the righteousness of the flesh or the Law properly speaking. Likewise from the disputations of the scribes with Christ we can see the situation. The Jews of our day draw from the ideas of the Pharisees that opinion which they openly express, that they would not seek from the Messiah, even if He were to come today, the remission of sin, grace, or life eternal, because these things can be gained by the works of the Law. It is worthy of careful study to note in the apocryphal books, which were added to the Old Testament after the time of Malachi, when the succession of prophets had come to an end, that these books which were written outside the canon deal only with matters of morality, but there is no sure or clear mention of the doctrine of the Gospel. Some unsatisfactory statements are made in the books of Tobit and Maccabees regarding the article of justification.

And Philo, who is generally regarded as the most learned of the Jews, took great pride in the fact that he had received his teaching in the form of occult secrets and traditions handed down from the elders of his nation who always hid something in their ancient writings (for these are his very words). He makes no clear mention of faith or of justification by grace, but those sweet promises of the Gospel, as the entire New Testament treats them, he transforms into allegories and Platonic philosophy, so that the serpent, for example, is interpreted as earthly pleasure, Eve as the senses, and Adam as mind. He cites the traditions concerning the origin of circumcision: (1) in order to prevent tumors on the foreskin; (2) because dirt clings to the foreskin; (3) because the foreskin has a similarity to the heart, in an allegorical sense; (4) because it makes for fertility in that the semen is more easily ejected. And although he wrote a complete book on sacrifices, he did not make one clear reference to the true Victim, but only dealt with allegories. In another place he says that the Jews had three advocates and intercessors before God: (1) the goodness of the Father; (2) the ancient founders of the nation, who because of their pure minds were held in honor by the Father, so that their prayers for their sons and daughters, in some undefined way, were efficacious and readily heard; (3) the effect of their penances. From this we can understand what the doctrine of justification was among the Jews after the time of the Babylonian captivity. Warnings of this come from the stories of the Old Testament.

2. Controversies in the New Testament
at the Time of Christ and the Apostles

It is obvious that many different kinds of disputes took place between Christ the Savior and the scribes and Pharisees concerning the article of justification. But lest this discussion of the history get too lengthy, I want to gather these disputes together and set them forth in a few main points:

1. The Pharisees in Luke 7:39 and 15:2 seem to be arguing that manifest sinners must not be received even if they are repentant and concerned about their sins.

2. They trusted in themselves that they were righteous, Luke 18:9, that is, they were defending their inherent righteousness and justification by good works.

3. The scribes in Matt. 9:3 seemed to have taught only a general faith which, when applied in a specific case, involved doubt. For the teaching that announced the remission of sins on earth, in specific instances to individuals who were repentant and believed, this they pronounced to be blasphemy.

4. In Matt. 3:9; John 8:33; and Rom. 9:7 they glory over the blood of Abraham, saying, "We have Abraham as our father," that is, they have done away with the doctrine of original sin.

5. It is evident that among the sects there were conflicts over which was the greatest commandment in the Law, that is, which kind of righteousness was most important before God, whether that which comes from observance of the ceremonial laws or that which comes from obedience to the moral law, as much as a person is able to do, or indeed that which is based on supererogation in observing human traditions. The idea of supererogation is clearly described in Matt. 19:20 and Luke 18:11–12.

6. We must also consider that Christ not only had trouble with His adversaries but also with His own disciples, so that He had to refute their idea regarding good works following justification, so that they would not mix them in with the article of justification, Matt. 19:27ff.; 20:25ff.; Luke 17:10.

In the same way later on the apostles had many different controversies regarding the doctrine of justification, not only with their adversaries but also particularly with false brethren. Let us sum these up, too, in a few points.

1. Some contended that the observance of the ceremonial laws of Moses was so necessary for salvation that it was impossible to be saved by faith in Christ alone without these ceremonies, Acts 15:1.

2. Others pursued the moral law, which they called "the law of righteousness," Rom. 9:31 [KJV]. Some contended that obedience to this law, without faith in Christ, was sufficient for a person for salvation, Rom. 9:32; 10:3. Others attributed justification to faith and works of the moral law, both at the same time, Gal. 2:4ff.; 5:1ff.; and Phil. 3:2ff.

3. From Col. 2:8 it is evident that at the time of the apostles some had mixed philosophical disputations into the doctrine of justification.

4. The apostles also had conflicts with those who were misusing the doctrine of reconciliation by grace as a cover for wickedness, 1 Peter 2:16. "They use their liberty as an opportunity for the lust of the flesh," Gal. 5:13, condemns the notion that since we are saved by grace alone no new obedience must follow, but that those who are justified can be justified freely and with impunity indulge in whatever lusts of the flesh they wish, cf. Eph. 5:6; Rom. 3:8; 6:1, 15. Many statements and even entire apostolic epistles, such as Peter, John, James, Jude, etc., are written in opposition to these Epicurean Christians.

It is useful, and can be done with a reasonable expenditure of effort, to see what the fountains of corruption were which in the time of the apostles had pervaded the church. Paul says, Gal. 6:12, that the false apostles mixed legal elements into the article of justification "that they might not suffer persecution for the cross of Christ." In 1 Cor. 1:23 he says that the preaching of faith is foolishness to the gentiles. Because of this a mixture of philosophy with the doctrine of faith was produced, Col. 2:8. Thus the zeal to reconcile the doctrine of the Law and the teaching of philosophy with the Gospel is the source and origin of all errors.

It must also be noted that in the first period of the preaching of the apostles arguments were raised regarding the discipline of the Law, but when the course of the Gospel could not be undermined by this line of reasoning, then the devil foisted Epicurean philosophy upon the church. And from this we find a difference in the writings of the apostles, so that the earlier epistles are contending against the belief in the righteousness of the Law, while the later ones are promoting the fruits of repentance and refuting Epicurean notions regarding licentious living. These points give a picture and preview of all the controversies of all later ages.

3. Controversies Regarding This Article after the Time of the Apostles

[I]

First. Following the categories we have given above, we shall speak of the manifest heresies which arose in the primitive church against the article of justification.

These heresies against the true doctrine of justification were not only of several varieties, but they were also monstrous and prodigious. They arose immediately after the times of the apostles in opposition to the true doctrine of justification, as has been fully described in the writings of Irenaeus, Tertullian, Clement, Eusebius, and Epiphanius. We shall note only a few statements from these writers, which will be seen to fit in with our premise that the doctrine of justification was vigorously opposed in different ways and for different reasons, and we will see from which sources these corruptions arose. This observation will be most useful.

1. Ebion and Cerinthus taught that faith in Christ alone does not suffice for justification, but that the observance of the Law is also necessary for salvation. Almost all the ancient writers make note of this fact. But they pass over what is most important of all, namely the reasons for which they were unwilling to attribute justification alone to faith in Christ. The matter can be discovered thus: They imagined that Christ was not true God but that He had divinity dwelling within Him, as in one of the prophets, although on a more exalted level. Therefore they said that faith in Christ was not sufficient for salvation. Eusebius even notes that Ebion had said that Christ Himself was justified by His own works; therefore He was not able to justify others without works and only by faith. We should carefully observe, because of the controversies of our own time, what the rationale was whereby Ebion and Cerinthus were not willing to concede that laying hold on Christ by faith is sufficient for a person to gain righteousness and salvation.

2. But when this lunacy of Ebion and Cerinthus had been refuted on the basis of the true, fundamental teaching that Christ is indeed true God, in whom "was life," John 1:4, and "of whose fullness we have all received," v. 16, then the devil immediately spread another blasphemy in order that he might render the doctrine of faith suspect and detested. For Simon Magus began to make the blasphemous assertion that he was able to give men salvation not by righteous works but by grace through the acknowledgment of his Helena or Selene, who

was a courtesan whom he had abducted from a brothel. These are truly devil-ish mockeries by which he wounds the heel of the Seed. Simon also added that there was no reason for the Law, but that men are free by saving grace, so that they may do whatever they wish. He defined salvation as being a liberation from the slavery by which men are compelled to good actions by the command of God and not permitted to do what they want to.

These diabolic seeds of Simon were immediately accepted and fostered by many people. For Basilides taught that because we are saved by grace alone, therefore all activities, indeed every kind of lust, can be practiced as a matter of indifference. Carpocrates added this blasphemy, that the pollution of lustful actions is necessary for salvation.

3. Whole groups of heretics called themselves Gnostics because of their outstanding knowledge, which they arrogated to themselves by revelations and other shameful mysteries, unknown to ordinary Christians; and they said that they were saved only by their knowledge because of the excellence of their faith and were so spiritual that they could not fall from grace, no matter what sins they might commit. The rest of the people, who were weaker in faith, they called "natural" or "earthly" (*psychikoi*), and they said that these were saved by faith and good works together. Here begins to appear the seed of the Anabaptists in regard to reconciliation and of the papists in their thinking about the contem-plative life. They also laid down the hypothesis that not all are justified and saved in the same way, but in several ways. We should note particularly that the Gnostics used the term "justification by faith" on account of the excellent, superior, and worthy quality of their faith. But in people who have a weak faith, in whom there is scarcely "a smoldering wick" [Matt. 12:20], there, they said, a supplement and addition of good works was necessary.

4. The Manichaeans detracted from justification by faith because . . . they understood faith only in the sense of historical knowledge. But the arduous, rare, difficult things, such as living a celibate life, forsaking everything, etc., these things, they said, were the way of righteousness, salvation, and perfection.

In this listing I am not following the chronological order, but I wanted to show the numerous ways, reasons, forms, and pretexts by which the doctrine of justification by faith alone has been opposed. (1) According to Ebion, Christ was not sufficient, etc. (2) From this teaching follows the breakdown of disci-pline and the cloak of maliciousness. (3) Faith is a weak quality; therefore how can it alone justify? (4) Also the ungodly can have historical knowledge; there-fore faith does not justify.

5. Basilides and Valentinus imagined that certain people by nature were to be saved, elected, and faithful, while others they called "material" (*hylikoi*). These, they said, were created so that they could not be capable of faith, knowledge,

righteousness, and salvation. That is, they corrupted the purity of the doctrine of justification by arguments regarding providence and predestination.

6. Marcion said that believers who lapsed could be rebaptized three times for the remission of sins. And he tried to prove this by the fact that Christ was first baptized in the Jordan; then in Luke 12:50 He says, "I have a baptism to be baptized with," and for the third time He says in Acts 1:5, "You shall be baptized with the Holy Spirit." Following him came the Hemerobaptists, who day by day repeated Baptism for each individual lapsed person. The Montanists opposed them in that (as Jerome says) they entirely took away repentance from their midst. Tertullian, in a special treatise on repentance, approves and defends this notion. After this the Novatians or the Cathari gave to the lapsed no opportunity for repentance after Baptism, even if they had done everything required for repentance. Their opinion was that faith justifies only once, at the first conversion.

7. Basilides said that not all sins were forgiven by faith in Christ but only those which were involuntary or committed through ignorance. Hence the Montanists and the Manichaeans piled up all kinds of traditions necessary for the remission of sins and salvation.

8. Eusebius [*Historia Ecclesiastica*, 5.13, MPL 20.460–61] writes that Apelles, a Marcionite, had said that we must absolutely not inquire into doctrine, but each should remain in what he believed. For he asserted that all who trusted in the Crucified One would be saved, if only good works were found in them. Thus Philostratus wrote of a certain rhetorician who said that all sects were correct and would be saved.

I do not want to produce a catalog of errors in later times, for the same errors, with some slight changes in the external coloration, have been repeated. But I have noted these controversies in the ancient church because they contain a picture of all the aberrations that have followed in later times regarding this article, about which a person can easily judge on the basis of these comments.

[II]

Second. We shall note certain points regarding adulterated traditions and spurious writings.

The chief points of this distinction we have expounded above, at the beginning. Now we want to add some explanation. It is evident from Acts 15:1 and Gal. 1:7 that, while the apostles were still living, certain people of authority among them had, under the pretext of tradition, opposed the teaching of Paul regarding justification by faith. . . . They did not, like Paul, attribute righteousness and salvation to the grace of God alone, which was laid hold of by faith in Christ, but rather they added the observance of the Law as necessary for justification and salvation. This figment of the imagination was refuted in the public council of the apostles, Acts 15:23ff.

After the death of the apostles various traditions of the apostles were under discussion, as fanatics dreamed up one notion after the other to favor their ideas that what they were teaching had been learned and received from the apostles themselves or their disciples in private conversations and meetings. From Irenaeus and Tertullian we can see how these figments were refuted by complete and correct books. In Clement's *Stromata* [7.17, MPG 9.547] Basilides glories in the fact that he had for his teacher Glaucis, who had been an interpreter of Peter. Valentinus tries to confirm his teachings by saying that he had learned from Theodulos, a friend of Paul, who is even said to be mentioned in the Second Epistle of Ignatius. Marcion brags that he held and defended the teaching of the apostle Matthew.

Because, even while the apostles were still living, ideas of this kind began to be spread abroad, so that the church might not be tossed about by every wind of doctrine and tradition [Eph. 4:14], Irenaeus fittingly says that the apostles had reduced to writing the things they had taught, so that faith might have a sure and certain foundation and a strong citadel.

Against these canonical writings the fanatics wrote opposition documents, which went under the titles of traditions, and they brought in many other and different teachings which they alleged the apostles had taught in public meetings and private discussions with their followers whom they claimed as living witnesses. But Irenaeus and Tertullian prove from the form of the churches founded by the apostles that the true traditions or teachings of the apostles were not different but were absolutely the same as those signed by them and included in the apostolic writings. Therefore the form of the traditions in the apostolic churches in every way agrees with the apostolic writings. In this way the reliable canon of the New Testament Scriptures was established. But very quickly spurious writings began to be spread. However, those who were true disciples of the apostles exercised their judgment and rejected these adulterated writings.

But we are speaking only of the article of justification. Adulterated and spurious writings under the names of the apostles and those who had listened to the apostles were spread around, and these included manifest errors in the apostolic doctrine regarding justification by faith. In the judgment of the earlier and purer and true church, these writings had always been rejected and placed among the apocrypha, and yet they had attracted many people by using the name of apostles and those who had heard them.

There is extant a certain writing under the name of James the brother of the Lord, the bishop of Jerusalem, to which has been given the glorious title of *The Protevangelium*, that is, the basis, the foundation, the rule that anyone else who writes an account of the Gospel must set for himself and follow. Even the writings of the evangelists had to be judged and censured on this basis. But it contains many fables which are in disagreement with the writings of the evangelists. At this moment we are dealing only with the article of justification. In the very beginning this writing brings in Joachim, the father of Mary, saying, "My substance shall be for the benefit of all my people, that I may find mercy from God for the remission of my sins."

Paul in Rom. 16:14 mentions a certain Hermas who was his follower. Three books circulated under the name of this man, *Visions*, *Commands*, and *Similitudes*,[16] in which Hermas is depicted as an angel to bring certain special revelations, which he is to announce to the church. However, in these revelations are manifest errors regarding the doctrine of justification . . . which are presented in such a way that unsuspecting people may be led away from the teaching of the apostles by a twofold trap: (1) Because the revelations are given by an angel. (2) Because Hermas was a follower and disciple of Paul. We want to make some comments on this matter.

In *Vision* 2.25 he says, "Your single-mindedness and your outstanding continence have saved you." In *Vision* 3.10, "Leave off praying only for your sins now; pray also for righteousness, that you may receive a share in it."

In *Commands* 1–4, "I have heard from certain teachers that there is no other repentance besides that of Baptism . . . and after that we must sin no more." V. 23, "I know that if I shall not hereafter add any more to my sins, I shall be saved." In other words, there is remission for your prior sins, if you keep the commandments. If anyone after Baptism sins, he has one repentance. But if he sins beyond that and is repentant, there is no benefit for such a man.

In *Command* 12.14ff. Hermas says, "I do not know if these commandments can be kept by man. But the angel replied vehemently and angrily, 'God has given to man that he shall rule over all. Therefore he can fulfill these commandments. Put the Lord in your heart and you will understand that there is nothing easier than these commandments. . . .'"

Similitude 5.52, Christ, "having blotted out the sins of His people, showed to them the paths of life, giving them the law which He had received from the Father." Again, v. 25, "Keep the commandments of the Lord and you shall be approved and shall be written in the number of those who keep His commandments. But if, besides those things which the Lord has commanded, you shall add some good thing, you shall be in greater favor with the Lord than you would have been otherwise."

Similitude 6.6, "The commandments can bring a man salvation."

---

[16] These are all part of the *Shepherd*, MPG 2.

Similitude 7 deals with the question of why those who repent are afflicted with punishment. And the answer is that you should not think that the sins of the repentant are abolished. But it is necessary that the repentant constantly afflict his soul, that he load on it many different vexations and that he suffer all things which have been prepared for him, and then perhaps God will be moved with compassion toward him and give him some remedy; and this will happen if He sees that his heart has been purified by acts of penance and by various kinds of works.

Similitude 9.113ff., "No man shall enter into the kingdom of God by any other way than through the name of His Son . . . for He is the only way of coming to God. . . . Therefore he who bears the name of the Son of God and the rest of the virtues, such as abstinence, patience, etc., shall enter into the kingdom of God. But he who only bears the name of the Son of God shall see the kingdom but shall not enter it."

The reader should observe how this writing of Hermas is obviously in opposition to the teaching of Paul in the article of justification in these respects: It asserts (1) that the true use of the Law is to bring life and salvation; (2) that the fulfillment of the Law is not impossible in this life, and that man can satisfy the Law with perfect obedience; (3) works of supererogation; (4) human satisfactions for sins; (5) merits; (6) the corruption of the doctrine of repentance; (7) faith as only historical knowledge; (8) that we are not justified by faith alone, indeed the name of Christ alone does not save us. These points are diametrically opposed to the teaching of Paul, as is obvious.

Similarly in Phil. 4:3 Paul calls Clement [of Rome, MPG 2] his "co-worker" (*synergos*), and they say that Peter made him the bishop of Rome. Under his name there are extant 10 books of *Recognitions* in which Clement is depicted as reciting the summary of the teaching he had heard and learned from Peter. In these books are so many corrupt and false statements that Rufinus, who translated them, says that he did not want to do so because they were so obviously spurious. For our part we shall only call attention to certain manifest perversions of the apostolic doctrine concerning righteousness by faith which were spread around in these books under the pretext of the authority of Peter. And we must note, because an objection can be raised, that although the writings of the apostles do not set forth this form of teaching, yet immediately in Book 1 he depicts Peter as having clearly said these things orally, but his writings are not so clear. They cannot be understood without an interpreter when they are read.

In Book 2 he says that it seems to be sufficient for salvation to have a kindly feeling toward the unbegotten God the Creator. Again, when Peter is disputing with Simon Magus he says that above all we must inquire as to what "the kingdom of God and His righteousness" are. And he explains God's righteousness as meaning that we teach people to live properly; and it is His kingdom to know what the rewards are.

In Book 3 he explains the term "the righteousness of God" in Matt. 6:33 and Rom. 1:17 by saying that God will be a righteous judge who renders to each according to his works.

In the same book he says, "If anyone desires to be baptized, he must strip off his former evils, and then he is an heir to heavenly blessings because of his good actions which come from his own activities."

In this book he also makes a completely crass defense of free choice and calls faith a work, so that he is in opposition to Paul, who says salvation is "through the law of faith" and not "through the law of works."

In Book 4 he says that we are saved not only by knowing Jesus but by doing His will.

In Book 5: "While unbelief does not believe in the coming judgment of God, it thus gives permission to sin. But faith, by believing that the judgment of God is coming, keeps men from sin." Note how he understands faith and in what sense faith justifies.

Peter over a period of three months instructs Caesar and not once does he mention Christ or faith. Rather Clement cites these main points of a sermon by Peter: "There is one God and a future judgment where God will render to each man according to his works; therefore God through His apostles announces to the gentiles that they must worship God by their works in order that they may attain salvation." But where is the Gospel, where is Christ, where is faith?

Book 7, "The salvation of your mother is reckoned as a reward for her purity."

Book 10, "The philosophers plainly taught the same things, but they did not know God, the rewarder of good and evil works." Note what kind of a difference there is between the doctrine of the Gospel and the philosophers.

In this book Peter also says that a work is good even if it is performed by those who err in faith. But where is the passage: "Whatsoever is not of faith is sin," Rom. 14:23? The reader can observe for himself how Satan tried to overturn the doctrine of Paul regarding the righteousness of faith by using the name and authority of Peter.

Clement [of Alexandria] in Book 6 of his *Stromata* [6.5, MPG 9.262–64] can find no Scriptural testimonies to support his contention that philosophers can be saved through philosophy. Indeed he sees that Scripture diametrically opposes the idea. Thus he contends and tries to prove on the basis of the apocryphal books of Peter and Paul that just as the Jews in the Old Testament were saved by the Law and just as Christians in the New Testament are saved through the Gospel, so the Greeks are saved through philosophy.

I think this rehearsal of statements has been useful to show how the spirit of lies has tried to corrupt the true teaching concerning the righteousness of faith by adulterated and spurious writings under the name and title of apostles and their followers. This point shows that the same errors which later on invaded the church and even now are rampaging through it had begun their work at the very beginning of the Gospel and the infant church. And indeed through this argument all things that are set forth in spurious writings must be suspect.

III

Third. [We must take note of certain] unfortunate statements of the fathers.

We have made the point regarding the reading of the history of the church so that we might consider how the ancient writers, when they were involved in controversies on other articles of faith, failed to deal with the doctrine of justification carefully and circumspectly. For often, when they were occupied with something else, they made many unfortunate statements that later on gave occasion for a gradual and serious departure from the purity of this article. There are extant a great many imprecise, inadequate, and injudicious statements regarding this article in all of the writers, so that it would be an easy matter to put together a long list.

But it is not our purpose to be like Ham, who uncovered his father's shame. Thus we shall not deal with the lapses of those by whose labors we have been aided and whose gray hairs we ought to honor, but we will refer to them only as warnings so that we may be cautioned by their examples to be more careful and diligent in preserving the purity of this doctrine, so that we never give occasion to anyone to follow in these footsteps. Therefore we shall only call attention to the chief reasons for these infelicitous statements among the ancient writers regarding the doctrine of justification. This will serve as a warning to us and will be beneficial for the easier and more correct demonstration of the sources of the explanations of those statements which the papists, citing the ancients, are accustomed to use against the doctrine of our churches. In keeping with our practice, we shall divide the subject into certain categories.

1. They departed from the proper, evangelical, and apostolic (as I may say) meaning of the terms through which the Holy Spirit revealed the doctrine of this locus in Scripture, terms such as "to justify," "righteousness," "righteous," and "grace," etc. They used these terms either in the legal sense or in the popular sense. Thus, by an improper use of the word, they referred the testimony in Paul's writings regarding justification to a different meaning, the renewal of the Spirit. Although this meaning in itself was not false or irreverent, and thus this misuse seemed to have no negative implication, yet from it the doctrine of

Paul was little by little obscured, as our examples will show when we come to the terminology.

2. They very often understood the term "faith" as only a historical knowledge and assent to what was contained in sacred Scripture. In this sense many statements from the ancients are read which take away and detract justification, salvation, and eternal life from "faith alone." We shall later supply examples of this. From this we can evaluate many of the statements used by the papists.

3. The confusion of Law and Gospel was widespread in the church, and even if we speak charitably, the statements are very unfortunate. They did not distinguish accurately enough as to what kind of righteousness the Law was describing, nor the purpose of the Law, nor did they define what the doctrine of the Gospel is, properly speaking, or what the righteousness of faith before God is, and why we must have another kind of righteousness than that of the Law.

The very early writer Theophilus [of Antioch] says in his *Ad Autoclium* [2.35ff., MPG 6.1107ff.], "God communicated the Law and the holy precepts to us, and if a man lives according to them, he will achieve salvation, and when he rises from the dead, he will find his incorruptible inheritance." Cyprian in his *Sermo de Baptismo*[17] says, "Because we know what must be done and can do what we know, command me, Lord, to do what pleases You. This I can and must do." Again in Book 4, Epist. 4 [New 7 (65), MPL 4.247], "The heavenly commandments have been given us for our salvation. . . ." Again in his *Sermo do Patientia* [5 MPL 4.619], "God in the Gospel has given commandments unto salvation." Hilary, *Canon 7 in Matt.* [MPL 9.955], "The salvation of the gentiles is all by faith, and the life of all men is in the commandments of the Lord." Origen, *Contra Celsum* [4.7, MPG 11.1038], "Jesus gave the Law, and he who establishes his life in keeping with it shall obtain salvation." Again in his *Homilia 6 in Lev.* [MPG 12.468], "The law of God is that which washes you, cleanses away your filth, and if you heed it, it will wipe away the blemishes of your sins." So as not to prolong the list, even Irenaeus, Tertullian, Origen, and Eusebius, when they tried to distinguish the righteousness of the Law and the Gospel, only refer to the doctrine of works and only distinguish according to what is greater and what is less. As Clement says in his *Stromata*, 6.18 [MPG 9.398], the righteousness of the Pharisees was rejected because they only refrained from evils. And in Book 7 he says, "The Law prohibits only evil actions, but the Gospel also prohibits evil thoughts." We can read similar ideas in Irenaeus [*Adversus Haereses*, 4.42, MPG 7 (1). 932], Tertullian, *Adversus Marcionem* [4.9, MPL 2.374–77], Eusebius, *Demonstratio Evangelica*, 4.2 [MPG 22.415], and Chrysostom, *Homilia 16 in Matt.* [MPG 57.239ff.].

---

[17] There is no work by this name attributed to Cyprian.

4. They did not place the doctrine of good works in its place in the category of the fruits of faith, but often mixed it in with the article of justification itself. And because they saw that among worldly men a great sense of security, a neglect of good works, and the breakdown of discipline in a person's entire life result from preaching the gracious reception to eternal life, therefore, in order to repress this sense of security and to arouse and encourage more ardent and effective zeal for good works (so it seemed to them), they often bent the article of justification in the direction of works and merits—burying Christ and His benefits.

Thus Chrysostom in Homily 32 makes this extravagant statement, "No one will deliver you from the eternal fire unless you receive aid from the poor whom you have benefited." Homily 33, "Almsgiving bestows eternal life and snatches us from death." Homily 37, "God enters into a kind of agreement with us: Give alms and I will give you eternal life." Again, "On Judgment Day this will be our excuse, if we can prove that we obeyed the commandments of God; and thus we shall escape hell." Hilary, *Canon 4 in Matt.* [MPL 9.932], "The glory of the joy to come must be merited by the works of the present life." *Canon 6* [MPL 9.953], "This blessed eternity must be earned by our effort." Ambrose, *De Poenitentia*, 2.5 [MPL 16.527], "David proclaimed that he is blessed whose sins are remitted through Baptism and he whose sins are covered by his works." Again, in *Epistle* 44 [new numbering 41.22, MPL 16.1166] he uses the similitude of the two scales, in one of which are placed evil works and in the other good. Judgment is made according to the scale which weighs the most. Clement [of Alexandria], *Stromata* [MPG 16.1166], 6.6, "When we hear the words, 'Your faith has saved you,' we do not understand this in the absolute sense that those are or are going to be saved who in some way or another believe, unless they have also done the works which follow. Only to the Jews who kept the law and had lived without blame did He say these words, for all that remained for them was that they have faith in the Lord." . . . Again, "The wise virgins said to God, 'We have left undone none of those things which You commanded; wherefore we ask for Your promises'" [7.12, MPG 4.247]. Statements like these cannot be excused or defended. They are most inadequate.

5. They made public spectacles out of satisfactions for sins, which were performed with great severity in the church in order to arouse a true recognition of sin and hatred for it and to determine publicly the intentions of the penitent. These promoted and confirmed the idea of merit and righteousness by works.

For example, Cyprian in Book 4 of his epistles [7 (new 65), MPL 4.247] often speaks about meriting God. Again in Epistle 2 [*Epist. 10 ad Ant.*, MPL 3.793] he says, "Wring your hands, lament, weep day and night, and do good works with liberality in order that you may wash away your sins and purge them out."

Epistle 4 [.2 new 7.65), MPL 4.247], "We who have not made satisfaction before God for our sins will feel the whips." Again, in his *De Simplicitate Peccatorum*,[18] "It is necessary for righteousness that a person is meritorious before God, who is the Judge." And in his *Sermo de Eleemos*.[19] "He makes satisfaction to God by his righteous works, and his sins are purged away by his meritorious acts of mercy." Thus Jerome says that he obtained mercy for himself through his tears and his fastings.

6. When they were first disputing with the gentiles, lest the doctrine of the church seem even more unpalatable to them, they bent it in the direction of philosophical disputations. They believed that in this way they could win more from among the gentiles. Thus Athanasius, in his *Contra Idola*,[20] treats the entire teaching concerning the Fall and original sin more as a philosophic rather than a theological matter. And Clement in *Stromata*, 2 [MPG 8.943], is very well satisfied to say that he can accommodate the teaching of the church regarding faith to the disputations of the philosophers concerning such subjects as knowledge, wisdom, and spiritual aptitudes. Likewise in his *Paraenetico ad Gentes* [MPG 8.198] he says, "Although it is permissible for you to purchase with your own treasure the most precious salvation, with charity and faith of life, which indeed is the proper price which God freely accepts . . ." In the same way Theophilus, *Ad Autolycum Gentilem* [2.35ff., MPG 6.1107ff.] speaks only in legal and philosophic terms about the gaining of salvation.

7. An excessive amount of admiration for outward discipline and for natural human powers in the unregenerate brought great darkness over this article. Thus Irenaeus, 4.30 [new 4.16, MPG 7(1).107], says, "The fathers before the promulgation of the Law were righteous by the natural law." Tertullian, *Adv. Judaeos* [2],[21] says that Noah and Abraham were righteous under the righteousness of the natural law. Justin in *Apologia* [2.13–14],[22] "Those who lived with the Word were Christians; but they believe that even if they had not known God, such men as Socrates and Heraclitus among the Greeks would be saved." Epiphanius and Clement of Alexandria echo the same thought. Tertullian, *Contra Marcionem* [4.37, MPL 2.451] says that the cause for the conversion of Zachaeus was that even in his ignorance he had fulfilled the statement of Isaiah 58:7, "Share your food with the hungry." Clement, *Stromata*, 5 [MPG 9.15–18], "We are saved

---

[18] No work by this name is attributed to Cyprian.

[19] Cyprian, *Opuscula de Opere et Eleemosynis*, MPL 4.628

[20] No work by this name is attributed to Athanasius.

[21] MPL 2.600. This is a spurious work.

[22] MPG 6.465–7. This is not an exact quote.

by grace, but not without good works. For we cannot achieve the perfection of good without the free choice of our mind. For it is necessary, since we are prone toward this by nature, to demonstrate a zeal for the good." In short, Pelagianism was built out of many unfortunate statements of this kind.

To these categories, I believe, can be referred all the statements the papists are accustomed to cite from the fathers in opposition to justification by grace. And the explanations can easily be taken from these reminders. These observations also have this value, that we are made more cautious lest by any kind of good intention or in any respect we undermine the purity of this doctrine; but let us love what is correctly, simply, and fitly spoken. For without due diligence in speaking, the substance of the matter cannot be retained as it has been divinely revealed to us.

[IV]

Fourth. [We shall see] through whom and how the corruptions of this article were refuted.

We have said that in the history of the church we must especially note that God in all periods has raised up witnesses who testified against these errors and led the church away from the pharisaic and philosophical swamps to the fountains of Israel, so that to the doctrine of this locus, based on prophetic and apostolic foundations, its purity has been restored uncorrupted, as it has been divinely revealed. In making this observation we should particularly consider on what occasions and how marvelously in an indirect way (so to speak) He once again kindled the genuine light of this doctrine, when it seemed almost completely extinguished. We shall call attention to only a few of the many examples which are extant.

The older writers judged that with severity of discipline in receiving the lapsed, people could be held to the work of pious devotion and be deterred from security and levity which lead to sin. So they would at times speak with greater harshness and rigor about repentance after falling and about the remission of sins, as we can read in the book of the *Shepherd*, cited above. Irenaeus, 4.45 [4.27, MPG 7 (2). 1036ff.], cites the statement of a certain elder who had heard the apostles preach: "To those of former times the death of the Lord was the cure and remission of their sins, but in the case of those who sin now, Christ does not die for them any longer, but the Son will come as a judge. Therefore we ought to fear lest after knowing Christ we do something which is not pleasing to God, for we do not have the remission of sins again, but shall be excluded from His kingdom." These statements of this elder are sufficiently hard and unyielding. But Clement in his *Stromata*, 2 [MPG 8.995–96] says, "Repeated and continuous penances are of no value. Therefore it is evident that it is not repentance to seek forgiveness for those things wherein we sin often," etc.

Thus some of them granted only one public and solemn repentance to anyone. And they tormented the souls of the penitent over a period of several years with their teachings regarding satisfactions before they were received back into the church. Hence the true doctrine of repentance, grace, faith, and the free remission of sins was greatly obscured, something the fathers failed to notice because of their overconcern with discipline.

Therefore the Montanists first, and later Novatian with his Cathari, began to deny entirely to those who lapsed after Baptism any repentance or remission of sins, even if they had true contrition and faith. There is extant a book by Tertullian regarding repentance where he simply cuts off all hope of forgiveness to those who lapsed and then returned to the faith. In a frightful and Montanistic spirit he wipes out the sweet consolations of Luke 15 regarding the lost sheep, the lost coin, and the prodigal son.

The Novatians called themselves the Cathari [the purified ones]. They imagined that they had no need for repentance because they were clean of sins. As to the rest of the people, who were contaminated by sins, even if in true acknowledgment and detestation of sin they fled in faith to the throne of grace, seeking forgiveness, the Novatians simply denied that there was any hope of grace and remission of sins for them. Afterward (as Ambrose tells us) they softened their stand and said that God could, to be sure, remit sins to penitents of this kind, but that man must not determine this for himself on the basis of the Word of God with any degree of certainty, or announce it to another person; but when they had done everything required for true repentance, it must be referred to God whether He is willing to remit the sin, and thus the penitent believer must remain in a state of doubt.

When consciences were horribly disturbed by these controversies, which destroyed hope and brought shame upon Christ, the fathers, warned by these events, began to pay attention to that which they had not noticed when they were concerned only about discipline. They began more carefully to look into the teaching of Scripture regarding sin, repentance, grace, faith, and remission of sins and to study the unfortunate statements they and others had made which supplied the seeds for Novatianism. They retracted these statements and corrected them according to the norm of the Word of God. This can be noted in at least one of Cyprian's writings. In this way, marvelously, at that time some light of the true doctrine concerning repentance, faith, and remission of sins was again restored, a doctrine which, by turning in the direction of overly severe discipline, would have altogether become extinct if through Novatian the fathers had not been aroused to consider the Law and the testimony.

Afterward statements that were more oratorical and extravagant than pious and correct rang out in the churches concerning free will, minimizing original sin and extolling the efficacy of the Law and the perfection of the righteousness of works, even of works of supererogation, and the righteousness of faith lay there in obscurity. Then God, in order to open the sleepy eyes of the doctors of the church to look more diligently at the teaching of Paul, permitted the church to be so disrupted by Pelagianism that it appeared that the very foundations of the entire Christian religion were about to collapse. At this point Ambrose, Jerome, and Augustine recognized what they had not noticed before, namely that while they themselves and the other ancient fathers had been so preoccupied with stirring up zeal for good works, they had made many statements which did not agree with the analogy of faith. Augustine retracted many such statements. [*Retractiones*, MPL 32.583ff., also many English editions] Jerome in his *Dialogus adv. Pelagianos* [MPL 23.495ff.] condemned many statements which we can read not only in the writings of the ancients but also in the very books of Jerome himself. Thus in an indirect way God again restored some light to the doctrine of the free remission of sins and other articles which otherwise would have been completely lost in the progress of time.

Augustine states in regard to Psalm 101 that the pagans condemned the teaching of the church by saying, "You have destroyed discipline and perverted the morals of the human race by giving to men an opportunity for repentance and by promising immunity for all sins; and thus men do evil, secure in the fact that all things will be forgiven them when they have been converted." Such objections some people tried to refute by changing the doctrine so that they restricted grace and in hyperbolic language extolled other teachings to the skies. But Augustine, after he learned his lesson from the Pelagian controversy, came to realize that the church was not being helped by this kind of thinking and that the truth was only being perverted and ultimately lost. For just as they should not do evil that good may come of it, so they should not teach falsely in order that the truth might be defended and retained.

Augustine is correct and truthful when he says in *De Civitate Dei*, 16.2 [MPL 41.477], "Many points pertaining to the catholic faith have been stirred up by the cunning trouble-making of heretics, so that we have had to defend these points against them, consider more carefully, define more clearly, and preach more powerfully. The question has been raised by the adversary, and the opportunity is present for better learning." This point is certainly most true in church controversies.

It is also useful to observe that the ancient writers spoke with the greatest security (as Augustine says)—and most unfortunately—concerning this article when they were engaging in general rhetoric in sermons and homilies, or when they were carrying on a debate with heretical adversaries. But when they were forced to deal with those passages in which we find the *sedes doctrinae* of the matter, then the actual evidence of the divine revelation convinced them to explain this doctrine more correctly and properly, as we can see in the commentaries of Origen, Ambrose, Chrysostom, Augustine, and others.

Particularly noteworthy is the fact that sometimes even monks who had preached at great length on merits and the righteousness of works learned the correct understanding of the article of justification, not in their idle contemplations, their sharp disputations, or their rhetorical declamations, but in serious trials, when the conscience was pressed down by a true sense of sin and the wrath of God, as if it had been dragged before His tribunal. For there, as the conscience worriedly looks around and wonders how it can escape the judgment of damnation and stand in the sight of God, it learns to understand Paul's statement in Rom. 3:28.

Thus Anselm [1033–1109, English theologian] and Bonaventura [1221–74, Italian theologian] speak entirely differently regarding the article of justification in their disputations than they do in their meditations. There are some lovely statements in the meditations of Augustine and Anselm and in the *Soliloquy* of Bonaventura. Bernard [of Clairvaux, 1091–1153, famous French abbot] also speaks far more fittingly than the others about the article of justification, because he is not carrying on some idle debate but is presenting his conscience before the judgment of God as if it were to state its case, and from this come the most beautiful thoughts in Bernard's writings. There is also in existence a little book which sometimes goes under the title of *Contemplations of an Uneducated Man*, and it is my opinion that this book was written, since the doctrine of justification had been changed in various ways, in order that uneducated people might know the best way of understanding the true meaning of this locus, if their consciences were troubled by an examination of the divine judgment. For there all other concerns, no matter how sharply and splendidly argued, immediately vanish away.

It is in recent memory, and ought to be noted for all posterity, by what events God in our own age brought the doctrine of justification out of densest darkness back into the brilliant light of His Word. For when Christ and His benefits had been quite buried, the impudent trafficking in Masses, indulgences, merits, and invocation of saints ruled in the church, together with sophistic and unending disputations regarding satisfactions. This memory won the minds of many good people over to Luther from the very beginning when, by presenting the torch of divine revelation, he uncovered these impostures and showed the true fountains of comfort.

This has been a historical survey of the controversies on this locus. I have taken more time than I should have, perhaps, but I believe that these observations shed a good deal of light on the many disputes pertaining to this locus.

They help us judge correctly and sharpen our diligence and care in teaching and preserving the sound doctrine. Now let us proceed to the remaining points.

CHAPTER II: THE TRUE AND PROPER POINT AT ISSUE IN THIS TOPIC

This is a useful and absolutely necessary consideration. For the sophists, the hirelings of their patron ruler the pope, try to hide under clouds and shadows the clear light of Paul's doctrine concerning the free acceptance unto eternal life, by faith, for the sake of the Mediator. In so doing they change the point at issue.

[Johann] Gropper [1503–59, German Roman Catholic theologian, active at Council of Trent], for example, argues at great length that Christ by His obedience did not merit only the remission of sins but also the Spirit of renewal; and that God remits sins to no one without at the same time renewing the spirit of his mind [Eph. 4:23]. He also contends that faith in Christ lays hold not only on the benefit of reconciliation but also that by faith the Spirit of renewal is received, etc. Thus justification does not consist only in the remission of sins and free reconciliation, but it also includes the renewal of the mind and the will through the Spirit.

[Albert] Pighius [ca. 1490–1542, Dutch Roman Catholic theologian] immediately changes the doctrine in this way: He concedes that the obedience of Christ is the only satisfaction for sins and alone merits remission of sins and life eternal. But he argues that these merits of Christ do not apply to those who live without contrition, repentance, good intention, etc. Because John says: "He who does not love remains in death" [1 John 3:14], he is pointing out that he who does not have love does not have eternal life. From this he infers that therefore faith alone does not justify.

Vicelius [Georg Witzel, 1501–73, former Lutheran pastor who returned to Roman Catholicism but tried to bring about reforms] so perverts the point at issue that he says: Those who are justified by faith alone lose the grace of God when they give in to their evil desires and slip into actions against conscience. Again, he says that God requires a zeal for good works from those whom He has freely justified. Therefore those who have been freely justified do not attain salvation and eternal life by faith alone.

These are the subterfuges of those who transform themselves into angels of light. They see that the impudence of the scholastics is too crass when they state the *status controversiae* thus: Christ has made satisfaction only for original sin. Others say only for mortal sin. Some contend that it was only for those sins preceding conversion, but that the rest of our sins require satisfaction on our part, if we want to receive remission. Still others argue that Christ has merited for us only the first grace, so that through it we ourselves might merit remission of sins, salvation, and eternal life.

They recognize that these enormous deviations cannot be defended in the face of such clear light without total shamelessness. Therefore they are now seeking other deceptions.

The point at issue in this locus is being confused in three principal ways. [1.] The argument is directed at the matter of outward discipline, that is, regarding the righteousness of the flesh or the honorable works preceding true conversion. [2.] The argument concerns itself with the initial stages of conversion, which precede faith itself or are concurrent with it, such as contrition, detestation of sin, the sorrows of recognizing God's wrath and judgment against sin, good intentions, etc. [3.] Or the argument hinges on the matter of renewal, that is, it deals with the good works that follow reconciliation. We must carefully note and distinguish these points.

Many people, not out of malice but out of a certain prudence, are disturbed or involved in these errors because they are charmed by irrelevant arguments and are led away from the real point at issue. For the papists argue in a very insidious way as if the point at issue were whether these things of which we are speaking ought to be present or follow. They make mighty efforts to prove points that are not in controversy.

Aeschines in his *Oratio Contra Demosthenem* ["On the Embassy," #147ff.] says that just as boxers fight to retain the position in which they are standing, so orators must fight to prove the point of their speech and not yield to their opponent or permit the debate to get beyond the bounds of the subject. We must observe this rule particularly in the case of this locus. In order to establish the point at issue correctly, we shall state it both negatively and affirmatively. We do not deny that unregenerate men must be coerced by external discipline. Nor do we dispute in this article as to whether contrition ought to be present in those who are to be justified, nor that some change in the mind and will, or renewal or new obedience, ought to follow. We have professed with a loud voice that all of these things do take place in a true conversion. Therefore the controversy is not whether these things should take place, are present, or follow.

The point at issue is this: When the mind is terrified by the recognition of sin and a sense of the wrath of God, (1) What is that entity on account of which the sinner, condemned before God's judgment to eternal punishment, obtains remission of sins, is absolved from the sentence of condemnation, and is received into eternal life? (2) What is the instrument or means by which the promise of the Gospel, that is, the promise of grace, mercy, reconciliation, salvation, and eternal life, is received, laid hold upon, and applied? For these two things are sought in the article of justification: the merit or satisfaction and the application of it to oneself.

Now we should put in order these points mentioned which take place in conversion, namely the discipline of the Law, contrition, change of the mind and will, faith, new obedience, etc. We must also determine whether remission of sins, absolution from the sentence of damnation, and acceptance to eternal life take place on account of our works—whether preceding or following or concurrent—or on account of the obedience, satisfaction, and intercession of the Son of God our Mediator.

Next we should examine the individual points, because among these is the means whereby we lay hold on or apply to ourselves the promise of the Gospel, or of mercy, promised for the sake of Christ. Beyond all controversy, it cannot be the discipline of the unregenerate. Contrition has as its object a sense of sin, wrath, judgment of God, and condemnation. But we are asking about laying hold on the promise of grace. Also the new obedience cannot be the application of the promise, because it is concerned with its object, which is the Law, that is, the commandments of God. And Paul simply excludes the Law from justification. Therefore faith is that instrument and means. But to what degree and in what respect? Not insofar as it receives the Spirit of renewal, not insofar as it works through love; but insofar as it lays hold on the promise of grace and eternal life in Christ. For this is the question: What is the instrument that lays hold on the promise of the Gospel of the remission of sins for the sake of Christ?

When the point at issue is stated in this way, both negatively and affirmatively, then it is easy to note and beware of the traps and pitfalls of our adversaries. The explanation of the matter will be much clearer and simpler, so that we do not mix in irrelevant material or in an indiscriminate and counterproductive way upset things which in themselves and in their own place are perfectly correct.

CHAPTER III: THE VOCABULARY OF JUSTIFICATION

"To Justify," "To Be Justified," "Righteous Act," "Acquittal," "Righteousness of God and of Faith"

We ought to love and magnify the linguistic description of the terms used in the chief loci of the heavenly doctrine. For the church, in its interpretation of these terms, has not produced new dogmas, but has scrutinized, learned, and accepted the things taught and revealed by the divine voice. Just as the concepts themselves have been revealed in Scripture by the divine voice in the Word, so they cannot be properly understood except from the true and genuine meaning of the words which the Holy Spirit used in handing down the heavenly doctrine.

Nor is this merely a grammatical war (as it is called), but in the principal loci of doctrine the greater the error in the terminology, so much the greater the loss in the concepts themselves.

In this locus the example is particularly illustrative. For when the correct terminology was lost, immediately the light of the purer teaching was also extinguished; and when in our time the correct grammatical meaning of the words in this locus was restored, the purity of the doctrine was also restored. Nor can we be the guardians of the doctrine of this locus, which has again been divinely purified, unless we learn and love the terminology involved.

Therefore, in order that we may more warmly love, more diligently learn, and more correctly understand these explanations which, because of their delicate nature, are often corrupted at the hands of careless people, we shall set them forth in a definite order point by point for our consideration.

I. In the entire history of the church it can be observed how much damage the contempt for and ignorance of the correct terminology has done to the church in the case of this article. In all periods the light of sound doctrine concerning justification has first been weakened, later increasingly obscured, and finally almost lost and extinguished—chiefly because there was a departure from the genuine meaning of the words of this locus, words which are peculiar and proper to Scripture.

Augustine is often convinced by the testimony of Paul that the term "to justify" is interpreted with reference to the remission of sins. But later in his life, deceived by the similarity of the words "to sanctify" and "to justify," he shifted the emphasis in the direction of sanctification, having the new qualities, desires and actions of the Spirit. Especially this became the case when he saw that this interpretation of the words "to justify" fit quite well with the case which he was arguing against the Pelagians. Thus in his *De Spiritu & Litera*, 26 [31, MPL 44.233–34], in treating the word of the apostle, "Being justified freely by His grace," Rom. 3:24, he says, "We are not justified through the Law, or through our own will, but through grace; not that this takes place without our will, but the weakness of the will is shown through the Law, in order that grace may restore the will, and the will having been restored, may fulfill the Law." *De Natura & Gratia* [58, MPL 44.281], "As a result of faith the Holy Spirit is given, who pours out love upon us by which, together with faith, they are righteous who are righteous." Likewise, *De Praedestinatione* [7, MPL 44.969], "Man is said to be justified by faith and not by works because faith is given first, and as a result of this other things are demanded which are properly called works and in which the righteous shall live." This improper use of the words on the face of it does not seem to produce any problem. For the facts are true that the Holy Spirit does renew the mind and will in those who have been reconciled, and does cause them to will and to do. But as time went on, this misuse showed what a problem was created by even a slight twisting of the words in the heavenly doctrine. Shortly after this Sedulius[23] corrupted the lovely statement in Romans 4 to mean that God justifies those who have entered upon the new life by following the example of His resurrection. And Lombard [*Sententiae* 3, dist. 19 (MPL 192.795)] gives both of these definitions: (1) "We are justified by the death of Christ because only by the shedding of His blood the charges against all their sins have been blotted out for believers. Previously they had been held in bondage by the devil because of them. (2) We are said to be justified through the death of Christ in a second sense in that there is commended to us the love of God, and because of this we are moved to love God and through this we are justified, that is, we are freed from our sins and made righteous. Therefore the death of Christ justifies us in the sense that through it love is aroused in our hearts." He seems to approve of this meaning. The scholastics afterward followed in his tracks and with their terminology corrupted the doctrine itself. For in their summaries they argue this way: Just as heating brings motion to warmth, and just as white-washing adds force to the whiteness of an object—things which are applied to something in a positive way—so, they say, justification refers to a force and righteousness. From this Thomas concludes that justification is a moving from the state of unrighteousness to the state of righteousness. And just as in the case of any other kind of motion, there is a departure from the place one has left (*terminus a quo*) toward the place where one is going (*terminus ad quem*), so in the case of justification they posit an expulsion of guilt and an infusion of grace. Thomas says that righteousness means the certainty by which the weaker powers are made subject to the stronger or to God Himself. This certainty is removed through mortal sin and regained through grace, which works love. And just as the light drives out the darkness, so the infusion of grace drives out guilt or mortal sin. Durandus[24] says it this way: Just as man is said to be unrighteous when he ceases to be obedient to God, so when he returns to obedience he is said to be justified.

From this kind of thinking, which arose out of ignorance of the true meaning of the words, the actual content of the article of justification became totally corrupted. They do indeed retain from the glosses to Romans 8 such a definition as this: "Justification is the remission of sins and the total fulfillment of good

---

[23] Christian poet who wrote about 430. He translated his work into prose also, which was more specific in its theology.

[24] Durandus, Durand of St. Pourcain, d. 1334, wrote a commentary on the *Sentences* of Lombard.

works." But they even pervert this. Thomas, for example, in 1.2.113[25] argues whether an infusion of grace is required for the remission of guilt. To be sure, he does see in Ps. 32:2 that remission of sin comes under the category of divine imputation, but he goes on to add that God cannot be made favorable in regard to the offense unless the sin is expelled and into its place is poured the attitude or quality of grace, which God has respect for in order that He may remit the offense. In the same place he says, "We are justified by faith, in this way: Because the will is not moved by something it has not considered but rather is moved by something it recognizes, therefore faith is required as something which directs the will to love God, and by this love we are formally righteous." This is a horrible corruption of the doctrine of faith and the remission of sins, and it arises principally from a misunderstanding of the meaning of the word "justification." I have cited these examples in order to show how important it is to retain faithfully the correct linguistic description of these terms and how much damage can be done to the purity of teaching by even a very slight twisting of the words away from the proper and genuine meaning in this locus.

We must also add this point, that God has kindled the light of the doctrine of faith by rescuing these terms from the barbarism of the papacy and restoring their true, genuine, and apostolic meaning. There is no need for a long discussion of this point, for the matter is perfectly clear, unless we want to consider how great the difficulty was for the church, which had learned its terminology from the barbarians, to reconstitute these words on the basis of the true fountains. Luther in the preface to his first volume tells of himself that although he had a correct understanding of the subject of the free remission of sins, yet he was often troubled by the terms, because he could not establish the concept of the righteousness of faith in relation to his training, for the meaning which at that time was resounding in the schools and temples, that righteousness is a quality, pressed down upon his mind.

Furthermore, it is useful to observe in what a bad light these linguistic studies put the papists, as Gropper clearly shows when he attacks the *Scipio* of Philipp so mercilessly.[26]

There is no doubt that if the linguistic interpretation again falls into neglect or is lost in regard to these terms, the light of this doctrine, even though it is very clear at present, will again be obfuscated and extinguished, just as in the Osiandrian controversy God warned the church with a serious reminder that it should not play games with these words.

---

[25] Thomas Aquinas, *Summa*, 1.2.113 (2), Blackfriars Ed., v. 30, p.167.

[26] Gropper had attacked Melanchthon and Luther, but we have been unable to locate any work by Melanchthon with the title of *Scipio*.

[II.] In order that we can establish what the word "to justify" properly means in the doctrine of the Gospel, we shall show how this word was used in common, ordinary speech. The papists cry that in the usage of no languages does the word "to justify" mean "to absolve" or "to impute as righteous," but rather "to make righteous," by the giving or infusing of new qualities.

In the common Greek language the word *dikaioō* is simply a forensic or declarative word having two meanings. (1) It means to evaluate or pronounce something to be righteous, not in the sense of one's private opinion but in the way that those who hold a public office make a pronouncement. Plutarch says in his *Agesilaus* [23.608]: "Agesilaus, after announcing the war, compelled all to stand before those on whom the Persian had pronounced judgment" (*hois ho Persis edikaiōse*). In his *Brutus* [45.1005] he says, "Upon those who had scoffed at the murder of Cassius, when they had been accused in court as pretended captives, Messalas Corvinnus pronounced the judgment (*edikaiou*) that they should be beaten with rods and sent naked to the camp of the enemy." A commentator on Sophocles' *Oedipus Coloneus* uses the expression "to judge against the righteous" (*anti ton dikaion krinein*). Suidas [Kuster Ed. 996] speaks of "calling someone righteous" (*dikaion nomizein*). And he cites Herodotus, "Pronouncing them righteous for having defended against the Scythians, with whom they had broken a treaty toward the Athenians who had given them aid." Appian [ibid., 994], "To make a treaty with those whom they pronounced to be brothers" (*symbaseis poiein eph hois an . . . dikaiōsin*). Suidas adds that Lysias calls acts of "doing justice" "pleas for justification" (*dikaiōseis tas dikaiologias*). And from Josephus he cites, "Those who had been reckoned righteous (*tēn dikaiōsin logizomenoi*) by reason of their insolence when their arms were broken, fled for refuge" [ibid.] (2) The term means "to inflict punishment (*kolazein*), not in the way private individuals punish but as when a person is punished by a legal decision after a case has been judged. Suidas uses words of this kind to explain it: "one who has been sentenced" (*dikaiomenos*), "one who has been punished" (*kolazomenos*), "to pay the penalty," "condemnation" (*dikaiōsis*), "judgment" (*dikaiomenos*). And from Thucidides he cites "judgments in place of punishments" (*dikaiōseis anti tōn kolaseōn*). He adds an example from an author who is unnamed, "He was punished lightly, but when all the brothers of the great Zeus are punished, the punishment shall be most appropriate" [ibid.], Cicero, *In Verrem* [3.4.9], uses the term "they were punished" (*edikaiōthēsan*), and he interprets it as meaning they had punishment inflicted upon them.

Therefore it is clear that among the Greeks this was simply a forensic or legal term. The apostles used the word in the same sense in the article of justification as was known from the legal use of the word in popular Greek. The Septuagint had used the word *dikaioō* to translate the Hebrew concept of which we are now speaking. But we must note the difference; there is not total agreement. Scripture uses the term "to justify" for "to pronounce righteous," almost always with reference to people. But the Greeks used it also for legal cases or matters of business. To the Hebrews the term "to justify" refers to one who has been absolved, to defend him and to adorn him with rewards for his righteousness. But the Greeks used the term also in the negative sense, with reference to condemnation or to punish the condemned person. This sense is not used in Scripture.

In the common Greek language the word *dikaioō* is never used with the meaning the papists attach to it of infusing righteousness as something positive and inherent. In Aristotle, *Ethica*, 5 [*Nicomachean Ethics*, 5.1136a], the forensic use of the term is transferred from the specific to the general meaning. The term *dikaiousthai* is used when someone receives what is his (*dem recht geschicht.*) But this meaning likewise gives no support to the papists.

The scholastics judge the word *iustificare* (to justify) by its composition, like *vivificare* (to make alive) or *calefacere* (to make warm), involving the idea of expelling one quality and putting in another. But the age of Cicero and the other Latin writers knows nothing of this usage of the word. In the period of Augustine it seems that the term was used in keeping with the practice of Scripture. *De Bono Conjugali*, 14 [MPL 40.384], "If a person, after unjustly taking over someone's field, makes large alms, that does not justify robbery." Thus the papists cannot establish the meaning which they are trying to give to the word "justify" on the basis of the use in the time of the purer use of Latin. Thus the papists cannot from the time of the purer use of Latin establish the meaning for the word "justify" for which they are contending.

The Germans use the term *rechtfertigen*, following the Greek practice, as a legal and forensic word. In legal actions it is still common to use the word "justify" in this sense, following either the German or the Greek custom.

Thus no language in its more polished use supports the papists, but all bear testimony that the word "justify" is a forensic term.

III. We mentioned at the beginning that words used in explaining the doctrine of the church are of three kinds. Some are taken from the common usage of the language; some are peculiar or proper to Holy Scripture; and some are taken into use for certain reasons in a special meaning, such as the word "person" or "sacrament." The word "justify" in the teaching of this topic, although it has some relationship to the usage of the Greek language, nevertheless is doubtless a term peculiar to sacred language. Thus we must gather some examples from Scripture from which we can establish with certainty the true, proper, and genuine meaning. In order that this might be more expeditiously accomplished, we shall now take some examples of what meaning the word "justify" has in other passages, unrelated to the doctrine of justification. Thus later on an accommodation can skillfully and easily be made to the locus on justification.

It is manifest and beyond denial or doubt that among the Hebrews the word is a forensic term, and this can very evidently be proved in two ways.

First, the word is clearly used with references to courts and legal cases and actions. In 2 Sam. 15:4 Absalom says: "If only I were appointed judge in this land! Then all who have a complaint or a case could come to me and I would get them justice [*justificem*, "justify them"]." Deut. 25:1: "When men have a dispute, they are to take the case to court and the judges will decide it, acquitting [*justificent*, "justifying"] the innocent and condemning [*injustificent*, "unjustifying"] the guilty." Both words have the same derivation. In Ps. 82:3 God addresses judges thus: "Defend the poor and the fatherless; do justice to [*justificate*, "justify"] the afflicted and needy" [KJV]. Is. 43:9, 26: "Let them bring their witnesses, and let them be justified. . . . Let us plead together; tell Me if you have anything to justify yourself."

Second, the antithesis shows it clearly. Often the terms "to justify" and "to condemn" are put in opposition to each other. Prov. 17:15 states: "He who justifies the wicked and he who condemns the righteous are both an abomination before God." Deut. 25:1: "They shall justify (*justificabunt*) the righteous and condemn the wicked" [KJV]. 1 Kings 8:32: ". . . condemning the wicked . . . and justifying (*justifices*) the righteous" [KJV]. Is. 50:8: "He who justifies me is near at hand. Who will then bring charges against me? Who will condemn me?" Matt. 12:37: "By your words you will be justified, or condemned." Thus we read in Rom. 8:33–34: "It is God who justifies; who is he that condemns?" Rom. 5:16: "The judgment was by one to condemnation, but the free gift is from many offenses to justification."

The word "to justify" with this meaning includes these three aspects, as the examples clearly show. (1) It means to absolve the person who has been accused and brought to judgment of the crime with which he was charged, so that he not be condemned by the legal process or that he be restored to his state of innocence. (2) It means to account, pronounce, receive, and accept a person as righteous or innocent. The term is used in this sense without distinction as to whether the cause is a just or an unjust one, as in Is. 5:23: Woe to those who "justify the wicked for reward and take away the righteousness of the righteous from him." Compare Prov. 17:15. (3) The term also includes the fact that Scripture attributes to those who have been justified the praise, the testimony, and the rewards owed to the righteous and the innocent, and it treats them not as guilty convicts or even as suspects, but as righteous and innocent. This Scripture clearly includes in the word "justify." Ex. 23:7: "Do not kill the innocent, for I will not justify the wicked." In 1 Kings 8:31–32 we have this clear example: "If anyone trespasses against his neighbor, and an oath is laid on him . . . then hear in heaven, and act . . . condemning the wicked, to bring his way on his head, and justifying (*justificans*) the righteous, to give him according to his righteousness." And because he has been absolved in the judgment, he is freed from the Law, the power, the violence, and the oppression of his adversary. Hence Paul in Rom. 6:7 says: "He who has died has been freed [*justificatus*, "justified"] from sin." This observation will be useful later, as we apply the meaning of the word to the locus on justification.

This is the forensic or legal meaning of this word. But just as is the case in all languages, words are transferred from the specific to the general. Thus "justify" is sometimes used to approve, testify to, recognize, acknowledge, confess, and celebrate the fact that someone is righteous—granting, conferring, and attributing praise to his righteousness. Luke 7:29: "The people and the publicans justified God, but the Pharisees spurned the counsel of God." Luke 16:15: "You justify yourselves before men." Luke 10:29: "The scribe, wanting to justify himself . . ." Jer. 3:11 and Ezek. 16:51: "You have justified your sisters." 1 Tim. 3:16: "He was manifested in the flesh and justified in the Spirit," that is, the humility of His flesh offended many, and He was crucified as a misleader and a seditious man; but because of His divine works and the sending of the Spirit, He was declared and approved as the Son of God and the Messiah. Matt. 11:19 and Luke 7:35: "Wisdom is justified by her children." This statement is interpreted by the opposite phraseology, that is, "to master or condemn" (*meistern oder Unrecht geben*) or, as the Germans say, "to justify everyone" (*jedermann rechtfertigen*). But the passage can also be interpreted in a positive sense: The children themselves are forced to testify to the wisdom of God, because He has overlooked nothing, as the saying goes: "What must I still do which I have not done?" Thus wisdom is justified, that is, excused and absolved, by her children.

This meaning is in keeping with the forensic definition except that it has been changed from the specific to the general.

Because this forensic definition does not support the definition established by the papists, they anxiously seek examples by which they can render it probable that justification must be understood as making a person righteous by giving new qualities. They cite Dan. 12:3: "Those who are wise will shine as the brightness of the firmament; and those who turn many to righteousness [Latin, "justify many"], like the stars for ever and ever." But it is certain that the wise cannot pour into people new qualities of righteousness. Therefore Jerome renders it: "Those who instruct many to righteousness." Luther: "Those who show the way to righteousness" (*Die da weisen zur Gerechtigkeit*). What this righteousness is must be learned from the Gospel. Thus this passage from Daniel is beautifully brought back to the proper meaning of the word "justify." For God justifies, just as He binds, looses, and remits sins, etc., but He uses as His means or instrument the ministration of the Word, 2 Cor. 5:18, 21: He "gave us the ministry of reconciliation . . . God making His appeal through us." Therefore, just as pastors bind, loose, remit, and retain sins (Matt. 18:18; John 20:23; and 1 Tim. 4:16: ". . . you will save both yourself and your hearers"), so Daniel is saying that "the wise justify," that is, they are those who proclaim the remission of sins, who absolve many from their sins, spread the light, etc. Thus the papists get no support from Daniel.

They also pretend that the statement in 1 Cor. 6:11 supports them: "You are washed, you are sanctified, you are justified." They think that from this they can prove the meaning for which they are contending, because "justified" is placed after the washing and the sanctifying. But the antithesis declares what Paul is trying to say. For in opposition to the washing is put filth; in opposition to sanctification is put pollution or contamination; in opposition to justification is put guilt, which is expressed thus: "They will not inherit the kingdom of God" [v. 10]. Because Paul immediately adds: "You are justified in the name of the Lord Jesus," he is clearly showing the meaning. For salvation and remission of sins are given in the name of the Lord. Therefore this passage does not show directly or clearly that the word "justify" means an infusion of new qualities.

Up to this point they have not been able to offer a witness or an example that supports their position. There is a unique passage in Rev. 22:11: "He that is righteous, let him be righteous [Latin, "justified"] still" [KJV]. It is not wrong to explain it this way: There is always need for absolution or remission of sins for the righteous or regenerate. But because connected with it are the expressions, "He that is unjust, let him be unjust still . . . he that is holy, let him be holy still," the sense of the passage seems to be that just as the obstinate are not improved through the ministration of the Word but are hardened and more contaminated by filth and iniquity, so the righteous and the holy increase and progress in the holiness and righteousness of the new obedience through hearing the Word.

Just as the doctrine of the Law is one thing and the doctrine of the Gospel is another, which must not be confused, so "justify" means one thing when Scripture is speaking of the divine commandments, and another thing when it speaks of the gracious promises of the Gospel. Now we need to consider whether the statement in Revelation pertains to the Law or to the Gospel, and in this way we can make a determination regarding the meaning of the word in this passage.

We must still make this point, that in the entire Scripture it is impossible clearly to prove by a single example that the word "justify," when it speaks of God's justifying, is ever to be understood as referring to renewal by the infusion of new qualities. We do not deny the renewal that takes place through the Spirit, but now the question is what the word "justification" means in Scripture. Even if we granted the verse in Revelation 22 as an example, yet Paul most clearly declares how he wants the word "justify" to be understood. Certainly for the sake of one individual example, which itself is not demonstrably precise, we must not depart from the great and clear meaning of the rest of the passages.

Their quoting of Ps. 73:13, "In vain have I justified my heart" [Vulgate-Douay], proves nothing. For David did not infuse new qualities into himself. In the Hebrew the word "justify" is not used in this passage.

What we have said up to this point regarding the many different meanings of the word "justify" can be very easily explained and understood from the conjugations of the Hebrew verbs. The Greeks often expressed different meanings by the use of a particular form of a word, but the Hebrews made a distinction as to the diversity of meanings by changes in the conjugation. This is also a source of the errors in the doctrine of justification.

Osiander[27] apparently wanted to construct his tragic error from the Hebrew conjugations, namely because the word "justify" belongs to the third conjugation, the Hiphil. He divided up the meanings of the conjugations like this: In the first conjugation the verbs refer to having a certain quality. In the second they use this quality. In the third they attribute this quality to someone else, so that it passes to another person. In this way he developed his examples. In the first conjugation it is: "He shall be made good." In the third, "Make your ways good," Jer. 7:3. Again, the first conjugation would be "He was right," and the third, "He made it right." Again, "He was a wise man," "He made someone wise." Again, "to live," "to make alive." Similarly, he contended that in the first conjugation it would be "to be righteous," and in the third, "to make righteous."

But the examples from Scripture very clearly refuted him, as has been mentioned above. For if an unjust judge in justifying or acquitting a guilty man would pour into him the quality of righteousness, he would not be "an abomination before God," Prov. 17:15; nor would the Lord say, "Woe!" as in Is. 5:20ff. And Paul explains justification in terms of imputation. Therefore Osiander's rule is false if it is understood in a general and exclusive sense. The grammarians are more correct in their judgment that the verbs of the third conjugation indicate that the quality of the first conjugation is attributed to another person or to the thing itself, either by permission (as is said in the passage regarding hardening) or by judgment, by words, by testimony, by assertion, by declaration, and as Paul says, by imputation. The examples regarding the word "justify" fit with this rule. The rabbis themselves, although under their veil (2 Cor. 3:14) they do

---

[27] Andreas Osiander, 1498–1552, Lutheran reformer, pastor, and professor; his position on justification was condemned in Article III of the Formula of Concord.

not understand how God justifies the guilty, yet do not dare to attribute to the word the meaning given by Osiander and the papists. Rather they corrupt the passage in Is. 53:11, "By His knowledge shall My righteous Servant justify many" [KJV], to mean that the Messiah will have the understanding that He will know how He must justify the righteous and condemn the guilty.

The conjugations of the Hebrew verbs could be more usefully applied in order to show the difference when "justify" refers to the Law and when it refers to the Gospel.

In the first conjugation it refers to having righteousness, to being righteous in a positive sense, as in Ps. 19:9: "The judgments of the Lord are true and righteous altogether" [KJV]. Ps. 51:4: ". . . that You might be righteous in Your Word." Ps. 143:2: "Enter not into judgment . . . for in Your sight shall no living person be righteous." Dan. 8:14: "The sanctuary will be righteous"—that is, after it has been purged from the pollutions of Antiochus, the true and righteous worship of God will be restored.

In the Book of Job there is frequent reference to the righteousness within us, which is the righteousness of the new obedience and a good conscience. Job 13:18: "I have ordered My cause, and I know that I will be righteous." In 34:5 Job says: "I am righteous, and God has taken away my judgment." We must carefully note in the story of Job that the righteousness of the Law, or inherent righteousness, was pressed down by the cross and temptations so that he would not clothe himself in the opinion of the Pharisees but might learn to seek the righteousness of the Gospel. Job 9:20: "If I justify myself, my own mouth will condemn me." Again, in v. 15: "Though I were righteous, yet I would not answer, but would make supplication to my Judge." Job 10:15: "If I am righteous, I will not lift up my head, for I am full of affliction." This refers to doing justly. Job. 33:9, 12: "You say, 'I am clean . . . and there is no iniquity in me.' . . . Behold, in this you are not justified" (*Daran hast du nicht recht getan*). Job 35:7: "If you are righteous, or if you act justly, what will you give to Him?"

The word is used once in this conjugation with reference to the righteousness of faith, Is. 45:25: "In the Lord all the seed of Israel shall be justified and shall glory." It is a most fitting observation that with respect to us the righteousness of faith is in the third conjugation, that is, it is imputed, but with respect to the obedience of the Mediator it is positive, that is, in the first conjugation—but not in regard to us but in regard to the Lord, as the preceding verse, Is. 45:24, says: "In the Lord I have my righteousness." Paul seems to be imitating this expression in 2 Cor. 5:21: ". . . that we might be made the righteousness of God in Him" [KJV], and also in 1 Cor. 1:30: "He is made our righteousness."

In the second conjugation "justify" refers to arrogating righteousness to oneself or attributing it to another, as in Job 32:2, where Elihu is angry because

Job justifies his own soul. Job 33:32: "If you have something to say . . . speak, for I desire to justify you." Jer. 3:11: "Israel has justified her own soul . . ." Ezek. 16:51: "You have justified your sisters by your own abominations." Likewise Matt. 12:41: "The Ninevites will condemn this generation."

In the third conjugation "justify" has a forensic or legal connotation, of which we have already shown examples above. In the article of justification it is used in this conjugation, cf. Is. 53:11.

In the fourth conjugation it refers to pleading in court (*dikaiologia*), to bringing arguments or testimonies to the merit of a case. It is used once, in Gen. 44:16, where the brothers of Joseph say, "How shall we justify ourselves?"

I think this comparison has been useful and sheds considerable light on the subject. But because the Greek of the apostles must be evaluated by taking into consideration the apocrypha and the Old Testament, we will devote a few words to how the word "justify" is used in Sirach [Ecclesiasticus]. Ecclus. 1:22: "Unjust anger cannot be justified." Luther renders this "does not please God." Ecclus. 7:5: "Do not justify yourself before God, nor display your wisdom before the king." 10:29: "Who will justify the man who sins against his own soul?" 13:22: "A rich man . . . speaks words, and they justify him proud." 23:11: "If a man swears needlessly, he will not be justified." 31:5: "He who loves gold will not be justified." 42:2: "In judgment do not justify the ungodly."

All of these examples agree with the forensic meaning of the word, of which we have been speaking. Note Ecclus. 26:29: "A tradesman will not be justified from sins." There is a similar example in Rom. 6:7: "He that is dead is freed (*justificatus, dedikaiōtai*) from sin" [KJV]. Luther renders this, *sich vor Sünden hüten*. The Consensus Tigurinus[28] says: "He will not lack guilt or be free of sin." Ecclus. 18:22: "Do not put off till the time of death to be justified" [Vulgate]. Luther translates this *fromm zu werden*, but the term can simply be understood in the proper sense as it is in other passages. For it speaks of reconciliation with God at the time of death, that conversion should not be put off until death or the danger of death. Thus all the passages are in agreement.

IV. Now we must apply these points to the article of justification. We have noted these things with reference to the use of the term. Paul everywhere describes the article of justification as a judicial process wherein the conscience of the sinner, accused before the tribunal of God by the divine law, convicted, and subject to the sentence of eternal damnation, flees to the throne of grace and is restored, absolved, and freed from the sentence of condemnation and received

---

[28] The Consensus Tigurinus, a Reformed confession, was drawn up in 1549 by Calvin and Bullinger. It brought together the Calvinistic and Zwinglian views regarding the Lord's Supper.

to eternal life for the sake of the obedience and intercession of the Son of God, our Mediator, which is laid hold of and made one's own through faith.

Rom. 3:19–20: The Law places all under sin, so that "every mouth may be stopped and the whole world may become guilty before God, for by the works of the Law shall no flesh be justified before Him." We are justified freely. Rom. 5:10: "When we were enemies, we were reconciled to God . . ." [KJV]. Again in v. 16: "For the judgment was by one to condemnation, but the free gift is from many offenses to justification." Again, v. 19: "Through the disobedience of one man many were accounted as sinners, and through the obedience of One many were accounted as righteous." The word "to account" (*constituo*) is used in order to show that this takes place before the judgment seat of God. Rom. 7:9: "When the Law came, sin revived and I died." V. 24: "Wretched man that I am, who shall deliver me from the body of this death? I thank God . . ." [KJV]. Rom. 8:1–2: "There is now no condemnation. . . . For He has set me free from the law of sin and death." Vv. 33ff.: "Who is to accuse? It is God who justifies. Who is to condemn? It is Christ who . . . intercedes for us. . . . In all these things we are conquerors. . . ."

All of these points are clearly forensic and in the realm of Law. Most beautiful is the statement in Rom. 10:3: "They tried to stand in their own righteousness and did not submit to the righteousness of God." This means that they tried to set up their own righteousness before the judgment seat of God and were unwilling to humble themselves and seek that other righteousness which God has established.

In 1 John 1:9 we read: "If we confess our sins, He is faithful and just to forgive us our sins" [KJV]. Again in 1 John 2:1–2: "If anyone sins, we have an advocate . . . and He is the propitiation . . ." 1 Cor. 4:3–4: "I am not judged by man, but He who judges me is the Lord. Therefore, although I am not aware of any charge against myself, yet I am not thereby justified." Gal. 3:22: "Scripture has imprisoned all under sin, that the promise might be by faith." V. 10: "It is written, 'Cursed is everyone who does not continue,'" etc. Vv. 13–14: "Christ redeemed us from the curse of the Law . . . that . . . the blessing," etc. Gal. 4:4–5: "Made to be under the Law, that He might redeem those who were under the Law." 1 Cor. 15:55–57: "O Grave, where is your victory? O Death, where is your sting? But thanks be to God, who has given us the victory." Eph. 2:3–5: "When we were dead in sins . . . and by nature children of wrath . . . by grace you have been saved." Luke 18:13–14: "The publican did not dare to lift up his eyes, but beat on his breast saying, 'God, be merciful to me, a sinner.' . . . This man went down justified." Therefore Scripture sets up the antithesis of "before God" and "before men," cf. Luke 16:15; Rom. 3:20.

Thus it is manifest that Paul is using the word "justification" in the forensic or legal sense when he deals with the doctrine of the article of justification.

It is useful to observe why Paul in the explanation of this article so often prefers the forensic or legal word "justification" when the other apostles seem to use synonymous terms, such as "to save," "to remit sins," etc. The reason doubtlessly lies in the fact that profane, self-sufficient, and Epicurean persons believe that the matter and action of the justification of the sinner is a very unimportant matter, and therefore they are not greatly concerned about sin and do not seriously seek nor desire to retain reconciliation with God. When the human mind is puffed up with pharisaic opinion and indulges in its own ideas regarding justification, or judges by comparing itself with others, then it is easy to become persuaded of the value of its own righteousness, whatever that may be. But when the doctrine of justification is presented and considered under the picture of a divine judgment, examination, and tribunal, through a judicial process, so to speak, then the basic points of the true meaning are more correctly understood and can more easily be shown and taught to others, and purity of doctrine can be retained against both pharisaic and Epicurean opinions.

Paul himself shows this with a most beautiful statement in 1 Cor. 4:3–4: "I am not aware of any charge against me, but in this I am not justified." He adds the reason for this: "Because I am not judged by a human court, nor do I judge myself. . . . It is the Lord who judges me." And in Rom. 4:2: "If Abraham was justified by works, he has something to boast about, but not before God."

Thus, the use of the legal term "justification" refutes the ideas of the Epicureans. For it shows that the justification of the sinner is not some insignificant or perfunctory thing, but that the whole human being stands before the judgment of God and is examined both with respect to his nature as well as his works, and this according to the norm of the divine law. But because after the entrance of sin a human being in this life does not have true and perfect conformity with the law of God, nothing is found in this examination, whether in the person's nature or in his works, that he can use to justify himself before God; rather the Law pronounces the sentence of condemnation, written by the very finger of God Himself.

Now God does not justify the ungodly by some kind of mistake, as a judge often makes a faulty decision by failure to examine the evidence sufficiently or by wrong thinking; nor through indifference, as if He did not care about the transgression of His law; nor through wickedness, as if He approved of our iniquity, connived with it, or were in collusion with the impious. A justification of this kind God Himself pronounces to be an abomination, Ex. 23:1; Is. 5:23; Prov. 17:15. God cannot retract the sentence of condemnation revealed in the Law, unless it is perfectly satisfied or fulfilled, Matt. 5:18.

Thus righteousness and satisfaction are required where God is to justify. Luther is correct when he says that God remits no sin unless the Law has been satisfied with regard to it. In the case of human judgment, to be sure, guilt is absolved either because of some preceding merit (for they are accounted worthy who deserve to be forgiven), or with respect to present righteousness and innocence either of the cause or of the person, or with respect to a satisfaction which the guilty party promises to make either to the judge or to his opponent in the case. But before God's judgment man can put up nothing in his own defense in order that he might be justified, as many very clear Scripture passages declare.

Therefore, because God does not justify out of frivolity, unconcern, error, or iniquity, nor because He finds anything in man whereby he might be justified before God; and yet the just requirement of the Law must be fulfilled in those who are to be justified, Rom. 8:4, therefore a foreign righteousness must intervene—the kind of righteousness which not only with payment of penalties but also with perfect obedience to the divine law made satisfaction in such a way that it could be a propitiation for the sins of the whole world. To this the terrified sinner, condemned by the voice of the Law, flees in true faith. This he desires, begs for, lays hold of; to this he submits himself; this he uses as his defense before the judgment seat of God and against the accusation of the Law. By regard for this and by its imputation he is justified, that is, he is absolved from the comprehensive sentence of condemnation and receives the promise of eternal life. This is what Paul is saying in Rom. 3:31 : "The doctrine of the righteousness of faith does not destroy the Law but upholds it."

Paul clearly describes the act of justification in this way in Romans 3:

1. The conscience of the sinner is through the Law placed before the judgment tribunal of God (who is a consuming fire and in whose sight not even the stars are pure), is accused, convicted, and condemned, so that it is afflicted and pressed down by a terrifying sense of the wrath of God, Rom. 3:19: ". . . that every mouth may be stopped and all the world may become guilty before God" [KJV].

2. The heart thus contrite does not entertain Epicurean thoughts but anxiously seeks whether and how it can be freed from the comprehensive sentence of condemnation. From such thoughts come such passages as Ps. 130:3: "If You should mark iniquities . . ."; Ps. 143:2: "Enter not into judgment . . ."; Rom. 7:24: "Who shall deliver me . . . ?" Paul, by listing these points, shows that if anything can justify before God, it necessarily would be either the ethical system of the philosophers, according to the teachings of men, or the works of the divine law, because the Law has the promise of righteousness and eternal life. But Rom. 1:18ff. shows that the teachings and ethical principles of philosophers cannot

justify. And Rom. 3:20 says: "By the works of the Law shall no flesh be justified." For the Law shows and accuses the sin present even in our good works, because "the Law is weak through the flesh," Rom. 8:3.

3. Therefore God, "who is rich in mercy" [Eph. 2:4], has had mercy upon us and has set forth a propitiation through faith in the blood of Christ, and those who flee as suppliants to this throne of grace He absolves from the comprehensive sentence of condemnation, and by the imputation of the righteousness of His Son, which they grasp in faith, He pronounces them righteous, receives them into grace, and adjudges them to be heirs of eternal life. This is certainly the judicial meaning of the word "justification," in almost the same way that a guilty man who has been sentenced before the bar of justice is acquitted.

It is manifest how much clarity this gives to the discussion of justification. The fathers in disputing this matter often spoke inadequately about justification. But in their devotional writings, when they were looking at the picture of the divine judgment or the divine judicial process, they handled the doctrine of this article very well.

The example of Bernard [of Clairvaux, 1091–1153] shows this clearly, because he was not involved in idle speculations but was exercising himself in the serious matter of repentance based on the doctrine and testimony of Paul. Gerson[29] has some wonderful thoughts about the tribunal of God's justice and the throne of His grace. For if we are discussing our common position before the tribunal of God, we are all subject to the tribunal of His justice; and because before Him no living person can be justified but all are condemned, therefore God has also set up another tribunal, the throne of grace. And the Son of God pleads for us the benefit of being called away from the tribunal of justice to the throne of grace. Therefore the Pharisee, because he was not willing to use the benefit of this calling, but wanted to enter into judgment before the tribunal of justice, was condemned. But the publican, who was first accused at the tribunal of justice, convicted and condemned there, later by faith called out to the throne of grace and was justified [Luke 18:9–14].

All these points so beautifully illustrating the doctrine of justification come from the correct linguistic understanding of the word "justification."

V. Having established the foundations on the basis of Scripture, it is useful for us now to add this observation, that the ancient writers, although they often used the word "justification" in the way we have said above [as an infusion of good qualities], yet, convinced by the clear testimonies of Paul, they understood and knew this true and genuine meaning of the word which we have shown thus far.

---

[29] Jean de Gerson, ca. 1363–ca. 1429, French churchman who worked to end the papal schism.

Augustine in *Contra Julianum* [2.8.23, MPL 44.689ff.] cites Ambrose, "He to whom all his sins are remitted through Baptism is justified from his sin." And Augustine himself in treating Romans 5, where "to be justified" is explained in the text as meaning "to be reconciled," calls the attention to this fact and cites and gives approval to this meaning. And in his *Contra Julianum* [2.13, MPL 44.672–73] again he says that justification is given us in this life when our sins are remitted to us in Baptism, and afterward when we gather together our sins and say, "Forgive us our trespasses." Again in his *De Civitate Dei* he says that our righteousness consists in the remission of sins rather than in the perfection of our virtues.[30] Again, on Psalm 32 Augustine says, "If the ungodly is justified, from an ungodly man he is made into a righteous one. But how does this take place? You have done nothing good and the remission of sins has been given to you. There stand your works. And they are all found evil. If something is lacking in those works, God judges that the person should be condemned. Then what happens? God does not give you the punishment you deserve, but He gives undeserved grace. He owes us punishment. He gives indulgence." In his *Tract.* [42] *in Johannem* [MPL 35.1706]: "It was foreknown that they would not believe in that faith by which alone they can be freed from the debt of their sins." Hilary on Matthew [*In Matt.* 8, MPL 35.1706] says, "The scribe takes away from man the remission of sins because the Law could not free him. Faith alone justifies." Cyril, *In Johannem*, "Faith brings salvation and grace justifies; but the commandments of the Law condemn."[31] Oecumenius[32] in citing the ancient explanation of Romans 3 says, "The righteousness of God is the justification by God, the absolution and the deliverance from sins, from which the Law itself neither could nor would absolve us." Again, "How does justification take place? Reply: Through the remission of sins which we obtain in Christ Jesus." A gloss on the passage in Rom. 8:30, "Those whom He called He also justifies," explains the statement thus: "He justifies by the remission of sins." Gregory says, "It seems righteous for a man to take revenge for a hurt done him, but the righteousness of God is to forgive the offense of one who confesses it." And Bernard in *Sermo de Annunciatione* [MPL 183.383–84] says, "The apostle believes that man is freely justified through faith, if you believe that your sins cannot be remitted unless by Him against whom alone you have sinned. But he adds at this point that you

---

[30] Augustine, *De Civ. Dei*, 19.25, MPL 41.657. The reference to Psalm 32 is found in MPL 36.262–63, *Enarratio in Psalmum 31*.

[31] Cyril, *In Joh.* 6. Cannot locate. Inadequate reference.

[32] Oecumenius is a rather shadowy 10th-century author who produced a commentary, by the use of catenas, on the non-Gospel portions of the NT. See MPG 118–19.

should also believe . . . because the Holy Spirit also presents to our hearts the message: 'Your sins are forgiven you.'"

VI. Furthermore, we should not overlook the other synonymous words with which Paul himself explains the word "justification," as in Rom. 4:3, 5, "to impute or count for righteousness," or "faith is counted for righteousness" [KJV]. Again he explains justification on the basis of Ps. 32:1–2 as "covering iniquity" or as "not imputing sins," cf. Rom. 4:7–8; 2 Cor. 5:19. In Rom. 5:10 the word "to be reconciled" is clearly a synonym for "to be justified." Titus 3:5–7 joins these three expressions: to justify, to save, and to become heirs of eternal life, as being synonymous, each of which explains the other. Gal. 3:9–10 and Acts 3:25 explain justification in terms of the blessing in opposition to God's curse. In Acts 13:38–39 Paul says: "Through Him is preached to us the remission of sins, and all who believe are justified from all things from which they could not be justified by the law of Moses."

It is also noteworthy that Peter and John in their writings, even when dealing with this doctrine, do not use the word "justification." They did this, no doubt, not because they disapproved of Paul's terminology, but because they saw that certain people who were not accustomed to Hebrew expressions were disturbed by the word "justification," and some were even skillfully distorting it. Therefore they repeated the same doctrine by using better-known synonyms, in order that by this comparison they might show the true meaning in Paul's line of argumentation. For this reason, without doubt, God gave John a particularly long life, so that if he noted any less correct understanding of this matter, he might leave to the church a sure explanation.

John, therefore, often speaks like this, John 3:16–18: "He who does not believe is condemned already. . . . He who believes shall not be judged. . . . He does not come into judgment [John 5:24]. . . . He sent His Son not to judge the world, but that the world might be saved through Him . . . that whoever believes in Him should not perish but have everlasting life." It is clear that these expressions are paraphrases of the word "justification" and have the same meaning we have been speaking about. Cf. 1 John 3:14: "We have passed from death to life." This is similar to the statement in Col. 1:13: "He has brought us, freed from the power of darkness, to the kingdom of His Son." 1 John 1:9: "He is faithful and just to forgive us our sins," etc. [KJV]. It is manifest that John wants to use other terms to express the same concept as Rom. 3:26: "That He might be just, and the justifier . . ." [KJV]. 1 John 1:7: "The blood of Christ cleanses us from all sins." Paul says this in Rom. 5:9: "Justified by His blood . . ." 1 John 2:12: "Your sins are forgiven you for His name's sake." Paul says the same thing in 1 Cor. 6:11: "You are justified in the name of the Lord Jesus."

In Acts 2:38 Peter says: "Be baptized every one of you . . . for the forgiveness of sins." These words are applied to the locus on Baptism in Titus 3:5; a comparison shows the explanation. In Acts 10:43 Peter says: "To Him all the prophets bear witness that all who believe in Him receive forgiveness of sins through His name." An explanation of this is given in Rom. 3:21, where Paul says: "The righteousness of God . . . has been testified to by the Law and the prophets." Acts 3:19: ". . . that your sins may be blotted out." And Paul in Col. 2:14 says: "The handwriting has been blotted out." He is doubtlessly alluding to that judicial process of which we have been speaking.

Mark 16:16: "He . . . will be saved; but he . . . will be condemned." These terms are clearly put into the same kind of juxtaposition as the terms "to justify" and "to condemn" are in Paul. Matt. 9:2: "Be confident, your sins are forgiven you." Paul says this in Rom. 5:1: "Being justified by faith, we have peace," etc. Matt. 1:21: "He shall save His people from their sins." Paul in Acts 13:39 calls this "justify." Peter uses the word "save" in the same sense in Acts 4:12: "There is no other name . . ." Acts 15:1: "Unless you are circumcised . . . you cannot be saved." Likewise v. 11: "But we believe we will be saved through the grace of the Lord Jesus, just as they will." Paul expresses the same thought in Gal. 2:16 through the word "justify": "We have believed in Christ in order to be justified." Paul himself explains it this way in Eph. 2:5: "By grace you are saved."

In Matt. 16:19 and 18:18 Christ speaks of "loosing" and "binding" sins. These are judicial terms, for the guilty man, when he stands condemned before the tribunal, is bound; cf. Acts 26:29. Christ paraphrases the article of justification thus: ". . . that they may receive the remission of sins and 'an inheritance among all those who are sanctified' [Acts 20:32] by faith that is in Me."

This comparison explains, illustrates, and confirms the meaning of the word "justification."

VII. At this point we must also explain the proper meaning of the term "the righteousness of God" in the article of justification. Cf. Rom. 1:17; 3:22; 2 Cor. 5:21; 2 Peter 1:1; Matt. 6:33. In the usage of the languages with which we are familiar, it seems to mean that God examines all our actions according to the norm of the righteousness which is in Him, and He renders to each according to his works, as, after they are examined in keeping with the norm of His righteousness, He discerns whether these actions are in conformity with His righteousness or in conflict with it.

Varinus says that the word "righteousness" is derived from "the righteous judgment which is given, directed by, and in keeping with God's will."

We commonly say that we pray that God will not deal with us according to His righteousness but according to His mercy. Luther also, in the preface to the first volume of his works, confesses that although he held to the article of justification, yet he was troubled by the word and did not gladly hear the statement "In the Gospel is revealed the righteousness of God" [Rom. 1:17], because he understood it as referring to the judicial and severe righteousness by which God enters into judgment with us.

Augustine also noticed that this meaning did not agree with the teaching of Paul regarding justification, and therefore he interpreted the statement to mean that, just as we speak of the salvation of God and the power of God [Rom. 1:16], because they are gifts of God, so also those who believe are renewed and through the Spirit receive new qualities. This, Augustine says, is called the righteousness of God. But this idea, although it is true in itself, yet is not said in this passage and does not explain it, but only confuses and obscures Paul's meaning.

Therefore it is useful to show on the basis of the correct foundations what the term "the righteousness of God" properly means in this article. It is absolutely clear that the correct meaning in this passage is not the one about which we have now spoken. For this kind of "righteousness of God" is revealed in the Law, and Paul says that, apart from the Law, the righteousness of God is revealed in the Gospel.

We have said that the sum and substance of the Gospel is that we are exempted from the rigor of the tribunal of stern righteousness and that we flee to the throne of grace. And what the proper meaning of the Gospel of justification is cannot be understood nor correctly taught if we understand "the righteousness of God" in a legal sense; indeed, the most pernicious corruptions follow. . . . It seems indeed to be taken in the legal sense in Rom. 1:32: "Though they know God's decree [or righteousness, *dikaiōma*], that those who do such things deserve to die, they not only do them but approve of those who practice them." But the words are different. The *dikaiōma* of God refers to the rule of righteousness in God as revealed in the Law. It is used this way in Rom. 1:32; 2:26; and 8:4. The word *dikaiōsis* is used in Rom. 5:18 in opposition to condemnation; hence, it is manifest what it means.

In the passages with which we are dealing, however, the word for "righteousness" is *dikaiōsynē*. When this word is used in an absolute sense, it is beyond argument that it means that which is in agreement with the norm of divine righteousness, as in Lev. 19:15: "You shall judge in righteousness." Again in v. 36: "You shall have . . . just weights." Prov. 8:15: "By me . . . princes decree justice." Ps. 15:2: "He who works righteousness." And if it is used with reference to human righteousness, it has the same meaning. Cf. Gen. 30:33: "My righteousness shall answer for me"; Ps. 17:1: "Hear, O Lord, my righteousness" [Vulgate].

This meaning is not now at issue. Rather, the question is what the term "the righteousness of God" means in the article of justification. Because we neither can nor should establish the meaning of this term from the usage of ordinary speech, for the meaning is peculiar and proper to sacred Scripture, therefore we must seek illustrative and suitable examples by which the proper and genuine meaning can be declared.

Ps. 51:14: "Deliver me from bloodguiltiness and my tongue will exalt Your righteousness." Ps. 69:27–28: "Let them not come into Your righteousness, and let them be blotted out of the book of the living." Ps. 71:1–2: "In You, O Lord, do I put my trust. . . . Deliver me in Your righteousness." Ps. 143:1–2: "Hear me in Your righteousness, and do not enter into judgment," etc. Ps. 40:9: "I have preached the good news of Your righteousness." And in vv. 10–11 he explains this by the terms "salvation" and "mercy." In these examples it is obvious that "the righteousness of God" can mean nothing else than the goodness and mercy of God, whereby He does not enter into judgment but absolves, receives into grace, redeems, frees, and defends. In Rom. 1:16–17 the explanation is clearly shown, namely that the Gospel is "the power of God to salvation for everyone that believes . . . for in it the righteousness of God is revealed . . . as it is written, 'The just shall live by faith.'"

This is so evident that the translator, noting that in Latin ears the term "the righteousness of God" means something else, often substituted for it "the mercy of God," as in 1 Sam. 12:7: ". . . concerning all the mercies of the Lord which He has done for you and for your fathers" [Vulgate]. The text here has "concerning the righteousnesses of the Lord." Ps. 103:6: "The Lord shows mercy" [Vulgate]. Here the Hebrew has "righteousness." Dan. 9:16: "For the sake of all Your righteousnesses, turn away Your anger," etc.

This Hebraism was so familiar to the Septuagint translators that where the Hebrews had "mercy" they often rendered it *dikaiōsynē* as in Gen. 19:19; 20:13; 21:23; and 32:10: "I am not worthy of the least of all Your mercies," which the Septuagint rendered with the term *dikaiōsynē*. Although this is unfamiliar to Latin ears, yet the passages are correct and clear. Luther in a very learned way discusses this meaning in his translation of this word in a sermon for the First Sunday in Advent.[33]

In certain passages, however, it is not so appropriate to render this concept with the word "mercy," as in 1 Cor. 1:30: "Christ is made unto us righteousness by God"; 2 Cor. 5:21: ". . . that we might be made the righteousness of God in Christ"; Jer. 33:16: "The Lord is our righteousness"; Is. 45:24: "In the Lord I have righteousness"; Rom. 5:21: "Grace will reign through righteousness"; Ps. 24:5: "He shall receive . . . blessing from the Lord, and righteousness from the God

---

[33] As noted earlier, Chemnitz has many citations from Luther which are difficult if not impossible to locate.

of his salvation" [KJV]. In these passages the term "the righteousness of God" means the righteousness acceptable before God unto life eternal, and this is the obedience of our Mediator, which God imputes to believers for righteousness if they lay hold on it by faith. Thus Paul in Phil. 3:9 speaks of "the righteousness of God which is by faith."

This meaning is closely related to the previous one and depends upon it. For this righteousness is in believers by imputation; but in a formal sense and positively it is in Christ the Mediator, and the Father by His goodness and mercy communicates and imputes to us that foreign righteousness. Luther [in Rom. 1:17] translates it *die Gerechtigkeit, die vor Gott gilt*, or "the righteousness which is of value or avails before God." Osiander objected to this, but Luther gives the reasons for his translation, namely that it sounds different in our ears when we use the expression *Gottes Gerechtigkeit* ("God's righteousness").

This way of expressing it is familiar and well known in other places in Scripture, for example in Rom. 4:2: "He has something to boast about, but not before God" [RSV]; Luke 1:75: "In righteousness before Him"; Rom. 3:20: "No flesh shall be justified before Him"; Luke 16:15: "You justify yourselves before men." In Phil. 3:9 Paul interprets "the righteousness of God" as "the righteousness from God" [RSV], so that the way of speaking ("the righteousness of God") is similar to John 12:43: "They loved the praise of men more than the praise of God," that is to say, it was of value among men but not before God. Thus Luther is correct in rendering the term *justitia Dei* into German as . . . *die vor Gott gilt*. This interpretation goes back to those simple fundamentals that we have already demonstrated. For if the question is asked: What is this righteousness *die vor Gott gilt* ("which avails before God"), the answer is the Gospel, the grace, mercy, or goodness of God by which He imputes the obedience of His Son the Mediator to believers for righteousness.

Therefore all things have become clear as to what "the righteousness of God" means in the article of justification. Nor are there examples in Scripture in opposition to this. James (1:20) once uses the word in the legal sense: "The anger of man does not work the righteousness of God" [RSV]. But the same James also applies the word "justify" in another sense. In an absolute sense, with reference to the Law, it means the new obedience, 1 John 3:7: "He who does right is righteous" [RSV]; Rom. 6:16: "The servants of obedience unto righteousness"; 2 Tim. 2:22: "Follow righteousness."

Thus we have shown up to this point the basic interpretation in this Pauline proposition: "In the Gospel is revealed the righteousness of God . . . in that He Himself is righteous and the justifier of him who is of faith in Christ" [Rom. 1:17; 3:26].

[E.] The Word "Faith"

We must carefully consider the term "faith" and see what Paul is doing when he says that we are not justified by our works but by faith in Christ. This is new language to Roman ears, and we must at the very beginning seek the genuine and simple interpretation of it. To be justified by works means to obtain forgiveness of sins and to be righteous or accepted before God by reason of our own virtues or deeds. On the other hand, to be justified by faith in Christ means to obtain remission of sins, to be counted as righteous, that is, accepted by God, not because of our own virtues but for the sake of the Mediator, the Son of God. When we understand this word this way, then we can see how this proposition that we are justified by faith, which is the voice of the Gospel, is used by Paul in opposition to the other concept, which is the voice of human reason or the Law, that we are justified by works. As the Baptist cries, "Behold the Lamb of God who takes away the sin of the world," John 1:29, so Paul wants to present this doctrine to us, and he teaches that remission of sins and reconciliation are given to us for the sake of the Son of God and not for the sake of our virtues.

Thus, when he says that we are justified by faith, he wants you to behold the Son of God sitting at the right hand of the Father as the Mediator who intercedes for us, and to understand that your sins are forgiven you because you are considered or pronounced just, that is, accepted, for the sake of His own Son, who was the Sacrifice. Therefore, in order that the word "faith" may point to this Mediator and apply to us, "faith" refers not only to historical knowledge but also to trust (fiducia) in the mercy promised for the sake of the Son of God.

Thus, this statement that we are righteous by faith must always be understood as correlative, that is, connected with being righteous by trusting that we have been received by mercy for the sake of Christ, and not because of our virtues. This mercy is laid hold on by faith or trust. Paul says this in order that he may present to us this Mediator and Lamb, take away from us our glorying in our own righteousness, and testify that we have been received by God for the sake of this Propitiator.

There is no doubt that this is Paul's thinking, and it is absolutely clear in the church that his opinion is correct and true. All the saints confess that even if they have new virtues, yet they do not receive remission of sin or reconciliation because of them but only for the sake of the Son of God, the Propitiator. Therefore we must understand the statement, "By faith we have remission," to mean that by this trust we are received for the sake of God's Son.

But there are those who reply to this discussion that it is absolutely ridiculous and meaningless to say that "having been justified by faith we have peace with God," Rom. 5:1. They do not understand what it is to have a struggle of conscience with fears and doubts, when one is anxious about the remission of his sins; and they do not know the tremblings which take place in true repentance. If they would consider these things they would know that terrified hearts seek consolation outside themselves, and this consolation is the trust with which the will rests in the promise of mercy given for the sake of the Mediator. Faith embraces both trust in the mercy of God and knowledge of the historical events, that is, it looks to Christ, of whom it is necessary to know that He is the Son of the eternal God, crucified for us, raised again, etc. The historical facts must be applied to the promise or the effect of His work, as it is set forth in this article, namely: "I believe in the forgiveness of sins." Again this article warns that faith must be understood as trust. For to him who does not trust that his sins are forgiven him, the words "I believe in the forgiveness of sins" are useless.

I have been speaking in regard to the understanding of the proposition: "We are justified by faith," and now I will add testimonies to show that faith in the doctrine of the Gospel means trust in the mercy promised for the sake of Christ. Some argue about the word "faith" (pistis) and will allow no other understanding than that it is a statement of doctrine, a profession of a creed, as when we popularly say that the Nicene faith is our doctrine or collection of dogmas. But it is evident that to the Greeks the word "believe" (pisteuō) has several different meanings. And there is no doubt that the Hebrew uses interchangeably the words which mean to believe and to trust, as we see in Ps. 2:12: "Blessed are all those who put their trust in Him." Here the Hebrew has the word chasah. When Paul [Rom. 9:33] cites Is. 28:16, "He that believes shall not be confounded," the word in Hebrew is aman. The same word, which means "believe," is often used with the meaning of "trust" in the Hebrew, as in Dan. 6:23: ". . . because he trusted in his God." In Ps. 78:22 two synonymous words are used together: "Because they did not believe [aman] in God or trust [batach] in His salvation." There are also clear statements in the words of Christ: "O woman, great is your faith," Matt. 15:28; and again: "Your faith has made you whole," Matt. 9:22. In these and similar passages it is evident that by the term "faith" (fides) is meant "trust" (fiducia).

There is no doubt that Paul follows the Hebrew usage. There are also countless examples among the Greeks where the word pisteuō (believe) simply means to trust in something, as it occurs in the popular verse of Phocylides: "Do not put your trust (pisteue, credas) in the people, for the multitude is deceitful."

In his fourth Philippic, Demosthenes says, "But if he puts his trust (pisteuei) in the goodwill of his allies, he also builds up his armaments." And in his Contra Androtionem *he says, "Put your confidence in yourself" (sautō pisteueis). . . . It is not hard to pile up a large heap of testimonies.*

Let us therefore retain the force of the word pisteuō (to believe) and understand that it means both to assent to something and to put trust in something. The Greeks were very wide-ranging in their use of the word pistis (faith). But we should understand that in the church it means a firm assent and also confidence or trust, which is

also called pepoithēsis (a persuasion or belief). This definition of faith is a true one:
Faith (fides) is assenting to the entire Word of God as it is given to us, particularly to
the free promise of reconciliation given for the sake of Christ the Mediator, and it is
trust (fiducia) in the mercy of God promised for the sake of Christ the Mediator. For
trust is an action of the will which of necessity responds to the assent, or an action
by which the will rests in Christ. When this takes place, it is illuminated by the Holy
Spirit and by new light, as shall be described later.

It is common to use the word pistis (faith) for a firm assent, the opposite of an
uncertain opinion. Plato says that human beings do not have a steadfast or stable
assent (pistis) to the idea of the good. For although people understand the right, yet
because of the stubbornness of their heart and their corrupted desire, their assent
is minimized.

Similar in meaning is the word "trust" (fiducia), as we see in the verse from
Theognis: "I lost my property because of my trust (pistis), and I saved it by my distrust (apistia)." And in Hesiod both trust and distrust are deadly. But there are other
meanings, the most important of which is that pistis is the equivalent of fidelity, that
is, it is a term to describe the virtue of keeping a treaty. Where this meaning has a
place in the sacred writings it must be diligently considered. For in judging ecclesiastical controversies where we are seeking the correct meaning of the words in a
certain passage, we must look at the parallel meanings. The study of languages is
important for this purpose.

As I have said, the word pistis often means "fidelity" or "faithfulness," as in
the verse of Sophocles: "Faithfulness (pistis) dies and unfaithfulness (apistia) ger-
minates," or "faithfulness perishes." It is used in this way often in other places, as
in Polybius, Bk. 2: "They distinguished themselves by their faithfulness (pistis) in
keeping the treaty," or, to say the same thing, by the "faith," that is, the reputation
attributed to them, that they were faithful, just, and men of goodwill in keeping the
treaty. There are many derived meanings from this, which do not pertain to Paul's
point. . . .

Sad to say, the church almost, as it says in the Greek verse, learned to speak
the native tongue among barbarians. The monks overturned the true meanings of
the word and thought up a new kind of doctrine. For this reason godly people must
go back to the prophets and the apostles and again learn the proper language of the
church and restore it. That Paul wants trust in the mercy of God to be understood by
the word "faith" is clear from the passages we shall discuss. In Rom. 4:16 the promise is related to faith in a correlative sense: "It is freely by faith, that . . . the promise
might be sure." Here Paul clearly asserts that we should give assent to the promise;
and in order that we might be able to assent, he says that it is free, for if the condition of fulfilling the Law were added, then despair would follow at the statement:
"You will please God if you satisfy the Law." But Paul says that the promise is free,

so that it might be firm for the believer. Therefore he wants us to assent to the promise. This assent is really this trust which lays hold on the promise. This explanation is unassailable.

[I.] Further, we must consider the power of the Gospel promise, for if there is no need for assent, then the promise is an absolutely useless noise. However, it has been given in order that we should assent to it; and so that we can assent to it, it is free. Likewise, why does John say: "He who does not believe God has made Him a liar" [1 John 5:10]? And Paul says: "Abraham did not waver in distrust, but with firm faith and giving glory to God he was sure . . ." [Rom. 4:20]. These passages clearly show that it is required that we assent to the promise. Finally, why does this word ring out in the church: "For the sake of the Son of God your sins are remitted to you," if you say that assent is not required? What else is this than, as John says, calling God a liar?

II. Rom. 5:1: "Justified by faith, we have peace . . ." But the historical knowledge of this matter does not bring peace; indeed, it only increases our trembling and hopelessness, as is the case with the devils [James 2:19]. For what could be a more terrible sign of the wrath of God than that He could not be satisfied with any sacrifice except the death of His own Son? The devils see that they have been rejected; they know that the Son of God has been made their judge and they will suffer eternal punishments. And men in true terrors see not only the many other signs of God's wrath against sin, such as death and other incalculable calamities, but they see also this sign, that God cannot be placated except through His Son. The historical knowledge of this only increases our anxieties, if our faith is not a trust and confidence that applies this blessing to us—if it is not established that the Son of God suffered in order that there might be forgiveness for you, even though you have been undeserving, etc. This trust comforts the terrified mind and brings it peace.

III. The explanation of many other passages is similar—for example: "The just shall live by faith" [Hab. 2:4]. It is certain that no one shall live merely by historical knowledge of this fact, for this only increases torment. Nor shall anyone live by knowledge of the Law: "If you have sufficient virtues, you will please God." Thus it is necessary that faith be understood as that which assures us that God is favorable toward us and as that which rests in the promises of mercy. We must understand the following passage in the same way: "Everyone who believes in Him will not be put to shame" [Rom. 9:33]. Likewise Ps. 2:12: "Kiss the Son. . . . Blessed are all they that put their trust in Him" [KJV]. Here the Hebrew word has the very appropriate meaning of "to confide, to trust."

IV. Eph. 3:12: "In Him and through our faith in Him we dare to approach God confidently." Here Paul describes the nature of faith by three very significant words: "we dare," "to approach," and "confidently." It is a great thing to approach God as the Judge who is truly and horribly angry at sin. Here again the mere historical knowledge deters us, unless we have determined that the Son is our Leader and

Propitiator and that through Him we are led to the Father. This acknowledgment is the trust of which we have been speaking. Likewise, Rom. 5:2 says: "Through Him we have access by faith. . . ." And Heb. 4:14, 16: "Having such a high priest . . . let us come with confidence to the throne of grace." From this passage we learn both that this confidence is presupposed in prayer and that "faith" in similar passages must be understood as "confidence."

But many cry out in opposition because they do not understand this very worship of God, namely faith, as being involved in prayer, and they imagine that there is no sin in doubting whether we are received by God or heard by Him. But how great a sin this is and how harmful to us is seen when there is a genuine spiritual struggle, because it rejects the promise of God and calls Him a liar.

Acts 15:9: ". . . purifying their hearts by faith." If faith only refers to knowledge, such as even the devils have, this statement would be utterly inane. But it is evident in this very passage that that argument pertains to justification, and it is established beyond debate that hearts are not purified by the righteousness of the Law, but in another way, namely, "if they believe that they will be saved through the grace of our Lord Jesus Christ" [v. 11].

We can add a mountain of testimonies in which the word "faith" is used to denote "trust," such as: "O woman, great is your faith!" [Matt. 15:28]. Again in Luke 7:50: "Your faith has saved you." 2 Chron. 20:20: "Believe . . . and you will be established." In statements of this kind it is apparent that "faith" is called a trust that expects consolation and help from God; regardless of how different the outward circumstances are, yet the first and chief object of faith is always a reconciled God, according to the promise of reconciliation. Then David prays for and expects help in war, when he has determined that he has a God who is favorable toward him. So great a variety of outward objects and perils surrounds us that there is an opportunity to exercise our faith and at the same time to grasp the spiritual blessings, as that common prayer teaches us. For after we have said, "Give us this day our daily bread," the prayer immediately continues, "and forgive us our trespasses." Our mind in seeking material things would flee from God unless at the very same time it understood that we are forgiven, that we have been received into grace and thus are heard and protected.

To understand many passages it is useful to consider that faith regarding reconciliation often becomes evident in prayers and hopes for physical things. Thus Abraham sought an heir from God, and he believed the promise which assured him of posterity. But at the same time Abraham realized and was confident that he was forgiven by God, that, although unworthy, he was received by God through mercy for the sake of the Liberator who had been promised to the fathers. The promise and comfort which precede testify that this is the force of "he believed" in Gen. 15:6; cf. Gen. 15:1, "Fear not, Abraham, I am your Protector and your very great Reward." In this most sweetly comforting passage God bears witness that He is favorable toward

Abraham, that He is his Defender, his Helper, and Savior. In looking at this promise Abraham trusts that he is received into the grace of God. Therefore concerning this faith it is said that "it was imputed to him for righteousness," Gen. 15:6; Rom. 4:3.

Finally, the definition of faith given in the Epistle to the Hebrews [11:1] testifies that the word "faith" means "trust" when it says: "Faith is the substance of things hoped for." It is evident to those who understand the language that the word "substance" (hypostasis) refers to something hoped for, that is, an expectant trust.

I have reviewed testimonies from the prophets and apostles which are clear and which I hope will satisfy those who are skillful in judging. But I must confess that later many writers, such as Origen and others, have taught another kind of doctrine, an inadequate one; but some of the more learned agreed with us on the substance, although also they in some places spoke very well and in other places rather unfortunately.

In Augustine from time to time there are some excellent statements. In his De Spiritu et Litera [30, MPL 44.233] he says, "By the Law we fear God; by faith (fides) we flee to Him for mercy." Again, faith (fides) says: "Be of good cheer; your sins are forgiven you" [ibid.]. If these statements are correctly understood, they cannot be applied to anything except to trust (fiducia) in God's mercy.

Even clearer is the statement of Augustine regarding Ps. 32:1 [Enarratio in Psalmum 31, MPL 36.262], "Blessed is he whose transgression is forgiven." He says, "Who are the blessed? They are not those in whom no sin is found, for it is found in all; for 'All have sinned and fall short of the glory of God.' Therefore if sins are found in all, it remains that they are not blessed unless their sins have been remitted. Therefore the apostle says, 'Abraham believed God, and it was imputed to him for righteousness.'" Here certainly Augustine understands fides as fiducia, the trust by which a person receives the forgiveness of sins. And he clearly understands the statement in Gen. 15:6 and of Paul in Rom. 4:3 as we have interpreted them.

I will also add the testimony of Bernard [Sermo 1, MPL 183.383–84] which is found in his sermon on the Annunciation. He says that it is necessary first of all to believe that you cannot have the remission of sins except through the kindness of God; but he adds that you must believe also this, that by Him sins are forgiven you. This is the testimony which the Holy Spirit gives to your heart, saying: "Your sins are forgiven you." For the apostle believes that man is justified freely through faith. In this statement we have a clear and concise position of the belief of our churches. And similar testimonies are extant in the writings of this author.

Basil also very correctly states our position in his Sermon on Humility [MPL 31.529], regarding the passage "Let him who glories, glory in the Lord." He says, "Christ is made unto us wisdom from God, righteousness, sanctification, and redemption, as it written, 'He who glories, let him glory in the Lord.' For this is the perfect and complete glorying in God, when a person does not bring forward the offering of his own righteousness but recognizes that he needs the true righteousness and that he is justified by faith alone in Christ."

Finally, let us consider the matter itself. The voice of the Gospel is better understood in the circumstances of immediate struggle than when, as wicked and secure men, we listen to long disputations. How do you comfort yourself when your mind is really overrun with anxiety and fear of God's wrath? Must you not in this consternation flee to Christ the Mediator and say to yourself, "I truly believe that you are forgiven for the sake of this Victim!" Just as the Gospel everywhere orders us to believe that the Son of God died for our sins, as it says m Rom. 4:24–25, so we must consider also this: Through the Son is access to God, Rom. 5:2. Also, this faith by which you are comforting yourself is undoubtedly the trust which rests in the Son of God. Certainly one must not think like this: "I already love God, I already have the virtues and merits; therefore God will receive me." So we who see this struggle and this comfort understand that these anxieties do exist and that our minds are raised up by the trust which looks to the Son of God, and we will want to speak these things with whatever words we can, but the prophets and apostles used the term "faith" in this matter.

In the same way all godly people consider their daily prayer, that as often as you begin to invoke God your many-faceted unworthiness gets in the way and your fears prevent your prayers. Is any comfort to be found here? Certainly you must not think: "I already have virtues worthy to make my prayers acceptable." But you look to the Mediator who has been given for us. You think of the passage: "Come to Me, all you that labor and are heavy laden, and I will give you rest" [Matt. 11:28]. Or: "Whatever you ask the Father in My name He will give you" [John 15:16]. Likewise Heb. 7:25: "He always lives to make intercession for them." Therefore you believe that your prayer is pleasing to God and is received, on account of this High Priest who makes intercession along with you. To believe this is certainly trust which raises up and comforts the mind.

As we contend about this matter, about this comfort, we only desire to retain the content, regardless of what words others may use. Those who differ obstruct the content itself, destroy it, and order us always to be in doubt; they even bury Christ, because they absolutely will not teach people to seek comfort from Him or direct them to use His benefits. For if faith is not the trust that looks to Christ and finds rest because of Him, then certainly we will not apply His benefits to ourselves or use them. Therefore it is necessary that by faith we understand the trust that applies to us the benefits of Christ.

Thus when we say that we are justified by faith, we are saying nothing else than that for the sake of the Son of God we receive remission of sins and are accounted as righteous. And because it is necessary that this benefit be taken hold of, this is said to be done "by faith," that is, by trust in the mercy promised us for the sake of

Christ. Thus we must also understand the correlative expression, "We are righteous by faith," that is, through the mercy of God for the sake of His Son we are righteous or accepted. We know the nature of the related terms, such as love, fear, and other terms, which are the names for the emotions relating to what we have said. Such a term is "trust." Nor am I intimidated by any of the foolish criticisms leveled against this term by unlearned men.

Some people object that to this trust must be joined love. I do not contend against this, but when we say that we are justified by faith, we point to the Son of God sitting at the right hand of the Father, interceding for us; and we say that because of Him reconciliation is given to us, and we take away the merit of reconciliation from our own good works, whatever they may be.

To summarize, when we are criticized for saying in this dogma that a person is justified by faith, we are only being criticized for saying that we receive reconciliation for the sake of the Son of God and not because of our worthiness. We must believe this as well as that the benefit must be laid hold on by this faith or trust, and the merit of Christ must be put up against our sin and damnation. In this faith or trust, which looks to the Son of God, God is to be invoked. It is absolutely certain that these statements are the very voice of the Gospel and the perpetual consensus of the true church. Nor do I doubt that good and pious people have known this explanation as Paul's correct teaching and have clung to it with a grateful mind. Concerning this entire matter I appeal to the consensus of the church, that is, of the skilled and pious. I judge that the testimony of that church carries the greatest weight.

Many others insanely cry and contend that by the word "faith" nothing is meant except the historical knowledge, and they look for countless arguments to prove their point. But the godly remember the voice of Paul, who says in Rom. 9:31: "Israel pursued the righteousness which is based on law but did not succeed in fulfilling the Law." Human reason understands the righteousness of works and marvels at it, but the things said regarding the righteousness of faith it strongly hates, because they are foreign to civil matters. We should know that the righteousness of works has its place, but in seeking reconciliation there is need for a far different consolation.

I have made these brief remarks regarding the word "faith," which are uncomplicated and unsophisticated and in agreement with Hebrew terminology. Therefore let this be the definition of "faith": [1] Faith is to assent to the entire Word of God as it has been set forth for us, [2] and particularly to the free promise of reconciliation given for the sake of Christ the Mediator. [3] And it is trust in the mercy of God promised for the sake of Christ the Mediator. [4] For trust is an action or movement of the will which necessarily responds to assent. [5] Faith is also the power of laying hold on the promises and applying them to oneself. [6] It quiets the heart, as these words teach clearly enough: "Therefore, being justified by faith, we have peace with God through . . . Christ, by whom we also have access by faith to this grace . . ."

[Rom. 5:1–2]. But when we speak of assenting to the promise, we include the knowledge of all the articles. In the creed all the other articles are related to this statement: "I believe . . . in the forgiveness of sins . . . and the life everlasting." This is the sum of the promises and the goal to which the other articles relate. For the Son of God was sent, as John tells us, "that He might destroy the works of the devil" [1 John 3:8], that is, take away sin and restore righteousness and eternal life.

[CHAPTER I]: THE WORD "FAITH"

Thus far we have discussed the word "justification." But Paul's proposition not only affirms that we are justified but adds that we are justified by faith; indeed he calls the righteousness of which the Gospel speaks "the righteousness of faith." Therefore it is necessary to have a true, proper, and genuine explanation of the term "faith." Faith is the unique means and instrument through which we lay hold on the righteousness of Christ, receive it, and apply it to ourselves, as it says in Heb. 4:2: "The message which they heard did not benefit them, because it with faith was not mixed."

For this reason the devil is so hostile to the doctrine of faith: Since he cannot block the decree of God regarding the redemption of the human race—although he tried to do it with miraculous tricks against the house and family from which he knew the seed was going to come—therefore he puts all his artfulness to work to snatch away or harm or corrupt the instrument and means whereby God's work is applied. He knows that without faith there is no benefit for us, either from the decree of redemption or from the preaching of the Gospel, because "He who does not believe will be condemned" [Mark 16:16].

Therefore the doctrine of justifying faith has been revealed in Scripture by sure, well-known, and manifest testimonies, as one that God wanted to stand out most plainly and conspicuously in the church, not only for the wise but also for the unwise, Rom. 1:14. In our time, by the blessing of God, this teaching has been again brilliantly brought to light on the basis of the true foundations. We must be aware that we need to exercise great care to retain and defend against errors those things which have been correctly taught, for the father of lies, sowing his tares, is particularly attacking the doctrine of faith. Therefore we shall note the main points under dispute concerning the word "faith."

First. From the history of the church of all ages we shall make certain observations, for the sake of warning, showing how in various ways the proper and genuine meaning of the word "faith" was distorted, obscured, and finally corrupted. We shall point out what tragic darkness has overtaken this doctrine of justification from perversions that seem only grammatical and matters of terminology. This point will demonstrate how necessary it is that we are careful to retain the Biblical (so to speak) and ecclesiastical meaning of this word.

This cannot be done unless we point out its true sources. This study will also instruct us regarding the reasons or occasions for these errors and ravings in the article of justification.

These corruptions began at the very time of the apostles. James in ch. 2 tells of those who, upon hearing Paul's statement that we are justified by faith, took up a senseless opinion which received the name "dead faith." Therefore in 2:14 James does not say, "If anyone has faith," but "If anyone says he has faith." To this "faith" they attributed justification. For he says in v. 19: "You believe that there is one God; you do well. Even the devils believe," and yet they are not justified, for "they tremble."

The book called *The Shepherd* [by Hermas, *Mandatum*, 1.1, Hefele Ed., p. 350] understands the Christian faith in exactly the same way: "I believe that there is one God who made all things."

Clement [of Rome, *Recognitiones*, 5.3, MPL 1.1332] does recognize that "unbelief does not believe that the judgment of God is coming, and it gives a license to sin. But faith does believe in the coming judgment of God, and it does restrain men from sin." Clement of Alexandria in his *Stromata* [2, MPG 8.943] compares the disputations of philosophers regarding feeling, understanding, opinion, knowledge, and preconception (*prolēpsis*) and applies these ideas to the doctrine of the church regarding faith, with the result that "faith is a voluntary preconception, the assent of piety." And he says, as the Stoics do, that only the wise man is blest and is king. Thus he says that Scripture attributes to faith the state of blessedness, salvation, and eternal life. Again he says, "Just as, in philosophy, an action is born in our ability to make a free choice (*proairesis*), and this really arises out of knowledge, so in the case of justification a choice of the will is the main point of the action, and faith is the foundation of a wise choice; and for this reason faith justifies, because it is the mother of good works" [ibid., MPG 8.59ff.]. Again, "Repentance is the work of faith, for unless a person believes that there is sin and that punishment is awaiting sinners, but that there is salvation for him who lives by the precepts, he will not repent" [ibid., MPG 962]. Again, "He is faithful who does not break the Law but keeps the precepts which have been handed down, particularly the doctrine concerning God and the commandments, including the observance of the precepts. We believe in Him in whom we have confidence that He is true, and thus trust precedes faith; the first inclination toward salvation is faith, and charity together with faith makes a person faithful. Faith is to know the precepts of God, to believe them, and to follow them." These statements are from Bk. 2 of his *Stromata* [MPG 8.962ff.]. In Bk. 5 [MPG 9.12–13] he says, "Faith is the assent by the rational use of free choice." In Bk. 6 [MPG 9.325], "The righteous man is faithful, but the faithful man is not immediately righteous. The promise is the occasion for seeking obedience, and through this comes salvation. It is called faith in matters of piety through the observation of the works which are required." Thus Clement.

Thomas explains Paul's statement that we are justified by faith in this way: "Righteousness is in the will, but the will is not applied to something unknown, but is moved by a power which has knowledge; and thus faith is required as something which guides us to love God." Again in regard to the Epistle to the Galatians he argues that righteousness is that which each person attributes to himself, and faith attributes to God, because He is the Highest and the Greatest, that is, the Truth; and in this sense faith justifies.

Gregory in a certain homily says, "He has true faith and truly believes who shows by his work that he believes."

Aetius and Eunomius understood faith as an Epicurean concept, that God is so good that He imputes sin to no one, even to the impenitent. Basil and Gregory of Nazianzus opposed this statement.

We have already spoken concerning the ideas of the gnostics. The papists understand the profession of the Catholic faith, inasfar as it is distinguished from the Turkish Koran, and they interpret the verse, "Whatsoever is not of faith is sin," in this sense: If any heretic does something good outside the Catholic faith, this is a sin. And they make many philosophical statements about faith without reference to Christ, but no mention is made of applying this faith.

To put the matter in a nutshell, there are numerous errors regarding the word "faith." Some understand it only as an assent to the historical account, which in a general way asserts that the things revealed in Scripture are true. Some look only at the quality of the faith and how strong it is, and because it is imperfect and weak, they think something must be added to faith, which is done when a person adds, like weights on a scale, merits and worthiness which can justify him. From this comes the notion of the *fides informis* [faith without love; dead faith] and the *fides formata* [faith with love and works]. Others err in regard to the object of faith, because they make as the object of justifying faith the whole of Scripture including the precepts of the promises and the threats of the Law. Some rave in that they confuse the effects or activities of faith, by which it is shown to be true and living, with the object or formal cause because of which faith justifies. Thus Augustine says that to believe in God is to love by believing, and to go to God by loving. He has many statements like this. Others understand justifying faith to be an idea, an opinion, a figment of one's own brain concerning freedom from punishment for any crimes whatever, even without repentance.

Among those who understand the word "justify" differently than Scripture speaks of it, it follows that there is also a perversion of the word "faith." Their understanding is that faith justifies in this way, that by faith the Holy Spirit is received, who renews the mind and begins the new obedience. Therefore, according to these people, we are justified initially by faith but in a formal and complete way by love.

Philosophic thoughts about knowledge, prudence, free choice, etc., have also greatly upset the purity of teaching regarding justifying faith. These points can be demonstrated by examples from writers of all eras, but for the sake of brevity I have noted only a few of them.

Second. Because this doctrine has been corrupted by various errors, particularly because the statement of the point at issue has been turned upside down, therefore we must note the ways in which the genuine and apostolic meaning of the word "faith" as used by Paul can be easily and correctly investigated, understood, demonstrated, taught, and explained, so that we can offer it in the face of all corruptions for those who desire to consider it at length. It must be our chief concern that the point at issue be correctly stated. Therefore we shall cite three ways and then discuss the Biblical testimonies later.

1. The word "faith" is illustrated by the true interpretation of the word "justify." For the question is not what virtues follow faith, so that it may be efficacious through love. But this is the question: How and in what respect does faith justify, that is, when in the real struggle our minds are terrified by the feeling of the wrath of God and seek firm consolation so that they may be freed from the sentence of condemnation and be received unto eternal life, to what must faith, in the midst of this agony, look and what must it grasp? In sum, in the dispute about faith the question concerns the application of the merit and obedience of Christ for righteousness and the salvation of everyone who believes. When the *status controversiae* is stated in this way, then the meaning of the word "faith" becomes self-evident.

2. The antithesis Paul uses shows us the surest method for investigating the interpretation of the word: We are justified, that is, absolved from our sins and accepted as righteous, not by our works but by faith in Christ.

3. There is no better and surer method than to take the interpretation and establish it on the basis of the object with which justifying faith properly is concerned and to which it looks, which it grasps and applies to itself, with respect to which, by its merit and worthiness, the believer is justified. Paul clearly denies that the Law and works are the object of justifying faith. Rom. 3:21: "Now without the Law the righteousness of God is revealed." V. 27: "Boasting is not excluded by the principle of works but by the principle of faith." Rom. 10:5 "The righteousness of the Law says, 'He who does these things shall live by them'... but the righteousness of faith says...'" Gal. 3:12: "The Law is not of faith" [KJV]. But Paul describes the true and proper object of justifying faith in the sweetest words in Rom. 3:24: "Justified freely by His grace...'"; Rom. 4:24:

". . . to us who believe in Him who raised Jesus . . ."; Rom. 10:6: "The righteousness of faith says . . ."; Phil. 3:9: ". . . that I may be found in Him, not having my
own righteousness which is from the Law, but that which is by faith in Christ,
the righteousness from God which is by faith."

Third. Because they shout that this interpretation of the word "faith" conflicts with the usage of all languages, we must show that the grammatical
treatment we are using is not in conflict but is in complete agreement with the
Pauline position taught in our churches. In order that the lining up of examples
may be of some help, we will cite examples first from the Old Testament, then
from the New Testament, and finally from common linguistic usage.

The point at issue is to show that "faith" is having in our mind the kind
of knowledge that, in the case of true faith, produces an assent in our will and
a moving of our hearts, a desire and a trust which lay hold on and apply to
oneself the object of faith, because it has been shown to be so good that our
mind relies on it. Thus we shall note certain examples to show that in the Old
Testament all these activities are included under the one word "believe." This
can also be noticed from the antithesis, for it is opposed to doubting, trepidation, and distrust.

Gen. 45:26–27: When Jacob heard the message that Joseph was alive and
prospering, his heart fainted because he did not believe it. But later, when he
saw the chariot Joseph had sent, his spirits revived. Job 9:16: "Even when He
answered me, I did not believe that He was listening to me." Job 15:22: "The
godless person . . . does not believe that He can return out of the darkness." Ps.
27:13: "I believe that I shall see the goodness of the Lord in the land of the living." Deut. 28:66: "Your life shall hang in doubt before you; night and day you
shall be in dread, and have no assurance of your life" [RSV]. Job 24:22: "When
He rises up, no man is sure of life." Dan. 6:23: "So Daniel was taken up out of
the den of the lion, and no hurt was found upon him, because he had trusted
in his God." 2 Chron. 20:20: "Believe . . . and you will be established" [RSV]. Is.
28:16: "He who believes will not be in haste" [RSV], or disturbed.

Then we must note examples from the Old Testament in which the words
chasah and *batach* (believe and trust) are combined in the same statement. It is
customary in Scripture that often in the same verse two equivalent words are
used to describe the same thing, as in Ps. 78:22: ". . . because they had no faith
in God and did not trust His saving power" [RSV]. Micah 7:5: "Put no trust in
a neighbor, have no confidence in a prince." Job 39:11–12: "Will you depend on
him . . . ? Will you have faith in him . . . ?"

The following observation also sheds much light: Where the New Testament
requires "faith," there, the Old Testament commands "trust"; and in the New
Testament the same things are associated with faith and believers that in the Old

Testament are attributed to trust and those who have confidence. From this it is most appropriate to conclude that "faith" in the article of justification according to the language of Scripture means not only "knowledge" but also "trust." As the New Testament says: "He who believes . . . will be saved" [Mark 16:16]. Ps. 2:12: "Blessed are all those who put their trust in Him." Ps. 34:8: "Blessed is the man who trusts in Him." Rom. 5:1: "Justified by faith, we have peace with God." Isaiah expresses this in 26:3: "You keep him in perfect peace whose mind is stayed on You, because he trusts in You." Heb. 10:39–11:1: "Faith does not shrink back but is the assurance of things we wait for." Thus Ps. 112:7–8 says: "His heart is firm, trusting in the Lord . . . he will not be afraid," etc. And Ps. 125:1: "Those who trust in the Lord are like Mount Zion, which cannot be moved."

In the New Testament the grace and mercy of God is the object of faith. The Old Testament makes trust the object. Ps. 13:5: "I have trusted in Your mercy." Rom. 10:10: "A person believes with the heart unto righteousness." Acts 8:37: "If you believe with your whole heart . . ." Thus it speaks of trust: Ps. 28:7: "My heart trusted in Him." Ps. 112:7: "His heart is prepared to trust." Prov. 3:5: "Trust in the Lord with your whole heart."

In Rom. 5:2 Paul attributes "the glory of God in which we rejoice" to faith. In Rom. 14:17 he attributes joy. Ps. 5:11: "Let all those rejoice who put their trust in Him." Ps. 64:10: "The righteous shall rejoice in the Lord and trust in Him." John 1:12: ". . . who believe in His name." Ps. 33:21: "We trust in His holy name." Is. 50:10: "Let him trust in the name of the Lord and rely on His God." John 20:29: When Thomas says, "My Lord and my God," Christ replies, "Thomas, you have believed. . . ." Thus in Ps. 91:2: "My God, in whom I will trust." Rom. 10:11: "Whoever believes in Him shall not be ashamed." Ps. 31:1: "In the Lord do I put my trust; let me not be put to shame. Deliver me in Your righteousness." The New Testament requires faith for prayer; the Old Testament requires trust. Ps. 37:5: "Commit your way to the Lord and hope in Him." Ps. 62:8: "Hope in Him . . . pour out your hearts before Him."

Most noteworthy is the fact that the word "amen" is derived from the word "believe." It is a verb of hoping, a word whereby we apply something to ourselves. For prayers and invocations are ended with this expression, not only to show that in a general way we approve of the prayer but also that it may be applied to us personally. Jer. 11:4–5: "You shall be My people . . . that I may keep My oath. . . . And I answered and said, 'Amen, O Lord.'" Deut. 27:15: "Let all the people say, 'Amen.'" 1 Kings 1:36: "Amen, and thus may the Lord God say also." Neh. 8:6: "And Ezra blessed the Lord . . . and all the people answered, 'Amen, Amen,' lifting up their hands" [RSV]. Likewise, Num. 5:22: "And the woman shall say, 'Amen.'" Compare also Ps. 41:13. These examples of application to oneself are very illustrative.

We must also now add some examples from the New Testament. Those which indicate that faith means knowledge are obvious, and because this point is not under controversy we shall not cite any instances. But we shall note only those passages where faith clearly means trust. In Matt. 9:22, when the woman with the issue of blood conceived in her heart the confidence or trust that she would be healed if only she might touch the hem of His garment, Christ says: "Your faith has healed you." Thus Acts 14:9: "Seeing that the lame man had faith to be healed . . ." Luke 5:20, regarding those who had brought the paralyzed man on a stretcher, it says: "Seeing their faith . . ." 1 John 5:13–14, "I write this . . . that you may believe in His name, and this is the confidence which we have in Him . . ."

This point is understood even more clearly from the antithesis. Matt. 8:26 and 14:31: "O you of little faith." In Luke 8:25 He says in the boat: "Where is your faith?"

The word "believe" (credere) is used expressly in Luke 16:11: "Who will entrust [Vulgate: credet] to you the true riches?" John 2:24: "Jesus did not entrust [Vulgate: credebat] Himself to them." Acts 27:25: "Take heart, for I believe God, that it will turn out exactly as He told me."

This is even clearer in the passive voice. Rom. 3:2: "To them were entrusted [Vulgate: credita sunt] the oracles of God." Gal. 2:7: "The Gospel was entrusted [Vulgate: creditum est] to me." Cf. Titus 1:3 and 1 Thess. 2:4.

Up to now we have principally gathered only those passages in which the word is used in this way but without reference to the article of justification. Later on we shall add those testimonies which do refer to the article of justification.

Finally, we must show that this meaning of the word "faith" is not in conflict with the common Greek usage. There are many instances where it is used in the sense of "trust." Erasmus already saw and noted this in his treatment of Hebrews 10 and Romans 1, where he says that the Holy Scriptures frequently use "faith" to express the idea of "trust" in God, so that the meaning is nearly the same as "hope."

Budeaus[34] in his commentaries says, "Faith means not only the belief in something, but a trust in a matter which has been experienced and explored." Again, "We call the belief in matters pertaining to God what the chief theologians have called a persuasion, something we trust in (pepoiēthēsin).

Aeschines, Contra Ctesiphontem [1], "I am persuaded (pepisteukōs) first by the gods, and then by our laws and by you."

---

[34] William Bude, 1468–1540, French humanist, sought to reform the church before Luther. Wrote commentary on the Greek language.

Diodorus [Siculus, *Historia* 16.4.4], "He marched with his army against the enemy, trusting both in the victories which had already been won and in the manliness of the Illyrians." Plutarch [*Plutarch, Pompey, and Agesilaus Compared*, 5.664] says, "It is dangerous to entrust (*pisteuein*) such important matters to the fortune of one man." And in his comparison of Pompey and Agesilaus he says at the end, "Pompey trusted (*pisteusas*) in the treaty, but Agesilaus was trusted (*pisteutheis*) and deserted to the enemy."

There are many clear examples in the *Loci*. In other examples various changes in names and changes in the meaning of the word "faith" are involved. But the point at issue is not whether other different examples can be adduced, but first we must determine from the context itself what Paul is trying to have us understand when he asserts that we are justified by faith; and when we have done this, then we must apply the suitable examples. With regard to inappropriate and irrelevant uses, we must caution that they not be referred to Paul's argumentation.

Fourth. Because we are dealing with a matter of great importance, namely what that faith is by which Scripture affirms that we are justified (for "he who does not believe will be condemned" [Mark 16:16]), and because many are under the persuasion of a false or dead faith, and thus are doing themselves injury of eternal life and salvation; therefore a matter of this importance must not be left only in the hands of those who dispute grammatical points. It is necessary to set forth the clear, firm, and solid foundations from which the substance of the doctrine of justification is drawn, by which our conscience, in this great diversity of opinion and harshness of controversy, can rest securely.

This diligence is necessary both for our own sake as well as that of our adversaries, who in order to detract something from the doctrine of justification by faith, corrupt the correct meaning of the term. For since the formula for justification before the judgment of God is this: "Your faith has saved you" [Luke 7:50], there surely must be no ignorance or uncertain opinion as to what this faith is. This more careful study of the testimonies also has the value of showing the nature of justifying faith more quickly and more fully. Therefore we shall note certain general points to which these passages may be very appropriately applied for a better understanding.

1. We must carefully consider the weight of the testimonies which clearly show that "faith" in the article of justification must be understood not only as knowledge and general assent, stating in a general way that the promise of the Gospel is true, but that at the same time it includes the activities of the will and the heart; that is, it is a desire and a trust which, in the struggle with sin and the wrath of God, applies the promise of grace to each individual, so that each person includes himself in the general promise given to believers. In this way

he raises himself up so that he determines without hesitation that the promise of the Gospel is firm for him also. From this he gains comfort and life in time of temptation.

These testimonies and examples show that this applies in a beautiful way to individuals (so to speak). Thus in Gal. 2:16 Paul first lays down the general principle that "a man is not justified by the works of the Law but through faith in Jesus Christ." Second, in vv. 15–16 he makes the special application: "We . . . who are Jews . . . have believed in Jesus Christ, in order to be justified" [RSV]. Third, in vv. 20–21, in applying this teaching, he gets down to the level of the individual: "I live by faith in the Son of God, who loved me and gave Himself for me. I do not set aside the grace of God." Phil. 3:8–11: "That I may . . . be found in Christ, not having my own righteousness, which is of the Law, but that which is from God, which is the righteousness of faith, and that I may know Him and the power of His resurrection . . . that I might attain to the resurrection." He adds in v. 15: "Let those of us who are mature be thus minded." See also Rom. 4:16: ". . . that the promise may . . . be firm to all his descendants." Again in vv. 23–24: "This was written not only for the sake of Abraham but for us also, to whom it will be imputed as believers," etc. In 1 Tim. 1:15–16 an example of application to individuals who come to faith is shown and described. Rom. 8:35, 38–39 is a beautiful example showing how the faith of the individual is involved and includes both the general and the specific aspects. "Therefore who shall separate us from the love of Christ? . . . For I am certain that . . . no creature shall separate us," etc. Rom. 5:2: "By faith we have access into the grace in which we stand, and we rejoice. . . ."

The very form of the Apostolic Profession of Faith clearly shows that faith is the means by which this application takes place, for we say: "I believe in God," etc. And this is most definitely proved from the correct use of the sacraments. Note the form of absolution the Son of God uses in Luke 7:50: "Your faith has saved you; go in peace." Cf. Matt. 9:2: "Jesus, seeing their faith, said to the paralyzed man, 'Be confident, son, your sins are forgiven you.'" Gal. 3:27: "As many of you as were baptized . . . have put on Christ" [RSV]. 1 Peter 3:21: "Baptism . . . [is] the answer of a good conscience. . . ." Likewise in the Lord's Supper the assurance is given to individuals who in faith partake of the Sacrament: "Take, eat, this is My body; this is the new covenant . . . ."

2. We should also note in these passages which properties or effects Scripture attributes to justifying faith, such as, it brings remission of sins, adoption, absolution from the accusation of the Law, access to God, peace of conscience, purification of heart, victory over the world, salvation, and eternal life.

It is not necessary to write out all of these testimonies, for they are well known. But it is certain and obvious that these effects and others like them cannot be attributed simply to knowledge or a general assent. For the knowledge possessed by the devils is doubtlessly far greater; and the hypocrites, Matt. 7:22–23, were certainly not lacking in knowledge, for they had disseminated prophecy, that is, their interpretation of Scripture. Yet they heard the words: "Depart from Me," etc. These above-mentioned merits and blessings of the Mediator, the Son of God, are bestowed upon and given to those who by faith lay hold on and apply the promise to themselves. Thus it is clear that justifying faith has as its correlative the promise of grace, so that it grasps it as an instrument or a means, receives it, and applies it to itself.

3. We have already said that we must establish the proper and principal object of faith insofar as and with respect to which faith justifies, namely the promise of grace for the sake of the Mediator. Likewise we must determine how faith in justification relates to its object. Because Christ is the propitiation for the sins of the whole world, and yet not all are saved through Christ, therefore it is necessary that there be an application of those things which Christ by His obedience has merited and acquired, an application to each individual who has been ordained to eternal life.

It is certain that this takes place by faith, but not in the way or in the sense that when there is faith it works through love. Then the object of faith would have to do with the works of the Law, and the application of the free promise does not take place by works. Nor does the application take place through some kind of general assent found even in the devils. Thus it is manifest that justifying faith is concerned with its object, which is the promise of grace, and not with a general apprehending, but with the application of this promise to individual believers—and in regard to this it justifies. The testimonies above have been noted. And this is the heart of the whole discussion.

At this point we are discussing an objection for which an explanation is needed. It can disturb the uninstructed, but if it is handled skillfully, many disputes can be cleared up.

Hebrews 11, throughout the entire chapter, describes various and different objects of faith, such as the article of creation, the prediction of the coming flood, the hiding of Moses, the institution of the passover, the crossing of the Red Sea, the falling of the walls of Jericho after Rahab hid the spies, the battles of the judges and of the kings of Judah. In summary: "Through faith they conquered kingdoms, stopped the mouths of lions, overcame the camps of their enemies, out of weakness were made strong, extinguished the force of fire. . . . Women received their dead restored to life. They were tortured . . . stoned, killed, destitute, afflicted," etc. [Heb. 11:33–37]. In the Gospel account, where faith is commended, very often its objects are described in terms of the curing of sickness or of physical deliverance.

Likewise in the example of the faith of Abraham, which Paul cites in Rom. 4:3, it seems that Gen. 15:5 speaks of physical fertility, of the external or bodily seed.

In the light of this, the papists try to force us to the conclusion that the promise of mercy for the sake of the Mediator is not the proper or principal object of justifying faith, but that it is in general the whole content of the Word of God with which faith is concerned in several different ways. All these points are brought into the discussion to the end that the doctrine of justifying faith may be corrupted or at least confused and obscured.

There is a simple and true explanation for this objection, which confirms and illustrates the meaning we have given above.

We do not deny that there often are various external objects with which our faith has to do, but the question now is: In respect to what object does faith justify? In the story of the nine lepers it is evident that the external objects of their faith did not bestow on their faith the power to justify, as Christ Himself argues with reference to faith in miracles, Matt. 7:22, and Paul in 1 Cor. 13:1–2. Thus we must allow a distinction. In some places Scripture speaks of the object of faith in a general sense, and in other places it sets up that object with respect to which, by grasping it, faith justifies before God. Later on there is the further question concerning the exercises of faith under the cross, in obedience, in prayer, and the expectation of bodily and spiritual blessings, when the person is reconciled by faith, in regard to this question the Epistle to the Hebrews discusses how faith after justification exercises itself through suffering and receives various gifts and benefits, as the text itself shows.

Besides this, when "faith" is concerned with external objects, it obviously signifies "desire," "trust," "expectation," and "petition" for a mitigation or for aid or deliverance. The same will be the nature and meaning of "faith" when it has to do with justification as its object.

From this the correct meaning is confirmed that even when faith is concerned with external objects, yet in order that the promise may be sure and the confidence of our hope firm, that faith which relies on the promise of mercy for the sake of Christ must always shine forth. For unless faith first establishes that God is favorable toward us and has been reconciled, no peace of conscience can be sought or aid be expected. When calamities bear testimony to the wrath of God, and particularly when He delays in hearing us, then the conscience is in anguish above all over the question: "Is God favorable toward me?" This question is the beginning, the middle, and the end in our petitions and expectations in regard to physical things. Then faith can calmly and patiently wait, when it has determined that God has been reconciled. Therefore this diversity of objects is never a hindrance for the proper and principal object of faith to be the promise of grace. Certainly there is a difference between the faith that lays hold on Christ, who is "the end of the Law for righteousness for everyone who believes," Rom. 10:4, and the exercises of faith which have to do with other objects. Yet these exercises of faith always presuppose, as their foundation, that God is reconciled by faith, and to this they are always led back, so that faith may be certain and the promise sure in regard to these other objects.

This explanation is confirmed by the brilliant statement of Paul in 2 Cor. 1:20: "All the promises of God in Christ are yea and amen, to the glory of God through us," that is, the promises concerning other objects of faith have only then been ratified for us when by faith in Christ we are reconciled with God. The promises have been made valid on the condition that they must give glory to God through us. Therefore faith in Christ both causes the promises to be made certain and governs them. For Paul uses two words, *nai* and *amen*; one of these pertains to the assertion that the promises have been ratified, cf. Matt. 5:37: "Let your word be yes (*nai*) . . ."; Matt. 11:9: "Yes (*nai*), I tell you, more than a prophet." The second word [*amen*] refers to an expectation in sure confidence, as we have said about the word "Amen."

In the same way the example of Abraham is to be explained on the basis of the correct foundations, not as an implicit faith (*fides implicita*), or as a formed faith (*fides formata*) that was later fabricated as if it were restricted only to one object, the carnal seed. The text of Gen. 15:1 is very clear, for when God promises, "I will be your Protector and your great Reward," Abraham immediately replies, "What will You give me, since You have not given me the Seed?" You see that Abraham could not in true faith grasp the rest of the promises unless they were connected with that object which had been promised, concerning the Seed. When the Seed was mentioned, the patriarchs always looked back to the first giving of the promise in Gen. 3:15. Therefore the blessed Seed was the proper and principal object in this promise in Gen. 15:5, that from his posterity according to the flesh there was going to be born to Abraham the Seed in which all the nations of the earth would be blessed, and it was because of this Seed that God made the promise of such posterity to Abraham.

This explanation has clear testimonies in the New Testament, e.g., Rom. 4:17: ". . . that he might be the father of many nations." But this was not to come about in the physical seed, but in Christ, Gal. 3:8ff. Matt. 8:11 explicitly interprets the promise as given in Gen. 12:3; 15:5; and 22:17–18. Paul takes the time in Gal. 3:16 to say: "It does not say, 'and to seeds,' as of many; but 'in your Seed,' which is Christ." Again in Gal. 3:29: "If you are Christ's, then you are Abraham's seed, and heirs according to the promise." Therefore the promise of Genesis 15, which is the same as that in Genesis 12 and 22, is not speaking primarily of the land of Canaan. For in Heb. 11:10 the text says that Abraham was looking for a city to come in the future and a better fatherland, a different resting place, into which not Joshua but Jesus would lead the people [cf. Heb. 4:8ff.]. Therefore in this "wrapping" involving posterity according to the flesh and the land of Canaan, the end, the goal, and the final fulfillment was that blessed Seed, as Christ Himself affirms about Abraham, that he "saw My day," John 8:56. And in Rom. 9:7 and Gal. 3:29 they are called the seed and the children of Abraham who hold to the promise concerning Christ. Thus in Rom. 4:7–8 the faith of Abraham is explained by citing Ps. 32:1–2: "Blessed is he whose sin is forgiven . . . ."

These passages clearly show the object of Abraham's faith, with respect to which and in laying hold on which he was justified. Through these objections, therefore, the true meaning of justifying faith is more fully and clearly confirmed.

4. What the word "faith" properly means in the article of justification can most beautifully be gathered and demonstrated from the other names attributed to justifying faith in Scripture. For the apostles with great care selected words which were not in common use but were special and very meaningful, in order to arouse diligence in us in studying the sources of the terms and to put before our eyes with one unique word the whole force of the term "faith." Emphasis on these words plus a little diligence will be very enlightening.

a. In Heb. 11:1 the word *hypostasis* ("substance") is used. The commentators on the *Sentences* [of Peter Lombard] wondrously rack their brains as to how, since faith is a quality, one can in its definition take a general term (*genus*) from a "substance." Many reply that the definition is based on the similarity of words, so that just as a substance has been subjected or placed beneath all accidents and is the cause of their existence, without which no accident can be or subsist, so faith is the foundation and basis for the entire spiritual edifice, for all virtues proceed from it. Likewise, since faith is the first principle of the virtues produced, it is called a substance, because "substance" is said to be the first entity (*primum ens*) on which all other things depend.

But Thomas [Aquinas], because the text does not say "the substance of virtues," but "the substance of things hoped for" [KJV], calls attention to the fact that this is not said in this passage and that it was not the intention of the apostle to explain it in this way. And because it has no linguistic support, he suggested something different, such as an object or reward which it contains in itself by another power, and thus also faith can be defined as a substance because it contains in itself "the things hoped for." These bizarre disputations arose out of lack of knowledge of the languages.

Greek scholars do not interpret this passage in the same way. Theophylact and the Greek scholiasts interpret it by saying that "the things hoped for" are *anhypostata*, that is, they are things which are not yet present, but faith is the basis (*hypostasis*) for them, so that for the person who has faith they become as things which now subsist and are present, which do not yet exist in the nature of things, as Paul says in Rom. 4:17, "God calls those things which are not as though they were."

Others interpret the word *hypostasis* as a possession, for the things which belong to faith are not comprehended by human reason or the senses or experience, and yet faith is as certain as if one could hold in his hand and before his eyes those things which are promised in the Word.

Others interpret it as the basis or the prop or the foundation on which "the things hoped for" rely for support in the Word. For the promise is the object of faith.

By far the most appropriate and satisfactory interpretation is Luther's, "Faith is a sure expectation" (*eine gewisse Zuversicht*).

We must note the fundamental points in this interpretation, so that we thereby can understand and support the thrust of it correctly. In popular speech this meaning is not at all common but seems to be peculiar to the Bible. For example, Heb. 3:14 uses it this way: "We share in Christ, if only we hold our first confidence (*hypostasis*) firm to the end" [RSV]. V. 6 in the same chapter explains the same meaning thus: "If we hold fast the confidence and the rejoicing of the hope . . ." [KJV]. 2 Cor. 9:4 and 11:17 speak of the "confidence or basis (*hypostasis*) for boasting." Many argue about the subject matter of the boasting, but the term simply means an immovable confidence of the mind which surrenders to no one.

The meaning of this term is undoubtedly taken from the usage of the Septuagint. For in Ps. 39:7, "And now, what is my hope except in the Lord?" and "My hope is in You," it uses the word *hypostasis* [in the second part]. There are two words in this verse, one of which means cheerfully to await something with ardent desire; but the second word refers to a waiting connected with pressure or effort involving great anxiety. Thus in Ezek. 19:5 the Septuagint renders the words "Her hope was lost" by the word *hypostasis*. In Micah 5:7 the Septuagint uses *hypostē* to describe "the grass which does not wait for man." The etymology of the Hebrew root that we have been talking about correlates beautifully with the Greek word *hyphistēmi*. It is a military word meaning "not to yield or give way to a charging enemy but to stand firm, to receive the force of the attack and sustain it." Plutarch, "They spared those who surrendered, but those who stood firm (*hyphistamenous*) they slaughtered." Again, "When he had conquered the rest, one who had stood firm (*hypostas*) thrust a spear into him." In his *Demetrius* [25.900] he says, "When none of his enemies stood facing him, but all had fled and were leaving the towns, Synesius was the first who stood (*hypostas*) stripped of all his arms." It is also used this way in other places.

Plutarch in his *Lysander* [27.449] says, "Pausanias did not stand firm (*hypostas*) to receive his punishment, but fled (*wolts nicht ausstehen*). Suidas equates this word with "to be fearless" (*tharseō*), and he cites as an example: "He who dares to advance voluntarily (*hypostas, wers wagen dürffte*). Budaeus cites an example from Polybius, *De Cochlite*, "While the enemy stood by in wonderment, his only power was his willingness to face danger, his presence of mind, and an unterrified guard who yielded to no one." Suidas cites from Diodorus, "They sent a message ahead to him to gather support (*hypostasin sumbaleisthai*)." Again, "He conducted himself with steadfastness (*hypostatikōs*) in danger, and as a result he received praise as a man of courage."

This meaning beautifully depicts the struggle of faith. And then Paul in 1 Tim. 6:12 speaks of "the good fight of faith"; Eph. 6:16, "the shield of faith"; 1 Thess. 5:8, "the breastplate of faith"; and 1 Thess. 1:3 speaks of the "work (*ergon*) of faith," referring to the struggle of faith in the midst of various difficulties. This emphasis, rightly considered, offers many beautiful thoughts to ponder.

b. Also attributed to faith is "full assurance" (*plērophoria*), Rom. 4:21; Col. 2:2; Heb. 6:11; and 10:22. There is no doubt that *plērophoria* is a very important word and that it would be useful to highlight suitable examples by which it can be illustrated. Suidas and Varinus have no examples of its use. Budaeus cites only one instance, from Isocrates: "Confidence (*plērophoria*) has failed me when there are many hearers," and here the term refers to the great certainty which goes with knowledge of a matter.

Luke 1:1 speaks of "the things which have been most surely believed among us" (*pragmata peplērophorēmena*). These are things which have been established by such incontrovertible testimonies that they cannot be called into doubt without great wickedness. It is the "full assurance" (*plērophoria*) of faith which through the certainty of the Word and the promise brings about a firm and immovable conviction in the mind, so that the will with the whole mind is borne up by what the understanding has demonstrated in the Word. Here it is appropriate to study fully the etymology of the word *plērophorēsthai*. Certain secular writers interpret this word as "to encourage," "to cause trust and assurance," but they do not give examples.

There are, however, some examples in the New Testament, and by comparing these we can establish the meaning and emphasis of the term. Rom. 4:21: ". . . being fully persuaded (*plērophorētheis*) that He who had promised could also deliver." Rom. 14:5: "Let each one in his own mind be fully persuaded (*plērophoreisthō*)" that he is doing nothing with a doubting conscience, but can say with Paul in v. 14: "I know and am fully persuaded that in Christ Jesus nothing is common." Col. 2:2 speaks of "the full assurance of understanding (*plērophoria syneseōs*)," a knowledge producing such emotions in our minds. 2 Tim. 4:5: "Make full proof (*plērophorēson*) of your ministry." Erasmus translates it "render it approved." Luther, more meaningfully, has "perform it sincerely (*richte . . . redlich aus*)," so that a person is moved by a serious intention in his mind to accomplish his ministry. Thus 2 Tim. 4:17: ". . . that the proclamation might be fulfilled (*plērophorēthē*) and all the nations might hear." More significantly, in 1 Thess. 1:5 *plērophoria* is coupled with the Holy Spirit and with power (*dynamis*): "Our Gospel came to you not only in word, but also in power and the Holy Spirit and with full conviction (*plērophoria*)" [RSV]. Heb. 6:11: "We desire that every one of you show the same diligence to the full assurance (*plērophoria*) of hope to the end; that you do not become slothful but followers of those who through faith and patience inherit the promises." This statement can establish for us the meaning of the "full assurance (*plērophoria*) of hope," etc. Heb. 10:22: "Let us draw near with a true heart in full assurance (*plērophoria*) of faith (*in völligem Glauben*)" [KJV].

From these examples it is manifest that *plērophoria* pertains not only to the mind but also includes those emotions of the soul which follow from a sure persuasion. This meaning casts light on the word "faith."

c. Also attributed to faith is "confidence" or "boldness" (*parrēsia*), Eph. 3:12; 1 John 2:28; 3:21; 4:17; 5:14; Heb. 3:6; 4:16; 10:35. This word, meaning "to speak and act freely, without fear and trembling," is very well known. There are also many examples of the verb *parrēsiazomai*. The loveliest meaning relates to justifying faith, which brings such peace to the conscience in its relationship with God that it does not tremble at the accusation of the Law and is not terrified at its own unworthiness or the fiery darts of the devil. Nor does it flee God, but because it has the surest trust in the love of God toward it, it freely comes to God, and as the ancient church says, "We dare to say, 'Our Father,' etc." Luther in a beautiful way translates this *Freudigkeit*. Its precise force can be understood from the Biblical passages cited. 1 John 2:28: ". . . that when He shall appear we may have confidence (*parrēsia*) and not be ashamed before Him at His coming" [KJV]. 1 John 3:21: "If our hearts do not condemn us, we have confidence (*parrēsia*) before God" [RSV]. 1 John 4:17: "We have confidence in the day of judgment." 1 John 5:14: "This is our confidence . . . that if we ask anything . . . He hears us." Heb. 10:19: "We have confidence in the blood of Christ to enter the sanctuary." Heb. 4:16: "Let us then with confidence draw near to the throne of grace." Note also Eph. 3:12.

d. Also attributed to faith is "trust" (*pepoithēsis*), Eph. 3:12. In Phil. 3:3–4 he puts trust in the flesh in opposition to faith and glorying in Christ. Varinus says that while the word is not used in Luke 18:9, yet the meaning of the term is seen here, "They trusted in themselves that they were righteous." Matt. 27:43,

"He trusted in God that He would deliver Him." Ps. 2:11, "Blessed are all who put their trust in Him." Likewise Homer says in *Iliad* [1.423], "By nodding the head she indicated she trusted." *Iliad* [5.299], "The lion trusts in his strength" (*pepoithōs*). Demosthenes, *Phil.* [2.28], "These are the promises in which you trusted" (*eph hals epeithēte*). Luke 18:9: "They trusted in themselves that they were righteous." Matt. 27:43: "He trusted in God; let Him deliver Him . . ." Ps. 2:12: "Blessed are all who trust in Him."

e. The Scriptures also use the word *tharseō* when they are speaking of faith as opposed to fear, trepidation, and doubt. Matt. 9:2: "Son, be of good cheer." Mark 6:50: "Be of good cheer; do not be afraid; it is I." John 16:33: "Be of good cheer; I have overcome the world." 2 Cor. 5:8: "We are of good courage, and we would rather be away from the body and at home with the Lord" [RSV]. Indeed, he says that "we are always of good courage (*tharroumen*), even when we are away from the Lord."

f. Also attributed to faith is the concept of "boasting" (*kauchēma* and *kauchēsis*), Rom. 5:2–3.

g. Also these phrases illustrate the word "faith": "To keep [*tērein*] the Word of Christ," John 8:51; 14:23; "To guard [*phylassein*] the Word," Luke 11:28. Varinus rightly says: "To keep as an entrusted deposit." Thus, in a very significant way, this means to apprehend and apply the Word. Also these metaphorical terms appear: to thirst, to drink, to eat, to be filled, John 4:14; 6:35, 51; 7:37; Rev. 21:6. John interprets "believing" by "to come to the Father" [John 14:6].

h. Also attributed to faith is the concept of "sealing." John 3:33: "He who has received his testimony has set his seal that God is true." Eph. 1:13–14: "You who . . . have believed in Him were sealed with the promised Holy Spirit, which is the Guarantee of our inheritance" [RSV]. 2 Cor. 1:21–22: "It is God who . . . has sealed us and given us the guarantee of the Spirit." Rom. 8:16: "The Spirit bears witness with our spirit."

i. There are also other illustrative words, which are put in an antithetical position, such as "to doubt" (*diakrinesthai*), Rom. 4:20; James 1:6; and Mark 11:23. Budaeus correctly states that those who cling to Him themselves are like those who are alternately the accused and the accuser, Rom. 14:1, where a person who does something with a doubtful conscience is said to be "judged" (*diakrinesthai*). Acts 10:20, "Go with them, doubting nothing" (*diakrinomenos*).

Matt. 14:31 uses the word (*distazō*), "O you of weak faith, why are you in doubt?" In Matt. 28:17 some "believed," and some "doubted" (*edistasan*). Aristotle uses this word in *Ethica*, 7.2 [*Nic. Eth.*, 7.2,1146a] to point out that when the mind is pushed by its desires hither and thither, it does not remain of one opinion but is like a traveler who is going in both directions. Varinus describes it as a "mind with two opinions."[35]

The term "you of little faith" (*oligopistoi*) as used in Matt. 6:30; 8:26; 14:31; 16:8; Luke 12:28, clearly shows that Christ by the term "faith" understands "trust." Thus the statement in Rom. 4:18, "Against hope he believed in hope" proves that faith is not only a knowledge in the mind.

In Luke 12:29 the word "to be in doubt" (*meteōrizesthai*) is used. Certain people on the basis of astrology bring in this term and use it in the sense of "being puffed up with arrogance." Demosthenes, *De Syntaxi* [13.12], equates (*meteōrisis*) with (*physēsis*), "to be puffed up." Plutarch in *Pericles* [4.154] says that "he was greatly elevated (*emeteōrise*) in his mind. But his meaning does not apply to the statement in Luke 12 where it is used in antithesis to faith, what Matthew calls "lack of faith" (*aligopistia*). The word *meteōrosk* is often used with this meaning. Thucydides [*Historia*, 4.14.] says that "all Greece was puffed up (*meteōros ēn*)." For just as those who are up in the air are easily pushed here and there, or just as a ship which sails far from shore out into the deep is tossed by the waves (for this is what the word *meteōros* means, and in an antithetical sense this applies very nicely to the statement in Heb. 6:19 concerning the anchor), so those who lack true confidence in Christ run first here and then there with doubt, with their mind up in the air, as they face prosperity and adversity.

There are also some other words which pertain properly to the distinction between faith and doubt, but from these which we have studied I believe that the argument concerning the word "faith" can be properly illuminated.

In the fifth place, to confirm the true and correct meaning of justifying faith it is useful also to have before us some of the testimonies from antiquity as supporting statements, both in order that our consciences may be strengthened by their agreement with the correct meaning as well as that the clamors of the papists may be put to silence, when they say that this is a new understanding of faith, a special teaching (as they call it) without any corroboration from antiquity. The papists do cite many differing statements from the ancients, which in a tricky way they place before the unsuspecting in opposition to our teaching, and many people are disturbed by this array of differing opinions. But the clear and simple determination of the position of the ancients can be seen from this distinction: at times they speak concerning general historical knowledge and assent such as is found even in the ungodly; at times they speak about the external profession of faith which can also be found in hypocrites; at times they describe faith by the fruits or consequent effects by which it is proved to be true

---

[35] Varinus, also Phavorinus or Guarinus, even Barius, 1370–1460, classicist, teacher of Leo X, compiled Greek lexicon.

and living. For often the topic under discussion is the point that the Spirit of renewal is received, and from Him arise truly good works. Therefore a diversity of ideas regarding the purpose of faith is not surprising. The fathers spoke differently in different situations in regard to faith. These points which we have cited should be discussed in their proper context, but they do not properly pertain to the genuine teaching regarding justifying faith. Therefore we must be selective in citing statements from the ancients, so that those statements are used which properly pertain to the subject at hand, that is to say: (1) are they clearly describing that object which in true contrition faith lays hold on and looks to, by which it governs and sustains itself? and (2) How does faith lay hold on this objective and apply it to itself, so that it thereby receives remission of sins and life eternal? From the many statements I shall cite only a few.

Cyprian [*De Mortalitate*, MPL 4.605–7] in a sermon on death says, "This is the beginning of the reward of life and the joy of eternal salvation. What place do anxiety and worry have here? Who in this place is troubled or sad unless he lacks faith and hope? The man who fears immortality is he who does not want to go to Christ; and he who does not want to go to Christ is he who does not believe that he shall begin to reign with Christ. For it is written, 'The just shall live by faith.' If you are just and live by faith, if you truly believe in God, why shall you not be with Christ and be secure in the promises of the Lord, clinging to the fact that you are called to Christ? If an honorable and praiseworthy man promises you something, you have faith in the person who makes this promise." Again, "God has promised immortality and eternal life to you when you leave this world. Or do you doubt it? To doubt it is not to know God at all. It is to assert that in the church, in the house of faith, there is no faith. If we believe in Christ, we have faith in His words and promises, that we do not die forever but will come in safety to Christ, with whom as Victor and Ruler we shall always live in joy" [ibid., MPL 4.607–8].

Again in his *Ad Demetrianum* [MPL 4.583], "Although you are at the very end of your life and at the very close of your temporal existence, you can still pray to God regarding your sins, that He will give you an opportunity for confession and for begging Him for faith and for the chance to confess your sins; you can ask that He be indulgent toward the believer and out of His divine goodness grant you absolution."

Origen on Romans 3 [MPL 38.605], "The thief said to Christ, 'Remember me,' and Christ did not reply to him by asking what works he had done, but solely by reason of his faith He said to him, 'Today you shall be with Me in paradise.'"

Ambrose, on 1 Corinthians 1 [v. 4, MPL 17.195], "Grace is given in Christ Jesus in such a way that it is thereby established by God that he who believes in

Christ shall be saved, without works, by faith alone, freely receiving the remission of sins.

Augustine, *De Verbis Domini*, Sermon 7 [(new 100), MPL 38.605], "Now I ask, O sinner, do you believe in Christ? You reply, 'I believe.' What do you believe? If you believe that all your sins can be freely remitted to you through Him, you have what you have believed.

Hesychius, on Leviticus, 4.2 Bk. 4 [.2 (new 4, L14), MPL 93.956], "Grace is obtained by mercy through faith alone, without works."

In the sixth place, this warning should be added: The true meaning of justifying faith is understood best of all in serious exertions of repentance, as the meditations of the ancients show. The diversity of opinions arises mostly from this, that without the struggle of temptation, idle and secure disputations, joined with the philosophical opinions of human reason, have disturbed the minds of men. But this exertion, illustrating the doctrine of faith more than all commentaries, is undertaken chiefly in two ways—either the conscience places itself before the tribunal of God . . . or it finds itself under cross and temptation, in petition and expectation, both spiritual and corporal. . . .

[CHAPTER II]: THE DEFINITION OF JUSTIFYING FAITH

Before we complete a definition, we must precede this with the division of the name (so to speak), for because the word "faith" is used in different ways, we cannot, unless an accurate distinction is applied, establish a correct definition of the word without some serious deviation. In many of the descriptions of "faith" extant among the fathers, it is easy to see which ones should be objected to, because, when the distinction is applied, they can easily and correctly be judged.

There is a certain general faith, which we commonly call historical faith, not only because it deals with the Biblical stories but because it holds in a general way that the things revealed in the Word of God are true, in the sense of the simple knowledge which historians use. Thus King Agrippa in Acts 26:27 believes the prophets and yet he is not a Christian.

There is the faith of miracles, as in 1 Cor. 12:10; 13:2; Matt. 17:20. Acts 3:16: "Faith which through His name has given him this health." To this Titus 1:4 opposes "common faith." There is also the faith that accepts miracles, as the lepers in Luke 17:19. In Acts 14:9 Paul looks at the lame man and sees that he has faith to be healed. But this faith in itself does not justify, Matt. 7:22; Luke 10:17–20.

Then there is dead faith, James 2:17. This faith is hypocritical or false and pretended. 1 Tim. 1:3–5; 2 Tim. 1:5; and Titus 1:16 speak of confessing with words but denying by deeds. Matt. 13:21 speaks of enduring "for a while," that is, some are convinced by the evidence of outward signs and the greatness of miracles, so that they cannot contradict them but are forced to conclude that the facts are true. The scholastics call this an "acquired faith," a knowledge which human reason can establish by its own powers from reading or hearing the historical account. It is only an external profession and persuasion that the Epicureans put together from it.

There is also a legal faith. If I may say so, it is also an evangelical faith. This is a faith concerned only with the temporal promises, etc.

If all these are thrown together into one pile without making any distinction, it is manifest that there can be no correct definition.

We must also observe here that there is a difference between a definition referring to the name and one referring to the substance. For there are many etymological definitions, or general descriptions, which should not be passed off as complete definitions of the subject under discussion.

Thus, for example, Augustine, *In Joh. Tract.*, 34, [wrong reference] "Faith is a virtue by which the things are believed which are not seen yet are necessary for salvation." Or, "What is faith except to believe that which you do not see?" [idem.]. Likewise, *Contra Cresconium* [4.28, MPL 43.567. Not an exact quote.], "Faith is the first enlightenment of the mind leading to the highest truth." . . . *De Spiritu & Litera* [31, MPL 44.235], "What is it to believe except to assent that what is believed is true?" *De Civitate Dei*, 15.8 [MPL 41.455–56], "Faith believes the Holy Scriptures—the Old Testament and the New Testament, which we call the canonical Scripture."

Athanasius says, "The catholic faith is this . . . ." In the same sense we speak of "the Nicene faith."

Dionysius, *De Div. Nominibus* [MPG 3.872], "Faith is the one foundation of the believers, calling them to the truth."

John of Damascus, *De Orth. Fide*, 4.3 [inadequate or erroneous reference], "Faith is not a searched-for consensus concerning the first cause."

Hugo, "Faith certainly concerns things which are absent, beyond human opinion, and above our knowledge."[36]

Suidas says, "Faith is hope regarding things which are not evident to the senses."

Varinus distinguishes the terms this way: "A refutation (*elegchos*) pertains to things which are seen (*blepomena*); knowledge pertains to things which can be understood (*kateilēmmena*); but faith pertains to things which are not evident to the senses (*adēla*)." Again he says, "Proof (*apodeixis*) seeks the reason for a thing, but faith is assent to the simple truth, the persuasion of that which

---

[36] Hugo of St. Victor, *De Sacramentis Fidei Christianei*, 1.10, MPL 176.330.

is simple truth. Others say that faith is complete assent to things which cannot be seen. Varinus likewise says that faith is of two kinds: one comes from the hearing of the Word, which all can possess; but there is also a kind of faith which is more steadfast or reliable than the good things hoped for, which only the righteous have.

It is clear that these are etymological descriptions and very general. They have a valuable use, as we shall soon show, but yet from these it is impossible to establish or set forth what justifying faith is.

Our task is not to set up general descriptions but to define what justifying faith properly is. Nor is the question at this point how faith exerts its power in renewal or how it is efficacious through love, but we must define how and for what reason and in what respect faith justifies.

This definition cannot be more correctly set forth or better understood or more fully explained than if it is considered through use of the kinds of causes that are customary in causal definitions. Therefore let us by analysis resolve the customary definition of faith into its parts.

In the common definition [Melanchthon's definition at the end of the section quoted some pages back], the first part is this: Faith is to assent to the entire Word of God as it has been given to us. Many have debated as to whether this part really ought to be placed in the definition of justifying faith. But there are true and serious reasons why the definition was made up this way, and a consideration of them will teach us much. For justifying faith presupposes and includes general faith, which establishes with a sure conviction and without any doubt that the things revealed in the Word of God are absolutely true because God Himself is the Author, who is to be praised for His truthfulness because He is beyond all limitation. When this general foundation begins to vacillate, then the firm confidence in the promise of the Gospel cannot take root or be retained in time of spiritual struggle.

Justifying faith has many properties in common with general faith, in that it involves things which are not seen, that it does not rely on the judgment of our senses or a rational demonstration or proof, that it is not made up of things which can be comprehended by human reason, and yet is not a mere opinion but a sure conviction which has only the divine revelation in the Word as the cause of its certainty against the judgment of our senses and our reason and even against our own experience. These are obviously important reasons. There are others also.

The papists keep up a constant attack on our doctrine as if we were depicting faith as something partial, so to speak, which is not catholic because it is removed from the other articles of faith and the total Word of God, and is restricted to only that one part concerning Christ the Mediator, as if assent to the other parts of the Word of God were not necessary but a matter of choice. In order to refute this charge, we have put this declaration at the very beginning of the definition: We do not exclude the other parts of the heavenly doctrine when we say that the proper object of justifying faith is the promise of grace. But the sum, the end, the goal, and the boundary of all Scripture is Christ in His office of Mediator, Luke 24:27, 44; Rom. 10:4; John 5:39, 46; Ps. 40:7; Heb. 10:7.

Thus, when faith assents to the entire Word of God, it looks at the goal of all of Scripture and refers all the other articles of faith to the promise of grace for the sake of Christ the Mediator. As Augustine says, *On the Trinity*, 2, the Christian faith differs from the faith of the devils in the last articles of the Creed: "I believe in the forgiveness of sins, the resurrection of the body, and the life everlasting." In vain does faith concern itself with the other objects of Scripture if it does not hold firmly to the Head of Scripture, which is Christ, Col. 2:19. For this understanding it is correct to add these parts to the definition of faith. For the article of redemption cannot be solidly understood without preceding knowledge of the remaining parts of the Word of God. Yet it is to be firmly retained that faith justifies only with respect to that one object, which is Christ. It is necessary to add this reminder in discussing the general parts of the definition, so that the cause of our justification is not divided up among the other objects outside of the unique Object, Christ.

Besides the general statements, a special clause is put in the definition of justifying faith in order to remove the error of Apelles the Marcionite, which we have previously noted in the statement of Eusebius. For if this error or corruption in the other necessary articles or parts of the Word of God is permitted, there can be no true justifying faith. It is for this reason that Paul in Titus 1:13 requires "that they . . . be sound in the faith." And the ancients spoke correctly when they said that the doctrine of the faith is one connected unit.

These points about general faith are opposed to the dreams of the papists concerning implicit faith, wherein they say that we must assent to all the things that are brought in outside of and even contrary to Scripture under the title or pretext of traditions.

This clause shows the means through which faith is kindled by the Holy Spirit, nourished, preserved, and increased, namely the Word of God.

For these reasons I believe that this part has been correctly and usefully included in the common definition, as long as we add the reminder that the one and only object on which justifying faith lays hold is the promise of grace for the sake of Christ the Mediator. . . .

The second part of [Melanchthon's] definition describes the material principle, that is, the proper and principal object in which justifying faith seeks reconciliation, remission of sins, and eternal life. This can be nicely shown by listing the chief parts of the Word of God . . . namely the Law and the Gospel. But in that aspect of the Law which shows and condemns sin and which contains the divine threats, faith cannot seek grace and reconciliation. Nor can faith find grace in that aspect of the Law which commands obedience and contains the promises of reward for our works. For Paul expressly says in Gal. 3:12: "The Law is not of faith, but he who does them . . . "; Rom. 10:5–6, 10: "Moses describes the righteousness of the Law thus, that he who does these things shall live by them. But the righteousness of faith . . . believes with the heart unto righteousness"; Rom. 3:21: "The righteousness of God has been manifested apart from the Law"; again in v. 27: "Boasting is excluded, not through the law of works, but through the law of faith."

There remains, therefore, the doctrine of the Gospel, which instructs us concerning the twofold benefit of Christ, namely, reconciliation and sanctification or renewal. It contains the promise of the remission of sins, free reconciliation, adoption, and acceptance unto eternal life, for the sake of Christ the Mediator. It also contains the promise of the Spirit of renewal, who works in us both to will and to do, so that after we are justified we can also begin the new obedience. Therefore, because justifying faith seeks reconciliation with God, forgiveness of sins, adoption, and acceptance unto eternal life, it is manifest what the proper and principal object of faith is, namely, the promise of grace for the sake of the Mediator. In respect to this and by laying hold on it we are justified.

These things are confirmed by sure and clear passages of Scripture which establish that the object of justifying faith is not the Word of God in general, but the promise of the benefits of Christ the Mediator, Rom. 3:22, 26; 4:24; 10:9; Phil. 3:9; Acts 10:43; 13:39; John 3:15–18, 36; 17:3; 1 John 4:2, 15; 5:13, etc.

In order that this object of justifying faith may be set forth as in a well-lit place for our consideration, we must resolve questions about it through the use of analysis. I think the most expeditious way of doing this is to divide it up according to the article of the Trinity, as Scripture celebrates: (1) the grace, mercy, love, kindness, compassion, and blessing of God the Father; (2) all the benefits of the Son of God in His entire office of Mediator, in the incarnation, the crucifixion, the resurrection, ascension, and sitting at the right hand of the Father—all of which have wide ramifications; (3) the fact that the Holy Spirit sets forth these promises, offers, distributes, applies, and seals them by faith, through the Word and the sacraments, in the hearts of believers.

Then how many blessings come to us along with this object of our faith: free reconciliation, remission of sins, imputation of the righteousness of Christ, free acceptance before God, adoption, freedom from the law of sin and the Law, liberation from the curse of the Law, propitiation for our sins, salvation, eternal life, communion with God, the inheritance of life and salvation, peace, joy, and hope of the glory of God! These are the words of Scripture. When in this way the object of justifying faith is unfolded before us, the entire matter becomes clearer.

There must be a continuous progression from Sinai to Zion, so that the object of justifying faith does not become Epicureanism or, as Peter says, "a cloak for maliciousness" (1 Peter 2:16).

In the third part of [Melanchthon's] definition [of faith] we have a description of the formal cause or principle, namely, how justifying faith relates to its object. The answer is: not with a general or superficial assent or with some Epicurean persuasion, but in such a way that with a true and earnest desire of the mind, the will, and the heart, it desires, seeks, grasps, receives, and applies personally to individual believers the promise of free reconciliation for the sake of Christ the Mediator, so that it may find rest in it unto righteousness, salvation, and eternal life.

The papists quibble that we are borrowing from the Stoics a (*katalēpsis*), which Cicero calls a *comprehensio*, or a direct apprehension of something by the mind. But Scripture itself uses words which are extremely significant, e.g., John 1:5: "The darkness did not comprehend [*katelaben*] it"; vv. 11–12: "And His own received Him not. But as many as did receive Him, to them He gave power to become the sons of God, to those who believe in His name." Scripture uses three very important words: *elabon, katelabon, parelabon* [all meaning "received" or "took"]. Col. 2:6: "As you received (*parelabete*) Jesus Christ the Lord. . . ." Demosthenes explains that this Word means to take to oneself that which is offered or given by another. Compare Matt. 1:20 and 2:20, where Joseph is commanded to take to himself Mary and the child. John 17:8: "I have given them Your words, and they have received them and have known . . . and have believed." Rom. 5:11: "We have received reconciliation." V. 17: "To receive abundance of grace and . . . righteousness." Gal. 3:14: ". . . that we might receive the promise of the Spirit through faith" [RSV]. Heb. 9:15: ". . . that they might receive the promise of the inheritance."

Therefore this apprehension or acceptance or application of the promise of grace is the formal cause or principle of justifying faith, according to the language of Scripture. This is not all that Scripture says about faith, but it also describes how and by what impulses this apprehension or application takes place. Such an explanation is very useful, for an analysis or synopsis of these points will clarify the nature of the matter and, so to speak, the practice of justifying faith, and thus each person can determine whether he has true justifying faith.

Much of the quibbling of our adversaries can be refuted by dividing the matter up in this way. It is helpful to make even clearer the difference between true justifying faith and the idle or Epicurean opinion of those who think that in the midst of wickedness they are nevertheless acceptable to God without any conversion. I shall list the degrees of faith in a very simple way, as they are described in Scripture and discovered in the exercise of faith.

1. First, Scripture calls faith a knowledge or an understanding, Luke 1:77; Is. 53:11; Col. 2:3; Eph. 3:19. The decree and history of redemption, the gracious and universal promise that God for the sake of that Victim wants to receive sinners who flee to the Mediator in faith—these teachings are to be shown to faith and inculcated from the Word of God.

2. But because many who hear, understand, and know this either neglect or doubt or reject it, or are turned away and even persecute the faith, therefore it is necessary that to this knowledge be added assent, not indeed just a kind of general assent but that firm persuasion which Paul calls the full assurance of faith (*plērophoria*) whereby each person should determine that the universal promise applies also to him, personally and individually, and that he also is included and comprehended in that universal promise—that our Lord God thereby means me (*Dass unser Herr Gott auch meine Person damit meine*). The testimonies already cited prove this.

3. Then from this knowledge and assent in the mind, by the working of the Holy Spirit, the heart or will conceives a groaning or desire so that, because it feels very earnestly that it is burdened down with sins and the wrath of God, it wills, prays, and seeks that these benefits be given to it which are set forth in the promise of the Gospel. This desire burns within "with groanings which cannot be uttered" [Rom. 8:26 KJV], and it exercises itself in prayer, Rom. 10:13: "Whoever calls on the name of the Lord will be saved"; and "Forgive us our trespasses."

4. When in this way you turn away with your mind, your will, and your heart from looking at your sins and feeling the wrath of God and begin to look to the Lamb of God, who takes away the sin of the world, that is, when from the sentence of damnation pronounced upon you through the Law you flee to the throne of grace, to the propitiation the heavenly Father has set forth in the blood of Christ, it is necessary to add trust. With firm persuasion it concludes from God's Word that God gives, communicates, and applies to you the benefits of the promise of grace and that you in this way lay hold on and receive unto righteousness, salvation, and eternal life those things which the free promise of the Gospel offers. This trust struggles in time of trials with doubt, with the anxieties of a troubled conscience, even with sin, death, the devil, and hell itself.

[5.] Finally, from this faith there follows a confidence (*parrēsia*) which has access to God, Eph. 3:12; peace of conscience, Rom. 5:1; "the joy of the Spirit," Rom. 14:17, so that the heart, feeling the new life and joy in God, happily rests in the promise of grace, even under the cross, in persecution, finally in death itself; and it has an undoubting "hope of the glory of God," Rom. 5:2.

This is a somewhat rough analysis of "faith," yet it is simple and correct. Its use can be noted both in teaching and learning, but especially in the earnest exercise of repentance. I shall add a few brief points showing the use of this description.

1. We must understand that in these individual levels of faith God's "strength is made perfect in weakness" [2 Cor. 12:9 KJV]. For justifying faith is not always or in all people a brightly burning light; often it is a scarcely smoking flax. It is not always a loud noise, but often an obscure desire and a hidden groaning. Here this distinction is pertinent: There is a great faith, such as in the centurion and the woman of Canaan; there is a weak faith as in Matt. 14:31. Faith is strong and robust; it is weak and infirm, Rom. 14:1. This weakness may be in the area of knowledge, as when the apostles did not sufficiently understand several articles of faith; or it may be in the area of trust, Matt. 6:30; 14:31. Yet Scripture says that the smoking flax is not put out [Matt. 12:20], the groanings are unutterable, Rom. 8:26, that is, weak faith is still true faith, and it justifies.

We must note the foundations. For we are justified by faith, not because it is so firm, robust, and perfect a virtue, but because of the object on which it lays hold, namely Christ, who is the Mediator in the promise of grace. Therefore when faith does not err in its object, but lays hold on that true object, although with a weak faith, or at least tries and wants to lay hold on Christ, then there is true faith, and it justifies. The reason for this is demonstrated in those lovely statements in Phil. 3:12: "I apprehend, or rather I am apprehended by Christ," and Gal. 4:9: "You have known God, or rather have been known by God." Scripture shows a beautiful example of this in Mark 9:24: "I believe; help my unbelief."

2. We must note that these individual grades or levels of faith are not always equally brilliant in believers, but faith has more difficulty now on this level, now on that; and yet it is still faith, so long as it clings to the true object. For spiritual struggles, whether in the area of assent or in desire or in trust, are not signs of unbelief, but true marks of living and efficacious faith, which takes captive both the mind and the will in obedience to God.

3. We must not determine the status of our faith on the basis of our feeling of comfort or spiritual joy. Because this fifth level follows faith, it is not of the essence of faith; and God often takes away this feeling of peace from believers. But when the true object is firmly centered in the Word and when the predicted emotions follow, or at least the attempts and the desire, then there is true faith. These instructions have great value, so that we do not think of faith as some ideal state of perfection. . . .

In the fourth part of [Melanchthon's] definition we must explain in what subject justifying faith inheres. It is manifest that this is not an attitude or activity of the body but of the soul. We have said that faith is in the mind and in the will or heart. Here our adversaries, particularly Pighius, scream that faith is a monstrosity or something imaginary if it is located in only one particular subject but in several at the same time, such as the mind and the will, because things differing in their subjects differ in their nature or reality. We shall not engage in nitpicking as to whether and how the powers of one and the same soul, namely the mind and the will, differ as to their subject. Scripture simply attributes to the heart both trust and attitudes, and at the same time also knowledge. In Psalm 119 the man of God stores up things in his heart. Acts 8:37: "If you believe with all your heart . . ." Mark 16:14: "their hardness of heart." Luke 24:25: "slow of heart." Ps. 33:11: "the precepts of the Lord make glad the heart." Prov. 3:5: "Trust in the Lord with all your heart." Ps. 20:4: "the desire of your heart." Ps. 119:20: "My soul is breaking with longing." The Hebrew language does not have a special word for "mind" and "understanding." Therefore we can protect ourselves against this attack by the simplicity of Scripture and say that he who walks in simplicity walks in safety. But if someone tries to use technical language, the best answer is taken from what is perfectly clear: Whatever applies to the subject, the emotions, and the powers of the mind applies equally to the will, so that whatever the knowledge and assent are in the mind, there are the same kind of emotions in the will. . . . This question was recently under dispute among the scholastics themselves, such as Bonaventura[37] who asks whether faith is a cognitive matter or something which pertains to the emotions. He also says, "Because hope is defined as something which is a sure expectation, the question is asked, how does this fit in since certainty is in the mind and expectation is in the will?"[38] The answer is that both faith and hope, as is the case also with other powers, are located in the mental activity of man, as they call it when the intellect is joined to the appetitive part of man's makeup. And Bonaventura adds this rule: "There is no impropriety in placing one attitude both in the mind and in the will." Therefore this is a childish caviling which has already been refuted and exploded by the scholastics themselves.

The fifth part of the definition, which deals with the efficient cause of faith, must be added because faith is not a work of our nature or natural free will, but it is a gift and work of the Holy Spirit, who kindles, nourishes, increases, and preserves knowledge and firm assent in our mind and trust in our will. Also

---

[37] Bonaventura, *Sententiae*, Bk. 3, *dist.* 23, *art.* 1, *quaest.* 2, p. 463, Peritoni Ed., Florence, 1949.

[38] Ibid., 3.26.1.5, pp. 558ff.

pertaining to the efficient cause is the means through which the Holy Spirit works faith, namely the Word of God and the sacraments. For these two concur: (1) God offering, giving, and pouring out in Word and sacraments; and (2) faith apprehending and receiving, as has been said. When these two are joined together, then we truly have justifying faith.

Finally, in the definition we must also mention the final cause or goal of justifying faith, as Peter says in 1 Peter 1:9: ". . . the end of your faith, that is, the salvation of your souls." Rom. 10:10: "With the heart a person believes unto righteousness." Rom. 1:17: "The righteousness of God is revealed from faith to faith." Rom. 5:1, 11: "By faith we have peace with God through . . . Christ . . . through whom we have now received our reconciliation" [RSV]. John 1:12: "We are the sons of God." Eph. 1:7: "We have redemption . . . the forgiveness of sins." Eph. 3:12: "We have . . . access." Rom. 8:15: "We cry, 'Abba, Father.'" Heb. 11:5–6: We please God. Gal. 3:9: We "are blessed with faithful Abraham." We achieve all of these things through faith, through faith we possess them and through faith we retain them. Heb. 3:14: "We share in Christ, if only we hold the beginning of our confidence firm to the end." Therefore this part also pertains to the definition of justifying faith.

Let this be the analysis of the principal parts in the definition of justifying faith, which is not so complicated but simple and somewhat lacking in refinement, yet true and clear. It gives instruction in many respects and casts a great deal of light on these discussions.

But the papists contend that in the definition of justifying faith we must add this clause: Faith which has added to it hope, love, and the other virtues justifies. And since it is true that justifying faith is fruitful unto good works (for it works "through love," Gal. 5:6; is not "dead," James 2:17; and love comes from faith, 1 Tim. 1:5), the question is asked as to why this part should not be added to the definition.

The answer, however, is plain. It is one thing to speak of the parts which constitute the definition of justifying faith as integral or substantive parts, that is, things required for faith, or of which faith must consist in order to have the power to justify. It is another thing to speak of the fruits or the effects of faith; likewise, to speak of the marks by which faith is determined to be genuine and living. For there are three elements in faith: (1) the general assent; (2) the laying hold on Christ the Mediator, or the application of the promise of grace; and (3) the efficacy of faith through good works.

If the question is in what respect or by what power and strength faith justifies, then the scholastics reply that faith obtains this power and efficacy to justify from love, and this they call "the faith formed by love" (fides formata). But Scripture affirms that faith justifies because it lays hold on Christ and applies to itself Him "whom God made our . . . righteousness," 1 Cor. 1:30 [RSV]. Because the papists, in order to establish their notion about faith formed by love, contend that this clause which we have just mentioned must be added to the definition, it is absolutely correct not to add it when we set about to define justifying faith. If in our reading we find that these words have been added to descriptions of faith, as often happens, then we must add this explanation, that love is only an effect or a mark of justifying faith, and that it is not involved with justification as a part or a cause, that is, that faith does not receive from love the power or efficacy of justifying.

On the basis of this solution of the definition we can also evaluate those criticisms which Pighius makes regarding the different descriptions of faith which are found in the writings of our theologians. For it is obvious that for illustrative purposes our writers from time to time will emphasize one part of the definition of justifying faith above the others. But these statements are only passing remarks and not proper definitions. But because these points can be judged by careful analysis, I shall cite only those definitions which Pighius criticizes. This comparison of the different definitions will help to clarify matters.

Luther somewhere[39] says that faith is believing those things which have been divinely revealed and promised. In his formal statement he says that faith is that which believes that it has obtained grace in the absolution of the Eucharist, etc. In his work *Concerning Vows*[40] he says that faith does not apply to things past but only to the future. In his little book *On Faith and Good Works*[41] he says that faith is a lively thing, an opinion past all doubt by which a man above all certainty is sure that he is pleasing to God, that he has a God who is favorable toward his good works and forgiving toward his evil ones. In his *Christian Liberty* [*The Freedom of a Christian*, Amer. Ed., 31.361] he says that he who has faith is thereby free from the whole law and out of this pure freedom he does freely all the things which he does without any concern for his favor or his salvation, that is to say, he already is rich and saved by the grace of God through his faith, and he seeks only this one blessing of God. Pighius says that these statements contradict one another.

Pomeranus[42] in his Danish Church Order for Ordination defines faith as that by which we believe with certainty that Christ is our righteousness before

---

[39] Luther, *The Defense and Explanation of All the Articles*, or the *Assertio Omnium Articulum*, Amer. Ed., 32.44–45.

[40] We have not been able to locate this statement.

[41] We have been unable to find a writing with this title.

[42] Johann Bugenhagen, 1485–1558, Lutheran reformer. Officiated at Luther's wedding and preached at his funeral. Reformed the church in Pomerania, Denmark, Schlesuig, Holstein, and elsewhere.

God the Father, our sanctification, redemption, and eternal life; and He who has freed us from the Law, from sin and death, has established us under grace and caused us to know and worship the Father. Or faith is that by which we believe in the remission of sins through Christ, who was conceived, born, suffered, and was glorified for us. Or, again, faith is the trust whereby we lay hold on Christ in good conscience before God and we lay hold on the Father in Christ. Pighius really attacks this last definition in an unbelievable way.

Calvin says that faith is the firm assurance of divine benevolence toward us, the knowledge by which the truth of the free promise in Christ is revealed through the Holy Spirit to our minds and sealed on our hearts.

The Augsburg Confession, Art. 4 [Tappert, p. 30], says, "Men . . . freely are justified . . . when they believe that they are received into favor and that their sins are forgiven on account of Christ, who by his death, made satisfaction for our sins." And in Art. 5 [ibid., p. 31], "The Holy Spirit produces faith, where and when it pleases God, in those who hear the Gospel. That is to say, it is not on account of our own merits but on account of Christ that God justifies those who believe that they are received into favor for Christ's sake." The Apology [4.45, Tappert, p. 113] says, "This faith . . . when a man believes that his sins are forgiven because of Christ and that God is reconciled and favorably disposed to him because of Christ . . . obtains the forgiveness of sins and justifies us. In penitence and the terrors of conscience it consoles and encourages our hearts. Thus it regenerates us and brings us the Holy Spirit, so that we can finally obey God's law. . . ." Again [Art. 4.46, ibid.], "This faith is the true knowledge of Christ." Again [Art. 4.48, ibid., p. 114]. The faith that justifies, however, is no mere historical knowledge, but the firm acceptance of God's offer promising forgiveness of sins and justification. To avoid the impression that it is merely knowledge, we add that to have faith means to want and to accept the promised offer of forgiveness of sins and justification." Nor does it suffice for justifying faith to believe that sins are forgiven to a person and that for the sake of Christ he has received grace or to desire this, but it must also be received.

These are the definitions which Pighius criticizes as disagreeing [with one another]. I have written them down so that [his] insolent carping may be manifest, and because a comparison of these different descriptions, if properly done, has considerable value.

All these points will be clearer if we consider carefully the descriptions of faith cited here and there in Scripture. For example, in Rom. 4:20–21 faith is directed to the promise of God, and it does not hesitate because the promise was unbelievable, but gives glory to God with great assurance that He who had made the promise could also bring it to pass. Col. 2:2–3: "Faith is the knowledge of the mystery of God the Father and of Christ, because in Him are hidden all the treasures of wisdom and knowledge." In vv. 2 and 5 there is "assured understanding" and "firmness of . . . faith in Christ" [RSV]. 1 John 3:21, 19: Faith is trust toward God by which we persuade our hearts in the sight of God for the sake of the name of His Son. 1 John 5:10–11: Faith is to believe in the witness which God has borne concerning His Son, that in Him He has given us life eternal. 1 Peter 1:13 says that faith is to have strong hope in that "grace which is brought to us when Christ is revealed to us." John 1:12: Faith is to believe in the name of the Son of God. John 12:44: "He who believes in Me does not believe in Me but in Him who sent Me." John 17:3: Faith is to know the Father and that Jesus, whom the Father has sent, is the Christ. Is. 53:11: Faith is the knowledge of Christ as the servant of God, that is, obedient to the Father even unto death. Is. 26:3: Faith is knowledge that is strengthened and supported because God will preserve peace to those who hope in Him. Ps. 112:7–8: Faith is trust in the Lord whereby the heart is so prepared and strengthened that it is not moved. Eph. 3:12: Faith is the "boldness and confidence" whereby we come through Christ to God.

James gives us a double definition of faith, each, from a different standpoint. In 1:21, 18, and 6, faith is that which "in meekness receives the engrafted Word," that is, the Word by which we are grafted into Christ, "which is able to save our souls"; and it is this Word with which God by His kindness has begotten us. This faith without any hesitation can demand of God His blessings promised in Christ. But in 2:14ff. James describes faith from the standpoint of its effects, whereby it produces good actions.

The definition of faith in Hebrews 11 has earlier been noted and partly explained.

[CHAPTER III]: FAITH IS A SURE CONFIDENCE, CONTRARY TO THE POPISH DOGMA OF DOUBT

Luther says on Genesis 41 [*Luther's Works*, Amer. Ed., 7.155]: "It was a horrible blindness and an error which must be execrated by all means, even if there had been nothing else in the papal doctrine than the fact that they taught us to be unsure and to waver in indecision and doubt about our salvation. For this uncertainty removes from me my Baptism and grace."

Yet so enormous is the arrogance of our adversaries that even under the most brilliant light of the Gospel they do not hesitate in the public decrees of the Council of Trent to foist upon the church this pernicious and blasphemous dogma under the denunciation of the anathema.

These are their words [Session VI, Justification, Chapter IX]:

Although it is necessary to believe that sins are not remitted nor have ever been remitted except freely, by divine mercy, on account of Christ, nevertheless it dare not be said that sins are forgiven or have been forgiven to anyone who boasts of his confidence and certainty of the remission of his sins and relies solely on this, since it can happen among heretics and schismatics, yes, in our time it is happening, that this one confidence which is far removed from godliness is being preached with great contention against the Catholic Church. But neither is it to be asserted that those who are truly justified must without any doubt whatever settle in their own minds that they are justified and that no one is absolved and justified from sins except the person who confidently believes that he is absolved and justified, and that absolution and justification are wrought through this faith alone, as if he who does not believe this therefore doubted concerning the promises of God and concerning the efficacy of the death and resurrection of Christ. For as no pious person should doubt concerning the mercy of God, the merit of Christ, and the power and efficacy of the sacraments, so everyone, when he looks upon himself and his own infirmity and indisposition, can be in fear and dread concerning his own grace, since no one can know with a certainty of faith which cannot be in error that he has obtained the grace of God [*Proceedings of the Council of Trent*, Art. 11, Kramer trans., 1.549].

Again in [Session VI,] Canon 13, the council says:

If anyone says that it is necessary for every man, in order to obtain remission of sins, to believe certainly and without any doubt arising from his own infirmity and indisposition that his sins are remitted to him, let him be anathema [ibid., Art. 13, Kramer trans., 1.551].

We must carefully note the true point at issue in this discussion. For our people have in common with all other truly pious people the concern that true faith is often tried in the weakness of the flesh with great difficulty in believing, in often experiencing great doubt, and in being so weak and trembling in temptation that faith itself, by reason of its infirmity, needs the remission of sins. For we are not justified because of our faith (*propter fidem*), in the sense of faith being a virtue or good work on our part. Thus we pray, as did the man in Mark 9:24: "I believe, Lord; help my unbelief"; and with the apostles: "Lord, increase our faith," Luke 17:5.

We teach that the struggle with doubt must go on constantly, and we contend valiantly against the security of the flesh. Those who without conversion continue in their sins and devise for themselves a vain persuasion that their sins shall go unpunished we confront with the statements of Paul in 1 Cor. 6:9–10;

Eph. 5:5–6; and Gal. 5:19–21, which do not command such people to doubt whether they are in a state of grace, but thunder with a terrifying denunciation: "Make no mistake, do not let anyone deceive you with empty words . . . for I said to you before and I say to you now that those who do such things do not have a portion in the kingdom of God and of Christ." We carefully warn those who have been justified that they not abuse their confidence in the grace of God to establish carnal security and arrogance of the flesh, which we want always to be curbed and repressed by the bridle of the fear of God. Likewise, when we look not only at our weakness but also at our new qualities or virtues, we do not develop from this any confidence in our reconciliation before God. This is the arrogance condemned in the Pharisee. Indeed, we not only doubt our own powers but we openly confess with Paul in 1 Cor. 4:4: "I am not thereby justified," and with Isaiah in 64:6: "All our righteousnesses are as filthy rags" [KJV].

There is no controversy concerning these parts of this dispute about doubting. I have recounted them here because I see that the papists, in a callous and insidious manner, are mixing them into the argument in order to confuse the unwary reader.

The point at issue between us and the papists is that they teach that the sinner cannot and must not stand in sure confidence that he is in grace and that his sins have been remitted to him—even when in earnest repentance and true faith created in us by the Holy Spirit on the basis of the Word of God he lays hold on the promise of grace and at the same time upon the Mediator Himself, the Son of God who is our righteousness. To be sure, they say, he can and must have a strong hope for the good things promised him out of the mercy of God, and yet these things must be left without any sure confidence in the midst of fluctuating doubt. This doubt they include not among the sins and infirmities of our flesh but among the virtues of faith, so that unless this doubt is present to adorn and commend our faith, such trust is only the empty confidence of heretics and is not justifying faith.

But because they see that to believe and to doubt are diametrically opposed to one another and that Scripture speaks in an entirely different way about faith, they come up with the notion that faith in a general way establishes that the divine promises are true and that in a general way we are not to have doubt concerning the mercy of God, the merit of Christ, or the efficacy of the sacraments, but concerning the special application to individual believers, as to whether I who believe am a participant in those blessings, here faith must not establish anything certain even when it relies on the Word of God, but remains suspended in doubt.

Thus the Jesuits of Cologne say that faith is concerned only with general propositions, but the personal application pertains to hope. This new concoction they explain in this way: They hope resolutely and with courage for grace, remission of sins, and eternal life, but this is not a matter of belief. For faith is not able to fail, but hope may. When we hope we are in a state of uncertainty. Thus say these new academics.

These arguments of the papists arise primarily from confusion of Law and Gospel. For they teach that the grace of the remission of sins must be merited or at least applied to us by our works. Others, such as Pighius, try to be more subtle in their philosophizing and say that the blessings of justification are certainly free and are given to us out of mercy for the sake of the merit of Christ, but are given to those who dispose themselves in a worthy manner by contrition, love, and other virtues.

Thus they really teach only and totally Law, that is, that merit or at least the application of the remission of sins and eternal life to ourselves, depends on our own works. But because the conscience can never determine that it has sufficient works for the promise of grace to be merited or applied, not only does it remain in constant doubt, but finally in real agony it must take the route of despair. Because the Law requires works, whether for merit or for application, it always accuses and works wrath. Thus the Cologne theologians expressly say that since we cannot determine with certainty that we have correctly fulfilled all the conditions required for repentance, we must remain in perpetual doubt.

They contend so vociferously for this dogma because they realize that all the trafficking in popish business relies on this foundation. For the conscience that seeks some sure and firm comfort hears that faith itself, when it lays hold on Christ in the promise, ought to remain in a state of doubt and endlessly pile up all kinds of good works. Hence they have not been content with the divinely mandated works, but specially selected forms of worship have been thought up without end and without rhyme or reason, with the result that we have pilgrimages, invocations of saints, works of supererogation, the trafficking in Masses, indulgences, the selling of merits, and the whole morass of papistic superstitions. For consciences seek some certain and firm consolation, and when they see faith denigrated, they think that they will pile up so many kinds of works that if one kind does not help, then many kinds will. And when in its struggle the conscience does not find solid comfort in all of these, a purgatory is dreamed up and prayers for the dead are proposed. They are trying to institutionalize this horrible slaughtering of consciences and bring it back into the church when they carry on their attacks in favor of their dogma of doubt with such great contentiousness. They see that all these things will fall into disuse if faith in the promise of the Gospel finds and possesses a sure and firm comfort.

Therefore, because this battle is not an unimportant one but concerns weighty and serious matters, namely how consciences can possess sure and firm consolation, it is useful always to keep before us the chief points which surely and clearly demonstrate that justifying faith is not some wild dream and does not toss around in a sea of doubt, but is the trust and confidence that brings peace to the conscience, that is, sure and firm comfort for all who truly believe.

We also wish to note the main points in a brief way so that we can obtain strong and clear testimonies against the papists.

1. From the nature of the free promise. Confidence in our salvation does not rely on the idea that our own human reason by its own acumen can penetrate the heaven of heavens and scrutinize what has been concluded about me in the hidden counsel of God. For it is written: "Who has known the mind of the Lord?" Rom. 11:34 [RSV]. But it relies on this foundation that God, proceeding out of His secret light, has revealed His will to us in His Word, so that Paul does not hesitate to affirm in 1 Cor. 2:16: "We have the mind of Christ." Indeed, in the Law the will of God is revealed thus: "He who performs them shall live in them" [Rom. 10:5]; again: "Cursed is he who does not remain in all . . ." [Gal. 3:10]; and "He who . . . offends in one point is guilty of all" [James 2:10]. If we could attain eternal life through doubt, there would be no more appropriate promise than that of the Law. For because of the attached condition, namely perfect fulfillment, it leaves consciences in perpetual doubt; indeed, the Law finally drives them to despair, because it is "the ministration of death," 2 Cor. 3:7.

But because not doubt but faith justifies, and not he who doubts but he who believes has eternal life, therefore faith teaches the free promise, which relies on the mercy of God for the sake of the sacrifice of the Son, the Mediator, and not on our works, as Paul says in Rom. 4:16: "Therefore it is of faith, that the promise might be sure according to grace." Moreover, God has told us about this free promise not through angels but through the Son Himself, who is greater than any possible limitation to the promise, as it says in Heb. 2:2–3: "If the word spoken by angels was valid," etc. God confirmed that promise by various miracles and stupendous signs and wonders, certainly not so that we should be tossed about by doubt but so that with firm confidence I might be able to determine "not what I should think about God but what God thinks about me," as Luther says. That the free promise does not speak only in generalities but that it embraces the application to individual believers has been shown above. Heb. 6:17–18 has a long and beautiful statement which says that God in His free promise has confirmed His counsel "by an oath, that by two immutable things, in which it was impossible for God to lie, we might have a strong consolation, who have fled for refuge to . . . the hope that is set before us" [KJV].

The fathers have shed wonderful light on this statement for example, Augustine on Psalm 88 [*Enarratio in Psalmum 88*, MPL 37.1123] points out this progression: (1) God spoke; (2) He promised; (3) He established a covenant with us; (4) He confirmed it by an oath. The words of Augustine are these, "God said this; He promised this; and as if this were not enough, He swore to it." The statement of Tertullian is well known, "How blessed are those whose cause God has sworn to; how wretched we are if we do not trust Him when He swears it."

From this source, that is, from the free promise, many mighty arguments are created in opposition to the doubt of the papists. For to doubt concerning the promises of God is nothing else than calling God a liar. The uncertain mind which doubts His promises attributes very little to its faith, as 1 John 5:10 says: "He who does not believe God makes Him a liar." John is not speaking of general assent, because he adds: "I write this to you who believe in the name of the Son of God, that you may know that you have eternal life" [v. 13 RSV]. If I truly believe in the Son of God and yet doubt whether I have eternal life, it is certain that I do not believe this promise: "He who believes in the Son has eternal life" [John 3:36 RSV], but make God a liar.

2. From the nature of justifying faith many testimonies can be gathered. We have spoken above of the kind of activity faith is in the mind, the will, and the heart, and in what way it is the "substance" (*hypostasis*, [Heb. 11:1 KJV]) and the "full assurance" (*plērophoria* [Heb. 6:11; 10:22 KJV]) in knowledge, assent, and trust; so there is no need to repeat this here. In Heb. 11:1 [KJV] faith is also called the "evidence" (*elenchos*), a word in diametric opposition to doubt or uncertain opinion. It does not mean merely to show something with a degree of probability but to convince by arguments (*überweisen*) or, as Varinus says, to make manifest that which is indeed true but has been hidden or secret. Therefore the text says "the evidence of things not seen" [KJV]. The Greek scholia interpret this by the word *apodeixis* (proof, "demonstration" [1 Cor. 2:4]).

John deliberately speaks thus. 1 John 3:2: "We know that when He appears we shall be like Him" [RSV]; and in v. 14: "We know that we have passed from death into life." 5:13: "That you may know that you have eternal life . . . you who believe in the name of the Son of God" [RSV]; v. 19: "We know that we are of God." [Paul also speaks this way.] 2 Tim. 1:12: "I know whom I have believed." Most beautiful is the testimony in Rom. 8:38–39: "I am persuaded . . ." [KJV].

Pighius gets around this by saying that Paul is glorying in the certainty of his salvation, but he does not affirm that every believer in Christ has this kind of certainty. This is the grossest of slander, for Paul in this entire section is speaking in the plural. Thomas [Aquinas, ca. 1225–74] says that Paul had this certainty not because of the promise but because of a special revelation given to him. But Paul himself refutes this notion, for he says in Rom. 8:30: "Those whom He chose He also called." He also sets this forth as the foundation of his certainty, v. 34: "Christ died, yes was raised from the dead and, sitting at the right hand of the Father, intercedes for us." This is the very promise of grace.

Gal. 2:20: "The life I now live in the flesh I live by faith in the Son of God" [RSV], not by a special revelation. There are many statements like this. See 1 Peter 1:13: "Set your hope fully upon the grace that is coming to you" [RSV]. Heb. 3:6: "If we hold fast our confidence and rejoice in our hope to the end." Heb. 10:22–23: "Let us approach with a true heart in full assurance of faith . . . holding fast the confession of our hope without wavering."

In Heb. 6:19 he calls faith "the anchor of our soul, sure and steadfast." He adds the reason, that this anchor "enters the inner sanctuary behind the curtain," where Christ is, according to the order of Melchizedek. This is a lovely figure of speech, for an anchor, when it falls into sandy ground, cannot hold the ship firmly, but when it falls into a sea bottom which retains it firmly, then it cannot be dislodged. Thus, he says, the anchor of our faith has been cast into heaven itself, where Christ is our high priest according to the order of Melchizedek. Christ lays hold on, secures, and retains this anchor, as He says in John 10:28: "No one shall snatch them out of My hand" [RSV]. Phil. 3:12: "I apprehend . . . or rather I am apprehended."

These very lovely statements are cruelly corrupted by the papistic academicians. But Paul speaks thus in Rom. 5:1: "Justified by faith, we have peace . . ." And in v. 2 he says: "We stand in grace and rejoice in the hope of the glory of God." This certainly is not doubt. Particularly relevant here is Paul's statement in Rom. 4:16: "Therefore it is by faith . . . that the promise might be sure." He adds ". . . to all the seed," for the promise is sure in itself—our faith adds nothing to it, and our unbelief takes nothing away. But that the promise might be sure for both you and me, therefore it is by faith.

Again, if doubt were a virtue of faith, it would not only be in vain but would be ungodly to command that there must be spiritual struggles against doubt, nor would we be commanded to ask that our faith be increased or to pray: "Help our unbelief," etc. It is also a very strong argument against the papists that Paul in 2 Cor. 13:5 says: "Examine youselves, to see whether you are in the faith. . . . Do you not know that Christ is in you?—unless indeed you are reprobate." It should be diligently noted that he says that those who do not know that Christ is within them are reprobate. Here is pertinent the statement in 2 Peter 1:10: "Make your calling and election sure" [KJV]. Likewise: "The tree shall be known from its fruits" [cf. Matt. 7:16–20]. All of these statements are in error if the popish dogma of doubt is correct.

3. The strongest arguments against popish doubt are taken from the passages of Scripture which deal with the sealing of the believers through the Holy Spirit. Eph. 1:13–14: "After you believed, you were sealed with the Holy Spirit of promise, who is the Guarantee of our inheritance." 2 Cor. 1:21–22: "It is God who . . . has put His seal upon us and given us His Spirit in our hearts as

a guarantee" [RSV]. Eph. 4:30: "Do not grieve the Holy Spirit . . . in whom you were sealed for the day of redemption" [RSV]. John 3:33: "He who believes puts his seal on this, that God is true."

The emphasis of the words in these passages must be weighed carefully. It is beyond all argument that sealing is employed by those who want others, to whom it pertains, to be without doubt and as certain as they possibly can be. The term is not used to render doubtful and uncertain those things which are sealed, but that all doubt and hesitancy that can occur may be removed through this act of sealing. Thus in Esther 8:8 and 1 Kings 21:8 there is reference to sealing the letters of a king. And Isaiah, when he says, "Seal the Law among My disciples" [8:16], is certainly not asking that his disciples wallow around in doubtful and uncertain opinions regarding Isaiah's teaching. Most beautiful is the statement in Song of Sol. 8:6: "Set me as a seal upon your heart, as a sign upon your arm; for love is stronger than death . . . and many waters cannot quench love." John 6:27: "God the Father has sealed Him," that is, the Father has added to His Son the testimony, as if with letters and a sealing ring, that men shall have no doubt about His ministry.

This sealing by the Holy Spirit does not pertain only to a general faith, as the papists quibble, but Paul says that individual believers are sealed, as when Abraham received the seal of the righteousness of faith, so that he determined that the righteousness of faith before God was sure and ratified, not in a general way but for him personally. God for this very reason made use of the sealing of the Spirit, because "He knows our frame" [Ps. 103:14], that by nature such a great doubt clings in our minds that it does not wish either to approve or to confirm it when He shows us this seal, precious as it is, given through the Holy Spirit Himself. These points are clear and indisputable.

Another word is "guarantee," which is certainly Hebrew in origin. It refers to a pledge, a bond, or some kind of sign by which its issuing is ratified or confirmed, certainly not that there may be doubt but rather that the matter be regarded as something of unquestionable trust. This is a term for "hostages" in 2 Kings 14:14. In Gen. 38:17–18 it designates a "pledge" in the way Latin does, that is, a certain part of the price is paid as down payment, with the rest to be paid under a pledge.

This word shows the sweetest comfort. "We are saved, but in hope," Rom. 8:24. "We walk by faith, not by sight," 2 Cor. 5:7. In the meantime "they go forth weeping," Ps. 126:6. Lest for this reason we have doubts about God's will toward us, about grace, remission of sins, salvation, and eternal life, He has given us a guarantee, pledge, and down payment which is not an angel or some created thing, but the Holy Spirit Himself, who is consubstantial with the Father and the Son, so that we might be strengthened against all doubt. For because the

Father, the Son, and the Holy Spirit are one, as they cannot be divided or separated, thus no one shall separate us from the love of God, His salvation, and eternal life, Rom. 8:35. We are built upon the rock, Matt. 16:18. Therefore God wishes to render our faith sure and firm. It is a terrible insult against the Spirit of grace to defend the popish doctrine of doubt.

Lest the figures of sealing and of a guarantee might be somewhat unclear, the Spirit Himself gives us the obvious explanation. 1 John 5:10: "He who believes in the Son . . . has the testimony in himself" [RSV]. Rom. 8:16: "The Holy Spirit gives testimony to our spirit: that we are the children of God." 1 Cor. 2:12: "We have received the Spirit from God, that we may know what things have been given to us by God." Eph. 1:18: "Having the eyes of our understanding enlightened, that we may know what is the hope of our inheritance." Rom. 5:2, 5 gives us this wonderful statement: "We rejoice in the hope of the glory of God . . . because the love with which He loved us has been poured through the Holy Spirit into our hearts," so that from this we can gain firm and certain comfort.

4. The doctrine of the sacraments gives us highly persuasive arguments concerning the certainty of salvation for believers, counter to the doubt of the papists. it is certain that God has added to His gracious promise the institution of those signs which are called sacraments, not in order that through them the confidence of our faith might be weakened and rendered unsure and dubious, but in order that the weakness of our faith, which with the bare Word can hardly sustain itself "against hope . . . in hope" [Rom 4:18 KJV], might be raised up by the efficacy of the sacraments, as is so correctly said: "The sacraments have been instituted to strengthen our faith." Thus in Rom. 4:11 circumcision is called "a seal of the righteousness of . . . faith" [KJV]. In 1 Peter 3:21 Baptism is called "the answer of a good conscience" [KJV].

We are not discussing the certainty of the promise in only a general way in the use of the sacraments, but the application of this promise to the individuals who use the sacraments. Thus if doubt is a virtue of faith, the sacraments have been instituted in vain and are used contrary to a virtue of faith. These points are therefore so manifest that there is no need for more words among those who were correctly instructed in the basic principles of Christian doctrine. Godly people cannot fail to resist not only the violence done to this lovely comfort but also having the papists snatch it away altogether from consciences.

In regard to absolution, about which the Son of God so beautifully speaks: "Whoever's sins you remit . . ." [John 20:23], and "Whatever you shall loose on earth . . ." [Matt. 18:18], Gerson argues very correctly that absolution is not in the optative mood, but for the sake of certainty must be pronounced in the indicative mood. There is the prayer of Basil to be spoken before the reception of the Eucharist, where among other things he prays: "Grant that I do not receive this to my judgment, but as provision for eternal life and for a favorable defense before Your terrible judgment throne." John of Damascus prays thus: "Deign, O Lord, that I may receive this as a pledge of the life and the kingdom to come." If these statements are rightly considered, they show how full of blasphemy is the Babylonian dogma concerning the confused belief whose chief virtue is to be thrown into doubt.

5. Doubt is condemned in Scripture in plain words. Matt. 6:30: "O you of little faith." Matt. 14:31: "O you of little faith, why did you doubt?" Mark 11:23 and Matt. 21:21: "If you had faith and did not hesitate . . ." James 1:6–7: "Demand in faith, doubting nothing. For he who doubts is like a wave of the sea that is driven by the wind. Let that man not think that he shall receive anything from the Lord." Rom. 4:20: "He did not waver at the promise of God in unbelief." This should be diligently noted. The papists say that doubt is a virtue of faith, but Paul attributes it to unbelief (*apistia*). In Romans 14 Paul argues in many places that doubt is not only in itself a sin, but that it contaminates other works and makes them sins too. "For he who eats with a doubting conscience sins . . . for whatever is not from faith is sin," v. 23. He says that whatever a person does with a doubting conscience is "not from faith."

6. There are several clear testimonies from the ancients in which we can see that the popish dogma of doubt is a new adulteration of teaching. We shall only note, however, those in which can be seen that even in those times the same objections were raised against the confidence of faith which now are being raised in opposition by the papists. In regard to the objection of arrogance and pride Augustine says, Sermon 28, *De Verbis Domini*, "All your sins have been forgiven you. Therefore do not be presumptuous regarding your manner of life, but only regarding the grace of Christ. For 'By grace you are saved,' says the apostle. Therefore there is no arrogance here, but faith, to proclaim what has been received. It is not pride but devotion." Again, on Psalm 88, "God has said this, He has promised this; if that is not enough, He has sworn it. Therefore, because it is not by our merits but by His mercy that the promise is sure, no one ought with doubt preach about that of which there is no doubt." In regard to the objection that this causes pride, Augustine in *Tract. 22, in Johannem*, says, "It is necessary that we all stand before the tribunal of Christ, and will you dare to promise yourself that you are not going to enter into judgment? God forbid, you say, that I should dare to promise this to myself; but I believe the One who has made the promise to me, 'He shall not come into judgment,'" John 5:24 (Vulgate); "therefore I am not judged for my arrogance, but because of His promise I shall not come into judgment." Gregory of Nazianzus replies to these objections by quoting Joel and Jonah. He says this in his *Oratio Consolatoria in Grandinis Calamitate* [16.14, MPG 35.954], "Who knows whether he will be converted,

and then change his mind and lose the blessing? I know this clearly that I have the guarantee of divine clemency." Bernard beautifully replies to the statement of Solomon which is always used in opposition by our adversaries, Sermon 5 *In Dedicatione Ecclesiae* [MPL 183.533], "'Who then can be saved?' said the disciples. And He replied, 'With man it is impossible, but not with God.' In regard to the possibility we are already certain, but what shall we do about the will? Who knows if he is worthy because of his love or his hate? Who knows the feeling of the Lord? At this point it is clear that faith must support us, that truth must help us, so that what lies hidden from us in the Father's heart may be revealed to us through the Spirit, and the Spirit in bearing witness may persuade our spirit that we are the sons of God, and He persuades us by calling and justifying us freely by grace through faith." Again, *De Fragmentis Septem Misercordiarum*, Sermon 3 [MPL 183.344], "I believe that there are three areas in which my entire hope rests: God's loving adoption, the truth of His promise, and the power of His return. My poor weak mind murmured at how much it wanted, saying to me, 'Who are you, or how much glory do you have, what have you done to merit what you hope for?' But I reply in confidence, 'I know whom I have believed, and am certain that He adopted me in great love, that He speaks truthfully in His promise, that He is powerful in demonstrating what is to come.' This is a triple cord which is difficult to break, which has been sent from our Father's home down into this prison, and if we hold on to it firmly, it will raise us up, draw us onward, and carry us along until we see the glory of our great God."

Finally we must add also this point. The scribes in Matt. 9:3 accused Christ of blaspheming in the support of this doctrine, because He promised unconditional remission to the paralyzed man and ordered him to "be of good confidence," that is, of a good and peaceful mind. And the *Historia Tripartita* Bk. 9 [8.9 CSEL 71.487] says that the error of the Novatians was their belief that "we should indeed invite the lapsed to repentance, but remission of sins must be left entirely in the power of God." Ambrose, *De Poenitentia* 1.2.6 [MPL 16.487] says, "The Novatians say that they reserve to God alone the power of remitting sins. But Christ commands His disciples to loose sins." And in ch. 6 [ibid., MPL 16.497], he says, "I have forgiven you in the person of Christ . . . 2 Cor. 2:10." And in 2.5 [MPL 16.527–28] he says [that the Novatians point to Acts 8:22, where Peter says], "Repent . . . if perhaps the iniquity of your sin might be forgiven you." They say that in this passage Peter is not affirming with certainty that their sins will be remitted to those who repent. Ambrose replies that Peter spoke this way because Simon Magus did not believe with a true faith, but was only thinking in terms of wickedness. And with regard to this passage Ambrose says, 'I do not say that Peter doubted, nor do I believe that so important a matter should be cut off by the judgment of one word. For Christ also says Matt. 21:37,

'Perhaps they will reverence my son.' And in John 8:19 He says, 'If you knew Me you would have known My Father.' Nor could Peter doubt concerning the gifts of Christ, who had given him the power to remit sins. . . ." These points must be noted in order that it can be demonstrated from which errors the papists get their notion of doubt. But there is also another little book under the title and name of Ambrose, *De Exhortatione ad Poenitentiam*, where he says, "When a person does penance, does he gain complete security from this? I am not sure. I can do penance, but I cannot give a guarantee. I do not say such a person is damned, but I do not say he goes free. I do not presume, I do not promise, indeed I do not know anything certain about the will of God. Does He forgive you, or does He not forgive, what shall happen to you?—these things I do not know."[43] These statements are clearly contradictory to the statements which we find in the books of Ambrose regarding repentance. Therefore these spurious books have been interspersed among the writings of the fathers in order to impose [errors] on the unsuspecting under the appearance of antiquity.

These are the main points from which we can draw and construct the confirmation of the truth and the refutation of error in this controversy.

We also ought to note the points which the adversaries use to tear down the certainty of faith, so that we may have firm and immovable refutations before us, because by the use of the antithesis the correct understanding is more brightly illuminated and a good opportunity is given to explain the objections more fully.

Before we speak about the passages of Scripture which the adversaries use, we shall summarize their objections under certain headings, so that it does not become necessary to repeat the same things under each of the individual points.

[1.] In the first place, they put together many of their arguments from the teaching on humility, the fear of God, the recognition of our weakness and unworthiness. They speciously expand on these points and try to show how dangerous it is if without proper consideration and acknowledgment of our own unworthiness and (as they say) indisposition we proceed into the presence of God. They also talk about how pleasing a virtue it is to God that we have true humility of mind, without which there can be no true faith.

But the true and simple answer to this is taken from the distinction between Law and Gospel. For the imaginings of the adversaries have their origins in the idea that God has indeed promised grace, salvation, and eternal life, but that this applies only to those who are worthy either by merits or by attitude. But because

---

[43] We have not found this.

the Law always accuses us and convinces us of our unworthiness, nothing can follow from this teaching but perpetual doubt.

We not only grant this, but we say more. If in the matter of justification we look at the promises of the Law, which have the condition of perfect fulfillment attached to them, there must not only be doubt about our salvation, but there must be absolute despair. For Paul says in Rom. 8:3: "It was impossible for the Law," etc. And in Gal. 3:10: "All who rely on works of the Law are under a curse" [RSV]. Of the works of the regenerate Paul says, not doubtfully but categorically, 1 Cor. 4:4: "In this I am not justified." Of the Galatians he says in Gal. 5:2, 4: "You have fallen from grace. . . . Christ is of no profit to you . . . who want to be justified by the Law."

For this very reason the promise of the Gospel was revealed, as Paul says in Rom. 4:16: "Therefore it depends on faith by grace, that the promise might be certain to all the seed." This is the true solution.

But they say: Is not your faith then without true humility? I reply: True faith always has humility attached to it, which comes from the earnest recognition of our own unworthiness, as it says: "Whoever humbles himself will be exalted" [RSV], Matt. 23:12; Luke 14:11; 18:14. But this humility does not cast doubt over our faith or cause it to waver, because it does not keep the conscience in the Law so that it sets its view of its own worthiness against the judgment of God. Rather, it impels and urges it to seek another promise, in which, for the sake of His Son the Mediator, the Father freely gives to believers the benefits of reconciliation. And because man cannot find in himself that on which he can safely rely in the face of God's judgment, he lays hold on that Mediator in whose wounds there is firm and safe security for those who truly believe, as Bernard says. Therefore true humility does not tear down faith, but brings it about that faith seeks more eagerly the confident assurance of the gracious promise, lays hold of it, retains and protects it all the more firmly, and does not allow anyone to take it away.

Thus the humility of our faith is far more notable and genuine than that which the papists brag about. For their humility opposes the judgment of God with their own worthiness. And because it sees some weakness in this worthiness, it only doubts but does not plainly reject that notion, and therefore does not flee to the free promise. But even though it doubts and also fears, yet it continues to hope with respect to its own worthiness. But the true humility which Scripture proclaims recognizes its own unworthiness and considers that in no way would it dare to bring this before the judgment of God when it comes to justification. Rather, before the judgment seat of God it despairs totally of its own worthiness, works, and attitude, and it seriously determines and openly confesses from the heart: "Do not enter into judgment," not only with the ungodly

but also "with Your servant, because in Your sight shall no one living be justified," Ps. 143:2.

Therefore faith does not cling, either with assertiveness or with doubt, to
its own worthiness or attitude; but outside itself, in Christ, it seeks the true
righteousness which it can safely place in opposition to the judgment of God.
Thus Scripture does not speak doubtfully but exclusively when it says: "He has
saved us, not of ourselves, not by works of righteousness which we have done,
but freely, through grace, according to His mercy, for the sake of the redemption
in the blood of Christ" [cf. Titus 3:5]. Thus it is false when the papists boast of
their humility, which doubts whether the things are true which Scripture with
such great emphasis proclaims concerning our unworthiness, namely that of
ourselves, by our own works, we cannot be saved. These are true and clear fundamental points, from which many explanations can be taken.

2. Many things are proclaimed about the presumptuousness of the Pharisees.
Our adversaries say that it is intolerable pride and arrogance for a most wretched
sinner, who is terribly corrupted in many ways, to assert without any hesitation
that he is an heir of eternal life.

The answer to this is easy. If our confidence relied upon our merits, works,
or right attitude, then they would be correct in what they say. But to be in doubt,
as the papists teach, as to whether or not we can stand on our good works before
the judgment of God, this smacks of Pharisaism. For Paul in Rom. 10:3 says:
"They sought to establish their own righteousness before God." But because our
confidence relies on God's free promise and the merit of Christ, Scripture speaks
in a far more appropriate way. Cf. Jer. 9:24: "Let him who glories glory in this,
that he . . . knows Me" [RSV]. Likewise Rom. 5:2: "We glory in the hope of the
glory of God." It is certainly not Christian modesty to accuse God of lying in
His promise of grace, as John says in 1 John 5:10, or to doubt the value and the
worthiness of the sacrifice of the Son of God, as the Academics do. Therefore,
with respect to ourselves, we are the lowest of the low, but with respect to Christ
the Mediator and the free promise, we have confidence and boldness; indeed,
we even boast.

3. They cry that by our doctrine carnal security is fostered and confirmed,
and men cease to be concerned about repentance when they are persuaded that
they can be certain about their salvation. Likewise they assert that many who
live profligate lives and continue in their iniquities have arrogated to themselves
this certainty of eternal life, etc.

The answer to this is that we must keep the precept of Paul about "rightly
dividing the Word of truth," 2 Tim. 2:15 [KJV]. For we do not put these comforts
before the impenitent; indeed, we do not speak to them in a hesitant manner, but
as Paul says in Eph. 5:5; Gal. 5:21; 1 Cor. 6:9–10; Col. 3:5–6. But to those who

thus recognize their sins, so that they feel the wrath of God and in faith flee to the throne of grace, we propose, with Scripture, not doubt but faith.

Because in believers there is the flesh and the Spirit, the old and the new man, the encouragements must always be inculcated in believers that they not misuse the promise of the Gospel to establish the security and insolence of the flesh, according to Paul's statement in 1 Cor. 10:12: "Let anyone who thinks he is standing take heed, lest he fall."

Therefore the faithful Christian, when he looks within himself at his own flesh and sees the great temptations he has because of his security and pride to drive out his faith and tread the Spirit of grace underfoot, then he surely must in the fear of God restrain, repress, and even crucify and put to death his flesh with its lusts and set before himself statements such as 1 Cor. 10:12: "Let anyone who thinks he is standing . . ."; Phil. 2:12: ". . . with fear and trembling." This fear of God does not tear down or drive out the trust and assurance of faith; but this impels it, that faith may not be lost or destroyed but may firmly cling to the promise of grace. When the believer, by the leading of the Spirit or the new man, looks up to Christ and the promise of grace, then he does not doubt or tremble, but glories, Rom. 5:2. "I am persuaded . . ." Rom. 8:38 [KJV]; "God is faithful . . . who has begun . . ." 1 Cor. 1:9 and Phil. 1:6.

These statements are plain and true. And the objections give us an occasion to show how this doctrine is to be "rightly divided," so that it can be presented with fruitfulness.

4. Our adversaries also say that the universal experience of all the godly conflicts with our doctrine. For all people feel great doubt. They even pretend that those who are weaker in faith are upset by this teaching and are driven to despair. For when in times of temptations, in great weakness, their faith becomes even more listless, they cannot feel a sure and absolute certainty and think they do not have true justifying faith; and because "without faith it is impossible to please God" [Heb. 11:6], nothing else can follow than complete despair.

In response to this we say that also this objection gives us an opportunity to make a useful and necessary declaration. We are not speaking of a certainty of faith which is a kind of Platonic idea, which in the weakness of the flesh is not at all tempted by doubt, which languishes in no weakness, feels no trepidation, where there is never any difficulty in believing. For as long as we live in this flesh, the flesh will always contend against the Spirit, who is also the Spirit of faith, and in this warfare the flesh often seems to prevail, as Paul says in Rom. 7:23: ". . . bringing me into captivity" [KJV]. In 2 Cor. 1:8 he says: "We were . . . unbearably crushed" [RSV].

But these things are not of the nature of faith, much less the virtue of faith, but they pertain to the statement in Rom. 7:18: "In my flesh dwells no good thing." Likewise, v. 21: "When I want to do good, evil is always present with me." Faith does not boast of these blemishes before God, as if they were virtues, but it acknowledges that faith itself, insofar as it is considered a work or a virtue, is not perfect; and it seeks to have these faults washed out of the flesh by faith, covered and forgiven. Nevertheless, because of the object which this weak faith lays hold on, it has a sure and certain comfort, as we have said above in discussing the weakness of faith.

But, you ask, since this is the case, why do you promulgate this doctrine of certainty? I reply: that they may learn that doubt is not to be indulged, but we are to fight against our doubt and uncertainty, and whatever has become weak, so that we may always strive for certainty and not allow our confidence to be driven away. Indeed, in order that this sluggish faith may have sure and firm comfort in the very midst of its infirmity, God has set forth the remedies of the Word, the sacraments, and prayer, cf. Mark 9:24; Luke 17:5. Indeed, "The Spirit aids our infirmities," Rom. 8:26, so that faith can prevail and "the smoking flax not be quenched," Is. 42:3.

If doubtfulness were a virtue, there would be no need for this struggle, no remedies would be placed before us to strengthen our faith. In order that in the midst of this weakness faith may still have sure and firm consolation, Paul is accustomed to speak like this: "I apprehend, indeed I am apprehended," Phil. 3:12; "I know God, or rather I am known by Him," Gal. 4:9.

The points the papists are accustomed to make can just about be reduced to these headings. We shall now examine those passages of Scripture which the papists cite in favor of their doctrine of doubt, and we shall briefly show the sources from which they can be explained.

1 Cor. 10:12: "Let anyone who thinks that he stands take heed lest he fall" [RSV]. Phil. 2:12: "With fear and trembling work out your salvation." Rom. 11:20: "Do not become proud, but stand in awe" [RSV]. Prov. 28:14: "Blessed is the man who fears the Lord always." 1 Peter 1:17: "Pass the time of your sojourning here in fear" [KJV].

To these statements there is the general response: They are warning against degenerating into carnal security by which faith itself would be suffocated and extinguished, or against indulging in wicked passions under the delusion that we are certain of salvation. For unless by faith we remain in the goodness of God, we shall be cut off, as were the Jews, Rom. 11:20. Faith does not remain in those who without repentance indulge in wicked passions. Therefore these statements are not proclamations in favor of doubt, but exhortations that we do not allow our faith to grow drowsy in idleness, to go to sleep, and thus finally be extinguished, but that it be always exercised in the struggle against the flesh, which must continue in anxious fear, lest it forfeit grace and the Holy Spirit. This is the correct answer.

Then Scripture always inculcates and places before the eyes of believers their weakness, unworthiness, and many faults, not in order that it may cast doubt or uncertainty upon their faith, but so that believers do not become insolent because of confidence in their gifts. The recognition of their weakness is to instruct them so that they do not depend on their gifts but totally on the Lord, and it should impel them to cling more ardently and vigorously to the mercy promised for the sake of Christ.

They pile up many statements from the ninth chapter of Job. V. 28: "I feared all my works" [Vulgate]; v. 20: "If I would wish to justify myself, my mouth would condemn me"; vv. 30–31, "If I be washed with snow water . . . You shall plunge me into filth"; v. 15: "Even if I were innocent, yet I would make supplication to my judge." Prov. 20:9: "Who can say, 'My heart is pure'?" Ps. 19:12: "Who can understand his sins?" Jer. 17:9: "The heart of man is corrupt . . . who can know it?" James 3:2: "We all offend in many points." Luke 17:10: "When you have done all these things . . . you have only done your duty." 1 Cor. 4:4: "I am not thereby justified." Ecclus. 7:5: "Do not justify yourself before God." To all these passages there is one brief and plain reply: With regard to the righteousness of the Law or of works it is true that consciences can never thereby have certain and sure comfort but will remain in perpetual doubt. Indeed Paul says, not doubtingly but expressly: "I am not thereby justified." Indeed the Gospel is set forth for this reason, that the promise might be by faith, that it might be according to grace, that "the promise might be sure" [Rom. 4:16].

Eck [Luther's opponent, 1486–1543] had the practice of citing the statement in Ecclus. 5:5: "Do not be without fear about sin forgiven" [Vulgate]. Thus, he said, even after remission has been received we must still be in doubt. There is a fallacy in this form of speech, for Sirach has "Do not be without fear about pardon" (*peri exilasmou mē aphobos ginou*), which has been translated: "Do not be without fear about forgiveness of sins." The monks had put a gloss in the margin which said "about sin forgiven." This Eck seizes upon. But Sirach clearly explains himself, for he says in the preceding [v. 4]: "Do not say, 'I have sinned, and what harm has befallen me?'" and in the verses which follow [vv. 5–6]: "Be not without fear . . . so that you add sin upon sin because you say 'the mercy of the Lord is great.'" The passage is a warning against carnal security, and the meaning is that we should not foster security or pile up sins without repentance, just because forgiveness of sins is set before us. Or, do not be so secure that you put off reconciliation; but if you have been dominated by sins, you should make haste to become reconciled. Thus Sirach is saying nothing at all about doubt.

There remains that oft-repeated statement in Eccl. 9:1–2: "The righteous and the wise and their works are in the hand of God, and man does not know whether he is worthy of love or hatred, but all things are kept uncertain for the future." Therefore [they say] in this life believers are uncertain whether they are under God's love or His hatred, but this will only be made manifest in the coming age.

But this passage does not read this way in the Hebrew, the Greek, in Jerome's translation, nor among the ancient writers who commented on the Book of Ecclesiastes. The sense is entirely clear. For the author adds this because things turn out equally for the righteous and the ungodly, for the good and the evil, that is, we must not and cannot determine on the basis of the outcome whether we are pleasing to God. But it does not follow, because we cannot make a determination from the outcome, that therefore faith on the basis of the Word of God must remain uncertain.

In another place in the same book [3:19] there is this statement: "The spirit of man is mortal, just as the spirit of beasts." He is saying that on the basis of external events it is impossible to know whether the spirit of man differs from that of an animal, because the death of both is the same. Bernard explains: Reason of itself cannot know this, but faith, the truth of the Word of God, and the Spirit help us. And so in the same chapter Solomon soon says: "Your works are pleasing to God" [9:7].

But what is more horrible than to doubt whether the crimes of the Sodomites are displeasing to God! And how could the martyrs bear their atrocious torments if they had to be in doubt as to whether they were under the love or hatred of God?

Finally, when all their other bastions have been captured, they take refuge in this, that they say that in regard to present grace there can indeed be certainty, but no one can be sure whether he will persevere to the end. They cite Augustine, *The City of God*, Bk. 11, ch. 12 [MPL 41.328]: "Although they are certain of their reward for their perseverance, yet those who are unsure are pressed down concerning their perseverance. For what human being knows that he will persevere unto the end?"

Reply: It is manifest that many do not persevere but fall from grace. But this is not because God does not will that believers, whom He at one time received into grace, should persevere unto the end, but it comes from the fact that many drive out the Holy Spirit and trample their faith underfoot. And looking at the traps of the devil, the evil of the flesh, and the frightful examples of those who have lapsed, we ought to disintegrate with fear and trembling for our salvation. But when we look at the will of God revealed in the Word, and at Christ the Mediator, we can and must declare: "Who shall separate us? . . . For I am certain

that neither . . . things present nor things to come . . . shall separate us . . . ,"
Rom. 8:35ff. We have been called to fellowship with Christ, not in order that
He would again want to reject those whom He has received. But He is our ever-
lasting Savior. We are called to eternal fellowship with Christ. He is the eternal
Father, and the gifts and the calling of God are without repentance on His part.
"No one shall snatch them out of My hand" [John 10:28]. Therefore, as it pertains
to God, the perseverance of the godly is sure; and because it has been revealed
in the Word, faith must believe this.

But Paul says in Rom. 11:22: ". . . if you continue in the goodness of God";
Heb. 3:14: ". . . if only we hold our . . . confidence firm to the end" [RSV]. I
reply: John says: "I write this to you . . . that you may know that you have eternal life. . . . But we know that when He appears we shall be like Him" [1 John
5:13; 3:2 RSV]. Phil. 1:6: "I am persuaded that He who has begun the good work
in you . . ." Likewise 1 Cor. 1:8. And David says in Ps. 31:1: "Let me never be
ashamed." Therefore we are commanded to pray for perseverance, because God
has promised it. Prayer always requires a promise in order that it may have no
cause for hesitancy, James 1:6. But we pray and struggle that the pride of the
flesh not stifle the gift of perseverance. This distinction will help in understanding the question of perseverance.

[F.]: THE WORD "GRACE"

[MELANCHTHON'S TEXT]

*Even the philosophers saw that outstanding virtue cannot exist without divine
motivation, as in the case of the bravery of Alexander, which they believed was caused
by divine impulse. Following this idea, the monks understood grace only in the sense
of new virtues or powers stimulated by the Holy Spirit. When it is said that we receive
the remission of sins through grace, they interpreted this to mean that remission is
received on account of these virtues. This interpretation is in direct conflict with Paul.
Likewise in regard to faith or trust in Christ, or trust in the free imputation, they had
nothing to say. Their notion was in large part a philosophic concept and obscured the
benefit of Christ and the doctrine of free imputation. Therefore the word "grace" in
the true, correct, and proper sense of the word means much more than this.*

*In Romans 5 there are two terms: "grace" and "the gift through grace." "Grace"
is the free remission of sins, or mercy, or free acceptance. "The gift through grace,"
then, means the giving of the Holy Spirit and eternal life, that is, the new and eternal
righteousness and life which begins here in this life and is brought to completion hereafter. This is the way John speaks in 1:17: "The Law was given by Moses, but grace
and truth came by Jesus Christ" [KJV]. Here also "grace" means the free remission of
sins, or acceptance for the sake of the Mediator. "Truth," then, is the true light, that*

is, the true knowledge of God, true and eternal righteousness and life, which begins in this world but is completed hereafter. This is said in regard to the entire benefit of Christ, as if to say: You have indeed heard the Law, but it does not take away sin nor the blindness in our minds, that is, the doubts concerning God and our raging against God as our Judge. Likewise, the Law does not bring true and eternal righteousness, but only the outward discipline which dies with us, which is not eternal or durable or perpetual righteousness.

But through the Messiah these marvelous gifts are given: first, grace, that is, the free remission of sins and the imputation of righteousness. Then also truth, that is, the true light, the knowledge of God, and true and eternal righteousness and life. Therefore, although the word "grace" means the remission of sins or the free mercy of God, yet we also confess that the gift of the Holy Spirit is added, and with a clear testimony we condemn the error of Pelagius, who absolutely did away with the distinction between philosophy and the Gospel and devised the notion that in philosophy men could also without the Holy Spirit satisfy the law of God, that this outward discipline is the righteousness of the Gospel, and that there is no need for the gift of the Holy Spirit. We condemn these ravings because it is a certainty that there is a need here for the beginning of the new and everlasting life, which cannot take place without the Holy Spirit, as the heavenly voice cries out over and over again in the Gospel and the prophets.

Therefore let this be the definition of "grace": Grace is the remission of sins, or the mercy promised for the sake of Christ, or the free acceptance which necessarily accompany the giving of the Holy Spirit.

Nor is it difficult to judge regarding this word, whose Hebrew usage is known. The Hebrew word often means "favor," at times also "gift." Now I shall add some testimonies which bear witness to the fact that "grace" in this context refers particularly to free mercy or free reconciliation. Rom. 4:4: "Now to him who works, his wages are not reckoned according to grace." Here Paul clearly understands "grace" in the sense of free benevolence or imputation. For it is an antithesis: For those who work, there must be wages, but "to the one who believes," even if he brings no merit, nevertheless there is the free imputation of righteousness.

In the same way it is said later on: "It is from faith . . . according to grace, that the promise might be sure" [v. 16], that is, that the reconciliation might be certain. It does not depend on the condition of our own worthiness, but it is freely given. For if you judge that you have remission only if you are worthy and pure, then endless doubt and despair will follow.

Rom. 6:14: "You are not under the Law but under grace." Here Paul is dealing with this very thing, that we are pleasing to God for the sake of His Son, not because of our worthiness, since indeed great weakness and sin still cling to the regenerate. Therefore "grace" means the free mercy promised because of the Son.

Rom. 5:20: "Where sin abounded, grace did much more abound" [KJV]. Although sin has been condemned by the frightful wrath of God, which no creature can understand adequately, yet grace abounded, that is, the mercy promised for the sake of Christ, by which remission comes to us, along with reconciliation and grace, is much greater, that is, God wills that we trust in the promised mercy. Therefore we must not understand this passage as referring to our virtue or our obedience, in which we surely must not put our trust.

Likewise it says in Heb. 4:16: "Let us . . . come boldly unto the throne of grace, that we may obtain mercy and find grace to help in time of need" [KJV]. He understands the throne of grace to be the Mediator Himself, as though he were saying: "the throne which placates the wrath of the Father."

Since the Hebrew expression is well known to the learned, there is no need for a longer discussion. But this we must very diligently consider, that the exclusive particle "freely," often repeated by Paul, is included in the definition of grace. This exclusive particle means that reconciliation is given for the sake of the Son of God, the Mediator, and not because of our worthiness, not because of our merits, not because of our virtues or deeds. To be sure, this particle does not exclude the virtues themselves, but it does exclude them as a condition for worthiness or merit, and it transfers the cause of reconciliation solely to the Son of God. In Peter's confession [John 21:15–17] there had to be repentance and faith, by which a person knows that he is forgiven, and it is necessary that these virtues follow; and yet the proposition is true, and must be retained, that our sins are forgiven freely, that it was not because of Peter's virtues that his sins were forgiven, but because of the Son of God.

Because the correct understanding of this exclusive particle is so important, I shall set forth four reasons why we must retain and defend this matter. First, in order that the honor due to Christ is given to Him. Second, that the conscience may retain its sure and firm consolation, and the pestilential error of those who command us to doubt be destroyed. Third, that true prayer can be offered. Fourth, that the distinction between Law and Gospel may be observed. I shall discuss each of these causes briefly, so that we may keep them in mind at all times. Each of them must be carefully considered.

The first is this, that the honor due to Christ be given to Him. Those who transfer the cause of the remission of sins from Christ to our works sin doubly: (1) They mitigate the wrath of God and sin; and then (2) they take away from the Son of God the honor due Him. For human blindness and self-security do not understand the enormity of the wrath of God against sin, and therefore this blindness imagines that this wrath can be assuaged by human discipline. Thus it embraces Christ as a teacher of this discipline, or as a legislator, but not as the Sacrifice for sin, although John the Baptist cries: "Behold, the Lamb of God, who takes away the sin of the world!"

[John 1:29]. And Isaiah says: "He gave His soul as an offering for sin, and He shall see His seed."

The second reason is that the conscience may have sure and firm consolation. Paul also teaches this in Rom. 4:16: "Therefore it is freely by faith . . . that the promise may be certain." This statement will be much clearer to the person who is undergoing the genuine struggle of a terrified mind. We know from the Law and from natural reason that God is good and merciful, but toward those who are not guilty. Therefore in true anxiety the mind does not ask whether God is merciful, but this is the torment of the struggle: whether He will forgive you who have been contaminated by sin and guilt, and for what price. Here it is necessary to hear the voice of the Gospel concerning the exclusive words and the Mediator, that God really wants to receive you freely, that is, not on account of your worthiness or merits, but for the sake of the Son of God.

This we must believe. If the exclusive words are ignored, doubt is strengthened; that is to say, if you think that your sins are not forgiven unless you have enough worthy contrition or love, doubt will cling to you, which sometimes produces contempt for God and at other times hatred and despair. This can easily be determined by godly people. For even if doubt is innate in the minds of men, yet we must know that we are not to have doubt about our reconciliation for this reason: The Son of God has brought from the bosom of the eternal Father the clear and sure promise of reconciliation, to be put in opposition to the judgment of human reason, as it says in John 1:18: "The Son, who is in the bosom of the Father, He has made Him known to us."

Therefore doubt is to be rejected and faith must be encouraged, the faith that God truly wills to receive you for the sake of His Son and to hear your prayers. We must refute the impious error of our adversaries, who in their ignorance of the Gospel, and following only the judgment of human reason, command us to doubt; and they imagine that doubt is not a sin. This pernicious error must be removed, for it is surely a sin not to accept the promise. Likewise it is a sin not to attribute to God, when He makes this promise, the praise He deserves for being truthful, as John says in 1 John 5:10: "He who does not believe God makes Him a liar." It is the height of blasphemy to despise the voice which sounded from heaven: "Hear Him," Matt. 17:5.

The third reason arises out of the previous reasons and concerns prayer. We must distinguish between the prayer of the heathen and that of Christians. The heathen pray, but they are in doubt as to whether God respects and receives them and their prayers. So in the poems there are frequent complaints that those who are struck by calamities are not noticed or heard by God. But in true sorrow, when the mind flees from an angry God, as Saul did, it surely does not call upon Him. On the other hand, the Gospel teaches the kind of prayer in which faith shines forth. And even if your unworthiness disturbs you as often as you begin your prayer, still faith looks to the Son of God, the Mediator, and assures you that your prayers are received for *the sake of that High Priest, as it is written: "Whatever you ask the Father in My name He will give you" [John 15:16]. Again: "Through Him we have access to God" [Rom. 5:2; Eph. 2:18].*

Such prayer is proper for the true church but absolutely unknown to those who do not know the doctrine of free remission or of this exclusive particle "freely," of which Paul repeatedly speaks. Thus also Daniel prays in 9:18: "We do not pray in our own righteousness but in Your great mercy," for the Lord's sake. We do not wish by means of this exclusive particle to say more or teach anything different from what Daniel says. There are many examples in the Psalms which speak so sweetly to the godly, if we understand them as referring to free reconciliation. "With the Lord there is mercy" [Ps. 130:7]. If you add "toward the worthy," or "toward those who are sufficiently meritorious," that will be the voice of the Law striking terror. But if you understand this Psalm according to the Gospel, as Paul teaches and the psalmist feels—mercy receiving us freely for the sake of the Mediator—then this word brings comfort and calls the fleeing soul back to God and encourages it to true devotion.

The fourth reason is that we may clearly see the distinction between Law and Gospel, for even though the Law has a promise, yet it does not freely promise the remission of sins or reconciliation or imputation of righteousness, but pronounces only him righteous who offers complete obedience and is without sin, as these passages show: "Cursed is he who does not continue in all the things which are written in the Law" [Deut. 27:26; Gal. 3:10]; "He who does these things shall live by them" [Lev. 18:5; Gal. 3:12]. But the Gospel shows us the Son of God, the Mediator, and it proclaims to us that reconciliation is freely given to us for His sake.

Therefore the particle "freely" causes a very great difference between the Law and the Gospel. If this is lost, a great darkness must come over the Gospel. For as soon as the notion crept in that remission was given for the sake of our works—by the admission of this error the doctrine of faith, of the true honor of Christ, and of sure consolation of consciences went to ruin.

I have explained how important it is to retain the exclusive terminology, but we must also see that it is correctly understood. For when Paul says, "We obtain remission freely, by faith, for the sake of Christ," he does not thereby want to say that there should be no contrition in those who are converted or that the other virtues should not follow. Indeed, he wants them to be present. But he excludes the condition of our merit or worthiness; he denies that our contrition and virtues are causes for reconciliation, and he testifies that the real cause is the merit of Christ the Mediator. The meaning is that reconciliation is freely received by faith for the sake of the Son of God, and not for the sake of our own worthiness. These statements are clear, true, without any sophistry, and they contain nothing complicated, nothing intricate.

Nor are our theologians trying to say anything else when they say that we are justified by faith alone than what I have just said, namely that we attain the remission of sins freely, by faith for the sake of Christ, not by our own worthiness. Nor does the particle "alone" (sola) exclude contrition or the other virtues, as if they should not be present, but it denies that these things are the causes of reconciliation, and it transfers the cause to Christ alone. We must understand these expressions as being correlative: By faith (fide), that is, by our trust in Christ, we are righteous. In other words, we are righteous for the sake of Christ—freely, that is, not because of our own worthiness. We must believe this in order that we may lay hold on the benefit of Christ and find our rest in the mercy which has been promised for the sake of Christ.

Now I shall add some testimonies from Paul, showing that this is truly the doctrine of the Gospel which I have set forth concerning justification, namely that we must be sure that for the sake of the Son of God we freely, by faith, attain the remission of sins and are accounted as righteous, accepted by God unto eternal life. Further, it is beneficial for us to have these testimonies before us not only in order to refute our adversaries, but much more to strengthen ourselves and to build up our faith in all our invocation. For God particularly requires this worship and this work. This worship gives true honor to the Son of God, namely when we invoke God for the sake of this Victim and this Placator, and believe that through this High Priest our prayers are carried to the eternal Father.

In Romans 3 the substance of this discussion is treated in many words: "All have sinned and fall short of the glory of God. But we are justified freely by His grace through the redemption which is in Christ Jesus, whom God has set forth as the Propitiator, through faith in His blood" [vv. 23–25]. At the beginning, in order that he might show that men are not righteous by their own purity, he says: "All are guilty and fall short of the glory of God," that is, the wisdom and the righteousness which God approves or considers as His glory. Then he goes on to add how we are to be reconciled, when he says that we are justified, that is, we attain the remission of sins and are accounted as righteous, or are received freely by His grace, that is, by His free mercy for the sake of Christ, whom God set forth as a propitiation. He adds that we are justified "in His blood," that is, the wrath of God is assuaged through the death of His Son.

But this benefit must be applied by faith. You must understand that for the sake of this Propitiator, and for the sake of His death, God is favorable toward you, not because of your own worthiness. This faith is the trust or confidence which brings peace and life to our hearts, as we have said above in regard to faith; and it finds its rest in Christ.

Then Paul in Romans 4 undertakes to confirm this proposition and cites testimonies and arguments. The first testimony is taken from Gen. 15:6. In order to show that this has always been the doctrine of the church, he quotes the very first statement in existence regarding the method of justification, written by Moses. He also refers to that man who is set forth, in order that from him others may learn the promises and the true worship of God: "Abraham believed God, and it was imputed to him for righteousness" [Rom. 4:3].

But here, before I add other arguments of Paul we must refute certain criticisms by those who try to escape Paul's statements. For there are many profane men who treat Paul with contempt and cry that he is using irrelevant statements to support his position, and twisting them either through ignorance or sophistry, and for this reason they do not honor either Paul's writings or his authority. But these ungodly judgments arise from their own ignorance. Since they do not understand the struggles of faith that occur in the midst of real anxieties, it is not to be wondered at that they do not see how suitable are the statements from Paul here cited.

People are accustomed either to hate or proudly to condemn what they do not understand. But the pious know the voice of the apostle as the voice of God, which sounds from heaven and must be heard. They know that Paul is not playing tricks or speaking falsely but understands his own position and explains it correctly. They also know that the doctrine of Paul agrees with the writings of the prophets. Let us be the disciples of the apostles, not their detractors.

Moreover the adversaries, in order to escape the passages concerning faith, devise their own interpretation and say that there is a synecdoche here for the fides formata, as they themselves put it, that is, a faith that has joined to it various virtues that agree with its profession. Thus they understand faith as historical knowledge, and in reality they believe that man is not righteous by faith but by these other virtues.

But that this synecdoche conflicts with Paul himself can clearly be shown. For Paul over and over again repeats the particle "freely," that he might show that we do not achieve reconciliation because of our own virtues but for the sake of the Mediator. Thus he says "by faith" in order to urge us to keep our eyes on that Mediator and to convince us that for His sake and not because of our virtues we are the sons of God. These words clearly conflict with the synecdoche of our adversaries.

Further, their synecdoche yields endless doubt. You please God if you have sufficient merits. But also this doctrine of doubt is in clear opposition to the teaching of Paul: "Justified by faith, we have peace with God" [Rom. 5:1]. Doubt brings hopelessness and hatred of God.

We have said these things by way of prefacing the other testimonies, because in them is expressly contained the exclusive particle "freely," refuting the synecdoche. Likewise, we have mentioned that faith conflicts with doubt. Nor have we made up any interpretation for Paul, but we retain the proper meaning of his language, not subjecting the literal word to criticism or fanaticism, having studied the entire argument, having compared all the epistles of Paul, having compared even the sayings of the prophets, and finally having compared the judgment of the true church as to how it understood the doctrine of the remission of sins and the exercise of faith.

Our adversaries admit that they depart from the words, because they say that "by faith" means "by faith which is formed," that is, not by faith but by other virtues; and they brag that they know the "mind" of Paul. But since their interpretation is without doubt opposed to Paul himself, it has to be removed and repudiated; for every sophistry must be removed from our whole life, and especially from the doctrine that deals with God. Therefore let us in good faith retain those teachings that God has given through His prophets and apostles, and we shall properly and precisely explain them.

What can be said that is plainer and simpler than this? Even if there must be repentance in our hearts, yet we must firmly hold that we are received by God not on account of our virtues but for the sake of the Son of God, the Mediator, and that in this way we please God. What is so absurd about this statement? It demands that good works be present, and yet it transfers the cause of our reconciliation over to Christ, it attributes to Christ the honor due Him, and it shows pious hearts their firm consolation. On the other hand, the interpretation of the adversaries contains many obvious errors.

It embraces two absurdities: It commands men to be in perpetual doubt concerning the remission of their sins, and in the meantime it says that men earn remission by their own worthiness. Thus it takes away from Christ the honor due Him, and the conscience is left in doubt. This is clearly a heathenish notion. For there is no difference between Paul and Atticus, if both have equal doubt as to whether God regards them or hears their prayers; indeed, the adversaries say repeatedly that this doubt is not a sin. Further, they say that the regenerate are righteous by reason of their own worthiness, and that sin is not that inner darkness of the mind, doubts about the providence of God and reconciliation with Him, or the stubbornness of the heart which fears only a little bit, which does not love God with the warmth that it ought to have, and which has many erring desires and wicked thoughts. These things they extenuate, and even dare to say that evils such as these do not conflict with the law of God.

Therefore, since this synecdoche contains such manifest errors, let us leave the interpretation of our adversaries and return to Paul. Let us skillfully hold to the literal word and learn the doctrine of the remission of sins and of faith from Paul himself, and not bring in human notions of our own. In these arguments of Paul we shall understand the refutation of that synecdoche.

In Romans 4 Paul gives the most important argument in this area, and he takes it from these very sources: If the promise of reconciliation should depend on the condition of the Law as its cause, it would be uncertain. But it is necessary for this promise to our consciences to be certain. Therefore it is necessary that there be a free promise of the remission of sins and reconciliation, and that it be received by faith and not because of our own merits.

Paul's major point is that "the Law works wrath" [Rom. 4:15], that is, since no one can satisfy the Law, the Law accuses us all, and thus our conscience must always be in doubt and fall into despair, if it has to believe that we can be received by God only after we have satisfied the Law. Now although secure and idle minds are not moved by this argument, yet in true terrors of conscience we confess that we are guilty. Therefore it is necessary to hold to the idea of free reconciliation, as Paul says: "Therefore it is of faith, freely, that the promise might be certain" [Rom. 4:16].

He stresses the particle "freely" in order to refute that very synecdoche. You have the remission of sins freely, not because of your fulfillment of the Law, as the synecdoche says. Indeed, you cannot arouse any love for God unless you first by faith are assured that the wrath of God has been placated, as it says in Rom. 5:2: "By faith through Christ we have access to God." The subject matter shows that in this argument that synecdoche is refuted.

Furthermore, you will observe that the same passage teaches that by "faith" is meant not only the knowledge of the historical facts, such as the devils possess, but the assent whereby we believe the promise, and the confidence in God's mercy offered in the promise. For He commands that the promise be received by faith, and He commands that you be sure that God truly wants to forgive you and receive you, and He urges you to believe this, and by this faith to invoke Him. Such faith is not only the knowledge of the history or the commandments, which only brings greater terrors to our souls, as James [2:19] correctly says regarding this knowledge: "The devils . . . believe, and tremble" [KJV]. They know the Son of God but do not accept the promise; indeed, they are tormented with horrible fear of the judgment to come.

Eph. 2:8: "Freely you have been saved, through faith, and this not of yourselves; it is the gift of God, not of works, lest anyone should boast." Clearly he is excluding our worthiness and affirming that we have been reconciled by faith. Therefore we must not allow this statement to be corrupted by that synecdoche, but insist that the apostle means what he says, namely that by faith for the sake of Christ we have been received into grace.

Gal. 2:16: ". . . knowing that man is not justified by the works of the Law but by faith in Jesus Christ; and we have believed in Christ Jesus, so that we are justified by faith in Christ and not by the works of the Law."

Various people try to get around these statements with various sophistries. Some say that only the ceremonial law of Moses is excluded, and others admit that justification by works is taken away from the unregenerate. But these cavilings can easily be refuted by sane and godly people who love the truth. For sane people must agree that neither the ceremonial law nor the moral law, whether the works precede or follow regeneration, merit the remission of sins.

Finally, although we have brought together many statements concerning faith, such as "Justified by faith, we have peace . . ." [Rom. 5:1]; again: "With the heart we believe unto righteousness" [Rom. 10:10], and others of this kind, the adversaries contend that all of these have been spoken incorrectly and imprecisely, and they dream up an interpretation out of their own human reason. But we, having gathered and compared all the passages of Paul dealing with this dispute, and the testimonies of the prophets, judge that Paul meant what he said: By faith we human beings are accounted righteous, that is, for the sake of Christ the Mediator we receive remission of sins and reconciliation, by confidence in the mercy promised for His sake, and not because of our own worthiness.

Then, to make the matter even clearer, we also teach that when our hearts are in this way sustained by the voice of the Gospel and are raised up by faith, they receive the Holy Spirit, as Paul says in Gal. 3:14: "That we might receive the promise of the Spirit through faith." Therefore we are not talking about some idle knowledge, and those who are inexperienced make a mistake in thinking that the remission of sins comes to the idle, without any emotion of the soul, without struggle, without trust which comforts the soul.

Since the Holy Spirit in this work of giving comfort brings new desires and a new life, this conversion is called "regeneration," John 3:5, and it is necessary that obedience follow, as I will say later.

When the conscience seeks the remission of sins, questions about predestination should be laid aside. For just as the preaching of repentance pertains to all people, so the promise of grace is universal and brings reconciliation to all. At this point it is helpful to keep before us some of these universal statements, so that we truly include ourselves in them and understand that God truly wants to forgive also us, to hear our prayers, and to receive us. Matt. 11:28: "Come unto Me, all you that labor. . . ." John 3:16: ". . . that whoever believes in Him should not perish." Acts 10:43: "To Him all the prophets give testimony, that through His name we receive the remission of sins, all who believe in Him." Acts 13:39: "In Him everyone who believes will be justified." Rom. 3:22: ". . . the righteousness of God through faith in Jesus Christ in all and upon all who believe." Here the particle which refers to universality is repeated, so that we may know that this did not accidentally escape the writer. Rom. 10:11–13: "Whoever believes in Him shall not be put to shame. For there is no difference between the Jew and the Greek, for the same Lord of all bestows His riches upon all who call upon Him. For everyone who calls upon the name of the Lord shall be saved."

"God has consigned all under disobedience, in order that He might have mercy on all," Rom. 11:32. This is the way we should also understand the statement: "God wants all people to be saved," 1 Tim. 2:4. But we are not to judge otherwise concerning the will of God than the Gospel teaches, which has been brought from the bosom of the eternal Father, that the will of God may be revealed clearly to us. We must also carefully consider that it is the universal mandate of God that all should hear His Son, as He says: "Hear Him," Matt. 17:5, and that all should believe the promises *of God. If a person wishes to explore this subject, he will come to understand that salutary doctrine and comfort have been given to godly people.*

Concerning free will we have said elsewhere that since in conversion our will must be moved by the Word of God, this Word must certainly be heard, and since with the Word of God the Holy Spirit does His work, raising up and helping our hearts, we are to sustain ourselves with faith. Nor should we idly indulge in mistrust or other vices against conscience, nor trouble the Holy Spirit, but rather give assent to the Word of God and follow the Holy Spirit. In this spiritual struggle we feel that our will in contending against doubt and other vices is not idle.

Paul instructs us about this very thing when he says in 2 Cor. 6:1: "We entreat you not to receive the grace of God in vain." He wills that the Gospel be heard, He wills that we assent to it and follow it, not indulging ourselves in wickedness contrary to our conscience. Furthermore, in Luke 11:13 it says: "He will give the Holy Spirit to those who ask Him." It does not say, "to those who spurn Him, or grieve Him, or resist Him." Therefore He wills that we struggle with our infirmities. He wills that we acknowledge our sins and seek deliverance, that we do not cling to them contrary to our conscience. Thus the will is not an idle thing.

I have set forth the doctrine of the Gospel concerning the remission of sins and reconciliation or justification, as correctly and properly as I could. I have no doubt that this is the thinking of the learned fathers, even though from time to time they spoke with unfortunate language. There is nothing complicated, nothing puzzling, nothing tricky, nothing sophistic in this statement which I have dealt with, or in our explanation of the subject. For what more simple statement can be made than that man receives the remission of sins and reconciliation for the sake of Christ the Mediator, by faith, that is, by trusting in the promise of God's mercy for His sake and not because of our human virtues? This statement is easy for all pious minds to understand and judge in the true exercises of repentance and in daily prayer, which could not take place if faith did not look to the Mediator for whose sake our prayers are heard. Therefore I call upon the judgment of the church, that is, I address it to godly people, learned and intelligent, in their struggles with repentance and prayer.

[CHAPTER I]: THE WORD "GRACE"

Here again we must deal with a linguistic explanation, for it is very important in our teaching of the heavenly doctrine. The Holy Spirit, with singular wisdom, did not wish in the article of justification to use terms taken from the common usage of people, but many terms are of such a nature that they are neither used nor known with this meaning in other kinds of speech, but are idiomatic, proper, and peculiar to Holy Scripture. Just as the content in this article is not known to human reason, so also the words are peculiar; in fact, I might call them sacred, not secular or commonly used.

I believe this is the case for two reasons: (1) that the very words might instruct us that there is a difference between the doctrine of the church and the opinions of philosophers, based on reason, regarding justification. Nor should we be surprised that our human reason recoils at the heavenly doctrine of the righteousness before God, since the very words show that there is a mystery here, something placed far above and beyond the purview of human reason. (2) The Holy Spirit wanted not only the contents of this article but also the terms themselves to have a special meaning, distinct from philosophical language, so that no similarity or relationship between the terminology would give occasion for confusion or intermingling of the ideas themselves, that is, that the very names of things might serve as warnings that the ideas of philosophy must not be mixed in with the article of justification and that we must seek no conformity or reconciliation between these two kinds of teaching.

The true light of this article was lost when the vocabulary began to lean toward the philosophical meaning of the terms. And the purity of the doctrine was restored in this way, that the words were once more recalled to the source, the Word of God, and separated from the philosophical usage. I am mentioning these things in order that no one will despise this linguistic care, for it is so necessary that without it the sound teaching on this locus cannot be preserved. The adversaries at the present time are doing especially this, that when they do not dare openly to corrupt a word, they little by little turn it to another meaning. Thus the "Formula of the Interim" insidiously plays with the word "grace."

Therefore we shall divide our treatment of the word "grace," in keeping with our practice, into various parts.

First. It is useful for the sake of instruction to cite certain examples which show how in various ways the genuine meaning of the word "grace" was always corrupted, and what corruptions followed from this in the article of justification.

In order that we may learn as much as possible from the Pelagian controversy, we point out that Pelagius, in the early stages of this controversy, imagined that "grace," in the writings of Paul in the article of justification, meant the goodness of nature, that is, the gifts bestowed on human nature at birth. The word "grace" to some degree lent itself to this interpretation, because "grace" means that which is given to us and bestowed on us by God without any preceding merits. And because before we existed we could not deserve even to exist, it is correct that grace be called a blessing of the article of creation.

He [Pelagius] amplified this in a brilliant sermon in which he stated that we were created, without any preceding merits, that we might not be like a corpse which has no life, nor like a tree which has no feelings, or an animal which does not have intelligence, but as rational human beings who have been endowed with powers of the mind, the will, and the heart. To this concept he applied the statement of Paul in 1 Cor. 4:7: "What have you that you did not receive?" [RSV]. Augustine quotes this idea of Pelagius in his Epistle 95 (177), *Ad Innocentium* [MPL 33.765ff.] and again in 105 and 106 [*ad Paulinum*, MPL 33.815]. Erasmus in his *Hyperaspiston.*[44] says that it also redounds to the glory and praise of God if by the powers of free choice the unregenerate contribute something in their actions toward their salvation, because these things also are gifts of God and included under grace.

Augustine rightly says that the good in our nature can properly be called "grace," because it is given by the free goodness of God without merits, especially because after the Fall God wanted something of those natural gifts to remain in this depraved nature. Concerning this blessing we ought to give thanks to our Creator. But we do not read, says Augustine, that this gift is called "grace" in any legitimate writings of the prophets, evangelists, or apostles, for it is common to all who use their reason, whether ungodly or godly. Indeed, these gifts of nature are often more brilliant in the ungodly than in the godly, as is written in Luke 16:8: "The children of this world are in their generation wiser than the children of light" [KJV]. Likewise Luke 10:21: "These things have been hidden from the wise and revealed to babes."

But grace is attributed unto salvation only to the godly and believers. Likewise Paul says that grace is given in Christ and for the sake of Christ. Furthermore, Christ did not die for those who did not exist, in order that they might be created, but He "died for the ungodly" [Rom. 5:6]. Therefore it follows that Christ died in vain if by our nature and condition we have that grace by which Paul says we are saved.

Augustine, *De Verbis Apostli*, Sermon 11 [26.12, MPL 38.176], says, "If it is grace that we were created when we merited nothing, how much more is it grace that although we merited only evil we were saved freely through His grace!" This statement of the apostle, "What do you have which you did not receive?" (1 Cor. 4:7), Augustine proves must not be understood as referring to natural gifts but to spiritual ones, for Paul adds in the same verse, "Who makes you different from anyone else?" That is, who singles you out from the common mass of mankind and makes you more outstanding? We must note this, because the adversaries treat this statement of Paul in an entirely Pelagian way with regard to the natural powers of our will.

Later on, when Pelagius saw that his notion regarding the good in our nature as being common to both the ungodly and the godly could not be defended from Scripture with even the appearance of probability, he began to change himself

---

[44] His *Diatribe Against Luther*, 1526. Clericus edition of Erasmus's works, Hildesheim, 1962, Vol. 10.

into another form and say that the grace of God in Christ Jesus, by which we are justified and saved, consists only in this, that since human reason by nature did not know the counsel and decree of God, He Himself came out of His secret dwelling place in light and revealed His will to us in the Law and in Scripture. But when this grace of divine revelation had been given and received, then human beings by the powers of their own nature can apply themselves both to believing and doing the things set forth in Scripture. Thus Vitalis says to Augustine in Epistle 106 [MPL 33.816–18], "God works in us to will only to the extent that He has revealed His will to us."

Pelagius was able to give this opinion some appearance of credibility. For in Rom. 1:5 Paul says with regard to the ministry of the Word: "We have received grace and apostleship." And the doctrine of the Gospel is called "the Word of grace," Acts 14:3; 20:24. Chrysostom even interprets John 1:16 ("We have received grace for grace") to mean that the first grace was the giving of the Law, as it says in Ps. 103:6–7: "Showing mercy the Lord . . . made known His ways unto Moses" [Vulgate]. The later grace is the revelation of the doctrine of the Gospel. Pelagius at least could plausibly enlarge on what an immeasurable blessing of God it is that in the great darkness and blindness of our minds He has kindled for us the light of His Word, in which He reveals the true teaching concerning His being and His will, a benefit of God which Psalm 103 along with others gratefully celebrates. But finally, as the dog returns to its vomit, Pelagius held that man can by his own natural powers do what he has learned from the Word and by nature fulfill the good that he needs for salvation.

Therefore, did Christ die so that the Law might be promulgated on Mt. Sinai? To be sure, "the Law . . . was in the world," Rom. 5:13, but because it could not take away sin, it was necessary that the Son of God die, so that through Him we might receive grace unto life everlasting. And so that this grace might be shown to us, therefore Scripture was given, and therefore the Gospel is called "the Word of grace."

In this way Pelagius philosophized about grace. But the scholastics and now the papists argue that this grace, by which we are justified and saved in Christ Jesus, is a supernatural gift bestowed by God upon man, by which the mind is enlightened and the will is healed, so that man can now produce love toward God and his neighbor with the perfection required in the commandments of God.

And this they call "grace which makes a person pleasing" (gratia gratum faciens). They imagine that man, because of this new, inherent conformity with the law of God, has remission of sins and is acceptable to God unto eternal life, without making any mention of trust in Christ the Mediator. Indeed, they do not even consider this grace as completely acceptable to God. For they say that

Christ merited for us only the first grace, and that our free will, aided by that first grace, can elicit from us the attitude of love toward God and our neighbor, and that through this attitude men are righteous and saved before God.

Thus says Bonaventura [1221–74]: "Sin is a deprivation, but a deprivation is not removed except through filling the void with a *habitus* (right attitude). Therefore, just as sin, that is, the deprivation, displeases God and causes us to displease Him, so the new attitude pleases God and causes us to please Him. And they are anxious in this dispute to determine whether grace is indeed the same thing as this attitude of love, or whether they really have to be distinguished.

Thomas [Aquinas, ca. 1225–74] and Richard[45] say that certain people receive grace because of the blessing and the free love of God by which He chooses men, calls, adopts, and justifies them. And they admit that Paul does speak this way about grace in Eph. 1:6–7. But yet they prefer the other meaning of which we have just been speaking, embrace it, and give it their approval. We shall speak later regarding the true foundations of this teaching, but for the moment we are only citing opinions.

The Jesuits of Cologne do not hesitate to affirm that it is the grace of God in Christ Jesus by which we are justified and saved, that is, that God has promised those who observe His law that He will give them eternal life. And they say that it is grace because the master in Luke 17:9 owed nothing to his servants who worked for him, but that he gave to them only out of his grace. This new sect of the pope entirely takes away the whole Gospel. The Law is not a doctrine which contains the promise of eternal life under the condition of an imperfect fulfillment of the Law. Therefore what is the purpose of the Gospel? What does this statement mean, "We are not under the Law but under grace?" Thus Paul's axiom will be false in Rom. 4:4, "To one who works, his wages are not reckoned as a gift but as his due."

I wanted to cite these statements as examples of the corruption of the word "grace." What horrendous perversions in the article of justification follow the misuse of this word is shown by the doctrine of Pelagius and the Roman Antichrist.

Second. In order that the matter may be even clearer, we must note the division in the terminology, as the dialecticians speak. For just as the benefit of Christ bestowed upon believers is twofold, namely reconciliation and renewal, so the word "grace" sometimes means the free benevolence of God, which receives believers for Christ's sake unto eternal life. Sometimes it means also the very gifts of renewal through the Holy Spirit. Rom. 12:6: "Having gifts differing

---

[45] Richard of St. Victor, d. 1173. Pupil of Hugo and supporter of Becket in his conflict with Henry II of England. Contended against the use of Aristotle in theology; influenced Bonaventura.

according to the grace that is given to us . . ." [KJV]; 1 Cor. 15:10: "The grace of God . . . toward me was not in vain, for I worked harder than any of them."

We must take a thoughtful look at the meaning of the word "grace" with reference to the article of justification, that is, in such passages as: "We are justified by grace," Rom. 3:24; "We are saved by grace," Eph. 2:5, 8; Acts 15:11. It is certainly true that both are benefits of Christ, that both are given to believers, and it is also true that no one is reconciled to God who at the same time is not renewed. But the question is: What is that grace by which we are justified and saved? For the source and origin of many of the errors under this locus is the fact that these meanings were not distinguished with the proper care.

For the sake of instruction it is helpful to tell some of the history of the controversies of Augustine on this matter. Pelagius, after he had been dislodged from his original position where he had opposed the doctrine of grace, then attacked the meaning of the word which was in agreement with Scripture and said that the grace of God availed only for the remission of sins we had already committed. But for putting to death the law of sin in our flesh and beginning the new obedience, there was no need for the giving of the Spirit, or for the special grace of God; but man by the powers of his free will could perform this and satisfy the law of God. Since this dogma is false and pernicious (for it uproots and mutilates the entire benefit of Christ), Augustine sharply opposed Pelagius and so did many others, and they rightly contended that the benefit of Christ and His merit does not consist only in the fact that past sins are remitted, but that also the giving of the Spirit of renewal is a gift of God for the sake of the merit of Christ, and that man cannot be reconciled without the giving and grace of the Holy Spirit, that he cannot mortify the deeds of the flesh and walk in newness of life by the powers of his own free will.

To support this viewpoint are many writings of Augustine concerning grace. In the proceedings of the Council of Milevis[46] there is this canon: "Whoever says that the grace of God by which we are justified through our Lord Jesus Christ avails only for the remission of sins which have already been committed and is not afterward necessary as an aid, lest they be committed again, let him be anathema." There is also this statement from De Consecrat., dist. 4, "Grace, which is given through Christ, not only brings remission of sins but also causes the Law to be fulfilled, our nature to be freed, and sin no longer to rule over us."[47]

---

[46] Or Mileve (in North Africa), A.D. 416. Augustine took part, cf. his Epistles 176–79 in MPL 33. See also Denzinger, *Enchiridion Symbolorum*, p. 52, canon 3, cf. MPL 20.582b.

[47] The reference to *De Consecratione* pertains to the famous decrees of Pope Gelasius. This reference comes from *Pars Tertia*, which is entitled *De Consecratione ecclesiarum et quod missae non sunt alibi celebrando quam in locis Deo sacratis, Distinctio IV*, found in *Corpus Iuris Canonici*, Richter Ed., Graz, 1955, col. 1362–1412. Also includes Gratian's decrees.

These statements speak of the entire benefit of Christ. There is another statement of Augustine regarding the consummation of the benefit of Christ, *Contra Julianum*, 2, "The Lamb of God takes away the sin of the world by forgiving the sins which have been done and helping us so that they do not occur and leading us to life, where sins can no longer be committed."[48]

But, you say, what is the problem with this line of argumentation by the fathers, as long as they were correct on the substance of the matter?

I answer: The use of the word "grace" to describe the gifts of renewal is so common in Augustine and others that the grace of remission of sins or free acceptance by God is rarely mentioned in these discussions, and then only by the way and in passing, although this is the chief point of the heavenly doctrine. The reason for this is that it was not the main point of controversy with Pelagius as to whether our sins are forgiven us by the grace of God. Pelagius conceded this, and it is customary in disputes to refer only in passing to those points which both parties profess.

Afterward, when the Pelagian controversy had cooled down, the later generations did not carefully enough consider the causes and reasons for the statements and picked up only the one meaning for the word "grace," namely the gifts, of which such frequent mention had been made in the fathers. They attached this meaning to the article of justification in such a way that they clearly removed the primary and principal meaning, that is, the free mercy which accepts believers for the sake of Christ unto life everlasting, as we have shown previously. Indeed, Chrysostom, in *Homilia in Matt.* [Hom. 18, MPG 57.267], distinguishes the Law and grace or the Gospel in this way: "The Law is the bare precept, but grace is the power of God because it commands that something be done and gives the power to the one who is working to accomplish it in us."

Another problem is that Augustine and the others did not distinguish accurately enough those passages of Scripture where the word "grace" refers to free acceptance by God and those passages in which the word means "gifts." Nor did they teach the necessary distinction as to which meaning of the word "grace" applies to this doctrine of how we are justified, that is, how we are reconciled with God and how we are saved. They were preoccupied only with the Pelagian controversy.

From this confusion many corruptions in the article of justification arose among later generations. Indeed, there is no point in hiding the fact that Augustine in his conflict with the Pelagians used the word "grace" only in the sense of gifts. In this he was very wrong and certainly misinterpreted Paul's statement in Rom. 6:23: "The gift of God is eternal life." For this is what he says in

---

[48] We have been unable to locate this.

Epistle 105 (294), to Sixtus [MPL 33.816–18], and in his *Enchiridion*, 107 [MPL 40.282]: "Eternal life is a gift and a grace, because the merits for which it is given are gifts of God, who is working in us, and thus grace is given on top of grace." Again: "Merits are not produced by us through our own sufficiency, but they are produced in us by grace; and thus eternal life is called 'grace' (*gratia*), because it is given freely (*gratis*) and is not given because of merits, for even the merits themselves, for which life is given, have been given to us."

These historical facts show how useful and necessary the correct distinction of the meanings of the word "grace" is, and they shed a great deal of light on many disputes. The reader who has not been forewarned can easily be upset by the reading of Augustine, as is obvious in the collected writings of many people in which the disputations of Augustine concerning grace are often very poorly applied to the doctrine of our churches.

Third. Just as justification is one thing and renewal is another, so we must distinguish between the meaning of the word "grace" in the article of renewal and in the article of justification. We have to determine what is its proper and genuine meaning in the article of justification, that is, in such passages as Rom. 3:24: "We are justified freely through His grace"; and Eph. 2:5, 8: "By grace you are saved." Here the term does not mean the gifts of renewal through the Holy Spirit or the new qualities, as if for the sake of these we are justified and saved, but it means the free goodness of God, His favor, His benevolence, and His mercy, by which not according to our works and worthiness but out of sheer mercy, for the sake of Christ, God receives into grace sinners who are repentant and flee in faith to the Mediator, and He accepts them into eternal life with their sins forgiven and the righteousness of Christ imputed to them.

The usage of sacred language shows that this is the correct, primary, proper, and genuine meaning. The Greek and Latin languages seem in some way to allude to this meaning in several instances, but it is beyond all doubt the proper and special usage of Scripture, and therefore the word cannot be rightly understood except from this source.

Yet I do want to gather some examples from secular usage before proceeding, and this for two reasons: (1) To show that because the interpretation of the word "grace" was not sought in the fountains of Holy Scripture but in secular speech, occasion was given for the intrusion of error into this matter; and (2) To show that the true meaning of the word "grace" which we use is not so absurd, but does have some basis in popular speech. The same has been shown to be the case with regard to the word "faith."

Thus Suidas and Varinus show by example from Sophocles that "grace" (*charis*) means a "gift" and "the acknowledgment of a gift." Likewise when the expression *logōn charis* is used, it means pleasure or enjoyment, that is, a quality which produces favor (*gratiam*). And the word *charizomai* they interpret as meaning "to be presented with something (*dōroumai*)," or "to do something pleasant to someone (*to xarin tini poiein*)," or "I have done this in order to be pleasant or gracious to you (*xarizomenos soi*)," that is, "for your happiness or your pleasure (*pros charin kai hēdonēn*)." In an adverbial sense *charis* means "for the sake of (*eis xarin*)," and is distinguished from *heneka*, which means the same thing, but when the purpose is not that something pleasant (*gratia*) may be undertaken. They give definitions such as this: Grace (*charis*) is the giving of something beneficial, or the repayment of a loan, or a good deed done willingly, or prompt payment for good services. Thus far the lexicographers. They show how easily an occasion for error could arise in the church.

I have often noticed, especially in reading Plutarch,[49] his use of the word *charis*, for example in his *Timoleon* the term *charis tēs aretēs*, "the grace of moral virtue." Likewise, "that he might add a certain grace or gain favor (*charis*) for all his actions." Here the word refers to the quality of bringing pleasure or favor. In his *Philopoemon* he says, "I hoped the restoration of the fugitives of the Lacedaimoneans would not take place by the favor of the Romans or of Flaminius but by the kindness or grace (*chariti*) of the Greeks," that is, that when this was done they might come into favor. In his *Pyrrhus* the word is used in the sense of "for the sake of." In *Phocion*: "He was silent for the sake of (*chariti*) Nicanor." In *Cimon*: "Ephialtes dissolved the court on the Areopagus for the sake of (*chariti*) the people," that is, in order that he might gain the favor of the people for himself. Likewise in his *Gracchi*, Micipsa writes that he is going to send food as a favor (*chariti*) for Caius Gracchus. Budaeus has gathered some examples of the expression "grace for grace," that is, to add something which gains favor. These examples do not apply to the article of justification, and if the word is understood in this sense, there will obviously be a corruption in the teaching of justification.

But I have also observed certain instances which are in close agreement with the Scriptural usage. In *Cato Uticensis* [34.775] we read. "If I wished to preserve my life for the sake of (*chariti*) Caesar. . . ." In *Demosthenes* [27.859], "Financial penalties were levied against Demosthenes, and he was not permitted to be freed from the punishment even by grace (*chariti*)." This agrees very well. Related also are such statements as *Phocion* [26.753], "It was necessary to show favor (*charis*) to Phocion." In Euripides [*Suppliants*, 380], "Theseus as a suppliant demands of you grace (*pros charin*) to bury the dead."

---

[49] Plutarch: *Timoleon*, 3.237 and 35.253; *Philopoemon*, 1 21.368; *Pyrrhus*, 21.395; *Phocion*, 31.756; *Cimon*, 10.485.

In the Latin language Cicero says in his *De Inventione* [2.22] that it is grace in which is contained the desire to reward friends or officers in memory of something they have done. Thus we speak of giving thanks (*agere gratias*). This has nothing to do with our discussion, however. But closer to it is the concept of gaining favor, to increase in favor, to return to favor, to be in favor, to bring back or restore to favor, to put into a favorable position, to seek or enter favor, to send away with good grace, or to cut off from favor.

Likewise in the German language: "to have a gracious Lord is to add grace to grace." (*einen gnädigen Herrn haben/begnaden/mit Gnaden gewogen sein*).

There are thus certain allusions in the citations from secular literature, but the true foundation and the proper and genuine meaning must be sought in the language of Scripture. Therefore we shall gather some selected passages and illustrative statements from the Old Testament.

Just as there is a relationship between cause and effect, so the word *charis* refers to giving something out of grace, as in Gen. 33:5, "These are the children whom God has graciously given me." But the second main meaning agrees with the article of justification. For the Septuagint and the Latin translations in many places translate this word by "showing mercy" or "sparing." Thus it is not so easy to see this Hebrew word in some of the versions. But it is correct to say that grace is mercy. For the word *chānan* is translated this way by the interpreters, and the word "to have mercy" is often joined with the Hebrew *chānan*. In 2 Kings 13:23, when the Syrians had long afflicted Israel, it says, "God was gracious to them and had mercy on them." In Rom. 9:15 Paul cites Ex. 33:19, and he uses the word "I will have mercy" (*oikteirō*). Is. 30:19: "He will be merciful to you at the sound of your cry." Ps. 6:2: "Have mercy on me, Lord, for I am weak." Ps. 123:3: "Have mercy on us, for we are filled up with contempt." Ps. 77:9: "Has God forgotten to be gracious, has He in anger shut up His tender mercies?" Ps. 102:13: "You shall arise and have mercy on Zion, for it is time to show mercy." There are many such examples in which the word *chānan* is translated by "mercy" or is joined with the concept of mercy. And we should note that the word *chānan* does not involve the idea of marvelous gifts or virtues as the basis, as the dialectitians call it, which gains favor with God, but the Psalms use such expressions as "because I am weak," "because I am filled up with contempt," "because I am afflicted."

But the following examples properly pertain to the article of justification: Judges 21:22: "If a person wants to enter into judgment with us, we shall say, 'Receive them into grace' [or 'have pity on them']." Amos 5:15, where God is threatening, it goes on: "Perhaps He will have mercy [or be gracious] to the remnant of Joseph." Deut. 28:50: "They will not show favor (*kein Gnad erzeigen*) to the young." Num. 6:25: "The Lord make His face shine upon us and be merciful to us."

The passive use of the term in Prov. 21:10 and Is. 26:10 does not mean an infusion of qualities, but as the German has it, "to find favor" or "to be blest" (*Gnad erlangen/begnadet werden*).

This is particularly enlightening because the same word in the fourth conjugation means "to pray for grace which is to follow," as in 2 Kings 1:13, when the fire had consumed two groups of 50 soldiers, he who was sent with the third group came as a suppliant before the prophet, that they not be devoured by the fire.

The word is used this way also in Gen. 6:8, "Noah found grace in the eyes of the Lord," and Gen. 39:21, when Joseph was thrown into prison, "The Lord gave him grace [or favor] in the eyes of the keeper of the prison." This expression can very properly be understood with reference to the passage, "The Lord make His face to shine upon you and give you grace." Jer. 16:13: "I will cast you out . . . and will not show you grace." Joshua 11:20: ". . . that they should be left without grace." Ezra 9:7–8: "We have been cast out . . . but now suddenly grace has been shown by the Lord our God to leave us a remnant."

There is also an adjectival aspect of this word which is attributed only to God. Ex. 22:27: "I hear the poor, for I am gracious." Ps. 86:5 and 112:4: "The Lord is merciful and gracious."

Both the verb and the noun from time to time refer to supplication for grace. Jer. 42:9, Dan. 9:18: "We present our supplications before You for Your great mercy." Zech. 12:10: "The Spirit of grace and of prayers." Here is a very beautiful play on words, and the Greeks, misled by this, rendered it "the Spirit of grace and compassion." Ps. 55:1: "Do not hide Yourself from my supplications." Jer. 36:7: "Perhaps their supplication will come before the Lord." This is a beautiful parallel, for it shows the correlation between how the grace of God, by which we are justified and saved, is received and applied.

These grammatical points are helpful in understanding the article of justification. The main ideas are these: (1) It is translated by the word "mercy." (2) It is joined with the concept of showing mercy. (3) It is used in the sense of supplying strength, "because I am weak and loaded down with contempt." (4) Grace is shown although we deserve something else. (5) We must note the correlation with supplication and prayer.

Moreover, just as there are cognate words related to the meaning of one aspect, especially from cause to effect, so the word "grace" is used with reference to gifts. Ps. 45:2: "Grace is poured upon your lips." Prov. 1:9: "ornaments of grace upon your head." Prov. 3:22: "They shall add grace to your throat." 31:30: "Favor (*gratia*) is deceitful and beauty is vain." Also, Col. 4:6: "Let your speech be always with grace, seasoned with salt." Eph. 4:29: "That it may impart grace to the hearers."

But the question is, what is the proper and genuine meaning of the word "grace" in the article of justification, that is, what is the grace of God by which we are justified and saved?

In the New Testament the Greek reflects the Hebrew sources.

There are two words: *charizomai* and *charitoō*. In Eph. 1:6 one of the words is equivalent to the Qal conjugation, and the other to the Piel. In Luke 1:28 the passive is used, which cannot be precisely explained except on the basis of the Hebrew conjugation.

The word *charizomai* means "to bestow gifts," as in the Hebrew (*chānan*). Rom. 8:32: "How shall He not give you all things?" 1 Cor. 2:12: "We have received the Spirit that we might know the things which have been given to us."

But we must particularly note the meaning of the word *charizomai*, which beautifully describes the word "grace." Luke 7:42: "When they could not pay, he forgave (*echarisato*) them both." 2 Cor. 2:10: "Anyone whom you forgive I also forgive." 2 Cor. 12:13: "Forgive me this wrong." Eph. 4:32: "Forgiving one another as God in Christ has forgiven (*echarisato*) you." Col. 2:13: "Forgiving us all our trespasses." Col. 3:13: "As Christ has forgiven you, so you must also forgive." Thus it is correct to say that grace means the forgiveness of sins, as can very properly be seen from the meaning of the word.

We must also consider the meaning of the term in Acts 27:24: "God has given you all them that sail with you in the ship," that is, those who were going to perish in the shipwreck were saved for the sake of Paul. In the same way God gives to His Son sinners who were about to perish. Cf. Ps. 2:8 and Gal. 3:18: "For the inheritance is not by the Law . . . but God gave (*echarisato*) it to Abraham by the promise."

In regard to the term *charis* we have gathered only those examples which confirm and support its genuine meaning in the article of justification. Acts 25:3: When the Jews could not attack Him by the Law, they "sought favor against Paul." Acts 15:40: ". . . being commended to the grace of God." In these passages the term certainly cannot refer to a quality which is inherent in us. Gal. 5:4: "You have fallen from grace." The Latin expresses the same concept. Titus 3:4: "The grace of God has appeared." Heb. 2:9: "that by the grace of God He might taste death for every man." Gal. 2:21: "Do not nullify the grace of God." God wills that His grace be efficacious toward all believers, but because they seek in the Law for a way to please God, they nullify the grace of God which in the Gospel is freely offered for the sake of the Mediator. Jude 4: ". . . who pervert the grace of God into licentiousness." Note also these ways of speaking: Luke 2:40: "The grace of God was upon Him." Acts 4:33: "Great grace was upon them all." 2 Cor.

9:14: "The grace of God in you." 1 Peter 1:13: "Set your hope upon the grace that is coming to you at the revelation of Jesus Christ." 2 John 3: "Grace be with us." Note also that for the Hebrews the same word means both "gift" and "grace," cf. Paul in Rom. 5:15–17, where as synonyms for *charis* are *dōrēma, dōrea,* and *charisma,* "the free gift, after many offenses, brings justification, and they who receive the abundance of grace and the gift of righteousness shall reign in life." Rom. 6:23: "The free gift (*charisma*) of God is life eternal." Eph. 2:8: "By grace you are saved, not by works; it is the gift (*dōron*) of God."

I have wanted to discuss these expressions rather fully because they are helpful in our disputations and show the foundations of the matter.

Fourth. Thus far we have shown that the explanation of the word "grace" taught in our churches is in agreement with the usage peculiar to Holy Scripture. Because these examples show that the word is used for both the cause and the effect, that is, for mercy and for gifts, therefore we must add some stronger and more illustrative testimonies . . . which clearly prove and demonstrate with certainty that when Paul says: "We are justified freely through the grace of God," or "You are saved by the grace of God," we are not to understand that we are justified and saved either entirely by our own newness of life or by a combination of God's mercy and our own newness within us, but that in the article of justification before God the word "grace" means only the mercy of God, which is the remission of sins and free acceptance to eternal life for the sake of the Mediator.

Gifts, such as the Spirit of renewal, follow after this acceptance by God, and thus these two matters cannot be torn apart, as John so strongly confirms in his First Epistle, 3:14: "He who does not love remains in death"; and again in 4:20: "He who says that he knows God and does not love his brother is a liar." Therefore we are not rejecting the gifts of renewal when we contend, in keeping with the Scriptural principle, that "grace" in the article of justification means only "the mercy of God." But we do distinguish between these two, and attribute to each the place which Scripture assigns to it, that is to say, to the article of justification the mercy of God, but to the article of renewal the gifts of newness. We do so for this reason, that faith in the remission of sins and reconciliation with God might not rely on our qualities but solely on the mercy of God, and thus "the promise might be sure," Rom. 4:16 [KJV].

Now we shall note some of the chief fundamental testimonies showing that "grace" in the article of justification must be understood as referring only to the free mercy of God.

1. Scripture itself clearly distinguishes between grace and the gifts given through grace, Rom. 5:15–17. Likewise grace and truth, John 1:14. Yet both are certainly given through Christ. But when Paul says that we are justified and

saved by grace, he understands that grace which Scripture distinguishes from the gift through grace and from truth, that is, he understands it not as our renewal but only as the mercy of God or His acceptance.

2. The strongest testimony is the fact that in the article of justification Paul puts grace into opposition to good works, not only those which human reason performs apart from the Holy Spirit, but also those which are the gifts and fruits of the Spirit. For Abraham, Rom. 4, performed good works not from free will but from faith, Heb. 11:8, and yet Paul puts justifying grace in opposition to the working of Abraham, Rom. 4:4: "To him who works the reward is not imputed according to grace"; Titus 3:5: "Not by works of righteousness which we have done, but according to His mercy He saved us" [KJV]. He is clearly saying that those who have done works which are true, righteous, and pleasing to God are not saved by reason of these works, but by the mercy of God, Rom. 11:6: "But if it is by grace, it is no longer on the basis of works; otherwise grace would no longer be grace" [RSV]; Eph. 2:8–9: "By grace you are saved, through faith, and this not of yourselves" (that is, not by something inherent in you); "it is the gift of God, not of works."

From these passages it is possible to put together a definition of justifying grace. If with respect to some quality inherent in us (Eph. 2:8) or with respect to the "works of righteousness which we have done" God justifies us, that is, having forgiven us our sins, receives us on this basis unto salvation and life, then it is no longer grace but wages or debt, Rom. 4:4; 11:6. But grace is justifying because God is most kind toward us in Christ Jesus, even when "dead in sins," without respect to any quality or works in us, and has "made us alive together with Christ . . . raised us up . . . and made us sit with Him in heavenly places in Christ Jesus," Eph. 2:5–6 [RSV]. No amount of human rationalization can get around these testimonies, for they clearly show that justifying grace and salvation are not the newness in us, but only mercy and goodness in Christ Jesus.

3. There is also the brilliant testimony of Jer. 31:33, where the gifts of renewal are described in this way: "I will write My law in their hearts." Compare also Ezek. 36:27: "I will cause you to walk in My precepts." Paul in treating the article of justification uses this antithesis, Rom. 6:14: "You are not under the Law but under grace"; Gal. 5:4: "You have fallen from grace, as many of you are justified by the Law." Thus it is completely false when the papists teach that love is the grace which makes us pleasing to God; for love is the fulfilling of the Law, and we "are not under the Law but under grace."

4. The following testimonies should clearly convince us that justifying grace is not a quality or some newness inhering in us, but that the foundation, as the dialecticians say, is in God. 2 Tim. 1:9: "He has saved us, not according to our works but according to His own purpose and grace which was given us in Christ

Jesus before time began." Thus this cannot mean that there is something in us, because we did not exist "before time began." Thus in Eph. 1:9: "He set forth His plan according to His good purpose." Rom. 11:5: "There is a remnant according to the election of grace" [KJV]. Also Eph. 1:4: "He has chosen us before the foundations of the world were laid," when we did not yet exist.

5. It is also useful to consider the words coupled with the term "grace" in the article of justification, and what synonyms it has, as in the salutations in 1 and 2 Timothy and Titus: "grace, mercy, and peace." Cf. 2 Tim. 1:9; Titus 3:4–5, 7; Eph. 2:7; 4. In v. 5 he adds the parenthetical expression: "By grace you have been saved." Also note what is written in Heb. 2:9: ". . . that by the grace of God He might taste death for all." In Rom. 5:8 Paul asserts: "God has demonstrated His love for us in that while we were still sinners Christ died for us." These passages shed much light.

6. From the following testimonies we can confirm and illustrate the true and proper meaning of the word "grace." Heb. 4:16: "Let us . . . draw near to the throne of grace, that we may receive mercy and find grace to help in time of need" [RSV]; Rom. 5:2; Eph. 1:4–6; Gal. 1:15. Rom. 5:20–6:1: "If grace abounded over sin . . . shall we therefore remain in sin that grace may abound yet more?" Clearly there would be no place for this objection if grace in the article of justification meant renewal, as is clear from Heb. 2:9: "By the grace of God He tasted death." Here the term "grace" can in no way mean a newness which inheres in us.

7. Ambrose interprets the apostolic salutation in Rom. 1:7 thus: " 'Grace,' because we are absolved from sins; 'peace,' because we have been reconciled from being ungodly." Previously we noted that Thomas and Villanus admitted that the ancients to a certain extent interpreted "grace" as God's good will and love, by which He chooses, calls, adopts, and justifies us, Eph. 1:4–5, 11.

In my judgment the true, genuine, and proper meaning of the word "grace" in the article of justification is summarized in these fundamental points.

[CHAPTER II]: THE TERM "FREELY"

In order that the exclusive aspect of the term "grace" may be seen more clearly and fortified more strongly in the face of all corruptions, Paul in Rom. 3:24 adds the particle "freely" (*gratis*): "We are justified freely by His grace." Therefore we also need to take note of the explanation of this word. The Hebrews derive both "grace" and "freely" from the same root. This is the same in the Latin language [*gratia* and *gratis*]. But the Greeks, because they could not make an adverbial form of *charis*, took another term, *dōrean*.

Because a comparison of the terms in different languages is useful, we shall say a few things about the use of this adverb in ordinary speech.

Suidas and Varinus simply have nothing. Plutarch in his *Philopoemon* [15.365] uses the term in this way: "It was decreed to give him freely (*dōrean*), or as a gift, 120 talents." *Phocion* [36.758], "When the poison ran out and the executioner was unwilling to prepare more unless he were given money, Phocion said, 'Among the Athenians a person cannot even die free of charge (*dōrean*).'" *Demosthenes* [18.749], "He paid the ransom freely (*dōrean*)." The word is used the same way in 1 Macc. 10:33, "I freely set them at liberty."

In Latin the word means either "without money" and "without paying the price," or "without hope of reward" and "with respect to usefulness." Cicero, *De Officiis* [2.23.83], "To live at no cost or free in the home of someone else." *In Verrem* [2.5.19], "The ship cost me nothing (*gratis*)." *Pro Cluent.* [26.71], "To serve someone without pay." *De Finibus* [2.26.83], "They freely love all virtues for their own sake." *Pro Roscio* [*Comoeda Oratio*, 10.27], "The common action was done without charge; it should have been done for a price." Ovid [*Epistulae ex Ponto*, 2.3.14], "He was sorry to be upright for nothing (*gratis*)."

The particle *gratuito* is used in this way: Cicero, *De Off.*, "To defend the cases of many people, happily and without charge (*gratuito*)." *De Legibus* [1.18.48], "What is liberality? Is it free or is it done for a reward? If it is done out of kindness and without charge, it is free (*gratuita*); if it demands pay, it is something hired." *De Finibus* [2.36.98], "There is born in man a goodness which is free, not borrowed, not evoked by pleasures or rewards."

In one way or another these examples relate to the particle *gratis* as Paul uses it. Yet we cannot form a definite and sure explanation of the word on the basis of these instances, since they are subject to various interpretations, just as is the expression, "They hate me freely." Augustine says, "He hates freely who does not seek an advantage from his hatred or flee a disadvantage." Thus the ungodly hate God freely and the godly love Him freely so that they look for no other good besides Him, because He will be all in all. We shall shortly see how fitting this explanation is.

The true emphasis of the word *gratis* must be looked for in the language of Scripture, and because of its exclusive aspect its use is great and necessary. This work will not be painful to us.

The rabbis, because of the letter *mēm*, interpreted this word with reference to good favor. But the examples of Scripture clearly show the meaning and emphasis. The word is used especially in a threefold sense, and I think it will be helpful to note the distinction.

1. It is used in opposition to the payment of a reward. Gen. 29:15: "Should you serve me for nothing? What wages do you want?" Ex. 21:2: "He shall go out freely, without payment," that is, he shall find favor so that he will be sent out as a free man without paying money. Num. 11:5: "We ate the fish for nothing."

2 Sam. 24:24: "I will not offer burnt offerings to the Lord which cost me nothing." Matt. 10:8: "Freely you have received." 2 Cor. 11:7: "I have preached the Gospel without cost to you." Rev. 21:6: "He shall receive the water of life freely." Luther renders this *umsonst*.

2. It means "without just cause," "rashly," "out of frivolity or insolence." Ps. 35:19: "They hate me without cause," cf. 69:4. Ps. 120:7: "They fought against me without cause." Ps. 119:161: "They persecuted me without cause." Prov. 24:28: "Do not be a witness against your neighbor without cause." Prov. 26:2: "A curse that is without cause . . ." Gal. 2:21: "Christ is dead in vain." Luther: *vergeblich, ohne Ursache*.

3. It is used in opposition to merit, whether good or evil. 1 Sam. 19:5: "Why will you sin against innocent blood by killing David without cause?" In 25:31 Abigail says: ". . . that you shed blood without cause." 1 Kings 2:31: "Take away . . . the blood . . . shed without cause" [RSV]. Ezek. 6:10 and 14:23: "I have not spoken without cause. . . . I have not done this evil without reason." Ecclus. 29:6 speaks of those who by lending money have acquired enemies for themselves: "He shall acquire an enemy without cause." Again in v. 7: "Many are afraid to be defrauded without cause," that is, when they are deserving of something else. Jer. 15:13: "I will give your treasures as spoil without price," that is, to those from whom you did not deserve such treatment. Lam. 3:52: "They have hunted me like a bird, without cause," that is, those to whom I gave no cause (. . . *nicht verschuldet*). 2 Thess. 3:8: "We did not eat anyone's bread without paying, but with toil . . . " Luther: *ohne und wider Verdienst*.

In these examples the Septuagint always renders the Hebrew word with the particle *dōrean*. Hence there is no doubt that the true meaning and force of the particle "freely" can be correctly and beautifully determined in the writings of Paul. For just as the enemies of David are said to have hated him "freely" (*gratis*), but the cause of the hatred was not in David but in the malevolence of his enemies, therefore when God says that we are freely justified, He means that the cause of our acceptance is not in us but in the free goodness of God Himself. Thus Ezekiel says that God does not punish *gratis*, that is, He does not punish those in whom He finds no cause to punish. But He justifies "freely." It is manifest in these examples that the word *gratis* has two aspects. (1) The merit or cause is not in David that his adversaries persecute him. (2) His enemies actually find in David a reason why they should not hate him.

From this, therefore, it can be beautifully understood why Paul in Rom. 3:24 adds the particle "freely" to the word "grace": "We are justified freely by His grace." For in Gen. 39:4 the text says of Joseph: "He found grace in the eyes of his master." It is added that he was a fortunate man; that is, because of the outstanding virtues Potiphar saw in Joseph, he was very fond of him and promoted him. Lest anyone think that we are justified and saved by the grace of God in this same way, Paul adds the particle "freely" ("we are justified freely through His grace") in order to show that God in the article of justification does not regard worthiness, merit, cause, form, or anything inherent in us by whatever name you call it as the reason for receiving us into grace.

Although He found in us a cause why He could damn us, He by mere free goodness receives us to eternal life. This is what it means "to be justified freely through the grace of God." So these two points cover the things of which we have spoken above: (1) In us there is nothing meritorious, no worthiness or cause for justification and salvation. (2) Because our nature is contaminated in many different ways by sins, we deserve the wrath of God and merit eternal damnation, and yet purely out of the mercy of God for the sake of His Son the Mediator, we have been accepted by God. This is what it means to be "justified freely." As the psalmist says: "He has not dealt with us according to our sins," Ps. 103:10. Luther often expresses these two concepts beautifully with the words *ohne und wider unsern Verdienst.*

This emphasis, which beautifully illuminates the entire locus on justification, cannot be understood on the basis of the Greek or the Latin. Therefore it is necessary to learn from the original sources. There are those who do not wrongly interpret the particle "freely" in this way: We are justified only by the gift and the liberality of God. But this line of reasoning will not sufficiently explain the emphasis of Paul's use of the particle, when he says: "not by works, not of ourselves, He justifies the ungodly without works, eternal life is the gift of God"; it is opposed to the idea of a payment.

Ambrose explains the particle "freely" in Romans 3 thus: "We are justified by faith alone as a gift of God, ourselves doing nothing and not rendering any payment in return," that is, we merit nothing from our works which preceded our conversion, nor are we paid for those which follow. Augustine comments on the Psalm verse: "For nothing shalt Thou save them" [56:7 Vulgate] in a very appropriate manner: "You find nothing in us as a cause for saving us, but You find much reason for condemning us; and yet out of Your mercy for the sake of Christ You receive us." This is the sum and substance of the explanation of the word "freely."

[CHAPTER III]: THE WORD "IMPUTATION"

Several times in Romans 4 Paul repeats the word "imputation." In v. 3: "Abraham believed God and it was imputed to him for righteousness." V. 6: "David describes the blessedness of the man to whom God imputes righteousness without works." Again in v. 24: "It is written for our sakes, to whom it shall be imputed as believers." Yet again in v. 4 he attributes the imputation to grace; he takes it away from works and puts it in opposition to a debt.

Thus we must hold to the correct explanation of this word, as to what "imputed righteousness" properly is, how it can be understood and defended, and how it is opposed to inherent righteousness. The papists interpret it this way: Faith formed by love and other virtues is imputed for righteousness; that is, God accepts the works, which in themselves are not worthy, as being worthy in believers for the sake of Christ. This righteousness is such that it brings reconciliation with God, peace of conscience, blessedness, and eternal life. The Jesuits contrive an entirely new interpretation, namely that the expression "faith is imputed for righteousness" means that God considers the faith found in man to be worthy, and to this faith is given and conferred the inherent righteousness through which we are saved. This is a clear perversion of both the word and the substance, whereby the term "imputed righteousness" is interpreted as "inherent righteousness."

Therefore the true foundations of the proper and genuine meaning of this term must be considered. An analysis (*divisio*) of the term or word is useful. In Rom. 5:13 we read: "Where there is no law, there sin is not imputed." In 2 Sam. 19:19 Shimei says: "Let not the king impute iniquity to me." Ps. 106:30–31: The action of Phinehas "is imputed to him for righteousness." 2 Tim. 4:16: "All have left me. May it not be imputed against them!"

In these examples (to use the language of the dialecticians) is established the "basis" (*fundamentum*) inherent in those to whom something is imputed. There is also the "goal" (*terminus*), either guilt or reward. Between these two points the imputation itself, either to guilt or to reward, is what they call the "relationship" (*relatio*), which takes place by reason of or with respect to the "basis."

Now the question is whether the same line of reasoning is relevant when Paul discusses imputed righteousness. The papists vehemently contend for this and say that there is only one meaning, and no other, for the word "imputation," which it absolutely must have. But we, through analyzing the term, have established a second meaning for the word "imputation," namely that God, out of His free mercy for the sake of Christ, regards the believers, whose nature is still contaminated by various sins, as righteous. And as righteous He awards them salvation and eternal life, not with respect to inherent righteousness but imputed righteousness.

Because this matter is important and difficult, we must show the firm and unshakable foundations of what Paul means by the word "imputation" in the article of justification. Indeed, Paul clearly sets forth the analysis (*divisio*) of the term (as the dialecticians say), when he says in Rom. 4:4–5: "To him who works, his reward is reckoned as a debt, not as grace or a gift. But to him who does not work but who believes in Him who justifies the ungodly, his faith is imputed for righteousness." That is, there is a certain imputation which has and looks to a basis in the person who works, to whom the imputation is made, and this does not take place in terms of grace but as a debt. But there is another kind of imputation, which does not have or look to a basis in the person to whom it is made; its basis is in the grace and mercy of God, who justifies the ungodly. Therefore, when he says that the ungodly person is justified by this imputation, he is showing that in the believer to whom this free imputation is given the basis is the very opposite, that is, to this ungodly person righteousness must not be imputed, but guilt, if God should will to enter into judgment with him.

Thus Paul distinctly and clearly shows that he wants the word "imputation" in the article of justification to be understood in the second sense and not in the first. Further, he will soon show in a broader sense and prove from David the blessedness of the man to whom God imputes righteousness without works. Therefore the basis of this imputation of which Paul is speaking is not in him to whom the imputation is made, for he says, "apart from works." In Eph. 2:8 he expressly says: ". . . and this not of yourselves." He adds that in this imputation sins are forgiven, iniquities covered, sins not imputed. Therefore in believers to whom this free imputation is made there is an opposite basis, if God should wish to enter into judgment with them.

We must also carefully note this point, that Abraham, whose imputed righteousness Paul is discussing in this passage, at the time did have inherent righteousness. He had been adorned, through the renewal of the Spirit, with many outstanding virtues and works. But this inherent renewal or righteousness Paul clearly says is not the basis with respect to which or by reason of which there was imputed to Abraham this righteousness unto blessing. He adds the reason: because this inherent righteousness is imperfect and unclean, for sin still dwells in the flesh of Abraham and evil still lies close at hand when he wants to do good. If God should wish to enter into judgment with him, this sin would be imputed to him unto the guilt of eternal punishment. Therefore this imputation of righteousness consists in the grace and mercy of God, which for the sake of Christ covers the inherent "basis" (*fundamentum*), namely sin, so that it is not imputed to him; and a "basis" not inherent in the believer is imputed to him out of grace, as though the perfection he owes were inherent in him.

These points are very clear from Paul: The free imputation in the article of justification is the grace of God, which for the sake of Christ does not impute against us the sins inhering in us, 2 Cor. 5:19, and imputes to us (as though it actually did inhere in man) the perfect righteousness which does not inhere in us and which is worthy of eternal life. I am happy to use these terms of the dialecticians regarding the "basis" (*fundamentum*), the "goal" (*terminus*), and the "relationship" (*relatio*), because I believe this line of reasoning is most satisfactory for explaining and understanding the correct and genuine meaning of the word "imputation" in the article of justification.

There are many examples in which the word *chāshab* or *logizomai* establishes the "basis" not in the one to whom something is imputed, whether for good or for evil, but in the relationship, that is, the thinking, the judgment, and the will of the one who imputes. In Gen. 31:15 the daughters of Laban say: "We are accounted as foreigners by him." In Num. 18:26–27, in regard to the Levites who did not have a threshing floor from which they could offer first fruits, He says: "From the tithes you shall offer a heave offering . . . and it shall be reckoned or imputed to you as an offering of the first fruits, as though it were grain from the threshing floor." Lev. 17:3–4: "If a man kills an ox . . . and does not bring it to the door of the tabernacle to the Lord, blood shall be imputed to that man, as if he had shed blood, and he shall perish." There is a brilliant example in Ps. 144:3–4: "What is man that You have regard for him, or the son of man that You take account of him? Man is like a breath."

You see that the "basis" of this imputation is not in man but is located in the grace of God. Mark 15:28: "He was reckoned with transgressors." Rom. 2:26: "Will not his uncircumcision be regarded as circumcision?" [RSV]. Rom. 8:36: "We are accounted as sheep for the slaughter" [KJV]. Rom. 9:8: "The children of the promise are reckoned as descendants" [RSV]; but he is speaking of the gentiles.

These examples are clear, and in each of them there is the word *chāshab* or *logizomai*. Therefore, in order that the promise of imputed righteousness may be sure, its "basis" is not located in the qualities inherent in us but in the judgment and thoughts of God, which are infallibly true. And Paul says: "I am not aware of anything against myself, but I am not thereby justified, because He who judges me is the Lord," 1 Cor. 4:4. Therefore when His judgment attributes righteousness to us, when He thinks thoughts of peace toward us and not thoughts of affliction or wrath, then our justification has the best and firmest foundation. Our faith, when it lays hold on that judgment and on the thinking of God revealed in the promise of the Gospel, is rightly said to be imputed unto righteousness. These very true and comforting points appear from the linguistic explanations of the word "imputation."

Thus we can now draw three conclusions from these true fundamental points pertaining to the word "imputation" in this article. (1) The "basis" by reason of which and in respect to which righteousness is imputed unto blessedness does not lie in the believers themselves, not even in Abraham after he was adorned by the Holy Spirit with outstanding gifts of spiritual renewal. (2) A contrary "basis" is found if God should wish to enter into judgment. This must be covered so that sin is not imputed to us. (3) This imputation is also a "relationship" of the Divine mind and will, which out of free mercy for the sake of Christ does not impute their sins to the believers but imputes to them righteousness, that is, they are considered before God at the tribunal of His judgment as if they had perfect righteousness dwelling in them, and therefore salvation and eternal life are given to them as righteous people.

But there is a fourth point, which also pertains to imputation, for what it is and why it is to be added can be understood from this: Scripture says concerning human judgment that when a judge because of his relationship imputes the sentence of "righteous" to a guilty person without a "basis" (I am retaining the use of the language of the dialecticians), it is an abomination, Prov. 17:15; Ex. 23:1; Deut. 25:1; Is. 5:23; 1 Kings 8:32. Some people reply that God is a completely free agent, and therefore He can justify whom He wills and in any way He wills. But God has revealed His will in the Law, and this cannot be annulled. For it is easier for heaven and earth to pass away than for the least jot or tittle of the Law to be done away with so that it is not fulfilled [cf. Matt. 5:18].

Therefore, in keeping with His revealed will, God does not will to justify a person without righteousness, that is, not unless satisfaction has been made for sin in keeping with the Law and unless the Law has been fulfilled by perfect obedience. In Rom. 3:31 Paul says that when faith is imputed for righteousness the Law is not destroyed but established. That is, to use the language of the dialecticians, the "relationship" (*relatio*) of the Divine mind imputes to the believer the "goal" (*terminus*) of righteousness unto eternal life, but not without a "basis" (*fundamentum*). This "basis," however, is not in the believers, as we have said above. But God has set forth His Son as our Mediator, made under the Law, for which He has made satisfaction both by bearing our sins and by His perfect obedience. This was not done on His own behalf but, 1 Cor. 1:30: "He was made righteousness for us by God," and 2 Cor. 5:21: "that we might be made the righteousness of God in Him" [KJV]. Rom. 5:21: "By the obedience of the One many are accounted as righteous." Rom. 8:4: "That the righteousness of the Law might be fulfilled in us" [KJV]. Is. 45:24: "Therefore he shall say, 'In my Lord are righteousness and strength.' "

Thus we will have a complete "relationship." The "basis" is in obedience and redemption, in Christ Jesus our Lord. The "relationship" is the grace and mercy of God. The "goal" is the believing person, to whom for the sake of Christ's righteousness his sins are not imputed; but through Christ he is reputed as righteous before God unto eternal life, by the imputation of the righteousness of Christ. Faith, laying hold on this righteousness of Christ and thereby on the grace and mercy of God in the promise, is said to be imputed for righteousness, not insofar as faith is a virtue inhering in us, but because by this means or instrument the "relationship" of God applies this "basis" to the "goal."

This explanation casts light on the entire doctrine and refutes many cavilings. [Friedrich] Staphylus [1512–64] says: "The Lutherans set forth the righteousness of faith by speaking of a relationship, but a relationship involves an entity of minimal importance, as the dialecticians say. And it must be a matter of great and serious import to which is attributed salvation and eternal life." The Jesuits say that to talk of a relationship without a basis is an inane fantasy and illusion, as if Crassus would be greeted as a rich man when he was loaded down with someone else's copper. This is what imputed righteousness is, they say, which does not have a basis inherent in us.

These cavilings can be completely refuted by the points we have made. We do not teach that God out of some kind of capriciousness without any basis imputes righteousness to believers, but we affirm from the Word of God that there must be the firm, solid, entirely pure, and totally complete and perfect foundation of the free imputation, so that even the righteousness which dwelt in Abraham and David cannot be the foundation of this relationship and imputation, Rom. 4:2, 6, ". . . because sin is present," Rom. 7:21. But it was necessary that the Son of God become incarnate and be "born under the Law" [Gal. 4:4], in order that His completely pure satisfaction and perfect obedience might be the firm, solid, and immovable "basis" of this imputation.

Therefore the righteousness of faith is not "an entity of minimal importance" but something very significant, for Christ is our Righteousness. Nor is it "an inane fantasy," for it is the thinking and the judgment of God. From this also comes an entirely correct understanding as to how these two points are to be reconciled: "He who justifies the guilty is an abomination before God," Prov. 17:15, and "To him who . . . believes in Him who justifies the guilty . . . ," Rom. 4:5.

These points regarding the word "imputation" are true, simple, and uncomplicated. The objection is raised that it is written in Ps. 106:31 that the act of Phinehas was imputed to him for righteousness. But we said at the outset that Paul himself sets forth two kinds of imputation, one of works and the other of faith. In the article of justification he clearly says that the imputation of righteousness takes place apart from works. We should note that Paul in Romans 4 deals with how a person is justified before God unto blessedness through imputation, and he says that this takes place through faith without works. For no person can be justified unto eternal life before God on the basis of one act such as Phinehas performed. Concerning the righteousness of works it is written in Gal. 3:10: "Cursed is he who does not continue in all . . ." Likewise James 2:10: "He who falls short in one point is guilty of all."

But the next question is: How do the works of the justified please God? It does not appear that this action of Phinehas could be at all probable as God-pleasing. In external appearance it seemed to be a savage act, but God declared that it was a righteous action by decreeing for him and his posterity the reward of a priesthood. This act of Phinehas also seemed to have something of lawlessness attached to it, for he was not a magistrate bearing the sword, nor was he acting at the command and authority of a magistrate, but out of a kind of private zeal. Therefore it is said that God imputed this deed to him for righteousness, that is, He accepted it as a righteous work, covering and remitting the stains with which it was tainted. But the person of Phinehas was certainly not thereby, as a result of this work, justified before God unto eternal life, so that because of his person, justified by faith, God would accept as righteous this work which in itself was imperfect and impure.

This action of Phinehas was an individual one, not set before us for imitation. But in regard to the imputation of Abraham, Paul says: "This is written for our sake, to whom it will be imputed" [Rom. 4:23–24]. And the psalm says: "It was imputed to Phinehas for righteousness unto all generations." But Rom. 4:12 says that it will not be imputed to all who are descended from Abraham, "but to those who walk in the steps of his faith." Therefore the statement of the psalmist does not overturn the points made thus far regarding imputation. The psalm is speaking of the action and work of Phinehas, but Paul is saying that for believers righteousness is imputed without works. Therefore the questions in Romans 4 and Psalm 106 are different. I believe these points regarding the word "imputation" have not been noted down in vain.

[CHAPTER IV]: THE WORKS OF THE LAW

Paul often and with great emphasis affirms and repeats that "without the Law the righteousness of God has been revealed," Rom. 3:21; ". . . not having my own righteousness which is of the Law," Phil. 3:9; "By the Law no one is justified," Gal. 3:11; "By the works of the Law no flesh shall be justified," Rom. 3:20. He says in a simple way and without any addition in Rom. 4:6: "without works"; and in Eph. 2:9, "not of works"; 2 Tim. 1:9, "not according to works." Therefore it is a great and difficult question: What is this Law and what are these works which Paul repeatedly and emphatically excludes as a cause for justification?

In order that we can clearly show the true foundations, against all cavilings, we shall set forth the point in question. The question does not pertain to the effects or fruits following justification by faith, of which Jeremiah writes in 31:33: "I shall write My law in their hearts"; Ezek. 36:27: "I will . . . cause you to walk in My statutes"; Eph. 2:10: "In Christ Jesus we are regenerated unto good works, which God prepared beforehand that we should walk in them." From these effects or fruits of justification the Law and the works of the Law should in no way be excluded. But in this argument the question pertains to the cause or the form (or whatever word you choose to use) of justification by faith, or in what the righteousness of faith before God unto salvation and eternal life actually consists, or what things are required and necessary for this righteousness which brings the remission of sins, adoption, salvation, and eternal life. From this cause or form of justification Paul explicitly excludes the Law, the works of the Law, and works in general.

The absolute heart of the article of justification is this maxim of Paul that the Law with its works is excluded. Because this maxim manifestly differs from the judgment of human reason and the disputations of the philosophers concerning righteousness, various cavilings or sophistries have been thought up by which the very clear statements of Paul regarding the exclusion of works can be eluded, lest the entire credit for our justification be attributed only to the free mercy of God in the merit of Christ alone, as grasped by faith alone; but rather that something of our own must be added. We shall point out the principal opinions on this.

First. Some contend that Paul by the term "the works of the Law" understands only the ceremonial laws of Moses, and that he is excluding these from justification in this way because the Jews at that time held to the persuasion that they were righteous in the sight of God if they observed the statutes regarding circumcision, festivals, sacrifices, foods, and other ceremonies, in a purely external way without any true spiritual inner feelings. They say that only this ceremonial righteousness has been excluded by Paul from the article of justification, so that the meaning is that there is no need for us in the New Testament to have this ceremonial righteousness, but that we are justified without the ceremonial law and without the ceremonial works. In no way do they mean that Paul, by this exclusion, was thinking of the works of the moral law.

This opinion has some great and prestigious authors and patrons. Origen argued this way, and Ambrose followed him, along with Jerome and Chrysostom, when they were interpreting these exclusions made by Paul. The principal arguments by which they were led to this opinion, and by which they wished to prove it to others, are the following.

1. The ceremonial laws of Moses have been so abrogated that there is no need in the New Testament to observe them, for they have been excluded. But works of love or the moral law have not been so abrogated. These things are commanded in the New Testament and by many exhortations are required of believers. Therefore Paul by this exclusion understands only ceremonial works and not moral ones.

2. The question and the point at issue in Acts 15 and Romans and Galatians concerned circumcision and other aspects of the Mosaic ceremonial law. In Rom. 4:9ff. Paul brings in the matter of circumcision explicitly; in Gal. 4:10 he deals with new moons, sabbaths, and festivals; in Col. 2:16, 21 he deals with foods, "Do not taste, do not touch." Therefore when he says, "without works," we must understand this only with reference to ceremonial precepts but not moral ones. These are the main arguments they bring up.

We reply that what they say in this way about the exclusion of the ceremonial laws is indeed true. But the question at issue is whether Paul wishes his exclusion to be understood only of the ceremonial laws, so that he includes and requires the moral laws as necessary for justification.

We shall respond in a correct and simple way to the authority of the ancients. Pelagius had used these statements of the ancient fathers to confirm his error, and in this circumstance Augustine was compelled to study accurately and closely Paul's true and genuine meaning when he said: "without the works of the Law."

Augustine rejected and specifically refuted the opinion of which we have just spoken, and contended that Paul was speaking of the entire Law and of the works of the entire Law, in his book *On the Spirit and the Letter* [*De Spiritu & Litera*, 33, MPL 44.239] and in his *Exposition of the Epistle to the Galatians*, ch. 3 [*Expositio Epist. ad. Gal.*, MPL 35.2118].

When Jerome was dragged into the Pelagian controversy, he concluded that his earlier interpretation concerning the ceremonial laws did not properly convey Paul's meaning [*Dialogus adv. Pelagianos*, MPL 23.495ff.]. In his *Epist. ad Ctesiphontem* [132.8, MPL 22.1156] in reference to Paul's statement, "A man is not justified by the works of the Law," he affirms that this is spoken not only of the Mosaic ceremonies but of all the commandments which are contained under the general heading of "law." To confirm this position he cites Rom. 7:22, "I delight in the law of God in my inmost self."

Ambrose on Romans 4 [re Rom. 4:7–8, MPL 17.83] interprets Paul's exclusion ("without works") in this way: "Clearly they are blest whose iniquities are remitted and sins brought under control without labor or work, with no work of penance required of them, except that they believe." Now it is a certainty that works of repentance are not merely matters of the ceremonial law.

Origen himself in discussing Romans 3 [MPG 14.952] affirms that the thief and the adulterous woman were justified by faith alone; and he adds that the boasting of the Pharisee came from the works of the Law, but this is excluded; and the Pharisee is obviously referring to the Sixth and Seventh Commandments. In the same passage Origen explains Paul's exclusion in Gal. 6:14 [MPG 14.953] thus: "God forbid that I should glory except in the cross . . ." and he adds, "You see that Paul does not glory in his own righteousness, chastity, wisdom, or other virtues and actions, because this glorying is excluded, not through the law of works but through the law of faith."

Therefore it is clear how much we must attribute to the opinion of some of the ancients, that opinion of which we have been speaking. They themselves knew that Paul's statements require more than the exclusion of only the ceremonial law.

We must take note of the arguments by which it is demonstrated that Paul is speaking not only of the ceremonial laws of Moses but also of the entire Law when he says, "without the works of the Law."

1. The argument of Augustine is this: Paul in Rom. 3:20 shows that he is speaking of the works of that law through which we are made aware of our sins. But in Rom. 7:7 he says: "I would not have known covetousness if the Law had not said, 'You shall not covet.'" Therefore it is manifest and certain that Paul in this discussion understands particularly the moral law.

2. In Gal. 3:12 Paul cites this statement regarding the works of the Law: "He who does them shall live by them." Likewise in v. 10: "Cursed is he who does not continue in all . . ." Therefore it is absolutely clear that these statements pertain not only to the ceremonial laws but to the entire Law, and particularly to the moral law. Look at least at Deut. 27:26 and Luke 10:28: "This do, and you shall live."

3. In Gal. 3:21 Paul says: "If a law had been given which could make alive, then righteousness would indeed be by the Law." This statement can in no way stand if Paul is trying to take justification away from only one part of the Law, namely the ceremonial. Therefore it is completely manifest that Paul by this exclusion understands the whole Law. No amount of sophistry can get around this argument.

4. Paul in Romans 10 and Galatians 3 distinguishes between the righteousness of the Law and the righteousness of faith. He makes an antithesis, not between doing the ceremonial and doing the moral law, but simply between "doing" and "believing." In regard to the "doing" he uses the same line of reasoning seen in Luke 10:28, which clearly refers to the works of the moral law.

5. In Romans 2 Paul says that he is speaking of that law whose work is written in the hearts of even the gentiles, which in no way can be understood of the ceremonial laws of Moses. Thus in Rom. 3:19–20 he says that "the whole world is guilty before God, because by the works of the Law shall no flesh be justified." But the Mosaic ceremonies applied only to the Jewish people. Therefore it is certain that Paul is speaking of the works of that law which pertains to all human beings and which is neither ceremonial nor civil but moral.

6. To the Ephesians, in 2:8, Paul says: "By grace are you saved . . . not of yourselves . . . not of works." Then in v. 12 he says that the Ephesians had been "aliens from the commonwealth of Moses," that is, they had not had the ceremonial law. Thus in Titus 3:5 he says: "not by works . . . which we have done . . ." [KJV]. But in Galatians 2 he says that Titus had never received the ceremonial [circumcision] of Moses. Thus it is obvious which works Paul understands.

7. Abraham was justified before the giving of circumcision and 430 years before the Law was promulgated. Yet he had works of which Paul says: "not of works, without works," etc.

8. If Paul in these discussions were talking only about the ceremonial law, it would follow that he is discussing only such sin as is in conflict with the ceremonial law of Moses. It would also follow that the remission of sins would pertain only to sins against the ceremonial law and not those against the moral law. Thus the fruit of the death of Christ would contribute nothing to the gentiles, who were not bound by the ceremonial law; but only the Jews would be freed through Christ, and from nothing more than their slavery to the ceremonies. In this doctrine these things are correlative: the Law, sin, and the remission of sin because of the death of Christ, so that the Law, sin, and the Lamb who takes away the sin of the world are placed against one another, and what Paul speaks about the Law cannot be restricted only to the ceremonies.

We must also add something regarding the arguments by which, as we have said above, Origen and the others were motivated to interpret Paul as speaking only of the ceremonies of Moses.

The answer to the first argument is taken from the doctrine of the abrogation of the Law. As to what pertains to justification, all parts of the Law have been similarly and equally abrogated. For no law was given which could make alive [cf. Gal. 3:21]. But as to what pertains to obedience there is a difference. The civil and the ceremonial laws were abrogated in such a way that now in the time of the New Testament their observation is not required of believers. But there is a different rationale for the moral law. The articles of justification and of the new obedience are separate and distinct. Thus it does not follow that because the works of the moral law are commanded of believers, therefore they are necessary for justification by faith.

To the second argument this is the correct reply: The question arising in Acts 15 dealt primarily with the ceremonies of Moses, and Paul in many places speaks of these ceremonies. But in this discussion the apostles were moving from a part of the Law to the whole Law, for this reason. The question about the necessity of observing the ceremonial laws of Moses involved this error: It denied that we are justified only by trust in the grace of God for the sake of Christ the Mediator, but taught that it was necessary for justification that there also be observance of the Law. Because the Decalog is the principal and most significant part of the Law, therefore if the ceremonial law is necessary for salvation, the moral law will be even more necessary. For in Matt. 23:23 Christ criticized the Pharisees because they praised certain works of supererogation in the area of the ceremonial laws and in the meantime neglected "the weightier provisions of the Law," that is, things of greater value and importance. Likewise in Acts 15:10 Peter says that the argument concerned "a yoke of the Law which neither we nor our fathers have been able to bear." Christ Himself in Matt. 23:23 clearly affirms that the moral aspects in the Law are more serious, and in Gal. 5:3 Paul says that he who receives circumcision under the notion of its necessity for justification "is a debtor to observe the entire Law."

From this it is clear and can be understood how the apostles in this discussion moved from the part to the whole and from the specific to the general. They used examples which were clearly from the moral law, as we have said above.

Although it is obvious that Paul, when he speaks of "the works of the Law," cannot and must not be understood with reference only to the ceremonial laws, so that also the fathers noticed this, yet Vicelius undertakes the defense of this opinion and believes that he will be able to deceive the reader into agreeing with his idea that Paul is condemning the fact that the Jews under the outward covering of the ceremonial law were establishing righteousness for themselves in the eyes of God, and again that in the New Testament there is no necessity for us to observe the Mosaic ceremonies but that we can be saved without circumcision and the other ceremonial works. These points are true, and there is no controversy here. But the question is: Does Paul exclude only the ceremonial law and include and insist upon the moral law for justification when he says: ". . . not by the works of the Law" or: ". . . to whom God imputes righteousness without works"?

Second. There is the opinion of those who contend that "the works of the Law" in the writings of Paul must be interpreted only of the virtues of the heathen, that is, the works of those who have not been reborn by the Holy Spirit but are presenting certain works solely by the powers of their free will. There are many discussions to this effect in the writings of Augustine, to which Augustine was driven by the situation of the times. For the Pelagians were contending that those works which an unregenerate man performed by the powers of his own nature, without the Holy Spirit, and before faith and renewal, were either the very righteousness availing before God or surely deserved justification. In refuting this error Augustine was accustomed to use the statements of Paul concerning "the works of the Law."

The position which Augustine defended against the Pelagians is correct, that the works performed without faith by the unregenerate not only are not righteousness before God, nor merit righteousness, but that the virtues of the heathen in the eyes of God are vices and sins. In his *Against Julian*, Bk. 4, ch. 3 [.30, MPL 44.753–54], Julian raises the objection, "If a heathen has clothed the naked, freed someone in danger, treated the wounds of the sick, and could not be impelled to false testimony even by torments, would this, because it is 'not of faith,' be sin?" But Augustine replies vigorously, "To the degree that it is not of faith, it is sin." To prove this point, Augustine applies the statement about the works of the Law which Paul himself makes in Phil. 3:6, where he says concerning his manner of life in Pharisaism before the renewal of the Spirit: "according to the righteousness which is in the Law, blameless." And the Jews contended that they, apart from faith in Christ, could be saved solely by the works of the Law.

Up to this point we have no problem with [Augustine's] position [against the Pelagians], but the question is involved here as to whether in the discussion of Paul regarding the works of the Law we are to understand nothing else than only those works of our reason which are performed without faith and the Holy Spirit. The papists strongly contend for this statement, but they do not retain the position of Augustine regarding the works of unbelievers. They say that the statement of Lombard is cruel in which he affirms with Augustine that the entire life of the unbeliever is sin. The Cologne theologians say that this statement of Augustine is "too paradoxical," and on the basis of the works of the unregenerate they construct the concept of the merit of congruence. The Council of Trent [Session VI], Canon 7 [*De Fide*, Kramer Ed., 1.550], decrees: "If anyone says that all works which are performed before justification, in whatever way they may be done, are truly sins, or that when a person strives mightily to dispose himself toward grace he is only sinning more grievously, let him be anathema." In these points the papists are in total disagreement with the arguments of Augustine about the works of the Law, and yet they pass themselves off under the mask and pretext of antiquity.

Gropper interprets "the works of the Law" as those which are forced out of us by the fear of punishment without any consent by our inner feelings. He says that such are not truly good works, much less righteousness in the eyes of God, or worthy of Him. On this point we agree. But the question is, when Paul makes his exclusion regarding "the works of the Law," does he wish to exclude only those forced works, and does he wish to include the rest, which come from a renewed will, as works necessary to justification?

Third. We must set forth and confirm the correct statement of the case. The papists, as we have said above, seize on the discussion of Augustine, omitting the cause and reason for that disputation, and want Paul's statement "through the works of the Law" to be understood with reference only to the external behavior of human reason in the unregenerate. These "works of the Law" are distinguished from the works which they call "works of faith, grace, and love," as Jerome also argued.

Thus they contend that Paul's exclusions ("without works, not by works") are not to be understood with reference to the works of the regenerate coming from faith, but only with reference to the works of human reason preceding faith and regeneration. They exclude from the cause and form of justification only the works of the unbelieving, but not the works of the regenerate, which they are so anxious to make a matter of necessity that they are at the same time to be set forth as a substantial or integral constituent part of our righteousness before God unto salvation and eternal life.

Therefore, because the main element in the article of justification depends on the true explanation of this exclusion concerning "the works of the Law," we shall gather a few sure and clear testimonies which bear witness that Paul, when he says: "We are justified by faith without the works of the Law," is excluding from justification not only the ceremonial laws of Moses, not only the works of the unregenerate or the unbelieving, but we must understand that he also excludes the works which follow, that is, the works of the regenerate performed out of faith. These works which follow are to be excluded, not so that they will not follow justification, but so that they will not be the cause or merit, the form or a part of justification, that is, lest anyone should think that the righteousness before God which brings life eternal is divided between the merit of Christ, apprehended by faith, and the works of the regenerate—as if justification in part consists of these and relies on them—but that the praise and glory of our righteousness before God unto eternal life may remain entirely with the obedience and merit of Christ the Mediator, and the application of His merit be attributed to faith alone.

The papists realize that they have been put in a corner by this exclusion of Paul, if it is correctly explained; therefore they are looking for various cracks through which they can slip away. Some want to argue only about the ceremonial laws, some only about the works of unbelievers.

Vicelius feels that this point is very shaky and uncertain; therefore he is looking for other objections. He says that we are saved without our works, that is, we do not deserve by our works that the Father should give His only-begotten Son for our sins, and Christ accomplished the work of our redemption alone on the cross, without any works on the part of men, either preceding or subsequent. In this sense, he says, Paul made his exclusion. But it is not Paul's meaning, he says, that our applying of Christ's work should take place only by faith without works. But because he noticed that the light of Paul's discussion is too bright to let itself be obscured by this reasoning (for it is absolutely manifest

Vicelius

that Paul in Romans 4 is speaking of the application), he takes refuge in the distinction that in the first justification there is a place for Paul's exclusion but not in the second justification, that is, the regenerate man, if he has fallen into sin and lost his righteousness, is not justified a second time without works; or as Vicelius says, he who is justified by faith without works is later on righteous in the sight of God both by his faith and his works. Again, he says that we are justified by faith, to be sure, but in the Last Judgment eternal life will be given according to our works. These cavilings will all be refuted by the very clear testimonies we shall cite.

Particularly illustrative is the testimony in Romans 4, where Paul in setting forth a universal model (so to speak) of justification, uses the case of Abraham, whom for this reason he calls the father of the faithful, because both Jews and gentiles are to be justified by faith in exactly the same way. He uses Abraham as an example of justification, not with reference to his first conversion, when he was called out of the idolatry of Chaldea, Gen. 11:31; Joshua 24:2; for if this were the case, the exclusion ("without works") could be restricted only to those works which he had done before conversion, while still in idolatry and unbelief. But he refers to Abraham when Abraham after the first call was obedient to God by faith, from Genesis 11 to Genesis 15, 10 years more or less, that is, when he had already been renewed by the Holy Spirit and been adorned by good works and the fruits of the Spirit, as Scripture affirms in Heb. 11:8ff.

As can be demonstrated from the history in chs. 11–15, Moses in the Old Testament mentions many outstanding examples of the new obedience in Abraham in that course or life of good works which Abraham performed; and Paul in the New Testament poses the question as to what the righteousness of Abraham before God was at that time, in what his inheritance of benediction and blessing consisted. To this Abraham, now regenerate and adorned with many works, Paul applies these statements in Rom. 4:2: "If Abraham was justified by works, he has something to boast about, but not before God" [RSV]. Again in v. 5: "To the one who does not work but believes in Him who justifies the ungodly, his faith is imputed for righteousness." To this same Abraham he also applies this statement in v. 6: "David says, 'Blessed is the man to whom God imputes righteousness without works.'"

This testimony is so clear that it cannot be escaped by any line of reasoning. All the sophistries of Vicelius lie prostrate. It is manifest that Paul is speaking about the application, and it is absolutely clear that the discussion does not deal only with the first justification, as they say. It is very false to conclude from this what Vicelius contrives, namely that justification is imputed to faith without works but that salvation is given according to works. For Paul says that the inheritance and the blessing of a man are the same thing. Likewise: "By grace are you saved through faith" [Eph. 2:8]. It is not true that there is a second blessing and salvation which will be revealed at the Last Judgment, different from the one now received through faith. We are saved now, but in hope, and only the manifestation of it remains to take place.

Therefore this testimony is absolutely certain, that Abraham at the time of which Paul is speaking did have faith and also truly good works. But Paul says that he was not justified by his works, but that faith was imputed to Abraham for righteousness. At that time Abraham was both a believer and a doer of good works, and Paul asks whether the imputation took place on the basis of his working or his believing, or both at the same time. Paul replies: "To the one who does not work but believes . . ." [Rom. 4:5]; and he adds the reason: because it is grace, not a debt. Likewise, Abraham at that time had both faith and works, but righteousness unto blessing was imputed to him without works.

Paul in Rom. 4:4 mentions a reward according to debt and a reward according to grace, because in Gen. 15:1 God says: "I am your great Reward." Paul explains this to mean that because Abraham's faith was imputed to him for righteousness, therefore the reward which God promised him must not be understood as according to debt but according to grace. Lest a connection between this reward and the merit of works be set forth, Paul says that the imputation took place without works. This is Paul's explanation of the word "reward."

Therefore Paul's testimony is firm and clear in every respect as to what we must understand by "the works of the Law." And it should be noted that Paul in this discussion about Abraham does not call them "the works of the Law," but he simply speaks about "works": "by works," "without works," "to him who does not work," etc.

Writing to the Galatians, Paul opposes the righteousness of the Law to that of faith, faith to works, believing to doing. The question is: Is he speaking only of the works of unregenerate unbelievers which took place before conversion? The answer to this question lies in the chronology. For the Galatians had been converted to the faith at least six years before Paul wrote this epistle, as Theodoret suggests. Paul is discussing the works of the Galatians. There was no controversy in the Galatian church concerning the works preceding faith, whether they were to be admitted as the reason for righteousness before God; but the argument centered on the works of the regenerate, as to whether they were to be joined with faith in the matter and concern of justification before God. Paul makes the pronouncement that they have fallen from grace when they contend, in the article of justification, that to faith must be joined the righteousness of the Law, which consists in doing something.

The Galatians who were performing works were already regenerate. We must note the state of affairs. In Rom. 10:3 the Jews were arguing that only by works, without faith in Christ, they could establish righteousness for themselves in the eyes of God. But the Galatians were not contending about works alone, without faith; rather they were trying to join both of these in the article of justification. Nor was the dispute about works which had preceded faith, but about those performed out of faith by the regenerate through the Holy Spirit. For Paul says in Gal. 3:2, 5 that the Spirit had been supplied to them. It is about this controversy that Paul is speaking in his Epistle to the Galatians.

It is worth the effort to look at the mounting degrees, or the increasing force of this exclusion in Paul's writings. He says to the Romans in 11:6: "not by works"; in 3:28 and 4:6: "without works"; to the Galatians he says in 5:2, 4: "You have fallen from grace, Christ is of no value to you"; and to the Philippians he says in 3:8: "I count my own righteousness as dung."

We must also note that on the basis of the example of the Galatians there is a very clear refutation of the position of the papists that the regenerate, when they fall from grace, are not justified again by faith alone. For Paul says of the Galatians in 4:19: "My little children, with whom I am again in travail until Christ be formed again in you . . ." Yet it is crystal clear what method of justification Paul is setting before them.

In Philippians 3 Paul in his own person excludes from the article of justification: (1) The works which he had performed in his days in Pharisaism before his renewal. (2) He goes further and explains in what the righteousness before God unto eternal life consists at the time when he is writing the epistle. He even adds what will be his future righteousness before God when he will appear at the resurrection of the dead. Furthermore, this passage relates to the statement in 1 Thess. 4:17, where Paul writes of the Last Day: "We shall be caught up into the clouds to meet with the Lord." And he says: ". . . that I may be found in Christ, not having my own righteousness which is of the Law, but that which is imputed by God through faith" [Phil. 3:9]. Thus he uses not only the perfect tense "I have considered" (*hēgēmai* [Phil. 3:7]) but also the present "I consider" (*hēgoumai* [v. 9]). In 1 Cor. 4:4 he says: "I am not aware of anything against myself" (which unquestionably refers to the works which came after Paul's faith), but he also adds, "yet I am not thereby justified."

This exclusion occurs in the same way equally clearly in the Old Testament. Dan. 9:18: "We do not present our supplications before You on the ground of our righteousness." Here he is surely not speaking of the works of unbelievers but of those which Daniel as a regenerate man had done in obedience to the commandments of God. Likewise David in Ps. 32:2 says: "Blessed is the man to whom the Lord imputes righteousness," without works; and he says this not at the time when he had fallen into adultery but when God had borne witness to him, cf. Acts 13:22: "I have found in David . . . a man after My heart" [RSV].

These testimonies are clear and firm. Paul has two universal, fundamental points for this position of his. The first is that in the article of justification the righteousness of the Law and the righteousness of faith are opposed to one another, cf. Rom. 10:5[ff.]; Gal. 3:2ff.; and Phil. 3:9. Works are required for the righteousness of the Law, for it consists in doing. Opposed to this is the righteousness of faith; indeed, it is put in opposition in the way which Paul expressly describes in Gal. 3:12: "The Law is not of faith" [KJV].

Therefore whatever is of works and whatever is involved in doing, whether before or after regeneration, pertains to the Law and is excluded from faith in the matter and the article of justification. Thus what Vicelius and the rest say is false, when they dream that there are some works of the Law which Paul wants to be understood as belonging under his exclusion, but that others are works of faith which are an essential part of the righteousness of faith. For Paul, as is entirely evident, simply excludes our "doing" from faith in the matter of justification.

But if the works following are established as part of the righteousness of faith, the Pauline antithesis between believing and doing cannot stand. In Rom. 11:6 Paul says in a simple way: "If it is of grace, it is not of works," clearly a universal statement. For the Law is the doctrine embracing all things commanded by God. Therefore the works following faith, if they are commanded by God, are works of the Law. And "the Law is not of faith" [Gal. 3:12 KJV]. Jeremiah clearly says in 31:33 that the Law has been written through the Spirit into the hearts of believers; yet it is still Law.

The Law according to Paul must not be allowed a part in the righteousness before God. For Paul is arguing that faith does not justify in this way, that it prepares or aids us in obtaining the righteousness which consists in "doing" or in works, which is the righteousness of the Law. Thus he says in Rom. 1:17: "In the Gospel is revealed the righteousness of God," "not by faith unto works," but "by faith unto faith." Gal. 2:16: We have believed in Christ, not in order that by faith we may acquire the righteousness of works, but "that we may be justified by faith . . . and not by works. . . ."

In this article in the writings of Paul there is always an antithesis between the righteousness of the Law and the righteousness of faith, and between the righteousness before and after conversion. "If the inheritance is by the Law, faith is made void and the promise done away," Rom. 4:14. Again: "If the inheritance is from the Law, it is no longer from the promise," Gal. 3:18. The Law also has promises, requiring works as the condition for their fulfillment. Paul separates these from the free promise of the Gospel. To the converted Galatians Paul says in 5:4: "You have fallen from grace, because you are being justified by the Law."

We will be able to understand this fundamental point more correctly when we consider the reasons for Paul's careful and earnest distinction, in the article of justification, between our doing and our believing. The Law demands for salvation that our works be done with the completeness and obedience which the norm of the Law prescribes. But because this way of justification was impossible for the Law, "in that it was weak through the flesh," Rom. 8:3 [KJV], and yet at the same time it was impossible for "one jot or one tittle" to "pass from the Law" without being fulfilled, Matt. 5:18 [KJV], therefore God, by sending His Son, did what was impossible for the Law; He made Him subject to the Law so that justification by the Law might be fulfilled in us. Therefore our righteousness before God is not our doing; but the perfect obedience of Christ, by which He fulfilled the Law—by this "many were made righteous," Rom. 5:19.

This obedience of Christ by which He fulfilled the Law for us is not something infirm or mutilated or imperfect, to be patched on our "doing" so that we might have a full and complete righteousness before God consisting in part of the obedience of Christ and in part of our own. This is an insult to the merit of Christ, as if it were insufficient for our righteousness before God. Therefore, in order that the praise may be and remain solidly and wholly with Christ for our justification, Paul does not want our "doing" to be mixed in with Christ's obedience, but when we by faith lay hold on this obedience, then we have solid, perfect, and complete righteousness before God.

Paul makes this distinction so accurately between the Law and faith in the article of justification because by the grace of God justification is moved from the area of Law to the area of faith in Christ. Those who do not want to use this blessing of God and keep looking to the Law for their justification, so that they seek their righteousness in it, either in whole or in part, have lost Christ and fallen from grace. This antithesis warns and instructs us that those who are justified by faith in Christ are not justified by the Law; but those who wish to be justified by the Law are not justified by faith in Christ. For these two elements cannot be confused or mixed, but are separated, as it were, by a perpetual contradiction. From this fundamental point the entire discussion can be understood most correctly. Now the question is not whether in believers, through the Spirit, the new obedience is begun in keeping with the Law, but the question concerns the article of justification.

The second fundamental point is this: The works of the regenerate in the weakness of this flesh of ours are always such as Scripture describes in Rom. 7:21: "When I want to do good, evil is present with me"; Is. 64:6: "All our righteousness is as filthy rags"; Ps. 130:3: "If You, Lord, should mark iniquities . . ." Therefore the very works of the regenerate need remission, so that their uncleanness and imperfection may be covered with the perfect obedience of Christ, that

merit of Christ

is, speaking in the Pauline manner, that they may be justified, as Luther says in the Smalcald Articles [3.3, Tappert p. 309. This is not an exact quote.].

But if even these are justified, then they cannot justify the person, that is, they cannot be a part of the righteousness of faith before God. From this fundamental point Paul interprets the statement of Ps. 32:1: ". . . whose transgression is forgiven, whose sin is covered" [KJV] this way in Rom. 4:6: "to whom the Lord imputes righteousness without works," that is, where there is need for covering sin there is no justification by works.

It would be pleasant to expand on this idea a little more fully, because the main point in the article of justification is this exclusion, which is eluded by various sophistries on the part of the papists. Correctly understood, it illustrates the entire doctrine, and for this reason I have with some care investigated these fundamental points.

Moreover, the fathers themselves, although they often disputed regarding the ceremonial laws and the works preceding renewal, yet also have statements regarding the works following faith and regeneration in which they lead confidence of salvation away from these and transfer it to the free mercy of God for the sake of Christ the Mediator.

Origen, on Romans 3 [re v. 27, MPG 14.952; re Gal. 6:14, MPG 14.954] in explaining the statement of Rom. 3:27, "Boasting is excluded, not through the law of works but through the law of faith," uses the example of Paul in Gal. 6:14, "God forbid that I should glory," and says, "You see Paul does not glory in his own righteousness, his own chastity, his own wisdom, or his other virtues and actions." These words must beyond all argument be understood with reference to Paul's new obedience. And Origen says this concerning the passage where Paul over and over again attributes justification to faith alone.

Augustine, *Contra Duas Epistolas Pelagiani*, 1.21 [MPG 44.569], "Although great righteousness is predicated of the saints in both the Old and New Testaments, yet this does not save them, but only faith in the Mediator who poured out His blood for the remission of sins."

Hilary, on Psalm 51 [MPL 9.322], "For these very works of righteousness do not produce sufficient merit for perfect blessedness, unless the mercy of God effects a change in the will of men toward righteousness and does not count our sins against us. There must be hope in the mercy of God forever and ever."

Basil on Psalm 114 [115, MPG 30.109–12], "For there remains an eternal rest for those who in this life have made a genuine struggle, but not on the basis of the merit of their deeds but because of the most munificent grace of God in which they hope."

Gregory, "Not in deeds, not in tears, but in the pleading of our Advocate do we place our confidence."

Therefore it is evident what Paul wants us to understand by his exclusion ("without works") in the article of justification.

The objection is raised that Paul does not simply mention "works" but adds the restriction "the works of the Law." Therefore [they say] there will be certain works which are not of the Law but of faith, grace, and love, which are not involved in Paul's exclusion.

The answer to this is obvious, and from it we can shed some light on this doctrine. Paul often simply mentions "works" in an exclusive manner, without the addition of the word "Law," e.g., in Rom. 4:6; Eph. 2:9; 2 Tim. 1:9; Rom. 11:6; and in Titus 3:5 he speaks of "works done in righteousness."

Paul often uses the term "the works of the Law," not in order to ascribe to certain other works of ours, if not the whole, then nevertheless some part of our justification, but in order to take away from our works, in the highest degree and universally (from all of them, of whatever kind, even the most outstanding), the credit for our justification and to claim it for faith alone. For the Law is the doctrine of works, Rom. 3:10ff. And when God says concerning His law: "You shall not add anything or take away" [Deut. 4:2], it means that the doctrine of the Law is so perfect that nothing is worthy of the name of a good work which is not included in it. Therefore all good works necessarily must be works of the Law. For things not having the mandate of God are included in the statement in Matt. 15:9: "In vain do they worship Me, teaching as doctrines the precepts of men" [RSV]. Likewise: "Who has required these things?" [Is. 1:12]. See Luther in his book *On Translating* [*An Open Letter*, Amer. Ed., 35.175ff.]. Thus there are three primary causes for Paul's use of the term "the works of the Law," which he excludes from justification.

1. In those days many works were being touted which were actually matters of tradition, and many people put them on a higher level than the works which had been commanded by God, cf. Matt. 15:3; Luke 18:11–12. Therefore Paul uses the term "the works of the Law" as if he were saying: If any works were to justify, they doubtlessly would be those which God Himself commanded with His own voice and wrote with His own finger, that is, which He "prepared beforehand, that we should walk in them," Eph. 2:10 [RSV]. But if no one is justified by the works of the Law, much less will anyone be justified by the works of traditions.

2. Many people pass off the hypocrisy of outward works as righteousness. Paul argues against this and says that the Law requires inner and spiritual activities; indeed, it is necessary that it be written by the Holy Spirit in the hearts of believers, Jer. 31:31–33, in order that what Paul says in Rom. 7:22 may be fulfilled: "I delight in the law of God according to the inner man." If such works,

which belong to the Law, do not justify, much less will an external hypocritical appearance.

3. In regard to works per se, offered by the creature to the Creator, Christ says in Luke 17:10: "We have been unprofitable servants, for we have done only what was our duty." But in the Law God adds a promise to the works. Therefore that reward promised to the works is not in them of itself but comes from the divine promise which is added to the Law. Yet by these works to which God in the Law has added His promises "no flesh shall be justified" [Rom. 3:20] because "a law has not been given which could make alive" [cf. Gal. 3:21]. Thus the question of "the works of the Law" is explained.

[CHAPTER V]: THE EXCLUSIVE EXPRESSIONS

We must note three points with regard to these exclusive expressions. 1. What they are and how many. 2. In what sense they are to be received in the article of justification. 3. The reasons for which they are to be used and retained. We shall note a few things regarding these points.

First. Paul does not use only one exclusive expression, but several, in explaining the article of justification. He does so because he wants to protect this doctrine against all errors and pitfalls, so that it not be tampered with in any way; but that, after removing and excluding all errors, the credit for our justification be given to the free mercy of God alone, through the merit of the obedience of Christ the Mediator alone, and the application of all this be attributed to faith alone. So we shall list the principal points to which I think all these exclusive particles can be referred. Some of them speak about the cause, some about the merit, and some about the application of justification.

1. The word "grace" (*gratia*) with its equivalents. Rom. 3:24: "We are justified by the grace of God"; Eph. 2:8: "By grace are you saved"; Rom. 11:6: "If by grace, it is no more by works"; Titus 3:5: "according to His mercy"; Ps. 71:2: "In Your righteousness deliver me"; v. 16: "I will praise Your righteousness, Yours alone." In this passage, for the sake of greater emphasis, he doubles it: "Your righteousness, Yours alone." Cf. 2 Tim. 1:9; Eph. 1:9. It is evident that the following expressions are exclusive because they are added in each individual instance: "without works," "not by works."

2. The particle "freely" (*gratis*) with its synonyms. Rom. 3:24: "We are justified freely . . ."; 6:23: "The gift of God is eternal life" [KJV]; Eph. 2:8: "Salvation is the gift of God"; Gal. 3:18: "If the inheritance comes from the Law, then it is no longer from the promise. But God by His gracious favor gave it without cost to Abraham through the promise."

3. The designation "one." Rom. 5:15: "The grace of that one man, Jesus Christ, abounded for many" [RSV]; v. 17: "They . . . shall reign in life by One,

Jesus Christ" [KJV]; v. 18: "By the righteousness of One, righteousness came upon all"; v. 19: "through one man's obedience . . ." Therefore the grace, righteousness, and obedience of no human being except that one man, Jesus, shall prevail unto justification before the judgment seat of God. Cf. 2 Cor. 5:14; Gal. 3:16; 1 Tim. 2:5; Heb. 10:14; Luke 10:42.

4. The word "Law." Rom. 3:21: "without the Law"; Gal. 2:21: "not through the Law"; 3:21: "not from the Law."

5. Rom. 4:6: "without works"; Titus 3:5: "not from works"; 2 Tim. 1:9: "not according to works"; Eph. 2:8: "not of yourselves"; Phil. 3:9: "not having my own righteousness"; Rom. 10:3: "one's own righteousness."

6. The word "imputation," which Paul uses 11 times in Rom. 4: vv. 3, 4, 5, 6, 8, 9, 10, 11, 22, 23, and 24. He uses it in three ways: to impute faith unto righteousness, to impute righteousness without works, and to impute according to grace. 2 Cor. 5:19: "not imputing their trespasses to them."

7. "That we might be made the righteousness of God in Christ," 2 Cor. 5:21; "That I might be found in Him," Phil. 3:9; "He has risen with us and made us sit in heavenly places in Christ," Eph. 2:6; "I no longer live, but Christ lives in me," Gal. 2:20.

8. The word "faith." He uses this in many different ways. Rom. 4:5, 9: "Faith is imputed unto righteousness"; Luke 17:19: "Your faith has saved you." Cf. Acts 3:16; Rom. 3:28; Acts 26:18; 15:9; Rom. 5:2; 3:30, "He justifies the circumcision by faith, and the uncircumcision through faith." The terms "by faith," "through faith" are repeated several times. In Gal. 2:20 he says: "The life which I now live in the flesh I live in the faith of the Son of God. . . ." Heb. 10:22: "Let us draw near . . . in full assurance of faith." Phil. 3:9: "the righteousness . . . which is through the faith (*tē pistei*) . . ." 1 Tim. 1:14: "The grace of our Lord Overflowed with (*meta*) faith . . . in Christ." Titus 1:1: "according to (*kata*) the faith . . ." Heb. 11:13: "They died according to the faith." Matt. 9:29: "Let it be done according to your faith." Heb. 4:2: "The Word . . . was not mixed with faith." Rom. 4:13: "He was made an heir through the righteousness of faith."

That "faith" is exclusive is obvious from the fact that there is added "faith without works," Rom. 3:28; "through faith . . . not by works," Eph. 2:8–9. Rom. 3:27: "boasting is excluded, not through the law of works but through the law of faith."

In Gal. 2:16 there is a peculiar exclusion which must be noted in the language: "We know that a man is not justified by the works of the Law, unless by faith" [Vulgate]. In the Latin language the terminology seems to mean that works in themselves alone without faith cannot justify a man, but they can do it if they have faith joined to them, as if I should say that a natural inclination of people cannot produce artists unless they are instructed. Thus in 1 Tim. 5:19, "Against an elder receive not an accusation, except before two witnesses." In this verse the meaning is clearly that if an accusation can be proved, it must be received from two witnesses. Thus Hosius[50] devised this interpretation for Paul's statement: The works of pious people in themselves are, to be sure, imperfect and unclean and cannot justify, but through faith these works are sprinkled by the blood of Christ, and hence are worthy of a reward, virtue, and worthiness to justify, that is, they are worthy of meriting remission of sins, salvation, and eternal life. The Latin terms seem to permit this meaning that works do not justify except through faith. But Paul's discussion and the context itself do not permit this. For if it had been necessary that there be added the words, "We believed, so that we might be justified by works through faith," there would have been an inclusive expression, as the Latin seems to be saying, but Paul adds, "We believed in Christ, in order that we might be justified by faith in Christ and not by the works of the law" [also in Gal. 2:16].

Therefore it is absolutely clear that the particle "except" (*ean mē*) is for Paul exclusive of the words which precede it. The common practice in Scripture when a certain statement is made about two or more things is to use the particle (*ei mē*) and (*ean mē*) to remove or exclude the preceding words, as when in Latin we use an adversative particle. Note Rev. 9:4; "They were told not to harm the grass of the earth or any green growth or any tree, but only (*ei mē*) those people who have not had the seal of God on their foreheads." Again Rev. 21:27: "Nothing unclean shall enter, nor anyone who practices abomination or falsehood, but only those who are written in the book of life of the Lamb." Mark 13:32: "Of that day and hour no one knows, not even the angels in heaven, but only the Father." Gal. 6:13–14: "They glory in the flesh, but God forbid that I should glory, except in the cross." In these examples the expression (*ei mē*) is used. But here Paul has (*ean mē*). John also uses this expression in 15:4, "Just as the branches cannot bear fruit of themselves, unless (*ean mē*) they remain in the vine, likewise neither can you, unless you remain in Me." In this instance it is clear that the first part of the statement is completely excluded. For it is not the meaning that when the branch remains in the vine, it can bear fruit by itself. John 6:44, "No one comes to Me" (that is, by his own powers) "except (*ean mē*) My Father draw him." It is certain that the meaning here is not that a man, when he is drawn by the Father, can come to Christ by his own reason or strength, for this would manifestly be Pelagianism.

Therefore we have shown from the context of Paul's discussion, from his very statement and language, that the particle "except through faith" is exclusive.

---

[50] Hosius, Stanislaus Hoss, 1504–79, Roman Catholic controversialist. Began the Counterreformation in Poland and was active in efforts toward this end also in Rome and other places in Europe.

And Augustine clearly has borrowed this expression when he says, "No matter how great the righteousness of the saints was, yet it did not save them, but only the blood of the Mediator. "Here is pertinent the story of Thammer"[51] who was in a terrible sweat over Galatians 2, as he himself tells us.

[CHAPTER VI]: THE TERM *SOLA*

We find that these exclusive particles clearly have their place in Scripture. Thereafter all antiquity used the expression, "We are justified by faith alone," and it has been received by frequent use in our churches. It has also been viciously attacked by our adversaries on the pretext that Scripture does not have in so many letters and syllables the word *sola*, "alone." But the substance of the matter is clear beyond all controversy, when it is shown on what basis the exclusive terminology, "We are justified by faith alone," is used and for what reasons it has been accepted.

These are not some foolish wars over words [1 Tim. 6:4; 2 Tim. 2:14] in which we are contending about letters and syllables not found in Scripture, but we are anxious to retain and we will defend the content of this matter, which is so usefully set forth and explained by this exclusive expression. Our theologians desire nothing else, when they say that we are justified by faith alone, than what Paul is teaching by his many and varied exclusive expressions. When we contend for the word *sola*, we only desire to retain that all-important doctrine of Paul concerning free justification and the very sweet comfort which comes from it.

If the question is asked why we fight so hard over the word *sola* and are not content rather with those exclusive terms found in Scripture, we reply that we have true and important reasons. The church in all ages has freely used its own modes of speaking, so that the substance of the matter can be clearly set forth, explained, defended, and retained in the face of the various traps of the adversaries. So also in the article of justification we give first place to the exclusive particles of Paul. But there are true and important reasons why we want to use and retain the word *sola*; and it is profitable to keep the main ones in view, for in this way the use of this word will be better understood and it will be clear when and how we contend for it.

1. We are not correcting the wording of the Holy Spirit, as if we thought that we could speak better and more meaningfully regarding these great mysteries than Scripture speaks. But because there is a different line of reasoning in our languages, we surely must make every effort to set forth as clearly as possible

---

[51] Theobald Thammer, d. 1569, German Lutheran who defected to Catholicism and defended the concept of salvation without Christ.

the meaning of Scripture to our people in languages familiar to us, so that it can be rightly understood by everyone without ambiguity.

It is manifest, when Scripture speaks of two or more things in such a way that it affirms only one but denies the rest, that in our common languages, particularly in German, we cannot translate this easily or in the most meaningful way other than through the use of exclusive expressions such as *sola* (alone) and *tantum* (only). For example, John 1:13: They are the sons of God who "are born not of blood, or of the will of the flesh, or of the will of man, but who are born of God." This statement is best translated into our languages by saying: "Only those. . . ." or "Those alone are the sons of God who are born of God." Likewise in Jer. 9:23: "Let not the wise man glory in his wisdom, nor the mighty man in his might, nor the rich man in his riches, but he who glories, let him glory in the Lord." We express this thought correctly and meaningfully by rendering it: "He must glory only in the Lord." Rom. 3:4: "Let God be true but every man a liar." This thought is popularly translated: "God alone is true." 1 Peter 1:18–19: "We have been redeemed not with gold, not with silver, but with the precious blood of the Lamb." That is: "We have been redeemed by the blood of Christ alone."

Thus when Paul says: "You have been justified and saved, not of yourselves, not of works, but by faith" [Eph. 2:8–9], if the question is asked how this statement can be set forth and explained without ambiguity among our people and in our common language in a brief, easy, and meaningful way, it is clear that this cannot be done more conveniently than through the terms *sola* (alone) and *tantum* (only), as these examples show. And because the language of Scripture is to be so rendered and explained that it can be understood, it is necessary and right that we do this. The church has always used such liberty of speaking in regard to terms not found in Scripture, as in the examples we have noted. Just as no one finds fault when we say: "By the grace of God alone," or "God Himself alone is the righteous One and the One who justifies," or "Let God alone be true," so there is no substantive reason for raising so odious an uproar over the term *sola fide*.

2. Experienced translators have rendered this so freely that they have added the term "alone" or "only" when it is not in the original text in order to be able to render and express the emphasis of the concept correctly and meaningfully. For example, 2 Chron. 20:12: "Since we do not know what we should do, we have this alone as a refuge . . ." [Vulgate]. The word "alone" is not in the Hebrew text, but it is altogether necessary for expressing the meaning in the Latin language. These things are clear. The Septuagint renders Gen. 3:11 thus: "Have you eaten of the tree of which alone I commanded you not to eat?" The Hebrews do not expressly use the exclusive particle, but because the Septuagint was trying to give the meaning in the clearest possible way, it was correct in adding the

exclusive term "alone" (*monou*). The same line of thinking is in our suggested wording: "We are justified by faith alone."

3. In Scripture itself there are examples showing that in one place a term is used with a simple affirmative or negative connotation, but in another place it is explained through the addition of exclusive particles. Deut. 6:13–14: "You shall not go after other gods, but you shall worship the Lord your God and serve Him." Christ explains this statement in Matt. 4:10 thus: "And Him only shall you serve." He was trying to express the emphasis of the statement. Deut. 4:35: ". . . that you may know that the Lord is God and there is no other beside Him." This statement is thus explained in Deut. 32:39: "You see that I am the only One; there is no other beside Me." Thus what is written in Ps. 51:4: ". . . that You may be justified in Your judgment . . ." is interpreted in Ecclus. 18:1: "God alone will be justified." Mark 13:32: "No one knows . . . except the Father"; Matt. 24:36: ". . . except the Father alone." Such examples establish our suggestion: "We are justified by faith alone."

4. Lest any doubt remain, Scripture itself adds an exclusive expression to the word "faith" when it speaks of the application of the benefits of Christ. In Mark 5:36, to the servants who announced to Jairus that his daughter was dead, Christ says: "Do not be afraid; only believe (*monon pisteue*)." Luke 8:50: "Do not fear; only believe, and she shall be well." We have already shown that the particle *nisi* ["unless"; English versions have "but"] in Gal. 2:16 [Vulgate] is definitely exclusive.

5. Paul uses many and varied exclusive words, each of which we have looked at, as has been seen. But the term *sola* includes all of those ideas which Scripture uses, and it does so very meaningfully. For if it is by faith alone, then it is "without the Law," Rom. 3:21. "For the Law is not of faith," Gal. 3:12. "Therefore it is of faith that it might be by grace," Rom. 4:16. "By faith, not by works of the Law," Rom. 3:28. "Faith is imputed without works," Rom. 4:5–6. Therefore, when brevity does not allow us to cite in order all of the exclusions of Paul, we do want to include these briefly, as in a kind of bundle, and say as meaningfully as possible: "We are justified by faith alone, that is freely, by grace, without the Law, not by the Law, without works, not by works," cf. Rom. 4:16.

6. The papists have learned to get around all of these exclusive expressions of Paul (even the clearest ones) by their cavilings, so that they are not easily caught. They mouth the words of Paul: freely, through grace, by faith, without the Law, without the works of the Law. To those words they attach their errors, and under them hide their traps, concerning synecdoche, faith formed by love, the ceremonial law, and works preceding conversion. In the Formula of the Interim they often planted words about grace alone and about the blood and merit of Christ alone, but they always avoided the proposition of faith alone as

if it were a dangerous reef. They interpret grace with reference to inherent love, which is a grace which makes a person pleasing. Now because the most important aspect of this discussion centers on the means of application, they are trying to fool the reader by saying a great deal about the merit of Christ; and soon, when the discussion comes to application, they will corrupt this also.

Therefore the point at issue at this time, in opposition to the papists, can best be understood by means of the question: Are we justified by faith alone? In this way the traps of the adversaries can be detected, and Paul's statement, in opposition to all the tricks and corruptions, can be clearly and meaningfully set forth. Therefore it is right and necessary that our churches use, defend, and retain this exclusionary expression. In doing so, they are acting in accordance with the example of the ancient church, which in a similar situation, against the traps and corruptions of the adversaries, always used its liberty in modes of speaking, to the edification of the people. The wild clamors of the adversaries demonstrate how important it is to retain this exclusionary expression, for it is not without cause that they are so enraged against the proposition that we are justified by faith alone.

7. The expression "by faith alone" in the article of justification was not dreamed up as something new and for the first time by our theologians, but it was always used in the complete consensus of all antiquity in connection with this article, as examples from the writings of the fathers testify.

These statements have been gathered from the writings of Robert Barnes, Aepinus, Bullinger, and Otto Corber.[52]

Ambrose repeats this exclusion 15 times in discussing Romans 1, 3, 4, 5, and 10, as well as 1 Corinthians, and Galatians 1 and 3. Origen on Romans 3 [MPG 14.954], in one place repeats it seven times.

Basil, *Sermo de Humilitate* [MPG 31.529], "Thus the statement of the apostle, 'He who glories, let him glory in the Lord,' " relates to the statement, "Christ is made unto us wisdom and righteousness and sanctification and redemption," so "He who glories must glory in the Lord." And this glorying in the Lord takes place not when a person is exalted by his own righteousness, but recognizes that he is justified unto true righteousness only (*monē*) by faith in Christ: Thus Paul glories, despising his own righteousness and seeking through Christ the "righteousness of God which is through faith."

---

[52] Robert Barnes, 1495–1540, English churchman who converted to Lutheranism. He served Henry VIII in the English Reformation but was burned at the stake by him for his strong Lutheran stand. Aepinus (Joh. Hoech) 1499–1553, Lutheran reformer and controversialist, superintendent at Hamburg, got into controversy on Christ's descent into hell; Heinrich Bullinger, 1504–75, Swiss Reformer, successor to Zwingli, was active in efforts to unite Lutherans and Reformed; Otto Corber, or Koerber, German or Swiss Reformer, wrote on Mary's conception and Gen. 3:1.

Hilary, *De Trin.*, 6 [.30, MPL 10.181–82], "Faith alone reveals the Son of God and merits the glory of all His blessings"; *Canon 8 in Matt.* [MPL 9.961],"He instructs the scribes that sin is remitted by man; for they were looking only at the manhood in Christ, and the forgiveness which the Law could not grant; for faith alone justifies."

Chrysostom, regarding Rom. 8:20–21 [MPG 60.532], ". . . in the hope of being delivered . . ." says, "For we receive only this one gift from God which we believe will be given to us by Him who promised it, and by this way alone we are saved." Again in his *De Fide & Lege Naturae* [MPG 64.124] he says, "I cannot prove that he who works the works of righteousness without faith has life, but I can show that he who believes, apart from works, both has life and gains the kingdom of heaven. For without faith no one has life. The thief believed, and he was justified by the mercy of God. And at this point do not say to me that he lacked the time in which he might live righteously and perform honorable works; for I would contend and I would assert that faith alone by itself saved him. For if he had survived and yet neglected his faith and his works, he would have lost his salvation. But we must not ask questions of this type or raise such a point, because faith in itself saved him, but works in themselves in no way justify those who work them."

Gennadius, on Romans 3, "Because all who believe in Christ are freely justified, bringing only their faith . . ."[53]

Theophilus, in regard to Galatians 3, "The apostle clearly demonstrates that faith by itself or faith alone by justifying us has power in itself."[54]

Bernard, *Sermo Super Cantica*, 22 [MPL 183.881–82], "He who feels remorse over his sins and thirsts for righteousness must believe in You who justify the ungodly, and he is justified only through faith, and thus will have peace with God."

Haymo[55] on Romans 1, "Paul shows in many ways that righteousness and salvation are not through the Law but through faith in Christ, with the result that he took them away from the Law and established them in faith in Christ alone." Likewise in the Gospel for the day of the circumcision of Christ he says of the gentiles, "They were saved only by faith, as it is written, 'The just shall live by faith.' "

---

[53] This reference is found in Augustine's *De Iccl. Dogmatibus*, MPL 58.979ff. which has the works of Gennadius.

[54] We have been unable to locate this.

[55] Haymo. This may be a reference to Haymo of Faversham, d. 1243, an English Franciscan theologian.

Bonaventura, on the *Sentences*, 4, dist. 15, q. 1 [pp. 333–34, Perintoni Ed.], "Because man could not make satisfaction for such great offenses, therefore God gave him a Mediator who was to make satisfaction for these offenses, from whence in faith alone in His suffering all guilt might be remitted, and without faith no one is justified."

Lyra[56] on Galatians 3, "For what was the Law useful? [It is] as if he were saying, 'If the Law does not justify, but faith alone, then why was it given and laid down?'"

The ordinary gloss on the Epistle of James reads, "Abraham was not righteous through the works which he had performed, but by faith alone; his sacrifice is a work and testimony to his faith and righteousness."

Therefore we can correctly say with Erasmus: "This word *sola*, which has been attacked with so much noise in the era of Luther, was reverently heard and read among the fathers."

The papists noisily assert concerning Augustine that he did not use the exclusive particles. But there is one in a sermon for Quadragesima,[57] and in his exposition of the passage "Abraham believed God . . ." he says, "Note that justification is by faith without the works of the Law, and whatever can be bestowed by this observance of the Law, faith alone gives completely." Again, "What Abraham believed in his heart about God, this is in faith alone." In *Johannem 8, Tract.* 42 [MPL 35.1706], "For those of whom it had been foretold that they were not going to believe in faith, by which alone they could be freed from the bondage of their sins . . ." *Contra Duas Epist. Pel.*, 3, [MPL 44.599], "Thus for all the godly in this corruption of the flesh and the weakness of this life of tears there is one hope, that we have an advocate with the Father and that He Himself is the One who makes supplication for our sins." *De Verbis Domini*, Sermon 40,[58] "The medicine of the soul, for all wounds, and the one propitiation for all sins is to believe in Christ."

Note the clear use of the exclusive concept in Irenaeus [*Adv. Haer.*], 4:37–38 [MPG 7 (1). 1031–46], "Men are saved from the ancient serpent in no other way than that they believe in Him."

Cyril, *In Joh.*, 9.30 [Basel Ed. of Cyril, p. 448], regarding the verse, "You believe in God; believe also in Me," John 14:1, says, "He lines up strong soldiers and gives them arms with which they shall prevail over all adversity, for we are saved through faith and in no other way."

---

[56] Nicolas de Lyra, 1270–1340, French exegete, greatly respected by Luther.

[57] We have been unable to locate this.

[58] This is an incorrect reference.

But even though we have omitted a rather long list of such passages, it is useful to show that the ancients definitely used the particle *sola* in the same way that we do in our churches. The papists, who in the early stages of the controversy clamored that this statement, "We are justified by faith alone," was a new and entirely unheard-of voice in the church, now, because they see that in all periods this statement has sounded forth in the church, seek all kinds of sophistic escape hatches whereby they may elude the statements of the ancients and snatch away the correct meaning from the church. They are asserting that although the ancients did indeed use the term *sola*, yet it was in a far different way and with a different meaning than we do. The most important of those "escapes" which I have been able to note are these:

1. They say that the ancient fathers, to show the difference between the Christian faith or religion and that of the Jews, heretics, heathen, etc., said that only the Christian faith justifies, not the faith of heretics or Turks, as when Haymo says that Paul took the people away from the Law, that is, from Judaism and established them only in faith in Christ.

2. With respect to the works preceding faith and regeneration, they say that the fathers attributed justification to faith alone because the gentiles did not by their works merit being called to Christianity. They also say that they did not want to admit the works of unbelievers into the accounting of righteousness before God, as when Chrysostom, on Colossians, Homily 5 [MPG 62.331–32], says, "It is certainly evident that this is a great glory in this mystery as it pertains to the rest of mankind, but it is particularly great in the case of the gentiles. For men who are harder than stones are suddenly raised to the level of angels, by the simple words 'faith alone,' without any addition of works. This is truly the glory and the riches of this mystery."

3. They pretend that the ancients used the particle *sola* in those passages where they were disputing about justification in the first conversion of unbelievers, but that it is another matter as to how those who now have been made believers are justified before God or how believers who have fallen are to be justified, as Ambrose argues in his exposition of Psalm 32 regarding the passage in v. 1, "Blessed are they whose sins are remitted," saying that this does not pertain to the person of the repentant by whose labor and groaning remission of sins must be acquired, but only to those who are first baptized.[59]

4. They say that in the writings of the ancients "faith alone" is put in opposition to the ceremonial law as when Ambrose says regarding Romans 4 [v. 5, MPL 17.83] that when the Law ceases, only faith alone is required for grace unto salvation.

---

[59] We have been unable to locate this.

It obviously cannot be denied that there are different meanings among the ancient fathers. But yet I shall demonstrate, in opposition to these sophistries, that the ancients clearly did teach the position of our churches regarding the particle *sola*.

[First.] The first sophistry is the most easily refuted, for it is evident that the particle *sola* is always placed in opposition to works, as in the statements cited above. And we should note well that when these statements are speaking about the application, acceptance, or apprehension of grace and the remission of sins, they affirm that this does not take place by works but by faith alone. Ambrose in regard to 1 Corinthians 1, [v. 4, MPL 17.185] says, "This has been established by God, that he who believes in Christ is saved without work, by faith alone, freely receiving the remission of sins." There is also this beautiful statement of Hesychius: on Leviticus 1.2 [(4.14), MPG 93.956], "God had mercy on the human race when He saw that it had been weakened in fulfilling the works of the Law, and that man could not be saved by his works; but He willed that he be saved through grace. But this grace comes from His mercy, is apprehended by faith alone and not by works."

It is manifest that by the term *sola* the fathers did not exclude only the Mosaic ceremonial law. For example, Ambrose, regarding Romans 4 [vv. 6–8, MPL 17.83] says, ". . . in order that we may be justified before God without work and any observance of the Law, by faith alone." Again, "No works of repentance are required of them, but only that they believe."

The ancient fathers show that they understand the particle *sola* to apply to both the works preceding conversion and those following. Thus Chrysostom, *Oratio 4 Contra Judaeos* [MPG 48.873], "Not by our good works, our labors, nor as payment, but He justifies our race by grace alone." Thus also Ambrose regarding Romans 3 [v. 24, MPG 17.79], "Those who work nothing, who do not repay, are justified by faith alone by the gift of God." They undoubtedly understand this payment and paying back as referring to the works which follow conversion. And it is even clearer that Origen on Romans 3 [MPG 14.953] says regarding the thief, "The Lord did not inquire as to what he had done previously, nor did He look forward to what work he was going to fulfill when he had come to faith, but as he was about to enter into paradise, He took him as His companion, justified solely by his confession of faith." Again, in regard to the sinful woman in Luke 7:37ff. to whom Christ Himself gave the witness, "She loved much," Origen says in the same writing [ibid.], "Jesus said to her apart from any work of the Law but through faith alone, 'Your sins are forgiven you. Your faith has saved you.'"

But Origen shows that they are not using the exclusive particle *sola* only with reference to the first conversion when he introduces the example of Paul in Galatians 6 [MPG 14.954], clearly many years after his circumcision: "You see that the apostle is not glorying in his own righteousness, his own chastity, his own wisdom, or other virtues or actions of his own." And he adds the reason: "For who can rightly glory over his own chastity, when the prophet says, 'Who will glory that he has a pure heart?' Or over his righteousness, when he hears God saying through the prophet, 'For all your righteousness is as filthy rags'? Therefore the only righteous glorying is in faith in the cross of Christ, which excludes all that glorying which comes from the works of the Law." Likewise Ambrose, *Liber de Jacob et Vita Beata*, ch. 2 [MPG 13.648], ". . . we are not justified by our works but by faith, since our fleshly weakness is an impediment to our works, but the clarity of faith which merits the forgiveness of sins overcomes the error of our works."

This is clearly the sum and substance of the doctrine of our churches in regard to the particle *sola*.

On the other hand, Origen says that when a person hears this, he perhaps may relax and become negligent in well-doing [cf. Gal. 6:9], if indeed faith alone suffices for justification. To this objection we will reply that if a person acts unrighteously after justification he has doubtlessly spurned the grace of justification. Nor does a person receive forgiveness of sins so that he will think that a license to sin again has been given him. For the indulgence of forgiveness is not given for future sins but for those which are past. In this mind Chrysostom writes of the thief: "If he had survived, and would have been negligent in faith and works, he would have cut himself off from salvation."

This reminder in the explanation of the word *sola* is frequently and diligently being set forth and inculcated in our churches. So we have agreement with the ancient church, not only with regard to the words but also in the fact that they understood and explained the word in quite the same way that we do in our churches.

I have given a somewhat copious treatment to the word *sola*, for several reasons. For in both the colloquy at Ratisbon and at the time of the Interim there was wide discussion by many people that we must not contend for the particle *sola*, since it is not found in Scripture. But I do hope that the true fundamental points can be sufficiently understood on the basis of this discussion. This has been the first observation regarding the exclusive particles.

Second. We must take care that the exclusive particles are correctly understood. Therefore we must show in what sense they are used and accepted in the article of justification, so that some strange interpretation is not foisted upon them and that they are not twisted in the direction of carnal security. For when Paul says that we are justified and saved without works, he is not excluding repentance or contrition as something which precedes, nor does he exclude the other virtues as things which must be present or follow.

There is a great difference when Paul says in Phil. 2:14 and 1 Tim. 2:8 that we must pray and do all things without murmuring and wrath. By this statement he clearly is excluding all present sinfulness, that murmuring and wrath should not be present and should not follow. But when he speaks of the blessedness of the man to whom God imputes righteousness without works, he takes the example of Abraham, who at the very time when he is said to be justified by faith, apart from works, had been adorned with the most outstanding virtues, which were the fruit of the Holy Spirit. Our people, when they say that faith alone justifies, do not understand this as meaning that without repentance or contrition they have been promised immunity from punishment even if they continue in sins. Nor do they understand faith as being solitary, sterile, or dead, something which produces no good works or can stand before God with mortal sin.

Therefore, in order that it can be correctly and clearly taught and understood as to what the true and sound meaning of the exclusive particles is in the doctrine of justification, I believe it is a useful method if the matter be so divided that those exclusive terms in the article of justification refer to the following three points. 1. The exclusive terms refer to the object of justifying faith, i.e., the promise of reconciliation with God, which faith must lay hold on for eternal life, must not be sought in the Law which either condemns sin or gives precepts concerning good works, but it must find this in the Gospel, which sets forth and offers the free mercy of God for the sake of Christ the Mediator. 2. The terms refer to what causes or what merits reconciliation. They exclude our merit or worthiness as a condition, they prohibit our works as a cause of reconciliation, and they transfer this function solely to the Son of God, the Mediator. 3. The terms refer to the means or the organ of application, for not by any works, but only by faith, is the free promise of reconciliation for the sake of Christ the Mediator apprehended, received, and applied. And this application so pertains to faith alone that it neither can nor ought to be attributed to any other virtues.

The position of the papists that we are justified by works cannot include the application or the reception of the free reconciliation, for it means that we would be pronounced righteous on the basis of our own innocence. But Scripture pronounces that the free promise of reconciliation is apprehended not by works but by faith. It is manifest that works pertain to the law of works: "He who does them shall live in them" [Gal. 3:12]:. But faith pertains to the promise. Paul also distinguishes from justifying faith the promises of the Law regarding the reward of our new obedience, when he says: "The Law is not of faith, but he who does them . . ." [Gal. 3:12].

I will cite a most beautiful quotation found in Luther's commentary on Genesis 15, in which he very precisely explains in what sense the term *sola* is to be received in the article of justification. He says: "I know that the other virtues are marvelous gifts from God. I know that faith without these gifts does not exist. But the question is: What is the characteristic of each? You hold in your hand various seeds, but I do not ask which are related to which. I ask, which virtue is characteristic of each? Now state clearly what faith alone does, not with what virtues it is closely connected. Faith alone lays hold on the promise. . . . This is the proper function of faith alone. The other virtues have other concerns." Again he says: "We know that faith is never alone but brings with it love and many other gifts. . . . It is never alone, but it should not for this reason be confused with other matters, and that which belongs to faith alone must not be attributed to other virtues" [cf. Amer. Ed., 3.24–25]. Thus Luther.

Thus it is true, and useful for shedding light on the many discussions, when it is commonly said that in the statement "faith alone justifies" the particle *sola* does not govern the subject, but the predicate. The same is the case with such expressions as "faith justifies without works" and "faith without works is dead." It is a fallacy of putting together and separating, In the first expression the particle "without works" pertains to the predicate; but in the second it pertains to the subject.

This point is useful in making correct judgments regarding some of the statements of men like Chrysostom, who in speaking of the foolish virgins argues that it was not sufficient for salvation that they only made a profession of faith; and Theophilus in regard to Matt. 7:21ff., "Lord, Lord . . ." says, "This passage teaches us that if we have faith without works it will be of no value to us." Also cf. Augustine, *De Continentia*, 14 [MPL 40.370], "The apostle even frightens them in a salutary manner, so that they do not think that believers can be saved for the sake of their faith alone, even if they continue to live in these evils."

These fathers are fighting against two pernicious errors: 1. Some people understand the exclusion as if without repentance and contrition, while persevering in iniquities, a dead faith which is not working through love, that is, an intellectual persuasion of one's immunity to punishment, suffices for salvation. 2. There were those who understood faith as only knowledge and the external profession of the dogmas of the church, as is the case in many ungodly and hypocritical people. The fathers acted correctly in rejecting and refuting this corrupt interpretation of the exclusive particles and of the article of justification.

This kind of argument is manifestly the case in Augustine's *De Fide et Operibus* [1, MPL 40.197], which he says he had written after some laypeople had sent him questions in which they were discussing the point: If people seek Baptism and confess the faith, even if they are unwilling to change their wicked and shameful life known for its scandalous and dissolute behavior and openly and avowedly declare that they shall continue in it, are such to be admitted to Baptism . . . ? Then they also were discussing whether those who live criminal and shameful lives and continue to live in the same way, and only believe in Christ and receive His sacraments, will come into eternal life. To confirm this error they used these statements of Scripture: John 17:3, "This is life eternal, that they might know You . . ."; Wisdom 15:2, "Even if we sin, we are Yours." Against these pernicious ideas Augustine wrote this little book, and in ch. 14 [ibid., .211] he says, "They must not destroy their salvation by an evil sense of security, by thinking that faith alone suffices to obtain it and by neglecting to hold on to the way of God by good works and well-doing." Again, "The canonical epistles vehemently affirm that faith without works profits us nothing" [ibid.]. In ch. 22 [ibid., .223], "Let no unconcerned person be deceived or think that he has known God if he confesses Him with a dead faith, as the devils do, and thus has no doubt that he will come into eternal life, because the Lord says: 'This is life eternal, that they know You. . . .'" Ch. 27 [ibid., .229–30], "Eternal life is promised to believers in such a way that a person believes he can come to this life not through a dead faith which cannot save without works, but through that faith in grace which works through love."

On the basis of quotations like these many of the statements of the fathers which the papists marshal against the exclusive particle "sola" can be rightly understood and evaluated. For we also condemn it as false and pernicious if a person attaches a meaning of this kind to these particles. Here are pertinent also those points which at the beginning of this locus on justification we cited regarding the monstrous errors of Simon Magus, Basilides, Carpocrates, and the gnostics, in which we showed how they foully perverted the exclusive particles in the doctrine of justification.

This explanation is also useful because it refutes many of the criticisms with which our adversaries have tried to bring hatred and antagonism toward the doctrine of our churches, as if they were perverting it by rejecting repentance for sins and presumptuously promising immunity from punishment and attributing justification to dead faith. Thus when the Münster Anabaptists came with their proposition "Faith does not require or demand any good work from you," Urbanus Rhegius wrote a learned treatise against them regarding this statement, showing wherein it was true and wherein false with reference to the matter of justification.

Third. In regard to the exclusive words we should note and demonstrate the reasons why the doctrine of justification is not something which can simply be affirmed, but that the antitheses must be stressed through these exclusive terms, and why these terms cannot and must not be omitted but have to be retained in teaching the doctrine of justification. These correct reasons will be more fully explained in their own locus, so that there is no need for a lengthy explanation. Because this grammatical explanation of the words used in the article of justification would delay us considerably, we shall make an end at this point.

[CHAPTER VII]: THE TESTIMONIES OF SCRIPTURE

**The Methodology of the Doctrine of Justification, That Is,
the Passages of Scripture Pertaining to the Article of Justification:
The Order in Which They Are to Be Distributed,
So That We Can Comprehend, Set Forth, and Perceive
the Complete Body of Doctrine Concerning Free Reception before God
unto Eternal Life, with the Proper Order of the Individual Parts**

Because no one should fashion for himself in this primary article (which has been revealed in the divine Word alone and is beyond the purview of human reason) his peculiar method of interpretation, let us follow that method which beyond all controversy is the best and surest, which Paul himself has both demonstrated and prescribed for us in Romans 3, where he gives us the fullest presentation of the entire matter. The main points of Paul's method are these: 1. "All have sinned and come short of the glory of God" [v. 23]. Likewise: ". . . that every mouth may be stopped and the whole world become guilty before God" [v. 19]. 2. "By the works of the Law shall no flesh be justified" [v. 20]. 3. "They are justified freely through His grace" [v. 24]. 4. ". . . through the redemption which is in Christ Jesus, whom God put forward as a propitiation . . ." [vv. 24–25]. 5. ". . . through faith in His blood" [v. 25]. Likewise: "This righteousness is revealed in the Gospel apart from the Law" [v. 21]. 6. ". . . on account of the remission of sins . . ." [v. 25]. Again David describes the blessedness of that man "to whom God imputes righteousness without works: 'Blessed are they whose iniquities are forgiven . . .'" [4:6–7]. 7. ". . . to show His righteousness . . . that He Himself might be righteous . . ." [vv. 25–26]. 8. "This righteousness is witnessed by the Law and the Prophets" [v. 21]. 9. ". . . for all and upon all who believe; for there is no difference" [v. 22].

These main points of the Pauline position show beautifully the complete and correct method for studying the doctrine of justification. We did not want to cite or explain each individual passage, for many of them have been discussed in preceding chapters. We only want to show some reminders as to how, in keeping with these points of Paul, the testimonies of Scripture are to be gathered and applied in the article of justification.

First. Because those who either do not understand or do not feel the sickness of sin do not care for or seek a doctor, nor use his services as they ought, Paul has prepared the road to justification by showing that apart from Christ all men are under sin, and because of sin they are under the wrath and curse of

God, and unless through Christ they are reconciled with God, nothing remains for them but the horrible expectation of judgment and eternal fire, Heb. 10:27. Thus this righteousness of which the Gospel speaks is necessary for all who do not want to remain and perish forever under the wrath and curse of God.

This doctrine of sin and the wrath and curse of God properly pertains to the Law. Yet from here the Holy Spirit begins His work of bringing the doctrine of justification, for the following reason. The hearts of men by nature are either pharisaic or Epicurean. For the Pharisees the doctrine of the Gospel is something unpleasant, because they believe that by their own purity they are righteous before God and therefore there is no need for that righteousness of which the Gospel speaks. From such people we must on the basis of Scripture take away all trust in their own righteousness before God, and they must be confined by the Law under sin [Gal. 3:22]. But the Epicureans, when they hear about the righteousness of the Gospel, are not seriously concerned, and do not seek or embrace or cling to it, because they are convinced of the idea that what we are like and how we live are of no importance before God, whether we are reconciled with God or not. If we immediately set before them the promise of the Gospel, it accomplishes no more than casting pearls before swine. Therefore we must denounce such people as sinners on the basis of the Word of God, for he who has not been reconciled with God through Christ is under the frightful wrath and curse of God, he is in the kingdom of Satan and in the power of darkness, and nothing is more certainly expected for him than the judgment of eternal damnation.

This is the preparation for grace, as Luther says in discussing Galatians 3, for which the Gospel uses the ministry of the Law, so that both repentance and remission of sins will be preached in the name of Christ. We must preserve this order in teaching the doctrine of justification, so that all, whether Pharisees or Epicureans, might be moved by the Holy Spirit not to despise, neglect, hate, or attack the righteousness of the Gospel, but might hunger and thirst for righteousness, that is, that they might love, seek, embrace, and hold fast the grace and mercy of God which the Gospel offers and shows to us in Christ. The Son of God Himself used this method both in His formal teaching (as in Mark 1:15, "Repent and believe the Gospel"; cf. Matt. 4:17) as well as in His pastoral practice, so to speak, as when He treats Mary Magdalene one way and the Pharisee another [Luke 7:36ff.]. It is worthy of note that the same question is asked in Matt. 19:16; Luke 10:25; Acts 2:37; and 16:30: "What must I do to be saved?" But because in Acts the question is asked by those who are contrite, while in the Gospels by Pharisees, therefore the answer is not the same, and yet the purpose is the same in both cases.

The ministry of John the Baptist clearly demonstrates the use of this same order, Mark 1:4; Matt. 3:2; Luke 3:3. In John 1:29 and 36 he says to his disciples: "Behold, the Lamb of God. . . ." But in Matt. 3:7ff. to the Sadducees, when they were coming to him for Baptism, he began to preach about repentance and the wrath of God and the unquenchable fire. He admonished the Pharisees for being a brood of vipers, that is, they were descendants of the original corruption and thus were called the seed of the serpent, Gen. 3:15. "He who sins is of the devil," 1 John 3:8. And he adds: "Do not say within yourselves, 'We have Abraham for our father'" [Matt. 3:9]. He refers here to the final purpose of all this when He says that they should "flee from the wrath to come" [Matt. 3:7]. John 3:36: "He who does not believe in the Son . . . the wrath of God remains over him." Paul's method is so well known that there is no need for a long discussion of it; cf. Romans 1–3; Galatians 2–3; Ephesians 2; Titus 3. The word "justification" itself shows that this method must be preserved, as its meaning has been pointed out above.

We will not labor to pile up testimonies, but I believe it will be quite useful to observe how Paul uses the testimonies pertinent to this point.

1. As regards original sin, he shows that there is no difference between Jews and gentiles. Gal. 2:15: "We are by nature Jews and not Gentile sinners." Eph. 2:3: "We also" (that is, we who came from the circumcision and were faithful) "were by nature the children of wrath, just as were other people."

2. Regarding actual sin he condemns both groups, because among the gentiles there were many who walked in a "reprobate mind," Rom. 1:28, and in open sins, Eph. 2:17ff.; and "we (Jews)" also once walked this way, Eph. 2:3 and Titus 3:3.

3. Among the unregenerate, certain of the gentiles governed their morals with honorable discipline, Rom. 2:14, and from among the Jews some were zealous for the Law, Rom. 2:17–18. They had a zeal for God, and they sought righteousness, Rom. 9:31; 10:2–3. Yet Paul in Gal. 3:10 shows that, because they were outside of Christ, both were under sin and the curse, because it is written: "Cursed is he who does not continue in all . . ."

4. Paul is now a regenerate man who rejoices in the law of God, and yet he says in Rom. 7:18: "In me, that is, in my flesh, dwells no good thing, but only sin." Again, in regard to Abraham, who was now converted and regenerated, Paul says in Rom. 4:5: ". . . who . . . believes in Him who justifies the ungodly . . ." David, now in the regenerate state, summarizes justification as having our sin covered and not imputed [Ps. 32:1–2]. Therefore, also in the case of the regenerate in this life, the righteousness of faith is necessary.

5. He not only condemns sin in a general way, but contends against the infraction of each individual precept, and he shows this and describes it both in

a positive and a negative manner. Rom. 3:12ff.: "They have gone out of the way, they have become unprofitable, there is no one who does good . . . they are full of cursing and bitterness. . . ." Rom. 7:18 and 23: "I do not find how to accomplish the good. . . . The law of sin rebels, brings me into captivity," etc.

6. He has set up a kind of anatomy of the entire man and scrutinizes every hidden part and crevice of both the soul and the body, in order to show that everything is imprisoned under sin. In Eph. 2:3 in a kind of catalog he lists "the lusts of the flesh and of the mind," and specifically mentions the lusts and the wishes, including both the superior and the lower parts of the mind. In Eph. 4:17–19 he includes at the same time both the sins of omission and the sins of commission. Among them are "ignorance within themselves, hardness of head, vanity of the mind, darkness of understanding"—because of these things they had delivered themselves over to the work of uncleanness, etc. Rom. 7:23: "I perceive in my members the law of sin. . . ." In Rom. 3:13ff. he enumerates the throat, tongue, lips, mouth, feet, eyes, and as if breaking in on this list of physical parts, he adds a reference to "the way of destruction," that is, the actions of a person's entire life.

7. Yet he not only sets forth this catalog of sins, but he sets up a kind of judicial proceeding against unreconciled sinners before the tribunal of God, where the accused sinner is convicted and condemned; and he shows in Rom. 3:9 and 19 what sentence is going to be executed upon him: "For all have been condemned as under sin . . . so that every mouth may be stopped and the whole world may be judged guilty before God." Gal. 3:22: "He has confined all under sin"; Eph. 2:3: "the children of wrath"; cf. John 3:36; Rom. 2:8–9; 6:23; 5:18; Gal. 3:10; Eph. 4:18. This is the Pauline preparation for the article of justification, and I believe that a classification like this will be helpful.

Second. We must not patch this idea on, as if the righteousness of faith is only one among the many ways to achieve justification before God, and perhaps an easier way, as Pelagius suggested; but the praise for our acceptance before God unto eternal life belongs solely and only to the righteousness of faith. Scripture takes away from all of those ways (which could have some appearance of righteousness) the praise and credit for our justification before God unto eternal life, in order that by the principle of faith all boasting may be excluded [Rom. 3:27] and that "he who glories may glory only in this . . ." [Jer. 9:24]. . . .

There is no question about whether sins justify before God. But if something besides the righteousness of faith can make a person accepted unto eternal life, it would be either the integrity, excellence, or goodness of one's nature, or obedience to the natural law, or the works of the divine law, or *ethelothrēskia*, that is, the worship of God according to one's own choosing which is undertaken with a good intention apart from the Word of God.

The doctrine of original sin, however, removes the first item from this list, Eph. 2:3: ". . . by nature the children of wrath"; Matt. 3:7: "Generation of vipers!"

Regarding obedience to the natural law, Paul specifically argues in Romans 1 and 2 that the Gentiles knew only a part of the Law, that which pertains to external and civil matters, and that the truth which had been written in their heads was "suppressed in unrighteousness," Rom. 1:18. In brief, the whole discipline of human reason, even though Scripture does attribute to it some importance, is completely eliminated in the article of justification by the thunderbolt of divine judgment, because apart from faith and outside of Christ even those things which seem to be virtues in the unregenerate are vices and sins before the tribunal of God in the article of justification, John 16:8–9; Rom. 14:23; Heb. 11:6; Phil. 3:7.

In regard to the works of the divine law, we have noted above and have explained passages which show that neither before renewal nor after the reception of the Holy Spirit and the beginning of the fulfillment of the Law in this life do these works constitute our righteousness before God unto eternal life. The reason is not that the divine law is a teaching that is less holy, as is the case with man-made traditions, or that it is imperfect, as is the case with our natural knowledge; but it is "weak through the flesh" [Rom. 8:3], even in the saints, insofar as it pertains to perfect obedience. The sentence of the Law (remaining in force upon all) is that "those who are of the works of the Law are under the curse," because they do not "continue in all the things which are written in the Law" [Gal. 3:10].

In regard to self-chosen religion the Lord says in Is. 1:12: "Who has asked these things from your hands?"; Matt. 15:9: "In vain do they worship Me with the commandments of men"; Deut. 12:8, 32: "You shall not do every man what is right in your own eyes . . . but what I command you, this only shall you do." In Col. 2:23 *ethelothrēskia* (self-chosen religion) is condemned by name.

Therefore, because neither our nature, nor obedience to the natural law, nor the works of the divine law, nor self-chosen religion can justify us before God, there remains only the one and only true righteousness before God unto eternal life which is revealed in the Gospel.

Christ used this method of teaching against the Pharisees in a special way, not only by words but also, as it were, by actions. When the Pharisees heard the dogma that perfect fulfillment of the Law is impossible in this flesh, they thought it was a kind of Stoic paradox. Therefore Christ put the Law before them in such a way that they would try, exert themselves, and use all their powers in outward performance of the Law. And lest they presumptuously imagine that they could quite easily fulfill the Law perfectly or even do works of supererogation,

He explained what the norm of perfection in the divine law is, so that in the very attempt, even when they worked with the greatest zeal and desire for the Law, they might see, feel, and experience that they could not reach the goal prescribed in the norm of the Law. The conditions attached to the Law must always sound in their ears and their mind: "Cursed is he who does not continue in all . . ." [Gal. 3:10], or "He who falls short in one point is guilty of all" [James 2:10]. Therefore the conscience must always be left in doubt concerning the sufficiency and the perfection of works.

So Christ says: "Do this and you shall live," in order that in the very attempt they may condemn themselves and be convinced that they cannot be justified by the Law, but that there is need for another kind of righteousness before God unto eternal life. Thus Christ sets forth His standard of righteousness with reference to the First Table in Matt. 19:21, and the Second Table in Luke 10:3ff. There is a beautiful example of this in Mark 12:34, where Christ says to the Pharisee: "You are not far from the kingdom of God." Paul would certainly never have extolled the righteousness of faith so highly unless he had in fact learned what he writes in Phil. 3:8–9.

Third. When the way has thus been prepared, as the Baptist says, then we must bring in the doctrine of justification itself, which because of its magnitude cannot be divided more suitably than if, without sophistry and just for the sake of teaching, the proof passages are categorized under the various genera or orders of causes. In this way many of them can be set forth more clearly and many misunderstandings can be refuted, such as the cavilings of Osiander that we have countless kinds of justifications, such as the grace of God, the blood of Christ, the remission of sins, all of which he says are our justification before God. The position of Cochlaeus [1479–1552, Roman Catholic opponent of Luther] can also be judged on this basis, when he says: "It is certain that God justifies us; but God is love, not faith; and therefore not faith but love justifies."

In regard to the efficient or working cause (*causa efficiens*) of justification, we should note at the outset those passages which affirm that God justifies and saves believers freely—by His free kindness alone, Titus 3:4; by His grace, Rom. 3:24; by His mercy, Eph. 2:4 and 1 Peter 1:3; by the good pleasure of His will, Eph. 1:9; by His love or charity, 1 John 4:9–10; Rom. 5:8; Eph. 2:4; Titus 3:4. Concerning this efficient cause the papists use precisely the same words we do. But their understanding and interpretation is that God is the principal efficient cause of our justification because by grace He pours into us the quality of love by which we are afterward righteous before God.

Therefore we must add this statement: Scripture makes the grace of God the efficient cause of our justification, with this exclusion, that there is nothing in us which God sees on account of which He justifies us, that is, absolves us from our sins and the sentence of damnation and receives us into eternal life. (This is the meaning of the word "justification," and it helps to clarify things in this discussion.) Thus Scripture speaks. Is. 43:25–26: "I even I am He who wipes out your iniquities for My own sake. . . . Tell Me if you have anything whereby you might be justified." Ezek. 36:25, 32: "I will wash you from all your iniquities. . . . I am not doing this for your sake, let it be known to you, says the Lord. Be ashamed and blush for your behavior. . . ." Here are pertinent also the other exclusive expressions which we have noted above.

It is not only in a general way that our voices have been sounding forth about the grace or mercy of God, for Scripture does not speak only generally. But so that it may be possible in some way to show the indescribable riches of the glory of the grace of God, it in many and various ways sets this efficient cause of our justification before us for consideration in our justification, referring to redemption and referring to distribution or application. (These are general terms which I am setting forth as headings, in order that the listing not become tedious by dividing it into too many parts.)

Regarding our redemption.—God, before the worlds were made and before the foundations of the earth were laid [1 Peter 1:20], when He foresaw the misery which would befall the human race, out of pure grace, mercy, and love made the decree concerning the sending of His Son as the Mediator, that He might be the Victim and the Propitiation, 2 Tim. 1:9 and Titus 1:2. And in Him He chose and predestined us, Eph. 1:4–5. He demonstrated His love toward us, whereby in the fullness of time He sent forth His only-begotten Son and delivered Him up for all, Rom. 5:8; 1 John 4:9. Luke 1:78 and 54: "through the bowels of His mercy . . . in remembrance of His mercy." John 3:16: God accepted the sacrifice of His Son as satisfaction and propitiation for the sins of the whole world. 1 John 4:10 and 1 Cor. 1:30: He was made for us by God our redemption, righteousness, etc. 2 Cor. 5:19: "God was in Christ reconciling the world unto Himself."

Regarding the distribution or application of this to the believer.—The grace of God is commended in many ways as the efficient cause of our justification. "He set forth His Son as the Propitiation . . . ," Rom. 3:25; ". . . in the presence of all the people," Luke 2:31; ". . . establishing and preserving to us the ministry of reconciliation," 2 Cor. 5:18; "The God of all grace . . . calls us to His glory . . . ," 1 Peter 5:10; cf. Gal. 1:15; Rom. 8:28; 2 Tim. 1:9; Col. 1:12; Acts 5:31; 1 Tim. 1:14; 2 Thess. 2:16.

Concerning the actual acceptance unto eternal life, Paul says in Eph. 2:4, 5, and 8: "God, who is rich in mercy, for the sake of His great love with which He loved us, when we were dead in sins, has made us to live with Christ . . . for by grace you have been saved. . . ." Eph. 1:7: "We have the remission of our sins through the blood of Christ according to the riches of His grace." 1 John 3:1:

"You see what love the Father has for us, that we should be called the children of God"; cf. Col. 1:13; Acts 5:31.

Then we are commended to the grace of God in order that we might be saved and preserved in grace unto life eternal, Rom. 5:2; 1 Peter 5:10; Acts 14:26; 15:40; 20:32. In these last three passages the lovely words "commending" or "committing" are used, as when a person who cannot himself keep a treasure commits it to the care of a faithful friend. In this sense we are committed to the grace of God. Finally, the grace of God is life eternal.

By dividing the term in this way we can to a degree get an understanding of why Paul calls the grace of God "the riches of His glory" [Rom. 9:23; Eph. 3:16]; "God, who is rich in mercy," full of mercy, Eph. 2:4, 7. We can never exhaust the quarry of these riches; indeed, we cannot even get a full look at them. Yet Scripture sets them before us for our consideration, even if "we see only in a glass darkly and know only in part" [1 Cor. 13:12]. It teaches us what Paul is saying in Eph. 3:8: These riches are "unfathomable."

Because the works of the Trinity toward objects outside Itself are indivisible, we can gather some special testimonies regarding the individual Persons, for example, regarding the Father, 1 John 3:1: "See what love the Father has given us. . . ." There are also many passages of this kind regarding the Son, Gal. 2:20: "He loved me and gave Himself for me"; Eph. 5:25: "Christ loved the church and gave Himself for her"; 2 Cor. 8:9: "You know the grace of our Lord Jesus Christ, that . . . for us He was made poor. . . ." In regard to the Holy Spirit note 1 Peter 1:2: "You are chosen according to the foreknowledge of God the Father by the sanctifying work of the Spirit"; Rom. 5:5: "The love of God has been poured out within our hearts through the Holy Spirit, who has been given to us"; cf. 1 Cor. 6:11.

Further, because the will of God is the first cause (*prima causa*), we must not seek any other cause prior to or beyond the grace of God, Paul warns, when he mentions God's "purpose or predestination or predetermination before the foundation of the world"; likewise when he speaks of "the counsel of His will" and the "good pleasure of His will . . . to the praise of the glory of His grace" [Eph. 1:4–12].

The Gospel proclaims that "God loved the world" even "when it was dead in sins," John 3:16 and Eph. 2:5, and that "He commended His love toward us while we were still sinners," Rom. 5:8; and yet the sentence of the Law is immovable: "Cursed is he who does not continue in everything which is written in the book of the Law" [Gal. 3:10], and again: ". . . showing mercy to . . . those who . . . keep My commandments" [Ex. 20:6].

There are some people who in a rather irreverent way argue that God is a completely free agent, subject to no law, not even His own, and therefore God can by grace and mercy take sinners to Himself, even if the sentence of the Law rules to the contrary. But in this way they are attributing to God two contradictory wills, which is impossible, for it is written in Mal. 3:6: "I am God, and I do not change." We must include this caution, so that our minds are not carried off into Epicureanism by worldly thoughts of this kind, as if God does not care about sin, is not wrathful against it, but loves sinners and by His grace accepts them as they are in themselves.

To summarize, it is as if that which the Law proclaims about sin were no longer valid or true, even though Scripture affirms that it is impossible for the law of God to be dissolved or "pass away," Matt. 5:18, or be "made void," Rom. 3:31. If the mercy of God were the way they imagine, there would be no need for the obedience and the sacrifice of the Son of God, whereby He satisfied the Law. Outside of Christ, therefore, there is no grace or mercy of God toward sinners, and it cannot and must not be understood as correct to believe that if the Law is not dissolved or destroyed or annulled it is impossible for us to be saved. For Paul always adds to the words "before the worlds began" the words "in Christ." In this way the fundamental points of this doctrine can be rightly understood.

Obviously we cannot investigate or penetrate the secret counsel of the Trinity in regard to our redemption, for grace and mercy preceded the decree concerning the sending of the Mediator, but it nevertheless remains as an established fact that outside of Christ there is no grace or mercy of God toward sinners. When this matter is under discussion people can become troubled, but this statement is simple, true, and useful for edification.

In opposition to the papists, who place in us certain qualities which cause God to receive believers unto life eternal, this observation should be helpful: The preceding cause (or whatever it is called) for the grace and mercy of God toward us is described in Scripture as the hopeless misery of the human race, from which men cannot free themselves. It is the absence of this element in the statement of the papists that makes their position incorrect, e.g., Acts 13:39: ". . . because you could not be justified by the law of Moses"; Acts 15:10: ". . . because no one could bear the yoke of the Law"; 1 John 3:8: "The Son of God came to destroy the works of the devil"; Rom. 8:3: "What was impossible for the Law because of the flesh . . ."; Gal. 4:5: ". . . to redeem those who were under the Law . . ."; cf. Heb. 2:15; John 3:16; Eph. 2:4–5.

Fourth. There is a second efficient or working cause for our justification, namely Christ in and with His whole work as Mediator. We must consider on the basis of the Scriptural sources what the rationale is for considering Christ as an efficient cause in the matter of justification and how this differs from the other efficient cause, of which we have just spoken. In so doing we can make this doctrine clearer.

There is no argument about the absolute power of God, as to whether He can justify a person without true righteousness. But we must judge this point on the basis of the revealed Word. The Law promises mercy to those who love God and keep His commandments (that is, the Law requires righteousness in those who are to be justified), but upon those who do not "continue in all the things which are written in the Law," it pronounces an eternal curse. The norm of this righteousness in God which has been revealed in the Law is eternal, immovable, and immutable, Matt. 5:18. Therefore God neither will nor can justify without the intervention of a true righteousness. For He says that it is an abomination before God to acquit or justify the guilty without righteousness, Prov. 17:15; Is. 5:23. He cannot deny Himself [cf. 1 Tim. 2:13]. We do not have that righteousness of the Law for which eternal life is promised, nor are we able to supply it in this life; and yet God determined to justify us by His grace. But there can be no annulling, destroying, or doing away with the Law, Matt. 5:18; Rom. 3:31.

Therefore there was a transference of the Law, Heb. 7:12, to the Mediator, that is, to the Son of God. It took place in this way: He was "made under the Law" [Gal. 4:4] and satisfied the Law for us, in two special ways, namely by removing the punishments for the sins of the whole world and by giving perfect obedience to the Law, that there might be true and perfect righteousness according to the norm of the divine will, by which the grace and mercy of God would justify believers, that is, receive them unto eternal life. But because this satisfaction of the Law must be sufficient for redemption and righteousness for the whole world, therefore it was necessary that the person of the Mediator be at one and the same time both God and man, so that the price might be of sufficient value.

On this basis we can explain the rationale for saying that Christ the Mediator, with His work, is the efficient cause of our justification. So that the whole subject can be better understood and the testimonies more appropriately applied, we shall divide it in this way: There are three especially important points to be considered about the work of the Mediator as the cause of our justification.

1. The merit which God the Father regards and on account of which He justifies believers freely through His grace. Here belong the passages of Scripture which clearly speak of merit, such as Rom. 4:25: "He was put to death for our sins and raised for our righteousness"; 1 Cor. 15:3: "Christ died for our sins"; Rom. 5:6: "Christ died for the ungodly"; 1 Peter 2:21, "Christ suffered for your sins"; 1 John 4:10: "He is the propitiation for our sins." Also with regard to the ransom which Christ paid, note the entire article of the Creed: "He suffered . . . was crucified," etc. Concerning the perfect obedience note Rom. 5:19; Heb. 10:14; Philippians 3; John 14:31; 6:38.

We have cited these testimonies to demonstrate that Christ alone has made satisfaction for all our sins, for guilt, and for punishment, so that there is nothing remaining for us to suffer or to make satisfaction for in expiating our sins. The passion of Christ and His being made a curse for us are substituted for our punishment, Gal. 3:13. The obedience of Christ is substituted for our guilt, for "He was made sin for us," 2 Cor. 5:21. We should carefully note this division of these points, Is. 53:6: "The sins of all were laid upon Him"; John 1:29: "He takes away the sins of the world"; Rom. 8:32; 1 John 2:2; Rom. 5:15; Titus 2:14. 2 Cor. 5:14: "If one died for all, then were all dead." Augustine uses this argument against the Pelagians. Gal. 4:4–5: ". . . made under the Law, to redeem those who were under the Law"; therefore He has redeemed us from all sins, because sin is only that which is in conflict with the law of God. 1 Cor. 1:13: "Has Paul been crucified for you?" Acts 4:12: "There is no other name given . . ."

Here are pertinent those passages which say that the Father justifies believers for the sake of His Son the Mediator, e.g., 2 Cor. 5:18: "He has reconciled us to Himself through Jesus Christ"; Eph. 1:3: "He has blessed us . . . in heavenly places in Christ"; 1 Cor. 1:9: "God is faithful, by whom we were called into fellowship with His Son"; Rom. 3:24; Rom. 5:10, 17; Eph. 1:7; 2:16; Col. 1:13. In this way the work of the Mediator is considered as a merit in our justification.

2. Christ is Mediator and Savior not only from the standpoint of merit, but also from the standpoint of efficacy. For His merit does not mean that the things pertaining to our justification should be brought about through us or through others, but He also effected them and still effects those things in which our justification and salvation consists, such as our deliverance from sin, the devil, death, and the wrath of God and the application of these blessings to our hearts. Therefore this is deservedly called an efficient cause.

The testimonies from Scripture are the following. 1 Peter 1:18–19: ". . . redeemed . . . in the blood of the Lamb"; 2:24: "By His wounds you are healed"; 1 John 3:8: ". . . that He might destroy the works of the devil"; Gen. 3:15: "He shall bruise the head of the serpent"; Heb. 2:14; Rev. 5:9; Gal. 3:13; 1:4; Heb. 1:3: ". . . having made purification for sins . . ."; Heb. 9:12; 1 John 1:7: "The blood of Christ cleanses us . . ."; Rom. 5:9; Eph. 5:23.

Regarding His all-pervasive influence, note Eph. 4:12; Col. 2:10; Rom. 8:37: "We are conquerors through Him who loved us"; 1 Peter 2:25; John 10:27–28; Rom. 8:34: "He intercedes for us"; 1 John 2:1: "If anyone sins, we have an advocate with the Father"; Heb. 7:25; Col. 3:13: "Christ has been kind toward us"; John 12:32; Phil. 3:12; John 1:16: "Of His fullness all have received"; 1 Cor. 15:22; John 10:28: "I give them life eternal."

These testimonies must be studied so that we can in some way understand the blessings of the Son of God, the Mediator, in our justification.

3. The meritorious work of Christ does not mean that we are righteous before God unto eternal life for some other reason, but that the obedience or satisfaction of Christ is the very thing which is imputed to us for righteousness, or, that it is our righteousness before God unto life everlasting. This observation is necessary because of the papists. Jer. 23:6: "Jehovah our righteousness"; Is. 45:24: "In the Lord is my righteousness"; 1 Cor. 1:30. 2 Cor. 5:21: ". . . that we might be made the righteousness of God in Him." It should be noted that he not only says "through Him" but "in Him." Thus in Rom. 5:9: "We are justified in His blood." It is clearly a Hebraism to use "in" in place of "through." But there is an emphasis here, in that Scripture sometimes says "through Him" and sometimes "in Him." Rom. 8:4: ". . . that the righteousness of the Law might be fulfilled" not "by us" but "in us"; cf. Phil. 3:9; Rom. 5:19; Gen. 12:3 and 22:18.

This is a fairly adequate explanation to show the blessings which the Son of God, the Mediator, has opened up; and it is useful to study it.

Once we have explained these matters in this way the application of the terms is simple. There is a twofold efficient or working cause (*causa efficiens*) for our justification: 1. the grace of God, which is the common work of the three Persons. 2. the merit of Christ, which is the peculiar property of the Mediator. Because the grace of God is the efficient cause of our justification in one way and the merit of Christ in another, learned men have tried to indicate and explain this difference by using the language of the dialecticians. I shall mention these terms in order that educated people may be able to judge how to apply them to the technical words.

When the work of Christ as Mediator is considered from the standpoint of merit, it is called a meritorious cause, a term the dialecticians describe as a motivating cause, which in turn pertains to the efficient cause.

Since Christ is our Savior and our righteousness not only because of His merit but also because of His efficacy, He is called the efficient cause of our justification. In order that this difference can be demonstrated, they call the grace of God the principal or primary efficient cause. They call Christ the Mediator, with His work, the secondary efficient cause, because Christ was sent to achieve the work of our redemption. Others note this distinction: The Trinity makes the decree concerning our redemption, and sends the Son; but the Son is obedient and is sent. Thus they distinguish between the commanding cause and the obeying cause. This rationale for designating the terms is more acceptable to me than instances taken from the realm of the physical or secular world, as when the will commands certain of its members, or if a certain king gives a command to his servant to lead captives out of prison.

Because the papists understand and interpret this meritorious and efficient cause in this way, that Christ merits and accomplishes only that we are justified by something else, namely by new inherent qualities, therefore we must clearly show that it is absolutely necessary that true righteousness be involved when we are seeking to be justified, and that this righteousness consists in the obedience of Christ—that this itself is the very thing which is our righteousness before God unto eternal life.

Some have called the obedience of Christ the material cause of our justification, but because the term "material cause" perhaps is not particularly helpful, since the dialectitians argue about the material and formal causes in these relationships, I believe it is better simply to call the obedience of Christ the material cause of our justification when the term is applied to the end or goal, namely the person to be justified, and to call the acceptance of the person unto life everlasting the formal cause of the relationship.

Now do not think that this is useless nitpicking about some technical words. For these points are necessary in order to distinguish and to explain things better.

Furthermore, we can now undertake a useful comparison of those points which were discussed by the scholastics. Thomas says that the acts and sufferings of Christ were performed for the salvation of the human race in an instrumental way because the humanity of Christ is the instrument of the Deity. Likewise he says that the Father is the cause of our justification through His authority and Christ through His ministry. He made a distinction between the commanding cause and the obeying cause. Bonaventura says that the suffering of Christ is not properly the cause of our justification. Also that properly we cannot attribute to Him the cause of our justification. For He relates to no kind of cause. Yet He has some characteristics of a cause through the mode or fact of intervening merit, which has the reason of disposition or intention and leads to a material cause. In this way he explains that when sin has been driven out by the merit of Christ's passion, a subject or person is rendered suitable to receive the first grace or the beginning of grace. Richard speaks of the meritorious cause, because Christ by His passion has merited for us the first grace which makes us pleasing to God. From this we can understand why the papists make Christ only a meritorious cause and why we have to add other terms.

Fifth. It is absolutely necessary that there be an application of these causes to the person who is to be justified. "For as many as received Him, to them He gave power to become the children of God," John 1:12; 3:33. The method or means of applying or apprehending the benefits of Christ is for the sake of clear teaching called the instrumental cause (*causa instrumentalis*).

There is a twofold instrumental cause: 1. teaching, revealing, offering, and demonstrating the benefits of justification, through which God bestows these good things upon us. This is the voice of the Gospel and the use of the sacraments, or as the ancients said, "the oral and visible Word." 2. Receiving or laying hold on these blessings, by which we apply to ourselves these good things offered in the Gospel, so that we are made participants or sharers in them. Thus it is as if the hand of God is giving and the hand of man receiving that which is given. Above we have noted and explained the passages which witness that faith alone, and not other qualities or works in us, is the means for this application.

The instrumental cause is related to the efficient cause, and this is beautifully illustrated at this point. The preceding efficient causes show their efficacy in the instrumental cause. God is efficacious through the voice of the Gospel, and through it He enlightens the mind, kindles faith, and as Paul says: "To you it is given . . . to believe . . ." [Phil. 1:29].

The controversy regarding the instrumental cause is one of the most important. The devil attacks this doctrine in a hateful way because he fully understands that the efficient causes, without the application, profit nothing toward our salvation. Indeed, "This is the condemnation, that light came into the world, but men loved darkness," John 3:19. Thus he sows various corruptions: that the application takes place by works, either our own or someone else's; through the means of our merit, right attitude, or worthiness; or by faith and works at the same time.

Gropper is compelled to admit that in regard to the instrumental cause the laying hold on the promise is a work which is peculiarly the property of faith. For, says Gropper, faith is distinguished from hope and love in this one respect, that properly speaking it is the role of faith to believe, and by believing a person seeks to receive what God has promised in the gift of justification. Hope trusts that it will receive. Love is a work, but it does not work before or unless you by faith believe that you have achieved peace with God. For we cannot judge that we have been justified in any other way except in receiving the promise in faith. Thus Gropper. It is true, for by works the application cannot take place except through the means of merit, as Paul says in Rom. 4:4, "To him who works the reward is reckoned as a debt."

Pighius argues about the instrumental cause in a very sneaky way. He says that the question is how must they to whom the benefits of Christ are to be given dispose themselves. And he asks: Are those who without repentance indulge themselves in the lusts of the flesh made sharers in the merits of Christ? Again: Does a false or dead faith which is not efficacious through love receive the gift of justification? Scripture replies, "No indeed." From this Pighius infers: Therefore faith alone is not the means which disposes the person for the reception of the grace of God, but there must be repentance, faith, love, and a chorus of virtues. We have explained this above in the discussion of the exclusive expressions. We do not deny that in conversion these things must be present. But the question is not with what things faith must be joined but what is the characteristic of each of these entities.

It is false to say that the subject or the person is prepared for the acceptance of reconciliation by the virtues following reconciliation. For it is absolutely necessary that faith which lays hold on Christ, and grace and reconciliation with God in Christ, precedes love and the other new virtues. In repentance the Law kills and puts to death, but this surely is not the beginning of eternal life. This is the order which God observes in giving justification. We all know the marks of a true or false faith, but the application remains only and solely the property of faith.

The Council of Trent asserts that the sacrament received in fact or in desire is the instrumental cause of justification, but they do not add their explanation, namely what sacrament they are referring to and in what way it is an instrumental cause. They hide this pitfall to allay doubts. For they actually teach that the merits of Christ and the saints are placed in the treasury of the church and distributed by the power of the keys in the sacrament of penance, where satisfactions are imposed regarding the works which must be performed, that is, works of supererogation; and they try to make this the means of bestowal or application [of the benefits of Christ], namely the work of contrition, confession, and satisfaction, and the trafficking in indulgences and prayers for the dead, without even mentioning faith. Likewise they imagine that in the Mass there takes place a distribution and application of the merit of Christ from the external performance of the act, without even any good intention on the part of the participant. They conceal these traps and speak in a general way about the sacrament. Thus we must take note of these subterfuges, so that the doctrine of application be clearly and properly taught.

Sixth. There is a very acrimonious controversy between ourselves and the papists regarding the formal cause (*causa formalis*) of righteousness, that is, as to what constitutes our righteousness formally before God unto eternal life, or what enables us to stand in the judgment of God, so that we are not condemned by the sentence of the Law but rather are received unto eternal life. Because the form (*forma*) represents the thing (*res*) itself, and the form preserves the thing in its existence, therefore the question is: What is it by which, when we have it, we can be certain that we are righteous before God unto life eternal, and by the loss or nonpossession of which we do not have righteousness before God unto eternal life?

The papists argue this way: In other matters described by their qualities the form is a quality which inheres in the thing itself; so that if it is asked what is the form of a white wall, it is certain that it is the whiteness which inheres, not in some other subject, but in that wall which is thus called white. Thus, because their understanding of justification is the expulsion of one quality and the introduction of a new one, they believe that the new obedience toward the commandments of God, which begins in believers through the Holy Spirit, is the form or the formal cause of our justification before God to eternal life. Some call this love, and others call it the grace which makes men pleasing to God. The Tridentine Council calls it the righteousness of God, not that by which He Himself is righteous, but that by which He fills believers with new infused qualities.

This description of the form has two faults: 1. Justification by faith does not pertain to a quality but to a relationship, as we have shown above. If the question were asked about renewal, as to what its formal cause is, then this would be a correct answer. But we have demonstrated that there is a different rationale in the case of justification. 2. The form of our righteousness before God unto life eternal must be that by which we can stand before the judgment seat of God in the face of sin, the accusation of the Law, the devil, death, and hell. The new obedience has been begun in believers, to be sure, but because of the sin dwelling in us, this obedience is neither pure nor perfect.

The papists have realized that in itself this obedience cannot stand in the judgment of God; much less can we, through it, stand in a formal way before God's judgment for eternal life. But because they have asserted as an absolute that this righteousness must be something inhering in us and because they see that by these new qualities we do not fit the description or characteristic of the form, because of our imperfection, they seek various subterfuges.

Lombard recognized that our love cannot bear the burden of the form of the righteousness before God unto eternal life, and thus he had the idea that it was not a quality in us, but the actual essence of the Holy Spirit. This was Osiander's speculation also. For when he was trying to make our righteousness before God something inherent in us and considered the pollution and imperfection of our inherent renewal, he took refuge in the essential righteousness of God.

Gropper says that because our works of love are imperfect, therefore the formal cause of our righteousness before God cannot be established in them. Thus he says we must consider this love as a gift of God and a work of the Holy Spirit, and in this way love is the formal cause of our righteousness. But although there are certain gifts of the Holy Spirit even in the lost, Matt. 7:22, and although the work of creation is seen in all men, yet we must not say that it is the good in our nature or those things which are mentioned in Matthew 7, when we are considering to what extent our formal righteousness before God is a gift and work of God, because all these gifts have been polluted by sin.

Hosius says that the works of love are imperfect, to be sure, but the attitude or disposition (*habitus*) to love in believers is perfect, and this is the formal principle of our righteousness. But the clearest refutation of this notion comes from the Scriptural sources. The aptitude or disposition toward love is the renewal of the will, but this must be renewed every day, and the old nature of the flesh must be put to death through our whole life. Therefore it is false to say that the aptitude to love is perfect, for if this were the case, then the mandate could be fulfilled perfectly in this life: "You shall love God with all your heart." And because the works of love are imperfect, the result is that the aptitude or disposition to love is also not perfect, but increases, is augmented, and only after this life is brought to fulfillment.

Others say that what is lacking in our works whereby they are not pure and perfect is supplemented and supplied through the suffering and obedience of Christ. And thus good works not in themselves, but inasfar as they have been dyed in the blood of Christ, are the form of our righteousness into life eternal. This opinion can be enlarged upon in marvelous ways. But if the question is asked whether Christ as Mediator is only a supplement or addition to our own righteousness, the answer is simple. For Paul argues this point clearly and straightforwardly in writing to the Galatians: Christ the Mediator did not come into this world in order that we might be justified by that righteousness of which the norm, rule, and sum is: "He who does the laws shall live in them," Gal. 3:12. Indeed when there was an argument among the Galatians, the question was not: Could they without Christ be justified by their works alone, but rather could they be justified by Christ and works together? But Paul states the point of the controversy this way: Is it within our power to accomplish the righteousness of the law? And because it was impossible that we could through our own ability be justified before God, God has made a transference, and in the place of our works, He has placed this burden on Christ for righteousness, since He has done those things through which man might live. Paul says that this transference was made in such a way that Christ profits nothing for those who wish to add something of their own to Christ toward their righteousness before God unto eternal life. Likewise, such people have been cut off from grace. Thus it has been demonstrated that the opinions of the papists cannot support their notion of the formal principle of the righteousness before God unto life everlasting.

But how are we to understand what the formal cause really is?

Response. We have established two points above: 1. Justification is a matter of relationship. 2. The righteousness which is imputed to us, or on account of which we are accepted to eternal life, is not something inhering in us, either in whole or in part, but it is firmly rooted in the obedience of Christ alone. Therefore, in the simplest terms, the formal cause can be stated this way (as we state the formal cause in relationships): It is the very application of the foundation to the purpose, and the justification of the sinner comes from this application as its result, so to speak.

Therefore, when this application of all these causes of which we have spoken thus far takes place, so that they accomplish what belongs to our justification, that is, absolution from our sins and reception unto life eternal, then it is certain that we have what is required to stand before the judgment seat of God, that is, formal righteousness. They can dispute these points as minutely as they wish, but the simple faith of the fisherman, which sets forth these matters bluntly and simply, yet correctly, truthfully, and clearly, is more appropriate for explaining the apostolic teaching.

Thus if we bring this proposition through all these kinds of causes, whether beginning with the primary cause or the instrumental cause or the acceptance, it is certain that we have the formal cause of justification, with nothing foreign mixed in with it; but if one of these points is lacking, it is certain that we do not have true righteousness before God. This is a description of the form of our righteousness and of its peculiar nature: The grace of God does not impute our sins to us when it applies and imputes to us the righteousness of Christ the Mediator, through faith, and when faith lays hold on Christ the Mediator in the Gospel, in Christ apprehending the grace and mercy of God unto righteousness and eternal salvation. Or, to put it another way, the remission of sins or our acceptance unto life eternal is given freely, by the grace of God, through and for the sake of Christ in the Gospel, and it is apprehended by faith. This is our formal righteousness before God unto life eternal.

I approve of this simple statement of the case, because many disputes can be settled on the basis of it. Some suggest that the formal cause is faith, some Christ, others the mercy of God, others forgiveness of sins or acceptance. These ideas are often held by inexperienced people as if these points were in conflict with one another and different. This, of course, is exaggerated by our adversaries.

But the matter is clear. Faith in itself, as a quality, without Christ, is not our formal righteousness. And Christ, unless He is apprehended by faith, is not your (*tua*) righteousness. But if faith lays hold on Christ, but does not in Him also lay hold on the grace and mercy of God, it does not thereby establish that it will receive forgiveness of sins or acceptance, and it is certainly lacking the form of righteousness before God. For justification is absolution or acceptance.

Thus when all of these are included at the same time, in their own order, then nothing is lacking from our righteousness before God. This is the formal cause of justification.

From this we can also formulate our reply to the sophistry of Stapulensis that the relationship (*relatio*) is a matter of least importance among all of these things which have been stated. For, he says, if justification is a relationship, then it is a matter of minor importance, indeed, next to nothing.

But relationship has a foundation (*fundamentum*) and purpose (*terminum*) and an application (*applicatio*) or a relationship (*relatio*). Now the foundation of our righteousness before God unto life everlasting is the Son of God Himself, our Mediator, in His entire work. The relationship is the grace and mercy of God which imputes. The purpose or goal is the acceptance of the believing persons, the absolution of his sins, his deliverance from the devil, death, and hell. Does Stapulensis say that these things are matters of "minor import"?

Therefore you see what this righteousness is in God the Father, what it is in Christ, what it is in those who are reconciled.

I also want to note this point: Pighius is forced to concede something to the truth in this area of the discussion. For he says that if we are speaking with reference to the formal principle, we are not justified before God either by faith or by love, but by the one righteousness of God in Christ, by the one righteousness of Christ which is communicated to us, by the one mercy of God which forgives us our sins.

But Gropper insidiously comes with this kind of weapon: The form of a thing is that entity by which, when it is taken away or lost, the thing itself is lost or taken away. But with the loss of the new obedience the righteousness before God is lost. For "if they walk according to the flesh they shall die." And "those who do such things shall not inherit eternal life." Therefore, he says, the renewal is the formal principle or the form of our righteousness before God. But the fallacy here can be caught from his distinction. It is one thing when we say that when the form is lost the thing itself is taken away. But [it is another] when we say that when the effects are lost or cease to exist in their individual or undivided state, then the cause itself actually ceases and vanishes. For the causes or conditions or even the loss of a thing does not depend upon its effects, but the opposite is the case. When the individual effects cease, it is a sign or a testimony and a proof that the cause had previously ceased; for otherwise the effects would not have ceased. Thus it is foolish to conclude that the effects are the form of the cause. From this we can understand the sources for the explanations of Gropper's argument. And these are the chief points in the proposition concerning the necessity of good works for salvation.

Thus we must cite testimonies concerning these individual points: that our righteousness before God unto eternal life is Christ, that it is faith which lays hold on Christ, that grace is apprehended by faith, the free imputation, the remission of sins, and the acceptance of faith for the sake of Christ. Rom. 4:7: "Blessed are they whose iniquities are forgiven"; Rom. 3:25: ". . . for the remission of sins"; Acts 13:38: ". . . through this Man is preached to you the remission of sins . . . from all the things from which you could not be justified by the law of Moses"; Rom. 4:8 and 2 Cor. 5:19, regarding imputation; John 1:12, regarding acceptance and adoption. We have already noted the testimonies in regard to the other aspects of this.

Seventh. We still need to cite some testimonies in regard to the goal or final cause (*causa finalis*) and the effects of justification, and we shall add them both out of a desire for brevity and because certain of them describe the goal of justification in a clear and simple way, for example, Rom. 3:25, ". . . to show His righteousness"; v. 4; Eph. 1:6; 1 Peter 2:9; 1 Cor. 1:31; Rom. 3:27; 1 Tim. 1:16.

Certain passages speak at the same time regarding both the final cause and also the effects of justification. 1 Peter 1:9: "Receiving the end or outcome of your faith, the salvation of your souls." Peter alludes here to what I shall note in passing. Ps. 126:6; Matt. 11:29; Rom. 6:22; 1 Peter 5:4; Titus 3:7; Rom. 5:1; 1 Peter 1:8; Gal. 5:22; Rom. 8:30; 2 Cor. 5:15; Eph. 2:10: "We are His workmanship, created in Christ Jesus unto good works." The words are clear and illustrative of what is said in Gen. 2:3, "He created that He might make. . . ." Titus 2:12, 14; 1 Peter 2:24: ". . . that we should live to righteousness"; v. 21: ". . . that you should follow in His steps"; Luke 1:74–75; 1 Cor. 6:11, 19; Gal. 4:6; John 14:23. Note here also the testimonies concerning the other gifts of the Spirit.

The doctrine of the goals and effects of justification is clear and easy, but it is useful and necessary to repeat it at this point in our study of justification, for several important reasons. 1. That justification is received by faith should serve as a constant warning regarding the end or goal of the doctrine of justification, so that we do not misuse this teaching in order to cultivate or confirm licentiousness, as the Epistle of Jude admonishes in v. 4: "transposing or transferring or perverting the grace of God into licentiousness." 2. Just as we have a uniting of causes and effects in nature, so when we have the causes for our justification, we should have no doubt concerning the effects, namely salvation and eternal life. 3. That believers might know how to perform good works; and so that they will not seek a pretext to avoid doing them, Scripture says that renewal is an effect or result of justification. 4. Christ says in Matt. 7:16–20 that we are to judge a tree by its fruits. Paul in 2 Cor. 13:5 says: "Examine yourselves to see whether you are holding to your faith"; cf. 2 Peter 1:10: "Make your calling sure." We judge the cause by the effects. 5. This distinction between causes and effects is also useful for showing that sanctification or renewal is to be distinguished from justification, and that the new obedience is not a cause or an essential part of our justification, because it is an effect or a result. 6. By means of this distinction we can also answer the difficult question: When the believing heart in its trials feels no joy, peace, or happiness, is faith at that time, when it lays hold on Christ in the promise and tries to sustain itself with comfort, able to determine that it has the true righteousness unto life eternal? There is a difference between the causes, or the form of our righteousness before God and its effects. When the form or formal cause of our righteousness has been established, as described above, then faith ought to be assured of the acceptance of our person before God, unless it wants to make Him a liar. Indeed, the effects show the cause, and when the effects cease, then we may conclude that the cause does not actually exist either.

In the case of our justification, which is the full and perfect acceptance of the believer unto eternal life, certain effects in our life, such as the new obedience, follow rather slowly because of the weakness of our flesh. Some effects follow the way Scripture says, 2 Cor. 5:7: "We walk by faith and not by sight." Likewise Rom. 4:18: "In hope he believed against hope." Col. 3:3: "Our life is hidden with Christ in God"; Ps. 31:19: "You have laid up good things for those who fear You."

Augustine uses this distinction in his response to the Pelagians in speaking of the perfection of our righteousness on the basis of Eph. 5:27, ". . . that He might present to Himself a glorious church, not having spot or wrinkle." For finally this statement and this blessing have their beginning in this life, but are brought to perfection only in the life to come. He washes His church in Baptism, He cleanses away the filth, purges out the dross by constant repentance in this life, and all these things work toward the end that He may present to Himself a glorious church in that day. Thus the conclusion of Coelestius is false that in this life the church is without spot or wrinkle and perfect.

I think these are the chief parts of this study. We have spoken earlier regarding related and conflicting matters, and other problems. The doctrine of justification has been established by this mode of procedure on the basis of those sources of which we have spoken, and we need to add . . . only this warning: Never at any period did Scripture teach, nor did the true church use any other method of justification before God unto life everlasting . . . but from the beginning (after the Fall) in the Old Testament, and up to the end of the world in the New Testament, there has always been one and the same way of justification before God unto life eternal—the one we have set forth. It is a clear confirmation of the doctrine of justification that it has the testimony of all the books of Holy Scripture and the consensus of all the saints from the beginning of the world. It is truly, rightly, and properly called a catholic or universal doctrine.

It is pleasant to observe how the apostles and even the Son of God Himself, carefully sought testimonies to the doctrine of justification from almost every book of the Old Testament. For their adversaries disassociated themselves in horror frown the teaching of Christ and the apostles with the accusation that they were bringing in upon the people of God some new, strange dogmas, never before heard in the world. Thus in Mark 1:27, "What new teaching is this?" John 8:52: "Abraham is dead and the prophets, and You say, 'If a man keep My saying he will never see death.'" Thus Christ says in John 5:39, 46, "Search the Scriptures, for in them you think you have eternal life, and they are they which speak of Me. . . . If you had believed Moses, you would also have believed in Me. For he wrote of Me." John 8:56: "Abraham saw My day." In Luke 24:44, in bestowing His ministry upon the apostles, Christ says, "Thus it is written in Moses, the Prophets, and the Psalms concerning Me."

Also on Acts 26:22, when Paul is hatefully accused of a new teaching before Agrippa, he says, "I teach nothing other than what Moses and the prophets wrote."

Peter in Acts 3:21ff. says, "God through the mouth of His prophets from the beginning from Moses . . . to Samuel, and . . . from Samuel and those who came after him, has announced these days." Acts 10:43: "To Him all the prophets bear witness. . . ." For this reason John often repeats, "I do not write a new commandment to you, but that which has been since the beginning," [1 John 2:7–8; 2 John 5]. This confirmation, which he has established from the consensus of all of Scripture, Stephen uses in his counterargument to the accusation of the Jews in Acts 7. Note Paul in Acts 13 and 17. And he uses the same line of argumentation at the apostolic council in Acts 15. Also in Rom. 1:2 he speaks of "the Gospel which God has promised through His prophets in the Holy Scriptures." 1 Peter 1:10 and 2 Peter 1:19, "You have the more sure prophetic word." Cf. Heb. 13:8, "Christ today, yesterday, and forever."

Scripture, in order to sharpen our diligence in this investigation, shows the method for seeking these testimonies to the doctrine of justification in the individual books of the Old Testament. Christ sets forth this kind of division: "from Moses, from the Prophets, from the Psalms concerning Me." And how these testimonies are to be adduced from the individual books of the Old Testament is shown in the examples in Hebrews 13 and Acts 3, 7, 13, and 15.

I shall only point out how the New Testament not only in general but also in each individual case seeks out the testimonies from the Old Testament books regarding justification.

Because Moses is thought to be in the greatest conflict with the doctrine of free acceptance, testimonies have been diligently sought from New Testament writers in regard to Abraham. Note Romans 4 and Galatians 3. The whole history of Genesis is rehearsed in Acts 7 and Hebrews 11. And lest anyone think that this doctrine only began in the time of Abraham, Rom. 5:12ff. connects the account of the fall of Adam with the blessing of Christ. In Heb. 11:4ff. Abel, Enoch, and Noah are made part of the story. In Rev. 13:8 the Lamb "has been slain from the foundation of the world." The Epistle to the Hebrews clearly applies all the figures of the Levitical priesthood to the work of the Son of God, the Mediator. But because the moral law is seen as clearly contrary to the doctrine of the Gospel regarding justification, Paul also seeks testimonies from the moral law, as in Rom. 3:21: "The righteousness of the Gospel has been revealed apart from the Law, being witnessed by the Law and the prophets." Cf. Gal. 3:22: "Scripture has imprisoned all men under sin, that the promise might be given to believers by faith." V. 8: "If righteousness were by the Law, there would be no need for the promise of the Gospel," and in v. 7 he says that the promise of the blessing came before the promulgation of the Law. He is clearly drawing these testimonies from the books of Moses: Rom. 9:15: "I will have mercy on whom I will have mercy" [from Ex. 33:19]; Acts 3:22: "He shall raise up another prophet" [from Deut. 18:15]; and Rom. 10:6: "Do not say in your heart . . . the Word is near you" [from Deut. 30:12ff.]. Thus these testimonies are cited from the individual books of Moses.

From the books of Joshua, Judges, Kings [including the books of Samuel] and Chronicles are cited such testimonies as Acts 7:42ff. and Hebrews 11.

From the prophets: Isaiah 53 is cited in Acts 8:32, 1 Peter 2:22 and 24, Matt. 8:17 and 26:54. In Rom. 10:11 is cited the statement from Isaiah [28:16]: "He who trusts in Him shall not be put to shame." In Rom. 15:12 there is reference to the "rod of Jesse in whom all the nations shall hope" [Is. 11:10]. Is. 40:6ff. is re-echoed in 1 Peter 1:24: "All glory is like grass." 1 Peter 2:25: "All we like sheep have gone astray" [Is. 53:6].

Jeremiah 9:23ff. is cited in 1 Cor. 1:31: "He who glories, let him glory in the Lord." Jer. 23:6, "The Lord Jehovah our righteousness," [is referred to in 1 Cor. 1:30]. Also compare Heb. 10:16 [and Jer. 31:33]: "the new covenant."

From Ezekiel [34:11ff.], Christ cites in John 10:11 the statement regarding the good shepherd who lays down his life.

Daniel [2:44; 7:14–27] and ch. 9 are referred to in Matt. 24:15 and Luke 1:33: "Of His kingdom there shall be no end." Compare also the Epistle to the Hebrews.

Hosea [11:1] is cited in Matt. 2:15: "Out of Egypt have I called My Son." Rom. 9:25, "I will call My people those who were not My people," [is quoted from Hosea 2:23]; 1 Cor. 15:55: "O death where is your sting?" [Hos. 13:14].

The statement of Joel [2:28–32] concerning the sending of the Spirit is cited in Acts 2:16ff. [Joel 2:32] in Acts 2:21: "Whosoever shall call upon the name of the Lord . . ."

Amos [5:25] is cited in Acts 7:42 and [Amos 9:11ff.] in Acts 15:16 in connection with the Council of Jerusalem.

The figure of Jonah is used in Matt. 12:38–40, as well as in 16:4.

Micah [5:2] is quoted in Matt. 2:6: "And you, Bethlehem . . ."

Nahum [1:15] is cited in Rom. 10:15: "How beautiful are the feet of those who preach the Gospel. . . ."

Habakkuk [2:4] is quoted in Rom. 1:17: "The just shall live by faith."

Haggai [2:6] is cited in Heb. 12:26: "Yet once more . . ."

Zechariah [9:9] is cited in Matt. 21:5: "Behold, your King is coming. . . ." Also Luke 1:78: "The Day Star from on high" [cf. Zech. 8:7 (Vulgate)].

Malachi [3:1] is quoted in Luke 1:17 and Matthew 11 with reference to the Messenger of the covenant.

Many testimonies are drawn from the Psalms: Acts 2:25, 30, 31, and 34; Rom. 4:7; Matt. 27:35, 43, 46, and 48; Rom. 3:4, 10, 13, 14, 16, and 18; Acts 4:25 and 13:33–35. Likewise to the statement in Ps. 143:2, "In Your sight shall no living person be justified," reference is made in Romans 7, Galatians 3, and 1 Corinthians 4. . . .

Finally, lest speculations about predestination disturb the doctrine of justification, universal statements are to be noted and considered. There are these points:

1. The Son of God, the Mediator, "gave His life as the ransom for all," 1 Tim. 2:6. 1 John 2:2: "He is the propitiation for the sins of the whole world."

2. It is the will of God the Father "that no one should perish," 2 Peter 3:9, but that all should be saved through Christ, 1 Tim. 2:4. He also adds the reason, because "there is one God and one Mediator between God and men . . . who laid down His life as a ransom for all," vv. 5–6. Therefore, since He wants all to be saved, He did not lay down His life only for certain classes or certain kinds of individuals. It is incorrect to say that the words "He wants all to be saved" means that He wants some out of each of the orders or classes of people.

3. The Holy Spirit in His ministry universally announces repentance and remission of sins to all. We should note that Paul joins these two concepts together in Rom. 11:32, "For God has imprisoned all under disobedience that He might have mercy on all." Therefore in the same way that He wants to have mercy on all, He also has confined all under sin, that is, just as the sins of all are condemned by the Law, and just as the wrath of God accuses all, so also the promise of grace is universal.

4. It is the universal command of God that all should hear the voice of the Gospel and embrace the promise in faith. Peter also affirms in 2 Peter 3:9 that it is the will of God that "all should come to repentance," and Paul says in 1 Tim. 2:4: ". . . all should come to the knowledge of the truth." Also in Ezek. 33:11 God confirms by an oath that it is His will that "the wicked shall turn from his ways and live."

5. All who believe in Christ, without discrimination and exception, receive forgiveness of sins and are saved.

It is also useful to observe how Scripture sets forth the concept of universality and explains and develops it. Cf. Rom. 3:22; 10:12; Matt. 11:28; John 3:16; 1 John 4:14; John 3:17; Mark 6:15; Col. 1:23; Gen. 22:18; Matt. 28:19. In Rev. 5:9, 7:9, and 11:9 this division is noted: "You have redeemed us to God with Your blood out of every tribe and people and nation and tongue." Acts. 3:25: "All the families of the earth shall be blessed." For a "people" (*gens*) is divided into tribes and families. Cf. John 1:12; Matt. 22:9; 2 Peter 3:9; Matt. 18:14. Rom. 2:11, 3:9, 4:12, and 10:12: "There is no difference between Jew and Greek." And we should note that just as there is no distinction in the preaching of repentance, so there is none in the promise of grace. And just as there is the same Lord of all, so He is rich toward all. Cf. Gal. 3:28; Col. 3:11; Rom. 10:2–3. Eph. 2:3 and Titus 1:10: There are Jews who live licentiously. Rom. 1:28 and 2:14: There are gentiles of reprobate mind and those of honorable behavior; cf. Phil. 3:6; 1 Tim. 1:15; Gal. 2:1.

These observations which involve words denoting universality, show us a great deal.

Let this be the explanation of the locus of justification by way of instruction and equipping us for the battle. But the refutation of the errors cannot be better accomplished than by first dealing with the doctrine of good works, to which we shall now proceed.

To God alone the praise and glory forever and ever! Amen.

The end of the second part of the Loci Theologici
of Dr. Martin Chemnitz.

Third part of the *Loci Theologici* of the reverend and notable theologian
Dr. Martin Chemnitz, at one time most vigilant superintendent of the
church of Brunswick

Edited in the name of his heirs by Polycarp Leyser doctor of sacred
theology and successor to Dr. Chemnitz

Published by Johannes Spies, Frankfurt am Main, 1592

To Men Most Illustrious and Outstanding for Piety, Wisdom, Learning, and Virtue, Our Lords the Members of the Councils and Senates of the Famous Cities of Hildesheim, Halberstadt, Göttingen, Hannover, Eimbeck, and Hameln, Masters and Patrons Most Honorable: Dr. Polycarp Leyser Brings Greetings to You in Christ Jesus:

The royal psalmist King David, in that golden jewel of his psalms which is truly called a treasury for teaching and a storehouse for all doctrines necessary in our Christian life, prays this earnest and ardent prayer for the church in its old age: "You have taught me, O God, in my youth, and to this day I declare Your marvelous deeds. Even when I am old and gray, do not forsake me, O God, till I declare Your right arm to the next generation, Your might to all who are to come," Ps. 71:17–18.

This prayer, most endowed and famous men, honorable lords, if it ever seemed necessary to offer this prayer to God by the true members of His church, I believe that in these times in which we live and into which we have fallen it is most necessary. For if we rehearse in our memories the status of the church from the time of its youth and consider in our minds what its condition was in all ages, we shall plainly understand that this situation was never a happy one, for the church always had great enemies by whom it was under incessant attack. First the heretics and false teachers tried to adulterate the teaching of the truth in the church, then tyrants tried to overturn her by force of arms. Then the leaders of the church themselves who should have been eager to advance the common upbuilding of the church with the highest efforts of their minds, when strife arose, they attacked each other with divided opinions and laid waste the church which was flourishing prior to these quarrels. Then both the teachers and the learners offended many by their shameless and scandalous living, so that, as Peter says, (2 Peter 2:13), they are "blots and blemishes" on the body of the church, not an honor but a burden to it. Then others brought further troubles upon the church, as the poet sang about certain godly people:

    "The godly are never lacking in wars or controversies,
      The pious mind always has reason for being in conflict."

This can be said even more truly concerning the entire history of the church. And it certainly would take a long time to enumerate all of the unfortunate events and tribulations which have befallen the church of Christ since the beginning, since there has never been a time in which she has not been afflicted by thousands of torments and agonies. But at least we must set up a list of this kind (at least a few such instances): the bondage in Egypt, the constant attacks of the people of Canaan against the Israelites, the atrocities of the Assyrians against the people of God, the blasphemous words of Sennacherib against the worship of the true God, the cruelty of the Babylonian exile, the persecutions of the Roman emperors. Some of these are well known from the sacred writing and some from the history of the church.

Furthermore, it is true what has been stated concerning the stages in the lives of individuals, that each stage has its own adversities and troubles, but finally all calamities befall the old. The gentile poet is correct when he says, "Fear old age. For it never comes alone." And the wise man says [in Eccl. 12:1], "Remember your Creator in the days of your youth, before the time of trouble comes and the years approach when you will say, 'I find no pleasure in them.'" Thus in the whole church we can see the same thing, that evils and troubles one by one from the beginning until now befall her, and now in the final old age of the church they attack her together and en masse, with one concerted effort. In the years just past we have seen the precise example of this happening in neighboring churches which profess the Augsburg Confession.

For as if it were not enough that outside enemies and the papists were persecuting the true church of Christ with sword and flame and trying to bring it to total extinction, as if it were some kind of game or joke that faithful preachers of the church are compelled to stand day after day on the line of battle and defend the purity of the evangelical doctrine with danger to their heads and their honor against every kind of fanatical enemy of the majesty of Christ and His sacraments, the devil, in the midst of this torment of the church and in the very place from which in the time of our greatest men the beginnings of the sound proclamation of the Gospel had arisen, has raised up new men who in their pride have introduced into the church bald-faced heresies and the spreading theology of Calvin without the knowledge of our teachers, which has always been severely repudiated by them and rejected on the basis of the Word of God. So great has been their hypocrisy and deception that they have not only misled the highest magistrates with their trickery and fraud, pretending to teach one thing and actually doing something else, but they have also implanted their ideas in many good people so that they have brought the whole matter of religion to a position of emptiness or danger in this most present conflict, while the rest of the people were not on guard against their stealth.

As a result of this, terrible persecutions have arisen against honorable teachers, including the imprisonment of some and the sad and frequent exile of many, so that many despaired of even having a place to live. They also brought frightful confusion to many of the churches, some of which were deprived of faithful pastors either by deceit or violence, some even against their will were overcome by fanatic teachers. Other churches were incited, forced, and driven to repudiate their old free ceremonies and take up new and strange ones. The whole situation was sad and mournful and things were daily going from bad to worse; love was growing cold, iniquity abounded, faith was dying; and finally everything was in such a turmoil that the genuine doctrine and confession of Luther seemed almost at the point of destruction. Nor was this danger confined within narrow boundaries, but the bold army which was forcing this false religion upon people had set up its garrisons far and wide, and in some places it found some who favored their errors with the result that the fear of them pervaded many regions, not only because of the tragic exiles where every pulpit was taken over, but even internally there seemed to be concern over the sound teaching of the doctrine of the church.

Thus we surely must repeat these prayers of the church from the psalm: You, O God, have preserved Your church from the beginning through all the ages of the world so that the very gates of hell could not prevail against her, and thus she must marvel at Your deliverances which she has experienced and which shall continue forever. Now, I pray You, do not desert her when by Your blessing she has come to old age and to gray hair. Do not deliver over to the beasts those who entrust their lives to You. Do not ever forget the life of Your turtle dove. But keep for Yourself Your Seed through which in ages to come Your power may be proclaimed to posterity (if indeed there is any future for this world), in order that they may be converted unto You, confess You, and learn to glorify You forever.

To these prayers which David prescribed for the godly in his statement in the book of psalms, the Lord Himself answered in Isaiah in a loving and fatherly fashion, Is. 46:3–4, "Hearken to Me, O house of Jacob, all the remnant of the house of Israel, whom I have upheld since you were conceived and carried since your birth, even to your old age I am He and to gray hairs I will carry you. I have made you, and I will bear you. I will carry you and I will save you." This is certainly a marvelous promise which He has given to us, to whom is given all power in heaven and on earth with respect both to the bodies and the souls of men, as far as it pertains to this life. Through all the stages of life He will save us as He wills, so that not a hair of our head will fall without His will; so that His church which He has chosen from eternity and preserved through all the different calamities and troubles from the beginning of time down to this day, He will preserve, the church which He brought into being with His own blood and which He holds dearer than the apple of His eye, even unto gray hair and to the end of the world, He will preserve it and nourish it in His bosom. This same point is depicted in the imagery of John, the beloved disciple who foretold what was to be seen in the future, Revelation 12. The dragon rose up against the woman intending to devour the little male child which she had brought forth, so that the woman was compelled to flee. But God has always prepared a place in the wilderness for this woman, His church, where she may find refuge for herself, watch over the preaching of the Gospel, and be able to perform actions which are pleasing to God, until at last she passes from this vale of sorrow.

He did not make this promise only with words, nor did He prefigure it with mere shadows. But in all ages He has actually proved that He has the highest concern for the entire church and for individual godly people. It would take too long to list the examples which occur both in the sacred writings as well as in the history of the church and in secular writers by which He has borne witness that He would never desert His church. But what is the need to seek instances in antiquity, when this most recent affliction of the church and the marvelous demonstration of the *changelessness of His almighty right arm give a more illustrative and clear example of His divine protection and presence than can ever by denied by anyone? The hellish dragon raged in fury and tried with every effort to extinguish the light of the Gospel and to devour alive the true parts of the church and the purity of its teaching, so that not only did earnest teachers have to flee from place to place, but many lived in doubt as they wandered from one insecure dwelling place to another, unable to find any fixed domicile, indeed in fear that they would have to fight for their lives and forced to live in exile with hunger and starvation.*

But behold, the almighty Lord of heaven had already prepared for His faithful servants a place where they could go and bring forth new spiritual children, where they could fruitfully serve God until the tempest blew over. That place was found particularly in glorious Saxony and in your highness' honorable cities. Hildeshelm deserves great honor for her kindness to the church from of old, under the leadership of Dr. Nicolas Selnecker and Master George Schroeter, men pious and learned; Halberstadt, under that most famous theologian Dr. Martin Mirus; Göttingen, under Master Theodosius Fabricius and Master Felicianus Clarus, men of great distinction in age, in wisdom and in teaching; Eimbeck under Master Martin Forchamann offered, with notable zeal for confessing the doctrine, shelter and honorable sustenance and even promoted a refugee to the principal office of the churchly ministry. This hospitality of yours toward servants of Christ is surely worthy of everlasting commendation and remembrance, by which when many others because of fear were surrendering, you by this reception of the exiles also revived the spirits of the saints in the Lord and made public testimony before the whole church of Christ that you would not depart a hairsbreadth from the genuine confession of Augsburg in the face of any man, however powerful. And the cities of Hannover and Hameln deserve no less praise from later generations, even though they did not receive any of the exiles, for it was not that they lacked the will but because at that time there were no vacancies in the ministerial office. But in the meantime they embraced those who had been thrown out and purged from here and there and accepted them, just as you did, as equals, as those who were beloved of God and of whom the world was not worthy.

The storm did pass, and with God hearkening to the groans of His faithful, this terrible persecution of good people did come to an end, so that many were able to return to their former homes, if they desired. But the memory of your kindness and godliness has not passed away, nor shall it ever pass away. Yea, on that great day of the Lord when Christ Jesus, the Head of the church, shall repay him who gave the cup of cold water to His people, there is no doubt that your kindness in which you received and comforted the exiled Christ Himself in these members of His, before the whole church in heaven, not only will this worthy action be received, but also it will be repaid generously for all eternity.

Although in the meantime there is no lack of those who were displeased by your kindness toward our brethren of the Augsburg Confession, yet for my part (and I speak for many other good men) I am so impressed with love and admiration for you that I have held you above all others in my prayers, that we may live in continuing close fellowship with the ministry of your churches, and from this time hence I will seek every occasion to bear public witness to my affection for you. I believe that it is a satisfactory offering on my part as I was about to publish this third tome of the Loci Theologici of the reverend and famous theologian, Dr. Martin Chemnitz, of pious memory, in the name of his heirs, that I should make the determination as to the patrons to whom this work is to be dedicated. Wherefore, most noble lords, I desire to choose you above all others for these important reasons:

In the first place, that this address of mine may serve as a public testimony to my gratitude to your lordships for those acts of kindness in which during the recent torment of the church you supported and nourished these fellow workers in the same Confession who had been driven out of the churches which had been committed to their care. This kindness was as pleasing to me as if it had happened to me personally.

In the second place, that at the same time there might be a testimony of my love and a public notice of what was owed to your churches in the name of constancy and loyalty. Indeed it is clear that you in your cities during the times of trouble and under the rule of men who were attached to a different religion, held firmly to the sound teaching of the Gospel, and to this very day have preserved it and given the hope that you also will defend it courageously.

Finally, that this may be a close bond with which I may be even more closely bound to the teachers of your churches, with many of whom I have already developed the most cordial relationship because of our common confession concerning God and the Christian faith. Sad to say there are now not a few who increase the dissensions and the disturbances in the minds of people in the church by seeking material from perfectly correct statements and writings and actions of others as causes for conflict and stirring up people. Thus they are in the habit of further afflicting and troubling the church which has already been more than sufficiently afflicted. Far different were the practices of the ancient fathers of the church who were anxious to give a charitable interpretation and careful explanation and defend from criticism even those statements which were unfortunately worded and were sometimes not helpful to the church, so that right-thinking people would not be disturbed and no occasion given to the avowed enemies of the church to subject her to ridicule and evil rejoicing. If some people would do the same in our day and draw their swords against the common enemies of the church rather than prefer to cut the guts out of their own church itself, perhaps we might have some relief in these very tragic troubles in these last times. But, O good God, how far we have departed from this integrity and uprightness! For nothing can be written so precisely and spoken so carefully that they cannot try to *pervert it in keeping with their innate desire to carp and slander. But each must carry his own burden and render an accounting before his righteous and stern Judge.*

For my own part, just as I have given very special effort to living with the other teachers of the churches of Saxony in the closest fellowship and to cultivating God-pleasing harmony with them, so I confess that I will preserve the same bond of unity with the orthodox teachers of your churches in our common confession of the Book of Concord. And I have no doubt that there will be a greater benefit for the public edification of the church as a result of our agreement than will come from zealous search by some people for controversies by which they disturb many, enlighten few, and build nothing. "But they will not move forward, for their mindlessness is evident to all." The more they spread dirt, the dirtier they become.

In conclusion, I pray God that He out of His fatherly kindness and immeasurable power will richly bestow upon your lordships and upon your cities every kind of blessing, as the royal prophet prays, "that He would strengthen the bars of your gates and bless your sons, give peace in your borders, fill you with the finest wheat, and cause the word which He has sent to run swiftly to all your posterity," Ps. 147:13–15, and finally neither leave nor desert any of us in this old age of the church and in this tired old world, but by the Spirit of His power, goodness, and wisdom, guide and strengthen us, so that we may remain faithful in the work of our calling and do things which are pleasing to Him and beneficial for ourselves and our posterity. Amen.

Written in Brunswick on August 14 in the year of the last age of the world 1592.

[We are omitting a poem written in honor of Polycarp Leyser by Conrad Rittershusius.]

LOCUS [XIV]

Good Works

[MELANCHTHON'S TEXT]

After we have explained the doctrine of reconciliation and faith it is necessary to add the doctrine concerning good works or the new obedience. Therefore I want to say clearly and plainly that our obedience, that is, the righteousness of a good conscience or of the good works which God has commanded us, must necessarily follow our reconciliation. For Christ clearly gives command regarding repentance, and Paul says, "We are debtors not to live after the flesh," Rom. 8[:12]. Also 1 Cor. 6[:9], "Do not be deceived; neither fornicators, nor adulterers, nor idolaters, nor thieves . . . will inherit the kingdom of God." 1 John 3[:7–8], "Let no man deceive you. He who does righteousness is righteous. He who commits sin is of the devil. . . . For this purpose the Son of God came that He might destroy the works of the devil." Thus we are born again in reconciliation so that the new obedience might be begun in us. Likewise it is written to the Ephesians, 2[:10], "We are His workmanship created through Christ Jesus unto good works which God has prepared that we should walk in them." This statement contains the teaching and the comfort which we need, for regarding the necessity of this teaching, it first says that we "have been created unto good works." Then there is comfort in the fact that he says that God has prepared beforehand these good works in the church, just as He prepared beforehand in Samuel, David, Isaiah, Jeremiah, and others the marvelous works through which He both calls, governs, and preserves His church; and as He says in another place, "Strengthen, O God, that which You have wrought in us," Ps. 68[:28]. Likewise Paul says that these good works have been prepared by God, that is, not only commanded, ordained, and begun by Him, but also aided and established. Although the church struggles under great difficulties, as the afflictions of Jeremiah, Paul, and others demonstrate, yet the church does many important and salutary things for others, even if the world does not in any way understand them. But we ought to understand our own calling so that we may perform the works which have been prepared by God. There are five chief questions pertaining to good works. They are the following:

1. *What works must be done?*
2. *How can they be performed?*
3. *How are they pleasing to God?*
4. *Why must they be performed?*

5. What is the difference among sins, since in this life we must confess that sins remain in the saints?

The First Question: Which Works Must Be Done?

Those works must be performed which have been commanded us in the Word of God and summarized in the Decalog. In regard to this matter we need to know that not only the external works of the Decalog must be done which can be imitated even by the ungodly, but there must be a beginning of the inner obedience. And the inner works which pertain to the First Commandment are that we must believe the Word of God, fear God, and trust in God. The fear of God is seen in our contrition. Faith is seen more clearly when it guides us in our terror over sin. These virtues must continue and be exercised throughout our whole life. And faith assures us that we have already been received by God because it knows the goodness of God toward us and it produces the love for God by which we submit ourselves to the will of God. Then follow the other good works which are performed in keeping with all the commandments.

The adversaries want to appear to be treating the doctrine of works as something very important, although they actually are speaking only of external hypocrisy or human ceremonies. But they do not know the works of the First Table and they bury the real source of good works. They say nothing about faith which is trust in the mercy and the free reconciliation of God, nor of the necessity of praying to Him in all situations. And when this faith is taken away then doubt prevails which either despises God or flees His wrath and does not call upon Him. Further, the hypocrites give approval to this doubt and support it while denying that faith must be understood as confidence and trust in the mercy of God. They say that faith only refers to the kind of knowledge that the devils have. It is certainly most lamentable to pervert the doctrine of the prophets and apostles in this way and actually to subject it to the most terrible torture rather than to yield to statements such as these: Faith means trust in the mercy of God, "Abraham believed God . . ." Gen. 15[:6]; "Therefore being justified by faith, we have peace with God," Rom. 5[:1]; "Through Christ we have access by faith . . ." Rom. 5[:2]; "I now live by the faith of the Son of God," Gal. 2[:20]. We must not allow these passages to be perverted or ignored, for we certainly must know that they were spoken to us with regard to trust in God's mercy and we must learn in all of our prayers that we can approach God in trust as His children and that we are not received by Him because of our own worthiness.

Therefore the most important good work is faith or trust in the mercy of God which must be exercised in all the perils of our life and in every prayer. When David was involved in his struggles he believed that he was pleasing to God because of God's promise; and because he knew that he had been called to this obedience in discharging his duties, he was obedient, he prayed and he looked to God for guidance in his troubles. *Here the inner worship distinguishes the true church from the common multitude of humanity. Cicero lived an honorable life, he was well-deserving among the whole race of mankind for his role in governing the republic, indeed he even understood that there was a god, one definite eternal mind which was the cause of good, as Plato had defined him. And those graven images which the public worshiped had nothing of the divine about them. And yet, later on, the mind of Cicero was overwhelmed with doubt about providence, because he did not know the promises of God, and he doubted that he and others were heard or helped when they prayed, especially in times of calamities in which they felt that they were deserted by an angry god. The same was the case with Saul.*

Therefore there is a difference between Cicero and Jeremiah. Jeremiah served his country, but faith enlightened this work. Jeremiah was assured that he was pleasing to God, and that his prayers were heard, and that he was under God's protection, even if he saw a great mountain of calamities threatening him—his fatherland destroyed, his fellow citizens scattered, many things which had been preserved by the clear blessing of God now cast off by Him, his own people engaged in bloody slaughters among themselves, and finally his own death. When Cicero saw such things befalling him, they overwhelmed him in darkness and unending doubt. The human mind cannot without faith know anything other than that which is said by Lucan:

> *"Is nothing certain but the uncertain wandering of chance which goes this way and that, and do the affairs of mortals have a goal?"*

But Jeremiah overcomes such doubts and with great constancy believes that he is pleasing to God and in this faith he seeks and awaits the happy outcome of His guidance which would follow after 70 years.

Christ gives us a precept concerning this inner worship when He says in John 4[:24], "They who truly worship the Father will worship Him in Spirit and in truth," that is, with truly spiritual motives, fear, repentance, faith, prayer, and things of this kind. Paul calls this kind of worship "our reasonable service," Rom. 12[:1], that is, the mind understands God and recognizes the wrath of God, and on the other hand sustains itself by faith, and faith even beholds the Son of God and acknowledges that we for the sake of Christ the Mediator have been accepted by God. In regard to this inner worship, Isaiah in 66[:2] attacks the hypocrites who think that worship is the outward obedience and the observance of the ceremonies of the temple, saying, "Thus says the Lord, 'To whom shall I look? I shall regard the man who is humble and contrite in spirit, who trembles at My Word.' " Likewise, in Ps. 50[:15], He admonishes the superstition of external worship and demands the worship in the heart and true invocation, "Call upon Me in the day of trouble."

The Second Question: How Can Good Works Be Performed?

I have often said that we must not indulge in the idle human notion that we can govern our outward behavior by human diligence and human powers and that God demands this kind of diligence, as it is written, "The Law is given for the unjust," 1 Tim. 1[:9]; or "Do not grieve the Holy Spirit," Eph. 4[:30]. But the inner obedience cannot be begun without knowing the Gospel and without the Holy Spirit. For, in the first place, love for God cannot exist before the hearing of the Gospel regarding forgiveness. The mind which does not know reconciliation either despises God or flees from His wrath. Therefore love cannot be begun unless one first hears the voice of the Gospel of reconciliation. These points are very clear. Therefore, in order that love may arise, faith must precede, that is, trust in God's mercy of which we have been speaking. And we also must understand that when our terrified minds are guided by faith, then at the same time the Holy Spirit is given who arouses in our hearts new desires which are in harmony with the law of God. And in this way, in Gal. 3[:14], Paul teaches that the Holy Spirit is given, "that we might receive the promise of the Spirit through faith," and Zechariah describes this forgiveness and these chief works of the Holy Spirit in these beautiful words [in 12:10], "I will pour out the Spirit of grace and supplication upon the house of David." He calls Him the "Spirit of grace" because He testifies in our hearts that God is favorable toward us, that is, He moves our hearts so that they assent to His promise and we know that we have been received by God. Then when we know the mercy of God, we invoke Him, love Him, and subject ourselves to Him. Therefore He calls Him "the Spirit of supplication," and he includes as the main aspects of our worship the universal sources of our obedience, namely, faith and supplication.

Thus, from this passage we draw our teaching and our encouragement. We should also remember that in this passage we have been commanded to perform this worship in order that we may believe in God and call upon Him. Therefore the Holy Spirit is driven out and grieved when faith has died and our prayer life upset through lapses of an evil conscience.

After the fall of the human race a great weakness came upon us, and the traps of the devil, who strives in hatred toward God against the human race and is eager to increase his own position against God through his stubbornness, shamelessness, blasphemies, drives mankind into various kinds of sins because of man's weakened nature. He arouses depraved thoughts which in turn devise opinions contrary to the Word of God. He scatters the church and involves the kingdoms of the world in unjust wars. He drives the church from places where it is well received in order that he may divide and destroy it. Thus he caused Cain to burn in malice and hatred against his brother and thus inflicted not only murder upon Abel but anguish upon his parents, yet God upheld them. These examples of the most tragic calamities occur daily among the race of men. What a wretched end there has been for the majority of mankind,

Saul, Jonathan, Hector, Priam, Achilles, Ajax, Pompey, Caesar, and countless more. Finally, we know the complaints about ill fortune, the sudden ruination of good fortune. You do not know what this very night will bring. And suddenly, by accident, all the things which we value shall vanish away.

Therefore, although the entire human race lives in constant perils, yet the church is attacked much more furiously, for the devil opposes it even more vigorously, as is said at the very beginning of Genesis, "The serpent shall wound His heel," Gen. 3[:15]. With what savagery he has moved about in the church after the Mohammedan fury came upon us 90 years ago! What ruin of the churches followed! What else can be imagined except that in a brief time the rest of Europe will be overcome by the Turks!

Therefore, since the condition of things clearly shows that the devil is loose and prowling around laying traps for us, and since the weakness of human nature is manifest, shall we oppose the aid that is shown us in the Gospel? God forbid!

The Son of God promises that He will be with us and will destroy the savagery of the devil. Thus John says, 1 John 3[:8], "For this purpose the Son of God appeared, that He might destroy the works of the devil," sin, death, blasphemies, and the destructiveness which the devil creates. Thus Adam and Eve were saved in their struggle when they kept their eyes on the promise and sustained themselves by their faith and sought from God another offspring through whom the true doctrine might be propagated. The Son of God protected them against the devil and by the Holy Spirit He raised up their downcast minds. Thus Jacob says of the Son of God, "May the angel who has rescued me out of all my troubles bless these boys," Gen. 48[:16], for it is the proper work of the Son of God to bless and to free from all evils, from the wrath of God, from eternal death, and from the other punishments which accompany the wrath of God. In Isaiah 7[:14] Christ is called Emmanuel, that is, God with us, because He is with us with all His riches. He keeps watch over us and drives away the devil.

Furthermore, He pours His Holy Spirit into the hearts of those who pray for Him. Thus in John 14[:18], "I will not leave you comfortless." Again, [vv. 14, 16–17], "If you ask anything in My name, I will do it. . . . And I will ask the Father and He will give you another Comforter . . . the Spirit of truth." We will truly find this help, if we stand against the corrupt maneuvers and traps of the devil and in these struggles pray to God with trust in His Son, our Mediator, just as He has specifically said, "If you ask anything in My name. . . ." For there must be a difference between the true prayer of the people of God and the prayers of the Jews or Turks. For in every prayer faith at the very outset assures itself of two things, namely, that you believe in this eternal God and invoke Him who is the Father of our Lord Jesus Christ who was crucified for us and raised again. And in the second place, faith is certain that for the sake of this Mediator God truly accepts and hears your prayers. The godly should note this carefully, for this prayer makes a tremendous difference between the church and the heathen who are fighting against the Gospel.

The teaching concerning the second question must always be kept before us so that we may know with certainty that the Son of God is our helper and defender, as Paul also says when he tells us that He was with the people in the wilderness, 1 Cor. 10; and also that we may know with certainty that the Holy Spirit is given to those who ask for Him, as it is written in Eph. 4[:8], "He ascended on high and gave gifts to men." And He rules in such a way that He can give His gifts, righteousness, life, good counsel, governance, successes, and other good things. In order that we may believe this concerning God's help, we must strengthen ourselves with the testimonies of the Gospel and drive away the darkness from our human minds which imagine that God is idle and unconcerned about individuals, in the same way that Homer imagined that Jupiter, when they looked for him in heaven, was away at a banquet in Ethiopia [Iliad, 1.423]. These odd suggestions indicated what kind of thoughts men have about God, and I have cited them in order to refute them and to kindle the true knowledge of God, His wrath and His mercy.

The Third Question: How Do Good Works Please God?

It is evident that godly minds are tormented and also hopeful that their obedience may be pleasing to God, but in this terrible weakness of ours they see that our obedience is crippled, impeded, imperfect, corrupt, as Paul says in Rom. 7[:15]. Therefore godly minds ask how they may please God.

Hypocrites judge this matter one way, and anxious and troubled minds another. The hypocrites think that they do satisfy the Law, that they are righteous, that is, that they have been accepted by God because of their own worthiness or their fulfillment of the Law, as the Pharisee says in Luke 18:9–12. There are always people like this who admire their own virtues, who give long tributes to their own wisdom and righteousness, especially in secondary matters which are showy, which they think they can govern by their own ideas and which they choose to accept as the divinely given fruits of their own virtues and diligence, since things are peaceful. Therefore they tout themselves above others because of their wisdom and righteousness, as Nebuchadnezzar did, who after some important things had happened, said, Dan. 4[:30], "This is Babylon, that is, the kingdom established by my strength." Likewise Saul believed that the kingdom of Israel had been established by his power, although he should have known that both this power and the successes were blessings from God, and that he could not have accomplished or ruled over such things by himself, and that he must serve God in fear lest he be deserted by Him. But he became even more confident because of these successes and took unto himself the privilege of attacking other people, killing priests, etc. This is the picture which many hypocrites project, and there are not a few who are like this, self-confident, pleased with themselves because of their gifts, applauding their own wisdom, minimizing the divine doctrine, and from this exalted position ridiculing the Gospel by trickery, fraud, and power, oppressing that part of the teaching to which they are opposed, covering up valuable books because they are boasting that they are contending for the glory of God and for the truth, that they are the most steadfast pillars of the church, members of the people of God, because they are fighting for the established order and its power which has been accepted for a very long time. The priests who opposed the apostles were like this and we ourselves see the same kind, many of them, in recent years, such as Vicelius and others. But others are troubled. They recognize their weakness and they are struggling with despair, as Peter when he was cast down, cried, "Depart from me, O Lord . . ." Luke 5[:8]. Therefore at this point we must do both: we must attack arrogance and show true consolation to those who are troubled.

But first of all we must establish this point: Although in the regenerate there must be a beginning of obedience and the righteousness of a good conscience, yet sins still remain in them, that is to say, the disease which is born in us, the doubts, the ignorance of many things; or in other words, that they do not fear God as they ought nor burn with love toward Him as the Law demands. There are also many actual sins, many fires of illicit love, hatred, lust, vindictiveness, jealousy, hatred, and greed. Many fall in their calling. There are examples of manifest neglect, frightful complaints against God in times of adversity; often human refuges are sought under the cover of honorable behavior, while at the same time the individuals are acting out of defiance of God. We often witness people taking on religious duties which are neither necessary nor in keeping with their calling, confidence in one's own wisdom or power, as when Josiah provoked an unnecessary war against the Egyptians.

Finally, the mountains of sin which cling to the regenerate are far greater than can be comprehended by the judgment of any man. Thus we must not think that the statement, "Who can understand his sins?" of Ps. 19[:12], is a matter of little importance. It would take too long to list all the kinds of sin which remain in the saints, but Paul summarizes the matter in Romans 7 when he speaks of his inner conflict with all sins. But these proud hypocrites do not understand these secret sins. The monks even teach that these doubts concerning providence, the wrath of God, His mercy, our wicked desires, unless there is consent to them, are not sins; and they are not arguing about terminology but about the substance of the matter itself. They deny that these wicked things are in conflict with the law of God. This extenuation is false and demeaning toward the law of God. It brings only darkness over the doctrine of grace and the righteousness of faith and confirms the false idea that the regenerate can satisfy the law of God.

Therefore, in order that this arrogance may be brought under control, I shall cite testimonies which show that the regenerate, in this life, do not satisfy the law of God and that sin remains in this mortal nature of ours. Ps. 143:2, "Do not enter

into judgment with Your servant, for in Your sight shall no living person be justified"; 1 John 1:8, "If we say that we have no sin, we deceive ourselves, and the truth
is not in us"; Ps. 19:12–13, "Who can understand his sins? Cleanse me from hidden
faults and spare Your servant from the sins of others"; Rom. 7:23, "I see another
law at work in my members waging war against the law of my mind and making
me a prisoner to the law of sin which is in my members." Now, although the sophists get around this passage and say that there has been a shift in the word "sin,"
and that here the word refers to "the punishment of sin," the tendency to sin which
has come from the fall of our first parents, yet Paul himself refutes this sophistry
in his definition of sin itself, when he says that it is an evil in our members which
is at war with the law of God.

Furthermore, we have discussed in regard to this article whether the wickedness which remains in our nature is something which is in conflict with the law of
God. Human judgment excuses this corruption, but Paul uses very graphic words
to describe this terrible thing. He says that the corruption is at war in his members,
that it is viciously contending against the law of his mind, confirming his carnal security or his righteousness which is at odds with God, filling his mind with pride in
his own virtues and arrogance, kindling lusts, hatred, desire for revenge, and urging
him to seek forbidden help; and finally it takes him captive, because it overthrows
the antagonisms of his mind by fears and brings him to the point of despair, so that
he flees from God. These are not unimportant evils, as human philosophy believes,
but they harshly torment the saints, just as Moses became weak and cast down with
sudden uncertainty and doubt at the episode at the rock, Ex. 17:4, and just as David
fell into sin when he commanded the census of the people, or as his human pride
was overly puffed up, so that he might demonstrate that his kingdom had increased,
or that by human wisdom and without the command of God he was going to make
a new ordering in the kingdom.

In Matt. 6:12 Christ teaches the saints to pray, "Forgive us our trespasses."
Therefore through our whole life there are sins present in us for which we need to ask
forgiveness. He teaches the same thing when He says, Luke 17:10, "When you do all
the things which have been commanded, then say, 'We are unprofitable servants.' "
Note also 1 Cor. 4:4, "I am conscious of nothing against myself, yet I am not thereby
justified," which teaches us that there is need for the righteousness of a good conscience, but yet it says that this still is not the thing on account of which I am certain
that I have the remission of sins and that I am reconciled with God; but rather God
accepts me for the sake of His Son the Mediator by faith. Ps. 103:3, "If You, Lord,
should mark iniquities, O Lord, who would stand?" By this statement the psalmist
is recognizing that sin is present and he does not try to excuse it; but acknowledges
that the wrath of God is so great that it could not be borne unless God forgives it by
His immeasurable mercy for the sake of His Son. For human nature cannot endure

the wrath of God and the punishments which it rightly deserves, as Hezekiah confesses, "As a lion He will break my bones," Is. 38:13; and Job in ch. 9 says that no one can resist the wrath of God.

Therefore, although sins are present with us and the godly to some degree recognize the wrath of God, yet they believe that they are pleasing to God because of His promised mercy, and they sustain themselves with this comfort, as Ps. 33:20ff. says, "My soul sustains itself in His Word . . . my soul hopes in the Lord, for with the Lord there is mercy"; Ps. 32:5–6, "I said I will confess against myself my transgression unto the Lord, and You forgave the iniquity of my sin; for this shall every one who is holy pray unto You." He clearly says that the saints seek the remission of sins. Ex. 34:7 (Vlg.), "No man of himself is innocent before You," that is, even if a person cannot be condemned or convicted by human judgment, yet You can accuse him. Dan. 9:7–9, 18–19, "To You, Lord, belongs righteousness, but to us confusion," that is, we acknowledge that You are righteous and that we are punished justly. "To You belong, Lord our God, mercy. . . . Therefore we do not pray to You because of our righteousness but because of Your great mercies. . . . Hear us for the Lord's sake," that is, for the sake of the promised Mediator. This passage is a very clear testimony to the general consensus of the prophets and apostles. Indeed, Daniel teaches the same thing for which Paul so copiously contends, when he says that we understand that the nature of man is wicked and does not satisfy the Law, but that we are accepted by God through His mercy for the sake of the promised Lord. For Daniel specifically adds the words, "for the sake of the Lord," v. 19. We should compare testimonies like this with Paul in order that we may see that there is one ongoing belief by the universal church of God, the patriarchs, the prophets, Christ, and the apostles, and we must cling to this consensus and not depart from it, even if the disturbance caused by some recent monks creates a division which in a wicked way has mixed philosophy in with the doctrine of the Gospel.

In 1 Cor. 1:31, "He who glories, let him glory in the Lord," that is, we cannot be glorified or exalted because we are without sin, but we glory in the Lord, that is to say, in the Lord who promises us mercy. Just as it is said in another place, "God has imprisoned all under sin that He might have mercy on all," Rom. 11:32. Likewise Rom. 3:9, "We have said that all are under sin." At a later point in v. 19 the assertion is added, ". . . that every mouth may be stopped and all the world may become guilty before God." He often repeats this concept of universality, so that there should be no doubt that He is accusing all. Therefore we should acknowledge our own weakness and confess that also in the regenerate there are sins, such as the depravity of our nature and the many sinful desires; and we must stand in shame in the knowledge of the wrath of God against these evils and grieve that there is still in us so much hostility toward the will of God; and there must increase in us true repentance. The admission of our own weakness will counteract our pride, make us subject to God, encourage us to fear God, to implore His mercy and seek His help.

But after our pride has been put under attack, pious minds must still learn about faith, lest they fall into despair. We must teach how our beginning obedience may be pleasing to God. In this locus we shall always join together these three points:

First, the regenerate person must be assured that he is reconciled with God by faith for the sake of the Son of God, as is often said, that our person is accepted by God for the sake of His Son, by faith, freely.

Second, the regenerate person must recognize that in this life sin and weakness still remain in those who have been born again, and he must truly lament that he still has this darkness, corruption, disorder, and wicked desires against the law of God.

Third, he must also be assured that obedience and the righteousness of a good conscience must be begun, and that this is far from the perfection of the Law, and yet in the case of those who have been reconciled, it is pleasing to God for the sake of His Son the Mediator who presents our prayers and our worship before the Father and overlooks our weakness. Thus for the sake of Christ a person is first reconciled, then his works are accepted, and his faith sheds light on both of these points. Therefore Peter says in 1 Peter 2:5, "Offer up spiritual sacrifices acceptable to God through Jesus Christ."

We must think about these three points every day in regard to our works. For we must not dream that God is not concerned about our works, for He really does care. He demands obedience and with horrible penalties, both temporal and eternal, He punishes the evil behavior which is contrary to good conscience. Therefore it is necessary to possess the good righteousness of a good conscience and to know how it pleases God. For a doubting and corrupted conscience cannot call upon God. We must carefully inculcate these teachings in our minds. For faith struggles in these exercises, and true knowledge of God and spiritual renewal increase in these struggles.

Faith is trained in good works in two ways. First, it determines that its obedience is pleasing to God, as I have said above. Then it also seeks aid, as David understood, when he realized that his rule was being hindered and endangered; but he believed that his labors were pleasing to God because of the promise of God's mercy. Then he sought God's help and labored in the defense of his people and in controlling the conduct of his citizens as best he could. There is no doubt that this is a worthwhile instruction for godly minds, which, although they are anxious to obey God, yet they recognize the darkness of their nature, and their various sins, and they are so sorry for them that they almost fall into despair. But what sweeter comfort can be given them than these words of Paul in Rom. 8:1, "There is therefore no condemnation to those who are in Christ Jesus . . ."? That is, even though the regenerate are not without sin, yet God has received them and pronounced the believers righteous for the sake of His Son. In so doing He also accepts their obedience for the sake of His Son.

In Col. 1:28 it says, "You are presented perfect in Christ Jesus," that is, even if the regenerate do not yet fulfill the Law, yet they are righteous and pleasing to God for the sake of His Son. Here we should confess and celebrate the fullness of the mercy of God, that in those who have been reconciled, this obedience which is incomplete, imperfect, unclean, and corrupted by many wicked desires, is still accepted by God, not indeed because of the worth of our virtues but because of the Son of God, Rom. 6:14, "You are not under the Law but under grace." At this point the question is asked: Does our obedience please God when it does not satisfy the Law? Paul replies that it does please Him because "we are not under the Law," that is, we are not condemned by the Law; but we are under grace, that is, we have been reconciled or accepted into grace, Rom. 8:34, "Who will condemn us? It is Christ who died for us and rose again, who is at the right hand of God and intercedes for us," that is, the saints are pleasing to God because of the intercession of Christ. Rom. 3:31, "We establish the Law through faith." This is a very brief statement, but it teaches exactly what we are saying, that obedience cannot be begun in us, nor does it please God unless faith is added which determines that the person and the beginning obedience are both pleasing to God for the sake of the Mediator. Thus, says Paul, "We establish the Law," we do not minimize obedience, but we insist upon it and we reassert it; and in order that it might be retained, we teach how this obedience can be rendered and how it can please God.

Now, after we have said how this obedience may please God, which we all recognize is far from a perfect obedience to the Law, then we shall add testimonies which clearly tell us that the works of the saints or their beginning obedience are pleasing to God. From these passages we surely are aroused to a zeal for well-doing, and at the same time we instruct ourselves in regard to the immeasurable mercy of God who not only approves of our defective obedience but even adorns it with honor and rewards. For we should take a look at ourselves and realize what a rare thing an outstanding virtue is. There are certain pictures of this kind of virtue in men, but they are weak and fleeting and can never satisfy the law of God which requires far greater fight and order in the nature of man than is there, and yet these pictures or attempts are received by God, as the passage says, for the sake of His Son who earnestly intercedes for us. Likewise, in Rom. 10:10 it says, "With the heart we believe unto righteousness, and with the mouth confession is made unto salvation." When God demands confession He wills that our whole life be a confession. Therefore our whole life must be directed to honoring God, to showing what we profess, and to adorning the Gospel, as the passage says, "Let your light shine," Matt. 5:16. For example, that a prince may show what he believes, he calls upon God in times of danger to show that he is rendering obedience; that he may serve God, he destroys ungodly religions, that the banners of his confession may fly far and wide. In the same way, let each of us in our calling have the signs of our confessions. Let the scholar show his belief, let him call upon God in every turn of his life which is so filled with dangers, let him refute all ungodly ideas and in governing his desires, let him demonstrate that he is rendering such great obedience in order that he may serve God and adorn the Gospel. The life of man is so intertwined with others that both in our life and conversation our confession must shine forth in all of our duties.

But why does it say, "Confession is made unto salvation"? The answer is brief: Even if we are righteous for the sake of Christ, that is, even if we have been received unto eternal life, yet it is necessary that this newness follow. He wills this to be present when he says, "Confession is made unto salvation." Note also 2 Cor. 5:2–3, "Desiring to be clothed upon, if being so clothed, we not be found naked," that is, it is necessary in this life that conversion take place and that the renewal begin at the same time. This conversion began in the robber on the cross. He was repentant. He recognized that he was being punished by God justly; and then by faith he acknowledged his Savior and begged salvation from Him. Thus he heard the clear absolution and the announcement and the promise of eternal life. Furthermore, in order that he might give a sign of his confession, he refuted his fellow criminal who was cursing Christ.

This memorable example of these important matters serves as instruction to us that God is so concerned about His church that He raises up witnesses to His teaching, even when she has been deserted by her great leaders. The apostles in their consternation were struck dumb, and scarcely a spark of faith remained among these enormous storms of doubt. At this point, God produces new witnesses and warns men by the unexpected eclipse, the earthquake, and the resurrection of some dead people, so that no one should think that this is some ordinary punishment or that they were forgotten by God, and this thief is raised up who is made an apostle to speak for a moment from the cross and affirm that this is the Messiah, the giver of eternal life. Then this story particularly teaches us that this is truly the meaning of the Gospel, that we are accepted by faith for the sake of the Son of God, even if we do not supply the necessary merits. Likewise, it teaches us regarding the nature of faith that it is not merely the knowledge of the facts, but a trust which seeks eternal life from the Son. When this flame has been kindled, he shows us that this is something far different from human reason. The sight of these torn and dying bodies does not frighten the thief from determining to entrust his life and to believe that those who flee to this Lord will have eternal salvation. But the others who despise this Lord, he realizes, will be in eternal torment. Because he believes that God is favorable toward him, he subjects himself to Him and loves Him. He understands that he is not being punished by some accident, but he gives thanks to God because he has been called to the knowledge of God and of his Lord. He wants to obey God even in enduring this punishment, he is not angry at the judgment of God, he realizes that the human race is being punished by God under this mountain of troubles because of sin and not as the philosophers think that we encounter death and other calamities only as accidents, and thus we must understand the wrath of God and seek deliverance. Therefore, in regard to his suffering, he perceives that we must be willing to obey God in bearing our afflictions. The thief is instructed in this conversion in regard to sin, the wrath of God, his punishment, the remission of his sins, and his righteousness, in order that he may understand that the wisdom of the saints is something far different from the wisdom of the Pharisees or of human reason. For in their afflictions the godly learn, as it says in Ps. 119:71, "It is good for me that You have humbled me, that I might learn Your righteousness." Finally, the thief came to his confession, in which he proclaimed that this is the Messiah, nor was he frightened by the spectacle of the punishments, but rather he condemned the other thief who with poisonous sarcasm has excoriated the punishment of Christ and condemned Him for being on the cross, just as the world arrogantly spurns Christ and His church because of their weakness. We must carefully examine this illustration of mockery. For just as this man ridiculed in the midst of death and subjected Christ to further shame, so the ungodly, even in the midst of their furious ravings, do not realize their own sins and bring additional shame upon Christ, even while He is offering them deliverance.

I have cited this example because it teaches us about several points and also shows that in a true conversion there is the beginning of the new obedience which also demonstrates itself in many upright actions, which, as I have said, are pleasing to God. Thus in Rom. 14:17, "The kingdom of God is not meat and drink, but righteousness, peace, and joy in the Holy Spirit." He who serves God in these respects is pleasing to Him and has the approval of his fellow men. Heb. 13:2ff., "Be not forgetful of kindness and generosity . . . which are pleasing to God." Of Noah it is said in Gen. 8:20ff., "God smelled a sweet odor," that is, He was pleased with the sacrifice of Noah, his prayer, his thanksgiving, his praise, and his teaching. There is a wonderful figure of speech in the word "to smell an odor," which is derived from the ancient ritual whereby through the sacrifices a sweet smell was said to be offered to God when the burnt offerings were made. This was a special testimony that the people were pleasing to Him and accepted by Him. Furthermore, in a general way the sacrifices were compared to sweet smells, and incense was added, because in all of their works there was supposed to be an odor, that is, the message from God was to be spread far and wide as a sweet-smelling fragrance, that is, the sacrifices were part of the act of celebrating and honoring God, so that other people might be invited by this good teaching and these good examples.

The Fourth Question: Why Are Good Works to Be Done?

There are many reasons: necessity, worthiness, and rewards. First, necessity is of different kinds. There is the necessity of command, the necessity of debt, the necessity of retaining faith, and the necessity of avoiding punishment. For although it is one thing to speak of compulsion, yet there does remain in force the eternal ordering of the immutable God that the creature shall render obedience to the will of God. This immutable ordering is the necessity of command and the necessity of debt, as Paul says in Rom. 8:6, "We are under obligation to God, not to the flesh." And Christ says in John 13:34, "This is My command that you love one another," cf. 1 Thess. 4:3, 8.

There is the necessity for retaining our faith, because the Holy Spirit is driven out and grieved when we permit sins against conscience. Thus it clearly says in 1 John 3:7–8, "Let no one deceive you; he who commits sin is of the devil." And Rom. 8:13, "If you put to death the deeds of the flesh, you will live; if you live according to the flesh, you shall die." That faith is cut off through sinful works is witnessed by this statement of Paul in 1 Tim. 5:8, "If a person does not provide for his own, especially those of his own house, he has denied the faith and is worse than an unbeliever." Further, faith cannot be present in those who indulge in depraved lusts and do not repent, for it is written, Is. 66:1–2, "Where does the Lord dwell? In a contrite spirit and one which trembles at My words." Likewise, when faith brings peace to our conscience, it cannot at the same time be present in a person who intends to retain his sin, because faith condemns this conscience. Thus Paul says, Rom. 14:23, "Whatsoever is not of faith is sin."

Thus David drove out his faith and the Holy Spirit when he laid hands on another man's wife, and he troubled the Holy Spirit in several ways, first in his own heart by which he was urged on to his adultery, and then in many of the saints, to some of whom his offense brought sorrow, and to others an occasion for mischief. The same was the case with those poor women who were violated by Absalom and his soldiers, 2 Sam. 16:21ff.

The necessity of avoiding punishment ought to move our minds, since we see the whole history of the world filled with the saddest events which surely are the punishments for sins. But so great is the blindness of men that they think all these things happen only by accident. This insanity must be removed. We must understand that all these sad events of mankind are truly punishments, both for the first fall and for other sins. As Ps. 38:2ff. says, "Because of his sins You crush man." Indeed, since all present things are of short duration, present punishments do not correspond to the eternal wrath of God, but are witnesses to the judgment to come. God warns us to wait for another judgment in which we are not dealing with transitory and passing matters, but with matters of eternity. We must also keep this judgment in mind and instruct ourselves concerning this judgment, as often as we witness present punishments.

Further, we must resist this intellectualized caviling by which the blessings which come from fear of punishment are held up for criticism. The answer is simple for the godly who know that there are many causes and reasons for the same action. They know that we must do the right thing for the sake of God rather than because of the punishments. But they also know that God wills that His will and His wrath be acknowledged in the punishments we undergo, and that He wills that we fear present punishments as well as future ones. All punishments are very obvious; often sins are punished by sins and many people are implicated in sins and calamities. Often one person is guilty of all these evils, as in the case of the fall of David. What a terrible crime he committed, what hopelessness, blasphemy, and sadness he brought on all!

The worship of idols was permitted by Solomon, and this was the cause of the destruction of the kingdom of Israel. This invasion of idolatry brought religious controversy and unending wars. God wants us to consider these examples in order that we may fear His wrath and have a reason for concern for our own salvation and that of others. But the blind mind of man does not perceive the greatness of sin or the wrath of God. Indeed, it is not even sufficiently affected by present punishments, as in the case of the unrepentant thief who in the midst of his calamity was still mocking and deriding Christ.

Furthermore, the godly must learn, as has been said, to recognize the wrath of God in the enormous number of calamities which befall mankind and they must learn also to avoid the wiles of the devil, who little by little, one step after the other, coerces man and weaves the long thread of many miseries, so that finally he may force man to despair, as it is written, "The devil walks about as a roaring lion, seeking whom he may devour," 1 Peter 5:8.

The next cause is worthiness. Here again I caution you that we must not attribute any worthiness to our virtues, as if because of them a person has the remission of sins, or because of them he is satisfying the law of God, or as if they are the price of eternal life. But faith must shine forth and fully understand that we are pleasing to God because of the Son of God, as we have said above. But afterward, after conversion, also for the sake of this Mediator, our worship is pleasing to God who does not will that the whole human race perish. Therefore He wills that there be the church in which He is confessed, invoked, worshiped, whose obedience He accepts for the sake of His Son; and He calls those works "sacrifices" by which God judges that He is treated with honor. Thus Peter says, 1 Peter 2:5, "Offer up spiritual sacrifices." This is the worthiness of one's vocation, not his person, as when a magistrate or apostle must stress and consider the importance of his own work, that these are very significant things, through which God rules our lives and gives eternal life. Therefore he will do everything in his power to be governed and aided by God, and for this reason.

Thus when any member of the church believes that it is the highest calling of all that he be a member of the people of God, he will pray to God for himself and for others; he will offer sacrifices, that is, every kind of good works which has been commanded by God. This worthiness of our calling must be understood and considered in this context: You must know that your study of Scripture and the uprightness of your life are truly very important matters and pertain to the glory of your calling and the need of others. Therefore God demands and approves this, as we have said, and governs and aids it. Therefore you shall perform the duties of your station with eagerness.

[The final cause deals with] rewards. In order that we may have certainty concerning the remission of our sins and our reconciliation, rewards are given to us freely for the sake of the Son of God and they must be received by faith. For they would be uncertain matters if they depended on the condition of our merits. But in those who have been reconciled, after conversion, their good works, since they are pleasing by faith for the sake of the Mediator, as we have said, do merit spiritual and physical rewards in this life and after this life, as the parable of the talents in Matthew 25 clearly shows, v. 29, "To him who has shall be given . . ."; and in 1 Tim. 4:8, "Godliness . . . has promise of this present life and of the life to come"; cf. Mark 10:30; Matt. 10:42; Luke 6:38; Ex. 20:12; Is. 33:16; 58:10–11. Finally Scripture is full of promises of this kind concerning both spiritual and physical rewards; for in this life there is need for both. Individuals cannot keep their faith without practicing it; and without these spiritual gifts the true teaching cannot shine brightly nor the church and good government be preserved. Also, since God wills that in this life His doctrine be proclaimed, He gives a certain protection to those who teach and those who learn, and He preserves His church in a wondrous way, just as He preserved the ship in which Paul was being carried to Rome. Thus He promises blessings also for this present life. Although the church has been terribly tormented, yet there is always a remnant of the godly, just as victory comes even though many are killed on the battle line.

Therefore we must learn that there is a need for both kinds of good works and that the rewards have not been promised by God in vain, but there is the need for constant practicing of our faith, that it may grow and that we may labor more diligently even though we are undeserving of the rewards.

Further, faith is exercised in three different ways. First, when something else is going to be requested, faith always from the very beginning will think about the remission of sins, as David, when he could not seek victory unless he knew that he was pleasing to God.

Second, faith knows that good things do not happen by mere accident, as when the ungodly in Paul's ship imagined that the ship had been saved by an accident. But faith knows with certainty that we are cared for by God, defended and aided by Him, and that the promises have been given concerning His blessings in order that the Epicurean opinion, which believes that good and evil happen only by accident, may be thrust out of our minds. But we should learn that God truly gives good gifts and we must seek them from Him.

Third, faith is busily engaged in seeking aid and reward so that he who gives alms may also enjoy his own possessions and see that there will be something for his family, and if God has not taken care of them, faith seeks and awaits help and reward. In order that we may better understand these matters, we should look at the antithesis and examine our own sins. Therefore you may be less diligent in good works if you think that you are laboring in vain because you are displeasing to God. This figment of the imagination is in conflict with the first exercise of faith. You may be less liberal in the second exercise, if you think that these matters have been relegated to human diligence and are of no concern to God. This error conflicts with the second exercise of faith, for God demands this diligence on the part of man in order that He may will this activity of ours to be governed by His Word, as is the case with our other virtues. You must be diligent, but in keeping with the precepts of God; you must work, but not in performing useless and unnecessary things, but you shall devote yourself to things which are necessary and useful for the church and for the poor. In the third place, you would be less generous if you thought that God will not compensate and that your own loved ones will be in want. This hesitancy is in direct opposition to the third exercise of faith. Therefore, in order that faith may be kept in trim and grow, God has set forth many different kinds of works and He has added promises of aid and reward, so that there may be an opportunity for prayer on our part. For how will you look for eternal salvation from God if you do not look for a piece of bread from Him? Therefore we must fight against this lack of trust on our part and do the works which have been commanded; and even though they may be difficult, we must arouse thereby our faith and our prayer; we must also look to the rewards and be concerned about the universal church, the government, and our salvation. For the sake of these goals we must be more diligent in our calling, in controlling our morals, etc.

All of these points are depicted in the example of the widow of Zarephath and Elijah, 1 Kings 17. Elijah knew that he had been called by God to teach the people and that until God wanted him to carry out his ministry, he would not lack something to eat. With this confidence he sought and awaited his food and he went to the widow, and although he was worn out with his labors, yet commanded that food be brought to him. The widow told him of her poverty. At this point the prophet added the promise. The woman believed the word of the prophet that the God of Israel was truly the Creator and Savior, that He gives good gifts, that He would supply food for the future. Therefore, although she saw that this would take away food from herself and her son, because there was another mouth to feed, yet she fed the prophet first. Rewards followed this faith and this work. The family was fed for a long time, and it was without doubt by the blessing of God. Their home became a meeting place for the church where the prophet taught the whole area. Affliction followed this great glory. The son died. But new rewards followed again and the son was raised to life. By this example the woman was strengthened in her faith and the teaching of Elijah was spread far and wide. Therefore, understand how many great and good works this first duty which the woman performed in feeding the prophet produced and consider the mountain of rewards she received. For not only was the family fed, but it

1067

was instructed by the prophet concerning the true worship of God and eternal life and in many ways it was protected against the devil. The son was raised from the dead and became a disciple of the prophet, and he doubtlessly utilized his services for the church later on. Even small insignificant works are adorned with rewards far greater than is owed. It is necessary that all the saints should confess with Jacob in Gen. 32:10, "I am not worthy of the least of Your mercies."

But although it is necessary that there be a beginning of the new life, as Paul says in 2 Cor. 5:2–3, "We desire to be clothed upon with new clothing, so that we not be found naked," yet our heart must always recognize what the psalmist says, Ps. 143:2, "In Your sight shall no flesh be justified"; Ps. 19:12, "Who can understand his sins?" Our heart must know that our virtues are not the price of our eternal life, but that this is certainly given for the sake of the Mediator, as Paul says in Eph. 2:8, "The gift of God is eternal life." Christ says in John 6:40, "This is the will of the Father, that everyone who sees the Son and believes in Him has eternal life." The pious mind in true repentance must meditate upon this statement and with certainty await eternal life for the sake of the Mediator. Nor can faith rely on two things, the Mediator and our merits, as an experienced conscience can easily judge.

The Fifth Question: What Is the Difference among Sins?

Although we have said that sins remain in the regenerate, it is still necessary that we deal with the difference among sins. For it is a certainty that those who fall into sins which are against conscience do not remain in grace, do not keep their faith, their righteousness, or the Holy Spirit; and faith cannot stand with evil intentions in the face of conscience, that is, faith which is confidence in our acceptance by God. For these desires are absolutely opposed to one another, and true prayer cannot exist with a bad conscience which flees from God, as it says in 1 John 3:21, "If our heart does not condemn us, we have confidence toward God."

Therefore we must retain the rule that it is necessary in those who have been reconciled that there be this righteousness of a good conscience, as it says in 1 Tim. 1:5, "The sum of the commandment is love out of a pure heart, of a good conscience, and of genuine faith."

In the same chapter it says in vv. 18–19, "Fight the good fight having faith and a good conscience." 2 Cor. 1:12, "This is our boast, the testimony of our conscience." 1 Peter 3:16, ". . . having a good conscience."

But many passages testify that those who allow themselves to sin against conscience are cut off from grace and drive out faith and the Holy Spirit, and become guilty of the wrath of God and eternal punishments. For example, Gal. 5:19–21, "The works of the flesh are manifest, adultery, fornication, uncleanness . . . idolatry . . . they who do such things shall not possess the kingdom of God." He is speaking of manifest works which are done against our conscience. 1 Cor. 6:9–10, "Do not make any mistake: neither fornicators nor idolaters nor adulterers . . . shall inherit the kingdom of God." Here Paul mentions by name, v. 11, that although some of them had previously been guilty of such vices, now they had mended their ways. He commands them that they must keep a good conscience and he bears witness that they shall perish if they continue in their previous iniquities.

Rom. 8:13, "If you live by the flesh, you shall die, but if through the Spirit you put to death the deeds of the flesh, you shall live." Here Paul is dealing with this difference. Many inner evils do remain in the regenerate, that is, a kind of darkness and corruption which is born in us. For although there is a beginning of light and a beginning of obedience, and although faith still does shine forth as a small spark in this thick darkness which is valiantly struggling with doubts and fighting against them, yet the fear of God, trust, and love are not as great as they should be. Then there are many wicked desires, such as admiration for ourselves and self-confidence, and different kinds of emotions, the flames of lust, a burning unrighteous anger and deception, such as were found in Miriam and Aaron against Moses. Finally, many sins still remain in the saints, sins of omission, as they are called, that is, neglect of our duty and mistakes in the home, the government and the church, which nevertheless are not done in violation of conscience on the part of the godly, who do demonstrate faith and show as great diligence as they can. But because the saints fight against their evil desires and believe that for the sake of the Son of God their weaknesses are forgiven, therefore they do remain in grace and keep their faith and the Holy Spirit. This is Paul's meaning when he says, "If you put to death the deeds of the flesh, you shall live."

This is a very unusual emphasis when he says, "Through the Spirit you put to death the deeds of the flesh." He is calling us to a bitter contest, he wants us to fight against our evil desires, and to do this by the Spirit, that is, with the true desires, the fear and faith which have been kindled by the Holy Spirit through the Word of God; it must consider how great a thing the wrath of God is, it must remember the examples of those who have fallen, such as Saul and others who were not restored to grace. Our mind must understand that countless sins and offenses flow even from one lapse. Again it must believe also that our obedience is pleasing to God and it must seek aid and guidance, as it is written, "Without Me you can do nothing," John 15:5. Likewise, "Ask and it shall be given to you," Matt. 7:7. "How much more shall your heavenly Father give His Holy Spirit to them that ask Him," Luke 11:13. And as it says so often in the psalms: "Help me and I shall be saved"; and again, "Do with Your servant according to Your mercy and teach me Your righteousness"; Ps. 51:10, "Create in me a clean heart, O God," that is, a heart which rightly believes that it has been purified by God through faith. And "renew a right spirit within me," that is, a spirit which is strong and does not doubt that a renewal has taken place "within me." V. 11, "Cast me not away from Your presence, and take not Your Holy Spirit from me," that is, the Spirit who guides all my actions. V. 12, "Restore unto me the joy of Your salvation, and uphold me with Your free Spirit," that is, give me a willing spirit which does not flee from conflict and dangers and "strengthen me."

Thus Joseph repelled the illicit approaches of his master's wife; thus Jonathan strengthened himself against burning jealousy against David. Thus David kept himself in check from killing Saul and thus he sustained himself from being shattered by despair when he was driven into exile. Thus Paul teaches in Rom. 6:12, "Let sin not reign in your mortal body," and this seems to be taken from the word in Gen. 4:7, "Sin is lying at the door, and it desires you, but you must rule over it." For the word "to rule" does not mean something idle and cowardly, but it refers to the power of the Holy Spirit and the diligence of our will. Joseph saw the commandment of God and the punishments attendant upon it, the scandals and the other destructive involvements which would follow, and he rejected her sinful advances. He sought divine guidance and added to it his own determination. He ruled his eyes that they not wander lustfully, he controlled his loneliness and the opportunities which were offered him lest he be caught in the devil's snares. Godly people must learn to understand this precaution and to practice it, realizing that there is good reason for the statement, "You must rule over it . . . let not sin reign." When sin takes control it brings with it all kinds of troubles and the wrath of God and eternal death. On the other hand, when sin does not reign over us, the godly keep the righteousness and faith which have been given to them, and thus Paul can say, "If by the Spirit you put to death the deeds of the flesh, you shall live."

I have mentioned which sins remain in the regenerate, namely, certain inner evils against which they must contend. But when we permit sins which are against conscience, then the Holy Spirit is driven out and grieved, grace is lost and faith destroyed, that is, the confidence in the mercy of God. Paul is trying to say this when he says in Rom. 8:13, "If you live according to the flesh, you shall die," that is, if you obey the wicked desires of the flesh, you will be guilty of the wrath of God and eternal death. In the same chapter he says, v. 14, "Those who are led by the Holy Spirit, they are the sons of God." But those who go against conscience, drive out and grieve the Holy Spirit and therefore cease to be the sons of God, as also the passages cited above testify, such as 1 Cor. 6:9, "Do not be deceived; fornicators . . . shall not inherit the kingdom." Also John says in his First Epistle, 3:8, "He who commits sin is of the devil, that is, he is already a captive of the devil, guilty of the wrath of God and eternal punishment, driven by the devil into many more sins. These terribly tragic statements should encourage us to contend against the raging wickedness which battles against us, lest we fall from the grace which has been given to us. It is not necessary at this point to bring in the arguments concerning predestination, but rather we must simply form our judgments on the basis of the will of God which has been clearly found in the Word of God.

Good Works

We continue by considering the order of the presentation of these matters. Up to this point we have explained the following loci: (1) Who the true God is, whom man must recognize in keeping with the precept of the divine Word and, when He is known, worship Him. This God is one in essence and three in persons, the Father, the Son, and the Holy Spirit. (2) How this true God created (in addition to the angels and the other visible creatures) man in His own image and likeness. (3) That this man himself did not long remain in the innocence and righteousness in which he had been created at the beginning, but he fell into sin. (4) What a horrible corruption fell upon all the powers of men as a result of this fall. (5) Hence, the voice of the Law is heard, revealing, condemning, and damning forever the whole depravity of human nature along with all of its fruits, at the judgment seat of God. (6) But because God does not want what He created to perish, He joined to the Law the teaching of the Gospel, which deals with the locus of justification, that is, it teaches how our situation, which has become corrupt and lost because of our sins, can stand before the judgment of God, certainly not because of any of our works or merits, but freely, out of His sheer mercy for the sake of the death and resurrection of the one Jesus Christ, the Son of God.

Now therefore, in keeping with the best order, the locus on good works follows, partly because no one should think that in the locus on justification good works have been so excluded that there must be present a statement that they cannot and must not be involved in justifying, and that they do not follow justification; and partly because true faith is not an idle thing but, as it says in Gal. 5:6, "Faith works and is efficacious through love." Therefore, in order to close the mouths of slanderers who say that we (by this teaching of the free remission of sins and the reconciliation of sinful man with God for the sake of the merit of Christ) have opened all the doors and windows to every kind of impiety and have introduced a relaxation of discipline and an intolerable confusion of morals, and at the same time that our people need to know clearly how their saving faith is distinguished through good works from a false faith, it is absolutely necessary that we also explain and establish this locus of Christian doctrine from the prophetic and apostolic Scriptures.

Furthermore, we shall observe our usual method of explaining things by dividing the entire subject into its parts. In this way we shall aid the memory of those who learn and add light to the explanation.

The Terminology

As we begin this study of the locus on good works, we must first note the terms. This is a useful device because from the very term "good works" there sometimes develops a corruption of the purer teaching of this locus. The papists understand the term with reference to any external debts and works of supererogation, only that they be performed with the good intention and the purpose of serving God. From this they seize the opportunity of perverting the doctrine of the free justification of sinful man. For they say that good works do not justify, that is, external actions and those which we owe, but faith, that is, the internal obedience, this justifies. Some of them understand this only with reference to works beneficial to others, as in Acts 9:36, where it is written concerning Dorcas, "She was rich in good works and the giving of alms." And Paul in 1 Tim. 5:10 requires of a woman who is truly a widow that she be properly adorned with "the testimony of good works," and then he goes on to explain what kind of works these should be, "that she be hospitable, that she wash the feet of the saints, that she take care of the afflicted."

Therefore we must cling to the fact that the term "good works" is not used in only one way. For sometimes in Scripture it is used to describe a certain kind of work, such as in 1 Tim. 2:10 where Paul wants the women "to profess godliness with good works"; and in 2 Thess. 2:17 where he prays for the Thessalonians that "God would establish them in every good word and work"; likewise, Heb. 10:24 prescribes that the godly "stir up and provoke one another to love and good works." There are some who look for a distinction between good works which are *agatha* and those which are *kala*; and suggest that the former are external and the latter internal. But in the Scripture this distinction is not observed. Sometimes the term "good works" is a general one which includes the whole teaching of this locus. Thus in Titus 2:14 the apostle testifies that "Christ has purified unto Himself a peculiar people, zealous of good works." And in Titus 3:1 he writes, "Direct them that they be zealous to observe good works, those who believe in God"; Eph. 2:10, "We are God's workmanship, created in Christ Jesus unto good works, which God has prepared beforehand that we should walk in them." It has become a matter of common usage that when we wish to discuss the summary of the doctrine of this locus, we use the term "good works." In the following citations faith and good works are put in opposition to each other. Note how Paul in Rom. 4:3ff. shows by the example of Abraham that "to him who does not work, but believes in Him who justifies the ungodly, his faith is imputed to him for righteousness."

Furthermore, in order that this term may be more correctly understood, we must add the other words which pertain to the teaching of this locus. We shall list the principal terms in which it is useful to observe the individual passages from which the language is derived.

I. There are many words which are taken directly from Scripture itself, such as, regeneration, vivification, love, renewal, and others. These can be divided among themselves, so that some are referred to the efficient cause, such as, the word "sanctification," "the gift through grace," Rom. 5:15; "the new creature in Christ," 2 Cor. 5:17 and Gal. 6:15. Some of the terms refer to the formal cause, such as, "newness or renewal," in Eph. 4:23, "Be renewed in the spirit of your mind"; Col. 3:10, "Put on the new man who is renewed in knowledge according to the image of Him who created him"; Titus 3:5, ". . . the washing of regeneration and the renewal of the Holy Spirit"; cf. Rom. 6:4; 7:6; Ps. 51:10; Eph. 2:15; 4:24; Col. 3:10; Rom. 9:1; 1 Tim. 1:5; Heb. 11:39. 2 Cor. 9:2 speaks of their "eagerness and readiness to help all." In 2 Cor. 9:7 the words "purpose" and "intention" are used, "Let each do as he has purposed in keeping with the intention of his heart." In Titus 3:5ff. regeneration and vivification include both the efficient cause and the formal cause. Certain terms refer to the objects of good works, such as, "the works of the Law," Rom. 3:28; Gal. 2:16. Some refer to the effects of renewal such as, "good works," "worship of God," "the fruits of the Spirit," "the fruits of repentance or conversion," "putting to death the flesh," "the love of God and one's neighbor," "walking in the ways and commandments of the Lord," "putting to death the deeds of the flesh," "presenting our members as the arms of righteousness," "being led by the Spirit of God," "abstaining from sins." James 3:13, "good conduct"; cf. 1 Peter 2:12; 2 Peter 3:1; 1 Tim. 4:12; Rom. 16:19; 1 Tim. 4:8; 2:10; 2 Peter 1:5; Rom. 12:1, "Present your bodies as a living sacrifice, holy, acceptable to God, your spiritual service," cf. Acts 23:1; Rom. 1:9; Phil. 4:8–9.

These terms concerning good works I have wanted to cite briefly from Scripture, not as if there were no more of them in both the Old and the New Testaments, but because these are all very important. For the sake of memory I have divided them into these categories which if any one wished to examine more closely he will perhaps have some reason for criticism, but for those who are learning this method of distribution there will be no problem. I am not unaware that in some instances one word can be referred to different categories. For example, the word "sanctification" in 1 Cor. 1:30, "Christ is made unto us sanctification . . ." is used in an affective sense. Compare 2 Thess. 2:13, "We must give thanks to God . . . because He has chosen us from the beginning unto salvation through sanctification of the Spirit"; and 1 Peter 1:2, "Beloved by the foreknowledge of God . . . because He has chosen us from the beginning unto salvation through sanctification of the Spirit." Sometimes the word is used in a formal sense, as in Rom. 6:19, "Yield your members as servants to righteousness unto sanctification." 1 Thess. 4:3, "This is the will of God, your sanctification." In the same way the word "holiness" is used in a formal sense in 2 Cor. 7:1, ". . . perfecting holiness in the fear of God"; 1 Thess. 3:13, ". . . that He may establish your hearts blameless in holiness before God." It is worth the careful study of pious and learned men to pay attention to these points, but for us it suffices to have given this brief instruction.

II. The words treated thus far are Scriptural terms. But in our disputations with the papists other words have also been used, such as, "new qualities," "spiritual movements," "infused attitudes," "inherent righteousness." To these some others could be added.

The term "merit" is used by the fathers and is called *meritum*, that is, a work which is commanded by God, performed by the regenerate in faith, which has promises attached to it either in this life or the life to come. But because of the misuse of the term and the snares which accompany it, and finally because it is only a word from the unwritten tradition, it is not used by those who are more earnest in their concern for doctrine.

But a consideration of these terms is useful because a comparison of them sheds some light on the subject and gives additional instruction. Furthermore, it teaches us this: If there is consensus as to the substance of the matter, we must not create unnecessary controversies over the words.

These points which I have noted regarding the terminology will suffice. But the explanation of the matter itself cannot be dealt with more expeditiously than by following the order of the questions which have been posed.

THE FIRST QUESTION: WHICH WORKS MUST BE DONE?

Our method of presenting this matter requires that first of all we deal with the question as to whether good works must be performed. But because among all true Christians it is beyond controversy, therefore our author [Melanchthon] has omitted this question. But yet because the papists now for many years have slanderously accused our churches of condemning a zeal for good works, and of deluding ourselves in our teaching of the righteousness of faith into thinking that we have been freed from the observance of the commandments of God, therefore it is worth the effort to include this question in the doctrine of good works. The fact that the teaching heard in our churches day after day will present a very clear testimony before the whole world that the papists are slandering us and attributing something false to us. Yet in order that godly people may have proof at hand whereby they may repudiate this calumny, I shall cite the main points in the exhortations with which we encourage our hearers to be zealous for good works.

I. Our people are taught that God gives to the justified and the regenerate no permission or license by which they might dare rashly and freely to indulge in their depraved desires, or to conform themselves to the unclean world, to serve the devil, to seek after sins, or boldly to violate the commands of God. For Paul's word is, "God has not called us to uncleanness but to sanctification," 1 Thess. 4:7. Also note vv. 3–5, "This is the will of God, your sanctification, that you should abstain from fornication . . . not in the lusts of concupiscence, as the gentiles do who do not know God." Also Rom. 3:8, "Some say, 'Let us do evil, that good may come.' These people are rightly condemned."

II. Our people are also instructed to teach that God demands good works or the fruits of faith from the justified and the regenerate, and He will not endure their being idle and without good works. Matt. 3:10 and 7:19, "Every tree which does not produce good fruit is cut down and cast into the fire." Matt. 20:6, "The owner of the vineyard rebuked them for their laziness: 'Why do you stand here idle all day?' " 2 Peter 1:8, "If these things be in you, they make you so that you are not idle or unfruitful in the knowledge of our Lord Jesus Christ." The entire Scripture is filled with statements like this which urge the regenerate to be zealous for good works. See Ps. 34:14; Eph. 4:22–24; Rom. 13:12; 2 Cor. 5:15; Eph. 2:10; Titus 2:14; 1 Peter 2:24.

III. Furthermore, it is taught in our churches that God does not merely advise this new obedience to the regenerate and the justified (as the papists say), nor treat it as a matter of adiaphora or indifference or our own free choice, but that He requires it as something necessary because of His command and will. For these are the statements of Scripture: Luke 17:10; John 15:12; Rom. 8:12; 13:8; 1 Thess. 4:3; 1 John 4:21.

IV. From Scripture we want to add the fact that faith which is not active in love is not a true faith but dead, Gal. 5:6, "Faith works by love"; cf. 1 Tim. 5:8; James 2:17; John 2:4.

V. Finally, in our churches we place before violators of the commands of God the threats of punishments, physical, spiritual, and eternal, as we find them in the following passages: Ps. 89:31–32; Rom. 8:13; 1 Cor. 6:10; Gal. 5:21; 1 Thess. 4:6; Col. 3:6; 1 Tim. 1:19; 2 Peter 1:9.

These are the principal points of our exhortations given to those who hear our sermons, in order that they may be stirred up to do good works. Thus it is a slander if someone accuses our churches of prohibiting good works because we teach that the promise of the Gospel concerning the remission of sins and eternal life do not depend on the condition of our good works or our observance of the divine commandments, but on the free mercy of God for the sake of the obedience and merit of Christ the Mediator, as if we had no other reasons for doing good works if we exclude them from the article and the discussion of justification. The prophets and apostles themselves (as we have shown previously) have taught that out of the free mercy of God, by faith, for the sake of Christ the Mediator, without works we are justified, and yet they do not forbid or condemn us to be anxious to perform good works. Thus it is a papistic fantasy by which they are persuading themselves that if good works were not to be done in order to merit adoption and eternal life, then they should be entirely omitted. Thus they publish the notion that they do not want to serve God, as becomes obedient children, out of a free and spontaneous spirit, but insist that our works be done in a slavish manner for a reward and the hope of a reward. This idea should be the farthest thing from the mind of true Christians. Thus Luther taught that we should draw our sound teaching from the Word of God in such a way that although good works are kept separate from the article of justification, yet they are not thereby absolutely removed from the Christian church, but must keep their place among those who have been justified.

It was necessary to mention these matters concerning the question whether good works must be performed, partly because it will help to refute the slandering of the papists; partly because of Epicurean people who obviously have no concern about good works and yet we encounter them from time to time; and partly in order that the younger generation may understand from which passages of Scripture they must draw the main points of their exhortations to good works, by which they may encourage themselves and others to a zeal for godly living.

Now we must take a further look at this question: Which works are to be performed? For it has often developed that even those who have the intention of doing good have gone astray over this question.

The correct explanation of this question is established by exploring three main points. First, we need to study the controversies and errors by which the true teaching on this question has been obscured and distorted in all eras of the church. Then, the true interpretation must be developed and set forth on the basis of sure and immovable testimonies of the sacred Scripture. Finally, the objections and arguments of our adversaries must be considered and refuted. We shall note the principal points concerning all of these questions.

The First Point: The Controversies

[I.] In the Old Testament there were various controversies by the prophets against self-made cults which the Jews, who then were the true people of God, were following contrary to the Law and without the warrant of the Word of God. For they persuaded themselves that whatever was done with good intention was a good work and pleasing to God, even if these things had no command of God. Moved by this persuasion the people forced Aaron, in Ex. 32:1, to make gods who would go ahead of them in the journey. In Judg. 8:27, Gideon out of good intention made an ephod out of the booty of the Midianites, which brought his own house into ruins. On the basis of this the worship of Baal and other gods flourished among them, although Gideon had established it on the excuse that the people were really desiring to serve the true God. For the same reason kings who were not blatantly ungodly did not tear down the high places because they contended that this was done with good intention, and thought that this worship was leaning toward honoring the true God.

The prophets fought valiantly against this notion and, first, showed that it was useless for men to worship God by using the commandment and teachings of men, Is. 29:13. Therefore in Is. 59:4, 8, in regard to those who trust in their man-made worship, he makes the pronouncement: "They trust in vanity and speak lies; they conceive mischief and bring forth iniquity . . . they do not know the way of peace, and they have made crooked paths for themselves, and whoever walks in them shall not know peace," cf. Zech. 7:5–6. Second, the prophets taught that men of this kind, who out of good intention had gone off on their own into their own forms of worship, were not serving God but the devil, Deut. 32:17, "They sacrificed to demons which were no gods, to gods they had never known"; cf. Ps. 106:37; Amos 5:25–26. Third, God also has shown by manifest punishments that He is provoked to wrath by worship of this kind. As Ps. 106:39 says, "They angered God by their experimentations and He poured down ruin upon them." As a result of this, Solomon was removed from his kingdom because he instituted worship outside of the Word of God. Afterward the 10 tribes were carried off into endless captivity and the remaining two tribes were sent into a 70-year exile, because they wanted to worship God apart from and contrary to the Law which had been given to them.

II. In the New Testament Christ our Savior had several conflicts with the Pharisees concerning "the traditions of the elders." For they devised several works which were not mandated by God, using as their excuse that it was a worship designed for righteousness and merit. In Matt. 15:1ff. Christ objects to them because they had made the commandment of God an empty thing by their traditions. He also cites Is. 29:13, "In vain do they worship Me, teaching the doctrines and traditions of men." In Matt. 23:23 Christ raises the objection that they tithe of mint and anise and cumin, and meanwhile neglect the weightier points of the law." In v. 25 He criticizes them for "cleaning the cups and the platters but inside they are filled with extortion and uncleanness." Therefore, He calls them back to the observance of the Law and leads them to the works commanded in the Decalog, Matt. 19:18ff., "You shall not kill, you shall not commit adultery, you shall not steal, you shall not bear false witness, honor your father and your mother. You shall love your neighbor as yourself." In Matt. 22:37ff., He cites a brief summary of the whole Decalog, "You shall love the Lord your

God with all your heart and with all your mind and with all your soul. This is the first and great commandment. And the second is like it: you shall love your neighbor as yourself."

III. At the time of the apostles there was a serious controversy concerning the works of the Law. False apostles were asserting that the works of the Law were necessary for salvation and saying that it was impossible for a person to be saved without performing the works prescribed in the law of Moses. Thus in Acts 15:1 we see their position, "And certain men who came down from Judea taught the brothers and said that unless you be circumcised according to the custom of Moses, you cannot be saved." This opinion is refuted in Acts 15 by Paul and Barnabas and thus ultimately by the entire Council of Jerusalem. Paul also in his epistles to the Romans, the Galatians, the Ephesians, to Timothy, and to Titus, contends very strongly against this error. The apostles also taught clearly that the remission of sins, righteousness, and eternal life come to us not because of our observance of the Law and its works, but only for the sake of the merit of Christ which we receive and apply to ourselves by faith. Note also Acts 4:12, "There is no other name given among men whereby we must be saved"; Acts 10:43, "All the prophets give testimony to Him, that through His name all who believe in Him receive the remission of their sins"; cf. 15:11; Rom. 3:20; Gal. 2:16, "By the works of the Law shall no flesh be justified," although this passage properly pertains to the next point.

IV. Soon after the times of the apostles a flood of empty-minded men came in the train of Simon Magus, blasphemously raging that believers did not have to pay any attention to the law of God or be concerned about what was forbidden or commanded, but each could do freely whatever he wished. Magus defined salvation as being the liberation from that servitude in which men were bound by the prescriptions of the Law to certain works and not allowed to do what they wanted to do.

It would be difficult to believe that such abominable filth could be brought into the church and mixed with its doctrine at the very beginning of the Gospel, if we in our own age had not experienced almost the same things in the case of the Anabaptists. Lest anyone think that we are doing them an injustice, we shall quote the words of the fathers with which they described the aberrations of their own era. Irenaeus [*Adversus Haereses*, 1.23 (new 24), MPL 7.678], discusses the statements of Basilides and his shameless life, and among other things he says that Basilides was indifferent to the practice of lust. Irenaeus, in discussing the heresy of the Carpocratians, says [ibid., 1.24 (new 25) MPL 7.682], "They are so uncontrolled in their raving that they say they can do whatever irreligious and ungodly things they want to do. They say that good and evil are only matters of human opinion, since by nature nothing is evil." In 1.32 (new 29) [MPL 7.691], he describes the wild lusts of Basilides and Carpocrates thus: "Some people take the occasion from their association with Basilides and Carpocrates to practice promiscuous sexual relations, enter into multiple marriages and the neglect of their own families, and they say that such things as eating meat sacrificed to idols is a matter of indifference to God." Augustine in his *De Haeresibus ad Quodvultdeum*, ch. 1 [MPL 42.25], says in regard to Simon Magus, "He deceived many people with his magical lies. He also taught that the detestable practice of immorally using women communally was a matter of indifference." In ch. 7 [MPL 42.27], he refers to the Carpocratians as teaching that the rulers need not pass or avoid any kind of shameful activity, every experimentation with sin, and that there is no sin in this which prevents advancing to a higher heaven. Theodoret, in his *Hereticarum Fabularum Compendium*, ch. 1 [MPG 83.345], describes the heresy of Simon Magus thus: "He commanded those who believed in him to disregard the prophets and to have no fear for the threats of the Law, but as free people they should do whatever they wished to do. For they would obtain salvation through grace and not through good deeds. For this reason those who followed him gave themselves over to every kind of lust and excess and practiced every kind of incantation and magic, certain kinds of free love by skillfully devised allurements, and pursuing different other kinds of magic and incantation and religious mysteries." These were the dogmas or rather the monstrous fictions of these men. What more foul and more abominable wickedness can Satan pour out upon this world?

V. The papists attach great importance to works which are not owed, and in these they establish their ideas of satisfactions and supererogations, by which they are acting in direct contradiction to the express word of Christ in Luke 17:10, "We have done what we ought to have done," but they boast that they can do more than the law of God requires, and these actions can be applied to others for their righteousness and salvation. Thus the fathers at Trent are always mixing together the commandments of God and the mandates of the church. Indeed, they do not even set forth the mandates of the church as referring to those things which the church through the ministry of the Word prescribes and sets forth on the basis of Scripture, but these are matters which the church commands, even though they have no express testimony or command in the Word of God. To strengthen this position they cite the statement of Matt. 23:2, 3, "The scribes and Pharisees sit in Moses' seat. All things which they say to you, therefore, you should observe and do." Hence the argument goes thus: If in the Old Testament not only were the things which Moses commanded to be observed, but also what the scribes and Pharisees, who were the successors of Moses, ordered, therefore now much more in the New Testament obedience is owed to the pope, the successor of Peter and the rest of the leaders! To these works they apply the term "worship," and they pretend that it often happens that those who break these commandments of the church are involved in a greater sin than those who transgress the commandments of God, especially if something is done which displeases the clerical leaders.

VI. Among the Anabaptists there was the peculiar sect of the Libertines who believed almost the same things regarding the freedom from the Law that Simon Magus did, and yet they did these things under the pretext that Scripture says that those who have been born again are led by the Spirit of God. They imagined that whatever proceeded from the inspiration of the Holy Spirit which His impulse suggested to each person was a good work, whether it was outside of or even contrary to the Word. Some also concocted various divine revelations, as in the case of Münzer, of whom those who are interested can read an excellent history in the German language by Johannes Schleidanus. For just as in the Old Testament the Holy Spirit often fell upon the prophets without tangible means, so they boast that the same thing has happened to them. For this reason Luther calls them the "heavenly prophets."

VII. In our era the antinomians are trying to overturn the accepted teaching regarding the third use of the Law which asserts that the Law has been given to the regenerate so that it might be a norm which shows the works by which God wills that we exercise obedience. In order that they might have some pretext for their mischief, they twist certain statements of Luther to say what he did not intend. More on this later.

The Second Point: The Correct Opinion . . .

Holy Scripture sets forth the correct understanding of the matter in both an affirmative and a negative way. We shall limit ourselves to certain statements, and the prudent and careful reader can easily determine where the individual points are to be referred. Deut. 12:32, 8, "Each man shall not do what seems right in his own eyes . . . but whatsoever I command you, this you shall observe to do it; you shall not add to it or take away from it."

Ezek. 20:18–19, "Do not walk in the statutes of your fathers, nor observe their judgments . . . ; I am the Lord your God; walk in My statutes, and keep My judgments and do them." It should be noted that He is not speaking about the manifest iniquities of the fathers but of their lofty ideas as to where they should center the highest worship of God. In the psalms it is also said that we should "walk in the way of the Lord," and this is explained as meaning, Num. 15:39, that we should not follow our own thoughts and covetous eyes, but rather we should remember the precepts of the Lord and that those who do them will be holy unto God. Matt. 15:9, "In vain do they worship Me with commandments which are taught by men." Is. 1:12, "Who has required this of your hand?" The prophet speaks in this passage about the situation in which a person devises something false on the basis of the commandments of God. In the New Testament this man-made religion is condemned in Col. 2:23.

In the statements cited above we should note the emphases of the words. For the Holy Spirit teaches the following: (1) Our judgment does not lie in our senses or our eyes. (2) He also rejects the wisdom or thinking of the heart, meaning that which others call "good intention." (3) Likewise, no one should be led astray by the examples of the fathers. (4) When someone cooks up some man-made idea and attaches it to the commandments of God. (5) In regard to all of these items Christ pronounces, "God is worshiped in vain."

Therefore Paul in Eph. 2:10 says, "God has prepared beforehand the good works in which the godly should walk." For the same reason in Romans 12, in the teaching about good works which are to be done, he says in v. 2, "that you may approve what is the good and acceptable and perfect will of God." Thus in regard to our works we must see to it; (1) that they are good; (2) that they are a worship pleasing to God; (3) that they be perfect, and we do not find any works more perfect or better than those prescribed in the Decalog. Hence in the following chapter, when he is going to show how this good will of God is to be approved, he mentions the Law and recites the words of the Decalog word for word, Rom. 13:9, "You shall not commit adultery, you shall not steal, you shall not kill, you shall not bear false witness, you shall not covet; and if there be any other commandment, it is contained in this word, 'you shall love your neighbor as yourself.' " In Gal. 5:14, he says that love which is the sum of all good works is nothing else than "the fulfilling of the Law." On the basis of this Augustine says, "Have love and do what you wish." This statement must not be treated as a license to do whatever a person wants to, but it teaches that this love must look to the purpose of the Law and the prescriptions of the commandments of God. 1 Tim. 1:5, "The purpose of the commandment is love that issues from a pure heart, a good conscience, and sincere faith."

Therefore God has set forth His commandments as a norm for our good works, and indeed, as He affirms, this norm is absolutely perfect. For He says, "You shall not add anything to My words, nor take anything from them," Deut. 12:32, cf. Prov. 30:5–6; Deut. 5:32–33. Also, in Joshua 1:7, the law of God is commended to the people of God for their guidance, and they are commanded "not to turn from it to the right hand or to the left," that they may understand all things which it directs.

But the teaching prescribing which works have been commanded by God for us to do, properly speaking, is not the Gospel but the Law or the Decalog, which must be understood according to the interpretation of the prophets, of Christ, and of the apostles, as we have at some length set forth this interpretation above in the locus concerning the Law. This divine law, therefore, must be and remain the norm for our good works, so that it may teach us concerning our imperfection, even those of us who have been born again. For in these man-made religions the human mind can easily create for itself the persuasion and conviction of the perfection and even the supererogation of its own works, and this notion will absolutely vanish away when we examine our actions in keeping with the perfection of God's law

For not only must the outward works of the Decalog be performed, but we must also add to them—indeed, they must be preceded by—the inner obedience of the First Commandment, as we have already shown in our exposition of this point.

The Third Point: Refutation of Certain Arguments

Now that we have established the correct understanding of this matter, it will be useful to consider some of the chief arguments used by our adversaries, and also to give some thought to the correct explanation of these arguments. We shall note some of them briefly.

I. What is the purpose of saying that it is the worship of God to give Him honor and obedience? But things which are undertaken with a good intention, even if without the command of God, are done for this purpose; therefore, things done with good intention are the worship of God.

I reply: This definition of divine worship is incorrect. For in order that something may be the worship of God, there is required for it not only the final cause or purpose that it certainly be directed toward the honor of God, but also the material cause is needed, namely, that the action be commanded by God. But in addition to this formal cause is also required that the action be done in faith. Finally, it must be performed by a regenerate person, and for this the efficient cause is required, namely, the Spirit of regeneration and renewal. Therefore, since all of these must come together in the work or deed by which men desire to give to God a worship pleasing to Him, they absolutely fail to achieve this when they only attribute to their good works their own good intention outside of and without the prescription of the Word.

II. There is also a second limitation to this argument that a good intention produces good deeds, namely, that whatever comes from a good intention is a good work in the eyes of God.

I reply: We must establish our definitions correctly, and when we do this, the fallaciousness of this argument will be seen. It is truly a good intention or resolve to want to obey God in keeping with His commandments. He who refuses to be ruled by the commandments can never boast of his truly good intention.

III. Love is the rule and form for good works; therefore, those acts which take place out of love, even though they are not mandated by God, are good works.

I reply: "Love is the fulfilling of the Law," as Paul testifies in Gal. 5:14, and "It is the summary of the commandment," 1 Tim. 1:5. Therefore, things which do not have the testimony of the Word of God and are not included in His law, these cannot be said to be performed out of love. Thus, those who do not use the Sacrament under both kinds, on the grounds and under the pretext of love for the church of Rome, do not have true love, because they do not show respect toward the Word of God.

IV. They argue that there had been accepted in the Law not only those sacrifices offered because of commandment but also those special sacrifices offered voluntarily and as part of a vow. We can see instances of this in Lev. 7:16, "If the sacrifice of his offering be a vow or a voluntary offering . . ."; Likewise, Lev. 22:18, 21; Num. 15:3 and ch. 30 in its entirety, and Deut. 12:11. Therefore, they argue, works can be the worship of God even though they do not have the express command of God.

I reply: In the Law there are certain ordinances dealing with voluntary sacrifices, because they can take place; likewise, there are ordinances as to how they should be performed and where and when they must be done, as the passages cited show, if we look at them carefully. Therefore in the Old Testament such voluntary oblations were not works performed without testimony from the divine Word. In the New Testament voluntary works of this kind were not commanded but forbidden. For in Col. 2:23 man-made religion is condemned specifically.

It is a different thing, however, when in our own day Christians say with David in Ps. 54:6, "I will freely sacrifice to You, and I will confess Your name, for it is good"; or in Ps. 119:108, "Accept, O Lord, the freewill offerings of my mouth"; and with Peter when in 1 Peter 5:2, he joins to the ministry of the Word "to provide for the feeding of the flock," the idea that this has been committed to ministers "not by constraint," but "with a ready and willing mind" in keeping with God's plan. These words are not saying that each person may devise his own works for himself according to his predilections and choose the ways in which he shall serve God, but, as Paul explains to Philemon, in v. 14, ". . . that our goodness might not be by compulsion but with a free and voluntary spirit." This will become clear in the statements which follow.

V. They argue that the regenerate are "led by the Spirit of God," Rom. 8:14, and "they should walk in the Spirit," Gal. 5:16. But the Spirit is a completely free agent; therefore the obedience of the regenerate is not bound to the Word which stands in Scripture.

I reply: Although the regenerate are led by the Spirit, yet the Spirit does not guide them without means, for the Word of God is the "ministration of the Spirit," as Paul teaches in 2 Cor. 3:3. In the Old Testament in Jer. 31:33 God promises, "I will put My law in their inward parts and I will write it in their heart." From this it is evident that the Spirit of the Lord leads the believers to the law of the Lord, and He guides and directs their works according to its prescription.

VI. Many pile up examples, for instance, when Paul ministered at no cost to the Corinthians, 1 Cor. 9:18; the woman with the box of ointment who anointed Christ in Matt. 26:7; David dancing before the ark in 2 Sam. 5:16. They use other examples also. But because these and other points including supererogation have been explained previously, I shall not dwell on them now, but only refer the careful reader to the earlier loci.

However, because of the quibbling of our adversaries, I do want to add this: When we speak of the law of God, we must not be deceived and understand it only as being just those brief lines which we call the Decalog, but rather it is a norm for those good works which have been taught and interpreted in Scripture by the prophets, by Christ, and by the apostles. Therefore at the same time we understand all the points included and covered in this divine norm. From this it will be evident that many works of the saints, which the papists pass off as being merely matters of human choice, were actually commanded by God Himself and thus we must not come to the false understanding which the papists have invented. Thus the example of Paul preaching at no charge was done in order that he might not give any offense to the Gospel.

VII. The papists, in order to assert the commandments of the church and its leaders, bring in arguments above and beyond the law of God: Christ says in Luke 10:16, "He who hears you hears Me, and he who rejects you rejects Me." Therefore the command of Christ is that we should hear the leaders of the church just as we would also hear Him.

I reply: Christ did not give to the ministers of His church a kind of limitless power to put forth, to establish, or to command whatever they want to, with or without the command and testimony of the Word of God in Scripture, nor is the church bound to such obedience. But He gave them a limited power. Hence not only in Matthew 10 and Luke 10 did He give to the apostles and the 70 disciples, whom He had sent forth, certain definite commands, but even afterward He said to the apostles in Matt. 28:20, "Teach them to observe all the things which I have commanded you." And in John 10:21, "As My Father has sent Me, I also send you." In John 14:31 He explains how He Himself was sent, "As My Father has given Me the command, so I do with you." Thus we are not to receive everything which may be set forth to us under the guise of being a command of the church or its ministers. But "the spirits are to be proved, as to whether they are from God, because many false prophets have gone out into the world," 1 John 4:1. Indeed, Paul teaches that both he himself and the rest of the apostles are bound to the prescribed form of the divine Word, so that if an apostle or even an angel from heaven come and teach another Gospel, "let him be anathema," Gal. 1:8.

VIII. In opposition they bring in the notion that Christ had not commanded that the converts from the gentiles were to abstain from blood, from things strangled, and from fornication. Paul even asserts that these were ancient rites from the old law, and yet the apostles in Acts 15:29 impose this regulation upon the gentiles. Therefore the church has authority for creating laws, even in those matters which have not been taught by Christ or even have been abrogated.

I reply: The apostles never on their own authority, without divine mandate, would have made such a decree, for they clearly added, "It seemed good to the Holy Spirit and to us." For even if their decrees had sure foundations in Holy Scripture, it is clear from the speech of James and Peter what the decisions were. Here it is certain that in the article concerning the calling of the gentiles and their free justification the burden of the Law was not to be laid on their consciences, as is proved both from Holy Scripture and from the miracles of the Holy Spirit. However, since fornication was regarded as a matter of indifference among the gentiles, the apostles at first had not prohibited it, but it had been forbidden by God Himself under the threat of the most serious punishment. But insofar as we are talking about ritual laws, they were truly rendered obsolete through the death of Christ, although the observation of them had not totally been prohibited, both since the thinking of the weak Jews considered them meritorious and lest they be offended while they lived among the gentiles who boldly used their Christian liberty. Therefore the apostles issued this decree to direct them so that those who had been converted from the gentiles would not use their liberty for the present time in those rituals which to them were matters of adiaphora so that they might not offend the weaker Jews and so that through love they might invite them to faith in Christ.

IX. In the most ancient and accepted councils there were many decisions observed most religiously by the entire church. Therefore the church has the power of producing laws beyond and outside of the Word of God.

I reply: We do not condemn godly and useful ordinances if they work to edify the church. But we must beware that they do not become snares for consciences or hinder our Christian liberty, as we have shown elsewhere at considerable length.

The Second Question: What Kind of Good Works Should the Regenerate Perform, and How Can They Be Done?

In the locus on good works we must teach not only what works are to be performed, but particularly also what kind of works they must be and how they can be done. For the things which have been commanded by God not only must be done, but they are to be done in the way which God has prescribed. Although we must grant a place to the educative element for the sake of external discipline, yet it is absolutely necessary that we teach the doctrine of good works in such a way that we call attention to the distinction between the ancient philosophers and their idea of virtues, together with the good works of the Pharisees on the one hand and the truly good works of the regenerate on the other hand, not only with regard to the material cause but especially with reference to the efficient and formal causes.

However, the entire doctrine cannot be rightly understood unless we look at the antithesis. Thus, in brief we shall note how Augustine in opposing the Pelagians and later Luther in his controversy with the papists explained this question on the basis of the Scriptural foundation. For from this study certain controversies of our own time will be better understood.

The Pelagians taught that since the guidance of external discipline is to some degree within our own power, therefore the Law alone and by itself can by the powers of our free choice, by commanding, forcing, warning, threatening, and coercing, draw or extort from us truly good works. But Augustine from many passages of Scripture, both Old and New Testament, replied to these ideas regarding the Law, grace, the Holy Spirit, and the letter of Scripture. If the law by itself contends with the unregenerate will, even if it can draw some good works out of it, yet all that happens is some outward hypocritical action without any true spiritual inner motives. But because the Law is spiritual, requiring that the heart and the inner desires conform with the divine law, therefore in order that a particular good work be pleasing to God, it does not suffice that there be some outward hypocritical action, but the inner obedience is required which "delights in the law of God," Rom. 7:22, "the sum of which is love," 1 Tim. 1:5. But man in the corruption of his nature does not possess this kind of conformity in his mind, his will, or his heart, nor can his free choice by its own natural powers, even with the help of the Law, accomplish this. But the gift of the Holy Spirit and His working in our renewed nature accomplishes what Paul describes as "delighting in the law of God."

Therefore we must develop a method for teaching the doctrine of good works, so that we understand that first the Holy Spirit is received and He renews man. Further, the Spirit of regeneration is received not as some kind of attitude developed out of frequent actions or "the works of the law," Gal. 3:2, but "by the hearing of faith." Yet the beginning must be made by the Law to rouse us to repentance. For the Law shows our sins and it works wrath, from which comes contrition. But in order that this contrition may be salutary, faith must be added to it. Thus to the Law must be joined the doctrine of the Gospel or reconciliation for the sake of the Mediator. But since the teaching of reconciliation is connected with the bestowal of the Holy Spirit who renews the mind and arouses new desires in the heart which are in agreement with the law of God, man now begins to love God and "delight in His law." When the Holy Spirit in this way writes the Law into the hearts of believers, then truly good works begin to take place. "For when the tree is made good," Matt. 12:33, "then its fruits are good," which grow from the good root. From this was taken the distinction used by the ancients between the works of the Law and the works of grace, which Augustine also appreciated very much.

In a similar situation and in the same manner Luther was involved in a controversy over this question with the papists, of whom the complaint was always made that above all they wanted to be seen as encouraging good works as well as doing them. Indeed, they even urged the outward show of such actions even if there were no true inner motivation for them. From a comparison of these matters we can correctly understand Luther's expressions and lines of argumentation when he speaks of "the doctors of the letter," the works of the Law extorted from us either by fear or by the coercion of the Law, even when we are unwilling and our will is in direct opposition to the Law. For Luther showed the same point that Augustine tried to show using precisely the same method, namely, that the doctrine of good works is to be set forth and used in the church so that through the work and help of the Spirit, the new and true obedience could be undertaken and accomplished. This meaning has clear testimonies from Scripture: 2 Cor. 9:7; Philemon 14; 2 Cor. 8:12; 1 Cor. 9:17; 1 Peter 5:2; Ps. 110:3. In sum, Scripture requires not "the oldness of the letter but the newness of the Spirit," Rom. 7:6; 2 Cor. 5:17, "a new creature"; Ps. 51:12, "a new heart"; Rom. 12:2, "a renewed mind"; Eph. 4:24, "the new inner man." But these things are produced in the reconciled person by no laws, no powers of the soul, but only by the renewal and work of the Holy Spirit, as Paul so beautifully includes this way of speaking in the clear statement in 1 Tim. 1:5, "The sum of the commandment is love from a pure heart, a good conscience, and true faith."

The Third Question: Whether, Why, and How the Good Works of the Regenerate Please God

For the sake of good order we shall divide the explanation to this question into particular sections.

I. In regard to the works of the unregenerate, even those works which are good in a general way and are not wicked, we must take issue with the opinion of the papists who have produced the idea of congruent merit and the preparation for grace. Yet the position of Scripture is abundantly clear: Matt. 7:18, "An evil tree cannot bring forth good fruit"; Heb. 11:6, "Without faith it is impossible to please God"; Rom. 14:23, "Whatsoever is not of faith is sin"; cf. Ps. 109:7; Is. 1:13–14; 66:3.

We also must distinguish among the different kinds of works. There is the substance itself of the works (so to speak) which are performed by an evil person and thus contaminated and rendered an abomination. The virtues of the gentiles in themselves are good, but wickedness is added because the person by whom these works are performed has not been reconciled with God. Therefore, because of his original sin which clings in the wicked heart of the unregenerate, his actions are contaminated, rendered filthy, and iniquitous. Concerning the substance of such good works, see Augustine, *Contra Julianum* [4.3], where he very expertly argues this point. Younger people should take note of this rule: good works are not to be judged by the nouns but by the adverbs, that is, when someone does a good work but does not do it well, it still is not a good work.

II. Some people attribute too little to the works of the regenerate in the discussion of this question, and this must be avoided by those who are concerned about being honest, and all matters must be referred to the norm of Scripture. But other people have completely torn out of context the points which Luther has made regarding good works under the article of justification and thus created fantasies and inconsistencies, such as, that God is more offended by the good works of the regenerate than by the sins of the unregenerate, and that good works must be done only for the sake of and in the presence of our neighbor but not for the sake of or before God. When Luther deals with this subject that God does not need our good works, cf. his remarks on Ps. 16:2, "You have no need of my good things" (Vulgate), and in his treatment of the article of justification, he says that we must retain the exclusive particles; but outside of the article of justification and in the locus on good works Luther teaches that the good works of the regenerate are pleasing to God. He strongly criticizes the Anabaptists for saying without reference to the article of justification that all their good works were not worth a penny.

Furthermore, it is useful to cling to the testimonies of Scripture which clearly confirm both the fact that good works do please God and what kind of works they are to be, likewise what good works are to be done before God and for the sake of God. Note Eph. 5:8–10; Col. 3:20; Rom. 12:1; Heb. 13:16; Ps. 119:108; 1 Tim. 5:4; 1 John 3:22; 2 Cor. 4:2; Rom. 12:17; 2 Cor. 8:21; Gen. 17:1; 24:40; 48:15; Ps. 17:15; 56:13; 116:9.

Because Scripture says that we must do good works for the sake of God, that is, because of the command and will of God, therefore honor and obedience are to be given to God. Compare Rom. 8:36, "For Your sake we are put to death the whole day"; 1 Peter 2:13, "Be subject for the Lord's sake to every human institution." Again, v. 19, "This is thankworthy, if for the sake of conscience toward God a man endures grief, suffering unjustly."

III. Now that it is established as sure and certain on the basis of Holy Scripture that the good works of the regenerate are pleasing to God, we must also add from Scripture the meaning of this doctrine, namely that this acceptance by God does not take place because of the perfection, the purity, or the worthiness of our works, as if they were the perfect fulfillment of the Law. For Scripture shows that the obedience of the regenerate is only beginning in this weakness of the flesh, and that it is sluggish, imperfect, crippled, impeded, and contaminated, as the testimonies of Scripture, cited and explained in the different loci, demonstrate. Because of this the saints in their efforts to perform good works acknowledge and confess that they are sinners.

Therefore we must correctly distinguish in the regenerate between that which is the activity and fruit of the Spirit from the evil which still remains in his flesh. As Paul says in Rom. 7:21, "When I want to do good, evil is present with me." For these very works of ours, insofar as they are the fruits of the Spirit and insofar as they proceed from a pure heart and a good conscience, are not sins. Nor does a righteous person sin in that he is beginning to be obedient according to the norm of the divine Word. For up to this point, because these things are from God and are done in God, they are good, John 3:21. But evil is present with this good, because it dwells in our flesh, and it is not merely something idle, but it is at war with the law of our mind. In Heb. 12:1 sin is called "a besetting evil," which does not cling only in one part, but is present with us everywhere. Hence Paul himself is overcome in Rom. 7:25, "With my mind I serve the law of God, but with my flesh the law of sin." Although this disease of sin which clings even in our good works cannot be understood even by our reason, yet it is useful to keep in mind those points which have been listed and explained in the loci regarding venial sin, not that we may be turned away from a desire to perform good works, but in order that our self-confidence may be reproved in our efforts to do good works and we may be turned toward true humility of soul.

We read in Scripture such passages as the following: Ps. 119:1, "Blessed are the undefiled"; Matt. 5:8, "Blessed are the pure in heart, for they shall see God"; Phil. 1:10, ". . . that you may be sincere and without offense till the day of Christ"; Rev. 14:4, "These are they who are not defiled;" and v. 5, ". . . without fault before the throne of God." These must not be understood in the sense that the regenerate in the eyes of God are so perfect that no uncleanness is found in them any longer. For this Christ will bestow upon them in the life to come, when "He will present to His Father His glorious church, not having spot or wrinkle or anything of this kind," Eph. 5:27, at the same time as there will be a great crowd of hypocrites who will profess to be the reborn children of God and who think that it is sufficient if they have belonged to the external congregation, but meanwhile have shown no zeal for faith or good works in obedience to God. Therefore we shall hear that sincere obedience is opposed to this kind of hypocrisy and this obedience itself is a gift of the Holy Spirit and received by God for the sake of Christ.

IV. It is commonly said in our churches that the good works of the regenerate are pleasing to God through faith, through and for the sake of Christ, in believers. This statement has clear foundation in Scripture: Heb. 11:4, "By faith Abel gave a better sacrifice to God than Cain"; and in 1 Peter 2:5, the apostle says that we are "a holy priesthood which should offer spiritual sacrifices acceptable to God through Jesus Christ." We must understand this common and true explanation correctly, for the meaning is not that it is necessary to believe that our good works are perfect: and that through our faith they are pleasing to God. Nor does it mean that for the sake of Christ we are pleasing to God even if we fall into sin against conscience even though we profess to believe. But the meaning is this: first, a person is reconciled to God by faith freely, for the sake of Christ the Mediator; second, we are led by the Spirit so that we may walk in good works. Then, we should acknowledge and deplore our many filthy sins by which our good works are both hindered and contaminated. Finally, faith must seek and determine that this obedience has made a beginning, although it is far from the perfection of the Law, and yet in those who have been reconciled it is pleasing to God because of His Son the Mediator who by His most holy obedience has covered our infirmities and brings our worship to the Father. Thus faith always and everywhere has its genuine exercises both in conversion and in the newness of life, and thus it obtains the twofold acceptance both of the person and of his works.

V. Finally, pertinent also to the explanation of this question is how or by what rationale are the good works of the regenerate pleasing to God? That is to say, it is not because through and on account of these works that the person is rendered acceptable to God for the remission of sins and life eternal. For it is absolutely necessary that the person first be reconciled to God and be accepted by faith, for the sake of the Mediator, before he can perform anything good which is pleasing to God, as we have said above and have shown from Scripture, regarding the works of unbelievers. But there is totally absent the idea that a person is made acceptable unto eternal life by his works, because these very works, even those of the regenerate, must obtain from elsewhere the ability to please God, namely that the person has been reconciled with God through faith for the sake of the Mediator. Thus in Hebrews 11, where the efficacy of faith through works is described, yet it is not attributed to works but to faith that the saints obtain the testimony that they are pleasing to God.

After the reconciliation or acceptance of the believers, their works which unquestionably are pleasing to God and accepted by Him, must still not be referred to in the sense of placing confidence in them, in whole or in part, that because of them the person has been accepted by God unto eternal life. For undoubtedly it was pleasing to God that Paul carried out his ministry with a good conscience, and yet Paul says, "In this I am not justified," 1 Cor. 4:4. In Rom. 4:5 he says of Abraham, "To him who works not but believes in Him who justifies the ungodly, his faith is accounted for righteousness," according to the gift of the grace of God. Here the apostle is discussing the acceptance of the person, and he distinguishes between Abraham as the believer and Abraham as the worker, and clearly testifies that Abraham even while working was not pronounced righteous because he worked, but because he believed. Job 9:28, "I am afraid of all my works, knowing that You will not hold me innocent."

Therefore, in the person who is accepted unto eternal life by reason of something from elsewhere, that is, by faith for the sake of Christ, his good works become pleasing to God and accepted by Him, as in "obedient children," 1 Peter 1:14.

THE FOURTH QUESTION:
WHY ARE GOOD WORKS TO BE DONE?

This question poses many other important and useful questions, and it explains best those points which in our age have come into dispute regarding the necessity of good works. Hence, it is fitting that those who are anxious to be godly should give careful attention to this question.

The First Point: The Necessity of Good Works

First, the explanation of this question of the necessity of good works is pertinent without reference to justification and salvation. That is, we are dealing with the question whether good works are necessary. The antinomians declared war on this point even while Luther was still living, but at that time they were put down by his authority. But afterward the controversy flared up again. Even in public writings this question was shamelessly agitated and blown in all directions. Such words as improper, absurd, adulterated, pernicious, dangerous, scandalous, destructive, ungodly, and blasphemous were used.

The simplest method of explaining this point is that, first, the word "necessity" is used with different meanings. It is not our purpose at this point to start a discussion over this word as to what it means and how it is used in other languages or other sciences; but our concern is only how Scripture uses the term "necessity." Scripture uses the word "necessity" in four senses:

I. It is used to describe that which is required for righteousness and salvation. It is used in this sense in Acts 15:5, "Those who were of the sect of the Pharisees argued that it is necessary to observe the Law," cf. Gal. 2:4 and 6:12.

II. The word "necessity" in certain passages of Scripture means something either forced or involuntary, as when a certain outward work is forced from the unwilling or those who will not cooperate, in opposition to the opinion of their mind. 2 Cor. 9:7, ". . . not grudgingly or of necessity"; Philemon 14, ". . . that it not be a matter of necessity to do good to you."

III. Scripture uses the word "necessity" for something which is not an adiaphoron or a matter of free choice, but something which is done because of the command or will of God. Acts 13:46, "It was necessary that the Word be spoken first to the Jews"; cf. 15:28; Rom. 13:5; 1 Cor. 9:16.

IV. Very often the term is used in a general sense to describe the necessity of consequence, which they call immutability. Heb. 7:12, "Since the priesthood was changed, there was a necessity for a change in the law"; 9:16, "For where there is a testament there must of necessity be the death of the testator." Likewise, for that which has sure and serious causes, as to why it should not be omitted, but rather it must be done. See also Phil. 1:24; 2:25; Heb. 7:27; Luke 14:18; Jude 3.

In all of these passages of Scripture we find such words as *anagkaion*, *anagkaioteron*, or *anagkē*. There is another expression, "to have need," which is used commonly in the New Testament, but it has the concept of "being in want for something," for which there is some need. Thus those who are concerned about the truth must be very careful not to be misled by the improper use of these expressions.

There is also some benefit in considering how other writers used the term. Cicero, the father of Latin eloquence, writes in his *De Part. Orat.* [24.83], "But this is necessary and without it we could not be saved or free." *Octa*, "I would not have acted so freely, except by necessity."[1] *De Leg.* [3.18.41], "It is necessary for a senator that he know the state." *De Nat. Deorum* [2.60.151], "We mine iron from caverns in the earth which is necessary in order to plough the fields.

---

[1] Cannot locate this quotation.

But all the things in the past were necessary because they were immutable." *De Universo* [43], "He pointed out the laws which were decreed and necessary." *De Nat. Deorum* [1.20.55], "The fated necessity of things to come"; "The first speech was necessary; this one will be voluntary." In one of his epistles he says [Epistle 4.9.3, *Ad Fam.*], ". . . so that even if they were not that way by nature, they were compelled to be such by necessity." *Pro. Quincto* [51], "To make a person who is unwilling do a certain thing when he is compelled by force and necessity." *Pro Cluent.* [20.57], "I did this under the compulsion of force and necessity" *De Invent.* [2.57.170], "Necessity is that to which no force can be placed in opposition and that which cannot be done in any other way." *In Tog.* [16.60], "The cause in which there is present the necessity of accomplishing something." Epistle 17 [*Ad Fam.*, 1.9.25], "It is the duty of the consul to uphold the law passed by the assembly; it was not necessary for him." *De Offic.* [1.4.11], "Seek all things which are necessary for living." *De Domo Sua* [105], "Why was it necessary for you, O man of the temple, to visit this sacrifice?" *Pro Syl.* [7.22], "But here also what was not really necessary for me, this you wanted to be very elegant." *De Offic.* [1.5.17], "For the other three virtues the necessities were set forth in order to prepare those things by which the activity of life is contained." *Pro. Syl.* [12.35], "The necessity of saying many things about myself is laid upon me, a necessity which has been imposed by him." *In Phil.* [*Phillipicae Orationes* 10.12], "But the necessity was laid upon me of saying a few things about his opinion." I must come to an end in citing the many statements from Cicero about this subject.

Gabriel Biel, "We must note that the idea of necessity has many facets. There is absolute necessity, or to put it in simple language, a necessity of which the opposite includes contradiction. Then there is the necessity of violence or coercion, such as occurs when the necessity of a rotten log is thrown into the fire, and the log is destroyed violently by the fire. Third, there is the necessity of purpose, or a conditioned necessity. Something is necessary for a purpose, without which there can be no purpose."[2]

In the realm of the physical, things are always said to happen of necessity which do not have any natural impediment according to the common course of their nature to prevent their happening, such as the movements of the heavens, the setting of the sun. Things are said to happen by contingency which have some kind of hindrance.

Augustine, in discussing Ps. 54:6 ("I will sacrifice to You voluntarily"), says, "This is not of necessity. For if you praise God for the sake of something else, you are praising Him out of necessity. If it is necessary for you to love God, then

---

[2] *Sententia* 3, dist. 16, *Collectorium circa Quattuor Librorum Sententiarum*, Ruckert ed., Tuebingen, 1973. s.n.

you do not praise God." On Psalm 78 he says, "They should serve God not out of necessity but voluntarily." Seneca says, "Although it may be a most honorable thing to give thanks, yet it ceases to be honorable if it comes out of necessity." Again, "Virtue does nothing out of necessity, but it does all things voluntarily, freely, gladly, honorably."

Suidas, regarding the word *anagkaion*, says [Kuster Ed., 276–77], "They explain 'necessity' in two ways: one, those things which follow the order of nature, as when we say that of necessity fire is red and milk white; and two, that happens of necessity when we say that the power of fortune is a matter of necessity."

Once we have established and explained the meaning of the word "necessity" and the different uses of the term, it is easy and simple to evaluate the conflict. For the chief points of those who oppose us lie in this area of discussion.

Luther's rule is this: "We must use sound language to discuss sound matters, language which uses precise, holy, sober, and spiritual words, words which unquestionably are drawn from Holy Scripture."

But Scripture does not want to use the word "necessity" in the sense of coercion or for that which is necessary for justification and salvation, or with reference to the relationship with the works of the regenerate, Gal. 2:4; 2 Cor. 9:7. Therefore we must simply reject and condemn the use of the word "necessity" in our teaching concerning the good works of the regenerate.

I reply: This is a false and simple misuse of the context. For Scripture in other loci clearly uses the word "necessity" in other meanings with reference to the works of the regenerate. Thus we cannot simply forbid the use of the word "necessity" in the church, or words like it, such as, something is owed, or must, or determined. But the correct conclusion is that words used in more than one sense in Scripture must have a true and clear interpretation. For when it is taught that good works are necessary for justification and salvation, or that they are necessary in the sense that although people have no inner movements of the Spirit and their mind is unwilling and the will is fighting against God, nevertheless their works are good in the sight of God, it is a certainty that Scripture itself condemns this kind of necessity. The Augsburg Confession [Art. VI, Tappert, p. 31] adds a very clear statement as to how we should teach that works are necessary, not for justification or salvation, nor are they necessary because of the necessity of coercion, but out of the necessity of a debt, what we owe God, that is, that the new obedience in the regenerate is not an adiaphoron or a matter of free choice, but we owe it to God because of His will and command.

This opinion is absolutely certain because it pertains to the substance of the matter: I. First, it is certain because God does not give to those who are reconciled immunity from His commandments, or the license that they can freely and safely indulge in their own desires contrary to the mandates of God. For Scripture says, 1 Thess. 4:3–5, "This is the will of God, your sanctification, that you should abstain from fornication and each of you know how to take unto yourself a wife in holiness and honor, not in the lust of concupiscence, as the gentiles who do not know God"; Rom. 6:13, "Do not yield your members as instruments of iniquity unto sin; but yield yourselves unto God as those who are alive from the dead and your members as instruments of righteousness unto God."

II. It is also certain because God does not want His believers to be slothful, but to exercise themselves in godliness. 2 Peter 1:8, "For if these things are yours and abound, they keep you from being slothful and without fruit in the knowledge of our Lord Jesus Christ." Therefore God wills that His people turn away from evil and do good, Ps. 34:15 and 1 Peter 3:17. "They should die unto sin and live unto righteousness," 1 Peter 2:24; "Put off the old man and put on the new," Eph. 4:22.

III. It is also certain because God does not suggest this obedience to the reconciled in the way that the papists devise so that they can regard it as a matter of indifference or free choice. But Scripture affirms that this obedience is the will and command of God. 1 Thess. 4:3, "This is the will of God . . ."; 1 John 4:21, "We have this commandment from God that he who loves God loves also his brother." Scripture pronounces that those who have been reconciled are debtors to such a degree that they are obligated to perform this obedience. See Rom. 8:12; 13:8; Luke 17:10; 1 John 4:11.

It cannot be denied that this is the ongoing teaching of Scripture because it pertains to the substance of the matter. But if the question pertains to evaluating carefully the different ways of speaking, then it is manifest, when we want to state the teaching of Scripture in one brief statement, properly and meaningfully, that we must separate ourselves from the antinomians and libertines, which can easily be done when we say that in the regenerate good works are not a matter of free choice or adiaphora but necessary and something we owe. Scripture itself uses the word "necessity" in this sense with reference to the works of the regenerate, cf. Rom. 13:5; 1 Cor. 9:16; Acts 15:28. Yet it remains fixed what we said under the second question regarding the willing and voluntary obedience of the regenerate, and also that at the same time we must teach and explain our meaning when we say that good works are necessary. In the Augsburg Confession and particularly in the Apology we find these very well-known expressions: good works are necessary; it is necessary to do good works; good works of necessity must follow reconciliation; of necessity we must do the good works commanded by God. It is not true, as some dream, that Luther disapproved and condemned this form of speaking. For in the disputation against Eck he used this method of speaking over and over again.

In this statement of the case we must preserve the "form of sound words" of which Paul speaks in 2 Tim. 1:13. Nor is this an expression which only recently came into use, but from the very beginning of the purifying of the teaching it has been used in our churches and in those writings which prescribe the form of doctrine for us and are contained in the public symbols of our churches. In the Augsburg Confession and its Apology we find these very common statements. For example, in the Confession, Art. 20.27 [Tappert, p.45], "Our teachers also teach that it is necessary to do good works, not that we should trust to merit grace by them but because it is the will of God." In the Apology [4.189, Tappert, p. 113] it says in regard to the arguments of our adversaries, "Good works must be done because of the command of God, likewise to exercise faith and for the sake of confession and to give thanks; for these reasons it is necessary that good works be performed." Again [4.214, Tappert, p. 136] "We believe and teach that good works of necessity must be done. For the beginning of fulfillment of the law must follow faith." Again [4.222, Tappert, p. 137], "Love is necessary, just as it is necessary not to steal." Under the title *De Dilectione*, "We confess that it is necessary that there be begun in us the fulfillment of the Law, and that this grow increasingly."[3]

They raise the following points in objection: (1) Necessity conflicts with something voluntary. (2) It also conflicts with Christian liberty. (3) Luther rejected this concept of debt. Because response to these arguments shall be made later in this locus, for the sake of brevity we shall pass over the matter now.

However, the statement that is said of Luther that he disapproved and condemned this form of speaking is a figment of their imagination, as we must demonstrate in this locus. In his *Disputat. Contra Eccium* he says, "Eck knows that I am not suggesting that it is not necessary to do good works."[4] Again, concerning Galatians 5, "If we teach works alone, faith is lost; if we teach faith alone, immediately carnal men go to sleep in the thought that works are not necessary."[5] In his little booklet *On Monastic Vows*, Luther says, "The works of the divine law which are commanded in the Decalog do not justify, nor are they necessary for salvation and righteousness, since Paul says, 'By the works of the Law shall no flesh be justified.' Yet they are necessary and they cannot

---

[3] Apol. 4.136, Tappert, p. 126, under the title "Love and the Keeping of the Law," cf. footnote 9 in Tappert, p. 124.

[4] *Weimar Ausgabe*, 2.649. Not in Amer. Ed.

[5] *Lectures on Galatians*, re Gal. 5:13, Amer. Ed., 27.48.

be omitted, even when faith is present which alone justifies, since they are the fruit of justifying faith."[6] Ibid., "Those things which have been commanded are necessary, as the fruit of righteousness, even if they are not necessary for righteousness itself, which comes from faith alone. Nor does the Gospel give us the freedom to omit the commands of God." In *Disputat. de Operibus Legis et Gratiae* [*Weimar Ausgabe*, 39(1).202] he says, "All works are necessary, both of the law as well as of grace." Again, "The righteousness of works is necessary, but not out of the necessity of the law or of coercion, but out of the necessity of consequence or immutability."[7]

The Second Point: The Impelling and Final Causes

The second chapter of this fourth question contains the teaching concerning both the impelling and the final causes, or reasons, on account of which good works are necessary and must be performed. For those people are in error who say that it is perfectly proper for the regenerate to ignore all reasons, whether impelling or final, for good works, and to give them no thought. For God in His Word has revealed and often repeated them. Thus this aspect of the teaching pertains to the statement of Paul in 2 Tim. 3:16, "All Scripture is useful, that the man of God may be perfect, equipped for every good work."

Therefore, that we must draw these reasons or causes from the Word of God is a matter beyond controversy. But because not even all sound teachers have dealt with these reasons for which we must do good works in the same way on the basis of the Word of God, the result has often been controversy, but to support this aspect of the doctrine and for the sake of harmony, these two points can be very usefully observed: First, do not let the enumerating of these causes deal with justification or give occasion to Pharisaic pride and presumptuousness. Second, in order to show concern we must retain and observe, also in this aspect of the doctrine, the commonly received, sound, and true formulas for speaking, of which we shall at this point note a few briefly.

The Augsburg Confession, Arts. 6 and 20 say [Tappert, pp. 31–32, 45], "Our people teach that good works must be done because they have been commanded by God, not that we should trust in them to merit grace but because of God's will." The Apology explains the same point [4.189, Tappert, p. 133]: "Works must be done because of God's command." Again [ibid.], ". . . in order to exercise our faith." Again [ibid.], ". . . for the sake of confession and the giving of thanks. For these reasons good works of necessity must be performed."

---

[6]   *The Judgment of Martin Luther on Monastic Vows*, Amer. Ed., 44.298.

[7]   Inadequate reference. Cannot locate.

Urbanus Rhegius in his little book on the forms of careful speaking lists these reasons:

I. We owe obedience to what has been commanded by God. Again, good works are a kind of thanksgiving to God for His blessings.

II. The heavenly Father is glorified in us through this obedience.

III. Our faith is exercised through this and moved, so that it increases and grows.

IV. Good works are a testimony to our neighbor concerning our faith and by these works our neighbor is strengthened and aided in his own needs.

V. Through good works my "calling is made certain" for me, 2 Peter 1:10, that is, certain that my faith is not false.

VI. Even if good works do not merit salvation, yet out of the free promise of God they do merit physical and spiritual rewards both in this life and hereafter, 1 Cor. 4:5.[8]

The following reasons have been gathered from Luther's writings:

I. From his *Postilla Maiori. de Festis*, fol. 33, "God does not need our works, but yet He wills that you present them to Him as your service, because this is His good will and this He requires."[9]

II. In the same place he also says, "Works are to be done, not that we through them merit heaven, but that we may be pleasing to God the Father who gave His Son for us."[10]

III. In *Parte Aestivali.*, fol. 68, "The reason why good works must be done is, properly speaking, our own necessity, lest we live according to the flesh and lose our spiritual and eternal blessings."[11]

IV. "Lest the name of God be blasphemed, but good works also serve the advance of the Gospel."[12]

V. Folios 164 and 247, "Good works are a testimony to faith and righteousness, not only before men but also to our own selves. For because many devise for themselves a false faith, Scripture shows the outward difference between true and false faith, so that false faith can be rebuked and removed. Therefore, the righteousness of faith becomes known to others not only by the good works which follow it, but also it makes it certain for people themselves that their

---

[8]   This work was published in 1535, cf. Hauck, *Real Encyc.*, 16.740, Leipzig, 1905.

[9]   It has been impossible to locate many of the items which Chemnitz cites from the Wittenberg Ed. of *Luther's Works*, cf. Tome 2, Locus 6, note 32.

[10] Ibid.

[11] Ibid.

[12] Ibid.

faith is a true faith. For if works do not follow, it is certain that the faith is not true."[13]

VI. He also states this in regard to Genesis 17, "Works do not make a person righteous, but a righteous person does righteous works, and yet the works demonstrate that faith is living in those people, and through it, in a sense, faith grows and shines. For the works are testimonies that grace is working in us and that we are the called and elect. On the other hand, a sluggish faith which is not kept busy, quickly dies and is quenched."[14]

VII. Luther in a great many places argues for convergence of cause and effect. That is, the nature or property of faith, regeneration and renewal is such that of necessity it produces good works.

VIII. Frequently we see in the writings of Luther that good works are to be performed in such a way that we serve our neighbor and invite him to godliness.

In the *Loci* [of Melanchthon] the causes are listed as follows:

1. Good works are necessary because we owe this obedience and it is commanded.

2. Lest faith and the Holy Spirit be driven out.

3. The concern to avoid punishment.

4. The worthiness of our position as those who have been called, because God accepts the obedience of believers because of His Son and He calls this obedience a sacrifice, that is, God judges that these works honor Him and He adorns them with His promises concerning physical and spiritual rewards, both in this life and in the life to come.

5. Good works are necessary because of the close connection of cause and effect, as it is said, "Those who are led by the Spirit of God are the sons of God," Rom. 8:14.

Those who are concerned about being godly have gathered for themselves many statements of this kind, in order that they can have this matter under their constant purview. This is the accepted form "of sound words" in this aspect of the doctrine, and in this we may safely put our trust. Yet in passing, we must note that the question has also arisen as to whether it is correct to say that faith is retained through good works, because under the second cause, the impelling cause, it is said that good works must be performed lest faith be cut off. Therefore we must also realize that our faith is retained in us by Christ through the Word and the sacraments, as it says in 1 Peter 1:5, "You are kept

---

[13] Ibid.

[14] *Lectures on Genesis*, re Gen. 17, Amer. Ed., 3.78ff. Not exact.

by the power of God through faith unto salvation." Therefore faith is conceived and also retained through these same means, namely the Word and the sacraments. Nor are these means only treated as the custodians or guardians for good works, but through them a person lays hold on Christ, rather, he is "laid hold" on and "known" by God, 1 Cor. 13:12, cf. Phil. 3:12. Therefore it is in no way the "form of sound words" if a person says that faith is retained through good works, even though faith is driven out and cut off by evil works. Therefore it is much better to say that good works are necessary in order that faith might not be cut off and the Holy Spirit driven out, because this statement is far less open to sophistic arguments. Yet if a person believes that his faith is exercised, cultivated, increased, and witnessed by good works, I do not have any quarrel with him. For Luther often spoke this way, too, that faith shines through good works. This is Peter's statement: "Be diligent to make your calling sure through good works," 2 Peter 1:10.

Moreover, once we have accepted this "form of sound words" which is taught in our churches regarding the impelling and final causes of good works, then we must fortify these many different statements by sure and clear passages of Scripture. Certain statements are said regarding the impelling causes and others regarding the final causes, and these must be distinguished from each other. They can be divided into different parts. The distribution made by Luther seems to me to be very helpful because of its brevity and ease of memorization. He broke down the whole doctrine into three chief parts which can later on be further subdivided.

I. Certain passages of Scripture speak of those impelling and final causes of good works which have reference to God Himself, such as, that it is the will and command of God that we do good works, that God may be glorified by them, that we may be imitators of God, that we may walk worthily of God; or out of consideration for the blessing from the Father, the Son, and the Holy Spirit.

II. Certain passages of Scripture speak of causes which relate to the regenerate themselves. For because they have been born again, therefore they must be new creatures. They are the sons of light, therefore they must not walk in darkness. Again, that they may have the outward testimony that their faith is genuine and has received justification, and that they can distinguish dead faith from the newness of life. Again, that faith be not cut off or the Holy Spirit, grace, and salvation lost. Here are pertinent also the statements which deal with the punishments for sins and the rewards for obedience.

III. Certain passages of Scripture speak of the causes which pertain to our neighbor, such as, the service to our neighbor. Or, that by our example some may be drawn to godliness, and that we give no offense, but that we close the mouths of our adversaries by our well-doing.

Because we will speak at length on all of these matters in treating that part of the locus which has been added to this teaching, under the eighth question, therefore we shall not repeat for the second time points which may tire the reader, but will omit a fuller treatment now. We will give the reader a fuller explanation of this question later.

The Third Point: Whether Good Works Are Necessary for Salvation

Third, to the question regarding the necessity of good works pertains the explanation of the discussion over the proposition: Are good works necessary for salvation for those who have been justified, so that a person will never be justified without good works?

In all of these debates it has become customary to say that the same thing happens in every controversy. Some people contend that the controversy is about words. But others turn too far away from the propositions under discussion and take positions beyond the boundaries of the simple truth, and rush off in another direction, so that, in this case, they contend that good works simply are not necessary in those who have been justified, and understand the term "necessity" in this sense.

Therefore in this discussion a person who desires to keep his steps on the royal road of the truth must walk between the extremes of Pharisaism on the one hand and Epicureanism on the other. He must keep these two propositions before him:

First, as always, when these propositions regarding the necessity of good works for salvation are disproved, then at the same time this warning must be added, so that no antithesis is expressly established or tacitly approved, as if in the case of those who have been justified good works simply are not necessary even if after their conversion people obey their evil lusts, and affirm, possess, and retain their intention to sin, and permit acts contrary to conscience and yet assert that they nevertheless are righteous and saved and can remain so. Against ideas of this kind it is necessary in the church that the voice of true teaching be proclaimed loudly, as it is taught in Rom. 8:12–13, "We are not debtors to the flesh to live after the flesh. For if you live according to the flesh, you shall die"; cf. 1 Cor. 6:9–10; Gal. 5:19–20; Eph. 5:5; Col. 3:5–6. All these testimonies bear witness that men do not retain but cut off faith and the Holy Spirit, grace, righteousness, and eternal life, and bring down upon themselves the wrath of God and eternal punishments if they are not converted to God.

Second, in this discussion we must carefully build our defenses so that the doctrine of good works and its causes, whether impelling or final, in no way impinge on the article of justification, either as merit or as the application, cause, part, form, or means of application or preservation, but rather that works are treated in such a way that the teachings concerning the free justification by faith for the sake of Christ, without our works, will stand and be preserved in their saving and complete purity.

When we have fortified ourselves on both sides of this matter, then the determination of the controversy will not be difficult or obscure, as long as we retain these two propositions: (1) "the form of sound words" and (2) the form and sense of sound and pure teaching.

Therefore, because these propositions with the form of sound words, which has also been developed both in Scripture and in the body of teaching of our churches, are in direct conflict with many points, as can be demonstrated by perfectly clear evidence, we shall therefore note a few items.

I. Paul in Rom. 4:3–7 joins together righteousness and salvation and clearly pronounces on the basis of the statements of Moses and David, that is, the Law and all the prophets, "Blessed is the man to whom the Lord imputes righteousness without works." Thus the antithesis is also set up, and it will become manifest, that these statements affirm points which are directly contradictory. That is, for him who is justified by faith without works unto salvation, good works are necessary. Indeed, it is impossible that the blessing of God comes to any man without good works. This argument is very strong and very clear.

II. The position of the false apostles among the Galatians, against which Paul is contending so strongly, Luther has epitomized in ch. 1 of his *Commentary on Galatians* this way: In addition to faith in Christ the works of the divine law are also necessary for salvation. Luke, in Acts 15:1, quotes the false apostles as saying, "Unless you are circumcised and observe the Law, you cannot be saved." These words certainly state the proposition clearly, namely that it is impossible for a person to be saved without observing the Law, that is, without good works. For in Acts 15 the dispute concerned the whole Law and not only good works, as we have shown under that locus.

III. The Augsburg Confession, in Art. 6 [Tappert, p. 32], cites and approves the statement of Ambrose: "It has been established by God that he who believes in Christ is saved without works, by faith alone, freely receiving the remission of his sins." Therefore it is in conflict with "the form of sound words" as well as the Confession and the purer ancient church to teach that it is impossible for a person to be saved without good works.

IV. Luther, in a great many places in dealing with the question as to what is necessary for righteousness unto salvation and eternal life, rejected and condemned these propositions. See his disputation of 1536, item 22, and his writing on Galatians 1, as well as his sermon on the Gospel concerning Mary, who "chose the better part," because "one thing is necessary."

V. Now for over 40 years the papists have wielded the sword regarding the exclusive particle, "Justified by faith alone," and have always opposed it by saying: "Good works are necessary for salvation." Thus, they say, we are not justified and saved by faith alone, or, we are not justified by faith alone because good works are also necessary for salvation.

VI. In the sect of the Anabaptists there was also this article that good works are necessary for salvation, even though they did teach that trust was not to be placed in the merit of good works. This position of the Anabaptists was condemned and attacked by our people at great length. This refutation is found in the writing of Menius against the Anabaptists, to which has been added as a preface Luther's statements in the Wittenberg edition, 2.326.[15] The same thing was done with a statement from Luther regarding Genesis 22. The Münsterites also rejected this statement: "Faith makes us holy without good works" (*der Glaube seelig mache ohn gute Werck*) and substituted for it, "Faith makes us holy but not without good works" (*der Glaube selig mache/aber nicht ohn gute Werck*). Urbanus Rhegius refuted them. This refutation is found in *Luther's Works*, 2.443.[16]

VII. In the Formula for Intereligion (which later came to be called the Interim), when the papists saw more clearly that the doctrine of free justification in our church was established and corroborated by the Word of God and they could not overturn this teaching by a single thrust or tear it from the minds of the faithful, then they insidiously made propaganda for this statement: Good works are necessary for salvation. For they noticed that by the use of this expression, which had been allowed and received, they could easily bring about the ruination of the doctrine of free reconciliation. Although this statement had been prepared by the tricks of the popish Interim, yet it made some progress in our churches during this controversy and thus the God-fearing reader can easily determine what he must believe in regard to this matter. Many people were pretending that they were supporting this expression so that Epicureanism might not be introduced into the church while at the same time they believed that they were holding to the correct faith in Christ. But insidiously another thing was creeping in, namely that little by little there was too much omission of the word *sola* when they said that "we are justified by faith" and too little caution about merit.

The first point we wish to make shows clearly that these statements

---

[15] Cf. Luther, "Infiltrating and Clandestine Preachers," Amer. Ed., 40.383, note 2, where reference is made to Justus Menius, whose work on the Anabaptists had been approved by Luther, who had written a preface to it; cf. W. A., *Geheimnis aus heiliger Schrift widerlegt durch Justum Menium* 1529.

[16] Cf. W.A. 38.338–40, entitled *Widerlegung der Münsterischen neuen Valentinianes & Donatisten Bekenntnis ... durch Urb. Rheg.*, 1535. Luther also wrote the foreword to this work.

regarding the necessity of good works for salvation do not preserve the "form of sound words" but conflict with it almost diametrically.

Second, if these propositions are compared with the form of sound teaching regarding the substance of the matter, it will be clear that they are in conflict with the very fundamentals of the faith. For it is beyond controversy that the distinction of Law and Gospel is the basic foundation of the correct article of justification. But not only the Gospel but also the Law is preached with reference to righteousness, salvation, and eternal life. See Deut. 30:16; Matt. 19:17; Luke 10:28; Rom. 2:13; 7:10; 10:5.

But Paul shows this distinction: The Law, to be sure, does set forth righteousness, it promises salvation and eternal life, but only on the condition that "he who does these things shall live in them," Rom. 10:5; Gal. 3:12. The testimonies from Scripture which we have cited, Matt. 19:17; Luke 10:28; Rom. 2:13, all show this same thing, that is, the Law requires our works for righteousness and salvation. But because this is impossible for the Law on account of its weakness through the flesh, Rom. 8:3, the Law has become the ministration of sin, death, and condemnation, 2 Cor. 3:7.

Therefore the Gospel gives us righteousness, salvation, and eternal life without our works, freely, for the sake of the obedience of the Son, the Mediator, which is to be received by faith alone. Rom. 4:5, "But to him who does not work but believes in Him who justifies the ungodly, to him his faith is imputed unto righteousness, according to the giving of the grace of God," cf. Rom. 10:6, 11; Gal. 3:22. Paul immediately establishes the diametric distinction between the Law and the Gospel in Rom. 11:6, where he is speaking about salvation, and he affirms, "If it is by grace, then it is no more by works, for otherwise grace would not be grace. But if it be by works, then it is no more by grace. Otherwise work is no more work." Therefore the teaching that our good works are necessary for salvation is a manifest confusion and distortion of the distinction between Law and Gospel and clearly in conflict with Paul's doctrine.

But the promoters of these statements try to make this exception by saying that salvation must be distinguished from justification, so that our good works are necessary not for justification but for salvation to those who have already been justified by faith. But if this argument is examined on the basis of the analogy of faith, the matter will become clear. For if it is established that we are actually justified without works but not saved without good works, then it will of necessity follow either that Christ by His obedience did not promise to us righteousness before God or salvation, or that the promise of righteousness is received without works by faith, but the promise of salvation and eternal life is not received without works but by faith and works at the same time. Then it must be said that the exclusive terms do not pertain to salvation but only to justification. But this is a false statement. For Scripture does not permit our works as meriting or causing either our salvation or our righteousness, and attributes this to Christ alone; likewise, in respect to the means by which the promise is received and laid hold on, both of salvation as well as righteousness, Scripture states that the means is faith, not our works. For Scripture itself adds the exclusive particles not only to justification but also to salvation, whether in speaking of merit or the application of God's promise. Thus according to Scripture it is one and the same thing by which we are justified and by which we are saved, whether we are speaking of cause and merit or of application. Eph. 2:8, "By grace are you saved, through faith, not of works. . . ."; 2 Tim. 1:9, "He saved us . . . not according to our works but according to His own purpose and grace"; Titus 3:5, 7, "Not by works of righteousness which we have done, but according to His own mercy He has saved us . . . that we might be justified by His grace and made heirs of eternal life." Thus in Rom. 4:7 they are called "blessed," whose "iniquities are forgiven and whose sins are covered." Also Rom. 11:5, "The remnant according to the election of grace shall be saved."

This controversy is not concerned with mere inconsistencies in Paul's terminology, but he gives us some very important reasons in Rom. 4:16, "Therefore it is without works, according to grace, by faith, in order that the promise might be certain." But what is the promise? Does it pertain only to justification? He speaks with certainty regarding the promise of the inheritance, which he asserts would be made uncertain for us if it were taught that it depends in part on our works.

Nor is it true, as some imagine, that although our good works are not necessary for the earning or obtaining of salvation, yet they are necessary for the retaining or keeping of it. For the formula of the apostolic doctrine is that as the beginning is, so is the preservation, that is, the beginning, the intermediate, and the end of our justification and salvation must be attributed to the grace of God, without our works, for the sake of Christ the Mediator. This grace, just as it is received by faith also is retained by faith and preserved by it, Rom. 5:2. Through faith we first have access to grace; second, by faith we stand in grace; third, by faith we rejoice in hope of the glory of the Son of God. According to Paul, therefore, we do not receive salvation in one way, and once it has been received, retain and keep it in another way; but grace and faith are the beginning, the middle, and the end. 1 Peter 1:5, "We are kept by the power of God through faith unto salvation, ready to be revealed in the last time," that is, you hear that the preservation of your salvation until it is revealed in the last day is attributed to the power of God through faith. Again, 1 Peter 1:9, "Receiving the end of your faith, the salvation of your souls." And in Gal. 2:20, Paul, who had been justified many years before, if he should be asked how his righteousness was preserved, replies, "That life which I now live in the flesh, I live by faith in the Son of God who loved me and gave Himself for me."

It is correct at this point to apply the statement of Paul in Rom. 4:14, that if the preservation of our salvation depends on our fulfillment of the Law, that is, on our works, then "faith is made void and the promise abolished." Therefore, in order that the promise of salvation might be firmly established, not only must it be received but it must also be preserved by faith. Therefore salvation is given without works by faith according to grace.

These fundamental points demonstrate that these propositions concerning the necessity of works unto salvation are not in keeping with the formulations, statements, or teachings of the apostles, but they must be avoided as a corruption of the purity of the article of justification and not given our approval. The substance of the matter shows that this fear is not imaginary. For in the heat of the controversy these corruptions have been spread by those who have received patronage or support for their propositions as we know from their public writings, namely that justification consists of two parts, the remission of sins and the renewal with its fruits; or that the application of righteousness and salvation takes place by faith plus the work of confession.

Finally, in regard to the arguments on the other side, which they customarily use regarding the statement of these supporters, we must note a few points, for this kind of instruction will prove helpful. For the sake of brevity we shall cite only the main points from which we can reconstruct their arguments.

I. The most common slander is to say that those who reject these propositions, in so doing believe that the new obedience is simply not necessary for those who have been justified but is entirely a matter of free choice. Or, they say that because it is necessary, therefore it is necessary for salvation. But the answer to this is obvious from those things which we have said in connection with the first and second section of this fourth question. Because they are hindering by sowing and defending errors under the pretext of refuting the antinomians, we must clarify this matter.

II. They say that because it is certain that the two benefits of Christ, reconciliation and renewal, are so closely connected, therefore no one is saved without renewal. Because justifying faith is not without works, but faith which is without works is dead, therefore many people are trying to defend these propositions. But Luther replies in commenting on Genesis 15, "The question is not what is connected with what, but what belongs to each."[17] Again, "There is one question, namely, what are external signs which are taken hold of to determine

---

[17] *Lectures on Genesis*, re Gen. 15:6, Amer. Ed., 3.24.

whether faith is true and living; but the other question is, from whence does faith derive the power to justify and save?"[18]

III. They say that in the great carnal security of this world, our minds seem to be more readily stimulated to zeal for good works if they are taught as necessary for salvation. The answer to this is that there is no better or more compelling reason for exhorting the regenerate to be zealous for good works than that which is set forth in Scripture for us, namely by showing the reasons on account of which the Holy Spirit teaches that good works and the new obedience are necessary. But the very point which we are trying to make is called a figment of the imagination. The fathers often used long exhortations in praise of good works. But as a result of this the purity of the article of justification was lost. If a person says that the world is indifferent to these exhortations, this problem should be commended to God, but we should not for this reason depart from the form of sound speaking. For "He who is filthy, let him be filthy still," Rev. 22:11.

IV. The chief objection which they raise, which I think has some appearance of truth to it, is this: Those who have been justified by faith, if they later permit actions contrary to conscience, do not retain their salvation, but lose it; and if they persevere in this sin, they will not be saved, Rom. 8:12; 1 Cor. 6:9; Gal. 5:10; Eph. 5:5; Col. 3:5. When David took the wife of another man, he lost the Holy Spirit. Thus, they say, good works are necessary for salvation. To this argument there is no answer in the position of the antinomian Anabaptists who say that those who have been justified cannot lose salvation in this life even if they reject repentance, permit crimes against conscience, and drive out the Holy Spirit. This point has been often repeated and inculcated with the sternest language of God. But we do need to explain why David, when he took the other man's wife, did not possess righteousness and salvation, or therefore must it happen that faith which lays hold on and possesses Christ does not suffice for righteousness and salvation because works are also necessary for salvation? But Paul loudly denies this, as we have said. Thus, as Luther and the Apology explain, it is true that David did not have or keep his faith and the Holy Spirit, but lost them and drove them out. For faith does not remain in those who refuse to repent. But we are justified and saved by faith. Therefore, when faith is lost, then righteousness and salvation are not retained but are lost and driven away.

Thus Paul in 1 Tim. 5:8 says, "He who is not concerned about his own household has denied the faith and is worse than an infidel." In Col. 3:5 are listed the sins against conscience, and Paul adds, "Because of these things the wrath of God comes upon the children of disobedience," v. 6; 2 Peter 1:9, "He who lacks these things is blind . . . and has forgotten that he was purged of his old sins."

---

[18] Ibid., p. 22.

Again, 1 Tim. 1:19, ". . . those who have rejected a good conscience have made shipwreck concerning their faith."

Thus it says in the Apology [20.13, Tappert, p. 228] regarding the statement in 2 Peter 1:10: "Peter is speaking of the works which follow the remission of sins. He teaches why they are to be performed, namely 'that your calling may be certain,' that is, so that they do not fall away from their calling by sinning again. Do good works, he says, in order that you may continue in your calling and not lose the gifts of your calling, which he previously had established not because of the works which follow but which now are retained by faith and faith does not remain in those who lose the Holy Spirit, who refuse to repent." So far the Apology. Luther himself, says in the Smalcald Articles [3.43–44, Tappert, p. 310], "It is necessary to know and to teach when the saints fall into manifest sins, as David did, that then faith has been lost and the Holy Spirit has been lost. For the Holy Spirit does not permit sin to have dominion to the point of taking complete control, but He fights back. But when sin does what it wishes, then the Holy Spirit and faith are not present."

V. They raise in objection Rom. 10:10, "With the heart man believes unto righteousness, but with the mouth confession is made unto salvation." The answer to this argument is not difficult, if we keep the basic points in mind. For we are asking the question whether Paul in this passage is distinguishing between righteousness and salvation in such a way that he is attributing to our works the righteousness of faith in a way contrary to what he had said in Rom. 4:6. But the context most clearly testifies that Paul in this passage—when he is discussing righteousness and life or salvation, the law of works and the Word of faith—is making the same point and believing the same thing, that is, that faith and works insofar as they relate to the article of justification, are diametrically opposed to one another and are two separate things. Paul explains himself clearly, that his statement relates to the Word of faith and to the righteousness which is from faith. He is amplifying his statement, "If you believe in your heart, you will be saved," by putting before it the idea of confession and then he adds faith with it, in order to show that he is talking about the Word of faith.

But, you say, what is the meaning of Paul's statement "Confession is made unto salvation"? I reply: We must retain that most uncomplicated explanation which is given in the Apology [4.384, Tappert, p. 166] with the words, "Paul speaks in this way in order to show what kind of faith obtains eternal life, namely, a firm and efficacious faith. But it is not a firm faith which does not show itself in confession." Thus Paul's meaning is the same as Christ's when He says in Matt. 10:32, "He who confesses Me before men, him will I also confess before My Father who is in heaven"; and again in v. 22, "He who endures to the end shall be saved."

So much for the substance of the matter. Yet, if a person wants to look more closely, he would be correct if he studied the lies of the adversaries on this subject. The word "I confess" is used with reference to teaching by a minister, cf. 1 John 4:2, "Every spirit which confesses that Jesus Christ has come in the flesh is of God," and in 2 John 7, "Many deceivers have gone out into the world who do not confess that Jesus Christ has come in the flesh"; Heb. 3:1, "Consider Jesus Christ, the apostle and high priest of our confession," that is, of the doctrine which we profess. Heb. 4:14 and 10:23, "Let us hold fast to our confession without wavering," that is, "without neglecting" your profession. For faith is not some confused persuasion, but it has a sure and certain object which lays hold without question on that Word of God which is proclaimed, as Paul adds, "How shall they believe unless they are preached to?" Rom. 10:14, that is, "the Word of faith which we preach," v. 9. Thus Paul in this passage is not speaking this way with regard to confession as if it were a work, as if he is putting faith and works into opposition to one another, but he is speaking of the preaching of the Word which has faith joined to it. If we compare Paul's statement with the dictum of Moses in Deuteronomy 30, the matter will be even clearer. In the Law there were three points which Moses required: (1) to teach it; (2) to hear and understand it; and (3) to obey it. The first two points are easy, but the third is impossible for all men. Therefore Christ came, who is the completion or end of the Law, and He took upon Himself to obey it. This fact is proclaimed and preached to us through "the Word of faith," 1 Cor. 10:8, and this work is "the power of God unto salvation to everyone who believes," Rom. 1:16. For faith, when it lays hold on this "power" and gives this "confession" or profession without wavering, leads us to salvation.

Thus the expression "unto salvation" does not always indicate the cause on account of which a person receives this salvation, but it may refer to the ordinance of God whereby He accomplishes our salvation in certain steps and it may refer to how we proceed from one step to the next. Thus in Rom. 6:21 it says, "The end of sins is death, but the end of our holiness is life eternal." It is not that our sanctification or holiness is the cause of our eternal life, for immediately afterward in v. 23 he adds, "Eternal life is the gift of God." But it is a fact that these steps in our conversion do finally lead to life eternal. Thus in Acts 13:47 Paul says of himself and the other apostles that they "have been sent . . . for the salvation of the gentiles unto the ends of the earth." Thus in Rom. 1:16 the Gospel is called "the power of God unto salvation," that is by the ordinance of God, cf. 2 Cor. 7:10; Phil. 1:19; 2 Tim. 3:15; Heb. 9:28; 1 Peter 1:5. None of these statements point to the cause for which we gain salvation, but to the ordinance of God by which He brings us to salvation.

Further, because in the church at this time this proposition has been suggested and spread abroad that the good works of the regenerate are harmful and dangerous to salvation, therefore the question is this: What must we believe on this proposition? It is easy to judge this matter if we keep before us the correct and necessary distinction. For when we add to good works the idea of merit and trust in them for our righteousness and salvation before God, that is, when they are injected into the article of justification and we are taught that it is by good works that we merit heaven, then Luther is correct when he says that they not only have no value and profit nothing toward righteousness and salvation, but they are actually harmful and dangerous. This "form of sound words" is taught by the Holy Spirit in Scripture. This is stated and repeated three times in one passage in Phil. 3:7–8, "But what things were gain to me, those I counted as loss for the sake of Christ. Indeed, I count all things as loss for the excellency of the knowledge of Jesus Christ my Lord, for whom I have suffered the loss of all things and count them but dung, that I may gain Christ."

But the Scripture which we must carefully study does not use propositions such as this in simple and unaccompanied form, but adds the clear and plain explanation as to when and how good works are a detriment or a loss. In Phil. 3:4 it says, "Though I had confidence in the flesh, I consider this also a loss." Luther explains clearly when and how works are dangerous. He says that he is speaking only of the addition, which he calls a leviathan, that is to say, when it is added and taught that they are necessary for righteousness and salvation. The Apology says the same thing, "We do not condemn good works in themselves, but the idea of merit and trusting in them for righteousness and salvation—putting this power in works, we condemn."[19]

THE CONTROVERSY AS TO WHETHER THE GOOD WORKS OF THE REGENERATE ARE NECESSARY

[LEYSER'S COMMENTS][20]

To the Pious Reader: This is a brief explanation of this "Theological Locus," in which if a person feels some lack because of its brevity, the following treatise may be consulted, in which other points are more fully dealt with and explained.

We do not want you to be unaware, godly and learned reader, that at almost the same time, about 27 years ago [1565], when our beloved Chemnitz was dealing

---

[19] This statement is a summary of the entire Art. IV of the Apology.

[20] Leyser as editor of Chemnitz's work here is simply adding to the *Loci Theologici* an essay prepared by Chemnitz in a different connection, which as he tells us had never been published because the furor quieted down. In doing this Leyser is helpful to the reader, just as he is when he earlier added the treatise on angels. This section thus was not originally a part of the *Loci*.

with this subject in his Loci Theologici, *there had arisen a controversy in certain churches concerning the commonly stated proposition: Good works are necessary. It became evident that the forerunner of this controversy was Dr. Andrew Musculus, at that time a professor of the University of Frankfurt. Therefore, since this controversy disturbed our author, because of the name attached to it, because he saw that the churches of his native land were greatly troubled about the matter, partly under the leading of the Holy Spirit and partly at the request of others, he was moved to produce a special treatise dealing with the whole controversy. However, although a little later, the whole argument quieted down and even Dr. Andrew Musculus himself rejected his previously held opinions and confirmed by the subscription of his own hand the* Formula of Christian Concord *and made it manifest to the whole Christian world; yet because many points are explained more fully and more accurately in this treatise than in the notes just presented (wherein our author was anxious to be brief) we want to add the treatise itself to this commentary. For each additional explanation is very useful and beneficial for those who are anxious to be dutiful toward God, especially because this treatise has never prior to this time been published.*

First, those who are compelled to rehearse church controversies will have here an example from which they can determine, if they wish, how, without pride, bitterness, or personal attacks (by which articles of faith are not actually explained but rendered more complicated) controversies of this kind must be conducted. Fare well, dear reader. We desire that our zeal for publishing useful writings of our beloved Chemnitz may promote the common building up of the church of God. Consult it well.

[End of Leyser's Comments.]

[The Controversy: Are Good Works Necessary?]

The doctrine of the new obedience which must follow in those who have been justified by faith alone, freely, for the sake of the Son of God our Mediator, because it is necessary, and why and in what sense it is necessary, is so clearly set forth on the basis of so many firm Scriptural foundations, that I am frank to confess amazement at how such complaints, with no reason, have been circulated, as if there actually are people who deny and want to destroy the statement which has been received in all the churches, that good works are necessary. Thus I was particularly saddened when I first heard a rumor and afterward saw in some tracts which were flying here and there, that this unfortunate tragedy was being enacted in the midst of the church to the great consternation of people both in the schools and the churches. I thought that if people were seeking the simple purity of the doctrine and the blessed peace of the churches, it would not be difficult to judge and settle this matter in a clear and comprehensible way. But I see that the church is being troubled and punished for its ingratitude by the fate which the Son of God and the apostles with great sadness predicted for the last times. By nature and by the particular situation of my life I love peace and harmony and do not rush hastily into controversies, but yet, because I felt that this controversy troubled me personally, not only because of my ministry and my conscience but also for several other reasons, I began to write down a few main points as to what I believe we should understand and assert in a simple way about this dispute according to the analogy of faith, on the basis of the Word of God, especially if a person is not seeking conflicts or battles but simply the God-pleasing truth which is helpful to the church and beneficial for our consciences, and is truly anxious for godly harmony in the church.

I shall not undertake a complete explanation of the locus on good works, but only those points which I believe pertain to the sum and substance of this controversy, and I shall divide them up into definite sections so that the explanation may be simpler and clearer. Further, we must demonstrate in this controversy that prudence which is necessary for the settlement of all conflicts in the church; that is, the disputes about the substance of the matter must each be kept in its proper place and correctly separated from matters of terminology so that our judgment is not confused. Those points which are true and stated correctly must be distinguished from erroneous statements which have been patched onto the truth, when what is said is twisted contrary to the intention of the author.

The First Question

How can the regenerate perform truly good works and what kind of works must they be?

I am putting this question in first place, for many of Luther's clear statements in which he accurately and beneficially explains this question in opposition to the papists are being gathered by some people and twisted out of their correct meaning in order to overturn the true and useful teaching regarding the necessity of the new obedience which the regenerate ought to perform. Many of our readers have been disturbed by this piling up of Luther's statements. For this can easily happen to the inexperienced reader in that kind of extravagant language which Luther used, if he does not keep in mind the useful rule of Hilary: "The meaning of what is said is shown to the reader by the reasons for speaking."

Further, it is entirely clear that the thinking and suggestions of Luther in all these statements were that in opposition to the teaching and savage attacks of the papists concerning good works he might correctly show what kind of good works the regenerate must do and how they can be done. The explanation of this question, if it is clearly and correctly taught from the true foundations of Scripture, is not an idle matter but useful and necessary, so that not only is the new obedience urged upon us as something we owe and is necessary, but at the same time we must carefully teach how this obedience which we owe is to be begun and can be performed. For the doctrine of good works absolutely must be taught in the church in such a way that in the very method itself there is and is demonstrated the difference between the virtues of the philosophers and the works of the Pharisees on the one hand and the good works of the regenerate on the other. It is profitable for both learners and teachers to hold to those points the Holy Scripture presents to us as the method which we in turn must set forth to others as well as to ourselves, so that the new obedience, under the working and aiding of the Holy Spirit, can be rightly begun and completed. But these points can be so taught that there is no need to overthrow the accepted and sound form of doctrine or to disturb and condemn churches which believe correctly.

But Luther was not the first nor the only person to treat this question in this way, for in all antiquity, in many statements of the fathers, there are testimonies to this fact. Augustine in several disputations explains this treatment of the matter, particularly in his book *De Spiritu et Litera*, his *De Gratia Novi Testamenti*, his *De Natura et Gratia*, and his three books *Contra Duas Epistolas Pelagianorum*, and also in many other places. Luther in his *Disputationes Adversus Antinomos* confesses that he had always followed the opinion of Augustine regarding good works. Therefore I judge that these expressions of Luther regarding the works of the Law which the Law exacts of us either by fear or coercion and the other points can be easily and correctly understood if we note that several of the statements which are pertinent here are taken from Augustine. Thus we shall point this out as briefly as possible. For when this question has been correctly handled, the other points in the controversy will be clearer and more easily understood.

The Pelagian controversy gave occasion to Augustine to deal with this question in great detail. For the Pelagians set forth this method of teaching concerning good works, as we read their words in *De Spiritu et Litera*, ch. 2 [MPL 44.202]: "God created man with free choice of will, and then in giving him the commandments He taught him how he should live, so that man might know what he ought to avoid and what he ought to seek in his works, whereby through his free choice, which had been grafted into him by nature, he might enter the way which has been shown to him, and by godly and righteous living deserve to come to that blessed life in eternity." But Augustine takes sharp issue with this statement of the Pelagians, saying in ch. 3 [MPL 44.203], "Free choice has no power except to commit sin, if the way of truth is hidden from it. And since it does not learn what it must do and on what it must rely, it begins to reveal itself, and unless something charms and is loved, the will is not led to it, does not accept it, and does not live properly. And in order that it may learn to love, the love of God is poured into our hearts, not through our free choice which rises up out of ourselves, but through the Holy Spirit who is given to us."

But the Pelagians object: Is not the Law by its commanding, its forbidding, its threatening, its promises, its urging and compelling able to produce truly good works in the will of men without the Holy Spirit? To this objection Augustine replies that the Law, if the Law is directed to the unregenerate will, as it exists in its own natural strength and powers, without the Spirit of renewal, cannot cause the new obedience or good works which are really pleasing to God to be undertaken or accomplished, even if with the greatest legal powers, strength, or force it works in the unregenerate will with its threats, urging, and compulsion. For the divine law, according to Paul's teaching, if it is applied to the human heart where the life-giving Holy Spirit is not present, is "the letter which kills" and "the ministration of death," 2 Cor. 3:6–7. Augustine shows this by the way he divides the subject: For either the concupiscence of sin, because it is opposed to the will of God, is made more wrathful by the Law, or if the Law does press out and extort something from the unregenerate will, whether by the carnal fear of punishment or the earthly desire for rewards or by the compulsion of the Law, so that it is bound to its task, performs certain hypocritical external actions without any true and spiritual inner desires. But when things take place in this way, they are not the truly good works which are pleasing to God, who looks into our hearts.

Augustine devotes a complete treatise to this subject. We shall cite several statements from him. De Spiritu et Litera, ch. 4 [MPL 44.204], "The Law by its prohibition increases our evil desire, just as the force of water, if it does not cease to drip on one certain part of my body, becomes a very serious problem and the cumulative effect of this, when it has reached a high proportion, puts a person flat on his back. I do not know how something which is lusted after can become more enjoyable as long as it is forbidden." Ch. 14 [MPL 44.217], "If the command is obeyed out of fear of punishment and not out of love for righteousness, if it is obeyed in a slavish manner and not freely, it is nothing. For no fruit is good which does not grow out of the root of love." Ch. 19 [MPL 44.221], "The Law by its ministration, where the life-giving Spirit is not present, does not produce good works but liars, either to the point of producing an evil work, if the flames of lust outweigh the restraints of fear, or at least in the will alone, if the fear of punishment overcomes the allurement of lust." Ch. 32 [MPL 44.236], "Fear is compelled to have in its work that which is lawful, although it has something else in the will, by which it prefers, if it were possible, to allow what is not allowed." In his Contra Duas Epistolas Pelagianorum, 3.4 [MPL 44.593] he says, "He who fulfills the commandments out of carnal fear of punishment or worldly cupidity without doubt does it unwillingly, and therefore does not act from his heart. For he certainly prefers not to do them, if he could get by with impunity and thus in his very will he is guilty inwardly where God, who has given the precepts, sees our inner qualities."

Thus this was the practice of the Pelagians in the doctrine of good works, which Augustine so rightly condemned and disapproved on the basis of the teaching of Scripture. But he himself had another position which was in agreement with the Word of God, and this he established and set forth: Because the Law is spiritual, requiring the agreement of the inner desires of the heart with the divine law, therefore truly good works must grow out of this root, so that not only external actions, whichever form they may take, must be in keeping with the norm of the divine law, but particularly there must be in the mind, the heart, and the will a love for God, and He is loved by meditating on and by doing His will as it has been revealed in His commandments; and "iniquity does not love God, even if it went unpunished," as Augustine says in his *De Gratia Novi Testamenti*.[21] But man does not have a will like this by his own natural powers in his corrupted nature, nor does he have free choice without the Holy Spirit, even with the help of the Law, and thus he cannot effect that conformity of his will with the divine law. For the law of God, which is spiritual, and the unregenerate will of man are two bitter enemies. As Paul says in Rom. 8:7, "The carnal mind is enmity against God, nor is it subject to the law of God, neither can it be." But what Paul says, "I delight in the law of God according to the inner man," Rom. 7:22, is the gift and working of the Holy Spirit.

Therefore this is the way to teach the doctrine of good works and to establish and preserve it: First the Holy Spirit is received, who is to renew our hearts, free our will which has been in captivity, and in sum to create a new man who delights in the law of God. For in this way truly good works can be presented to God; and in the law of God there will also be good fruits, when the tree has been made good. But indeed the Holy Spirit who gives life is not received either from "the ministration of death" or "the works of the law," as Paul says in 2 Cor. 3:6–7 and Gal. 3:2, for they are "the letter which kills" and "the ministration of damnation." Yet by the ministration of the Law, the beginning must be made in this way: The Law by teaching, threatening, compelling, and urging, attacks or oppresses the old man, so that when he is presumptuous regarding his own power, he comes to understand in the very attempt and the doing of the work, that he cannot produce that inner and spiritual obedience which the Law urgently demands. It is for this reason that the Law thunders and storms that man must obey the whole Law and that in one lapse he becomes guilty of all, James 2:10; cf. Rom. 3:19; Gal. 3:10. But "the Law is our schoolmaster unto Christ," Gal. 3:24, in order that faith in the Gospel may seek the grace of Christ,

---

[21] MPL 33.560, Epistle 140 *ad Honoratum [De Gratia]*, 21.53.

by which a person is liberated from the curse of the Law. Since with this reconciliation has been joined the giving of the Holy Spirit, who renews the heart so that it may begin to love God and delight in His law according to its inner man, therefore into the hearts of the believers the Spirit writes the Law which is proclaimed through the public ministry, Jer. 31:33. In this way good works can really be performed and also the fruits of faith which spring from this kind of root. The fulfillment of the Law, as Paul says, is not some outward activity, but love which does not arise out of our nature, a gift and work of the Holy Spirit whom we receive through faith, Gal. 3:2. Hence we make the distinction between the works of the Law and the works of grace.

Thus also Augustine says in his *De Spiritu et Litera*, ch. 13 [MPL 44.214], "What the law of works commands by threatening, the law of faith accomplishes by believing. By the law of works the Lord says, 'Do what I order you to do'; by the law of faith we say to God, 'Give what You command, and command what You will.' " This is the sum and substance of Augustine's argument which he set forth on the basis of the passages in Paul regarding "the letter which kills" [2 Cor. 3:6] and "the old covenant" [vv. 7ff.], and regarding "the oldness of the letter" [Rom. 7:6]. I wanted to outline this briefly and not increase the size of my book by more citations. I have wanted this statement of Augustine on the matter of good works to be understood, for it is certain that it applies to the article of justification and that the works of the Law must be removed from the article of justification, but Augustine in his discussion of the point does not correctly or sufficiently express the mind of Paul. This point belongs under another locus.

This comparison shows the reason for the expressions which Luther also used concerning the forcing of the works of the Law by fears or legal coercion. For just as the Pelagians gave occasion to Augustine, so also the papists gave occasion to Luther to explain this question in different ways and with great care. For the whole kingdom of the papists resounds with the cry of works, and the whole religion of the pope is nothing else than the doctrine of works. They viciously attack our churches and accuse them of neglecting, rejecting, and prohibiting all good works. For this reason Luther undertook to demonstrate from the Word of God that the papists do not teach correctly regarding good works. Indeed, said Luther, they are really not good works at all with which the whole pontifical realm is preoccupied. He proved on the basis of Scripture the same thing which Augustine had shown in his disputations. For the papists do not teach that man must first seek reconciliation with God through faith in Christ, in order that having been justified by faith and renewed by the Holy Spirit he might begin to perform good works. But they teach that the beginning proceeds from the works, so that through them a man is justified and reconciled with God. They raise many points about the actions which come from free choice, through the Law, actions which are produced without the Holy Spirit, by which a man in doing what is within his own power merits grace. Luther argues these points most vigorously on the basis of Scripture, just as he is equally emphatic in teaching the opposite position, namely that when the works of the Law have been commanded, they are accomplished in two ways: sometimes through our natural power of free choice and sometimes through the Holy Spirit working in the believers and the regenerate. To be sure, Luther says, the unregenerate man can to some degree perform the external work of the Law without Christ and the Holy Spirit, but those things which are proper or peculiar to the divine law, that is, the emotions of the heart toward God commanded in the First Table, cannot be accomplished without Christ or without the Holy Spirit. For the love of God, from which all things must flow in order to be truly good works, cannot exist unless we first hear the voice of the Gospel and lay hold on it by faith, the Gospel of free reconciliation with God for the sake of His Son the Mediator. For the mind which is ignorant of the reconciliation either despises God or flees His wrath. Therefore, in order that the love for God may come forth, it is necessary that trust in the mercy of God for the sake of Christ comes first, for in this way God is actually the object of our love. For when we hear the Gospel and receive the remission of our sins, we are led by faith and at the same time the Holy Spirit is given, who has written the law of God in the hearts of believers, that is, the Spirit arouses new emotions in our heart which are in harmony with the law of God. The things done by the regenerate, in keeping with the Law, are truly good works.

But the papists teach nothing about the need to seek and receive the free reconciliation with God for the sake of Christ the Mediator by faith in the Gospel; nor do they even deal with the matter as to what the promise of the Spirit is and how it is to be received by faith, Gal. 3:5. Rather, by means of only the unadorned Law they urge and compel men to good works, and when in this way through the Law, by the natural powers of their free choice, they have elicited some outward appearance of work, or rather extorted it, they then brag that these works are so good that they can merit the grace of God and justification. Luther sharply attacks and refutes this idea, showing that works of this kind are not truly good or God-pleasing. For the man who has not been reconciled with God by faith for the sake of Christ and has not been renewed by the Holy Spirit, can indeed, under the urging and compulsion of the Law, be bound under the works of the Law to the extent that he seeks to obey the sum and substance of the Law by his own powers. But when the Law, without the Holy Spirit, contends with the unregenerate will, whatever works are performed under these circumstances, with the Law drawing, driving, urging, or compelling, are not really good works, but they are sins in the eyes of God. For these works are performed and offered up unwillingly and thus by a will which is opposed to the Law. The Law by its own strength and with all its power can work nothing in unregenerate man without the Holy Spirit except a certain external conformity of actions of this kind. But the will itself, in order that it may voluntarily obey the Law, cannot be pushed by the Law to do anything. For no one can make his will perform voluntarily without the grace of God. Therefore in no way are works good when the Law is kept only with hatred of the Law, or when the will chooses and does one thing inwardly and pretends to do something else outwardly, for that person is sinning who performs external works without the Holy Spirit. To be sure, the law does demand conformity also in our inner desires, but it does not supply the power to produce it. Therefore Luther is correct when he pronounces that works which are extorted from our old nature by the Law in this way without the Holy Spirit are false, imaginary, and not good works, because they come from an unwilling and contrary will. Luther also asserts that such people are teachers of the letter in the church and not of the Spirit, who although they do not deny free justification and renewal through the Holy Spirit, yet insist upon good works on the part of the old man and think that it is sufficient if some kind of obedience is forced out of unwilling people by the Law. But those works are not to be called good works which are done unwillingly and with a contrary mind, with the Law forcing this obedience. These are Luther's precise words.

Thus this method which the philosophers, the Pelagians, the Pharisees, and the papists use in teaching the doctrine of good works Luther condemns for these reasons and in this way, and in so doing he is correct. Philipp uses almost the same approach in his teaching and speaking in his locus on the Spirit and the letter. For he says that without the knowledge of the Gospel the Law produces only the external discipline of the philosophers and sheer terror of conscience. He adds that this teaching (however you designate it) of our thoughts, habits, discipline, good intentions, and the very works and acts of the Law itself, without the Holy Spirit, are a dead letter, indeed a letter which kills. It is obvious that this is the concept which we have cited from Augustine, namely that we must understand that in the case of the unregenerate their whole will is in rebellion against God. For in the case of the regenerate who delight in the law of God in the inner man, there remains this statement of Christ to Peter, John 21:18, "They shall take you where you do not want to go." Compare Rom. 7:23, "I see another law in my members warring against the law of my mind." This statement must be understood as not referring to the political or civil use of the Law, which forbids transgressions in a particular situation or order, or which may be abolished and rejected. But at this point the question is: How can truly good and God-pleasing works be performed and what kind of works must they be?

Thus on the basis of this foundation Luther showed that the papists who contended that they were almost the only church to profess the correct doctrine of good works did not teach the correct or true doctrine and that the works with which the whole papacy is preoccupied are not really good works. At the same time, he also instructed those who teach that when they wish to prepare their hearers for undertaking and performing truly good works, they must contend against the old man, not by the Law alone without the Gospel, and they must clearly understand whether it takes place because of fear of punishment or material desire for rewards, by the compulsion of the Law, or whatever it may be it is a work which is pulled out of an unwilling and rebellious will. In civil life this sociopolitical use of the Law has its place and is absolutely necessary and has been instituted by God, as Luther says on Galatians 3.[22] But now the question is this: What works are to be regarded as good works in the church? For people are not to be taught that they are doing good works when they do something external while inwardly the desires of their hearts do not agree and even fight against it. Therefore what is the true principle or way which Scripture teaches we must apply in order that with the work and aid of the Holy Spirit the new obedience can be begun and demonstrated? Reply: First, from the Law we must show that human nature in this state of corruption, when it utilizes all its powers and the greatest efforts, cannot make satisfaction by true inner obedience to the law of God. For "the carnal mind is enmity against God, for it is not subject to the Law of God, nor indeed can it be," Rom. 8:7. Thus when all have "been or imprisoned under sin," Gal. 3:22, "every mouth is stopped and the whole world made guilty before God," Rom. 3:29, even those who are of the works of the Law are "under the curse," Gal. 3:10.

Second, faith in the Gospel must seek and lay hold on Christ, "the Lamb of God who takes away the sin of the world," John 1:29, who "was made under the Law, to redeem us who were under the Law," Gal. 4:4, from the curse of the Law, by the imputation to us through faith of His holy and perfect obedience by which He fulfilled the Law for us.

Third, with this reconciliation is joined the gift of the Holy Spirit who takes away our stony heart which is inimical and opposed to the Law and gives us a new heart which, because of this renewal, puts on new desires so that it begins to love God and delight in His law. In this way works are produced which are good in the eyes of God, as Ambrose says: Faith is the mother of a good will and a righteous action. This is what Luther so correctly states: "Forced service is not pleasing to God, but that which is done freely and voluntarily, things which indeed are works of the Law but they are not extorted by or through the Law. For Christ, who dwells in our hearts through faith, rules the will of the

---

[22] *Lectures on Galatians*, re Gal. 3:19, Amer. Ed., 26.308.

regenerate through the Holy Spirit, so that without the coercion of the Law, but willingly and beyond the Law, men with joy and delight advance in works of spontaneous good will. These are the truly good works by which those things commanded by the Word of God are accomplished by grace in a wonderful way, with a willing heart which is happy and joyful, a will which acts gladly, readily, easily, and happily. For God seeks free and joyful givers who serve Him not by the compulsion of necessity but out of pure good will."

These are Luther's words which are taken from clear statements of Scripture, 2 Cor. 9:7; 1 Peter 5:2; Philemon 14; 2 Cor. 8:12; 1 Cor. 9:17; Ps. 54:6; 110:3. In sum, Scripture requires "a new heart," Ps. 51:12; "a renewed mind," Rom. 12:2; a "new inner man," Eph. 4:24; Col. 3:10; Rom. 7:22; "a new creature," 2 Cor. 5:17; Gal. 6:15; "that we may be God's workmanship created in Christ Jesus unto good works," Eph. 2:10. But these things cannot be accomplished by any laws or powers of our nature, but only by the renewal and working of the Holy Spirit. Paul covers this entire matter in a brief but illustrative statement in 1 Tim. 1:5, "The sum of the commandments is" not the pretense of performing external actions, "but love," that is, a ready will, a happy and spontaneous love for the law of God. This love is not natural, nor does it arise out of our free choice, but from a pure heart which has been renewed and purified by the Holy Spirit. This renewal does not take place until the conscience has first been made free from the curse of the Law, which takes place for the sake of Christ, if we lay hold on Him by faith. Therefore Paul sets forth these categories: (1) love; (2) a pure heart; (3) a good conscience; (4) true faith which also covers the sins which cling to the obedience of the regenerate. Thus Luther also says in regard to Psalm 110, that because our nature by its own powers cannot present to God true obedience, and yet God wills that the Decalog be obeyed, therefore He first justifies the person, then He renews his corrupt nature and bestows a new heart which by its own will is happy, anxious, and willing to begin to obey the Law. Such must be the true good works of the regenerate, because in this way they can both begin good works and present them to God. But these points must be so understood to mean that this renewal in this life is not perfect and complete, but only beginning, as we shall show under the next question.

These matters can be handled in a very useful way to show what the truly good works of the regenerate must be like and how they can be done, so that before God they may be distinguished from the virtues of the philosophers and the works of the Pharisees. When our zeal for good works is either lacking or languishing, it is helpful to know the principle of Scripture which we must set forth for others as well as ourselves so that the new obedience, with the work and aid of the Holy Spirit, may begin and be carried on, that is to say, that the mind through repentance may be led to the point of acting on or applying the article of justification. For the promise of the Spirit is received by faith, Gal. 3:2, and He stirs up and increases new desires in the heart which conform with the law of God.

In this necessary doctrine, if a person either by repetition or illustration can give useful instruction from the Word of God, we owe him great thanks. But it is not necessary (because all the churches do teach the correct and godly doctrine that good works are necessary) to disturb and torment them with all this clamor, as if this doctrine had been lost and become extinct. For in the Augsburg Confession, Art. 20 [Tappert, p. 41], and in the Apology under "Love and the Fulfilling of the Law" in [Melanchthon's] locus on the Holy Spirit [in Vol. I], and in [Luther's] *The Freedom of a Christian* [Amer. Ed., 31.327ff.], the question of how good works can be done is treated. Even the very titles show this, for it is not only called "obedience" but "new obedience"; they are not only called "works" but "good works." And in the teaching of the catechumens in all the churches this instruction is repeated, that the First Commandment is the foundation of all the rest, that the works and obedience to all the rest of the commandments depend on it and arise from it. This is explained simply and comprehended under three headings in the First Commandment, namely the fear of God, the love of God, and faith in God. (1) The fear of God shall not be servile but filial, so that the heart in earnest and childlike reverence subjects itself to the will of God as it has been revealed in His commandments. (2) The love of God, that is, that he who has been reconciled with God by faith, when he has considered the goodness and mercy of God toward us in Christ does with truly voluntary motives and serious feelings in his heart want to try to do those things which he knows from the Law are pleasing to God and he does this with pleasure and happiness in God toward his primary goal of giving honor and obedience to Him. (3) This kind of fear and love arises out of the knowledge of and confidence in the mercy of God which has been promised and revealed to us for the sake of the Mediator, and by this faith this fear and love are pleasing to God, both the inner emotions and the outward good works of the regenerate. This faith must therefore enlighten all the works of God's precepts.

Therefore, in the case of this first question, I know of no one in the churches which hold to the doctrine which from the Word of God is confessed in the Augsburg Confession, who does not accept and make his own the teaching which Luther drew from the fountains of Holy Scripture, so that there is no need for all these tragic controversies. But I did want to repeat briefly the explanations of this matter at the beginning because statements of Luther have been cited and I am of the opinion that Luther sheds a good deal of light on this argument. The other points will be explained in the following chapter.

The Second Question

Are the good works of the regenerate in this life so perfect that they satisfy
the divine law or even do more than is commanded (supererogation)?

In the teaching of the church in regard to good works we must strongly
insist and teach from the Word of God that this renewal which must take place,
as we have said, or this new obedience which is begun in the regenerate through
the Spirit of renewal, is not in this life perfect, complete, or absolute in all
respects and hence in itself pure and above reproach. Rather, because of the law
of sin which dwells in the flesh and members of the regenerate, Rom. 7:23, in the
weakness of this life under the burden of the sinful flesh there is a small, crippled, hindered, imperfect, unclean, and contaminated newness which in itself
does not satisfy the Law but is far away from the perfection of the Law, as many
clear statements of Scripture testify. See Ps. 19:12; 32:6; 130:3; 143:2; Rom. 7:23;
1 Cor. 4:4; 1 John 1:8. For as long as the remnants of the original sin with which
we are born remain in the regenerate, no one fears God as he ought; no one is
on fire with love for God as the Law prescribes. When the Holy Spirit stirs up
our inner desires and outward actions so that they are in agreement with the
law of God, the regenerate feel in their flesh the weakness, the heedlessness,
and the slothfulness, so that they do not eagerly follow the leading of the Spirit.
In their will is felt a kind of aversion, in their heart a stubbornness; and corrupt
thoughts, evil inclinations, various kinds of erring lusts of their desires are all
kindled. There are many kinds of ignorance, neglect, omissions. Who can comprehend in his mind or describe in his speech the whole mountain of sin which
still clings in the regenerate in this life, since David says, "Who can understand
his faults? Cleanse me from secret sins," Ps. 19:12?

The honest acknowledgment of this weakness and imperfection and the
humble confession of it (as Augustine says) is earnestly required in Scripture on
the part of all the regenerate in this life. We are not to extenuate our uncleanness
which still remains in the flesh of the regenerate, as Lindanus[23] does when he
mixes excuses in with his enticing words: "The little sins of our daily lapses are
spots and warts which like little dust spots lightly sprinkle the life of Christians
but they do not make us corrupt."

But, you say, what does this question have to do with the explanation of
the present controversy? The answer is that certain people have gathered from
Luther many statements which seemingly could be used to support the perfection in good works by the regenerate in this life. For they cite them out of context
and clearly add nothing to the explanation as to the occasion and the sense in

---

[23] Van Der Linden, 1525–88, Bishop of Ghent, Catholic moderate controversialist.

which these statements were made. I know that many readers who desire to be learned will be upset by these half truths which add nothing to the clarification of the matter. Therefore an explanation is right and necessary. They cite such statements as these: The Christian does not need the Law to teach, urge, and compel him to do good. The good tree does not need any instruction or rule in order that it may bring forth good fruit, for it does so by nature which is without any law or teaching, but it produces good fruit by its nature. Again, it would be most foolish to prescribe a book full of laws to an apple tree, as to how it must not produce thorns, since by its very nature it does this better than can be prescribed or commanded in all the books. Thus all Christians through the Spirit and through faith completely possess this nature, because they can do more good and right things than can be taught by all the laws. Likewise the righteous or just man has more than the Law can give him. The righteous man has the Holy Spirit and a pure heart, and thus he does all the things which the law requires. This can be understood from the expression "*Wenn ein Ding gehet wie es gehen soll/darf es niemand treiben*," (When a thing goes as it ought to go, then no one should push it). Or, when a person does what is asked, there is no need to command, to prescribe, or to prohibit. There is no need to command the sun that it should shine, water that it should flow, fire that it should burn. He would be foolish who wanted to command such things. Again, the Christian does all the things which the Law requires, *ist schon also gemacht/wie es sein soll* (what should be has already been done), so that he wills and does nothing else, because he has the Holy Spirit through whom the heart is kindled with love for all good works. Just as it cannot be compelled of a man that he become a male, nor of a woman that she become female, because they have been created such and can do nothing else by nature, so you cannot command a Christian *fromm zu sein* (to be pious), because if you want to demand this of him, I will call you insane because you are compelling what has already been accomplished, and you are prohibiting that which he cannot accomplish. Again, the righteous person does good works even beyond what is required, freely and willingly, and he so lives that he has no need of the Law which admonishes, condemns, and coerces him.

I see these and similar expressions quoted from Luther in this controversy. But I do not believe that anyone is so insane that he dares to attribute to Luther the opinion that the good works of the regenerate in this life are so perfect that of themselves they satisfy the law of God or that they do even more than the Law requires. I lament (to speak freely) that the church is mocked and consciences disturbed to the point where one person has drawn up statements which sounded like pure antinomianism, and then has written to his church organizations that he had done this to irritate his adversaries, and if anyone spoke against him he said that he wanted to use such statements as exist in Luther and that they could be correctly understood in a correct sense. But what perversity it is to use statements which are correct in such a way that they can be rightly understood and yet use them to create a quarrel!

Therefore I could not permit anyone to be praised for this activity of spreading statements of this kind from Luther, out of context, without any explanation as to the occasion or the sense in which they were spoken, neither among the learned nor among the common people, since many good men were convinced and thus greatly disturbed. To be sure, these statements—out of context and by themselves and piled up without any explanation—would seem to sound as if the renewal of the regenerate in this life is as perfect as it is natural for the sun to shine, fire to burn, or a good tree to bring forth good fruit; and that thus the regenerate in their obedience do satisfy the Law, indeed they do more than the Law requires. If these things are true, then what hinders us from being justified by our love and from rendering works of supererogation? Some from among the Anabaptists so perverted these statements of Luther that they tried to establish from them their opinion concerning the perfection of the righteousness of our works in this life. I remember also in the rebuttals which the papists gathered from the writings of Luther that they used these same statements, with the correct interpretation removed, to show that he was inconsistent when he said a man who was righteous in every respect still was a sinner, that he seemed to attribute to the regenerate complete fulfillment of the Law, even more than the Law required in this life. Therefore it is not an insignificant matter that I am lamenting the fact that many people are being disturbed and offended over the way in which these statements are being piled up, out of context, without explanation, and in abbreviated form; and since it would be a simple matter to explain them, these people ought to give some thought to the great earnestness with which the Son of God threatens that "He who offends one of these little ones who believe in Me, it would be better for him that a millstone . . . ," Mark 9:42. For the teacher of the church is obligated to teach not only the wise but also the simple, Rom. 1:14. Even when the doctrine is taught as simply and plainly as possible, many still can scarcely be instructed, so that plainly there is no need for this kind of deception in the church.

Thus it is our task to show on what occasion and in what sense Luther spoke this way. I would prefer that this task be undertaken by those who were known to be very familiar with Luther's method of speaking, so that the reader might have less reason for concern that he can truly and more easily acquire the true and genuine meaning of Luther's statements. I shall set forth my thoughts with simplicity and care, and the more learned readers may understand the occasion for the statements so that they can explain them more fully. I hope that my points will be simple, true, and accurate.

I. In the first place, we must establish what I hope no one is so foolish as to disagree with, namely that the continuous opinion of Luther is that which is repeated and explained in the Apology of the Augsburg Confession in the chapter on "Love and the Fulfilling of the Law," namely that the good works of the regenerate in this life are far from the perfection of the Law and the new obedience in us is minor and impure, which cannot be pleasing to God nor accepted by Him for its own sake. For our fulfilling of the Law is only beginning and is not perfect fulfillment of the Law. But it is necessary that faith be present in Christ, so that what is lacking in our fulfillment of the law not be imputed against us. Luther himself, in his second *Disputatio*[24] on the passage in Romans 3, uses this axiom in opposition to the papists: There was no example, there is no example now, and there will be no example of complete fulfillment of the Law in any of the saints in the entire holy catholic church. For the voice and confession of all the saints and of the whole church is, "If we say that we have no sin, the truth of God is not in us." I can prove this opinion from many other statements of Luther. But I believe this suffices. For our churches will not endure it if anyone tries to depict the doctrine of Luther and the Augsburg Confession as being in conflict with one another. Thus it is certain that these statements of Luther must not be understood as if the works of the regenerate in this life arrive at that stage of perfection that they satisfy the Law with complete perfection; or that they can fulfill even more than is commanded.

This would suffice for me in my simplicity, even if I could say nothing further. But I shall also say that I believe that I have comprehended the universal consensus of understanding regarding the *Disputationes* of Luther. Luther teaches that the law without the Gospel, without Christ and the Holy Spirit does not have the power, the strength, or the efficacy either to justify or renew man. But the Gospel brings to believers both Christ and the Holy Spirit. Those who believe in Christ have through imputation the perfection which the Law requires before God. For "Christ is the completion of the Law unto salvation to everyone who believes," Rom. 10:4. Indeed, those who believe in Christ have more than the Law requires. For "through the obedience of one many were made righteous," Rom. 5:19. But this obedience is the obedience of the person who is God and man, a person who owes nothing to the Law, since the Law requires perfection from men who are subject to the Law. In regard to this statement Luther is correct in saying that those who believe in Christ have as much

---

[24] For example, Apology 4.136, Tappert, p. 126. We have not located Luther's *Disputatio* on Romans 3.

as the Law requires, indeed they have more, by imputation through faith. For the Apology [4.178, Tappert, p. 131] speaks the same way when it says that the death and satisfaction of Christ which have been given for our benefit must be placed far above our own purity and far above the Law itself. This is the one way to explain these statements of Luther.

II. But Luther not only spoke this way about the renewal through the Holy Spirit but also about the statement "The fulfillment of the commandment" or what the Law requires, that is, according to Paul's statement in 1 Tim. 1:5, "love out of a pure heart, a good conscience, and sincere faith." But those who believe in Christ have "a good conscience," Heb. 9:14 and 10:22; and "a heart purified by faith," Acts 15:9; and are renewed by the Holy Spirit, from whence love remains and overflows along with works of love. Therefore believers who have been renewed through the Spirit have that which the Law requires, namely "love from a pure heart, a good conscience, and sincere faith." But the question is, do the regenerate have that perfection which the Law requires and as the Law prescribes? Here Luther certainly is not speaking of love and the good works of the regenerate in themselves. For he says that Paul deals with this "sincere faith" in such a way that what is lacking in our good works toward the fulfillment of the Law is not imputed to us, for the sake of Christ, just as in such a remarkable way he also treats the simile of Gerson regarding the calling from the throne of justice to the throne of grace, in his explanation of this statement of Paul, cf. Luther, Tome 6.[25] Therefore this is the same as that which Paul is saying in Rom. 8:4, "that the righteousness of the Law might be fulfilled in us, who do not walk according to the flesh but according to the Spirit." But how, then, is the Law fulfilled? Is the obedience of the regenerate in itself perfect? In no way, says Paul, Rom. 7:25 and 8:13, "With the mind I myself observe the law of God, but with my flesh the law of sin; but there is no condemnation for those who are in Christ Jesus. . . . For what the Law could not do in that it was weak through the flesh, this God accomplished by sending His Son. . . ." Thus the righteousness of the Law is fulfilled in the regenerate but in an incomplete beginning and by imputation, as we commonly and correctly say. These points are true, uncomplicated, and plain. It is manifest that this is the meaning of Luther, as his words themselves demonstrate on ch. 5 of Galatians [Amer. Ed., 27.96], "The righteous do willingly what the Law requires, if not perfectly with holy works at least with the remission of sins through faith. Thus the Christian inwardly is fulfilling the Law by faith. For Christ is the fulfillment of the Law to everyone who believes, without works and by the remission of sins." On ch. 3 of Galatians [Amer. Ed.,

---

[25] We have not located this reference, but it is well known that Luther was influenced by Gerson and read him thoroughly.

26.260] he says even more clearly, "Through Christ we are made doers of the Law. How? First, through the remission of sins and the imputation of righteousness, because of our faith in Christ. Second, through the gift of the Holy Spirit who produces the new life, new desires in us. Thus in a formal way we do fulfill the Law, but what has not been done is forgiven for the sake of Christ. Then whatever of sin remains is not imputed to us."

III. Luther in explaining the passage of Paul, "The Law was not given for the righteous but for the unrighteous," 1 Tim. 1:9, discusses the use of the Law which in his commentary on Galatians he calls the civil use, that is, the unregenerate are coerced by external discipline to abstain from manifest crimes. Under this civil use the Law is satisfied when it forces some degree of external discipline from the unregenerate. But for the righteous and the regenerate the Law was not laid down in this manner or for this purpose. For such people already have through their renewal more than this civil use of the Law requires. It is clear from the whole discussion that Luther wanted this interpretation to be given to this passage in Paul. But to twist these words out of context into a generalization concerning the perfect fulfillment of the entire Law does not explain, but only distorts, the position of Luther.

IV. Luther himself handles the interpretation of his position through his distinction between the new and the old man and by showing that the Holy Spirit is the efficient cause of the renewal in the regenerate. That this renewal in this life is not perfect is not brought about by the defect or out of the weakness of the efficient cause, but because of the flesh or the old man who is crucified, to be sure, and mortified, but he is not put down except through death. Therefore, that the new obedience of the regenerate in this life is imperfect and impure is not the case because the Holy Spirit works something impure in us. But the imperfection and impurity come not from the new man but from the old, and to him must the blame be given. Thus Luther says on ch. 2 of Galatians [Amer. Ed., 27.231–32], "The Spirit of the righteous person through faith is without sin, and owes nothing to the Law; but the body still has something alien and rebellious attached to it against which it works. . . ."

In this sense I do not see that it is correct to say that the renewal and newness in the regenerate in this life are perfect. I also know and understand that the apostolic doctrine and "the form of sound words" do not permit this understanding. For, first, Scripture clearly affirms that the renewal of the regenerate in this life must increase and grow, 2 Cor. 4:16, "The inward man must be renewed day by day"; cf. 2 Cor. 3:18; Eph. 4:15; Phil. 1:9. Second, Luther clearly teaches that the renewal of the regenerate in this life is not perfect but imperfect. Thus on ch. 17 of Genesis [Amer. Ed., 3.79] he says, "The fact that the name here is plural, *thāmīm*, 'that you may be a man of perfect actions and integrity,' means that you are correct in speaking of a twofold righteousness.

"The first and perfect righteousness is that by which we are righteous before God by faith. The second is imperfect and is that by which we are righteous before both God and men in regard to our morals and reputations." And on Genesis 1 [Amer. Ed., 1.64] he says, "But we are born again not only to life, but also for righteousness, because faith lays hold on the merit of Christ and through the death of Christ makes us free. Hence, our second kind of righteousness comes into being, that newness of life by which we are anxious to obey God, instructed by His Word and aided by the Holy Spirit. But this righteousness in this life is only a beginning, and it can never be perfect while we are in the flesh. Yet it is pleasing to God, not as perfect righteousness or as the price to be paid for our sins, but because it comes out of our heart which in confidence relies on the mercy of God through Christ." Third, I see Pope Hosius arguing this way: Although our works of love are imperfect, yet our attitude of love is perfect in the regenerate in this life, and therefore we can be justified by our love. Therefore it is certain that he is not teaching "the form of sound words," because he is saying that the newness of the regenerate in this life is perfect.

V. In regard to this subject Luther used the similes of the sun, the tree, and others which have been discussed under the first question and can be understood in that context. The scholastics teach that through actions which are elicited out of free choice with the encouragement and urging of the Law, and often repeated, the attitude or aptitude for love can be generated and formed in us, as Aristotle argues regarding the attitude of virtue. But Luther, in opposition to these ideas, teaches, as he says regarding John 15,[26] that love, renewal, or the new obedience of the regenerate are not generated or formed from outside, through habit or discipline, as actions of free choice (*wird nicht von aussen eingetragen*), but when through faith we are grafted into Christ who is the true vine, we are made participants in His fullness and sweetness, that is, when the Holy Spirit is given who renews the heart and makes the new creature, so that truly good works proceed from that root to which they are attached. In explaining this doctrine Christ Himself uses the simile of the tree in Matt. 12:33, "If you wish to make the fruit good," do not begin from the outside, but first "make the tree good," and then the fruit will be good. Augustine in writing to Simplicianus on this subject [MPL 40.113] uses this simile: A wheel does not revolve in order that it might become round; but because it is round, therefore it revolves. Lest a person confuse in the new obedience the works of the regenerate with the grace of renewal and free choice, Luther opposes this part of the simile that there is

---

[26] *Sermons on the Gospel of John*, Amer. Ed., 24.226; a rather free translation here by Chemnitz.

no need by the Law to compel a good tree to bear good fruit because the regenerate have within themselves the seed of God from which come forth love, new obedience, or good works, and there is no need to add the cooperation of free choice, but rather we must attribute to the Holy Spirit the blessing of renewal. For this is the correct teaching of Scripture.

But these points are not to be understood as if the gifts of renewal by the Spirit can be preserved in this state of becoming, without any zeal on our part, diligence, or effort, so that there is no need for spiritual exercise. For both elements must be retained and correctly taught.

In the first place, we are not "sufficient of ourselves to think anything of ourselves," 2 Cor. 3:5; cf. Phil. 2:13; John 15:4–5; 1 Cor. 4:7. Thus Augustine is right when he says that holy thoughts, good intention, the zeal or desire to do good, do not begin or emerge from the powers of the unregenerate will, but they are a grace, a gift, and the work of the Holy Spirit. In his *De Spiritu et Litera*, 13 [MPL 44.214], he says that the argument as to the kind of good works the regenerate should perform and how they can be performed is a necessary debate in order that he who is given a command, if he cannot do it, may know what he must seek and from whom and how he may get it. But if he is able and does perform the task obediently, he also ought to know who gives him the power to perform it. In his *Contra Duas Epistolas Pelagianorum*, 3.4 [MPL 44.591, 597], he says: "We say that the Holy Spirit is not our only aid, because the Pelagians by this doctrine think that it is sufficient that He be the true giver of virtue, but then they deny this to Him by attributing virtue rather to free choice."

In the second place, we must also add the teaching which Augustine explains so beautifully in his *De Gratia et Libero Arbitrio*, 16 [MPL 44.906], "It is certain that we in the regenerate state do the willing when we will, but He who causes us to will makes it happen that we do will. It is certain that we act when we do something, but He who works in us efficaciously brings it about that we perform the action." Again in *De Correptione et Gratia*, 2 [MPL 44.918], "They must understand, if they are the sons of God, that they are led by the Spirit of God so that they do what must be done, and when they have done it they must give thanks to Him by whom they have been led. For they are led that they might act, not that they should do nothing." *De Dogmat. Eccles.*, 32 [MPL 58.988], "God works in us that we might will and do; nor does He produce useless things in us which He gives us to do as exercises, or things which may be neglected."

Thus it is correct to say that there are three causes of a good action or of good works: the Holy Spirit, the Word, and the regenerate will.

For in the controversy regarding free choice the point at issue was not whether in conversion and renewal there must be present and follow new desires in the mind, the will, the heart, and the complete new man. For it is beyond all argument that where no clear change has occurred, where no new desires are clearly present and follow, so that there is a good desire, a good intention, zeal, diligence, effort, a struggle with evil lust, then no conversion or renewal has taken place or is present. But the question is this: Whence does a man possess those things which must take place in a true conversion, and how does he acquire them? Do they come from the natural powers of his free choice, and are they the gifts and workings of the Holy Spirit; or does the regenerate man possess these new desires partly from the Holy Spirit and partly from free choice? The fuller explanation of this question belongs under the second locus, but these points ought to be made now in regard to the simile of the sun and the tree which Luther used, and, which we have pointed out, correctly apply to the doctrine of renewal and the new obedience. Nor do we need to prolong the discussion except to state the mind of the author which seems contrary to simple truth. In the sun there is nothing which is in conflict, but its entire nature is caused to shine, in keeping with the ordinance of God. But Paul in the state of regeneration says, "I see another law in my members which is at war with the law of my mind and which takes me into captivity under the law of sin," Rom. 7:23; "The flesh and the Spirit are opposed to one another, so that you do not do what you want to do," Gal. 5:17. The good tree bears good fruit without thought, without any inclination of the will, without effort, zeal, diligence, or struggle, by its own natural power. Unless we really want to be insane, we must establish a difference between those things which we do by nature and those things which are the voluntary actions of the regenerate. For we will in an absolute sense when God works in us to will. But a good tree cannot produce evil fruit, and the regenerate person, insofar as he is regenerate does not do evil, as Paul says in Rom. 7:20, "It is not I who does the evil, but sin which dwells in me." Yet he says, "Let him who thinks he is standing take heed lest he fall," 1 Cor. 10:12, and "I keep my body in subjection, lest I become a castaway"; and again, Rom. 7:25, "With the mind I observe the law of God, but with the flesh the law of sin."

I believe that this is a simple and correct explanation as to the occasion and sense of the statements of Luther cited above, which have been brought into this controversy. But if those to whom this kind of talking on the part of Luther is familiar want to bring forward a better interpretation of his statements, I will happily concur with them, as long as the principle remains firm and immovable that the good works of the regenerate in this life are not perfect and absolute but are far from a perfect fulfillment of the Law, so that without remission of sin they cannot be pleasing to God. For we must not pretend that Christ ceases to be our Mediator after we have been renewed, so that after we have been renewed we please God by our own fulfilling of the Law.

The Third Question

Must the Law be presented to the regenerate in such a way that it is the norm and rule for the good works in which God wills that we carry out our obedience to Him?

The confession of faith of our churches, which was given to the Emperor Charles at Augsburg in A.D. 1530, says this in Art. 20 [20.1, Tappert, p. 41], "Our people are falsely accused of prohibiting good works. For their writings which are still extant regarding the Ten Commandments and other points testify with a similar line of argument that they taught usefully and properly concerning all kinds and duties of life as to which kinds and which works in any individual vocation were pleasing to God." That is, the Law must be set before the regenerate in order that it may teach certain works in which God wills that we carry out obedience to Him.

Certain people are clearly gnawing away at our common and accepted teaching. For they are citing such statements as these: It is not the task of the Law to govern our works; the righteous person does not need the Law to instruct him or admonish or push him to live a good life; the Christian who lives in faith does not need something to teach him regarding good works, but he does what occurs to him and all is completed; he does not permit himself to be charged with any particular work, but is completely indifferent to all and free to do what he wishes; the Christian wants to do nothing to which he is pushed by the Law. Therefore he does not act because he has been commanded, but because it is pleasing to him, even if it is not prescribed. In the New Testament there are no commands which push us. I do something freely, I do not care whether there is a precept for it or not; where the Holy Spirit is, there is no need for doctrine or the Law, and yet what must happen does happen. Just as he is foolish and crazy who wants to prescribe to a good tree what kind of fruit it must bear and wants to command or at least to admonish the sun to shine, so also is he who wishes to instruct or admonish righteous men or prescribe something to them regarding good works.

But, you say, these are the statements of Luther. I know and confess it. This is what causes many good people to grieve that the church is upset and disturbed in these last times by things of this kind. For certain people are either themselves tearing down and corrupting certain necessary points in the received form or body of doctrine, or at least they are indifferent when these teachings are overthrown and destroyed. On the other hand there are those who, when unnecessary controversies arise regarding the form of doctrine as it has been established simply and properly, are shamefully twisting and turning this way and that, and all this under the pretext of the authority of Luther, whose statements they do not hesitate to put into opposition to the Augsburg Confession. I see and grieve over the fact that this has taken place in this controversy. For what is simpler, what is plainer, what is more useful than this doctrine that the Law or the teaching of the Decalog must be set forth in the church of the regenerate, in order that there may be a definite norm to show what the works are in which God wills that the regenerate demonstrate their obedience.

It is completely true that the Holy Spirit renews the heart and causes us to will and to give obedience to God. Therefore, does God will that the regenerate by their own private wisdom and intention or out of human traditions think up self-made religions and peculiar works which they present to God as the obedience due Him? The answer is a definite no! For Paul expressly condemns "man-made religions" in Col. 2:23. We know the statements in Deut. 12:8 and 32, "You shall not each of you do whatever is right in your own eyes . . . but what I command you, this only shall you do unto the Lord. You shall not add thereto nor detract anything"; cf. Ezek. 20:18–19; Is. 1:12; 29:13; Matt. 15:9. Therefore God wills that the whole life of the regenerate be ruled by His Word, not only in regard to our faith but also in our good works themselves, as it says in Ps. 119:105, "Your Word is a light unto my path." But now the Gospel does not establish new laws, but when the heart has been renewed, so that it wills and tries to obey God, then to answer the question what those works were which "God has prepared beforehand that we should walk in them," Eph. 2:10, then it sends us back to the divine law which is the law governing our actions or works, Rom. 3:27. Thus when Christ was asked what a person must do, He replied in Luke 10:26, "What is written in the Law? How do you read?" When Paul in Rom. 12:2 has undertaken to explain what "the good and perfect will of God" is in the doctrine of good works, he immediately in the next chapter, 13:9, quotes the precepts of the Second Table of the Decalog. In Gal. 5:14, love is the root and summary of all good works, and Paul says that this is nothing else than the fulfilling or completion of the Law. The Law, therefore, must be the norm of our good works, so that at the same time it may warn us of our imperfections. For in man-made religions the human mind can easily persuade itself that it is perfect or does even more than is required. Thus the church is correct in teaching the catechumens that in the regenerate God approves this kind of life, and those works which have been set forth and commanded in His Word and are correctly said to be "sanctified by the Word of God," 1 Tim. 4:5. The doctrine which sets forth, prescribes, and demands certain works which have been commanded to us by God, properly speaking, is not the Gospel but the law of God or the Decalog, which must be understood in keeping with the interpretation of the prophets, of Christ, and of the apostles.

Beyond all controversy these points are certain, unless a person wishes to overturn and destroy everything. The Word of God must be the norm for good works. Both Christ and the apostles expressly call the law of God, which is the teaching of the Decalog, the "Word." These things must be clearly taught in the church. The Spirit of renewal does not act through enthusiasts who have been caught up without the means of grace, but through His doctrine which He has written in the hearts of men and which sounds forth in the proclamation of the ministry. Jeremiah explains what this doctrine is in 31:33 when he says, "I will write My law in their hearts." The Apology also says [4.136, Tappert, p. 126], "It is necessary that the Law have a beginning in the regenerate and increase more and more." And Luther says in his *Disputatio de Operibus Legis et Gratiae* [*Weimar Ausgabe*, 39(1).202–03], "The works of grace are those which come from faith, with the moving of the Holy Spirit who regenerated the will of man. And yet it is necessary that the will be instructed and aroused through the Word and the outward sign, that is, by threats or promises. For it pleased God through the ministry of the Word and the sacraments to give and increase the Spirit." Thus Luther. There is no doubt that to good works also pertain these spiritual exercises so that the body be held in subjection to the Spirit and brought back into captivity, so that the flesh might be crucified with its lusts, so that the old man might be put down, and the actions of the flesh mortified. These are the words of Scripture. There is no doubt that these are the actions of the Holy Spirit, as Paul says, "If you through the Spirit mortify the deeds of the flesh," Rom. 8:13. But the question at issue is this: Does the Holy Spirit work this through enthusiasm without the ministration of the Word? The answer is that God has set forth His law, prohibitions, instructions, promises, and examples of both punishments and rewards in order that through the ministration or means of the Holy Spirit He might mortify and crucify the old man. But if this law is to be removed from the church of the regenerate in this life, a great part of Scripture will be mutilated.

Rather, because this obedience which has been begun by the regenerate in this life is imperfect and impure, and does not keep busy, does not grow or increase by enthusiastic raptures, without thought, exercise, effort, or struggle, therefore the regenerate must avoid these raptures so that they may love, use, and exercise that ministration through which the Holy Spirit mortifies the old man, so that the inner man may be renewed from day to day. The Spirit is received through "the hearing of faith," Gal. 3:2. From the article of justification are given exhortations, admonitions, and supplications, so that the gifts of the Holy Spirit which have been begun may be stirred up, retained, increased, and augmented. Furthermore the doctrine of the Decalog still has its own use in this matter, as we have already said. For Deut. 6:6–7 and 11:18, "These words which I command you shall be in your heart. You shall teach them to your children, you shall talk of them when you sit in your house, when you walk in the way, when you sleep and when you rise," pertain not only to the unregenerate nor only for the knowledge of sins, but God repeated these words to Joshua in 1:8, "The book of the Law shall not depart out of your mouth, but you shall meditate on it day and night, that you may observe and do all that is written in it." Ps. 1:2 and Psalm 119 say many things regarding the meditation on the Law. Indeed, the word "Law" includes the entire ministration of the Word under this one general term. But Ps. 119:15 clearly says, "I will meditate on Your precepts." Therefore we are not to teach the regenerate that when they have received the first stirrings of the Holy Spirit, they are already secure and at ease, without any further thought or meditation on the Word, without any concern or effort or spiritual struggle to be expended, until, through some enthusiastic and violent inspiration, they are carried up into good works.

This opinion which we have stated is the constant and undeviating position of Luther, which can be testified by many clear statements. In regard to Psalm 130 he says, "There must be godly exercises and our works must be governed by the Word of God; for this purpose God has left the law for us."[27]

In his *Disputatio 2 Contra Antinomos* [*Weimar Ausgabe*, 39(1).349] he says, "Since the Law requires obedience toward God, they are enemies of the law, that is, those who are taking away the Law, and they also take away obedience toward God."

Luther in a sermon on good works presupposes this as axiomatic: There is no good work unless God has prescribed it, just as there is no sin unless God has forbidden it. Therefore, when I set out to perform good works, there is need for nothing except I know that it has been commanded by God. Again, in his account of Noah he says that even when it had become dry on the earth, Noah did not dare to come out of the ark before he had received a command from God, so that it might be demonstrated that there is no good work in the sight of God which He Himself has not commanded.[28]

In Tome 5, folio 521, Luther says, "The devil stirs up tragedies, for he does not permit us to remain under the material cause and the final cause, but leads us from that which has been commanded of us to other things which seem more important."[29] And in Tome 6,[30] in explaining the statement of Paul in 1 Tim. 1:5, "The fulfillment of the Law is love . . . ." There is a long *disputatio* by Luther on

---

[27] Inadequate reference. Cannot locate.

[28] *Lectures on Genesis*, re Gen. 8:15, Amer. Ed., 2.112.

[29] Inadequate reference. Cannot locate.

[30] Ibid.

this point: "Put the Word of God in your heart and govern yourself by it and your heart will be pure." Again, put this word before you: "You shall love your neighbor as yourself," that it may be your norm, and you will see your self-love purged away. Thus the servant will not only look to his pay, but if he is a Christian he ought to be moved to say: "I will not serve only so that my master will give me something or not give it, but because the Word of God says to me, 'Servants, obey your masters,' " Eph. 6:5. This is truly a good work out of a pure heart. Thus under the ministration of the Word the heart must be affected in this way because God calls me to this ministration and commands that I diligently and faithfully obey it, and therefore for the sake of the Word I perform this from my heart. In this way the Word is the cause, the foundation, the font and origin of love and all good works. Likewise, although the righteousness of a good conscience cannot stand before God, yet we ought to have such a heart that we can comfort ourselves before God and say, "God has commanded and prescribed this and therefore from my heart I do it. Whatever I say and do has been commanded and ordered by God."

In his first *Disputation* regarding the statement of Paul in Romans 3, Luther says, "When we have Christ, we easily condemn laws and yet do all things rightly. Indeed we shall make a new Decalog, as Paul says throughout all his epistles, and Peter also, and particularly Christ in the Gospel. Yet because we live with an iniquitous spirit and the flesh is lusting against the Spirit, it is necessary also, because of these erring spirits, that we cling to the sure commands and writings of the apostles, so that the church is not torn up, for we are not all apostles."[31]

In his explanation of the Epistle for the 19th Sunday after Trinity, Ephesians 4 [*Weimar Ausgabe*, 22.311–12], where Paul is clearly coming to his exhortations to good works on the basis of the Fifth, the Seventh, and the Eighth Commandments, Luther at great length confirms this position we are maintaining. We shall cite some of his words: "Those who willingly hear the Word of God and intend to live according to it, yet must daily be admonished, so strong is the old sinful flesh. For this reason there is great need for preaching in the church, not only for the unlearned but particularly for those who know well how they should believe and live. Preachers are to awaken and admonish so that the hearers do not become lazy and sullen and weary. Thus Paul also gives this admonition so diligently to his Christian so that he may shine forth in all his actions. Everywhere he urges strongly that no one be so unwise that he does not know himself, or is so careless and forgetful that he does nothing voluntarily, but only by force. But he should know also that the Christian has

[31] Cannot locate this citation.

made a beginning, yet he is not nearly finished or perfect because he does not say or think anything perfectly. Indeed, it is enough that the doctrines be taught as to where the Spirit and faith are, from which comes the fruit of good works. For although the Spirit is there and is willing, the flesh is also still there which is weak and corrupt, through which the devil makes every effort, so that we must not allow the people to follow him; and we must urge that admonitions be given through God's Word for a godly life. God must act as a good father to His family and must not think that something will be performed because He has commanded once or twice what He wants done, or that He does not always need to exercise discipline and lay it on the backs of people. So also with us it has not yet come to the point that our flesh and blood leaps up with strength and a desire to do good works, things which please God, as the Spirit gladly wants us to do and faith knows. But when our faith gets to the point where it tries this and urges and pushes, even if it can scarcely produce it, then what happens is that a person wants this admonition and lets such encouragement help him to stand." I do not believe there is any need for more illustrations from Luther. For to the responsible reader these statements of the truth are sufficient.

But you say this: Others have gathered different statements from Luther which have a contrary thrust, such as we have cited above. I have repeated from time to time that I, along with many good people, am grieved that these statements, which can be easily explained, are industriously being spread abroad and discussed without the necessary explanation. That deserter Staphylus,[32] by his unique sycophant treachery, has proved to the papists that it was worthwhile to hire him to gnaw away at and distort statements from Luther by his deceptive ways of speaking. As a blind man he dulls the eyes of the blind with his obfuscation, as if Luther taught absurdities and was inconsistent both with himself and with the Augsburg Confession. His treachery is worthy of his rhetoric. But surely our people must not imitate him.

Quintilian says of Cicero, "He should know that he has reached the highest position in letters when Cicero pleases him." I am happy to say the same thing about Luther: "He should know that he has reached the highest position in theology when the writings of Luther please him." A young man should be invited to read good writings of this kind, but he should absolutely be deterred from, rather than invited to imitate, the trickery of this kind.

When I first read this discussion in pamphlets which were being circulated, it immediately came into my mind what Luther said in his German writing against the antinomians. Even if such statements are found in his writings, as

---

[32] Frederick Staphylus, 1512–64, Catholic who converted to Lutheranism and later returned to Rome. Became noted controversialist at Ingolstadt.

the antinomians allege, yet he is acting in an evil way who tries to attribute to Luther the idea that the Law or the teaching of the Decalog should be forbidden in the church of God, since he will see that actually Luther carefully encouraged the teaching of the Law in the church in his Catechism, his sermons, his hymns, his prayers, and finally even in pictures. Furthermore, in regard to this controversy let me say that when I see that Luther in the church treats the doctrine of the good works of the regenerate on the basis of the Law or the Decalog in his Catechism, his sermons, hymns which sounded in the churches every day, I do not believe that the true and genuine teaching of Luther is, that in the question of good works, the Law or the doctrine of the Decalog were not to be set forth to the regenerate, as we have just explained. Indeed, it is well-known from the Anabaptists that certain people have so perverted the teaching of both Scripture and Luther as to say that those who have been born again of the Spirit are not bound to the works which God with definite word has commanded, but are so free that whatever the Spirit suggests to them (as they imagine), even if it is beyond and even contrary to the commands of God, yet this is clearly and properly a good action. These people have also been called libertines, but they do harm both to Scripture and to Luther. There exists a book of prayers of Luther [Amer. Ed., 43.200] in which, among other things, he prescribes by his own example the rationale for exercising in these meditations the teaching of the Decalog on the part of the regenerate, that is to say, first we gain from them instructions as to what God in each of the individual commandments requires of us. Second, we add the giving of thanks. Third, we join to it our confession of sin, and, finally, we form prayers on the basis of the individual precepts. I am acquainted with this method of explaining the Decalog through the use of a meditation and I know that it is very profitable in the true practice of repentance.

Therefore in regard to the position of Luther there is no doubt. But what shall we reply to those statements which we have cited above as quoted from Luther? I confess that I am not entirely satisfied that someone, when he does not understand the occasions and reasons for Luther's speaking as he does, exclaims that this teaching of Luther is only a mere hyperbole and exaggeration. Rather, on the part of serious people it is worthy of careful study to seek out the understanding for this method of speaking. In regard to the statements of Luther cited in this locus, it is easy to establish the difference from those cited under the preceding questions. For he was contending against those who, when the Spirit of renewal was not present, wanted good works to be forced and compelled through the Law, and when because of the rigor of the Law, without true emotions of the mind, they do something and think that it is a good work. Therefore Luther, in opposition to these ideas, taught with Paul that "the fulfillment of the commandment is love," 1 Tim. 1:5, "from a pure heart," and not when they use power or legal force to compel obedience to the precepts of the Law, as this is more fully explained under the first question. To this point Luther correctly says, "The regenerate perform good works, not because the precept forces them, but because it pleases them to do so." In his book *On Monastic Vows* [Amer. Ed., 44.302] he argues that God does not will that the works commanded in the Law be performed only in external matters without any inner desires or with a reluctant and rebellious will. This he calls the works of the Law, the doctrine of the Law, and the letter of the Law. In regard to this opinion he says in this book, "Just as the works of the Law must be omitted, so also the doctrine of the law must be omitted." Again he says [ibid.], "The rationale for teaching the letter of the Law and its works is ungodly." I want this point to be carefully noted. For many statements of Luther can be correctly understood on the basis of this as to the sense in which they are spoken.

Second, Luther clearly says that the old man must be forced, oppressed, pushed, and compelled by the Law so that he not do evil, but the new man has the grace of renewal by which without coercion he begins to delight in the law of God.

Third, under the article of justification Luther teaches that the conscience must not be ensnared by the Law, and he says it with this meaning: Because the new man allows me only to cooperate with the Law. Further, Luther's statement is noteworthy on Galatians 4 [Amer. Ed., 26.365], "Outside of the locus on justification we must with Paul believe reverently regarding the Law and give it the highest praises, call it holy, righteous, good, spiritual, and divine. But it is otherwise in the locus on justification."

Fourth, Luther in many places discusses the civil or condemnatory use of the Law which it possesses and exercises among the unregenerate. It is clear that the civil use of the Law, which coerces the ungodly with threats and force to bring about external discipline aside from any true feeling of the mind, has no place among the regenerate insofar as they are regenerate. For the Spirit has already renewed the heart which begins to delight in the law of God, begins to will and to try to obey with the mind. Similarly, those who have been justified have been freed from the accusation and condemnation of the Law through faith for the sake of Christ. Now it is certain that because of the antinomians Paul calls the civil and political use of the Law "the Old Testament," "Moses," or "the ministration of the Law," 2 Cor. 3:7, 9, 14–15; 1 Tim. 1:9. Just as Paul correctly says in regard to this concept, "The Law was not given for a righteous man," 1 Tim. 1:9; and "The Law was done away," 2 Cor. 3:7; "We are dead to the Law," Rom. 7:6, so also Luther has much to say in regard to the idea that the righteous have no need for the Law insofar as they are righteous. But if someone should infer from this that therefore the Law for the regenerate must not be a norm for good works, then he is surely in error and has simply gotten his logic wrong.

Thus Luther says in his Preface to the books of the Old Testament [Amer. Ed., 35.244], "With the coming of Christ the Decalog ceased, not because it must no longer be set before us, but because the work and ministration of Moses ceased." This concept of Luther, along with the explanation added at this point in great detail, should be carefully studied in this controversy. Therefore the Law, insofar as we are dealing with the new obedience, does not apply to the regenerate with its heavy hand, so that "He who does not continue in all points of the Law is cursed," but as Luther says in regard to Psalm 51, "We want to keep the Decalog and set it forth, but in a larger context, that is, in the framework of the Gospel."[33]

Thus according to Luther's teaching the Law is not to be pushed upon the regenerate. However, in his *Disputat. 2 contra Antinomos* [*Weimar Ausgabe*, 39(1).349–50], he says, "The law, as it was before Christ, certainly accuses us, but under Christ the law has been satisfied through the remission of sins and then completely fulfilled through the Spirit. Thus after Christ it will remain fulfilled in the future life. Therefore the Law will never for all eternity be done away with, but it will remain either to be fulfilled by those who have been damned or remain already fulfilled among the blessed. Thus those disciples of Satan seem to think that the Law is temporal, something which had ceased under Christ as circumcision was." Again, Luther says on ch. 3 of Galatians [Amer. Ed., 26.202ff.], "They misuse the law, first, all the works-righteous and the hypocrites who dream that men are justified by the Law. They also misuse the Law who want Christians to be totally freed from it, as the sectarians hold; and when they voiced their opinions, they stirred up the revolt of the peasants. Today many of our people are also dreaming that Christian liberty is a license to the flesh to do whatever you want to do. Finally there are those who misuse the Law by failing to understand its terrors, which must only harden them toward Christ."

Fifth, in regard to the simile of the sun and the tree I make the same reply as I did previously: Luther had in mind, as he himself clearly shows in his book *On Monastic Vows*, those disputations which had been carried on by the scholastics on almost the same level as we see in Aristotle's *Ethica*, 2 [Nic. Eth., 2.1.1103a]. For example, Aristotle says that in those qualities which are in us by nature we have natural powers from which then proceed good actions, but in ethical virtues as well as in artistic abilities first actions precede and are multiplied, from which later on attitudes are developed. Thus Aristotle. Because the scholastics disputed in almost the same way in regard to the obedience of the regenerate,

---

[33] Cannot find this reference.

Luther is teaching that the heart cannot be renewed by the works of the Law and the actions of free choice, without the Holy Spirit, so that the works become good works. But first and above all we must be concerned that we receive the Holy Spirit who will renew our heart, and thus from within shall proceed good works, and we must not try through good works from the outside to seek the renewal of the will. In regard to this point Luther correctly says that he who attributes this ability to good works is blaspheming against the Holy Spirit, for it is His work alone to renew the heart. But there is a far different reason when the Holy Spirit writes the Law in the hearts of believers.

Sixth, because Luther says that the Christian is not bound to certain works but is indifferent to what kind he performs, we need to know the occasion for saying this. The monks were binding themselves by special peculiar vows and rules to certain works as being more outstanding, so that the other things which had been commanded in the Word of God, particularly in the Second Table, they were neglecting and even rejecting in their self-confidence. Luther is refuting this position in the words which we have already cited. But good men judge and lament the statement that the Christian can be indifferent as to which of the works he is to perform, when it is used out of context, as a generalization, without any explanation as to the occasion for saying it, and then spread abroad as it is among the people.

Further, there is a similar disputation about the Law in the writings of Augustine, and a comparison of the two will be helpful. In his *De Spiritu et Litera*, 10 [MPL 44.210], he says, "The unrighteous has a proper use for the Law as well as the righteous; but when he has used it in this way, he still is not using it as a vehicle to arrive at his destination, or rather as a teacher to instruct him." Why, therefore, has the Law not been given to the righteous, if it is also necessary for the righteous? He explains his statement in his *Contra Duas Epistolas Pelagianorum*, 3.4 [MPL 44.559], "Who is so ungodly as to say that he does not observe the moral precepts of the Law because he is a Christian and has been placed under grace and not under the Law? Certainly no one doubts that this law of God was to be established for right living not only for the people in those days but also for us now. But it is a far different thing when they who have been placed under the law do something by legal coercion and when we who have been placed under grace do it out of love." These statements of Augustine can be understood when we know the reasons for saying them; and I do not see why this should not be the case with the statements of Luther, unless perhaps we are afraid that then there will be no occasion for controversy. Certainly the very sad example of the libertarians among the Anabaptists and the terrible crimes which took place among them as a result of a warped understanding of freedom from the Law, that is, from the commandments of God, ought to warn us.

The Fourth Question

The doctrine and the term "liberty"

The doctrine of Christian liberty is one of the most important loci of the heavenly teaching, but we do not need at this point to give a complete treatment of it. We shall note only a few points concerning those aspects which properly pertain to this controversy.

First, therefore, the highest degree of Christian liberty is that by faith, freely, for the sake of the Son of God, we are freed from sin, from the wrath of God, from eternal damnation, from the accusations of the Law against us, and from merit as a condition. Even more has been set before us and given to us, on account of which we receive the remission of sins and are pronounced righteous, namely the Son of God our Mediator, not the Law, not our merit. Properly speaking, in this controversy this degree or grade of liberty is not in controversy.

But the question at issue is this: Whether and how in the substance of the doctrine of good works or the new obedience is there any room for the doctrine and even the word "liberty"? For it is certain that both the doctrine and the word "liberty" neither can nor must be excluded from the doctrine of the new obedience. For Philipp in his *Loci Communes* establishes the second grade or degree of Christian liberty as the giving of the Holy Spirit which kindles new light in the mind and new emotions in the will and the heart. He adds, "Although this second degree is joined with the first, yet for the sake of teaching we must distinguish between them, so that whenever we speak about liberation from the Law we understand not only the aid [of the Spirit] as Augustine often says, but also the free imputation of righteousness. Augustine in several places says that we have been freed from the Law, that is, we are helped by the gift of the Holy Spirit, so that we may obey the Law, and so that we do not rely on it in vain when we are forced by the Law." Thus Philipp.

Luther in his little book, *Christian Liberty*, [Amer. Ed., 31.349–50], says, "It is clear that faith is sufficient for the Christian man for everything, that he has no need for works in order to be justified; but if he does not need works, then he does not need the Law. And if he does not need the Law, he certainly is free from the Law, and it is true that 'the Law was not given for the righteous,' 1 Tim. 1:9. This is Christian liberty, our faith which acts, not that we may be sluggish or live an evil life, but a person does not need the law or works to obtain righteousness or salvation." Again he says [ibid., p. 356], "We are not free from works through faith in Christ, but from works-righteousness, that is, from the ridiculous presumption of seeking justification through works." In his *On Monastic Vows* [Amer. Ed., 44.298], he says, "The liberty of the Gospel is the liberty of conscience by which our conscience is freed from works, not that they should not be done but that there should be no trust in them." Again in the same work he says, "The pious conscience is free from all works, not from doing them, to be sure, but from their accusations and defenses."

Again in his book on Christian liberty, Luther often says that the works of the Decalog should be performed freely, by our spirit, in liberty, that works of liberty are performed by a free conscience, and their fruits are freely produced. Luther himself explains these expressions [ibid., p. 361]: "It is not the liberty of the Gospel to omit God's commandments. For through faith we do not destroy the Law but we establish it." But the term "liberty" means that there is no need for works to obtain righteousness and salvation. This is because things are not to be done out of love for our ease or glory or out of fear of punishment. But especially they are not to be done to seek and to produce righteousness, peace, satisfaction, remission of sins, and salvation. Luther says that this is doing works freely and gratis with a view only to divine blessing.

Luther also speaks in another way regarding liberty or the liberation from the Law which has important significance for this controversy. In his *Preface to the Epistle to the Romans* [Amer. Ed., 35.376] he says, "Liberty or the liberation from the Law is not the carnal liberty to do nothing, but it is a spiritual liberty which does not remove the Law but gives and offers what is required by the Law, namely that we obey the Law with love and delight without the coercion of the Law. For example, a person who owes a debt and is unable to pay it can be made free of his creditor in two ways: either the creditor himself can tear up the bill and demand no payment, or if a good man pays it for you and gives it to you or advances you the money by which you can satisfy the bill of the creditor. This second method Christ Himself used in freeing us from the Law." Likewise in *Epistola Dominicali*, on Gal. 4:3, he says that we were "kept in bondage, locked up under the Law," but it is a vastly different thing to observe the Law and to be in bondage to the Law. Thus faith makes us free from the prison of the Law, not that we may do evil, but that we may freely do the good which the Law compelled, that is, above and beyond, with joy and delight. He explains this by the use of a simile: He who is in prison can be liberated in two ways. First, if someone comes and physically tears down the prison so that he can go wherever he wishes. Second, if someone so adorns the prison and makes it such a pleasant place, he will change your mind and your intention, so that you do not want of leave, but you will prefer to stay there not as in a prison but as in paradise. Thus Christ liberates us from the Law spiritually, not by breaking or taking away the Law, but He changes our heart and thus makes the Law a delight to us, so that the new man exercises himself in it with joy and pleasure. Likewise in his explanation of the verse in the Gospel, "He leads his sheep and they follow him," John 10:27, Luther says, "Christian liberty is not that the sheep wander about freely without the care of the shepherd according to their own desires, but that they are no longer penned in and held in captivity under fear, terror, and the coercion of the Law, but with joy and delight they follow their shepherd. Likewise, we are not liberated so that we may do whatever pleases the flesh, but we have been delivered out of the prison of the Law, under which we were doing nothing good of our own free will." In another place he says, "We have been delivered from a will which is turned away, rebelling and opposed to the Law, and there has been given to us a new heart which delights in the law of God."

This is certainly Luther's teaching. Nor is it necessary to say that Luther used the word "liberty" with reference to the new obedience in an improper and infelicitous manner in regard to this point. But there is no doubt that in the church the "form of sound words" is properly used as it was stipulated by the Holy Spirit in Scripture. Philipp also confessed regarding the first and second degrees of liberty, as we have mentioned above, that the statement of Christ, "If the Son shall make you free, you shall be free indeed," John 8:36, must be understood in this sense. Paul in 2 Cor. 3:17, where he is dealing with the doctrine of the letter and the Spirit who writes in the hearts of the believers, v. 3, says, "Where the Spirit of the Lord is, there is liberty." In Rom. 7:6, where he is arguing that believers are dead to the Law and delivered from the Law, that we should serve in newness of the Spirit, not in the oldness of the letter," he uses the word "liberty." See James 1:25 and 2:12 which speak of "the law of liberty" with this meaning.

Therefore up to this point the word "Christian liberty" and the teaching related to it have this meaning and are used in this way and have this position in the doctrine of the new obedience of the regenerate. Augustine often uses the term "liberty" in his *De Spiritu et Litera*, which deals with the same subject.

But the position of others who not only are discussing this matter, to which we have just given our approval, but who have also shamefully removed the long accepted proposition that good works are necessary and have substituted in its place the liberty of the new obedience and that they can do good works as a matter of freedom, this position regarding the word "liberty" I cannot approve, and for three very important reasons:

First, because the antithesis itself clearly shows the importance of the matter. For when I say that good works are not necessary but a matter of freedom, then all sane people will ask: Who shall teach us to speak correctly and get us to make the proper confession, who shall make the proper decision as to the meaning of a precept as to whether it should be done or omitted? In the same way, when Augustine was speaking of traditions which were matters of adiaphora, he said, "This whole subject can be viewed in any way you wish." This meaning in this kind of antithetical statement was used also by Luther. He says in regard to Psalm 51 [Amer. Ed., 12.398], "Although the ceremonial laws are now matters either of liberty or they have been abrogated, yet under the Law they were not matters of liberty, but necessary." In his book *On Monastic Vows* [Amer. Ed., 44.273], he says, "Vows are not matters of faith if they arise from necessity and are perpetual, or if they are not matters of freedom as to whether they can be done or omitted." Again he says [ibid., pp. 310–11] in the same work, "Those works are free in the eyes of God which you do of necessity in the eyes of men. For God did not will that there be celibacy but ordained that it be a matter of freedom, and He did not will that anyone who marries is guilty of sin. The vow of chastity must include with it the freedom to be broken. I vow freely, that is, that I may be able to change my vow when it seems best." Luther was accustomed to speak this way when he was discussing the precepts and counsels. There is a very clear instance of this on ch. 3 of Genesis, "Man does not have the kind of liberty which enables him to do what God prescribes or not do it. For man is not free as it pertains to the commands of God, but he must obey the voice of God or sustain the sentence of death. But liberty belongs to those things which God does not command, in external functions. Man is free to sit at the table and eat a pear or an apple, to dress in white or in black. In such things he has a choice, and it is certain that the worship of God takes place out of free choice if we walk in faith."[34] It is useful to teach these points, but it is false, even blasphemous, in this kind of antithetical statement and explanation of the meaning to teach that the good works of the regenerate are free, that is, a matter of free choice. But it is a far different thing when Luther says in his book *Christian Liberty* [Amer. Ed., 31.363, cf. p. 356], "Those who assert that works are necessary for righteousness and salvation, have lost both their liberty and their faith."

Second, I am much impressed by the fact that I could not determine that those who were contending had established any difference between Christian liberty in moral works and liberty in adiaphora. For he who will set out to prove a liberty in the new obedience, brings in testimonies, such as 1 Corinthians 9 and 10, where it is clear that Paul is speaking of those things which are not commanded at all but a person can have a good conscience whether he does them or omits them. For Paul says, "I have the power, but I have not used it . . . whatever is set before you, eat it . . . for why is my liberty judged?" Note Gal. 2:4 where Paul speaks of the liberty regarding circumcision after Christ has been glorified. Luther says of this passage that it is not a controversy concerning the works of the Law but it concerns the necessity or liberty of the works of the Law. For after Christ came He abrogated the works of the Law in such a way that they can be regarded as matters of indifference. It is clear that in matters of adiaphora, aside

---

[34] We have been unable to locate this quotation.

from giving offense, there is the freedom to do or to omit or to do the very opposite, as Luther explains in his *On Monastic Vows* [Amer. Ed. 44.311]. On ch. 2 of
Galatians [Amer. Ed., 26.85] he says, "I do not prohibit the Jews from circumcision; I permit those who wish to be circumcised, as long as they do it with a free
conscience." Likewise [ibid., pp. 85–86], "Thus we leave it a matter of freedom
for each person to wear or not wear the cowl, to eat meat or be a vegetarian, as
long as he does it freely and without offense to conscience and with consideration for his brother and with an example of love, but not as a matter of faith."
Again [ibid., p. 92], "I shall eat, I shall drink, I shall wear the cowl, I shall do
whatever the pope wills, as long as he permits all these things to be matters of
liberty." The Augsburg Confession [28.54–56, Tappert, p. 90], under the heading of ecclesiastical power says, "Ecclesiastical ordinations are matters of such
freedom that it should not be judged a sin if they are broken without offending
others." Now let us use the title for these discussions, "Concerning the freedom of good works and the new obedience," and to this should be applied the
testimonies which deal with adiaphora which tie in with the approval of this
opinion, and let the reader judge whether it follows from this that the works
commanded of the regenerate in the Decalog are matters of freedom in the same
way that matters of adiaphora are, so that they may be done or omitted or we
may do even the contrary—it is all the same.

But these people shout that we are doing them an injustice, that they do
not believe this way, that we are eagerly causing confusion over things which
must be distinguished in order to overturn the doctrine of necessity and then
we shout that we are being injured! Rather, why do we not distinguish only the
degrees of liberty and teach more precisely what Christian liberty is in the case
of moral works and what it is in the case of adiaphora? Luther in *On Monastic
Vows* [Amer. Ed., 44.310] certainly made a very careful distinction on this point
when he said, "Whatever is not commanded by God or has been abrogated is
given in liberty." But in regard to the commandments of God he says [ibid., p.
298], "The freedom of the Gospel is not omitting the commandments of God;
we are not free from doing these works."

Third, in this controversy we must also carefully note that the word "liberty" was not correctly explained or understood and this gave occasion to those
among the Anabaptists who are called libertarians, to dream up for themselves
a liberty under which they were not bound to obey the commandments of the
Decalog, but were free to omit them and even do things contrary to them without sinning. This blasphemous figment doubtlessly arose from the fact that they
did not distinguish between the Christian liberty which pertains to works of
morality and that which applies to adiaphora. Immediately after the time of the
apostles the church was troubled over the use of the term "liberty." Irenaeus

[*Adv. Haer.*, 1.9, MPG 7.518–19] says that the Valentinians did everything in freedom because they believed that because of the redemption they would not go into judgment. In ch. 12 [ibid., 1.12 (23), MPG 7.671–72], Simon teaches those who put their hope in him and in Helen who accompanied him that they could do freely whatever they wished. For through his grace men are saved and not according to righteous works. For there are some righteous things and some unrighteous, not by nature but by accident, because the angels through the commandments have led men into servitude. These are the ancient seeds of antinomianism, and it is useful to be aware of them. Again in ch. 24 [MPG 7.680], the Carpocratians say that they have the authority to do all irreligious and ungodly acts. For it is only a matter of human opinion which makes us call some works evil and some good. Theodoret, in his *Compendium of the Notions of Heretics* [MPG 83.345], lists the blasphemies of Simon Magus and says that he ordered those who followed him not to pay any attention to the Law, not to fear its threats, but as free men to do whatever they wished. These are the very words of the antinomians.

Therefore it is appropriate that the church requires a clear and careful explanation of this matter. It disapproves carelessness and imprecision in the article and terminology of Christian liberty. The apostles surely would not have discussed Christian liberty in such a way as to show that they did not care how it was received by their hearers. Peter surely warns his hearers when he says, "As free men, do not use your liberty as a cloak of wickedness," 1 Peter 2:16. Paul in Gal. 5:13 says, "You have been called into liberty, but do not use your liberty for an occasion to the flesh, but by love serve one another." This same word "liberty" is not used in Scripture in only one way. For in regard to matters of adiaphora which are not mandated but can be omitted, the term is used in 1 Cor. 9:19 and Rom. 6:20 where Paul says, "When you were the servants of sin, you were free in regard to righteousness." The Greek proverb has it this way: "They were free from the fields." But certainly the regenerate are not free from good works in this way.

The Fifth Question

Is the new obedience of the regenerate a matter of something we owe or is it a matter of free choice?

Before we come to the words "necessary" and "owed," we shall speak of the subject itself which is designated and explained by these terms. For in the settlement of all controversies it is useful, first, to establish the correct understanding of the matter from the Word of God and to point out the antitheses, so that contrary and conflicting opinions may be disproved and condemned. For after we have done this the rationale for the terminology will be easier and better understood. This kind of care is more necessary, because the usual trick is that when a conflict appears imminent over the substance of a matter, then arguments arise over the ways of speaking. For as long as the majority of the people think that these are merely wars over words, they are less concerned and the machinations of our adversaries are less noticeable; and thus when the purity has been lost, corruptions are patched on to many articles of the heavenly doctrine, contrary to what had been expected.

In this controversy there is no more expeditious way and method for settling it than by demanding and setting forth a simple, plain, and unambiguous explanation of these matters. For in this way the clouds of sophistry regarding the methods of speaking can more easily be swept away. In a clear matter there is no need for a long explanation; and thus we shall briefly set forth the main points from the Word of God.

First, it is absolutely certain that God does not give to believers and the regenerate the license to indulge their lusts to the extent they can and dare to do so, or to conform themselves to the world, or to serve sin and the devil. In this way the article of redemption is nothing else than a privilege to indulge in shamelessness. The church would truly be a school for sin, 1 Thess. 4:7, "God has not called us unto uncleanness but unto holiness"; cf. Titus 2:11–12; Rom. 6:15; 3:8.

Second, this is also a certainty that God does not will that we be sluggish and without good works, as the householder says in Matt. 20:6, "Why do you stand here idle the whole day?" Note also the statement of the Baptist in Matt. 3:10. Christ also in Matt. 7:19 says, "Every tree which does not bring forth good fruit is cut down and cast into the fire." See also 2 Peter 1:8.

Third, there are also these statements of Scripture which are neither doubtful nor unclear: Titus 2:14, "Our Savior Jesus Christ gave Himself for us that He might redeem us from all iniquity and purify to Himself a people who are His own, zealous of good works"; and v. 11, "For the grace of God has appeared . . . teaching us that we should deny ungodliness and live soberly, righteously, and godly in this world." Also Eph. 2:10, "We are His workmanship, created in Christ Jesus unto good works, which God has prepared beforehand that we should walk in them"; 2 Cor. 5:15, "Christ died for all that they who live should not henceforth live unto themselves but unto Him who died for them and rose again." In brief, the entire Scripture is filled with statements of this kind, the sum of which David states in a few words in Ps. 34:14, "Depart from evil and do good." Rom. 6:6 and 1 Peter 2:1 sum it up this way: We should die to sin and live to God with righteousness, cf. Eph. 4:22; Rom. 13:12.

Fourth, God does not only counsel this new obedience, as the papists imagine, but it in no way is a matter of indifference to Him. Scripture says that it is the will and command of God that we who have been liberated shall serve Him in righteousness and holiness before His face. See 1 Thess. 4:3; Rom. 12:2; John 13:34; 1 John 4:21. Therefore I do not believe that the church will be persuaded of what a certain antinomian is spreading around, that what Christ and John call the commandment "to love" is a Hebraism, or perhaps a commandment is the same thing as free license.

Fifth, in no way has God willed that this obedience be a matter of free choice on the part of the regenerate, so that nothing which has been set forth has any reference to their arbitrary notions even in the article of renewal, so that it may be observed or omitted. But Scripture pronounces that the regenerate are debtors, they owe something. See Rom. 8:12; 1:14; 15:27; 13:7–8; Luke 17:10; John 13:14; 1 John 4:11.

However, we must distinguish between a debt which is a mere matter of the Law of which Paul speaks in Gal. 5:3, "He is a debtor to keep the whole Law," and the statement in Luke 13:4, where Christ wishes to point to the guilt and punishment for sin and there uses the term "debtors," cf. Matt. 18:34. For that debt for which the Law accuses and condemns us is forgiven for the sake of Christ by faith in the Gospel. When this debt has been forgiven, believers are not thereby absolved from the debt of giving obedience to God; but God ministers to them through the Spirit, so that they can make a beginning in the new obedience; and because in this new obedience they are still imperfect and unclean, for the sake of Christ He does not impute the debt, but forgives it. Therefore the debt of obedience on the part of the regenerate does not arise out of obligation to the Mosaic law, that is, out of the necessity of meriting righteousness, salvation, and eternal life, so that we are forced to be exposed to the accusation of the Law unto eternal condemnation if anything is lacking from our perfect fulfillment of it. For from this obligation of the Law, or from this debt Christ has redeemed us, Gal. 4:4, by being made under the Law and this debt has been forgiven to believers.

In the meantime there remains that immutable order that the creature owes to his Creator reverence and obedience, as it says in Ezek. 20:19, "I am the Lord your God; walk in My precepts"; cf. Matt. 1:6. Not only does this obligation remain in a general way, but many additional serious reasons for the debt have been added to the regenerate to bring about the new obedience. For example, God the Father loved us even before sending His Son "to reconcile the world unto Himself, not imputing our sins unto us," 2 Cor. 5:19. The Son gave Himself for us that He might redeem us from all iniquity. The Spirit has sanctified us; we are freed from sin that we might serve righteousness. "We have been buried with Christ through baptism into death, that we might walk in newness of life," Rom. 6:4. We must walk worthily of God, worthily of the Gospel, worthily of our calling. Later on, when we talk about the causes for our need to do good works, these points will have to be repeated and illustrated with many testimonies.

For the present, we must show that the regenerate are debtors and that the new obedience is not a matter of free choice but a debt and something which we must not simply assert; rather, we need to explain what kind of debt it is and whence the obligation arises, so that we do not nourish any Epicurean notions or again impose upon the believers "the broken rod of the oppressor," Is. 9:4. Therefore to all believers pertains what is said in the parable in Matt. 18:32, "I forgive you all the debt," and yet they are still debtors, as Paul explains in Rom. 6:18, "Having been made free from sin, you have been made the servants of righteousness"; to whom you show yourselves as servants unto obedience, "for you are the servants of him whom you obey," v. 16. The regenerate are instructed in Scripture regarding the debt through teaching, supplication, exhortations, and precepts. Note Titus 2:15, where after he has treated the entire subject of the good works of the redeemed, he concludes by saying, "Speak: these things and exhort and rebuke with all authority," cf. Titus 3:1; 1 Tim. 6:17ff.; 1 Thess. 4:11; 1 Tim. 4:11; 5:7; Col. 1:28; Rom. 12:1. Everywhere in Scripture statements like this are found which teach that it is not a matter of free choice or indifference whether or not those who have been reconciled follow after the new obedience. But this pertains to the question why we must perform good works.

We must also note that the new obedience in this life is insignificant, tired, imperfect, and impure on the part of the regenerate, and thus the reborn should not be comforted when, because of this imperfection, they are still tempted to think that God does not care about our works, because they are not necessary. Indeed, the Son of God commanded the apostles to pray every day, "Forgive us our trespasses."

These are the main points included under the common statement of the subject when we say that good works are necessary. These points we must retain in our minds firmly and unshakably. For contrary views are not only false but they are manifestly Valentinian, Carpocratian, indeed blasphemous. When there is a controversy about such serious matters, it is clear that this is not some useless war of words, nor must we agree that the noise has to do only with terminology, but there is a hidden and corrupt teaching involved here regarding these matters. We must seek a clear explanation of these things so that contrary opinions can be expressly rejected.

The Sixth Question

Is "the form of sound words" preserved in the commonly used statement: Good works are necessary?
All the churches which hold and confess the doctrine included in the

Augsburg Confession teach and set forth this doctrine which we have explained under the preceding question, using these commonly accepted points:

It is necessary to do good works.

Love and good works must necessarily follow reconciliation.

We must of necessity do the good works which have been commanded by God.

Good works are necessary.

It is necessary to do the good works commanded by God.

These points are found in the public confessions and are used in the writings of individuals, in lectures, in sermons. They also are found in those writings which contain "the form of sound doctrine" of our churches. When the correct explanation is added, the following propositions are taught in the church: Good works are necessary, not by the necessity of coercion nor because they are necessary for righteousness and salvation, but they are taught as being necessary in the sense that they are something we owe because of the will and command of God.

But by the use of these propositions the Antinomians, even while Luther was alive, from time to time tried to make war, but when they revealed their ideas they were repulsed and put down. In our time, however, the controversy has been renewed on the part of certain people. However, they do not simply now disapprove of these statements, but they have forbidden them to be used in the city of God by shameful names and ideas. For they call them absurd, pernicious, ungodly, most shameful dogmas, the murder of conscience, propositions which are inappropriate, illegitimate, adulterated, dangerous, scandalous, destructive of pious consciences, godless, blasphemies against the merit of the death and suffering of the Son of God.

This is certainly a monstrous charge against all the churches, schools, confessions, writings, and sermons in which these propositions have been accepted and used with a true and godly understanding. So great is their craving and madness for conflict against righteous men that they do not hesitate to vomit out this kind of obscene language: In the teaching of the Augsburg Confession and the Apology the authors of the Confession had reason for their time in history (but not for the sake of the truth) to speak as they did, but they had not given sufficient thought to the inconveniences they caused for future generations and the absurdities which would follow; and hence it came about that in the Confession statements were made which according to the clamor of these people are ungodly and pernicious. They dislike the great praise which all of these churches heap upon the Confession and that all these churches use these expressions in the true and godly sense. In fact, they do not fear to play shameful games with absolutely clear statements of Scripture. What Peter and the apostles say in Acts 5:29, "We must obey God rather than men," they pervert by saying that it does not pertain to those who are under grace but to those who are under the Law, as if only the ungodly and those who have not been reborn must obey God rather than men, although it is perfectly obvious that the apostles are speaking of their own obedience, and a comparison shows that the term "we must" does not mean some kind of coercion by force. For in Acts 4:19 the apostles make the same statement: "Whether it is just or right before God to heed men rather than God, you judge." The Augsburg Confession in Art. 16 [1–5, Tappert, pp. 37–38] expressly applies this statement to Christians.

Thus, what Paul says in Rom. 13:5, "It is necessary that you be subject to the magistrate not only because of his wrath but also for the sake of conscience," they pervert to mean that Paul is speaking only of civil necessity and of the consciences of other people who might take offense. Therefore, aside from the matter of offense, is it really not necessary, but only a matter of free choice, whether we shall obey the government? They saw that what is done for the sake of someone else's conscience in itself is a matter of liberty, and except for the matter of offense can freely be done or omitted without any wounding of one's own conscience, 1 Cor. 9:19 and 16:2. This interpretation is seditious, for Luther in a marginal note explains that this is not a matter only of the conscience of another person but of our own, because the government is "ordained by God."

But they say that these words are Law words: necessary, we must, we ought; and they mean that: something is forced out of unwilling and rebellious people by coercion. But they confess that faith is necessary, which of necessity must be voluntary. Thus they soon turn the argument against themselves and say that whatever is necessary unto salvation is necessary But Luther loudly replies in explaining the Gospel in Luke 10, "To eat and to drink are necessary; to sleep, to dress, to stay awake are necessary. But it is a different question when we ask what is necessary for salvation."[35] In his *Disputatio* of the year 1536 [*Weimar Ausgabe*, 39(1).214–15], he says, "Many things are necessary—a heart, a will, the Law, repentance, the tears of Peter, and so forth, but it does not follow that they are necessary for salvation." In his book *On Monastic Vows* he clearly repeats the same thing, as we shall note in citing some of his statements.

This argument is somewhat specious and requires an explanation, because Scripture does want the good works of the regenerate to take place not out of necessity but joyously and with a free will, 2 Cor. 9:7, "Let each give as he purposes in his heart, not grudgingly or out of necessity, for God loves a cheerful giver"; cf. Philemon 14; 1 Peter 5:2. Indeed, if Scripture used the word "necessity" only in this sense, the "form of sound words" would absolutely require

---

[35] Inadequate reference.

that the word "necessity" not be used in the church with reference to the new obedience of the regenerate in the church. Augustine has correctly said, "The philosophers use words which pertain to freedom, but since for us in the church it has been prescribed, we must speak according to a definite rule." In a short while we shall show that Scripture uses the words "necessity," "we must," and "we ought or owe," also when it is speaking of the works of the regenerate. Thus we cannot permit as a consequence the argument that Scripture when it uses the word "necessity" in the sense of coercion does not want us to speak of the works of the godly; therefore the use of this word must simply be condemned even if Scripture in other places and with another meaning does use the word with reference to the good works of the regenerate. But it correctly follows that therefore he is acting against Scripture who teaches that good works are necessary in the sense that although they are done with an unwilling and rebellious mind, without any inner desires prompted by the Spirit, nevertheless before God they are good works. This also correctly follows that to these words regarding necessity we must add a clear and simple explanation. For in Scripture the words are not used in only one sense but with certain definite meanings.

If those terms are used of good works, they are condemned in Gal. 2:16 and Acts 15:5, when they are taught as necessary for righteousness and salvation; likewise, when the term "necessity" signifies coercion which forces something external out of the unwilling, 2 Cor. 9:7; 1 Peter 5:2; Philemon 14.

The science of dialectics, to be sure, teaches us to distinguish and explain ambiguous usages. Thus it is not fitting that pious and learned men play games with these ambiguities in meaning and disturb and condemn all the churches with sharp and tragic controversies. There are many clear explanations that good works should be taught as necessary not for salvation, not out of coercion, but out of the necessity of the fact that we ought to do good because of the will and command of God. In this meaning Scripture uses the word "necessity" with reference to the obedience of the regenerate.

Therefore, whence and why have these outrageous and enormous perversions of this statement arisen and been used in all the churches regarding the true and godly explanation of it? Luther in one of his *Disputations* says, "It is a crime, when you know the godly and sound meaning of something to make an error by the use of badly chosen words; for heresy does not consist in the words but in the sense." Thus Jerome, when he was exasperated by his attackers, asked by what name we are to call the virulent disease of a statement in which nothing is said properly. But these are the words of Scripture, and they are spoken correctly and reverently. For we must absolutely maintain the rule of Luther: "In regard to sacred matters we must speak with the sound, sacred, sober words of the Holy Spirit, as given to us in Scripture."

Therefore it is certain, and no one must deny it, that the word "necessity" in Scripture is sometimes used to indicate coercion. It is also certain that in this meaning it is not correct to say that good works must be done out of necessity, that is, even if they are done by an unwilling and rebellious will without true inner emotions or desires, they still are good works. Nor do I know any sound person who believes and says such things. I do believe that it is worthy to note that Scripture, when it speaks of coercion, does not simply say that good works are not necessary, but they must not be done out of necessity, or according to necessity, or by force. Thus the fathers often in this way used the concept of "voluntary" in opposition to "necessity." Luther also, in regard to 2 Cor. 9:7, did not render it in his translation with "*auss Noht*" (out of necessity), as he had translated Rom. 13:5 with "*Seyd auss Noht unterthang*" (it is necessary to be obedient), but he translated it "*auss Zwang*" (out of compulsion). Thus he is distinguishing between "*auss Noht*" and "*auss Zwang*." And in 1 Peter 5:2 he has "*nicht gezwingen*" (not out of compulsion), and in Philemon 14 "*nicht genotiget sondern freywillig*" (not forced but out of a willing mind). In the German language there is a great difference when I say "*es ist nicht noht oder notig*" (it is not out of need or necessity) and when I say "*es ist nicht genotiget*" (it is not out of compulsion). I marvel at the fact that some of these people after they have beaten this proposition (good works are necessary) with various and frightful punishments, then will say in another place that they do not approve of saying that good works are not necessary. Thus these two contradictory precepts are both false in their dialectics. According to this interpretation, if something is necessary, it means that something is extorted from an unwilling and rebellious mind, it is certainly true that it is not a good work which is done in this way. But such an argument is so ridiculous in the face of the manifest truth that afterward, regardless of what methods it has used to pervert the accepted teaching on this point, yet our very ears would be horrified if such a notion that good works are not necessary were to be taught in the church. The reader should carefully note this point.

So much for these interpretations. I repeat that we must absolutely reject the dogma which says that good works are necessary for salvation. On the other hand we absolutely must teach that truly good works which are only acts of hypocrisy are devoid of true inner desires. These things have been taught, are being taught, and can be taught so that there is no need to pile up a body of teaching to show that the public confessions and all the churches which believe in a godly way and speak correctly, condemn such ideas.

It remains that we show in a few words that the true and godly statement which is used and correctly explained in all our churches is this: Good works are necessary, not for salvation, not out of the necessity of coercion, but necessary because of the will and command of God.

For when I wish to produce a meaningful statement with only one proposition and express this idea, then it comes out about like this: God does not permit those who have been reconciled freedom to be able to omit the works which have been divinely commanded or to commit that which is contrary to them, but it is the will and command of God that obedience to His commands be begun in this life. Negatively, the statement is this: The good works which have been divinely commanded of the regenerate are not matters of free choice, adiaphora, or indifference.

All right thinking and right speaking people acknowledge and admit that the antithesis to this proposition cannot be stated affirmatively more briefly and more appropriately and meaningfully than it has been used in all the churches, namely: "It is necessary to do the good works commanded by God; we must do the works which have been divinely prescribed; good works must of necessity follow reconciliation."

Scripture uses these terms in this sense and also teaches this doctrine concerning the good works of the regenerate. For when Paul says in Rom. 13:5, "It is necessary to be subject to the government, not only because of the wrath but also for conscience' sake," beyond all argument and despite all objections, it is certain and clear that Paul in this verse is in the area of good works. He is making a general statement regarding all good works, both of the regenerate and the unregenerate, when he says in v. 1, "Let every soul be subject to the government." Yet he is clearly showing in this passage to whom he is giving this instruction regarding good works, that is, those who have love and a good conscience, and these people are certainly regenerate. Thus Paul even regarding the works of the regenerate uses the word "necessity." In this statement of Paul we should note both the use and the explanation of the word "necessity" as it pertains to the works of the regenerate. For just as he speaks in a general way regarding giving obedience to the civil government on the part of both the regenerate and the unregenerate, so he gives two reasons for the necessity of this obedience, namely wrath and conscience. Therefore the unregenerate are subject to the government out of necessity and with an unwilling mind, and only because they fear the wrath and sword of the magistrate. They would act far differently if they could do so with impunity. But he wills that the regenerate "for the sake of conscience," even if they do not have to fear the wrath of the magistrate, are to give obedience, that is, that the conscience may recognize that because of the command and ordinance of God it is obligated to render obedience, and therefore willing and out of a willing mind does so without coercion. This is the difference between the obedience given to the government by the regenerate and the unregenerate. In regard to the forced obedience of the unregenerate, the statement of Paul in the other passage applies, because this obedience takes place out of necessity, is not voluntary, and is not a good work.

Now the question is this: In regard to the obedience of the regenerate which is presented from the heart for the sake of conscience, is it correct to use the term "necessity"? Certain people deny this with great vehemence and rhetoric. But Paul says very simply, "It is necessary to obey the government, not only because of wrath, but for conscience' sake," something which describes the regenerate. Therefore does this mean that the method, the reason, the cause for this necessity for obedience is the same in the regenerate and the unregenerate? The answer is "NO," for the fear of punishment is what lays necessity upon the unregenerate, so that even with an unwilling mind, they are still forced to be in subjection. But the regenerate render obedience to the government out of a willing mind.

Because this obedience of the regenerate is not a matter of free choice or an adiaphoron, but something they owe, Paul gives it the name "necessity." In what sense he wishes the term "necessity" to be understood he very nicely explains in the context. For in a short time he is going to explain what he means by "subjection," when he says in v. 7 of Romans 13, "Render to the government tribute, fear, and honor." He calls this "their due." Therefore to Paul in this passage "necessity" means that which we owe or is due. The reason for this, whether we call it necessity or a debt, can be determined from the context, for when he says, "because it is necessary to obey," the particle *dio* (because) in v. 5 refers to the statement which precedes in v. 1, "because the powers that be are ordained of God," and in v. 4, "the minister of God." Therefore there is a necessity or an obligation to obey for the sake of conscience, because of the following reasons: (1) the conscience is obligated to obedience because of the command and ordinance of God; and (2) because in matters of adiaphora, except for the sake of scandal, there is no sin, and the conscience is not harmed, whether such things are done or not, but in those matters which are necessary because of the command and ordinance of God, their omission or violation does injure the conscience and cause shipwreck, 1 Tim. 1:19. I am only noting down the main points briefly which the reader may consider more fully. Thus there is in this passage of Paul both a confirmation and a statement of the traditional proposition that good works are necessary, and the context clearly shows that this explanation is not something new and strange but the natural, simple, and genuine meaning of the context.

There is a similar statement in 1 Cor. 9:16–17, "Even if I preach the Gospel, I have no reason for glorying, for necessity is upon me. Woe unto me, if I do not preach the Gospel. For if I do this willingly, I have my reward, but if unwillingly, it is still a position of trust which has been committed to me." They become very upset with this passage, as if Paul is attributing necessity only to those who are forced and do not willingly do the work of their ministry or calling. But the whole context of the passage shows that Paul is speaking of himself now in the regenerate state and he is speaking of the work of his ministry. Therefore it is correct to say that he is speaking of the works of the regenerate when he says, "Necessity is laid upon me." This passage shows the most beautiful explanation of this word "necessity," of which Paul is speaking. For when he says, "If I preach the Gospel, I have no reason for glorying, for necessity is laid upon me," he clearly is trying to state the point found in Luke 17:10, "When you have done all these things, say, 'We are still unprofitable servants, because we have done only what it was our duty to do.'" Therefore what Christ says, "It was our duty to do," this Paul renders by the words "necessity is laid upon me." Why he calls it "necessity" he explains in two ways: (1) Because "a duty or dispensation has been committed to me"; and (2) "Woe unto me if I do not preach the Gospel." Hence we can very correctly establish a definition of the term, as to what the word "necessity" means to Paul, when he uses the word "necessity" with reference to the works of the regenerate.

But the further contention that the word "necessity" must be restricted only to the second part of the passage (namely, "if I do this against my will") is proved to be false by the very context; for he states that the necessity of preaching the Gospel has been "laid upon" him, and he adds two options: "If I do this willingly," but "If I do this against my will." Thus "necessity" applies to both parts of the passage, and he even puts the reference to the voluntary aspect after the mention of the necessity. When he says, "If I do this willingly," the word "this" refers to the preceding general statement regarding "preaching the Gospel" which "necessity lays upon me . . . if I do this willingly." Therefore what has been divinely committed to us and must be done can take place in two ways, either voluntarily or with an unwilling mind. If these things are done with an unwilling mind, they are not truly good works. For God wills that they be done voluntarily. That this is the simple and true interpretation of this passage is clearly shown by the context. Again, therefore, we have apostolic confirmation and explanation for the additional understanding. Further, what Paul says in Acts 13:46 applies to this point, "It was necessary that the Word of God should be spoken to you Jews first," that is to say, it was necessary because of the ordinance and command of God.

Acts 15 deals with things which by their nature are matters of adiaphora, the practice of which the apostles for the time being, because of love, were not willing to make matters of free choice or liberty; but they commanded that the gentiles who had been converted abstain from them, as the apostolic council says in v. 28, "It seemed good to the Holy Spirit and to us to impose no greater burden upon you than these necessary things, that you abstain . . ." Now we are not arguing with the fact that these burdens for the time being had been imposed on the gentiles, but it suffices for us that the Holy Spirit and the apostles in the first and most famous council called this a necessity, because the council had certain reasons why this should be done and must not be omitted, that is, the apostolic synod put necessity in opposition to free choice or what was freely permitted. But there is added in the decree of the apostles also the reference to fornication. For the gentiles thought that promiscuous intermingling of the sexes was a matter of indifference which could be indulged in freely without sin or damage to the conscience. The Holy Spirit and the apostles opposed this notion by speaking thus: "It is necessary to abstain from fornication." These testimonies of Scripture most properly render and confirm the traditional proposition that good works are necessary. I pray that the reader will carefully consider that the point at issue in this council was: Are good works necessary to salvation? The apostles most seriously rejected this opinion at this synod. Yet they still made the decree that it is necessary to abstain from fornication.

The whole matter is perfectly clear, if we get rid of our desire to cavil. Therefore I shall not add any more than we find in the many other examples in Scripture where the word "necessity" does not mean coercion or that works are necessary for salvation, but simply that it has sure and serious reasons why something must not be omitted but done, as in 2 Cor. 9:2; Phil. 2:25; 1:24; Heb. 7:27; Jude 3; Luke 14:18.

Very commonly in Scripture the idea of the necessity of consequence is also used; Heb. 7:12, "With the change in the priesthood, of necessity there was also a change of the law"; cf. 9:16. Acts 13:46 means that God with a definite counsel has ordered or arranged and commanded, "It was necessary that the Word of God be preached first to you Jews." I do not see by what kind of quibbling anyone can get around this testimony. The second meaning, which indicated the necessity either of coercion or that good works are necessary for salvation, is seen in 1 Cor. 12:22, "The feebler members of the body are even more necessary"; cf. Titus 3:14. I have only called attention to these instances, in order that those who are taking a contrary position may see that they do not have reason for arguing that the word "necessity" in Scripture is used only for coercion or for that which is necessary for salvation. For they cite such passages as 1 Thess. 1:8, "it was not necessary to say anything to you"; 4:9, "It was not necessary to write to you"; 1 John 2:27, "You have no need that anyone teach you." This text does not have the word "necessity," but a different expression, "to have need." But to these people on the basis of a comparison of these passages which they are accustomed to cite to support their contention that it is permissible to follow their line of thinking, we can refer to Ecclus. 38:12, "His works are necessary." But the question here pertains to the word "necessity."

Furthermore, I have observed certain examples as to how and in what sense the word "necessity" is used in other languages and other areas of discussion. I believe there is no need to detain the reader with a long pilgrimage. Here is the status of the controversy: Is the traditional proposition that good works are necessary in keeping with the "form of sound words" which was set forth beforehand by the Holy Spirit in Scripture? This has already been clearly demonstrated, unless we might like to add the statement of Phormio, "Nothing has ever been said so well that it cannot be torn apart by wrong speaking." I only want to cite this one statement from Luther regarding Galatians 3 [Amer. Ed., 26.235], "God cannot deny His own nature, that is, He cannot not hate sin and sinners; and He does this of necessity. For otherwise He would be unjust and would love sin."

We must also add this consideration which can serve as a warning. The good works of the regenerate must be done out of a ready, a happy, a spontaneous and willing mind, as we said under the first question. But to this teaching regarding the word "necessity," because it seems to our ears to involve something unpleasant and contrary and thus can be judged not to be appropriate, I reply most simply that we must make our judgments not by our ears but by Scripture itself. For Paul speaks of what Augustine so eloquently calls "free servitude" when he joins together freedom and servitude in such passages as Rom. 6:18 and Gal. 5:13; just as Peter does in 1 Peter 2:16 where he joins freedom with subjections. Likewise, as we have been explaining, Paul shows that necessity is not in conflict with the readiness and joy of the will, for in Rom. 13:5 he calls the obedience of inferiors toward their superiors, which has been established by the ordinance of God, necessary, and yet in 1 Peter 2:16 the very same kind of obedience is described as "liberty." In Eph. 6:6–7 Paul calls the obedience of servants "doing the will of God from the heart, with good will doing service," while in v. 5 he had previously said, "Be obedient, with fear and trembling." In 1 Cor. 9:16 Paul says, "Necessity has been laid upon me to preach the Gospel," and yet right afterward in v. 17 he adds, "I do this willingly." In 1 Peter 5:2 in regard to the elders upon whom, according to Paul's statement, "The necessity has been laid to preach the Gospel," Peter writes, "Feed the flock, not under duress, but willingly." Thus also Rom. 6:18, "Being freed from sin, you became the servants of righteousness." Rom. 8:12 says in regard to those who did not receive the Spirit of bondage but of adoption, "We are debtors." Therefore good works are necessary, not only that they should take place but that they should take place in the way which has been described under the first question, that is, by the Spirit of liberty. For in Scripture under the true meaning of this term there is no conflict, as we have demonstrated: liberty and bondage, necessary and voluntary, but they are joined together as free bondage and voluntary necessity; and on the other hand freedom serves in love, and a ready will is bound to obedience by the necessity of the divine command. Nor should we submit these paradoxes to our own human cavilings, for Scripture has joined them together and ordered this arrangement. Thus this also is plain that in Scripture these two concepts are not in conflict with one another: The good works of the regenerate are necessary, and the good works of the regenerate are voluntary, but it is necessary that the good works of the regenerate be done voluntarily. For we have shown that Scripture speaks this way, and against the language of Scripture no cavilings are permitted.

I do not believe that there is need for a longer discussion, for the substance of the matter is clear, namely that the word "necessity" is sometimes used in Scripture with the idea of coercion and with reference to something necessary for salvation. In this sense Scripture disapproves, rejects, and condemns both the sense and the word "necessity" regarding the good works of the regenerate. But there are in Scripture many examples where "necessity" refers to a debt or an "obligation" because of the will and command of God, or that it is not a matter of free choice, but Scripture has definite and serious reasons why obedience must not be omitted but rather given. In this meaning Scripture uses the word "necessity" with reference to the good works of the regenerate. Thus, when this explanation has been added, it is true, godly, and in agreement with Scripture to say that the good works of the regenerate are necessary, not by the necessity of coercion nor that they are necessary for salvation, but by the necessity of a debt or an obligation for the sake of the will and command of God.

This statement is confirmed also by the fact that Scripture in the same subject matter uses synonymous or equivalent words, as in Rom. 8:12, "We are debtors"; 13:7, "Pay to all their dues." Among these "dues" there is not only a tribute but also fear and honor, cf. Luke 17:10; Matt. 18:33; 23:23, "These you ought to have done and not have left the other undone." This passage shows the explanation of the meaning of *dei*, "ought," that is, not by coercion, but simply that something ought not to have been omitted but done, cf. 1 Thess. 4:1; 1 Tim. 3:15; Titus 1:7. I cannot sufficiently marvel at the fact that anyone would stir up a controversy over this matter and these terms. But, someone says, it is the position of Luther that these expressions of the Law do not refer to the regenerate, such as, that the believer is obligated or ought to do good works, just as it is not correct to say that the sun ought to give light or a good tree ought to produce good fruit, or that three and seven ought to make 10.

I have often repeated that good men properly detest the arrogance of those who treat statements of Luther which both must and can be correctly and usefully explained in such a way that they do not hesitate to put them into opposition to the Augsburg Confession and even Scripture itself, so that when the Apology says that good works necessarily ought to follow reconciliation and when Scripture says that we ought to love one another, they put this opinion of Luther in opposition to it, and say that he not only spoke wrongly but foolishly, when rather they ought to be showing on what occasion and with what meaning Luther said these things. For he certainly had no intention of condemning the Augsburg Confession or trying to reform the language of the Holy Spirit, or to say that John was speaking foolishly when he said concerning the regenerate, "We ought to love one another," 1 John 4:11. But Luther himself adds the meaning of his expression, namely that he is speaking of something which we owe, which is certainly a legal term, which he calls a legal expression, for this debt has been forgiven us by the "cancellation of the record of our debt . . . which was nailed to the cross," Col. 2:14. Yet believers are debtors, as we have shown under the preceding question. Luther everywhere argues that true faith is not a snoring or sluggish quality, so that he who freely by faith for the sake of Christ has been truly justified is to be and remain without any renewal or good works, so that the newness of life must be brought in from the outside, as it were, by the coercion of the Law.

The nature or property of true faith is that it brings with it and receives the Holy Spirit, who renews the heart, and thus true faith is working through love. Thus Luther says in his *Disputatio 4 Contra Antinomos* [*Weimar Ausgabe*, 39(1).354], "Faith alone fulfills the Law; faith alone produces good works without the Law. Faith alone receives the remission of sins and willingly does good works through love." Thus it is true that after justification good works spontaneously follow, without the Law, that is, without the Law pushing or forcing. For it is just as Luther says in his *Disputatio de Operibus Legis et Gratiae*, "Man can do nothing alone by his own powers toward righteousness before God, but even when he is aided and instructed by the Law and works are forced out of him through the Law, he only becomes worse." In his *Prima Disputatio de Dicto Pauli Rom. 3* he explains this passage in several ways and says, "Even when we have been justified freely, we do not do the works, rather Christ Himself does all things in us, but if the works do not follow, it is certain that the faith in Christ does not dwell in our heart but it is dead, that is, a faith which relies on itself. We confess that works ought to follow faith, indeed they do not follow as a matter of obligation but they freely follow, just as a good tree does not produce good fruit as a matter of obligation but of its own free will. And just as good fruits do not make the tree good, so good works do not justify the person; but good works are done by a person even before he is justified through faith, just as good fruits are produced by a tree even before it is good by nature."[36]

Therefore, just as Luther says elsewhere, "Good works are necessary, but not by the necessity of compulsion but by the necessity of immutability or consequence." Thus Luther's expression is this: The faithful ought not to do good works by the debt of compulsion but by the debt of immutability or consequence. If these terms are explained, they can be understood and yet that which Scripture says remains absolutely unchanged: We are debtors; we owe it that we love. We are obligated to show compassion. Luther himself in his Catechism often uses the word "debt" or "we ought," not only in the explanation of the Decalog, but also in his explanation of the Creed. In his treatise on Christian liberty he says, "Faith redeems our conscience because we understand that our righteousness does not lie in our works, although good works cannot and ought not be absent."[37] On Psalm 51 [Amer. Ed., 12.365] he says, "That the new life ought to follow does not pertain to the matter of satisfaction but to obedience and what we owe." Again [ibid., p. 381], "Mortification, or the new obedience, ought to follow in the justified." On Galatians 2 he says [Amer. Ed., 26.16.9], "Works must be done as the fruits of righteousness, not that they may make us righteous. For as those who have been made righteous we ought to do these things, not that while unrighteous we may be made righteous through them." In his *Disputatio Contra Eccium* he speaks in opposition to the insanity of the papists regarding counsels, "Men are debtors to obey the will and precepts of God."[38] Therefore the word "debt" or "something owed" is commonly used by Luther with this meaning.

Therefore, because the proposition which we have just been discussing has so firm, clear, and solid a foundation in Scripture, it is used in public confessions, theological books, private writings, sermons, and lectures. This is so manifest and well known that our adversaries themselves openly admit that this statement is received and used in all the churches which adhere to the Augsburg Confession. It is worth the effort for godly people, for the sake of concord, to use the same language that the church does and we must reject that zeal for hairsplitting by which the formulas which have been received for good reasons and with true authority are being attacked and overturned. What arrogance it is to take unto oneself one or another kind of terminology so that as a result churches

---

[36] Cannot locate this quotation.

[37] This is not a direct quotation of the book but the theme of the entire treatise.

[38] While there are several *Disputationes contra Eccium*, we have not been able to locate this quotation.

which have a godly faith and speak correctly are condemned to loud disputes, not because of any ungodly or erring dogma but only because they are saying things which are in agreement with Scripture and express points which are really necessary and important and have been received by all!

Therefore I believe that the church must defend and retain this form of speaking also because of the antinomians and libertines, whose pernicious and blasphemous error makes the new obedience in the regenerate a matter of free choice. Certain people are agitating this question because once the language has been changed, they can more easily spread the seeds of their antinomian and libertine teaching. They can be rightly refuted.

But one of these people is saying that although all the churches do use this language, yet it actually is correct and proper to destroy this proposition because Luther did not want to speak this way and really disapproved of and condemned the idea. But for my part, even if I had no witness to the contrary, this would be sufficient, that while Luther was still living this statement was used by everyone. But Luther did not condemn the writings nor the teachers nor the churches; indeed, he was well acquainted with the Augsburg Confession and the Apology, in which this statement is repeated over and over again, and he gave highest praise to these documents and publicly commended the whole church.

Nor is it true that Luther in his writings shrank from using this terminology in the sense in which we have described it, for the matter of necessity to salvation and necessity of coercion are different areas of concern. In his *Disputatio Contra Eccium* [*Weimar Ausgabe*, 2.649, Art. 12], he says, "Eck knows that I do not believe that good works are not necessary." Again, regarding ch. 5 of Galatians [Amer. Ed., 27.62–63] he says, "It is difficult and risky to teach that we are justified by faith without works, and yet at the same time to demand that good works be done. For here, unless they are prudent dispensers of the mysteries of God who rightly know how to divide the word of truth, immediately faith and works are confused. Each locus, the doctrine of faith and the doctrine of works, must be carefully taught and inculcated, and yet in such a way that each retains its own sphere and limits. For otherwise, if works alone are taught, we fall back under the papacy and faith is lost; and if faith alone is taught, immediately carnal men go to sleep by thinking that works are not necessary."

In his book *On Monastic Vows* [Amer. Ed., 44.298] he argued strongly for these two points: (1) No works are necessary for righteousness, the remission of sins, or salvation. (2) Those things not commanded by God must not be done as matters of necessity but left in the area of freedom. Here he adds this statement, "The works of the law of God which are commanded in the Decalog do not justify, nor are they necessary for righteousness and salvation, since Paul says, 'By the works of the Law shall no flesh be justified,' yet they are necessary,

as Christ says in Matthew 18, 'If you wish to enter into life, keep the commandments.' " Note in what sense Luther affirms that good works are necessary, for
he adds [Ibid.], "For good works cannot be omitted, even when faith is present which alone justifies, since they are the fruit of justifying faith." Again he
says [Ibid.], "Those things which have been commanded are necessary as the
fruits of righteousness, even if they are not necessary for righteousness itself
which comes alone from faith. For it is not the freedom of the Gospel to be able
to omit the commandments of God." Throughout the entire book, in discussing the counsels and precepts, he says that freedom is one thing and necessity
another. Likewise in the Augsburg Confession [15.1, Tappert, p.36] they distinguish between adiaphora and necessary worship.

In his *Disputatio de Operibus Legis et Gratiae* [*Weimar Ausgabe*, 39(1).202]
Luther says, "All works are necessary, both of the Law and of grace." Later he
explains that the works of the Law are necessary in order to maintain external
discipline and peace, but the works of grace are necessary, as he also explains
[ibid., pp. 202–4], "Because the Law has not been abrogated so that it has become
nothing or that there is no obligation for acting in accordance with it. But the
justification by the Law must be fulfilled in us through the Son of God, as Paul
says in Romans 8. Therefore, even if we are justified apart from the Law and
the works of the Law, yet we do not live in faith without works." To this point
he also says regarding ch. 8 of Genesis [Amer. Ed., 2.114], "Noah did not sacrifice only out of his freedom, but it was also a necessity, and he did what he
did out of his calling." Again, "The righteousness of works is necessary, but not
out of the necessity of the Law or coercion but out of the free necessity of consequence or immutability."[39] On ch. 53 of Isaiah [Amer. Ed., 17.222] he says,
"We can permit good works to be commended and encouraged, as the necessary fruits of faith which have great rewards, also in eternal life, so long as the
merit of the suffering of Christ is not ascribed to them, for His suffering alone
takes away our sins, makes satisfaction for them, and gains reconciliation and
remission for us."

I do not think there is any need to cite more statements of Luther on this
point. For these will clearly show to the intelligent reader that Luther used the
accepted terminology on this subject, namely that good works are necessary,
and he also expressly disapproved of and condemned the contrary notion that
good works are not necessary. These testimonies also show in what sense Luther
taught that good works are necessary.

Therefore there is no true reason for rejecting this terminology. There are
many true and weighty reasons for defending it and retaining it in the church

---

[39] Cannot locate this statement.

in the correct sense. For the form of teaching in our churches, which is also included in the Augsburg Confession and the Apology, is to be preserved as a heritage, so that the freedom is not given to anyone to pervert this teaching with corrupt understanding or overturn it by unnecessary controversies. For true and appropriate is the simile of Philo that the body of the doctrine of the church is like a building, where, if a certain kind of cement was not used in the construction or was removed, the remaining mortar, although it did not immediately collapse but was considered to be strong and firm, yet where the process of giving way began, gradually the parts began to collapse and brought others with them, and thus the whole structure in various places begins to crack.

The Seventh Question

What are we to believe concerning those propositions which affirm this: To those who by faith have been justified, good works are so necessary to salvation that, just as through evil works no one can be saved, so also it is impossible for a person to be saved without good works?

The doctrine of good works must indeed be taught in the church, but so carefully that the purity of the article of justification is retained in complete integrity. For in this article, as Luther says on ch. 3 of Galatians [Amer. Ed., 26.282], are included all the articles of our faith; and if this article is kept intact, the rest are also safe; but if it is lost, the whole Christian doctrine is lost. Again, on ch. 2 of Galatians [ibid., p. 176], "I often say that there is no way to resist the sectarians except by this one article of Christian righteousness. For when this is lost, it is impossible to resist any other errors or schisms." Again, on ch. 2 of Galatians [ibid., p. 137] he says, "We grant that we must teach concerning good works and love, but at the proper point and time, that is, when it is a question of works apart from this principal article of justification. For the point at issue is this: By what are we justified and by what do we attain eternal life? Here we reply with Paul: Only by faith in Christ are we pronounced righteous and not by the works of the Law or by love. Not that we reject works or love, as our adversaries accuse us, but by means of the point at issue we want to overturn what Satan is trying to accomplish." Thus, when we are dealing with the common matter of justification, we reject and condemn works. For this locus does not bring forth or permit a discussion of good works. Therefore in this proposition we simply pass over all laws and all the works of the Law. Thus Luther.

Therefore, in this discussion concerning the necessity of the new obedience or good works, it is mandatory that we explain whether works are necessary to salvation, lest the doctrine of works be encouraged to the detriment of the article of justification. This is very important, because in our churches the controversy concerning the necessity of good works for salvation began to be stirred up at the most unfortunate time of the persecution, when the papists, during the stranglehold of the Interim, both by force and by guile were undermining the purity of the doctrine of our churches.

This controversy does not come from a sinful desire for dissension or a zeal for conflict over idle and meaningless questions or wars of words in regard to these propositions, but we are discussing this matter in order that the purity of the article of justification might stand and remain, that is, that the good works of the regenerate might be kept within their proper bounds and limits and remain as they have been delimited in Scripture, so that they are not mixed in with the article of justification.

However, the principles by which these propositions are to be judged will be entirely clear and will preserve the "form of sound doctrine or words," if we consider the distinction between Law and Gospel. The Gospel speaks of righteousness, salvation, and eternal life. The law of Moses clearly says in Deut. 30:19, "I have set before you life and death, blessing and cursing"; cf. Rom. 7:10. These statements must not be understood as applying only to the concerns of this life, for in Luke 10:25ff., when the scribe says, "What shall I do to gain eternal life?" Christ replies, "What is written in the Law . . . this do and you shall live."

Therefore, what is the difference between the doctrine of the Law and that of the Gospel? I reply: Various differences can be mentioned, but at this moment we are only discussing the question as to how the Law and the Gospel are directly contrary to one another. The Law sets forth righteousness, salvation, and eternal life, to be sure, but on the condition that "he who does these things shall live by them," Rom. 10:5; cf. Matt. 19:17; Luke 10:28; Rom. 2:13. Therefore it is the heart of the doctrine of the Law that good works are necessary for salvation, so that without them it is impossible for a person to be saved.

Because this is impossible for the Law in that "it was weak through the flesh," Rom. 8:3, and thus had become "the ministration" of sin, death, and condemnation, 2 Cor. 3:7, therefore the Gospel offers us righteousness, salvation, and eternal life apart from our works, freely, for the sake of the obedience of the Son of God our Mediator, to be received by faith alone, Rom. 4:5 and Gal. 3:22. This distinction between the Law and the Gospel Paul immediately establishes as being in diametric opposition, as in Romans 11, where he expressly speaks of salvation (for, v. 7ff., he says, "The rest were saved by the election of the grace of God") and affirms that these two entities, grace and works, are not compatible with one another (to use a popular term) in the article or work of justification and salvation, but that when one has been laid down, the other is excluded. For he says in v. 6, "If it is by grace, then it is no more of works; for otherwise grace is not grace. But if it is from works, then it is no longer grace; otherwise work would not be work." Thus there is a manifest confusion and corruption of the distinction between Law and Gospel and there is a clear conflict with Paul's doctrine when a person teaches that good works are necessary for salvation. This fundamental principle is sure, certain, and clear.

Our adversaries take exception and say that they are not speaking only of good works by themselves or of men who need to be justified, but of those who by faith have already been justified. Therefore the propositions, according to this interpretation, read this way: For those who by faith alone, freely, for the sake of the Son of God the Mediator have been justified, for those people good works are still necessary for salvation, so that it is impossible for a person to be saved without works, even if he has been justified by faith. If according to this interpretation we undertake an analysis or breakdown of these propositions, an evaluation of them will be clearer. For the righteousness of faith by this method of interpretation must be distinguished and separated from salvation and eternal life, so that we are justified, to be sure, without works, by faith alone, freely, for the sake of Christ, but yet not without works on our part. Therefore we are not justified and saved by the same thing. The exclusive expressions, "without works" and "not by works," according to this interpretation, will pertain to justification but not to the matter of salvation and eternal life. For these propositions say to those who have been justified that it is impossible for a person to be saved without good works, although they do concede that we are justified by faith without works.

When the point at issue is stated in this way, so that there is no alternative, then it is simple to evaluate. For Vicelius and certain others who desire to appear among the more moderate of the papists, plainly teach that the sinner and the ungodly persons who are lacking entirely in all good works are indeed justified without works, by faith alone, freely, for the sake of Christ; but it is another question in regard to their salvation and eternal life, for those who have been justified are not saved without good works by faith alone, but for those who have been justified, good works are necessary for salvation in addition to faith.

These statements should be examined in the light of the analogy of faith, and the matter will become clearer. For if it is established that we are justified indeed without works, but not saved without good works, then of necessity one or the other follows: either that Christ by His obedience promised us righteousness before God but not salvation, or that the promise of righteousness is received without works, by faith, but the promise of salvation and eternal life is not received without works, but by faith together with works, so that exclusionary expressions such as not "to salvation" but only "to justification" must be said to apply here. But this is wrong.

For Scripture, just as it rejects our works as meriting or causing our righteousness and salvation and attributes this to Christ alone, so also Scripture makes faith and not works the means by which this promise of righteousness and salvation is apprehended and received. It adds certain exclusionary expressions both to salvation as well as to righteousness, whether it is speaking of merit or of the application of merit, so that according to Scripture we are justified and saved by one and the same thing, and this must be said with reference to cause or merit or the application of this merit. Compare Gal. 3:11, "The just shall live by faith," but that which the law teaches, "He who does them shall live in them," is not of faith. Eph. 2:8, "By grace you have been saved, through faith, not of works"; cf. 2 Tim. 1:9; Titus 3:5–7; Rom. 4:6ff. describes the blessing, according to David's statement, of the man to whom God "imputes" righteousness without works.

Therefore the apostolic teaching is this: Just as we are justified without works, by faith, freely, for the sake of Christ the Mediator, so also we are saved without works, by faith, freely, for the sake of the Son of God the Mediator. As I said above, Paul in Rom. 11:5–6 speaks of salvation, "There is a remnant which is saved according to the election of grace." In this matter of salvation, Paul does not simply use only an exclusionary term, but he affirms that in the case of our salvation grace either excludes works or works exclude grace, for he says, "If it is by grace, then it is no longer by works; but if by works, then it is no more by grace." When we compare these apostolic principles with these propositions, it is manifest what our judgment must be. Or, is it the apostolic form of teaching to say that for those who have been justified by faith, good works are necessary for salvation, so that it is impossible for a person to be saved, even if he has been justified by faith, without works?

The false apostles in Galatians and Acts 15 certainly did not entirely proscribe faith in Christ from the article of justification and salvation, so as to remove faith and attribute justification and salvation to works alone. But their position was, as Luther reconstructs it in ch. 1 of Galatians, that in addition to faith in Christ they also insisted that the works of the divine law were necessary for salvation. Thus Luke in Acts 15:1 cites their words, "Unless you are circumcised and observe the law of Moses, you cannot be saved." This certainly means that it is impossible for a person to be saved without the observing of the Law. And in Gal. 3:3 Paul says, "Having begun by the Spirit, are you going to complete it with the works of the Law?" But in opposition to these statements Paul vigorously takes up the sword regarding this teaching and pronounces that this idea "makes vain the grace of God and that Christ has died in vain," if for justification and salvation in addition to faith in Christ we determine that works are necessary, Gal. 2:21. In Gal. 5:4 he states that for those who believe and teach this notion, "Christ is become of no effect and they have fallen from grace." Nor is this for Paul only a quarrel over words, but he gives serious reasons why he must remove and exclude the Law and works from the article of justification and salvation, cf. Rom. 4:16, "Therefore it is without works, by faith, that the promise might be sure according to grace." But what is this promise? Is it the promise of righteousness only? It certainly speaks in this passage also of the promise of the inheritance which would be made uncertain to us, if it were taught that in part the inheritance depended upon our works. Therefore, in order that the promise both of righteousness and salvation or the eternal inheritance might be sure and certain for believers, these propositions must be destroyed which affirm that good works are so necessary for salvation that it is impossible for a person to be saved without good works.

Nor is it true what they concoct when they say that although our good works are not necessary in order to merit or achieve salvation, yet they are necessary in order to retain and consummate our salvation. For the form of the apostolic doctrine, just as the beginning, so also the preservation and consummation or completion, the beginning, the middle, and the end of our righteousness and salvation, attribute to the grace of God, without our works, for the sake of Christ the Mediator, which is received, retained, and preserved by faith alone. Note Rom. 5:2, "Through faith we not only have access to grace, but by faith we also stand in this grace, and by faith we rejoice in the hope of the glory of God."

In this statement of Paul's position we have a description of the beginning, the middle, and the end, that is, the coming revelation of the glory of God. He is not saying one thing about justification, another about salvation, or that we receive salvation in one way and retain and preserve it in another. But he speaks only of faith and grace. Thus also in 1 Peter 1:5, we read, "We are kept by the power of God through faith unto salvation which is ready to be revealed in the last time." Please hear this: The preservation of our salvation until it is revealed in the last time is attributed to the power of God through faith. Compare Gal. 2:19–20, where Paul, who many years before had through faith received salvation, says, "I am dead to the Law . . . and the life which I now live in the flesh I live in faith in the Son of God"; cf. 1 Peter 1:9; Col. 1:22–23; 2:10. We can correctly apply here the statement of Paul in Rom. 4:16, cited above. But if the preservation and consummation of our salvation depends on our own implementation of the Law and on our own works, then faith is gone and the promise done away. Therefore, in order that the promise of salvation may remain firm, not only for the acceptance of it but also for its continuance, it must be without works, by faith, and according to grace. These fundamental principles demonstrate that the form of doctrine in these propositions is in no way apostolic, but rather that they present an opportunity either for despair or Pharisaic boasting.

It is clear from these many reasons that "the form of sound words" is not being observed in these propositions: (1) We have shown that the false apostles used the expressions that besides faith in Christ, the works of the law of God were necessary for salvation and that it was impossible for a person to be saved without observing the Law or without works. (2) Paul clearly says in Rom. 4:6–8, on the basis of David, "Blessed is the man to whom the Lord will impute righteousness without works." But these propositions clearly assert the contrary, namely, that it is impossible for any man to be blessed without good works. (3) The Augsburg Confession, Art. 6 [2–3, Tappert, p. 32], cites with approval the statement of Ambrose, "This has been established by God that he who believes in Christ is saved, without work, by faith alone, freely receiving the remission of sins." But these propositions on the contrary teach that he who by faith alone freely receives the remission of sins, that is, is justified, is not saved without good works. Therefore these statements are in conflict with the "form of sound words" as set forth in Scripture and the Augsburg Confession. (4) Luther very strongly in many places raises this question: What is necessary for righteousness, for salvation, and for life eternal? He clearly rejects and condemns these propositions. (5) The papists for over 40 years have waged war against the exclusionary concept regarding justification by faith alone, and have always raised the antithesis in opposition and in so many words, over and over again: Good works are necessary for salvation All the books of the adversaries are filled with such expressions, and if a person will look only at their notations, which they call marginal notes, and the warnings in these writings, he will see that this proposition concerning the necessity of good works for salvation is always and everywhere raised against the exclusive terms in the article of justification and eternal happiness. Now in public writings our adversaries boast that those who are using these statements regarding the necessity of works for salvation are willing little by little to depart from the teaching of Luther and to return to the bosom of the popish church in regard to the article of justification. (6) In the sect of the Anabaptists there was also this one article that good works are necessary for salvation, although we must not place our confidence in the merit of works. This Anabaptist position was publicly attacked and condemned by our people. The refutation appears in the writing of Menius against the Anabaptists, to which a preface by Luther has been added, cf. Tome 2, folio 326.[40] Luther, also, on ch. 22 of Genesis [Amer. Ed., 4.170], condemns and refutes their sophistry, when they say that although we demand works as necessary for salvation, yet we do not teach that one must trust in his works. Even the Münsterites rejected this statement, *"Dass der Glaube selig mache ohne gute Werck"* (faith makes holy without good works), and substituted one of their own, *"Dass der*

---

[40] We have been unable to locate this reference.

Glaube selig mache/aber nicht ohne gute Werck" (faith makes holy but not without good works). But Urbanus Rhegius refutes them very precisely. His reply is in Tome 2 of Luther's works, p. 443.[41] Stenckfeld to this day still contends that we must enter into life not by faith alone for the sake of the Son the Mediator, but through faith together with good works. (7) In the time of the Interim, when the more astute bishops saw that the doctrine of justification had been so well established and fortified by the Word of God in our churches that they had no hope of overturning it by one line of attack or of tearing it from the hearts of the pious, they insidiously argued for the proposition that good works are necessary for salvation. For they noticed that if we should permit or receive this statement, then the fall of the doctrine of gracious reconciliation would automatically follow. Since this concept came into controversy in our churches as a result of the poison of the popish Interim, the godly reader can determine for himself what he must judge in regard to it.

Thus, because in these statements neither the form of the apostolic doctrine nor the hypotyposis of sound words is preserved, it is correct to attack and disapprove of them. How necessary this is for the church can be judged from what has been said. We must reject these propositions because corruptions are being spread abroad asserting that for the completion of the gracious justification before God these two elements pertain and are required, namely the remission of sins and the renewal with its fruits. Again, they are saying that the application of the free promise, righteousness, and salvation takes place by both faith and the work of confession. Therefore we must reject all of these circumlocutions by which the essence of these propositions is insidiously retained and defended. This is particularly necessary in this discussion concerning the necessity of good works. For this doctrine must be taught in such a way that the purity and integrity of the article of justification remains in every way uncontaminated and unimpaired.

At the same time we must also carefully see to it that these discussions do not veer off beyond the boundaries of truth into the opposite direction and give support to Epicurean security. For Basil is correct in his warning that it often happens in arguments of this kind that the same thing that takes place in tree grafting often happens when men who are anxious to correct the direction in which a tree leans, often bend it too far in the opposite direction. In the churches it is not fair to attack only those points in which we err in one direction and meanwhile cover up those things which depart in the other direction from the form of the apostolic doctrine and sound words.

Therefore, when these statements concerning the necessity of works for

---

[41] Ibid.

salvation are rejected, it is necessary at the same time to add the caution that we do not set up an antithetical position, either expressly or tacitly, by some dissimulation which gives approval to the notion that a person who had already been justified by faith, if he later on gives in to his evil lusts, takes on, possesses, and retains the intention of sins and permits actions contrary to his conscience, and if there is no repentance, no change of the mind or the will for either the present or the future, such a person in no way is or remains righteous and saved, but he only is under the illusion that he believes that Christ died and rose again. This illusion is simply ungodly and false and must be removed; as Luther says in the Smalcald Articles [3.42, Tappert, p. 309] that there are many fanatics whom he calls raving, maniacs who imagine that those who have once received faith, remission of sins, and the Holy Spirit, even if they later permit lapses contrary to conscience, nevertheless remain in faith and such sins do not harm them. "And they also cry: Do what you wish. If you believe, it is of no account. Faith removes all sin." Thus Luther.

Therefore it is necessary in the church to proclaim this word of doctrine that those who have been justified, if later on they permit the rule of sin in their mortal body, so that they obey their evil lusts or in their external actions, knowingly and willingly, contrary to their conscience, rush headlong against the law of God when confronted by sin, do not retain their faith, but lose it and drive it away along with the Holy Spirit, grace, righteousness, and salvation, and bring down upon themselves the wrath of God and eternal punishments, unless they are again converted to God. For Paul says to those who have already been justified and born again, in Eph. 5:6 and Col. 3:6, "Let no one deceive you with empty words, for because of this the wrath of God comes upon the children of disobedience," cf. Gal. 5:21. In Rom. 8:13 regarding those whom "the law of the Spirit of life has freed in Christ Jesus from the law of sin and death," v. 2, he says, "If you live after the flesh, you shall die; but if through the Spirit you mortify the deeds of the body you shall live." The very sad lapses of many people testify to this same thing, as they are described in Scripture. I had in mind to say this, when first the controversy arose over these statements. But this argument has gone too far and these propositions do not restore the teaching of which we have been speaking, but, as it has been demonstrated, they conflict with both the form of the apostolic doctrine and with "the hypotyposis of sound words."

At this point we must make this explanation: David beforehand had been justified and blessed by faith, Rom. 4:6; but when he seized the wife of another man, it is a certainty that at that time he was neither justified nor blessed. Why did he not retain and possess his righteousness and salvation? Is it not that good works are necessary for righteousness and salvation and that it is impossible to be justified and saved without works? Paul with sure and strong voice denies this, as we have shown above. But just as Luther and the Apology of the Augsburg Confession explain this doctrine from the Word of God, David at the time when he laid hands on the other man's wife did not have righteousness and did not keep his salvation because he did not keep his faith, but he lost his faith and drove out the Holy Spirit. For where there is not a hatred but rather a desire for sin, there is no true repentance. Where the mind, the will, and the heart turn themselves away from Christ and God and are not concerned about deliverance from sin, but rather seek occasion for sinning, there it is certain that there is no true faith. True faith in Christ does not seek occasions or permission to sin, but seeks the remission of sin and deliverance from it. Likewise, where sin rules and there is no struggle against our corrupt desires, there it is certain that the Holy Spirit is not present. For "the Spirit struggles against the flesh," Gal. 5:17, and "the actions of the flesh must be put to death by the Spirit," Rom. 8:13. Therefore, where the Holy Spirit is not present, there there can be neither repentance nor faith. And faith does not remain in those who reject repentance, as the Apology states [20.13, Tappert, p. 228]. Furthermore, by faith we are justified, saved, and preserved unto eternal life. Thus if faith is lost, grace, righteousness, the remission of sins, salvation, and eternal life are not retained but also lost and driven away. Thus the Apology says regarding the statement in 2 Peter 1 [3.43, Tappert, p. 310], "Peter is speaking of the works which follow the remission of sins, and he is teaching why they must be performed, that is to say, 'that their calling may be certain,' [v. 10], that is, that they may not fall away from their calling by sinning again. Therefore he says, 'Do good works,' that you may continue in your calling, that the gifts of your calling may not be lost which were given to you previously, not because of the works which follow but which had already been retained by faith, and faith does not remain in those who lost the Holy Spirit and rejected repentance." Thus the Apology. And Luther in the Smalcald Articles says, "We must know and teach that when the saints fall into manifest sins, as David did, then faith has been lost and the Holy Spirit has been lost. For the Holy Spirit does not permit sin to rule, so that it may accomplish its goal, but He fights back, and when sin does as it wills, then the Holy Spirit and faith are not present."

Therefore true faith lays hold on Christ who is "the fulfillment of the Law unto righteousness to everyone who believes," Rom. 10:4, and there is "salvation in no other," Acts 4:12. True faith is not without works, James 2:17, but "is efficacious through love," Gal. 5:6. But because faith justifies and saves, it does not gain and possess from this that it produces good works and works through love, but because it lays hold on Christ who is our righteousness and salvation. But the next question is, by what testimony does it understand this and grasp whether faith is present, and is it a true faith, so that we are not deceived by a dead imitation of false faith? At this point it is correct to say that faith is alive and well which "works through love," Gal. 5:6. And "faith without works is dead," James 2:17. In this sense the Apology correctly notes [4.250–51, Tappert, p. 143], "Faith which is without good works does not justify." We must and can assert this, so that there be no departure from the boundaries set by the apostles in either direction. There must be this godly and reverent note of wisdom to all our posterity, that although at the Colloquy at Ratisbon, the proceedings stated that the sinner is justified through faith which works, yet our theologians upon the advice and urging of Luther were unwilling to accept this statement because of the obvious ambiguity involved. They said that the statement could easily be twisted to mean that the term "faith which works" or "a working faith" implies that a man is justified by faith together with works.

Further, it is not in keeping with "the form of sound words" received in our churches what certain people are arguing that when Paul says that believers are both justified and saved without works, we are not to understand this only in an exclusive sense that works are not meritorious, not a cause, not a form, not a part, not a means of application in the matter of our justification and salvation, but that the entire presence of good works is to be excluded so that they are not even present. For then it would follow that those who wanted to retain and preserve the accepted understanding concerning righteousness and salvation would have to avoid, beware of, and flee the very presence of good works. Because "faith without works is dead," it would follow that we are saved by a dead faith, or that when faith has been adorned with good works it could not justify or save, if the exclusionary expression should exclude the very presence of good works. But Paul appears to have adopted the example of the justification of Abraham with great care, and applied it not to the time when first he was called out of the idolatry of the Chaldeans, but to the time 10 years later, when he had been obedient to God through faith and had increased and endured in his obedience, as Heb. 11:8ff. shows. At the latter time Abraham's faith certainly had with it a heavenly multitude of very lovely virtues. But Paul, on the basis of Moses, poses the question as to how and why Abraham at the time when he was flourishing in virtues and good works was declared righteous and saved before God. And Paul's reply is, "It is not to him who works but to him who believes in Him who justifies the ungodly, that is, his faith is imputed to him for righteousness," Rom. 4:5. Again, "Blessed is the man to whom the Lord imputes righteousness without works," Rom. 4:6–8. In these passages the exclusionary expression does not exclude the actual presence of works, but it excludes only the fact that the works of Abraham were not meritorious, not a cause, not a part, not a means of the application whereby a man is righteous before God and saved, so that

Abraham, even at that time when he had the most outstanding good works, yet was justified in the eyes of God and saved without works.

Therefore Luther also translates it *"ohn zuthun der Werck"* (without perform-ing works). Again, *"Der nicht mit Wercken umbgehet"* (which happened without works). And on ch. 15 of Genesis [Amer. Ed., 3.24] he has this beautiful state-ment, "I know that the other virtues are notable gifts of God; I know that faith without these gifts does not exist. But the question is this: What is the property of each of these entities? You are holding in your hand various seeds, but I do not ask which is joined with which, but which are the powers proper to each. Here, say clearly what faith alone does, and not with what virtues it has been joined. For faith alone lays hold on the promise. This is entirely the work of faith alone; the other virtues have other concerns with which they deal." Again [ibid., pp. 25–26], "We know that faith is never alone, but brings with it a group of lovely virtues, but for this reason we are not to confuse things and attribute to the other virtues what belongs to faith alone. For faith is a kind of mother from which these other virtues are born as children; but unless faith is first present, love and the other virtues are not present either." And on ch. 3 of Galatians [Amer. Ed., 26.272–73] he says, "Faith always justifies and makes alive, and yet it does not remain by itself, that is, it is not idle. Not that it does not remain alone in carrying out its work or in its importance, for it alone always justifies; but it is not and does not remain idle or without love."

But these points can be explained simply and clearly by merely pointing out this distinction: (1) Abraham was established in his position while still in idolatry, Joshua 24:2. Paul in the very act of persecuting the church was laid hold on, and neither of these men was without good works. Thus the question is this: How were they justified? (2) David, who had been justified previously, took the wife of another man, lost his faith, the Holy Spirit, righteousness, sal-vation, and whatever good works he had. Ezek. 33:14, "When he turns again to God . . ." the question is this: How then is he justified? Abraham and Paul were in the very flower of their virtues and good works, as when Paul says, "I labored more abundantly than the others," 1 Cor. 15:10; and "I am not aware of anything against myself," 1 Cor. 4:4, and thus the question is this: Were they righteous and saved before God thereby? The papists restrict the exclusionary particles to only the first level; at the second level they require satisfactions, and at the third level they put the merit of worthiness (*meritum condigni*). But Paul in a simple way teaches that the only way of justification and salvation for gentiles and Jews is in the first conversion. After the fall of the Galatians and upon Abraham in the very flower of his good works, Paul pronounces Abraham as being accounted as righteous before God and saved without works, by faith, freely, because of the promised Seed, and not at that time only when he was first called out from idolatry and obviously had no good works, but also at that time when he was richly adorned with many beautiful works, he was accounted as righteous and saved without works, by faith, freely, for the sake of the Mediator.

By the use of this distinction of levels the argument can be easily understood and explained regarding the consequences and presence of good works. For the rule of Augustine is correct: "Good works do not precede the act of justification but follow in the one who is justified." Luther says, "Faith must first be implanted. For it is necessary that it be present before all good works, because it is the mother of good deeds." Therefore in this discussion we must beware of both extremes: that works are not mixed in with the article of justification and that the concept of a dead faith not be insinuated into men's minds. Thus Luther on ch. 2 of Galatians [Amer. Ed., 26.155] says, "We also say that faith without works is nothing and empty. By this the papists and the fanatics understand that faith apart from works does not justify, or that faith, if it does not have works, is not true faith and has no value. This is false. But faith without works, that is, a fanatic idea and mere vanity, the dream of the heart, is a false faith and does not justify."

Therefore it is false to say that faith, in order that it may receive and have the power or strength to justify and save, of necessity requires the presence of good works. For this is the essence of the "faith formed by love" of the papists. But the next question is this: How is true faith to be distinguished from dead and false faith? At this point it is certainly true that faith without works is dead. Urbanus Rhegius in his reply to the Anabaptists of Münster warns that these propositions must not be circulated in a bare or truncated form but explained accurately and corroborated: "Faith must involve no good work per se" (*Der Glaube möge keine gute Werck bei sich vertragen*). In the very useful little book on the forms of speaking carefully and without scandal, Urbanus criticizes those preachers who by using bare and incomplete statements, omitting the necessary explanation, tear down rather than build up, saying, for example, "Our good works are nothing. They accomplish nothing; they stink before God. He does not want them." I need the counsel and example of a man like this in this time of conflict, so that there may be a diminishing of the contentions.

There has been developed and spread around in the church in this time also this idea: The good works of the regenerate are evil and dangerous to salvation. I have seen many good and pious men shaking in horror both physically and spiritually when they read such a statement out of context and unexplained, that the good works of the regenerate are evil and pernicious, and not simply pernicious but dangerous to salvation itself. The refuse coming from this is the blasphemy of the antinomians that Christians need to beware more of doing good works than of doing evil. But they make the exception that they do not believe what the statement out of context seems to say. Why, then, cannot that which we believe correctly not be set forth clearly, explicitly, and plainly, so that it can be understood without ambiguity by the wise and the unlearned (as Paul says) without offense to godly ears? Or are we making fun of the church of God? For surely this statement in its bare form is not the "form of sound words" in our churches. There is a great difference between a statement taken out of context and a simple, straightforward statement. How easily they could set their ideas forth and explain them, so that they can be understood by all! They are unwilling to do this, but rather want to seek a cause for an argument, call it by whatever name you want to.

The true teaching is also the "form of sound words," namely that when to good works is added the idea of merit and trust in our own righteousness for salvation before God, when these ideas are mixed in with the article of justification, as if they are necessary for righteousness and salvation, so that without them, faith in laying hold on Christ cannot justify and save us; when, I say, good works are taught with this notion and are done with this idea, or when the question is this: How are we reconciled with God and received into eternal life, then Luther is correct when he says that good works are of no value and profit nothing, but rather are dangerous and harmful. This is the "form of sound words" taught in Scripture by the Holy Spirit Himself. For this point is repeated four times in one passage in Phil. 3:7–9, "What things were gain to me, those I reckoned as a loss for the sake of Christ . . . I count all things but loss for the knowledge of Christ for which I have suffered the loss of all things, that I may gain Christ," cf. Gal. 5:2–4; Is. 66:3; Rom. 9:31.

We must carefully note that Scripture does not put these expressions down in a bare and truncated condition, as if Christians, since they must beware of all things which are harmful and dangerous to their salvation, simply must beware of the most outstanding good works on the grounds that they are dangerous to salvation. But Scripture adds the plain and clear explanation as to when and how good works are a detriment, as, for example, in Phil. 3:4, 7, "Though I might have confidence in the flesh . . . this I counted as a detriment," Again, in vv. 8–9, ". . . for the knowledge of Christ, that I might be found in Him, not having my own righteousness . . . therefore I reckon all these things as a detriment," cf. Rom. 9:31–32; 11:7; Gal. 5:4; Is. 66:3. Therefore it is the "form of sound words" not to set forth and teach these points in their bare form and out of context, but with some explanation, so that they can be correctly understood. Thus Luther very explicitly teaches when, how, and with what line of reasoning works are dangerous. He says that he is speaking of that addition which he calls "Leviathan," when it is taught that works are necessary for righteousness and salvation.[42] The Apology says, "We do not condemn good works themselves. But we do condemn the idea of merit and confidence in the righteousness and salvation which looks to our good works." Luther on ch. 5 of Galatians [Amer. Ed., 27.10] says, "Paul is not dealing with the work itself and in itself, which without trust and the idea of righteousness is no hindrance, but he is dealing with the confidence and righteousness which is added to our work. For it is necessary that we understand Paul in keeping with the subject he is discussing." Likewise [ibid., p. 11], "He does not say that works in themselves are nothing, but that confidence in works and the righteousness of works are nothing. For this makes Christ of no avail." By the same line of reasoning we must and can clearly set forth the statement: Good works, if they are patched on to the article of justification or if they are done with the idea of merit and trust in our own righteousness and salvation by our own efforts, with this purpose, that we judge that we cannot be saved without them, at that time and in this way good works are pernicious and dangerous to salvation. It clearly can be seen and properly said that it is not the works themselves but a false concept and a false trust which are harmful and dangerous. But I see that Scripture speaks this way concerning works themselves, when it is avoiding this erroneous notion and rejecting it, for example, in Phil. 3:7; Gal. 5:4; and Is. 66:3.

Thus it is correct and in keeping with the "form of sound words" to teach and say these things, but it does not follow that good works in themselves are dangerous, and that thus we should assert without any explanation that the good works of the regenerate are harmful and dangerous to salvation. For, first, something else must be said concerning the works performed by the unregenerate apart from faith. Second, something else must be said regarding good works per se and considered without the remission of sins. Third, something else must be said regarding works when they impinge upon the article of justification and salvation. Fourth, outside of and beyond the article of justification, something else must be said which is quite different regarding the works of those who have been justified, when without any notion of merit and without any confidence for righteousness and salvation good works are performed and presented through the Holy Spirit in true humility, with full confession of our imperfection and in true faith, seeking to have our blemishes covered for the sake of Christ. Under these circumstances it certainly is not correct to say that the good works of the regenerate are harmful and dangerous, particularly that they are dangerous to salvation. For Paul in Phil. 1:28 says, "It is a clear token of our salvation, if we are faithful in times of persecution and willing to suffer" and persevere in our confession. Luther says that good works are a testimony of our faith and that we

---

[42] For detail on Leviathan compare Luther's *Lectures on Galatians*, Amer. Ed., 27.161.

have received salvation. Therefore good works are not dangerous to salvation. In the second German volume of the Wittenberg edition, folio 306, Luther cites a statement of the Anabaptists, "All our good works are not worth a penny."[43] It is a certainty that this statement can be better explained and defended than the other one which we quoted, but still Luther disapproves of it and rejects it because outside of the article of justification and salvation such a thing must not be said regarding the good works of the regenerate, works which God Himself works in us and which are far more outstanding than all the good works of this world. The careful reader can see the whole statement of Luther for himself, for he gives a great deal of instruction pertinent to this discussion. On ch. 3 of Galatians [Amer. Ed., 26.334] he says, "Except as it applies to our justification no one can sufficiently praise a good work. Or who can describe the usefulness and fruitfulness of one good work which a Christian does as a result of faith and in faith? For such a work is more precious than heaven and earth."

On the basis of these foundations it is possible to judge what we must assert regarding this proposition that the good works of the regenerate are harmful and dangerous to salvation. For it is absolutely necessary that in the church we use care to speak correctly, properly, and clearly about these important matters. For people's minds are disturbed when such statements are made by their teachers in a fuzzy and general way, learners are upset, the weak offended, and a pretext is given to the flesh for arrogance and license. Therefore we should believe and speak accurately and clearly so that we may edify the church under the blessing of the Holy Spirit. Note Augustine's excellent statement: "A person must keep his opinion but correct his tongue."

Luther under the article of justification teaches that works are not to be done before God for the purpose of righteousness and eternal salvation. Some people corrupt this statement by simply asserting that good works must not be done before God but only before our neighbor; or that they are not to be done for the sake of God but only for the sake of the neighbor. But, if this is the case, what shall we say about the inner works of the First Table? What shall we do with the well-known statement that we must love our neighbor for the sake of God? Will we not be permitted to follow the "form of sound words" given by the Holy Spirit in Scripture? For in many places it says these things, for example, Matt. 10:39; 1 Peter 2:13; 1 John 3:22; 1 Tim. 5:4; 2 Cor. 4:2; Luke 1:74. Surely the chief purpose of good works is to give honor and obedience to God. But where will this purpose remain if good works, aside from the article of justification, are not to be done for the sake of God and before God, but only for the sake of our neighbor and before him? But the next question is this: What is required in the sight

---

[43] Cannot locate this citation.

of God in the article of justification and salvation? These points can and must be set forth and explained, in order that we can avoid and resist both extremes which do not comply with the form of sound words. For in the church it is a false and dangerous error to make generalizations out of context.

The Eighth Question

Why must good works be performed?

It is not correct to say that it is entirely satisfactory for the regenerate to be ignorant of all the reasons for doing good works, or what causes them or results from them. For God certainly did not reveal them in His Word in such a way that it would be satisfactory to be ignorant of them; but He willed that that doctrine be repeated in many statements of Scripture, because it is a means and instrument through the hearing of which and the meditation on which He might stir up, kindle, preserve, confirm, increase, and cause to grow a zeal for the Spirit of renewal, or as Paul says, a zeal for good works in the hearts of the regenerate. What Paul says must remain in the church as ultimate truth, 2 Tim. 3:16, "All Scripture is given by inspiration of God and is useful for teaching, for reproof, for correction, for instruction in righteousness, that the man of God may be perfect, equipped unto all good works." Therefore we must love this part of the doctrine and teach it so that when we feel that the zeal for good works either is lacking in us or begins to grow weak or decrease, we may use it as that instrument through which it is a certainty that the Holy Spirit wills to work efficaciously in us and in others by instructing, encouraging, and causing us to meditate upon it.

In treating this part of the doctrine we must all the more carefully avoid the following: (1) that the causes, both impelling and final, for good works, in no way impinge on the article of free justification; (2) that we do not produce supercilious, Pharisaic pride which admires our own virtues and is unduly pleased with one's self because of our gifts, so that our conscience, because of these works or virtues, begins to grow drowsy and we despise others more than ourselves and seek and gain the applause of men. For it is far more necessary that there be a zeal for humility while we are on the very course and in the flower of our virtues or good works, so that the left hand as it cooperates does not know what the right is doing; so that when we have done all, we still may say, "We are unprofitable servants," who are debtors, and we have not acted perfectly or purely or with the whole heart, mind, and strength; just as the elect in Matt. 25:37 are not willing to acknowledge their good works before the tribunal of God, and when they stand before the whole congregation of men and of angels, they will be marvelously praised and commended by the Son of God Himself. There is a lovely description in Rev. 4:10–11 where the golden crowns are given to the 24 elders, but when they come before the One seated on the throne, as they are about to adore the One who lives forever, they throw down their crowns before the throne, saying, "You are worthy, Lord our God, to receive glory and honor and power. . . ."

With these words of instruction, it is correct and useful to teach that for these reasons we must perform good works. In this we must always repeat the word of Paul which is a means through which the Holy Spirit by teaching, warning, encouraging, testifying, reproving, and correcting . . . that the man of God may be prepared and established for every good work, 2 Tim. 3:16.

Therefore the Augsburg Confession says in Art. 6 and 20 [Tappert, pp. 31–32, 45], "Our people teach that it is necessary and obligatory to do the good works which have been commanded by God, not that we should put our trust in them to merit grace, but because of the will of God."

The Apology says [4.189, Tappert, p. 133], "Works are to be done because of God's command; likewise in order to exercise our faith; likewise for the sake of confession and giving thanks. For these reasons it is a matter of necessity that good works must be done."

Urbanus Rhegius in his book on the formulas[44] for careful speaking cites these reasons why good works must be done: Our good works are absolutely necessary, for they have this function: (1) They are the obedience which we owe to God and which has been commanded by Him because we as creatures owe this to our Creator. They are the giving of thanks for God's blessings and a sacrifice which is pleasing to God because of His personal faithfulness to us. (2) The heavenly Father is glorified in us through these works, Matt. 5:16. (3) Through good works our faith is exercised and moved so that it may increase and be nourished. (4) Good works are testimonies to our faith over against our neighbor, testimonies by which our neighbor is built up, provoked to imitate us, and helped in his need. (5) Through good works my calling is made certain. For when I love my neighbor and pour blessings upon him, I find that my faith is not false and that I am a Christian. (6) Our good works, even if they are immeasurable treasures, do not merit the remission of sins, justification, deliverance from death and the devil, for this alone Christ accomplishes; yet out of the free promise of God they do merit rewards both spiritual and temporal both in this life and in the life to come. Not that God owes us anything, but because He promises out of His mercy and is true to His word.

Philipp lists these reasons: (1) The necessity of paying the debt or obeying the command. (2) That faith and the Holy Spirit not be driven out. (3) The concern to ward off punishments. (4) The worthiness of our vocation, because

---

[44] *Formulae Caute Loquendi*, Wittenberg, 1535.

God accepts the obedience of believers for the sake of His Son and calls it a sacrifice, that is, the works by which God judges that He has received honor; and He adorns these works with the promise of rewards, both physical and spiritual, in this life and hereafter. (5) Because of the consensus of cause and effect, according to the statement, "Those who are led by the Spirit of God are the sons of God," Rom. 8:14.

From Luther we can gather these reasons: 1. In his *Postilla Maior de Festis*, folio 33, "God does not need our works, but yet it is His will that we present them to Him, as a service, because this is His good will, and He requires it."[45]

2. Ibidem, "Works must be performed, not that we thereby may merit heaven, but that we may be grateful to God our Father who has given us His Son."[46] In many places he teaches that the merits or benefits of Christ must invite us to show obedience to God.

3. In the spring sermon for the third Sunday after Easter, folio 68, he says, "The reason why we must do good works is properly our own need, lest we live according to the flesh and obey our base desires and lose our spiritual and eternal blessings. For our lusts contend against our soul."[47]

4. Ibidem, so that the name of God not be blasphemed, but that seeing our good works people may glorify God and thus the good works of the regenerate serve to advance the Gospel.[48]

5. The good works of the regenerate are testimonies to our faith and righteousness. Therefore, because many people devise for themselves an empty faith, Scripture teaches the doctrine of good works that it may demonstrate the outward difference between true faith and false faith. Just as false faith can be recognized and removed, thus James says in 2:17, "Faith without works is dead," that is, because the works do not follow the faith, it is a sure sign and testimony that faith is not present but a dead intellectualization and a dream. Therefore the righteousness of faith is not only recognized from the other works which follow faith, but also it is rendered certain for its own benefit, that it is true faith. For if works do not follow, it is a certainty that it is not true faith. Therefore let no one boast that he has life if he remains without love and the fruits of faith.

"For he who does not love remains in death," 1 John 3:14. Luther explains this passage at length in his *Postilla* in folios 164 and 247. In regard to the Second Epistle of Peter, 1:10, he says, "Our calling and election are indeed certain in

---

[45] Cannot locate this quotation.

[46] Ibid.

[47] Ibid.

[48] Ibid.

themselves, but in your own mind they are not yet firm. Therefore Peter wills that we make this calling and election sure by our good works."[49]

6. Luther in a great many places, on the basis of the consensus of cause and effect, urges us to perform good works, that is to say, it is the nature or property of faith, regeneration, the renewal of the Holy Spirit that faith of necessity produce good works.

7. He also gives this reason on ch. 17 of Genesis [Amer. Ed., 3.169–70], "Works do not make a person righteous, but a righteous person does righteous works; and yet the works demonstrate that faith is being exercised in doing them, and through them it increases and shines forth. For while Abraham showed his obedience, his faith is described as trusting in the promise of God who receives us. Thus Peter commands that we should make our election certain through good works. For they are a testimony that grace is working efficaciously in us and that we have been called and elected. On the other hand, a sluggish faith which does not exert itself dies and is quickly extinguished. Thus through the very works of repentance I come to understand that I am one of those who has been snatched from the burning of Babylon. In this way, even if this obedience does not justify us, it still certifies and in a way illuminates so that our justification can be observed. Thus the Book of Revelation says, 'He who has been justified is still justified,' Rev. 22:11. For just as those who are busy with the works of unbelief become more and more unbelieving, and sin in a sense receives strength from this diligent exercise, so on the other hand those who are busy with godliness become stronger in faith by these activities, so that they establish as a matter of fact that they belong to the church." Thus Luther.

8. This statement is frequently found in Luther: Good works must be done in order that we may serve our neighbor, help him, and invite him to godliness.

These are the chief points regarding the reasons for good works which I have noted in Luther, to which perhaps others can be added. But I have noted these because I believe it is useful for the church that in this aspect of the doctrine we receive and preserve the sure, commonly used, and received form of teaching. But we must not create a war if someone lists a different set of reasons for good works, so long as the understanding be the same and the form of apostolic doctrine be preserved.

Furthermore it is useful always to keep in mind the chief passages of Scripture in which this doctrine (namely the reasons for doing good works) is contained. For there is a very sure reason which can neither err nor deceive, for setting forth and explaining why we should do good works, as Scripture teaches.

---

[49] Ibid.

These statements of Scripture can be divided into several different parts. Some speak of the impelling causes and others of the final causes for good works and others can be added and applied to the main points which we have already touched on.

I have noted in Luther, for the sake of brevity and easy memory, that the chief Scripture passages which speak of the reasons, both the causes and the effects, can be divided into three main categories which in turn can be further subdivided: (1) Certain passages speak of the reasons for good works as over against God Himself. (2) Certain speak with regard to the regenerate. (3) Certain speak with regard to the neighbor.

Luther demonstrates this very simple division. For he often says, "Good works must be performed to glorify God, to testify to our faith, and to serve our neighbor." I will not note all the passages of Scripture which apply to these points, but only certain ones which can be applied to the rest.

I. Therefore, in the first place, certain passages of Scripture speak of those reasons for good works as they apply to God Himself. These are numerous and varied and we shall note only the main ones:

1. There is the command of God. See John 15:12; 1 John 4:21; 1 Thess. 4:2; 2 Thess. 3:4.

2. There is the will of God. See 1 Thess. 4:3; 1 Peter 2:15. Even a child could set up a division here in keeping with the article of the Trinity.

3. God is our Father so that we should be His obedient sons. See 1 Peter 1:14, 17; 2 Cor. 6:17–18; 1 John 3:2–3; 4:11; Luke 1:74; 1 Thess. 4:7.

4. "The Son of God gave Himself for us, in order that He might redeem us from all iniquity and purify for Himself a peculiar people, zealous of good works," Titus 2:14; cf. 1 Peter 2:24; 1:18; 2 Cor. 5:15; Eph. 2:10; Rom. 6:4.

5. Good works are "the fruit of the Holy Spirit," Eph. 5:9, cf. Gal. 5:25; Eph. 4:30; 1 Thess. 4:8; Rom. 8:14.

6. That God may be glorified through our good works, Phil. 1:11; 1 Peter 4:11; Matt. 5:16.

7. That we may be "imitators of God," Eph. 5:1ff.; 1 John 2:6; 1 Peter 2:21; Eph. 4:32; Col. 3:13; Rom. 15:7.

8. Here is pertinent also the statement in Col. 1:10, "Walk worthily of God"; cf. Phil. 1:27; 1 Tim. 6:1; Titus 2:10.

II. In the second place, certain statements of Scripture speak of the impelling and final causes or effects of good works which apply to the regenerate themselves.

1. Because they have been born again, therefore they must be new creatures. See Rom. 6:2, 16, 18; 7:6; 1 John 3:9; 2 Cor. 5:17.

2. Because they are the sons of light therefore they are not like the gentiles

who walk in darkness, cf. Eph. 5:8, 11; 4:1; 1 Cor. 6:11; Rom. 12:2; Eph. 4:17; 1 Thess. 4:5; 1 Peter 1:14.

3. That the regenerate might have a witness to the fact that their faith is genuine and that it has been accepted by God unto righteousness and salvation, cf. 1 John 4:7, 12, 16; 2 Peter 1:8, 10; Matt. 7:16; Gal. 5:6.

4. So that they can lay aside an imaginary and dead faith and see clearly so that they can avoid this kind of faith and not deceive themselves; cf. 2 Peter 1:9; 1 John 3:6, 14. Herein are manifest the sons of God and the sons of the devil, cf. 1 John 2:4; 1 Tim. 5:8; James 1:22, 26; Matt. 7:26; James 2:17.

5. So that faith not be cut off, the Holy Spirit not lost, along with grace, righteousness, and salvation. See 1 Tim. 1:19; 2 Peter 2:11; 1 Tim. 5:8; 2 Peter 1:9; Rom. 8:13; Col. 3:6; 1 Tim. 6:9; 2 Peter 2:20; Eph. 4:30; 1 Thess. 4:8. The very tragic example of David testifies to the same point, when he prays in Ps. 51:11, "Take not Your Holy Spirit from me."

6. Here are pertinent many passages which teach that we must beware of sin and must perform good works in order that we may avoid the punishments of God both for this life and the future, cf. 1 Cor. 6:10; Gal. 5:21; Eph. 5:5; Col. 3:6; 1 Thess. 4:6; Matt. 3:10; Luke 6:37–38; Matt. 22:7; 25:30; Ps. 89:31–32.

7. Likewise, the promises of rewards must arouse in the regenerate a zeal for well-doing. Hence we can understand how pleasing to God are the good works of the regenerate. Our works do not merit grace, righteousness, salvation, or eternal life; but they have other rewards both in this life and in the future, not out of the worthiness of our works but because of the grace of the promise. See 1 Tim. 4:8; 2 Cor. 5:10; Gal. 6:9; Eph. 6:8; 2 Tim. 4:8; Matt. 5:3, 12; 6:4; 10:32, 42; Mark 10:30; Matt. 25:21, 35; Luke 14:14; 6:38. But the complete teaching regarding the rewards for good works belongs to another locus.

III. In the third place, certain Scripture passages speak of the impelling and final causes of good works as over against our neighbor.

1. That the neighbor may be helped and served. See Luke 6:37–38; 14:13; Rom. 14:1; 1 John 3:16–18; Prov. 24:11.

2. That others may be invited to godliness by our example. See Matt. 5:16; 1 Peter 3:1.

3. That we give no one a cause for offense. See 1 Cor. 10:32; Phil. 2:15; Heb. 12:15.

4. That by blessing we may shut the mouth of our adversaries, cf. 1 Peter 2:12; 3:16; Titus 2:8.

I wanted to cite and distribute these Scripture passages in this way, for the doctrine of the cause of good works must be set forth in such a way that it can be included in these categories. And because in these statements of the causes, even when they have in them nothing improper or false or ungodly, one contends against the other, so that nothing can be said so carefully that it is not taken up in various derogatory ways, and the most simple and sure method is to set forth the doctrine in the very terms which Scripture itself uses.

Furthermore there were certain things at this point which had to be said in regard to this question. For those against whom we are here disputing confess indeed that we must not take away the true impelling and final causes from good works, yet they immediately add that it is alright if the regenerate are not aware of them. They add that it is wrong and improper to say that good works are necessary as things which have been commanded by God, as expressions of gratitude, in the way that an effect follows a cause. Again they argue that it is wrong and improper to say that good works are necessary for the glory of God and for the benefit of our neighbor. I do not think that they really believe what they are saying, but if anyone still does believe this way he clearly believes something ungodly. But if he believes one thing and says something else, I do not understand what kind of theology he has. But this I do know, that he does not have a fisherman's faith (as Ambrose so beautifully describes the simplicity of the apostolic faith) nor does he have the faith of the church, but rather a "craftiness," if we may call upon Paul in Eph. 4:14 for a name. Irenaeus says truthfully and accurately that it is proper for the church to believe and to speak the same way that it believes, but to fanatics he attributes the speech of monsters. . . . It is impossible to retain the purity of doctrine in the church without concern for speaking simply and properly.

To the extent that I am able to judge, these are the chief points in this controversy, and I have tried to explain them in simple fashion according to the norm of the "form of sound words," which is drawn from the Word of God and used in the Augsburg Confession, which even while Luther was still alive was used and accepted in all of our churches. For he who desires that this form of doctrine be overturned or upset, in my opinion departed from the simple language which I use. But if in handling this matter he misuses this treatment of the subject, the reader should know that he has given unworthy treatment to me. I pray God, the eternal Father of our Lord Jesus Christ, with my whole heart that He would heal the wounds of His church and rule us all by His Holy Spirit, so that we may believe the same thing and speak the same thing in our Lord, so that in our beloved Germany He may gather His eternal church in the simplicity and purity of His Word.

THE ARGUMENTS OF THE ADVERSARIES

[MELANCHTHON'S TEXT]

We teach plainly and clearly that there must be in man the knowledge of the articles of faith; likewise, that there must be contrition, good intention, and the beginning of love. Our adversaries contend against these points which we, however, confess must exist in man himself. And we say that faith must also be added, that is, confidence in the mercy of God, that for the sake of the Son of God we have remission of sins, but not because of our virtues. The adversaries, on the other hand, say this must be a matter of doubt and they add that you will have remission of sins when you are worthy, that is, because of your own virtues. They also devise the notion that men can satisfy the law of God.

But since we retain all the things which they demand, and want to add the faith which attributes His honor to Christ and which gives sure comfort to terrified minds, we certainly are not teaching anything ridiculous. Yet without cause they so savagely attack the concept that has been set forth in our churches regarding justification, which undoubtedly is the very essence of the Gospel and the consensus of the holy patriarchs, prophets, apostles, and all godly people in all ages who have brought light to this subject. All people have believed that there must be in us repentance and that good works must follow, but yet that the remission of sins is given for the sake of the Mediator and not because of our own worthiness and that we please God for the sake of the Mediator and that this takes place by faith, that is, by trust they call upon the mercy of God, do not flee from Him, and do not rage against Him. Therefore Paul often uses the particle "freely." Likewise Peter says in Acts 10:43, "To Him all the prophets give testimony, that through His name all who believe in Him receive the remission of sins." This consensus is the true witness of the church, and the experience of all the pious support this viewpoint. For our minds cannot without this comfort find rest in true contrition or in the midst of real terrors. For when these things are absolutely certain, no sane person in the church can contradict them.

But the monks have written otherwise because they did not distinguish between Law and Gospel and spoke of justification in the philosophic way. Particularly they cited the thinking of Plato and Aristotle, that Achilles was a brave man because he had strength and a certain divine power; and thus they said that Paul was a righteous man because of his virtues and the divine power, but they say nothing about the Mediator, the promises, the Gospel, of faith or trust in the Mediator; indeed, they command us to be in doubt about our reconciliation, that is, they command us to destroy the Gospel and the promise and to bury Christ. Therefore, as often as the argument about this subject comes into our minds, we should direct our eyes to this point: When it is actually and correctly said that repentance is necessary, and yet that we for the sake of the Son of God have remission, that we please God and that our prayers are heard, then we must attribute to the Son of God His honor; and in this faith or confidence in the promised mercy of God, I will call upon Him, as it is said, "Whatsoever you ask the Father in My name," that is, in trust in the Son, John 16:23; and again, "Through Him we have access to the Father," Rom. 5:2. And in order that there may be more eager instructors to refute the arguments of the adversaries, I shall cite and explain in order the principal points.

I

The word "righteousness" means obedience according to all the commandments: Faith of which we are speaking is properly not the work of all the commandments: Therefore we are not justified by faith.

I reply to the major premise this way:

The major premise is true, in regard to the righteousness of the Law, for the righteousness of the Law is properly obedience according to all the precepts. But because this corrupt nature does not satisfy the Law, therefore another thing has been revealed and given, which is our acceptance for the sake of the Son of God which is followed by the giving of the Holy Spirit. Therefore the word "righteousness" in the major premise means one thing and in the conclusion it means another. When Paul says in Rom. 3:28 that we "are justified by faith," he understands that by faith we obtain the remission of sins or the acceptance by God for the sake of the Mediator, freely, as he says in Rom. 4:3, "His faith was counted to him for righteousness." This explanation clearly shows that our position is not destroyed by this argument. Therefore we must carefully consider the sources. Many arguments have been developed by our adversaries by the judgment of reason or the Law, dealing with discipline, on which the eyes of all have been fixed, as Paul says, "Seeking to establish the Law of righteousness, they did not arrive at righteousness," Rom. 10:3, nor did they distinguish between Law and Gospel, nor notice that the Gospel in this question is not speaking of civil life but of reconciliation before God. These mysteries must be distinguished from our normal civil life in society. Therefore those who are careful students must dispel the darkness and the clouds, that is, the confusion of the Law and Gospel and the confusion of civil righteousness with reconciliation before God; and they must pay attention to the question which is under discussion.

II

It is impossible for knowledge alone to make a person just. Faith is the only knowledge: Therefore it is impossible to be made righteous by faith alone.

I shall first reply to the minor premise.

The word "faith" does not mean only knowledge, such as the devil possesses, of which James says, "The devils believe and tremble," James 2:19; but the word "faith" signifies knowledge in the mind and an assent to the promise concerning Christ, and in the will a trust by which the will desires and receives the offered mercy and rests in it. As when Cicero heard that safety had been promised to him by Caesar, knowledge followed in his mind and trust in his will by which he desired and received the offered kindness, and he remained content in this promise. Therefore faith is not only a knowledge but that trust, as we have said, by which the promise is laid hold upon; as the fourth chapter of Romans clearly testifies that faith is understood as that which accepts the promise which must be understood as trust in the mercy which has been given. But this argument also arises out of the imagination of our reason which always seeks some virtue of our own by which we should recognize that we are righteous, although in this situation it should not be said that we are righteous by faith, because the virtue in us is, in one way or another, such that we would have to conclude that there must be some virtue in us. But for this reason we say that we are justified by faith because faith lays hold on the promise and makes us understand that we have reconciliation for the sake of the Mediator.

Thus we must refute this argument that faith means trust: In trust there is love: Therefore we are righteous by love. I agree that in trust there is love and that there must be both this virtue and many others, but when we say that we are righteous by trust, this must not be understood to mean that we receive worthiness because of this virtue rather than through God's mercy for the sake of the Mediator, which must be laid hold on by faith. Therefore we make this correlative statement: Through mercy for the sake of the Son of God we have been reconciled to God, and it is necessary that this be received or established by faith, so that the will may find its rest in the propitiation which has been set forth.

Moreover the pious reader should understand how absurd and unworthy it is not to distinguish the faith of devils from that faith in which the church calls upon God, by which she approaches God and gains peace, as it says in Rom. 5:1–2. Likewise Rom. 10:11, "He who believes in Him shall not be ashamed"; Gal. 2:20, "I live by the faith in the Son of God." No one can fail to see how absurd a notion it would be if a person should believe regarding such passages that faith means nothing else than the kind of knowledge the devil has. For the knowledge of devils runs away from God, does not call upon Him nor draw near to Him. Thus the statement of James 2:19 that "the devils believe and tremble" is not to be confused with Paul's position. Paul is speaking of one kind of faith and James of another. And it is easy for a sane man to understand that the faith of the church which calls upon God is not like the faith of the devil who flees from Him.

III

"He who does not love remains in death." Therefore it is impossible to say that a person is righteous by faith alone.

I agree with the above if you understand that faith must not be alone. But it does not follow from this that love is the cause for the remission of sins, just as it is necessary to add patience to faith, but it does not follow that our patience is a cause of our remission of sins. The exclusive particle does not exclude our virtues from being present, but it does exclude them as being the cause of our reconciliation, and this *exclusionary idea does mean that the merit of Christ alone is the cause of our rec-onciliation. And we must also understand that it is necessary to remove our human imaginings from the righteousness of the Law which arises out of love for God. If human nature were without sin, it could truly love God, but because it is covered over with sin, it must first receive the remission of sins, and love cannot be kindled unless the remission of sins has been recognized and laid hold upon. And those who think that this can be received without the struggle of faith are thinking too weakly regarding the remission of sins.*

IV

We are righteous by faith: Faith is a work: Therefore we are righteous because of our works.

I reply to the major premise this way:

The major premise must be understood in a correlative sense: that is, we are righteous by faith, that is, through mercy for the sake of Christ we are righteous, not because faith is a virtue which merits the remission of sins by its own worthiness. But we must concede the expression which is added, that faith is a work. For it is a work, just as love, patience, and chastity. And just as these are weak and faltering, so faith is very uncertain and is upset by many doubts. Therefore we do not say that we are righteous by faith in the sense that this is a worthiness of such great power that it merits remission, but in the sense that there must be some instrument in us by which we lay hold upon our Mediator who intercedes for us, and on account of whom the eternal Father is favorable toward us.

V

We are righteous by grace: Grace is the love which is poured into the heart: Therefore we are righteous by infused love.

We must reply to the minor premise.

"Grace" in the proper sense of the word means free mercy or the free acceptance of us for the sake of Christ. For when it is said that through grace we have the remis-sion of sins, you must understand this to mean that because of the virtues which have been given to us we have the remission of sins, a statement which clearly over-turns the entire position of Paul and takes all true comfort from our consciences. For we must not look at our own qualities when we are troubled over the remission of our sins, but we must flee to our Mediator. In this struggle our hearts are also aided by the Holy Spirit, as Paul says, "He has given us the Spirit in whom we cry, 'Abba Father,'" Rom. 8:15, and He teaches us that the Holy Spirit is given to us in such a desire of faith, Gal. 3:14, "That we might receive the promise of the Spirit through faith." Therefore with this acceptance is joined the giving of the Holy Spirit, and yet it does not follow that we have reconciliation through these new virtues.

VI

It is impossible for us to know the will of God toward us: To believe that we are in grace is to affirm something regarding the will of God toward us: Therefore we seem to be affirming something impossible when we say that we must believe that we are in grace.

I reply:

The major premise is true regarding the will which has not been revealed through the Word of God. But it is certain in the Gospel that the Son of God has declared from the bosom of the eternal Father the command that we should affirm that God is favorable toward us for the sake of the Mediator. But the human mind, pressed down by the darkness of its nature, thinks under the rule of works-righteousness that that man is insane who affirms that he has a God who is favorable toward him. As over against these imaginings you should know that this is the Word which is given us in the Gospel, that the Son of God has been sent, and the promise given that we should believe in Him and affirm this fact.

But you say that the condition of the fulfillment of the Law has been added. I reply: Although repentance is necessary, yet the remission of sins does not depend on our worthiness, but is sure because of Christ. David after his fall repented and determined that he had truly been received back into grace upon hearing these words, "The Lord has put away your sin." The administration of the Gospel brings the same word to individuals who are repenting, and the commandment is immutable that we must believe in the Son of God. "Hear Him," Matt. 17:5. Therefore, although this statement seems absurd to the human mind, yet we should oppose the imaginings of our reason with the promise and command of God, so that we truly learn to call upon Him. For where this faith, which believes that we are received by God and heard by Him for the sake of our Mediator, is not present, then there is no worship. Therefore the doctrine which commands us to doubt is a heathen doctrine which takes away true worship.

VII

No one is pleasing to God unless he has new attitudes which have arisen from the Holy Spirit: No one can affirm that he has these attitudes because they can be virtues similar to those which come from human reason: Therefore no one can affirm that he pleases God.

The minor premise must be denied.

For although we must not make a determination regarding our reconciliation on the basis of our own attitudes but on the basis of the sure promise of God, yet when our heart is guided by faith in its fears and repentance, new spiritual desires truly are created by which in our prayers we cry, "Abba Father," and yet our trust fixes its eyes on the Mediator and not on our renewal. I always add this other point also *so that our will does not persevere in its desires contrary to conscience. For this reason John says in 1 John 3:21–22, "If our heart not condemn us, we have confidence in God that whatever we ask we shall receive from Him."*

VIII

The theological virtues, faith, hope, and love, are separate and distinct: If "faith" means "confidence," then it is the same as hope: Therefore the distinction of these virtues is lost.

I reply:

We confess that these virtues must always be joined together, and when we say that a man is justified by faith, we have already said above that this is to be understood in a correlative sense. It does not mean that we are righteous because of the worthiness of this virtue, but because of the Mediator. Therefore, just as faith differs from the other virtues because it is that which lays hold on and applies the promise to us, likewise it differs because it wills to receive the reconciliation which is present. But hope looks forward to the future deliverance. If we keep this in mind that we are saying that through the Mediator remission of sins is given to us, as all the godly certainly confess, then the explanation is easy and the way of avoiding these tricky points of casuistry is easy. If they include among the theological virtues that there is a need not only for knowledge, such as the devil himself has, but also faith by which we draw near to God and call upon Him in prayer, we, however, do not draw near in true sorrows if we judge that we must forever remain in doubt. For this doubt puts us to flight and creates hatred toward God, as it says in Romans 7 in regard to the sins which take place through the Law.

IX

Evil works merit eternal punishments: Therefore good works merit eternal life. The consequences seem to be valid because the points are contrary.

I reply:

The consequences would be valid, if the contrary points were completely comparable. Many things are completely in opposition to the law of God, and even when they are good they do not satisfy the law of God. For there remains in the saints a great weakness, even when there is no blemish in a person's outward obedience and there are many outstanding virtues present, as in Isaiah and other men. Yet there remain many inner evils, doubts in our prayer, many wicked drives, false confidence, and lack of trust. Likewise there are the specters which the devil raises to oppose us, to hinder our prayers, things which Paul calls "the fiery darts of the devil," Eph. 6:16, by which even those who excel in goodness are injured, so that they prefer to die rather than endure their wounds, as Paul complains in 2 Corinthians 12 about the thorn in the flesh which he had received from the devil; or note his words in Romans 7, "O wretched man that I am, who shall deliver me from the body of this death?" In these miseries the godly recognize their own weakness and see that they do not satisfy the law of God, that they are never without sin; and in this humiliation they take refuge in the One who has made propitiation. The hypocrites know nothing of such struggles for they dream that outward behavior is the fulfillment of the Law.

X

Sin is hatred of God: Therefore righteousness is love of God.

We must agree with the entire argument, but we also have to consider at the same time that these contrary points are not completely parallel. For our love is weak and still hindered by many spots and blemishes and, as I have said above, "the fiery darts of the devil" come upon us which also hinder our worship, as happened to Moses at the rock. Therefore our love does not satisfy the law of God, nor does it please God because of its own perfection, but our love pleases Him because of the Mediator, as said above.

Therefore, when they say that love is righteousness and therefore we are righteous by our love, the answer has to be this: This is the case if the expression "we are righteous" means that we have virtue, which, as the philosophers say, validates the consequences; but if the term means receiving the remission of sins, then it does not validate the consequences. For the term "righteousness" cannot be understood in the first statement as referring to something which merits the remission of sins, but as referring to a virtue, as if I should say: to pay a merchant is righteousness: therefore he who pays a merchant is righteous. Such lines of argumentation can be easily evaluated by thinking people.

XI

Righteousness is in the will: Faith is not in the will: Therefore we are not justified by faith.

The same point has been dealt with above by merely changing a few words, yet I am stating the case in this form in order that the learned may give the matter careful thought. First, we must deny the minor premise. For "faith" means to assent to the promise of God which is in the intellect, and with this assent there must of necessity be joined trust in our will which wills to receive the promise of reconciliation and rests in the Mediator who has been shown to us. For unless at the same time we will to receive and do receive the promise of reconciliation, flight and shame remain with us, and peace and quiet in our conscience and heart do not remain. Therefore by the term "faith" we embrace the Gospel and will to receive the promise which is offered.

Now, although this idea is displeasing to our adversaries who are contending sharply that by the term "faith" is understood nothing except the kind of knowledge that devils have, yet it is impossible for such knowledge to be in agreement with the statement, "Having been justified by faith we have peace," Rom. 5:1, or "He who believes in Him shall not be put to shame," Rom. 9:33.

Next, I want to give this warning again, which has been stated over and over again: The righteousness which is in us is in the will. But "to be justified" in this context means to obtain from God the remission of sins and acceptance unto eternal life. These things come to us for the sake of the Mediator who sits at the right hand of the eternal Father, but yet these blessings must be received by faith. And at the same time the Holy Spirit is given who begins in us new light and new virtues by which we subject ourselves to God and by which there is begun in us eternal life, as Christ says, John 17:3, "This is life eternal, that they might know You, the only true God, and that the Jesus whom You have sent is the Christ."

Some people imagine that we must be in a state of doubt concerning our reconciliation, and they say that a man is righteous by reason of his own virtues, but this is a heathen notion and they do not draw near to God in trust in the Mediator, since God does not want to be worshiped and is not willing to hear in any other way than by those who invoke Him through trust in the Mediator.

XII

James 2:24, "You see, therefore, that a man is justified by works and not by faith alone."

I reply without any sophistry:

It is evident that "faith" in this passage in James refers to the knowledge of the historical facts such as the damned also possess. For he says, v. 19, "The devils believe and tremble." Furthermore it must be confessed, and we do clearly confess, that a man is not righteous by this knowledge. But Paul, when he is speaking of faith, understands confidence in God's mercy which relies on the Mediator and for His sake receives reconciliation. Therefore we must understand "faith" in one sense in Paul, when he says in Rom. 10:10, "With the heart man believes unto righteousness," and in another way in James 2:19, where he says, "The devils believe." Therefore James is not in conflict with Paul but is speaking about something else and refuting the error of those who imagine that they are righteous on account of their profession of the dogmas, as this opinion can easily take over the minds of inexperienced men. In the same way the Jews imagined that they were righteous on account of their profession of their doctrine and their ceremonies. It is necessary to refute this error.

Nor does this refutation conflict with Paul, when James adds, "A man is justified by works," for he is speaking of the righteousness or works which Paul also proclaims with great emphasis as being necessary; but he denies that remission of sins is given on account of this righteousness. Therefore the word "to justify" should not be understood as being the equivalent of reconciliation, but as we have often said elsewhere, it means "to be approved." A man is justified by his works, that is, he has *a righteousness of works which is approved and which pleases God. That obedience is necessary in the reconciled and how it is pleasing to God has been said above. The person is not righteous or pleasing or accepted if he lacks this obedience and if sins against conscience remain. Therefore the statement that a man is obliged to have the righteousness of works must be confessed by us. But in the meantime the hearer must also learn some other things, namely that he does not receive the remission of sins because of his works, or that they are pleasing to God, for they do not satisfy His law, but they are pleasing only for the sake of the Mediator. It is clear that he must add these points.*

Thus it is very apparent that James is not disputing about the entire matter but has spoken about only one aspect; he is demanding the righteousness of works and refuting those who imagine that they are righteous merely on the basis of their profession. But with regard to reconciliation and how our imperfect obedience is pleasing to God—of this he does not speak at this point, but above in ch. 1:18 he alludes to this matter a little when he says, "Of His own will God begot us with the Word of truth, that we should be the first fruits of His creatures."

XIII

1 Cor. 13:2, "If I have all faith, but do not have love, I am nothing."

The reply to this is straightforward, easy, and clear: I grant the entire point. For we clearly affirm that love must be present, but it does not follow from this that we receive reconciliation on account of our love and that our love is pleasing to God on the grounds that it satisfies the Law. Indeed, love cannot exist unless faith precedes it, and it is by faith that we receive remission of sins and learn to recognize God's mercy and to determine that we have been accepted by God and are heard by Him. Thus love is kindled and the will subjects itself to God. But this love and subjection are still weak and still stained by many blemishes. Thus it is a far different thing that Christ has made propitiation and on account of Him a person determines that he has sure and certain reconciliation. We look to Him and not to our own qualities.

Thus both points are true: Love must be present and yet a person must have reconciliation on account of the Son of God. We can use this simple response to avoid longer quarrels when we see them coming. For here it is customary also to debate other points, such as, that "faith" means the gift of performing miracles or that "love" means only the love for our neighbor. But I am omitting these ideas, since they are already sufficiently clear.

XIV

Matt. 19:17, "If you wish to enter into life, keep the commandments." Therefore it is possible to satisfy the Law and our obedience merits eternal life.

I reply:

Our adversaries have established their errors by the use of this passage that man can satisfy the law of God and that the wickedness which is born with us is not an evil which is in conflict with the law of God and that because of our fulfillment of the law the price of our eternal life has been paid. These errors have arisen because they did not distinguish the Law from the Gospel. The Law requires complete obedience, and it promises life on the condition of complete obedience, as it has been said, "This do and you shall live," Gal. 3:12. But it is evident that no one satisfies the law of God, as Paul clearly testifies in Romans 7 and 8. Therefore we must compare the passages under discussion here with other statements which properly apply to the Gospel: Rom. 6:23, "The gift of God is eternal life through Christ." And John 6:40, "This is the will of Him who sent Me that everyone who believes in the Son shall have eternal life." This is a different voice from the statements of the Law which are to be interpreted out of the Gospel. For although there is a difference, yet the law is not abolished, but as Paul says, "We establish the Law through faith," Rom. 3:31. For although our weak nature does not satisfy the law of God, yet God wills for the sake of His Son to receive us and to make us heirs of eternal life, and this takes place through faith. And when we are received, then the new light and the new obedience do begin which are in agreement with the law of God. And although this beginning does not satisfy the law of God, yet it is pleasing to Him for the sake of the Mediator, as said above. Thus it is obligatory that the commandments of God be observed, and to this same point Paul says in Romans 3, "We establish the Law through faith," that is, when we are by faith grafted into Christ, our obedience is pleasing to Him and our love toward God is begun.

Therefore to all the words of the Law add the Gospel. "If you want to enter into life, keep the commandments," that is, according to the voice of the Gospel or according to the spirit which the Gospel adds. You cannot begin to love without a knowledge of Christ and without the Holy Spirit. Nor does our obedience please God because it satisfies the Law, but on account of the Mediator, and yet this beginning is necessary, as Paul says, "We are clothed with our heavenly body, and thus are not found naked," 1 Cor. 5:3. Likewise Christ says in Matt. 5:20, "Unless your righteousness exceeds that of the scribes and Pharisees, you shall not enter into the kingdom of heaven." The Pharisees were teaching outward discipline. But the voice of the Gospel which speaks of repentance adds more; the righteousness of the godly must abound and exceed in these six areas: repentance, faith, renewal of spirit, true worship, advancing in our calling, and contending against the devil. For this new light is the beginning of eternal life which is and will be the kind of life, the kind of wisdom and righteousness which the Law demands, that is, a full knowledge of God and pure love for Him. Therefore it is said in Jer. 31:33, "I will put My law into their hearts," that is, I will kindle true light and obedience unto salvation, which will be for them eternal wisdom and righteousness.

XV

Forgive and it will be forgiven you, Matt. 6:14: Therefore our forgiving spirit merits remission of sins.

I reply: This statement preaches of repentance, like many in the prophets: Is. 1:17–18, "Cease doing evil . . . though your sins be as scarlet, you shall be whiter than snow"; 58:7–8, "Break your bread to the hungry . . . and the glory of the Lord will gather around you." These and similar statements contain two parts: One is the word of command ordering us to change our ways and the other is the promise of the remission of sins. And now in regard to the promise we must listen to the Gospel. Isaiah does not say that we should cease doing evil things and remission will be given you because of your virtues. Indeed, in another passage he clearly says of Christ, "Truly He has borne our griefs," Is. 53:4.

Thus in this statement, "Forgive and it shall be forgiven you," the first part is a commandment. The second part contains the promise; but it is not added that because of your forgiving spirit your sins are remitted to you. But rather if this condition must be added, then the promise is rendered uncertain as one can easily understand. Thus, when we have heard the promise, then our mind should look at the teaching regarding the remission of sins which has been promised freely for the sake of Christ. It means that this work is required, namely our forgiving spirit, that just as our other works are pleasing to God, as said above, not because there is then no evil in our mind, but because the pious mind fights against evil desires and hatreds because of the commandment of God and for the sake of harmony in the church, and it knows that this behavior is pleasing to God because of Christ.

Almost the same idea is found in Dan. 4:27, "Free yourself from sins by righteousness and alms for the poor, and there will be a cleansing of your iniquities." The whole speech preaches repentance in which the first part demands a changing of ways and does not speak only of alms but of a complete conversion: "Free yourself from sins through righteousness," that is, become righteous, acknowledge the true God who has revealed Himself in His Word which He has given to His people Israel and promised remission of sins for the sake of the coming Lord. Then as a result your governing also becomes righteous; you should be diligent in your justice, prohibit evils, punish the delinquent, defend the upright, do not be cruel to the church and the people of God. And finally all duties of a fair and beneficial government are included, then he says, "give alms to the poor," that is, give benefits to the poor. This first part is the voice of the Law which commands concerning the conversion of the king.

The second part, "There will be a cleansing of your iniquities," is a promise which must be received by faith. Therefore when He makes the promise, He also requires faith by which we believe that God makes His promise through mercy, not because of our worthiness. Nor was this some fleeting instruction, for when the king inquired how Daniel knew the will of God and from whence he could affirm with certainty that sins were truly remitted, Daniel without the slightest hesitance explained the promise which had been given by God regarding the future liberation and also in regard to eternal life, and he showed that this promise also pertained to the gentiles. Therefore he did not command certain ceremonies in order that he might thereby signify that reconciliation is given not on account of the Law but on account of the promise.

Therefore, although this account in Daniel is brief, yet the promise of remission itself instructs the godly reader regarding the universal promise of reconciliation and eternal life. And the thoughtful reader will understand that the account in Daniel is in agreement with the Gospel. The first part deals with the precepts concerning the amending of one's life and the later part is the promise which must be received by faith, by which we are assured that we have been received by God's mercy. These points are clear and sure for pious people and are entirely free of sophistry. Nor am I using this story to support the notion that good works merit the remission of present sins, even if it is true that Daniel was not talking only of the remission of the penalties but first of the remission of guilt. But Scripture often speaks of the remission of present penalties, for example, "alms deliver from death," Tobit 4:11 and 12:9, that is, our alms-giving merits that we are not pressed down by dangers. Honoring your father also brings about a placating of your sin, that is, insofar as it pertains to present punishment, if you will be kind toward your parents, teachers, rulers of the church, God will also mitigate your punishments.

XVI

The greatest virtue justifies most greatly: Love is the greatest virtue: Therefore, love justifies most greatly.

I reply: The major premise concerning the righteousness of the Law is true, that is, if we fulfill the Law satisfactorily, we would be righteous on account of our virtues, and the greatest virtue would contribute the most, so that we can truly say of Christ that He was righteous particularly because of His perfect love. But because we do not satisfy the Law, we are accepted before God on account of the Mediator and not on account of our own worthiness or our own qualities. Therefore the major premise is not valid in regard to our reconciliation. The greatest virtue reconciles most greatly; indeed, only the Mediator reconciles. It is the greatest virtue of all to burn with love for God, but even the regenerate and those who have advanced far scarcely believe that the smallest spark has been kindled in them since in their own minds faith struggles with doubt and the devil is upsetting their worship by various false ideas; so that in our heart the love for God still languishes, as we can sense in our prayers in which our heart either believes that it is negligent or even flees God, and wicked desires and love of pleasure, glory, and our own life rush in upon us.

Therefore, although love for God must exist in us, yet we acknowledge the enormous weakness in us and we know that our person has been received by God, heard by Him, and is righteous, that is, our person has been reckoned as accepted by God on account of the Mediator by faith. Thus it is one thing to speak of reconciliation and God's mercy toward us; it is another to arrogate these virtues to ourselves. For there is no question that love is the greatest of all virtues, and the Law requires it as the highest virtue, "You shall love the Lord your God with all your heart. . . ." But where is this burning flame of love? Scarcely a spark shines in the saints and it is retained with difficulty. If we consider these points, we will understand more clearly why it has to be said that we are justified by faith. Now if a person wishes to compare these virtues and to consider the individual definitions of each, there is some value to be gained from this. The first virtue is faith, which is to know the Word of God and to assent to the promise of grace. There is also trust, by which for the sake of Christ we determine that God is favorable toward us, so that we may rest in confidence. Therefore knowledge lays hold on the promise, and trust quiets our heart for the sake of the Mediator. Then follows love. For it is necessary that the knowledge of God's mercy comes first, since the heart truly senses the wrath of God and again by faith recognizes that God is favorable toward us for the sake of Christ. By this light the darkness of Epicureanism and the Academicians is driven away and our mind, aided by the Holy Spirit, determines that God really is concerned about us and that we are received by Him. Thus the heart begins to submit to God and love toward God begins. But in this life the kind of flames are not burning which we owe to God, but there is a certain degree of beginning obedience by which the heart does subject itself to God and rejoices in knowing and obeying Him. As it says in the canticle in Luke 2:14, "Glory to God in the highest, and on earth peace and happiness or good will among men." Thus John, in order to show in some way what our love toward God should be, says in 1 John 5:3, "This is the love of God, that we keep His commandments." To these virtues we add, in the third place, hope which is properly the expectation of the coming deliverance promised by God. Hope differs from faith in two ways. The first is a noteworthy and significant difference. Faith lays hold on the promise and applies the Mediator to us. Hope is not like this, but awaits the future outcome. From this we can easily understand why it is not proper to say that we are justified by hope, because it is not the purpose of hope to demonstrate or apply the Mediator as when we say we are justified by faith. The second difference is this: Faith receives the present benefit, the present reconciliation without which there can be no calling upon God. Hope expects in advance the future events which have been promised by God.

XVII

"Her sins, which were many, have been forgiven her because she loved much," Luke 7:47: Therefore remission of sins takes place on account of love.

I reply: There is a twofold absolution. One is private, directed to the conscience which is struggling with the wrath of God. In this absolution we must understand that remission is received by faith and not on account of our virtues. Thus Christ says, "Your faith has saved you," Luke 7:50. Our faith does not rely upon our love but only on the mercy which has been promised, as is evident. Nor can love exist unless remission be received. The second kind of absolution is public, before the church. This takes place on account of good works which are testimonies of a person's conversion, as when Christ here explains to the Pharisee why He had received the woman, namely because there were evident testimonies to her conversion.

This entire account is a picture of the church. There are always two congregations. The one is hypocritical, puffed up by the authority which has been given to it and its reputation for righteousness, because it seems to be carefully observing the doctrine of discipline and the Law. And although this congregation does not cling to the Gospel, yet because it holds governance of the church, therefore Christ sat at its table, that is, he used its platform as a place to preach. The second congregation is the one which hears the Gospel, truly repents, and with true faith calls upon God, recognizes the Son as the Mediator, and proclaims the Gospel. To this congregation, although the other group has the outward appearance of works, Christ still gives in this passage praise for their love, a love which the hypocrites had taken for themselves by arrogating to themselves the righteousness of the Law. But Christ transfers this honor to this poor woman: the righteousness of the Law is pleasing here where there is the true knowledge of Christ. And in this congregation there is true worship, that is to say, repentance, faith, true calling upon God, love, kissing Christ's feet and washing them, that is, adorning and defending the ministry of the Gospel and the necessary zeal for the church, enduring dangers in confession and labors, and hatred in teaching. On the other hand, the hypocrites are without repentance or the fear of God because they think that they are righteous by their own behavior or their own ceremonies. Then they are also without faith, because they either trust in their own righteousness or remain in doubt. They are without love because love for God and true worship cannot exist unless there first be a knowledge of remission of sins. They do not honor the Gospel but try either to destroy or repress it. In this passage Christ sets before the godly His comfort, He sharply refutes the Pharisee and takes away from him all praise for his righteousness in order that He may show that He defends His church against the unfair judgments of the congregation of hypocrites.

But if this idea of the twofold absolution does not please you, then use another illustration. The idea of synecdoche has been suggested. Her many sins were forgiven her because she had been converted. Statements such as this occur in many places and yet the synecdoche must be explained. Although it is necessary that the many aspects of conversion do come together at one and the same time—contrition, faith, love or good intention—yet remission of sins is not given because of our worthiness but through mercy which is grasped by faith. This explanation is taken from Paul in his contentions for the term "freely, by faith for the sake of Christ."

XVIII

Eternal life is called a reward: Therefore it is owed to us because of our works.

My reply is very brief: Eternal life is a reward because it brings blessings even if it is given for another reason, namely for the sake of Christ. Just as an inheritance is a reward for a son, even if it comes to him for another reason. This reply is brief and simple and it satisfies the objection of our adversaries who are exaggerating the word "reward" out of all proportion and are drawing some ridiculous conclusions from it, such as placing works and reward either in the realm of the marketplace, or making the price and the reward equal. Thus they come up with the notion of equalizing our obedience with our eternal life, and speak of the obedience of the merit of our worthiness (meritum de condigno); they imagine that men can satisfy the Law and they mix it all up with works of supererogation. And in regard to faith which does not look to our worthiness but to the Mediator and which receives the remission of sins and the inheritance of eternal life for the sake of Christ—of this they say nothing. Indeed, they teach the very opposite when they say that hope is the expectation of eternal life which comes from our own merits. Finally, the word "merit" has created many arguments, and Bernard, when he could not solve this problem, finally said, "It is sufficient to know regarding the word 'merit' that merit does not suffice." Thus the knowledge of his own infirmity compelled him to take refuge in Christ.

Therefore our explanation of this matter is simple. We say that it is necessary for salvation that there be repentance, faith, the beginning of obedience or love; and yet because there is still in our flesh a great darkness and weakness which conflicts with the law of God, we must acknowledge what David says, "In Your sight shall no flesh be justified," Ps. 143:2. We must flee to Christ and determine that eternal life is given to those who repent and believe for His sake. As He Himself says, "This is the will of the Father, that everyone who believes in the Son shall have eternal life," John 6:40. It is insanity to imagine that it is possible for the regenerate to satisfy the law of God and that they are thus without sin. Therefore, in order that our hope of eternal life may remain strong, we should know that it is given to those who repent and believe for the sake of Christ.

Meanwhile, however, because God does receive our obedience, even though our good works do not merit the remission of sins and the inheritance of eternal life, yet they do merit other rewards both physical and spiritual in this life and in the future, as Christ says, "Great will be your reward in heaven," Matt. 5:12. These things which I have said satisfy the wise and pious consciences.

This reply is also true: The statements, "The reward will be eternal life," Matt. 5:12, and "It shall be rendered to each according to his works," 2 Cor. 5:10, are *statements of Law which speak of righteousness as well as of our own worthiness. And yet the faith which receives reconciliation determines that we are not pleasing to God because of anything else or because of our virtues, because no one satisfies the Law, and in this weakness of our nature many sins still remain. It is necessary to add an explanation from the Gospel which causes us to understand that merit is a compensation, but we must not understand that reconciliation is given on account of our worthiness, and that our beginning obedience is not pleasing to God in itself, but it is pleasing for the sake of the Mediator in those who have been reconciled. The compensation for good works only comes after this reconciliation.*

But we must destroy the argument which some make that men will become slack and lazy toward well-doing if we take away from them the idea of merit. I have said above that the reasons for the necessity and obligation for good works are much more serious than this. Besides, we must maintain the difference in the promises. The promise of reconciliation and eternal life is a free promise; while the promises belonging to the Law are additions made for the sake of good works, such as the promise, "He who gives a cup of water shall not lose his reward," Matt. 10:42. Thus, even though good works do not merit reconciliation and are not the price of eternal life (for reconciliation must precede these things in order that our obedience may please God), yet they do merit some rewards, as we have said.

Further, what has been said regarding sluggishness must be refuted by raising the danger of doubting. If we must be in doubt regarding eternal life, as the teaching of these points regarding merits leads us to believe, then doubt will even more weaken our zeal for doing good. But I am passing over this point. There is a great darkness upon the human mind and a horrible weakness. Very few people understand what it is to serve God. But the pious have some degree of light. They thank God who has received us to Himself for the sake of His Son and that for the sake of the Mediator He has given His approval to this weak and corrupted obedience of ours and adorned it with rewards and aroused us to the exercises of faith and good works. For in these exercises these questions can easily be judged.

I have discussed this entire controversy regarding justification or reconciliation. And although many people oppose this position, yet it is the task of the godly mind to see what really is at issue so that the matter can most easily be judged, that the church of all ages may be alerted, and the experience of the saints carefully considered. We say that repentance is necessary, and we add that people must believe that the remission of sins is freely given for the sake of the Son of God, not on account of our own worthiness. Likewise the mind must not fall prey to doubt but in faith conquer doubt. Further, we are saying that it is necessary that there be the beginning of obedience, but that this does not satisfy the law of God, but is pleasing to Him in the reconciled for the sake of the Mediator; and indeed sins do remain in the regenerate, but yet we are to distinguish sins which are contrary to conscience from those which remain in the saints. For we are saying that grace is lost when the law of God is violated against conscience. Not only are these ideas correct, but in fact they are in agreement with the consensus of all the saints from the very beginning.

Think of David when he was accused by Nathan. Here David acknowledges the wrath of God and is truly ashamed and grieves. Again, when he hears the Gospel, "The Lord has taken away your sin," he is governed by this word and does not think that he has the remission of his sin because of his virtues. But he believes the word and understands concerning the promises which have been given to the fathers, he struggles with his doubt and conquers in faith. What happens then? Does he later come to the conclusion that he is satisfying the law of God? Indeed he recognizes that his weakness is far removed from the perfection of God's law. He therefore says, "In Your sight shall no flesh be justified," Ps. 143:2, and he knows that still through mercy this righteousness of a good conscience is pleasing to God in those who have been reconciled, as he says, "Those who love Your law have great peace," Ps. 119:165.

Our minds must carefully note these statements which are constant and irrefutable, in agreement with the consensus of the saints of all ages. Nor will it be difficult to refute the arguments which are used against them, if we keep these points before us and use them in our daily prayers. For there can be no true prayer unless we understand the doctrine of faith. For we must draw near to God in trust in the Mediator, Rom. 5:1, "Through Him we have access . . ." and Heb. 4:14ff., "Having such a high priest, let us draw near with confidence."

THE ARGUMENTS OF THE ADVERSARIES

Although in the above quotations the true teaching concerning the justification of sinful man before God has been established and confirmed by the surest testimonies of the sacred writings, yet it is also useful and necessary to examine the arguments of those who oppose us and to refute them by solid debate. (1) That no uncertainty disturb the true teaching on this. For the sure confidence of faith requires that the mind be certain. Therefore it is necessary that not only do we hold to the correct teaching, but also that we seek to overcome the opposition to it, so that the true opinion is not again overturned. (2) That we may be able to "convince the gainsayers." For Paul in Titus 1:9 sets forth the second task of the ministry, to "refute those who speak against the truth," that is, the minister of the Word must not only deny things that are false, but also refute this error by valid arguments. (3) It is useful, even necessary, to consider these opposing arguments in order that we hear not only the true voice of Christ, but also that we can beware of strange and erring positions. For the purity of the article of justification cannot withstand the admission of any error in any of its aspects. (4) The antithesis sheds a great deal of light because it calls attention to things which are otherwise not noticed. It is useful to observe and hold fast to the fundamental points which solve these problems. For these arguments are not all answered in the same way. Many unfortunate statements have arisen in solving certain problems which afterward have been the cause of great trouble in the church in times of controversy. Thus it is worth the effort to consider the sources of them.

In the Colloquy at Ratisbon, Contarini[50] said to Philipp: Your doctrine is stronger in its affirmative aspects than in refuting negative problems. For your arguments move me, so that I am not able to contradict your position easily, but when you have the task of dealing with points which contradict you, I see that you work very hard and present your case, but your solution does not always satisfy me. Luther correctly replied: If I cannot solve all problems as well as they might be, yet for this reason I must not give up the affirmative aspect of what I am contending for which has the firmest Scriptural basis. And thus I shall retain this major point that the merit of Christ by the grace of God is my justification, because this is communicated to me through the Word and the sacraments, and this I lay hold on by faith.

However, so that it is not necessary to set forth and analyze all the individual arguments which our adversaries are accustomed to raise in opposition (which seems to be an enormous and fruitless endeavor), I think it will be useful to present only the main points of the explanation. And a comparison will be helpful when we note how one and the same argument is resolved by different methods, so that we do not belabor each of them, nor feel that our own explanations are the only correct ones, but are given only for the sake of example. Indeed, Aepinus, whose learning, even during his lifetime, was well known, but after his death was even better known during the time of the Interim, has shown us the way in this area.[51] And I know that Dr. Philipp gave such high approval to the work of Aepinus in refuting the arguments of the adversaries that he more often preferred Aepinus' suggested solutions than his own.

And we ourselves also having entered on this path shall set up certain classes of arguments as general headings to which we shall compare the arguments of our adversaries. And we shall show in each individual case the sources and foundations of the correct explanations. When a person has learned these

---

[50] Gasparo Contarini, 1483–1542, Italian cardinal, used by the pope in diplomatic endeavors, mild and evangelical in spirit. Attended Colloquy at Ratisbon in 1541 as papal delegate but failed in peace proposals.

[51] Johannes Aepinus (Hoeck), 1499–1553, Lutheran theologian and superintendent at Hamburg, friend of Luther, Melanchthon, and Bugenhagen. Prolific writer in support of the Reformation.

general explanations to a fair degree, then by private study he can apply these points to each of the arguments of the adversaries which are raised.

Class 1

They argue that because conversion does not consist only in faith, but has three parts which are connected in an orderly manner, it is necessary that there be in those who have been converted not only faith but also contrition and the new obedience. Likewise those who have been converted receive for the sake of Christ not only remission and reconciliation but also renewal or sanctification. Therefore from this fountain various arguments are drawn and developed by the adversaries to which many passages of Scripture are applied.

The answer to these points is true and simple. I agree with everything, but I have to deny the consequence which is drawn from these points in opposition to free justification, because it is a fallacy to stipulate something as a cause when it is not a cause. This solution to the problem can be demonstrated in three ways in keeping with their different arguments.

1. Insofar as it pertains to merit or the cause of our justification, these virtues do not merit and are not the reason that the remission of sins is given to us; but it is necessary that we be sure that the free mercy of God relies only on the free merit of the Mediator. For the real point at issue here and the chief question in this matter is this: What is the cause on which our faith must rely in determining for itself that our sins are remitted, that is to say, is it Christ or is it our works? Thus there can and must be present both contrition and the new obedience, but we cannot rely on these before the judgment seat of God.

2. Insofar as it pertains to the means of applying grace, these three parts of conversion are connected with each other, but if we maintain the individuality of each of the three parts as well as the order of each, then it is the property of faith alone to lay hold on and apply to itself the promise of the Gospel, the merit of Christ, and the grace of God. It is necessary that the person be first reconciled by faith, and then works follow which are also pleasing to God.

3. Insofar as this pertains to the form of justification, our renewal is, to be sure, a blessing of Christ, but because in this life our renewal is never perfect but contaminated by sin which dwells in our flesh, therefore, in order that the promise of justification might be certain, we must add here the matter of our reconciliation which is entirely a free thing for the sake of the Mediator. If we maintain the distinction in this way, the points which cannot be separated in our justification will not be confused, and the entire matter will be clearer.

Class 2

On the basis of the example of civil righteousness and the notions of philosophy and the Pharisees, human reason has developed many arguments in opposition to the righteousness of the Gospel. Here applies the statement of Paul in Rom. 2:14, "The gentiles who do not have the Law, do by nature the things contained in the Law."

But the true solutions to these problems are taken from those passages of Scripture which show that the kind of righteousness which can stand before men is not the righteousness which can stand before God in heaven. See Matt. 5:20; Rom. 4:2; 1 Cor. 4:3–4.

But because the divine law is the norm for perfect and absolute righteousness, not before men but before God, and has the promise not only of physical reward but also of eternal life and blessing, therefore Scripture raises many statements in opposition which speak of the idea of righteousness, as it is prescribed in the law, such as, Matt. 19:17; Lev. 18:5; Gal. 3:12; Luke 10:28; Rom. 2:13; Deut. 30:19.

These objections are dealt with in different ways, but Scripture shows the true and fundamental solution as coming from this source, which Christ and Paul both answer by conceding that the righteousness which is prescribed in the Law is such that if we could obey it in this life with that perfection which is prescribed in the Law, we would be totally justified through it and would live by it. See Luke 10:28; Rom. 2:13. But Christ convicts the Pharisees; and Paul on the basis of Scripture proves that it is impossible, Rom. 8:3; Gal. 3:21–22. And since the Law pronounces the sentence of condemnation upon those who do not remain under it in all respects, Deut. 27:26, in order that we not be condemned, we must have another righteousness, namely, that which is revealed in the Gospel.

Class 3

Because the Scripture in this doctrine uses the words "justification," "righteousness," "grace," "imputation," "faith" and the like in a particular meaning which is not used this way in common speech, therefore various arguments have been devised by our adversaries to demonstrate that these words in the doctrine of the Law, the philosophers, civil righteousness and popular speech are used in a different way.

But all these arguments which are peculiar to Scripture can be correctly explained and resolved on the basis of the true and genuine meaning of the words.

Here are pertinent also the words of James 2:17, and other passages, the entire understanding of which consists, as the text shows in using the words "faith" and "justification," in a different sense than Paul uses them, that is, James is speaking of one kind of faith and one kind of justification and Paul of another. For James is saying that if a person says that he has faith and yet has no works, he does not have saving faith but an empty persuasion. The word "justification" is used in different ways in different passages of Scripture: for example, in 1 Kings 8:32, "You, O God, judge from the heart Your servants, condemning the ungodly and justifying the righteous, giving to each according to his righteousness"; Ps. 51:4, ". . . that You might be justified in Your words and prevail when You judge"; 1 Tim. 3:16, "The Son of God was justified in the Spirit."

Class 4

This solution can be applied to many of the objections which have been raised: There are many statements in Scripture in which the cause of our justification, or the means of applying grace, or the form of our justification before God are not described, but rather a description is given of the quality or character (so to speak) of those who have been justified. John has many statements of this kind in his first epistle: 1:6–7; 2:3, 6, 9, 29; 3:3, 5–7.

But we also have to consider how this solution can be correctly applied to the different objections. Because many people have adopted the Epicurean notion of impunity for sins without repentance and have misused the doctrine of free justification for false security and carnal license, Scripture in many places sets forth and demonstrates with definite statements and outward signs or testimonies, from which results or fruits we ourselves and also others can compare and judge whether we are justified by true faith or whether our faith is false and merely an empty picture of justification. Here pertain those statements from the epistle of John which we have just cited. See also Luke 7:47; 2 Peter 1:5, 8.

Thus also in many Scripture passages the character of those who have been justified is described by their fruits, not as the cause or the reason for which eternal life has been given to them, not to those who are shameless or disobedient or who possess only a sluggish profession of faith, but to those who repent and bring forth fruits worthy of repentance. Here we can apply such passages as Matt. 5:3ff., "Blessed are the poor . . . those who mourn . . . the merciful . . . the pure in heart." Christ here is not speaking of the cause of this blessedness but He is showing who they are who possess this blessedness. Thus in Matt. 20:9, in regard to the pay which is given to the workers, He is not speaking of the cause for which those who did not labor were paid, nor of the proportion which they were paid, but from the outward signs which were given He shows who they are to whom the pay is given, namely those who went into the vineyard, who labored, who did not complain, even though they "bore the heat and burden of the day," and who finally remained in the vineyard. Note also Matt.

24:46 where He says, "Blessed is the servant, whom his Lord, when he comes, shall find so doing." Their fruits show to whom the heavenly inheritance is given or not given. For the eternal Father has received His family for the sake of Christ. But He wills that in this family we be diligent in living according to the word of Scripture: "He who now says in his heart, 'The Lord delays His coming,' and begins to mistreat his fellow family member," shows in his actions that he is unworthy of the grace of God. And when the Lord returns, "He shall cut him off." But he who has given proof of his faith, him shall the Lord receive and keep in his household. In the same way in Matt. 25[:34–36], in the forum of the last judgment, He shows to the others who could not see it in any other way, that on the basis of their fruits those who had been faithful and believing had truly been justified. The same is the case in Psalm 15 where He is not describing the cause of our justification or the means of apprehending righteousness, nor the form wherein our righteousness actually consists, but He is describing it by its fruits and who they are who have attained true righteousness and dwell in the church of God. Thus 1 John 3:10, 14. And Paul in Eph. 4:20–21, after he has described the great and immeasurable wickedness in which the gentiles are sunk and which Christians must avoid, adds, "You did not come to know Christ that way if you have heard Him and been taught by Him."

Likewise many passages of Scripture teach concerning those who do not have or keep righteousness and salvation, who permit actions contrary to their conscience. See John 5:29; Rom. 6:12; 8:13; Gal. 6:8; Heb. 6:4.

But this point must be carefully and correctly explained, not, indeed, as if it is a matter of justification and salvation, but because true faith is especially known by these signs, namely that in repentance "faith is efficacious through love." Further, because those who reject repentance and love certainly do not keep their faith. See 1 Tim. 5:8; 2 Peter 1:9; Col. 3:6.

Thus we must carefully investigate the fact that Scripture does not treat this article the same way in all cases. Sometimes Scripture describes justification by its fruits or outward proofs, so that it might draw secure men away from an Epicurean idea of faith. Again, in other places, it describes the cause on account of which justification takes place, by what means it is accepted, in what it consists, and in which passages the *sedes doctrinae* is truly located. Thus in Ezek. 18:21, where both of these concepts occur, God speaks through the prophet, "If the wicked will repent of all the sins which he has done and keep all My statutes and do what is lawful and right, he shall live and not die." But here the question arises—Shall the ungodly live on account of his renewal? The answer is no. For Ezekiel immediately adds in v. 22, "All the transgressions which he has done I shall not record." And thus our righteousness consists in the fact that the Lord has not kept a record of our sins and does not impute them against us, as is explicitly stated in other passages of Scripture. And yet, because this does not take place apart from true repentance, therefore the righteousness of faith is designated by these definite signs or indicators. Thus in Is. 1:16–17 it says, "Put away evildoing; learn to do well, relieve the oppressed, defend the cause of the fatherless, plead the case of the widow." And the promise is added in v. 18, "If your sins be as scarlet, they shall be whiter than snow; and if they be red like crimson, they shall be as wool." But is righteousness given because of these works? Absolutely not! For the prophet himself says in 45:24, "In the Lord is my righteousness," and in v. 25, "In the Lord shall all the seed of Israel be justified and saved." Therefore what is he teaching in chapter 1? Is he contradicting himself? Not at all, but he is exhorting us to repentance. And how reconciliation with God takes place he explains elsewhere. Thus note also Matt. 6:14 and Mark 11:25 where Christ says, "If you forgive men their sins, your heavenly Father shall forgive you your sins." Does this mean that justification is given us because we forgive others and that our sins are remitted for this reason? No. For Christ Himself explains more fully in Matt. 18:23, in the parable of the unmerciful servant, where He shows us poor sinners, the servants of God, that our debt has been forgiven purely out of His mercy. But because that servant later went out and was unwilling to forgive the debt of his fellow servant, he lost again the forgiveness of his sins because he had lost his faith. For if he had had faith, he certainly would have forgiven the debt. This account shows how justification, when it has been received, can be either retained or lost, but not how justification is to be attributed to these fruits.

To this class also is pertinent the solution which is used in the Apology, namely that Scripture in its exhortations to repentance adds promises of grace and salvation. But for what reason this promise is given and how it is grasped and in what it consists, this the Scripture teaches in other passages. But the correct understanding must be drawn from those statements of Scripture in which this doctrine is clearly treated.

Class 5

Certain statements of Scripture do not speak of the remission of guilt and eternal punishment but of the remission of temporal punishment which is turned away sometimes through a complete repentance, as the following Scriptural examples clearly prove: Jer. 18:7–8, "I shall suddenly speak against a people and against a kingdom, to pluck it up, to destroy it and to break it down; yet if that nation shall repent of its evil against which I have spoken, I will repent of the evil which I have intended to do it." From this we see how God remits outward penalties when men earnestly repent. Likewise in Luke 13:6–9 Christ brings in the simile of the tree in the garden. The householder had decided that he wanted to cut it down because for three years he had found no fruit on it and he believed that it was encumbering the ground uselessly. But the gardener interceded for the tree and promised to care for it, and then if it produced nothing, he agreed to cut it down. This serves as an illustration for us as to how God remits the temporal punishment for those who are repentant, or at least He mitigates the punishment. Likewise, Paul says in 1 Cor. 11:31, "If we judge ourselves, we would not be judged by the Lord." Yet this is not a perpetual or universal situation, so that whoever repents will immediately have his temporal punishments removed. For surely David in 2 Sam. 12:14 was not delivered from his punishment, for even after he repented his son died; nor did the sword depart from his house [2 Sam. 12:10]. Hence the people in Micah 7:9 humbled themselves under temporal punishment before God, because they recognized that they had deserved it because of their sins, and they said, "I will bear the wrath of the Lord, for I have sinned against Him." In many cases temporal punishments are inflicted even upon those who have been reconciled as a warning concerning their sins and to mortify their flesh, as we have seen from examples.

Thus the fundamental basis for the resolution of this problem is the doctrine of the causes of the calamities which are imposed upon believers even after they have been reconciled with God or, for that matter, are remitted to them. And the solution to this is so definite that the adversaries themselves use it, as Gopper himself writes: "The remission of guilt is one thing and the mitigation of punishment is another."

Here is appropriate the account which we read in 1 Kings 21:17ff. where the prophet Elijah is sent to the godless King Ahab to announce to him that because of his unjust killing of Naboth and his other crimes, God wants to punish him and his whole house so severely that not even one male child shall survive. Yet because the king, after he had heard this frightful curse and the announcement of his punishment, did humble himself and put on sackcloth, God then took away the sentence of death [v. 29], "Because Ahab has humbled himself before Me, I will not bring the evil judgment in his days, but in the days of his son I will bring evil upon his house." This was surely fulfilled in Jer. 18:7–9 where even then under the condition of repentance a turning away of the temporal punishments was promised.

In Joel 2:12–14 the prophet says, "Turn unto Me with all your heart with fasting, with weeping, and with mourning. And rend your hearts and not your garments and turn to the Lord your God, for He is gracious and merciful, patient, and of great kindness, and He relents from sending calamity. Who knows whether He will not turn and relent and leave a blessing behind Him?" The adversaries use this passage to contend against placing our confidence in faith and they argue for the idea of doubt, because the prophet says, "Who knows whether He will not turn and relent?" They say that the remission of sins is conditioned upon our "fasting, weeping, and mourning," and since these are not perfect, we must remain in doubt regarding the remission of sins. But the actual situation is far different. The prophet is announcing the temporal punishments of the Jews with which God wills to visit them because of their sins. And the prophet adds the concept that if you want these punishments to be taken away or at least mitigated, then turn to Him. But what is the rationale for true conversion? He adds, "Do not rend your garments," as the hypocrites do, but "rend your hearts," that is, let your conversion be a genuine one and show this by the fruits worthy of repentance. He uses a promise which has an element of doubt: "Who knows whether He will not relent?" For in the area of temporal punishments we must humble ourselves under the mighty hand of God and let God be free either to punish or withhold punishment, totally or in part. Thus the whole prophetic statement seems to be dealing with the remission of temporal punishments.

Jonah 3:10, "And God saw the works of the Ninevites, how they turned from their evil way; and God was merciful regarding the evil which He had said He would do to them, and He did not do it." From this passage the adversaries infer that God had respect for the works of the Ninevites. Thus we do not lay hold on forgiveness by faith alone, because God did not look at their faith but their works, and thus works also play a part in the action of justification. But the answer to this problem is simple and correct, and the circumstances of this text show it. God wanted to announce to the Ninevites through the prophet, v. 4, "Forty days from now Nineveh will be destroyed." The king believed this message, descended from his throne, proclaimed a fast, and directed everything so that men might turn away from their evil ways and from all ungodliness, and he adds in v. 9, "Who knows, God may yet relent and turn from His fierce anger, so that we do not perish." He is speaking here of external and physical punishment which God could turn aside if He so willed, and if not he was willing to endure the wrath of the Lord. Therefore God had respect for their works and saw that each of them turned himself away from his evil; and He in turn was merciful and turned away this outward punishment.

Jer. 5:1 says, "Run through the streets of Jerusalem and look and search high and low to see if you find a man who does justice and seeks fairness, and I will be gracious toward the city." Thus the adversaries infer that righteousness and salvation are to be attributed to our works, contrary to the fact that the propitiation for our sins is not our works but the blood of Christ. But the text itself shows the solution to the problem. For this entire chapter is an announcement of temporal punishments. Yet in this very announcement He promises that He will be favorable, that is, He will either remit or lessen the punishments, if they will turn away from their sins. Thus in v. 7 he adds, "How can I pardon you? Your children have forsaken Me and sworn by those who are not gods," that is, when they have piled up sins and continued in them. But if there were going to be some who acted righteously and practiced judgment, and thus were converted from their evil ways, then for the sake of those few good people God promises that He would mitigate their punishments." Likewise in Gen. 18:26 God says to Abraham, "If I find in Sodom 50 righteous in the city, I will spare the whole place for their sake."

Thus in Matt. 3:7ff., the Baptist says to the Pharisees and Sadducees, "Who has warned you to flee from the wrath to come? Bring forth fruits that prove you have repented. . . . Already the axe is laid at the root of the tree." From this the adversaries conclude that we through the fruits of our repentance escape the wrath of God. But pay attention to what the Baptist is saying about this wrath, namely, he is speaking of the physical and external overthrow of the Jewish state by which God had determined to punish that nation. But how could they escape this punishment? Through true repentance which is not pretended or hypocritical. They must show this repentance by true fruits and actions.

They raise in objection the statement in Dan. 4:27, which seems very harsh against the idea of free imputation, for Daniel says, "Let my counsel be acceptable to you, O king; redeem your sins by giving alms to the poor, and perhaps the Lord will forgive your iniquities" (Vulgate). Thus, the adversaries conclude, the prophet himself places the redemption from sins not only in the blood of the Messiah but also in alms and works of mercy toward the poor. The text itself shows what the prophet was intending. Nebuchadnezzar in his dreams (vv. 10ff.) had seen a tree growing toward heaven and (vv. 13ff.) he had heard a messenger of the Lord crying, "Cut down the tree and scatter its fruit." All these things Daniel explained in v. 25, "The Lord will take from you your kingdom and you will wander as a beast in the field; but a root shall still remain, so that when you recognize that it is the Most High God who gives kingdoms, you shall be restored." This is clearly an announcement of punishment and at the same time a mitigation of it, if the king repents. Thus he says, "Let my counsel be pleasing to you—stop your sinning and give alms." These words have no other intent than this: God will take away your kingdom unless you repent. Therefore do this: Repent! Because this is your sin that you have exploited the poor and the oppressed, therefore in order that there may be a witness that you have seriously repented, then make this testimony by giving alms and benefits to the poor. Who knows? Perhaps God will be slow to wrath, perhaps He will not punish you in keeping with your sins, but if you repent, after these seven years, you will return to your kingdom. This is very common in Scripture, that when it speaks of the mitigation of physical punishments, it almost always uses formulas which express this kind of uncertainty: perhaps, or, who knows? Physical punishment is not always taken away through repentance but often is mitigated.

At this point we must also note that in the sacred language we do not have the word which Scripture uses in other places, when it says, "God will redeem Israel" or that "He is your Redeemer, O Israel." But Scripture uses the word *parak* which means to snatch something from destruction or danger, as when the psalmist says, "Deliver my soul," Ps. 6:4, or "There is no god who will snatch you from My hand," Dan. 3:15. Thus the prophet speaks of deliverance and redemption, not from sin but from danger and adversities.

Thus in Prov. 16:6, "Iniquity is redeemed by mercy and truth" (Vulgate). Luther translates this *"Durch Gute und Treue wirt Missethat versohnet."* Thus they say that expiation of sins consists of mercy. But this is the mercy of Christ alone. Why, therefore, does Solomon speak this way? Luther in a marginal note shows us the true meaning here: God indeed does turn away punishment if the person repents. Therefore there is in mercy the expiation not of guilt but of temporal punishment. For just as in Deuteronomy 21, in the early part of the chapter, there is instruction regarding what to do in the case of the guilty shedding of innocent blood in a place outside the city, that is, how the wrath of God and His punishment can be averted, namely when the elders of the nearest city are called to view the body of the murdered man, they are to bring a calf, wash their hands, and proclaim themselves innocent of the shedding of blood. Then there was redemption and expiation for the shedding of the blood, that is, the guilt and punishment were taken away. So also Solomon uses this kind of language and bears witness that their iniquities have been redeemed by God's mercy.

They also bring in the passage from Tobit 4:11, "Alms deliver us from all sin and death and do not permit the soul to go into darkness." I reply, first, that this book is found among the Apocrypha, and hence in proving and establishing dogmas it is not of great authority in the church. But so be it. We shall not belabor this argument, for this statement has nothing in it which is contrary to the doctrine of free justification. For in the Greek it does not have the expression "delivers from sin," but simply reads "acts of kindness snatch us out of death and do not allow us to enter into darkness." But what does this mean? The same as we see in Ps. 41:1–2, "Blessed is he who considers the poor: the Lord will deliver him in the time of trouble. The Lord will preserve him and keep him alive . . . and will not deliver him over to the will of his enemies." Thus, as we have said above, the text is speaking only of the mitigation or turning away of physical punishments, that is to say, in the midst of their troubles they will feel the reward for their kindnesses. But the same idea is repeated in Tobit 12:9, where the additional point is made, "alms purge away sins." This must not be understood as referring to the elimination of the merit of the blood of Christ which is the one and only thing which cleanses us from all sin, 1 John 1:9. But the passage is simply judging that while a man is zealous to show kindness he is minimizing many sins, such as greed, avarice, lack of humanity, and things of this kind.

Class 6

Certain Scripture passages speak not of kindness, salvation, and eternal life, which are given freely for the sake of Christ and received by faith. As Paul testifies in Rom. 4:5, "To him who does not work but believes in Him who justifies the ungodly, to him his faith is accounted for righteousness," according to the decision of God's grace. In Gal. 3:13–14, "Christ has been made a curse for us . . . that we might receive the promise of the Spirit through faith." God says to Abraham, "In your seed shall all the nations of the earth be blessed" [Gen. 22:18]. But these statements speak of other physical and spiritual rewards by which God out of His grace crowns the gifts of good works in those who already by faith, for the sake of Christ, have been made heirs of eternal life. This is in keeping with the sweet statement of Augustine, "God crowns nothing in us except His own gifts." Because Paul in 1 Tim. 4:8 says, "Godliness has the promise of the life that now is and of the life to come," thus we must study separately these points which speak of the rewards of this life, whether physical or spiritual, and distinguish them from the rewards of the life to come. For after eternal life has been freely given for the sake of Christ, then in that life there will also be the reward for good works, as Scripture so carefully points out. With regard to rewards of this life, Deut. 6:25 (Vulgate) says, "Our God will be merciful, if we keep and do all His commandments before the Lord our God, as He has commanded us." This is not a statement of Law, but it is speaking of the mercy which God bestows on the godly in this life. The entire chapter is a recitation of the rewards for godliness in this life, because God rewards godliness. Moses also calls it mercy because it is not given out of merit but out of grace, cf. Leviticus 26 and Deuteronomy 28. Moses throughout these chapters is referring not only to the physical rewards which God will give to those who live a godly life according to the prescription of the law of God, but He also is promising spiritual rewards. For the Lord says in Lev. 26:11–12, "I will place My tabernacle among you, and My heart will not reject you. I will walk among you and be your God and you shall be My people"; cf. Is. 1:19–20; 33:15–16; Luke 19:26, "To every one who has it shall be given, and from him who does not have even what he has shall be taken away." This is in keeping with the statement of Augustine, "Love merits an increase of love." For he who rightly uses the gifts of the Holy Spirit, upon him they are increased. Acts 10:4, "Your prayers and your alms come up as a memorial before God," that is, when Cornelius used well the gifts which he had already received from God, these gifts then came as a reminder before God that they should be increased and new ones added besides.

Furthermore, in regard to the rewards in the life to come, Scripture speaks very carefully, as we can see in Matt. 5:12, "Great is your reward in heaven." It does not say that heaven will be your reward but that your reward will be in heaven. But how do we get to heaven? Through Christ and for His sake. And now, since we gain heaven freely through Him, then also good works shall have their reward there. The statement in Matt. 19:21 has the same meaning, "Sell what you have and give it to the poor, and you will have treasure in heaven"; Luke 14:13–14, "When you make a feast, call the poor, the maimed, the lame and the blind who cannot repay you, and you will be blessed, for you shall be recompensed at the resurrection of the righteous." Therefore it is presupposed that we are righteous in the resurrection, and since there will be a remuneration for our kindness to the poor; 2 Cor. 5:10, "We must all appear before the judgment seat of Christ, that each may receive good or evil, according to what he has done in the body." Before the tribunal of Christ the free inheritance of eternal life is given for the sake of Christ, but then also the rewards for our good works, as they have been evaluated, shall be added, as in Matt. 25:34, where Christ says to those believers whom He has freely judged as the heirs of the heavenly inheritance, "Come you blessed of My Father. . . ." But whence were they blessed, unless from the blessing of the Seed, as Paul says in Gal. 3:14. Therefore because of Christ we freely possess the kingdom of heaven, but after this inheritance has been given to us, then He celebrates and honors our good works and promises for them a reward in eternal life which has already been freely given.

The fundamental answer to this question depends on the distinction among the promises of the Law. For the promise of the Law regarding eternal life, because it has attached to it the condition of the full implementation of the Law, which in this life because of the flesh is impossible for us, has been rendered worthless, and thus must be transferred onto Christ. But the rest of the promises concerning other rewards are made certain for us by faith on account of Christ, for God accepts the obedience of believers, even though it is impure and imperfect. For whatever imperfection still inheres in us is covered through Christ. Hence the statements of Paul in Gal. 6:8, "He who sows to the Spirit shall reap eternal life"; 2 Thess. 1:6–7, "God deems it just to repay with affliction those who afflict you and to grant rest to us who are afflicted, when the Lord Jesus is revealed from heaven"; 2 Tim. 4:8, "There is laid up for me a crown of righteousness which the Lord the righteous judge will give to me on that day, and not to me only but to those who love His coming." He calls it a "crown of righteousness" not in the sense that it is attributed to our righteousness, for God has gone before us with His blessings when He bestows the crown upon us, cf. Ps. 20:4.

In Revelation 4, when the elders had received their crowns, they took them off again and cast them at the feet of the Lamb, confessing that He alone was worthy. But Paul understands the crown of the righteousness of God as meaning that to him who has promised freely to serve Him for the sake of His righteousness, Heb. 6:10, "God is not so unjust as to overlook your work and the love which you showed for His sake in serving the saints, as you still do."

They raise the objection that God calls Himself "the reward" of Abraham in Gen. 15:1, "Do not be afraid, Abram: I am your shield and your very great reward." Eternal life is presented as a remuneration in Matt. 19:29 and Luke 18:30, "Everyone who leaves his home or his brothers or sisters in the field for My name's sake shall receive a hundredfold and he shall possess eternal life." Thus they say that not only temporal goods but also eternal life itself is given as payment for good works.

There is no need to scratch up an explanation for Scripture itself is very clear on this point. First, indeed, from the negative side, it is not called a reward in the sense that our works are worthy of eternal life. For Paul in Rom. 4:3, in commenting on the statement in Genesis 15, expressly affirms that our works are not the meritorious cause of our salvation, nor is salvation laid hold on by works. Therefore he says in v. 14 that the inheritance does not come from the Law but is by faith, so that, according to grace, "the promise might be sure," v. 16. Again in v. 5, "To him who does not work but believes, his faith is imputed to him for righteousness." Thus in the parable in Matt. 20:8 the denarius which many understand as eternal life is called a reward or their pay. But He adds the explanation to show that this does not relate to merit and that the idea of a reward is not under discussion. For some of them had borne the heat and burden of the day; others had worked only one hour, and yet they all received the same pay. Was any harm done to them? Not at all. For the agreement with them had been for a denarius. God has willed that those who come at the 11th hour, that is, at the very end of their lives, should receive equal to those who had labored throughout the entire day, in order that He might show that He is not paying for the labor but is demonstrating the goodness of His own divine blessing.

Second, from the affirmative side, the explanation is given that the compensation and remuneration for works does not always follow in this life, and that it is accompanied by tribulation or persecution, as we read in Mark 10:30. Yet lest the believers lack an opportunity to war or suffer for Christ, Scripture leads them to a consideration of life eternal in this way, 2 Cor. 4:18, "We do not look at the things which are seen but at those which are not seen; for the things which are seen are temporal, but the things which are not seen are eternal." Therefore, although eternal life is given as a free gift (as Christ in Matt. 19:29 uses the word "inherit"), yet at the same time there will be a compensation. As

Paul says in Col. 1:4ff., "You have love toward all the saints because of the hope which has been laid up for you in heaven, which you have heard of in the Word of the truth of the Gospel." For this hope has been laid up in heaven for us freely for the sake of Christ, as we are taught in the Gospel, namely that for the sake of this hope we should exercise ourselves even more strongly in love toward the saints. Thus Paul in Rom. 8:23, while under great persecution, holds before his eyes the reward of the coming glory, so that he might strengthen himself with this hope, even when in this life he sees nothing in the way of recompense.

Therefore no one should be upset by the word "reward" when it is attributed in the holy writings to eternal life. For it is not used in the sense of a debt owed to us, but is given as a promise. Thus, although in Gen. 12:3 and 18:18 the promise of the Seed is given freely to Abraham, and on the other hand in Gen. 22:18 it is put in the setting of a reward, and also in 15:1 where He says, "I am your very great reward," yet He does not say that Abraham merited this reward by reason of his works, but as in the parable in Matt. 20:8 it is called a reward because it is given by a promise, although it is not paid out in proportion to the work done. Surely in laboring I have not lost my reward, but in pouring out the riches of His kindness on those whom He has chosen apart from their works, as also the others who are sweating in great labor and yet receive no more, they must understand that they are receiving a gift of grace and not a reward for their works. Thus in Ps. 127:3 children are called "a heritage of the Lord and the fruit of the womb a reward," and yet at the same time it is most noteworthy if when the work is completed this follows and it is called a reward, cf. Prov. 23:18; Jer. 31:17. Thus since no crown is given except to one who is striving, 2 Tim. 2:5, this is also called a reward. Paul, further, in Rom. 6:23 speaks very carefully and accurately. He calls death "the wages of sin," yet he does not want to call eternal life a wage, but it is "the gift of God in our Lord Jesus Christ." In the preceding verse he uses the term *telos* (end) from the Hebrew *'achrīth*, that is to say, "the end," the final blessing which we await.

Class 7

We must note the distinction; where Scripture speaks of the righteousness of faith and where it speaks of the righteousness of the new obedience or of a good conscience. For the new obedience of the regenerate in this life, although it cannot stand before God according to the rigor of the Law since it is imperfect and impure, yet because for the sake of Christ it is pleasing to God and received before Him in keeping with the passage in 1 Peter 2:5, "offer up spiritual sacrifices, acceptable to God for the sake of Jesus Christ"; cf. 1 John 3:22; 1 Tim. 5:4; Luke 1:74–75. Luther expresses the emphasis of this verse when he translates it *"in Heiligkeit und Gerechtigkeit die ihm gefallig ist"* (in holiness and righteousness which belong to Him). Thus certain statements of Scripture honor also this blessing of God that, after the person freely and by faith for the sake of Christ has been received unto eternal life, now also by faith and for the sake of Christ, the obedience of the godly, even though it is weak and impure, is accepted in the sight of God and adorned with the name of "righteousness." Yet this righteousness cannot justify the person before God so that he thereby should think that he is pleasing to God and given the title of "righteous" on the grounds of this obedience.

Luther used and expressed this way of solving the question in a few places where he says that there is a twofold kind of justification: one of the person, the other of his works.

Here pertain the statements in Deut. 6:25, "This will be our righteousness before God, if we keep His precepts as He has commanded us." Some say that this passage is speaking of the righteousness before men. But this interpretation is in direct conflict with the text. For it speaks of the righteousness before God, just as Zechariah does in Luke 1:75, cf. also 1 John 3:22. Others say that he is speaking of legal righteousness or justice. This is a correct solution, to be sure, but the most helpful solution is this which interprets Moses this way: If you permit yourselves to be led by the Holy Spirit so that you have a beginning obedience, even though it is imperfect and weak and impure, yet God will accept it in order to adorn it with the name of "righteousness."

Deut. 24:13, "Give his pledge back to a poor man and you will have righteousness before the Lord your God." To give a pledge back to the poor is certainly a good and righteous work, and yet it is not such a work that—if measured by the rigorous standard of the Law—would merit the title of "righteousness." For as Augustine correctly writes to Coelestius, "The perfect fulfillment of the Law has its basis in the first and last commandments. If anything is lacking in either of these, even though in the others there has been something very excellent, the obedience is not perfect nor does it merit the title of 'righteousness.'" Hence, because the person has already been justified, the term "righteousness" has already been assigned to him, but not in the sense that this work has justified the person.

Ps. 106:31, "That was accounted unto Phinehas for righteousness." Indeed, if God had wished to judge according to the Law, Phinehas would not have been perfect, much less could he of himself have possessed the title "righteousness." In fact, because Phinehas was not the high priest and did not even hold the office of magistrate, it was possible that this action of his had been an evil act, as Christ says in Matt. 26:52, "He who takes the sword shall perish by the sword." But because Phinehas committed this action out of a kind of godly zeal, and against an evil man who did not hesitate to commit the sin of fornication in public, therefore it was accounted unto Phinehas for righteousness, as to one who had done a righteous action.

Acts 10:35, "In every nation he who fears God and does righteousness is accepted by Him." The Holy Spirit is speaking correctly, for in Rom. 14:17 it is said, "The kingdom of God is righteousness." Therefore Peter also states in Acts 10 that he who serves God among the people is pleasing to Him.

Under this class of objections we must also note that Scripture from time to time speaks of works of this kind in the abstract. Col. 3:20, "It is well-pleasing to the Lord that children obey their parents"; cf. Phil. 4:18; Heb. 13:16; Rom. 12:1. Sometimes Scripture speaks in the concrete, namely that those who do these things are pleasing to God: Matt. 25:23, "Well done, good and faithful servant. You have been faithful over a few things. I will put you in charge of many things. Enter into the joy of your lord"; Rom. 14:18, "For he who serves Christ in these things" (righteousness, peace, and joy in the Holy Spirit, v. 17) "is acceptable to God and approved of men"; cf. 1 Cor. 7:32; Col. 1:9–10; 1 Thess. 4:1; Heb. 11:6; 12:28. This observation is profitable to distinguish correctly: Certain good works are in themselves pleasing and accepted; but they are not pleasing if they are performed by corrupt people. But if the person has already been reconciled with God through the free remission of his sin, then his works are also pleasing to God.

Thus, properly speaking, there are two kinds of acceptance: (1) the acceptance of the person (who has been condemned on account of his sin) unto adoption and life through this free remission. Of this kind Eph. 1:6 says, "He has made us accepted in His beloved Son in whom we have redemption through His blood and the remission of sins, according to the riches of His grace." (2) There is the acceptance of the works in the reconciled person when he walks in faith and renewal according to the image of God and is anxious to please God in his whole obedience. Under this class we must also observe whence and why it happens that our works merit the title of "righteousness." (1) Because the very commandments of God by which works are commanded are called "righteousness," Deut. 27:10, "Hear the voice of God and do His commandments and the righteousnesses which I command you"; Ps. 19:8, "The righteousnesses of the Lord are righteous, rejoicing the heart." (2) Because the Holy Spirit who is the Spirit of righteousness works these actions. Rom. 6:13, "Yield yourselves to God as those who are alive from the dead, and your members as instruments of righteousness for God." (3) Because our works are accepted freely by God as being performed by those who have been adopted by Him. The prophet says in Is. 58:7–8, "Break your bread to the hungry and receive the homeless poor into your house; when you see a person naked, cover him, and do not hide yourself from your own flesh. Then your light shall break forth like the dawn and your healing shall spring up speedily; and your righteousness shall go before you and the glory of the Lord shall be your rearguard"; 2 Cor. 9:9 cites Ps. 112:9, "He scatters abroad, He gives to the poor; His righteousness endures forever."

Class 8

The adversaries are in the habit of raising a great objection to our position by citing such passages as Ps. 7:8, "Judge me, O Lord, according to my righteousness and according to my innocence"; cf. 35:24; 18:20ff.; 1 Sam. 26:23; Is. 38:3; Ps. 139:23–24. In statements of this kind the saints seem to put their own righteousness or innocence in opposition to the judgment of God, and ask that they be judged according to it; and thus they seem to be trusting and boasting in the righteousness of their own works even when they are dealing with God.

The simple and correct explanation is this: When the saints speak this way, they are not speaking of the righteousness of their own person on the day of judgment before God but of the righteousness of their cause. For what pertains to the righteousness of their person the saints confess fully and openly, "If You will to mark our iniquities, O Lord, who shall stand?" Ps. 130:3; cf. 143:2; 71:16; Ex. 34:7; Rom. 3:27; 1 Cor. 1:31. But when they compare their cause which they know is just and has been laid upon them by God with the evil endeavors of the ungodly, they see that they are innocent in this matter and are falsely condemned by men. Thus they put the cause of goodness and the testimony of a good conscience in opposition to the perverse judgment of the world and the unproved accusations and crimes of their adversaries. But because men do not see this, the saints before God Himself and His judgment put their own good works in opposition to the evils of their enemies. Thus Paul in Acts 23:1 says, "I have lived in all good conscience before God until this day." And in 2 Cor. 1:12, "Our boasting is this, the testimony of our conscience that in godly simplicity and sincerity, and not with carnal wisdom, we live in this world"; and 2 Cor. 4:2, "We have renounced hidden things of dishonesty . . . commending ourselves to every conscience of men in the sight of God." The circumstances of David in the psalms also clearly demonstrate that he is not speaking of the righteousness of his person but of his cause. For he composed these psalms against the wicked charges of Shimei and others, who had rebelled openly against him in the sedition of Absalom in order to see that he might come into the kingdom and might escape the just punishments for his wrongs. But David himself did not only look at the righteousness of his own cause, but he also commended it to God and prayed that He would judge between him and his accusers on the basis of this cause.

For the goodness of his cause and the testimony of a good conscience produce a boldness which confirms his expectation of help and divine deliverance, it makes his heart tranquil, so that a man has no doubt at all that God is with him and hears his prayers. Thus 1 John 3:19–22, "In this we know that we are of the truth and shall assure our hearts before Him. For if our heart condemn us, we have confidence in God; and whatever we ask, when we do those things which are pleasing in His sight, we shall receive from Him." A murderer cannot pray or hope for divine aid, because his own heart condemns him. But he who has a good cause, his heart increases under adversities and he has good confidence that he shall receive divine help.

In addition, the believers themselves are strengthened by their works as fruits, signs, and testimonies; and later they are assured that they have truly been adopted into sonship, justified, born again, and finally glorified. Thus our calling and election are made sure, as Peter says in 1 Peter 1:10, "Brothers, be diligent that through your good works you make your calling and election sure." When we have this certainty in our hearts, then also we will not doubt that on the great day of the Lord our works shall be honored and rewarded by grace by the Son of God. This is what John is saying in 1 John 4:17, "Herein is our love made perfect, that we have confidence in the day of judgment." Paul says in 1 Thess. 2:19, "What is our hope, our joy or our crown of glory? Is it not that you are in the presence of our Lord at His coming? For you are our glory and our joy." There is no doubt that Paul placed his hope of salvation on the day of God's judgment in Jesus Christ only and alone, as he testifies in many places, Phil. 3:7. But yet because he had come to understand by experience that the labors of his calling and his ministry were not empty things, from this fact he gained a sure sign and thus had a certain hope that would be fulfilled for him in eternal life.

Class 9

This correct explanation can be used and applied to many passages of Scripture: We are saved freely in this life through faith, not by our works, Eph. 2:8; "We are heirs of God and joint-heirs with Christ," Rom. 8:17. 1 John 3:2, "Now we are the sons of God"; 1 John 5:11, "He has given us eternal life"; v. 12, "He who has the Son has life"; v. 13, "I write this to you that you may know that you have life eternal, you who believe in the name of the Son of God." But this life is "hidden with Christ in God," Col. 3:3; "For we are saved by hope," Rom. 8:24; and "This hope is laid up in heaven," Col. 1:5; for "This inheritance is incorruptible, undefiled, and does not fade away. It is reserved in heaven for you . . . ready to be revealed at the last day," 1 Peter 1:4–5, when the elect shall be sent openly into the possession of the kingdom, cf. Matt. 25:34. "When He shall appear, we shall be like Him," 1 John 3:2. But to that possession or manifestation God leads as His heirs those who have been justified, who in the sure course of this life have been led by His Holy Spirit, because Scripture speaks of "walking" in the way of the Lord, in patience, that is, under the cross, in a zeal for godliness or good works, each in his own calling. The end or completion of this road is eternal life, Rom. 6:22, which is freely given through faith and not by reason of works, Rom. 4:16.

Scripture in many places describes this order of consequences and it does it so carefully that the purity of the article of justification and salvation might stand and remain firm on this foundation: freely, by faith, according to grace, "that the promise might be sure for all the seed," Rom. 4:16. Note also 1 Peter 1:5, "You are kept by the power of God through faith unto salvation"; and v. 9, "The end or goal of your faith is the salvation of your soul"; And Rom. 6:22, ". . . the return you get is sanctification and its goal eternal life," not as a payment but "as a gift of God."

On this basis we can correctly explain these and similar passages of Scripture: Matt. 7:14, "Narrow is the gate and hard is the way which leads to life," for, Acts 14:22, "we must through much tribulation enter into the kingdom of God"; Luke 13:24, "Strive to enter by the narrow door, for I say to you, there are many who will seek to enter and will not be able"; cf. 2 Peter 1:8, 11; John 5:29; 1 Tim. 6:19; Phil. 1:12; 1 Thess. 5:6ff.; Rom. 8:17; 1 Tim. 2:11; Gal. 6:8; Heb. 10:35ff.

Ps. 119:35, "Lead me in the path of Your commandments, for I delight in it"; 139:24, "Lead me in the eternal way"; 143:10, "Let Your good Spirit lead me into the land of uprightness." These statements are not speaking of the means of application of righteousness and salvation, but of the method and order by which God brings salvation to those who have been justified.

Here pertains also the statement of Paul in 1 Tim. 2:15, "The woman shall be saved through bearing children, if she continues in faith and love and holiness with modesty." The pains in childbearing have been imposed as a punishment for sin. Yet the woman should know that this is not a sign of divine wrath and thus lose heart, says Paul, if she bears her difficulties with patience and remains in faith, she can be saved, even if her troubles are a punishment for sin.

Class 10

This explanation can also be correctly applied to certain statements pertaining to the Law in the Old Testament. For the ceremonial washings were not only signs but figures of the person and work of the Messiah through which were set forth, offered, and applied to believers the promise of grace for the sake of the coming Seed. Thus mercy, blessing, and life were set forth for those who kept the commandments, the testimonies, and the ceremonies. Deut. 5:32–33, "Observe and do what the Lord your God has commanded you, that you may live and that it may be well with you"; cf. 7:12–13; 11:26–27; 30:19. In this way certain statements in Moses which pertain to the Law include also the promise concerning Christ and faith in Christ. There is great value in the solution to this problem, if we simply keep in mind that the statements which speak of works include faith in Christ.

Thus in the Levitical sacrifices there is the expiation and remission of sin; Lev. 4:35, "The priest shall burn the offerings upon the Lord's altar of incense, and he shall pray for him and for his sin, and it shall be remitted to him." Lev. 5:18 teaches the same thing. Note also Lev. 16:30, "On that day your expiation will take place, and you will be cleansed from all your sins before the Lord"; Num. 15:25–26, "They shall offer to the Lord a burnt offering for themselves and for their sin and their error; all the people of the children of Israel shall be forgiven, and also the strangers who dwell among them, for the guilt of all the people is because of their ignorance." In regard to this and similar sacrifices they [the opponents] judge that this sacrifice had to be made only to expiate civil and political punishment, so that they not be punished by the magistrate. But this is puerile. For the text is speaking of a true expiation of sin before God, not indeed by the mere doing of the act (*ex opere operato*) but out of faith in the promise of the coming Seed whose death and suffering were prefigured in the sacrifices. Yet because, as is so often the case, many people, in the performance of these ceremonies, sought remission by the mere doing of them, therefore the prophets in many places and the entire Epistle to the Hebrews refute this idea and take away the expiation and remission of sins from the mere outward performance of the Levitical ceremonies. David in Ps. 51:2, 7, shows the true use of these ceremonies when he says in both verses, "Wash me." He is showing by these words that he is looking forward in faith to the passion of the promised Seed, by whose blood he wants to be washed from his sins. Later on he adds: "Purge me with hyssop and I shall be clean," by which he indicates that this is the proper use of these ceremonies, namely, that through them the merits of the Messiah are applied, and faith confirmed and sealed, as happens with us in the case of the sacraments.

Class 11

When Scripture says in Ecclus. 1:27, "The fear of the Lord drives out sin," and Tobit 4:11 and 12:9, "Alms purge away sin," also Ecclus. 3:30, "As the burning fire is extinguished by water, so sins are extinguished by alms"; Prov. 15:27, "Through mercy and faithfulness sins are purged: but through the fear of the Lord everyone turns away from evil," such passages are not speaking of propitiation or satisfaction for sin, as when John says in 1 John 1:7, "The blood of Jesus Christ, God's Son, cleanses us from all sin," or Heb. 1:3, "Christ by Himself made a purging for sins and sits at the right hand of God," but these passages are saying that through repentance and zeal for godliness our sins may be avoided and we may beware of them, and the root of sin may be put to death and crucified.

The term "purging of sin" is also used when habitual sinning, as it occurs in our nature, becomes the object of careful purging and cleansing, so that the cause of sin is cut out, destroyed, and it is cured by effective remedies. But it is most important if we work against the sins which have already been committed.

Scripture speaks regarding such statements in this way. Ecclus. 1:28 adds, "For he who is without fear cannot do justly. For the anger of his boldness is his ruin." Prov. 15:27 (Vulgate) adds, "Through the fear of the Lord everyone declines from evil." Thus we must understand the statement in 1 Peter 4:8 which cites Prov. 10:12, "Love covers a multitude of sins," and James 5:20, "He who converts a sinner from the error of his ways shall save a soul from death and shall hide a multitude of sins."

These are the chief answers which can be raised in opposition to almost all the arguments of the adversaries. If our young people will remember that in these objections they can have at hand the means whereby it will not be easy for our adversaries to lead them away from their sincere faith. I wanted to divide these points into the above classes or categories, not so as to take away from learners the well thought out labors of others, but that I might show to our young people in a summary fashion how they can retain, without a great deal of labor, the true meaning of some of the most important Scripture passages and not be disturbed by any of these allegations. Now let us move on to other matters.

The Difference Between the Old and New Covenants

[MELANCHTHON'S TEXT]

There is one ongoing church of God which has existed from the creation of man and the giving of the promise after the fall of Adam down to the present day, but the spreading of the teaching of the church has taken place in different places and under different kinds of government. It is profitable to consider in a chronological order the history and the testimonies in which God has revealed Himself from the very beginning and showed His wrath against sin and has declared His mercy to those who have turned to Him. For in order that we might know that the doctrine of the church is the only, the first, and the true doctrine, God in His special blessing willed that from the beginning this ongoing history should be put in writing and preserved, and to this book which was written through the work of the patriarchs and the prophets, He has added testimonies, along with the demonstrations of the great miracles, in order that we might understand whence and how the doctrine of the church has been spread abroad from the beginning of time. But later on the religions of the heathen arose, which here and there in an ungodly manner developed new gods and new forms of worship, when they had departed from the original teaching. Nor did the Greeks and other writers, who were of their religious persuasion, know the true God, but daily dreamed up horrible licentiousness, sometimes dealing with Bacchus and other times with Diana.

Thus we should understand that it is a great blessing of God that He has given to His church a certain Book, and He preserves it for us and gathers His church around it. Finally, the church is the people who embrace this Book, hear, learn, and retain as their own its teachings in their worship life and in the governing of their morals. Therefore where this Book is rejected, the church of God is not present, as is the case among the Mohammedans; or where its teachings have been suppressed or false interpretations set forth, as has happened among heretics. Therefore we must read and meditate upon this Book so that its teachings may be retained, as we are often commanded regarding the study of it, e.g., 1 Tim. 4:13, "Devote yourself to reading"; Col. 3:16, "Let the Word of Christ dwell in you richly." The Holy Spirit testifies that it is His will that the doctrine and the divine testimonies be put in writing, e.g., Ps. 102:18, "This shall be written for the generations to come, and the people who shall be created shall praise the Lord."

Therefore we should love and cultivate the studies of this divinely given Book. First, we should know its substance and that there are two kinds of teaching contained in the entire Book, the Law and the promise of grace, which is properly called the Gospel. This distinction is a light to the entire Scripture and was taught even before Moses.

The Law is the knowledge planted in the mind of man in the creation, teaching that there is one God, the Creator of things, and that we must worship Him and render Him obedience in keeping with the difference between what is honorable and what is shameful and subject to punishment, which God Himself has impressed on the mind. For the image of God was in man and this image was the sure and certain knowledge of God and the knowledge of the Law, and in his will there was a turning to God. But although after the Fall the will was turned away from God and the knowledge in his mind was darkened, yet there did remain a knowledge that there is an eternal and immutable judgment of God against sin which testifies that God is angry with sin.

But after the Fall the promise of reconciliation is not the knowledge which has been inserted into our nature, but it is a voice brought from the hidden bosom of the Father which was previously unknown to all creatures, by which voice God testifies that He does receive men into His grace, that He will destroy sin and death, and that He will restore righteousness and life for the sake of the coming Seed of the woman. The proclamation of His birth began in paradise. The voice of the Law is the accusation against our disobedience. But the promise was this: "The Seed of the woman shall bruise the head of the serpent." After this came the patriarchs, such as Adam, Seth, Enoch, and others who, by a legitimate call of God, exercised the priesthood and spread the true doctrine.

The Law which prohibits murder is expressly proclaimed in the preachment to Cain and later in the word repeated to Noah. The Law which prohibits vagrant lusts is sanctified in paradise and later the testimony is given concerning the judgment of God in the Flood and the destruction of Sodom. Likewise the promise becomes increasingly clearer, as when it is said to Abraham, "In your seed shall all the nations be blessed," Gen. 22:18.

Therefore what do we properly call the old covenant and the new covenant? For it has always been necessary to proclaim both the Law and the Gospel, and the voice of each has been the ongoing ministry in the church. I reply: The old covenant in the most proper sense is the promulgation of the Law, or the pact by which the people of Israel were bound to the Law and to this form of civil life for this purpose, that in this civil arrangement the promise of the coming Messiah might be preserved and propagated, and for this reason in this people there was also the true church of the elect.

We must carefully consider this purpose which the ignorant multitude among the people of Israel failed to understand, for they fell into three errors:

1. Just as they saw the promise of the land as being the possession of a certain piece of real estate and a certain government as being purely physical, so they believed that the promised Messiah would increase this land area and strengthen it. They did not understand that He was sent to be the sacrifice, to abolish sin and death, and that through this government or nation He would give righteousness and eternal life to those who believed.

2. They did not understand the principal reason for the promulgation of the Law. For it was given not only as the civil law by which this nation should be ruled, but that it might be the voice of God given by sure and clear testimony by which the judgment of God was revealed as something eternal and immutable in its opposition to sin, so that the promise of the Messiah might be sought when the wrath of God became understood. But the great majority was entirely ignorant of this and thought that the Law was only a matter of civil obedience and that the law of God was satisfied by this external obedience. They did not understand inner sins or doubts about the wrath and mercy of God; they did not know about genuine shame or ardent faith and love; they did not understand about trust in God for divine help in their prayers or their doubts as to whether God really receives their prayers. They had countless erring notions. They believed that many of these things were not sinful and were not in conflict with the law of God.

3. They believed that sins and lapses were compensated for by sacrifices and that they merited the remission of sins by the killing of bulls and other ceremonies. Under this opinion they piled up sacrifices. Indeed, they even dreamed up new ones or took them over from the gentiles. They sacrificed their own children in order that they might merit more good things in times of great and difficult troubles. Human blindness is prone to such errors as this, so that it imagines that works which we ourselves have created out of our imagination are particularly pleasing to God. These three errors were widely spread among the people.

Yet God in this civil arrangement always preserved some true church, that is, a gathering of those who truly believe, as Isaiah says in 1:9, "If the Lord of hosts had not left us a remnant, we should have been as Sodom." Thus the true church attacked errors and called some back to the true worship of God; it taught that this civil structure had been established in order that there might be a definite and a sure place for the church, until the coming of the Messiah, with the result that in the meantime in this place the promise might be preserved and spread abroad. The church also bore witness that the Messiah was sent that He might make sacrifices for sin and give righteousness and eternal life, but not a worldly empire in this mortal life.

Furthermore the church taught regarding the Law that external obedience and discipline do not satisfy the law of God nor please Him, unless the true foundation has first been laid, that is, that we know the promise of the Messiah and for His sake receive the remission of sins and reconciliation. They taught in their worship that God for the sake of this Messiah truly did receive them and hear their prayers. By this faith they taught that there must be a beginning of obedience to this Law in the heart, that is, the statements of the Decalog concerning love, worship, and the fear of God.

They proclaimed the same in regard to the ceremonies, that they were not merely given in order that they might be the price for the remission of sins; but that they might be signs of the coming Messiah and testimonies of their profession of faith and exercises which served as instruction regarding faith and worship; and they were not of value unless the foundation was first laid down that they knew the promise of the Messiah and had received the remission of sins and that there was the beginning of obedience to the first part of the Law, namely the Decalog.

So also with regard to the third part of the Law, that is, the judicial aspects, they taught that the civil law was pleasing to God when the true foundation had been laid, namely knowledge of the promised Messiah and reception of the remission of sins and the beginning in the heart of the first part of the Law, that is, the Decalog, in order that trust in divine aid and for the glory of God and love of our neighbor, the civil duties must also be performed, not as Alexander, Sulla Marius, and others carried out the laws—with contempt for God and solely for the sake of their own power and purposes.

In this way the prophets showed the promise and the use of the Law, and on the other hand attacked superstitions, as we read in Jer. 7:22, "I did not give command to your fathers regarding burnt offerings"; Ps. 51:16, "You do not desire sacrifice." These and similar passages seemed to be in open conflict with the Law and gave reason for ungodly kings and priests armed with the pretense of the Law to inflict cruel persecution on the prophets. But it was the will of the prophets that the ceremonies be not commanded unless there was also with them the knowledge and trust in the Messiah, repentance, or as it is said in common language, that the ceremonies not be done merely as a formality (ex opere operato) and accompanied by other errors which the ignorant multitude dreamed up.

That this establishment of the civil structure by Moses is properly called the old covenant is confirmed by such statements as these: Gal. 4:24ff., "These are two covenants, the one from Mount Sinai which bears children for slavery," that is, which binds men to this civil structure, which even though it was a great blessing (for it was most beneficial to know for certain that the church was there), yet there was slavery there, that is, the highest good had not yet been made known, the new and eternal life which was to be demonstrated as the true liberty in the new covenant. But there was the ministration of the Law preaching God's wrath against sin and compelling obedience, instructing the people by certain types and shadows regarding the blessings to come.

Thus Hebrews 7 shows that the old covenant was abrogated because it was weak and useless. It does not speak of the promise of the coming Messiah. This covenant was not useless to the patriarchs, but the Law was weak and useless, that is to say, for justification or for abolishing sin and death, for it was the purpose of the Law to do this. Although it was a great benefit that a definite location be given to the church on earth and that a beautiful civil structure and outward discipline be established, yet all these good things were things which perish, subject to death, and they were not righteousness or eternal life.

Jer. 31:31ff. clearly calls the old covenant a treaty which was made when the people were being led out of Egypt, and in a very skillful way he distinguishes between the old and the new covenants. The old was the promulgation of the external law and a pronouncement of judgment against sin; it was the establishment of a political structure so that there might be a definite seat for the Word and testimonies of God. But the new covenant was not an external promulgation of the Law, but new and eternal life, light, and righteousness while the Law burned warmly in the hearts [by the abolition] of death and sin. Jeremiah includes the whole scope of the new covenant just as many of the prophets do when they speak of the blessings of the Messiah, and they not only instruct concerning the beginning but of the complete restoration of man's nature. Thus there is a clear distinction between the new and the old covenants, since the new covenant speaks of the heavenly and complete nature freed from all evils; and this is bestowed on our old nature which had been subjected to the Law and to death.

Here also we should refer those titles which have been applied. It is called the old covenant both with respect to time and because of the subject, for the promulgation of the Law preceded in time the restoration of our nature, something which begins with the resurrection of Christ and is to be completed when the entire church is raised and adorned with His glory. Second, it is called "old" because of the subject, because this old nature is pressed down by the judgment of the Law and must be coerced by the discipline of the Law. Just as our nature remains in this life, so the Law remains and the enormous burden which the Law denounces with its curses, that is, the eternal wrath of God remains, unless remission of sins is received through the Gospel. Further, there also remain the great calamities which are punishments by which God punishes the sins of all who are outside the church and in the church. Wars are created, diseases, poverty, devastations, exiles, injuries, desertions, betrayals, troubles on the part of friends, and finally countless sorrows. We should know that these chastenings do not happen by accident but they are the constant voice of the Law which is admonishing this wretched nature of ours regarding the eternal wrath of God and restraining and coercing our nature so that we should not think that by the destruction of the Mosaic civil structure the judgment of God and His curses against sin are no longer in effect. To be sure, the blessing and deliverance are begun in those who believe the Gospel and are thus freed from the eternal wrath of God; but as long as the old corruption of our nature remains, the punishments also remain.

For the voice of the moral law and the curses have been revealed not only to the people of that time, but that there might be the testimony and judgment of God against sin in all places against the entire human race. Therefore the old covenant is called a burden because it crushes the entire old nature, not only in the ungodly but also in the saints before their full deliverance. But for the saints there is consolation, help, and mitigation offered in the Gospel and to the same degree the curse is abrogated. But the ungodly perish in keeping with the curse, without deliverance, so that even many very outstanding men have perished horribly, crushed both by calamities of this life and the eternal wrath of God, men such as Saul, Pompey, Caesar, Crassus, and Cato, who are before us daily as examples in keeping with the whole history of the world. For since the nature of men is guilty, it is pressed down by the curses of the Law.

From these citations which I have quoted we can sufficiently understand how the nomenclature of the old and new covenants square with one another if we take into account the time of the promulgation of the Law and the matter of the complete restoration of our nature, especially if we take into consideration the fact that our old nature is crushed and coerced up until the time of its complete restoration. When we understand this, then individuals should realize that their troubles are a testimony to the Law by which we are instructed about the wrath of God in order that we may seek the Messiah; and they should also realize that a bridle has been put upon us to curb this old nature of ours.

The new covenant is the proclamation of the remission of sins and the giving of eternal life, and the giving of new righteousness with the destruction of sin and death, for the sake of Christ the Mediator. When it is called the new covenant we understand the beginning of this in every proclamation of the Gospel, from the very beginning of the giving of the promise, and we understand that this is brought to fulfillment in the entire church when it has been raised from death and puts on eternal glory.

The apostles saw an example of this great glory above their heads and upon some of their members when they witnessed the ascension of the risen Christ. For there they saw that mortality had been completely abolished, they saw the new nature shining with divine light, new righteousness, and life. Jeremiah speaks this way concerning the new covenant, including not only the preaching of the Gospel before the resurrection but the complete blessing, 31:33–34, "I will put My law in their hearts, and I will be their God and they shall be My people; and no longer will each man teach his neighbor, saying, 'Know the Lord,' for they will all know Me . . . for I will forgive their iniquity and remember their sin no more." Here He seems to be contradicting Himself, for first He says, "I will make a new covenant," but the covenants are made with a certain terminology and speak in the language of ministration or a ministry through which God reveals His will, and often in other places it is said that in the new covenant a new word must be proclaimed. For example, Is. 61:1, "The

Spirit of the Lord is upon me to preach good tidings to the afflicted. He has sent me,"
but later we read in Jer. 31:34, "No longer will each man teach his neighbor." Here
He is saying that the ministry of the word preached by man will cease. These points,
if properly applied, are in agreement.

For the new covenant begins in this mortal life through the ministry of proclaiming the promise in all ages, but it is entirely completed when the light has been shed abroad, along with righteousness and eternal life, in which the ministry of teaching the commandments to men has ceased and we rejoice before the sight of the eternal God. But in the meantime even if the new covenant is beginning among the regenerate, yet because our old flesh remains, as said above, it is terribly oppressed by the curses of the Law, that is, by calamities of every kind, in order that the wrath of God against sin may be understood and the Mediator sought; likewise, that sin may be crushed and punished. Therefore, as we have often said above, the church is oppressed with very great troubles because particularly in the church God wants His wrath against sin to be seen clearly. Thus in the end the church will completely strip off its sin and be freed from all penalties and adorned with eternal life and glory, as shown in these words: "Their sin will I remember no more," Jer. 31:34.

Likewise in 2 Corinthians 3, Paul distinguishes the new covenant from the old and brings us the most important teaching and the sweetest comfort. The teaching is that he calls the old covenant "the letter" and "the ministration of death," vv. 6–7, that is, the Law in its accusation and condemnation of man. But he calls the new covenant "the ministration of the Spirit," v. 8, that is, the proclamation of the Gospel through which the Holy Spirit is given, who begins in the heart the new light, righteousness, and life, as it also says in Rom. 8:15, "You have received the Spirit of the adoption of sons whereby we cry, 'Abba! Father!'"

When we know mercy through the Gospel, our minds no longer flee from God but draw near to Him as to a Father, and as they draw near they are helped by the Holy Spirit, they pray, they believe, and rely on the promises, since they look upon God as having joined Himself to human nature by an eternal and immutable covenant when His Son was born of the virgin, that is, when the two natures, the divine and the human, were joined together in the Son, they hold evident testimony which shows that the human race is a matter of concern to God, when they hear His Son has been sent to be the sacrifice and the author of new and eternal life, as Isaiah says in 9:6, "the everlasting Father," to whom they flee for refuge; and this is the voice of the Gospel which is "the power of God unto salvation to every one who believes," Rom. 1:16, that is, through this power the Holy Spirit is given along with the beginning of the new and eternal righteousness.

This comfort is added: Someone may wonder why the glory of the new covenant is so greatly celebrated by the prophets, when that gathering known as the church which took place under the apostles never has such a settled order, such significant leaders, such great victories and miracles as are seen in the exodus from Egypt and the establishment of the Jewish civil state.

Paul supplies the answer to this: All this glorying took place in order that there might be testimonies not only to the civil government which was going to perish but also to the promise of the future eternal reign. They teach in order that we may believe that since God was with that nation which was going to perish, much more shall He be with His eternal kingdom. Human judgments stumble when they see the church as a dispersed and wandering flock without any human supports, without powerful rulers, and finally without any order. Then people are tormented by this weakness and ask what is the benefit of the Gospel and the name of Christ when we feel nothing in ourselves of these new and wonderful gifts. Further, we are left in the midst of our troubles, just as the rest of the condemned people in this world.

Paul puts this point in opposition to these doubts: If the civil structure which was going to perish was the ministration of glory, "how much more glorious will be this ministration of eternal salvation," 2 Cor. 3:9, that is, it will be efficacious in those who receive the Gospel and it will be preserved in marvelous ways. We suffer in our hearts in the midst of so many tumults of human affairs; we are anxious for the church, for its doctrine, and the destruction of its learning. These dangers instruct us that the church is not preserved by human plans but by divine actions among the great overthrow and ruination of kingdoms. God wants us to consider these things and He wants us to seek His protection so that we are not torn apart in our hearts. He gives us the promise that His church shall remain on earth to the end of time, as Christ clearly says in Matt. 28:20, "Lo, I am with you always, even unto the end of the age." Now, since the church will remain, the Gospel must be glorious, that is, efficacious; the church must be protected by the marvelous works of God; the study of theological literature must remain even if in this last age of the world all things are weaker and more out of shape. We must comfort ourselves with these thoughts and continue in prayer.

There are in many places in the prophets several descriptions of the new covenant which we must mention along with the sufferings of Christ and His blessings, the remission of sins, and the eternal kingdom, that is, new and eternal righteousness and life, as Isaiah 53 says; cf. Dan. 9:24, "Seventy weeks are decreed concerning your people . . . to put an end to sin . . . to show everlasting righteousness." Again, v. 26, "The Lord shall be cut off." In these passages there is a brief summary of the points which are comprehended in the new covenant.

Likewise it says in Zech. 9:11, "You also by the blood of your covenant have sent forth your prisoners out free from the waterless pit" (Vulgate). This is a short statement and there are many like it in the prophets, but by means of comparison they become very clear. He calls the blood of the sacrifice the "blood of the covenant" through which we must establish and confirm the covenant regarding matters of eternal significance, that is, the blood of Christ. For the prophets knew that sins were not taken away by the blood of animals but that these sacrifices were signs of another Victim. "You have led out your prisoners," he says, "from the waterless pit," that is, from eternal death. The captives were those who were Your people and You led them out by means of blood, that is, by the sacrifice which had been promised, so that eternity might be restored to us, namely, God's wrath assuaged by the death of the Son of God. Thus this passage includes the death of Christ and eternal blessings.

Next in ch. 12 Zechariah explains what kind of kingdom this is and what particular kind of actions it will produce. V. 10, "I will pour out upon the house of David the Spirit of grace and prayer." Here He speaks of good things which belong to the new covenant. The Spirit of grace is the Holy Spirit by whom our hearts are aided so that they may know Him when they hear the Gospel and believe that they have been received into grace and may be assured that the wrath of God has really been assuaged. But afterward, when they come to know His mercy, they pray and he particularly calls it prayer because this is the worship which belongs to the church alone and is absolutely unknown to all those who do not know the Gospel

At the same time that this teaching and comfort is being given to us, we are instructed that we must pray; and this means that our worship is pleasing to God and will not be in vain. These descriptions and others like them in the prophets are very useful and give us instruction regarding the new covenant and its blessings which we must look at closely, since we may apply these marvelous comforts to our needs and thus we will call up the Spirit of prayer.

When they speak of the new covenant, most of the prophets preach at the same time of present and eternal punishments of the ungodly, for example, Amos 9:8–9, "Behold, the eyes of God are upon the sinful kingdom, and I will destroy it . . . but I shall not utterly destroy the kingdom of Jacob. For lo, I will give the command and I will shake the house of Israel among all the nations, as wheat is shaken with a sieve, yet not a grain shall fall to the ground. All the sinners of My people shall die by the sword. In that day I will raise up the tabernacle of David . . ." that is, while I am gathering for Myself the church, at the same time with frightful punishments I shall declare My wrath against the ungodly; and when their kingdoms have been destroyed, I will rescue and preserve a small select group. Thus when Jerusalem has been destroyed and the nation of the Jews dispersed, a remnant shall be rescued by the preaching of the apostles and afterward, when even the Roman Empire has been destroyed by civil and foreign wars, still the church will be gathered. And now the most frightful actions of kingdoms and murders are the fatal punishments of the world, among which God still rescues His church and He will also glorify the whole church at the same time that He casts the ungodly into eternal punishments.

Isaiah 65 describes the new covenant in these words regarding prayer and proclamation, "I said, 'Behold Me,' to a nation which did not know My name," v. 1. Then in regard to the punishments of the ungodly he says, vv. 11–12, "You are those who have forsaken the Lord . . . you shall bow down to the slaughter." Yet He also says, "I shall save the church, so that if one grape is found, I shall not destroy the whole place." In regard to the fulfillment of the new covenant He adds, v. 17, "I create new heavens. . . ."

These statements of the prophets must be studied in order that we may distinguish between the beginning and completion, so that we not be torn apart by the sad sight of these empires rushing to their destruction and think that the church of God no longer exists. Rather we should understand that in the midst of these horrendous confusions we must still seek and retain the Word of God, and that those who join themselves with the true church by their faith, their will, their prayers, and their confession, are members of the people of God wherever they may be, even if they are crushed by slavery and death among the overthrowing of kingdoms. In this present day they all understand that this comfort is necessary for the godly. For even sane people are often troubled by this kind of trial: Has God completely rejected those nations where church structure no longer exists? Here many people fall into despair when they see a few godly people struggling in an overwhelming contest. Describing sorrows of this kind Hosea says in 13:13–14, "The sorrows of a travailing woman shall come upon them . . . I will redeem them from the power of death, O death, I will be your death." What he calls "the sorrows of a travailing woman" reasonably intelligent people can understand when they are troubled at the sight of the Turks with their pillage and their other attacks and uproars in many places; but comfort is added which will encourage the godly to take refuge in the promise of the new covenant; "O death, I will be your death," and again, "Every one who calls on the name of the Lord will be saved," Joel 2:32.

I have said what the new covenant is and shown that we must consider which statements are speaking of the beginning and which of the consummation. For it is called the new covenant both because of the promise which was given after the fall and because of the beginning of new and eternal righteousness and life, blessings which will be given to us in their completeness after the resurrection. But now the church in the weakened condition of our nature is subject to the cross and all the empires of the world are attacking it with frightful punishments, and this will continue to the end. Therefore even if the state of Israel has been destroyed and with it the ceremonies and civil laws have been brought to extinction, yet the voice of the Law which judges sin, that is, the voice of the Decalog, always remains in force, and the punishments also remain, but they are mitigated for the godly.

Just as in the civil structure of Israel God promised peace to the people and other blessings if they would obey, so the church, although it is a little flock in a hopeless condition and has neither power nor any definite geographical center, yet because it *needs food and shelter for this life, it has the promises not of a definite location but of shelter and nourishment of a general kind.*

Therefore we should prudently apply the examples of the punishments and blessings of Israel to our own life, so that just as they were polluted by idols, lusts, and other crimes and were punished, so now punishments fall upon all those who have become polluted because the judgment of God against sin is the same in all ages and the examples which have been given are universal for all the human race as the voice of the Law; and they speak to all ages and urge us to repent. Then also David, Isaiah, and many others in calling upon God are heard and defended in their calling. So also now we should understand that God will give shelter to His church when it is scattered, just as in days gone by He gave to Elijah in his exile the place of refuge at the home of the widow of Zarephath.

Yet we must realize that there is a difference, that no kingdom has been promised to us, no special location in this world has been promised, but we do know in a general way that God in this life will give shelter to His churches and to the studies of His Word, just as to Christ at the time of His birth lodging was given in the manger. On this point Paul says in 1 Tim. 4:8, "Godliness has the promise of the life which now is and of that which is to come."

It is profitable to understand why the promises of bodily blessings were given. We can mention three reasons:

First, that the ravings of the Epicureans might be refuted, that is, so that we do not get the idea that physical blessings come to us either by accident or by the natural order of things, without the help of God; but may determine correctly that God is concerned about these good things and that God does give us shelter, government, our home, peace, food, success in our endeavors. Often such instruction as this is given, as is found in Ps. 127:1, "Except the Lord build the house . . ."; and in Ps. 128:1–2 we read, "Blessed are all who fear the Lord. You shall eat the labor of your hands"; 37:19, "In the days of famine they shall eat their fill." Christ says in Matt. 6:33, "Seek first the kingdom of God . . . and all these other things shall be given to you in addition." He even commands us to ask for daily bread, and in Deut. 8:3ff., God afflicted the people with want and gave them bread, in order that He might show that "man does not live by bread alone but by every word which proceeds out of the mouth of God." Of Isaac it is said in Gen. 26:12–13, "He sowed in that land and received in the same year a hundredfold, and the Lord blessed him and he was greatly enriched." Gen. 28:20, "If God will be with me, and keep me and give me bread. . . ." Finally, testimonies are spread everywhere regarding the help which God gives to this physical life of ours to defend us and to aid us with necessities.

The second reason that the promises of physical blessing have been given to us is that we may know that God will protect His church in this life. For in the great number of dangers which surround us we need this comfort.

The third reason is that our faith and calling may be strengthened in asking and waiting for these necessities, that our knowledge of the goodness and presence of God may increase along with our gratitude. Thus Paul says in Rom. 5:3–5, "Tribulation works patience and patience experience and experience hope, and hope is not put to shame." When Paul sees in the ship that his prayers were heard and that all the men were saved, even though the ship was destroyed, he recognized the presence of God and by this testimony his faith burned more brightly and he was moved to give thanks.

Thinking of things like this trains us also in praying for physical blessings. Let us also train ourselves in giving thanks. Although it is necessary that as individuals we be prepared for all calamities, yet in this practice of prayer there are two objectives. We pray for the whole body of the church and for ourselves. We ask that the entire church not be destroyed by wars, and we beseech God's blessings on the entire group throughout the world. Although evil is not always taken away from every individual, yet we pray that it may be mitigated. Thus when the people prayed for David's army, they prayed first that the entire army might be saved and then they prayed for individuals who had prepared to obey even if they died in the struggle; but still they prayed for mitigation so that many might be saved or at least that they might have comfort from God, as was the case with Jonathan, who, although he was killed, yet was adorned and strengthened by God, and the side which Jonathan himself had hoped would win was finally victorious. I mention these points in order that we may learn in our praying to include not only ourselves but the entire church and all governments and by these practices men must always be instructed.

I have explained the distinction between the old and the new covenants because it is useful in the church to have a good understanding of this point. But finally the reader must be warned that the political structure established by Moses has been destroyed, so that the ceremonial and the civil laws have also been abolished (unless they are part of the natural law), and they have no more relevance for us than the laws of Solon. But just as the nature of man remains, so natural laws remain, such as the fact that people who are in the first or second degree of consanguinity should not marry. The Decalog is among these natural Laws. It is the chief part of the law, the basis on which the rest is established. For God willed that the Decalog be promulgated in order that there might be a sure testimony that the clear light of divine judgment against sin is in force over against the entire human race. Thus the people were led out of Egypt with so many miracles and were miraculously protected for so many years in the desert, in order that the presence of God might be seen and all these marvels recognized as the voice of the Decalog which was not abolished but is the eternal and immutable judgment of God against sin.

Their sins are forgiven for those who take refuge in Christ because sin is displeasing to God, just as the eating of pork was to Him who had then forbidden it.

This voice of the Law remains and is eternal: "God does not take pleasure in wickedness," Ps. 5:4. But He has poured out His great wrath against sin upon His Son who was put to death for us and paid our penalty. By the intercession of this payment we are received. But those who do not flee for refuge to the Son remain under condemnation by the voice of the Law and will perish. We shall explain these points more fully later on.

But even though the Levitical ceremonies have been abolished, yet they contain images of many of the blessings of Christ, but they require careful treatment. For under a corrupt imitation of the Mosaic law many errors have taken root. In the Law the establishment of the order of priests was a very honorable thing. The high priest was established; some families were set apart for sacrifices, others in their turn were on hand for other special tasks relating to the tabernacle or the temple; they instructed the people, performed sacrifices, settled controversies on doctrine; they were well versed in sacred studies. Finally, there was no group of people in the entire human race which was more honored and venerated than this priestly society. For although there were often among them ungodly people and finally the Pharisees and Sadducees, yet because God had given to the family of priests His promises, there were always some godly men remaining among them, such as Jeremiah and later Simeon, Zacharias, and many others.

This example of a group who were the most honored of any people through the whole world certainly shows that in the church there has always been and will be the ministration of the voice of God through which He is efficacious and imparts eternal life. Likewise He instructs us that this ministry must be treated with reverence. But the principal function of this group is to set forth the Gospel, as is said in Mal. 2:7, "The lips of the priest should preserve knowledge and they should seek the Law at his mouth for he is the messenger of the Lord of hosts."

Just as at one time the gentiles kept certain ceremonies although the teaching of Noah, Shem, and Japheth was lost, so the unlearned in these later times devise, in keeping with the image of the Levitical priest, a kingdom of priests in which even though the light of the Gospel has been darkened, they still give authority to the priest, to establish laws for their new worship; and in order to allude to the Levitical sacrifices they turn the Lord's Supper into a sacrifice of a certain order which they imagine is profitable for both the living and the dead by merely going through the motions (ex opere operato), that is, without any good intention on the part of the participant. These perversions and this zeal for wickedness must be condemned and we have to ask the question: What was the original use of the sacrifices and what did they really signify?

However there are many lovely images in the ceremonies which can give instruction to pious people regarding many points, but we need to be cautious that our interpretation is correct. There is a very appropriate picture of the church of all times, namely, the ark located in the Holy of Holies. This was called the "ark of the covenant."

Therefore first it was called "the ark of the covenant" to signify that this was the only people with whom God had made a pact by express word. Therefore when the Word was lost, then the people ceased to be the church of God; and finally only a few are truly the members of the church when they cling to the covenant by faith and in a sense enclose or fortify themselves in this ark in which they are not merely to contemplate the walls. But this term "covenant" or "treaty" means that in a sense God has made a pact with us and that we have been accepted by Him. You can thus see that by this term is signified the fact that it is the church which clings to the covenant, that is, to the Word of God.

Second: In the ark were gathered the tables of the Decalog by which is signified that the church must always be the guardian of those books of the prophets and apostles in which God reveals Himself. Therefore where the books do not exist there it is impossible for the church of God to exist, and the ark must be preserved for the sake of these books. Thus a church will always be preserved which will act as a guardian of these books. For first the profession and the guardianship of the book signifies that we are invited to preserve and read this book. Then it signifies what the church of God really is, as distinguished from the rest of the human race. The knowledge of God given to us in the Word shines in the minds of this group, and there is the beginning of obedience, and some day this obedience will be complete. Such will be the eternal people of God keeping Him in their minds, and when their nature has been completely restored, continuing to hold to the Decalog; the church will burn with love for God with its whole body and whole mind, free from all evil desires.

Third: The ark was covered by a golden table which was called the mercy seat. This term signifies that the whole church is protected against the wrath and terrible judgment of God by our Mediator Christ, for whose sake—because He is the one who makes propitiation for us—God spares us, receives us, and keeps us. Without this shelter the nature of man would be crushed under the terrible burden of God's wrath.

There is also added the promise concerning this propitiation in Ex. 25:22: From this mercy seat God was going to speak to the people and there He would answer their prayer. Thus this table had the name of mercy seat or place of propitiation because there God wished to be invoked, and He gathered the people there so that new arks and temples would not be erected in other places. There are several types which apply here. Just as the mercy seat is the seat of God, so Christ is the seat of God, because in Christ the divine nature truly exists and before Him the church is gathered; and our prayers are not heard except for His sake, as it is written in John 16:23, "Whatsoever you ask the Father in My name He will give it to you." Therefore those who pray without knowledge of Christ or trust in Him will be rejected by God, as will all those who do not know the Gospel.

Above this mercy seat stood two cherubim with wings joined and facing one another. These signify the ministry of teaching under both the old and the new covenants. The wings are touching one another and the faces looking at each other, signifying the consensus of teaching in both covenants. The message of the prophets and the apostles is the same in regard to sin, the deliverance through Christ, eternal life, and finally the true knowledge of God and the true worship of Him. The whole ceremonial aspect of the ancient sacrifices typified the one sacrifice of the Son of God who was made a victim for us, endured the wrath of God which was poured out upon Him as if He Himself had committed our sins. No angels and no men can adequately describe the enormity of this wrath, sorrow, shame, and ignominy, but yet our minds must be moved to think of such things. Further, these cherubim instruct us that there is no church where the ministration of teaching the doctrine of the prophets and apostles is not present. The carrying of rods and the rings also signify the ministers, teachers and scholars of the church. Although this service on our part is imperfect and far inferior to the government of the ungodly, yet we should know that it is pleasing to God and necessary for the human race and that it is marvelously defended and aided by God among the terrible torments of life. Thus it is full of genuine dignity, and when we think of the importance of this work of ours, we should be eager to adorn our activity with diligence, patience, and modesty; and in the face of all perils we should sustain ourselves with the promises, "Behold, I am with you always, even to the end of the age," Matt. 28:20, and "Upon this rock I will build My church and the gates of hell shall not prevail against it," Matt. 16:18.

Furthermore, although we are, as Paul says in 2 Cor. 4:7, "earthen vessels," wretched men, weak, needy, poor, yet "we are ambassadors for Christ," as Paul says, 2 Cor. 5:20, a role which God will surely defend as He declared in the calling of many of the prophets and apostles, indicating that this work is important to Him. Note the great miracles attached to the call of Isaiah, Jeremiah, John the Baptist, and Paul These things did not happen by mere accident, nor did they apply to those men only, but these testimonies are useful for the whole church for they show that the Gospel is truly the voice of God and that God is concerned about His servants. This is sufficient instruction regarding the Levitical ceremonies to enable us to understand that these types refer to great things, and for the correct interpretation we absolutely must have a true understanding of the Gospel.

Finally, although the civil laws in no way pertain to us, yet in a general way they do instruct us that God is pleased with orderly civil life, contracts, the concept of government officials, courts, and punishment for crimes; and they demonstrate that godly people must exercise their faith, their confession, their patience, and their love in carrying out such duties. For as we said, above and beyond these works of civil *righteousness we must hold to the foundation, namely the knowledge of the promises and faith and the beginning of obedience to the Decalog.*

Because the Mosaic political structure is the highest ideal and best form of civil order in this corrupt state of our human nature, it is useful for wise rulers to study this form of government. The laws of the gentiles were less stringent in two areas, in the matter of punishing blasphemies and in controlling our vagrant lusts. The law of God established serious penalties against the worship of idols, blasphemies, ungodly teachers, and likewise against our erring desires. Therefore the will of God in regard to these sins must be studied by prudent rulers in the divine law itself.

THE DIFFERENCE
BETWEEN THE OLD AND NEW COVENANTS

It is certain, on the basis of Scripture, that the covenant or treaty or pact or testament between God and man can be divided so that there is the old and the new covenant. Matt. 26:28, "This is My blood of the new covenant or the new testament"; Jer. 31:31–32, " 'Behold, the days are coming,' says the Lord, 'and I will make a new covenant with the house of Israel and the house of Judah, not according to the covenant that I made with your fathers when I took them by the hand and led them out of the land of Egypt, a covenant which they broke . . .' "; 2 Cor. 3:6, "Christ has made us able ministers of the new covenant"; Gal. 4:24; Heb. 7:22; 8:6; 10:28–29; 12:24; 13:20; Rom. 9:4; Eph. 2:12.

What, properly, is the old covenant and what is the new, and how may we distinguish between them? This point is under great dispute. Therefore, in order that the whole subject can be more simply understood and explained, we shall review the main passages dealing with this so that the antithesis may show what statements they are and how and why errors occur and what truth each passage contributes and which points are in agreement with the simplest and clearest statements of Scripture.

The confusion which has arisen in this discussion seems to have come from the common practice of dividing the books of Holy Scripture into the Old and New Testaments. The time from the beginning of the world up to Christ has been called the period of the Old Testament or the old covenant, and the time after the coming of Christ is called the period of the new covenant. Therefore, they argue, the teaching should be judged in accordance with whether it was given in the time of the old covenant and is contained in the books of the same covenant and thus the Old Testament must be understood with respect to this disjunction of time; and in turn that teaching must be regarded as pertaining to the new covenant which temporally is contained among those writings which were produced after the coming of Christ.

1. Therefore the first thing that happened is that the Pelagians imagined

that the men in the Old Testament before the time of Moses were justified and saved by the natural law, but afterward by the law of Moses, and in the New Testament men were justified and saved by the law of Christ.

We should look at some of the individual opinions as to whence and by what erring principles they arose and thus how they can be refuted.

Pelagius was of the opinion that men by their own free choice and their own powers could perfectly fulfill the law of God and therefore under the old covenant there was a different way of justification than is now the case under the new. Nor was Pelagius the first to teach this, but before him in the writings of Epiphanius and Clement the same idea is found repeatedly for which Pelagius was condemned. For they said that there were different eras and that men were justified in all eras, but not in the same way. For those who lived before the giving of the Law were justified by the leading of nature; but after God had promulgated the Law He had added ceremonies by which men were righteous; and now after the birth of Christ a new law has been given by which we are saved. Because even Justin, the oldest of all the fathers, thinks that Christ was called the Word because those who lived according to their reason before His advent were justified the same way. Indeed, Pelagius latched on to these statements and attacked Augustine most vigorously with them because Augustine had attacked statements which he found in the ancients. But Augustine divided the authority of the ancients and some he excused and testified that they had spoken less carefully because Pelagius had not yet arisen, and at the same time he showed that the position of Pelagius was at variance with sacred Scripture.

For there is one and the same church, one and the same faith, Eph. 4:4–6, and one way of being justified by which all who would be saved have been justified from the foundation of the world. Therefore the Epistle to the Hebrews in 13:8 does not limit the work of Christ only to the time of the New Testament but extends it also to the Old Testament, for this "Christ is the same yesterday and today and forever." Hence in John 8:56 Abraham saw Christ's day and rejoiced. Paul in Rom. 4:1ff. carefully adduces the example of Abraham and David in this discussion of the article of justification to show that all, as many as have been justified from the beginning of the world, have been justified in no other way than through faith in Christ. But if anyone carefully looks at the speech of God to Cain in Gen. 4:7, he will come to understand that even before Moses, the moral law, and before the birth of Christ, the doctrine of the free remission of sins had been taught. For in regard to curbing lusts God said, "Your lust shall be under you" (Vulgate). In regard to the free remission of sins He says, "If you do righteously," that is, by faith in the Messiah who is to come, "there will be a lightening or the remission of your sins."

II. The scholastic teachers and even some of the fathers understand both the New as well as the Old Testaments as being the doctrine of the Law, with this difference that Moses brought to the people of the ancient era commandments which were imperfect and dealt with external and carnal matters, and this is the old covenant; but Christ gave to the new people more perfect precepts, which were much more difficult and pertained to inner and spiritual virtues, and this is the new covenant.

Augustine had more light than the rest of the fathers and restored many teachings. Before him nearly all asserted that Christ in the new covenant had given even more difficult commandments than were found in the old covenant, and that we are saved by observing them. We should consider where this opinion came from. Christ says in Matt. 5:17, "I did not come to destroy the Law and the prophets but to fulfill them," a word which they took as meaning that the Law and the prophets were not complete or perfect, but Christ would make up the deficiency and would lay down precepts which were more arduous and more outstanding. They called this a supplement or an addition. Thus in the Old Testament it was said, "You shall not kill," but in the New Testament Christ adds something even harder, "You shall not be angry." Therefore they created the antithesis between the law of Moses and Christ, that is, the law of Moses was satisfactory to set before the simple people that they should not kill nor commit adultery; but Christ has wanted even our desires to be held in check. Thus Eusebius says in his *De Demonst. Evang.*, 1, "Moses judged that it was sufficient for men in those times that they not commit murder, but I am giving you something more perfect, that you shall not even be angry." Chrysostom in regard to Matthew 5 says that the teaching of Christ was a supplement to the law of Moses and thus its observance was of far greater value, because the observance of the Law was recompensed by the promise of the land of Canaan, but the observance of the teaching of Christ will be recompensed by the possession of heaven.

If it can be shown that Moses and the prophets also gave commandments regarding inner and spiritual worship, then this opinion will be refuted. For the ancient church fathers did not correctly evaluate the text of Matthew 5. For Christ is not there setting up an antithesis between the teaching of Moses and His own, as if Moses had prohibited only outward murder, but He Himself was prohibiting also anger. Rather He was pointing out the difference between His own explanation of the teaching of the moral law in Moses, which was correct, and the traditions of the Pharisees. For the Pharisees interpreted the Law as applying only to external matters, an explanation which Christ attacked as being inadequate, and He went on to add the correct interpretation which dealt also with our inner morals. This was not something new and previously unheard of, but it had already been expressed in the very writing of Moses himself. In Deut. 32:35 the Lord says with certainty, "Vengeance is Mine. I will repay." Lev.

19:18, "You shall not seek vengeance nor bear a grudge against your fellow citizen," and v. 17, "You shall not hate your brother in your heart; you shall publicly rebuke him, lest you have sin because of him"; Ex. 23:4–5, "If you come upon your enemy's ox or his donkey gone astray, bring it back to him. If you see the donkey of a person who hates you lying under its burden, you should not pass it by but help him to lift it up."

They object: Why, therefore, does Christ say in John 13:34, "A new commandment I give you, that you love one another"? I reply: He does not say "new" as if it had not been in existence before, for, as John so correctly says in 1 John 2:7, "I am not writing a new commandment to you, but an old commandment which you have had from the beginning. The old commandment is the word which you have heard from the beginning." But Christ says it is new, (1) Because it is given in a new way. For Moses says, "You shall love your neighbor as yourself," but Christ says, "As I have loved you so you shall love one another," John 13:34. (2) Also because this command is not given to the old man, as if he out of his own powers can love his neighbor as himself, but it is given to the new man who has been renewed through the grace of the Holy Spirit and has begun to "walk in newness of life." For he also has begun to love his neighbor as himself for the sake of Christ. For these reasons it is called "a new commandment," or a commandment of love, even though it had also been given to the ancients.

III. The papists also follow this notion. But some of them add new colors with which they are anxious to paint the old statements. For example, Gropper writes that when the Law is put before the old man to the point where sin increases, then he is called the old man, but when the Spirit writes the Law in the mind which has been renewed, thus beginning the new obedience according to the Law, then it is called the new covenant. Although these points are true, yet they are twisted insidiously to pervert justification by faith, and we must carefully consider the true explanation of the matter. In 2 Cor. 3:7ff. the old covenant is called the ministration of wrath, sin, and death; but the new covenant is called the ministration of righteousness, the Holy Spirit, and life. Gropper mixes up these things, saying that the renewal of the Holy Spirit which takes place under the new covenant is the benefit through which we achieve salvation. But in a very unwise manner he confuses matters which must be kept separate. For there is a twofold benefit of Christ under the new covenant: reconciliation and renewal. When we are discussing the distinction between the old and the new covenants and the question is asked how under the new covenant we are justified and achieve grace, then is it sanctification or renewal which brings it about? Gropper replies that there absolutely must be the beginning of the new obedience in order that we may be justified. But he is in error. For Paul teaches again and again that the imputation of the obedience of Christ and the free reconciliation with God is our justification.

Lindanus and Asotus imagine that the distinction between the old and the new covenants lies in the fact that the old covenant was given through the letter or in writing, but the new covenant is life given orally without writing. Here they drag in Jer. 31:33, "I will write My law in their inward parts and in their hearts." They do this because they want to corroborate their own unwritten traditions and establish that not all things were put in writing which must be taught to Christians. But we have refuted this erroneous teaching of theirs elsewhere.

IV. The Anabaptists imagine the kind of distinction in which the fathers under the old covenant had only physical, external, and temporal promises (as if they were all Sadducees); but only under Christ or in the new covenant era the spiritual and eternal promises were given for the first time. But it is evident that spiritual promises of eternal life had been given under the old covenant. Lev. 18:5, "He who does these things shall live by them," certainly must not be understood of this physical life only or of external tranquility, but of life eternal, which the patriarchs also believed. Therefore these notions in no way can stand.

V. Bucer, Calvin, and those who follow them use the word "pact" (*pactum*) or "testament" (*testamentum*) to refer only to the doctrine of the person and benefits of Christ the Mediator. Just as this teaching was revealed and set forth in the time of the patriarchs, Moses, and the prophets, dressed and shrouded in various shadows of the ceremonies, they call this the old covenant (*testamentum*). When the veil of the figures had been taken away, then just as the teaching of the Gospel was given by Christ and the apostles, they call this the new covenant. Thus, in fact, insofar as it pertains to the matter or substance of the covenant, they assert that there are not two different covenants but the old and the new are one and the same, but there is a difference only insofar as the mode or form of the revelation and its completeness and the extent of the blessings is concerned. That is to say, the doctrine of the Gospel (1) was given less clearly in the old covenant and explained more clearly in the new; (2) was shrouded by the various shadows of the ceremonies in the old; (3) was presented to one people in one place on earth, particularly the land of Canaan, but now to all nations in the world; (4) in the old covenant the promises pertained to the Messiah who was to come, but in the new the Gospel deals with the Christ who has been shown; (5) in the old covenant there were many promises which pertained to earthly matters which were determined by certain circumstances; (6) in the old covenant, although certain people had been equipped with most outstanding gifts, yet in general the measure of the gifts of the Spirit was less than those which are now poured out under the new covenant, in keeping with the promises, for example, in Joel 2:28, "After these times I will pour out My Spirit upon all flesh, and your sons shall prophesy and your daughters, and your old men will see dreams and your young men visions; and upon My servants and handmaids in those days I will pour out My Spirit." Jer. 31:33–34, "'And this shall be the covenant which I will make with the house of Israel after these days,' says the Lord. 'I will put My law in their inward parts and I will write it in their hearts, and no longer shall each man teach his neighbor and each his brother, saying, "Know the Lord," for they shall all know Me, from the least to the greatest,' says the Lord."

Their chief arguments are these: The ancients were not justified by merits and the works of the Law, but by the grace of God no less than we are; they did not have any other Mediator than Christ through whom they were reconciled, than we do; they had the same promise of the Gospel given through the holy prophets in Holy Scripture. Rom. 1:2 and 3:21, "The righteousness of faith is testified by the Law and the prophets"; in Rom. 4:1, 6 the examples of Abraham and David are adduced to establish the doctrine of justification by faith and the true Gospel. From these passages it is evident that they had the same doctrine, the same faith, the same righteousness, and the same salvation that we do. John 8:56, "Abraham rejoiced to see My day and he saw it and was glad"; Rev. 13:8, "The Lamb was slain from the foundation of the world"; in Luke 1:73–74 Zacharias sings of "the oath which He swore to Abraham our father that He would grant to us . . ."; in Gen. 17:7, God says to Abraham, "I will be a God to you and to your seed"; and v. 8, ". . . I will be their God"; and in Jer. 31:33 the Lord says, "I will be their God," and He testifies that this is the new covenant itself. From these statements they assume that it is correct to say that insofar as their substance is concerned the two covenants are one and the same, and the only difference is this: (1) There are more earthly promises in the old than in the new; (2) The old covenant was a type, clothed in shadows and sacrifices all of which were accidental or added to the treaty, but in the new covenant these ceremonies have been abrogated; (3) In the old covenant something was done with a view to the Messiah who has been manifested; (4) The old covenant was more obscure because it was only a schoolmaster and like the rising sun where the ancients saw the Messiah from afar, but in the new all things are clearer; (5) In the old the grace of the Spirit was given sparingly, but in the new He came in richer supply; (6) The old covenant was given to one people in one place, but the new to all the people of the world.

Hence they conclude that now also in the sacraments of the new covenant nothing more is given than was the case in times past. But just as they once had types and figures of the Christ who was to become incarnate, so now we have figures of the body and blood of Christ as He was made incarnate and put to death. But the benefits and fruits of both are the same.

To be sure, the substance of this opinion (that there is the same Savior Christ, the same Gospel, as we commonly say, the same faith, the same justification of the saints under the old and the new covenants) is true, but the question at this point is what Scripture properly understands when it differentiates between the old and the new covenant.

Furthermore, the differences between these two covenants are clearly treated in Scripture, and from them it is easy to get the correct understanding of what the old covenant properly is and what the new covenant also is, and whether the substance and matter of each is the same, as Calvin and the others try to assert.

I. The first difference relates to the time of the promulgation. The old covenant as it was promulgated was written in the time of the deliverance of the Israelites from Egypt. Jer. 31:33, ". . . the pact or covenant which I made with your fathers in the day in which I took their hand to lead them out of the land of Egypt." The promulgation of the new covenant is predicated for the future, in the last days, that is, in the days of Christ, Is. 2:2; Micah 4:1, "In the last days it shall come to pass that the mountain of the house of the Lord shall be established on the top of the mountains and it shall be exalted above the hills and all the people shall flow to it." From passages such as this the apostles acquired their terminology. 1 Cor. 10:11, ". . . upon whom the end of the ages has come"; 1 John 2:18, "Little children, it is the last time."

II. The second difference pertains to the place. The old covenant was promulgated on Mt. Sinai, Ex. 19:18; but the new covenant came from Mt. Zion and Jerusalem, Is. 2:3; Micah 4:2, "The Law shall go forth from Zion and the Word of the Lord from Jerusalem"; Gal. 4:24–26, "These are the two covenants; the one from Mt. Sinai which bears children for bondage, which is Hagar [for this Hagar is Mt. Sinai in Arabia] who is in bondage with her children. But the Jerusalem which is above is free which is the mother of us all." Heb. 12:18, 22 show that Mt. Sinai and Mt. Zion are opposed to one another. From this it is clearly evident that the matter and substance of these two covenants are not the same. For the teaching of the old covenant is the Law but of the new the Gospel.

III. The third difference relates to the effects. The old covenant is the letter which kills, the ministration of death and condemnation, which produces children for bondage, and the teaching of the old covenant or the Law was given on two tables of stone. But the new covenant is the life-giving Spirit, the ministration of righteousness of the Spirit and of life, writing the law of the Lord in our hearts. 2 Cor. 3:6–9, "God has made us able ministers of the new covenant, not of the letter, but of the Spirit; for the letter kills, but the Spirit gives life. But if the ministration of death which was engraved on stones was glorious, how much more glorious will be the ministration of the Spirit? And if the ministration of condemnation be in glory, much more does the ministration of righteousness abound in glory"; Gal. 4:24–26, "The covenant on Sinai produces children for bondage . . . but the Jerusalem which is above is free."

IV. The fourth difference pertains to the Mediator. The mediator of the old covenant was Moses. For the people said to Moses in Deut. 5:26–27, "Who is there of all flesh who has heard the voice of the living God who speaks out of the midst of the fire, as we have heard, and been able to live? Go even closer and hear everything which the Lord our God shall say to you, and tell it to us, and we will hear it and do it." But the mediator of the new covenant is Christ, Heb. 8:6, "Christ has obtained a better ministry, since it is the ministry of a better covenant"; cf. 9:15; 12:24.

Therefore it is most certain that in the exodus of the people of Israel, on Mt. Sinai there was the solemn promulgation of the moral law and the establishment of the political and ecclesiastical life of the Israelites. Nor is there any doubt that this is the very same old covenant which is also the ministration of death, of sin and condemnation, which brings forth children for bondage and has Moses as its mediator. But from Zion and Jerusalem came the word of the Gospel or the word of faith and free justification for the sake of Christ the Mediator, who is the mediator of a better covenant. Therefore shall I follow Calvin when he says that there is actually only one covenant? Or shall I follow the Scripture which testifies that the new covenant is better than the old? Let us proceed.

V. The fifth difference deals with the promises or blessings. The old covenant has promises regarding the definite position of the kingdom of Judah and the preservation of it as a political entity. It also has promises which are spiritual and eternal but on the foundation of the observance of the Law which was called weak and useless, Heb. 7:18, "The former commandment is set aside because of its weakness and uselessness"; 8:7, "For if the first covenant had been faultless, there would have been no need for the second." But what was lacking Paul indicates in Rom. 8:3, "For what the law could not do in that it was weak through the flesh . . ." but the new covenant has the free promise of righteousness and eternal salvation which must be laid hold on by faith for the sake of Christ the Mediator.

VI. The old law was written on tablets of stone, Ex. 31:18 and 34:1; Deut. 9:10, but the new covenant is inscribed through the Spirit of God in the hearts of believers, Jer. 31:33, "I will put My law in their inward parts and write it in their heart"; and 2 Cor. 3:3, "You are the epistle of Christ ministered by us, written not with ink but with the Spirit of the living God, not on tablets of stone but in the fleshly tables of the heart."

VII. The old covenant has been abrogated. The new remains forever. Heb. 7:20, "Some became priests without an oath . . . but concerning this One the Lord took an oath and will not change His mind, 'You are a priest forever.'" Heb. 8:13, "In speaking of the new covenant, He is saying that the first one has become obsolete. And what is becoming obsolete and growing old is ready to be done away"; cf. 9:12; 10:9, 14.

VIII. The old covenant was ratified by the blood of animals, but the new by the blood of the Son of God. Ex. 24:5, "Moses sent young men of the children of Israel and they offered burnt offerings and sacrificed twelve oxen as a peace offering to the Lord. And Moses took the blood and sprinkled it on the people and said, 'This is the blood of the covenant which God has made with you regarding all His words'"; Heb. 9:12, "Christ did not take the blood of goats or sheep but with His own blood He entered once for all into the Holy Place"; cf. 10:4, 19, 22; Zech. 9:11.

Also in regard to this point the old and new covenants are distinguished from each other by Christ. Note Matt. 9:16; Mark 2:21; and Luke 5:36, where He gives this simile to the disciples of John: "No one tears a piece from a new garment and puts it onto an old one, for he will tear the new and not match to the old that which has been torn from the new. And no one puts new wine into old wineskins; otherwise the new wine will burst the skins and will be spilled and the skins ruined; but he puts new wine into new skins, and thus both the wine and the skins will be preserved. And no one, after drinking the old wine wishes for the new right away. For he says that the old is better."

Therefore the determination of what is properly the old covenant and properly the new is not derived from the common division of the books into the Old and New Testaments or from the times of the two covenants, but it is manifest and certain from the basic points which we have shown that in the exodus of the Israelites from Egypt and on Mt. Sinai there the old covenant was solemnly established with horrendous signs of the wrath and judgment of God, with Moses as the mediator, that it was written on tables of stone and shown first as the Decalog; and then when the Decalog had been solemnly set forth with dramatic testimony, there was also added the establishment of a certain form of civil government and ceremonial laws for the people of Israel, with the added promises under the condition of obedience. This is the old covenant according to the clear demonstration of Scripture.

Likewise it is also a matter of certainty that the word which was set forth from Zion and Jerusalem which went out into all the world is the doctrine of the Gospel or the Word of faith concerning free justification, the giving of the Spirit, salvation, and eternal life for the sake of Christ. Or to put it briefly, it is the doctrine of the benefits of Christ the Mediator. For "the law out of Zion" and the "Word from Jerusalem" have been spread into all the world. Therefore this is also the definition of the new covenant according to Scripture.

Now having laid this sure foundation, it is no longer difficult for us to apply these ideas and understand why the one is called the old and the other the new covenant. We shall briefly note the main points:

1. The first reason for this designation is clear: The solemn promulgation of the whole Law preceded in time the public promulgation of the Gospel. For this reason note Jer. 31:31 and Heb. 8:8 as to why the one is called the old and the other the new: " 'Behold, the days are coming,' says the Lord, 'and I shall make a new covenant with the house of Israel and the house of Judah, not like the covenant which I made with your fathers in the day when I took them by the hand to lead them out of the land of Egypt, a covenant which they violated.' "

But the sense of these passages is not that before the appearance of Christ, the teaching concerning the free reconciliation of God for the sake of Christ had not been given, or that now after Christ has appeared the doctrine of the Decalog is no longer to be taught; but that we should know that the teaching of the Law, insofar as it is the ministration of death and condemnation, wherever it is found in Scripture, pertains to the old covenant. The teaching of the righteousness of faith in Christ, wherever it exists in Scripture, pertains to the new covenant. The Calvinists indeed raise this objection against us that since the new covenant was not promulgated from the beginning, therefore it was not known to the patriarchs. But this is false. For it made itself known to them through revelation and the announcement of God, just as the life to come is already known to us. For unless the new covenant had been known to them, how could Abraham and the other faithful men have possessed the Holy Spirit and eternal life, since it is the new covenant which is the ministration of the Spirit and life? Therefore, although both kinds of teaching were in existence from the beginning of the world, yet by reason of their promulgation and the difference in time there was a distinction.

2. The second reason for this designation is that the covenant which God entered with Abraham contained two parts. The first was the promise of the increase of his posterity, of a definite dwelling place, and a certain realm for the people; likewise it dealt with the protection and preservation and blessing of the realm and the posterity. The second part, which came later and was added to the first part, was the promise of the spiritual blessing in the blessed Seed, Christ. Therefore, with respect to these two parts which were given, because of the time difference, the one is called the old and the other the new covenant. This rationale is clear when we compare such passages as Gen. 12:2; 17:7; and 22:16–17, " 'I have sworn by Myself,' says the Lord, 'because you have done this thing and not withheld your only-begotten son for My sake; I will bless you and

multiply your seed as the stars of the heaven and as the sand on the seashore, and your seed shall possess the gate of his enemies and in your Seed shall all the nations of the earth be blessed.'" In the Hebrew language the first and the last part of a statement are put in opposition to each other, with reference to the name and designation of the old and the new. Ex. 1:8, "A new king rose up in Egypt." He is called a new king with respect to the previous king. Thus in Deut. 24:5, "When a man has taken a new wife . . ."; Is. 42:9, "The former things have come to pass, and new things I now declare."

3. The third reason for this designation is that the teaching of the Law was implanted in the mind of man in the very act of creation along with the command regarding the forbidding of the fruit of a certain tree, at a time which preceded the promulgation and revelation of the promise of the Seed. In Gen. 2:17, before the Fall, it is said, "Of the tree of knowledge of good and evil you shall not eat. For in the day that you do eat thereof, you shall surely die." And after the Fall, in Gen. 3:15, He says, "I will put enmity between you and the woman and between your seed and her Seed; and it shall bruise your head and you shall bruise His heel."

4. The fourth reason is given in Heb. 8:13 where He promises a new covenant and thus indicates that the other one which came first is old, and "What is becoming obsolete and growing old is ready to be done away." But it is called "new" because it is vigorous and flourishing. And this concept is derived from the word *kālāh*, which means that something has become old, worn out by age, and in a sense deteriorated, just as garments wear away when they get old and are rendered useless by constant wear. See Ps. 32:3; Deut. 8:4; 29:5; Josh. 9:4; Is. 38:17; Ps. 102:26; Is. 51:6.

This is not some idle disputation and a vain war of words over the oldness of the old covenant and the vigor of the new, or the fact that it has been substituted for the old. For Jer. 31:32 says that the fathers had first broken this pact, that is, they had rendered it void, and hence from that point on there was need for another promise, unless God wanted the entire human race to perish. Therefore in Christ we are "new creatures," 2 Cor. 5:17, "For the old things have passed away and behold all things have become new." From this arises the distinction between the old and the new man, concerning the first and second Adam. Thus he is called the "old man," because he has been perverted by his corrupt nature and condemned to eternal perdition; therefore he must be crucified, put to death, and destroyed. But the term "new man" is used to show that he has been restored by the imputation of Christ's merit, by the bestowal of the Holy Spirit, and by the beginning of the new obedience, so that he may live and flourish forever. Here also is pertinent the statement of Rom 7:6, "We should serve God in newness of the Spirit and not in the oldness of the letter."

5. The fifth reason is that just as there is an old and a new man, so the Law exercises control over the old man or his nature, coerces, crushes, and mortifies it by outward discipline, punishments, and threats; but the consolation of the Gospel pertains to the new man and indeed produces the new man. For it is the ministration of renewal through which, when the man is outside he is brought low and when he is inside he is renewed from day to day. This is from the Hebrew *chādash* or *garash* which means to restore that which has fallen. Ezek. 18:31, "Make a new heart and a new spirit."

Finally, it remains for us to consider how the chief arguments against this position are commonly used to support other opinions and how they can be refuted:

1. The most common argument raised in opposition is that the doctrine of Christ was known to the saints before His time and was contained in the books commonly called the Old Testament. The answer to this argument has already been explained. In the use of it they err greatly in thinking that the voice of the covenant is not speaking of the Law but only the promise of grace. This is false. For in Heb. 9:19 the book of the law is called the book of the covenant, the pact, or the treaty.

2. The third argument seems more difficult because on Mt. Sinai through Moses not only was the Decalog given but also the ceremonial laws together with the entire institution of the Levitical priesthood which contained types and figures of the person and work of Christ, that is, of the doctrine of the Gospel. The Epistle to the Hebrews, when it discusses the abrogation of the old covenant, particularly is dealing by name with the Levitical ceremonies. Thus it appears that the old covenant is actually the doctrine of the Gospel insofar as it is involved with types and shadows.

Reply: From Paul we know that "Christ is the end of the Law," Rom. 10:4, and that the "Law is our schoolmaster to Christ," Gal. 3:24. But the term "end" does not pertain to the substance of the matter of which it is the end. Thus also the Law, properly speaking, pertains to the old covenant, the end or fulfillment of which teaching is Christ. In order that this end might be demonstrated, certain things pertaining to the Gospel or the new covenant were taught also by Moses, with the result that the primary and principal work of the Law was and remains a legal matter, which, however, is not rightly accomplished unless at the same time it correctly points to Christ as the end or the fulfillment of the Law. Thus in Deut. 18:15 the promise is given of another prophet and mediator who shall be raised up from the tribe of Judah. Acts 3:22ff. explains this prophecy as referring to Christ and the teaching of the Gospel. In Ex. 33:19 God shows Moses all His goodness and says, "I will show mercy on whom I will show mercy," a statement which Paul in Rom. 9:15 applies to God's free mercy in the Gospel. Yet the ministry of Moses is different from that of Christ. John 1:17 shows that the Law is one thing and the end or fulfillment of the Law, which is Christ, is another thing.

Further, we should consider the Levitical ceremonies from two standpoints; (1) as fleshly and external ordinances which teach us the works by which we shall preserve the members of the group in some kind of outward and physical purity, and thus these ordinances relate to the Law. For the end or purpose of this civil law was that the people were kept under the promise that from them should come the Messiah who was going to rule over the whole world. Again, these ceremonies should be considered as proclamations and confessions of sin, of the wrath of God and divine punishments, and each in a certain way pertained to the Law. But because Christ is the end or the completion of the Law, therefore: (2), these ceremonies should also be considered as types of Christ and as such pertaining to the Gospel. Furthermore we should at this point note that insofar as they are types, the ceremonial laws which look forward to Christ were not first given on Mt. Sinai. For these ceremonies were also known and used by the patriarchs before the flood. In 2 Cor. 3:14 Paul teaches that this understanding is the true focus and use of the entire law, but when this end or purpose is not considered [and] they bring in only ideas regarding external discipline and [the idea] that the mere performance of the work justifies (*opus operatum*), then he calls this a veil. The proper focus of the one is Moses; of the other, Christ.

3. The third objection is that the Decalog has not become obsolete as the other laws of Moses, both civil and ceremonial, have become; for under the new covenant it not only is taught but also inscribed in the hearts of the regenerate, Jer. 31:32. Thus the Decalog does not pertain to the old covenant but to the new. The answer to this is that insofar as it pertains to condemnation and justification the Law is completely obsolete, for the Law has no power to condemn those "who are in Christ Jesus," Rom. 8:1 and "By the works of the Law shall no flesh be justified," Gal. 3:11; cf. Rom. 3:20. But insofar as it pertains to the new obedience the Decalog is absolutely pertinent to the new covenant; for the new covenant includes two concepts: (1) the remission of sins and (2) renewal. Therefore as regards the condemnatory work of the Decalog it does pertain to the ministration of Moses and to the old covenant, but insofar as it is the rule for righteousness in God in whose image we were formed at the beginning and which is now restored in us, to this extent it is part of the new covenant. For then obedience to the Decalog is beginning to take place in us through the Spirit, and it is written in the hearts of the regenerate. For we are new creatures in Christ, "created unto good works," which have been prepared for us in the Decalog, Eph. 2:10. From this it is possible to judge what we ought to believe about the

idea of those who want to remove the Law entirely from the new covenant and who contend that it has no relevance for the new man.

4. They raise in objection the statement in Ex. 24:7, where the book of the old covenant was read and then sprinkled with the blood of the sacrifices. But because the tables of the Law had not yet been written by God, they say that it was the book of Genesis in which were contained the promises concerning Christ. Therefore these promises also pertain to the old covenant. The answer to this is that the Epistle to the Hebrews in 9:19, when every commandment of the Law had been read, "Moses sprinkled the people and the book with the blood of the calves and goats, with water and scarlet wool and hyssop." Thus this passage must not be understood as referring to anything other than the book of the Law. For as the account in Exodus 24 clearly teaches, Moses, in descending from the mountain, told the people all the words and judgments of God and wrote them in the book. Therefore he very soon took up this book and sprinkled it with the blood of the sacrifices, and he showed that the people were bound to the teaching of this book. Therefore this historical account in no way conflicts with our position on this matter, but rather confirms it.

5. Many of their arguments are answered by the fact that not only is the promise of the Gospel clothed and wrapped up in types and figures, but the precepts of the Decalog itself were not so clearly taught at that time, but were mixed in with the civil laws with their own peculiar, secular, and outward observances. For example, it was prohibited for them to wear clothing made of wool and linen woven together, Deut. 22:11, cf. v. 10, "You shall not plow with an ox and an ass together"; or the fact that there was a prohibition against the eating of certain animals, fish, and birds. Note the whole of Leviticus 11, or that a mother bird sitting with her young should not be taken with her young, Deut. 22:6. Thus temporal promises of this kind were involved with certain outward circumstances. In the same way the old covenant was to be involved with types or figures as well as to be established with reference to things still pertinent to the period of the old covenant.

6. They raise in objection Is. 43:19 and 2 Cor. 5:17, "The old things have passed away and all things have been made new," and say that therefore to the old covenant pertains nothing except those abolished ceremonies and the types. I reply that these two passages properly speaking are not discussing the status of the church as it now is, when only a beginning has been made, and we are still in great difficulty with the old Adam; but they are talking about the complete restoration and completion of the full deliverance and perfection which will take place in eternal glory, as the application of these passages shows. Note Rev. 21:5, "And He who sat upon the throne said, 'Behold I make all things new.'" Thus these people are too prone to cite passages which do not apply and

use them constantly to support their preconceived false opinions. But from the points which I have made the kind reader may learn to understand the correct viewpoint on these matters.

Here we could attack the errors of the following: (1) the Jews, who still to this day have a bulldog grip on the Old Testament and the ceremonies to the extent that they can observe them living among gentiles, and they still await the Messiah; (2) the evil of the papists by which they are moved to bring into the church of Christ many of the ceremonies of the Jews and mix darkness with the body of the church; and (3) the Anabaptists who desire to reintroduce the Jewish civil laws, as if the Gospel does not permit any nation to live under the good laws of their own ruler. But there will be a locus on this matter later. [There is no such locus.]

The Difference Between Mortal and Venial Sin

As Paul says in Rom. 7:9, "I was once alive apart from the Law," that is, I did not feel that I was being accused by the Law, nor was I ashamed, nor did I sense the wrath of God against sin. I did not consider how great the guilt of my sin was or the anger of God. Thus the great majority of men are secure and do not even give a passing thought to how great the guilt of their sin is, how great God's wrath is, although the penalties for the first fall and the enormous calamities of the whole human race are a daily reminder to us of the magnitude of the wrath of God; and even though the intercession of Christ along with His death is a witness that God is seriously and truly angry at sin. The hearts of the godly to some degree are moved by these witnesses, for they feel the greatness of His anger to some extent and do seek a mitigation of the punishments, such as in the statement of Ps. 6:1, "Do not rebuke me, Lord, in Your anger"; or Hab. 3:2, "In Your wrath, Lord, remember Your mercy"; Jer. 10:24, "Correct me, O Lord, in judgment but not in Your anger, lest You reduce me to nothing." To some degree they understand the difference between venial and mortal sin. Men who are carnally secure, drunk with pleasures, do not understand this difference and therefore many writers are hallucinating on this subject.

Moreover, although the magnitude of the wrath of God cannot be described in words, yet for the sake of teaching this subject, we must hold to these definitions: Mortal sin in a general sense is the defect or inclination or action contrary to the law of God, which offends Him, which is not forgiven, but merits the wrath of God and eternal punishment. Thus in the unregenerate there are mortal sins, the very disease of our origin and all wicked desires and perverted actions. Although the virtue of Pomponius Atticus and Seneca was very great and they did not want to harm anyone, indeed were very kind and did not pollute themselves with lusts, did not defraud in their business dealings, yet in their minds they had doubts concerning providence, they did not call upon God but actually railed against Him when they saw that in the great trouble of this life, the good were often overlooked. This darkness in their heart is a great sin which men still do not recognize. Since their hearts are turned away from God, even the virtues of such unregenerate men are polluted and not properly governed. Atticus does good, but not for the sake of God. The bravery of

Alexander was a gift of God along with his other outstanding virtues, and the things he did were aided by God, but Alexander himself did not have as his goal that he should serve God or that the true knowledge about God should be spread under his guidance. Indeed, he did not actually believe that his own hand was guided by God in his warfare, but was of the opinion that the Macedonians had arisen by accident and by their own power. Therefore he neglected God and thought too highly of himself, wanted to be worshiped as a god, killed his friends when he did not think they sufficiently admired him, and fell into shameful lusts. These disgraceful things show how impure the heart of man was. Thus the impurity of their hearts corrupted their virtues and later produced manifest crimes.

Furthermore, although Nero and Epicurus sinned much more grievously than Cato, yet they all were crushed by horrendous mortal sins and by the eternal wrath of God. It is not necessary for the unregenerate to inquire into the distinction between mortal and venial sins, because "whatsoever is not of faith is sin," Rom. 14:23. Cato is without light in his invoking of a god, he flees God, he rages against Him when he sees that although his cause is more righteous (as he sees it), yet he is passed by. At this point all his belief regarding a god is swept away. Therefore all his actions are condemned. But for the regenerate it is necessary to ask the question who has venial sins and why the fall from these are called mortal sins.

Therefore, although the regenerate, in whom has been kindled the knowledge of Christ, faith, and the true prayer and in whom the new obedience has been begun, are righteous, are pleasing to God, and have His Holy Spirit, yet in them there still remains in this life a great infirmity, that is to say, a darkness in the mind regarding God and in the will and heart a corrupt inclination and many wicked desires. Perverted doubts come into our mind about God; and trust, fear, love, and all the other virtues are much weaker than they ought to be. Meanwhile we make more of ourselves than we should and we produce in ourselves pride and self-confidence. By this pride and self-confidence of ours we irresponsibly start to move things which ought not be moved, as in the case of Josiah, a godly and holy king, who declared war on Egypt when Egypt was offering peace. The saints often burn with unrighteous anger and hatred, with flames of lust and wrath which they should repress. Likewise there are many sins of ignorance and omission among the saints, as David cries out: "Who can understand his sins?" Ps. 19:12. There is no function of man, ecclesiastical, civil, or domestic, to which our human infirmity is equal.

These evils in the regenerate are contrary to the law of God, as Paul testifies in Romans 7; and godly men in their true sorrows to some degree do understand how great this perversion is and the magnitude of the evils. But because the person who is received when knowledge of Christ is kindled in his mind and faith in his heart and the Spirit given, and because the person also recognizes his weakness, deplores it, is ashamed at the knowledge of God's wrath against his sins, seeks pardon, and fights back against the first flames of desire, for him these evils are venial sins, that is, they are forgiven, with the result that they do not drive out the Holy Spirit and faith, and the person remains in a state of grace. Paul clearly teaches this in Rom. 8:1, "There is therefore no condemnation to those who are in Christ Jesus," that is, even if sins are present in them, this weakness which I have mentioned, and evil desires, yet the person has been received by God and his condemnation taken away, as Paul says previously, "You are not under the Law, but under grace," Rom. 6:15.

But the statement is made: Nothing is sin unless it is an act of the will, but the darkness, doubt, sins of omission, the sudden unexpected desires which precede an act of judgment and an assent are not acts of the will or voluntary. This sophistry can be easily refuted, for the statement, "Nothing is sin unless it is an act of the will or voluntary," is speaking of civil law but not of the judgment of divine law. For the fact is that the darkness in the mind, the doubts, great and numerous omissions, and the many and unexpected and sudden flames of desire are sins, even if they are not voluntary, as Paul says, "The evil which I do not want to do, that I do," Rom. 7:19. John is speaking of the same things when he says, "If we say that we do not have sin, we are liars," 1 John 1:8; for he is speaking of the weakness and wicked emotions which occur in the regenerate, not of their actual falls which are against conscience, that is, when they voluntarily indulge in corrupt desires.

Thus Paul also makes a distinction between the sins of those who remain in grace and those who reject grace, Rom. 8:13, "If you live according to the flesh, you shall die, but if through the Spirit you mortify the deeds of the body, you shall live," that is, if your will gives in to depraved lusts and turns itself away from God knowingly and willingly is contrary to the commandment of God, refuses to repent, to fear God, and to believe Him, which is pleasing to God, your will does harm to your mind, so that it cannot call upon God and with the loss of grace and the Holy Spirit it again turns back to death, that is, it draws down upon itself the wrath of God and eternal punishment, just as Adam and Eve, when they fell, lost grace and brought upon themselves the terrible anger of God. But if by the Spirit you mortify the deeds of the flesh, you shall live. He calls the depraved desires and negligence of our wicked nature "the deeds of the flesh." But then he continues by saying that we shall be victorious, that is, we shall retain grace and the Holy Spirit, if we contend against these wicked desires. This point is explained more clearly in other passages, where it is prescribed that there be in the regenerate the righteousness of a good conscience. 1 Tim. 1:5, "The purpose of the commandment is love that issues from a pure heart, a good conscience and sincere faith."

Therefore we should fight back and be on guard that we do not knowingly or willingly give way to evil desires or indulge ourselves with them. There is in us an impenetrable darkness which grieves us very much, and there are many evil forces which precede our will or capture it for a while, as Paul says in Rom. 7:23, "I am brought into captivity by the sin which wars in my members." At this point if you fight against sin so that you do not give way against your conscience, you shall retain grace and the Holy Spirit.

These sins are not perplexing and there is no need in a subtle or Stoic manner to measure the degrees of consensus. For the weak will is captured even before it realizes it, but we must look at this fact (which can be easily understood and judged) so that we do not indulge in this knowingly but fight against it; and Paul adds in Rom. 8:13 the words "by the Spirit," that is, if we live with the true desires to repent, to fear and to love God, and if our will is ashamed when it learns of the wrath of God, deplores its weakness, fears the traps of the devil, seeks pardon for the sake of Christ, asks also for the aid of the Holy Spirit, recalls the promises and prepares itself as for a great battle, then it will not give way to these allurements but will vigorously repel them and will avoid opportunities for sin. The regenerate have the Holy Spirit and they do not trouble Him by cultivating and kindling depraved desires, but understand that He has been given to guide us and indeed He wants to guide us and help us, if we do not drive Him away but fight against our wicked desires. Therefore, it is said in 2 Cor. 6:1, "We beseech you that you do not receive the grace of God in vain." David was able to keep the Holy Spirit and would have been aided by Him if he had not wanted to expel Him and wanted to give room to the burning lust which had arisen in his mind.

We have given many examples of some of the greatest people who fell because of their security and brought down punishment upon themselves and their posterity, such as Adam, Eve, Aaron, David, Solomon. Of the whole people it was said, "My people sat down to eat and to drink and rose up to play," Ex. 32:6, that is, when their stomachs were full and they felt at ease, they forgot all about God and became negligent and wanton. We are familiar with the common saying: Our minds have an abundance of thoughts about unimportant matters. The devil walks about looking for opportunities to entrap the unwary in lapses from which they cannot escape. He has created a long spear and he sees that many evils follow one fall. What a mountain of sins and calamities resulted from the fall of Adam, David, or Solomon! These examples and the daily calamities characteristic of our nature are always before us to warn us about the frightful wrath of God against sin. Therefore our prayers should be used to drive away carnal security, as Solomon says, "Blessed is the man who always fears the Lord," Prov. 28:14; and "Watch and pray that you do not enter into temptation," Matt. 26:41.

Therefore, although the vestiges of this disease still cling in the regenerate in this life, and our wicked desires have not been diminished and evils still must be condemned, such as the darkness and the many doubts about God, carnal security, errant flames of lust and hate, many great errors of ignorance and sins of omission. These are not only a disorder which is beside the law of God, as the monks imagine, but are *truly against the law of God, yet a good conscience and faith still do remain in the regenerate and the Holy Spirit also remains. Our confidence certainly does not rely on our own worthiness, but on Christ, and we establish for ourselves on the basis of the promise that we are really in grace because of Christ, and we do contend against these wicked desires and we seek forgiveness. In the same way also we retain our ability to call upon God, as it says in 1 John 3:21, "If our heart does not condemn us, we have confidence toward God and whatsoever we ask we shall receive, because we keep His commandments," that is, we believe in Christ and keep a good conscience. It is necessary that we know that the conscience is governed by the Word of God.*

I have been speaking of venial sin. But when those who have been born again knowingly and willfully break the law of God, as when they take up ungodly opinions or establish them by their own authority or indulge in hatred, ambition, lusts, avarice, or other outward infractions which are counter to the law of God, as David did when he seized the wife of another man and caused the husband to be killed in a subtle manner, such actions are mortal sins which are against conscience, and the person who allows them loses grace, faith, and the Holy Spirit and brings upon himself the wrath of God; and unless he is again turned to God, he will be lost in eternal punishment. Because his conscience then has the intent of sinning, he despises God and flees from Him and cannot call upon Him.

The testimonies on this point are manifest: Eph. 5:5–6, "Know this, that no fornicator or impure person . . . has any inheritance in the kingdom of God. Let no one deceive you with empty words, for it is because of these things that the wrath of God comes upon those who are disobedient." It is clearly stated that God is wrathful against such people as long as they have the desire to do such things.

Ezek. 33:18–19, "When the righteous man turns from his righteousness and commits iniquity, he shall die; but if the wicked man turns from his wickedness and does what is lawful and right, he shall live."

In the same way we should understand the statements in 1 Cor. 6:9, "Neither fornicators nor idolaters nor adulterers shall inherit the kingdom of God."

Gal. 5:19ff., "The works of the flesh are manifest . . . adultery, fornication, idolatry. . . . Of these things I say to you that those who do such things shall not inherit the kingdom of God." He uses the word "manifest" in regard to these works because in regard to them the conscience of the person who does them is surely able to judge from the law of God and understand that the evil he is intending is displeasing to God. Likewise, 1 John 3:7–8, "Let no one deceive you; he who does righteousness is righteous . . . He who commits sin is of the devil." Further, it is totally manifest that the Gospel demands a good conscience.

In 1 Tim. 1:5, it speaks of "love out of a pure heart, and of a good conscience and of true faith." In the same chapter, vv. 18–19, it mentions the "good soldier who has faith and a good conscience." In 2 Cor. 1:12 Paul says that his "boasting is the testimony of our conscience"; Gal. 6:4, "Let every man prove his own work, and then he shall boast in himself and not in another," that is, let each person be concerned that he does his own work properly, so that he can have the personal satisfaction of work well done, that is, the testimony and approval of his own conscience which each person needs, and then he will not go chasing after the compliments of others to his shame, nor will he depend on the judgments of others. 1 Peter 3:16, "Having a good conscience . . ."

Likewise it is impossible that a man who clings to his intention of sinning can please God because it is clearly said, "As I live, I do not will the death of the sinner, but that he should turn from his way and live," Ezek. 18:23. The oath should be referred to both conversion and reconciliation. The person who has fallen does not please God as long as he keeps his intention of sinning.

Isaiah teaches the same thing in 66:2, "To whom shall I look except to him who is contrite in spirit and trembles at My word?" In 57:15 He says, "I live with him who has a contrite and humble spirit so that the humble spirit and the contrite heart may live." O what sweet comfort and promise! We must inscribe it in our inner heart, but it pertains to those who feel shame, that is, those who do not cling to the intention of committing sin, but fear the wrath of God.

Finally, it is impossible for these two to exist at the same time, an evil conscience, that is, the intention of committing sin, and faith which is trust in the mercy of God which has been promised for the sake of Christ; because he who harbors the intention to sin despises or flees from God and does not draw near to Him. But trust in His mercy does draw near to God under the intercession of Christ. Wounded consciences find that they are frightfully driven away from prayer and overwhelmed with contempt for God or hopelessness. Thus Paul says, "Whatsoever is not of faith is sin," Rom. 14:23, that is, the matter has been condemned by God. But many have explained this passage "whatsoever is not of faith" as meaning that whatever is against conscience "is not of faith," that is, whatsoever is contrary to the law of God, "is sin." But we should recognize that both the law and the Gospel are included here. A work must be in keeping with the Law of God and at the same time faith must be present, that is, trust in the promised mercy of God for the sake of Christ. In the case of Nicodemus there was no intent to do evil, but yet before his conversion faith was absent, that is, confidence in the mercy of God which had been promised for the sake of Christ, which was the determining factor making his deeds pleasing to God.

From all these points it is clear that we must make a distinction between those who have fallen contrary to conscience and those who have done so out of their weakness and the infirmities which still cling to the saints. This distinction must be maintained in the church. Paul speaks of sin "ruling" or "having dominion" over us, Rom. 6:12.

Furthermore, although it is not an argument about words, yet a comparison of terms will shed some light on the matter. There is a particular emphasis in the expression, "sin rules over us," namely the idea of the savageness and effective power of sin, which absolutely dominates us if we do not resist it. It produces horrible results, it piles up crimes and by various means it brings with it great ruin and merits God's anger and His terrible punishment and drives the guilty into eternal destruction. This was the case of Saul who had been given the Holy Spirit, adorned with marvelous powers and great victories. He, however, did not retain these marks of distinction but fell prey to jealousy. At first it was easy for him to resist this emotion, as Aaron repressed similar lusts, but Saul fed his fury. Therefore the sin which ruled over him first drove him to try to kill David, enticed him away from God, and greatly increased his raging. In his madness Saul rushed from here to there, killing priests and increasing in his anger at God, as the sin dominated him and caused him to become even more savage. Finally God turned him and his army, and even his pious son Jonathan, over to his enemies to be slaughtered. All these concepts are included under the term "sin has dominion or rules over a person."

It is apparent that Paul took this expression from Genesis 4, where a brief statement is made summarizing the doctrine of the Law. First, it speaks of the judgment of God, v. 7, "If you do well, you will be received, and if you do evil, sin lies at the door until it is revealed, waiting to attack you, but you must rule over it."

These few verses cover a great area. First, they teach that outward worship pleases God if the heart is right. Then, the sinners are threatened with punishments. There is a warning about delaying lest carnal security is strengthened by the delay of punishment. The passage also refers to the coming judgment at the end of this life. It is a marvelous description. The secular security of the whole world is signified by one verse, "Sin is lying at the door" or is quiet until it is revealed. The sin of Judah lay quietly until he felt the punishment. Then he followed the precept: There are within you depraved desires and "you must rule over them." This means that in men there still remain wicked drives, but we must oppose them. This obedience pleases God when we fight against our sins in recognition of Him. On the contrary, those people have been rejected by God who have allowed sin to rule over them.

According to this statement, Paul says in Rom. 6:14, "Sin shall not have dominion over you." Although the attacks are vicious, the doubt great, and the fires of hatred and the desires for the possessions of others very great, yet it must not rule over us, that is, as he interprets his own words, we must not obey sin. But when people are ruled by it, they are torn away from God and later driven into all kinds of crimes and encounter punishment both in this life and hereafter. Therefore when we speak of sin as "mortal," or as Gregory of Nazianzus says "murderous," sin can certainly be described as ruling or having dominion.

There is no need to prolong this discussion with regard to such things as election, for we must judge things according to the Word of God in which He clearly states His will. Nor are we to seek any other will of God outside His Word. He clearly shows us the example of our first parents, that although they were elect, yet when contrary to conscience they fell, they lost grace and drove out the Holy Spirit. For it is certain that Adam and Eve had lost grace and the gifts which they had possessed. Thus their posterity were born as the children of wrath, that is, separated from grace, living in darkness, their will turned away from God, and filled with terrible stubbornness. Indeed, the enormity of the punishment for Adam's fall warns us how great God's wrath is and how many evils follow upon this one fall. We must know how to set before ourselves the many aspects of the doctrine of the church of all ages regarding the very notable instructions the account of the fall of Adam gives us.

Therefore we must not flatter ourselves or excuse our falls, but acknowledge that God is very angry against sin, and we must keep in mind the passages which I have cited which speak of God's anger and judgment against sin and His punishments, as it is said, Col. 3:6, "Because of these things the wrath of God comes upon the children of disobedience." Our minds must blush with shame and reject the intention of sinning and return to God, remembering His oath, "As I live, I do not want the death of the sinner, but that he may turn and live," Ezek. 18:23. We must keep in mind the falls of Adam, Aaron, David, and Manasseh, their punishments and their conversions. We must learn to deplore the terrible weakness of human nature and be vigilant against the allurements and traps of the devil; we must remember that even our individual sins deserve immediate death, just as adulterers and murderers are often put to death in the very act of their crime; and yet by the immeasurable mercy of God an opportunity has been given to us so that we can return to God, as it is said so sweetly in Is. 30:18, "The Lord will wait that He may be gracious to you," and in Luke 13:6ff., the parable of the fig tree means the same thing.

We must not misuse this kindness, but if we fall, we must accuse ourselves by our groaning, as David says in 2 Sam. 12:13, "I have sinned against the Lord." We must keep our eyes on the Son of God as our Mediator and return to God with confidence, again calling upon Him and seeking to be forgiven, received, and cleansed. Then we will recognize the gentle voice, "There is joy in heaven over one sinner who repents," Luke 15:7. We will also hear the voice of the Gospel by which we are publicly received into the church, we will be strengthened in this testimony so that we may stand more firmly in the confidence that we have been received even though we have fallen. There must come into our minds the witness of the universal church which always has received the fallen, just as Peter the Bishop of Alexandria cited over against the Cathari. Finally, we must give careful attention to the universal teaching concerning repentance which teaches the pious regarding the most important matters and removes from our thinking all thoughts about election.

Finally we must add this point: When we say that mortal sins are lapses which take place against conscience, we are including sins of ignorance and sins of omission, *as we commonly say. For we want to assert and confirm that those who are unwilling to learn the Gospel with its statement, "Hear Him," which God has commanded to the whole human race, we must hear Christ; and for this purpose He has spread His Gospel among all nations; and He has added testimonies which do not fail.*

Thus all atheists, Turks, Jews, and others who reject the Gospel are guilty of mortal sin, even if they admit that they had not learned the Gospel or understood it. Such was the sect of the Pharisees to whom Christ says, "If you were blind, you would not have sin; but now you say that you see and therefore your sin remains," John 9:41.

There were also the cults of idolaters among the gentiles who were living in ignorance because they had voluntarily lost and rejected the doctrine of the Gospel and did not seek it again in the church and had taken up ideas which were in clear conflict with the natural knowledge of God, which shows that there is one God and that He is not to be worshiped as God in any obscene way, as practiced among the Bacchanals and others.

Concerning the matter of omission, Paul says, "Woe is me if I do not preach the Gospel," 1 Cor. 9:16; and Matt. 25:30, "Cast the unprofitable servant into outer darkness." Let each person consider this sad statement as it applies to his own calling. For although a great deal of ignorance and involuntary omissions remain in the regenerate, as was the case with the apostles before Pentecost, yet there is in a person's calling the will or the zeal to do well and to perform everything correctly. Paul has established this level of concern: First, he confesses in 2 Cor. 3:5 that human powers are not strong enough to accomplish the ministry of the Gospel. He says, "We are not sufficient of ourselves to claim anything as coming from our own powers," that is, to explain the teaching or to govern with good counsels or to supply the right words in settling controversies. All who are wise, even if it be in some minor function, still recognize that they are lacking in good judgment. The father of the household often gives poor instruction to his children and deprives them of true hope. In 1 Cor. 4:1 he says, "The prime requisite of a minister is that he be faithful," that is, that such men have the unfailing desire to do good and do not indulge in idleness but study, learn, and work hard and do nothing but the duties of their office; for diligence flees vice, sloth, and putting our noses into other people's business.

The Difference Between Mortal and Venial Sin in the Regenerate

In order that the fundamental teaching of the distinction between mortal and venial sin in the regenerate can be correctly understood and studied, we shall show the chief points which we must note in this treatment.

CHAPTER I: THE SCRIPTURE PASSAGES UNDERLYING THIS DOCTRINE

First of all, we must note the *sedes* of the matter (as they say in the schools), that is, in which passages of Scripture the doctrine is established. For just as the students in law schools are directed to the chapters and titles of their subjects in which they can find the complete treatment of this matter, so also it is possible to prove each point by a passage of Scripture, but the choosing of the proper statements must be carried out so that there is always a confirmation or a rebuttal appropriate to the subject.

For example, in the teaching of the Anabaptists there are some who clamor that this distinction between mortal and venial sin is a device of the scholastics. But Scripture does have certain very clear illustrations of this distinction, so that it cannot be denied. I shall produce some of these statements in which both kinds of sin are included: Ps. 19:12, "Who can understand his errors? Cleanse me from secret faults." Here he uses a word derived from *shāgag*, which refers to doing something without knowing it and without considering it; it gives the idea of something done through ignorance or lack of prudence or without thinking it through. The Greeks use the word *paraptōmata* (trespasses). German: *Wenn einer nach eineem Dinge greifft/und einen Fehlgriff thut* (when a person reaches for something and commits a blunder). "Keep Your servant from presumptuous sins," which in the Vulgate reads *ab alienis*, that is, "from the sins of others." In the Hebrew the root is *zūd*, which means "he boiled over" or "puffed up," or "he did it out of pride and malice." The LXX says *apo allotriōn*, "Spare me from the attack of strangers." They were trying to express that the sons of the kingdom are opposed by strangers. Matt. 17:25, "who are not Jews but strangers." Note also Job 19:27, where the word *zār* is used, "The others shall not see God." Therefore they took note of those sins which made us aliens or strangers to the kingdom of God and by which our adoption as the sons of God is lost. Thus David made a distinction between "errors" which happen through thoughtlessness and those sins which are committed out of pride, audacity, and presumptuousness. He prayed to be removed from this stubbornness, and adds, "Then I shall be upright and innocent of great transgression," that is, I will have a good conscience and know that the rest of my sins are covered. Here he uses the Hebrew root *pāshaʿ*, a term which means to walk faithlessly, to break the Law maliciously, and to lie wickedly.

In Num. 15:27 and 30 there is a distinction among the sacrifices, when the soul has sinned in error or ignorance and when it has sinned through pride or obstinacy "with presumptuous hand" and neck stretched high, without repentance. For to bow the head is a sign of contrition. Luther renders this "*auss Frevel und Muthwillen,*" "wickedness and wantonness." God Himself wanted to show this distinction by the public ceremony.

Ps. 32:1, "Blessed are they whose iniquities are forgiven and whose sins are covered." This shows that sins are indeed also present in the regenerate because the word "covered" is used, but there is a distinction among the sins. Some are covered, that is, under our repentance, but others are uncovered when there is no repentance, in order that they may be manifest.

1 John 1:8, "If we say that we have no sin, we deceive ourselves and the truth is not in us"; and yet he says in 3:6, "Whoever sins has not known God." These statements seem to contradict each other, but they are easily reconciled. In ch. 1 he is speaking of those who have been washed in the blood of Christ but still have sin in them. But in ch. 3 he is speaking of premeditated sins which thus are a different kind of sin. Again the same John says in the same epistle, 3:8, "He who commits sin is of the devil," and in v. 9, "Whoever is born of God does not sin." Thus John is demonstrating that there is a difference between having sin and committing sin. The latter is more serious than the former, although sometimes they are treated as one. For sin still clings in all of us, and no one can say that he is absolutely pure of all sin. Yet the godly through the grace of the Spirit resist sin. But he who carries out his calling and brings evil lusts into his work in a sense is training himself in the art of sinning. Of him Christ says in John 8:34, "Whoever commits sin is the servant of sin"; and in Matt. 7:23, "Depart from Me you workers of iniquity." Christ does not want to send away from Himself all those who have iniquity (for if He "should mark their iniquities, who would remain standing?" Ps. 130:3), but only those who commit iniquity, of whom the prophet Ezekiel pronounces in 18:24, "When the righteous man turns himself away from his righteousness and commits iniquity and does according to all the abominations which the ungodly man does, shall he live? All the righteousness which he has done shall not be mentioned and he shall die for his sins." Paul in Rom. 7:23 and 8:1 says, "I see another law in my members warring against the law of my mind and bringing me into captivity to the law of sin which is in my members . . . but there is no condemnation to those who are in Christ Jesus, who do not live according to the flesh." Therefore there is sin dwelling in us which tries to keep us in captivity, and those who hold hands with it and are overcome by it are led to damnation. But if they fight against it and are in Christ Jesus, even though sin is still in their members, yet for them there is no condemnation. This is venial sin. But Paul goes on to add in Rom. 8:13, "If we live according to the flesh we shall die." It is obvious that he is speaking here of the regenerate. For of the unregenerate he says in Eph. 2:1 and Col. 2:13, "You were dead in your trespasses and sins." But after they through faith had been converted to Christ and born again, they were at the same time also brought back

to life, so that they might be reconciled and live. But those people will again die if they continue to live according to the flesh, that is, when they lose their life, they rush headlong into eternal damnation.

1 Cor. 6:10 and Gal. 5:21, "Those who do such things cannot inherit the kingdom of God." The Greek uses the word *klēronomein*, a term which is applied to the regenerate. For here they are "heirs of God and co-heirs with Christ," Rom. 8:17. But those who commit these terrible crimes and the works of the flesh lose again their inheritance, adoption, and blessing, and as Eph. 5:5 says, "They have no inheritance in the kingdom of Christ and of God." Thus it speaks in the present tense, "they have not," because they have lost it. By the term "kingdom of Christ" is understood the kingdom of grace of which 1 Cor. 15:24 speaks when it says that the kingdom of God shall be delivered to the Father and he calls this the kingdom of glory in this life. What he is saying is this: Many who commit these sins promise themselves immunity, but they have deceived themselves with false persuasions. For those who do such things have no place either in the kingdom of grace in this life, nor will they dwell in the kingdom of glory in the life to come.

Col. 3:6, "Because of these things the wrath of God comes upon the children of unbelief." Concerning these unbelievers who have not been converted, John the Baptist says in John 3:36, "He who does not believe in the Son . . . the wrath of God remains upon him." By this he means that they are already under the wrath of God. But Paul says here that "because of these things the wrath of God comes." Thus they had been previously under grace, but because of "these things" the wrath of God will come back over them. Thus those who are under grace, if they return to actions which are contrary to conscience, can so offend God that His wrath returns upon them. In order that the regenerate do not return to such actions, the apostle carefully warns them: "For on such people comes the wrath of God." It is as if from the heart of God is poured out His wrath which previously had been taken away by faith. Unbelief includes both impenitence and lack of faith. As it says in John 3:36, "He who does not believe in the Son shall not see life," and Deut. 21:18 speaks of a stubborn and rebellious son, an adjective often attributed to the Israelites in the Old Testament. Note also Num. 14:9; 20:10; Deut. 9:24 and elsewhere.

From all of these citations it is clear that the distinction between venial and mortal sin has a sure basis in Holy Scripture.

CHAPTER II: THE TERMS BY WHICH THIS DIFFERENCE IS EXPLAINED

In the second place, therefore, we should consider the terms by which the distinction between mortal and venial sins is indicated, taught, and explained.

It is worth the effort for the godly student to note the following: (1) This difference is indicated in the Scripture of the Old Testament by the terminology. (2) It is taught by certain words in the New Testament. (3) There are ecclesiastical terms which have been used and accepted to explain this doctrine. For those who want to pervert something in the doctrines themselves begin by perverting the terminology, and for this reason we should keep a sharp eye on them. Because we need only some helps for our memory and some brief instruction, I shall keep these points brief.

I. In the language of the Old Testament there are distinct words which contain and demonstrate the difference and the definition of mortal and venial sin. Thus the word *zaddon* shows that a sin is committed out of the pride of the heart, without fear of God, out of an evil intention. The term is derived from the idea of boiling in the process of cooking something. Thus he who perpetrates an action out of the intentional malice of his mind, has cooked it over in his heart and has heated it with the flames of his lusts. From this follows the overflowing, and evil thoughts begin to boil up and harm others. The LXX renders this word with *itamia* (fierceness of heart), Jer. 49:16; with *hybris* (pride) in Ezek. 7:10, and with *hyperēphania* (arrogance) in 1 Sam. 17:28.

Mered (rebellion). This word includes both the malicious intent and the outcome, for it refers (1) to rejecting the authority of one's superior, as when it says in Ps. 2:3, "Let us break their chains asunder and cast off their yoke from us"; and Luke 19:14, "We will not have this man rule over us"; and (2) to grieving the Spirit of God, as when it says in Ps. 95:8, "Do not harden your hearts as in the rebellion in the day of testing in the wilderness." The term thus has reference to arrogant maliciousness and includes also the effect because the Spirit is not only saddened by such insolence and rebellion, but He is also irritated by it so that He swears, "He shall not enter into My rest," Heb. 3:11. We also read in Dan. 9:5, "We have sinned and committed iniquity, we have done wickedly and have rebelled." The initial word in this verse relates to *hamartia*, which also means "sin."

'Asham means a guilt which is an abomination to God, drawing down desolation upon itself. It includes both the material and the formal aspects of sin. The LXX translates it by *plēmmeleiai*, Gen. 26:10[1], and Ps. 69:5, that is, a deed which renders one guilty and which requires expiation.

Rasha' means "to act in an ungodly way" and to condemn the godly as being ungodly. The LXX uses several terms to express this idea: in Job 9:29 with *asebēs*, "ungodly"; in Dan. 9:5 with *adikein*, "we have done iniquity"; and in Ps. 37:21 with *hamartōlos*, "sinner."

---

[1] Gen. 26:10 in the Hebrew has *'āshām*, but the LXX does not have *plēmmeleiai*.

Shāgag refers to something which is not committed out of a deliberate malice but from error, ignorance, or some weakness. Ps. 19:12, "Who can understand his errors?" Numbers 15 speaks of the institution of separate sacrifices, one for him who has sinned "with a presumptuous hand" or with pride, v. 30; and the other for the person who has sinned "through ignorance or by mistake," v. 27.

This distinction is clear from the statements of the Old Testament where the difference is being treated. For example, Ps. 19:12, "Cleanse me from secret faults." Here it is called a secret sin which has been cleansed, or as the emphasis of the word *nakah* has it, a sin which is not subject to the curse, but the person is absolved from condemnation; or, as it says in Ps. 32:1, it is a sin which is covered and not imputed; or again in Ps. 19:13, "Let sins not have dominion over a man." Compare Gen. 47:4, "Sin is waiting at the door to attack you but you must have dominion over it."

II. In the New Testament there are also separate words which pertain to the difference and definition of mortal and venial sin. Rom. 6:13 uses the word "unrighteousness" (*adikia*), "Do not yield your members as instruments of unrighteousness," that is, of sin. 2 Tim. 2:19, "Let everyone who names the name of Christ depart from unrighteousness."

Apeitheia (stubbornness), Eph. 5:6 and Col. 3:6, "The wrath of God comes upon the sons of disobedience," which means disobedience, stubbornness, and disbelief which oppose repentance and faith.

"Godlessness (*asebeia*), *ein Gottloss Wesen*. 1 Tim. 1:9 and 1 Peter 4:18, "sinners" and "godless men" are coupled together. Because in the Gospel account "sinner" is a title applied to those who are known and notorious for their sins, as Mary Magdalene is called a sinful woman in Luke 7:37, therefore the term "godless" involves a very flagrant sin, something irreligious, scandalous, ungodly, and a crime.

"Defection" or "hostility" (*defectio, apostasia*), Heb. 12:3; or a falling away or a departure from the living God, 1 Tim. 4:1, "They shall depart from the faith," when their entire religion is rejected or they permit errors which attack the very foundation of faith, which is the highest degree of sin.

"Trespass" and "sin." These words are most commonly used of the sin which dwells in the regenerate. They refer to lapses or errors which arise out of our weakness. Gal. 6:1, "Brothers, if a man be overtaken in a fault (*paraptōma*) . . ."; 1 John 1:8, "If we say that we have no sin (*hamartia*) . . ."; Rom. 6:14, "Sin (*hamartia*) shall not have dominion over you"; 8:10, "If Christ is in you, the body is dead because of sin (*hamartia*)." Jerome regarding Ephesians 2 says, "If we ask what the difference is between *paraptōma* and *hamartia*, they reply that *paraptōma* are in a sense the beginnings of sin when the mind quietly creeps into sin and it has not yet pulled us down to destruction; but *hamartia* is that sin which, when something has been done, brings it to completion." Origen also says that *paraptōmata* are those sins which are permitted to occur because of negligence or thoughtlessness, but *hamartia* is the sin which a person knowingly and willingly commits. Erasmus, however, correctly noted that Paul uses these two terms interchangeably in Romans 5. Therefore we should not draw too precise a distinction between them. For the correct way to speak in the church is more easily lost when we fail to imitate the simplicity of the fisherman, as Ambrose puts it. After the time of Origen, Clement of Alexandria and others were called to their task by dealings with philosophers, and they introduced philosophical language and subtleties into the church. Soon the truth was obscured and changed into philosophical strife.

In regard to these words we must also note that illustrative terms used in describing the differences between mortal and venial sin are commonly found in the New Testament. For here are pertinent not only the words all by themselves but also coupled with modifying terms. Thus in 1 John 1:8 and 10, he uses the term "to have sin" and "to do sin." In Rom. 7:23 and 8:1, there is a sin which "dwells in my members . . ." which yet is not "a condemnation to those who are in Christ Jesus." Gal. 5:24, "Those who are in Christ have crucified the flesh with its passions and desires." Therefore the regenerate are not without sin, but they still do not want to be ruled by it, but rather they crucify it. Rom. 8:13, "Mortify the deeds of the flesh by the power of the Spirit." This mortifying is not of our own powers because "we have been united with the very death of Christ," Rom. 6:5, "that therefore the death of Christ is efficacious in us through the Spirit and works its power, so that the sin in us is put to death lest we be condemned for it." Rom. 6:6, ". . . that the body of sin might be destroyed," or abolished, be deprived of its muscle. What does this mean? Does he want our body to be hung up on a gibbet? If sin were a physical substance, some might argue halfway in jest that this would be a rather appropriate consequence. But Paul here is not speaking of the physical abolition of sin, but that our corrupt flesh cannot retain its power to do its work. For the sin in our body always wants to exercise its powers and these must be kept under control so that sin cannot function. This is what it means when it says in Rom. 7:5, "Our sinful passions were at work," the passions of our sinful flesh at work "in our members to bear fruit unto death." Among medical doctors there is a difference between *pathos*, "suffering," and *pathēmata*, "passions," so that if a person is troubled with pains from heat, that is called *pathos*; but if he begins to get warm in his work, that is *pathēma*. Thus when we have fevers, the person who suffers from the heat has a fever, but when the heat boils over, then it is called a passion or heat. Thus the suffering because of sin is present in all of us, but when it goes to work, then there are passions. Rom. 6:12, "Let not sin reign in your mortal body that you should serve it or obey its desires." Gal. 5:19 and Eph. 5:6, "The works of the flesh are manifest," bringing down the wrath of God and excluding from His kingdom. James 1:13–15, "When lust is illicit, it draws us away and produces sin, and sin, when consummated, produces death." 1 Tim. 1:19, "They put away a good conscience and then follows the shipwreck of their faith." Rom. 6:13, "Do not yield your members as instruments of wickedness unto sin." This is the meaning of Ps. 69:27, "They add iniquity to iniquity," *Auss einer Sünde in die ander fallen.* These expressions clearly show the distinction between mortal and venial sin.

III. Finally, we must consider the ecclesiastical terminology. The terms "mortal" and "venial sin" were used and accepted among the scholastics. The sententiaries were not the first to think them up, but took them from ancient usage. Tertullian, who is the oldest of the Latin writers, in his book *De Pudicitia* says [MPL 2.986], "Certain sins are major or mortal, and we are all attacked by these every day, so that if none of them were venial, there would be salvation for no one. A sin becomes venial through Christ's intercession for us." By the term "major" (*capitalia*) sins Tertullian does not understand those sins upon which others depend, but just as in the study of law there are the kinds of sins which are not punished by the magistrate in a civil court setting but in criminal court; so he applies this to the same end in the church. In the same work he speaks of *remissibilia* sins and those which are *irremissibilia*. Also he says [MPL 2.585], "God weighs every sin as either deserving the favor of correction or the punishment of condemnation." Thus Augustine, *Contra Jul.*, 2, and *De Spiritu et Litera*, 28, distinguishes between sins "which are deadly and those which are venial or deserve favor" [MPL 44.571ff.; MPL 44.230–31]. In Epist. 89 he says [MPL 33.675], "There are certain sins which are called crimes and certain which do not deprive of life."

Augustine, in reference to our weakness or daily falls, calls them sins which do not deprive us of eternal life. He also speaks of sins of rebellion, sometimes of light sins or small sins. Likewise in his sermons he uses the term *capitalia* or "major sins" and he speaks of those "which do not destroy the soul." But in the writings of Augustine there is no specific place where he particularly deals with the subject of mortal sin. He calls it *lethale* or *capitale* because it kills the soul. Theodoret, in his *Dial.*, speaks of "the devil as the father of sin and sin as the mother of death." In the Apology [4.79, Tappert, p. 118] this term is used to describe mortal sin, "sin against conscience," or "the sin which lays waste or destroys the conscience."

It is easy to see from which passages of Scripture these designations are drawn, as we have cited them. Rom. 1:32, "Those who do such things are worthy of death"; 7:5, "The passions of sin bear fruit unto death"; 8:13, "If you live according to the flesh, you shall die"; James 1:15, "Consummated sin produces death"; 1 John 5:16, "There is a sin which is unto death. I do not say that he should pray for it"; v. 12, "He who does not have the Son does not have life." Ps. 32:1, "Blessed are they whose transgressions are forgiven and whose sins are covered." He does not call these sins free from punishment, but he says that pardon follows the sins. Rom. 14:1, "Receive him who is weak in faith"; Prov. 24:16, "A righteous man falls seven times in a day and rises up again, but the wicked falls into evil"; Ezek. 43:22, "They shall offer a goat for sin every day."

CHAPTER III: DEFINITION OF THE MATTER

Next we must consider the definition of this matter. What is mortal sin? What is venial sin in the regenerate? The usual definition is that mortal sin is those kinds of actions which cut off those who permit them from the grace of God and thus they cease to be righteous, and as a result they are condemned unless they change their minds. But venial sins are not of this nature, since out of the pure grace and mercy of God they are forgiven for the sake of the Son of God our Mediator to those who repent, and in the case of these sins, their sins are covered.

In another place we have shown that in setting up correct definitions we must keep our eye on two things. The first is that in the main parts of a definition we must include those elements necessary for an understanding of the subject. The second is that they must have the foundations for each part of the definition drawn from the testimonies of Scripture.

Therefore in defining mortal sin we must indicate the chief aspect of this kind of sin, in order to understand it. These are:

I. The difference between mortal and venial sin is derived not from the subject of sin as it is considered in itself in keeping with the Law. For although one kind of sin may be greater or less than another kind, cf. John 19:11, "He who betrays Me has the greater sin"; Luke 12:47–48, "The servant who knew the will of his master and did not prepare himself and did not act in keeping with his will, will be beaten with many stripes, but he who did not know and did commit things worthy of stripes, he shall be beaten with few"; Matt. 11:24, "I say to you that it shall be more tolerable in the day of judgment for the land of Sodom than for Capernaum"; yet according to the Law, if God should enter into judgment with sin, all sins in themselves are mortal, guilty of or subject to the wrath of God and worthy of the curse and eternal death. That is to say, there is no sin, even if it seems to be insignificant, which in itself according to the Law and outside of Christ, if God should enter into judgment with it, that is not worthy of eternal death. Deut. 27:26 and Gal. 3:10, "Cursed is every one who does not continue in all the words of this law, to do them; and all the people shall say,

'Amen.'" Therefore in the definition we must include the concept that "all sins in the unregenerate are mortal." For "he who does not believe in the Son shall not see life, but the wrath of God remains over him," John 3:36. This is what Luther is saying on Galatians 5 [Amer. Ed., 26.76], "Mortal sin and venial sin are distinguished from each other not on the basis of the substance of the deed involved or according to some difference in the sin committed, but on the basis of the person or because of the difference of those who commit the sins."

We must note this aspect of the matter thoroughly. For the error of the Pharisees in the time of Christ pertained to the matter of big and little sins. This idea, however, is refuted at length in Matthew 5. On the other side, Jovinian contended that "all sins are equal," something which Jerome refuted. Likewise in our own day Sebastian Frank, an unlearned and arrogant man, has asserted the same thing. But Luther is correct when he says, "As far as guilt is concerned, all sins are equal unless reconciliation takes place." Thus those people are in error and need to be corrected who think that certain sins do not deserve death. But it is a certainty that all sins, even those which in our eyes seem minor, are worthy of the eternal curse. Augustine uses this simile: It is insufficient to make this comparison between these two kinds of sin and simply say that whether a person is on the shore or sinking in the depths of the sea, they are both dead. There will be some difference among those who are saved, just as there is a difference among stars in their brilliance, 1 Cor. 15:41, and there are also degrees among the damned because of the difference in their sins. Yet all are in damnation.

Thus also this is not a recent but an old controversy in regard to the virtues of the gentiles. Augustine at one time believed that Socrates and Heraclitus lived according to the Word, that is, they abstained from vices and controlled their living, and for this reason they were saved. He says that because Christ is called the Word or the Logos, that they lived in keeping with the Logos, and thus they had lived according to Christ. Thus it is certain that the ancients often spoke very inappropriately. Clement of Alexandria, who is celebrated for his learning, says that the philosophers were justified according to the natural law because they had no other. Thus also Epiphanius stated that many among the gentiles were saved by the law of nature. Pelagius believed the same thing. Yet Augustine, in thinking more carefully on this matter, rejected it. In Epist. 95 he says that the virtues in the gentiles do please us with a certain peculiar quality which they have by nature, so that it is not easy for us to condemn them. We would hope that they might be delivered from eternal torment. But human desires are one thing and the sentence of divine judgment and the righteousness of our Creator are something else. Their virtues in themselves are not evil but good, as when a person is moved by mercy toward his poor neighbor, covers his nakedness, gives him something to drink, things which in themselves are not evil. But the voice of judgment says, "Whatsoever is not of faith is sin," Rom. 14:23. Augustine is correct in saying, "Not only must they do good things, but they must do well. There are many good works, but they are rendered unprofitable because the people by whom they are done do not do well. Our works are not to be judged by our actions but by our intentions, for an action must be compared with a righteous purpose." Thus the formal cause and the final cause make the difference between the good works of the regenerate and the virtues of the gentiles. "An evil tree cannot bring forth good fruit," Luke 6:43. Prosper, in his book *De Vocatione Gentium* [MPL 33.764ff.], says, "Without the worship of the true God that which appears as virtue is sin, because nothing can please God without God." Lombard cites the statement of Anselm, "The whole life of unbelievers is sin." We must make a distinction between the gifts of God and the impurities which inhere in us by reason of which even the virtues of the gentiles are contaminated, so that they are sin.

II. Because in the definition of mortal sin mention is made of lapses or falls contrary to conscience, we should note that this is a Scriptural expression: Acts 24:16, "I am always anxious to have a conscience without offense toward God and men"; Rom. 13:5, "Be obedient for the sake of conscience"; 1 Tim. 1:5, "The purpose of this commandment is love which issues from a pure heart, from a good conscience and from sincere faith"; Heb. 10:22, "Purify your hearts from an evil conscience"; 1 Peter 3:21, "the covenant of a good conscience." The conscience is called the judgment of the mind regarding what has been done or ought to be done, as it says in Rom. 2:15, ". . . their conscience bears witness concerning their thoughts which accuse or excuse them"; or Col. 2:14, where "the written accusation which was used against us" is referred to conscience. Therefore whatever evils we commit against our own conscience, these are quite properly called mortal sins. Thus 1 John 3:21, "If our hearts do not condemn us, we have confidence before God."

But it is not an easy matter to show in the case of the individual precepts the difference between mortal and venial sin. Yet Luther's explanation is simple, and it shows how mortal sins in the regenerate can be seen and recognized, namely, when the regenerate refuse to repent, do not fight against sin but indulge in wicked lusts and knowingly and willingly act upon them. For where there is no repentance, there there is no faith and no grace. When a person refuses to repent, at the same time the Holy Spirit is driven out and faith is lost. Hence the Apology [4.353, Tappert, p. 161] correctly says, "There must also be faith, and it must increase in repentance." Thus Christ says, "Unless you repent you shall all perish," Luke 13:3, cf. Jer. 5:5, "Even the great men have broken the yokes and burst the bounds. 'Shall I not visit them?' says the Lord."

The teaching regarding the degrees of conscience gives some help to this consideration. For example in James 1:14–15, these grades or steps are mentioned: (1) our own original concupiscence; (2) the temptation by our concupiscence, when it begins to urge us to evil and gives us evil thoughts; (3) the inviting enticements. For we are lured by these enticements, just like birds and fish. In the same way our original lust invites us by these lures; (4) the enticing occurs when our will through the fires of evil desires is unexpectedly seized to bring it to obedience. Even the regenerate person can fall into this position. For Paul in Rom. 7:23 laments that he is made captive, but while he still remains in Christ he resists and damnation is still not upon him, Rom. 8:1; (5) an evil intention is conceived, a plan to do wrong. When wickedness progresses to this point, repentance and faith are driven away; (6) "Lust brings forth sin," that is, when this work is completed which was undertaken, then sin produces death.

From this passage in James we can see the distinction used in the ancient church, as we see in Lombard, Bk. 2, dist. 24 [MPL 51.647–722], where he cites Augustine.

1. The first degree or step is the evil suggestion.
2. The enticement.
3. The consent. When the will agrees.
4. The planning or scheming.
5. The evil deed itself.

To these steps of Augustine later scholars, such as Gregory the Great and Isidore, added others which can be listed in this way: from evil activity comes the habit of sinning; from the habit of sinning comes the excusing of sinning; from this comes the defense of sinning. Later comes an obstinacy, and then a glorying and exulting in it. Note Prov. 2:14, "He rejoices in evil things"; Ps. 52:3 (Vulgate), "Why do you glory in malice, you who are mighty in iniquity?" Is. 3:9, "They revel in their sin as Sodom. They do not hide it." For the Sodomites in Gen. 19:9 were such shameless sinners before God, as if they actually saw God before them and yet they did not blush to make an open admission of their crimes. They continued to act this way until they were cast into destruction. For after boasting and glorying in sin, there finally followed the "reprobate mind" of which Paul speaks in Rom. 1:28, "God gave them up to a perverted mind," from which comes the final step, the sin against the Holy Spirit.

The study of these steps is useful, for it shows how repentance is first delayed because of our lust, then little by little broken down and finally destroyed, conquered, and ultimately rejected and driven away, until it is utterly crushed and leads into the sin against the Holy Spirit.

But we must also note the steps or degrees of concupiscence. For in Paul even in his regenerate state there were the fires of depraved lusts in which his flesh delighted and which took his will captive; and yet because he mourned over this, resisted it and kept a good conscience, we must not consider him to have committed mortal sin.

God Himself shows these steps in concupiscence in the Decalog in the Ninth and Tenth Commandments. For in Deut. 5:21 in the Ninth Commandment *chāmad* is used, which is derived from the idea of the heart burning with original or innate lust or emotions. The word includes the root of this concupiscence, the idea of our being pushed into it and enjoying it. The Latin translator tried to express the force of this term through the word, "You shall not covet," but he could not quite get the emphasis of the word. Luther, in the German language which sometimes can express ideas of this kind better than the Latin, renders it, *"Du Solt dich Nicht lassen Gelusten"* (You shall not allow yourself to hanker after something). In Ps. 51:5 David uses the cognate word which is taken from the root *yācham* or *chāmam*, and means that the conception of lust has taken place in heat. This word includes the first or original lust, when the flesh burns in its desires. From this we can to some degree estimate the force of the term which concurs with the ideas set forth in Rom. 7:7, "They would not have known lust if the Law had not said, 'You shall not covet.'"

In the Tenth Commandment the fourth conjugation verb (*'āvah*) is used which means that a person lusts or desires eagerly. But in the fourth conjugation there is a reciprocal aspect involved, which reflects an action toward the person performing the action. That is, the person causes himself to lust eagerly which clearly includes by this emphasis the other steps in concupiscence. Thus in Gen. 3:6 it says of the forbidden tree that it was "desirable and something that a person would lust after." Thus in the Ninth Commandment is the first step of concupiscence, but in the Tenth are the rest of the steps, when I am really helping my lust along (*wann ich der Lust so weit bringt*), so that I am now planning and thinking about my lust. Num. 11:4 has, "The people had a strong craving for meat," of which it speaks in 1 Cor. 10:6. Sirach in Ecclus. 18:30–31, seems to be emphasizing the same thing when he says, "Do not give free rein to your lusts, but control them; do not indulge the desire of your soul, for lust will make you a joy to your enemies." And Paul says in Rom. 6:12–13, that when sin so reigns in a man he is "obedient to its lusts and yields his members as instruments of wickedness." Note also Rom. 7:8, "Sin through the commandment worked in me all kinds of covetousness"; Gal. 5:16, "Do not gratify the desires of the flesh"; Ecclus. 9:9, "Lust is kindled like a fire"; Prov. 6:18, "The heart devises plans for lust."

The explanation of Luther for discerning mortal sins is this: When repentance has ceased, when faith has been crushed, then a man is in a state of mortal sin. We have already spoken of the refusal to repent, but it is not out of the question to say something about the loss of faith also, for "without faith it is impossible to please God," Heb. 11:6; and "He who does not believe shall be condemned," Mark 16:16; and "The wrath of God remains over him," John 3:36.

The loss of faith is shown by four very simple signs:

1. As the common definition says, when a person assents to an error in a fundamental article of faith. For the articles of faith are the objects of justifying faith. Eph. 2:20, "We are built upon the foundation of the apostles and prophets, Jesus Christ Himself being the chief cornerstone." Thus a person who does not know the number of years that Methuselah lived or the dimensions of Noah's ark is no worse off, as long as he retains the foundation of the faith. But if a person in regard to his salvation believes something other than what the Gospel teaches, for example, if he ignores the merit of the Son of God which is brought to him in the Word and the sacraments, so that he does not apply it to himself by faith, or if a person allows an error in the doctrine of the person or the work of Christ, such a person commits an error in a fundamental point. Hence matters pertaining to the sacraments are not adiaphora whereby each can believe whatever he wishes without any detriment to his faith. For not every kind of opinion regarding Christ or faith is correct, but only that teaching which lays hold on the promise of grace as it has been taught. But he who in opposition to this foundation commits an error, he has lost his faith and the grace of God. A false or heretical faith is not true faith but is contending against the foundation.

2. The loss of faith takes place when he who had been born again permits himself to take an action contrary to conscience and is not desirous of receiving remission in the Word and the sacraments. There are many who neglect the hearing of the Word and the use of the sacraments, and they persuade themselves that they can still keep their faith and the forgiveness of their sins despite this. But they have shamefully blinded themselves. For when faith does not grow in sinners or exercise its own qualities, but rather degenerates into Epicurean impurity, how can it continue to exist or live in a man? This point can be easily demonstrated and understood. For it is the characteristic of true faith that it clings to the promise of the Gospel with a sound mind and a contrite heart, and in Christ seeks the remission of sins or deliverance from sin. Further, it is the fruit of true faith that it does not live in sin but in righteousness. Therefore, when a person constantly shuts off either of these elements, how can he retain true faith?

3. Faith also is lost when the mind without repentance conceives and adopts the opinion or persuasion that it wants to and can continue and keep on in sin, and yet nevertheless for the sake of Christ can have and keep the grace of God. It is manifest that such faith is not true faith. For faith in Christ does not seek to be able freely to practice sin against conscience and to pile up sins, but rather to be freed from them.

4. From the fruit we also can learn whether faith is true or false. The fruit of true faith is not to serve sin but to live unto righteousness. Likewise the corrupt fruits also show that the tree itself has become evil because of the loss of faith. From these basic ideas it is simple to judge when true faith has been lost and trodden under foot. Consequently when sins take place and are mortal, it means that faith has been lost and destroyed.

III. The third part of the definition refers to mortal sin, that is, that through mortal sin repentance is crushed and faith driven out, the Holy Spirit grieved and tormented, the grace of God along with the remission of sins and the inheritance of eternal life lost and the person is again guilty of the wrath of God, eternal death, and condemnation.

We have a very good example of this situation in Judas. He "denied the faith" from the beginning, as Paul says in 1 Tim. 5:8. Although in words he said that he believes, yet he begins to be forgetful of the blessings of God, 2 Peter 1:9, and afterward he grieved the Holy Spirit who over and over again tried to lead him by His chastenings into the way of God's commandments and to cause him to mortify his flesh. Because faith is the means whereby the grace of God and the inheritance of eternal life are retained, 1 Peter 1:5, therefore when faith is lost, the person cannot retain grace but falls again under the wrath of God which clearly follows the judgment of God.

IV. To this definition of mortal sin also pertains the part which asserts that it is mortal sin if a person does not through repentance come back to God. We need to add this part, so that this doctrine does not drive away those who have fallen into despair or the feeling that they are reprobate. But in order that those who have fallen may be called back to repentance, at the same time that the hope of reconciliation is shown to them, if they repent, at the same time there is also shown to them what kind of repentance is required for mortal sins. Rom. 2:4, "Do not despise the riches of His kindness, His patience and His forbearance which is meant to lead you to repentance."

The Analysis of the Definition of Venial Sin

The definition of venial sin must be subjected to the same analysis. For in order that the sin found in the regenerate may be venial, that is, a sin on account of which grace is not lost nor the Holy Spirit and faith driven away, these aspects are necessary:

I. In order that the sin found in the regenerate may be and become venial, there must be repentance and faith over against the earliest stages of concupiscence, as described above, so that the regenerate will resist with repentance and fight against their depraved desires either in the pressures put upon them or in their pleasure or in consent, and not permit these desires to "rule over them" whereby they might "yield their members as instruments of sin," Rom. 6:13, or that they might "fulfill the lust of the flesh," Gal. 5:16.

II. In order that they might seek by faith and ascertain that these corrupt desires and the resulting fires through which they resist the Holy Spirit are pardoned and not imputed for the sake of Christ, and that they might ask the help of the Holy Spirit. They should not believe or feel in their hearts that God is unconcerned about their weaknesses, but they must understand that if God should want to enter into judgment with them they could not stand in His sight, Ps. 130:3 and 143:2. Because they know that they must resist these desires, they call upon the Holy Spirit that He would be present and help them so that they are not overcome but may live in Christ.

III. Therefore they must recognize their own lust and corrupt desires, even if there is no pleasure or consent regarding them and no action follows which in itself is sin according to the Law, since if God should will to deal with them in keeping with the rigor of His righteousness, no one could be justified. Therefore they should grieve because of these stains and they should seek and believe that they solely for the sake of Christ the Mediator are pleasing to God. With Paul they must say, "I am not aware of anything against myself, but I am not thereby justified, for He who judges me is God," 1 Cor. 4:4.

In the writings of Jerome the question arises as to whether the first stages of emotion are sin. From this a controversy arose concerning these first emotions which are suggested to the mind of the regenerate man in addition to his will. Thus Paul, when he says in Rom. 7:19, "The evil which I do not want to do that I do," understands these suggestions by which the pleasure and consent come, but he deplores them and struggles against them. This they call "the first stage of emotion." Concerning these, Jerome states that unless there is the addition of pleasure and consent, inclinations of this kind are not in themselves sins, but only natural emotions which are not involved with the divine law. Lindanus says that they are insignificant things, minor defects, little faults which cannot contaminate the works of the regenerate. The Scholastics also teach that in venial sins there is no need for contrition and there is no need to lament over them. They are things which in themselves are worthy of being overlooked and unworthy of God's wrath. But we must not judge about desires of this kind on the basis of our own human reason, for God says in Is. 55:9, "For as the heavens are high above the earth . . . so are My thoughts higher than your thoughts." When His law prohibits these lusts, there is no doubt that they are sin and that the godly must lament over them. Thus, in order that the promise might remain sure, the regenerate are not to trust in their own works nor rely on them, even though neither desire nor consent are added to their first emotions, but they must pray that they can remain in grace only for the sake of Christ.

IV. Even if the fires of depraved lusts in their great power take the regenerate as captives either to the point of consent or to the actual performance of some evil work, yet if they immediately repent in sorrow and in faith seek forgiveness, it is certain that the Holy Spirit has been grieved or hurt, but not yet crushed, and faith and the grace of God have not yet been lost. For the Holy Spirit works in the regenerate that he may rise again as a righteous person, even if he falls seven times in a day. Thus Paul says, Eph. 4:26–30, "Even if you are angry, do not sin, nor give place to the devil . . . and do not grieve the Holy Spirit in whom you have been sealed unto the day of judgment."

V. The reborn stand by faith, although they cannot in this life completely get rid of the stains of their original sin or totally put to death their evil actions, Rom. 7:24, and although these evils in themselves according to the Law are worthy of eternal damnation, yet because they have been born again and remain in Christ and do not walk according to the flesh, that is, because they keep their repentance and faith and practice them, they therefore do not have to experience condemnation, Rom. 8:1. And this is what is said in the common definition, namely that grace and the Holy Spirit are not lost because of venial sins. The reason is that those who repent and believe in Christ receive, possess, and retain grace and the remission of sins. But those who reject faith and repentance, such people lose the grace of God.

The Anabaptists, in opposition to this position which we take, try to defend their own peculiar notion that the regenerate cannot lose grace. They use two particular arguments:

1. The will of God is immutable, just as grace is in the courts of princes. For God has said in the prophet Hosea 2:19, "I will betroth you to Myself forever." Therefore they say that he who has once obtained the grace of God can never lose it in all eternity. But they fail to observe the additional words in Hosea, "In righteousness and in judgment, in mercy and in faithfulness, I will betroth you to Me"; or Col. 1:23, "If you continue in the faith established and settled . . ."; cf. Heb. 3:6; Rom. 5:2.

2. They argue that while faith remains, grace also remains. But the regenerate do not deny their faith in Christ, even though they sometimes fall into sins, and therefore they also retain the grace of God. For the explanation of their line of reasoning, which has misled not only the Anabaptists but almost the whole world, it is useful to note the point given above, which indicates the signs we can use to understand whether faith is still present or has indeed been lost. For there is no doubt that where there is true faith, there is also the grace of God. But where the first is lost, the second cannot be present. For (1) faith in Christ, which alone justifies, does not take pleasure in sinning, but when the foundation has been overturned, then justification is no longer present. (2) The

specific difference of faith is that it lays hold on Christ in Word and sacraments. Therefore, when you permit something to be done against conscience and are not concerned after the lapses have occurred to seek to be reconciled by the Word and the sacraments, then there is no faith present which may show itself and use its power; and the result is that faith no longer again lays hold on Christ. (3) A person who is involved with sins against conscience might adopt the opinion: I know, to be sure, that God does not approve of what I am doing, but because He is merciful, I believe that He will have mercy on me even when I am engaged in my sins. This kind of persuasion is not true faith. For it is the quality of true faith that it does not look for the opportunity to do something shameful, but with contrite heart seeks remission of sins in the Word and sacraments, for the sake of Christ (4) We can judge a tree from its fruits. The fruits of true faith are not to look for occasions to sin or to remain in our sins, but to mortify the flesh. Thus Luther says in the Smalcald Articles [3.43, Tappert, p. 310], "When sin contrary to conscience is permitted, faith is lost." And Augustine says, "It is unbelief which hangs on to all sins, so that they are not forgiven."

CHAPTER IV: THE BASES OF THE DEFINITIONS

In the fourth place, in explaining this locus we must observe and consider in which passages of Scripture the individual parts of the definitions have their foundations, as Scripture applies both to mortal and venial sin. We do this in order that the younger generation may understand the sources which confirm these points, may understand the explanations of the true meaning of the matter, and may learn from where refutations are to be taken.

There are passages which deal with the suppressing of repentance, such as Jer. 5:5, "I will go to the great men and speak with them; for they know the way of the Lord and the judgment of their God, but behold they have broken the yoke and burst the chains." It is obvious that He is speaking of the regenerate. For, because the common mass of men could not understand the sentence of God, He determined to go to the best people, that is, to those who were highest in the church and to whom the will of God was known. But these also turned faces to Him which were harder than stone and they cast off His bonds, cf. Ps. 2:3. From this we can see how people reject repentance in their mortal sin when even we who have been well instructed do not want to repent. And lest anyone think, after repentance has been refused, that God is still favorable toward him, He says, in Jer. 5:7, "Why should I forgive you?" Rom. 2:4–5, "The goodness of God leads you to repentance, but according to your hardness and the impenitence of your heart, you treasure up for yourself wrath and on the day of wrath comes the revelation of the righteous judgment of God." He is certainly indicating by these statements that our own thoughts are such that they will accuse our heart; 1 John 3:21, "If our heart condemn us . . ." then the wrath which has been "treasured up" for us will be poured out upon us. Compare 2 Peter 2:20ff., "If after they have escaped the pollutions of the world through the knowledge of our Lord Jesus Christ, they are again caught in them," their latter actions are worse than the first. They are "the dog who returns to his own vomit and the sow which had been washed and returned to her wallowing." Thus through mortal sin men again go back to that from which they had, by repentance, departed. And thus they are in worse condition than they were at first; they have brought greater shame down upon themselves than they had before their conversion, as Christ says in Luke 12:47, "The servant who knew his master's will and did not prepare himself to do it, shall be beaten with many stripes." In Rev. 2:16 it is written to the angel of the church of Pergamos in Asia that the church should repent for holding the doctrine of Balaam and the Nicolaitans, unless she wished to lose the seven golden candlesticks. For the fallen—unless they return to God through repentance—cannot retain the grace of God. Revelation 9, God invites those who have fallen to come to Him, not only through the Word but through calamities, and in vv. 20–21 He says they shall perish who see sins punished in others and yet do not repent themselves. Rev. 16:1 speaks of the angels who poured out the vials of divine wrath upon the human race. The reason is given in v. 11: "because they did not repent of their deeds." For the grace of God is turned away through impenitence.

It is evident that faith is lost through actions against conscience, as 1 Tim. 1:19 testifies, "Keep a good conscience, which some have put away and have made shipwreck of their faith." For when a good conscience is lost, so is faith; and when faith is lost, so is the grace of God. 1 Tim. 5:8, "If a man does not provide for his own and especially for those of his own household, he has denied the faith and is worse than an infidel." From this it is patent that he who acts contrary to the commandments of God whose image he bears and does not take care of his own family, this man not only has lost his faith but is worse than a gentile. For he who denies the faith sins more gravely than he who has always practiced the works of darkness. 2 Peter 1:9, "He who lacks these things is blind and has forgotten that he was purged from his old sins," for this is nothing else than losing one's faith. The regular recalling of the remission of sins is an exercise of faith. On the other hand, forgetfulness is the judgment for losing one's faith. 1 John 3:6, "Whoever sins has not seen Him or known Him"; that is, he does not have the knowledge of God and true faith. 1 Cor. 13:5, "Test yourselves to see if you are in the faith; prove yourselves. Do you not know your own selves, that Jesus is in you, unless you have become reprobate?" But from what source do the regenerate know that they have faith and the reprobate that they do not, except from the fruits? But if, however, the fruits contrary to conscience cut us off from faith, then we are cast off. These statements against the Anabaptists should be noted carefully, for they think that he who has once received faith can never lose it, even if he commits sins which are contrary to conscience. But these poor blind men do not know what true faith is, and they demonstrate this by the position they give to their vain opinions regarding Christ and the place of faith.

The remaining testimonies are in the first chapter, where we have discussed the *sedes doctrinae* and shown and explained the individual parts of the definition.

CHAPTER V: THE USE OF THIS DOCTRINE

In addition to what has been said above in the explanation of this subject, we must now in the fifth place note what the use of this teaching is, in order that the distinction between mortal and venial sin may be demonstrated and considered. The purpose of this discussion is not, however, only a matter of words or definitions, but of applying the teaching to a genuine use in the daily and serious exercises of repentance and faith. This consideration can include these parts:

1. That the regenerate may walk in the fear of the Lord and be so led and governed by the Holy Spirit that they do not give consent to any mortal sins or acts against conscience, but avoid them as diligently as possible and be aware of them and all the time consider that they must not grieve or torment the Holy Spirit, or neglect repentance, or lose faith, grace, and salvation, or give place to the devil, or run into any of his traps, from which so many can no longer extricate themselves. Thus Paul says in Gal. 5:16, "Walk in the Spirit and you will not fulfill the desires of the flesh"; v. 18, ". . . you are led by the Spirit"; v. 25, "If we live in the Spirit, let us also walk in the Spirit"; cf. Eph. 4:30, 27; 1 Tim. 3:7; 6:9; 2 Tim. 2:24–26.

2. That each person may carefully examine his own life, and if he discovers that he is taken up with some mortal sin to which he clings, that he may not in his false security continue in it or pursue it, imagining for himself the notion that he is under grace and has salvation; for from such a state of mind comes hardening, a reprobate mind, and the sin against the Holy Spirit. Therefore let such a man rise again through repentance and again turn back to God. Paul warns the Corinthians of this in 2 Cor. 13:5, "Examine and prove yourselves as to whether Christ and the faith are within you, unless you have become a castaway." Thus Tertullian says, "Many people sin in the hope of favor, but such people are brought down to destruction." Thus in Rev. 2:5 it is said to the angel of the church of Ephesus, "Remember from whence you have fallen; repent, and do the works you did at first. If not, I will come to you and remove your candlestick from its place, unless you repent." In Jer. 3:12, God complains about the

sins of the Israelites and testifies that He has rejected the entire nation, and with regard to the house of Judah which had imitated the sins of Israel, He enjoins the prophet, "Go and proclaim these words to the north, and say 'Return, faithless Israel,' says the Lord, 'and I will not turn My face from you,'" and in v. 14 He says, "Return, faithless children, for I am your husband and will take you up."

3. That we may understand that the repentance of those who have fallen does not consist only in recognizing or confessing their sins and certainly not in persevering or continuing in them, as Saul did in 1 Sam 24:17–18. When David had cut off a piece of Saul's garment in the cave and had shown it to him and thus proved his innocence, Saul wept and said to David, "You are more righteous than I am; you did good to me, but I am doing evil to you." Yet afterward Saul returned to his vomit and again persecuted David. Therefore, "We do not repent, but only pretend to do so," as Augustine says. Therefore, as Scripture says, we must certainly cease from evil and desist from sinning. For what kind of nonsense is it to devise for ourselves a license to sin and in our hearts to say, "It will do no harm as long as I say to myself that I am repenting." "This is the mere appearance of faith: it is not true faith," says Tertullian. And when we do not take this care, then it is a certainty that all kinds of corrupt actions follow, and false security is fostered, along with impenitence among those people who boast of the name of Christ and flatter themselves with the hope of grace and salvation.

4. That the regenerate may always keep before them the instruction as to how they must fight against the sin which dwells in their flesh, so that it may be and remain venial, that is, that it not be imputed to them for condemnation. Sad to say, when this indwelling sin begins to rage, we do not give it the attention which it requires but often give way to it, consent to it, even make plans for entering into sin, and thus permit sin to rule in our mortal bodies. Therefore it is beneficial that we always have before us this warning, for unless we support the Spirit in His struggle against the flesh, it will be easy for us to fall and lose our salvation. But by this admonition or the bridles of the Holy Spirit we can be kept under control so that we are not drawn into mortal sin. Therefore, just as in the earlier discussion of the degrees or steps in concupiscence we are showing how a venial sin becomes a mortal sin if we allow just the suggestion and the element of pleasure, so that there is the addition of our consenting to sin, and through our evil plans we are brought to the point of the deed itself. So we must be on our guard that we do not progress in this direction, but mortify our flesh. Otherwise, if we remain in our false security, we will fall into mortal sins, and from this will come hardening and finally the crushing of the Holy Spirit.

5. That the godly in the stains and weaknesses which cling to them and even in their lapses, may have remedies and comforts daily before them. But if

a man is "overtaken in some fault," Gal. 6:1, through the wickedness of Satan and the weakness of his own flesh, he must seek the remedy in this doctrine and rise again through repentance.

Chapter VI: The Antithesis to This Doctrine

The final section of this locus must consider the antithesis, or the opinions which are in conflict with the correct doctrine. We must consider how these ideas are to be refuted.

1. The scholastic doctors argued that venial sins derived their name from the fact that they have in them something by which they can achieve forgiveness, and thus they do not merit eternal punishment. Some of them establish this point by devising the notion that venial sins are not contrary to the law of God but belong to a kind of irregular status called "things which are alongside of (*praeter*) the law," because the intention of the law is not completely achieved.

The Pharisees had this same idea, yet they did not deny that such actions were against the law of God. But they came upon the distinction that some precepts are great, and others are minor. Thus some sins are great, which are contrary to the big commandments, and they have guilt; but others are minor, which are against minor commandments, and they do not condemn us. The scholastics do not accept this distinction but say that such sins are not against the law but only alongside or beside it, "*und machens also arger dann die Pharisae.*" Indeed, the crasser papists try to get to the point of saying that good works in the eyes of God do merit something, even though imperfectly, and they neither dare nor can deny that these many sins do cling to men, but they say that these stains do very little damage to our works, because our righteousness as we travel is such that if each does as much as he can, God is content. For, they say, the law does not obligate us to the impossible. And it is impossible in this life that a person be without blemishes and weaknesses.

Both the term "venial sin" and the subject itself are perverted by all these ideas. Hence it is called venial sin because it has in itself something which merits forgiveness. But, as Luther says on Galatians 5 [Amer. Ed., 27.76], "The difference between mortal and venial sins does not pertain to the substance of the sin but to the person committing the sin," insofar as he is repentant or rejects his sin, and on this ground an act deserves to be called mortal or venial.

Others among the papists distinguish mortal from venial this way: When a sensual emotion or desire of the flesh conceives some enticement to sin, to which the lower portion of our mind and thought (that is, some pleasure) gives some fleeting attention, but if the will (which they say is the superior portion of the mind) does not contribute the decision to complete the action, then they try to call this a venial sin, just as there are the primary emotions or those which arise out of some secret weakness or ignorance.

In this way Peter Lombard, who was the first writer of scholastic doctrine and whom the later scholastics followed (they themselves commented on "the Master of the Sentences," and where statements both of Scripture and of the fathers were lacking, they made up the deficiencies from the writings of the philosophers, this method of teaching had also been attempted in the school of Origen, both by himself and by Clement, but from the beginning it had been rejected by the church, and only afterward it was reestablished under the papacy), this man Lombard, in Bk. 2, dist. 24 [MPL 192.705], says, "From the standpoint of human reason every sin is treated as mortal, but not every one as venial, that is, a sin which exists only in the desire of our flesh." And Thomas says, "Mortal sin is in the reason, but venial sin is in our sensuality." Again, "An evil action in the area of morals which is unexpected, not planned, is a venial sin." But Augustine speaks more correctly, at least at times, "No sin is so pardonable or venial that it could not be mortal, if a person wanted to make it so."

The scholastics took occasion to make these distinctions from statements which the fathers had taught on the basis of Scripture regarding the degrees of concupiscence and that, quite correctly, some sins were greater than others. But they got so confused over these matters that they imagined that venial sins in themselves were not contrary to the law of God and did not have the quality of sin and therefore there was no need for contrition over venial sins. They could be easily expiated by using holy water, by the unction of the heart, by the blessing of the bishop, by wise counsels. And they said that venial sins were no hindrance to the regenerate for complete and perfect obedience in this life. Hence, in the hereafter they produced merit unto eternal life.

In the writings of the fathers we can read various statements on these matters which, if carefully explained, are in no way improper, but they have been distorted by the scholastics. Augustine: "A person can live without committing a crime, but if we say that he does not have sin, we are deceiving ourselves." Thus Bernhard says in his book *De Praecepto et Dispensatione*, 14 [MPL 182.875ff.], "To be angry at one's brother, while it is not a crime for which a man will go to hell, yet it makes him guilty of judgment. And if it brings guilt, it is therefore sin. Further, every sin is certainly against the commandment of God. Therefore venial sin is a transgression against the divine law, such as foolish talking, running at the mouth, idle talk, and deeds of this kind. Such things are always against the commands of God. And thus they are venial sins, not crimes, except that when they are indulged in by habit and with contempt, then not the outward appearance of the sin but the intention of the sinner should be examined. Indeed, the arrogance of the contemptuous person and the obstinacy of the man who will not repent, even in the matter of small sins, does not draw down small guilt but turns into a crime of genuine rebellion, and a little wart becomes a matter of plain transgression." These and other statements like them are not in conflict with what we have said; indeed, they explain and confirm it; but our opponents should be able to see how they concur with the doctrine of the scholastics.

2. In our time, among the Anabaptists certain people have argued that once grace has been received, it cannot be lost because of any kind of sins, unless a person refuses to believe. They have this understanding because of historical faith. Certain perverse men do not hesitate to attribute this fanatical opinion to Luther. For when he wrote that faith destroys all sins so that there is no sin by reason of the faith which precedes, where he adds that if it happens that a person commits adultery while he is in faith, this is not a mortal sin, these evil interpreters of Luther have ripped this out of context and treated it as if he were saying categorically that a person could keep his faith even if he sinned against conscience, although in Art. 13 of the Smalcald Articles [13.3, Tappert, p. 315] Luther clearly asserts, "We say further that where good works do not follow, there the faith is false and not true faith."

3. There are also some people who assert that he who falls into mortal sin has never had faith or the Holy Spirit, and thus they plant doubt in the hearts of all, since we all fall often.

But the main points of the refutation, insofar as they are individual notions, have been pointed out above.

LOCUS [XVII]

The Church

Let us always keep this statement of Paul in mind: "Whom He chose them He also called" [Rom. 8:30]. Whenever we think about the church, we should consider the congregation of the called, which is the visible church, nor should we imagine that somewhere else there are any chosen ones except in this visible assembly itself. For God wants to be invoked and known in no other way than as He has revealed Himself, and He has revealed Himself in no other place than in the visible church in which alone the voice of the Gospel is proclaimed. Nor should we devise some other invisible and silent church of people still living in this life, but the eyes and mind of the assembly of the called, that is, of those who confess the Gospel of God must be looked at, and we should know that the voice of the Gospel must sound forth among people publicly, as it is written, "Their sound has gone out into all the world" [Ps. 19:4]. We should understand that there must be the public ministry of the Gospel and public gatherings, as it says in Eph. 4[:8ff.], and to this assembly we should join ourselves. We are citizens and members of this visible gathering, as it is enjoined in Ps. 26:8, "I have loved the beauty of Your house"; and Ps. 84[:1], "How amiable are Your tabernacles, O Lord." These and similar passages speak not of a Platonic idea but of the visible church in which the voice of the Gospel rings out and in which the ministry of the Gospel is seen through which God reveals Himself and through which He is efficacious.

Nor should we heap praise upon those vagrants who wander about and attach themselves to no church because they nowhere find such an idea, in which something is not lacking in morals or discipline; but we should look for a church in which the articles of faith are correctly taught and idols are not defended and join ourselves to it and hear and love it as it teaches and add our own invocation and confession to its prayers and confession. Thus Cyrus and other godly men among the gentiles, though they were not at Jerusalem, nevertheless in their public profession they were in the assembly of the called, listened to the voice and ministry of the Gospel, were citizens and visible members of the visible church, joined and added their invocation and confession to that of the prophets and the whole company of the godly who were in Jerusalem which was the principal center of the ministry.

These points should be often and seriously considered in order that we may learn what the church of God is and where it is [and] how God is to be known. And we should genuinely attach ourselves to the church and learn to support it, so that no dissolutions take place. For where there are no congregations, the voice of the Gospel is stilled; for example, the Muslim tyrants have destroyed all the church buildings in many places, and no congregations, not even their own, are permitted to come into being. We should realize that such diabolic devastations and destructions are a huge and consummate evil. Hence we should pray God that He would preserve His congregations and we ourselves in all our work should support them.

Now this should be the definition: The visible church is the assembly of those who hold the Gospel of Christ and rightly use the sacraments, in which God, through the ministry of the Gospel, is efficacious, and He regenerates many unto life eternal. In this assembly, however, there are many unregenerate who nevertheless give their assent to the true doctrine, just as in the time of Mary the church consisted of Zacharias, Simeon, Joseph, Elizabeth, Mary, the shepherds, and many others like them who were in agreement regarding the pure doctrine and did not listen to the Sadducees or the other ungodly priests but to Zacharias, Simeon, Anna, Elizabeth, Mary and people like them. For God preserves some as His remnant among the ministers and gradually restores the ministry. And among these hearers of Zacharias and Elizabeth there were some who were not born again, having sins against conscience; and yet, because they consented to the true doctrine, they were citizens and members of the church in this life.

But meanwhile the priests, the Pharisees, and the Sadducees were in conflict with the Word of God; though they were in control, yet they were not members of the church, according to [Gal. 1:8], "If anyone teach another Gospel, let him be accursed," etc. Thus in the time of Elijah the church consisted of Elijah, Elisha, and their hearers, and the church was not without a ministry. For the prophets themselves were the ministers of the Gospel and there were some godly priests with them. For there was a fair-sized multitude of saints, as the text says [1 Kings 19:18], "I still have left to Me seven thousand," etc. Mixed with these were some whose morals were subject to criticism, who still, because they assented to the true doctrine, were members of the church in external association and in the function of the ministry. But in the meantime the priests of Baal and those like them who defended ungodly rites were not members of the church. These examples from history were written to teach the difference between the true and false church.

And now these words are part of the definition: "In which assembly God through the ministry of the Gospel, is efficacious." There are two noteworthy elements, not to be omitted, whenever a definition of the church is formulated. For we must not imagine the church without some knowledge of the promise concerning Christ and without the ministry; the church is not in an assembly where there is neither knowledge of the promise of Christ nor the voice nor the ministry of the Gospel. Therefore Aristides, Cicero, and others like them are not members of the church, even though they have outstanding civil virtues which God gives for the sake of rulers, for so long as He wills that the human race remain in this life. But these statements testify that there must be the knowledge of Christ in the church of God. See John 3[:18, 36]; 17[:17]; 1 Cor. 1[:21]; Rom. 10:14.

Eph. 4:11, Christ sitting at the right hand of God, "also gives some prophets, some apostles, some pastors, [and] some teachers," and He clearly says that the ministry of the Gospel must be preserved, so that "it be not tossed about by various winds of doctrine" [cf. v. 14]. Just as the gentiles, when they do not hear the Word of God, fall into frightful ravings and gradually devise other gods and many portents and many prodigious expressions of worship. The same thing happens to heretics, [such as the] Manichaeans, the Anabaptists, etc., because they abandon the Word of God.

Therefore we should know that the church of God is the assembly which is bound to the voice or the ministration of the Gospel. And outside of this assembly, where there is no voice of the Gospel and no invocation of Christ, there are no heirs of eternal life, as it is written, "There is no other name . . . by which we must be saved" [Acts 4:12]. Thus also Isaiah says in 8[:16], "Seal the law among My disciples," that is, I see that great darkness will follow, but I pray You, O God, that You preserve the hearers of [Your] prophets and seal in them Your doctrine given to the prophets, so that the Word and the true understanding of the Word not be quenched. Some churches remain and these are this assembly which retains Your Word uncorrupted which they have received from the prophets.

Therefore Isaiah in 8:20 [cf. Vulgate] adds the words, "To the law and to the testimony. They who do not speak according to this Word shall not have the morning light." For the will of God is not understood except through the Word which He has given, and God wills to be known and invoked as He has revealed Himself.

Then we must also add this, that God is efficacious through this ministry that is, through the voice of the Gospel [as it is] heard, read, and pondered He moves [our] minds by the Holy Spirit, wants us to assent, aids those who assent, and renews eternal life in them. Thus it is written in Rom. 1[:16], "The Gospel is the power of God unto salvation to every one who believes"; and 2 Cor. 3[:8], "The new covenant is the ministry of the Spirit." These points contain the saving doctrine and comfort, that is to say, when we know that the promise of eternal life is truly offered in this way through the Word.

Nor should we imagine that there was faith in Socrates, Plato, Xenophon, Cicero, and others like them, because they had a certain knowledge of the law of God. For this is still not knowledge of Christ. But the church is simply and completely bound to the promise of Christ. It is necessary above all things to call upon the name of Christ, and in all those who are capable of being taught there must be knowledge, invocation, and confession of the Son of God. The church has been such since the beginning, from [the time of] Adam, after the promise was given, an assembly sometimes large, sometimes small, which in confidence in the promise of God received the remission of sins and rightly called upon God.

But after this is established, that in the church there must be the voice of the Gospel and the ministry, then questions arise regarding the persons. Is the church bound to the bishops and their colleges, which are said to hold the office of the ministry? Likewise, is [the church] bound to a regular succession of bishops and colleges?

I reply: The church is bound to the very Gospel of God, because, in order that it may be proclaimed in the ministry, God raises up some men from time to time who teach correctly, as it says in Ephesians 4, even if, among these, some have more light, others less. But when the ministers or bishops or colleges or others teach things which are in conflict with the Gospel and the doctrine of the apostles, it is necessary to follow the rule of Paul: "If any one teach another Gospel, let him be accursed" [Gal. 1:8]. From this rule we can judge that the church is not bound to certain titles or a regular succession. For when those who hold the power of orders err, they must not be heeded.

This statement is correct, but unwelcome to political people who see disputes arising thence [and] therefore, with an eye on rulers and human states, transform the church by imitation into a kingdom. Just as the kingdom of France is the mass of people subject to the French king, who in their laws and places of law courts are distinct from other nations, fortified by garrisons, bound to a regular succession of kings and of necessity in the courts obedient to the laws and interpretation of the king, whose interpretation has validity because of [his] authority, so also many imagine that the church is the mass of people subject to the one Roman pope, distinct from other nations by ceremonies which the popes have established, and bound to a regular succession of bishops and to the interpretation of Scripture which the pope or councils have handed down. For since dissensions often arise regarding what has been written, they say that there must be another sure rule, that is the voice of a ruler, just as in a secular kingdom the voice of the king has the authority to interpret the laws. These things are plausibly said among rulers. For human reason loves this kind of picture of the church—a picture that is in agreement with secular opinions, and rulers understand that their authority is increased by this view, and they believe that this form is quite useful for peace.

The godly also know that in this imitation, or rather, unhappy imitation, there are many errors. We must agree that the church is a visible assembly, but it is not the kingdom of the popes but an assembly like a company of scholars. For God wills that the church not be absolutely hidden in secret places or that it be unknown, but He wills that it be listened to; He wills that His Son our Lord Jesus Christ be acknowledged; He wills that He be invoked always by some part of the human race; He wills to gather out of the human race an inheritance for His Son. Therefore it is written,

"Their sound has gone out into all the earth" [Ps. 19:4]. And Christ Himself says in Ps. 2[:7], "I will talk about the precept." Therefore the voice of the Gospel and of the ministry of the Word will remain, and there will be some visible assembly of the church of God, but it will be like a school assembly. There is order, there is a distinction between those who teach and those who hear, and there are grades: Some are apostles, others are pastors, others teachers, and it is correct to understand the words, "Tell it to the church" [Matt. 18:17], of a visible gathering. But first we must see who the members of this visible church are. For those who condemn the clear truth of the Gospel and exercise violence to establish manifest errors are not members of this gathering, of which it is written: "Tell it to the church." Nor, finally, should we accept this, that most of their decisions must be given preference. Because, although there are many who believe correctly and have kept the light of the Gospel, yet there are many more who openly contradict the Gospel either out of weakness or doubt, like the apostles themselves for a long time held on to the dream of a worldly empire. Therefore who will be the judge when a dissension arises about a statement of Scripture, since then there is need for the voice of one who settles controversy?

I reply: The Word of God itself is the judge and to it is added the confession of the true church. For some godly always follow the Word as the seat of authority, and with the confession of those who are stronger the weak are aided, as Christ says, "And you, when you are converted, strengthen your brothers" [Luke 22:32]. In this way controversies over doctrine are settled. And although the majority do not heed this true judge and the true confession, as also ancient examples show often happens, God, the judge of the church, finally settles controversy, destroying blasphemers, as when the greater part of the Jews opposed Jeremiah and later the apostles, blasphemers were finally destroyed.

There is, therefore, some difference between the judgment seats of the church and secular judgment seats. For in the civil realm either the monarch alone makes pronouncements by his own authority or the opinion of the majority prevails in the senate. But in the church the position which is in agreement with the Word of God and the confession of the faithful prevails, whether they are more numerous or less numerous than the ungodly. Thus the ancients condemned Paul of Samosata and later Arius. The judge was the Word of God, that is, testimonies brought from the Gospel in good faith and without sophistry which convinced all but a prejudiced judge; but still also the weak were then greatly aided in expressing themselves by the confession of the stronger, namely of those who had heard the apostles or their disciples, that is those of whom it was clear that they had been faithful guardians of doctrine, such as, Polycarp, Irenaeus, [and] Gregory [Thaumaturgus] of Neocaesarea. Their disciples [in turn] had heard from them that Logos indicates a person. Later they themselves, after comparing statements of the Gospel, acknowledged that this was the natural meaning [of the statement] which they had heard from [their teachers].

Some also not only learn from those who went before them but also are strengthened as by those who are stronger. Thus Peter of Alexandria refuted Meletius [and] cited the Gospel, which very clearly teaches that fallen ones who amend their lives should be received; but at the same time he was helped by the examples of the earlier church which had always received those who had previously fallen.

Thus we declare regarding the baptism of infants: We have clear testimonies in Scripture which affirm that outside the church there is no salvation. Therefore we bring infants into the church. Further, we are also aided by the testimonies of the early church. Thus the Word of God is the judge and to it is added the pure confession of antiquity. For God wills that in the church there be the ministry of the [spoken] word. Hence we must heed the church as teacher, but faith and prayer rely on the Word of God, not on human authority. We must learn from the church that Logos in the account in John 1 indicates a person, but we believe that the Son of God is by nature God, and we call upon Him because He Himself revealed this and taught it in the Gospel.

We must ponder this distinction, lest we despise the church when it teaches, and yet we must know that the judge is the Word of God itself. Thus we must beware of pitfalls in both directions: on the one hand, lest a tyranny of corrupt practice be established and yet on the other lest we give free rein to audacious minds which, if they will not heed the true church, devise notions which do not have the testimony of any era in the church, as in our time Servetus, Campanus,[1] the Anabaptists, and many others have done. Let us learn to love, respect, and honor the church when it teaches and seek the testimonies of the church in its periods of greater purity, as is indicated in a very lovely way in the allegory of Samson [Judg. 14:18], "If you had not plowed with my heifer, you would not have discovered [my riddle]," that is, unless you had heard the church, which is the guardian of the Word of God, working in the ministry, the Word of God would be entirely unknown to you. And Ps. 68:26, "Bless God the Lord in the congregations [churches] from the fountains of Israel," that is, from the ministry of the prophets and apostles.

I have spoken of the definition of the church and of the question as to where the church is to be sought, namely wherever the voice of the Gospel is proclaimed uncorrupted, especially where it pertains to the foundation, as Paul says, that is, where the articles of faith are taught in their wholeness and without corruption and where manifest cults of idols are not defended. Now, since there is a great weakness even in the saints in this life, some have more [and] some less light. Hence Basil, Ambrose, Epiphanius, Augustine, Bernard, and many others, even if they correctly held to the foundation, yet from time to time they said something ill-advisedly in regard

---

[1] Servetus and Campanus were both prominent anti-Trinitarians of the era. Campanus was also an Anabaptist. Servetus was put to death by Calvin for his views, and Campanus was imprisoned.

to human rites, so that by the practice of their era some of the contagion spread to all people. Therefore Paul commands that we consider particularly the foundation, and he indicates that many true members of the church have some weakness and some failings.

[In 1 Cor. 3:11] he says, "No other [foundation] can be laid than that which has been laid, which is Jesus Christ." In this statement he includes the uncorrupted knowledge of all the articles of faith and the prohibition of the worship of idols. Then there follows [v. 12] that one man builds on [the foundation] gold, another straw. Thus Polycarp built gold on the foundation, that is, he explained the necessary doctrine in his refutation of Marcion concerning the essence of God, the cause of evil, and many other articles, and he performed the acts of worship which had been commanded by God and, above all, he governed the church well and adorned [his] confession with marvelous steadfastness under torture. All of these things are included in the word "gold." But Basil and many others built straw on the foundations. To be sure, they did retain the articles of faith, but they still established monastic rites and preferred these practices to civil life and spread the notion in the minds of people, so that they thought that [such things] are the worship of God. And then many erred much more when they imagined that such ceremonies merit the remission of sins.

Furthermore, Paul says [in 1 Cor. 3:13], "Fire will test each one's work, of what sort it is." For he is alluding to building material. Gold is not consumed by fire, but straw easily succumbs to flames and quickly burns up. Thus doctrine, discussed and disputed in [a time of] testing, remains true and necessary and comforts minds, as now all the godly joyously embrace the tested doctrine of the righteousness of faith and perceive it to be a great comfort. But on the other hand, the monastic rites disappear because they are now perceived as not being profitable either for knowledge of God or for morals. I have mentioned these things so that Paul's statement may be carefully considered and so that human weakness which still is often observed in the true members of the church, may be lamented and that we may wisely judge the statements of writers and recognize what things are to be condoned and what things are not to be condoned.

In order that the difference between the church and [civil] states may be seen more clearly, let [this] comparison be made: In the empires of the world these three things are necessary: order, glory, and protection. Thus in the kingdom of France there is order, so that there is one king at whose death it is necessary to be subject to the one who succeeds in regular succession. Then there are certain laws and courts of certain places and ranks of the princes and the common people. The glory consists in the excellence of counsel and powers and in victories, because, since peace is never certain, as Plato says, in empires peace is an empty word. For either restless citizens or enemies always cause tumult. It is necessary that there be many glorious successes *and victories for those who govern; otherwise rulers are quickly overthrown. Defenses are armies and the means necessary for domestic rule and for waging war.*

These three things are different in the church than in empires.

1. There is order, because there is indeed one head, who gives life and eternal blessings to the church, namely the Son of God. But this Head is not now seen with physical eyes nor does He hold an assembly limited to some single place; and though there is no [ranking] order, there is always the ministry of the Gospel. And by divine law obedience is owed to ministers of the Gospel in all matters which the Gospel prescribes. However, this order is not bound to a regular line of succession, but when the bishops and ministers defend errors and idols, they are to be avoided. Further, there are degrees of gifts, as when Paul excels Barnabas. These degrees must be considered, so that we may love and honor individuals adorned with their gifts.

2. The church does not always have secular glory, that is, material victories such as it had when Saul at the time of David overcame hostile armies, but for the most part the church has been, is, and will be subject to the cross; and yet it has marvelous glory of wisdom and virtues and of many miracles which are not seen by the ungodly. Its highest honor is that it knows and prays to the true God. For there are always some true members of the church who keep the foundation, even if there is also a great number of weak people who, because they rightly invoke God, still have great honor. As for the rest, it was said above that they are not members of the church who stubbornly defend errors which conflict with the foundation, even if they use the name and title of the church as a pretext.

Then there are the great victories of all who rightly pray, because they are not destroyed by the traps of the devil, the terrors of tyrants, and other trials; and there are many daily miracles of frequent deliverance in great perils, many of which [deliverances] take place because of the prayers of the church; for example, Paul knows that he and his ship are saved by God, even if others thought that it was saved by chance.

A great glory is happiness in vocation, studies, counsels and judgments, just as on the other hand parricide of church or fatherland is the height of depravity and calamity and the turpitude to be avoided most of all.

3. Finally, there are no visible defenses of the church bound to certain places, that is, after the destruction of the [political] state of Israel the church in this life has neither kings nor armies nor any one certain or perpetual seat. Thus Christ says, "The Son of man has no place to lay His head" [Matt. 8:20]. For it is the will of God that the church be under the cross, that its cases be evaluated in a different court, which are not the writings of the philosophers, but only revealed in the Gospel.

Now, although God does from time to time raise up certain kings for a time for the defense of the church, as He raised up Cyrus, Constantine, and others, yet He did not always join kingdoms to the church to defend it, but wanted it to pray, and hope for the whole body's defense from heaven, as it says in Is. 46[:3–4], "I bear you in My womb. . . . I shall also carry the aging church." Hos. 1[:7], "I will save you not by bow nor by sword but by the Lord your God." What is sadder than this sight? The church is at loose ends and [its] scholars are in exile. And although God provides fair reception here and there, yet the power of the enemies of the Gospel is greater, and it is uncertain how strong the defenders are and how long they will last. Cyrus fostered the church; Cambyses and Darius oppressed [it]. We should ponder this form of the church in order to understand the dangers and at the same time to learn that the church is gathered, preserved, restored, [and] defended not by human counsels or defenses, but by the power of God, just as in Paradise Adam and Eve again were delivered from sin and the tyranny of the devil. Therefore there is always present the Son of God as the guardian of His church, as He said, "I am with you even to the end of the world" [Matt. 28:20].

Against the Donatists

We have described the visible church, in which we have said that there are many unregenerate mixed with the saints, but at this point it is necessary that the evil people be discerned. Some believe correctly in regard to doctrine and they are not enemies of the Gospel or heretics, but they only have some weaknesses in morals. If such people have not been excommunicated, even though they are called dead members, they still are in the outward fellowship of the church, and when they carry out the duties of teaching or administering the sacraments, the ministries are valid and efficacious and one is permitted to use them.

Therefore we must vigorously attack the error of the Donatists, who contend that neither the Gospel nor any sacrament is efficacious if the morals of the minister are corrupt. In opposition to this error one must cling to clear views.

In Matt. 13[:47–48] Christ compares the church to a net in which are both good and bad fish. Likewise He says that the tares will remain in the church even to resurrection [Matt. 13:40]. Again, "As in the days of Noah," etc. [Matt. 24:37]. From these statements it is clear that in the church there always was, is, and will be even to the resurrection a great number of evil people.

Therefore, since there are wicked people in the church and since hypocrisy cannot be recognized by human judgment, there can even be hypocrites in the ministry. Accordingly, faith would be made unsure if the power of the Gospel and the sacraments were to depend on the worthiness of the minister. Therefore we must understand that the Gospel and the sacraments are efficacious because of the promise of God [and] not because of the person of the minister. Christ therefore calls our minds and our faith away from the person of the minister to Himself when He says, "He that hears you hears Me" [Luke 10:16], as if He were saying that the Gospel is not yours and it is not your work to save the hearers, but it is God's work, who in this marvelous way, when the voice of the Gospel is spread, gathers to Himself the eternal church. As John also says, "I baptize you with water, but another will baptize you with fire and with the Holy Spirit" [Matt. 3:11], that is, the Gospel and the sacraments are efficacious because of Christ and through Christ. There is also cited this statement of Christ, "The scribes and Pharisees sit in Moses' seat," etc. [Matt. 23:2]. These words mean that even if there are hypocrites in the ministry, yet the function itself is valid, if only they sit in the seat of Moses, that is, they should teach the doctrine which has been given by God, they should not sit in another seat, and they should not set forth a doctrine which is in conflict with faith.

This whole case against the Donatists has been fully treated by Augustine in many books, and in [his] Epist. 166 [(105), MPL 33.400–401] he repeats this argument: If the power of the Gospel and the sacraments should depend on the worthiness of the minister, our faith would be made unsure. Therefore, in order that faith might be certain, it is necessary to reject and condemn the fanatic ravings of the Donatists.

This error was also refuted by Gregory of Nazianzus who used this simile: The shape of the little image is the same, whether it be engraved on a gold or an iron ring. Likewise the ministry is the same, he says, whether good or evil men hold [the office]. It is necessary to point out these things regarding the Donatists, so that [the godly] may be fortified against such ravings and may learn to understand the power of the ministry. For also in our age the Anabaptists revive the errors of the Donatists and impiously reject ministries while professing that they have established a church in which there are no evil people, just like the Circumcellions, while actually they have brought together a large rabble of the worst thieves, as the example of Münster shows, which is a good reminder that good minds should exercise great care and diligence that they not approve false notions, and that they should consider that from one error manifold and incurable ravings gradually arise. Therefore what is to be done? Should open sins of ministers of the Gospel be covered up? I reply: Those who are polluted with open sins should be excommunicated by the common voice of the church, as Paul in 1 Corinthians 5 put the incestuous man out of the church. And Christ in Matt. 18[:17] says, "Tell it to the church." And that strictness must not be relaxed, but if it is relaxed, yet the ministry is valid, as has been said.

Furthermore, the magistrates who bear the sword must use the laws to punish those crimes such as adultery, murder, and the like.

But in addition to public crimes there are weaknesses in the manners of all people; one is more wayward or more given to anger, another is more indulging or less temperate than he should be, another is more intent upon wealth, one is criticized for his pride, another for being dilatory. Finally all have some weaknesses of their own. In regard to these common behavior patterns, when [open] wrongdoing is not involved we should understand that the general rule for the godly person to follow is: Know [but] do not hate the manners of a friend. Again, "Forgive, and it shall be *forgiven you*" [Luke 6:37]. Again, "*Love covers all sins*" [Prov. 10:12]. And particularly must one be patient with the less-than-perfect manners of godly rulers and teachers, as Christ commands us to wash one another's feet [John 13:14], that is, to improve such weaknesses among us with mutual gentleness.

Now, it is common slanderously to exaggerate the faults of rulers; therefore the Holy Spirit so often commands us to honor them, as it is said so earnestly in the Epistle to the Hebrews [13:17] as if [the author] were saying that the task of governing in itself is difficult and troublesome, but when there is added to it the stubbornness of inferiors, the trouble doubles. For as Herodotus says, as much as war differs from peace, so much does sedition differ from war; thus it is harder for a ruler to fight both with his own [subjects] and with others, and in an otherwise difficult office he is hindered by the very ones by whom he should be helped. Therefore also Paul says in 1 Thess. 5[:12–13], "*We pray that you believe that those who rule excellently should be loved because of the ministry and that you should be at peace with them.*" Finally, there are many precepts which deal with this matter. Even as Ham was punished [Genesis 9] for ridiculing [his] father, so [people] should understand that they will all pay the penalties to God if they are troublesome to ministers who teach them correctly if there be some weakness in manners, as it was said to Abraham, "*I will bless them that bless you and curse them that curse you*" [Gen. 12:3]. This pattern undoubtedly pertains to the church and those who teach correctly. Therefore we should understand that a person should not leave the church over the morals of the teachers nor should a schism be created if there is no error in doctrine.

But there are other evil people, polluted with false ideas, who defend godless doctrine and oppose the truth and kill pious men because of [their] profession of the true doctrine. Thus at the time of Jeremiah, [Judas] Maccabaeus, [and] Christ there were priests [and] their followers who openly contradicted the true doctrine and killed the saints. With such a group, even if it holds its power through tyranny, the saints should have no fellowship, and they have the right to be guilty of schism, because God's command is, "*Flee idolatry*" [1 John 5:21]. Likewise, "*If anyone will teach another Gospel, let him be anathema*" [Gal. 1:8]. For this reason the apostles withdrew from Caiaphas and his company.

We must make a careful distinction here. The ministry is not changed, even if the morals of some are wicked, but when false doctrine is defended and idolatry supported, then the ministry itself is changed. Hence one must leave the ministry of those who corrupt the doctrine. And although the principal part of the ministry is teaching, yet sometimes also those who corrupt the doctrine possess a part of the ministry, such as the administration of one of the sacraments. Thus the Israelites retained circumcision, even though they later added ungodly practices. Caiaphas and the Pharisees retained circumcision, [and] although in other matters they embraced serious errors, still circumcision was valid, not because of these persons but because it was performed by the church.

We should say the same about the Baptism of those who were baptized in churches where false teachers were in control. For Baptism was valid because it was performed by the true church and the words of institution and their meanings were retained without idolatry in this sacrament. But the baptism of Paul of Samosata, the Manichaeans, and the Arians was not valid, because they did not retain the meaning of the words "I baptize you in the name of the Father and of the Son and of the Holy Spirit" [Matt. 28:19]. I have touched briefly on these things so that the faithful might be strengthened against the Anabaptists and to ponder that evil men often rule in the church. As Christ says, the church is like a net with good and bad fish in it. Therefore a ministry is valid which they retain in these sacraments, which they do not openly corrupt.

Now although the Baptism of those who retain the meaning of the words is valid, as I have said, yet because they teach wicked things about other matters, they give reason why the church should necessarily separate from them.

There is also a difference between persons who have sinned out of ignorance and those who are open blasphemers, such as Caiaphas and those like him were after the resurrection of Christ. Nor is there any doubt that one must depart from blasphemers and those who defend manifest idols, as it is written, "Flee idolatry" [1 John 5:21].

The Signs Which Point Out the Church, Which Others Call Marks

The marks which point out the church are the pure Gospel and the proper use of the sacraments. And although the church does not always flourish with the same glory, yet from time to time certain indicators of the Holy Spirit are added in [His] marvelous governance. Now, I have mentioned testimonies above that the Gospel is the sign which shows what gathering the church is, and these are sufficiently clear. See Eph. 2[:20–22] and Is. 59[:21].

Others, in unhappy imitation of human states, add to the church these signs: the regular succession of bishops and obedience in human traditions; and besides they arrogantly arm the bishops with two royal prerogatives, the power to interpret Scripture and the power to make laws and establish new forms of worship. But the pious are to be warned that they beware of these traps. For in all ages in the governing of the church, worldly people, ignorant of the doctrine of the Gospel, have pictured for themselves a church by such imitation of states, and in this way great errors are established.

Therefore, when you hear all these things: "the regular succession," "the power to interpret," and "the power to make laws," you should know that traps have been laid for the true teaching and a pretext is being sought to establish errors in the church. Therefore we must remove this notion of human states and change our views regarding the church. I have said above that the church is not bound to the regular succession of bishops, as they call it, but to the Gospel. When bishops do not teach correctly, regular succession has no relevance for the church, but one must of necessity separate from them.

But as to the power to interpret Scripture, we must understand that there is a great difference between a power and a gift. In the church there is the gift of interpretation, not bound to a certain order [of clergy], just as the Holy Spirit is not given because of position or title. This gift is not a power attached to an order or a title, to which we must be obedient on account of the order in the same way that we must be obedient because of order to a royal or imperial interpretation. For God has given to civil magistrates the power to establish laws which are in agreement with reason and to interpret them. But it is an entirely different matter in regard to the voice of the Gospel in the church. The Son of God has revealed this from the bosom of the eternal Father. And it is the correct understanding, placed above reason, concerning the knowledge of God, the wrath of God against sin, the enormity of sin, the righteousness given through the Son of God, concerning fear, faith, the cross, God's help, the resurrection, the church, eternal life, the two natures in Christ, and concerning the Father, the Son, and the Holy Spirit. Therefore, since God had commanded that we hear His Son and then the apostles were sent by the command of the Son so that we might hear them, we must keep the doctrine taught through the apostles and learn their doctrine [and] not devise interpretations which are in conflict with their sure and certain testimonies, as the Jews devised corrupt interpretations in order to escape the statements concerning Christ.

Further, those who want to be learners of the Gospel do not hear in order slanderously to distort, but in order to know God, honor Him, and be obedient to Him. When they assent to the Word of God with fear and faith, a light is kindled in them by which they are helped to distinguish the Gospel from human wisdom and knowledgeably to receive the articles of doctrine concerning God, sin, righteousness, Christ, the church, and eternal life.

Third, they are also aided by the testimony of the true church, as when Paul of Samosata was unwilling to interpret the passage, "In the beginning was the Word," etc. [John 1:1–14], as referring to a person, the faithful were aided by the witness of Irenaeus, who had heard Polycarp, a disciple of John. And they were also helped by Gregory of Neocaesarea and the testimonies of the church of Alexandria. These affirmed that this meaning was kept by the apostles, and the godly saw that the other testimonies in John and Paul were in agreement with it.

And although the church must be heard in keeping with the statement [Judg. 14:18], "If you had not ploughed with my heifer, you would not have found out . . . ," yet faith does not rely on the authority of the church but on the very voice of the Gospel. We call upon the Son of God because it is said, "And the Word was God" [John

1:1]; again, "My Father works until now, and I work" [John 5:17]; and, "Without Me you can do nothing" [John 15:5]; and Stephen says [Acts 7:59], "Lord Jesus, receive my spirit."

Also, when testimonies of the church are sought, one must consider where and what the church is, which ages of the church are purer, [and] which writers are more genuine. Thus we are aided against the Anabaptists. We know first from the Gospel that infants are born with guilt and subject to the sin of origin, and that this is remitted to those who are in the church, and that infants should become members of the church and be brought to Christ. Finally, add the testimony of the early church which, we know from our reading, baptized infants. Therefore we hold that one is in no way to yield to the raving of the Anabaptists, who try to expel so many thousands of infants from the church and destroy them—one error, with which they mix many [more].

Therefore the gift of interpretation is a light which the Holy Spirit kindles in the minds of those who assent to the Gospel, as Christ says in John 14[:26], "The Holy Spirit will teach you all things and bring all things to your remembrance which I have said to you." Here He binds the apostles and the whole church to what He has said, and He adds that the Holy Spirit will remind us of the gift [and] of this very word itself. And in John 6[:45] Christ quotes from Is. [54:13], "They will all be taught by God." On the other hand it is said of the ungodly that all the ungodly do not understand; cf. 1 Cor. 2:14; Is. 6:9.

These testimonies clearly show that interpretation is a gift of the godly and it is not bound to power or the majority, which is often ungodly, and indeed the chief penalty is the blindness of ungodliness, cf. Ps. 69[:23] and Rom. 11[:10]. The obvious ravings of the gentiles and of the Jews show that ungodliness is especially punished with blindness.

If the power of [clerical] orders or the majority would have the authority to interpret, the sentiments of the Pharisees should have had preference over the sentiments of Zacharias, Simeon, Elizabeth, Mary, Anna, and people like them. But the true church is often a small group dominated by a large multitude of godless people, as Isaiah says [in 1:9], "Unless the Lord had left us a seed, we would be as Sodom." Therefore we must absolutely not tie interpretation to the authority of a [clerical] order and to the majority. And we must beware of these traps when the adversaries try to establish errors under this pretext.

Furthermore, we must also recognize the gift itself and thank God that He has always so governed His church that, when the doctrine became obscured, He again restored it, as after Noah, Abraham was the interpreter of the promise, so after Moses, Samuel, David, and others in turn were sent. While the Pharisees and Sadducees were ruling the church, there still were people like Simeon, Zacharias, Anna, Mary, and many others in whom the gift of interpretation shone forth, in some more and *in others less clearly. Likewise later God kindled the flame of true doctrine in the church from time to time. We, therefore, must not extinguish this kindled [flame] under the fear of the multitude or of the power of [clerical] order which defends idols and errors.*

As for the rest, also those who at one time believed correctly can fall and those who believe correctly still have in them some darkness and their stubble, as [Paul] says [1 Cor. 3:12]. Therefore we must hold the views taught on the basis of the Word of God and carefully compared. We shall speak later about the similarity of traditions and about the laws of bishops. For the unity of the church must not be based on the similarity of human traditions, because we must cling to this position, that human traditions are not worship; likewise that people who otherwise believe correctly are not to be condemned because of them.

THE CHURCH

This is a very broad locus which contains many useful and necessary points of discussion, However, we shall not deal with all of them here, but we shall briefly touch on those which are especially necessary. And above all we must note the usefulness and the necessity of this locus.

1. In opposition to the papists. Among them this locus was the most important. Whatever the church decided, this was ratified, even if [it was] not only outside of but even contrary to Scripture. For in 1 Tim. 3:15 [the church] is called "the pillar and foundation of the truth." In John 16:13 the church is promised the "Spirit of truth" who will guide her "into all truth," cf. Luke 10:16; Matt. 18:17; Mal. 2:7; Matt. 16:18; Is. 59:21. Besides these statements of Scripture the popish orators know how to bring forward also many other statements and to embellish them with their own colors. They say that outside the church there is no salvation. They also claim the unity of their church and say that the [church] whose doctrine is received in all areas is catholic and that the church is visible and, though it has its defects, it is still like a net which brings both good and rotten fish to shore. And these points of dispute are discussed with great emotional contention, so that not only is the authority of the church placed above Scripture and to the church is attributed the authority to interpret the Scriptures but also all kinds of foolish traditions are peddled in the name of the church. And whoever does not adhere to these things is subjected to the anathema of excommunication as a gangrenous member. Even though all these things can be overturned by the single statement of the apostle Paul, Eph. 2:20, where he clearly builds the church on the foundation of the apostles and prophets, [and] does not, on the other hand, found the writings of the prophets and apostles on the church, yet we shall discuss this notion at greater length later.

2. We must also note the necessity of this locus because of the fanatics

who boast of their own inspiration and glory in the fact that they are the true church of Christ because the universal church is invisible. We shall point out at the proper place the reason why Luther and others held that the church of Christ is invisible.

3. Some imagine that the church is a jumble of all kinds of sectarian Anabaptists, Sacramentarians, Schwenkfelders, and others, provided they are not papists; and so they introduce a kind of all-in-one which is unknown to all Scripture. Thus many think that this man or that man is not to be condemned because he is a learned, eloquent man and endowed with similar gifts. But if we wish to include such people, why from the beginning are the papists excluded and condemned, for many of them were certainly endowed with gifts of great genius?

4. Because even among those who boast about the purity of the Gospel there are found some who persuade themselves (either because of the place in which the purity of doctrine arose at the beginning or because the doctrine was defended by their predecessors with great determination and strong spirit) that the true church is among them, although they have turned away to a great degree from the purity of teaching in major articles.

5. There are also many who, when they think about the church, seek out where the majority is or to what the more influential ones are inclined, or what the more learned ones decide, and then they also join that group and consider it to be the church of Christ.

6. Nor is there lack of those who attach themselves to no group, care for no church, and have no desire to be members of any church, but in all respects are loners, hanging on like bulldogs to certain preconceived notions of their own way of thinking, yet hoping for salvation. Because of each and every one of these and even more others, it is especially necessary to consider carefully and accurately this locus of Christian doctrine on the church.

Now, in keeping with our pattern, we shall divide it into certain chapters and briefly explain them for the sake of the younger generation.

CHAPTER I: THE TERMINOLOGY

First of all we must note the true rationale and explanation of the words [involved]. The Hebrews had especially two words to describe the assembly of the church. The one, *qāhal*, means "to gather together" and properly is used of a congregation of people formed by being called together. From this word some desire to derive also that Greek [term] *kaleō* (to call), and from that the term *ekklēsia* (church). The second [Hebrew word], *'ēdāh*, means a cyclical meeting, a gathering, or a coming together of people. It is derived from the root word, *yā'ad*, that is, "he appointed [place and time] by public authority; he announced with a solemn rite." In brief, it means to set a certain place and time for gathering and carrying on certain business, as customarily takes place in a synod and a convention of people. Thus, this latter term means a gathering of people who come together by solemn authority and public ritual at a certain indicated place and time to transact certain business. But *qāhal* indicates the whole multitude and the church that has no set place or time. Those two words are joined together in Prov. 5:14 and Lev. 8:3–4.

Joel 2:15 has the word *ʿătsārāh*, for that word means the kind of gathering of people that takes place with celebration or festivity, where the people are forbidden to work and must be gathered to celebrate a feast to the Lord.

The LXX translators use the Greek word *synagōgē*, which also occurs in the New Testament in the writings of the four evangelists and the Acts of the Apostles, whenever they speak of the congregation of the Jewish people. However, this is a more general word than is the word "church" (*ecclesia*). For in Gen. 1:9 it says, "Let the waters be gathered into one gathering" (*synagōgē* [LXX]), and this gathering is called seas, cf. Jer. 44:15 and 50:9. In Ezek. 38:4, 7, and 13 *synagōgē* [LXX] *megalē* (a large company) is taken for an army, whose burial place is called *polyandrion* [LXX] (the multitude) in Ezek. 39:15–16.

In the New Testament the apostles use this word, *ekklēsia*, in place of the word *synagōgē*. For it pleased the Holy Spirit to call by this name the universal assembly, called to eternal life, which professed the true religion of Christ. (1) By this name the apostles wanted to distinguish the company of Christians from the synagogues and congregations of the Jews. (2) Because the church of the New Testament is gathered from all languages and peoples and thus is catholic or universal, therefore they did not want to use the word "synagogue." (3) Because this word was in common use also among other nations to whom the doctrine of the Gospel was being proclaimed with reference to proper assemblies, gatherings, and called meetings. (4) Because this word also included the call by which a beginning needed to be made if anyone wanted to become a member of the church of Christ.

Yet James in his epistle, 2:2, uses the word *synagōgē*, cf. Rev. 2:9; 3:9; Heb. 10:25.

But note the difference in the cognate words:

Synklēsis is used of the most important people, magnates, consuls, and their meeting. Therefore, lest we think that only the great and the noble relate to the church, the apostles use another word.

Diaklēsis [is used] of the jumbled crowd of common people when there is a gathering from the countryside.

Ekklēsia [is used] of citizens when a citywide gathering is held of those who, bound together by certain laws, are citizens of one commonwealth.

But because the word "church" [*ekklēsia*] is a more general term which is applied also to civil and secular meetings, as in Acts 19:32, 39–40, therefore in order to distinguish the New Testament church from other gatherings, in Scripture the term "church of God" is used: Acts 20:28; 1 Cor. 10:32; 11:16; 1 Thess. 1:1; 2:14; 1 Tim. 3:15.

As for the rest, because the people of the Old Testament as well as the New were the assembly [*ekklēsia*] of God, as Micah the prophet says in 2:5, therefore in keeping with this distinction it is called the church [*ekklēsia*] of Christ, that is, [the assembly] which believes in the revealed Christ and confesses faith in Him, cf. Rom. 16:16; Col. 1:24; Matt. 16:18. And because in Micah 2:5 "the church of Jehovah" or "of the Lord" is mentioned, the church is also called *kyriakē* [the Lord's], which the Latins in Cyprian call *dominica*. And hence the Germans seem to have derived their term *Die Kirche Christi* from the Greek [*kyriakē*].

In the creed the church is called holy. For there is also a false church, indeed bearing the title of "church" but not having the pure Word of God or the true use of the sacraments. In Rev. 2:9 and 3:9 it is called "the synagogue of Satan," and in Ps. 26:5 it is called "the congregation of evildoers (*ekklēsia ponēreuomenōn, kᵉhal pᵉrēʿīm*). The Hebrew for "evildoers" is derived from a word that means "bitterness," because God was embittered and vexed by [their] disobedience. Thus in Ps. 106:33 it is said of the Jews that they "made the Spirit of the Lord bitter." In 1 Kings 13:26 it is said regarding the disobedient prophet that he made the mouth of the Lord bitter, that is, that he was disobedient to the voice of the Lord. Ezek. 2:8, "Do not be rebellious" (*perī*) that is, irritating or rebellious, "like that house of rebellion" (*haperī*). Therefore, as a result of its difference from this rebellious and irritating church, the church of Christ is called holy: (1) because in Scripture what has been separated from the common and profane and has been set aside and consecrated for the use or honor of God is called holy; (2) because in that assembly God sanctifies the believers by His Word, John 17:17. And in Rev. 11:2 and 22:19 it is called the holy city.

In the creed the church is also called catholic. The correct meaning of this word can be understood from the antithesis. For in the old covenant the church was ordinarily bound to one particular nation, a certain race and people, namely the Israelites, and thus [it was bound] to one certain place, so that all who wished to join the church had to attach themselves to this group. And these were called "proselytes," Acts 2:10, and "devout men," religious men, v. 5, who went up to Jerusalem to worship the true God or to offer sacrifices to Him. Such was the Ethiopian eunuch of Queen Candace, Acts 8:27, for, as Ps. 76:1–2 has it, "God is known in Judah, His name is great in Israel. His place is in Salem and His abode in Zion," cf. Ps. 147:19–20. Hence Paul says regarding the Jews of the old covenant, Rom. 3:2, that they had this advantage over all the gentiles that "to them had been entrusted the oracles of God"; cf. Rom. 9:4.

Therefore under the new covenant the church is called "catholic" by way of antithesis; for, without respect to or distinction of places, nations, languages, peoples, and persons, Christ ordered the Gospel to be preached in the whole world, among all nations, or to every creature, beginning at Jerusalem, "even to the ends of the earth," Acts 1:8, cf. Matt. 28:19; Mark 16:15; Luke 24:47; Acts 1:8; 2:5; Col. 1:6. Ps 19:4, "Their measuring line," or building standard for building the church, "has gone out into the whole world, and their words to the ends of the earth," cf. Matt. 26:13; Mark 14:9; Acts 9:31. From these [passages] we can understand what the reason is for using the name catholic.

Moreover, there is yet another reason for that term, why the church is called catholic, drawn from this, that there are many particular churches in the world, cf. Rom. 16:5; 1 Cor. 16:19; Col. 4:15; Philemon 2; Acts 11:22; 13:1. But because all these churches must be gathered unto one body into Christ, so that as members they might be gathered together under one Head, therefore, in line with its difference, the whole church, gathered from those particular ones as members, is called catholic. Thus the epistles of Peter, John, and James, because they are not addressed to certain particular churches and because the name of no particular region is attached to them to which they were specifically directed, but [they were addressed] in general to all believers, therefore they are called catholic, or universal and ecumenical [epistles]. Thus Augustine in Epistle 170 [(52), MPL 33.194] says, "The church, which is scattered throughout the whole world, is called catholic."

Yes indeed, the name "catholic church" includes this, that in all eras even to the end of the world there will be a church in the world and sincere and believing people will hold fast to that one and same doctrine of Christ at all times [and] in all places, cf. Matt. 28:20; 1 Cor. 11:26. Therefore it is correct to call the church catholic if it is looked at from the standpoint of (1) place, (2) time, (3) people, [and] (4) the form of doctrine. For in all these areas it must be considered catholic.

In this the papists berate Luther with the charge of removing the word "catholic" from the creed in the German language, in order that he might impose his own name also on the assembly of the church. But I reply that it is true that even before the time of Luther here and there this article was recited thus: *Ich glaube ein heilige Christliche Kirche* (I believe in one holy Christian church). Here the word "Christian" has the same meaning as "catholic," because the name "Christian" was spread throughout the whole world. And it is found this way in ancient manuscripts. Since Luther left the matter as he found it, he is falsely accused of fraudulently rejecting that word ["catholic"].

Further, so that no excuse for error be given because of the great number of errorists, the Nicene Creed adds the word "apostolic," namely that the true church is that one which, in whatever part of the world, "built on the foundation of the prophets and apostles," faithfully and purely preserves the doctrine of the apostles.

In the [Apostles'] Creed there is also the addition of the words *koinōnia tōn hagiōn* (the communion of saints). This expression the Augsburg Confession, arts. 7 and 8 [Tappert pp. 32–33], interprets as the assembly and congregation of saints or true believers. And this can be understood of the true and living members of the church of Christ; likewise of the church which still struggles under the cross in this life and which already triumphs in heaven after [these] conflicts. See Heb. 12:22.

And because in this communion of saints all are participants of the same blessings, as Christ says to Paul, Acts 26:18, cf. Col. 1:12, therefore some understand the "communion of saints" in the neuter gender and the ancients called it *"Eine Gemeinschaft der Heiligen"* (a sharing or communion of holy things), but in Acts 26:18 and Col. 1:12 and elsewhere the masculine gender is used, as also in 1 Cor. 14:33, cf. Eph. 1:18, ". . . that you may know what are the riches of the glory of His inheritance in the saints," that is, that you may know what a glorious inheritance Christ has prepared and will give to the saints.

There are some who try to distinguish between the article of the catholic church and the communion of saints. But in fact they are looking for a knot in a bulrush and are trying to involve the church of Christ in unnecessary controversies. Let us love simplicity and join these two parts of one and the same article together; in that way the explanation will be clearer and [the subject] will be full of consolation for us, if we consider and believe that we also have a share in the lot of the saints who are already glorious in heaven.

CHAPTER II: QUESTION: IS THERE A CHURCH?

In the question of method, which is usually called "Is there?" there are two things here:

1. The promises that God always wills, out of the offscouring of this world, through the ministration of the Word and sacraments, to gather the church and preserve it up to the end of the age somewhere in this world. The Scriptural testimonies are clear: Matt. 16:18; 28:20; 1 Cor. 11:26; John 10:16, 28. And in His last prayer, John 17:11, Christ most clearly prays that the Father will preserve in His own name those whom He has given to Christ, "that they may be one as He and His Father are one." And who will doubt that our heavenly Father has mercifully heard these prayers, when Heb. 5:7 affirms that "He in the days of

His flesh offered up prayers and supplications to His Father with a loud cry and tears and was heard for His reverence"?

2. The doctrine must also be considered that each person who is to be saved must be a member and a citizen of the catholic and apostolic church and that those who are outside the church are alienated from Christ, from God, [and] from His grace and are without hope of eternal salvation. For thus that great apostle of the Lord affirms in Eph. 2:12–13 and 19–21. Rom. 8:30, "Whom He chose [and] whom He will justify and glorify, those He calls," namely that they might be members of the church and in the church hear the voice of the divine will and use the sacraments for the strengthening of their faith. See 1 Peter 2:4–5 and 10: Eph. 4:15–16. On the basis of such passages it is commonly and correctly said, "Outside the church there is no salvation." Jude 19 calls those who "separate themselves" godless; cf. 1 John 2:19. Rev. 22:14–15: In the city of God are the saints, but outside, or outside the church, "there are dogs and sorcerers and unchaste and murderers and idolaters, and everyone who loves lies and practices deceit," cf. Matt. 8:12.

The picture of the spiritual building which God has built in the church is truly beautiful and pleasant. The blessed city of Jerusalem which is in the heavens is built of living stones. These stones by nature are unpolished, but they are polished by tensions and pressures and the various crosses on earth; they are each fitted in their own places and placed by the hands of the artisan. And the cornerstone and foundation is Christ Himself, sent by the heavenly Father so that the stones which in themselves are dead, set on Him, might receive from Him life and the Spirit. He also is the firm foundation of His church, so that not even "the gates of hell can prevail [against it]." And because He is the cornerstone, by connection with Him He firmly binds the walls together, so that the building does not fall apart and never ever can develop cracks. Let the godly think very carefully about this picture. It is sufficient for us to have given them occasion to think.

CHAPTER III: DEFINITION OF THE CHURCH

In [dealing with] the question, "What is it?" because the definition has been eruditely drawn up, one must by analysis consider the individual on what bases of Scripture, with what intent, and for what reasons it was put that way.

I. Note that the definition of the church must be so established and understood that it applies both to particular true churches in particular places and to the truly catholic church scattered throughout the whole world, which is one body. Hence in the definition as the genus it is stated that the church is an assembly. For now in the New Testament the church is not limited to the Jews or Israelites, as of old in the Old Testament, Ps. 76:1, but the assembly is catholic [universal]; it is gathered in any place, in any nation and tongue, and at any time.

II. God wills that we seek, know, and understand what and where the true church is, so that we join ourselves to it as members and citizens, and heed it. For it is like a city set on a hill and a light not hidden under a cover but put on a candlestick, Matt. 5:15. Hence the church should be known not only to God, who knows the things that are hidden and searches into the hearts [Ps. 44:21], but also to us. And for this reason it is defined as a visible assembly of those who embrace the Gospel of Christ and rightly use the sacraments. For these are the signs which show the church, cf. Acts 2:41–42; 1 Cor. 1:2.

1. But in this part [of the definition] we must carefully note that not only was it held by Wycliffe, Hus, and others, but also in the controversies of Luther against the papists that the church is not visible but is the number of those who have been predestinated, among whom "the Lord knows those who are His," 2 Tim. 2:19. Therefore, lest there seem to be a contradiction, we must consider why it was thus held at that time, namely because the papists formulated the definition of the church, [as an entity] which must be heeded and from which one must not depart, from an analogy like this: Just as the republic of Venice, the kingdom of France, [or] the German empire consists of a certain order of rulers and subjects [and] certain laws and customs, so among the clergy who are in the succession of orders the church of Christ is so bound that whatever they determine and believe must of necessity be accepted by all and one must under no pretext depart from them. For [they believe that] this assembly cannot err in doctrine in any respect, for the church is "the pillar and foundation of truth," 1 Tim. 3:15. Therefore, against this political figment of the imagination it was necessary to set this position, that the church is not such a visible assembly but rather that it is the flock of such sheep as, known by Christ and in turn knowing Him, can never be plucked out of His hands, as Christ Himself defines His church, John 10:14 and 28.

2. Because in this opinion [of the papists] many, persevering in sins, flatter themselves that since they are members of the visible church they cannot be condemned, the position that the church is not visible was taken also against this notion.

3. Because other assemblies often distinguish themselves in works, power, glory, learning, authority, outward appearance, and numbers, therefore it was said that the church is invisible lest it be judged by that outward appearance. That is, a poor group in which there are many weaknesses and which is not only oppressed by persecutions and the cross but also deformed by causes of offense and by scandals, may be the church, regarding which one should form

an opinion not on the basis of outward appearance but from the Word and judge according to the Word.

Therefore, in order that these things might be set forth clearly, a distinction was put forward. At this point we are not defining the church triumphant, a description of which is given in Heb. 12:22 and Rev. 21:2, but describing the church militant. Likewise, we are not defining here the church as a body in which all the members are true and living members who are known alone to God, 2 Tim. 2:19, but as a body in which there are also many gangrenous and dead members, among which, however, there is consensus in doctrine. Thus Luther also observes a distinction regarding the church. Sometimes he takes it for a mixed group in which all who gather under an external profession to hear the Word and use the sacraments are considered as the members of this church. But sometimes he takes it for the company of the elect, who are known only to God, who searches hearts. Eck indeed ridiculed this acceptance of the term "invisible" and said that the church is mathematical and ideals are Platonic. But let them ridicule as he wishes; what is an ideal for us and cannot be seen is not immediately therefore also hidden from God. Col. 3:3: Our life is hidden with Christ in God; yet our life is not therefore a Platonic ideal, that is, a fantastic [figment] of the imagination; but we know, v. 4, that when Christ, our life, will appear, we will also appear with Him in glory.

Yet meanwhile Luther completely disapproved of the ravings of the Anabaptists who also wanted to hide in secret under this pretext [and] went from house to house and wanted to establish little churches in them secretly, namely because the church is invisible. Against them Luther wrote an earnest warning in 1532 under the title *Wider die Winckel-Prediger* (*Against Clandestine Preachers*).[2] For in fact the true and holy church of the elect nevertheless remains invisible especially if it is described as an assembly not of some one nation, as was the Jewish or Israelite in the Old Testament, but as a catholic [universal] assembly gathered in whatever place, nation, tongue, and time, which with firm faith embraces the Gospel of Christ, uses His sacraments, and constantly fights under the cross for Christ unto life everlasting.

III. Because the papists define the church as the assembly which acknowledges the Roman pope as head and is subject to the rest of the ecclesiastical hierarchy, and approves and observes the things which have been taught, instituted, and commanded by them, and because many think that the assembly that has an excellent outward appearance of multitude, wisdom, power, learning, [and] glory is the church of God, therefore in the definition it is said that it is the assembly bound to the preaching or ministry of the Gospel, or that it

---

[2] *Luther's Works*, Amer. Ed., 40.379–94.

is the assembly of those who embrace the Gospel of Christ and correctly use the sacraments. And this clause is set against two errors. The first is that the papists promote a person for their seven-hilled Babylon [and] so tie the church to him that one who does not recognize its leader as the head of the church and does not subject himself in all respects cannot be a member of the catholic [universal] church. The second error is that many figure that every assembly is the true church of God, whatever doctrine and religion it may follow, provided it be done with the intent of worshiping God and the expectation of obtaining eternal life.

Therefore we must learn not only to say those words but also to think properly regarding the fundamental points, where this clause has its foundation and whence it was drawn, cf. John 10:5, 26–27; Eph. 2:20; 1 Tim. 3:15; John 17:17. The chief testimony is Matt. 28:19, "Teach all nations" or "call all nations to be My disciples" and thus gather the church to Me. And how? See Matt. 28:19–20; 18:18, 20; 1 Cor. 12:13; 10:16–17; 14:26. From these passages it is clear that the church of Christ is not bound to some certain seat or place in the world, but to the Gospel and the doctrine of Christ and the absolution pronounced in His name, to Baptism and the Holy Supper of the Lord instituted by Him. And all these things are to be done in His name, according to His precept and command.

IV. The fourth clause of the definition is that in this gathering God is efficacious through the ministry of the Word and regenerates many unto eternal life. This clause is set in opposition (1) to those who imagine that God saves, also without the ministry of the Gospel, many who have good intention, and (2) to those who think that because of the ungodly multitude they labor in vain in the ministry. The Anabaptists even have the notion that the Holy Spirit is not present with His grace in that group where there are a great many godless people. And it is true that where the depravity of those who contend against God and His Word is universal, there God takes away His Spirit, as it says in Gen. 6:3. And yet, nevertheless God set a limit of one hundred and twenty years; if that completely corrupted mass of people had repented by then, He would not have taken away His Spirit, and would not have destroyed the whole first world by the flood.

Therefore we must gather the testimonies which prove this clause: Rom. 1:16; 1 Peter 1:23; Eph. 5:26; Titus 3:5.

But here the question arises: Does God do this also in that place where there are ungodly people? And we reply: Absolutely! For the following passages prove it: Is. 55:10–11; 1 Cor. 15:58; Luke 8:8; Matt. 13:23, 27; 1 Kings 19:18; Is. 1:9; 6:13.

V. The fifth clause of the definition is that in this assembly of the church many are not saints. Here I prefer to use the term "not saints" rather than another. For if we should say that in this gathering many are ungodly, it could be understood of false teachers and those who are manifestly wicked, who, we know, should be excluded from the church and rejected. Likewise [it could be understood of] those who reject, violently oppose, and stubbornly deny the Word, whom no one would say are members of the church. But if we were to say that in this gathering there are many unregenerate, then it could be understood of those who have not been baptized. For Baptism is the normal means of regeneration, Titus 3:5. Therefore I say that in the external assembly of the church many are not saints.

Augustine proves this clause against the Donatists by many clear parables and similes from Scripture. For the church is the great house of God (1 Tim. 3:15); and in a great house there are vessels "not only gold of and silver but also of wood and clay and some indeed to honor but some to dishonor," 2 Tim. 2:20. Matt. 13:24–30: the church is the field of the Lord which bears not only wheat but also many weeds which absolutely cannot be eradicated before the last day. Likewise, vv. 47–48, the church is like a dragnet which catches and draws fish of every kind, good and bad, and the separation takes place at last at the shore. In Matt. 3:12 the church is like a threshing floor on which both wheat and chaff have been put. In Matt. 22:10–12 the church is like a wedding feast at which there are good and bad people, the bad ones not having a wedding garment. In Matt. 25:2 also foolish virgins are invited to the wedding. In John 10:1–5 the church is compared to a sheepfold in which there are not only sheep but also goats or kids. And although the Lord judges between sheep and sheep and between rams and goats, Ezek. 34:17, yet the complete separation will finally be on the last day, Matt. 25:32. In John 15:1–6 Christ also uses the parable of the vine. But just as in a vine there are many dry and sterile branches, so also in the body of the church many Christians in name are found, in fact, completely unfruitful. And the garden of God has not only "trees of righteousness," Is. 61:3, which, "planted beside running waters bring forth their fruit in their season," Ps. 1:3, but there are also sterile [trees] which God threatens to cut down, Luke 13:7. Indeed, just as one tree has some branches green and bearing fruit and others dry, so the church has some members living [and] bearing fruit to the glory of God, the upbuilding of the neighbor, and the promotion of their own salvation, but it has some members gangrenous or even completely dead. This was also foreshadowed of old in the church in the home of Abraham, Isaac, and Jacob, who each had in their circle of friends and even among their children people of this kind, who showed in many ways that they were not interested in holiness and thereby stirred up various scandals. In fact, even Christ Himself had among His own disciples an adversary who betrayed Him and who perished miserably.

Moreover, this clause is stated not only because of the Donatists, but also lest anyone think that a mere outward profession and communion suffices for salvation, 2 Tim. 2:19.

Furthermore, in this fifth clause of the definition also this is added, that still these evil people and nonsaints do agree as to doctrine, and thus they are members by outward profession, cf. 2 John 10–11. And those who defile themselves with open crimes should be separated from the visible church by excommunication. As it says in 1 Cor. 5:4–5, Paul determined in the name of the Lord to deliver to Satan the incestuous man at Corinth, for the destruction of the flesh. Therefore when ministers lack all zeal against sins, they should absolutely not fawn on their sloth with the result that they altogether lay aside the binding key, but they should rather use the power given them by Christ to the extent, of course, that the edification of the church in a particular place can bear it.

From this explanation of the definition we can easily see the doctrine of the causes of the church. The efficient cause is the Holy Spirit [working] through the Word and the sacraments. The material [cause] is the whole human race and all nations that are under heaven who now in the [era of the] new covenant, after the suffering and glorious resurrection of Christ, have been admitted to the fellowship of the church. The formal cause is the assembly [*coetus*] which embraces the Gospel of Christ and correctly uses the sacraments. The final cause or goal is that by this assembly people might be born again unto eternal life. Because these things can be clear from the definition, which is causal, I did not think it necessary to undertake a special discussion of them. Therefore let us move on to other things.

CHAPTER IV: TEACHERS AND HEARERS IN THE CHURCH

The fourth part in the doctrine of the church, to which part many things pertain, is about those who teach and those who learn in the church. For since the foundation of the church is the doctrine of Christ taught by the prophets and apostles, Eph. 2:20, the doctrine concerning Christ cannot be taught and cannot be proclaimed in the church unless there are teachers, Rom. 10:14. And since there are promises of the perpetual preservation of the ministry in the church, Is. 59:21; Eph. 4:11. Therefore the question is: Is the church simply, without any exception and limitation or restriction, bound to teachers or bishops who make up the ministry?

This question is indeed explained clearly enough in the *Loci*; yet we ourselves will also say a few words about it. Now, this entire doctrine can with some order be well divided so that there is an explanation of the five parts which (at least as regards the purpose) are required in a faithful teacher of the church: (1) a call; (2) the ability to teach; (3) faithfulness or constancy in teaching over against the wolves; (4) gifts; (5) piety of life. We shall say a few things on each of these.

I

Now then, with regard to the call, it is certain from the Word of God that no one should be heeded in the church who has not been lawfully [*legitime*] called, whether this takes place immediately or mediately. For Paul clearly says in Rom. 10:15 that they cannot preach (that is, lawfully, even though in fact they try it) "who have not been sent," cf. Jer. 23:21. In fact, the churches must not and cannot with profit hear those who do not have the testimonies of a lawful call. For the words of Paul are clear, Rom. 10:14–15: How can they hear, so that by hearing the faith which justifies and saves is conceived, if they do not have a preacher who has been sent? See Jer. 27:14–15; Heb. 5:4.

Therefore it was right to rebuke and reject the Anabaptists, whom Luther called *arge Schleicher* (wicked intriguers), who enter into homes and upset people in [their] faith. They even say that if anyone understands the doctrine of the Gospel, whether he be a cobbler or a tailor or a blacksmith, he should teach and preach.

And how much from these fanatics the Sacramentarians differ in this matter they themselves saw, who themselves also often teach without a call. When in France the papists once talked with the Sacramentarians about the call and asked them what kind of call they had, Beza replied that he had neither a mediate nor an immediate call, but an extraordinary call to teach in France. And I hear that they have this practice in Geneva, that they instruct some men in theology and then send them to France to teach. But such as a call is so also is [its] success. They rightly say of Origen that he thrust himself into the office of teaching without a call, and it happened as a result that he fell into so many errors.

But they object (1) that Paul in 1 Tim. 3:1 very strongly praises the man who desires the office of an overseer. The reply: To desire the office of overseer does not mean that one injects himself without a lawful call into ecclesiastical functions. But he who understands the fundamentals of the heavenly doctrine and has been equipped with the gift for teaching well, when he offers his work to God and the church, seeks nothing else than that God through some lawful call would declare whether, when, and where God wills to use his service in His church. And such a person must be so prepared in [his] mind that if a lawful call does not follow this petition he must not push his way in, but say with David [2 Sam. 15:26], "If He says, 'I have no delight in you,' I am ready; let Him do with me what is good in His sight."

They also object (2): But Christ has made all the faithful [to be] priests, Rev. 1:6; 5:10; 1 Peter 2:9. But the work of the priests, among other things was to teach the church, Lev. 10:10–11; Mal. 2:7. I reply: Paul in 1 Cor. 12:7–9 and 29 expressly writes that God does not give to all the gift of explaining the Scriptures, but He bestows the gifts of His Spirit variously for the benefit and upbuilding of the church (cf. Eph. 4:11–12). And Peter explains himself: All Christians are priests—not that all should carry out the function of ministry promiscuously, without a particular call, but that they should "offer up spiritual sacrifices" [1 Peter 2:5], which are described in Rom. 12:1; Heb. 13:15–16.

They object (3): Peter says that all the faithful are priests because they are to "proclaim the virtues of God," 1 Peter 2:9. And the heads of households have the general charge to instruct the members of their families, Deut. 6:20ff.; 1 Cor. 14:35. I reply: This is indeed a general call, common to all Christians, to speak among themselves about the Word of God, Eph. 5:19, to comfort one another with the Word of God, 1 Thess. 4:18, and to confess the Gospel, Rom. 10:9, and this is enjoined on heads of households by individual command. But to administer those things which pertain to the public ministry of the Word and the sacraments is not commanded to all Christians in general, as the two passages from 1 Corinthians 12 and Ephesians 4, cited above, teach clearly enough. Nor does the general calling which all receive in Baptism suffice to give a person the office of the ministry, but there is required a special call, as has been shown in the preceding testimonies, cf. James 3:1.

But it is worthwhile to ponder for what reasons it is so important that a minister of the church have a lawful call. Now, we must not think that this takes place out of some human arrangement or only for the sake of order, but the reasons are very weighty [and] consideration of them brings many things to mind:

1. Because the ministry of the Word is that of God Himself, which He Himself wants to carry out through ordained means and instruments in His church, Luke 1:70; Heb. 1:1; 2 Cor. 5:20, "We are ambassadors for Christ, as though God" [who is not far away from His ambassadors as king or ruler] "were appealing through us." Therefore it is absolutely necessary, if you want to be a faithful pastor of the church, that you be certain that God wants to use your labors and that you are such an instrument of His. For in this way you can apply also to yourself these statements of Scripture: such as Is. 59:21; 2 Cor. 13:3; Luke 10:16. And as John the Baptizer says in John 1:23, "I am the voice of one crying in the wilderness," which Luther renders thus: *Ich bin eine Stimme eines Rufers* (I am a voice of a crier), in order to indicate that it is another who is crying through John.

2. Very many spiritual gifts, but particularly divine governance and protection, are required so that the ministry may be carried out rightly and for the edification of the church. And one who has a lawful call can call upon God

with a serene conscience and expect a certain hearing in keeping with these promises. Through our ministry God wants to inscribe His law in the hearts of the hearers, 2 Cor. 3:2. But who is fit for these things? [2 Cor. 2:16]. See 2 Cor. 3:4–6; 1 Tim. 4:14; Is. 49:2.

3. The real heart of the ministry is that God by His Spirit and His grace wants to be present with the ministry and through it work efficaciously. And one who is lawfully called to the ministry and carries it out correctly, that man can certainly believe that these promises apply also to him: Is. 49:2 and 51:16; Luke 1:76; 1 Tim. 4:16; 1 Cor. 15:58. 1 Cor. 16:9 and 2 Cor. 2:12, "A door was opened for me." Why? Because the doorkeeper, the Holy Spirit, opened [it], John 10:3, through a lawful call.

4. The certainty of the divine call in the ministry is profitable also for this, that ministers with greater care, faithfulness, and readiness, in the fear of God may administer their office and not be easily deterred. In fact, this doctrine of the call also stirs up in the hearers true reverence and obedience toward the ministry.

Further, after we have once entered this topic of the call of ministers, we must also briefly touch on this question: Who properly has the right and power to call and send ministers of the Word and sacraments? For at all times there have been great and often bloody controversies on the right to call. But the true right to call, God claims for Himself. For, Jer. 23:21, He does not want those men to be acknowledged as true prophets who, to be sure, had a call from kings but had not been called or sent by God Himself. And it is interesting to note in Scripture that to each of the persons of the Trinity has been expressly attributed the right and handling of this matter. Regarding the Father, the Son says in Matt. 9:38, "Pray the Lord of the harvest that He would send workers into His harvest." And Paul says in Eph. 4:11 that the Son of God gives pastors and in 1 Cor. 12:28 that Christ places teachers in the church. Acts 13:2 and 20:28 affirm that they have been placed and sent by the Holy Spirit.

But as to how and in what way God ordinarily calls and sends, it is commonly taught that this is done in two ways. There is an immediate call [and] a mediate [call]. Let us consider both.

The immediate call takes place when a person is called to the ministry not by men or through men, as through the ordinary means, but by God Himself and through God Himself, without means. This does not take place in the way the fanatics boast that they have been called without means, when they imagine that they, by I know not what kind of inner moving of the Spirit, are driven to preach. But in the immediate call God Himself either appears or speaks directly and without means to those whom He calls in this way. The prophets and apostles were undoubtedly called in this way. Thus God calls Moses out of the burning bush without means, Ex. 3:4ff. Thus the call of Aaron without means was confirmed by God, Num. 17:8, when his rod sprouted flowers. Matthias also was called without means, Acts 1:26, because God showed His will through the casting of the lots. And Paul, Gal. 1:1, describes his own immediate call by saying that it was not issued by human beings or through human beings.

But someone wants to know how we are to discern a certain and immediate call of God from the imposture of the fanatics, who also boast that God appeared to them and that the Father gave them these commands. God Himself forewarns that these impostors should not be heeded, Jer. 14:14. Therefore those whom God calls immediately, them He also equips either with the gift of miracles or with other testimonies of the Spirit, so that they may prove and confirm their calling with them. Thus, Ex. 4:2ff., Moses is equipped with miracles, so that both the Israelites and Pharaoh with his people might believe that he had been sent by God. And although the magicians for a while emulated his miracles, yet finally, Ex. 8:19, they were forced to confess that, whatever Moses and Aaron did was done by the power of God. And Christ says of Himself, John 5:36, "The witness which I have is greater than John's, namely the works which the Father has given Me to accomplish." In Matt. 10:8, when Christ called His apostles without means, He added this testimony to them: "Heal the sick, raise the dead, cleanse the lepers, cast out demons." And in 2 Cor. 12:12 Paul calls the signs, wonders, [and] miracles testimonies of his apostleship.

John the Baptizer performed neither signs nor miracles. For this was reserved for the Messiah in order that He might thereby manifest Himself; and yet [John] had an immediate call, for it was confirmed by other testimonies of the Spirit and predicted many centuries before, Is. 40:3 and Mal. 3:1. Such was also the call of the patriarchs; although it was immediate and clearly divine, yet not all were equipped with the gift of miracles. But, on the other hand, miracles should not be ranked above the teaching which was confirmed by the miracles of Christ and the apostles. Hence, when the papists bring forward miracles of their saints to establish their idolatry, they are in no way to be accepted. For Christ, Matt. 24:24, also predicts that there will be many false Christs and false prophets who will perform miracles, but [says] that the faithful must not permit themselves to be drawn away through these from the doctrine of the apostles. Hence also God in Deut. 13:1–3 forewarns that if a prophet arises who proclaims another teaching, and, to confirm it, predicts signs and miracles, and these signs happen, yet this doctrine should not be accepted. For, you see, no miracles can prevail against the doctrine which has been revealed by God.

But if someone asks if immediate calls are to be looked for also in our age, I hold that one must answer him: It certainly does not behoove us to prescribe with boundless boldness anything to the free will and infinite power of God.

But yet we have no commandment, at least which applies to us, to look for an immediate call, nor do we have the promise that God wants at this time to send workers into His harvest through an immediate call. But rather, through the apostles, He has given and prescribed to the church a certain form how He now wants to send and call ministers, namely through a mediate call. For, you see, there is now no need for an immediate call. For God absolutely wills that to the end of the age the ministry be bound to that word of teaching which has been received from the Son of God and handed on to the church through the apostles who were directly called. See Gal. 1:8[–9]; 2 Tim. 1:14; Heb. 1:1. And thus absolutely no new kind of teaching is to be accepted. And if some arise who boast of a direct call and besides produce marvelous miracles and bring a new and diverse doctrine, different from that of Christ and the apostles, we are still not to believe them. For Christ foretold that the antichrist will arise who will put forth such miracles that, if it were possible, even the elect would be seduced into error [Matt. 24:24]. Paul bears witness in 2 Thess. 2:9 that the coming of "the son of perdition will be in accord with the working of Satan, with all power and signs and false wonders."

Now, we must also take note of the usefulness of this distinction between an immediate and a mediate call. It is this, and it is very great. For the prophets and apostles, because they were called immediately, have the testimony of the Spirit and of miracles that they did not err in doctrine, with the result that the other ministers of the church are obligated to take their doctrine from the prophets and apostles and prove it by them or be anathema. Nor has their ministry been bound to some certain church, but they have a command to preach everywhere. But they who do not have a direct call cannot claim these two things for themselves, nor should they be attributed to them.

The mediate call takes place when a certain minister is called to the ministry of the church not directly through God Himself, like the prophets and apostles, but by God through regular means in a lawful way.

And this mediate call has sure and solid foundations in the Word of God, for the apostles, through the vote of the church maintained elders in individual churches, Acts. 14:23. And the ministry of the church is committed to Timothy through the laying on of hands of the elders, 1 Tim. 4:14. For because of their call the apostles could not remain in any one place and teach only there, but it was necessary that they go also to other people and proclaim the Gospel to all nations. Yet meantime, wherever they planted a church they did not leave it without a teacher. Therefore what? Did they wait until they [teachers] might be called immediately by God? Not at all! But through the vote of the church they chose learned and suitable men and gave them their assignment. But this took place through the laying on of hands of the presbytery or by the assembly of elders, who were not only those who had labored in the Word but also other selected and honorable men, "*ein Ausschuß*" [a committee], to whom had been entrusted the business matters pertaining to the church in the name of the entire church.

Nor must we think that this mediate call rests only on examples without divine command. For Paul directs Titus and Timothy to ordain presbyters and how they should do it through means, Titus 1:5; 1 Tim. 2:2.

Even so, for let the younger people note well here that between an immediate and a mediate call there is no difference as if the prophets and apostles were called not by human beings but by God and on the contrary those who are called mediately have not been called by God but by human beings. For we have shown above that there is absolutely no true call except from God alone. Therefore Timothy was no less called by God than [was] Paul himself. But there is a difference in the manner of the call. For God called the prophets and apostles directly Himself. Certainly God indeed also Himself called Timothy and the rest, but through regular means established by Him for this purpose.

And that those who are lawfully called in this way through regular means have been called and sent by God Himself can be clearly proved from Scripture. Timothy was called not directly but through Paul and the presbytery, as we have just now said, 1 Tim. 4:14 and 2 Tim. 1:6, and he had a charge to ordain other presbyters, 2 Tim. 2:2. Yet Paul in Acts 20:28 says to all the presbyters of the church of Ephesus, "The Holy Spirit has made you overseers, to lead the church of God, which He has purchased with His own blood." And in 2 Cor. 5:18–20, an epistle to which Timothy also added his name, 1:1, Paul says not only of himself but in the plural, "God has given to us the ministry of reconciliation. Therefore we are ambassadors in the name of Christ, with God appealing through us." In 1 Cor. 12:28, therefore, Paul says, "God has appointed in the church not only apostles," who were immediately called, but also "teachers," who are mediately called.

But who can doubt whether the promises of grace, help, power, and divine efficacy in the ministry which God gave to the prophets and apostles also apply to those who have been mediately called? And regarding this we must know that the prophets and apostles who were called immediately indeed had many and great prerogatives. Nevertheless Scripture shows that the promises of divine grace and efficacy pertain also to a mediate call, 2 Tim. 1:6. And lest anyone think that this pertains only to those who were mediately called, to be sure, but through apostles, he says in 1 Tim. 4:14: "The grace [Vulgate] that has been given to you through the laying on of the hands of the presbytery." And in 2 Cor. 3:6, which Timothy also signed, Paul says, "God has made us able for the ministry of the new covenant." And in 1 Tim. 4:16 he says of Timothy, "You will save yourself and those who hear you." And it is noteworthy that when, in the church of Corinth, the effectiveness of the ministry is measured on the basis of the persons, whether mediately or immediately called, or on the basis of the gifts of the ministers, Paul says, 1 Cor. 3:5–8, "Who is Apollos? Who is Paul, if they are not servants through whom you believed, and that as the Lord gave to each? I planted, Apollos watered, but God gave the increase. Therefore neither is the one who plants anything, nor the one who waters, but God who gives the increase. Now, the one who plants and the one who waters are one." Here it is notable that Paul was called immediately and Apollos mediately. And yet Paul proclaims that, as regards the efficacy of the ministry and divine grace, they are one.

But it is worth the effort also to consider what these regular means are which God wills to use for a mediate call. And here we need to remember well that God does not ordinarily use the ministry of angels for a mediate call. Therefore, that spirits of the dead appeared at the time of Gregory the Great and that Nicephorus often mixed in with serious things those fables of appearances of spirits who said, "You will be here, but you [will be] bishop there," [these] were illusions of Satan by which the world was deluded. But Christ gave the keys to His church as His bride, Matt. 18:19, and He promised that whatever they would agree on on earth and request, it would also be given by His Father who is in heaven. To the same [church] He entrusted His Word and the sacraments, just as Paul proclaims regarding the ancient people, Rom. 3:2, that "To them were entrusted the oracles of God" and, Rom. 9:4, "To them belong the adoption as sons, the glory, the covenants, the giving of the Law, the worship and the promises," and to the church, Eph. 4:12, "the ministry." For, 1 Cor. 3:21–22, all things belong to the church, whether Paul or Apollos or Cephas. And therefore Paul, when in 1 Tim. 3:15 he has spoken of the mediate call, adds that the church is the pillar and the mainstay of truth.

But here the urgent question arises: Did the papists act correctly in excluding the magistrates and the rest of the church from the election and confirmation of bishops? For Gratian in dist. 62 and 63 cites the Canons of the Roman pontiffs in which a warning is given that the laity should not meddle with the election of the clergy, and particularly that the rulers should not claim for themselves the right to call or demand bishops. And there they tell how [Pope] Hadrian, out of very singular grace, granted to Charlemagne, and later [how Pope] Leo granted to Otto I, king of the Germans, the investiture of the Roman pontiff, archbishops, and bishops. Whether emperors still enjoy this privilege, they themselves would know. But because various sins are committed in this question which pertains to a lawful call and the ordination of ministers of the Word, I shall treat this matter somewhat more carefully and through certain parts.

1. It is certainly and clearly evident on the basis both of the commandments of Scripture and of examples, Titus 1:5; 1 Tim. 4:14; 2 Tim. 2:2; and Acts 14:23, that those who are now in the ministry and confess the sacred doctrine are to be employed when, through a mediate call, the ministry is to be entrusted to a certain person.

2. But because the ministers are not the whole church but only a part of it, Eph. 4:11, they are also not lords of the church but administrators and overseers, 2 Cor. 1:24; 1 Peter 5:3. Therefore they cannot and must not seize the mediate call for themselves alone, with the other members excluded. For not even the apostles did this, Acts 1:15–26; 6:2–6; 13:2–3; and 14:23.

3. But this call in no way pertains to the civil rights of the magistrate, which they call royal prerogatives. For the ministry of the Word pertains to the kingdom of Christ. And because Christ wants His kingdom and the kingdoms of the world with their functions to be separate and distinct, therefore the establishment of the ministry is not to be subjected to the civil power of the magistrate. For the apostles, where the ruler was a heathen or an ungodly man, did not in the call of the presbyters ask for the permission or authority of the ruler.

4. Therefore what? Should the ruler simply be excluded from the election and calling of ministers? When the ruler is a Christian or godly, he is a member of the church of God and has the command to love and support the doctrine of the divine Word not only privately for himself, Ps. 2:10; 47:9; 102:19–22, but God wills that the ruler by his office be a nourisher of the church, Is. 49:23. The gates of the world must lift up their heads that the king of glory may come in, Ps. 24:7. And in this sense this care of the church applies also to a godly ruler, so that the ministries of the church may be properly established and administered. Note also the examples of David, Hezekiah, Jehoshaphat, and Josiah.

5. However, it is not permissible for a Christian and godly ruler to call and establish ministers in the church without the will and consent of the ministry and the rest of the church. For just as the Roman pontiff with his [cohorts] committed sacrilege in that he took away the selection and calling of ministers from the church and took it for himself alone with his [court], so also is a ruler guilty of the same wrong when by excluding the ministry and the rest of the church he would claim for himself alone the authority to establish ministries in the church. For a godly ruler is not the whole church but only a member of it, Ps. 47:9 and 102:22, nor is he the lord of the church but its nourisher, Is. 49:23; indeed, he is only a servant, Is. 60:10, 12.

6. Thus the turbulent and seditious Anabaptists are certainly not doing right when by the word "church" [ecclēsia, der Gemein] they understand only the common multitude, with the ministry and the godly ruler excluded. For among them ignorance rules along with evil sedition. For the church is a body

which includes all the members of Christ, Eph. 1:22 and 4:12. Therefore the election and calling of the ministers of the church must not be subject only to the ministers or only to the ruler or only to the inexperience and temerity of the common multitude, but must be and remain with the whole church, yet with the maintenance of proper order.

For because God is not a God of confusion but of order, 1 Cor. 14:33, therefore so that "all things may be done decently and in order," 1 Cor. 14:40, the business of electing and calling of ministers both in the time of the apostles and after their time, in the older and purer church, was always handled with a certain definite order by particular members of the church in the name and with the consent of the whole church. Thus in Acts 1:15[–22] Peter proposes a directive as to the kind of person to be chosen; then the apostles choose together with the church. In Acts 6:2[–4] the apostles propose a directive regarding the selection of deacons who were to administer the outward goods of the church; they also describe what kind of people they should be, and the church chooses in keeping with this rule. And [the members of the church] submit to the judgment of the apostles those who had been chosen, who [the apostles] in turn by their approval confirmed the election. Often also the apostles themselves proposed suitable persons to the church. Thus Paul sent Titus, Timothy, Silvanus, and others to the churches, [and] the church later approved this selection by vote and consent, Acts 14:23, and in 2 Cor. 8:16, Titus is proposed, who, with a certain other man, was to bring the offering to Jerusalem, and the church concurred in [the choice of] his person. Thus undoubtedly the election nevertheless takes place through the church, but with a definite order.

In support of this position there are many old canons in Gratian. For example, in dist. 24 [*Corpus Iuris Canonici*, Richter ed., pp. 87–89] there is the requirement for "the counsel of the clergy." In dist. 23 and 67 [pp. 76–82, 253] there is required "the authority of the bishop and the assent of the clergy and the laity." Dist. 65 [p. 250] requires either the election or the consent of the clergy and the people. Dist. 62 [p. 234], "Ministers must be requested by the people, elected by the clergy, and ordained by the judgment of the bishops." And dist. 63 [p. 242], when the ruler embraces the doctrine of the Gospel, his vote, consent and authority are also required. Hence in dist. 62 [p. 234] the canons say, "In the ordination of ministers the vote of the citizens, the testimony of the people" (those who are outside, 1 Tim. 3:7), "the decision of the distinguished" (these are the magistrates), "[and] the election by the clergy are required." Again, "Let those who are going to be priests be requested by the bishops, [and] let the endorsement of the clergy, the testimony of distinguished ones, [and] the consensus of the people be obtained," (ibid.) Of this there still are residual words for nomination or request, presentation, consensus, and the confirmation or charging [of ministers]. And by these words, if they are rightly understood, the entire matter of the call is comprehended, and it becomes clear how that assignment was made among the orders of the church in the ancient church. For sometimes the common people by their desire and petition or request proposed a particular person. Hence even today bishops are said to be requested who indeed have been elected but have not yet received confirmation from the pope. Sometimes a godly magistrate was nominated bishop, as [we read] in Sozomon, 7.[7–]8. Gregory of Nazianzus and Nectarius were so chosen.[3] For the emperor nominated them and the whole synod indeed approved his nomination, but the people of Constantinople and the clergy ratified [it]. But more often the bishops who were able to judge more accurately about this matter proposed suitable persons. Thus Cyprian, in his third and fourth books [Epistle 24, MPL 3.294] proposed Saturus, Operatus, [and] Celerinus; Valerius [proposed] Augustine, and Augustine [proposed] Evadius. But this nomination or request was always set before the rest of the orders of the church, so that by their judgment or consensus it might be confirmed, as we can see from that very nice discourse in Augustine's 110th epistle [(213), MPL 33.966–68].

Those who are students of antiquity should also look at that epistle of Augustine, and they will find in it what the custom of the church was of old for proposing a suitable person for the ministry and how the acclamation and approval was given by the people, "He is worthy and righteous." Later the papists, as we can see in the *Pontifical* [service book], turned the matter into a mockery. For now, as the person who is to be confirmed in office enters the doors of the choir, [the people] shout and ask, "Is he worthy and righteous who is to be chosen and confirmed?" And someone stands in a corner and cries, "He is worthy and righteous." But this is a mockery of God and man.

Further, this also is worth considering: whether the church has full power to call to the ministry any kind of persons it wishes. For in the Old Testament the ministry was indeed hereditary, as it was in the tribe of Levi. Likewise the priesthood was hereditary in the family of Aaron. And yet when the priests departed from the Word, God removed them, as happened to Eli, 1 Sam. 3:12. Thus, when the Levites did not do their duty, God raised up prophets from other tribes who brought them back into line. But in the New Testament this does not happen. And yet the Lord of the harvest gave His church a formula, and, so to say, instruction [as to] how they must be like in doctrine and life who are to be chosen and called for the ministry of the Word, 1 Tim. 3:2–7; Titus 1:6–9. And this rule, which is to be followed, the church must set before itself in true

---

[3]   Sozomon, *Historia Ecclesiastica*, 7.7–8, MPG 67.1417ff.

fear of the Lord, if it wants the Lord Himself to call and send workers into His harvest through this means.

But what we have said above about the apostolic calling, that it should stretch into the whole world, we cannot say also now about those who are called mediately. For teachers, pastors, bishops, [and] presbyters are called to certain churches and do not have authority to teach everywhere or in all churches. Thus in Acts 14:23 elders are ordained for individual churches, and in Titus 1:5 Titus is left in Crete to establish churches in every city. And thus God, through a special call, ordinarily shows where He wants someone's labor to be used. Therefore by virtue of this call they do not have authority to teach in other churches to which they do not have a special call. Hence in the Council of Chalcedon, in Canon 6, and in Gratian, Canon 16 [*CIC*, p. 256, dist. 70], it states that absolutely no one should be ordained except to a specific and particular church. Yet Gerson says that the formula for the public preferment of teachers is this: "I give you authority to engage in disputation, to teach, and to lecture here and everywhere in the world." And Luther says that he very often drew comfort from his preferment because public authority was given him to teach the Gospel and to condemn errors. And though these things be so and, besides, good reasons may underlie, for which a person might also lawfully teach in several places, yet such preferment or license to teach differs for the most part from the apostolic call.

Moreover, just as there is a lawful method for calling someone into the ministry of the church, so also there is a lawful method for removing someone or for transferring [him] from one church to another. In the popish church the benefices and prebends were bestowed in such a way that one might enjoy them for life; meantime there was no concern for the upbuilding or the destruction of the church. And in our churches many also do not understand this matter correctly. For just as, when one hires a servant, he has the power to dismiss [him] when he wishes, so some think that they have authority also to dismiss a preacher, though they have no just cause. Thus there also are some who think that no preacher can with a good conscience betake himself from one place to another. We shall add also a few words on this matter.

Just as the one God properly claims for Himself the right to call even when the call takes place mediately, so also is it properly of God to remove a person from the ministry. Therefore, as long as God endures in the ministry of His minister who teaches correctly and lives blamelessly, the church does not have authority to remove someone else's servant. But when he no longer edifies the church by doctrine or life, but destroys [it], then God Himself removes him. Hos. 4:6; 1 Sam. 2:30. Therefore there are two reasons for which God removes unfaithful ministers from their office: (1) because of doctrine, when they teach error. For Mal. 2:7, "The lips of the priest should guard knowledge, and they should require the Law from his mouth." When he rejects this, then he in turn is rejected by God. (2) Because of life, when they act in such a way that the name of the Lord is blasphemed. Thus the life of the sons of Eli was shameful and scandalous and they caused the people to abhor the sacrifices of God. And although the church may tolerate such a one for some time, yet God finally removes [him], for He says, "They that honor Me I will honor," 1 Sam. 2:30. And then also the church not only can but also should remove such a one from the ministry.

For just as God calls, so also does He remove through means. But just as a call in keeping with the instruction of the Lord of the harvest, so also, when someone must be removed from the ministry, it is necessary that the church can show with certainty that this is the judgment and this is the will of God. And just as the call, so also does the deposition pertain to the whole church in a certain orderly way. Hence the ancient church with diligent inquiry and accurate judgment in its councils dealt with the reasons for deposition. And there are some ancient canons in Gratian which pertain to this matter, *Causa* 15, *Quaest.* 7 [*CIC, Decreti*, pp. 756–59].

On the basis of these foundations the second question can also be determined, regarding the transfer of some minister from one church to another. There are some useful canons on this matter [*Decreti*] *Caus.* 7, *Quaest.* 1 [*CIC*, p. 579]. Thus Pope Anthony replied to the bishops of Baetica and Toledo, "You should understand that the moving of pastors may take place out of mutual benefit and necessity, but not out of anyone's self-will or heavy-handedness. Saint Peter, our teacher and the prince of the apostles, for the sake of usefulness, was transferred from the city of Antioch to Rome in order that there he might be of greater service. Eusebius also was moved to Alexandria by apostolic authority from some small city. Similarly Felix, from the city in which he had been ordained, by the election of the citizens, because of the good doctrine and life which he had, by the authority of this holy see and the common counsel of the bishops and the rest of the priests and the people, was transferred to Ephesus. For he does not go from city to city, nor is he transferred from a smaller to a larger [place], because he does not do this out of unlawful striving for honor or self-will nor was he deposed either by force or by his own see, or compelled by necessity, but for the good of the place or the people he is transferred by others, not proudly but humbly. For the reason of good is one thing, [but the reason] of avarice and presumption and self-will is another." Likewise, Pelagius, a benign archbishop [*CIC*, p. 579], says, "You should know, most dearly beloved brother, that a case of necessity and helpfulness is one thing, [and] a case of presumptuousness and self-will is another. Therefore he does not change [his] location who does not change his mind; that is, he that does not move from city to city out of avarice or heavy-handedness, or self-will or his own pleasure, but he is moved because of necessity and benefit. For the benefit of the many is to be preferred to the benefit or will of the one. For it is one thing to move and another to be moved. For it is one thing to move willingly, another to come by compulsion or necessity. Hence, they do not change [their] city, but they are changed because they do this not willingly but under compulsion. Therefore they do not well understand the rules of the church who deny that because of necessity or helpfulness this can be done as often as common need and helpfulness make it the thing to do." Shortly after this, a long canon is added which declares one guilty of denying Christ who does not show mercy to those who suffer need: "Now, they deny mercy to those who suffer need, who need divine services and do not have their own bishop to instruct them, when in a case of necessity and opportunity, a man refuses to move from one city to another, even to a smaller place, which does not have a very learned or competent or important bishop, and is unwilling to transfer upon good counsel or the exhortation of the superiors" [ibid., p. 580]. And in the proceedings of the Council of Carthage it says, "The bishop or any of the lower clergy should not transfer from a humble place to a more important one out of ambition. It is obvious that if the benefit to the church demands it, by a decision of the clergy and laity the matter may be referred directly by the bishops to a meeting of the synod; nevertheless with another bishop substituted in his place. But the lower ranks of priests or the other clergy can, with the permission of their bishops, move to other churches" [ibid.].

What need is there for more words? The Lord of the harvest has the authority to transfer His ministers from one church to another. The church also has the same power, as long as all things are done lawfully. Thus Paul moves Timothy and Titus from place to place, but not out of his own impulsiveness or private judgment, not because of unlawful striving for honor or heavy-handedness, not out of pleasure or presumption, but for the benefit, the need, and the edification of the church. At one time there was an established punishment applied to those who changed location in order to look out for their own advantages: "Let him be without his own seat who strives for that of another." Again, "Let him be expelled from both." And yet people should not be so bound to one place that they cannot move to another when they see its clear benefit in the church. But in the ancient church it was the custom to refer the judgment about this matter to other churches.

Finally, we need to add something about this question: If a lawful call consists of these things which we have mentioned, then what does the rite of public ordination confer? For in the popish church this rite is performed without any consideration of a call. And if someone is ordained, they think it is enough, so that he has authority to teach, absolve, [and] administer the sacraments, though he lacks a lawful call. On the contrary there are those not only among the Anabaptists who reject this rite entirely but who sometimes also in other places debate very sharply about these things. For from time to time cases of this kind occur in which a man has a call and is prohibited from going to a more illustrious church in which he might receive the rite of ordination. Therefore the question is: Is his ministry annulled? Some say yes; others say no, since the rite of ordination is not necessary, so long as the call is lawful.

Nevertheless, because of those who run and have not been sent, a call ought to have the public witness of the church. And the rite of ordination is nothing else than such a public testimony by which this call is declared, in the sight of God and in His name, to be lawful and divine. And by that rite, as by a public designation or announcement, the ministry, with the consent and approval of the whole church, is entrusted to one who is called. Thus Paul, although called immediately, still is sent to Ananias, who was to lay hands on [him], that it might be evident to the church concerning [his] call, Acts 9:17; and later, Acts 13:3, when he was to be sent among the gentiles, he was made a regular teacher of the gentiles, again by the laying on of hands. And this rite was used so that his call might be publicly declared lawful; nor would others similarly glory in it. Therefore, thus if this rite was done in the case of him who had been directly called, how much more is it fitting to do it in the case of those who are mediately called? Therefore, although ordination does not make a call, yet, if a man has been lawfully called, this rite is a declaration and public confirmation that the call which preceded is lawful.

Also, by this very rite as by a solemn vow and obligation, he who has been called is bound before God, under the testimony of the church, to render the faithfulness in the ministry which God requires in His stewards, 1 Cor. 4:2.

But that rite is observed mainly so that the whole church may, with common and ardent prayers, commend to God the ministry of the one who has been called. And that those prayers offered with such a rite are not in vain, Moses testifies, Deut. 34:9. Joshua is filled with the spirit of wisdom because Moses had placed his hands on him, cf. 1 Tim. 4:14; 2 Tim. 1:6.

We must confess that there is in the Scriptures no command of God that this rite of ordination must be used, nor is there a promise that through this rite God will bestow grace, as in Baptism and the Lord's Supper. But the free and impartial use of it was introduced into the church by the apostles, not because they wanted in any way to bind grace to this rite regarding which they had neither command nor promise. Yet it has its foundation in the Word of God, Gen. 48:14. Jacob, about to bless the two sons of Joseph, Ephraim and Manasseh, holds out his hands and puts them on their heads. In Num. 27:18 and Deut. 34:9, when Moses designates Joshua as [his] successor, before the temple [and] in the sight of all the people, he lays [his] hands on him and by this rite indicates that he has been lawfully chosen by God, so that after his [Moses'] death he may lead the people. And in Mark 10:16 Christ engages in the laying on of hands when He blesses the little children who were brought to Him.

To be sure, when He sent out the apostles to preach, Matt. 10:5 and Luke 9:2, He did not use the external rite but was present with them only with [His] Word and grace. And later again, Matt. 28:19, He simply says, "Go into all the world . . . teach . . . and I am with you." Nor does He add any rite; nevertheless, John 20:22–23, when He gave the authority to loose and to bind sins, He "breathed on them."

There is no doubt that the apostles had reasons why also they themselves did not breathe, as Christ had done. For they certainly did not have a command, and lest anyone think that the Holy Spirit was bound to such a practice, just as the Holy Spirit proceeds in the substance of the Son, they rather retained the rite of the laying on of hands, received from the patriarchs, by free use in the church, Acts 13:3; 1 Tim. 4:14; 2 Tim. 1:6.

In the ancient church that simplicity ruled, so that in the ordination of the bishops nothing else was practiced but the laying on of hands. Thus in the *History* of Socrates we read of many examples of public ordination. In Socrates 2.11 [MPG 67.206] and Sozomon, 6.24 [MPG 67.1351ff.] nothing is said of Ambrose except that he was elected by the people with the confirmation of the emperor and the laying on of the hands of the bishops. Later many ceremonies were added, as, for example, a book was given to the one ordained by which he was admonished to "be attentive to reading," 1 Tim. 4:13. Later when everything had degenerated, unction was also adopted from the Old Testament, from the anointing of David, 1 Sam. 16:13, and because the Holy Spirit is called a chrism or unction, 1 John 2:20, as Peter Lombard points out. Yet in Dionysius the Areopagite, although in him there are many seeds of the papal reign, nothing is found regarding anointing, but only regarding the laying on of hands. But not content with these things, with the passage of time they always added trifles and ditties, as can be seen in the decretals and the *Pontifical*. And although there were not lacking those who objected to these things, they still did not stop, and out of the fraudulent Epistle of Anacletus they cite that unction is to be used because the grace of the Holy Spirit is added to the chrism with which the hands of the priests are anointed. Therefore the papists anoint the hands of their priests, so that they may receive authority to celebrate the Eucharist and offer the unbloody sacrifice for the sins of the living and the dead. The suffragan bishop also adds the insufflation, saying, "Receive the Holy Spirit," etc. And they say that in this way the indelible character is stamped upon him so that he has the power to save people. And in this way they lead their people away from the true foundation, as if the priests in themselves, because of this unction, had the power to remit sins and that it is not to be sought from God. Likewise, if they have not been anointed in this way by the suffragan bishop, then they have no power at all.

We in our churches simply and plainly retain the laying on of hands and according to the analogy of Scripture hold that these three things especially are indicated:

1. By this public rite we testify that though this act is mediate, yet it is truly divine, for the person is presented to God and it is pointed out that the person has been sent through lawful means by God Himself. For it is not our work but God's which we do; through us He calls and ordains this person. And he who is thus called is presented to God. In a sense he is delivered over to God for the ministry, just as when of old in the Old Testament hands were laid on the sacrifices, they were then devoted, as it were, to the service of God alone.

2. By this laying on of hands it is also brought to the attention of the church that it must also be instructed that God through this person and his ministry wills to teach, exhort, and console them, administer the sacraments, [and] to loose or bind sins. In sum, God wills to be efficacious through this man and lead people to eternal life. And just as God says to Moses, Num. 27:[18–]20, "Lay your hands on Joshua and you will give him a part of your glory," that is, the authority with which you have hitherto been adorned you will give to your successor, so also is authority publicly given before the church to him upon whom the hands are laid.

3. By the public prayers we are promising ardent prayers. James 5:16, "The prayer of a righteous man avails much," that is, it is efficacious and active. Therefore, in order that the godly might be encouraged to ardent prayers, the burdens of the office are to be shown to them as far as it concerns the flesh, Satan, and the world; and the more men understand that the grace of God and divine aid are necessary for this task, the more fervent they are in their prayers. Therefore the people are to be brought into the presence of God, as it were, and God through their prayers is admonished: You, O God, have established the ministry and You have promised that You will be present with Your grace. We bring before You this man who has been lawfully called through the instrumentality of Your church to administer the Word and the sacraments. And thus we pray that You, according to Your promise, may will to be present with Your Spirit and Your grace. Prayers of this kind are not vain, as the above examples show, Deut. 34:9; 1 Tim. 4:14; 2 Tim. 1:6.

I have been rather prolix in this discussion of the call into the ministry because it is useful material in itself and is necessary above all for theological students. Now let us proceed.

II

The second matter which the ministry must look out for in the church is the teaching. For the call to the ministry is not directed to the end that as "lazy bellies" they may enjoy the dignities of the office or in their sloth sit on their ecclesiastical emoluments as happened under the papacy. But, as the popular saying has it, "The benefit is given because of the work." For Christ also affirms that payment should be given, but to those who work, Luke 10:7. Paul says that ministers are "worthy of double honor," but again to those who "labor," 1 Tim. 5:17. Hence Christ in Matt. 9:38 speaks of "laborers in the Lord's harvest." Paul in 1 Tim. 3:1 says, "He who desires the office of bishop desires a good work," not leisure. 2 Tim. 2:15, "Show yourself to God . . . a worker who does not need to be ashamed," that is, a worker whose works are approved by God. In Phil. 3:18–19 he complains of those "enemies of the cross of Christ, whose God is their belly and whose glory is in their shame."

Scripture expressly states what kind of work it should be in which the ministers of the church should labor. 1 Tim. 5:17, "in the Word and in teaching"; 2 Tim. 2:15, "in dividing the Word of truth."

[1.] Therefore this question pertains to those who are lawfully called and hold the ministry in orderly succession: Is the church bound to such men and to their fellowship or organization, as if they cannot err and hence whatever they teach and assent must of necessity be received without question or discrimination?

Therefore we must understand that the arrangement which has been sanctified by divine institution in the church is this: There are classes of people or duties, that is, to be sure, there are some who teach and some who learn.

2. We must consider the promises regarding the ministry. For because the church will remain, therefore there will also remain both teachers and learners. Regarding the teachers we have promises: Is. 59:21, " 'This is My covenant with them,' says the Lord, 'My Spirit which is upon you and My Word which has been put in your mouth shall not depart from your mouth, or from the mouth of your seed, or from the mouth of your seed's seed forever.' " And in Jer. 18:18 they plot against Jeremiah, "The law shall not perish from the priest, nor counsel from the wise, nor the word from the prophet"; Matt. 28:20, "I will be with you always until the end of the age." In regard to those who hear, it says in 1 Kings 19:18, "I have left to Me seven thousand whose knees have not been bowed to Baal"; Is. 1:19, "The Lord God of hosts has left us a seed"; 6:13, "The holy seed shall be the stump which remains in the land"; Matt. 13:30, in the parable of the sower it is said, "Let it grow until the harvest and in the time of the harvest I will say to the reapers, 'First gather the tares and bind them in bundles to burn them, but gather the wheat into my barn.' "

3. Here pertains the doctrine of the duties and faithfulness of ministers in the church. For Paul in 1 Cor. 4:1–2 says, "In the work of the ministry it is required that the steward be found faithful." This fidelity involves several things:

First, that the minister of the Word correctly understand the fundamental points of sound doctrine; for in Mal. 2:7 it says, "The lips of the priest must guard knowledge and they shall require the law of the Lord from his mouth." Therefore he must be "able to instruct others," 2 Tim. 2:2, and be certain that he is speaking "the oracles of God," as Jeremiah says in 17:15–16, when the Jews accuse him of speaking lies, "Behold they say to me, 'Where is the Word of the Lord? Let it come.'" But Jeremiah replies, "I am not troubled being your pastor and I have not desired the day of disaster. You know that what comes out from my lips was right in your sight."

Second, related to this faithfulness in teaching sound doctrine is that nothing must be hidden, Acts 20:27, "I did not hesitate to proclaim to you the whole counsel of God." Nor is there to be any confusion regarding the "right division of the chief points of doctrine," 2 Tim. 2:15. This is not to take place in order to show off, but in proportion to the ability of the hearers, just as a nurse distributes bread to the children proportionate to their age because she desires all of them to receive it, cf. Heb. 6:1, those who were unlearned in Christ, among whom was being laid the foundation for their conversion to God, "for faith, for baptism, for doctrine, for the laying on of hands, the resurrection of the dead, and eternal judgment." And in Matt. 23:37, Christ says that He had often wanted to gather the citizens of Jerusalem as "a hen gathers her chicks under her wings"; 1 Cor. 3:1–2, Paul testifies that he had spoken with the Corinthians "as with children." He had fed them with milk, not meat, "because they were not yet able to bear it." The apostle also shows in other places how he was in the habit of accommodating himself to the capacity of his hearers, e.g., Gal. 4:20, where he hopes to be with them that he "might take on the voice of a father in order to gain them."

Third, the faithful minister of the Word must be so strong and faithful in the Word that "he may convince those who contradict him," Titus 1:9; that he can distinguish "the voice of the stranger from the truth," John 10:5; that he can "separate the precious from the vile," Jer. 15:19ff.; and "protect the sheep from the wolves," Acts 20:29. For God does not put watchmen in His house in vain, but "He will require from their hands and for their carelessness they shall perish," Ezek. 3:17ff. and 33:7ff. From this Luther concludes that the two primary duties of a pastor are "instruction and warning" (*lehren und wehren*).

Fourth, he is to set forth and apply from the Word of God those things which edify the hearers, 1 Cor. 14:12, "Seek to edify, that you may abound";

v. 19, "In the church I would prefer to speak five words with my understanding, that I might instruct others, rather than ten thousand words in an unknown tongue"; v. 26, "Let all things be done to edify." Thus the minister of the Word briefly brings forth all things which are beneficial and applies them to certain subjects which Christ includes under the summary statement, "Preach repentance and remission of sins," and "teach them to observe all things which I have commanded you," Luke 24:47 and Matt. 28:19; "baptize," Matt. 3:2, 8. And Paul in Acts 26:20 sums them up thus: repentance, faith, and works, or the fruits of repentance.

But Paul in Rom. 15:4; 1 Cor. 10:11; 14:31; 2 Tim. 3:16; Titus 1:9 refers to all these subjects more fully and pointedly, and divides them up for the benefit of teachers and learners. He also speaks of the following: (1) "Teaching" or "doctrine" (*didaskalia*), 2 Tim 3:16, which includes the explanation of the various dogmas. Likewise, this word demonstrates on which foundation these concepts are built and how to prove them (2) "Rebuke" (*elegchos*), Titus 1:9 and 2 Tim. 3:16. By this false doctrine is refuted and it is done on the correct foundations. (3) "Instruction" (*paideian*), 2 Tim. 3:16, a word which refers to the instruction for living our life toward God and men. (4) "Correction" (*epanorthōsis*), 2 Tim. 3:16, which includes admonitions and chidings by which we are corrected and restored in those things which have been neglected and fallen into disuse in our living, our morals, and our discipline. (5) He uses the term "admonition" (*nouthesia*), 1 Cor. 10:11, referring to advance warning either by instructions or examples and pointing out the pitfalls and punishments against which we must guard. Luther renders this with *Warnung*, which refers to the frequent instruction to the mind that we should not tempt God in this way and not fall or be punished. (6) Paul uses the word "exhortation" (*paraklēsis*) in 1 Cor. 14:3 referring to encouragement or an earnest entreaty, that that which is taught may be applied in repentance, faith, and new obedience, or that that which has been well begun may be continued and brought to completion. (7) "Consolation or comfort" (*paramythia*), 1 Cor. 14:3, so that under the cross "through patience and the comfort of the Scriptures we might have hope," Rom. 15:4. This faithfulness is described in Ezek. 34:16 under the beautiful picture of a shepherd, that the good shepherd "will seek what was lost and bring back what had gone astray, that he will bind up the broken, strengthen the weak, destroy the sleek and the strong."

Fifth, for the faithfulness of the minister it is required that he be an example to the flock, 1 Peter 5:3, "in life, in character, in faith, in purity," 1 Tim. 4:12. In these two passages, as also in Titus 2:7, is found the word *typos* (an image or type or pattern). This concept is also found in Ex. 25:40 where Moses on the mountain is shown the pattern according to which he must make the tabernacle. Faithful preachers must be like this so that their hearers may learn to see in them what kind of people they themselves ought to be in their speech and their life in keeping with the will of God. And just as in the art of printing, where the pieces of type impress a certain form of the letters, so also ministers in their lifestyle give a norm for piety. There are many statements on this subject among the fathers. For example, Gregory says, "His doctrine is despised whose life is looked down upon." Augustine, *Lib de Mor. Eccles* [MPL 32.1309ff.], "An evil pastor tears down with an evil life as much as he builds up with his teaching. If only he who lives an evil life would build up something! His teaching is cold who himself is not affected by the teaching which he presents in the place of God." Chrysostom, on Matthew 25 [*Homilia*, 79–80, MPG 58.718], says, "The teacher of the church by good teaching and good living instructs the people how they should live; but by evil living he instructs God how He ought to condemn him." Bernard complains of the shameless life of the clergy of his time, saying, "In our day we cannot say, 'as the prophet says, as the priests, so the people,' because now the priests are worse than the people."

Sixth, to the faithfulness of the minister of the Word applies the serious and ardent prayer that God by His Spirit and grace would be present and give the increase. For what else can he do than plant and water? But "God gives the increase," 1 Cor. 3:7. As Samuel prays in 1 Sam. 12:23, "God forbid that I should commit the sin of ceasing to pray to the Lord for you," so Paul prayed for all of his churches. Origen applied Ex. 17:11, where it is said of Moses who prayed while the people were advancing to battle, by saying, "Let the priests pray that the people may conquer their invisible enemies."

4. Related to the order established by God is that we should know that the will of God has commanded that the sheep hear the voice of their shepherd, John 10:4, and that the hearer should show reverence and obedience to the minister, 1 Tim. 5:17, "Those elders who rule well are worthy to be held in double honor, especially those who labor in the Word and teaching"; also 1 Thess. 5:12–13. Reverence is due them particularly for these reasons: (1) that the people might hear sermons and teaching, "My sheep hear My voice," John 10:4; (2) that they might obey the teaching, Heb. 13:17; (3) in regard to sharing our blessings with those who teach us, it says in Gal. 6:6, "Let him who is taught the Word share with him who teaches in all good things"; cf. 1 Cor. 9:14; (4) that they should live in peace, 1 Thess. 5:13; Heb. 13:17.

5. Here a great and difficult question arises which is dealt with in the *Loci*: Is the church simply gathered around the bishops and their co-workers who are said to hold the ministry? Or, to put it another way, is the church gathered around the ordinary succession of the bishops and their colleagues? While this question has been dealt with in the *Loci*, still I want to add a few points.

The papists describe the ordained succession of bishops thus: When in the principal see of the church, that is, Rome, bishops are elected in the canonical and lawful way and successors in an unbroken series follow them, and from this supreme see other bishops, and from them, in turn, priests in an ordered and continuous succession have been established in offices, then, they say, that all these one after the other, but particularly the pope and his entourage and particularly when they are gathered together in a convention or synod, by reason of the place [Rome] and the line of succession, have from Christ the privilege or honor that they cannot err in the faith or in teaching and determining concerning things which pertain to the Christian religion. And therefore they say that the church is so tied to such bishops and priests, or at least to their meetings or synods, that the people are compelled to obey them upon pain of the loss of salvation. But those who do not have this ordered and continuous succession must not be heeded, even if they proclaim the true doctrine. For this reason men are afraid to hear us if we are lacking this succession.

But for the true and faithful doctrine not only is a lawful call and succession required, but chiefly the quality of doctrine, that is, the church must not look only at the call and the ordained succession of the teachers, but especially it must be attentive to what message is proclaimed or what kind of doctrine is taught, 2 John 10. "Out of the treasure of his heart he brings forth good or evil," Matt. 7:15; Luke 6:45. Is his "the voice of the true shepherd, or the voice of a stranger?" John 10:5. And in order that we can distinguish the true and good from the evil and the alien, Scripture teaches that Christ is "the chief bishop and chief shepherd of our souls," 1 Peter 2:25 and 5:4; therefore the church is bound to His voice alone, John 10:27. But Paul affirms that this "voice" is "the doctrine of the apostles and prophets upon which we have been built," Eph. 2:20, which God willed to be included in Holy Scripture as far as it was necessary for the church, cf. John 20:31 and 2 Tim. 3:16, so that the church might cling constantly and firmly to this voice and for all posterity might be "the foundation and pillar of faith and truth," 1 Tim. 3:15.

Therefore the church has the mandate from God that "it not believe every spirit, but prove the spirit, whether it is from God," 1 John 4:1. Paul says in 1 Thess. 5:19–20, "Do not despise prophesyings. Test all things; hold fast to that which is good." Thus it is the will of God that the church hear and believe its lawfully called teachers and those who bring the word of sound doctrine. If this is not the case, the church should pay them no heed. Thus in 2 John 10–11 it is written in the form of a mandate or a prohibition, "If anyone comes to you and does not bring this teaching, do not receive him into your house or bid him godspeed. For he who bids him a farewell becomes a participant in his evil works"; cf. Gal. 1:8, "If anyone, or even we ourselves," that is, the apostles or a person who has been called immediately or mediately and is adorned with miracles, "or an angel from heaven," that is, a witness who appears in heavenly splendor and asserts by a miracle that he has been sent by God, if such a person brings something not only contrary but even alongside of the apostolic doctrine, "let him be anathema."

The anathema is an abomination to God and men, something to be detested, and thus we are in all ways to avoid their teachings and if they are received and used, the users become polluted and bear the burden of God's wrath. This great weight of words lies in the statement of the apostle, and a person should weigh these words carefully.

Some barbarian nations had noted this point carefully, as Irenaeus tells us, and shut their ears if anyone came to them bringing anything other than the doctrine of the apostles. Thus he writes in Bk. 3, ch. 4 [*Adv. Haer.*, 3.4, MPG 7.856], "This faith [the apostolic] they had believed, although they did not have it in written form since they were barbarians, both the words and the substance, the practices and the method of living, because of the faith through which they had become very wise and were pleasing to God, living in all righteousness and purity and wisdom. And if any people proclaimed to them ideas which had come from heretics, or which sounded like their words, they immediately closed their ears and fled far away so as not to hear those who upheld blasphemous talk. Thus through the old teaching of the apostles, they allowed no false messages to enter their minds or take root there, for they had neither an organized group nor established teaching."

We must also consider the arguments by which the papists try to prove their opinion regarding the authority of the succession of ordination, in order that we might be able to explain and refute these arguments. We shall note their chief arguments in order.

I. They use the simile of civil governments. Just as no organized society or government among men can stand unless there are interpretations of the laws, opinions, and mandates with reference to place and office which have validity and authority, so since the church is certainly a community established with the divine and thus the best order, and since many controversies have arisen which of necessity require some decision; therefore, so that intolerable confusion is not brought into the church and that out of disagreement and arrogance and constant contradiction we do not produce schisms by which the church is disturbed and ultimately overturned, but that there might be an end to the contentions, it is imperative that we establish and retain in the church the authority of the orderly succession, so that to those who are in this orderly succession we can refer controversies, whenever and wherever they arise, and thus hear the decision of the leaders and obey them.

But the explanation of this argument concerning the difference between the church and the civil state has been dealt with at length and with such clarity in the loci which discuss the kingdom of Christ and the kingdoms of the world, I think it superfluous to add anything more.

II. They cite the passage in Deut. 17:8–13 saying that God Himself established this arrangement in His dealings with His people in the days of old in order that there might be certainty, constancy, and consensus in religion, namely, "If a case arises that is too hard for you to decide, for instance, whether someone is guilty of murder when there is not sufficient evidence, or whether someone's rights have been denied him—you shall take the case to the sanctuary of the Lord to the priests and Levites, and the chief judge on duty at the time whom the Lord has chosen, he will make the decision. His decision is without appeal and is to be followed by turning neither to the right nor the left. The sentence he imposes is to be fully carried out. If the defendant refuses to follow the decision of the priest or judge appointed by God for this purpose, he shall die. You shall remove this evil person from Israel. And when the people hear what happened to the man, then none will swell up with pride." They try to apply this arrangement and ordinance of God to the church of the new covenant. God, they say, knows all things most perfectly and by His reasoning and order, certainty and consensus can be preserved in matters of religion. But He Himself has established the supreme tribunal for church matters and this we must therefore preserve. Likewise, they say, because the kernel of truth found in the shadows of the old covenant must be present under the new covenant, therefore in the new covenant there must also in the same way be established such a tribunal or court. Again, they say that Christ must have a better order under the papacy in the new covenant than the people had in the church of the old covenant. Therefore this kind of tribunal today can be omitted even less than in the old covenant. For if the order of the church of the old covenant was beautiful, how much more beautiful is it today under Christ?

We ought to give careful thought to the explanation and refutation of this argument.

I reply:

1. For instance, God Himself under the old covenant shows by many examples that His believers are not so bound in religious matters to that judgment tribunal that they could not from time to time depart from this procedure in legal cases. For the Sanhedrin often injected into the divine law ungodly forms of worship and corrupt doctrine and defended it. For this reason God raised up the prophets who condemned these activities. And although they condemned the prophets, the apostles, and Christ Himself, nevertheless we know that their condemnation of the abuses of the Jewish leaders was correct. Christ also had

something to say about this, "Beware of false prophets," Matt. 7:15. Lyra, a very learned man who was born a Jew, has written a useful book which explains the Old Testament; and concerning this point he says that even in our day among the Jews whatever is decreed by the rabbis must be accepted by everyone without contradiction. Thus if a rabbi says that right is left, they must believe this. But we very properly describe them as blind leaders.

2. There is a difference between the old and new covenants. In the Old Testament there was the rule of priests, that is, the church was regulated in the same way as the state. Hence in Heb. 9:1 it is said, "They had an earthly sanctuary," that is, a worldly or physical sanctuary. For the priests and Levites had civil duties attached to their office. But in the New Testament it is a royal priesthood, as Peter calls it in 1 Peter 2:9, where the church has officers who in their own special way are spiritual priests before God. Therefore Christ, because His kingdom is not of this world, John 18:36, says to His servants in Luke 22:25–6, "The kings of the gentiles exercise lordship over them . . . but not so with you." Therefore we have in this spiritual realm one Head, Christ, and to Him "all judgment has been committed by the Father," John 5:22.

3. Let us get closer to the matter. This statement in Deut. 17:8ff. is not speaking of the doctrine which has been commanded or of the dogmas of the faith or religious controversies, but of ceremonial and civil matters. For it clearly says that the judgment pertains to a person's rights or penalties, between different kinds of shedding blood or evaluating cases, that is, whether the penalty should involve death or not. For in civil and ceremonial cases of this kind the opinions pronounced by a higher court take precedence in authority. We appeal lawsuits from lower to higher courts and also of law which is divinely established or granted, just as in the Roman Empire in civil cases an appeal could be made to the imperial court. But this must not be understood of the decreeing of dogmas, as the examples of the prophets, of Christ, and the apostles show.

4. In the Vulgate, Deut. 17:10 reads, "You shall do whatever they say . . . and teach you according to the law of the Lord." From this it is clear that they did not have the authority for each to do whatever he wished, as the popes have assumed for themselves, but they were bound to the law of the Lord, and if they judged contrary to this, their decision was null and void. But Pighius contends that neither in the Hebrew, the Greek, nor the Aramaic language does it read this way, but rather, it only reads, in vv. 10–11, this way: "You shall act according to the word of the Law which they have taught you and according to the judgment which they shall tell you." He is trying to say that this must be believed absolutely without question. But he is in great error. For when it says, "The judges shall judge the truth for you," this he understands as if it were a kind of promise that they could not err, and it is a mandate as to what the judges must do. For

the future tense is used for imperatives, as is common in the sacred language, and it is especially evident in the Decalog. Likewise in the statement in Matt. 2:7, "The lips of the priest shall guard knowledge (in place of "must guard") and they shall require (in place of "should require") the Law from your mouth because he is the messenger of the Lord of hosts." Thus the meaning has to be that the judges must render a truthful judgment, and this cannot happen unless they follow the law of God and obey these laws. But if the high court, whoever they may be, pronounces contrary to the law of God, then Mal. 2:4–9 shows what must be done, for He says, " 'My covenant was with Levi,' says the Lord of hosts, 'a covenant of life and death and I gave it to him for fear. The law of truth was in his mouth and there was no evil found on his lips . . . but you have departed from the way and have caused many to stumble at the Law. You have nullified the covenant of Levi,' says the Lord of hosts. 'For this reason I am making you despised and humiliated before all the people, since you have not kept My ways and have shown partiality in handling the Law.' "

5. A consideration of the terminology in Deut. 17:8 will shed some light. Because of the difficult and ambiguous use of the word *pala'*, which means that something is hidden, and because things under a veil are hidden, this not only seems marvelous to us but also beyond our comprehension. Thus the Septuagint translated it to say, "If a matter is too lofty because it is beyond understanding and the common experience, then it must be referred to a higher court." Thus Prov. 30:18, "There are three things which are hidden or veiled from me"; Ps. 118:23, "This is the Lord's doing. It is marvelous in our eyes," that is, veiled and hidden.

Scripture also uses another word with this meaning and this we must also carefully ponder, v. 9, *nagad*, "They will show you the judicial decision." This showing is something public and in a sense is pointed out with the finger and shows what ought to be done when the man is brought to the position which is a public matter and against which he cannot contradict. But God did not will that His judgments be only court matters but things by which the Israelites were instructed concerning the will of the Lord.

From all these points it is clear that the papists are not able to demonstrate that their orders and arrangements, their succession and its overarching authority have been established by God, so that a person cannot refute or reject or repudiate them; because they themselves have turned aside from the way of the Lord and are making their pronouncements not only outside of but contrary to His Word.

III. Related to this argument is this point: It is impossible that Christ under the new covenant would provide to His church less certainty and assurance in matters of religion than in the old covenant which was given to the synagogue where the one supreme tribunal of judgment was established to ward off schisms and dissensions, and to this tribunal all could come with their most difficult questions. Therefore they say that just as there was at one time a tribunal in Jerusalem, so today we have the see of the vicar of Christ at Rome.

I reply: There is great diversity for the church under each covenant. At one time the whole church was in one definite geographical area and it was not yet so widespread that it was difficult to establish a form of tribunal where all could be governed by it. But today in the New Testament era the church is not so limited to a definite place or included under a definite line of thinking, so that, despised throughout the whole world as it is, it cannot be restricted to one such form of legal system or physical center. There is one Word of God to which we know that all Christians are bound.

IV. The opponents want Christ in the New Testament to have sanctified and confirmed this order of theirs, e.g., in Matt. 23:2–3 Christ says, "The scribes and Pharisees sit in Moses' seat, so practice and observe whatever they tell you." From this they infer that since it was necessary for the ancient Jews to believe and obey the scribes and Pharisees because they sat in Moses' seat and from among them came those of whom it is said, "The lips of the priest guard knowledge and they shall require the Law from his mouth," Mal. 2:7; likewise, "If he is not willing to obey, he shall die and the evil shall be driven from your midst," Deut. 17:11; even more, then, they ought to hear the Roman popes who sit in Peter's seat, the chief of the apostles and to whom Christ said, "I will give to you the keys of the kingdom of heaven and whatsoever you shall loose on earth shall be loosed in heaven . . ." Matt. 16:19; again, "Feed My sheep," John 21:17.

I reply: 1. Christ in the passage cited certainly establishes no judicial tribunal such as in ancient times had existed among the people with their counsel of the seventy elders. But as He undertakes to condemn the life and morals of the scribes and Pharisees and what a foul example they were setting for the people, He first distinguishes life from teaching. For they held the ordered office or duty of teaching and interpreting the Law and they read both Moses and the prophets to the people on every Sabbath in the synagogues. Thus, lest they offend the people by their life and at the same time spurn the Word of God and the teaching of the Law, Christ teaches this distinction: As regards the scribes and Pharisees sitting on Moses' seat, that is, as it concerns their teaching of divine truths which were in accord with the Law received through Moses, the people should hear them. But they should not follow their example as they applied these truths to their life and practices. But what a similarity there is between this practice and that of the papists for people who must simply obey and believe the seat at Rome in all matters which the popes determine and decree!

2. We must also understand that the seat has two aspects. One is "the seat

of the scornful" in Ps. 1:1, a term which they interpret in the sense of an evil word or deed by some person. The second is the "seat of Moses," where Moses' words are read and set forth in a simple way, as the scribes were accustomed to do. This, Christ, in undertaking to condemn the tradition of the scribes and Pharisees, along with their superstitions and life, first said this, lest He seem to be speaking contemptuously of their office itself. Therefore, insofar as they were in Moses' seat, He wanted them to be held in honor. But regarding the rest of their position He says, "Woe unto you," and "beware." Likewise Chrysostom says in his *Homilia* on Matthew 23 [73072, re Matt. 23:1, MPG 58.668], "Christ says, 'Do what they state must be done, for they are not preaching their own ideas but those things which God had commanded Moses.'" Therefore, since, as I said, there are two seats, we must consider on which seat a person is sitting. "For the seat does not make one a priest, but a priest makes the seat, nor can his location make a man holy but a man makes his place holy." But the Roman pontiffs have recently demonstrated that they are not sitting in Moses' seat, nor Peter's, but in "the seat of the scornful" and of "scoffers," as Peter calls them in 2 Peter 3:3. For what is taught in Scripture regarding Christ and eternal life is a farce and a joke to them. There are many earnest admonitions about this matter by many godly people which must not be despised.

V. They believe that in the New Testament through the call Christ has given the promise that the Holy Spirit will always be with all who are in the ordained ministry so that in establishing, treating, and judging things which pertain to religion, they can never err, cf. Is. 59:21; John 14:16–17, 26; 16:13; 1 Tim. 3:15; Matt. 28:20; Eph. 4:11–14.

I reply: 1. All these promises are general, that God will always in His church raise up faithful teachers through whom He wills to be present with His Spirit to teach, to treat, to spread, and to retain the truth of His Word in the church, and there will always be sound teachers everywhere. For in order that there may always be a church, so also there will always be true teachers, but these promises are not tied to certain persons, to a certain succession, or a certain seat. For Paul says to the Ephesian elders in Acts 20:30, "From among yourselves shall arise men who speak perverse things, to lead away disciples after them"; cf. John 10:12; Matt. 7:15; 2 Peter 2:1; Matt. 24:24. Thus John in 1 John 4:1 warns that he must not "believe every spirit, but test the spirits whether they are of God." And how are we to test them? Is. 8:20–22, "To the Law and to the testimonies; if I do not speak according to this Word, there will be no light of dawn for them . . . they will be cast into darkness"; cf. Gal. 1:8; Matt. 23:8, "You are not to be called rabbi. For one is your teacher and you are brothers." For of this Teacher who is called "heavenly," it says in Matt. 17:5, "Hear Him." 1 Peter 4:11, "If a person speaks, let him speak as the oracle of God." Therefore Paul says in

2 Cor. 1:24, "Not that we lord it over your faith." And 1 Cor. 14:29, "Let two or three prophets speak and let the others judge."

2. We must observe that these are promises which allow a certain limitation or restriction. For, to be sure, the Spirit is promised in the old covenant to the prophets, e.g., Is. 59:21, but on condition that they do not turn aside from the Word and doctrine of God. In the New Testament the promise is given in the same way to the apostles in John 14:16 and 16:13, namely, the Holy Spirit is promised, but not His fullness but only "the first fruits." For even in them the flesh remained. Thus Paul in Rom. 8:23 says, "We have the first fruits of the Spirit." The Spirit Himself is given to the apostles, not to use as they pleased, but "that He might lead them into all truth." And the word which Christ uses is "truth," John 17:17, and thus He also says in John 14:26, "He will bring to your remembrance all things which I have said to you." Christ also promises that He Himself will also be with the apostles and the church "always even to the end of the age," Matt. 28:20, but if they "teach them all that I have commanded you." Also it is said that the church is "the pillar of truth and the foundation of truth," but yet the bishop must know "how he must behave himself in the house of God," 1 Tim. 3:15. And finally Christ gives gifts to His teachers, Eph. 4:11, but they "must not neglect the gifts," 1 Tim. 4:14 and "rekindle" them, 2 Tim. 1:6. But by what things were they to be rekindled? By the things "which you have heard from me before many witnesses" and these things you shall "entrust to faithful men," 2 Tim. 2:2. The papists overlook all of these passages and take to themselves unlimited license to establish and command whatever tyranny they wish upon the church with no basis in God's Word.

VI. They contend that this privilege was given especially to the seat of the blessed Peter, that is, to the Roman pontiff, because it is written in Matt. 16:19, "I will give to you the keys of the kingdom of heaven and whatsoever you shall bind on earth shall be bound in heaven and whatsoever you shall loose on earth will be loosed also in heaven." To this passage they add this gloss or interpretation: "Whatsoever you bind," that is, whatsoever obligatory decree you make for the sake of religion and bind this on men on earth, shall also be bound in heaven. They use as proof texts Is. 8:16, "Bind up the testimony and seal the law among my disciples"; Matt. 23:4, "For they shall bind heavy burdens, hard to bear and place them on men's shoulders." "And whatsoever you loose," that is, even if it pertains to something established in Scripture, yet because of your authority, to whom you give a dispensation, that is done also in heaven. As proof texts they cite Matt. 5:19, "He who breaks one of the least of these commandments . . ."; Luke 22:31–32, Christ had predicted that Satan would "sift" the rest of the apostles, but, "I have prayed for you, Simon, that your faith does not fail and that you will comfort your brothers." And finally, in Matt. 16:18, they find that "the gates of hell shall not prevail against the church" which is built upon Peter.

I reply: 1. This is a false interpretation of Scripture, for what Christ had said of the orderly authority of the minister which consists in forgiving and retaining sins in the name of Christ, this they interpret of some unspecified power to make up laws and pass them off in the church in direct contradiction to Christ's clear explanation. And the words which Christ speaks to Peter pertain also to the rest of the disciples as the entire context of the account teaches. For Christ has asked them all who they say He is. Peter replies in the name of all of them and makes a confession of their common faith. Therefore what Christ said to him must be applied commonly to them all. Hence also in Matt. 16:18 He says to all the apostles, "Whatsoever you shall bind on earth shall be bound also in heaven and whatsoever you loose on earth shall be loosed in heaven." After the resurrection, when He showed Himself alive, He breathed on them and said, John 20:22, "Receive the Holy Spirit. Whosoever sins you remit, they are remitted to them and whosoever you retain, they are retained." From these passages it is clear that the keys of the kingdom of heaven were not given only to Peter, nor is the primacy and dominion of the Roman pontiff in any way established by this line of reasoning.

2. Church history testifies that this boasting by the papists that the Roman pontiffs in matters of religion cannot err is an empty idea. For of Peter himself it is shown that he could err and that he did indeed do so shamefully very soon afterward on that night, Luke 22:58, cf. also Gal. 2:11. It is told of Pope Marcellinus that he sacrificed to idols. Jerome writes that Pope Liberius had communed with heretics. Gratian writes the same thing regarding Anastasius in dist. 19 [*Decreti*, pp. 63–64]. The sixth general council condemned Pope Honorius as a Monothelete. In sum, the descriptions of the antichrist in 2 Thess. 2:3, whose coming will be with all deception of iniquity, and Rev. 17:1–9, the woman who "sits above the many waters and upon the seven hills," cry out against the papacy.

The canon lawyers and the scholastics all believe, dist. 40 [*Decreti*. p. 146], "If the pope is condemned for neglecting his own salvation and that of his brothers, is remiss and unprofitable in his duties and above all silent regarding the good, is a hindrance to himself and to all others even to the point where he takes with him countless hosts of people, leading them by his own hand to hell and he shall be beaten with more blows in eternity, yet no mortal presumes to condemn his guilty actions because he who will himself judge all is to be judged by none unless he is found to have strayed from the faith." Therefore they are confessing that the pope at Rome can err. Therefore in opposition to this boasting of the papists regarding the seat of Peter, it is correct to cite dist. 40, "It is not easy to stand in the place of Peter and Paul and to occupy the chair of those who rule with Christ. Thus it is said that they are not the sons of saints who hold the places of the saints, but those who do their works" [ibid., p. 145]. And *Causa* 2, Quest. 7, cites Jerome's letter to Heliodorus, "Not all bishops are true bishops. You hear Peter, but consider Judas. You support Stephen, but look at Nicolaus.[4] The worthiness of the Christian does not establish church practices. Cornelius the centurion was still a gentile when he was cleansed by the gift of the Holy Spirit; the youthful Daniel judged the elders. It is not easy to stand in the place of Paul and hold the high office of Peter, both of whom are now reigning with Christ. 'Salt which has lost its flavor is worth nothing but to be cast out and trodden underfoot.'"[5]

3. In regard to the statement "Upon this rock I will build My church," Matt. 16:18, I admit there are many different ancient interpretations. Some say the rock is Peter, such as Cyprian, Jerome, and Ambrose. But some say the church is not built on Peter but on Christ who is the rock and foundation of the church. For the apostle says, "No other foundation can anyone lay than that which has been laid down, which is Christ Jesus," 1 Cor. 3:11. But others understand this rock to refer to the faith and confession of Peter when he said, "You are the Christ the Son of the living God." In this variety of opinions among the ancients from which the papists prove their position, the first is preferable to the others. Indeed the text itself shows quite clearly what Christ wants us to understand. He says, "You are Peter" (*petrus*, a rock). Peter received his name from Christ the rock (*petra*, a rock base). And upon this rock base the church is built, as Peter himself interprets in 1 Peter 2:6, "Behold, I lay in Zion a stone, a cornerstone, chosen, precious," and v. 5, "You are built upon Him as living stones, a spiritual house, acceptable to God." Further, who with any real confidence can assert without hesitation that Christ could have laid for the foundation of His church a person whom, very quickly after, in the same chapter, Matt. 16:23, He would call "Satan"? But even if we grant that Christ said this about the person of Peter, what does this have to do with the Roman pontiffs? They are, they say, Peter's successors. And let them first prove on the basis of good authorities that Peter was even at Rome. Let them prove that Peter was made bishop by the rest of the apostles. Or why do they not at least grant the same privileges to the see of Antioch where Peter did live for certain? From all of these points it is much more certain that those who admire Rome so greatly can prove nothing sure or certain from this passage to establish primacy of their pontiff.

---

[4] Nicolaius, who some feel is referred to in Rev. 2:6, founded one of the many gnostic sects in Asia Minor and practiced immorality.

[5] The reference to Nicolaius occurs in Gratian's *Decreti, causa* 2, *quaestio* 7; *CIC*, 492.

VII. Even if the papists should agree that individual Roman bishops from time to time could err, yet they assert that the college of cardinals and their councils cannot err, because it is written in 1 Tim. 3:15, "The church is the pillar and foundation of truth"; and in Matt. 18:17, "Tell it to the church, if he will not hear the church, let him be to you a heathen and a publican."

I reply: Church history shows that heresies have often arisen from bishops themselves and from their colleagues, as in the case of Samosatenus, the bishop of Antioch, and Macedonius and Nestorius, bishops of Constantinople. It is also obvious that councils have often erred and not only in the case of particular men, such as Cyprian in regard to rebaptism, but also in general, universally and completely, as was the case with the Councils at Milan, Sirmio, and Ephesus II. And the papists cannot deny this. Note the statement of Augustine, *De Baptismo contra Donatistas*, 2.3 [MPL 43.127–28], "Who does not know that the sacred canonical Scripture, of the Old and New Testaments, with its own particular words contains that which has authority above all the subsequent writings of bishops, so that there can be no doubt or deception at all as to whether what is thus written in the Scripture is true or right? But the writings of the bishops which were or shall be written after the establishment and acceptance of the canon, and perhaps the wise sermon of someone who is more experienced and has greater authority and judgment than the other bishops and teachers, certainly can be criticized through a council if he has deviated in some way from the truth. And the councils themselves which take place in local regions and provinces are subordinate to the authority of the fuller councils which are universal; and even these plenary councils often correct previous decisions when experience discovers that what was previously unknown and had been hidden was correct. This is done without any ungodly pride or the puffed up arrogance of the stiff-necked person, without the contentiousness of jealousy, but with humility, with universal peace, and Christian charity."

We must also consider what Paul's statement in 1 Tim. 3:15 means. He says, "The church is the pillar of truth." Pastors alone do not make up the church. For, as Aristotle says in regard to a city, "A city does not consist of a doctor and a doctor or of farmer and a farmer, but of a doctor and a farmer." Likewise, the church also does not consist of pastor and pastor or hearer and hearer, but of teachers and learners. Therefore the voice of the church does not bind us to the bishops alone, as if they have the power to devise new dogmas by their own free choice which the rest of the assembly is compelled to accept without hesitation. But the voice of the church shows to us the whole assembly, hearers with the teacher. Now the church hears the voice of its shepherd who is Christ. His Word is the truth in which Christ prays that His sheep may be sanctified, John 17:17. Therefore where this Word is and this truth, there the church is. And the church must be the pillar of this truth and its foundation, that is, it must defend the truth by fighting and contending against errors. For the church is (as Irenaeus says) a kind of repository for treasures in which God brings and stores up the truth of His Word and He must preserve it. Therefore it is not Paul's meaning that whatever the church sets forth is thereby the truth. But Paul means that the church must firmly and faithfully guard the truth which has been committed and entrusted to it by Christ.

Up to this point we have shown the correct understanding regarding the orderly succession of bishops after their call.

III

Now comes the third main point of those things which we have said are required for the faithful teachers or ministers of the church. For he who has been lawfully called brings with him the true voice of doctrine if he himself does not indeed teach false doctrine, but refutes those who teach falsely, rebukes sinners and refutes them, warns his sheep to beware of the voice of the stranger and flee from it, does not remain silent or gloss things over or teaches pleasantries, Is. 30:10. Such a person is not a true or faithful pastor but is called a "hireling," John 10:12, or he is negligent by omitting a part of his ministry which consists of "rebuking the gainsayers," Titus 1:9; or he gives occasion for "the wolf to seize and scatter the sheep," John 10:12, because he causes harm by not prohibiting it when he could and should have done so. The statement of the lawyers is correct, "He who gives occasion for harm may be regarded as having done harm." God in the writings of the prophets calls such men "blind watchmen, . . . dumb dogs not able to bark," Is. 56:10; "those who whitewash walls," Ezek. 13:10; "those who sew cushions under the head of the sleeper and sew pillows under the elbow of the wrong-doer . . . for a handful of barley and a piece of bread," vv. 18–19. God also threatens them with temporal and eternal punishments.

Therefore, regarding the faithfulness of the minister of the church, God says in Jer. 15:19–21, "Thus says the Lord: 'If you return, I will restore you and you shall stand before Me and if you separate the precious from the worthless, you shall be as My mouth. Let them turn to you, but you shall not turn to them. I will make you for this people a brazen fortified wall. They will fight against you, but they will not prevail because I am with you to save you and deliver you,' says the Lord, 'And I will deliver you out of the hand of the wicked and redeem you from the hand of the strong.'"

IV

The fourth section on duties which belong to the teachers of the church pertains to the gifts of teaching. In general it is required in all that they "hold the foundation of sound teaching," 1 Tim. 3:9, "holding fast the sure Word as he has been taught." Of Timothy, Paul says in 2 Tim. 3:10, "You have followed my teaching." But not only must they hold to the sound teaching but they must also be "able to teach others," 2 Tim. 2:2, "Commit the things which you have heard from me among many witnesses to faithful men who are able to teach others." Paul does not want those "who do not understand what they are saying or asserting," 1 Tim. 1:7. To such can be applied the saying, "No one can teach what he does not know."

But still among these gifts there is a great diversity or difference. Thus the apostle Paul warns in 1 Cor. 12:6ff., "There are varieties of activities. . . . To each one is given the manifestation of the Spirit for the common benefit. To one is given through the Spirit the word of wisdom, to one the word of knowledge according to the same Spirit, to another faith in the same Spirit, to another the grace of healing, in the one Spirit the working of miracles, to another prophecy, to another the discerning of spirits, to another different kinds of languages, to another the interpretation of words. The one and the same Spirit works all of these, dividing them among individuals as He wills," Rom. 12:6ff.; 1 Cor. 14:26. In brief, one person has the gift of instructing the more unlearned, another the gift of exhorting the sluggish, another the gift of comforting the sorrowful, and so forth. And of these gifts some have fewer, some greater, some lesser, some are stronger, some weaker.

And when these added gifts are correctly explained, many disputes are settled which have arisen partly among the teachers [and] partly among the hearers. Thus it is beneficial:

I. that the church not think that the efficacy of the Spirit is tied to these gifts as if it were to be measured on the basis of the greatness or smallness of the gifts. Thus, when the Corinthians were disputing and some said, "I am of Paul," others, "I am of Apollos," [and] others, "I am of Peter," [then] Paul says, 1 Cor. 3:5[–7], "What is Apollos, or what [is] Paul? They are ministers through whom you believed as the Lord gave to each. For neither he that plants is anything nor he that waters, but God, who gives the increase." And God does this so that, when some are turned to God and believe, this should not be credited to eloquence or other gifts but to the power of God, 1 Cor. 2:4–5. Thus, when many wanted to prefer Peter to Paul, Paul says, 2 Cor. 11:30, "If I must boast, I will boast of the things that concern my weakness" . . . "so that the power of Christ may dwell in me," 2 Cor. 12:9; cf. Gal. 2:6[–8].

Therefore no one should puff himself up because of [his] gifts and despise others as beneath himself. Nor should anyone despair over his own ministry because of his lesser or fewer gifts but should in any case labor faithfully in both hope and prayer for divine blessing. Moerlin used to say, "Work honestly, speak truthfully and pray diligently."[6]

II. For the argument about the right of interpretation and the authority of synods can be very simply and most correctly settled on this basis. For those things stand not by praetorian (as it is called) authority and power but because God always opens the minds of some "so that they understand Scripture," Luke 24:45, that is, it is God's usual pattern to give to some in the church the gift of so searching and teaching the fountains and sources of interpretations: (1) from the words or tongues, (2) from the context, (3) from a comparison of statements, and (4) from the analogy of faith, so that on the basis of that information, the others, upon comparing passages of Scripture, may see that this is the native and true meaning, 1 Cor. 14:29, 32. Thus, when the opinions of many are compared in the councils, then through these discussions and instructions the sources and bases for settling controversies and refuting corruptions are pointed out in such a way that others, less trained, may therefrom know and see what is true [and] what [is] false. In this way, I believe, the rest of the firmer ones are instructed and strengthened. And to this end also the interpretations of the ancients are cited so that the agreement of the ancient church with ours can be shown. For the church is catholic, that is, God in all ages raises up some in the church and equips [them] with gifts, who defend the true belief; and yet it remains, as Augustine writes to Jerome in Epist. 19 [(82), MPL 33.277], "I read other writers in such a way that be they as strong as they may in holiness and doctrine, I would not consider it truth because they wrote this way, but because they were able to persuade me either through other canonical authors or through sound reasoning that they do not depart from the truth."

III. Since among the doctors of the church some are weaker, some purer in doctrine, [and] some have their warts—and they [are] either very dangerous, as when they touch on the very foundation, or more tolerable, as those who leave the foundation stand—Paul's rule regarding the foundation and those things which are built on it applies here, 1 Cor. 3:12–13. Therefore we should read the fathers with discretion, for each has his warts.

From this rule of Paul we can establish this: Which blemishes can be tolerated in the church and which are errors on account of which we must sever fellowship with them; and those who cling to those errors cannot be recognized as the true church. Certainly, when the false teachers of the Galatians attacked

---

6   Joachim Moerlin, 1514–71, Chemnitz's predecessor as general superintendent at Brunswick. He had served as Luther's chaplain and had great influence on Chemnitz. This reference is interesting, because it is almost the only personal reference in the entire *Loci*, and it is made only in passing about a man whom Chemnitz probably saw every day for most of his professional career.

the foundation, even though in other articles they did not believe incorrectly, yet [Paul] says, Gal. 5:12, "I wish those who trouble you were cut off," and in 4:11, "I fear that I have labored in vain among you."

V

The fifth main point is about the life and conduct of the ministers of the church. In this chapter we deal with the Donatist controversy. The very form of the election shows that piety of life, seriousness of conduct, and uprightness in the ministry are helpful for the edification of the church, Titus 1:7–8; 1 Tim. 3:2–4. And to the apostles and ministers of the Word applies especially what Christ says, Matt. 5:16: The light of their teaching must shine, that men may not only hear their voice but also see good works and glorify the heavenly Father. Cf. 1 Peter 2:12. For because ministers of the Word are exposed to many injuries, Peter does not want them to dispute much verbally with others, but that by piety of life and uprightness of conduct they may so adorn their ministry that the enemies are put to shame. And here it is correct to apply, from the lesser to the greater, what is written regarding servants and wives, 1 Tim. 6:1, "that the name of the Lord and [His] doctrine be not blasphemed"; cf. 1 Peter 3:1. But Paul speaks clearly about the ministry in 1 Tim. 4:12; 2 Thess. 3:9; Titus 2:7–8. Cf. 1 Peter 5:3.

We can read many well-put statements about this matter in the fathers. Jerome said, "The hearts of the weak are pierced by the life of an evil presbyter; those who live in carnal security fall more freely into sin." To Heliodorus he writes, Epist. 3: "Your (that is, a bishop's) home and life are set up as it were in public view; it is a teacher of public discipline; whatever you do, everyone thinks he should do. Beware lest you do either what some want to censure or what compels them to sin if they imitate you."[7] Gregory [says], "When something is censured in a priest, because of his sin, the very structure of our religion is disturbed." Leo, "Examples are better than words." Jerome writes to Nepotian [Epistle 52, MPL 22.533], "Do not let your works subvert your teaching, lest when you speak in the church someone gets angry and replies: 'Why do you not practice what you preach?'" Gregory, "The authority of teaching is overthrown when the word is not supported by the deed." Again, "Whose life is despised, his preaching will also be held in contempt." Jerome, "The life of a priest must be such that he grasps the truth with his mind and lets it show in his entire attitude, so that whatever he does and whatever he says becomes the teaching of the people." Gregory of Nazianzus, "He who teaches well and lives an evil life builds with one hand and tears down with the other."

Therefore if ordinary Christians polluted with sin are commanded to be

---

[7] This is an incorrect reference. We have been unable to locate it elsewhere.

separated by excommunication because "a little leaven leavens the whole lump," 1 Cor. 5:6, far greater severity should be applied in correcting the life and in cutting off the wickedness of a minister of the Word, because by their wicked life the Holy Spirit is grieved by the godly, they themselves offend the godly, [and] lead many astray by their example, and hamper the hearing of doctrine itself. For here applies especially what Christ says, Matt. 18:6. "Whoever causes one of these little ones who believe in Me to sin, it would be better for him that a millstone were fastened around his neck and he were drowned in the depths of the sea." Just as the severity of the ancient church in deposing or excommunicating clergy for public and scandalous sins is described in Gratian from the statements of many fathers and decrees of councils, so Augustine, "No one does more harm in the church than one who, acting perversely, possesses the name or rank of holiness and priest. For no one dares to condemn him as delinquent, and the guilt is greatly extended into examples when a sinner is honored out of respect of rank."

Now, from this the Donatists took occasion for their schism, which later turned into a heresy through stubbornness and the addition of erroneous opinions. This is a summary of the account, which is found recorded in many places in Augustine.

Before the times of Constantine the Great, in an extremely severe persecution, it was decreed under threat of death that individual Christians, but especially bishops, were to turn over sacred books to inquisitors to be burned. Then many, in fear of punishments, turned them over. Others, who were braver, were punished by imprisonments, exiles, and various penalties, and some were even put to death because they refused to give up their books. But when peace was restored to the churches under Constantine, the braver people accused those who had been weaker of "defecting" and excommunicated them. But particularly Caecilian, who had been bishop of Carthage during that persecution, was accused of being such a traitor. For so they called those who had given up sacred books at the command of the persecutors. And for these reason the people, under the instigation of Donatus, left the communion of that Caecilian and did not want to use his ministry, especially in the administration of the sacraments. Some chose for themselves a different bishop, establishing a separate ministry for themselves by building another altar and baptistry. But when Bishop Caecilian steadfastly rejected what was done, the case was brought to Constantine the Great, from whom many of the assembled bishops learned of the case. Therefore Caecilian was deemed innocent in the judgment of the bishops.

But the Donatists, with the separation once an [accomplished] fact, because they were unwilling to return to communion with Caecilian, then claimed that even if Caecilian had not been such a traitor, yet he had been ordained by a certain Felix, who had been such a traitor, and therefore he could not be a true bishop and could not perform the ministry beneficially. And so it began to be claimed that sacraments which were administered by ministers polluted with sin were not efficacious.

But when the churches in the rest of the world did not approve that line of thought of the Donatists, [the latter] proudly boasted that only in Africa among the Donatists were there still true churches left. As time went on, it began to be claimed: The true church is not present where ungodly people are tolerated in the communion, and those who do not leave such a group, if they come with them to the same altar, they are polluted by this communion and those polluted are damned. They also held that among heretics who err in any area of teaching, the true sacraments either are not given or those which had been received earlier were nullified. Thus they are called Donatists or Donatians who determine the efficacy of the sacraments on the basis of the worthiness and goodness of the minister and who dream that in this life the church is absolutely pure, without spot or wrinkle.

It is worth the effort to consider the principal arguments which the Donatists used in this controversy, for in this way light is shed on the whole conflict. We shall therefore gather and briefly touch on some things from Augustine. Those who are zealous for godliness can consult his lengthy writings on this matter in the seventh volume.

1. The principal point was this: What a person does not have, he cannot give to another. Godless ministers do not have faith and the Holy Spirit. Therefore when they baptize, preach, [and] absolve, they cannot give the Holy Spirit, faith, [and] the grace of God, for they themselves lack these gifts. Augustine replies and concedes the whole argument, namely that the ministry, whether good or evil, does not cleanse the conscience or bestow the Holy Spirit, faith, or grace. For these things belong to Christ. And Augustine draws the foundation for this reply from the statement of John the Baptizer, Matt. 3:11. Thus Augustine distinguishes between the visible administration of the sacraments and the invisible grace of God. As regards the visible administration, good [ministers] baptize and evil [ministers] baptize. But He whose is both the visible ministry and the invisible grace baptizes through them both. Thus he says, *Contra Crescon.*, 2.21 [MPL 43.482], "Good men and evil men can apply the water, but only He who is always good can wash away [sin]." Therefore we must understand that grace always belongs to God, that the sacrament always belongs to God, but that only the administration belongs to man. He that is good works with God, 1 Cor. 3:9, but if [the minister] is evil, God through him performs the visible form of the sacraments, but He Himself bestows the invisible grace. And here aptly apply Ps. 60:11; Jer. 17:5, 7; Ps. 3:8; Rom. 4:16.

II. Here they also wrested the statement in Matt. 7:18, "An evil tree cannot bring forth good fruit." [They say that] therefore if he who baptizes is evil, those who are baptized by him cannot be made holy. Augustine replies on the basis of another Scripture passage, 1 Cor. 3:7. To be sure, this statement does not apply completely to this point, yet it squares with it to a degree. For Paul also deals with the efficacy of Baptism, which some of the Corinthians wanted to measure by the worthiness and the gifts of the persons. For they contended among themselves in such a way that some said that Peter's baptism was better, for he had lived with Christ in this life while Paul was His enemy and persecutor. On the other hand, others said that the baptism of Paul was better and more efficacious, for he was in the third heaven, where Peter was not yet. But Paul rejects this contention and says [cf. 1 Cor. 3:5–8], "What are we but ministers of Christ by whom you believed? I planted, Apollos watered, but he who planted and he who watered are one." And so, if we consider the efficacy of Baptism or of the [other] sacraments, we must not fix our attention on the minister, but we must look to Christ, who is the Lord of the minister and efficacious through him.

III. The Donatists were especially agitated by the statement in Ecclus. 34:30 [Vulgate; literally translated it reads], "One who is baptized by the dead—what does his washing profit?" [*Qui baptizatur a mortuo, quid prodest lavatio illius?*] From this they concluded that because sinners and the ungodly are dead in the eyes of God, their baptism profits nothing. And they cried: What more evil thing can be said than that one who is polluted purifies another, [that] the unclean washes clean, [that] the impure cleanses, [that] the unbelieving gives faith, [and that] a guilty one makes one innocent? In refuting this objection Augustine goes to great pains in many places. But he keeps this basic position, that it is true and cannot be rejected for any reason, that the ministry is of God Himself, but the administration is of man. Hence Paul writes, Eph. 5:25[–27], that it is "Christ who loves the church and sanctifies it, cleansing it with the washing of water in the Word, that He might present it to Himself a glorious church. But how Christ Himself is neither polluted nor filthy nor impure nor unfaithful nor guilty.

Those things are indeed rightly said, but he who wants to have a complete explanation of that passage [Ecclus. 34:30] ought to look at the phrase. Sirach says, "He who is baptized from the dead" [*baptizomenos apo nekrou*]. Here he is not speaking of the New Testament baptism but he is using that word in a general way, which means "to dip," "to immerse," and "to wash away." And properly he is discussing the practice of the Jews that when they returned home from the body of some dead person, they were to purify themselves according to the law of Moses, in case they had touched anything unclean [cf. Num. 19:11–22]. Therefore the wise man [Sirach] does not say "by the dead (*hypo nekrou*)" but "from the dead (*apo nekrou*)." For the LXX translators and Scripture use that word *apo* in a different sense from that in which the Donatists understood it.

This will be clear from an example. Paul says, Acts 13:38–39, "Be it known to you, brothers, that the forgiveness of sins is proclaimed to you through him, . . . and from all the things (*kai apo pantōn*) from which you could not be absolved through the law of Moses, through Him every one who believes is absolved." Here the words *apo pantōn* do not refer to persons through whom we are delivered but to the troubles from which we are delivered. So to be washed clean *apo nekrou* does not denote a person through whom we are baptized, but it refers to the pollution and uncleanness into which they fell who touched dead bodies under the law of Moses, and to be cleansed from it. And therefore Luther is also correct in his translation, "*Wer sich wäscht, wenn er einen Toten angerühret hat*" [who washes himself when he has touched a dead person]. He did not translate according to the sense of the Donatists, "if he lets himself be baptized by a dead person" (*wenn sich einer von einem Toten taufen lässet*).

The Donatists also committed a fraud in this matter by not citing the complete statement, which is this: "If a person who is washed after touching a corpse [*a cadavere*] then touches it again, what does the washing profit him?" Likewise if a person fasts for his sins and then goes away, to do the same things again, who will hear his prayers? or what did his pain profit him? From this whole statement it is easily clear what the wise man meant. No doubt by that simile of washing he points out the levity and folly of those who relapse after repentance into former sins. Therefore just as Peter, 2 Peter 2:22, uses a proverb, "The dog returning to his vomit and the washed sow having returned again to the mire," with which he censures people who return to former licentiousness and sinful conduct, so Sirach uses the simile drawn from those washings and baptizings of the Jews which are also mentioned in the Gospel, John 2:6. So then this passage has absolutely nothing that might establish the error of the Donatists.

IV. They also cite Ps. 141:5, "Let not the oil of the sinner anoint my head." For in the time of Augustine oil was used in the administration of Baptism to show the efficacy of Baptism, that through it we are anointed and endowed with the Holy Spirit.

1. From this the Donatists drew the conclusion that if sinners must not anoint my head with oil, which is a part of [the ritual of] baptism, they must therefore also not anoint my head with water. But Augustine replies: If we must not be baptized by a sinner, then we can receive Baptism from no human being, cf. 1 John 1:8; Ps. 32:6. He also counters with these examples that Christ Himself used the ministry of Judas the thief, and that Paul, Phil. 1:15, does not condemn the ministry of those who "preach Christ out of contention, not [out of] a pure heart," and that in Phil. 2:21 he complains about unfaithful ministers who "seek their own interests, not those of Christ," and yet he does not add that [people] should not listen to them, but he leaves them in the ministry. Gregory

of Nazianzus also in this case uses this kind of a simile: If an image is pressed into wax, it makes little difference whether it was a gold or a silver or a wooden seal. For the material of the ring bestows nothing on the form of the image. Thus also in the ministry. But Augustine uses this simile: If water is rechanneled into gardens, then the water makes the earth fertile, whether it flows through stone or through wooden channels. Likewise, even if light, shines through impure places, yet it is not polluted and is received from pure [sources] unpolluted. Thus although ungodly men perform the ministry, yet the ministry itself is not changed nor is anything taken away from its efficacy. And if the ungodly simply cannot perform the ministry, where is there room for the statement of God? Ps. 50:16–17; cf. 1 Cor. 9:27.

And all these things are indeed rightly said. But if one wants to have a complete solution, he ought to look at the text, consider what precedes and what follows, and see whether it all applies to the present subject. And he will discover that David is discussing nothing less than what is said regarding the administration of the sacraments. For according to true Hebrew the text [of Ps. 141:5], reads thus: "Let a just man correct me and reprove me," and there will be this special oil, which will not "break [KJV] my head," that is, I have that correction as the greatest blessing. Therefore it is the same as if he had said: If a godly man smite me, this will be a greater favor to me than if some ungodly one wanted to anoint my head with oil to flatter me and thus to confirm me in wickedness. For when the godly upbraid us, they bring us back into the way, but when the ungodly sweet-talk us with their favors and flatteries, then they further deceive and finally destroy us.

Let this suffice regarding the unapproved manners of ministers and regarding the first error of the Donatists, who separated themselves from them and regarded their ministry as altogether fruitless. The Schwenkfelders and Anabaptists brought this notion back into the church.

2. The second error of the Donatists was that there is no true Baptism among heretics and schismatics, that is, among those who err in any part of Christian doctrine, and therefore those had to be rebaptized who, having been baptized by them, returned to the church. Augustine opposed this error with the principle that Baptism which is consecrated by the words of the Gospel (that is, if the institution is observed), regardless of where or by whom it is given and received, is the baptism of Christ, which is not changed or polluted by the wickedness of the administrators or the recipients. Therefore a distinction is made between the verity or integrity of Baptism and its power. For the integrity of Baptism it is not important what he who gives or receives [the Baptism] believes, but it is absolutely of great importance for the way of salvation that he who receives it believes, Mark 16:16. If the emperor gives his soldiers a military sign or imprints

on them such a mark as cannot be removed or washed off, then the sign remains, though one defects and becomes an enemy. And if he later returns to emperor, there is no need for a new sign. Thus also as regards Baptism, if it has once been properly performed, there is no need to repeat it.

But the Donatists, to support their error, cite those statements of Scripture in Matt. 7:15–17; John 10:10. But the correct explanation is that there is a difference between those who keep the foundation and build [with] straw on it and those who subvert the foundation itself. Likewise we must distinguish between these two: False teachers of this kind hold errors by which they deceive and destroy those who follow them; on the other hand there are also things that they teach rightly and administer correctly, but these are not false because of those errors. And [Augustine] says that Christ makes this distinction. For cf. Luke 12:1 with Matt. 23:2–3. That is, those things in which they err you are to flee and avoid, for through them they destroy those who have been deceived. But from this it does not follow that those things which they teach rightly and administer correctly are false. Augustine also cites John 13:10 against that rebaptism.

3. The third error of the Donatists was that they believed that a congregation in which some, whether many or few, are evil, is not a true church, even though the voice of true teaching is heard there and the sacraments are properly administered, and that one who in such a congregation, or who, among such and with such, used the ministry of Word and Sacraments was polluted by that communion or did not receive it beneficially.

And here they cited Ps. 1:1; 26:4–6; 50:17–23; 2 Cor. 6:14–18; 2 Thess. 3:6, 14–15; 1 Tim. 5:22; 1 Cor. 5:6–7; Rev. 18:4.

Now, to explain those objections we must note this distinction: When a certain assembly publicly approves and adopts false doctrine, practices sinful forms of worship, and reviles and intensely opposes true teaching, we must certainly leave its communion, lest we be partakers of other men's sins. And the following passages speak of this separation: Ps. 1:1; 26:4; 2 Cor. 6:14; Rev. 18:4.

But when, with purity of doctrine safeguarded, evil ones, whose life is wicked, are mixed with the good in the church, there is a difference, for sometimes wickedness lies hidden, covered by hypocrisy, and then the rule holds: "The church does not judge regarding hidden things." But sometimes wickedness is manifest, and then Paul commands that those who have become polluted with public sins be excommunicated and separated, 1 Cor. 5:4[–5]. And here the godly magistrate must punish such manifest wrongs. But if they fail to exercise the required severity, they certainly sin grievously and to this extent partake in the sins of others. Yet nothing is thereby lost to the ministry as regards its efficacy. The rest of the members of the church are not polluted by this. For it is like the kingdom of heaven, that is, the church in this life [is like] a net, Matt.

13:47, in which good and bad fish are caught; a field, Matt. 13:24[–30], in which wheat and tares grow at the same time, a mixture which Christ commands us to endure, if a change cannot be made without damage to the wheat; a threshing floor, Matt. 3:12, where the wheat lies mixed with chaff; a flock, Ezek. 34:17, where sheep and goats are together; a feast, Matt. 22:11, where the good take their places with the evil; a gathering, Matt. 25:1, where both wise and foolish virgins are together; a vine, John 15:1, in which there are both living and dry branches. And such indeed is the church of Christ in this world; but the complete separation and purging will take place finally on the last day.

Augustine has some very apt statements on this matter. For example, Epist. 152, "Whoever will live well in the church, the sins of others do not prejudice him, because, as the apostle says, 'Each will bear his own sin,' Gal. 6[:5]. Therefore the sharing of evils does not defile anyone by participation in the sacraments but by the consent of the perpetrators." And *Contra Cresconium Grammaticum*, 2.34 [Epistle 152 (141), MPL 33.579], "Cyprian wrote to the presbyter Maximus, 'The fact that we see tares in the church does not mean we should leave the church.' We must only work that we may be fruitful, so that when the grain begins to be laid up in the Lord's storehouses we may receive the fruit of our own work and labor. And the apostle says, 'In a great house are vessels of gold and vessels of clay, to honor and to dishonor,' 2 Tim. 2:20. Let us endeavor and labor as much as we can to be a gold or silver vessel. But to the Lord alone, to whom also the iron rod has been given, has been given the authority to break the vessels of clay. And let no one claim for himself what the Father has granted only to the Son, so as to think that he can now either use the threshing fan to thresh and clear the chaff away or separate all the tares from the wheat by human judgment." Again, Epist. 162, "Those to whom evil ones are pleasing in union, they share with the evil ones. But those who are displeased with evildoers and cannot change them share not their actions but the altar of Christ." Again, Epist. 164, "Even known evildoers are not lacking in the church if either the power is lacking to keep them from communion or if some reason to keep the peace stands in the way." Epist. 166, "What is there for us regarding the burdens of others except to correct either by rebuking or by some form of discipline? But those whom we cannot correct, but necessity compels that they share the sacraments with us, we still do not partake of their sins, which does not happen except by consent, support, or imitation."

LOCUS [XVIII]

The Sacraments

[MELANCHTHON'S TEXT]

At the outset let us establish a simple definition of the word. In current church terminology, "sacrament" of course means a ceremony established in the Gospel to be a testimony to the promise which belongs to the Gospel, that is, the promise of reconciliation or grace.

Profane people think that the sacraments are signs of profession which distinguish us from other people, [we] who have as it were joined this covenant, just as the toga distinguished the Romans from people of other nations; or [they think the sacraments] are symbols of certain functions regarding other people. For as at one time in making treaties it was the practice to eat meat of sacrifices together, so many now think in keeping with this human custom that the Lord's Supper is only such a mark of a mutual covenant among people. But although many purposes have been ordained for the sacraments, yet far at the head of all of these must be placed this chief purpose, namely that they might be signs of God's will toward us, that is, added testimonies of the promise of grace. And we must also consider the whole church, in which immediately after the fall of Adam, when the promise of grace had been given, ceremonies were added, namely the sacrifices of Adam which were kindled from heaven; a lamb was offered which was consumed by fire from heaven. This signified the passion of the coming Sacrifice, promise of which had been given [Gen. 3:15] and which was a testimony of reconciliation.

Then when the promise was renewed, a new testimony was added, namely circumcision. Finally, with the light of doctrine again restored, there was added the slaying of a lamb and other ceremonies. Thus in the church there were added to the proclamation of the Gospel the rites of Baptism and the Lord's Supper. I shall speak about others later. These rites are not human spectacles, like the tragedies of the Greeks, which were set up so that some kind of commemoration of things done might be handed down to posterity; but they have far higher purposes.

For first, they are signs of God's will toward us, or testimonies of promised grace. Hence Paul says of Abraham that he received circumcision as a sign of the righteousness of faith [Rom. 4:11], that is, testimony by which God testified that he had been received into grace. And because the sacraments are added to the promises, therefore just as the promise must be received by faith, so it is necessary in the use of the sacraments that there be added the faith which looks to the promise.

1355

Many purposes can be added thereafter: confession, distinction from other [religious] groups, celebration of a public gathering, [and] a reminder of a certain work. Thus the Lord's Supper is first a testimony of the grace of God toward us. It reminds us of the whole Gospel, [and] of the death and resurrection of Christ [and] bears witness that the benefits of Christ are given to us. And hence faith which believes the promise of grace must be added.

Then other purposes are added. Theodosius, in the Gospel, by this example publicly confessed what he believed. Likewise through this rite one is perceived as being separate from other [religious] groups

Third, because God wills that the church not lie in hiding completely unknown but wills that it be seen and heard, so that His name might be celebrated and [His] doctrine spread, therefore He also wills that there be proper assemblies. He wills that the Gospel be heard in the public meeting. Therefore, that confession might be made in such a meeting and there might be exercises of faith, He has always willed that there be certain public rites for which the church would publicly gather. And although the devil tries in various ways to scatter and spoil these meetings, yet God repeatedly cleanses and marvelously preserves them. Thus also the Lord's Supper was instituted for this use, that it might be a basic element in the public gathering.

Finally, the rite is also a reminder of many obligations. First, of giving thanks to God, then of mutual kindness of members of the church, just as those who made covenants partook together of things which had been sacrificed.

The Number of Sacraments

It is not the most ancient practice to list seven sacraments. There are disputes regarding this number; let this be their goal: that necessary things be retained and that they be distinguished from those which are not necessary. Ceremonies divinely instituted in the preaching of Christ must also be distinguished from other works which do not pertain properly to the new covenant.

If the general rule is that they want every work commanded by God to which some promise has been added to be called a sacrament, then prayer, patience under the cross, almsgiving, [and] forgiving of injury are sacraments. For to these works divine promises have always been added. There are well-known commands and promises regarding prayer: Ps. 50:15; Deut. 4:7; Matt. 7:7. It might be useful to include prayer among the sacraments, so that this very name might remind people about the promises and the benefits of this very great work.

There are promises regarding patience under the cross: Ps. 51:17; 116:15; 72:14. And in the Gospel there are many statements of this kind: Matt. 16:24; 10:30.

There are some very well-known statements regarding almsgiving: Luke 6:38; Is. 58:7.

Regarding the forgiving of injury [it says]: "Forgive and it shall be forgiven you,"

Luke 6:37. This is the glorious promise added to our forgiveness, not because our forgiving can placate the wrath of God, but to remind us of the Gospel, just as the other sacraments [do].

Therefore, if the name "sacrament" is to be applied not only to ceremonies but also to moral works, then marriage can also be called a sacrament, because it is both instituted by the command of God and adorned with a promise, such as Ps. 128:6. And it has been instituted for the spreading and conserving of the church. Moreover it is also an image both of the love of Christ toward [His] bride the church and of the afflictions and works of the church. Just as a husband who truly loves his wife and children fights for them and bestows his goods on them, so Christ truly loves the church [and] adorns it with His blessings, His righteousness, and the fellowship of eternal life. Paul indicates that this love and affection of an honorable husband is attached to nature for this reason, that it might be a picture representing the true love of Christ toward [His] bride, the church. Further, afflictions and domestic duties are a picture of the afflictions and duties of the church.

But when we thus use the term "sacrament" in a general way, we are speaking not only of ceremonies which were first instituted in the preaching of Christ but in one way or another of those works which we will always remember have been set forth in the Decalog as the sum of all the moral works which are necessary and have been commanded by God. Moreover let us seek everywhere for added promises and threats and examples of them.

We should also know that there is a difference between the promises connected with the Law and the promise which belongs to the Gospel, which is the promise of free reconciliation.

But when the word "sacrament" is understood of ceremonies instituted in the preaching of Christ, we list these sacraments: Baptism, the Lord's Supper, [and] absolution, which are external rites and are signs of the entire Gospel, and properly speaking are in fact testimonies of the remission of sins or of reconciliation, which is especially mentioned in the common definition: A sacrament is a sign of grace, that is, of free reconciliation, which is given for the sake of Christ and proclaimed in the Gospel.

In my opinion there is considerable merit in adding also ordination, that is, the call into the ministry of the Gospel and the public approval of this call, because all these things are enjoined as injunctions of the Gospel, e.g., Titus [1:5], "Appoint elders, as I have commanded," and there is added the promise which is the greatest of all and most worthy of recognition, which testifies that God is truly efficacious through the ministry of those who have been chosen by the voice of the church, as the universal statement testifies of the apostles and all who proclaim the Word which has been given through the apostles: "The Gospel is the power of God unto salvation for everyone who believes" [Rom. 1:16].

And Christ says in John 17[:20], "I do not pray for these only, but for all who will believe through their word." Note also John 20:23; Eph. 4:8ff.; Luke 10:16.

John 15:1ff.; 2 Cor. 5:19–20; 3:6. These and many other passages like them clearly testify that God is efficacious through this very ministry of those who teach the Gospel, which He wills to preserve in the church by the constant calling [of ministers]. For Paul is expressly speaking about the external Word or of the ministry that proclaims the Word of the Gospel when he says, "The Word is near you, in your mouth" [Rom. 10:8], and again, "He has committed to us the Word of reconciliation; therefore we are ambassadors for Christ," 2 Cor. 5:19–20. And the command has been given to the church that such ministers or ambassadors be chosen, as is expressly written to Titus.

Therefore the rite of ordination reminds us of this command and these promises, and we should give thanks to God for instituting and preserving this ministry and for receiving us in this way and freeing us from sin, the power of the devil, and eternal death and for restoring to us righteousness and eternal life. In this faith we should honor and uphold the ministry and use it, learn and hear the Gospel, exercise faith by the use of the sacraments, and understand that through this ministry eternal blessings are given to us. Likewise we should pray God that He would give able ministers and support them, as Christ enjoins us to pray that God may send out laborers into His harvest. And in Col 4[:3] Paul enjoins others to pray that God may aid him in his work.

There is also this great comfort, that since the ministry was instituted by God, even if in the world it is always variously tossed about and many people withdraw from it and perish, yet it cannot be completely overturned. For Christ says in Matt. 16:18, "On this rock I will build My church," that is, on this ministry, and "the gates of hell will not prevail against it." With this consolation the godly also in our own times sustain themselves and know that there will be remnants of the church and of the true ministry remaining even if empires fall. Yet this does not mean that the church will be without troubles, but such things are and always have been the punishments of the world, as Amos says [9:8–9]. Here the prophet sets forth threats and comfort at the same time. And it is no wonder that empires are punished, because, whereas they should have supported and upheld the ministry, as the psalmist says, "Open your gates, O you princes" [Ps. 24:7 (Vulgate)] the ungodly rulers try to destroy the churches. Others, indifferent, by their neglect deform [and] do not support studies, do not seek learned ministers, do not provide a fair living for them, and show no interest in being reconciled with them. Finally, they either neglect this part of the public estate, as of the lowest priority, or severely restrict it.

Basil laments that in his time the most unworthy, unlearned, and laziest of all the ministers were elevated to the governance of the church. Later, as wealth increased, ecclesiastical offices were prey for the powerful. But the ministry itself was neglected and was corrupted by unlearned mercenaries partly out of superstition, partly out of greed.

Now again also in those places where the true doctrine has been received, many unlearned and unworthy men are admitted to the ministry, because the leaders neglect the whole matter, do not support studies, and are not concerned that ministers have a living. Thus the church is afflicted with constant difficulties in this world, about which godly men must be concerned so that each in his own place may relieve them as much as he can and that God also would mitigate [His] punishments.

And indeed, God most strongly requires these duties which are beneficial for the preservation of the ministry, and He provides great rewards [Matt. 10:42]. There are notable examples: the widow of Zarephath, who took care of Elijah; Obadiah in 1 Kings 18, who defended and fed the 100 prophets who were hidden in caves; Hezekiah, who in 2 Chronicles 31 arranged for support of the priests and Levites; the Ethiopian who saved Jeremiah [Jer. 38:7–13].

The teaching on ordination, when it is listed among the sacraments, should remind us of all these things, of the efficacy of the ministry, of prayer for the ministry, of the functions that belong to the ministry, [and] of the punishments for spurning the ministry; and the rite itself, when we publicly witness the very ancient practice, undoubtedly approved by the earliest fathers, namely the laying on of hands, which was always a sign of something set aside for the worship of God, has also been a sign of His blessing. By this rite Jacob blessed the sons of Joseph [Gen. 48:14]. By this rite Moses appointed Joshua to govern the people of God, Num. 27[:18]. By this rite Christ blessed the children [Mark 10:13–16]. By this rite animals were set aside for sacrifice [Lev. 16:21], and sacrifices in a special way pointed to Christ. God the eternal Father laid [His] hands on Him, that is, He chose Him, blessed Him, anointed Him, and subjected [Him] to Himself; He loaded a great burden on Him and made Him a sacrifice for us. This rite of laying on of hands pointed especially to this.

But later the meaning [of the act] was applied to ministers. Christ the High Priest laid [His] hands on them, that is, He chose them by the voice of the church, blessed them, and anointed them with His gifts, as it is written, "He ascended on high [and] gives gifts to mankind, prophets, apostles, pastors, teachers," whom He adorns with the light of doctrine and other gifts [Eph. 4:8–12]. Then He makes them subject to Himself, so that they should teach only the Gospel and serve the kingdom of Christ alone, not seek power for themselves, nor set up empires under the pretext of religion, but should be sacrifices, that is, endure hatred, troubles, and torments for the sake of the true doctrine, as the psalmist says [Ps. 44:22].

Therefore, when you consider that this rite was used by the earliest fathers and the apostles, not by accident or in a meaningless way, the mind should be stirred up to recognize the efficacy of this function so as to honor it and to seek signs which remind us of Christ [our] High Priest and of the work of this function. But on the other hand we should consider also corruptions in the doctrine of ordination. The sacrificing priests who perform Masses for others imagine that ordination has been established so that power might be given to make sacrifices for the living and the dead; and they even say that they offer up the Son of God and by their sacrifice merit for others the remission of sins. They also add that without this sacrifice the death of Christ is of no benefit to the church. Now though some things were drawn from unhappy imitation of the Levitical priesthood incorrectly understood, yet they have added many other things from heathen notions. These errors must be rejected; they have spawned manifold idol madness, which is undoubtedly being punished by the Turkish tyranny. But for the sake of the work of preaching the Gospel and the efficacy of this gift, it must be retained and highly honored.

But the Anabaptists despise ordination along with the ministry [and] imagine that we are to await new revelations and illuminations from God and that they are to be sought by great torments of the body, as the monks and the enthusiasts of old imagined. These fanatic absurdities are to be abominated, for they arise out of false persuasions regarding the discipline of the Law and from ignorance of the doctrine of faith.

We, on the other hand, should know that God out of immeasurable goodness has revealed His will in the Gospel, and we are to seek no other enlightenments, but faith and prayer are stirred up when this Gospel itself is proclaimed to us. And God wills that there be the public ministry, and He wonderfully preserves and continually cleanses it so that we may know that the church is bound to this Gospel which is proclaimed. Paul says this in Eph. 4[:14] when he says that the ministry of the Gospel was established in order that the Gospel might be preserved, lest [the ministry] be "tossed about by every wind of doctrine."

Confirmation

In days gone by they used to have an examination of the teaching in which individuals recited a summary of the doctrine and showed that they dissented from the heathen and the heretics; and there was also the very useful practice of instructing people in how to distinguish between the profane and the godly. Afterward there was public prayer and the apostles laid hands on them. Thus they were given manifest gifts of the Holy Spirit. But in our day the rite of confirmation, which the bishops keep for themselves, is an absolutely useless ceremony. But it would be useful to have examination and profession of teaching and public prayer for the godly, nor would that prayer be in vain.

Unction

At one time, anointing with oil was a medical concern. For God, in order to invest the fathers and the prophets with some authority, therefore equipped them from the *beginning with the gift of healing, as in the case of Abraham, Isaac, Jacob, Isaiah, and men like them who were physicians by profession. And it is through these men that, together with the doctrine of the true religion, there was spread information about the physical world, things pertaining to plants, and other aspects of nature. Christ revived this ancient custom when He sent the apostles, ordered them to heal the sick, and equipped [them] with the gift of healing. This gift remained in the church also later, and it is certain that many are still healed by the prayers of the church. It is useful to point these things out so that we may learn that a healthy body is a gift of God which He gives us so that we might serve others. He wants this to be sought and fostered with some diligence. But the rite of anointing as it now exists is only a superstitious ceremony. And invocation of the dead was added, which is ungodly. Therefore this rite of unction with its additions is to be rejected.*

The Sacraments in General

Two things are required for the essence of a sacrament in the New Testament: (1) The express and universal command of God, covering the universal church of the New Testament, regarding some external or visible element or sure sign and a prescribed rite for administration and use. (2) The promise of the Gospel regarding the free mercy of God for the sake of Christ added to this rite in the Word in such a way that through it this [mercy] is offered, shown, applied, and sealed to individuals who use the sacraments in true faith. Therefore it is manifest that, properly speaking, there are only two such sacraments in the New Testament, namely Baptism and the Lord's Supper. It is also manifest why the sacraments of the papists must not and cannot be received into this number and order. And absolution, because in it a certain external rite, prescribed and commanded by the divine voice, is missing, is not properly a sacrament like Baptism and the Lord's Supper. But because it has this in common with the sacraments that through it the general promise of the Gospel is proclaimed, applied, and sealed to individual believers, the Apology [13.14, Tappert, p. 211], holds that in this respect it could in its own way be listed with the sacraments in order that its worth and benefit to the church might be more strongly commended. These things should be explained in such a way that the matters themselves are profitably set forth and unnecessary wars of words are not carried on.

Second, we need to be on guard that we do not, with the papists, attribute the power or efficacy of the sacraments either to the visible elements or to the external actions, 1 Peter 3:21, or believe that it depends on the worthiness of the administrators, 1 Cor. 3:7. Nor should we imagine with the scholastics that the sacraments justify or confer grace by the work performed [*ex opere operato*] without the good intention of the user, that is, without the faith of the users. For it is one thing, according to Augustine, to speak of the substance or integrity of the sacraments, which does not depend on our faith but only on the institution of God, but it is something different [to speak] of the power or value of the sacraments. For in the latter case we must join both together, the sacrament and faith in the sacrament, because the sacraments are like the hand of God by which He offers and holds out His benefits to us, but faith is like our hand by which we lay hold on and receive the blessings of God which are offered, Mark 16:16.

Third, we need to be on guard also against this, that we do not with the Sacramentarians reduce the real efficacy of the sacraments, as if they are only external signs which only remind of or testify to something before the church. But we must believe and speak according to Scripture that the sacraments are actions of God Himself, who through this outward ministry, by offering, showing, applying, and sealing His promise to individuals, works and accomplishes by His divine efficacy those things about which the promises connected with the sacraments speak. Therefore people are to be taught that in the sacraments they should not only see the external elements or the person of the minister and only his outward action, but by faith in the Word they should see God Himself present and working through the sacraments according to [His] promise. Then they must and can easily distinguish between the external action of the minister and the internal working of God, but they must not be separated. For it is God who saves, cleanses, and regenerates, but [He does so] through the washing of water in the Word.

LOCUS [XIX]

Baptism

Baptism is a complete action, that is, a washing (mersio) and the pronouncement of the words, "I baptize you in the name of the Father and of the Son and of the Holy Spirit." And the principal significance and purpose of Baptism is found in the promise, "He who believes and is baptized will be saved." Hence Baptism is properly called a sacrament because there has been added to this promise the testimony that the promise of grace truly does apply to the person who is baptized. And we should likewise believe regarding this testimony, as if God Himself with some new voice were testifying from heaven, that He receives him. Therefore when the baptized person learns the doctrine, he should exercise his faith [and] believe that he truly is received by God for the sake of Christ and is sanctified by the Holy Spirit. Baptism is to be used in this way throughout life. It should daily remind us: Behold, by this sign God testified that you have been received into grace. He does not want this testimony to be despised. Therefore you should believe that you have truly been received and you should call upon Him in this faith. This is the constant use of Baptism. In the same way circumcision was a constant testimony to Abraham, written upon his body, by which he was put in mind of the coming Seed and the blessing promised for the sake of the Seed, [and] as often as he thought about [his] circumcision, he rested in faith, believing that he pleased God and gave Him thanks and called upon Him.

Furthermore, in order that the fullness of the promise might be better seen, we must consider the words of Baptism, which include the sum of the Gospel and are a benediction by which we are consecrated to God and through which we invoke the name of God upon us. The minister says, "I, by the command of God and in the place of Christ, baptize you," that is, by this sign I bear witness that your sins are washed away and that you have been reconciled with the true God, who is the eternal God, the Father of our Lord Jesus Christ, and who has sent for you His Son with marvelous and indescribable wisdom, that He might remit your sins and begin in you the new righteousness and eternal life through the Holy Spirit. This blessing consecrates us to God and separates the church from all nations, because no other nation truly invokes God as He has revealed Himself, that is, as the Father of our Lord Jesus Christ, pleased [with us] through the Son, and sanctifying [us] through the Holy Spirit. And because the sum of the Gospel is contained in these words, the fullest consolations are offered to us here. For how pleasant it is to hear that you have so truly been accepted by God the eternal Father, because the benefits of the Son have been given to you, that God wants to rule you through [His] Holy Spirit, that He has rescued you from eternal death and from the chains of the devil! The more attentively you will consider the words of Baptism, the more will your mind be kindled with the knowledge of the mercy of God and strengthened by faith and moved to prayer.

Moreover, as the words put before us promise and comfort, so they in turn demand faith and this obligation, that we acknowledge the Father of our Lord Jesus Christ and the Son and the Holy Spirit as the true God. Peter says of this mutual covenant, in 1 Peter 3[:21], "Baptism, which is not the removal of filth from our physical body, but the assurance of a good conscience toward God through the resurrection of Christ . . ." For he understands a mutual obligation and a mutual covenant. God declares that He receives us; this the conscience believes and clings to, and in this faith it now truly knows God and calls upon [Him]. This correct understanding about God is called a "good conscience," that is, to know God rightly and to invoke Him rightly. And there is added, "through the resurrection of Christ," for [Peter] teaches that Baptism is efficacious because of the reigning Christ, and enjoins [us] to acknowledge by faith that this reconciliation has been granted for the sake of Christ.

The Signs

I said above that there are many signs in the sacraments, but one especially, namely that of grace, must be put in first place. The rite itself also gives us a picture of this, for the washing signifies that sins are washed away for the sake of Christ and that the benefits of Christ's suffering are applied to us when we are put into the water as into the death of Christ. Nor is it out of line to add other signs. Just as the passage of the Israelites through the Red Sea was a figure of the afflictions of the church and [its] deliverance, so the immersion in Baptism is a figure of afflictions and deliverance. But the other sign is preferable, which reminds us of the promise and of grace and requires faith.

Furthermore, just as it was sufficient to be circumcised once, when circumcision was commanded, so also is Baptism to take place only once, as this very weighty reason indicates: It is a sin to misuse the name of God and to reject true prayer. But those who rebaptize reject the first baptism [and] indicate that it was vain and useless. And so they reject the true invocation of God made for the person who is baptized. Therefore the ceremony itself is not to be repeated. As for the rest, we shall soon say more about the Anabaptists, who have mingled many pernicious errors with their Anabaptism.

The godly should also understand that Baptism once performed remains forever as a perpetual testimony and covenant. A new circumcision was not necessary for David after [his] fall, but that previous circumcision reminded him of both things, namely that this nature is circumcised because it is under sin and that one must come back to the promise of reconciliation for those who have fallen. Thus those who have *fallen must now understand that they should not repeat the ceremony, but, reminded by the covenant which was made before, in which the Son is mentioned, which is a testimony to the remission of sins, they should return to the reconciliation set forth. Thus Baptism brings great teaching and consolation to one who has fallen, because the very mention of the Son puts us in mind of repentance and the remission of sins and testifies that those who return become members of the people of God.*

The Baptism of John and of the Apostles

The entire ministry of John the Baptizer was the work of God and the beginning of a new ministry which was to follow after the Law. Therefore we should not think improperly of his baptism or that it was merely a useless spectacle. And as for some saying that it signified only repentance, not remission [of sins], this is absurd. For the preaching of repentance without remission is heathenish, and is a preaching of wrath and eternal death which is not proclaimed in the church without the preaching of remission. Hence Luke and Mark expressly say, ". . . preaching the baptism of repentance for the remission of sins" [Luke 3:3; Mark 1:4].

Therefore, although there was a difference on this point in that John preached of the Christ who was to suffer, whereas the apostles preached of the Christ who suffered and rose again, yet the ministry was the same and had the same effects in the believers. For John taught about both things, about the remission of sins and about the efficacy of the Holy Spirit in those who believed in the Son, as he says, [Matt. 3:11], "He will baptize you with the Holy Spirit." Again [John 1:16], "Of His fullness we have all received," where he testifies that the believers are not received in such a way that Christ is not efficacious in them, but he teaches that the new light and righteousness are begun in them.

But why does John make a distinction, saying, "I baptize you with water, but He who is about to come after me will baptize you with the Holy Spirit and with fire"? I reply: He is not distinguishing external ministries but persons. He wants them to understand the difference between the Messiah and ministers. Ministers only perform the outward ministry, but through it Christ is efficacious [and] for His sake and through Him is given reconciliation, the Holy Spirit, and eternal life. The ministers do not effect these things; for this reason it is necessary to differentiate the person of Christ from the ministers. Those who do not know the Gospel do not observe this distinction; they imagine that Christ is only a teacher, as the Pharisees thought, and they did not understand that He had been sent to be the sacrifice and to be the giver of new and eternal life and righteousness.

The Baptism of Infants

Paul most earnestly commands that we investigate the spirits [1 John 4:1], and Christ gives [us] the rule: "By their fruits you shall know them" [Matt. 7:16]. For it is a sure sign of a fanatic mind and one troubled by an evil spirit stubbornly to defend certain notable errors. Moreover the Anabaptists not only overthrow this one article of the baptism of infants, but they stir up many egregious errors. Their whole madness is a hodgepodge from the ravings of many ancient sects, from the Manichaeans, from the enthusiasts, and from the fables of recent Jews. They do not understand the difference between spiritual and civil righteousness. Therefore they deny that it is permissible for Christians to be a ruler, to function as a magistrate, to act as a judge, and to give an oath in court, and they contend that people must give up their personal possessions and must assign them to common ownership, and they say that spouses who are shocked at Anabaptist teaching must be abandoned.

These ravings can only arise from the devil and are the firebrands of seditions. Because they do not understand the chief point of the Gospel regarding the righteousness of faith but strongly contend that man is righteous because of his own works and harsh afflictions, as they themselves put it, therefore they devise for themselves other monastic works, so that they appear to be doing something new and difficult. The Anabaptists of Münster added much worse errors. They imagined, in keeping with Jewish custom, that there will be a kingdom of the godly before the resurrection, and in order to establish this kingdom, they took up seditious arms. This insanity was clearly demonic. It has forced sane people to conclude that they must flee the contagion of the Anabaptists. But even though some are more moderate, yet they retain seeds of similar ravings. Finally, they all err in regard to the sin of origin, the righteousness of faith and the external ministry. In manifest madness they abolish the doctrine of original sin and do not consider anything to be sin except external deeds or actions which are contrary to the law of God. Now I hear that new ravings are devised by them: Christ died not to do away with sin but to abolish physical death. This idea is not only wrong, it is stupid, because to abolish death is to do away with sin. For as Paul says [Rom. 5:12], "Through sin came death." Finally, it is never only one great error which is defended, but many must be added to the mixture. Therefore it is easy to render a judgment about fanatical ideas, once such marks are gathered. And since there are clear marks of an evil spirit in the hodgepodge of the Anabaptist teachings, we must avoid their contagion and not be moved by their hypocrisy.

Moreover the following statements demonstrate that the baptism of infants is not a recent custom, but approved by the testimony of the ancient purer church. I shall list them because I do not doubt that the pious are strengthened by the example of the purer church.

Origen, on Romans 6:3 [MPG 14.1047] writes thus, "Therefore also the Church has received from the apostles the tradition that baptism is to be given also to small children. For they, to whom had been entrusted the doctrines of the divine mysteries, knew that in all people there are the true stains of sin which must be washed away through water and the Spirit." These words of Origen contain a clear testimony concerning points, both original sin and the baptism of infants.

Cyprian writes that in a synod the opinion of a certain man was condemned because he did not want infants to be baptized before the eighth day. For the synod held that infants are to be baptized and that precept regarding the eighth day need not be observed.

Augustine, De Baptismo Contra Donatistas, 4, says in regard to the baptism of small children that the church universal holds to this, and it has not been established by councils but has always been held and handed down by apostolic authority [and] is most correctly believed.

First Argument

But we shall draw arguments also from the Gospel, and they of necessity must be valid because sound conclusions follow from absolutely sure statements And the first absolute certainty is this: The kingdom of God, that is, the promise of grace and eternal life do not pertain only to adults but in fact to infants who also have been implanted in the church, because Christ most clearly says of infants, "Of such is the kingdom of heaven" [Matt. 19:14], and again [Matt. 18:14], "It is not the Father's will that one of these little ones should perish." These lovely voices bear witness that children on whom the name of God has been invoked are a large part of the church. Hence we ought to love and uphold these statements and not allow them to be lost through cunning cavils, as the Anabaptists contend that nothing is promised to infants but that the command to baptize is given to adults in order that they may imitate the innocence of infants who do not yet have an inclination to do wrong. This sophistry should not hinder you from believing that these statements are faithful promises which testify that these children of whom He is speaking are pleasing to God, that is, infants implanted in the church.

This also is certain, that outside the church, that is, among those on whom the name of God has not been invoked through Baptism and who are without the Gospel, there is no remission of sins and a share in eternal life, as among the enemies of Christ, blasphemers, Jews, Mohammedans, and the like. This is clearly proved by this statement, "There is no other name given to mankind whereby [we] must be saved," except the name of Jesus Christ [Acts 4:12].

In Ephesians 5 Paul, in describing the church, says [vv. 25–26], "Christ loved the church and gave Himself for it, that He might sanctify it, cleansing it with the washing of water," [and] he defines the church as the kingdom of Christ which He sanctifies, and He gives to the church a sign to distinguish it from other nations [or peoples; gentibus], upon whom the name of Christ has not been invoked.

Again, Rom. 8[:30], "Whom He chose them He also called." Hence there is no choosing of those who are not brought into the church by an external calling. Likewise *in Matt. 18[:20], "Where two or three are gathered in My name, I am in their midst." Therefore in the assembly which is not gathered in Christ's name, Christ is not present. Hence we must cling very tenaciously to the statement: Outside the church there is no remission of sins and eternal salvation. When these two principles have been established that the promise of grace applies to infants but not to infants outside the church, the conclusion clearly follows that infants must be implanted in the church through Baptism, in which the name of God is invoked upon them. The invocation of the name of God is a great thing which is done through the ministry. Therefore Christ has joined these two: "Let the little children come unto Me, for of such is the kingdom of heaven." Of such, that is, of those who are brought to Me [and] upon whom My name is invoked.*

Therefore I have no doubt that all sane people will be convinced by this argument: Outside the church there is no salvation, that is, where the ministry of the Gospel is not proclaimed and the sacraments are not administered. To infants pertains the promise of salvation; therefore it is necessary that infants be implanted in the church through Baptism, in which is invoked upon them the name of the eternal Father, the Son, and the Holy Spirit. This argument is so firm that it cannot be overturned. For it can never be affirmed that salvation belongs to an infant outside the church, as the Anabaptists furiously contend without any testimony.

Second Argument

Infants are born with sin, and they are not made heirs of eternal life without the remission of sin. Now, God has established in the church the ministry of remitting sins and distributing remission through the sacraments. He wills remission to be given as we use its ministry. Hence this benefit must be given to infants through Baptism.

But because the Anabaptists completely deny the whole doctrine of the sin of origin, they display their madness even more. For if infants are without sin, Christ did not suffer for them. But we have collected in another place testimonies from the prophets and apostles which show that all who are born bring sin with them, e.g., Rom. 5[:12], "Death passed upon all people, because all have sinned," that is, they are guilty. Eph. 2:3, "We also were by nature the children of wrath," that is, guilty of or delivered over to wrath or condemned. Therefore, since there is no doubt that there is sin in infants, there must be some difference between the infants of the heathen, who remain guilty, and the infants in the church who are received by God through the ministry.

Third Argument

To whom the promise pertains to them also the sign pertains. For the sign was given for the sake of the promise. Furthermore, it is certain that the promise of grace pertains to infants. Therefore it is necessary that the sign be applied to them through the ministry by which the name of God is invoked upon them.

Fourth Argument

The command regarding baptism is universal and applies to the entire church. See John 3:5. Therefore it pertains also to infants that they might become part of the church. Nor is there any doubt that there have always been some signs by which infants in the church have been brought to God, e.g., there was circumcision of the males from [the time of] Abraham and other ceremonies by which both male and female infants were brought to God, that is, ceremonies in which the name of God was invoked upon them and the divine blessing promised to the fathers was applied to them. The patriarchs, even before Abraham, had other signs given to them by God, for it is necessary to hold to the position that infants who are in the church, upon whom the name of God has been invoked, are received into grace, not Turks [and] not Jews.

But the Anabaptists cry out [and] deny that Baptism benefits infants, since they do not understand the Word, and a ceremony without faith is worthless to those who receive it. To this I reply: It is certainly true that in all adults repentance and faith are required. But it is sufficient to hold this regarding infants, that the Holy Spirit is given to them through Baptism, and [He] effects in them new affections, new inclinations toward God in proportion to their condition. Nor is it rash to say this. For these things are certain, that infants are received by God through this ministry, likewise that the Holy Spirit is always given with the remission of sin, and that no one is pleasing to God unless he has been sanctified by the Holy Spirit, as Christ clearly says, "Except a person is born again of water and the Spirit he shall not enter into the kingdom of heaven." Again, 1 Cor. 15[:50], "Flesh and blood," that is, without the Holy Spirit, "cannot possess the kingdom of God." And Rom. 8[:14], "Those who are led by the Spirit of God, they are the sons of God." Therefore, since it is certain that these infants are part of the church and are pleasing to God, this is also certain, that God is efficacious in them, because eternal life must be begun in this life.

We should all consider these things regarding Baptism devoutly and diligently, in order that we may encourage ourselves and [our] elders with this pact and covenant, as I have said above. But particularly the young should be on their guard that they not discard the gift of Baptism nor lose the great glory which Christ proclaims regarding infants in the church: "It is not the Father's will that one of these little ones should perish" [Matt. 18:14]. Who can think of greater glory than that He affirms that these [little ones] are pleasing to God and of concern to Him? And parents with this faith regarding Baptism invoke God on behalf of their children and commend them to God; and immediately, when they can be taught, train them that they themselves call upon God and His Son, and gradually they teach them the sum of the Gospel.

Finally since the children are a large part of the church, parents and teachers should know that no small treasure has been entrusted to them. Therefore they should show faithfulness and diligence in teaching and governing the youth.

BAPTISM

From the *Loci*, catechisms, and other books of instruction we must seek statements which show how we should teach the doctrine of Baptism for the upbuilding of the faithful in the face of popish superstitions and Anabaptist ravings. We shall now briefly note other main points that seem to have some part in controversy.

I

Now, first, the Sacramentarians argue that the infants of believers, by the very fact that they are born of believing parents, even without Baptism and before they are baptized, are not children of wrath but children of God, not outside of but within the kingdom of heaven, and Baptism is only an external sign that they are heirs of eternal life in the first place. But because by this line of argument both the sin of origin is minimized and the salutary efficacy of Baptism is dangerously diminished, we must oppose it by firm and clear testimonies of Scripture regarding the regular means of regeneration. For believing parents also produce their carnal children not according to the Spirit but according to the flesh. Therefore this is a general statement which includes also the children of believers: "That which is born of the flesh is flesh, and unless it is born again by water and the Spirit, it cannot enter into the kingdom of heaven," John 3:5–6. Thus David, even though he was born of circumcised and believing parents, still confessed that he was conceived and born in sins, Ps. 51:5. And Paul says in Eph. 2:3, "We also," that is, we who were born of circumcised parents, "were by nature the children of wrath, even as the others." The promise of grace and of the kingdom of heaven, to be sure, pertains not only to the parents but also to their children, Gen. 17:7 and Acts 2:39, but the promise profits nothing unless it is applied, Heb. 4:2–3. Therefore Christ says, "That which is born of the flesh must be born again, or regenerated," John 3:5–6. The application of the promise and of regeneration does not take place by physical generation. For the judgment is universal, because "Through the transgression of one man sin passed upon all men unto condemnation," Rom. 5:18. But Baptism is the regular [or ordinary; *ordinarium*] means, that is, "the washing of regeneration," Titus 3:5, so that those who are born of the flesh and were not in the kingdom of heaven might be born again of water and the Spirit and thus enter the kingdom of heaven, John 3:5. For they are "baptized for the remission of sins," Acts 2:38, in order that the sins in which they were born might be washed away, Acts

22:16, and that they might be cleansed and saved by God through the washing of regeneration, Eph. 5:26; Titus 3:5.

What Augustine long ago already condemned in the Pelagians on the basis of Scripture in *De Baptismo Parvulorum*, 2.25 and 26, applies also to this opinion of the Sacramentarians. He explained Paul's statement in 1 Cor. 7:14, "Your children are holy," by the other statement in the same verse, "The unbelieving husband is sanctified through the believing wife."

Pastors should seek in the writings of Luther and Bugenhagen on this matter what words of comfort to offer godly parents in extraordinary cases regarding children who die either in the womb or at birth before Baptism.

II

Second, we must in no way concede that infants who are baptized are either without faith or have been baptized into the faith of another person, cf. Heb. 11:6; Mark 16:16; Hab. 2:4; Rom. 1:17. The faith of another person, whether of the parents or the sponsors, indeed brings the children to Christ in Baptism, Mark 10:13, and prays that they may be given their own faith. But through the washing of water in the Word there is no doubt that Christ works and is efficacious by His Spirit in the infants who are baptized, so that they may receive the kingdom of God, even though we do not understand how this takes place. For Baptism is "the washing of regeneration and of the renewal of the Holy Spirit," who is poured out upon the baptized, so that, having been justified, they are heirs of eternal life, Titus 3:5. And Christ Himself affirms that the little ones receive the kingdom of God, Mark 10:15. And this is called the faith of infants. For just as circumcision also of infants in the Old Testament was a sign of the righteousness of faith, Rom. 4:11, so, because in the New Testament infants who have been baptized are pleasing to God and are saved, they cannot and must not be rejected as unbelievers but rightly included among the faithful. And thus these words of Scripture pertain to these things: "He who believes and is baptized shall be saved," Mark 16:16. Likewise, through faith we obtain the testimony that we are righteous and that we please God, for "without faith it is impossible to please God," Heb. 11:6, although in adults who know, understand, and will, faith comes by hearing in a different way than in infants who do not yet have the use of reason.

III

Third, because certain Sacramentarians argue that Baptism is only an external reminder of and testimony to what God either before or outside of or without Baptism works within us, therefore from the Word of God we must emphasize that Baptism is an action in which God Himself, the Father, the Son, and the

Holy Spirit, through the external ministry, offers, applies, and seals to us the promise of grace. And because some begin to dispute whether what Luther says in his Catechism is correct that "Baptism works the forgiveness of sins, delivers from death and the power of the devil and gives eternal salvation to those who believe," since these benefits belong alone to Christ, [therefore] this statement must be clearly and distinctly taught, that this power and efficacy of Baptism should in no way be attributed either to the element of water or to the external action of the administrator. But because Baptism is the kind of action in which, through the washing of water in the Word, God the Father, for the sake of His Son the Mediator, saves us by the application and sealing of the promise of grace, Titus 3:5, the Son sanctifies and purifies, Eph. 5:26, [and] the Holy Spirit regenerates, John 3:5, so that by the grace of Christ, into whose death and resurrection we are baptized and whom we put on in Baptism, we who have been justified have the assurance of a good conscience before God and are heirs of eternal life, Titus 3:5; Rom. 6:3; 1 Peter 3:21. Therefore the power, work, and efficacy of Baptism is of God Himself, who works, gives, and effects such blessings not without means but through the washing of water in the Word.

Therefore, when I ask what Baptism profits, bestows, and works, it is the same as if I ask what the Father, the Son, and the Spirit work, give, and effect in Baptism and through Baptism. And Scripture speaks both ways, that God saves us through Baptism, Titus 3:5, and that Baptism saves us, but not by reason of the external washing, but because it is "the assurance of a good conscience toward God through the resurrection of Christ," 1 Peter 3:21. For we do not have Baptism without Christ, but we are thus baptized in the name of the Father, the Son, and the Holy Spirit because the whole Trinity is present in Baptism: the Father saves, the Son cleanses, the Holy Spirit regenerates, not without means, but through the washing of water in the Word, Titus 3:5; Eph. 5:26.

IV

Fourth, we must retain this distinction that the essence of Baptism consists in this action and in these words, "I baptize you in the name of the Father and of the Son and of the Holy Spirit," [and] that the other elements which are either spoken or which take place in the action of Baptism in our churches do not belong to the essence of Baptism itself, but even without these the Baptism is complete and perfect. But because the statements and reminders are brief and useful, setting before us the doctrine, efficacy, and benefit of Baptism, we must not rashly reject or condemn these rites but explain them in such a way that the church may be edified thereby, so that the unlearned may be able to call to mind the entire teaching on Baptism from seeing the baptismal ritual performed.

From these fundamentals the dispute about exorcism can more easily be cleared up, so that disruptions do not arise therefrom. For those who omit or reject exorcism under the notion and for the reason that the Anabaptists and Sacramentarians [give] because they think that infants either do not have sin and thus are not by nature the children of wrath and not under the power of Satan, or though they be born in sin, yet because of their physical birth from believing parents, even before Baptism and without Baptism they are not outside the kingdom of heaven and not under the power of darkness—they are deservedly to be censured and rejected because they deny original sin and its consequences and also the efficacy of Baptism, as if infants did not need to be delivered through Baptism from the power of Satan. But if this teaching regarding original sin, the power and kingdom of Satan and the efficacy of Baptism is granted by clear confession the essence, the integrity, and the efficacy of Baptism are not tied to this prescribed ritual of the words of exorcism, but the church has the freedom to set forth and explain this doctrine with other words which are in greater agreement with Scripture.

However, some reminder concerning the main points of doctrine in the baptismal ceremony either through exorcism or some other words is useful both because of the corruptions of the Sacramentarians and for the sake of those present in the service. In this way neither side will have just cause to condemn the other, since the things themselves remain intact and the church is not of necessity bound to such prescribed rites regardless of how old [they are]. But those who practice exorcism, because it was used in the most ancient times of the church and because (as Luther writes in [his] preface to the act of Baptism) it very earnestly portrays the wretchedness of the infant, the power of Satan, and the grace of God, who powerfully frees the infants from the kingdom and power of darkness through Baptism—these people are not to be condemned, as long as they do not attribute particular power or efficacy to exorcism beyond Baptism.

For some indeed claim that the words sound as if the infants had been possessed [by the devil]. We surely know that infants are not physically filled with the blessing of God. We also know in turn from the Word of God that it is much sadder and more perilous, that, banished from the kingdom of heaven because of sin, they are held as spiritual captives under the kingdom and power of darkness, from which they cannot be set free by the power of any creature. But God the Father by His divine power, for the sake of the Son, sets them free through the Holy Spirit in Baptism. Therefore, not without weighty reason, exorcism was both received in ancient times and retained by Luther, provided the liberty of which we have spoken, remain for the church.

LOCUS [XX]

The Lord's Supper

Omitted

═══════

LOCUS [XXI]

Marriage

Omitted

═══════

Theses [On Various Subjects]

Omitted

═══════

Scripture Index

OLD TESTAMENT

GENESIS

1	154, 255, 264, 267, 276, 585, 1128
1:1	58, 89, 90, 154, 277
1:2	58, 59, 89, 90, 213, 223, 225, 236, 237, 267, 274, 277
1:3	84, 90, 265
1:9	58, 1303
1:11	279
1:12	291
1:14	153
1:20	281
1:21	281
1:24	281
1:26	89, 90, 104, 105, 263, 267
1:27	291, 466
1:31	263, 268, 273, 314, 332, 466
2	701
2:2	526, 714
2:2–3	263
2:3	279, 632, 701, 1037
2:4	277
2:5	236, 279
2:6	282
2:7	264, 282
2:15	633
2:17	67, 359, 360, 851, 1250
2:24	633, 757
3	302, 586, 1144
3:5	90
3:6	332, 1275
3:11	1007
3:12	323, 381
3:13	323, 334
3:15	37, 67, 165, 230, 307, 489, 493, 633, 835, 839, 848, 917, 1020, 1028, 1155, 1250, 1355
3:16	341, 519, 757
3:18	344
3:19	281, 292, 536
3:22	90
3:23	281
4	633, 852, 1261
4:1	839
4:3–4	632
4:4	840
4:5	852
4:6	633, 740
4:6–7	852
4:7	469, 568, 634, 840, 852, 1070, 1241, 1261
4:9	634
4:10	576, 633, 748
4:12	749
4:13	852
4:13–15	633
4:20–21	725
4:21	334
4:26	37, 632, 840, 852
5:1	510
5:3	466, 510, 515
5:24	840
5:29	840
6	520
6–8	580
6:2	633
6:3	249, 343, 367, 373, 520, 633, 1310
6:4	685, 759
6:4–5	633
6:5	466, 520, 634, 640, 787
6:5–6	332, 372
6:5–7	673
6:8	975
6:12	173, 520
6:14	263
8	520, 521, 1163
8:15	1134
8:20	1063
8:21	431, 466, 489, 498, 520, 521, 580, 640, 787, 787, 840
8:22	286, 291
9	1297
9:2–3	744
9:5	749
9:6	737, 738, 744, 748, 796
9:25	731, 733
9:26	840
9:26–27	733
9:27	732
11–15	996
11:7	90
11:20	853
11:31	674, 996
12	917
12:1	67
12:1–3	841
12:2	1249
12:3	37, 778, 835, 853, 917, 1029, 1216, 1297
12:13	774
12:17	759, 760
13:14–15	749
14:18–20	841
14:22	692
15	917, 1015, 1106, 1174, 1215
15:1	835, 902, 917, 997, 1215, 1216
15:5	916, 917, 1215
15:6	834, 841, 902, 903, 960, 1052, 1106
15:13–14	373
15:14	1215
15:16	351, 373, 576, 1215

15:18	373, 841	26:10	482, 759, 1267	39:21	975
17	1099, 1127, 1182	26:12–13	1235	40:15	765
17:1	1089	26:28	692, 696	41	937
17:5	841	27:19	774	41:40	759
17:7	539, 631, 1245, 1249, 1370	27:27–29	841	41:43	725
		27:41	351, 739	42:7	774
17:8	1245	28:1	749	42:15	692, 695
17:9–10	841	28:9	853	43:12	482
17:14	675, 841	28:13–15	841	44:15	774
18:2	89	28:14	37, 165	44:16	887
18:18	1216	28:18	674	45:8	352, 725
18:20	576	28:20	841, 1235	45:26–27	910
18:21	288, 373	28:24	841	46:26	526
18:26	1211	29:15	980	47:4	1268
18:27	167	30	520	48:5	733, 760
19	759	30:1–2	670	48:14	1236, 1359
19:9	1274	30:2	741	48:15	1089
19:15	309	30:33	895	48:15–16	67, 122, 841
19:19	896	30:39	520	48:16	1055
19:24	84, 91	30:43	770	49:1	733, 841
19:33	755	31:2	740	49:3–4	733
20:2	774	31:13	67	49:4	759
20:3	759, 760	31:15	985	49:5–7	749
20:13	896	31:26	761	49:10	37, 623
21	853	31:30	674	49:10–12	841
21:1–2	294	31:36	482	50:20	352
21:10	734, 841	31:45	674		
21:17	309	31:52–53	696	**EXODUS**	
21:23	692, 696, 896	32:1–2	309	1:8	1250
21:33	631	32:10	841, 896, 1068	1:16	841
22	673, 832, 917, 1103, 1169	32:24	67	1:17	665
		32:29	71, 138	1:19	774, 775
22:5	776	32:32	617	1:21	673, 749, 774
22:12	665	33:4	351	1:22	841
22:14	149	33:5	974	2:6	498
22:16	692	34	759	3:4	1316
22:16–17	1249	34:1–2	755	3:7	576
22:17–18	841, 917	34:2	753	3:13–14	150
22:18	37, 165, 1029, 1042, 1216, 1226	34:30	749	3:13–15	71
		35:2–4	841	3:14	148
24:2	692, 695	35:9–12	841	3:19	365, 370, 382
24:7	311	37:28	765	4:2	1316
24:13	1217	38:9	738	4:11–12	227
24:40	1089	38:10	759	4:16	145
25:1–2	294	38:17–18	944	4:21	337, 338, 387
26	294, 391, 673	39:7	755	5:3	775
26:3–4	841	39:8	759	6	147
26:4	165			6:3	71, 685

7:1	115	20:11	649, 701	23:19	618
7:3	314, 337, 338, 387, 432	20:12	725, 727, 731, 1066	23:20	672
				23:20–21	91
8:19	1316	20:17	589, 651, 785	23:27	373
9:16	347, 361, 685	20:19	808, 842, 855	23:30	309
10:1	68	20:20	665	24	614, 1253
10:25	264	20:24	616	24:1	1247
11:2–3	351	21:2	620, 980	24:7	1253
11:8	741	21:6	631	24:14	630
12:3	725	21:7	765	25:8	710
12:14	631	21:12	748	25:17	616, 842
12:36	770	21:14	748	25:18	616
12:37	68	21:15	727	25:18–20	302
12:45	620	21:15–16	732	25:22	1238
13:9	707	21:16	769	25:23	616
14:16	294	21:18–20	738	25:31	616
14:19	308, 309	21:20	737	25:40	1331
15	691	21:22	738	26:7	616
15:3	71	21:23	738	27:2	616
16:7	147	21:24	738	29:9	631
16:20	741	21:29	738	29:19	617
16:23	650	22:1–3	769	29:20	617
16:29	650, 704, 706, 713	22:2	738	29:42	631
		22:3	620	31:2	418
17:2	147	22:6	766	31:3–4	221
17:4	1058	22:7	766	31:13	702, 708
17:5–6	294	22:10	766	31:14	713
17:11	1332	22:11	691, 695, 696	31:16	631
17:15	149	22:16	753	31:18	1247
18:21	777	22:16–17	620	32:1	1076
19	84, 630	22:18–20	737	32:6	251, 1258
19–20	636	22:23	576	32:19	741
19:6	809	22:25–26	768	32:25	741
19:8	600, 808, 842, 853	22:27	975	32:28	673
		22:28	115, 346, 577	32:34	309
19:18	1246	22:31	617	33:19	974, 1040, 1251
20	780, 809, 855	23	728	33:20	77, 148
20:1	648, 657	23:1	889, 986	34:1	1247
20:2	56, 656, 658, 664, 683	23:3	772	34:7	547, 554, 1059, 1219
		23:4	736		
20:3	663	23:4–5	1243	34:24	713
20:4	648	23:5	746	34:28	638, 650
20:5	373, 672, 684	23:6	772	34:30	134
20:6	657, 672, 673, 1025	23:7	546, 882	35:2	713
		23:9	620	35:3	706
20:7	683, 687, 690, 780	23:11	770	35:30	418
20:10	714	23:13	695	39:34	616

40	616
40:5	616
40:22–23	616
40:24	616

LEVITICUS

2:4	615
3:17	617
4:2	482
4:3	482
4:20	617
4:35	1222
5:18	482, 1222
7:16	1083
8:3	617
8:3–4	1303
8:12	617
10	699
10:10–11	1314
11	1253
13:2	616
13:45	616
14	617
14:33	616
14:35	617
15	616
15:2	617
15:18	617
16:21	1359
16:30	1222
17	301
17:3–4	985
17:7	301
17:12	617
18	647
18:5	779, 804, 837, 959, 1205, 1244
18:6	620, 754
18:22–23	754
18:25	754
19	621
19:3	665, 727
19:11–15	765
19:12	692
19:13	765, 768
19:15	895
19:15–16	772
19:16	771, 773

19:17	736, 1243
19:17–18	740
19:18	736, 1243
19:19	618
19:26	617
19:29	753, 755
19:31	699
19:32	725
19:35	765
19:35–36	765
19:36	895
20:2	727
20:3	688, 690
20:6	696, 699
20:9	727, 732
20:10	753, 759
20:11	754
20:14	754
21:1	617
21:5	617
21:9	759
21:10	617
21:17	617
22:14	482
22:18	1073
22:21	1083
23:8	705
23:14	631
23:21	631
23:22	747
23:31	631
23:41	631
24:3	631
24:4	617
24:10–11	689
24:14	690
24:16	688, 689, 690
24:17	748
26	1213
26:1	674, 676
26:2	710
26:2–4	713
26:11–12	1213
26:14	672, 713
27	482
27:26	779

NUMBERS

1:4	725
5:7	482
5:12	620
5:19	695
5:22	911
6:23–27	91
6:25	975
8:6	617
8:9	617
10:2	263
11:5	980
11:17	221, 244, 249
11:25	249, 250
12:6	636
12:8	636
13:25	249
14:6	249
14:9	1266
14:20	147
14:22	147
14:36–37	673
15	1268
15:3	1083
15:22–31	576
15:25	617
15:25–26	1222
15:27	1264, 1268
15:28	482
15:30	1264, 1268
15:32	713
15:39	1080
15:39–40	668
16:5	618
16:15	741
16:31	360
16:32	734
17:2	725
17:8	1316
18	612
18:9	482
18:26–27	985
19:11–22	1350
19:15	617
19:18	589
19:20	617
19:23	618

20:10	1266	5:31	630	12	619	
20:16	311	5:32–33	1081, 1221	12:8	1022, 1080, 1132	
21	749	6	614	12:11	1083	
21:7	575	6:1	613	12:19	713	
21:9	842	6:4	71, 82, 84, 91, 663, 664	12:32	1022, 1080, 1081, 1132	
22	351	6:5	396, 411, 589, 590, 657, 663, 664, 682, 683, 800	13:1	681	
22–23	749			13:1–3	1316	
22:22	309, 311			14:6	617	
22:28	452			14:21	617	
22:31	690	6:6–7	1333–34	15:7–8	747	
23:8	452	6:7	654, 709	15:8	768	
23:19	80, 156, 630	6:8	707	15:9	768	
25:1	759	6:12	665	15:10	770	
25:7	379, 738	6:12–13	693	15:12	620	
25:8	741	6:13	300, 657, 683, 691, 694	15:17	631	
25:11	741			16:18–20	772	
27:18	1326	6:13–14	664–65, 1008	17:2–5	672	
27:18–20	1328	6:17	613	17:6	770	
30	1083	6:20	1314	17:8	614, 748, 1337	
31:14	741	6:25	1213, 1217	17:8–13	1335	
35:6	620	7:2	673	17:9	617, 1337	
35:16	748	7:3	620	17:10	1336	
		7:12–13	1221	17:10–11	1336	
Deuteronomy		7:16	663	17:11	1338	
1:5	38	8:1	595	17:14	630	
1:16–17	728	8:2–4	636	17:18	728	
1:39	546	8:3	1233	18:10–11	699	
2:25	351	8:4	1250	18:13	607	
2:30	351	8:9	755	18:14	270	
4–6	621	8:19–20	672	18:15	180, 842, 855, 1040, 1251	
4:2	630, 1002	9:3	274			
4:7	1356	9:10	1247	18:18	623, 855	
4:10	665	9:19	665	19:10	547	
4:11	809	9:20	566	19:14	765	
4:12	77, 133, 638, 685	9:24	1266	19:15	770	
4:13	650	10:4	638, 650	19:18	771	
4:15–16	682	10:16	469	19:19	800	
4:25–26	672	10:20	663, 691, 693	19:21	738	
4:35	82, 84, 663, 1008	10:20–21	665	20:16	339	
5:3	636	10:21	693	20:16–18	673	
5:7	663	11:5–7	672	21	1212	
5:13	649	11:14	1275	21:1–7	696	
5:13–14	730	11:17	672	21:15	620	
5:15	704, 709	11:18	654, 1333–34	21:18	727, 1266	
5:21	651, 785, 1275	11:26	599	21:21	732	
5:22	630	11:26–27	1221	22:2	746	
5:25	600	11:28	672	22:5	618	
5:26–27	1247					

22:6	618, 1253
22:9	618
22:10	1253
22:10–11	618
22:11	1253
22:13	620
22:20–21	621
22:22	759
22:25	753
23:2	620
23:8	620
23:15	730
23:17	753
23:19–20	619
24:5	1250
24:7	765, 769
24:13	770, 791
24:19	770
25:1	748, 882, 986
25:4	618, 620
25:5	620
25:13–15	765
25:15	760
25:19	723
26:12	770
26:15	770
26:19	685
27:10	1218
27:15	672, 684, 911
27:16	727, 732
27:17	765, 769
27:18	1359
27:19	772
27:20–23	754
27:24	748
27:25	772
27:26	589, 596, 732, 831, 959, 991, 1205, 1271
28	1213
28:11	257
28:15	642, 672
28:23	295
28:32	672
28:50	974
28:66	910
29:2	433
29:3–4	430

29:4	411, 442, 832, 1250
29:5–6	636
29:18	570
30	1109
30–31	672
30:6	433, 469
30:12	467, 1040
30:15	468
30:16	1104
30:19	599, 837, 1165, 1221
30:20	257
31:9	630
32	609, 691
32:4	609
32:11	236
32:12	227
32:15	251
32:16	663
32:17	1077
32:21	148
32:35	1242
32:39	82, 84, 663, 1008
34:9	1326, 1328

JOSHUA

1:7	1081
1:8	707, 1134
2:4	775
2:12	695
2:13	340
2:14	778
6:25	340, 778
7:19	778
8:5	775
9:4	1250
9:18	696, 773
14:9	691
22	675
22:7	694
22:22	483
22:29	483
24:2	853, 996, 1174
24:14	674
24:19	90
24:26	675

JUDGES

2:1–3	309, 311
4:18	775
6:11	725
6:24	149
6:34	249
7:19	772
8:21	749
8:27	673, 1076
9:1	724
9:53	749
9:53–55	734
11:10	691, 696
11:20	975
11:29	249
11:30	694
12:4	734
13:5	842
13:8	498
13:15	264
13:18	71, 138
13:22	749
13:25	249
14:6	249
14:18	215, 1292, 1299
15:6	759
16	759
16:30	746
19–20	750
21	696
21:14	339
21:22	974

RUTH

2:12	770
3:10	770
4	620

1 SAMUEL

1:22	631
2	691
2:22	713, 759
2:23	1332
2:25	347, 575
2:29	673
2:30	347, 369, 1323
2:34	733
3:12	1322

4:11	733
5:1–4	813
7:3	608
7:12	675
8:3	764
10:6	249
10:26	433
12:7	896
13:11	673
13:11–12	378
14:24	695
15:7	642
15:22	655
15:23	642, 665, 769
15:24	673
16:5	775
16:13	249, 1327
16:14	245, 249, 344, 388, 395, 452
17:5–6	727
17:28	482, 1267
17:55	695
18:17	738
19:5	981
19:13	775
20:3	692
20:5	738
20:16	696
20:28	775
21:13	775
22:9	749, 773
24:7	733
24:11–12	724
24:17–18	1283
24:19	733
24:20	749
25:3	661
25:22	697
25:28	735
25:31	981
25:34	695
25:38	769
26:1	773
26:23	1219
26:25	749
27:12	631
28:7	699

2 SAMUEL

1:15	745
2:6	696
3:27	759
4:10	820
4:12	749
5:16	1084
6:16	773
6:20	773
7:12	165
7:12–14	842
10:12	725
11	759
11:4	755
12:10	1209
12:13	398, 555, 1262
12:14	1209
13:9	755
13:11	753
13:28	759
14:20	728
15:4	882
15:6	761
15:26	1313
16:2	759
16:5	352, 353
16:10	346
16:11–12	749
16:12	346
16:21	1064
17:1	773
17:14	351
17:19	777
17:23	733
18:9	733
18:22	819, 820
18:24	820
18:25	819
18:27	819
19	727
19:14	433
19:19	983
19:23	696
19:24	264
20:9	774
20:10	759
20:21	733

21:7	692, 749
21:17	692
22	691
22:8	265
22:16	265
22:50	688
23:2	91, 227
24	304
24:1	345
24:24	981

1 KINGS

1:5	733
1:36	911
2:8	346
2:19	733
2:29	749
2:31	981
3:9	432
3:19	738
4:20	755
7:36	674, 675
8:9	630
8:31–32	882
8:32	882, 986, 1206
8:55	432
8:65	755
11	856
11:4	673
11:11	672
12	856
12:12	351
12:15	351
12:26	673
13:4	355, 734
13:6	356
13:21	673
13:26	1304
14:2	774
14:9–10	673
15:3	608
15:13	608
16:18	733
17	1067
18	1359
18:12	249
18:21	663
18:23	264

18:44	295
19:5	309
19:18	1288, 1310, 1329
20:28	691
21:1	749
21:2	764
21:8	944
21:9–10	772
21:14	772
21:17	1209
21:29	1209
22:16	695
22:20	346
22:21–22	352
22:22	304, 346
22:23–24	388
22:24	249

2 KINGS

1:3	699
1:10	360
1:13	975
2:9	221, 244
2:12	724
2:21	295
2:23	773
2:24	734
3:5	773
4:13	770
4:38	713
5:7	670
5:13	725
5:27	734, 769
6:16	309, 310
6:17	303, 309
7:10	820
9:33	749
10:16	741
10:19	775
10:20	710
11:16	749
11:20	733
13:14	724
13:19	741
13:23	974
14:8	749
14:14	944
14:25	843

15:14	733
16:18	713
17	856
18:21	673
19:35	690
22:18–20	673
23:25	608
24–25	420
25	749
25:6	697

1 CHRONICLES

8:34	733
12:33	608
12:38	608
17:11	165
18–19	661
18:4–5	676
21:1	304, 335, 345, 388, 403
22:8	614
22:9–10	842
29:9	608

2 CHRONICLES

3:10	674
3:11–13	302
4:3	675
7:1	675
9:18	675
15:14	691
15:15	608, 673
16:12	673
18:25	713
19	728
20:12	401, 1007
20:20	902, 910
21:16	352
23–24	713
24–25	749
25	344, 347
25:16	347
25:20	351
28:21	765
31	1359
32:20	690
32:21	243
33:6	699

34:27	433
35:3	614
36	673
36:14	713
36:21	700

EZRA

1:5	725
6:22	433
9:7–8	975

NEHEMIAH

8:6	911
8:10–12	755
9:20	223
13	713
13:5	765
13:10	765
13:15	713

ESTHER

6:11	749
7:10	749
8:8	944

JOB

1	306
1:5	710
1:6	311
1:9–10	673
1:10–11	308
1:12	275, 345, 346, 351
1:21	85, 308, 345
2:6	351, 352
4:18	283, 301
5:2	749
5:13	351
8:13	672
9	1059
9:5–7	294
9:7	294
9:8	236, 266
9:15	886, 953
9:16	910
9:20	554, 886, 953
9:28	953, 1091
9:29	482, 1267
9:30–31	953

10:3	291	39:11–12	910	11:5	672
10:7	482	39:14	340	11:6	221, 222
10:8	282, 291, 542, 584			12:2	608, 773, 776
		PSALMS		12:6	853
10:10–11	526	1:1	421, 1339, 1353	13:5	911
10:11	291	1:2	334, 452, 609, 707, 1134	14:1	368, 667
10:15	482, 886			15	1207
10:18	291	1:3	1311	15:1–2	778
11:20	672	1:6	421	15:2	607, 895
12:9–10	285	2:1–2	377	15:4	673, 691, 696
12:10	282	2:2	843	15:5	620, 769, 770
12:24	351, 433	2:3	1267, 1280	16:3	333
13:18	886	2:4	377	16:10	163, 843
14:1	303	2:6	843	17:1	895
14:4	168, 498, 519	2:7	75, 89, 91, 129, 137, 155, 162, 821, 843, 1290	17:15	1089
15:22	910			18:1	665
15:35	785	2:8	260, 843, 976	18:2	482
19:25	179	2:9	349	18:4–5	178
19:26	586	2:10	1320	18:11	77, 260
19:27	1264	2:11	847, 921	18:20	1219
20:19	769	2:11–12	727	19	594
21:18	761	2:12	898, 901, 911, 922	19:4	1287, 1291, 1305
22:13–14	288			19:5	180
22:14–15	289	3:8	1349	19:7	821
24:18	759	4:4	662, 739	19:8	126, 592, 1218
24:22	910	4:5	654, 659	19:9	592, 886
26:13	249, 265	4:7	679	19:12	498, 503, 647, 743, 766, 953, 1057, 1068, 1122, 1256
27:8	769	5	333		
29:9	764	5:4	314, 333, 1237		
29:16	725, 772	5:4–6	333	19:12–13	576, , 1058
31:1	755	5:5	75, 333, 342, 387	19:13	482, 1268
31:10–12	759	5:6	333, 774, 778	20:1	686
31:15	265, 266	5:10	432	20:4	933, 1219, 1353
31:20	770	5:11	911	20:4–6	1353
31:39–40	765	6:1	1255	20:7	687
32:2	886	6:2	974	21:3	437
33:4	223	6:4	1212	22:1	131, 843
33:9	886	6:5	741	22:4–5	691
33:12	886	7:1	665	22:6	164
33:26	309	7:8	1219	22:10	291
33:32	887	7:14	785	22:22	685
34:5	886	8	843	22:25	718
35:7	886	8:3	265	23:2	822
36:26	70	8:4	1250	23:4	822
38:4	283	8:5	164	23:5	822
38:4–7	283	8:6	843	24:5	896
38:10–11	279	10:13	749	24:7	843, 1320, 1358

24:8	150
24:10	150
25:4	421
25:5	318
25:7	489, 498, 546
25:16	661
26:4–6	1353
26:8	1287
27:8	679
27:8–9	95
27:9	114
27:10	661
27:13	910
28:7	911
29:5	1250
31:1	673, 911, 955
31:19	1038
31:22	490
31:23	665
32	892, 1012
32:1	496, 563, 903, 1001, 1265, 1268, 1271
32:1–2	893, 918, 1020
32:2	879, 998
32:3	1250
32:5	836
32:5–6	554, 1059
32:6	604, 783, 1122, 1351
32:8	373
32:9	373, 800
33:4	332
33:6	89, 91, 105, 223, 227, 231, 237, 241, 255, 264, 267
33:7	279
33:9	237, 255, 263, 265
33:10	288
33:11	288, 933
33:13	257, 292
33:13–15	288
33:15	257, 525
33:15–16	1213
33:16	292
33:18–19	257, 292
33:19	779
33:20	1059
33:21	911
34:3	688
34:7	299, 307, 308, 309, 311
34:8	911
34:10	257, 269, 673, 770
34:14	778, 1075, 1147
34:15	1095
34:15–16	288
34:17	690
35:6	421
35:12	746
35:19	592, 741, 742, 981
35:24	1219
36:6	257, 286
37:4	298
37:5	258, 401, 421, 659, 673, 911
37:19	257, 1235
37:21	746, 768, 1267
37:23	317
38:2	1064
38:3	849
39:1	778
39:7	919
39:11	684
40:6–7	819
40:7	928
40:9	819, 896
40:10–11	896
40:13	843
40:16	665
41:1–2	1212
41:4	433, 521
41:11	843
41:13	911
42:5	711
42:7–10	68
44	704
44:21	1308
44:22	1359
45:1	821
45:2	165, 975
45:6	843
45:6–7	145
45:7	223, 843
45:11	58, 122, 128
45:13	843
46:1	79
47:5	151
47:7	843
47:9	727, 1320
49:6	672
49:13	323
49:20	323
50	512
50:8	855
50:15	217, 258, 683, 1356
50:16	441, 685
50:16–17	1352
50:17–23	1353
50:18	755, 765
50:23	690
51	245, 519, 1001, 1139, 1144, 1161
51:2	1222
51:4	482, 886, 1008, 1206
51:5	168, 482, 489, 498, 501, 520, 1275, 1370
51:6	524
51:7	482, 548, 1222
51:10	223, 230, 261, 262, 790, 1069, 1073
51:11	482, 1069–70, 1184
51:12	247, 249, 432, 433, 1070, 1087, 1120
51:14	896
51:16	1228
51:17	433, 618, 659, 1356
52	749
52:3	1274
52:6	665
52:7	673
54:5	1083
54:6	452, 1093, 1120
55:1	975
55:22	256, 770
55:23	749

56:7	982	76:1–2	1304	99:3	686
56:11	673	76:12	221	100:3	257, 292
56:13	1089	77:8	357	101	872
57:4	740	77:9	974	102:12	80
58	635	78	1094	102:13	974
58:11	459	78:5	709	102:16	843
59:10	437	78:22	898, 910	102:18	261, 1225
60:11	1349	78:38	178	102:19–20	1320
62:8	911	78:42	306	102:22	1320
62:10	768	78:47	744	102:25	265
62:11	764	78:49	306	102:26	1250
62:12	691	79	577	103	968
64:10	911	79:6	688	103:3	1058
66:2	688	80:13	344	103:6	896
67:6–7	89, 91	81:8–12	342, 388	103:6–7	968
67:29	387	81:9	344, 663	103:10	982
68	581	82:1	115	103:12	555
68:8	820	82:3	882	103:13–14	521
68:11	819	82:6	592	103:14	521, 944
68:17–18	145	82:8	145	103:18	707
68:18	843	84:1	1287	103:20	303, 308, 309
68:26	1292	85:8	227	103:20–22	322
68:28	1051	86:5	975	104	276, 322
68:30	749	88	941, 946	104:2	265, 278
69:1	843	88:13	459	104:2–3	278
69:4	741, 981	89:11	265	104:4	221, 222, 300, 302
69:5	1267	89:20	842		
69:6	482	89:31–32	1075, 1184	104:5	265, 278, 294, 322
69:23	1300	89:32–33	644		
69:27	512, 1270	89:37	265	104:6–7	278
69:27–28	896	89:52	151	104:8	265, 294, 322
71:1–2	896	90:2	154	104:8–9	278
71:2	1003	90:8	498	104:9	322
71:16	1003, 1219	90:11	431	104:10	279, 294
71:17–18	1044	91:2	911	104:13	279
72	153	91:11	305, 307, 308, 311	104:14	279, 292
72:1	843			104:14–15	280, 292
72:5	122, 128	91:12	309	104:16	280, 292
72:14	1356	91:14	673, 686	104:19	294, 322
72:15	122	94:8	288	104:20	280
72:17	153	95:8	1267	104:21	292, 293
72:17–19	128	96:1–2	819	104:22–23	280
73:3	329, 671	96:5	275	104:24	279, 280
73:11	288	96:6	679	104:25–26	281
73:13	885	98:3	843	104:27	292, 293
74:16	265	99	843	104:27–30	257
76:1	1307	99:2	151	104:30	106, 227, 231, 249, 267

105:15	843	118:22	180, 843	128:6	1357
106	988	118:23	1337	130	1134
106:6	547	118:29	332	130:1	68
106:30–31	983	119	592, 594, 595,	130:2–3	521
106:31	987, 1217		654, 688, 707,	130:3	604, 637, 835,
106:33	1304		805, 808, 821,		856, 890, 1000,
106:37	1077		933, 1134		1122, 1219, 1265,
106:37–38	547	119:1	1089–90		1278
106:39	1077	119:14	609	130:4	666
108:10	733	119:15	1134, 1356	130:7	959
109:6	304	119:20	933	132:11	165, 692, 842
109:7	1088	119:29	421	133:1	749
109:17	371, 672	119:31	222	135:6	75
110:1	56, 91, 128, 150	119:32	421	135:7–8	291
110:2	843	119:34	432, 433, 608	136:5	264, 280
110:3	91, 1087, 1120	119:35	251, 791, 1221	136:6	265
110:4	56, 128, 179, 692,	119:40	786	139:5	291, 526
	836, 843	119:41	843	139:7	226, 231
110:5	91	119:46	707	139:7–8	288
110:6–7	843	119:57	168	139:13	291, 526
111:1	608	119:68	332	139:15–16	526
111:5	673	119:69	608	139:16	291
111:7	332	119:71	1063	139:21–22	741
111:9	686	119:73	265	139:22	741
111:10	673	119:81	843	139:23–24	1219
112:3	770	119:90–91	332	139:24	1221
112:4	975	119:91	286, 288	141:4	327, 416
112:5	749, 768	119:105	793, 803, 1132	141:5	1351, 1352
112:6	770	119:108	1083, 1089	143:2	835, 847, 856,
112:7	911	119:109	463		886, 890, 950,
112:7–8	911, 937	119:113	741		1041, 1057, 1068,
112:9	1219	119:123	843		1122, 1200, 1202,
113:3	686	119:133	567, 785, 793		1219, 1278
114	1001	119:161	981	143:10	223, 247, 249,
114:7–8	294	119:165	1202		444, 1221
115:3	5, 366	119:166	843	144:2	723
115:8	672	119:174	843	144:3–4	985
115:13	673	120:7	981	144:5–7	68
116:1	665	123:3	974	145:13	631
116:3	178	124:8	261, 285	145:13–14	67
116:9	1089	125:1	673, 911	145:14	401
116:15	658	126:6	944, 1037	145:15	292
116:17	684	127:1	257, 292, 338,	145:15–16	257
118:1	332		401, 1235	145:18	401, 404, 690
118:8	671	127:3	1216	145:19	673
118:13	385	128:1–2	1235	146:4	221, 222
118:17	55, 60	128:2	292, 770	146:5–7	285
		128:3	732	146:6	268, 278
				146:8	444

147:3	67	6:25	786	16:5	661
147:4	67	6:29	759	16:6	1212
147:6	200	6:30–32	769	16:9	421
147:8	257, 291	6:32–33	759	16:11	762
147:8–9	292	6:33	759	16:32	749
147:9	292	7:10–13	754	17:2	732
147:10–11	292	7:22–23	759	17:5	743, 778
147:13	338	8	158	17:11	788
147:13–15	1049	8:13	665	17:13	743, 748
147:15	67	8:15	895	17:15	772, 882, 885,
147:16	67	8:17	672		889, 986, 987,
147:18	221, 236	8:22	89, 154, 157, 843		1027
147:19	67	8:24	268	17:22	221
147:19–20	1304	8:27–29	265	18:3	347
147:20	270	9:10	673	18:6	773
148	322	9:17	764	18:10	687
148:5	268	10:1	727, 732	18:20	778
148:6	265, 322	10:12	1223, 1297	19:5	778
148:8	291, 322	10:18	773	19:9	778
149:1	55, 60	10:19	778	19:17	770
		10:22	257	19:19	749
PROVERBS		11:1	769	19:26	727, 732
1:7	673	11:3	770	20:7	749
1:9	732, 975	11:12	746	20:9	554, 604, 953
1:24	467, 468	11:21	770	20:12	719
2:14	378, 416, 1274	11:26	765, 769, 770	20:15	778
2:16	759	11:28	672	20:17	764
2:18	759	12:13	778	20:19	773
3	727	12:14	778	20:20	733
3:5	911, 933	12:19	778	20:22	749
3:7	665	12:20	749	20:23	765, 769
3:10	770	12:22	778	20:24	422
3:22	975	12:27	778	21:1	351
3:29	577, 746	13:2–3	778	21:3	749
3:30	746	13:3	778	21:6	778
3:33	257	13:5	778	21:6–7	769
4:6	672	13:10	482	21:10	786, 975
5:3	759	13:24	726	21:13	768, 769
5:14	1303	14:27	673	21:21	749
5:20	754	14:29	749	21:23	778
6:6	64	14:30	748	21:28	778
6:11	769	15:5	727, 732	21:30	351
6:12–13	774	15:26	787	22:1	778
6:16	778	15:27	1222, 1223	22:4	673
6:18	785, 787, 1275	15:33	673	22:7	768
6:20	727	16:1	421, 438	22:9	770
6:23–24	732	16:4	347	22:16	769
6:24	759			22:19	759

22:24–25	749	30:3	138	1:17	716
22:28	765	30:4	138	1:17–18	1196
23:5	766, 769	30:5–6	138, 1081	1:18	467
23:13	726	30:8–9	767	1:19	467, 1329
23:14	732	30:10	730	1:19–20	1213
23:18	1216	30:17	733	1:22	762, 765
23:22	726, 727	30:18	1337	1:23	765
23:27–28	759	31:10	758	2:2	1246
23:29	755	31:30	763, 975	2:2–3	844
23:30	755			2:3	592, 819, 821, 1246
23:33	755	**ECCLESIASTES**			
24:11	729, 738, 1184	1:16	138	3:9	1274
24:15	786	3:14	631	4	844
24:16	1271	3:19	954	4:2	165, 843
24:17	743	3:21	221, 222	5:1	843
24:17–18	748	5:10	769	5:4	344
24:21	728, 729	5:10–17	768	5:4–6	344
24:21–22	733	6	770	5:5	311
24:28	774, 981	6:1	769	5:8	765, 769
24:30	769	7:9	743	5:11	755
25:9	773	7:25	466	5:12	65, 709
25:18	740, 772	7:29	466, 522	5:20	582, 885
25:21	736	8:8	482	5:23	772, 882, 889, 986, 1027
25:21–22	749	9:1–2	954		
25:27	70	9:7	537, 954	6:1	146
26:2	981	10:4	749	6:2	302
26:17	727	12:1	1045	6:3	89, 91, 220, 302
27:4	769	12:7	525–26, 584	6:9	1300
27:20	766			6:10	338, 339
28:2	482	**SONG OF SOLOMON**		6:13	1310, 1329
28:8	769	**(SONG OF SONGS)**		7:2	673
28:13	482	4:9	433	7:14	128, 145, 179, 498, 843, 1055
28:14	338, 952, 1258	8:6	944		
28:22	769			7:14–15	843
28:24	482, 727, 738	**ISAIAH**		7:16	498, 546
28:25	741	1	467, 1208	8:1	38
28:27	770	1:2	136	8:13–14	146, 150
28:28	769	1:3	322	8:14	844
29:1	338	1:9	1227, 1300, 1310	8:16	944, 1340
29:3	759	1:10	655	8:18	166
29:9	741	1:11	855	8:20	1289, 1339
29:19	730	1:12	911, 1002, 1022, 1080, 1132	9:4	1149
29:21	730			9:6	58, 109, 128, 145, 149, 165, 178, 1231
29:24	765	1:13	710		
29:25	672, 673	1:13–14	1088		
30:1	138	1:15	572, 653	10:1–2	765
30:2	138	1:16	468, 787	10:15	352
		1:16–17	1208	11:1	165, 843

11:2	224, 249, 432	37:28–29	373	44:25	351
11:3	844	37:36	309	45	348
11:4	223, 451	38:1	369	45:1	723
11:10	122, 843, 1040	38:3	1219	45:5–7	82, 85, 348
12:7	282	38:13	802, 1059	45:6	215–16
13:9–10	341	38:15	380	45:6–7	266, 274
13:17	341	38:17	1250	45:7	274
13:21	301	38:21	295	45:8	348
14:24	372, 377, 380	40	844	45:9	349
14:27	372	40:3	843, 1316	45:11	349, 364
16:2	1088	40:4	522	45:20	469
17:4–7	680	40:6	1040	45:21	152, 663
19:14	221, 351	40:9–10	819	45:21–22	82, 85
19:18–19	694	40:18	156, 682	45:21–23	147
20:5	672	40:25	156	45:22	469, 665
21:12	469	40:26	291	45:23	694
23:4	519	40:28	631	45:23–24	693
25	844	40:31	673	45:24	896, 986, 1029, 1208
25:8	714	41:4	150		
26	844	41:9	338	45:25	886, 1208
26:3	911, 937	41:17	152	46:3–4	1046, 1295
26:10	975	41:20	262	46:10	372, 380
26:16	470, 644	41:23	336, 364	48:4	432
26:18	519	41:24	268	48:12–13	150
26:19	438	41:26	364	48:16	89, 249
27	844	41:27	819	49	844
28	768, 844	42	91, 844	49:2	1315
28:11–12	592	42:1	196, 249	49:6	180
28:13	672	42:3	952	49:15	80
28:16	180, 898, 910, 1040	42:4	821	49:23	713, 727, 1320
		42:5	265, 525	50:6	844
28:21	274	42:6	180	50:8	882
29:13	608, 1077, 1132	42:8	148, 670, 681	50:10	911
30:1	249	42:9	1245, 1250	50:15	1053
30:10	1344	42:17	672	51:4	821
30:15	469	43:2	68	51:6	1250
30:18	1262	43:7	264	51:16	345, 1315
30:19	974	43:9	882	52	844
32	844	43:10	154, 156, 235	52:7	819
33:1	769	43:13	377	53	91, 836, 1040, 1163, 1232
33:16	1066	43:19	1253		
33:16–17	749	43:24–25	844	53:2	843, 844
33:22	91, 178	43:25–26	1024	53:2–5	157
34:14	301	43:26	882	53:3	162
35	844	44	844	53:4	169, 178, 1196
35:5–6	843	44:3	223	53:5	618
37:23	649	44:6	82, 84, 150, 663	53:6	178, 430, 836, 1028, 1040

53:8	115, 153, 156, 163
53:9	168, 553, 843
53:10	163, 178, 333, 836
53:11	196, 836, 847, 853, 886, 887, 931, 937
54	844
54:8	80
54:13	655, 1300
54:15	357
54:16	357, 418
54:17	357
55	844
55:4	178
55:6	321
55:9	1278
55:10–11	1310
55:11	250
56:2	714
56:4	714
56:4–5	620
56:4–7	713
56:10	1344
57:15	433, 1260
57:19	230, 261
58:2	855
58:3–4	713
58:3–5	855
58:4	653
58:7	716, 869, 1356
58:7–8	1195, 1218
58:8	770
58:10–11	1066
58:11	714
58:13	708, 714
58:13–14	713
59	844
59:3	572
59:4	672, 1077
59:8	1077
59:20–21	397
59:21	213, 217, 235, 236, 251, 1298, 1301, 1312, 1314, 1329, 1339, 1340
60	844
60:10	1320

60:12	1320
60:19	91
61:1	199, 223, 819, 1230–31
61:1–2	820
61:3	1311
62	844
63:1	844
63:9	308, 344
63:9–10	341
63:10	344, 791
63:11	213, 215
63:14	223, 225, 227, 232, 236
63:15	341
63:16	136
63:17	339, 341, 387, 389
64:4	672
64:6	310, 504, 605, 939, 1000
65	844, 1233
65:1	1233
65:11–12	1234
65:12	333, 354, 361, 363
65:16	694
65:17	1234
66	844
66:1–2	1064
66:2	1053, 1260
66:3	1088, 1176, 1177
66:23	649, 702, 714
66:24	480

JEREMIAH

1:6	337
1:9–10	802
2:10–11	799
3:11	883, 887
3:12	1281–83
3:14	1283
4:1–2	693
4:2	696
5:1	778, 1210
5:5	1273, 1280
5:7	695, 697, 755, 1211, 1280
5:8	754

5:22	279
5:25	672
5:27	765
5:29	759
7:3	885
7:7	769
7:8	672
7:16	685
7:21–23	855
7:22	1228
8:9	713
9:4–5	765
9:5	778
9:8	740
9:9	778
9:23	1007, 1040
9:24	664, 950, 1021
10:5–7	670
10:6	664, 686
10:7	664
10:10	90
10:11	152, 266
10:13	291
10:18	420
10:23	317, 353, 400, 419, 420
10:24	1255
11:4–5	911
12:3	643
14:14	346, 689, 1316
15:9	1330
15:13	981
15:18	522
15:19–21	1344
16:13	975
16:14	68
16:14–15	704
16:16	844
17:5	522, 670, 672, 1349
17:7	522, 673, 1349
17:9	489, 490, 522, 523, 564, 640, 787, 953
17:9–10	522
17:14	522
17:15–16	1330
17:21	704

17:22	706
17:25	713
17:27	713
18:4	349
18:6	349
18:7	349, 380
18:7–8	368, 372, 1208
18:7–9	1209
18:8	369
18:10	368
18:11	368
18:18	740, 1329
20:4–6	713
20:7	325, 336, 337
20:9	337
20:15	820
22:13	768
23	672
23:5	165, 844
23:5–6	91
23:6	71, 147, 148, 179, 1029, 1040
23:7	648
23:9	236
23:11	713
23:16	346
23:21	346, 1313, 1315
23:22	95
23:24	152
23:29	591, 635
23:30	762
26:1	385
27:2	700
27:6	723
27:8	728, 733
27:14–15	1313
27:15	346
29:7	725, 732
29:9	346
29:16	482
29:22–23	759
30:9	844
30:11	547, 644, 690
31	623
31:3	80
31:13	755
31:17	1216

31:18	469, 470
31:22	165, 262
31:29–34	548
31:31	822, 844, 1229, 1249
31:31–32	623, 1240
31:31–33	596, 630, 1002
31:32	856. 1250, 1252
31:33	432, 654, 789, 790, 805, 821, 826, 832, 978, 988, 999, 1040, 1084, 1116, 1133, 1195, 1244, 1245, 1246, 1248
31:33–34	1230, 1234
31:34	1231
32:19	70
33:14	821
33:15	165
33:15–16	91, 844
33:16	71, 127, 147, 179, 896
34:11	730
35	733
35:19	732
36:2–3	369
36:7	975
37	773
38:4	749
38:7	749
38:7–13	1359
39:17	749
42:9	975
44:14	1303
44:26	692, 693
49:16	1267
50:9	1303
52:24	713

LAMENTATIONS

3:24	168
3:52	981

EZEKIEL

1:10	302
1:20	220
2:2	249
2:8	1304

3:14	249
3:17	1330
6:9	433
6:10	981
7:10	482, 1267
8:16	616
10:14	302
11:17	844
11:19	338, 433
12:2–3	369
12:18–19	1344
13:10	1344
14:7	664
14:7–8	346
14:9	345, 346
14:9–10	346
14:23	981
16:4–5	498
16:47	577
16:49	755
16:51	883, 887
17:13	697
18:6	759
18:7	761
18:9	759, 770
18:10	761, 764
18:10–13	769
18:12	761
18:16	761
18:17	547, 620
18:20	547
18:21	1207
18:22	1207
18:23	1260, 1262, 1265
18:31	469, 482, 1251
19:5	919
20:8	853
20:9	688
20:11	804
20:12	708, 713
20:14	688
20:18	855
20:18–19	1080, 1132
20:19	469, 1148
20:20	702
20:25	856
20:27–28	708

20:31	690	3:25	309	12:7	692
20:47	713	4:3	661	**HOSEA**	
21:4	420, 421	4:10	1211	1:2	751
22:7	734	4:13	1211	1:7	91, 1295
22:15	734	4:25	1211	2:8–9	257, 292
22:21	713	4:27	770, 1195, 1211	2:12	292
23	754	4:28	690	2:16	669
23:16	755	5:3	691	2:18	844
23:38	713	6	304, 308	2:19	1279
23:47	713	6:6	773	2:23	1040
29:4	373	6:13	772	3:4	624
29:19	419	6:22	308, 309	3:4–5	844
30:24	338	6:23	898, 910	3:5	178
33:4	217	7	721	4:3	748
33:7	1330	7:8	721	4:6	1323
33:11	366, 370, 1041	7:9	682	4:11	759
33:14	768, 1174	7:10	302, 303, 308	4:12	221
33:15	768	7:13	165	4:15	693
33:18–19	1259	7:13–14	844	5:15	470
34:11	1040	7:14–27	1040	6	716
34:16	338, 433, 1331	7:25	721	6:2	844
34:17	1311, 1354	8:14	886	6:6	655, 844
34:23	165, 179, 844	9	1040	6:7	549
36:25	844, 1024	9:2–7	341	8:1	482
36:26	338, 432, 433, 469	9:5	547, 1267	10:3	672
		9:7–9	1059	11:1	844, 1040
36:26–27	443, 530	9:16	896	11:8–9	80
36:27	448, 605, 789, 978, 988	9:17	856	11:9	156
		9:18	959, 975, 998	13:4	668, 844
36:32	1024	9:18–19	1059	13:9	379
37:5–7	220	9:19	91, 1059	13:13–34	1234
37:12	844	9:24	844, 1232	13:14	179, 746, 1040
37:24	165, 178, 179	9:25	178	13:42	364
37:25	178	9:26	1232	14:5	844
37:26	710	9:26–27	844		
38:4	373, 1303	9:27	623, 630	**JOEL**	
38:7	1303	10	308	2:12–14	1209
38:13	1303	10:3	300	2:15	1303
43:22	1271	10:7	311	2:15–16	710
48:35	149	10:7–8	303	2:23	844
		10:13	299, 302, 304, 308, 309	2:28	59, 173, 214, 226, 244, 249, 563, 844, 1245
DANIEL					
2	844	10:20	101		
2:21	62	10:21	299	2:28–32	1040
2:37	734	12:1	299, 308, 845	2:32	686, 687, 690, 1040, 1234
2:44	1040	12:3	883		
3	673, 729	12:5–12	128		
3:15	1212				

Amos

1:3	482, 576
2:1	576
2:6	373
2:11–12	713
3:6	274, 348
4:2	692
4:7	295
4:10	274
5:15	974
5:22–23	713
5:25	1040
5:25–26	1077
7:15	200
8:5	765
8:6	765
8:10–11	713
8:14	695
9:8–9	1233, 1358
9:11	1040

Obadiah

1	672

Jonah

1:9	261
1:14	547
3:1	369
3:4	1210
3:9	1210
3:10	1210
4:1	369
4:11	292, 546

Micah

1:9	522
2:1	784
2:1–2	764
2:2	765, 788
2:5	1304
2:7	249
3:2–3	764
4:1	1246
4:2	819, 821, 844, 1246
4:3	769
5:2	75, 128, 153, 178, 242, 844, 1040

5:4	844
5:7	919
5:26	853
6:6–7	855
6:7	653
6:10–11	765
6:12	765
6:13	769, 778
7:3	729
7:5	910
7:9	1209
7:19	555, 844

Nahum

1:3	547, 554
1:15	820, 844, 1041

Habakkuk

2:2	38
2:3–4	844
2:4	901, 1041, 1371
2:6	769
2:8	764, 769
3:2	1255

Zephaniah

1	672
1:5	697
3:3	765
3:5	332, 387, 542
3:9	844

Haggai

2:6	845, 1041
2:7	179

Zechariah

1:3	469, 470
1:12	309
1:15	361
2	845
2:8	577
3:1	304, 845
3:8	165
6:12	165, 845
7	716
7:5–6	1077
7:7	213
7:10	786

7:12	225, 235, 236, 237
8	845
8:7	845, 1041
8:17	314, 334, 387, 778, 786
9:5	665
9:9	157, 845, 1041
9:11	704, 820, 1232–33, 1248
11:12	845
12	845, 1233
12:8	147
12:10	76, 147, 149, 173, 216, 218, 224, 242, 249, 251, 396, 440, 845, 975, 1054, 1233
13	845
13:1	845
13:7	845
14	845

Malachi

1:6	665, 690, 727
1:7	614
1:11	845
2:4–9	1337
2:7	614, 617, 1237, 1301, 1314, 1323, 1330, 1337, 1338
2:10	85, 266
2:14	619
2:15	517
2:17	329
3:1	178, 179, 845, 1041, 1316
3:3	853
3:3–4	845
3:5	748, 759
3:6	80, 158, 185, 189, 1026
3:15	329
4:2	839, 845
4:4	38, 809

Apocrypha

3 Ezra

10:5	695

TOBIT	
3:8	305
4:4	726
4:11	770, 1197, 1212, 1222
4:14	768
5:15	733
5:21	247, 311
6:7	305, 310
6:17	310
8:1–3	305
8:3	305, 309
10:10	100
12:9	1197, 1212, 1222
12:12	309, 311

JUDITH	
6:2	691
6:18	620
11:4	775
13:20	309
15–16	760

WISDOM	
1:7	226, 286, 821
1:11	714, 774, 775, 778
1:13	274
1:13–14	268
1:14	265, 273
2:23–24	268
2:24	333, 549
3:16–17	759
6:7	285, 577
6:7–8	290
7:22–23	224
7:25–26	134
8:1	289
9:7–9	158
11:25	286
12:13	290
12:18	286
14:3	285, 286
15:2	1017
16:21	95
18:15	133
19:1	362
19:4	381

ECCLESIASTICUS	
1:2	673
1:22	887
1:27	1222
1:28	1223
3	727
3:6	732
3:8–9	726
3:15	727
3:18	733
3:19	749
3:22	70
3:30	1222
4:1	770
4:30	773
5:1	769
5:4	953
5:5	953
5:5–6	953
5:6	311
5:14	769
6:1	778
6:5	778
7:5	887, 953
7:14	774, 778
7:23	730
7:25	466
7:26	759
7:27	726
7:29	466
7:36	770
8:4	773
8:20	773
9	754, 755
9:8	755
9:9	1275
10:9	769
10:15	577
10:28	732
10:29	887
11:10	769
11:14	274, 348
11:22–26	770
12:2	770
13:22	887
14	770
14:3	769

14:13	770
15:11	324
15:11–12	339, 341, 381
15:12	324, 333, 388, 389
15:14	401, 402, 466, 468
15:14–15	466
15:14–16	335
15:15	466
17:6	613
18:1	268, 277, 1008
18:22	887
18:30–31	1275
19:1	768
19:2	759
19:2–3	759
20:25	768, 769
20:26	778
20:28	778
21	778
22:27	466
23:9	693
23:10	689
23:11	887
23:24	759
23:29	364
25:21	786
25:23	548
26:12	755
26:13	755
26:20	759
26:29	887
27–28	749
27:15	693
27:28	778
28	778
29:4	768
29:6	981
29:7	981
29:15	770
29:25	768
30:26	749
31:5	769, 887
33:25	729, 730
33:27	730
33:30	730
33:31	730

34:21	768	1:20	166, 199, 227, 249, 302, 930	5:19	600, 641, 653, 736, 1340
34:22	768	1:21	179, 894	5:20	600, 739, 791, 1195, 1205
34:30	1350	1:23	145	5:21	734, 735, 736
35:4	770	1:25	137, 165	5:22	633, 739, 740, 741, 747, 748, 784
37:9	773	2:6	178, 1040	5:24	739
38:12	1158	2:15	1040	5:25	748
40:18	768	2:20	173, 930	5:26	739
41:3	731	2:23	842	5:27–28	752
41:9	733	3:2	38, 1020, 1331	5:28	642, 751, 755, 781, 784
41:26	770	3:7	1020, 1022, 1211	5:29–30	781, 788
42:2	887	3:8	1331	5:30	788
42:11	755	3:9	857, 1020	5:32	751
42:12	786	3:10	1075, 1147, 1184	5:33	695
43	65	3:11	223, 249, 1296, 1349, 1365	5:34	691, 692, 695
44–50	673	3:12	1311, 1354	5:34–36	695
46–48	691	3:15	200	5:37	778, 917
49:19	497	3:16	223, 228	5:39	753, 783
		3:16–17	88, 225	5:40	729

ADDITIONS TO DANIEL

		3:17	58, 211, 214, 842	5:43	744
13:36	772	4:1	221, 249	5:44	746
13:45	760	4:9	671	5:45	84, 291, 387
14:21	749	4:10	663, 668, 1008	5:46–47	270
		4:11	308	5:48	607, 632

1 MACCABEES

		4:17	1019	6:2	426
1:50	713	5	571, 638, 691, 695, 739, 748, 749, 777, 1242, 1272	6:3	865
3:20–21	725			6:4	770, 1184
9:29	713			6:5	419, 426
10:33	980			6:12	1058
		5:3	1184, 1206	6:14	749, 1196, 1208

2 MACCABEES

		5:5	732, 749	6:15	748
1:16–17	769	5:7	749, 770	6:16	426
3:7	765	5:8	788, 1090	6:24	652, 671
4:24	769	5:9	749	6:26	64, 105, 292, 293
7:22	528	5:11–12	690	6:28	64, 291
7:28	268	5:12	643, 1184, 1200, 1214	6:28–29	292
9:5	696	5:13	577	6:30	293, 923, 932, 946
10:22	770	5:15	1308	6:31	270
11:6	312	5:16	716, 718, 1061, 1180, 1183, 1184, 1347	6:33	894, 1235
14:37–46	745			7	501, 1033
15:23–24	312	5:17	589, 603, 614, 628, 691, 809, 1242	7:1	740, 773

NEW TESTAMENT

MATTHEW

				7:2	748, 778
1:1	165	5:18	231, 604, 790, 889, 986, 1000, 1026, 1027	7:7	400, 404, 805, 1069, 1351
1:6	1148				
1:16	167				
1:18	249				

7:11	80, 501	10:37	671, 727	13:30	1329
7:12	368, 592, 635, 799	10:39	744, 1178, 1356	13:35	265
		10:41	713	13:47	1353–54
7:14	1221	10:42	686, 712, 770, 1066, 1184, 1201, 1359	13:47–48	1295, 1311
7:15	1333, 1336, 1339			13:52	821
7:15–17	1353			14:7	694
7:16	1184, 1365	11	1041	14:10	182
7:16–20	943, 1037	11:9	917	14:24–25	169
7:17–18	569	11:11	164	14:31	912, 922, 923, 932, 946
7:18	426, 1088, 1349–50	11:13	592, 593, 624		
		11:19	169, 883	15:1	1077
7:19	1075, 1147	11:24	1271	15:3	638, 1002
7:21	1016	11:25–26	350	15:4	722
7:22	251, 916, 925, 1033	11:25–27	66	15:4–6	727
		11:26	350	15:5–6	653
7:22–23	915	11:27	61, 107, 656, 685	15:9	613, 667, 681, 803, 1002, 1022, 1080, 1132
7:23	570, 1265	11:28	122, 469, 904, 964, 1042		
7:26	1184			15:18	242
8:11	917	11:29	824, 1037	15:19	411, 571, 756, 763, 774
8:12	1307	12:1	705		
8:17	1040	12:5	705	15:28	898, 902
8:20	1294	12:6	705	16:4	1040
8:26	912, 923	12:7	614, 705	16:8	923
8:31	308	12:8	704	16:16	234
9:2	832, 894, 914 922	12:12	705	16:17	430
9:3	689, 857, 947	12:20	860, 932	16:18	945, 1239, 1301, 1304, 1306, 1341, 1342
9:4	739	12:28	199, 223, 226, 249		
9:13	614			16:19	894, 1338, 1340
9:17	591, 822	12:33	570, 1087, 1128	16:23	306, 1342
9:22	898, 912	12:34–35	569	16:24	658, 1356
9:29	1004	12:35	570, 582	17:5	217, 569, 660, 958, 964, 1190, 1339
9:38	1315, 1329	12:36	686, 778		
10	1084	12:37	882		
10:5	1327	12:38–40	1040	17:19	576
10:8	981, 1316	12:40	843	17:20	925
10:10	620	12:41	887	17:24–27	196
10:15	577, 713, 748	12:42	843	17:25	1264
10:16	292	13:3	661	18	1163
10:20	223, 226, 227, 232, 237, 241, 249, 250, 317	13:12	244	18:6	1348
		13:14	442	18:7	370, 375
		13:19	822	18:9	788
10:22	1108	13:21	925	18:10	301, 302, 303, 305, 308, 309, 311
10:28	282, 671	13:22	764, 768		
10:29	105, 288, 290	13:23	1310		
10:29–30	257	13:24	822	18:14	385, 1042, 1367, 1369
10:30	290	13:24–30	1311, 1354		
10:31	292	13:27	822, 1310		
10:32	690, 1108, 1184	13:27–28	304	18:15	575, 743

18:16	770	22:37	411, 651, 1077	25:37	1179
18:17	1291, 1296, 1301, 1343	22:37–39	641	25:40	686, 749
		22:38	652	25:41	589, 684, 769
18:18	884, 894, 945, 1310, 1358	22:38–39	478	26:7	1084
		22:39	468, 651, 655	26:13	1305
18:19	1319	22:44	175	26:28	1240
18:20	127, 152, 710, 1310	23	1339	26:37	175, 176, 177
		23:2	1296	26:38	131, 174, 177, 494
18:23	749, 1208	23:2–3	1079, 1338, 1353	26:39	174, 175–76, 185, 193
18:32	1149	23:4	1340		
18:33	1159	23:8	1339	26:41	1258
18:34	741, 1148	23:12	949	26:49	774
18:35	484, 748	23:14	69, 699	26:50	515
19:5	633, 757	23:23	478, 993, 1077, 1159	26:52	733, 748, 1217
19:7	629			26:53–54	379
19:8	619, 692	23:25	1077	26:54	1040
19:14	546, 1367	23:25–27	570	26:61	772
19:16	1019	23:27	1330	26:63	695
19:17	332, 1104, 1165, 1194, 1205	23:32	351, 576	26:63–64	692
		23:37	367, 452, 467, 468	26:65	689
19:18	1077			27:13	772
19:19	722	24:2	152	27:35	1041
19:20	600, 857, 1368	24:9	688	27:43	921, 922, 1041
19:21	1023, 1214	24:14	595	27:46	185, 193, 1041
19:27	858	24:15	1040	27:48	1041
19:28	163	24:24	345, 681, 814, 1316, 1317, 1339	27:50	221
19:29	1215			28:3	302
20	350	24:36	194, 302, 1008	28:17	922
20:6	1075, 1147	24:37	371, 1295	28:18	160
20:8	1215, 1216	24:38	714	28:19	120, 211, 225, 230, 246, 683, 1042, 1298, 1305, 1310, 1327, 1331
20:9	1206	24:43	761		
20:12	839	24:45	822		
20:22–23	163, 176	24:46	1207		
20:23	163	25	1332	28:19–20	1310
20:25	858	25:1	1354	28:20	158, 825, 828, 1084, 1232, 1239, 1295, 1305, 1306, 1329, 1339, 1340
20:28	173, 334	25:2	1311		
21:5	1041	25:21	1184		
21:21	256, 946	25:23	1218		
21:22	256	25:26	449		
21:31	805	25:29	244, 400, 673, 1066	**MARK**	
21:37	947			1:1	829
22:7	1184	25:30	576, 1184, 1263	1:4	829, 1020, 1365
22:9	1042	25:31	302	1:8	249
22:10–12	1311	25:32	1311	1:9	58
22:11	1354	25:34	265, 749, 770, 1214, 1220	1:10–11	88
22:21	729			1:12	249
22:30	302, 447, 714	25:34–36	1207	1:14	822
22:36	593	25:35	1184	1:15	38, 829, 1019
				1:27	821, 839, 1039

2:21	1248	16:15	1305	3:21	58
3:4	705	16:16	832, 894, 906,	3:21–22	88
3:5	494		911, 913, 1276,	4:1	249
4:19	781		1352, 1362, 1371	4:18	199, 223, 819
4:25	244			5:3	714
5:9	284		**LUKE**	5:6	770
5:36	1008	1:1	920	5:8	1057
6:15	1042	1:4	40, 711	5:20	912
6:49–50	169	1:10	711	5:26	1248
6:50	922	1:17	221, 433, 1041	6:31	635
6:52	432	1:28	976	6:34	768
7:10	722	1:30	308	6:35	749, 768
7:12	727	1:33	158, 179, 1040	6:37	773, 778,
7:21	242	1:35	137, 207, 227,		1296–97,
7:21–22	569		243, 249		1356–57
8:33	306	1:35–37	199	6:37–38	749, 1184
8:38	302	1:41	185	6:38	770, 779, 1066,
9:5	180	1:50	673		1184, 1356
9:16	1248	1:54	1024	6:41	773
9:24	388, 440, 932,	1:68	179	6:43	569, 1273
	938, 952	1:70	227, 1314	6:45	1333
9:42	1124	1:73	692	7:29	883
9:44	480	1:73–74	1245	7:30	369
10:7	757	1:74	820, 1178, 1183	7:35	883
10:13	1371	1:74–75	1037, 1216	7:36	1019
10:13–16	1359	1:75	897, 1217	7:37	1013, 1268
10:15	546, 1371	1:76	1315	7:39	857
10:16	1327	1:77	822, 931	7:42	976
10:18	161, 332	1:78	165, 845, 1024,	7:47	1198, 1206
10:19	722, 771		1041	7:50	902, 913, 914,
10:23	672	1:79	430		1199
10:24	768	2:9	134, 302, 308	8:8	1310
10:30	644, 1066, 1184,	2:11	179	8:11	764
	1215	2:14	1198	8:12	306, 310, 522
11:23	922, 946	2:22	593	8:14	781
11:25	1208	2:25–26	249	8:15	712
12:6–7	180	2:26	179	8:18	244
12:34	1023	2:30	179	8:25	912
13:9	595	2:31	1024	8:30	284, 300
13:32	161, 193, 194,	2:32	180	8:31	284
	1005, 1008	2:34	146, 150	8:50	1008
14:7	743	2:40	976	8:55	221
14:9	1305	2:51	727	9:2	1327
14:45	774	2:51–52	733	9:26	302
15:28	985	2:52	164, 174	10	493, 1084, 1151
16:5	302, 828	3:3	1020, 1365	10:3	1023
16:6	308	3:14	764, 765	10:7	620, 1329
16:14	522, 933	3:16	249		

10:16	700, 1084, 1295, 1301, 1314, 1358	13:8	250	18:20	722
		13:11	301, 305	18:22	770
10:17–20	925	13:14	1148	18:30	1215
10:18	301, 1104	13:15	705	19:2	441
10:21	249, 967	13:24	1221	19:8	768
10:22	160	14:5	705	19:13	449
10:24	786	14:11	350, 949	19:14	1267
10:25	469, 600, 1019, 1165	14:12	1184	19:26	244, 1213
		14:13–14	1214	19:42	152
10:26	593, 1132	14:14	770	20:13	369
10:28	805, 837, 991, 1104, 1165, 1205	14:18	1092, 1157	20:36	284, 302, 303
		14:22	1221	20:47	774
10:29	883	14:23	388	21:6	152
10:30	467, 746	14:26	652, 653, 727, 741	21:8	689
10:35	444	15	871	21:12	688
10:42	714, 1004	15:2	857	21:30	325
11:13	80, 153, 317, 332, 396, 399, 400, 403, 440, 501, 965, 1069	15:7	1262	21:33	34
		15:10	311	22:15	786
		15:11	441	22:25–26	1336
11:14	305	15:16	786	22:31	307
11:20	223, 228	16:1	762	22:31–32	1340
11:22	307	16:1–24	178	22:32	307, 1291
11:24	301	16:8	967	22:43	308
11:25	310	16:9	770	22:43–44	177
11:25–26	344	16:10	673	22:44	131
11:26	221, 302	16:11	912	22:46	310
11:28	922	16:15	883, 888	22:47	774
11:41	770	16:21	786	22:58	1341
11:47	724	16:22	309, 769	23:2	772
12	923	16:26	284, 302	23:24	250
12:1	1353	17:5	938, 952	24:4	308
12:6	288, 290	17:9	969	24:25	432, 741, 933
12:14	614, 759	17:10	563, 858, 953, 1003, 1058, 1075, 1079, 1095, 1148, 1156, 1158	24:26	375
12:15	769			24:27	839, 928
12:16	673			24:28	775, 776
12:20	153	17:19	925, 1004	24:31–32	442
12:28	923	18:4	772	24:37	221
12:29	923	18:8	814	24:39	221
12:47	577, 1281	18:9	857, 921, 922	24:39	166, 169, 300
12:47–48	1271	18:9–12	1056	24:44	592, 745, 928, 1039
12:48	546	18:9–14	891		
12:50	861	18:10	661	24:45	1346
13:3	1273	18:11–12	600, 857, 1002	24:47	38, 476, 818, 828, 848, 1305, 1331
13:6	1262	18:13–14	888		
13:6–8	351	18:14	341, 350, 626, 672, 949	**JOHN**	
13:6–9	1208			1	119, 1292
13:7	576, 1311	18:19	106		

1:1	122, 131, 133, 145, 146, 153, 154, 274, 283, 1299	3	240, 488	5:24	142, 893, 946
		3:2	180	5:26	135, 154, 160
		3:5	136, 397, 964, 1369, 1370, 1372	5:27	160
1:1–3	145			5:29	1207, 1221
1:1–14	1299	3:5–6	249, 546, 1370	5:30	174, 226
1:3	59, 119, 122, 123, 152, 255, 265, 267, 268, 273, 283	3:6	234, 543, 546	5:36	1316
		3:8	222	5:39	928, 1039
		3:13	152, 166	5:46	842, 928, 1039
		3:14	842	6:19–20	169
1:4	180, 859	3:15–18	929	6:27	944
1:5	430, 930	3:16	75, 122, 837, 964, 1024, 1025, 1026, 1042	6:35	922
1:6	146, 161			6:38	160, 174, 1027
1:7	771			6:40	127, 1068, 1195
1:8	771	3:16–18	893	6:44	397, 443, 469, 1005
1:9	106	3:17	759, 1042		
1:10	105, 124, 275, 276	3:18	494	6:45	398, 1300
1:11	160	3:18–26	1289	6:51	202, 922
1:11–12	930	3:19	672, 832, 1031	6:54	202
1:12	136, 934, 937, 1030, 1037, 1042	3:21	1089	6:55	822
		3:27	318, 400	6:57	202
1:13	136, 431, 1007	3:29	180	6:58	724
1:14	79, 121, 122, 129, 136, 137, 173, 242, 977	3:33	922, 944, 1030	6:62	127, 166
		3:34	249	6:63	153, 201, 202, 224, 233, 249
		3:36	391, 564, 832, 929, 942, 1020, 1021, 1266, 1272, 1276		
1:15	771			6:64	364, 443
1:16	859, 968, 1028, 1365			6:67	474
		4:14	223, 822, 922	6:68	822
1:17	816, 822, 827, 955, 1252	4:16	219	7	234
		4:23	249	7:11	705
1:18	61, 66, 77, 656, 685, 834, 958	4:23–24	109	7:16	241
		4:24	75, 220, 221, 222, 682	7:19	602
1:19	771			7:23	600
1:23	1314	4:34	822	7:37	922
1:29	179, 555, 826, 898, 957–58, 1020, 1028, 1119	4:38	813	7:38	223
		5:7	705	7:39	233, 234
1:30	161	5:8	704	8:11	759
1:32	88, 234, 235, 771	5:17	104, 152, 288, 289, 360, 526, 1300	8:12	180
1:33	211, 234, 235, 249			8:16	107
		5:17–19	126	8:19	948
1:34	771	5:18	136, 154, 159	8:28–29	107
1:36	1020	5:19	104, 131, 152, 160, 241	8:29	101
1:38	180			8:32	585
1:41	179	5:19–21	154	8:33	857
1:49	180	5:21	126, 152, 160, 227, 233, 276	8:34	407, 408, 417, 431, 512, 564, 570, 1265
2:6	1351				
2:19	162, 190, 203	5:22	151, 1336	8:36	407, 408, 409, 414, 447, 1143
2:21	162	5:23	57, 107, 241, 680		
2:24	912, 1075				

8:37	635	12:25	672, 744	15:4–5	1129
8:40	174, 203, 208	12:27	174	15:4–6	432
8:42	242	12:28	214	15:5	127, 153, 318, 397, 432, 433, 444, 1069, 1300
8:44	284, 301, 302, 304, 314, 331, 334, 345, 346, 388, 549, 570, 581, 778	12:31	275		
		12:32	1028	15:12	1075, 1183
		12:39–40	344, 370	15:15	196, 232
		12:40	339	15:16	904, 959
8:51	922	12:41	146–47	15:22	548
8:52	1039	12:43	897	15:25	592
8:54–55	107	12:44	937	15:26	212, 224, 225, 230, 241, 242, 249, 401
8:55	142	13:2	306, 335, 388		
8:56	918, 1039, 1241, 1245	13:3	242		
		13:10	556, 1353	16	241
8:58	125, 127, 150	13:14	1148, 1297	16:8	249
9:1	705	13:27	306, 395	16:8–9	480, 569, 831, 849, 1022
9:34	499	13:34	808, 1064, 1148, 1243		
9:41	1263			16:8–11	475
10	145	13:37	176	16:10	475, 476
10:1	762	14:1	1011	16:11	557
10:1–5	1311	14:6	63, 217, 922	16:13	212, 224, 226, 230, 232, 249, 1301, 1339, 1340
10:3	1315	14:8–9	56, 656		
10:4	1332	14:9	148, 149, 164, 656		
10:5	1330, 1333			16:13–14	225
10:10	1353	14:10	101, 104, 130, 226	16:14	104, 249
10:11	173, 179, 1040			16:15	104, 107, 117, 135, 155, 241
10:12	1339, 1344	14:13	127, 152–53, 161		
10:14	1308	14:14	1055	16:23	217, 656, 657, 687, 1186, 1238
10:15	1310	14:16	59, 212, 225, 229, 232, 249		
10:16	1306			16:27	672
10:17	127	14:16–17	88, 213, 1055, 1339, 1340	16:28	242, 275
10:17–18	153			16:32	107
10:18	162	14:17	224, 1218	16:33	922
10:21	1084	14:18	218, 317, 401, 1055	17:3	60, 66, 106, 107, 161, 663, 664, 853, 929, 937, 1017, 1193
10:26–27	1310				
10:27	1142, 1333	14:19–20	232		
10:27–28	60, 1028	14:21	665		
10:28	127, 152, 943, 955, 1028, 1306, 1308	14:23	108, 226, 245, 563, 665, 672, 712, 922, 1037	17:5	127, 130, 153
				17:6	160, 685
				17:8	930
10:30	106, 110, 164	14:24	142, 672	17:10	155
10:33	689	14:26	249, 251, 1300, 1339, 1340	17:11	275, 1306
10:34	123, 592			17:17	1289, 1304, 1310, 1340, 1343
10:34–36	146	14:28	130, 159, 164		
10:35	195	14:31	161, 177, 1027, 1084	17:20	1358
10:35–36	145			17:21	181
11:33	741	15	1128	18:4	364
11:51	452	15:1	1354, 1358	18:6	355
11:53	572	15:1–6	1311	18:36	1336
		15:4	1005	19:7	137, 593

19:11	577, 1271
19:26	731
19:26–27	725
19:37	147
20:17	160
20:22	127, 153, 223, 234, 249, 282, 439, 1341
20:22–23	1327
20:23	884, 945, 1358
20:28	126, 145, 179
20:29	911
20:31	151, 1333
21:15–17	957
21:17	1338
21:18	1118

Acts

1:5	249, 861
1:6	163
1:7	161
1:8	243, 249, 1305
1:10	308
1:15–22	1321
1:15–26	1320
1:16	371
1:18	176
1:26	1316
2:2	223
2:3	225, 228
2:4	76, 249
2:5	1304, 1305
2:10	1304
2:16	1040
2:17	439
2:21	1040
2:23	362
2:25	1041
2:30	165, 173, 1041
2:30–31	362
2:31	1041
2:32	162
2:33	214, 234
2:34	1041
2:36	161, 162
2:37	1019
2:38	246, 555, 894, 1370

2:39	550, 1370
2:41–42	1308
2:42	711, 712, 821
3	1039
3:12	152, 160
3:15	179
3:16	925, 1004
3:17	576
3:18	372
3:19	894
3:21	158, 1039
3:22	842, 1040, 1251
3:24	842
3:25	893, 1042
4:8	249
4:12	686, 830, 894, 1028, 1078, 1172, 1289, 1367
4:19	1151
4:24	372
4:25	1041
4:27–28	372
4:28	372
4:31	249
4:32	83, 97
4:33	976
5:2	765
5:2–3	765
5:3	306, 334, 335
5:3–4	227
5:6	772
5:20	822
5:29	652, 671, 729, 1151
5:31	1024, 1025
5:32	249
5:33	572
5:36–37	734
6:7	822
6:10	624
7	1039
7:2	839
7:3	67
7:38	594, 595, 809
7:38–39	602
7:39	853
7:42	1040

7:51	245, 249, 344, 358, 367, 372, 452, 792
7:53	593, 602
7:59	122, 127, 221, 1300
8:4	821
8:14	430, 821
8:15	249
8:16	1289
8:22	947
8:25	821
8:27	1304
8:32	1040
8:37	608, 911, 933
8:39	223, 249
9:14	688
9:15	685
9:17	1326
9:31	1305
9:36	770, 1072
9:40	770
10	1218
10:1	441
10:2	441
10:3–4	309
10:4	770, 1213
10:13	744
10:20	922
10:35	1218
10:36	821
10:38	223
10:40–41	250
10:43	894, 929, 964, 1039, 1078, 1186
10:44	249
10:45	249
11:22	1305
11:26	96
12:17	309
12:22	773
12:23	690
13	1039
13:1	1305
13:2	249, 1315
13:3	1326, 1327
13:12	822

13:14–15	711	16:30	1019	23:1	1073, 1219
13:20	842	16:37	772	23:3	593
13:22	998	17	356, 1039	23:8	300
13:26	822	17:11	430	23:9	249
13:33	137, 162	17:19	821, 839	24:5	772
13:33–35	1041	17:20	441	24:16	1273
13:38	1036, 1351	17:23	63	25:3	976
13:38–39	893	17:23–28	61	26:11	689
13:39	602, 929, 964, 1026	17:24	275	26:18	430, 432, 433, 1004, 1306
		17:24–28	285		
13:44	711	17:25	62, 353, 355	26:20	1331
13:45	689	17:25–26	291	26:22	1039
13:46	1092, 1156, 1157	17:26	62, 373, 517	26:23	180
13:47	1109	17:27	62, 63, 258	26:27	925
14:3	968	17:28	62, 115, 256, 270, 288, 355, 457, 572	26:29	894
14:9	912, 925			27:24	976
14:15	62			27:25	912
14:15–17	61	17:30	64, 373, 388, 430, 576	28:22	235
14:16	64, 388			28:26–27	432
14:17	62, 63	18	704	28:27	339
14:23	1317, 1320, 1321, 1323	18:3–4	704		
		18:6	689	**ROMANS**	
14:26	1025	19:2	235	1	674, 682, 795, 798, 799, 806, 912, 1009, 1010, 1022
15	990, 992, 1039, 1078, 1102, 1156, 1167	19:5	246		
		19:12–13	301		
		19:13	699	1–3	1020
15:1	858, 861, 894, 1102, 1167	19:32	1304	1:1–2	846
		19:37	649	1:2	235–36, 819, 1039, 1245
15:5	1092, 1152	19:39–40	1304		
15:6	623, 712	20:7	703, 711	1:3	167, 171, 179
15:9	433, 902, 1004, 1126	20:20	562	1:3–4	209
		20:21	829	1:4	137, 162, 224, 236
15:10	425, 594, 602, 609, 993, 1026	20:22	249		
		20:23	249	1:5	968
15:11	894, 902, 970, 1078	20:24	822, 968	1:7	146, 979
		20:25	822	1:9	821, 822, 1073
15:16	1040	20:27	562, 1330	1:14	906, 1124, 1148
15:16–17	844	20:28	145, 146, 181, 249, 250, 712, 1304, 1315, 1318	1:16	398, 678, 822, 895, 1109, 1231, 1289, 1310, 1357
15:21	711				
15:23	862				
15:28	249, 614, 1092, 1095, 1156	20:29	1330	1:16–17	822, 896
		20:30	1339	1:17	823, 824, 825, 827, 865, 894, 895, 897, 934, 999, 1041, 1371
15:29	649, 1085	20:31	712		
15:40	976, 1025	20:32	894		
16:3	626	20:33	786, 1025	1:18	61, 477, 484, 781, 793, 798, 802, 849, 890, 1022
16:6	249	21:24–26	626		
16:7	249	22:3	653, 781		
16:13	711	22:16	1370–71	1:18–19	418, 799
16:14	433, 443				

1:19	61, 62, 794, 798	2:21–22	714, 762	3:25	179, 842, 1018, 1024, 1036, 1037
1:19–20	61, 259	2:22	664		
1:20	62, 64, 258, 260, 261, 263, 277, 321, 417	2:23	484	3:26	893, 897, 929
		2:24	689, 712	3:27	592, 819, 822, 829, 831, 909, 929, 1001, 1004, 1021, 1037, 1132, 1219
		2:25	626		
1:21	64, 343, 411, 430, 432, 440, 441, 668, 799	2:26	895, 985		
		2:29	249		
1:21–22	442	3	892, 924, 982, 990, 1001, 1009, 1010, 1013, 1018, 1125, 1135, 1195	3:28	873, 998, 1004, 1008, 1073, 1187
1:23	64, 649, 682			3:29	1119
1:24	342			3:30	1004
1:25	773	3:2	595, 912, 1305, 1319	3:31	404, 628, 789, 804, 838, 890, 986, 1026, 1027, 1061, 1195
1:26	343, 754				
1:26–27	754	3:4	432, 1007, 1037, 1041		
1:27	343				
1:28	272, 341, 342, 412, 414, 418, 424, 442, 758, 799, 1020, 1042, 1274	3:8	858, 1075. 1147	4	878, 960, 962, 978, 982, 987, 988, 990, 996, 1004, 1009, 1012, 1013, 1039, 1188
		3:9	1021, 1042, 1059		
		3:10	431, 1002, 1041		
		3:12	1021		
		3:13	529, 1021, 1041		
1:29	484, 739	3:13–14	572	4:1	839, 1241, 1245
1:29–30	740	3:14	1041	4:2	889, 897, 987, 996, 1205
1:30	733, 773	3:15	572, 737, 738		
1:31	494, 727, 739, 773	3:16	1041	4:3	834, 893, 903, 916, 961, 982, 1004, 1072, 1187, 1215
		3:18	1041		
1:32	576, 738, 755, 765, 794, 895, 1270	3:19	592, 826, 890, 1018, 1021, 1059, 1115		
				4:3–7	1102
2	798, 806, 991, 1022	3:19–20	887, 991	4:4	956, 969, 978, 983, 997, 1004, 1031
2:1	805	3:20	402, 469, 599, 635, 638, 802, 805, 806, 830, 855, 888, 891, 897, 988, 991, 1003, 1018, 1078, 1252		
2:4	360, 367, 373, 643, 644, 1277			4:4–5	983
2:4–5	348, 1280			4:5	826, 893, 987, 996, 997, 1004, 1012, 1020, 1091, 1104, 1165, 1173, 1213
2:5	432, 522				
2:8–9	1021				
2:9	480, 570	3:21	592, 815, 822, 824, 826, 894, 909, 929, 988, 1004, 1008, 1018, 1040, 1245		
2:11	1042			4:5–6	1008
2:12	548			4:6	982, 987, 988, 996, 998, 1001, 1002, 1004, 1167, 1171, 1245
2:13	837, 1104, 1165, 1205				
2:14	419, 447, 467, 518, 798, 1020, 1042, 1205	3:21–22	1319	4:6–7	1018
		3:21–28	815	4:6–8	1013, 1169, 1173
		3:22	823, 894, 929, 964, 1042	4:7	1036, 1041, 1105
2:14–16	613	3:23	488, 510, 1018	4:7–8	893, 918, 990
2:15	61, 363, 368, 378, 479, 595, 632, 635, 794, 798, 799, 1273	3:23–25	960	4:8	1004, 1037
		3:24	877, 909, 970, 972, 979, 981, 1003, 1013, 1023, 1028	4:9	990, 1004
				4:9–11	629
2:16	821			4:10	1004
2:17–18	1020				

4:11	945, 1004, 1355, 1371	5:4	666	6:12	470, 484, 782, 788, 1070, 1207, 1260, 1269	
4:12	988, 1042	5:5	244, 249, 673, 945, 1025	6:12–13	551, 1275	
4:13	822, 1004	5:6	514, 967, 1027	6:13	484, 572, 788, 1218, 1268, 1270, 1278	
4:13–16	822	5:8	484, 979, 1023, 1024, 1025			
4:14	999, 1106	5:9	893, 1028, 1029	6:14	552, 553, 609, 628, 956, 978, 1061, 1147, 1261, 1268	
4:15	484, 594, 599, 635, 802, 806, 807, 826, 847, 855, 962	5:10	888, 893, 1028			
		5:11	930, 934			
		5:12	268, 274, 314, 333, 335, 336, 338, 349, 486, 488, 514, 517, 518, 524, 548, 549, 1039, 1366, 1368	6:14–16	593	
4:16	817, 900, 914, 941, 943, 949, 953, 956, 958, 963, 977, 1008, 1105, 1168, 1221, 1349			6:15	466, 858, 1257	
				6:16	897, 1149, 1183	
				6:17	224, 381, 444, 452, 821	
4:17	917, 919	5:12–13	484	6:18	407, 408, 447–48, 1149, 1158, 1183	
4:17–20	268	5:13	687, 784, 968, 983			
4:18	923, 945, 1038			6:19	551, 572, 1073–74	
4:19	294	5:14	484, 486, 516, 517, 549			
4:20	452, 901, 922, 946			6:20	408, 431, 1146	
		5:15	827, 1003, 1028, 1073	6:21	571, 1109	
4:20–21	936			6:22	1037, 1221	
4:21	920, 1018	5:15–17	977	6:23	971, 977, 1003, 1021, 1109, 1195, 1216	
4:22	1004, 1018	5:16	882, 888			
4:23	1004	5:17	548, 790, 930, 1003, 1028			
4:23–24	914, 988			7	472, 476, 477, 486, 488, 489, 491, 517, 531, 551, 560, 570, 604, 608, 611, 779, 785, 800, 1041, 1057, 1191, 1195, 1256	
4:24	162, 909, 929, 982, 1004	5:17–18	484			
		5:18	548, 565, 895, 1004, 1021, 1370			
4:24–25	904	5:19	484, 486, 549, 888, 1000, 1004, 1027, 1029, 1125			
4:25	1027					
4:25–26	1018					
5	484, 518, 536, 549, 892, 955, 1009, 1269	5:20	469, 566, 686–87, 784, 805, 957	7:2–3	757	
				7:4	628	
				7:5	354, 499, 511, 570, 594, 1269, 1270	
5–7	499	5:20–6:1	979			
5:1	894, 898, 901, 911, 931, 934, 943, 961, 963, 1037, 1052, 1193, 1202	5:21	484, 828, 896, 986	7:5–6	251	
		6	580	7:6	249, 628, 629, 1073, 1087, 1116, 1139, 1143, 1183, 1250	
		6:1	858			
5:1–2	906, 1188	6:2	1183			
5:2	800, 902, 904, 911, 914, 932, 943, 945, 950, 951, 959, 963, 979, 1004, 1025, 1052, 1105, 1168, 1186, 1279	6:2–6	1320	7:7	468, 498, 506, 553, 641, 642, 650, 781, 782, 804, 805, 806, 991, 1275	
		6:3	1366, 1372			
		6:4	1073, 1148, 1183			
		6:5	1269			
		6:6	433, 499, 551, 552, 609, 788, 1147, 1269	7:7–8	559	
5:2–3	922	6:6–7	553	7:8	429, 486, 570, 650, 687, 784, 1275	
5:3–5	1236	6:7	883, 887			

7:9	802, 888, 1255	7:25	530, 552, 592, 604, 808, 1089, 1126, 1130		1258, 1265, 1269, 1270
7:10	594, 599, 837, 1104, 1165			8:14	249, 334, 396, 1070, 1075, 1083, 1099, 1181, 1183, 1369
7:11	499, 511	8	171, 390, 488, 489, 491, 517, 560, 580, 779, 800, 878, 1163, 1195		
7:12	594			8:14–15	1138
7:13	477, 641, 802, 806			8:15	109, 136, 224, 249, 934, 1189, 1231
7:14	335, 429, 499, 543, 552, 590, 603, 604, 640, 780	8:1	553, 554, 562, 790, 791, 1060, 1252, 1257, 1265, 1269, 1274, 1279		
				8:16	212, 249, 922, 945
7:15	406, 465, 466, 554, 1056	8:1–2	888	8:17	1220, 1221, 1262
		8:2	224, 249, 591, 592, 628, 819, 822, 1171	8:18–21	828
7:15–22	553			8:20	292
7:16	552			8:20–21	1010
7:17	181, 486, 499, 503, 552, 553, 570	8:3	75, 168, 171, 414, 425, 591, 602, 603, 605, 789, 826, 837, 891, 949, 1000, 1022, 1026, 1104, 1165, 1205, 1247	8:21	407, 408, 447
				8:23	307, 644, 1216, 1340
7:17–18	181			8:24	944, 1220
7:18	438, 459, 519, 552, 603, 641, 951, 1020, 1021			8:25	666
		8:3–4	790	8:26	249, 251, 388, 452, 931, 932, 952
7:18–19	518, 553	8:4	553, 628, 789, 789, 791, 807, 890, 895, 986, 1029, 1126		
7:18–22	604			8:28	557, 1024
7:19	406, 467, 542, 553, 1257, 1278			8:29	165, 363, 658
		8:5	225, 230	8:30	328, 892, 942, 1037, 1287, 1307, 1367
7:20	486, 499, 503, 552, 1130	8:6	249, 1064		
		8:6–7	530	8:32	136, 163, 790, 976, 1028
7:21	499, 511, 553, 603, 604, 791, 952, 987, 1000, 1089	8:7	414, 425, 429, 431, 467, 488, 490, 499, 518, 553, 602, 609, 657, 779, 1115, 1119	8:33	888
				8:33–34	882
				8:34	161, 179, 942, 1061
7:22	444, 452, 552, 554, 609, 990, 1002, 1115, 1120			8:35	914, 945, 955
		8:8–10	519	8:36	985, 1089
7:22–23	782, 808	8:9	223, 249, 396	8:37	381, 1028
7:23	374, 380, 412, 488, 499, 511, 518, 519, 530, 552, 553, 564, 592, 650, 737, 783, 787, 951, 1021, 1058, 1086, 1122, 1118, 1122 1130, 1257–58, 1265, 1269, 1274	8:10	171, 172, 249, 1268	8:38	951
		8:11	162, 223, 241, 244, 249, 250	8:38–39	914, 942
		8:12	790, 1051, 1075, 1087, 1095, 1107, 1120, 1148, 1158, 1159	8:39	377
				9:1	1073
				9:4	1240, 1305, 1319
				9:5	126, 145, 146, 151, 208, 209, 1251
7:24	503, 519, 523, 552, 563, 604, 788, 888, 890, 1279	8:12–13	1101		
		8:13	221, 551, 553, 566, 604, 788, 1064, 1069, 1126, 1133, 1171, 1172, 1184, 1207, 1257,	9:7	857, 918
7:24–25	605			9:8	985
				9:9	822
7:24–8:1	554			9:11	692

9:15	974, 1040	10:17	451, 633	13:5	381, 613, 728, 732, 733, 1092, 1095, 1151, 1153, 1154, 1155, 1158, 1273
9:17	347, 361	10:18	643		
9:18	382	11	239, 1165		
9:20	156	11:2	362		
9:21	348	11:5	979		
9:21–22	349	11:5–6	1167	13:6–7	728
9:22	333, 373	11:6	978, 998, 999, 1002, 1003, 1104, 1105, 1165	13:7	725, 728, 768, 1155, 1159
9:23	333, 1025				
9:25	1040			13:7–8	1148
9:31	441, 604–5, 803, 855, 858, 905, 1020, 1176	11:7	1165, 1176	13:8	805, 807, 1075, 1095
		11:7–8	442		
		11:8	339, 343, 442	13:9	646, 650, 651, 771, 782, 1081, 1132
9:31–32	1176	11:10	1300		
9:32	858	11:11	342	13:10	570
9:33	180, 898, 901, 1193	11:16	519, 549	13:12	1075, 1147
		11:17	822	13:13	754, 755
10	991, 1009	11:20	952	13:14	286, 755
10:2	441, 855	11:22	955	14	946
10:2–3	822, 837, 1020, 1042	11:25	522	14:1	571, 572, 922, 932, 1184, 1271
		11:26	179		
10:3	419, 858, 888, 950, 997, 1004, 1187	11:32	803, 837, 964, 1041, 1059	14:4	445
				14:5	622, 703, 920
10:3–5	316	11:33	70	14:6	626
10:4	176, 658, 790, 791, 822, 826, 827, 842, 855, 917, 928, 1125, 1172, 1251	11:34	941	14:11	147
		11:36	90, 108, 112, 267	14:14	920
		12:1	626, 695, 1053, 1073, 1089, 1149, 1218, 1314	14:17	911, 931, 1063, 1218
				14:18	1218
10:4–6	593	12:2	412, 444, 530, 790, 807, 1081, 1087, 1120, 1132, 1148, 1184	14:20	349, 446, 792
10:5	804, 826, 909, 941, 999, 1104, 1165			14:23	380, 426, 427, 480, 572, 805, 831, 865, 946, 1022, 1064, 1088, 1256, 1260, 1273, 1320
		12:3	116, 443		
10:5–6	929	12:6	969, 1345		
10:6	467, 910, 1040	12:7	1089		
10:8	822, 1358	12:9	742, 743, 746	14:26	241
10:9	712, 929, 1109, 1314	12:11	249	15:4	175, 626, 666, 712, 821, 1331
		12:14	740, 742, 746, 773		
10:10	683, 911, 929, 934, 963, 1061, 1108, 1193			15:7	1183
		12:19	734, 739	15:8	846
		12:20	743	15:12	1040
10:11	911, 1040, 1104, 1188	13	718	15:13	249
		13:1	722, 723, 1154, 1155	15:16	249, 820
10:11–13	964			15:18	181, 197, 572
10:12	1042	13:2	723, 728, 733	15:26	241
10:13	931	13:2–3	1320	15:27	1148
10:14	441, 1109, 1289	13:3	728, 732	15:30	249
10:14–15	1313	13:3–4	727	16:1–2	712
10:15	345, 819, 1041, 1313	13:4	728, 1155	16:5	1305

16:14	40, 863	3:6	280	6:10	761, 769, 773, 884, 1075, 1184
16:16	1304	3:7	361, 1332, 1350, 1361	6:11	223, 249, 556, 884, 893, 1025, 1037, 1069, 1184
16:17	821				
16:18	671	3:8	83, 97		
16:19	1073	3:9	1349	6:12	407, 676, 695
16:25	106, 821, 822	3:11	180, 1293, 1342	6:13	758
16:27	106, 621	3:12	43, 1293, 1301	6:18	570, 575
		3:12–13	1346	6:18–20	752
1 Corinthians		3:13	1293	6:19	227, 249, 759, 1037
1	924, 1013	3:16	120, 190, 249		
1:2	1308	3:16–17	227	6:19–20	250
1:4	1013	4	1041	6:20	1266
1:8	106, 955	4:1	1263	7:2	757
1:9	951, 1028	4:1–2	1330	7:3	758
1:10	695	4:2	711, 719, 1326	7:3–5	757
1:12	713	4:3–4	604, 888, 889, 1205	7:4	753
1:13	1028			7:5	306, 756, 757
1:18	822	4:4	553, 563, 647, 939, 949, 953, 985, 998, 1058, 1090, 1122, 1172, 1278	7:9	756
1:21	56, 61, 65, 66, 657, 821, 1289			7:10–11	758
				7:12	757
1:23	858			7:14	519, 545, 549, 707, 1371
1:25	821				
1:30	147, 157, 179, 853, 886, 896, 935, 986, 1024, 1029, 1040, 1073	4:5	1098	7:16	758
		4:7	436, 437, 457, 967, 1129	7:18	627
				7:19	552, 626, 649
1:31	1037, 1040, 1059, 1219	4:13	235	7:27	757
		4:15	724, 731	7:29	757
2:1	821	4:21	224	7:30–31	768
2:4	249, 821, 942	5	1296	7:32	1218
2:6	430, 611	5:1	754	7:34	756, 757, 758
2:7	61, 821, 834	5:3	1195	7:36	415
2:8	150, 206	5:4	710, 1312	7:36–37	466
2:9–10	249	5:4–5	1353	7:37	375, 407
2:10	94, 226, 231, 249	5:5	754	7:39	757
2:11	107, 161, 223	5:6	499, 1348	7:40	249
2:12	242, 249, 945, 976	5:6–7	1353	8:1	649, 676
		5:7	179, 604, 626, 842	8:3	672
2:13	249, 821			8:4	116, 649, 675
2:14	397, 430, 438, 530, 780, 1300	5:8	499	8:4–6	82, 85
		5:11	713, 773	8:5	147, 275, 333
2:16	941	5:46	842	8:5–6	146, 662
3:1	711	6:6	772	8:6	111, 150, 226, 231, 266, 267
3:1–2	1330	6:8	1214		
3:4	713	6:8–9	764	8:8	552, 626
3:4–5	1345	6:9	754, 1051, 1070	8:13	768
3:5	726	6:9–10	801, 938, 950, 1068–69, 1101, 1106, 1259	9	1144
3:5–7	1345			9:2	1157
3:5–8	1319, 1350				

9:7	768	11:32	659	14:33	1306, 1321
9:9	292	12:2	441	14:34	758
9:10	763	12:3	234, 249, 432	14:35	757, 758, 1314
9:13	620, 626	12:4	224, 225, 230, 244	14:39	713, 1331
9:14	712, 1332	12:4–6	227	14:40	710, 1321
9:16	1092, 1095, 1158, 1263	12:4–8	249	15:3	1027
9:16–17	1155	12:5	231	15:10	101, 449, 467, 970, 1174
9:17	452, 467, 1120, 1158	12:6	227, 318, 336, 1345	15:12–20	169
9:18	1084	12:7–9	1314	15:14	170
9:19	1146, 1151	12:8	212	15:15	771
9:20	626	12:9	227	15:20	165
9:22	695	12:10	925	15:21	274
9:24	444	12:11	212, 224, 227, 233, 344	15:22	515, 1028
9:27	577, 756, 1352	12:13	224, 249, 1310	15:24	159, 284, 1266
10	1056, 1144	12:22	1157	15:25	158
10:4	128, 151, 232, 736	12:28	1315, 1318	15:28	164, 447, 828
10:5	736	12:29	1314	15:31	695
10:6	782, 786, 1275	13:1	302	15:32	508
10:7	649, 673, 755	13:1–2	916	15:33	270, 799
10:8	759, 1109	13:2	925, 1194	15:36	744
10:9	147	13:5	571, 739, 740, 1281	15:37–38	291
10:10	659	13:7	774	15:38	279, 361
10:11	712, 1246, 1331	13:10	468	15:40	116
10:12	951, 952, 1130	13:12	70, 181, 1025, 1100	15:41	1272
10:13	339, 388, 706, 745	14	712	15:47	166, 174, 325, 454
10:14	1312	14:3	712, 1331	15:53–54	523
10:16–17	1310	14:5	807	15:55	179, 1040
10:19	675	14:6	711	15:55–57	820, 888
10:20	669	14:9	713	15:56	594, 687, 784, 802, 807
10:23	676	14:12	1330	15:57	108
10:24	743	14:16	712	15:58	250, 1310, 1315, 1369
10:32	1184, 1304	14:19	711, 1331	16:1	712
11:1	1209	14:21	592	16:1–2	711
11:3	160, 164, 722, 757	14:22	711	16:2	703, 1151
11:5	758	14:23	711, 1273	16:9	1315
11:7	115, 510	14:24	712	16:19	1305
11:10	308, 309, 311	14:24–25	711	16:22	672
11:16	1304	14:26	710, 711, 1310, 1331, 1345		
11:17	710	14:28	712	**2 Corinthians**	
11:19	375	14:29	712, 1340, 1346	1:3	109
11:20	711, 712	14:31	712	1:8	951
11:26	1305, 1306	14:32	1346	1:11	718
11:31	644			1:12	1068, 1219, 1259–60

1:17	692	4:3	821	8:11	467
1:20	827, 917	4:4	272, 275, 306,	8:12	747
1:21–22	922, 943		335, 344, 430,	8:16	1321
1:22	223		432, 671, 822	8:20–21	765
1:22–23	692	4:6	278, 432, 433	8:21	1089
1:23	691, 692	4:7	814, 1239	9:2	1073
1:24	1320, 1340	4:13	224, 443	9:4	919
2:10	947, 976	4:16	433, 499, 556,	9:7	375, 381, 1073,
2:11	306, 310, 335		1127		1087, 1092, 1094,
2:12	1315	4:18	1215		1120, 1151, 1152,
2:15	822	5:2–3	1062, 1068		1153
2:16	1315	5:5	223	9:9	1219
2:17	762, 821	5:7	944, 1038	9:10	770
3	842, 1231	5:8	922	9:14	976–77
3:1	774	5:10	1200, 1214	9:17	1087
3:2	1315	5:14	514, 1004, 1028	10:5	83, 155, 350, 580
3:3	223, 1084, 1143,	5:15	1037, 1075, 1147,	10:6	672
	1247		1183	10:12	773
3:4–6	1315	5:16	205	11	452
3:5	235, 388, 430,	5:17	1073, 1087, 1120,	11:3	306, 334, 335,
	436, 443, 446,		1183, 1250, 1253		388
	447, 466, 478,	5:18	115, 884, 1024,	11:4	116
	719, 1129, 1263		1028	11:7	822, 981
3:6	225, 230, 232,	5:18–19	822	11:9	712
	233, 249, 439,	5:18–20	1318	11:13	768
	818, 822, 825,	5:19	893, 984, 1004,	11:14	301, 302, 310
	1116, 1318, 1358		1024, 1037, 1148	11:15	571
3:6–7	594, 1114, 1115,	5:19–20	1358	11:17	919
	1231, 1240	5:20	1239, 1314	11:30	1345
3:6–9	1246	5:21	168, 553, 884,	11:31	151, 692
3:7	134, 510, 599,		886, 894, 896,	12	1191
	602, 809, 826,		986, 1004, 1028,	12:7	306, 644
	941, 1104, 1136,		1029	12:9	444, 447, 448,
	1138, 1165, 1243	6	712, 743		452, 557, 745,
3:8	398, 826, 1231,	6:1	400, 448, 467,		788, 932, 1345
	1289		965, 1258	12:12	1316
3:8–9	822	6:3	711	12:13	976
3:9	594, 826, 1136,	6:7	304	12:14	726
	1232	6:14	484, 1353	12:19	692
3:11	628	6:16	227, 713	12:20	739, 740
3:13	848	6:17–18	1183	13:3	226, 232, 449,
3:14	441, 442, 855,	7:1	557, 1074		1314
	885, 1252	7:7	712	13:5	943, 1037, 1282
3:16	594	7:10	635, 1109	13:7	428, 791
3:17	212, 225, 226,	7:14	549	13:11	468, 607
	230, 231, 233,	8	452	13:14	106, 249
	249, 407, 408,	8:3	224		
	447, 1143	8:9	200, 1025	**GALATIANS**	
3:18	114, 124, 212,	8:10	437		
	510, 1127			1	1009, 1102, 1167
4:2	1089, 1178, 1219				

1:1	1316	3:5	998, 1117	3:27	914
1:4	1028	3:7	1040	3:28	624, 627, 1042
1:7	861	3:8	362, 819, 846,	3:29	917, 918
1:8	302, 1085, 1288,		917, 1040	4	1136
	1290, 1297, 1333,	3:9	934	4:1–2	725
	1339	3:9–10	893	4:2	702, 731
1:8–9	1317	3:10	477, 593, 599,	4:3	1142
1:12	552, 822		605, 642, 643,	4:4	826, 987, 1027,
1:15	979, 1024		779, 803, 804,		1119, 1148
1:18	302		826, 831, 837,	4:4–5	790, 888, 1028
2	992, 1006, 1127,		887, 941, 949,	4:5	592, 807, 1026
	1145, 1161, 1164,		959, 987, 991,	4:6	109, 114, 223,
	1175		1020, 1021, 1022,		227, 241, 244,
2–3	1020		1023, 1025, 1115,		249, 1037
2:1	1042		1119, 1271	4:8	65, 97, 145–46,
2:4	703, 858, 1092,	3:11	837, 988, 1167,		148, 663
	1094, 1144		1252	4:9	594, 627, 809,
2:6–8	1345	3:12	804, 832, 909,		932, 952
2:7	912		959, 991, 999,	4:10	624, 649, 702,
2:8	101		1008, 1015, 1034,		703, 713, 990
2:10	1252		1104, 1195, 1205	4:10–11	622
2:11	101, 624, 626,	3:13	627–28, 643, 790,	4:11	1347
	1341		1028, 1213	4:19	724, 726, 998
2:14	622, 825	3:13–14	888	4:20	1330
2:15	518, 1020	3:14	213, 398, 438,	4:21	592
2:15–16	914		439, 846, 930,	4:22	853
2:16	894, 914, 963,		964, 1054, 1189,	4:24	594, 1228, 1240
	999, 1004, 1005,		1214	4:24–26	1246, 1247
	1008, 1073, 1078,	3:16	165, 231, 846,	5	805, 1096, 1126,
	1152		917, 1004		1162, 1177, 1272,
2:17	831	3:16–22	822		1284
2:19	592, 628, 821	3:17	827	5:1	594, 858
2:19–20	1168	3:18	976, 999, 1003	5:2	622, 624, 949,
2:20	163, 181, 943,	3:19	308, 469, 625,		998
	1004, 1025, 1052,		805, 1119	5:2–4	1176
	1105, 1188	3:21	599, 602, 627,	5:3	993, 1148
2:20–21	914		643, 804, 838,	5:4	605, 626, 949,
2:21	603, 803, 976,		856, 992, 1003,		976, 978, 998,
	981, 1004, 1167		1004		999, 1167, 1176,
3	807, 831, 838,	3:21–22	822, 1205		1177
	991, 1009, 1010,	3:22	591, 599, 635,	5:5	249, 666, 828
	1011, 1039, 1041,		810, 826, 830,	5:5–6	1173
	1119, 1126, 1139,		837, 849, 888,	5:6	675, 934, 1071,
	1158, 1164, 1174,		929, 1019, 1021,		1075, 1172
	1178		1040, 1104, 1119,	5:10	1107
3:1	741		1165	5:13	858, 1146, 1158,
3:2	249, 397, 822,	3:22–24	598		1347
	998, 999, 1087,	3:23–24	594	5:13–14	807
	1115, 1116, 1121,	3:23–25	650	5:14	805, 1081, 1083,
	1133	3:24	316, 394, 618,		1132
3:3	1167		635, 731, 805,		
			848, 1115, 1251		
		3:25	807		

5:15	740
5:16	249, 499, 572, 782, 788, 1083, 1184, 1275, 1278, 1282
5:16–17	506
5:17	249, 250, 343, 465, 511, 551, 604, 650, 782, 788, 1130, 1172
5:18	249, 592, 593, 604, 628, 791, 1282
5:19	354, 498, 570, 754, 754, 782, 1259, 1270
5:19–20	1101
5:19–21	571, 939, 1068
5:20	738, 739
5:20–21	530, 735
5:21	562, 748, 758, 950, 1075, 1171, 1184, 1266
5:22	221, 245, 249, 438, 1037
5:22–23	759
5:24	506, 511, 788, 1269
5:25	249 1183, 1282
6	1013
6:1	224, 484, 576, 743, 1268, 1284
6:4	1260
6:5	1354
6:6	712, 1332
6:8	221, 1207, 1221
6:9	1014, 1184
6:10	743, 747
6:12	858, 1092
6:13–14	1005
6:14	990, 1001
6:14–18	1353
6:15	1073, 1120

EPHESIANS

1	535
1:3	1028
1:4	153, 265, 275, 979
1:4–5	318, 979, 1024
1:4–6	979
1:4–12	1025
1:5	338
1:6	976, 1037, 1218
1:6–7	969
1:6–9	827
1:7	934, 1024, 1028
1:9	979, 1003, 1023
1:9–11	822
1:11	979
1:13	224, 249, 822, 846
1:13–14	922, 943
1:14	223
1:17	224, 432
1:18	433, 945
1:19–20	197
1:21	284
1:22	1321
1:23	702
2	483, 517, 1020, 1268
2:1	431, 433, 452, 467, 483, 1265
2:1–3	551
2:2	181, 275, 284, 305, 334, 335, 344, 345, 354, 388, 395, 479, 484, 512
2:3	136, 182, 192, 431, 487, 488, 493, 499, 502, 518, 519, 543, 549, 570, 572, 787, 1020, 1021, 1022, 1042, 1368, 1370
2:3–5	888
2:4	891, 1023, 1024, 1025
2:4–5	1026
2:5	432, 433, 448, 894, 970, 972, 979, 1024, 1025
2:5–6	978
2:6	1004
2:7	979, 1025
2:8	443, 518, 827, 963, 970, 972, 977, 978, 984,
	992, 997, 1003, 1004, 1024, 1068, 1105, 1167, 1220
2:8–9	978, 1004, 1007
2:9	988, 1002
2:10	383, 387, 433, 599, 828, 988, 1002, 1037, 1051, 1072, 1075, 1081, 1120, 1132, 1147, 1183
2:12	432, 433, 992, 1240
2:12–13	1307
2:14	179, 625, 628
2:14–15	624
2:15	628, 1073
2:16	1028
2:17	551, 1020
2:18	249, 959
2:19–21	1307
2:20	51, 180, 1276, 1301, 1310, 1312, 1333
2:20–21	1298
2:21	349
3:3	39
3:4	822
3:5	249
3:7–9	106
3:8	1025
3:10	284, 302, 308
3:12	901, 921, 931, 934, 937
3:14	247
3:15	723
3:16	106, 232, 247, 249, 1025
3:16–17	106
3:19	931
4	979, 1135, 1290, 1314
4:1	1184
4:4	224, 747
4:4–6	1241
4:6	82, 85
4:7	432
4:8	145, 214, 557, 820, 1056, 1287, 1348

4:8–12	1359		1101, 1107, 1184,	6:15	822
4:11	35, 700, 1289,		1262	6:16	1191
	1312, 1315, 1319,	5:5–6	487, 939, 1259	6:17	249, 822, 822
	1320, 1340	5:6	223–24, 484,	6:18	249, 712
4:11–12	1314		566, 858, 1171,		
4:11–13	711		1268, 1270, 1371	**PHILIPPIANS**	
4:11–14	1339	5:7	576	1:6	245, 251, 388,
4:12	265, 1028, 1321	5:8	429, 432, 1184		437, 441, 442,
4:13	444	5:8–10	1089		444, 446, 461,
4:14	35, 862, 1185,	5:9	245, 429, 1183		951, 955
	1289, 1360	5:10	1184	1:8	692
4:15	1127	5:11	570, 571, 765,	1:10	1090
4:15–16	1307		1184	1:11	1183
4:17	1184	5:12	224	1:12	1221
4:17–18	343, 499	5:14	433, 438, 451	1:15	1351
4:17–19	430, 1021	5:18	576, 755	1:19	223, 249, 1109,
4:18	416, 432, 522,	5:18–19	249		1127
	530, 758, 1021	5:19	1314	1:24	1092, 1157
4:19	342, 424, 432,	5:22	757	1:27	822, 1183
	754, 756	5:23	180, 757, 1028	1:28	1177
4:20–21	1207	5:24	757	1:29	443, 1031
4:22	306, 499, 511,	5:25	1025	2:1	249
	1095, 1147	5:25–26	1367	2:2	712
4:22–24	1075	5:26	557, 1310, 1372	2:4	764
4:23	249, 433, 530,	5:26–27	557	2:6	154, 159
	874, 1073	5:27	468, 607, 1038,	2:6–8	129
4:23–24	412		1090	2:7	168, 170
4:24	283, 301, 321,	5:28–29	757	2:8	170, 174, 177
	433, 487, 1073,	5:29	747, 757	2:12	951, 952
	1087, 1120, 1282	5:29–30	169	2:13	36, 317, 361, 388,
4:25	771, 773, 774,	5:31	757		401, 417, 437,
	777, 778	5:33	757		443, 446, 467,
4:26	654, 662, 735,	6	500, 651		1129
	739, 740	6:1	723, 727, 731	2:14	740, 1015
4:26–30	654, 1279	6:2	651, 722	2:15	607, 1184
4:27	306, 307, 740,	6:3	648, 650, 731,	2:16	822
	788		732	2:21	1351
4:28	654, 767, 768	6:4	726	2:25	1092, 1157
4:29	572, 754, 778,	6:5	730, 731, 1135,	2:29	725
	976		1158	3	998, 1027
4:30	223, 245, 249,	6:6–7	1158	3:2	768, 858
	344, 740, 788,	6:6–8	731	3:3	249, 626
	791, 944, 1054,	6:8	732, 1184	3:3–4	921
	1183, 1184, 1282	6:9	729	3:4	419, 1110, 1176
4:31	735, 773	6:11	307	3:6	419, 426, 547,
4:32	742, 743, 976,	6:11–12	307		781, 994, 1042
	1183	6:12	275, 284, 300,	3:7	998, 1022, 1176,
5:1	1183		303, 306, 307		1220
5:4	689	6:13	310	3:7–8	1110
5:5	642, 671, 750,				
	758, 769, 950,				

3:7–9	1176, 1177
3:8	669, 998
3:8–9	1023, 1176
3:8–11	914
3:9	838, 897, 910, 929, 988, 998, 999, 1004, 1029
3:12	444, 468, 604, 607, 932, 943, 952, 1028, 1100
3:15	611, 914
3:17	712
3:18–19	1329
3:19	275
3:20	171
3:21	169, 171
4:3	712
4:7	659
4:8–9	1073
4:11	767
4:12	763, 767
4:13	447
4:14	712
4:18	1218

COLOSSIANS

1:4	1216
1:5	822, 1220
1:6	1305
1:8	249
1:9–10	1218
1:10	1183
1:12	284, 301, 1024, 1306
1:13	307, 335, 512, 820, 893, 1025, 1028
1:15	65, 119, 134, 165
1:16	90, 134, 152, 267, 283, 284, 300
1:16–17	124, 127, 137, 268
1:16–18	204
1:17	256, 265, 286, 355, 360
1:18	165, 180
1:20	204, 300
1:21	571
1:21–22	173
1:22	607

1:22–23	1168
1:23	1042, 1279
1:24	1304
1:28	468, 607, 1061, 1149
2:2	920, 937
2:2–3	936
2:3	931
2:5	937
2:6	930
2:8	798, 858
2:9	100, 121, 127, 181
2:10	284, 1028, 1168
2:11	499
2:12	530, 1083
2:13	431, 467, 976, 1265
2:14	594, 629, 699, 894, 1160, 1273
2:15	557, 820
2:16	613, 624, 638, 649, 650, 702, 703, 713, 990
2:17	618, 625, 702, 703
2:18	299
2:19	231, 928
2:20	627
2:21	990
2:23	633, 681, 708, 744, 1022, 1081, 1132
3:3	1038, 1220, 1309
3:4	1309
3:5	480, 572, 575, 671, 744, 754, 756, 769, 787, 788
3:5–6	950, 1101, 1107
3:6	480, 484, 487, 758, 1075, 1107, 1171, 1184, 1209, 1262, 1266, 1268
3:8	739, 754
3:9	571, 773
3:10	510, 732, 1073, 1120
3:11	627, 1042
3:12	743
3:13	976, 1028, 1183

3:16	711, 822, 1225
3:17	572, 687
3:18	757
3:19	757, 758
3:20	727, 731, 732, 1089, 1218
3:22	723, 730, 731
3:23	729
3:24	732,
3:25	733
4:1	729, 730
4:3	822, 1358
4:6	975
4:15	1305

1 THESSALONIANS

1:1	1304
1:3	920
1:5	921
1:6	249
1:8	1157
2:4	912
2:7	712
2:9	768
2:13	249, 430
2:14	1304
2:18	304
2:19	1220
3:5	334, 335
3:11	122, 127, 247
3:13	1074
3:19	671
4:1	1159, 1218
4:2	1183
4:3	864, 1064, 1074, 1075, 1094, 1148
4:3–4	545
4:3–5	1075, 1095
4:4	756
4:4–5	752
4:5	270, 499, 756, 1184
4:6	762, 765, 769, 1075, 1184
4:7	754, 1075, 1147, 1183
4:8	249, 1064, 1183
4:11	1149

4:11–12	767
4:17	998
4:18	1314
5:2	761
5:6	1221
5:8	920
5:12–13	1297, 1332
5:13	712, 1332
5:14	743
5:15	739
5:19	234, 244
5:19–20	713, 1333
5:21	712
5:22	756

2 THESSALONIANS

1:6–7	1214
1:7	302
1:8	672
2:2	681
2:3	484, 1341
2:4	671
2:8	223, 241, 451
2:8–9	304
2:9	1317
2:10	344
2:11	344, 814
2:12	1073
2:16	122, 1024
2:16–17	127
2:17	1072
3:1	712
3:6	713, 1353
3:8	712, 768, 981
3:9	1347
3:10–12	767
3:11	767
3:14–15	1353

1 TIMOTHY

1	806
1:3	711, 712
1:3–5	925
1:5	645, 934, 1068, 1073, 1081, 1083, 1086, 1087, 1120, 1126, 1134, 1136, 1257, 1259, 1273
1:7	645, 1345

1:8	804, 809
1:8–9	805
1:9	316, 394, 419, 484, 628, 727, 1054, 1127, 1138, 1141, 1268
1:10	754, 773
1:10–11	765
1:11	822
1:12–13	443
1:13	546, 576
1:14	1004, 1024
1:15	827, 1042
1:15–16	914
1:16	1037
1:18	821
1:18–19	1068, 1259
1:19	800, 1075, 1103, 1155, 1184, 1270, 1281
2:1	711, 712
2:1–2	728
2:2	304, 418, 722, 727, 729, 1318
2:4	964, 1041
2:5	75, 174, 179, 1004
2:5–6	1041
2:6	179, 334, 821, 1041
2:7	821
2:8	711, 1015
2:8–9	722
2:9	756, 758
2:10	1072, 1073
2:11	758, 1221
2:12	757
2:13	1027
2:14	334, 388, 484
2:15	758, 758, 1221
2:30	1324
3	712
3:1	786, 1313, 1329
3:2–4	1347
3:2–7	1322
3:3	767
3:4	727, 757
3:7	1282, 1321
3:8	767
3:9	822, 1345

3:11	758
3:15	1159, 1301, 1304, 1308, 1310, 1311, 1319, 1333, 1339, 1340, 1343
3:16	883, 1206
4:1	301, 345, 371, 484, 1268
4:1–3	304
4:3	758, 1183
4:5	549, 707, 1132
4:6	821, 822
4:8	643, 678, 1066, 1073, 1184, 1213, 1235
4:10	256, 286, 292, 354, 361
4:11	712, 1149
4:12	711, 1073, 1331, 1347
4:13	158, 1225, 1327
4:14	1315, 1317, 1318, 1320, 1326, 1327, 1328
4:16	884, 1315, 1318
5:1–2	725
5:3	725
5:3–6	731
5:4	577, 724, 726, 727, 758, 1089, 1178, 1216
5:6	755
5:7	1149
5:8	286, 577, 724, 726, 733, 747, 768, 1064, 1075, 1184, 1207, 1277, 1281
5:10	1072
5:11	755
5:13	758
5:14	758
5:15	306
5:16	768
5:17	712, 725, 1329, 1332
5:18	768
5:19	1004
5:21	284, 302
5:22	576, 713, 1353

5:24	576	2:21	332, 448	2:5	689, 758
6:1	689, 725, 1183, 1347	2:22	897	2:6	731
		2:24	743	2:7	711, 1331
6:1–2	730	2:24–26	1282	2:7–8	1347
6:3	583	2:25	385, 712	2:8	821, 1184
6:4	1006	2:25–26	305	2:9	730
6:5	430, 740	2:26	308, 310, 335, 388, 512, 564	2:9–10	731
6:8	767			2:10	712, 765, 822, 1183
6:9	306, 310, 671, 788, 1184, 1282	3:1–2	733		
		3:2	727	2:11	827, 1147
6:10	577, 764	3:3	739	2:11–12	1147
6:11	743	3:4	670, 738, 756, 1183	2:12	788, 1037
6:12	920			2:13	145
6:13	256	3:6	342, 343, 572	2:14	608, 609, 1028, 1037, 1075, 1147, 1183
6:15–16	106, 151	3:8	430, 432		
6:16	77, 80, 260	3:10	1345		
6:17	257, 292, 665, 764, 768, 1149	3:16	654, 712, 1097, 1109, 1179, 1180, 1331, 1333	2:15	712, 1149
				3	1020
6:18	767, 768			3:1	728, 1072, 1149
6:19	1221	4:2	712	3:2	740
6:20	116, 583	4:3	342, 371, 572, 712, 713, 821	3:3	432, 756, 1020
				3:4	494, 976, 1023
2 Timothy		4:4	345	3:4–5	979
1:1	846	4:5	921	3:5	433, 461, 556, 894, 950, 978, 992, 1002, 1003, 1004, 1073, 1105, 1310, 1370, 1371, 1372
1:3	549	4:6–8	176		
1:5	925	4:8	1184, 1214		
1:6	449, 791, 1318, 1326, 1327, 1328, 1340	4:16	983		
		4:17	821, 921		
1:7	224			3:5–6	249
1:8	822	**Titus**		3:5–7	893, 1167
1:9	153, 978, 979, 988, 1002, 1003, 1004, 1024, 1105, 1167, 1309	1	712	3:7	979, 1037, 1105
		1:1	1004	3:14	726, 1157
		1:2	153, 1024	3:15	232
		1:3	821, 912		
		1:4	234, 925	**Philemon**	
1:11	821	1:5	712, 1318, 1320, 1323, 1357	2	1305
1:12	942			14	375, 381, 452, 1083, 1087, 1092, 1120, 1151, 1152, 1153
1:13	40, 98, 711, 807, 1096	1:6	727		
		1:6–9	1322		
1:14	249, 1317	1:7	1159		
2:2	712, 1318, 1320, 1330, 1340, 1345	1:7–8	1347		
		1:9	54, 540, 712, 821, 1202, 1330, 1344	**Hebrews**	
2:5	1216			1:1	1314, 1317
2:14	740, 1006	1:10	1042	1:2	85, 105, 124, 137, 152, 180, 267, 276
2:15	264, 478, 562, 711, 822, 950, 1329, 1330	1:11	540		
		1:13	712, 771, 928		
		1:16	925	1:2–3	127
2:16	583	2:2	731	1:3	75, 96, 105, 119, 134, 135, 152,
2:19	484, 1268, 1312	2:4	758		
2:20	332, 1311, 1354				

	256, 286, 355, 360, 1028, 1222	5:4	131	9:16	375, 1092, 1157
1:4	161	5:5–7	842	9:19	1251, 1253
1:5–6	300	5:7	173, 200, 1306	9:24	563
1:6	198, 302	5:8	165, 200	9:26	497
1:8–9	145, 146	5:10	179	9:28	1109
1:9	209, 484	6:1	265, 571, 711, 1330	10	714, 912
1:10	76	6:4	249, 1207	10:1	593, 618
1:14	221, 300, 302, 307, 308	6:5	821	10:3	618
		6:10	1215	10:4	1248
2:2–3	941	6:11	920, 921, 942	10:5	265, 819
2:4	249	6:13–14	692	10:7	928
2:7	164	6:16	692, 694	10:14	1004, 1027, 1072
2:8	307	6:17–18	941	10:15	249
2:9	976, 979	6:18	610	10:15–16	227
2:10	179	6:19	923, 943	10:16	1040
2:14	165, 166, 1028	7	841, 1228	10:18	625, 627
2:15	1026	7:1–2	840	10:19	921, 1248
2:16	166, 167, 284	7:2	179, 853	10:22	920, 921, 942, 1004, 1126, 1248, 1273
2:16–17	165	7:9–10	515		
2:17	169, 179	7:11–12	624	10:22–23	943
3:1	179, 1109	7:12	593, 628, 837, 1027, 1092, 1157	10:23	1109
3:1–2	161, 200			10:25	710, 712, 1303
3:4	162, 265, 266	7:17	624	10:26	467, 576
3:6	919, 921, 943, 1279	7:18	622, 628, 643, 837, 1247	10:27	1019
				10:28–29	1240
3:8	338	7:18–19	625	10:29	224, 245, 791
3:10	432	7:19	687, 784	10:31	347
3:11	1267	7:20	1248	10:34	767
3:12	484	7:22	1240	10:35	921, 1221
3:13	499, 511	7:25	161, 904, 1028	10:39–11:1	911
3:14	919, 934, 955	7:27	1092, 1157	11	673, 852, 915, 937, 1039, 1040, 1091
3:18	673	8:2	179		
4	704, 714	8:5	618	11:1	34, 903, 918, 942
4:1	714	8:6	627, 1240, 1247	11:3	65, 263, 265, 268, 839
4:2	906, 1004	8:7	1247		
4:2–3	1370	8:8	1249	11:4	633, 840, 851, 852, 1039, 1090
4:3	265	8:13	623, 628, 1248, 1250		
4:3–4	275			11:5	840
4:4	650, 702, 842, 918	9:1	596, 1336	11:5–6	934
4:8		9:4	630	11:6	426, 441, 480, 790, 831, 951, 1022, 1088, 1218, 1275, 1371
4:9	650	9:9–10	842		
4:12	640	9:10	625, 630, 702, 705, 789		
4:14	902, 1109, 1202			11:7	265, 840, 852
4:15	131, 165, 168, 169–70, 172	9:11	179	11:8	853, 978, 996, 1173
		9:12	1028, 1248		
4:16	657, 902, 921, 957, 979	9:14	224, 571, 1126	11:10	917
		9:15	179, 930, 1247		

11:13	1004		1:6	571, 922, 937, 955		3:17	756

11:13 1004
11:19 268
11:20 841
11:21 841
11:22 841
11:23 842
11:26 842
11:28 842
11:32 842
11:33–37 915
11:39 1073
12 636
12:1 499, 580, 788, 1089
12:2 179, 201
12:3 1268
12:7 726
12:9 109, 221, 300, 724
12:14 756, 758
12:15 448, 499, 1184
12:18 1246
12:18–19 809
12:21 855
12:22 1246, 1306, 1309
12:24 179, 1240, 1247
12:26 1041
12:28 1218
12:29 563
13 1039
13:4 545, 750, 757, 758, 780
13:5 767
13:7 712
13:8 80, 150, 1039
13:9 589, 1241
13:11–15 626
13:15–16 1314
13:16 742, 768, 770, 1089, 1218
13:17 712, 1297, 1332
13:18 712
13:20 179, 1240

JAMES
1 486
1:2–3 654
1:5 446

1:6 571, 922, 937, 955
1:6–7 946
1:7 468
1:8 608
1:13 324, 339, 381, 388, 389, 666
1:13–14 334
1:13–15 1270
1:14 380, 416, 499, 511, 603, 738, 761
1:14–15 335, 506, 574, 782, 1274
1:15 486, 559, 785, 788, 1271
1:17 80, 106
1:18 136, 156, 937, 1194
1:19 743, 778
1:20 740, 897
1:21 937
1:22 1184
1:23–24 135
1:25 1143
1:26 778, 1184
2 907
2:2 1303
2:9 570
2:10 593, 609, 628, 831, 941, 987, 1023, 1115, 1187
2:12 822, 1143
2:13 748
2:14 907, 937
2:16 768
2:17 925, 934, 1075, 1172, 1173, 1181, 1184, 1205
2:19 441, 460, 907, 963, 1188, 1193
2:24 1193
2:26 221
3:1 1314
3:2 503, 572, 694, 773, 953
3:5 529
3:13 1073
3:14 739
3:15 430

3:17 756
4:1 530
4:5–6 788
4:13 424
4:17 576
5:2 769
5:4 576, 768
5:12 691, 695, 778
5:14–15 698
5:16 1328
5:20 1223

1 PETER
1:2 249, 362, 1025, 1073
1:3 136, 433, 1023
1:4–5 1220
1:5 445, 1099, 1105, 1109, 1168, 1221, 1277
1:8 1037
1:9 934, 1037, 1105, 1168, 1221
1:10 1039, 1220
1:10–11 213, 225
1:11 223, 227, 235, 236
1:12 167, 169, 177, 181, 302, 308
1:13 937, 943, 977
1:14 170, 788, 1091, 1183, 1184
1:15–16 632
1:17 952, 1183
1:18 623, 627, 1183
1:18–19 1007, 1028
1:19 179
1:20 265, 362, 1024
1:22 529, 743
1:23 1310
1:24 1040
2:1 1147
2:4–5 1307
2:5 655, 1060, 1065, 1090, 1216, 1314, 1342
2:6 1342
2:8 146, 150

2:9	626, 1037, 1313, 1314, 1336	4:18	484, 1268	2:20–21	577
2:10	1307	5:2	452, 1083, 1087, 1120, 1151, 1152, 1153, 1158	2:22	1351
2:12	1073, 1184, 1347			3:1	1073
2:13	613, 624, 722, 723, 728, 731, 1089, 1178	5:3	711, 1320, 1331, 1347	3:3	371, 1339
				3:5	265, 367, 576
		5:4	179, 1037, 1333	3:7	265
2:13–14	723, 729	5:5	350, 731	3:9	1041, 1042
2:13–15	732	5:6	341, 605, 659, 666	3:10	761
2:14	727, 728			3:16	445, 562
2:15	1183	5:7	770		
2:16	561, 858, 930, 1146, 1158	5:8	299, 304, 305, 308, 335, 756, 1065	**1 JOHN**	
				1	1265
2:17	725, 728	5:9	307, 310, 445	1:1	154
2:18	721–22, 723, 728, 730	5:10	445, 1024, 1025	1:2	146
				1:1–3	124
2:19	901, 1089	**2 PETER**		1:5	332
2:21	1027, 1037, 1183	1	1172	1:6–7	1206
2:22	1040	1:1	894	1:7	893, 1028, 1222
2:23	773	1:4	97, 181, 208, 226, 245, 788	1:8	495, 499, 604, 1058, 1122, 1257, 1265, 1268, 1269, 1351
2:24	1028, 1037, 1040, 1075, 1095, 1183	1:5	1206		
2:25	1028, 1040, 1333	1:5–7	666	1:8–10	609
3:1	758, 1184, 1347	1:8	1075, 1095, 1147, 1184, 1206, 1221	1:9	888, 893, 1213
3:2	758			1:10	1269
3:4	758	1:9	1107, 1184, 1209, 1281	1:12	467
3:5–6	757			2:1	1028
3:6	757, 758	1:10	943, 1037, 1098, 1100, 1108, 1172, 1181, 1184, 1277	2:1–2	179, 888
3:7	722, 757, 759			2:2	1028, 1041
3:8	742	1:11	1221	2:3	1206
3:10	572, 778	1:15	1073	2:4	1184
3:14–15	671	1:19	839, 1039, 1075	2:6	1183, 1206
3:15	688, 712	1:21	90, 227, 249	2:7	1243
3:16	712, 1068, 1184, 1260	2:1	1339	2:7–8	1039
		2:2	822	2:9	1206
3:17	1095	2:4	284, 301, 307, 334, 351, 673	2:12	893
3:18	791			2:16	268, 314, 332, 335, 336, 338, 342, 371, 529, 572, 755
3:19–20	852	2:5	497, 840, 852		
3:20	67, 373	2:7	754		
3:21	170, 914, 945, 1273, 1361, 1364, 1372	2:7–8	673	2:16–17	506
		2:8	571, 572	2:18	1246
3:22	300	2:9	788	2:19	1307
4:1	129, 206	2:11	1184	2:20	1327
4:8	1223	2:12	430	2:21	774, 775, 778
4:11	711, 1183, 1339	2:13	1044	2:23	662
4:14	249	2:14	755	2:25	822
4:15	720, 768	2:19	408, 512	2:27	223, 807, 1157
4:17	658, 659, 822	2:20	788, 1184, 1281	2:28	921

2:29	1206	4:9	1024		**JUDE**	
3	1265	4:9–10	1023	3	1092, 1157	
3:1	1024–25	4:10	665, 1024, 1027	4	976, 1037	
3:2	942, 955, 1220	4:11	1095, 1148, 1160,	5	691	
3:2–3	1183		1183	6	283, 284, 301,	
3:3	433, 1206	4:12	1184		334	
3:4	356, 499, 638	4:13	226, 232, 244	9	299, 304, 308,	
3:5–7	1206	4:14	1042		689	
3:6	1184, 1265, 1281	4:15	929	15	571	
3:7	897	4:16	749, 1184	19	430, 1307	
3:7–8	566, 1051, 1064,	4:17	921, 1220	23	788	
	1259	4:20	653, 977		**REVELATION**	
3:8	301, 302, 314,	4:21	1075, 1095, 1148,	1:5	165	
	334, 448, 504,		1183	1:6	1313	
	549, 557, 568,	5	238	1:7	150	
	801, 906, 1020,	5:3	467, 609, 791,	1:8	95, 148, 150, 151	
	1026, 1028, 1055,		1198	1:10	703	
	1070, 1265	5:6	237, 238, 822	1:17	150	
3:8–9	499	5:7	98, 106, 214, 226,	1:17–18	150	
3:9	1183, 1265		238	2:5	1282	
3:10	1207	5:7–8	231, 238	2:9	1303, 1304	
3:12	334	5:8	238	2:16	1281	
3:14	672, 874, 893,	5:9	238	2:18–23	137	
	942, 977, 1181,	5:10	901, 942, 945,	2:20	649	
	1184, 1207		950, 958	3:9	1303, 1304	
3:14–15	748	5:10–11	937	3:15	663	
3:15	641, 735, 739,	5:11	1220	4	1215	
	744	5:12	1220, 1271	4:10–11	1179	
3:16	738	5:13	665, 929, 942,	5:5	165, 179	
3:16–18	1184		955, 1220	5:9	1028, 1042	
3:17	768, 769	5:13–14	912	5:10	1313	
3:18	742, 743	5:14	921	6:9–10	748	
3:19	937	5:16	1271	7:9	1042	
3:19–22	1220	5:19	275, 629, 942	8:3	311	
3:20	265	5:20	107, 145, 818	8:3–4	309	
3:20–21	251	5:21	649, 1297, 1298	9	1281	
3:21	921, 937, 1068,			9:4	1005	
	1259, 1273, 1281		**2 JOHN**	9:20–21	1281	
3:21–22	1191	3	977	10:6	692	
3:22	1089, 1178, 1216,	5	1039	11:2	1304	
	1217	9	662	11:9	1042	
3:23	821	10	713, 741, 1333,	11:11	249	
3:24	101, 106, 108,	10–11	1312, 1333	12	307, 1046	
	226			12:7	299, 303	
4:1	712, 1084–85,		**3 JOHN**	12:8	309	
	1333, 1339, 1365	5	712	12:9	301	
4:2	249, 929, 1109	10	768	12:10	306	
4:6	224					
4:7	1184					
4:8	494					

12:11	307	16:14	151	21:4	702, 714
12:12	303, 305, 454, 814	17:1–9	1341	21:5	1253
		17:14	151	21:6	922, 981
12:13	303	18:4	1353	21:8	778
12:17	303, 305, 822	18:7	755	21:27	1005
13:8	179, 497, 1039, 1245	18:23	738	22	885
		19:9	180	22:8	299
13:10	748	19:10	224, 299, 822	22:11	606, 884, 1107, 1182
14:4	1090	19:12	107		
14:5	1090	19:13	151	22:14–15	1307
14:6	302, 822	19:16	151	22:16	166
16:1	1281	20:3	311	22:19	1304
16:11	1281	21:2	1309		

Subject Index

BY JAMES A. GAU

absolute will, 176

Absolution, 711, 876, 884, 892, 914, 924, 935, 938, 945, 1035–36, 1062, 1198–99, 1310, 1357, 1361

academic philosophy (comprising Middle Platonism and Renaissance Neoplatonism), 34, 368, 659, 667, 940, 943, 950, 1198

accident, 59, 70, 74, 78–80, 102, 255–59, 270, 277, 289, 296–97, 310, 405, 423, 464, 472, 494, 524, 536, 540, 545, 687, 689, 702, 730, 747, 794, 918, 964, 1055, 1062, 1064, 1066, 1146, 1229, 1235, 1245, 1256, 1359

action of God, general 266, 287, 297
  arguments concerning, 355–62
  in the godless, 351
  status controversiae on, 361–62

action of God, general and special, 78, 353–62, 435
  definitions of, 120, 256, 353–54
  distinction between, 353–55
  primary and secondary causes, 358–62

actions, despotic, 419
  preferential, 419

actual sin, 316, 332–33, 476–77, 483–87, 498, 515, 531, 536–38, 546, 551, 564–86
  categories of, 575–78
  Melanchthon on, 571

Adimanthus (Manichaean), 348

adultery, 384, 431, 535, 546, 569, 577, 600, 604, 619, 621, 637, 639, 642, 651, 695, 715–60, 763, 782, 793, 796, 802, 998, 1064, 1068, 1077, 1081, 1242, 1259, 1286, 1296
  spiritual, 714, 762

Aepinus, 1009, 1203

Aeschines, 875, 912

Aetius, 143, 908

affections, 393

Aginnensis, Phoebadius, 95

Alexander (of Alexandria), 142, 229

Alexander of Hales, 462, 513

Alexander the Great, 270, 315, 393, 475, 565, 661, 721, 750, 955, 1228, 1256

Algazel, Mohammed, 289

allegories, 17

Alphonsus de Castro, 474, 486

Ambrose, 24, 27, 29, 71, 74, 102, 134, 169, 175, 283, 292, 343, 356, 364, 374, 381, 385, 386, 413, 416, 427, 435, 442, 450, 466, 485, 501, 502, 505, 516, 520, 543, 552, 561, 573, 584, 651, 689, 738, 775, 868, 871–73, 892, 924, 947–48, 979, 982, 989–90, 1009, 1012–14, 1102, 1119, 1169, 1185, 1269, 1292, 1327, 1342

Anabaptist, xi, xiii, 35, 133, 144, 166–68, 233, 300, 396, 455–56, 494, 539, 546, 567, 591, 691–92, 807, 825, 860, 1017, 1078, 1080, 1088, 1103, 1107, 1124, 1137, 1140, 1145, 1169, 1175, 1178, 1244, 1254, 1264, 1279, 1282, 1286, 1289, 1292, 1296, 1298, 1300, 1302, 1309–10, 1313, 1320, 1326, 1352, 1360, 1364, 1366–70, 1373

analogy of faith, 13, 32, 53, 103, 337, 387–88, 470–73, 542, 559, 872, 1104, 1112, 1166, 1346

Andreae, Jacob, xiii, 16

angels, 22, 48, 58–59, 75, 79, 81, 87, 101, 113–14, 145, 161–62, 164, 166–69, 177, 181, 198, 217, 231, 234, 240, 255, 272–76, 283–85, 298–311, 314, 322, 334–35, 352, 383, 447, 598, 602, 673, 680, 692, 714, 716, 733, 823, 863, 874, 941, 944, 1005, 1012, 1055, 1071, 1085, 1110, 1146, 1179, 1239, 1281–82, 1319, 1334
  blessings of as comfort to Christians, 307–9
  "cherubim," 302
  condition of, 300–303
  conflict between good and evil, 303–7
  creation of, 283
  evil, 48, 301
  having free choice, 407–10, 470
  "seraphim," 302
  "spirits," 221–22
  value of doctrine, 310–11

anhypostatio, 140

Anomeans, 143

Anselm, 376, 478, 515, 538, 873, 1273
  on definition of sin, 478, 501–2, 506–10, 515, 529, 544

antichrist, 6, 671, 721, 814, 969, 1317, 1341

Antinomian, 592, 622, 804, 808–9, 828, 830, 833, 1080, 1091, 1095, 1106, 1107, 1136–38, 1148, 1150, 1162, 1175

Antinomianism, 439, 1123, 1146

Antoninus, Marcus, 721

Antoninus, Pius, 82, 329

Apelles, 861, 928

Apollinarianism, 172–74

Apollinaris, 172–74, 182

Apollonia, 745

Apology of the Augsburg Confession, 8, 24,
  415, 462, 504, 508–11, 550–51, 561, 573,
  828–29, 936, 1095–97, 1107–8, 1110,
  1121, 1125–26, 1133, 1150, 1160, 1162,
  1164, 1172–73, 1177, 1180, 1208, 1270,
  1273, 1361

apostles, teaching of, 38

Apostles' Creed, 17–18, 20, 22–23, 35, 39,
  40–41, 105, 215, 261, XXV, 285, 906, 928,
  1027, 1161, 1304–5

apostolic writings, 5

apostrophe, 29

Appian, 880

Aquinas, Thomas. *See* Thomas Aquinas

Arcadius, 669

Arcesilaus, 34

Arianism, 143, 229

Arians, 26, 28, 97, 99, 106, 115–16, 130,
  142–46, 153–54, 158, 163–64, 172–73,
  175, 177, 216, 243, 267, 275, XXI, 660,
  1298
  arguments of, 155–57
  positive response to, 155–57

Aristotle, 92–93, 220, 269, 275, 286, 293, 362,
  423, 481, 518, 533, 603, 781, 848, 881,
  922, 969, 1128, 1139, 1186, 1343

Arius, 27, 35, 95–97, 115, 126, 139, 142–44,
  146, 176, 193, 207, 229, 231, 1291

ark of the covenant, XV, 614, 616, 630, 674,
  679, 813, 1084, 1134, 1238

Asotus, 602, 1244

Aspasia, 735

Athanasian Creed, 17–18, 26, 111, 159, 165,
  180, 209, 240

Athanasius, 25–27, 85, 95–97, 99–100,
  109–11, 115–16, 159, 165, 172, 203–5,
  586, 680–81, 869, 926

atonement, xiii

Augsburg Confession, xii, 8, 43, 331, 389,
  391, 415, 435, 509, 550, 573, 578, 580,
  583, 587, XXV, 828–30, 936, 1045, 1048,
  1094–97, 1102, 1121, 1125, 1132, 1136,

1145, 1150–51, 1160–64, 1169, 1172,
  1180, 1185, 1306

Augsburg Interim, xi–xii, 438–39, 531, 814

August, elector of Saxony, 1

Augustine, 3, 13, 19, 22, 25, 27–32, 41–42, 45,
  50, 52–53, 66, 70, 73, 78–80, 84, 87, 90,
  92–93, 96, 99–102, 104, 107–9, 111–12,
  115–16, 133–35, 154, 157, 168, 170, 180,
  186, 188, 218–19, 222, 238–39, 241–43,
  262, 273–75, 277, 284, 286, 288–92,
  296, 323–29, 331, 336, 338, 340, 342–43,
  348–50, 352–54, 356–59, 361–68, 370–71,
  374–76, 378, 380–87, 389–90, 407–11,
  413–17, 419, 425–28, 431–38, 440–46,
  456–69, 471–74, 481, 485–87, 493,
  497–98, 500–502, 504–7, 510–12, 514–17,
  524–38, 540–46, 548–49, 552, 554–61,
  570–71, 574–75, 577, 579, 581–84, 596,
  601, 603, 606–8, 610, 625, 635, 651, 664,
  679, 681–82, 694–95, 697–98, 744–45,
  753, 766, 768, 774–77, 786–87, 813, 818,
  823–24, 838, 854, 872–73, 877, 881, 892,
  895, 903, 908, 925–26, 928, 941–42, 946,
  954, 967–68, 970–72, 980, 982, 990–91,
  993–94, 1001, 1006, 1010–11, 1016–17,
  1028, 1038, 1079, 1081, 1086–88, 1093,
  1113–16, 1118, 1122, 1128–29, 1140–41,
  1143, 1152, 1158, 1175, 1178, 1213, 1217,
  1241–42, 1270, 1272–74, 1280, 1283,
  1285, 1292, 1296, 1305, 1311, 1322, 1332,
  1343, 1346, 1348–54, 1361, 1367, 1371

Aurelian, 84, 92, 140–41, 324

Aureolus, Peter, 513

Ausonius, 140

autoousios, 117

Balbus Quintus Lucius, 62

Baptism, 22, 25, 31, 58, 60, 86, 88, 98,
  120–21, 163, 182, 211, 217, 225, 228–29,
  246, 495–96, 530–32, 540, 543, 549,
  550–52, 611, 745, 829, 861, 863, 868, 871,
  892, 894, 914, 937, 945, 1016, 1020, 1038,
  1148, 1298, 1310–11, 1314, 1326, 1330,
  1343, 1350–53, 1355, 1361, 1363–73
  blessings of, 60
  of Christ, 58, 86, 88, 211, 217, 225
  formula of, 228–29, 246, 225
  of infants, 495, 527, 536–39, 549, 550,
    1292, 1365–67
  of John, 1365
  and original sin, 554–59, 562–63, 579
  and promise, 60
  signs of, 1364–65
  as sum of Gospel, 120–21

Basil, 27–29, 49, 95, 116, 121, 133–34, 143, 195, 204, 213–14, 230, 232, 246–47, 281, 285, 330, 389, 398, 446, 462, 472, 534, 601, 677–78, 680, 903, 908, 945, 1001, 1009, 1170, 1292–93, 1358

Basilides, 83, 271, 274, 276, 860–62, 1017, 1078–79

Bede, 238, 461

Benedict, 461

Berenger, 507

Bernard of Clairvaux, 378, 380, 410, 413, 443–44, 461–62, 873, 891–92, 903, 947, 949, 954, 1010, 1200, 1292, 1332

Bessarion, 240

Beza, 1313

Biel, Gabriel, 1093

Boethius, 102–3, 287, 297, 327, 362, 366, 373–74, 376–77

Bonaventura, 27, 79, 175, 462, 487, 507, 539, 873, 933, 969, 1011, 1030

Book of Concord, xv, 578, XX–XXI, XXV–XXVI, 1049

Brenz, Johann, 148, 498, 667–68

Bucer, 531, 1244

Budaeus, Guglielmus. See Bude, Guillaume

Bude, Guillaume, 515, 920, 922, 973

Bugenhagen, Johann, 935, 1203, 1371

Burgensis, 89–90, 138, 147, 149, 153, 237

Burgos, Paul of. See Burgensis

Caecilian, 1348

Caesar, Julius, 128, 262, 317, 973, 1055, 1187, 1230

Caesars, 674, 729, 750, 772, 865

Caligula, 568, 718–19

call, immediate, 1313, 1315–17
    mediate, 1313, 1315, 1317–20

Calvin, xii, 86, 93–94, 355, XXIV, 781, 887, 936, 1045, 1244, 1246–47, 1292

Calvinism, xv, 12, 16, XXI, 887

Calvinist, xi, XXI, XXV, 1244, 1249

Campanus, John, 233–34, 1292

canon, rule and clarification, 2, 19–20, 37, 39, 41, 51, 240, 428, 462, 698, 754, 776, 856, 938, 970, 994, 1319, 1321, 1323–25, 1333, 1341

canonical Scriptures, xii, 6, 8, 13, 19, 23, 25, 31, 39, 153, 238, 535, 862, 926, 1017, 1343, 1346

capital sins, 503, 576–77

Carpocrates, 83, 860, 1017, 1079

Carpocratians, 1078–79, 1146, 1149

Cassian, John, 328, 436, 459–63, 584

Cathari. See Novatians

causes, primary and secondary, 256, 304, 313, 320–21, 354, 358–59, 361, 454, 687, 689

Cerdo, 83, 271–72, 329, 804

ceremonial law, 596, 612–26, 631, 650, 674, 676, 706, 754, 842, 855, 857–58, 963, 989–95, 1001, 1008, 1012–13, 1144, 1248, 1251–52

Cerinthus, 92, 121, 139, 141, 859

Charles V, xi

Chemnitz, Anna, 16

Chemnitz, Martin, ix–xvi, 1, 8–9, 11, 13–16, 18, XI–XII, XIX, XXIII, XXIV, XXVII, 607–8, 766, 781, 896
    disagreements with Melanchthon, xii–xiii
    method of Loci, 49–54
    schema of doctrine, 46–48

Chemnitz, Martin Jr., 1, 16

Chemnitz, Paul, 1, 16

Cheremonius, 459

children, duties of, 726

Christian, elector of Saxony, 1

Christian liberty, 2

Christians, duties of, 724–31, 792–93
    fruits of, 1207, 1277
    struggles of, 1058

Chrysippus, 296, 368

Chrysostom, John, 27, 30, 146, 243, 247, 275, 327, 331, 343, 350, 370, 374–75, 386, 398, 407, 436, 459, 473, 500, 505, 516, 535, 678, 680, 699, 741, 769, 776, 820, 867–68, 873, 968, 971, 989, 1010, 1012–14, 1016, 1242, 1332, 1339

Church, 33–36, 68, 141, 257, 1287–354
    definition in terms of Gospel, 397
    and formulation of dogma, 49
    invisible, 1287, 1302, 1308–9, 1349
    marks of, 1298–303
    misunderstandings of, 1298, 1301
    proclaims Word, 848–49
    protected by God, XXI–XXII
    relation with state, 1320
    suffers, XXII, 1055
    visible, 1287–88, 1291, 1295, 1308, 1312, 1349
    terminology for, 1302–6

Church fathers
  Pelagius's use of, 50, 471–74
  reading and use of, 19–32
  role in dogmatics, 49–54

Cicero, 44, 61–63, 69, 72, 86, 262–63, 267,
  269, 285, 287, 289, 291, 296, 317, 367, 376,
  378–79, 407, 411, 422, 438, 442, 450, 466,
  533, 597, 641, 745, 795, 816, 834, 880–81,
  930, 974, 980, 1053, 1092–93, 1136, 1187,
  1288–89

circumcision, 100, 502, 547, 552, 556, 593,
  615–16, 623, 626–27, 629, 631, 649, 675,
  703, 705, 737, 841, 857, 945, 985, 989–90,
  992–93, 1004, 1010, 1013, 1020, 1139,
  1144–45, 1297–98, 1355, 1363–64, 1369,
  1371

civil law, 330, 479–80, 547, 596, 598, 603–4,
  612–14, 619–31, 641, 648, 650, 761, 769,
  780, 789, 804–5, 808, 1227–28, 1234,
  1236, 1239, 1252–54, 1257

civil righteousness, 415, 442, 547, 590, 1187,
  1205, 1366

Claudius, 140

Clement, 1241

Clement of Alexandria, 24, 40–41, 330, 823,
  859, 862, 865, 867–70, 907–8, 1269, 1272,
  1285

Clement of Rome, 535, 864, 907

Cochlaeus, 1023

Coelestius, 415, 458, 467, 472, 505, 536, 543,
  579, 606–7, 1038, 1217

Coelius, 326

Colloquy at Ratisbon, 390, 439, 531, 574, 602,
  814, 1014, 1173, 1203

Colloquy of Regensburg, 439, 541

Colloquy of Worms, 520, 541, 550, 552, 558

Commandments, 633. See also Decalog
  First, 55–56, 425, 632, 639, 642–43,
    645–46, 648–49, 651–52, 655–76,
    682–84, 690, 698–701, 714–17, 732,
    742, 792, 795, 832–33, 1052, 1082,
    1121
  Second, 215, 632, 639, 642, 646, 649,
    651–52, 682–99, 707, 732, 761, 771,
    773, 795
  Third, 299, 632–33, 639, 645–46, 648–49,
    688, 699–714, 762, 795
  Fourth, 633, 646, 648, 650, 718–35, 737,
    743, 770, 780, 782–83
  Fifth, 633, 641, 652, 724, 734–49, 753,
    755, 760, 784, 795

  Sixth, 633, 639, 714, 749–60, 762–63, 766,
    774, 781, 784, 789, 796, 990. See also
    adultery
  Seventh, 633, 650, 652, 744, 760–70, 782,
    784, 796, 990
  Eighth, 633, 650, 740, 770–78, 797, 1135
  Ninth–Tenth, 634, 639, 647, 763, 778–89,
    1275

communication of attributes, 32, 129–30,
  140, 157, 159, 168, 183, 185, 187–88. See
  also Jesus Christ. See also Son of God

concupiscence, 310, 314, 334–36, 338, 342,
  378, 456, 470, 481, 486, 491–93, 495–97,
  503, 506–7, 510–13, 530–32, 538, 540,
  542–43, 550–64, 572–75, 603, 634, 639,
  647, 650, 654, 687, 756, 778–91, 832,
  1075, 1095, 1114, 1274–77, 1283, 1285

conditional will, 176

confession, 485, 503, 506, 519, 521, 563,
  610, 618–19, 627, 655, 679, 683, 687–88,
  692–94, 703, 715, 728, 924, 943, 957,
  1013, 1032, 1045, 1048

confirmation, 1360

Consensus Tigurinus, 887

Constantine the Great, 27, 140, 143, 222, 229,
  735, 1294, 1348

Constantinus, 676

Contarini, 1203

contingency, 84, 358, 427–29, 467, 1093
  and external freedom, 317, 424
  Melanchthon on, 313–17
  and necessity, 428
  in sins conflicting with external disci-
    pline, 422–24

continuous grace, 414,

conversion, xii–xiii, 46, 414, 433–34, 436,
  441–42, 604, 644, 861, 869, 874–76, 887,
  931, 938, 964–65, 982, 996–99, 1008,
  1012–13, 1031, 1062–66, 1073, 1090,
  1101, 1109, 1129–30, 1174, 1196, 1199,
  1204, 1210, 1260, 1262, 1281, 1330
  passivity of human will in, 446–53

cooperating grace, 444–49

corruption, 2, 4–5, 34–35, 37, 55, 83, 96, 98,
  123, 141, 144, 173–74, 203, 205, 233, 273,
  284, 315, 329, 332–33, 336, 350, 356–57,
  380, 401–2, 409, 431, 434, 461, 464, 469,
  471, 479, 487, 494, 502, 504, 506, 508,
  510, 513–14, 518, 520–21, 523–24, 530,
  539, 546, 562, 574, 579–81, 584–87,
  598–600, 603, 607, 634, 676, 688, 691–92,
  701, 704, 737, 770, 773, 788–89, 794, 796,
  813–14, 828, 830, 850–51, 858–59, 864,

870, 879, 895, 907, 909, 928, 966, 969, 971, 973, 979, 1009, 1011, 1020, 1031, 1058, 1060, 1069, 1071–72, 1086, 1106, 1119, 1147, 1166, 1170, 1229, 1292, 1346, 1360, 1373
of doctrine of original sin, 532–40

Council at Milan, 1343

Council at Sirmio, 1343

Council of Africa, 25

Council of Antioch, 141, 215

Council of Carthage, 1325

Council of Chalcedon, 102, 186, 324, 1323

Council of Constance, 462, 464, 513

Council of Constantinople, 215, 230, 232, 1341

Council of Ephesus, 32, 183–88, 215

Council of Ephesus II, 1343

Council of Florence, 240

Council of Jerusalem, 623, 1040, 1078

Council of Milevis, 428, 970

Council of Nicaea, 27, 115–17, 124–25, 215, 229, 676, 678–79

Council of Orange, 400

Council of Sirminum, 140

Council of Trent, ix, xi–xii, xiv–xv, 414, 439, 474, 498, 550, 555, 874, 937–38, 994, 1032–33

courts. See government, judicial system of

"create," metaphorical uses of, 262

"create" and "make," 261–65

creation, xiv, 2, 5, 46, 48, 58, 60, 62, 65, 67–68, 75, 104, 108, 114, 122–23, 127–28, 152, 179, 219, 227, 231, 248, 250, 252, 317, 321–22, 324, 326, 353, 358, 362, 387, 433, 463, 533, 541–42, 544, 572, 580, 584, XVIII, 649, 695, 701–3, 706, 709, 717, 915, 966, 1033, 1225
action of one God, 266
Church's doctrine of over against philosophical opinions, 269–71
completion of in six days, 276–85
description of, 268–69
doubts concerning, 257–59
God responsible for order in, 259–60
God's presence with, 255
God's revelation in, 255
goodness of, 268
intelligence and, 258–59
Law revealed in, 598, 611, 613, 629, 632–34, 647, 649, 798, 1226, 1250

limits of philosophical doctrines of, 269–71
Melanchthon on, 255–60
order and mode of, 276–85
order in nature a demonstration of, 258
out of nothing, 268
and preservation, 256, 268
proof from conscience, 259
proof from efficient causes, 259
proof from final causes, 259
proof from order in society, 259
proof from signs in nature, 259
proven through prophecy, 259
scope of, 266
Scripture's terms for, 261–65
the six days of, 276–85
souls transmitted or newly created, 524–30
and secondary causes, 256–57
statement of doctrine of, 266
Trinity active in, 59, 255, 266–67

cross, xv, 2, 5, 47, 130–31, 147, 161, 163, 177, 206, 492, 644, 658, 666–67, 677–80, 802, 843, 858, 886, 916, 925, 932, 990, 995, 1005, 1014, 1062–63, 1160, 1221, 1234, 1294, 1299, 1306, 1308–9, 1329, 1331, 1356

Crypto-Calvinism, xv, 16, 266

Cubricius, 327. See also Manes

Cyprian, 20, 25, 31, 39, 41, 133, 474, 500, 502, 505, 867–69, 924, 1304, 1322, 1342–43, 1354, 1367

Cyril of Alexandria, 32, 42, 78–79, 95–96, 101, 107, 141–41, 155, 157, 183, 677, 892, 1011
conflict with Nestorius, 182–207
refutation of Arius, 161–64

Damasus, bishop of Italy, 95, 232, 473

Darius, 304, 308, 623, 1295

Decalog, 3, 38, 346, 417, 470, 509–10, 547, 592–94, 598, 612, 614, 616, 619, 626, 628, 630, 632–55, 662–63, 665–67, 671–72, 684, 690, 701, 706–7, 710, 714, 717, 720, 722–32, 735–39, 747, 751–53, 760–62, 771–72, 779–85, 787, 789, 792, 797–99, 804–5, 808–9, 993, 1052, 1077, 1081–82, 1084, 1096, 1120, 1132–37, 1139, 1142, 1145, 1161–62, 1228, 1234, 1236, 1238, 1240, 1248–53, 1275, 1337, 1357. See also Commandments

Decemvirales Tables, 589

Democritus, 269
atoms, 296

Demosthenes, 222, 481, 899, 922–23, 930, 973

depravity, 379–80, 395–96, 402, 422, 425–29, 477, 484, 487, 489, 491–95, 497–98, 503, 505, 514, 520, 533, 536, 545, 574, 579, 585, 603, 634, 779, 788, 851, 1059, 1071, 1294, 1310

dialecticians, 169, 229, 356, 818, 969, 978, 983–84, 986–87, 1029, 1152–53

dialectics, 17, 142, 144, 373, 524, 645

Diet at Worms, 520

Diet of Augsburg, 389–90, 415

Diodorus, 204, 270, 913, 920

Dionysius, 336, 926, 1327

Dionysius of Corinth, 40

Dionysius the Areopagite (Pseudo-), 20–21, 49, 71, 77, 389

disorder (*ataxia*), 491–92

divine essence. *See* essence of God

Docetism, 168–72

doctrinal conflict, necessity of knowing about, 54

doctrine, fate of pure, 4
relation to piety, 54

Dominic, 462

Donatists, 25, 371, 700, 744–45, 1295–96, 1311–12, 1347–53

Donatus, 1348

doubt, 946, 949, 952, 963

Draconites, J., 133

Duns Scotus, John, 462–63, 507, 513

Durandus, 878

Dydimus, 146, 221, 234

Ebion, 92, 121, 139, 167, 859–60

Eck, John, 20, 35, 389–91, 552, 560–61, 573, 602, 639, 780, 953, 1096, 1162, 1309

ecumenical creeds, 17–18, 35

elect, 318, 328, 345, 357, 362–63, 366, 606, 618, 629, 814, 1099, 1179, 1220, 1226, 1262, 1309, 1317
Manichaean ravings, 455, 534
and (Melanchthon on) loss of grace, 565–67

election of angels, 284, 302

Empedocles, 326, 745

Emser, 430

Enthusiasm, xi, xv, 398, 437, 440, 446–48, 608, 1133–34, 1360, 1366

history of, 455–57

Epictetus, bishop of Corinth, 206

Epicurean, 217, 256–57, 430, XXVI, 591, 604, 606, 659, 667, 684, 689, 759, 781, 789, 858–59, 889–90, 908, 926, 930–31, 1019, 1026, 1066, 1076, 1101, 1103, 1149, 1170, 1198, 1206–7, 1235, 1276

Epicurus, 44, 270–71, 295–96, 1256

Epiphanius (bishop of Salamis), 17, 19–20, 22, 24, 26–27, 30, 66, 83, 92, 116–17, 139–40, 142, 158, 167, 173, 176, 230, 239–40, 271, 472, 545, 676, 823, 853, 859, 869, 1241, 1272, 1292

Epistle of Anacletus, 1327

Erasmus, 21, 67, 109, 115, 133, 238, 426, 447, 484, 515, 518, 544, 601, 806, 825, 912, 921, 967, 1011, 1269

Ernest (duke), 1

essence of God (*ousia*), 100–101, 122–23, 130, 211, 214–18, 262, 526
accepted modes of speaking about, 110–11
Apollinarian controversy, 174
Arian controversies, 156–64
autoousios, 117
communication, 100–103, 117, 119, 134–36, 160, 241–43. *See also* Jesus Christ, begotten of the Father
disputes, 288
early controversies, 83–84
heteroousioi, 142
Holy Spirit's essence and His gifts, 244–45
homoousios, 116, 146, 233. *See also* essence of God, communication
ineffable, 71, 80, 148, 155–56, 206, 222, 236, 239, 260
infinity, 152–54, 228, 277,
name of God. *See* God, name of
nonaccidental, singular, and definitive attributes of deity, 58–59, 67–68, 73–76, 79–80, 319, 405
as one systematic aspect of knowledge of God in theology, 45, 57–59, 155, 319
problems in distinguishing *ousia* from *hypostasis*, especially in Latin, 99–100, 102–3, 111–12, 220, 243. *See also* person
statements of essence versus statements of personal duty, 130–31, 157
sufficiency to predicate attributes of, 78, 100–101
synousios, 116,
uncreated, 266, 276,
unity of, 82–85, 239. *See also* external works of God

unity of and difference of person, 86, 91, 95, 112. *See also* person

warnings against scrupulosity over *agraphos* words related to doctrine of, 95, 109, 115, 497

worship of as one, 71, 107–9, 246, 251

eternal death or punishment, 120, 496, 515, 551, 554, 563, 589, 596, 598, 618, 638, 642–44, 672, 713, 750, 806, 868, 901, 909, 984, 1019, 1027, 1055, 1060, 1068, 1070, 1141, 1148, 1171, 1191, 1208, 1226, 1233, 1250, 1255–61, 1266, 1271–72, 1277, 1279, 1284, 1344, 1358, 1364–66

differentiation of eternal, spiritual, and physical punishment, 732, 747, 758, 1075

eternal life, 76, 126–28, 146, 151, 212–13, 311, 396, 460, 469, 550, 558, 598, 602, 612, 622, 629, 638, 641–44, 666, 672, 702, 714, 732, 775, 804, 818, 834–40, 846–47, 849, 856, 867–68, 874–76, 888, 893, 907, 913–15, 924, 928–31, 936–37, 940–50, 955–56, 960, 968–69, 982, 1005, 1017, 1025–26, 1032, 1036, 1062, 1065, 1067–68, 1076, 1078, 1090–91, 1101–5, 1108–9, 1148, 1163–69, 1172, 1176, 1184, 1193–97, 1200–1201, 1205–6, 1213–17, 1220, 1228–33, 1239, 1248–49, 1270, 1277, 1288–89, 1299, 1303, 1310, 1312, 1328, 1339, 1357–58, 1365, 1367, 1369–72

equated with knowledge of God, 60, 66, 128, 1017

glorification, 58, 68, 607, 1230, 1253

promise or gift of, 33, 54, 56, 59, 76, 87, 128, 152–53, 164, 216, 391, 476, 592, 599, 890, 971–72, 977, 982, 1003, 1015, 1017, 1025, 1027–28, 1062, 1109, 1244, 1367

and righteousness, 114, 120, 122, 127–28, 147, 216, 475, 568, 590, 599, 822–23, 827, 835–37, 855, 891, 897, 986, 995, 998, 1021–24, 1029–30, 1032–36, 1178, 1227, 1363

against the problem of guilt, 550, 558, 563

not inhering, 906, 984, 986–89

Euchites, 455–56

Eudoxius, 231

Eunomius, 97, 143–44, 193, 231, 908

Euripides, 973

Eusebius of Caesarea, 24, 27, 40, 66, 83, 92, 121, 124, 139–42, 215, 327, 330, 626, 669, 681, 824, 859, 861, 867, 928, 1242, 1324

Eusebius of Nicomedia, 142

Eusebius of Pamphilia, 677

Eutyches, 186–87, 207, 215, 460

Eutychians, 207

excommunication, 711, 713, 1295–96, 1301, 1312, 1348, 1353

exorcism, 689, 1372–73

external discipline, 24, 29, 63, 170, 380–81, 394–95, 401, 415, 466–67, 496, 509, 533, 564, 622, 641, 851, 875, 1086, 1118, 1127, 1138, 1163, 1252

in which is freedom, 417ff.

not able to save, 475

the old man, 499

problems of regarding sin as external shortcoming, 479

stimulus to Pelagianism, 457ff, 1086

external works of God, 60, 67, 83, 91, 103–10, 148, 154, 262, 270, 274, 315, 318, 324, 360, 385, 390, 444, 452, 493–94, 502, 534, 542–45, 719–20, 779, 1033

Fagius, Paul, 264

faith

absence of, 800, 805–6, 831, 837, 993–94, 1088, 1256, 1260, 1273, 1289

comprehended by creeds, 22, 39, 167

danger of sin, 1057, 1063–64, 1068–70, 1101, 1160, 1171, 1260, 1274, 1283

definition of, 34, 898–925, 960, 1052

degrees of, 293, 446, 449, 689, 1271

our weakness, 590, 653, 684, 689, 836, 1136, 1195, 1256

discriminated by careful statement of articles of, 22–24, 29–34, 40–41, 43, 49, 81, 96–97, 168, 171, 183, 232, 236, 337, 512, 569, 602, 850, 1164, 1186, 1287, 1292–93, 1360

explained by various theologians, 870–74, 1001

but of simple, resolute apostles or of fishers, 65, 67, 74, 77, 83, 97–98, 140, 159, 165, 174, 193, 210, 265, 336, 366, 528–29, 559, 965, 1185, 1269, 1334

and Law and Gospel distinction, 271, 643, 959, 1186

marred by rationalizing, 42–43, 67, 77, 155, 170, 184, 485, 506, 528, 540, 601, 626, 773, 798, 831, 1161–62, 1249, 1279–82

supported in *sedes*, 50–51, 141, 261, 528, 554

effects of, 106, 250, 311, 403–4, 426–27, 462, 480, 572, 590, 790, 792, 837, 986, 1054, 1071, 1075, 1090–91, 1096–97, 1116, 1123, 1126, 1128, 1207

falsity of doubt, 937–55, 1067, 1202,
1209–10
    superseded by grace, 958–60, 977
and fleeing, 803, 887, 890–91, 895, 902–4,
921, 931, 949, 951, 972
goal of, 251, 445, 453, 828, 1066
history of, 67–68, 839–46, 1055, 1249
    faith same in Old and New Testa-
    ment, 23, 619, 633, 1246–48
justifying, 26, 37, 42, 49, 63, 76, 163, 213,
217, 380, 426, 496, 547, 566, 610, 643,
665, 687, 779, 790–91, 800, 803, 813,
815, 822, 827, 829, 832, 835, 838, 847,
956, 964, 985, 988–89, 1078, 1125,
1128, 1141, 1148, 1198, 1214–15, 1245,
1247, 1355
    definition of, 925–37
    unknown to philosophers, 955,
    1053
law of, 592, 649, 819, 826, 829, 831, 991,
1116
loss of, 371, 383–85, 453, 484, 565, 576,
647, 660, 1054, 1266, 1268, 1270,
1275–77
misunderstandings, 235, 412, 414,
426–28, 438, 441, 456, 460, 511, 539,
548, 558, 701, 823–25, 838, 991,
1104–10, 1286, 1295, 1349, 1369
    history of, 851–61
    patristic errors, 866–70
    sophistries, 874–76, 961–63,
    983–84, 995–1000, 1029–37,
    1116–19, 1166–70, 1174–75,
    1187–89, 1191–94, 1243, 1333,
    1341, 1361
    spurious writings and traditions,
    861–66
nature of, 218, 293, 336, 397, 429, 439–41,
443, 452, 475, 496, 501, 540, 628, 646,
823–23, 836, 849, 957–58, 986–88,
1052, 1062, 1096, 1160, 1182
not a righteousness of works, 593, 815,
817–18, 832, 982, 987, 989–90,
995–1003, 1102–3, 1141–42, 1144,
1162, 1165, 1167–68, 1173–74, 1199,
1220–22, 1228
    exclusive terms, 1003–17
    though doing works, 978, 992, 995,
    1160, 1163–64, 1173, 1175,
    1178
and oaths, 688, 693, 696, 1144
and obedience, 605, 659, 666, 701, 707,
715, 731, 767, 789–90, 792, 803, 832,
1054, 1061, 1072, 1216–18, 1256
object of, 391, 610, 633, 822, 1292, 1295
one, true, or catholic, 23, 83, 114, 159,
218, 224, 234–35, 329, 458, 581,

piety or confession, 17, 38, 54, 59, 76, 114,
122, 127, 132, 174, 179, 201, 210, 212,
214, 217–18, 237, 246–47, 353, 388,
399–401, 446, 451, 525, 564, 645,
652–53, 655, 657–59, 662, 664, 698,
709, 712, 717, 1054, 1060, 1062, 1081,
1177, 1234, 1238, 1259, 1273, 1299,
1304, 1307, 1341, 1356
reckoning under First Commandment,
658–59, 662, 664, 683–84, 717, 832,
1121
sedes, 1017–29, 1040–42
source of, 43, 345, 396, 403, 437–40, 446,
449, 452, 465, 711, 803, 827, 1313,
1358, 1371
struggle of, 25, 174, 176, 214–15, 238,
250–51, 257, 268, 306, 353, 399,
445, 449–50, 540, 566, 666, 715–17,
731, 803, 961, 1060, 1066, 1098–99,
1180–81, 1184, 1202, 1236, 1239,
1279, 1309, 1363
unity of, 711, 743, 747, 1241
vocabulary of, 540, 822, 876–97, 959–60,
972

fall, 2, 7, 58, 76, 171–72, 174, 205, 272, 283,
302, 316, 333–35, 380, 382, 406, 418,
428, 447, 466, 469, 473, 477, 484, 487–88,
491, 493, 495, 504–5, 510, 523, 526, 536,
547, 565–66, 579, 585–86, 633, 638, 756,
793–94, 798, 806, 833–34, 839, 845, 851,
869, 967, 1038–39, 1054, 1064, 1071,
1225–26, 1250, 1255, 1258, 1262, 1355
cause of evil, 273–74
efficient causes of, 491, 524, 528
final cause of, 492
Pelagian corruptions, 536–37

false witness. *See* Commandments, Eighth

fate, 297–98, 319, 374–75, 381, 405, 407. *See*
foreknowledge, divine. *See* ordering

Father, 112–14. *See also* essence of God. *See
also* Holy Trinity. *See also* ordering
in relation to all three persons, 86–103

father, human. *See* parents

Faustus of Riez, 460

Festus, Sextus Pompeius, 263

First Article, 580

First Commandment. *See* Commandments,
First

First Table of the Law, 61, 64, 425, 484, 590,
614, 646, 650–53, 655, 717, 720, 733,
735, 762, 780, 782–83, 785, 787–88, 795,
799–800, 832, 1023, 1052, 1117, 1178

Fisher, John. *See* Roffensis

Flaccius, XXI

Flacius, 578–87. *See also* original sin

flood, 67, 332, 633–34, 673, 759, 796, 801, 840, 852–53, 915, 1226, 1252, 1310

foreknowledge, divine, 287, 327, 331, 362–73, 373–76, 379–82, 384–86, 400, 405–6, 1025, 1073
  and cause of sin, 362–63
  and causes, 365
  certainty of, 364
  consequences of, 364–65
  definition, 365,
  and determinism, 366–67
  extent, 364
  and freedom of God, 366–67
  and necessity, 364–65
  objections to, 365
  safest procedure concerning, 363
  terminology, 362
  three necessary classes of, 371–72

forgiveness, 25, 31, 33, 49, 114, 260, 341, 395, 428, 476–77, 532, 566, 569, 578, 625, 656, 665, 739–40, 751–52, 787, 792, 801, 822, 828, 834–36, 870–71, 898, 901, 906, 928–29, 934, 938, 953, 976, 1010, 1014, 1035, 1041, 1054, 1058, 1208, 1210, 1259, 1276, 1284, 1351, 1357
  Baptism and, 547, 555, 559, 894, 1372
  ceremonial sacrifices, 615, 619
  condemnation without, 480, 483, 487, 496, 503–4, 598
  natural human ignorance of, 55

Formula of Concord, ix–xiv, 16, 578, 586, 885

Francis, 462

Frank, Sebastian, 382, 762, 1272

Frederick, elector of Saxony, 1

free choice, 64, 72, 79–80, 589–90, 605–6, 620, 627, 789, 809, 865, 870, 907, 909, 967, 1075, 1086, 1092, 1094–95, 1106, 1113, 1115–17, 1120, 1128–30, 1140, 1144, 1146, 1148–49, 1151, 1154–57, 1159, 1162, 1241, 1343
  ability to commit sin, 416
  and attitudes of the heart, 396
  bondage and captivity of unregenerate, 429–31
  evangelical use of, 473–74
  in external discipline, 417–22
  freedom of glory, 468
  freedom of the regenerate, 408, 447–48
  "human powers" preferable to, 406–7
  includes both mind and will, 397–98
  Melanchthon on, 393–404
  and natural freedom (*exousia*), 407
  none in spiritual matters, 417
  outward freedom, hindrances to, 395, 400–402, 423–24, 428
  Pelagius and Augustine on, 31, 408–9
  refutation of arguments concerning, 464–74
  and role of Holy Spirit, 396, 399–400, 429
  scope of, 414–15
  scriptural argument concerning, 466–70
  and sins or wicked actions, 416–17
  and spiritual actions, 429
  status controversiae on, 404–6, 429

Fulgentius, 327–29, 333, 363, 374, 383, 387, 460

Galen, 64, 265, 499, 511

Gallienus, 140

Gasmer, John, x

Gelasius, 19, 27, 207–8, 681, 970

Gellius, Aulus, 296, 368

generation (of the Son), 115, 132–38

Gennadius of Marseilles, 41, 409, 460, 1010

George, duke of Saxony, 1

Gerhard, John, x, 16

Gerson, Jean, 464, 513, 891, 945, 1126, 1323

Gnesio-Lutheran, xii, 586

Gnostics, 82, 84, 297, 860, 908, 1017, 1342

God
  activity of, 68
  attributes of, 78
  as Creator, 123
  definitions of. *See also* God, name of
    by Albertus Novicampanus, 74
    by Ambrose, 74
    by Augustine, 73–74
    and catalog with Dionysius, 77
    by Cicero, 72
    enigmatic points of natural knowl-edge, 69–70
    by Iodocus Willichius, 75
    by John of Damascus, 72
    by Lactantius, 74
    Melanchthon's explanation, 76–77
    objections to, 70
    by Plato, 72
  essence of. *See* essence of God
  gifts of, 1213
  gives Law, 589, 632–36
  Melanchthon, on God in general, 55–59
  long-suffering of, 359–62
  modes of considering God and sin, 381–91
  name of, 122–23, 133, 1363. *See also* Com-mandments, Second

ambivalence: hidden or revealed, 71, 138
Christ and proper name, 91, 126–28, 145–51
Hebrew language for "God," 145
related to definite knowledge of God in this life, 71, 77, 133
natural knowledge of, 60–66
nature of, 609–10, 793–94
oneness of, 85. *See also* essence of God
works of. *See also* external works of God
internal, 103–5
rules concerning, 103–10
wrath of. *See* wrath of God

Godhead, modes of speaking concerning, 110–11
names applied to, 111–12

good action, causes for, 328, 359, 361, 397

good works, 324, 328, 366, 381, 387, 398, 406, 427, 448, 454, 462–63, 465, 470, 499, 504, 512, 550, 563, 572–73, 592, 595, 599–600, 604–5, 608–10, 641, 646, 766, 783, 787–88, 823–25, 868, 934, 1273, 1286, 1347
ancient controversies of, 1076–80
misunderstandings of, 1082–85, 1104–10, 1118, 1143–46, 1170, 1175–76, 1185–223
nature of, 1053, 1081, 1111–30
necessity of, 1063, 1074–76, 1089, 1091–101, 1149–64, 1179–85
norm of, 1097–101
in regenerate, 609–10, 641, 666, 789–93, 1066, 1089, 1112–30, 1146–49
relation to salvation, 1101–10, 1164–79
rewards of, 1066
source of, 1054, 1113, 1130
types of, 1052, 1088
vocabulary of, 1073

Gospel, 56, 125, 141, 154, 166, 235, 350, 371, 399, 440, 475, 490, 552, 569, 611, 620, 656–57, 660, 665, 677, 683–84, 687–88, 760, 801–3, 805–8, 816–18, 863, 865, 883, 886, 895, 897, 905, 929, 965, 968, 999, 1010, 1019
angels and devils regarding, 302, 305–6, 308, 330
in Christology controversies, 194, 204, 207
definition of, 818, 828–33, 899
distinct from natural knowledge, 260, 350, 475, 956
foolishness of belief, 350, 398, 430, 800, 851, 856, 858, 865, 898, 958
given and free, 56–57, 59, 114, 442–43, 492, 976, 981, 1015

light of, 35, 39, 56, 66, 217, 677, 698, 847, 853, 937, 968
ministry of, 35, 38, 54, 59, 66, 92, 99, 114, 120–21, 272, 371, 398, 489, 569, 708, 726, 799, 866, 880, 912, 956, 1022, 1030
nature of, 51, 123, 833–34, 846, 904, 906, 915, 958
power of God, 678, 699, 896, 901, 921, 936, 964
preaching of, work of Holy Spirit, 67, 397, 437, 440, 452, 455, 475–76
proclamation of fulfillment of Law by Christ, 590, 904, 959
promise universal, 213, 345, 397
promises of, 32, 37, 113, 211, 212, 217, 235, 398, 469, 548, 827, 834–35, 876, 901, 913–14, 927, 929, 931, 940, 949, 951, 953, 964, 985, 999
relation to Law, 23, 34, 260, 271, 308, 330, 397, 426, 467, 493, 590–95, 643–44, 701, 809–10, 826, 838, 848, 855, 884, 895, 929, 959, 969, 971, 1018–19, 1025. *See also* Law and Gospel
vocabulary of, 818–22

Gottfried, Jacob, x

government, 720–21
duties of, 727–28, 734–35, 737, 1296
judicial system of, 770–71
relation with Church, 1320

grace, 34, 42, 157, 399–400, 428, 450, 457–58, 496, 504, 511, 522, 526, 536, 548, 553, 563, 565–66, 576, 578, 611, 657, 666, 679, 757, 807, 831, 876, 887, 911, 914, 930, 935, 953, 965, 967, 995, 1019, 1024–26, 1042, 1057, 1091, 1096–97, 1100, 1133, 1168, 1198, 1202, 1207, 1215, 1218, 1221, 1226, 1271, 1277–79, 1281, 1307, 1315, 1345, 1355–56, 1363–64, 1369, 1372–73
Adam and Eve, 55, 60, 1262,
Augustine's teaching of, 428, 433–48, 450, 454, 458–59, 872, 946, 970–71, 1086–87, 1116, 1129, 1140
Cain's story, 852
cause of spiritual advances, 15–16, 25, 44, 234, 308, 389, 398, 410, 416, 426, 449, 452, 827, 1017, 1054, 1128, 1182
comfort, 7, 656, 805, 840, 913, 1001
definition of, 969–70, 972, 974, 977, 979, 1189
effects, 354, 518–19, 610, 733, 1099
explained by prophets, 809, 819
and freedom, 408–10, 413, 447, 936
in greetings, 1, 106
and humility or under harshness, 350–51, 830, 929, 1208

and imputation, 349, 403–4, 414, 931–32, 934, 978, 983–85, 1004, 1035, 1104, 1167

light or revelation, 63, 76, 114, 153, 937, 1147

and ministry, 1318–19, 1326–28, 1332

misunderstandings of, 398, 426–28, 447, 456–78, 529, 605–6, 806, 823, 829, 838, 847, 856, 858–60, 871, 874, 878, 938–40, 948–49, 954–55, 968–69, 971–72, 994, 997–99, 1013, 1023, 1030–31, 1037, 1088, 1117, 1151, 1189–90, 1243, 1251, 1276, 1281, 1286, 1310, 1349, 1361

nature of, 779, 810, 851, 879, 896–97, 924–25, 929, 936, 942, 944, 951, 956–57, 964, 975, 981–82, 1034, 1041, 1097, 1172, 1204, 1273, 1281–82, 1367–68, 1370

necessity of, 591, 598–99, 1101, 1118, 1120, 1163, 1180, 1276

obscured in papal superstitions, 21, 389–90, 529, 660

prevenient, 449–50, 452

reason for justification, 815, 827, 846, 870, 877, 888, 892, 894, 902, 909, 915, 928, 930, 947, 950, 960, 967, 992, 996–97, 1000, 1007–8, 1012–14, 1018, 1023, 1027, 1029, 1035, 1079, 1105–6, 1146, 1165, 1203, 1213, 1220, 1245

relationship (*relatio*), 986, 1036

sought, 792

source of, 79, 816, 861, 905, 978, 1003, 1026, 1115, 1216

Spirit of. *See* Holy Spirit, grace of

status of Christians, 646, 658, 737, 791, 805, 809, 826, 891, 895, 902–3, 921, 939, 943, 951, 963, 978, 1061, 1068–70, 1126, 1140, 1151, 1257–59, 1266

use of term or idea, 31–32, 50, 52, 457, 593, 606, 609, 997, 1002, 1206

versus hardening, 383–84, 449, 728, 1171, 1184

vocabulary of, 819, 955, 966–67, 973–76, 1003–4, 1205

Gratian, 42, 102, 376, 776–77, 970, 1319, 1321, 1323–24, 1341–42, 1348

Gregory, 677, 681, 741, 775, 892, 908, 1001, 1332, 1347

Gregory of Nazianzus, 27–28, 95, 97–98, 100–101, 104, 106, 115–16, 133, 135, 143, 157, 159, 174, 204, 228, 230, 237, 239, 243, 246–47, 267, 283, 505, 651, 908, 946, 1261, 1296, 1347, 1351–52

Gregory of Neocaesarea. *See* Gregory Thaumaturgus

Gregory of Nyssa, 232, 678

Gregory of Rimini, 463

Gregory of Tours, 463

Gregory Thaumaturgus, 28, 124–25, 239, 1291, 1299

Gregory the Great, 32, 577, 1274, 1319, 1322

Gropper, John, 544, 556, 825, 874, 879, 994, 1031, 1033, 1036, 1243

guilt, 323, 341, 466, 475–77, 512–13, 517, 531, 541, 558–60, 576, 581, 657, 661, 664, 690, 699, 703, 747–48, 826, 838, 851, 878–79, 882, 884–87, 890, 958, 983–84, 1011, 1028, 1148, 1197, 1208–9, 1212, 1222, 1255, 1267, 1272, 1284–86, 1300, 1348

Anselm's clear thinking on, 509, 538. *See also* Anselm

Baptism removing, 496, 501, 537

causes of studied, 328, 335, 405–6, 524, 526–27, 540–42, 547–49, 574

confession of, 341, 346, 519

evil of versus that of punishment, 273, 330, 333, 347

fate does not alter, 319

in our present condition, 275, 335, 386, 433, 487–92, 504, 506, 518, 551

as proper cause of punishment, 55, 64, 170–71, 554, 556, 565–67, 569

sinfulness, 480–83

too much formality, 508, 536, 539, 558

upon breaking one point, 593, 606, 609, 628

Hadrian, 329, 1319

Haymo, 1010, 1012

Heinrich II, x

Helmstedt, University of, x, xiv

Hemerobaptists, 861

Hemmingsen, Niels, 266

Henry of Navarre, x

Herman of Wied, 544

Hermas, 544, 863–64, 907

Hermogenes, 325, 327

Herodotus, 53, 628, 880, 1297

Hesiod, 35, 216, 817, 900

Hesychius, 426, 925, 1013

heteroousios, 84, 99, 116, 142. *See also* essence of God

Hexaemeron, 276–85

Hilary, 26–27, 69–70, 98–99, 111, 115, 117,
133, 159, 175, 186, 239, 275, 436, 458, 501,
505, 561, 867–68, 892, 1001, 1010, 1112

Hispanus, Alphonsus, 44, 553

Holy Spirit, 211–53, 594–96, 604, 606, 608–9,
623, 629, 635–36, 641, 643, 646–47,
653–55, 660, 665, 670–71, 682, 687, 692,
707, 724–25, 733, 735, 738–40, 746,
751–52, 754, 759, 782, 786, 788–92, 801,
806, 814–15, 818, 821, 827, 831, 849, 861,
866, 876–77, 893, 900, 903, 908, 921–22,
928–29, 931, 933–34, 936, 939, 943–45,
953–56, 964–66, 969–70, 972, 978, 985,
993–94, 996, 998, 1002, 1006, 1015,
1019, 1022, 1025, 1033, 1041, 1054–56,
1063–64, 1068–73, 1080–81, 1085–87,
1090, 1099–101, 1107–34, 1140–41, 1043,
1152, 1156–58, 1060, 1171–72, 1174,
1176–90, 1193, 1195, 1198, 1213, 1217–18,
1220, 1225, 1231, 1233, 1243, 1249–50,
1256–59, 1261–62, 1273–74, 1277–79,
1282–83, 1286, 1289, 1296, 1297–1300,
1303, 1310, 1312, 1315, 1318, 1327,
1339–42, 1348–49, 1351, 1360, 1363–65,
1368–69, 1371–73. *See also* essence of
God. *See also* God. *See also* person (*hypos-
tatis*). *See also* Holy Trinity
  activities of, 248, 250, 252
  benefits of in NT, 249–51
  benefits of in OT, 248–49
  as Comforter, 88, 212, 215, 218, 222–23,
  225, 229, 232, 234, 401
  constancy of need for (despite human
  efforts toward salvation), 444–45
  consubstantial with Father and Son. *See*
  homoousios
  controversies concerning, 222–48
    deity, 233–39, 246–47
    indwelling and gifts, 244–46
    procession, 239–43
    worship of, 247
  convicts world, 635
  creates obedience, 443
  definition of "spirit" illustrated
    by Augustine, 222
    exegetical thoughts on "spirit,"
    220–21
    by Melanchthon, 211
    with Virgil, 220
  definitions of, 218–22
    by Augustine, 218
    by John of Damascus, 219
  descriptive titles, names, and epithets of
  Third Person, 222–24
  efficacious through Gospel. *See* Gospel,
  preaching of

  grace of, 76, 216, 218, 224, 234, 236, 354,
  396, 414, 416, 426, 434, 438, 440, 444,
  792, 945, 951, 975, 1054, 1233
  grieving, 245, 251, 341, 449, 646, 654,
  740, 754, 788, 792, 944, 965, 1054,
  1059, 1070, 1277, 1279, 1282, 1348
  Melanchthon on, 211–17
  names of, 222–24
  in Old Testament, 236–37
  procession of, 48, 58, 66, 72–76, 78, 81,
  87, 94, 105, 107, 112, 114, 120, 147,
  212, 215, 219, 222, 225, 227, 229–30,
  239–243, 396
  received through faith, 404
  renews man, 604–6, 608–9, 629, 653,
  655, 706, 790–92, 807–8, 825–27, 866,
  874, 876–77, 884, 895, 909, 924, 929,
  969–70, 972, 977, 984–85, 993–94,
  996, 1033, 1069, 1073, 1082, 1086–87,
  1099, 1114–20, 1122, 1125–29,
  1132–33, 1137–38, 1140, 1160, 1179,
  1182, 1204, 1243, 1289, 1371
  as sanctifier, 49, 77, 87, 108, 113–14, 120,
  124, 126, 168, 179, 211, 218–19, 224,
  234, 362, 476
  Spirit of Christ, 203, 213, 223, 225, 227,
  235, 241, 396
  testimonies of Scripture, 225–28
  as Third Person of Trinity, 91, 112, 114,
  120, 212–13, 219–21, 225, 228,
  233–34, 237, 246

Holy Trinity, 4, 5, 23, 26, 28, 32, 38, 46, 48,
59, 70, 80, 86–88, 662, 818, 929, 1025–26,
1029, 1135, 1183, 1315, 1372
  biblical testimonies on, 88–89
    rules for reading Trinity, 89–91
  consubstantiality of persons. *See*
  homoousios
  controversies on, 91–94
  definition of, 112–14
  modes of speaking concerning, 111
  mystery of, 87
  plurality of persons, 90
  terminology on, 94–103
    and Church's use of, 96–97
    role in controversy, 97–101
    role in development of heresy,
    96–97
  three persons in, 103–5, 146, 211

Homer, 24, 66, 93, 297, 816, 820, 922, 1056

homoousios (consubstantiality with the
Father), 68, 74, 87, 91, 106, 114–17, 121,
138, 153, 155, 159–62, 172, 216, 225, 243

honor, of the Law, 717, 808–10
  of parents. *See* Commandments, Fourth

Hormisdas, 460

Hosius, 1005, 1033, 1128

Hostiensis. *See* Segusio, Henry of

Hugh of St. Victor, 287, 365, 487–88, 507, 513, 538, 926, 969

Hugo. *See* Hugh of St. Victor

human will
active in regenerate, 449–50
can resist Holy Spirit, 452
captivity and inborn depravity of, 425–29
as enslaved, 417
free in matters subject to reason or senses, 467
liberated through Holy Spirit, 452
summary on, 464–74

Hus, John, 464, 1308

hypostatic union. *See* personal union

Ignatius, 22, 626, 862

image of God, 55, 58, 60, 77, 89–90, 282–83, 301, 321–22, 466, 487, 509–10, 515, 541, 655, 658, 794, 796, 813, 851, 1071, 1073, 1218, 1226, 1252, 1281

images, 42, 55, 639, 645, 648–49, 651, 654, 660, 663, 668–70, 673–82, 697–99, 1053

incarnation, 59, 122, 125, 135, 141–42, 144, 168, 181, 185–87, 191, 195, 205–6, 208, 586, 843, 929

incommunicability, 86, 102–3

infant baptism, 538, 1292, 1300, 1365–71, 1373

inner depravity, 427

intercession, 67, 161, 215, 360, 602, 644, 676, 679–80, 876, 888, 904, 1061, 1237, 1255, 1260, 1270

Irenaeus, 22–23, 39, 81, 83–84, 125, 129, 132–33, 141, 169, 186, 271–72, 275, 285, 324, 336, 340, 374, 378, 381, 407, 470, 472, 500, 505, 859, 862, 867, 869–70, 1011, 1078, 1145, 1185, 1291, 1299, 1334, 1344

Irenaeus the Grammarian, 99

Isidore, 20, 292, 1274

Islebius, 828

Jerome, 19, 21–22, 24–28, 29–31, 40, 95, 99, 109, 134, 144, 151, 221, 229, 232, 238–39, 264, 289, 327, 331, 369, 374, 381, 385, 402–4, 406, 415, 435–36, 458, 461, 467, 472–74, 483, 501, 505, 518, 520, 522–23, 526–27, 543, 575, 601, 606, 608, 610–11, 625, 651, 681, 691, 693, 696, 699, 704, 775, 784, 824, 843, 861, 869, 872, 883, 954, 989–90, 995, 1152, 1268, 1272, 1278, 1341–42, 1346–47

Jesuits, 44, 463, 939, 969, 983, 987

Jesus Christ, 827
assumption of human infirmities, 131
begotten of Father, 134, 138
benefits of, 396, 403, 425, 431, 445–46, 458, 474–76, 478, 496, 557
communication of properties, 208
conceived by Holy Spirit, 113–14, 137, 168, 171–72, 199
confusion of two natures, 201, 203, 208
consubstantial with Father and Holy Spirit
with man. *See* homoousios
and creation, 152
divine nature, 98, 101, 113, 119, 121–63
eternity of, 154
human nature of, 131, 137, 159, 164–78
controversies concerning, 166–78
orthodox formulation of, 164–65
as image of the Father, 58, 65, 74–76, 82, 87, 112, 114, 119–20, 124, 127, 133–36, 138, 210, 216,
incarnation of. *See* incarnation
infinite essence of, 152
and justification, 127, 147
likeness to Father, denial of, 143–44
as Mediator, 2, 37, 49, 56–57, 75, 114, 160–62, 164, 174, 179, 215–18, 250, 399, 402–3, 446, 469, 476, 480, 490, 496, 503–4, 563, 569, 590–91, 598, 618, 644, 647, 652, 656, 658, 660, 662, 667, 683, 687, 751, 767, 788, 790, 800, 803, 809, 818, 824, 827, 832, 839, 845–46, 874, 876, 886, 888, 897–900, 904–5, 915–16, 927–31, 934, 939, 941, 949–50, 954–55, 957–59, 961–62, 964–65, 968, 972, 976–77, 982, 986, 992, 995, 1001, 1003, 1011, 1015, 1024, 1026–30, 1034–36, 1040–41, 1053, 1055, 1058–61, 1065–66, 1068, 1075–76, 1087, 1090–91, 1104–5, 1111, 1117, 1121, 1130, 1141, 1165–70, 1175, 1186–95, 1197–202, 1204, 1230–31, 1238, 1244–45, 1247–48, 1251, 1262, 1271, 1278, 1372
merit of, 7, 38, 548, 557
names of God applied to, 144–51
obedience of, 176
offices of, 178–80
personal union of two natures in. *See* personal union
personhood, denial of, 139–42
resurrection of, 137
sacrifice of, 201
as servant, 196, 200
sinlessness of, 168

state of humiliation, 137, 163, 170–71,
177, 193–94, 196–97, 201–2, 237
suffering of, 131, 176–78
titles of, 178–80
two natures in, 124, 129
virginal birth of, 137
as Word. *See Logos*
work of, 113–14

John of Antioch, 184, 204, 207

John of Damascus, 17, 42–43, 72, 95, 111, 135,
137, 174, 187–88, 219, 240, 243, 287, 378,
538, 679, 926, 946

John of Samosatenus, 215. *See* Samosatenians

Josephus, 651, 674, 880

Jovinian, 30, 426, 473, 1272

Julian law, 751

Julian of Eclanum, 28, 427, 458, 461, 472,
525, 532–35, 541–42, 545, 558, 560, 677,
994

Julian the Apostate, 143, 660

Julius (duke), x

justification, 49, 52, 245–46, 479, 507–8
as central doctrine, 814, 847, 1042
Christ alone, 858–59, 864, 960, 989,
1007–8, 1010, 1028, 1034, 1105, 1167,
1189, 1212, 1359
controversies over, before Christ, 851–57
definition of, 815, 818, 875–76, 885,
1023–24
early church controversies of, 859–74
goal of, 934, 983–85, 986–87, 1030,
1036–37
and good works, 550
nature of, 979–88, 1003–18, 1167
NT controversies of, 857–59
preservation of, 872
propter Christ, "sake of Christ," 403–4,
480, 504, 566, 652, 658, 687, 751, 779,
791, 817–18, 824, 826, 828, 832, 836,
847, 849, 876, 898–900, 905, 916,
928–30, 936, 953, 956–57, 959–60,
963–65, 967, 971–72, 982–84, 986,
992, 1001, 1015, 1035–36, 1053, 1060,
1062, 1076, 1090–91, 1102, 1105, 1110,
1117, 1120, 1126–27, 1138, 1148, 1160,
1166–68, 1176–77, 1189, 1198, 1200,
1204, 1207, 1213–14, 1216–17, 1230,
1243, 1247–49, 1258, 1260, 1276,
1278, 1280, 1357, 1361, 1363–64
relation to original sin, 563
Satan undermines, 814, 850
synonyms of, 893–97
vocabulary of, 815, 849, 876–97

without works of Law, 859, 925, 982,
984, 987–88, 990, 992–93, 995–98,
1001–4, 1008, 1014–18, 1076, 1102,
1104–6, 1126, 1162–63, 1166–69,
1171–75, 1181

Justin Martyr, 148, 187, 262, 267, 270, 327,
329–30, 371, 374–75, 381, 407, 418, 465,
470, 472, 535, 823, 869, 1241

Karlstadt, 133, 648

Kenkel, Dithmar, 208–10

Keys, Office of the, 883 84, 894, 1032,
1311–54

Kimchi, David, 264

Kirchner, Timothy, xiv

knowledge of God, 60–91
priority of words and works of God,
65–68
subordination of natural to divine, 65–68
and Word of God, 84–85

Koelpflin, Wolfgang, 339

Koran, 139–40, 143, 908

Lactantius, 25, 41, 74, 263, 681

Lanfranc, 507

Latomus, 67

Law, 38, 61, 395
demands complete obedience, 425
external acts of worship, 415
external compliance, 403
external discipline. *See* external discipline
fulfilling of, 426
internal works of, 415
schoolmaster, 316, 465–66, 594, 598, 801,
807, 810, 848, 1115, 1245, 1251. *See
also* honor, of the Law

Law, divine (locus), 589–813
attributes of, 589, 627
ceremonial and civil versus moral, 627–32
conditions of fulfillment and disobedience, 589–90, 593, 599–611, 638–39,
641, 643–44, 672, 705, 729, 755,
758, 765, 779, 782, 788–91, 801, 803,
807–8, 810, 816–17, 823, 831, 837,
847–48, 863–64, 877–78, 889–900,
905, 940–41, 949, 963, 968–69, 978,
986, 999, 1013, 1022, 1034, 1056,
1061, 1081, 1083, 1089, 1096, 1106,
1114–15, 1116, 1121, 1124–27, 1130,
1132, 1134, 1138, 1148, 1160, 1190,
1192, 1195, 1197, 1217, 1241, 1278,
1282
fulfillment and Christ, 627, 791,
826–27, 838, 918, 970, 1000,

1029, 1119, 1139, 1163, 1172, 1242, 1251–52
First Table of. *See* First Table of the Law
misunderstandings of, 592, 600, 804
nature of, 1086–87, 1118–19, 1226
Paul's teaching of, 780–89
relation to Gospel. *See* Law and Gospel
Second Table of. *See* Second Table of the Law
source of, 612–13, 629–36
taught by Holy Spirit, 788
third use of, 1131–40
threats of, 589, 598, 642–44, 649, 672, 684, 690, 694, 699, 713, 731, 747–48, 753, 758–59, 763, 779–80, 826
use of, 640, 800–808, 1081
vocables for, 593–96

law, human, 589, 596, 598, 611–13

Law and Gospel, 23, 34, 260, 271, 308, 594, 625, 711, 779, 808, 816–17, 823–25, 829, 837–38, 867, 929, 940, 948, 957, 959, 1104, 1165–66, 1186–87, 1226, 1260. *See also* Gospel, relation to Law

Leipzig Interim, xi

Leo, 1347

Leo I, 324, 385

Leo VIII, 1319

Leo X, 550, 923

Leo the Isaurian, 676

Leyser, Caspar, 16

Leyser, Polycarp, ix, 16, 298, 578, XI, XXVI, 1044, 1110

Libanius, 143

Libertines, 592, 807, 1080, 1095, 1137, 1162

liberty of Christian, 1141–45

Lindanus, 1122, 1244, 1278

Livy, 262, 323

Loci, proper order of, 51
relationships, 260–61

Loci Communes. See Melanchthon

Logos, 59, 103, 106, 119, 122, 123, 125, 133–34, 140, 173, 215, 595, 1272, 1291–92

Lombard, Peter. *See* Peter Lombard

Lord's Prayer, 109, 257, 339, 686–87, 698, 749

Lord's Supper, xiii–xiv, 63, 209–10, 701, 711, 887, 914, 1237, 1327, 1355–57, 1361
in one kind by Manichaeans, 324
real presence, 49

Loreottus, 276

Lucian, 322

Luther, ix–xii, xiv–xv, 6–78, 12, 15, 37, 43–44, 63, 67, 89–90, 95, 104–5, 107–8, 113, 133–35, 145, 147, 167, 188, 210, 236, 238, 241, 245, 264, 266, 268, 277, 293, 299, 302, 306–7, 310, 390–91, 425, 447, 454, 464, 499, 503, 511, 515, 519–22, 524, 528, 550, 573, 575, 580, 583–84, 586–87, 594, 608, 620, 627, 633, 641, 645, 648, 650, 663, 670, 780, 783, 791, 805, 807, 809–10, 814–15, 820, 825–26, 828–33, 838, 845, 852, 873, 879, 883, 887, 890, 894, 896–97, 912, 921, 935, 937, 941, 967, 981–82, 1001–2, 1011, 1016, 1019, 1023, 1045, 1076, 1080, 1086–88, 1091, 1095–97, 1099–100, 1102–3, 1106–8, 1110, 1112–13, 1116–28, 1130–31, 1133–45, 1150–53, 1158–64, 1167, 1169, 1171–78, 1181–83, 1185, 1203, 1212, 1216–17, 1264, 1272, 1275, 1280, 1284, 1286, 1302, 1305, 1308–9, 1313–14, 1323, 1330–31, 1351, 1371–73

lying. *See* Commandments, Seventh

Lyra, 29, 89, 277, 462, 744, 1101, 1336

Maccabees, 20, 268, 312, 324, 528, 745, 856

Macedonians (followers of Macedonius), 232–33, 246

Macedonius, 220–21, 229–31, 1343

Magnus (son of prince), 1

Magus, Simon, 272, 330, 859, 864, 947, 1017, 1078–80, 1146

Malvenda of Ratisbon, 439

man, attributes of, 793–94
obedience of, 1148–49

Manes, 84, 168, 318, 324, 326–27, 329

Mani, 168. *See* Manes

Manichaeanism, 168–72

Manichaeans, 23, 35, 50, 84–85, 90, 169–72, 175, 215–16, 268, 271–74, 313, 318, 324–27, 329, 332, 348, 356–57, 378, 381, 389, 398, 442, 450, 453–57, 471–73, 501–2, 518, 524, 534, 543–44, 551, 578, 584
doctrine of, 325–26, 453–55
history of, 453–57

Marcellus, 26

Marcion, 24, 35, 83–85, 166–67, 186, 215–16, 271–72, 324–25, 329–30, 381, 454, 622, 804, 861–62
refutation of, 84–85, 273, 1293

Marcionites, 167–168, 470, 624–25, 861, 928

marriage, x, 20, 30, 75, 180, 304–5, 415, 467, 540, 545–46, 549, 619–20, 637, 647, 670,

715, 718, 721, 750–54, 757–58, 760, 796, 1079, 1357
    forbidden degrees of, xiv

Mary, "mother of God" (*theotokos*), 183, 185, 189–90, 204

Mary Tudor, 414

Maxentius, John, 460

Maximinus, 66, 243, 669

Melanchthon, Philipp, ix, xi–xiv, xvi, 8–14, 25, 43–44, 54–55, 60, 66–67, 72, 76, 78, 82, 86, 88, 93, 119, 142, 158, 211, 255, 298, 313, 375, 389–90, 393, 404, 422, 475, 487, 499, 511, 564, 571, 578, 597, 741, 829–30, 879, 1118, 1141, 1143, 1180
    and *Loci Communes*, ix, 8–9, 11, 13, 19, 41, 44, 49, 54, 60, 62, 78, 88, 142, 144, 159, 176, 180, 287, 298, 390–91, 404, 429, 544, 577, 597–98, 655, 798–99, 804, 913, 1099, 1121, 1141, 1312, 1332, 1335, 1370. *See also* table of contents

Meletius, 142, 678, 1292

Menander, 99, 263, 381, 799

Menius, 1103, 1169

merit, 465
    of congruence, 390, 462–63, 529, 1088

Messalium, 455

Methodius, 17

ministry, 35, 85, 106, 114, 161, 197, 248, 250–52, 371, 391, 398, 438, 440, 455, 476, 489, 617, 633, 639, 645, 650, 683, 687, 700–701, 705–6, 710–12, 726, 742, 762, 765, 793, 819, 821, 828–29, 842, 844, 848, 884, 921, 944, 968, 1019–20, 1024, 1030, 1039, 1041, 1047–48, 1067, 1079, 1083, 1091, 1112, 1116, 1133, 1156, 1199, 1202, 1220, 1226, 1230–31, 1237, 1239, 1247, 1252, 1263, 1287–98, 1309–32, 1339, 1344–45, 1347–53, 1357–62, 1365–69, 1372

Moerlin, Joachim, xiv, 1346

Mohammed, 326, 721

Mohammedans, 35, 216, 656, 660, 668, 721, 846, 1055, 1225, 1357

Monarchians, 93

Monasticism, and monks, xiv, 6, 18, 28, 70, 270, 444, 459, 461–62, 492–93, 506–7, 590–91, 637, 701, 847–48, 873, 900, 953, 955, 1057, 1059, 1140, 1186, 1258, 1293, 1360, 1366

Montanism, 25

Montanists, 861, 871

Montanus, 24

moral law, 64, 270, 313, 319, 337, 369, 396, 415, 425, 462, 475, 479, 485, 518, 596–99, 612–14, 620–22, 624, 626–29, 632, 634, 639, 641, 649–50, 666, 672, 674–76, 691, 700–703, 705–6, 712, 726, 730, 793, 799, 805–6, 834, 836–37, 842, 847, 855–58, 872, 963, 973, 989–93, 1020, 1040, 1067, 1071, 1128, 1140, 1144–45, 1225, 1230, 1241–42, 1247, 1285, 1287–88, 1293, 1295, 1297, 1331, 1338, 1357

mortal sin, 427–28, 462–63, 483, 495, 560, 563–65, 567, 569, 574–75, 702–3, 739, 776, 786, 788, 831, 847, 874, 878, 1015, 1255–86

Moses Maimonides, 289

mother. *See* parents

Muenster, Sebastian, 249, 301

Muenzer, Thomas, 456, 1080

Munzer, 456

Musculus, Andrew, 1111

mystery, 208, 821, 834, 936, 966, 1012

natural knowledge of God, 33, 258–60, 611, 635, 647, 773, 794, 797–99, 1022, 1263
    appropriate use of, 65
    different from revealed knowledge, 60
    from effects, 62
    God's approval of, 64–65
    grafted into the minds of men, 60–62
    purpose of, 63–64

natural law, 369, 595–96, 611–13, 634–35, 640, 699, 725, 754, 789, 793–800, 823, 834, 838, 869, 1021–22, 1236, 1241, 1272

natural man, 397, 430–31, 438, 536, 780

necessity, distinction of, 373–81
    sources of distinction, 375
    status controversiae of locus, 377

necessity, of compulsion, 378
    of consequence, 319, 375–78
    freedom for external works of Law, 378–79
    of immutability, 378–80
    of obligation, 381
    to sin, church fathers and, 374
    two senses of, 377

neighbor, 589, 638, 641, 645–46, 651–53, 655, 675, 688, 691, 693, 696, 705–6, 716, 739–47, 754, 759, 761–88, 800, 807, 883, 910, 968–69, 981, 1073, 1077–78, 1081, 1088, 1098–100, 1135, 1178, 1180, 1182–85, 1194, 1228, 1230–31, 1243, 1245, 1272, 1311

Neofanius, Melchior, XXVII

Nero, 315, 318, 516, 568, 718–19, 1256

Nestorian controversy, 182–210

Nestorius, 32, 140, 215, 460, 1343. *See also* Nestorian controversy

Neuser, Adam, XXI

new obedience, 569, 603, 646–47, 654–55, 686, 790–91, 805, 807–9, 824, 858, 875–76, 884, 886, 897, 909, 929, 970, 992, 996, 1000–1001, 1015, 1033, 1036–38, 1051, 1063, 1075, 1094, 1106–7, 1111–14, 1119–22, 1125, 1127–30, 1139, 1141, 1143–49, 1152, 1161–62, 1164, 1195, 1204, 1216, 1243, 1250 1252, 1256, 1331

New Testament, 595–96, 617, 623, 634, 647–51, 675–77, 691–92, 701–4, 708, 710–11, 731, 755, 775, 787, 809, 830, 833, 842, 845–46, 856–57, 865, 910–12, 917, 920, 926, 976, 989, 992–93, 996, 1001, 1038–39, 1073, 1077, 1081, 1083, 1086, 1131, 1225–54, 1303, 1307, 1322, 1336, 1338–40, 1343, 1350, 1361, 1371

Nicaea II, 676–78

Nicene Creed, 17, 35, 88, 105, 215, 1306
   addenda of Council of Constantinople, 229–30
   "begotten" and "only-begotten," 135–36
      "before all worlds," 153
      "Light of Light," 109, 119, 135
      homoousios, 115. *See also homoousios*
   filioque, 239–40
   "and in the Holy Spirit," 229
      "incarnate by the Holy Spirit," 181
         "and was made man," 174
   "spoke through the prophets," 91, 238
   "who for us men, etc.," 167, 284

Nicephorus, 27, 40, 185–86, 232, 272, 285, 330, 1319

Nicholas of Lyra. *See* Lyra

Nicolaitans, 1281

Nicolaus, 1342

Noetians, 92,

Novatian, 25, 871,

Novatians, 861, 871, 947

Novicampanus, Albertus, 74

oaths, 683, 688–89, 691–97, 715, 771, 773, 795, 841, 911, 941–42, 1041, 1245, 1248, 1262, 1366
   Cicero denying providence for, 367, 466

obedience. *See* Law, divine

Oecumenius, 892

Old Testament, 4, 6, 23, 89, 122, 127, 234, 411, 442, 481
   comparison of Old with New, 84–85, 519, 1225–54
   definition of *homoousia* in, 153
   Hebrew words for sin, 482–83
   proofs of original sin in, 498
      and discussion of the heart, 411, 519–23
   rules regarding proofs of Trinity in, 89–91, 234–35, 237–38, 249

Onkelos, 149, 236

operating grace, 444–49

Optatus, 527

ordering (*dispositio*), 256, 296–97, 313, 362, 368

ordination, 935, 1145, 1319, 1321, 1325–27, 1334, 1357–60

Origen, 17, 24–27, 41, 125–26, 175, 221, 240, 327, 331, 340, 348, 364–65, 411, 459, 483, 500, 516, 533–34, 615, 651, 674, 707, 848, 867, 873, 903, 924, 989–90, 992, 1001, 1009, 1013–14, 1269, 1285, 1313, 1332, 1366–67

original righteousness, 487, 504, 506, 509–11, 530, 574

original sin, 23, 28–30, 293, 315, 329, 332–33, 389, 476–80, 483, 485, 487–513, 516–20, 524–26, 528–32, 534–36, 538–51, 555–56, 558–59, 564–65, 569–71, 573–76, 578–80, 583–85, 587, 634, 756, 783, 787, 857, 869, 874, 1020, 1022, 1088, 1122, 1279, 1366–67, 1373
   biblical testimonies, 488–90, 513–23
   definition in church fathers, 487–88, 503–13
   dialectical method and, 523–32
   effects of, 532
   efficient cause, 524, 526, 528, 534
   Flacius on, 578–87
   formal aspect of, 531–32, 536, 557–58
   and free will, 478
   German terms for, 503
   guilt of, 517, 559
   material principle of, 531–32, 539
   Melanchthon on, 487–96
   names for, 496–503
      in early and medieval theologians, 500–502
      in New Testament, 499–500
      in Old Testament, 498
   principal corruptions of, 532–40
   propagation of, 517–18, 524–25, 527, 534, 537, 541, 545

remnants of in regenerate, 550–64
sedes doctrinae, 514
subject of, 517
substance of, 536
the term, 497
transmission of, 537
unknown to reason, 542
use of doctrine of, 562

Osiander, Andreas, 134, 245, 558, 825,
885–86, 897, 1023, 1033

Ovid, 267, 269, 980

owners, duties of, 729–30

Papists. *See* Roman Catholicism

paradoxes, 355, 361, 382, 818, 994, 1022,
1159

parents, 795. *See also* Commandments,
Fourth
duties of, 726, 757–58

Patripassians, 93, 112

pattern of teaching, 5

Paul of Burgos. *See* Burgensis

Paul of Samosata. *See* Samosata, Paul of

Pauline method, 38–39

Paulus, Simon, XXVI

Peasants' War, 456

Pelagian controversy, 434–36, 456–61,
524–25, 535–36, 541, 543, 550, 552, 600,
606, 872, 966, 971, 1113

Pelagianism, 389, 409, 415, 432, 534, 438,
440, 446–47, 457–58, 461, 463, 473, 516,
535, 539, 579, 838, 870, 872, 967, 1005

Pelagians, 29–30, 50, 383, 389, 396, 414, 427,
434–35, 437, 445, 447–48, 453–54, 458,
460, 465–66, 469, 471–72, 490, 500–501,
514, 524–25, 535, 537–38, 540–42, 546,
553, 555, 557, 579, 584, 601, 606–7, 846,
854, 877, 993–94, 1028, 1038, 1086,
1113–16, 1118, 1129, 1240, 1371

Pelagius, 29, 31, 66, 192, 408, 415, 426,
428–29, 434–35, 437–38, 442–43, 452–53,
456–461, 464–65, 470–74, 485–86, 497,
500–501, 505–6, 515–16, 518, 524–25,
527, 536, 541, 543, 548, 551, 555, 579, 606,
838, 956, 966–71, 990, 1021, 1241, 1272

Pelagius, "benign archbishop," 1324

Pentecost, 113, 211, 225, 234, 330, 616, 1263

Pericles, 55, 735

perseverance, gift of, 384, 445, 955

person (*hypostasis*), 25, 72, 78–79, 86ff.,
266–67, 269, 276, 497, 918–20

personal union, 127–32, 174–75, 178–88. *See
also* Jesus Christ
Cyril's anathemas against Nestorius,
188–208
rule of Scripture concerning, 180

Peter De Soto, 414, 463

Peter Lombard, 10, 42–43, 57, 95, 111, 156,
239, 244–45, 261, 289, 361, 371, 409–10,
414, 427, 434, 461–63, 465, 476, 506–7,
513, 528–29, 538, 550, 556, 574, 776–77,
786, 806, 878, 918, 994, 1033, 1273–74,
1285, 1327
Sentences, 342, 362, 366, 878
sententiaries, 434, 462–63, 497, 507–8,
530, 565, 918, 1270

Pharisaism, 469, 563, 590–91, 605, 691, 798,
808, 847, 870, 889, 950, 994, 998, 1019,
1097, 1101, 1168, 1179

Pharisees, 4, 341, 469, 478, 499, 534, 570,
600, 605, 619, 630, 637–39, 641, 645,
647, 653, 661, 668, 692, 695, 704, 736,
738–39, 744, 746–48, 782, 789, 791, 803,
805, 808–9, 823, 847, 856–57, 867, 883,
886, 891, 931, 950, 990, 993, 1019–20,
1022–23, 1056, 1063, 1077, 1079, 1086,
1092, 1113, 1118, 1120, 1195, 1199, 1205,
1211, 1237, 1242, 1263, 1272, 1284, 1288,
1296–97, 1300, 1338–39, 1365

Phavorinus, 187, 219, 223, 406, 481

Philastrius, 66, 92

Philippists, xii

Phillip. *See* Melanchthon

Philo, 651, 856, 1164

philosophy, 33, 54, 83, 95, 260, 263, 269–71,
296, 313, 326, 367–68, 430, 475, 479, 496,
541, 589–90, 597–98, 600, 603–5, 640,
659–60, 663, 674, 717, 744, 761–62, 782,
787, 789, 793–94, 796–99, 846–47, 856,
858, 865, 869–70, 890, 907–9, 925, 940,
955–56, 966, 968, 989, 1058–59, 1062,
1086, 1113, 1118, 1120, 1152, 1186, 1192,
1205, 1269, 1279, 1285, 1294
and ignorance of Gospel, 61
method of, 33
role in Church, 83

Philostratus, 861

Phoclydes, 589

Phormio, 1158

Photinus, 96, 123, 126, 140

Pierozzi, Antonius, 458

Pighius, Albert, 35, 391, 412, 509, 520–21, 541–43, 549, 678, 874, 933, 935–36, 940, 942, 1031, 1036, 1336

Plato, 51, 61, 64, 69, 72, 82, 148, 319, 438, 745, 797, 900, 1053, 1186, 1289, 1293

Platonism, 77, 83, 260, 271, 290, 856, 951, 1287, 1309. *See also* academic philosophy

Pliny, 290

Plotinus, 290

Plutarch, 600, 624, 816, 820, 880, 913, 919–20, 923, 973, 980

Pneumatomachoi. See Macedonians

Polybius, 900, 920

Polycarp, 22, 84, 1291, 1293, 1299

Pomeranus, 935

Ponticus, Evagrius, 70

Praxeas, 23, 92

prayer, 14–17, 21, 26, 29, 32–33, 42, 54–57, 60, 66–68, 71, 76, 81, 107–9, 112, 114, 120–22, 125–28, 132, 152, 163, 173, 175, 181, 201, 212, 214–18, 224, 238, 244, 246–47, 251, 256–57, 295, 298–99, 306, 309–11, 318–20, 339, 341, 356, 367, 379, 385, 397–99, 401, 403, 405, 424, 426, 428, 431–32, 440–41, 444, 448–50, 453, 455–56, 459, 466, 468, 470, 490, 492, 503, 508, 527, 538, 547, 563–64, 566–67, 578, 607, 617–18, 631–32, 637–38, 647, 653–56, 661, 669, 671, 675–76, 678, 680–81, 683, 685–88, 690, 694, 698–99, 701, 709–12, 717–19, 726, 728, 746, 749, 756–57, 774, 786–88, 791–92, 794, 820, 841, 847, 848–49, 857, 863, 894, 902, 904, 911, 916, 924, 931, 938, 940, 943, 945–46, 952, 955, 957–60, 962, 964–65, 975, 1032, 1044, 1046, 1048, 1052–56, 1060, 1063, 1067–68, 1137, 1186, 1190–91, 1197, 1202, 1213, 1220, 1227–28, 1232–34, 1236, 1238, 1256, 1258, 1260, 1287, 1292, 1294, 1306–7, 1326, 1328, 1332, 1346, 1351, 1356, 1359–61, 1364

predestination, 287, 327–29, 350, 362–63, 371, 374–75, 382–85, 391, 406, 836–37, 851, 964, 1024–25, 1041, 1070, 1308

preparatory grace, 443, 449

Probus, 96

Procopius, 115

prolegomena, 1

promises, eternal and temporal, 18

prophets, 5–7, 12, 35, 37–39, 592–93, 598, 612, 619–20, 623–25, 634, 636, 639,

647–48, 655, 664, 673, 680, 684, 689–700, 710–13, 716, 718, 723–26, 736, 740, 745, 751–52, 765, 774–75, 782, 786, 799, 802, 809, 814, 816, 819–20, 823, 832, 834–35, 842–48, 850, 855–56, 859, 870, 894, 900, 903–4, 915, 917, 925, 956, 961–62, 964, 967, 975, 1014, 1018, 1039–40, 1049, 1052, 1059, 1067–68, 1071, 1075–81, 1084, 1102, 1132, 1186, 1196, 1207–12, 1218, 1222, 1225, 1228–29, 1231–34, 1238–39, 1242, 1244–45, 1251, 1265, 1276, 1279, 1283, 1287–89, 1292, 1301, 1304, 1306, 1312, 1315–18, 1322, 1329, 1332–33, 1335–36, 1338, 1340, 1344–45, 1358–60, 1368

propitiation, 32, 179, 548, 616, 815, 888, 890–91, 915, 929, 931, 960, 1011, 1018, 1024, 1027, 1041, 1188, 1192, 1194, 1210, 1222, 1238

Prosper of Aquitaine, 71, 328–29, 383, 409, 436, 458–61, 1273

providence, xiv, 8, 55–56, 67, 75, 105, 152, 259, 269, 271, 285–98, 311, 315, 358, 362, 397, 406, 495, 717–18, 737, 794, 861, 962, 1053, 1255
   biblical terminology concerning, 291–93
   comprehensive extent of, 290
   definition, 287–91
   grades of, 292
   secondary causes, 292–97

Pythagoras, 69, 267

Quasten, 19, 85

Quintilian, 1136

Rashi, Solomon, 237

rationalism, xi

Ratisbon. *See* Colloquy at Ratisbon

reason, 1–2, 4, 7, 12, 43, 54, 62, 65, 70, 88, 100, 155, 167–68, 261, 270, 287, 293, 296, 316, 323, 350, 355, 367, 369, 393–94, 396–97, 410–11, 417–18, 429, 438, 446, 457, 464, 467, 475, 477, 479, 486, 496, 498, 508, 512, 533, 535, 542, 569, 580, 584, XII, 596–97, 600, 629, 633, 640, 642, 647, 669, 761, 770, 780, 784, 795–800, 803, 817–18, 821, 826, 850–51, 898, 905, 919, 925–27, 941, 958, 964–66, 968, 978, 989, 995, 1018, 1022, 1062–63, 1190, 1205, 1278, 1285, 1290

rebirth, creative act of God, 433

reconciliation, unknown without revelation, 55

Reformed theology, xiii

renewal, progressive nature of, 449

repentance, 507, 591, 643–44, 646, 653–54,
658, 665, 742, 768, 802–3, 806, 816, 818,
828–33, 837, 848–49, 855, 859, 861,
863–64, 870–72, 874, 891, 899, 907–8,
925, 932, 939–40, 947–48, 950, 952–53,
955, 957, 962, 964–65, 990, 1013–17,
1019–20, 1031–32, 1038, 1041–42, 1051,
1053, 1059, 1068, 1073, 1087, 1107, 1120,
1137, 1151, 1171–72, 1182, 1186, 1190,
1195–96, 1199–201, 1206–12, 1223, 1228,
1262, 1264–65, 1268, 1273–84, 1331,
1351, 1365, 1369

Rhegius, Urbanus, 133, 382, 539, 628, 670,
845, 1017, 1098, 1103, 1170, 1175, 1180

Richard of St. Victor, 438, 969, 1030

righteousness, of faith, 815, 822, 824–25,
927, 829, 832, 837, 841, 851–53, 865–67,
872, 879, 886, 890, 905–6, 909–10, 914,
929, 944, 987, 989, 991, 999, 1001, 1004,
1020–21, 1023, 1057, 1074, 1098, 1108,
1166, 1181, 1208, 1216, 1245, 1249, 1293,
1355, 1366, 1371
of God, 629, 717, 740, 798–99, 815,
823–25, 827, 865, 876, 886, 892,
894–97, 909, 929, 934, 964, 986, 988
999, 1004, 1009, 1029, 1033, 1036,
1215
misunderstandings of, 1033
of works, 872–73, 905, 987, 999, 1097,
1163, 1177, 1194

Roffensis, 454, 463, 473–74, 520, 601

Roman Catholicism, x–xv, 14, 16, 21, 23–24,
35, 44, 49–50, 52, 63, 133, 299, 304, 382,
390, 405, 415, 427, 434, 438, 454, 461,
463–64, 466, 473–74, 485, 509, 528–29,
539, 541, 544, 550, 553–54, 559–62, 573,
602, 606–7, 609–10, 622, 639, 666, 668,
679–80, 814, 824–25, 828, 830, 860,
866–67, 870, 875, 879–91, 883–84, 886,
891, 908, 916, 923, 927–28, 930, 934–35,
937, 939–52, 968, 978, 983, 994–95, 998,
1001–17, 1023, 1026, 1029–30, 1032–34,
1045, 1072, 1074–76, 1079, 1084,
1086–88, 1095, 1102–3, 1112, 1116–19,
1124–25, 1136, 1147, 1161–62, 1165–66,
1169, 1174–75, 1203, 1243, 1254,
1284–85, 1301–2, 1305, 1308–10, 1313,
1316, 1319, 1322, 1327, 1329, 1333–35,
1337–38, 1340–43, 1361

Rosarius, 463

Rufinus, 24, 28, 39, 142, 516, 864

Sabbatarians, 650

Sabbath, 22, 299, 616, 619, 631–32, 639, 645,
649–50, 699–714, 729, 748, 762, 990,
1338

Sabellianism, 93, 96, 104, 228

Sabellius, 92, 95, 96, 98, 102, 117, 228, 389

Sabinus, 140

Sacramentarian, xi, 12, 14, 93, 539, XXV,
1302, 1313, 1362, 1370–71, 1373

sacraments, creation of faith, 935, 945–46
definition of, 1355–56
nature of, 1361
number of, 1356, 1361

Sadducees, 300, 856, 1020, 1211, 1237, 1244,
1288, 1300

Samosata, Paul of, 92, 123–24, 126, 139–44,
183, 187, 228, 231, 660, 1291, 1298–99,
1343

Samosatenians, 216

Saturninus, 83, 271

Scaevola, 621

Scholastics, 43, 45, 53, 69, 78, 80, 89, 103,
109, 176, 245, 285, 298, 354, 369, 371,
373, 375–76, 405, 422, 425–27, 429, 434,
436, 443, 465, 485, 509, 513, 529–32,
534, 538, 538, 572–73, 575, 586, 615,
619, 634, 678–79, 702, 736, 741, 777, 780,
784, 806, 823–24, 831, 839, 874, 878, 881,
926, 933–34, 968, 1030, 1128, 1139, 1241,
1264, 1270, 1278, 1284–86, 1341, 1361

Schwenkfelder, XXV, 608, 1302, 1352

Scripture, xiii, 1, 3–9, 47, 71, 77–78, 89–91,
95–98, 106–7, 115, 122, 133, 137, 141,
145–46, 150, 157, 159, 163, 170, 173, 180,
185, 200, 211–13, 220, 222–28, 231, 242,
244, 247, 249, 261–65, 267, 270, 286, 292,
299, 301, 309, 336–53, 369, 375, 388, 408,
411–12, 430, 433, 442, 451, 466–69, 471,
479–80, 482–87, 514, 520–21, 554–57,
562, 569–74, 580, 591, 594, 598, 601–4,
606–9, 611, 613, 617–18, 625–28, 631,
639–40, 643, 645–46, 650–51, 654–55,
662–63, 665–68, 670–71, 674–75,
677–80, 684–90, 692, 694, 698–99, 701,
706–7, 710–12, 714, 719, 722, 724–25,
727, 729–30, 732, 736, 738, 741, 744–48,
751–56, 758–78, 781, 784, 786, 788–90,
799–800, 803, 805, 815–17, 819, 821–23,
836–37, 839–40, 843, 845, 848–50, 853,
855, 862, 865–67, 871, 876–77, 881–82,
884–85, 888, 890–91, 896–97, 906–18,
922, 926, 928–36, 939, 943, 946, 948–53,
965, 967–68, 970–72, 974, 977–78,
980, 986, 996, 1000, 1005–8, 1014–15,
1017–19, 1021–29, 1031, 1037–40, 1042,
1065–66, 1071–73, 1075–76, 1079–80,
1083–100, 1102, 1104–5, 1107, 1110,
1112–13, 1115–22, 1127, 1129, 1133, 1137,

1143, 1146–54, 1157–62, 1166–67, 1169,
1171, 1176–79, 1181–85, 1197, 1205–8,
1211–23, 1226, 1240–41, 1245–49,
1264, 1266–67, 1270–71, 1280, 1283,
1285, 1290–92, 1298–99, 1301–2, 1304,
1307, 1311, 1314–15, 1318, 1320, 1326,
1328–29, 1331, 1333, 1337, 1339–41,
1343, 1346, 1350, 1353, 1362, 1370–73
  clarity of, 50
  interpretation of, 50–53
  use in formulating dogma, 50–51

Second Table of the Law, 442, 484, 509

Sedulius, 878,

Seed, 625, 630, 835, 839–43, 851–53, 860,
917–18, 1046, 1174, 1214, 1221–22, 1226,
1249–50, 1363

Segusio, Henry of, 754

Seneca, 67, 533, 1094, 1255

sensuality, 529

Servetus, Michael, 86, 93–94, 123, 126–27,
137–38, 140, 1292

Seventh General Council. *See* Nicaea II

Severus, 348, 458, 545

Siculus, Diodorus. *See* Diodorus

Sigebert of Bemblous, 327

sin, 475–587
  actual, 476–77, 483–84, 486–87, 495–98,
    503, 515, 531, 536–39, 546, 551,
    564–78
  against divine Law
  against Holy Spirit, 575
  categories of, 483, 486–87
  cause of, 313–91, 486
  cause of, and controversies concerning,
    323–31
    correct understanding, 331–36
    and divine foreknowledge, 363–64
    and human complicity, 335
    Melanchthon on, 313–21
    philosophy on, 367–68
    summary, 335–36
  church and philosophers regarding,
    478–79
  of commission, 576
  defect as material principle, 492
  definition of, 314, 485–86
  degrees of avoiding, 428
  evil effects of, 563–64
  existence of, 322–23
  explanation of terms, 480–85
  final cause, 480
  formal cause, 479
  in general, 475–87
    Melanchthon on, 475–78

God not cause of, 545
Greek terms for, 481
guilt as formal principle of, 491
of infants, 544, 546–48
Latin terms, 481
material cause, 479
mortal, 516. *See* mortal sin
nature of, 356
in Old Testament, 482–83
of omission, 576
original. *See* original sin
twofold deprivation in, 356
unbelief as basic sin, 548
venial. *See* venial sin
vocabulary of, 1266–71
will of devil the first cause, 334, 356, 581

Sirmians, 96

Sisinnius, 182

slaves, duties of, 730

Smalcald Articles, 503, 791, 830, 1001, 1108,
1171–72, 1280, 1286

Smalcald War, xi

Small Catechism, 6–8, 306, 580, 584, 1137,
1161, 1372

Socrates (church historian), 70, 92, 95, 99,
142, 229, 1327

Socrates (philosopher), 17, 423, 806, 869,
1272, 1289

sola fide, 1006–17

Son of God, 119–210. *See also* Jesus Christ. *See
also* Holy Trinity
  communication of attributes. *See* commu-
    nication of attributes
  language of Church concerning, 129–30
  names of, 126–66
  person of, 113–14
  as Redeemer, 113–14
  work of, 144

Sophists, 52, 122–23, 140, 143, 155–56, 211,
228, 242, 259, 261, 271, 423, 434, 438,
459, 488, 491, 520, 524, 531, 553, 573,
575, 582, 584, 586, 601, 653, 770, 772–73,
783, 813, 833, 873–74, 905, 959, 961–65,
989, 991, 996, 1001, 1012–13, 1023, 1035,
1058, 1100, 1147, 1169, 1193, 1197, 1257,
1291, 1367

Sophocles, 99, 481, 661, 880, 900, 972

soul, origin of, 525–27

Sozomon, 92, 1322, 1327

Spiera, Ambrose, 427, 463

Spirit. *See* Holy Spirit

Spirit of God. *See* Holy Spirit

spiritual actions, 429–33
and Holy Spirit, 429

spiritual man, 397, 527

Staphylus, XXI, 987, 1136

Stapulensis, Jacobus Faber, 146, 1035–36

Stenckfeld, 608, 610, 1170

Stephen (martyr), 245, 396, 594–95, 624,
1039, 1300, 1342

Stephen (pope), 20

Stoics, 131, 255–57, 269, 271, 295–97, 319–21,
363–64, 368–71, 374–76, 378–79, 393,
411, 478, 494, 566–67, 784, 848, 907, 930,
1022, 1258

substance (ousia), 98. See also essence of God

Succensus, 204–6

Suidas, 21, 95, 140, 143–44, 154, 173, 176,
183, 187, 229, 284, 326, 386, 484, 499,
515, 676, 880, 920, 926, 972, 980, 1094

Sulpicius Severus. See Severus

Symmachus, 348, 669

Tatian, 83, 545, 744

Terebinthus, 326–27

Tertullian, 23–25, 39, 41, 66, 83, 92, 99, 125,
133, 167, 186, 271, 273, 325, 327, 330, 348,
374, 381, 407, 470–72, 823, 859, 861–62,
867, 869, 871, 942, 1270, 1282–83

Tetragrammaton, 145, 148, 685

Tetrapolitan Confession, 339

Thamer, Theobald, 63, 67

Theodoret, 184, 188–203, 997, 1079, 1146,
1270

Theodorus, Vitus, 301

Theodosius the Great, 669, 1356

Theognis, 589, 900

Theophilus, 40–41

Theophilus of Antioch, 867, 869, 1010, 1016

Theophylact, 30, 175, 240, 918

Thirty Years War, xv,

Thomas Aquinas, 89, 266, 411, 462–63, 486,
510–11, 597, 633, 777, 878–79, 908, 918,
942, 969, 979, 1030, 1285

Thucydides, 100, 923

Torquatus, 44

Traducianism, 526, 528

transmission of soul, 530, 538

Trinity, persons of, 1025

Trismegistus, Hermes, 297

truth, 777. See also Commandments, Eighth

Turks, 56–57, 59, 217, 267, 667, 704, 721, 908,
1012, 1055, 1234, 1263, 1360, 1369

Ulpian of Emesa, 222

unction, 1285, 1327–28, 1360–61

"union," in personal union, 181

Valens, 143

Valentinian, 83, 169, 216, 324, 330, 669, 804,
809, 1146, 1149

Valerian, 92

Valerius, 1322

Valintinus, 82–85, 90, 166, 271–72, 274, 276,
329, 454, 622, 860, 862

Valla, Lorenzo, 21, 328, 393, 404–6, 414, 464,
538

Varinus, 176, 187, 262–63, 483–84, 499, 515,
597, 894, 920–23, 926–27, 942, 972, 980

Vatablus, 148

venial sin, 427, 462, 483, 512, 554, 560, 563,
565, 574–75, 607, 646, 672, 739, 756, 775,
786, 831, 1089, 1255–86

Vicelius, 825, 874, 993, 995–96, 999, 1057,
1166

Victor, Vincentius, 526

Vigilius of Thapsus, 26, 85, 97

Vincent of Lerins, 328

Virgil, 44, 220, 264, 298

Vitalis, 443, 968

will, human, 794

will of God, 45, 55, 57, 68, 71, 76–77, 155,
250, 260, 287, 297, 316, 318–19, 331–32,
334–35, 351, 353, 360–61, 366, 377, 379,
382–85, 387, 394, 398, 406, 412, 444, 475,
495, 577, 630, 644, 665, 667, 685, 726,
729–30, 733, 764, 808, 926, 941, 948, 954,
964, 1025, 1041, 1052, 1059, 1063, 1070,
1074–75, 1081, 1089, 1092, 1095–96,
1114, 1121–22, 1132, 1158, 1180, 1183,
1190, 1196, 1240, 1262, 1279–80, 1289,
1294, 1324, 1332–33

William of Occam, 463, 472, 490, 508

William of Paris, 27, 175, 462

William the Younger (duke), 1, 14–15

Willigis, Iodocus, 76

Wittenberg Confession, 830

Word, divine, as judge, 1292
as person, 124–26

Word and Sacraments, 113

"world," meanings of, 275–76

worship, 35, 55–61, 63–64, 66–69, 71, 76–77, 81–83, 87, 89, 94, 107–9, 120, 122, 128, 149, 152, 169, 198, 218, 228, 230, 233, 246–47, 250, 260, 266, 275, 290, 299–300, 307, 336, 347, 395, 402, 415–16, 426, 429, 443, 446, 478, 487, 495, 596, 613–14, 616, 620, 622, 626–27, 631–32, 637, 639, 641, 645, 649, 652–53, 655–60, 663–84, 692, 694, 697–98, 700–701, 703–8, 710, 715–17, 727, 745, 791, 793–96, 799, 803, 808, 836, 839, 846, 853, 855, 865, 886, 902, 936, 940, 960–61, 1002, 1008, 1021–22, 1044, 1053–54, 1060, 1065, 1068, 1071, 1073, 1077, 1080–83, 1090, 1144, 1163, 1190, 1192–93, 1195, 1197, 1199, 1225–27, 1233, 1237, 1239, 1240, 1242, 1256, 1261, 1263, 1273, 1289, 1293, 1298, 1301, 1304, 1310, 1319, 1335, 1353, 1359

wrath of God, 49, 131–32, 147, 163, 178, 313, 342, 347–48, 397, 399, 402–3, 428, 475–77, 480, 487–90, 493, 495, 512, 518, 537, 539, 551, 564–68, 590, 618, 637–38, 684, 728, 732, 736, 748, 750, 784, 786, 801–3, 831–32, 834, 840, 847–49, 887,

890, 909, 916, 931, 1020, 1041, 1053, 1057–59, 1062–70, 1101, 1107, 1141, 1171, 1198–99, 1202, 1211–12, 1227, 1229–31, 1252, 1255–60, 1262, 1266, 1268, 1270–72, 1276, 1277, 1299, 1357
    assuaged by Jesus Christ, 901, 960, 963, 982, 1028, 1055, 1233, 1239
    and fear of God, 665, 671
    and Gospel, 806, 830
    and judgment, 602, 605, 610, 690, 957
    and knowledge of sin, 855, 873, 875, 913, 951, 957

Wycliffe, John, 464, 1308

Xenophon, 17, 259, 269, 720, 795, 834, 1269

Zeno, 62, 270, 319

Zwingli, Ulrich, 63, 67, 133, 539, 1009

Zwinglians, xi, 49, 549, 648, 887